Mexico City Metro

G000122493

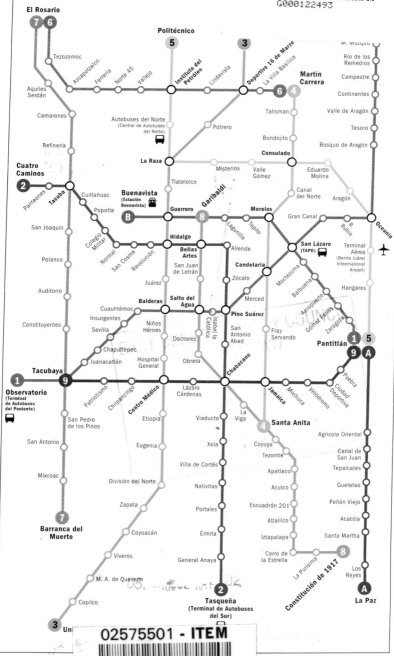

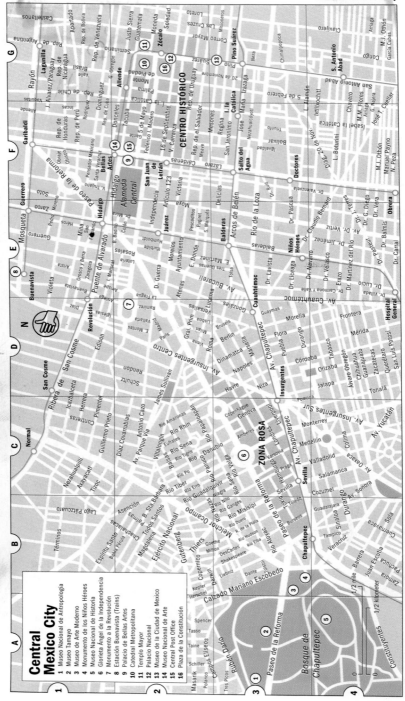

Central Mexico City

Central Mexico City

1 Museo Nacional de Antropología
2 Museo Tamayo
3 Museo de Arte Moderno
4 Monumento de los Niños Héroes
5 Museo Nacional de Historia
6 Glorieta Ángel de la Independencia
7 Monumento a la Revolución
8 Estación Buenavista (Trains)
9 Palacio de Bellas Artes
10 Catedral Metropolitana
11 Templo Mayor
12 Palacio Nacional
13 Museo de la Ciudad de Mexico
14 Museo Nacional de Arte
15 Central Post Office
16 Plaza de la Constitución

CENTRO HISTÓRICO

ZONA ROSA

Bosque de Chapultepec

N

1/2 mile
1/2 kilometer

 Let's Go writers travel on your budget.

"Guides that penetrate the veneer of the holiday brochures and mine the grit of real life."

—*The Economist*

"The writers seem to have experienced every rooster-packed bus and lunar-surfaced mattress about which they write."

—*The New York Times*

"All the dirt, dirt cheap."

—*People*

Great for independent travelers.

"The guides are aimed not only at young budget travelers but at the independent traveler; a sort of streetwise cookbook for traveling alone."

—*The New York Times*

"A guide should tell you what to expect from a destination. Here *Let's Go* shines."

—*The Chicago Tribune*

"An indispensible resource, *Let's Go*'s practical information can be used by every traveler."

—*The Chattanooga Free Press*

Let's Go is completely revised each year.

"A publishing phenomenon...the only major guidebook series updated annually. *Let's Go* is the big kahuna."

—*The Boston Globe*

"Unbeatable: good sight-seeing advice; up-to-date info on restaurants, hotels, and inns; a commitment to money-saving travel; and a wry style that brightens nearly every page."

—*The Washington Post*

All the important information you need.

"*Let's Go* authors provide a comedic element while still providing concise information and thorough coverage of the country. Anything you need to know about budget traveling is detailed in this book."

—*The Chicago Sun-Times*

"*Let's Go* guidebooks take night life seriously."

—*The Chicago Tribune*

Let's Go Publications

Let's Go: Alaska & the Pacific Northwest 2002
Let's Go: Amsterdam 2002 **New Title!**
Let's Go: Australia 2002
Let's Go: Austria & Switzerland 2002
Let's Go: Barcelona 2002 **New Title!**
Let's Go: Boston 2002
Let's Go: Britain & Ireland 2002
Let's Go: California 2002
Let's Go: Central America 2002
Let's Go: China 2002
Let's Go: Eastern Europe 2002
Let's Go: Egypt 2002 **New Title!**
Let's Go: Europe 2002
Let's Go: France 2002
Let's Go: Germany 2002
Let's Go: Greece 2002
Let's Go: India & Nepal 2002
Let's Go: Ireland 2002
Let's Go: Israel 2002
Let's Go: Italy 2002
Let's Go: London 2002
Let's Go: Mexico 2002
Let's Go: Middle East 2002
Let's Go: New York City 2002
Let's Go: New Zealand 2002
Let's Go: Paris 2002
Let's Go: Peru, Ecuador & Bolivia 2002
Let's Go: Rome 2002
Let's Go: San Francisco 2002
Let's Go: South Africa with Southern Africa 2002
Let's Go: Southeast Asia 2002
Let's Go: Southwest USA 2002 **New Title!**
Let's Go: Spain & Portugal 2002
Let's Go: Turkey 2002
Let's Go: USA 2002
Let's Go: Washington, D.C. 2002
Let's Go: Western Europe 2002

Let's Go Map Guides

Amsterdam
Berlin
Boston
Chicago
Dublin
Florence
Hong Kong
London
Los Angeles
Madrid
New Orleans
New York City
Paris
Prague
Rome
San Francisco
Seattle
Sydney
Venice
Washington, D.C.

Let's Go

MEXICO
2002

Angie K. Chen editor

Theresa A. Botello associate editor
Michelle S. Ybarra associate editor

researcher-writers
Carla Blackmar
Ashley Forde
Grainne Godfree
Ben Mathis-Lilley
Rei Onishi
Joel Walsh
Ben Wells

Noah Askin map editor
Brady R. Dewar managing editor

Macmillan

HELPING LET'S GO If you want to share your discoveries, suggestions, or corrections, please drop us a line. We read every piece of correspondence, whether a postcard, a 10-page email, or a coconut. Please note that mail received after May 2002 may be too late for the 2003 book, but will be kept for future editions. **Address mail to:**

Let's Go: Mexico
67 Mount Auburn Street
Cambridge, MA 02138
USA

Visit Let's Go at **http://www.letsgo.com,** or send email to:

feedback@letsgo.com
Subject: "Let's Go: Mexico"

In addition to the invaluable travel advice our readers share with us, many are kind enough to offer their services as researchers or editors. Unfortunately, our charter enables us to employ only currently enrolled Harvard students.

Published in Great Britain 2002 by Macmillan, an imprint of Pan Macmillan Ltd.
20 New Wharf Road, London N1 9RR
Basingstoke and Oxford
Associated companies throughout the world
www.panmacmillan.com

Maps by David Lindroth copyright © 2002, 2001, 2000, 1999, 1998, 1997, 1996, 1995, 1994, 1993, 1992, 1991, 1990, 1989, 1988 by St. Martin's Press.

Published in the United States of America by St. Martin's Press.

ISBN: 0-333-90593-8
First edition
10 9 8 7 6 5 4 3 2 1

Let's Go: Mexico is written by Let's Go Publications, 67 Mount Auburn Street, Cambridge, MA 02138, USA.

Let's Go® and the thumb logo are trademarks of Let's Go, Inc.
Printed in the USA on recycled paper with biodegradable soy ink.

HOW TO USE THIS BOOK

Mexico will inevitably enchant, enrapture, and seduce visitors with her wiles—from her breathtaking ruins to sinful resort towns to smoldering jungles, this country can be hot and hard to handle. Never fear, budget traveler, for here you have a complete guide to romancing Mexico. We'll keep your feet on the ground and pointed in the right direction, while serving as a beacon of sanity and practicality that will allow both you and your wallet to enjoy this steamy love affair.

ORGANIZATION OF THIS BOOK

INTRODUCTORY MATERIAL. The first chapter, **Discover Mexico**, speaks of Mexico in sweeping (some might say clichéd) terms. **Suggested Itineraries** suggest where and in what order one might discover Mexico, and about how long that discovery will take. The **Life & Times** chapter provides first-timers with a crash course in the art, culture, and history of Mexico, while **Essentials** does the dirty work, letting you know what you need to do to get to Mexico and back in one piece.

COVERAGE. The book's coverage, comprised of the diligence, sweat, and love of our seven researchers in the field, is divided by region into nine chapters, starting at the heart of it all in Mexico City, and ending on the wild and beautiful beaches of the Yucatán Peninsula. The **black tabs** in the margins will help you to navigate between chapters quickly and easily.

APPENDIX. The appendix contains handy **conversions**, a **phrasebook** of useful (and sometimes useless) phrases in Spanish, and a **glossary** of foreign and technical (e.g. architectural) words.

A FEW NOTES ABOUT LET'S GO FORMAT

RANKING ESTABLISHMENTS. In each section (accommodations, food, etc.), we list establishments in order from best to worst. Our absolute favorites are so denoted by the highest honor given out by Let's Go, the thumbs-up (🖐).

PHONE CODES AND TELEPHONE NUMBERS. The **phone code** for each region, city, or town appears opposite the name of that region, city, or town, and is denoted by the ☎ icon. **Phone numbers** in text are also preceded by the ☎ icon.

GREYBOXES AND IKONBOXES. Greyboxes at times provide wonderful cultural insight, at times simply crude humor. In any case, they're usually amusing, so enjoy. **Whiteboxes,** on the other hand, provide important practical information, such as warnings (⚠), helpful hints and further resources (🔍), border crossings (🛂), dangerous highways, etc.

UNIQUE AND USEFUL SECTIONS. Our 2002 edition bursts with new listings of **vegetarian restaurants** and **gay nightlife** establishments, and an expanded **glossary** of useful Spanish terms to help you find them. Movie buffs will enjoy our new **Film** section in the **Life and Times** chapter which notes popular (and surprising) films that were shot in various parts of the republic. Finally, our hardcore researchers have tramped through the jungles of the Yucatán and Chiapas, the barren peaks of central Baja California, and the depths of the Pacific Coast to bring you more detailed coverage of **national parks, outdoor activities,** and **fishing** opportunities.

A NOTE TO OUR READERS The information for this book was gathered by *Let's Go* researchers from May through August of 2001. Each listing is based on one researcher's opinion, formed during his or her visit at a particular time. Those traveling at other times may have different experiences since prices, dates, hours, and conditions are always subject to change. You are urged to check the facts presented in this book beforehand to avoid inconvenience and surprises.

CONTENTS

MAPS

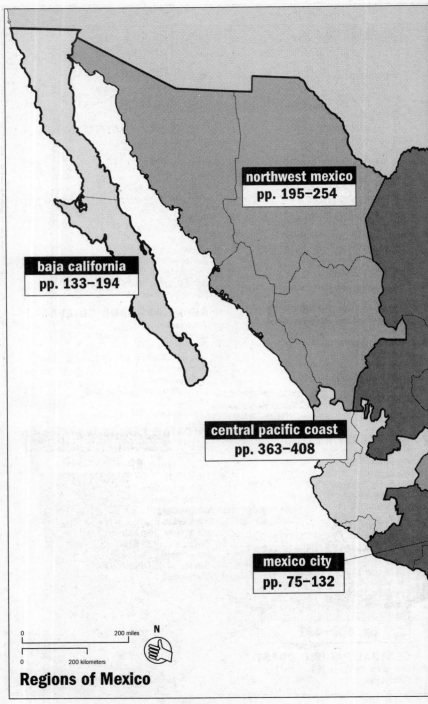

0   200 miles   N

0   200 kilometers

Regions of Mexico

x

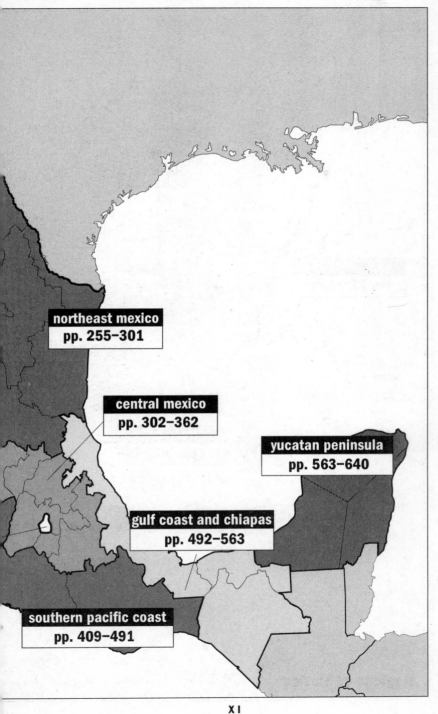

northeast mexico
pp. 255–301

central mexico
pp. 302–362

yucatan peninsula
pp. 563–640

gulf coast and chiapas
pp. 492–563

southern pacific coast
pp. 409–491

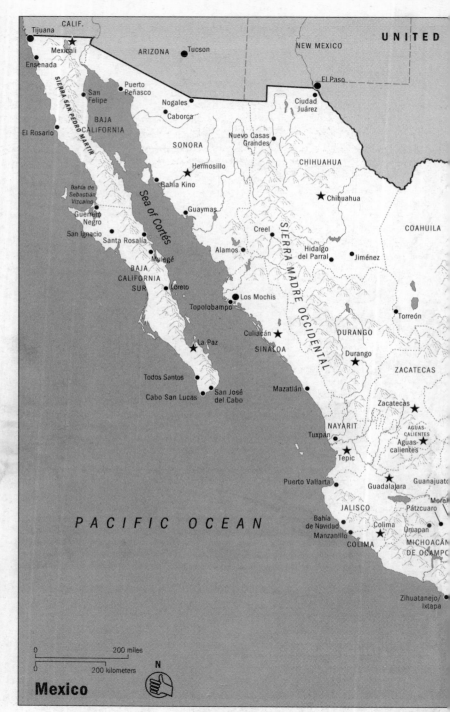

Mexico

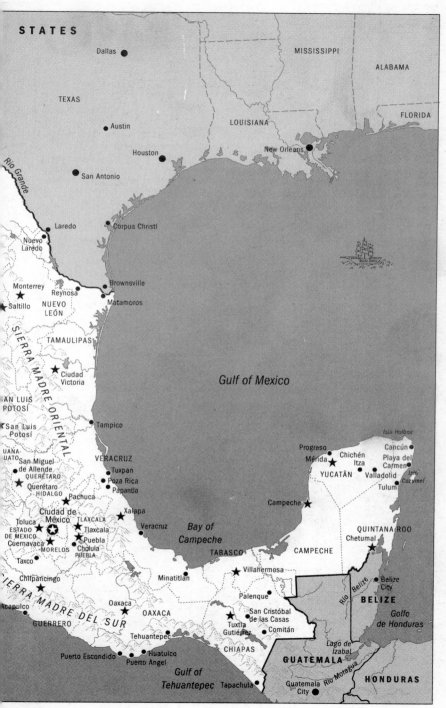

STATES

Dallas

MISSISSIPPI
ALABAMA

TEXAS

Austin

LOUISIANA
FLORIDA

Houston

New Orleans

Rio Grande

San Antonio

Laredo
Corpus Christi

Nuevo
Laredo

Monterrey
Reynosa
NUEVO
LEÓN
Saltillo
Brownsville
Matamoros

SIERRA MADRE ORIENTAL

TAMAULIPAS

Ciudad
Victoria

Gulf of Mexico

AN LUIS
POTOSÍ

San Luis
Potosí
Tampico

UANA-
UATO
San Miguel
de Allende
QUERÉTARO
VERACRUZ
Tuxpan
Poza Rica
Papantla

Querétaro
HIDALGO
Pachuca

Progreso
Mérida
Chichén
Itzá
YUCATÁN
Valladolid

Cancún
Playa del
Carmen
Isla Holbox

Isla
Cozumel

Tulum

Xalapa
Campeche

Toluca
Ciudad de
México
TLAXCALA
ESTADO
DE MÉXICO
Tlaxcala
Cuernavaca
MORELOS
Puebla
Cholula
PUEBLA
Taxco

Bay of
Campeche

Veracruz

QUINTANA ROO
Chetumal

TABASCO
CAMPECHE

Chilpancingo

Minatitlán

Villahermosa

Belize
Belize
City

SIERRA MADRE DEL SUR

Oaxaca
OAXACA

Palenque
San Cristóbal
de las Casas
Tuxtla
Gutiérrez
Comitán

Rio Belize
BELIZE

Golfo
de Honduras

Acapulco
GUERRERO

Tehuantepec
CHIAPAS

Lago de
Izabal

Puerto Escondido
Puerto Angel
Huatulco

GUATEMALA
Rio Motagua

HONDURAS

Gulf of
Tehuantepec
Tapachula

Guatemala
City

XIII

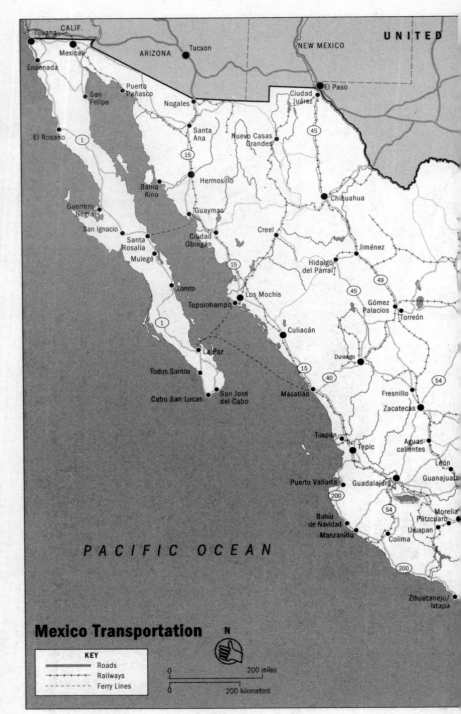

Mexico Transportation

KEY
- Roads
- +++++ Railways
- - - - - Ferry Lines

0   200 miles
0   200 kilometers

N

PACIFIC OCEAN

UNITED

CALIF.
ARIZONA
NEW MEXICO

Tijuana
Mexicali
Ensenada
San Felipe
Puerto Peñasco
El Rosario
Guerrero Negro
San Ignacio
Santa Rosalía
Mulegé
Loreto
Topolobampo
La Paz
Todos Santos
Cabo San Lucas
San José del Cabo

Tucson
Nogales
Santa Ana
Nuevo Casas Grandes
Ciudad Juárez
El Paso
Bahía Kino
Hermosillo
Guaymas
Ciudad Obregón
Creel
Chihuahua
Jiménez
Hidalgo del Parral
Gómez Palacios
Torreón
Los Mochis
Culiacán
Durango
Mazatlán
Fresnillo
Zacatecas
Aguascalientes
León
Guanajuato
Tuxpan
Tepic
Puerto Vallarta
Guadalajara
Morelia
Pátzcuaro
Uruapan
Colima
Bahía de Navidad
Manzanillo
Zihuatanejo/Ixtapa

1
15
45
49
54
40
200

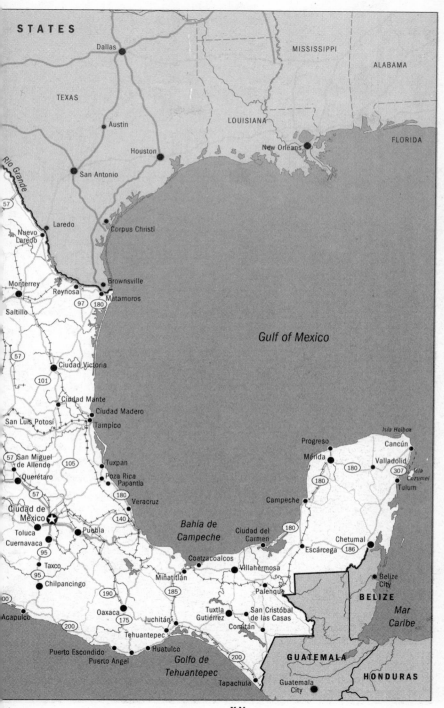

RESEARCHER-WRITERS

Carla Blackmar *Northwest Mexico, Nayarit, and Jalisco*

Carla loves Mexico, and we love Carla. Armed with a camera and the best of humors, this *Let's Go: Mexico 2000* vet shook out her brilliant red curls and kicked up hurricanes of dust in the northwest, leaving love-struck *vaqueros* and dazzled Mennonites in her wake. Throwing caution and itinerary to the wind, she revolutionized nightlife listings and regaled us with tales of adventure. Carla stormed through the Copper Canyon, danced her way into a wedding, filled her sketchbook with dead cockroaches, and won our hearts with her endless spirit.

Ashley Forde *Central Mexico, Colima, Michoacán, and Guerrero*

With her sexy southern drawl and passion for history, Ashley set out across the golden beaches of the Pacific coast in search of a good time. Two months, countless marriage proposals, and the occasional nudie bar later, she returned blissful, bronzed, and—to the despair of Mexico's male population—still monogamous. After reading through reams of Ashley's eloquent prose and examining stacks of her immaculate maps, we too were enchanted.

Grainne Godfree *Northeast Mexico and Veracruz*

Grainne charmed her way from the gritty Texan border to the salty beaches of Veracruz, swiveling her hips and nibbling grilled corn on the cob the whole way. A self-proclaimed city girl, she discovered a love for nature, hiking through forests, waterfalls, and mountain villages. Full of cheerful notes, *Tomb Raider* references, and sugary treats, Grainne's sweet copy batches always left us hungry for more.

Ben Mathis-Lilley *Oaxaca, Tabasco, and Chiapas*

Dripping with sarcasm and overflowing with wit, our very own "scrawny, under-motivated, super-genius" battled gunfire, cockroaches, and teenaged girls in his quest for the perfect copy. Ben delighted the office with his hilarious prose, winning widespread admiration and even a heart or two. Drawing on his newspaper past, this intrepid Michigander uncovered quite a few secrets in the southern jungles, and neither *Let's Go* nor Subcomandante Marcos will ever forget him.

Rei Onishi *Yucatán Peninsula*

Filling hundreds of neatly hand-written pages with evocative metaphors and detailed information, Rei brought a touch of class to the touristy resort towns and small villages of the Yucatán. Between dozens of ruins, a few moped crashes, and a traumatic sandal theft, he managed to work on his tan, dive colorful Caribbean reefs, and earn our undying appreciation. Dedicated, adventurous, laid-back, and enthusiastic, Rei may have redefined researcher-writer perfection.

Joel Walsh *Mexico City*

With an eye for cleanliness and a knack for marginalia, Joel eagerly took on the fearsome streets of big, bad Mexico City. He turned the capital inside out, unearthing everything from bargain laundromats to the hottest *discotecas*, always finding time for a nutritious vegetarian lunch. Joel felt so at home in *el D.F.* that his five-week itinerary turned into seven, and we had to beg for him to come back.

Ben Wells *Baja California*

The definition of cheerful crisis management, our beloved Ben never let anything wipe the smile from his increasingly hairy face. When the fates conspired against him, breaking first his laptop and then his car, he took it all in stride, bought a few 40oz. Tecates and settled in for the wait. A lover of animals and the outdoors, Ben revamped coverage of Baja's barren mountain parks and stunning surf and consumed cows by the kilogram to keep himself, and his perpetual grin, strong.

ACKNOWLEDGMENTS

The Let's Go 2002 series is dedicated to the memory of Haley Surti

WE THANK: Jam'n for the tunes. Our RWs for enthusiasm and *amor*. Ben for dancing and Leary for putting up with us. Brady for the late nights. Harris for answering our questions. Jean, Michelle B., and Erzulie for cheerfully pitching in. Carla for social visits and awesome edits. Noah for his patience. And, Justin for excellent *español* and keeping Angie sane.

ANGIE: Theresa, the Psycho, and Michelle, the Dark Force, for dedication and uncontrollable laughter. Erzulie and Michelle B. for understanding, and Jean for salads and creativity. Mui, Johanna, Ronkey, Frankie, Tato, and Anne for four great years. Patty, here's to an amazing (super-)senior year. My best friends, Zach and Becky, for always being there. Mary, Scott, and Wilson for pastoral vistas and good food. My crazy family, Mom, Dad, Albert, Gracie and Roscoe, for unconditional love and relaxing retreats. And, Justin *por todo*.

THERESA: Angie, for this chance and the gaffaws that made it super. Michelle, for your cuteness and (mother) wit. Mom and Dad, for love, guidance, and Spanish (slang/otherwise). My grandparents, for cheery words. Chicas, for being the best roommates/blockmates and this summer! The Botello and Sullivan clans, not enough words of praise. Tina, for being faboo! Jessica for living. Mike for calming. The Cummings, for showing me Salem. Emily for marianette madness.

MICHELLE: Evil Empress Angie, for ruling with a big smile and black heart, and Theresa for your infectious laugh—may we all catch your mental illness. Steph for crisis management and knowing just what to say. Zach for always treating me like a queen. Carla and Yuan for cuddling and the most precious friendships ever. Chris for big-brotherly advice and abuse. Suzanne for Spongebob. My parents and lil' sis for your love and sacrifices. And Jason, for the future, wherever you are.

Publishing Director
Sarah P. Rotman
Editor-in-Chief
Ankur N. Ghosh
Production Manager
Jen Taylor
Cartography Manager
Dan Barnes
Design & Photo Manager
Vanessa Bertozzi
Editorial Managers
Amélie Cherlin, Naz F. Firoz, Matthew Gibson, Sharmi Surianarain, Brian R. Walsh
Financial Manager
Rebecca L. Schoff
Marketing & Publicity Managers
Brady R. Dewar, Katharine Douglas, Marly Ohlsson
New Media Manager
Kevin H. Yip
Online Manager
Alex Lloyd
Personnel Manager
Nathaniel Popper
Production Associates
Steven Aponte, Chris Clayton, Caleb S. Epps, Eduardo Montoya, Melissa Rudolph
Some Design
Melissa Rudolph
Office Coordinators
Efrat Kussell, Peter Richards

Director of Advertising Sales
Adam M. Grant
Senior Advertising Associates
Ariel Shwayder, Kennedy Thorwarth
Advertising Associate
Jennie Timoney
Advertising Artwork Editor
Peter Henderson

President
Cindy L. Rodriguez
General Manager
Robert B. Rombauer
Assistant General Manager
Anne E. Chisholm

Editor
Angie K. Chen
Associate Editors
Theresa A. Botello and Michelle S. Ybarra
Managing Editor
Brady R. Dewar
Map Editor
Noah Askin

DISCOVER MEXICO

Mere words cannot do justice to Mexico's *sabor*. Something so unique and so pervasive, so subtle and so striking can't be found in any museum, beach, or ruin, and it certainly can't be found in any guidebook, no matter how solid the research, evocative the prose, or keen the insight. Mexico reveals its *sabor* only at rare times. When walking down the street, for example, you pause, look up from your worn and tattered map, and realize that all around you children are laughing and playing *fútbol*, elderly couples are engrossed in conversation, and young men are sitting outside a corner *taquería* and enjoying the air. It is then that a warm feeling of camaraderie embraces you and allows you to perceive a distinct *sabor* in the laughs, the smiles, and the humor of Mexico. This is the unexplainable element that defines Mexican life and its people. This is the unnameable thing that makes Mexico feel different than any other country The traveler who finds Mexico's *sabor* will surely fall in love with the place, and in falling in love, realize that this pervasive flavor allows Mexico to somehow surpass and transcend its beaches, its ruins, and its stereotypes of men in *sombreros* leaning over *cantina* counters. Those who have experienced Mexico and discovered its *sabor* will inevitably return time after time to seek out the same sensation and delight in its thrill. Take a good look around you, smell the smells, see the sights, climb the ruins. But once in a while, put the book down and truly discover Mexico.

WHEN TO GO

Mexico's lush jungles, golden beaches, and romantic deserts entice visitors year-round. Temperatures fluctuate widely throughout the country. Winters tend to be mild while summers vary from warm to excruciatingly hot, with temperatures in both the arid North and the moist Gulf regions soaring to more than 50°C (122°F). Exceptions to the rule of infernally hot summers are high altitude regions such as the Valley of Mexico and the Oaxaca Valley, which remain spring-like in any month. Rainfall, like temperature, varies greatly between the temperate north and the tropical south. While it seldom rains in the northern border states, rain falls abundantly in the humid south, sometimes exceeding 15cm per month. The official rainy season lasts from May to November, during which the soggy south receives an average of two to three hours of rain every afternoon. The best time to hit the beaches is during the dry season (November-May), when afternoons are sunny, evenings balmy, and nights relatively mosquito-free.

The peak tourist season (high season) encompasses December, *Semana Santa* (the week before Easter), and midsummer. Additionally, unless you want to spend your vacation rubbing elbows with hormone-charged, booze-seeking US college students, it's best to avoid resort towns such as Mazatlán, Cabo San Lucas, and Cancún during the waning weeks of March and the early weeks of April, traditional US spring break. Central Mexico and spots on the so-called *gringo* trail see the most tourist traffic during mid to late summer, when throngs of Spanish-language students hit both the books and the trendy cafes in search of "Spanish immersion." If you travel to Mexico during any of these times, you should expect to pay slightly higher prices at hotels and restaurants.

AVG. TEMP. (LO/HI), PRECIPITATION											
	JANUARY			APRIL			JULY			OCTOBER		
	°C	°F	mm	°C	°F	mm	°C	°F	mm	°C	°F	mm
Acapulco	22/31	72/88	1	25/32	77/90	0	25/33	77/91	27	24/32	75/90	18
Cancún	19/28	66/82	110	22/31	72/88	35	25/32	77/90	110	23/31	73/88	220
Guadalajara	7/23	45/73	15	14/31	57/88	8	15/26	59/79	257	10/25	50/77	54
La Paz	13/23	55/73	23	17/33	63/91	1	23/36	73/97	32	17/29	63/84	28
Mérida	18/28	64/82	60	21/34	70/93	148	23/33	73/91	122	19/29	66/84	269
Mexico City	6/22	43/72	8	13/27	5/81	19	13/24	55/75	129	9/23	48/73	44
Monterrey	9/20	48/68	18	20/31	68/88	29	22/34	72/93	62	12/23	54/73	78
Oaxaca	8/28	46/82	3	15/32	59/90	26	15/28	59/82	88	10/28	50/82	44
San Cristóbal	5/20	41/68	2	9/22	48/72	30	10/22	50/72	160	7/20	45/68	150
Tijuana	6/20	41/68	49	12/23	54/73	20	16/27	61/81	1	10/23	50/73	13

THINGS TO DO

Mexico has no end of attractions. From climbing age-old Maya temples to haggling for silver trinkets in colonial open-air markets to diving through coral reefs to dancing the *merengue* with margarita in hand, each region boasts its own cultural allure and culinary appeal. See the **Highlights of the Region** section at the beginning of each chapter for specific regional attractions.

THE GREAT CIVILIZATIONS

A journey through Mexico is like a whirlwind through time. The ancient Olmecs—known world over for their colossal carved heads—were the first to call Mexico home, settling the villages of **San Lorenzo** (see p. 522), **La Venta** (see p. 526), and **Tres Zapotes** (see p. 517) in the humid Gulf Coast around 1000 BC. Centuries later, a mighty empire rose in the Valley of Mexico at **Teotihuacán** (see p. 126), the ruins of which were so impressive that even the Aztecs thought the city had been built by the gods. Farther south, the Zapotec capital **Monte Albán** (see p. 468) rivaled Teotihuacán in greatness, occupying a stately hillside position overlooking the verdant Oaxaca Valley. To the east, in the lowland jungles of the Yucatán Peninsula, the Classic Maya built grand cities such as **Palenque** (see p. 551), which continue to dazzle visitors with their distinct Classic architecture and lush settings. Returning to central Mexico, admire the Tlaxcalans who drew the breathtaking murals at **Cacaxtla** (see p. 346), and the Totonacs who carved the Pyramid of Niches at **El Tajín** (see p. 504). After the fall of the Classic civilizations, Post-Classic powers like **Tula** (see p. 325), the birthplace of the feathered-deity Quetzalcóatl, and **Mitla** (see p. 465), whose intricate carvings and religious architecture are second to none, kept Mesoamerican traditions alive. Head back into the Yucatán for a rendezvous with the warring Post-Classic Maya trio of **Chichén Itzá** (see p. 591), **Mayapán** (see p. 579), and **Uxmal** (see p. 575). Finally, witness the great end of Pre-Hispanic Mexico in the Aztec capital of **Tenochtitlán** (modern-day Mexico City; see p. 101).

SAND AND SURF

Mexico's infinite stretches of sparkling golden and white beaches will please even the most discriminating beach-goer. Those in search of a crowd like to strut their stuff in **Cancún** (see p. 604), home to millions of bronzed bodies. If the glam tourist scene isn't your style, ramble down the turquoise coast toward **Tulum** (see p. 630), and cavort amidst the beachside ruins. The splendid shores of **Isla Mujeres** (see p. 612) promise a quiet respite from the insanity as do **Isla Cozumel** (see p. 623), where coral is king and scuba is queen, and **Isla Holbox** (see p. 616), quiet keeper of the most splendid sunsets in the Western Hemisphere. Those preferring golden sand to the harsh white stuff should make tracks to the Southern Pacific Coast. The surfing towns of **Puerto Escondido** (see p. 481), **Puerto Ángel** (see p. 476), and **Zipolite** (see p. 478) beckon with formidable waves and scantily clad beach bums. Farther up the coast sprawls the grand old dame of beach resorts, **Acapulco** (see p. 445), complete with men in tiny briefs plunging off high cliffs. The stately duo of **Ixtapa** and **Zihuatanejo** (see p. 438) host tons of sun-worshippers, as do always popular **Puerto Vallarta** (see p. 385) and **Mazatlán** (see p. 240). Bolder beachgoers might want to stray off the beaten track and head north to some of the most overlooked—and most spectacular—beaches in the country. Discover **San Felipe** (see p. 162), on the calm Sea of Cortés, or bask beneath the stars on beautiful **Bahía de La Concepción** (see p. 169), one of the most pristine beaches in the world. For those who like things shaken—not stirred—no trip to Baja California would be complete without a quick jaunt down the peninsula to rocking **Cabo San Lucas** (see p. 184).

COLONIAL LEGACIES

The influence of Mexico's colorful history has left its imprint on the constructed landscape. If they could speak, each brick in each church in each city would tell stories of treason, murder, and conquest. The best place to begin a historical investigation is of course, **Mexico City** (see p. 75), the sprawling megalopolis with a population (25 million and counting) nearly equal to that of a medium-sized country. Check out the stately **Palacio Nacional** (see p. 101), home to Spanish viceroys and Mexican presidents, and stop by **Coyoacán** (see p. 98), where Hernán Cortés established his government and tortured the Aztec Emperor Cuauhtémoc. Heading out of *el D.F.*, visit **Cuernavaca** (see p. 332), former home of Cortés, and **Taxco** (see p. 433), the colonial silver town whose narrow, winding streets recall visions of Spain. Skip down south to the faded limestone streets of **Oaxaca** (see p. 452), birthplace of the nation's first president with indigenous roots, Benito Juárez. Swing by meticulously planned **Mérida** (see p. 580), a large Maya center converted to a modern city by the Spanish. Frolic with mummies in **Guanajuato** (see p. 304), and don't miss artsy **San Miguel de Allende** (see p. 310) or its friendly neighbor, **Dolores Hidalgo** (see p. 316), where Father Hidalgo sounded the *Grito de Dolores* (the electrifying speech calling for Mexican Independence). Relax in **San Luis Potosí** (see p. 288), the nation's wealthy silver and gold capital, before coming back down through steamy **Veracruz** (see p. 505), the first city founded by the Spanish, Mexico's main port, and the site of numerous foreign invasions. Farther inland is **Tlaxcala** (see p. 339), the city-state that collaborated with Cortés to defeat the Aztecs. Neighboring **Puebla** (see p. 348) epitomizes colonialism, with its order and rigidity embedded in the city's gridded streets and cobblestone walkways.

■ LET'S GO PICKS

BEST WAY TO WARM YOURSELF UP: On a distillery tour in **Tequila** (p. 383), where three free shots times sixteen factories will definitely bring on a flush.

BEST MOUNTAINTOP VIEW: The dazzling vista of the calm turquoise Sea of Cortés, the frothy deep-blue Pacific, and the rugged Baja peninsula from Picacho del Diablo (3086m) in **Parque Nacional Sierra San Pedro Mártir** (p. 160).

BEST PLACE TO REVEL IN DRUNKEN, LOUD, OBNOXIOUS AMERICANISM: Wearing a sombrero and downing a beer while having a photo taken atop a donkey painted like a zebra in **Tijuana** (p. 136).

BEST ONLY-IN-MEXICO ICE CREAM FLAVORS: *Chicharrón* (pork rind), *elote* (corn meal), *aguacate* (avocado), and *cerveza* (beer).

BEST PLACE TO TAKE A VERY LONG NAP: On the long, isolated and unbelievably soft sands of Playa los Algodones in **San Carlos** (p. 212).

BEST TIME TO BREAK OUT THE SHORT SHORTS: Hurling yourself off a 35m cliff while emulating the famous, half-naked **Acapulco** (p. 445) cliff divers.

BEST PLACE TO LOSE YOURSELF IN THE CROWD: Amid the 25 million residents of big, bad **Mexico City** (p. 75).

■ LET'S GO PICKS

BEST ROYAL GATHERING: The annual meeting of more than 20 million monarch butterflies from at their winter sanctuary of **El Rosario** (p. 430).

BEST DRIED UP DEAD PEOPLE: The 122 naturally mummified residents of **Guanajuato**'s (p. 304) infamous Museo de las Momias, and their sugary, *sombrero*-wearing miniatures sold outside.

BEST THIGH-MASTER SUBSTITUTE: Climbing the massive Pyramid of the Sun in the ancient and sophisticated city of **Teotihuacán** (p. 126).

BEST PLACE TO OBSERVE WILD ANIMALS IN THEIR NATURAL HABITAT: Spy on the *bronzus americanus* romping in the **Cancún** (p. 604), **Mazatlán** (p. 240), and **Cabo San Lucas** (p. 184), ecosystems.

BEST PLACE TO ADMIRE REALLY LARGE HEADS: At Parque-Museo La Venta in **Villahermosa** (p. 522), where 33 gigantic Olmec sculptures collected from throughout the Gulf Coast stare at you along a winding jungle path.

SUGGESTED ITINERARIES

SEA OF CORTÉS (3 WEEKS) Get going on the raucous shores of **Puerto Peñasco** (see p. 199). Calm down in tranquil **Bahía Kino** (see p. 208) and groove with transvestites in **Guaymas** (see p. 209). Catch a ferry from **Los Mochis** (see p. 237) to **La Paz** (see p. 175), the capital of Baja California Sur. Swing down to **San José del Cabo** for a quick rest before partying with José's brother, **Cabo San Lucas** (see p. 184) and his spring-breaking chums. Say hello to the artsy expats of **Todos Santos** (see p. 181) and stroll along the *malecón* in **Loreto** (see p. 171). Soak up some rays on the beaches of pristine **Bahía de la Concepción** (see p. 169) before visiting pretty **Mulegé** (see p. 168). Cool off in **San Ignacio** (see p. 164), and marvel at the sunsets in **Bahía de los Angeles** (see p. 161). Then pack up the 4x4 and enjoy amazing views from **Parque Nacional Sierra San Pedro Martír** (see p. 160). Improve your tan on the endless beach of **San Felipe** (see p. 155), and sleep lakeside at **Parque Nacional Constitución** (see p. 151) before rejoining *gringos* in **Ensenada** (see p. 146) and **Rosarito** (see p. 144), home of *Titanic*. Finally, share stories of your spectacular trip with drunken tourists in bawdy **Tijuana** (see p. 136).

CENTRAL MEXICO (2 WEEKS) Begin your journey in action-packed **D.F.** (see p. 75), but don't dally too long. Travel north to

SEA OF CORTÉS

Tijuana
Rosarito
Ensenada
Parque Nacional Constitución
San Felipe
Puerto Peñasco
San Pedro Martír
Bahía de los Angeles
Bahía Kino
Guaymas
Mulegé
San Ignacio
Bahía de la Concepción
Los Mochis
Loreto
Ferry
La Paz
Todos Santos
San José del Cabo
Cabo San Lucas

CENTRAL MEXICO

San Miguel de Allende
Guanajuato
Morelia
Mexico City
Tlaxcala
Puebla
Cuernavaca
Taxco
Zihuatenejo/Ixtapa
Acapulco

peaceful **Tlaxcala** (see p. 339) before moving on to bustling **Puebla** (see p. 348), with its immense cathedral and colonial streets. Relive old memories at Cortés's palace in **Cuernavaca** (see p. 332), before practicing your haggling skills as you banter with silver vendors in **Taxco** (see p. 433). Cool yourself down and enjoy the bronzed bodies in sunny **Acapulco** (see p. 445), and continue up the coast to the beautiful beachside duo of **Zihuatenejo** and **Ixtapa** (see p. 438). Head back inland to the stately colonial city of **Morelia** (see p. 422), and kick back with backpacking language students in lively **Guanajuato** (see p. 304) before chatting it up with retired North American expatriates in the intellectual town of **San Miguel de Allende** (see p. 310). Finally, wrap it all up with a few more days in **el capital.**

YUCATÁN AND CHIAPAS (3 WEEKS)

Kick things off with some alcohol-drenched nights in **Cancún** (see p. 604), and recover on the peaceful shores of **Isla Mujeres** (see p. 612). Back on the peninsula, don't miss the cavernous *cenotes* of **Valladolid** (see p. 597) on your way to the ruins of **Chichén Itzá** (see p. 591). Rest those aching legs in hammock-filled **Mérida** (see p. 580). Traverse the **Ruta Puuc** (see p. 573) and dance in plazas within the walls of **Campeche** (see p. 566). Venturing south into the Chiapan jungle, summit the soaring temples of **Palenque** (see p. 551). Head

west to the sprawling capital **Tuxtla Gutiérrez** (see p. 534), home of the best zoo in Latin American and a base from which to explore the green walls of the **Sumidero Canyon** (see p. 539). Chat with fellow travelers and discover **San Cristóbal de las Casas** (see p. 540). Back on the Yucatán Peninsula, dally in **Chetumal** (see p. 637) and peruse its world-class museum, while mesmerizing **Tulum** (see p. 630) beckons. Toast the trip in lively **Playa del Carmen** (see p. 618) before returning to crazy **Cancún.**

BEST OF MEXICO (4 WEEKS)

Start your trip in **Chihuahua** (see p. 222). Ride the thrilling train through the **Copper Canyon** (see p. 232) and into **Los Mochis** (see p. 237). Hop on a ferry for a quick trip to **La Paz** (see p. 175) and skip down the coast to rocking **Cabo San Lucas** (see p. 184) before heading back across the Sea of Cortés to the golden sands of **Mazatlán** (see p. 240) and **Puerto Vallarta** (see p. 385). After relaxing for a second or two, take off for busy **Guadalajara** (see p. 369), and continue to **Zihuatenejo** and **Ixtapa** (see p. 438). Shop-till-you-drop in **Taxco** (see p. 433) and practice your Spanish in **Cuernavaca** (see p. 332). Stay for a couple of days in cosmopolitan **Mexico City** (see p. 75) before hitting equally sophisticated **Puebla** (see p. 348). **Veracruz** (see p. 505), Mexico's steamy port, is next. If things get too hot, head to stately **Oaxaca** (see p. 452). Coming back north, stop by **Palenque** (see p. 551), en route to colonial **Mérida** (see p. 580). Finally, swing through **Chichén Itzá** (see p. 591) before engaging in some **Cancún** (see p. 604) mischief.

YUCATÁN AND CHIAPAS

Cancún
Isla Mujeres
Mérida
Playa del Carmen
Chichén Itzá
Valladolid
Tulum
Campeche
Chetumal
Palenque
Tuxtla Gutiérrez
San Cristóbal de las Casas

BEST OF MEXICO

Chihuahua
Copper Canyon
La Paz
Los Mochis
Mazatlán
Cabo San Lucas
Cuernavaca
Mexico City
Cancún
Guadalajara
Puebla
Mérida
Chichén Itzá
Puerto Vallarta
Veracruz
Zihuatenejo/Ixtapa
Taxco
Oaxaca
Palenque

ESSENTIALS

FACTS FOR THE TRAVELER
DOCUMENTS AND FORMALITIES

ENTRANCE REQUIREMENTS
Passport (p. 6). Recommended for citizens of the US, Canada, and Japan. Required for citizens of Australia, Ireland, New Zealand, South Africa, the UK, and most other countries.
Visa (p. 9). Visas are not required for citizens of the US, Canada, and most EU countries. Citizens of countries in Eastern Europe, Africa, and Asia need visas, as do individuals entering the country for work or extended study.
Inoculations (p. 17). None required, but some are recommended for travelers to more rural and humid parts of the country.
Driving Licenses and Permits (p. 9). All foreign licenses are accepted. Insurance is recommended. A **Vehicle Permit** (p. 11) is required to bring an automobile more than 22km into Mexico.

MEXICAN SERVICES ABROAD

EMBASSIES AND CONSULATES
Embassies: Australia, 14 Perth Ave., Yarralumla, Canberra 2600 ACT (☎02 6273 3905; fax 6273 1190; www.embassyofmexicoinaustralia.org); **Canada,** 45 O'Connor St. #1500, KIP 1A4 Ottawa, ON (☎613-233-8988; fax 235-9123; www.embamex-can.com); **UK,** 42 Hertford St., London W1J7JR (☎020 7499 8586; fax 20 7495 4035; www.embamex.co.uk); **US,** 1911 Pennsylvania Ave. NW, Washington, D.C. 20006 (☎202-728-1600; fax 728-1698; www.embassyofmexico.org).

Consulates: Australia, Honorary Consulate Kevin F. Kelly, 58 Godfry Terrace, Erindale, SA 5066 (☎08 8331 3764; fax 8332 7443); **Canada,** 2055 Peel #1000, H3A 1V4 Montreal, QC (☎514-288-2502; fax 288-8287; www.consulmex.qc.ca); **UK,** 8 Halkin St., London SW1 X7DW (☎020 7235 6393; fax 7235 5480; www.mexicanconsulate.org.uk); **US,** 2827 16th St. NW, Washington, D.C. 20009 (☎202-736-1000; fax 797-8458).

TOURISM OFFICES
Chicago: 300 N. Michigan Ave., 4th fl., Chicago, IL 60601 (☎312-606-9252; fax 606-9012; mgtochi@compuserve.com).

Houston: 1010 Fomdren St., Houston, TX 77096 (☎713-772-2581; fax 772-6058; mgtotx@ix.netcom.com).

London: Wakefield House, 41 Trinity Square, London EC# 4NDJ (☎020 7488 9392; fax 7265 0704; mrc@jaruz.com).

Los Angeles: 2401 W. 6th St., 5th fl., Los Angeles, CA 90057 (☎213-351-2075; fax 351-2074; 104045.3647@compuserve.com).

Miami: 1200 NW 78th Ave. #203, Miami, FL 33126 (☎305-718-4091; fax 718-4098; mgtomia@gate.net).

Montreal: 1 Place Ville Marie, #1931, Montreal, QC H3B 2B5 (☎514-871-1052; fax 871-3825; turimex@cam.org).

New York City: 21 E. 63rd St., 3rd fl., New York, NY 10021 (☎212-821-0314; fax 821-0367; milmgto@interport.net).

Toronto: 2 Bloor St. W #1502, Toronto, ON M4W 3E2 (☎416-925-2753; fax 925-6061; mexto3@inforamp.net).

Vancouver (and Northwest US): 999 W. Hastings #1610, Vancouver, BC V6C 2W2 (☎604-669-2845; fax 669-3498; mgto@bc.sympatico.ca).

FOREIGN SERVICES IN MEXICO

EMBASSIES

Canada: Schiller 529, Col. Polanco, 11580 México D.F. (☎5724 79 00; fax 5724 79 80).

UK: Río Lerma 71, México D.F. 06500 (☎5207 2089; fax 5207 76 72).

US: Paseo de la Reforma 305, Colonia Cuauhtémoc, 06500 México D.F. (☎5209 91 00; fax 5511 99 80).

US CONSULATES

Ciudad Juárez: López Mateos 924 Nte. (☎(1) 611 30 00; fax 616 90 56).

Guadalajara: Progreso 175 (☎(3) 825 27 00; fax (3) 826 65 49).

Hermosillo: Monterrey, 141 Poniente (☎(6) 217 23 75; fax 217 25 78).

Matamoros: Primera 2002 y Azaleas (☎(8) 812 44 02; fax (8) 812 21 71).

Mérida: Paseo Montejo 453 (☎(9) 925 50 11; fax (9) 925 6219).

Monterrey: Constitución 411, Poniente 64000 (☎(8) 345 21 20).

Nogales: San José s/n, Fracc. Alamos (☎(6) 313 48 20; fax 313 46 52).

Nuevo Laredo: Calle Allende 3330, Col. Jardín (☎(8) 714 05 12; fax (8) 714 79 84).

Tijuana: Tapachula No. 96, Colonia Hipódromo (☎(6) 681 74 00; fax (6) 681 80 16).

PASSPORTS

Citizens of Australia, New Zealand, South Africa, the UK, and most EU countries need valid passports to enter Mexico and to re-enter their own country. Mexico does not allow entrance if the holder's passport expires in fewer than six months; returning home with an expired passport is illegal and may result in a fine. It is recommended that citizens of the US, Canada, and Japan carry a valid passport, but proof of citizenship (such as an official birth certificate, naturalization certificate, consular report of birth abroad, or a certificate of citizenship) and a photo ID will also be accepted. A passport, however, carries much more authority than does a birth certificate, makes returning home by air easier, and is mandatory for anyone traveling from Mexico to Central America.

PHOTOCOPIES. Be sure to photocopy the page of your passport with your photo, passport number, and other identifying information, as well as any visas, travel insurance policies, plane tickets, and traveler's check serial numbers. Carry one set of copies in a safe place, apart from the originals, and leave another set at home. Consulates also recommend that you carry an expired passport or an official copy of your birth certificate in a part of your baggage separate from other documents.

LOST PASSPORTS. If you lose your passport, immediately notify the local police and the nearest embassy or consulate of your home government. To expedite its replacement, you will need to know all information previously recorded and show ID and proof of citizenship. In some cases, a replacement may take weeks to process, and it may be valid only for a limited time. Any visas stamped in your old passport will be irretrievably lost. In an emergency, ask for immediate temporary traveling papers that will permit you to re-enter your home country. Your passport is a public document belonging to your nation's government. You may have to surrender it to a foreign government official, but if you don't get it back in a reasonable amount of time, inform the nearest mission of your home country.

NEW PASSPORTS. Citizens of Australia, Canada, Ireland, New Zealand, the UK, and the US can apply for a passport at the nearest post office, passport office, or court of law. Citizens of South Africa can apply for a passport at the nearest office of Foreign Affairs. Any new passport or renewal applications must be filed well in advance of the departure date, although most passport offices offer rush services for a very steep fee. Citizens living abroad who need a passport or renewal services should contact the nearest consular service of their home country.

Australia: (☎ 13 12 32; passports.australia@dfat.gov.au; www.passports.gov.au). Apply at a post office, passport office, or overseas diplomatic mission.

Canada: Canadian Passport Office, Department of Foreign Affairs and International Trade, Ottawa, ON K1A OG3 (☎ 800-267-6788; www.dfait-maeci.gc.ca/passport). Applications available at passport offices, Canadian missions, and post offices.

Ireland: Pick up an application from a *Garda* station, post office, or passport office and mail it to the **Department of Foreign Affairs,** Passport Office, Molesworth St., Dublin 2 (☎ 01 671 1633; fax 671 1092; www.irlgov.ie/iveagh).

New Zealand: Passport Office, Department of International Affairs, P.O. Box 10526, Wellington, New Zealand (☎ 0800 22 50 50 or 4 474 8100; fax 4 474 8010; www.passports.govt.nz; passports@dia.govt.nz).

South Africa: Department of Home Affairs. Passports are issued only in Pretoria, but all applications must still be submitted or forwarded to the nearest South African consulate. Processing can take 3 months or more. For more information, check out http://usaembassy.southafrica.net/VisaForms/Passport/Passport2000.html.

United Kingdom: (☎ 0870 521 0410; www.open.gov.uk/ukpass/ukpass.htm). Get an application from a passport office, main post office, travel agent, or online at www.ukpa.gov.uk/forms/f_app_pack.htm.

United States: (☎ 202-647-0518; www.travel.state.gov/passport_services.html). Apply at any federal or state courthouse, authorized post office, or US Passport Agency.

OTHER FORMS OF IDENTIFICATION

When you travel, always carry two or more forms of identification on your person, including at least one photo ID; a passport combined with a driver's license or birth certificate is usually adequate. Many establishments, especially banks, may require several IDs in order to cash traveler's checks. Never carry all your forms of ID together; split them up in case of theft or loss.

For more information on all the forms of identification listed below, contact the organization that provides the service, the International Student Travel Confederation (ISTC), Herengracht 479, 1017 BS Amsterdam, Netherlands (☎ +31 20-421 28 00; fax 421 2810; istcinfo@istc.org; www.istc.org).

TEACHER & STUDENT IDENTIFICATION. The **International Student Identity Card (ISIC),** the most widely accepted form of student ID, provides discounts on sights, accommodations, food, and transport. The ISIC is preferable to an institution-specific card (such as a university ID) because it is more likely to be recognized (and honored) abroad. All cardholders have access to a 24hr. emergency helpline for medical, legal, and financial emergencies (in North America call 877-370-ISIC), and holders of US-issued cards are also eligible for insurance benefits (see **Insurance,** p. 21). Many student travel agencies issue ISICs, including STA Travel in Australia and New Zealand; Travel CUTS in Canada; usit in the Republic of Ireland and Northern Ireland; SASTS in South Africa; Campus Travel and STA Travel in the UK; Council Travel (www.counciltravel.com/idcards/default.asp) and STA Travel in the US (see p. 31).

The card is valid from September of one year to December of the following year and costs US$22. Applicants must be degree-seeking students of a secondary or post-secondary school and must be at least 12 years of age. Because of the proliferation of fake ISICs, some services (particularly airlines) require additional proof of student identity, such as a school ID or a letter attesting to your student status, signed by your registrar and stamped with your school seal. The **International Teacher Identity Card (ITIC)** offers the same insurance coverage as well as similar but limited discounts. The fee is AUS$13, UK£5, or US$22.

ESSENTIALS

YOUTH IDENTIFICATION. The International Student Travel Confederation also issues a discount card to travelers who are 26years old or under, but are not students. This one-year **International Youth Travel Card** (**IYTC;** formerly the **GO 25** card) offers many of the same benefits as the ISIC. Most organizations that sell the ISIC also sell the IYTC (US$22).

VISAS AND PERMITS

Unless you're a North American tourist visiting for fewer than six months, it's a good idea to check with the nearest Mexican consulate or embassy for exact entry requirements. Checking beforehand is particularly important for those seeking to enter for human rights purposes; the political uprisings in Chiapas have made many Mexicans sensitive to meddling foreigners, and many have been detained, expelled, or deported for violating their tourist visa status or allegedly interfering in the country's internal politics. Also note that children traveling into Mexico may have to present special papers (see **Travelers with Children,** p. 39).

TOURIST CARDS (FOLLETO DE MIGRACIÓN TURISTICA)

All persons, regardless of nationality, must carry a **tourist card** (**FMT,** Folleto de Migración Turistica) on their person in addition to proof of citizenship. Most tourist cards are good for up to 180 days; some, however, are only good for 30 days or for a shorter pre-determined length. If you need to leave and re-enter the country during your stay, make sure your tourist card will enable you to do so; you might have to ask for a multiple-entry permit. US and Canadian citizens don't need the tourist card if they are staying in the country for less than 72 hours or intend to stay within the 22km US-Mexico border zone. When traveling into the country by plane, the US$18 tourist card fee is included in the airline ticket price, and the tourist card will be given to you to fill out during your flight. If driving into Mexico, you will be charged the fee at your point of entry. You can avoid any delays by obtaining one from a Mexican consulate or tourist office before you leave (see **Embassies and Consulates,** p. 5).

 DON'T LEAVE HOME WITHOUT IT. Because you may be asked to present your tourist card when leaving the country, you must keep it for the duration of your trip. Keep it along with your other valuables in a safe place.

TOURIST VISAS

Tourist visas are **not necessary** for citizens of Australia, Canada, New Zealand, the UK, the US, and most EU and Latin American countries for stays of up to 180 days; the tourist card is sufficient. Individuals with Eastern European, Asian, African, or Middle Eastern citizenship must procure a tourist visa from the nearest Mexican consulate before traveling; in order to do so, a valid passport, a valid I-94 form, three passport photographs, and evidence of a round-trip ticket are necessary. A consular fee of US$36 may also be charged, depending upon nationality.

BUSINESS VISAS

Under the North American Free Trade Agreement (NAFTA), US and Canadian citizens can enter Mexico to conduct business for up to 30 days with a **FM-N permit** (free). To do so, travelers must prove they are traveling on international business and that their pay is coming from a non-Mexican source; a letter from their company or firm in addition to a valid passport will suffice. Business travelers planning on staying longer than 30 days will have to apply for an **FM-3 permit** (consular fee of US$88), which is good for up to one year.

STUDENT VISAS

Students interested in studying in Mexico for longer than 180 days must obtain a student visa from their nearest Mexican consulate. In order to do so, they must submit the acceptance letter from the school they wish to attend along with sev-

ESSENTIALS

eral photographs, a statement proving economic solvency, and a certificate of good health. Those studying under a specific program must also submit a letter from the sponsoring organization. The consular fee depends on nationality and bureaucratic procedure; citizens of some nationalities might have to pay a US$28 fee. Note that students planning on studying for less than six months may enter the country with a normal tourist visa or tourist card.

RETIREMENT VISAS

Seeking a temperate climate and favorable exchange rates, many foreigners have chosen Mexico as their place of retirement. Those whose retirement income comes from abroad may seek the classification of **no immigrant-restista** (retired non-immigrant). Those interested in settling down in Mexico must contact the nearest consular office for an **FM-3 permit** (US$96) and present a valid passport, several photographs, proof of economic solvency, and other documents. The FM-3 visa will be good for 30 days, whereupon retirees must go to a immigration office in Mexico, prove solvency, and receive another stamp on their FM-3 permit, which must be renewed every couple of years. After 10 years, status changes to **FM-2** status, non-immigrant resident.

CUSTOMS

ENTERING MEXICO

BY CAR

Crossing into Mexico by land can be as uneventful or as complicated as the border guards want it to be. You may be waved into the country or directed to the immigration office to procure a tourist card (FMT) if you don't have one already. Make sure all papers are in order before proceeding; if there is anything amiss when you reach an immigration checkpoint 22km into the interior, you'll have to turn back.

If you plan on driving into Mexico, you will need to obtain a **vehicle permit** at the border. Permits are US$11 when you pay with a valid credit card. Those without credit cards will have to provide a cash deposit or bond worth thousands of dollars, depending on the value of the car. Your deposit will be repaid in full when you return across the border, but paying the minimal fee by credit card is strongly advised. To extend a vehicle permit beyond its original expiration date and to avoid confiscation, contact the temporary importation department of Mexican customs. The maximum length granted to tourists is six months. A vehicle permit is valid only for the person to whom it was issued unless another driver is approved by the federal registry. Violation of this law can result in confiscation of the vehicle or heavy fines. In order to get a permit, you will need an original copy and a photocopy of several documents: a state vehicle registration certificate and vehicle title, a tourist entry form (FME, FMT, FM6, FM3), a valid driver's license accompanied by either a passport or a birth certificate, and a Mexican insurance policy, which can be purchased at the border. If leasing a vehicle, you must provide the contract in your name (also in duplicate). **Vehicle permits are not needed if you do not plan to travel more than 22km past the border.** Furthermore, only legitimate drivers may purchase car-ferry tickets. Regulations change frequently; for updated information, contact a consulate.

 HAPPINESS IS A WARM GUN Mexico has severe penalties for those carrying weapons or firearms into the country, and many foreigners have been incarcerated for violating firearms regulations. If you are entering Mexico to hunt, you must contact the nearest Mexican consulate and your local police department *before* your visit to obtain written permission and proof of gun ownership. Trying to bring a weapon into Mexico is, however, more hassle than it's worth, and it can get you into big trouble. To ease your travels, please leave the gun at home.

BY AIR

Entering Mexico by air is somewhat easier. Dash out of your plane as fast as possible to beat the rush to *aduana* (customs). Beware that agents randomly examine luggage using a press-your-luck light system; unless you want the entire airport to see that rhinestone g-string, leave it at home—or, better yet, wear it.

Mexican regulations limit the value of goods brought into Mexico by US citizens arriving by air or sea to US$300 per person and by land to $50 per person. Amounts exceeding the duty-free limit are subject to a 32.8% tax.

LEAVING MEXICO

Upon returning home, you must declare all articles acquired abroad and pay a **duty** on the value of those articles that exceed the allowance established by your country's customs service. Goods and gifts purchased at **duty-free** shops abroad are not exempt from duty or sales tax at your point of return; you must declare these items as well. ("Duty-free" merely means that you do not have to pay a tax in the country of purchase.) To establish the value when you return home, keep receipts for items purchased abroad. Since you pay no duty on goods brought from home, record the serial numbers of any expensive items (cameras, computers, radios, etc.) you are taking with you before you begin your travels, and check with your country's customs office to see if it has a special form for registering them.

It's a very bad idea to take illegal drugs out of Mexico. If you have questions, call the **Mexican Customs Office** in the US (☎ 202-728-1669) or contact your specific embassy or consulate. In the north, especially along the Pacific coast, expect to be stopped repeatedly by burly, humorless troopers looking for contraband. That innocent-looking hitchhiker you were kind enough to pick up may be a drug peddler with a stash of illegal substances. If the police catch it in your car, the drug possession charges will extend to you, and your car may be confiscated. If you carry **prescription drugs** while you travel, it is vital to have a copy of the prescriptions themselves and a note from a doctor readily accessible at country borders.

Note that when entering the US, you may be hassled by immigration officers if you are a minority or resident alien of the US, or simply have a Latino surname.

MORE RESOURCES

Australia: Australian Customs National Information Line (☎ 1300 363 263; www.customs.gov.au).

Canada: Canadian Customs, 2265 St. Laurent Blvd., Ottawa, ON K1G 4K3 (☎ 800-461-9999; www.revcan.ca).

Ireland: Customs Information Office, Irish Life Centre, Lower Abbey St., Dublin 1 (☎ 01 878 8811; fax 878 0836; taxes@revenue.iol.ie).

New Zealand: New Zealand Customhouse, 17-21 Whitmore St., Box 2218, Wellington (☎ 04 473 6099; fax 473 7370; www.customs.govt.nz).

South Africa: Commissioner for Customs and Excise, Privat Bag X47, Pretoria 0001 (☎ 12 314 9911; fax 328 6478; www.gov.za).

United Kingdom: Her Majesty's Customs and Excise, Passenger Enquiry Team, Wayfarer House, Great South West Road, Feltham, Middlesex TW14 8NP (☎ 0845 010 9000; www.hmce.gov.uk).

United States: US Customs Service, 1330 Pennsylvania Ave. NW, Washington, D.C. 20229 (☎ 202-354-1000; fax 354-1010; www.customs.gov).

MONEY

If you stay in cheap hotels, diet rigorously, and avoid sights and attractions, expect to spend US$6-15 per person per day. A less stingy (but substantially happier) traveler, depending on his or her level of extravagance, might expect to spend about $20-35 traveling in less touristed areas and about $35-50 near the US border or in resort areas. Prices for hotels start at about $7 per night for a single and can increase dramatically. A basic sit-down meal will cost around $3.

CURRENCY AND EXCHANGE

The currency chart below is based on June 2001 exchange rates. For the latest exchange rates, check a newspaper or consult the internet (e.g. http://finance.yahoo.com, www.bloomberg.com, or www.letsgo.com/Thumb).

CURRENCY		
US$1 = 9.1 PESOS	1 PESO = US$0.11	
CND$1 = 5.9 PESOS	1 PESO = CDN$0.17	
UK£ = 13.1 PESOS	1 PESO = UK£0.08	
AUS$1 = 4.9 PESOS	1 PESO = AUS$0.21	
NZ$ = 4.0 PESOS	1 PESO = NZ$0.25	
ZAR$1 = 1.1 PESOS	1 PESO = ZAR$0.92	

International Currency Express (☎888-278-6628) delivers foreign currency or traveler's checks 2nd-day at competitive exchange rates for a US $12 fee.

Changing money in Mexico is easy in all but the most rural areas, where banks might be scarce or have limited hours. The more money you change at a time, the less you will lose to commission. Also keep in mind that while all banks exchange dollars for pesos, some might not accept other currencies; foreign travelers of all nationalities would be wise to keep some US dollars on hand. **Casas de Cambio** (currency exchange booths) may offer better exchange rates than banks and are usually open as long as the stores near which they do business. In most towns, the exchange rates at hotels, restaurants, and airports are extremely unfavorable. Avoid them unless it's an emergency.

TRAVELER'S CHECKS

Traveler's checks are one of the safest means of carrying funds in Mexico. Travel agencies and banks will sell them for a small commission. Each agency provides refunds if your checks are lost or stolen, and many provide additional services, such as toll-free refund hotlines abroad, emergency message services, and stolen credit card assistance.

While traveling, keep check receipts and a record of which checks you've cashed separate from the checks themselves. Also leave a list of check numbers with someone at home. Never countersign checks until you're ready to cash them, and always bring your passport with you to cash them. If your checks are lost or stolen, immediately contact the company that issued your checks to be reimbursed; they may require a police report verifying the loss or theft. Less-touristed cities may not have refund centers at all, in which case you may have to wait to be reimbursed.

Exchanging traveler's checks in Mexico is fairly easy. Remember however, that some places (especially in northern Mexico) are accustomed to US dollars and will accept no substitute. It might also be difficult to exchange traveler's checks in the more rural parts of Mexico and other less touristed places. Finally, it's probably best to buy most of your checks in small denominations (US$20) to minimize your losses at times when you can't avoid a bad exchange rate. Purchase checks in US dollars; many *casas de cambio* refuse to change other currencies.

American Express: Australia (☎800 25 19 02), New Zealand (☎0800 441 068), UK (☎0800 521 313), US and Canada (☎800-221-7282; www.aexp.com). *Cheques for Two* can be signed by either of 2 people traveling together.

Citicorp: (US and Canada ☎800-645-6556, elsewhere call US collect +1 813-623-17090.) Traveler's checks (available in US dollars, British pounds, and German marks) at 1-2% commission.

Thomas Cook MasterCard: (US and Canada ☎800-223-737, UK ☎0800 62 21 01, elsewhere call UK collect +44 1733 31 89 50.) Checks available in 13 currencies at 2% commission. Thomas Cook offices cash checks commission-free.

Visa: (US ☎800-227-6811, UK ☎0800 89 50 78, elsewhere call UK collect +44 20 7937 8091). Call for the location of their nearest office.

ESSENTIALS

ESSENTIALS

CREDIT CARDS

Credit cards are accepted by all but the smallest Mexican businesses. **Visa** (US ☎ 800-336-8472) and **MasterCard** (US ☎ 800-307-7309) are the most readily accepted. **American Express** (US ☎ 800-843-2273) is also accepted; holders may cash personal checks at AmEx offices abroad, access an emergency medical and legal assistance hotline (24hr.; call collect to the US +1 202-554-2639), and enjoy American Express Travel Service benefits. All major cards can be used to get **cash advances,** which allow you to withdraw pesos from networked banks and ATMs throughout Mexico. Credit card companies get the wholesale exchange rate, which is generally 5% better than the retail rate used by banks and other currency exchange establishments. Transaction fees and sky-high interest rates for all credit card advances (up to US$10 per advance, plus 2-3% extra on foreign transactions after conversion), tend, however, to make credit cards a more costly way of withdrawing cash than ATMs or traveler's checks. In an emergency, however, the transaction fee may prove worth the cost. To be eligible for an advance, you'll need to get a Personal Identification Number (PIN) from your credit card company.

ATM (CASH) CARDS

Automated Teller Machine (ATM) use is widespread in Mexico, and all but the smallest towns have ATMs in central locations, such as in the town *zócalo*, near commercial areas, or in large supermarkets. Most large banks (such as Bancomer and Serfin) also have ATMs outside their front doors or in their main lobbies. ATMs get the same wholesale exchange rate as credit cards, but there might be a limit on the amount of money you can withdraw per day (around US$500; check with your bank), and there is typically a surcharge of $1-5 per withdrawal. Be sure to memorize your PIN in numeric form since machines in Mexico often don't have letters on their keys. Also, if your PIN is longer than four digits, ask your bank whether you need a new number. The two major international money networks are **Cirrus** (US ☎ 800-424-7787) and **PLUS** (US ☎ 800-843-7587). To locate ATMs around the world, call the above numbers, or consult www.visa.com/pd/atm or www.mastercard.com/atm.

MONEY (THAT'S WHAT I WANT) While using ATMs is a convenient way to access money, travelers should take special care; thieves have been known to lurk around ATMs and rob individuals at the machine or shortly after they have used it. Exercise caution. Don't flash your ATM card. Use ATM machines during the day, inside commercial establishments or well-lit and busy areas. Transactions made outdoors or at night are much more likely to attract thieves.

GETTING MONEY FROM HOME

The cheapest way to receive money in Mexico is to have it sent through a large commercial bank to associated banks in Mexico. The sender must either have an account with the bank or bring in cash or a money order. If the sender can supply the bank with exact information on the recipient's passport number and the Mexican bank address, the cabled money should arrive in one to three days; otherwise, there will be significant delays. Other options are listed below.

AMERICAN EXPRESS. Cardholders can withdraw cash from their checking accounts at any of AmEx's major offices and many representative offices (up to US$1000 every 21 days; no service charge, no interest). "Express Cash" withdrawals from any AmEx ATM are automatically debited from the cardholder's checking account or line of credit. Green card holders may withdraw up to $1000 in any seven-day period (2% transaction fee: minimum $2.50, maximum $20). To enroll in Express Cash, cardmembers may call 800-227-4669 within the US; elsewhere call the US collect +1 336-668-5041. The AmEx number in Mexico is 5326 26 26.

WESTERN UNION. Travelers from the US, Canada, and the UK can wire money abroad through Western Union's international money transfer services. In the US, call 800-325-6000; in Canada, 800-235-0000; in the UK, 0800 83 38 33; in Mexico 5546 7361. The rates for sending cash are generally US$10-11 cheaper than with a credit card, and the money is usually available at the place you're sending it within an hour. For the nearest location, consult www.westernunion.com.

FEDERAL EXPRESS. Some people choose to send cash abroad via FedEx to avoid transmission fees and taxes. While FedEx is reasonably reliable, note that this method is illegal. In the US and Canada, FedEx can be reached by calling 800-463-3339; in the UK, 0800 12 38 00; in Ireland, 800 535 800; in Australia, 13 26 10; in New Zealand, 0800 733 339; and in South Africa, 011 923 8000.

US STATE DEPARTMENT (US CITIZENS ONLY). In dire emergencies only, the US State Department will forward money during normal business hours to the nearest consular office, which will then disburse it, according to instructions, for a US$15 fee. If you wish to use this service, you must contact the Overseas Citizens Service division of the US State Department (☎202-647-5225; nights, Sundays, and holidays ☎202-647-4000).

TIPPING AND BARGAINING

Ah, the age-old question: To tip or not to tip? In Mexico, it can be hard to know what to do. Overly eager tipping can be offensive (never, for example, throw a couple of pesos at someone you just asked for directions), but many people make their livings assisting tourists in exchange for tips. In general, anyone who offers a service and then awkwardly waits around afterward is expecting a tip. In a restaurant, waiters are tipped based on the quality of service; **good service deserves at least 15%.** Cab drivers are generally not tipped, as they do not run on meters. Regardless of the quality of service, never leave without saying *"gracias."*

In Mexico, skillful bargaining separates the savvy budget traveler from the timid tourist. If you're unsure whether bargaining is appropriate, observe the locals and follow their lead. A working knowledge of Spanish will help convince the seller that you are a serious bargainer, and you will be rewarded with a better deal. When hailing a cab, settle the price of the ride beforehand, lest you get pegged as a tourist and get charged exorbitantly.

KNOW WHEN TO WALK AWAY, KNOW WHEN TO RUN Buying quality crafts sometimes requires special knowledge. When buying **turquoise,** ask the vendor to put the rocks to the "lighter test." Plastic or synthetic material will quickly melt under the flame. When buying **silver,** examine the pieces closely and look for a stamp with the number **.925** on the underside. This stamp indicates that the silver is sterling (i.e. it is at least 925 parts per 1000 pure). If there's no number, the piece might be inferior silver—silver-plated or silver *alpaca* (nickel silver). If sterling's what you're looking for, walk away.

SAFETY AND SECURITY

Mexico is relatively safe, although, like many other countries undergoing economic recessions, dire circumstances have led to increased crime, particularly against tourists. While most is of the petty and annoying variety—pick pocketings, purse-snatchings, etc.—violent and brutal attacks on tourists are reportedly on the rise. Exercise caution; common sense precautions and heightened alertness can help you avoid dangerous situations.

VALUABLES. To prevent theft, don't keep all your valuables (money, important documents) in one place. **Photocopies** of important documents allow you to recover them in case they are lost or pilfered. Bring one copy separate from the documents and leave another at home. Carry as little money as possible, keep some aside to use in an emergency, and never count your money in public. **Don't put a wallet with money in your back pocket.** If you carry a purse, buy a sturdy one

ESSENTIALS

TRAVEL ADVISORIES. The following government offices provide travel information and advisories by telephone, by fax, or via the web.

Australian Department of Foreign Affairs and Trade: (☎2 6261 3305; www.dfat.gov.au).

Canadian Department of Foreign Affairs and International Trade (DFAIT): (800-267-6788; www.dfait-maeci.gc.ca). Call for their free booklet, *Bon Voyage...But.*

New Zealand Ministry of Foreign Affairs: (☎04 494 8500; fax 494 8511; www.mft.govt.nz/trav.html).

United Kingdom Foreign and Commonwealth Office: (☎020 7008 0232; fax 7008 0155; www.fco.gov.uk).

US Department of State: (http://travel.state.gov). For travel emergencies, call 202-647-5225. For a copy of *A Safe Trip Abroad,* call 202-512-1800. US citizens can also refer to the State Department's pamphlet, *Tips for Travelers to Mexico,* which is available by mail from the Superintendent of Documents, US Government Printing Office, Washington, D.C. 20402.

with a secure clasp, and carry it crosswise on the side, away from the street with the clasp against you. Secure packs with small combination **padlocks** that slip through the two zippers. A **money belt,** a nylon, zippered pouch with a belt that sits inside the waist of your pants or skirt, combines convenience and security; you can buy one at most camping supply stores. A **neck pouch** is equally safe, but refrain from pulling it out in public. Avoid keeping anything precious in a fanny-pack (even if it's worn on your stomach); your valuables will be highly visible and easy to steal.

ALCOHOL. Mexicans are fed up with foreigners who cross the border for nights of debauchery, so avoid public drunkenness—it is against the law and could land you in jail. Drinking is unsafe for other reasons. The US State Department warns of tourists—almost always traveling alone—at nightclubs or bars who have been drugged or intoxicated and then robbed, abducted, and/or raped.

DRUGS. Contrary to international opinion, Mexico rigorously prosecutes drug cases. A minimum jail sentence awaits anyone found guilty of possessing any drug, and Mexican law does not distinguish between marijuana and other narcotics. Even if you aren't convicted, getting arrested and tried will be long and incredibly unpleasant. The Mexican judicial process assumes you are guilty until proven innocent, and it is not uncommon to be detained for a year before a verdict is reached. Foreigners and suspected drug traffickers are never released on bail. Ignorance of Mexican law is no excuse, and a flimsy "Man, I didn't know it was illegal" won't get you out of jail. If you are arrested, there is little your embassy can do other than inform your relatives and bring care packages to you in jail. (For information on how to address those packages, see **Post and Communications,** p. 25.)

OTHER AREAS OF CONCERN

Mexico is a fairly safe country, provided you pay attention to your surroundings and take all common sense precautions. However, there are certain areas of the country where special care is advised.

MEXICO CITY. Mexico City, like most bloated metropolitan areas, has more than its share of crime; in fact, it has the highest crime rate in the country. But before you cancel your visit to *el D.F.*, keep in mind that most crimes against tourists fall under the category of **petty street crime**—muggings, pick pocketings, and purse-snatchings. Although the government has prided itself on reducing crime in the city, visitors to the capital should still exercise extreme caution, particularly on public transportation. For more information on safety in Mexico City, see p. 89.

CIUDAD JUÁREZ. Because of its position along the US border, the narcotics trade has flourished in Ciudad Juárez. Many foreigners involved in the trade have been kidnapped and/or murdered. The US State Department urges special caution for those visiting the entertainment district west of Av. Juárez.

CANCÚN. Cancún, an international tourist mecca, has drawn pickpockets and petty thieves from all over the country. Muggings, purse-snatchings, and hotel-room burglaries are on the rise. Use common sense and protect your valuables. A relatively new phenomenon are the sexual assaults and rapes that occur in the early morning hours in the Zona Hotelera. Intoxicated clubbers are separated from friends and then attacked. Such assaults, while few and far between, are on the rise. There have also been reports of increased police harassment and abuse.

CHIAPAS. Recent Zapatista activity has meant that tourists need to be especially careful when traveling in Chiapas. While the Mexican government has brought much of the area under control, armed rebels are occasionally active in the highlands north of San Cristóbal de las Casas, Ocosingo, and in the jungles east of Comitan. These rebels have in the past been openly hostile toward foreigners.

GUERRERO AND OAXACA. Due to political unrest in the rural parts of these states, visitors might encounter roadblocks and increased military presence. If your bus or car is pulled over, be prepared to show ID. There is no evidence, however, that the insurgent groups, the Popular Revolutionary Army and the Insurgent People's Revolutionary Army, have targeted tourists or will begin to do so.

BEACHES. Sadly, crime has infested even the most beautiful and pristine parts of the country, and tourists have not escaped attack. As tempting as it sounds, stay away from hidden or secluded beaches, unless they are known to be especially safe. If you are going to the beach, it's a good idea to go during the afternoon or during weekends, when families and visitors are more numerous and beaches aren't so empty. Several US citizens have been killed while frolicking alone on beaches; some of these attacks happened during the morning hours. Exercise caution.

HEALTH

Before you can say "pass the jalapeños," a long-anticipated vacation can turn into an unpleasant study of the wonders of the Mexican health care system. While you can't foresee everything, some careful preparation can minimize trips to the clinic.

BEFORE YOU GO

In your **passport,** write the names of any people you wish to have contacted in case of a medical emergency and list any allergies or medical conditions of which doctors should be aware. If you take prescription medicines, carry up-to-date, legible prescriptions or a statement from your doctor stating the medication's trade name, manufacturer, chemical name, and dosage. While traveling, be sure to keep all medication with you in your carry-on luggage.

IMMUNIZATIONS AND PRECAUTIONS

Visitors to Mexico do not need to carry vaccination certificates unless they are entering from South America or Africa, in which case proof of vaccination for yellow fever may be required. Despite Mexico's lax attitude toward inoculation, all travelers over two years of age should have their standard vaccines up to date and should consult a doctor for any additional recommended inoculations.

USEFUL ORGANIZATIONS AND PUBLICATIONS

The US **Centers for Disease Control and Prevention** (**CDC;** ☎877-FYI-TRIP; www.cdc.gov/travel), an excellent source of information for travelers, maintains an international fax information service. The CDC's comprehensive booklet *Health Information for International Travelers*, an annual rundown of disease, immunization, and general health advice, is free on the website or US$22 via the Govern-

ESSENTIALS

INOCULATION REQUIREMENTS. Mexico does not require visitors to carry vaccination certificates, nor does it require specific vaccinations for entry. It is advisable, however, to consult your doctor four to six weeks before departure. In addition to **booster shots for measles and tetanus,** consider the following vaccines and prescriptions:

Malaria Tablets: Chloroquinine is recommended for those traveling in rural and coastal areas in the southern half of the country.
Hepatitis A: Vaccine or immune globulin (IG).
Hepatitis B: Recommended for those planning long stays, those who might be exposed to blood, or those who plan on being sexually active.
Rabies: Recommended for those who might have contact with animals.
Typhoid Fever: Recommended for those traveling to rural areas only.

ment Printing Office (☎202-512-1800). The **US State Department** (http:// travel.state.gov) compiles consular information sheets on health, entry requirements, and other issues for various countries. For quick information on health and other travel warnings, call the **Overseas Citizens' Services** (☎202-647-5225), contact a US passport agency or a US embassy or consulate abroad, or send a self-addressed, stamped envelope to the Overseas Citizens' Services, Bureau of Consular Affairs #4811, US Department of State, Washington, D.C. 20520. For information on medical evacuation services and travel insurance firms, see http://travel.state.gov/medical.html. The **British Foreign and Commonwealth Office** also gives health warnings for individual countries (www.fco.gov.uk).

For detailed information on travel health, including a country-by-country overview of diseases, try the **International Travel Health Guide,** by Dr. Stuart Rose (Travel Medicine, $15; www.travmed.com).

MEDICAL ASSISTANCE ON THE ROAD

The quality of medical care in Mexico often varies directly with the size of the city or town. The same applies to the availability of English-speaking medical practitioners. Medical care in Mexico City is first-class, while care in more rural areas can be spotty and limited. Along with the town clinic or Red Cross, local pharmacies can be invaluable sources of medical help. Most pharmacists are knowledgeable about mild illnesses—particularly those that plague tourists—and can recommend shots or medicines. Wherever possible, *Let's Go* lists pharmacies open for extended hours. If none are listed, ask a policeman or cab driver.

If you are concerned about access to medical support while traveling, there are special support services you may employ. The *MedPass* from **Global Emergency Medical Services (GEMS),** 2001 Westside Dr. #120, Alpharetta, GA 30004, USA (☎800-860-1111; fax 770-475-0058; www.globalems.com), provides 24-hour international medical assistance, support, and medical evacuation resources. The **International Association for Medical Assistance to Travelers** (**IAMAT;** US ☎716-754-4883, Canada ☎416-652-0137; www.sentex.net/~iamat) has free membership, lists English-speaking doctors worldwide, and offers detailed info on immunization requirements and sanitation. If your regular **insurance** policy does not cover travel abroad, you may wish to purchase additional coverage (see p. 21).

ON THE ROAD

ENVIRONMENTAL HAZARDS

HEAT EXHAUSTION AND DEHYDRATION. Heat exhaustion, characterized by dehydration and salt deficiency, can lead to fatigue, headaches, and wooziness. Avoid it by drinking plenty of fluids, eating salty foods (e.g. crackers), and avoiding dehydrating beverages (e.g. alcohol, coffee, tea, and caffeinated soda). Continuous heat stress can eventually lead to heatstroke, characterized by a rising body temperature, severe headache, and cessation of sweating. Victims should be cooled off with wet towels and taken to a doctor. The risk of heat exhaustion is greatest in Baja California and northern Mexico, where the combination of heat and dryness can result in rapid water loss.

SUNBURN. Bring sunscreen with you and apply it liberally and often to avoid burns and risk of **skin cancer**. Nowhere in Mexico are you safe from sunburn, though the risk increases as you travel toward the equator and up in altitude. If you get sunburned, drink more fluids than usual and apply an aloe-based lotion.

AIR POLLUTION. Mexico City has recently earned the distinction of having the worst air in the world for children. It's not too great for adults, either. Fortunately, many of the possible effects—wheezing, tightness in the chest, bronchitis—tend to reverse themselves once exposure stops. Unfortunately, long-term exposure can result in serious problems such as lung cancer and heart disease. To protect yourself, heed daily pollution warnings. Pollution is usually worst during the winter and in the early morning hours.

ALTITUDE SICKNESS. Many places in mountainous Mexico, including Mexico City, are high enough for altitude sickness to be a concern. Symptoms may include headaches, dizziness, and sleep disruption. To minimize possible effects, avoid rapid increases in elevation, and allow your body a couple of days to adjust to a new elevation before exerting yourself. Note that **alcohol is more potent** and UV rays stronger at high elevations.

INSECT-BORNE DISEASES

Many diseases are transmitted by insects—primarily mosquitoes, fleas, ticks, and lice. Be aware of insects in wet or forested areas, and while hiking, camping, or climbing around ruins. **Mosquitoes** are most active from dusk to dawn and are rampant along coastal areas. Use insect repellents that have a 30-35% concentration of DEET (5-10% is recommended for children). Wear long pants and long sleeves (fabric need not be thick or warm; tropic-weight cottons can keep you comfortable in the heat) and consider buying a **mosquito net** for travel in rural (especially coastal or humid) regions. Natural repellents can be useful supplements: taking vitamin B-12 pills regularly can eventually make you smelly to insects, as can garlic pills. Calamine lotion or topical cortisones (like Cortaid) may stop insect bites from itching, as can a bath with a half-cup of baking soda or oatmeal.

MALARIA. Malaria is transmitted by *Anopheles* mosquitoes that bite at night. The incubation period varies from six to eight days to as long as months. Early symptoms include fever, chills, aches, and fatigue, followed by high fever and sweating, and sometimes vomiting and diarrhea. See a doctor for any flu-like sickness that occurs after travel in a risk area. Left untreated, malaria can cause anemia, kidney failure, coma, and death. If you are visiting coastal or rural areas of Campeche, Chiapas, Guerrero, Michoacán, Nayarit, Oaxaca, Quintana Roo, Sinaloa, Tabasco, or Yucatán, consider getting a prescription for **Chloroquine.** Chloroquine may have some side effects such as nausea, headaches, and vomiting; consult your doctor. Antimalarial drugs are not recommended for travelers to the major resort areas on the Pacific and Gulf coasts or travelers to the northern parts of the country.

OTHER INSECT-BORNE DISEASES. Filariasis is a roundworm infestation transmitted by mosquitoes. Infection causes enlargement of extremities and has no vaccine. **Leishmaniasis** is a parasite transmitted by sand flies. Common symptoms are fever, weakness, and swelling of the spleen. There is a treatment, but no vaccine. **CHAGAS disease (American trypanomiasis)** is another relatively common parasite transmitted by the cone-nose and kissing bugs, which infest mud, adobe, and thatch. Its symptoms are fever, heart disease, and later on an enlarged intestine. There is no vaccine and limited treatment. All three diseases are rare and limited in range to the tropical areas of Chiapas and the Yucatán.

ESSENTIALS

ESSENTIALS

FOOD- AND WATER-BORNE DISEASES

The biggest health threats in Mexico are food and water. ■**Traveler's diarrhea,** known in Mexico as *turista*, often lasts two or three days. Symptoms include cramps, nausea, vomiting, chills, and fever. Scientifically speaking, *turista* is a temporary reaction to bacteria in new food ingredients. In plain speak, *turista* will blow your bowels inside out. **Watch what you drink and eat.**

Dirty water is enemy number one. Never drink water straight from the tap or from dubious sources, such as water fountains. Don't brush your teeth with tap water, don't rise your toothbrush under the faucet, and don't keep your mouth open in the shower. Be suspicious of the most clever disguise of impure water—the treacherous ice cube. **Drink only purified, bottled water (agua embotellada).** If you must purify your own water, bring it to a rolling boil (simmering isn't enough) and let it boil for about 30 minutes, or treat it with **iodine drops or tablets.**

If impure water is enemy number one, food is enemy number two. Stay away from those tasty-looking salads; eating uncooked vegetables (including lettuce and coleslaw) is a quick way to get *turista*. Other culprits include raw shellfish, unpasteurized milk and dairy products, and sauces containing raw eggs. Peel fruits and vegetables before eating them. Beware of food from markets or street vendors that may have been "washed" in dirty water or fried in rancid oil. Juices, peeled fruits, and exposed coconut slices are all risky. Also beware of frozen treats; they may have been made with bad water.

> **THE GOLDEN RULE IN MEXICO.** Beware of food and water. Drink only bottled water *(agua embotellada)* or purified water *(agua purificada)*. Eat food that has been boiled, peeled, or cooked. Otherwise, forget it. Remember: a careful tourist is a diarrhea-free tourist.

If you have the misfortune of developing *turista*, try quick-energy, non-sugary foods with protein and carbohydrates to keep your strength up. Good things to eat are tortillas and salted crackers. Perhaps the most dangerous side effect of *turista* is dehydration and loss of electrolytes; drink lots of (pure) water with ½ tsp. of sugar or honey and a pinch of salt, uncaffeinated soft drinks, and bottled juices. If you develop a high fever or your symptoms don't go away after 4-5 days, consult a doctor; it might be more than just *turista*. More serious diseases with *turista*-like symptoms (diarrhea, nausea, and cramps) include:

CHOLERA. Cholera is an intestinal disease caused by a bacteria found in contaminated food and water. Though most cholera outbreaks occur in developing countries in Asia and Africa, several outbreaks have been reported in Latin America. The early symptom of the disease is mild diarrhea; symptoms of more advanced stages include profuse diarrhea, dehydration, vomiting, and muscle cramps. See a doctor immediately; if left untreated, cholera may be deadly. Antibiotics are available, but the most important treatment is rehydration. The best way to avoid cholera is to be careful with water and food. A cholera vaccine (50% effective) is available but not recommended; see your doctor for more information.

HEPATITIS A. The symptoms of this viral liver infection acquired primarily through contaminated water include fatigue, fever, loss of appetite, nausea, dark urine, jaundice, vomiting, aches, and light stools. Risks are highest in rural areas, but it may be found in cities. Ask your doctor about the vaccine (Havrix or Vaqta) or an immune globulin injection (IG; formerly called gamma globulin).

TYPHOID FEVER. Caused by the salmonella bacterium, typhoid is most common in villages and rural areas in Mexico. While primarily transmitted through contaminated food and water, it may also be acquired by direct contact with an infected person. Early symptoms include fever, headaches, fatigue, loss of appetite, constipation, and sometimes a rash on the abdomen or chest. Antibiotics are available, but a vaccination (70-90% effective) is recommended.

OTHER INFECTIOUS DISEASES

RABIES. Transmitted through the saliva of infected animals, rabies is fatal if untreated. By the time symptoms appear (thirst and muscle spasms), the disease is in its terminal stage. If you are bitten, wash the wound thoroughly, seek immediate medical care, and try to have the animal located. A rabies vaccine, which consists of three shots given over a 21-day period, is available but only semi-effective.

HEPATITIS B. Hepatitis B is a viral infection of the liver transmitted via bodily fluids or needle-sharing. Symptoms may not surface until years after infection. Vaccinations are recommended for health care workers, sexually active travelers, and anyone planning to seek medical treatment abroad. The three-shot vaccination series must begin six months before traveling.

HEPATITIS C. The mode of transmission of Hepatitis C differs from its similarly-named viruses. IV drug users, those with occupational exposure to blood, hemodialysis patients, and recipients of blood transfusions are at highest risk, but the disease can also be spread through sexual contact.

WOMEN'S HEALTH

While **maxi pads** are plentiful in Mexican pharmacies and supermarkets, **tampons** are harder to come by and, if available at all, come only in regular sizes. It might be wise to bring a supply along, especially if you are traveling to smaller cities. Contraceptive devices are also hard to find, with the exception of condoms, which are found in most large pharmacies.

Abortion remains illegal in Mexico. Women considering an abortion should contact the **International Planned Parenthood Federation (IPPF),** Regent's College, Inner Circle, Regent's Park, London NW1 4NS, UK (☎ +44 020 7487 7900; fax 7487 7950; www.ippf.org), for more information.

INSURANCE

Travel insurance generally covers four basic areas: medical/health problems, property loss, trip cancellation/interruption, and emergency evacuation. Although your regular insurance policies may extend to travel-related accidents, you should consider purchasing travel insurance if the cost of potential trip cancellation/interruption or emergency medical evacuation is greater than you can absorb. Prices for travel insurance purchased separately generally run about US$50 per week for full coverage, while trip cancellation/interruption may be purchased separately at a rate of about $5.50 per $100 of coverage.

Medical insurance (especially university policies) often covers costs incurred abroad; check with your provider. **US Medicare** covers travel to Mexico. **Canadians** are protected by their home province's health insurance plan for up to 90 days after leaving the country; check with the provincial Ministry of Health or Health Plan Headquarters for details. **Homeowners' insurance** (or your family's coverage) often covers theft during travel and loss of travel documents (passport, plane ticket, railpass, etc.) up to $500.

ISIC and its cousin, **ITIC** (see p. 7), provide basic insurance benefits, including $100 per day of in-hospital sickness for up to 60 days, $3000 of accident-related medical reimbursement, and $25,000 for emergency medical transport. Cardholders have access to a toll-free 24hr. helpline for medical, legal, and financial emergencies overseas (US and Canada ☎877-370-4742, elsewhere call US collect +1 715-345-0505). **American Express** (US ☎ 800-528-4800) grants most cardholders automatic car rental insurance (collision and theft, but not liability) and ground travel accident coverage of $100,000 on flight purchases made with the card.

INSURANCE PROVIDERS. Council and **STA** (see p. 31) offer a range of plans that can supplement your basic coverage. Other private insurance providers in the **US and Canada** include: **Access America** (☎800-284-8300); **Berkely Group** (☎800-228-

9792; www.berkely.com); **Carefree Travel Insurance** (☎800-323-3149); **Globalcare Travel Insurance** (☎800-821-2488; www.globalcare-cocco.com); and **Travel Assistance International** (☎800-821-2828; www.travelassistance.com). Providers in the **UK** include **Campus Travel** (☎01865 258 000) and **Columbus Travel Insurance** (☎020 7375 00 11). In **Australia**, try **CIC Insurance** (☎9202 80 00).

PACKING

Pack light. A good rule is to lay out only what you absolutely need, and then take half the clothes and twice the money. Not only does this facilitate running for buses and squeezing into *taxi colectivos*, but it also means fewer items to worry about losing and more room to take home souvenirs.

LUGGAGE. Unless you plan on spending most of your time in one location, a sturdy **internal frame backpack** is recommended. Shop carefully for a pack; if the fit isn't perfect your life on the road could be very miserable. Remember that packs may be strapped atop buses or otherwise exposed to the elements, so bring along a waterproof pack cover or trash bags. A smaller **daypack** will be helpful for carrying around daily necessities, such as bottled water and your copy of *Let's Go*.

CLOTHING. Mexican culture values neat and clean appearances, and visitors are recommended to do likewise, especially when dealing with officials at border crossings or military roadblocks. Shorts are rarely worn outside of beach towns and touristy ruins, and bathing suits are only appropriate on the beach.

Regardless of the season, those headed to into the great outdoors should bring a waterproof **rain jacket,** sturdy shoes or **hiking boots,** and **thick socks.** Cotton socks are not recommended as they tend to soak up and retain moisture. **Flip-flops** or waterproof sandals are crucial for scuzzy hotel showers and beach areas, and hiking sandals should be enough for any adventure in the hot, dry northwest. Keep the intense sun out of your eyes with a wide-brimmed **hat** or **sunglasses.** Those headed to the highlands or to mountainous national parks should pack a wool sweater or medium-weight fleece for the chilly nights.

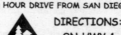

TOILETRIES. Basic toiletries are easy to find in most of Mexico, but those traveling in more rural areas should pack a supply of more specialized products. Contact lens wearers especially may want to bring along extra pairs and plenty of saline solution, as well as glasses and a prescription in case emergency replacements are needed. **Sunscreen** is essential, and those traveling in coastal areas or through the southern jungles will want a lot of **insect repellent.**

FIRST-AID KIT. The basis of your first-aid kit should be: **bandages, ibuprofen** or another painkiller, **antibiotic cream, a thermometer, a Swiss Army knife, tweezers, moleskin** for blisters, **a decongestant,** diarrhea or upset-stomach medicine (**Immodium AD),** an **antihistamine,** and **cortisone cream.**

ELECTRIC CURRENT. Appliances in Mexico use the same voltage and plugs as the rest of North America (110V, parallel plugs). Those with European appliances (220V) should visit a hardware store for an **adapter** (which changes the shape of the plug) and a **converter** (which changes the voltage). Do not make the mistake of using only an adapter, unless appliance instructions explicitly state otherwise).

FILM. Film in Mexico usually costs about 60 pesos for a roll of 24 color exposures. If you're not a serious photographer, you might want to consider bringing a **disposable camera** or two rather than a costly permanent one. Despite disclaimers, older airport security X-rays can fog film, so either buy a **lead-lined pouch** (sold at camera stores), or nicely ask the security guard to hand inspect it. Always pack film in your carry-on, as higher-intensity X-rays are used to examine checked bags.

OTHER USEFUL ITEMS. Many travelers like to store their essentials in a **money belt** and **padlock** their packs. A **sleepsack**—basically a full-size sheet folded over and sewn together—and a pillowcase can be useful in lower-end accommodations which sometimes have dirty sheets. A small absorbent **towel** or chamois will also come in handy when you tire of scratchy budget hotel towels. Definitely bring a **flashlight** if you are planning to camp or drive. Other handy items include: a **mosquito net,** a **water bottle,** a **travel alarm clock, earplugs** (hostels can be noisy inside and out); **toilet paper,** a **needle and thread** or duct tape for tears, a **clothes line,** a pocket **calculator,** resealable **plastic bags** (for damp clothes, spillable toiletries, a cockroach collection, etc.), and **laundry soap.**

ACCOMMODATIONS

HOSTELS

The few hostels that exist in Mexico are youth-oriented, dorm-style accommodations, often having large, single-sex rooms with bunk beds. Many have kitchens, laundry facilities, and storage areas, though they may inconvenience their patrons with curfews and daytime "lock-out" hours. Perhaps most importantly, Mexican hostels tend to be run-down and far from town. Although a bit cheaper than hotels—around US$5-6 per person—the money you save usually doesn't make up for the inconvenience. For more information about Mexican hostels, contact the **Red Mexicana de Alojamiento para Jóvenes** (☎5662 82 44; hostellingmexico@remaj.com; www.hostellingmexico.com), a hostelling organization affiliated with Hostelling International.

HOTELS

Bargain-seekers will not be disappointed with Mexico's selection of hotels. Although some (particularly in resort towns) are among the world's most overpriced, the majority of Mexican accommodations are affordable and convenient. Usually located within a block or two of a city's *zócalo*, the cheapest hotels (about US$7-10 per night) rarely provide amenities such as air conditioning, though they usually have hot water and private bathrooms. Higher priced hotels (about US$20 per night) are often located in the same district but are much better equipped, with telephones and the occasional television. Before accepting a room, ask to see it, and always find out whether the price includes any complimentary meals and if there are any extra surcharges before you pay.

All hotels, from luxury resorts in Cancún to rent-by-the-hour joints in Tijuana, are controlled by the government's **Secretaria de Turismo (SECTUR)**. This ensures that hotels of similar quality charge similar prices; you should always ask to see an up-to-date **official tariff sheet** if you doubt the quoted price. Many hotels post their official tariffs somewhere near the reception area. Although hotel prices are regulated, proprietors are not prohibited from charging *less* than the official rate. A little bargaining can work wonders, especially if you stay a number of days.

YOU CAN CHECK OUT ANYTIME YOU'D LIKE. Reservations are almost always necessary during Christmas, *Semana Santa* (the week before Easter), and local festivals. At most other times, even during the summer season, you need not worry much about having to reserve rooms in budget hotels.

CAMPING

Travelers accustomed to clean and well-maintained campgrounds may be in for a few surprises. By and large, Mexican national parks exist only in theory. The "protected lands" are often indistinguishable from the surrounding countryside or city and may be dirty, unappealing, and overrun with amorous teenagers. Privately owned **trailer parks** are relatively common on major routes—look for signs with a picture of a trailer, or the words *parque de trailer, campamento,* or *remolques.* These places often allow campers to pitch tents or sling up a hammock.

For those budget-minded individuals traveling along the coast, the hammock is the way to go. Most beach towns in Mexico are dotted with **palapas** (palm-tree huts). For a small fee, open-air restaurants double as places to hang your hat and hammock when the sun sets. At beaches and some inland towns frequented by backpackers, **cabañas** (cabins, usually simple thatch-roof huts) are common. For

the truly hard-core, camping on the beach can sometimes be an option. Lax permit laws and beach accessibility (every meter of beach in Mexico is public property) offer campers oodles of options.

 UNDER THE STARS. When camping on the beach, make sure safety is your number one priority. While all beaches in Mexico are public, not all of them are safe for camping. Hotel security in glitzy resort areas have a reputation for being unkind to beach campers. There have also been more serious reports of beachside robberies, rapes, and assaults. It's a good idea to check in with the local tourist office or police department to see whether camping is safe or permitted. Use common sense: don't camp on very secluded beaches or beaches near unsafe urban areas.

USEFUL PUBLICATIONS AND WEB RESOURCES

BOOKS
Backpacking in Mexico, Tim Burford. Bradt Publishing ($17).
Traveler's Guide to Camping in Mexican Baja, Fred and Gloria Jones. Foghorn Outdoors ($15).
Mexico: A Hiker's Guide to Mexico's Natural History, Jim Conrad. Mountaineers Books ($17).
Mexico's Copper Canyon Country, John Fayhee. Johnson Books ($17).
Traveler's Guide to Mexican Camping, Mike Church. Rolling Home Press ($20).

For topographical maps of Mexico, write or visit the **Instituto Nacional de Estadísticas, Geografiá e Informática (INEGI),** Calle Patriotismo 711, Torre A, Del. Benito Juárez, Col. San Juan Mixcoac, Mexico, DF, ☎5598 89 35. Available online at **Global Perspectives** (www.global-perspectives.com) and **Omnimap** (www.omnimap.com).

KEEPING IN TOUCH

MAIL

SENDING MAIL TO MEXICO
Mark envelopes "air mail" or "por avión" to avoid having letters sent by sea or land.

Australia: Allow 3-4 weeks for regular airmail to Mexico. Postcards and letters up to 20g cost $1; packages up to 0.5kg $12, up to 2kg $39.

Canada: Allow 2-3 weeks for regular airmail to Mexico. Postcards and letters up to 20g cost $1.05; packages up to 0.5kg $10.20, up to 2kg $34.00.

UK: Allow 3-4 weeks for airmail to Mexico. Letters up to 20g cost £0.3; packages up to 0.5kg £2.22, up to 2kg £8.22. **UK Swiftair** is a day faster for £2.85 more.

US: Allow 2 weeks for regular airmail to Mexico. Postcards/aerogrammes cost $0.50/ 0.70; letters under 1oz. $1. Packages under 1lb. cost $7.20; larger packages cost a variable amount (around $15). **US Express Mail International** takes 2-3 days and costs $19/23 (0.5/1lb.).

 WITH LOVE, FROM ME TO YOU. Address *Poste Restante* letters to:
Justin SKINNER (name)
Lista de Correos
Ortiz Rubio 40 (street address for post office, or leave it blank)
Tecate (city), Baja California (state), 21400 (postal code)
MEXICO

Additionally, **Federal Express** (US and Canada ☎ 800-247-4747; Australia ☎ 13 26 10; New Zealand ☎ 0800 73 33 39; UK ☎ 0800 12 38 00) handles express mail from most of the above countries to Mexico. Note that Federal Express will not deliver to post offices in Mexico, only to businesses and residences.

RECEIVING MAIL IN MEXICO

There are several ways to arrange pick-up of letters sent to you by friends and relatives while you are abroad.

General Delivery: Mail can be sent to Mexico through **Poste Restante** (the international phrase for General Delivery; **Lista de Correos** in Spanish) to almost any city or town with a post office. Mail sent via *poste restante* will go to a special desk in the central post office, unless you specify a post office by street address or postal code. Letters should be marked *Favor de retener hasta la llegada* (Please hold until arrival); they will be held up to 15 days. It's probably not a good idea to send valuable items to a city's *Lista de Correos*.

American Express: AmEx's travel offices throughout the world offer a free **Client Letter Service** (mail held up to 30 days; forwarding on request) for cardholders who contact them in advance. Address the letter in the same way shown above. Some offices will offer these services to non-cardholders (especially AmEx Travelers Cheque holders), but call ahead to make sure. *Let's Go* lists AmEx office locations for most large cities in **Practical Information** sections; for a complete list, call 800-528-4800.

Packages sent via Express Mail International, FedEx, UPS, or other express services might be held at a different office (often MexPost, see below). It's a good idea to not send anything particularly valuable via any sort of mail to Mexico.

SENDING MAIL HOME FROM MEXICO

Mexican mail service is painfully slow. **Airmail** from major cities in Mexico to the US and Canada takes anywhere from two weeks to one month; to Australia or New Zealand, one month; to the UK or Ireland, three weeks to one month; to South Africa, one to two months. Add another one or two weeks for mail sent from more rural areas. Mexican mailboxes are notorious for being infrequently picked up, but the bright plastic orange boxes labeled *Express* that have popped up around Mexico City and other large cities are quite reliable and are picked up every morning. Anything important, however, should be sent *registrado* (registered mail) or taken directly to the post office, at the very least. To speed service, it's a good idea to write Spanish abbreviations or names for countries (i.e., EE.UU. for the US). Also write "por avión" on all postcards and letter, lest they sit on a boat in the Atlantic for two or three months.

Packages cannot weigh more than 25kg. Keep in mind that all packages are opened and inspected by customs at border crossings; closing boxes with string, not tape, is recommended. You may also have to provide several pieces of information: your tourist card data, contents, value, and nature of the package ("Gift" works best), and your address and return address.

For the speediest service possible, **MexPost** works in collaboration with Express Mail International in the US and similar express mail services in other countries to deliver mail quickly and reliably. Three days is the official MexPost delivery time to the US, but allow up to a week. MexPost offices are usually found next to regular post offices, but if not, the post office staff can usually give you directions to the nearest MexPost office.

TELEPHONES

CALLING MEXICO FROM ABROAD

To call Mexico direct from home, dial:

1. The **international access code** of your home country. International access codes include: Australia 0011, Ireland 00, New Zealand 00, South Africa 09, UK 00, US 011. Country codes and City codes are sometimes listed with a zero in front (e.g., 033), but after dialing the international access code, drop successive zeros (with an access code of 011, e.g., 011 33).

2. 052 (Mexico's country code).

3. The city code (across from the city or town name) and local number.

CALLING ABROAD FROM MEXICO

The **LADATEL phones** that have popped up all over the country have revolutionized the way Mexico calls. To operate one, you'll need a colorful **pre-paid phone card,** available at most *papelerías* (stationery stores) or *tiendas de abarrotes* (general stores)—look for the "De venta aquí LADATEL" signs posted in store windows. Cards come in 30-, 50-, and 100-peso increments. Once you are armed with your precious LADATEL phone card, calling using various methods can be a snap.

INTERNATIONAL CALLS WITH A CALLING CARD. A **calling card** is probably the cheapest way to make international calls from Mexico. To use a calling card from Mexico, contact the operator for your service provider by dialing the appropriate toll-free Mexico access number. If your provider does not have a Mexico-specific access code, you should inquire beforehand as to the correct dialing procedures.

AT&T: ☎01 800 288 2872 (using LADATEL phones) or 001 800 462 4240.

Sprint: ☎001 800 877 8000.

MCI WorldPhone Direct: ☎001 800 674 7000 or ☎01 800 021 8000 (using Avantel phones).

DIRECT INTERNATIONAL CALLS. To call directly, insert your LADATEL card, dial 00 (to get an international line), the country code of the place you are calling, the area code, and phone number. You can then chat quickly (and nervously) while the seconds tick away. It is extremely expensive to make direct international calls. On average, a 10-minute phone call to the US will exhaust a 100 peso phone card.

ESSENTIALS

CALLING COLLECT. If you speak Spanish and can't reach the international operator, dial 07 for the national operator, who will connect you (sometimes even a local operator can help). The term for a collect call is a *llamada por cobrar*. Calling from hotels is usually faster but beware of exorbitant surcharges. Remember, however, that there can be a fee of 1-5 pesos for collect calls that are not accepted.

CALLS MADE WITHIN MEXICO. The entire Mexican telephone system has been revamped and reorganized in the last two years. Before, numbers were listed as five or six digits accompanied by a two- or three-digit city code. Now, all local numbers are **seven digits** (with the exception of those in Mexico City, which are eight), and all city codes are one digit. *Let's Go* uses the new system, but, if you should encounter a five- or six-digit number written using the old system, add digits from the end of the old area code until you have seven digits. For example, if you see a number listed as ☎6 98 36, and you know the area code was 314, then the correct seven-digit number would be ☎146 98 36, which you should use to call locally. Add the city code and you've got ☎(3) 146 98 36, the long-distance number, which you must dial in addition to an 01 prefix.

ESSENTIALS

EMAIL AND INTERNET

With many Mexican businesses, language schools, and individuals now online, the internet and the electronic communication it offers provide a cheap and accessible alternative to pricey phone calls and slow postal service. Cybercafes, included in the **Practical Information** of most town listings, are the most prominent form of internet access in Mexico. These cafes can even be found in some of the smaller Mexican towns; expect to compete for computers with gawky Mexican teenage boys and to pay US$2-10 per hour for access. For lists of additional cybercafes in Mexico, check out www.netcafeguide.com/mexico.htm or www.netcafes.com.

Some, but not all, internet providers offer telnet, Internet Relay Chat (IRC, pronounced "eerk" in Spanish), and instant messenger (IM) programs such as America Online Instant Messenger or ICQ. All internet providers maintain some sort of World Wide Web access, be it Netscape or Internet Explorer. Though in some places it is possible to forge a remote link with your home server, it is, in most cases, slower and more expensive than free **web-based email accounts** (such as Hotmail or Yahoo!); it may be a good idea to sign up for one before your trip.

GETTING THERE

BY PLANE

When it comes to airfare, a little effort can save you a bundle. The keys are to hunt around, to be flexible, and to ask persistently about discounts. Students, seniors, and those under 26 should never have to pay full price for a ticket.

DETAILS AND TIPS

Timing: The most expensive time to travel is between mid-June and August. Midweek (M-Th morning) round-trip flights run US$40-80 cheaper than weekend flights but are generally more crowded and less likely to permit frequent-flier upgrades. Traveling with an "open return" ticket can be pricier than fixing a return date when buying the ticket.

Route: Round-trip flights are by far the cheapest; "open-jaw" (arriving and departing from different cities) tickets tend to be pricier. Patching one-way flights together is the most expensive way to travel.

Round-the-World (RTW): If Mexico is only one stop on a more extensive globe-hop, consider a RTW ticket. Tickets usually include at least 5 stops and are valid for about a year; prices range $1200-5000. Try **Northwest Airlines/KLM** (US ☎800-447-4747;

www.nwa.com) or **Star Alliance,** a consortium of 13 airlines including United Airlines (US ☎800-241-6522; www.star-alliance.com).

Gateway Cities: Flights between capitals and regional or tourist hubs will offer the cheapest fares. The cheapest gateway cities in Mexico are typically Mexico City, Guadalajara, and Cancún.

Fares: The cheapest round-trip fares to Mexico City from New York usually range from $400-550; from London $500-750; from Los Angeles $280-350; from Sydney $1400-1550; from Cancún $200-400; from Monterrey $180-250.

Taxes: Be prepared to add $150 in taxes on plane tickets to Mexico. Taxes average $80.

BUDGET AND STUDENT TRAVEL AGENCIES

While knowledgeable agents specializing in flights to Mexico can make your life easy and help you save, they may not spend the time to find you the lowest possible fare. Students and under-26ers holding **ISIC and IYTC cards** (see p. 7), respectively, qualify for big discounts from student travel agencies.

usit world (www.usitworld.com). Over 50 **usit campus** branches in the UK (www.usitcampus.co.uk), including 52 Grosvenor Gardens, **London** SW1W 0AG (☎0870 240 1010); **Manchester** (☎0161 273 1721); and **Edinburgh** (☎0131 668 3303). Nearly 20 **usit now** offices in Ireland, including 19-21 Aston Quay, O'Connell Bridge, **Dublin** (☎01 602 1600; www.usitnow.ie), and **Belfast** (☎02890 327 111; www.usitnow.com).

Council Travel (www.counciltravel.com). Countless US offices, including branches in Atlanta, Boston, Chicago, Los Angeles, New York, San Francisco, Seattle, and Washington D.C. Check the website or call 800-2-COUNCIL for the office nearest you.

CTS Travel, 44 Goodge St., **London** W1 (☎020 7636 0031; fax 7637 5328; ctsinfo@ctstravel.com.uk).

STA Travel, 7890 S. Hardy Dr. Ste. 109, Tempe, AZ 85284 (☎800-781-4040; fax 480-592-0876 www.statravel.com). A student and youth travel organization with over 150 offices worldwide. Ticket booking, travel insurance, railpasses, and more.

Student Universe, 545 5th Ave., Suite 640, New York, NY 10017 (toll-free customer service ☎800-272-9676, outside the US 212-986-8420; help@studentuniverse.com; www.studentuniverse.com), is an online student travel service offering discount ticket booking, travel insurance, railpasses, destination guides, and much more. Customer service line open M-F 9am-8pm, Sa noon-5pm EST.

Travel CUTS (Canadian Universities Travel Services Limited), 187 College St., **Toronto,** ON M5T 1P7 (☎416-979-2406; fax 979-8167; www.travelcuts.com). 40 offices across Canada. Also in the UK, 295-A Regent St., **London** W1R 7YA (☎020 7255 1944).

COMMERCIAL AIRLINES

Most major international airlines travel in and out of Mexico City. Popular Mexican carriers include **AeroMéxico** (☎800-237-6639; www.aeromexico.com), which flies to practically every Mexican city with an airport, and **Mexicana** (☎800-531-7921; www.mexicana.com), North America's oldest airline, which flies to most major US and European cities.

To book a flight quickly or gauge the market price, try online ticket brokers such as Microsoft Expedia (msn.expedia.com) or Travelocity (www.travelocity.com). These offer no student or senior discounts and require membership, but pride themselves on being cheaper than buying directly from the airlines.

Taking **standby flights** requires considerable flexibility in arrival and departure dates and cities. Companies dealing in standby flights sell vouchers rather than tickets, along with the promise to get to your destination (or near your destination) within a certain window of time (typically 1-5 days). One established standby company in the US is **Airhitch,** 2641 Broadway, 3rd fl., New York, NY 10025 (☎800-326-2009; fax 864-5489; www.airhitch.org) and Los Angeles, CA (☎888-247-4482).

Another cheap option is to buy from **ticket consolidators,** or **"bucket shops,"** companies that buy unsold tickets in bulk from commercial airlines and sell them at

ESSENTIALS

discounted rates. The best place to look is in the Sunday travel section of any major newspaper (such as The New York *Times*), where many bucket shops advertise dirt cheap flights to popular Mexican destinations such as Acapulco and Cancún. Not all bucket shops are reliable, so insist on a receipt that gives full details of restrictions, refunds, and tickets; and pay by credit card (in spite of the 2-5% fee) so you can stop payment if you never receive your tickets. For more info, see www.travel-library.com/air-travel/consolidators.html or pick up Kelly Monaghan's *Air Travel's Bargain Basement* (Intrepid Traveler, US$8).

BY BUS OR TRAIN

Greyhound (☎800-229-9424 or 402-330-8552; www.greyhound.com) serves many US-Mexico border towns, including El Paso and Brownsville, Texas. Schedule information is available at any Greyhound terminal, on the web page, or by calling the 800 number. Smaller lines serve other destinations. Buses tend not to cross the border, but at each of these stops you can pick up Mexican bus lines (among them Estrella de Oro, Estrella Blanca, ADO, and Transportes Del Norte) on the other side. Guatemalan bus lines operate at Guatemala-Mexico border towns, including Talismán and La Mesilla. Buses usually stop just short of the border, and you can walk across to Mexico and pick up a local bus to the nearest town. Buses also operate between Chetumal (see p. 637) and the capital of Belize, Belize City.

By train your options are limited to the US-Mexico border. You can take **Amtrak** (☎800-872-7245; www.amtrak.com) to El Paso, walk across the border to Ciudad Juárez and use other forms of transportation to travel within Mexico. Amtrak also serves San Diego and San Antonio, where you can catch a bus to the border towns.

GETTING AROUND

BY BUS

Mexico's bus system never ceases to astound, amaze, and mystify. From most large cities, it is possible to get almost anywhere in the republic, and companies like **Autotransportes del Oriente (ADO)**, **Estrella Blanca**, and **Estrella de Oro** run cheaply and efficiently—as efficiently as is possible in Mexico, that is. Several types of bus services exist. Travel executive service, called **servicio ejecutivo** provides royal treatment: plush reclining seats, sandwiches and soda, sometimes too frigid A/C, and movies galore. Slightly less fancy are **primera clase** (1st-class) buses, which usually feature ridiculously bad movies and A/C. Significantly inferior in quality are **segunda clase** (2nd-class) buses, which are usually converted school buses or some variation thereof and are overcrowded, uncomfortable, and painfully slow. Buses are categorized as either *local* or *de paso*. **Locales** originate at the station from which you leave. **De paso** (in passing) buses originate elsewhere and pass through your station. Because they depend on the seating availability when the bus arrives, tickets cannot be purchased in advance. When *de paso* tickets go on sale, forget civility, chivalry, and anything that might stand between you and a ticket, or plan to spend the greater portion of your vacation in bus stations.

BY CAR

Driving in Mexico can be hazardous to your health. The maximum speed on Mexican routes is 100km per hour (62mph) unless otherwise posted, but, like most other traffic signs and regulations, it is often ignored. Mexicans are a rowdy bunch on the road. It's not unusual to hear drivers exchange such greetings as *"¡Baboso!"* (Drooling fool!), *"¡Eh, stupido!"* (Hey, stupid!), and, of course, the ubiquitous *"¿Donde aprendiste a manajar, menso?"* (Where did you learn how to drive, dumbass?). With enough practice, you'll be able to curse with the best Mexican driver. It's also not unusual for Mexican drivers to overuse their car horns; drive down any busy street, and you'll be serenaded by a harmonious chorus of horns. In such a climate, it's best to drive defensively. Please be careful.

Driving norms aside, it's a good idea to avoid driving during the rainy season (May-Oct.), when road conditions deteriorate. If you are planning on driving extensively between cities, check with local authorities or with your nearest consulate for updates on potential danger. In general, it is a good idea to avoid less secure freeways *(libres)* in favor of toll *(cuota)* roads. Also avoid driving at night, when chances of hijacks and other criminal acts are higher. While on the road, you may be stopped by agents of the Federal Public Ministry and the Federal Judicial Police for a search of your car and its contents. Be as cooperative as possible; they will usually just open your trunk, look around your car, and wave you through. For information about driving a car into Mexico and obtaining a **Vehicle Permit,** see **Entering Mexico By Car,** p. 11.

 FILL 'ER UP. Petroleos Mexicanos, more commonly, **PEMEX,** the national oil company, sells two types of gas: **Magna** (regular) and **Premium** (unleaded). Unleaded gas is now almost universally available in Mexico. Both *Magna* and *Premium* are extremely cheap by all but Saudi Arabian standards. PEMEX accepts cash and checks only.

If you're unlucky enough to break down on a major toll road between 8am and 8pm, pull completely off the road, raise the hood, stay with your car, and wait for the **Angeles Verdes** (Green Angels) to come to the rescue. These green-and-white emergency trucks, dispatched by radio and staffed by almost a thousand mechanics, are equipped for performing common repair jobs, towing, changing tires, and addressing minor medical problems. Your green saviors may take a while to show up, but the service (except for parts, gas, and oil) is free. Tipping is optional but a good idea. These guardian angels will assist you anywhere but in Mexico City, where you can contact the **Asociación Nacional Automovilística (ANA;** ☎ 5597 42 83).

Some credit cards cover standard **insurance.** If you rent, lease, or borrow a car, you will need a **green card,** or **International Insurance Certificate,** to prove that you have liability insurance. You can obtain it through the car rental agency; most include coverage in their prices. If you lease a car, ask the dealer for a green card. Some travel agents offer the card, and it may also be available at border crossings. Even if your auto insurance applies internationally, you will still need a green card to certify this to foreign officials. If you have a collision abroad, the accident will show up on your domestic records if you report it to your insurance company. Rental agencies may require you to purchase theft insurance in countries that they consider to have a high risk of auto theft. Ask your rental agency about rules applying specifically to Mexico.

BY TRAIN

The Mexican railroads are all owned by the government, with most lines operating under the name of **Ferrocarriles Nacionales de Mexico** (National Railways of Mexico, FFNN). The train system is not as extensive, punctual, cheap, comfortable, or efficient as the bus system, and, assuming they are on time, even the "fast" trains can take twice as long as buses to reach their destination. Other than the spectacular ride through the **Copper Canyon (Los Mochis-Creel,** see p. 234) you probably won't want to rely on trains unless you crave a leisurely crawl through the countryside.

BY PLANE

Flying within Mexican borders is a method of transportation usually overlooked by budget travelers. That said, time is money. As a general rule, whenever busing will take you longer than 36 hours, consider flying; chances are it will cost about the same or be only marginally more expensive, but save you many, many hours. If you are considering traveling by plane, visit one of the ubiquitous travel agencies that lurk on main streets; agents will be more than happy to help you find cheap, last minute fares. It's a good idea to mention it if you are a student or a senior citizen and ask about the possibility of standby seats. You can also check with Mexican airlines directly (See **Commercial Airlines,** p. 31).

BY THUMB

Mexicans who pick up tourists are often friendly, generous and well-meaning; in fact, people who *don't* pick you up will often give you an apologetic look or a gesture of explanation. However, you should always be careful. Women should never hitchhike, even when traveling in groups. Hitchhikers should size up the driver and find out where the car is going before getting in. Think twice if a driver opens the door quickly and offers to drive anywhere. Some bandit-ridden routes are particularly dangerous for hitchhikers (see **Traveling by Car,** p. 34). If you do decide to accept a ride, exercise caution and make sure you will be able to make a quick exit. Do not sit in the middle, for example, and try to keep all of your belongings easily accessible. If you have trouble getting out for any reason, affecting the pose of someone on the verge of vomiting has been known to work.

 COOL KIDS DON'T HITCHHIKE. *Let's Go* strongly urges you to consider the risks before you choose to hitchhike and does not recommend hitchhiking as a safe means of transportation.

SAFETY WHILE GETTING AROUND

BY BUS

While bus travel is one of the safest ways to get around in Mexico, travelers should still exercise caution. Mexican highways have a reputation for being unsafe, and hijackings of buses, while fairly uncommon, do occur. **To minimize risk, take 1st-class buses rather than 2nd-class buses.** First-class buses are more likely to take toll *(cuota)* roads instead of free *(libre)* highways, which have more reports of hijacking and incidents of crime. It is also a good idea to arrange your travel schedule so that any lengthy intercity bus travel is done **during daylight hours** when there is a lower chance of crime. Once on a bus—be it a local or intercity bus—keep your wits about you; stories abound about determined thieves who wait for travelers to fall asleep. Carry your backpack in front of you where you can see it or store it in the underside of the bus. In certain areas of the country, buses may be pulled over and boarded by humorless armed federal officials *(federales)* looking for drugs or illegal aliens. In such a situation, be quiet and cooperative.

BY CAR

Because the number of hijackings and robberies of non-Mexican drivers has increased, those who choose to drive on Mexican highways should be extremely careful. **Whenever possible, drive during daylight hours and with others.** Keep valuables out of sight, in your trunk if you can, and park your vehicle in a garage or well-traveled area. **Sleeping in your car** is not only often illegal, it is also extremely dangerous. If you absolutely must sleep in your car, do so as close to a police station or a 24-hour service station as possible.

Driving is unsafe for other reasons. Road conditions in Mexico are highly variable. The expensive *cuota* roads are not only the safest, but they provide the smoothest ride and the best road conditions. Free *(libre)* highways and local roads might have poor (or nonexistent) shoulders, few gas stations, and roaming animals. If you plan on spending a lot of time on the road, you may want to bring spare parts. Finally, it's always a good idea to use a little common sense and take extra preparation time. Learn local driving signals and customs, but keep in mind that they are frequently ignored by local drivers. Bring plenty of maps and have a good idea of the route you plan to take before you hit the road.

> **HIGHWAY TO THE DANGER ZONE.** According to the US State Department, the following highways are particularly unsafe, and those traveling on them should exercise caution: **Mex. 19** (Tuxtla to Tapachula and Tuxtla to Villahermosa), **Mex. 186** (Chetumal to Villahermosa), **Mex. 15** (Sinaloa), **Express Highway 1** (Sinaloa), the **Toluca Highway** (outside of Mexico City), and the highway connecting **Altamirano to Ixtapa/Zihuatanejo.**

BY FOOT

To avoid unwanted attention, try to blend in as much as possible. Respecting local customs—in many cases, dressing more conservatively and avoiding obvious tourist paraphernalia—may divert attention. It also helps to familiarize yourself with your surroundings. When walking at night, stick to busy, well-lit streets and avoid dark alleyways and other large, deserted areas. Look for children playing, women walking in the open, and other signs of an active community. If you feel uncomfortable, leave as quickly and directly as you can. You may want to carry a **whistle** or another noise-making device to scare off attackers and attract attention. Memorize the emergency number of the city or area. If you are traveling alone, be sure that someone at home knows your itinerary and **never admit that you're traveling alone.** Whenever possible, *Let's Go* lists unsafe areas; it still helps to ask about safety at tourist offices or at hotel reception desks. For more information on safety for **Women Travelers,** see below.

ADDITIONAL INFORMATION

SPECIFIC CONCERNS

WOMEN TRAVELERS

Mexican women seldom travel without the company of men, and to find foreign women doing so is surprising and draws attention. Moreover, Mexican men are notorious for their exorbitant *machismo*, a brand of Latin American chauvinism that translates into whistles, catcalls, and stares. Persistent men will insist on joining you and "showing you the sights." If you're fair-skinned or have light-colored hair, *"güera, güera"* will follow you everywhere; if not, expect to hear the typical mating call, *"¿Donde vas, mamacita?"* (Where are you going, babe?). The best answer to this unwanted attention is to offer no answer at all. Ignore it and avoid making eye contact. *Machismo* is usually more annoying than dangerous, but in real emergencies yell for help or draw attention to yourself and the situation. It might be a good idea to wear a **whistle** or some sort of noise-making device. Beware, however, that many police officers and uniformed officials are the biggest *machistas* of all; don't consider yourself safe from harassment just because men in uniform are nearby. Good allies are **local elderly women** or **nuns,** who command respect from men of all ages and may be able to help you in time of need.

Awareness of Mexican social standards and dress codes may help to minimize unwanted attention. Mexican women seldom wear shorts, short skirts, tank tops, or halter tops. To do so—and to wear any sort of clothing without a supportive bra—is to ask for additional harassment and stares. Shorts and tank tops are appropriate only in beach and resort areas or in towns with a high number of foreign students and tourists. More traditional areas of the country require even more conservative wear; bring a long skirt to wear in churches or in places like Chiapas, where locals are very religious. If you are traveling with a male friend, it may help to pose as a couple; this will make it easier to share rooms and will also chill the blood of Mexican Romeos. Wearing a **wedding ring** on your left hand or a **Catholic cross** around your neck may assist in discouraging unwanted attention, as can talking loudly and frequently about your muscular boyfriend *(novio muy fuerte)* or easily-angered husband *(esposo muy facilmente enojado);* some savvy women even carry pictures of these "boyfriends" and "husbands," gladly displaying them to prospective suitors. Most importantly, always look like you know what you're doing, even when you don't. Feigning confidence can deter potential harassers.

FURTHER READING

A Journey of One's Own: Uncommon Advice for the Independent Woman Traveler, Thalia Zepatos. Eighth Mountain Press ($17).

Gutsy Women: More Travel Tips and Wisdom for the Road, Marybeth Bond. Travelers' Tales ($13).

Nothing to Declare: Memoirs of a Woman Traveling Alone, Mary Morris. St. Martin's Press ($13).

OLDER TRAVELERS AND RETIREES

Mexico's temperate climate, natural and historical attractions, and favorable exchange rates lure older travelers and retirees alike. Thriving and tight-knit expatriate communities have popped up all over the country—in the center (San Miguel de Allende, Guadalajara, and Xalapa), north (San Carlos and Todos Santos), and south (Oaxaca, Puerto Escondido, and the breathtaking turquoise coast of Quintana Roo). For information on retiring in Mexico, see **Retirement Visas,** p. 11. Senior citizens just looking to travel in the country will be pleasantly surprised: Mexican culture fosters respect of one's elders, and seniors will receive among the best service and treatment. Don't be surprised if young people embarrass you by insisting you take their seat on the Metro or on the bus. In addition to preferential treatment, seniors are eligible for a range of discounts, from transportation tickets

to museums to accommodations. If you don't see a senior citizen price listed, ask and you may be rewarded. Many seniors also travel to Mexico to take advantage of the country's excellent language schools, many of which offer special discounts and programs for senior citizens (see **Studying Abroad,** p. 41).

Elderhostel, 11 Ave. de Lafayette, Boston, MA 02111 (☎877-426-8056; www.elderhostel.org). Organizes 1- to 4-week "educational adventures" in Mexico on varied subjects for those 55+.

The Mature Traveler, P.O. Box 15791, Sacramento, CA 95852 (☎800-460-6676). Deals, discounts, and travel packages for the 50+ traveler. Subscription US$30.

FURTHER READING

Living Well In Mexico: How to Relocate, Retire, and Increase Your Standard of Living, Ken Lubolt. Avalon Travel Publishing ($16).

Choose Mexico for Retirement, John Howells and Don Merwin. Globe Pequot Press ($15).

No Problem! Worldwise Tips for Mature Adventurers, Janice Kenyon. Orca Book Publishers ($16).

BISEXUAL, GAY, AND LESBIAN TRAVELERS

Mexico's conservative and Catholic character makes homosexuality frowned upon at best, violently despised at worst. Intolerance is especially rampant in more rural areas of the country, where displays of gay or lesbian affection might be the quickest way to attract violence. More urban areas are generally more accepting of homosexuality; there are fledgling gay-rights movements in Mexico City and Monterrey and a thriving community in Puerto Vallarta. However, the best rule of thumb is to avoid displays of homosexuality altogether—at least until you know you are in a safe and accepting environment, such as one afforded by gay and lesbian clubs and establishments (of which, interestingly enough, there are many). Whenever possible, *Let's Go* lists gay and lesbian establishments; the best way to find out about the many others that we do not list is to consult organizations, mail-order bookstores, and publishers that offer materials addressing specific gay and lesbian concerns. **Out and About** (www.planetout.com) publishes a biweekly newsletter addressing travel concerns.

Gay's the Word, 66 Marchmont St., London WC1N 1AB (☎020 7278 7654; sales@gaystheword.co.uk; www.gaystheword.co.uk). The largest gay and lesbian bookshop in the UK, with both fiction and non-fiction titles. Mail-order service available.

Giovanni's Room, 345 S. 12th St., Philadelphia, PA 19107 (☎215-923-2960; fax 923-0813; www.queerbooks.com). An international lesbian/feminist and gay bookstore with mail-order service (carries many of the publications listed below).

International Gay and Lesbian Travel Association, 4331 N. Federal Hwy. #304, Fort Lauderdale, FL 33308 (☎954-776-2626; fax 776-3303; www.iglta.org). An organization of over 1350 companies serving gay and lesbian travelers worldwide.

International Lesbian and Gay Association (ILGA), 81 rue Marché-au-Charbon, B-1000 Brussels, Belgium (☎/fax +32 2 502 2471; www.ilga.org). Not a travel service; provides political information, such as homosexuality laws of individual countries.

WEBSITES

Aquí Estamos: www.aquiestamos.com. Chat, personals, and an online guide (still under construction) to over 30 Mexican cities.

Gay México: www.gaymexico.com.mx. An all-purpose informational site.

Ser Gay: www.sergay.com.mx. A Mexico City-based site with chat forums and event listings in the D.F. area.

FURTHER READING

Spartacus International Gay Guide. Bruno Gmunder Verlag (US$33).

Damron Men's Travel Guide, Damron Road Atlas, Damron Accommodations, and *Damron Women's Traveller.* Damron Travel Guides ($14-19). For more info, call 800-462-6654 or visit www.damron.com.

Gay Mexico, Ferrari Guides' Gay Travel A to Z, Ferrari Guides' Men's Travel in Your Pocket, Ferrari Guides' Women's Travel in Your Pocket, and *Ferrari Guides' Inn Places.* Ferrari Publications ($16-20). Purchase the guides online at www.ferrariguides.com.

A Man's Guide to Mexico and Central America. Señor Cordova ($19).

TRAVELERS WITH DISABILITIES

Mexico is increasingly accessible to travelers with disabilities, most noticeably in popular resorts like Cancún and Cabo San Lucas. Northern cities closer to the US such as Monterrey and Saltillo also tend to be more wheelchair friendly. Money talks—the more you are willing to spend, the less difficult it is to find accessible facilities. Keep in mind, however, that most public and long-distance modes of transportation and most of the non-luxury hotels don't accommodate wheelchairs. Public bathrooms are almost all inaccessible, as are many ruins, parks, historic buildings, and museums. Still, with some advance planning, an affordable Mexican vacation is not impossible. Those with disabilities should inform airlines and hotels when making arrangements for travel as some time may be needed to prepare. The **Green Book** (http://members.nbci.com/thegreenbook/home.html) has a partial listing of diabled-access accommodations and sights in Mexico.

USEFUL ORGANIZATIONS

Mobility International USA (MIUSA), P.O. Box 10767, Eugene, OR 97440 (voice and TDD ☎541–343-1284; www.miusa.org). Sells *A World of Options: A Guide to International Educational Exchange, Community Service, and Travel for Persons with Disabilities* (US$35).

Society for Accessible Travel and Hospitality (SATH), 347 Fifth Ave. #610, New York, NY 10016 (☎212-447-7284; www.sath.org). An advocacy group that publishes free online travel information and the travel magazine *OPEN WORLD* ($18, free for members). Annual membership $45, students and seniors $30.

TOUR AGENCIES
   Directions Unlimited, 123 Green Ln., Bedford Hills, NY 10507 (☎800-533-5343).
Books individual and group vacations for the physically disabled; not an info service.

MINORITY TRAVELERS

Nearly all of the Mexican population is white, Indian, or a combination of the two.
This general homogeneity means that any minority traveler—regardless of skin
color—is bound to stick out, particularly when traveling in rural or less touristed
parts of the country. In general, the whiter your skin, the better treatment you'll
receive. (Unfortunately, light-skinned travelers are viewed as wealthier and therefore are more likely to be the targets of crime.) Travelers of African or Asian
ancestry will likely attract attention from curious locals and their gawking children, who may giggle, point, and stare. Asians may find themselves called *chinos*,
while African Americans are often called *morenos* or *negros*. None of these
words are meant to be offensive; to Mexicans they are simply descriptive terms. In
many rural areas, non-Spanish speakers may be viewed as a threat. It helps to try
to speak Spanish to help locals feel more at ease; a smile can work wonders.

TRAVELERS WITH CHILDREN

Mexicans love children and children love Mexico. Traveling with children requires
little more than a bit of planning and a lot of extra patience. When deciding where
to stay, for example, consider staying in more moderately-priced establishments.
Unless you want your children rubbing elbows with questionable backpacker
types, it's best to avoid the hard-core budget joints and hostels. It's also a good
idea to call ahead to make sure your hotel welcomes children. In choosing a restaurant, make sure that the establishment offers food your child will like. Some
children are finicky eaters, and the spicy (and sometimes unusual) food eaten by
many Mexicans may seem strange to them; offer them simple and tasty *taquitos*,
quesadillas, and *sopas de fideo* (yummy noodle soups). Unless your child has a
particularly adventurous palate, stay away from the *salsa picante*. Finally, be
very careful with food and water safety, as children's digestive systems are more
delicate than those of adults. Always give children plenty of bottled water to drink
(especially if it's hot out), and take them to a doctor if they develop any abnor-
mally severe diarrhea. When traveling by car between cities, make sure that your
car has a seat for young children (if it doesn't, request one from your rental company). Also keep in mind that many Mexican highways—particularly those connecting Mexico City to the coasts—are hilly and windy and have a tendency to
make children carsick.

BABY ON BOARD. In Mexico, children traveling by themselves or with only
one parent must carry a parental consent form that has been signed, in the presence of a notary public, by the parent not traveling. If the one parent is
deceased, then a death certificate or court order is required. These rules are
meant to curb the numbers of parents who try to flee with their children across
international borders. Although the rules are seldom enforced, some travelers
have been turned away at the border for not providing proper documentation for
their accompanying children.

   Perhaps the only truly child-unfriendly part of the country is Mexico City, where
the big-city noise, congestion, and pollution tend to affect children more than
adults. If staying in *el D.F.* with children, keep them indoors when pollution is at
its heaviest—generally in early mornings during the winter. Stay alert for pollution
index updates, which are frequently broadcast on radio and television. Outside of
the capital, Mexico is extremely child-friendly, particularly the coastal regions,
which offer children miles of golden beaches upon which to frolic and build sand
castle after sand castle. Remember to slather on the sunscreen, though—Mexico is
kind to children, but the Mexican sun can be harsh.

FURTHER READING

Let's Go Traveling in Mexico, Robin Rector Krupp. An illustrated journey through Mexico with the mythical Quetzalcóatl as guide. Ideal for children ages 4-8 years old. No relation to our favorite *Let's Go*. William Morrow Company ($17).

Backpacking with Babies and Small Children, Goldie Silverman. Wilderness Press ($10).

How to Take Great Trips with Your Kids, Sanford and Jane Portnoy. Harvard Common Press ($10).

Tropical Family Vacations: In the Caribbean, Hawaii, South Florida, and Mexico, Laura Sutherland. Griffin Trade Paperback ($17).

Have Kid, Will Travel: 101 Survival Strategies for Vacationing With Babies and Young Children, Claire and Lucille Tristram. Andrews and McMeel ($9).

Adventuring with Children: An Inspirational Guide to World Travel and the Outdoors, Nan Jeffrey. Avalon House Publishing ($15).

Trouble Free Travel with Children, Vicki Lansky. Book Peddlers ($9).

DIETARY CONCERNS

Vegetarians are rare in Mexico, and vegans are almost unheard of. Expect incredulous stares not only from your waiters, but also from concerned patrons at nearby tables. Oftentimes, it's best to blame your tastes on the weather ("It's so hot I only want to eat vegetables") or on illness ("I have *turista;* I will vomit on you if I eat lots of meat") rather than complicated ideology. A diatribe on animal rights will win you no converts and will raise more than a few eyebrows. With that said, the carnivorous nature of Mexicans can make it difficult for **vegetarian tourists** as almost all meals are prepared using animal products. Some popular vegetarian dishes available in most restaurants include *quesadillas* (melted cheese wrapped in tortillas), *chilaquiles* (strips of fried tortillas baked in tomato sauce with cheese and fresh cream), *molletes* (french bread smothered with refried beans and cheese), and *frijoles* (beans). Beware that nearly all flour *tortillas* and that many types of beans are prepared with *manteca* (lard). **Vegan tourists** will have a

harder go at it and may have to subsist on the old standbys of corn tortillas and rice. It may be a good idea to bring high-calorie protein snacks (such as granola bars and peanuts) to maintain your energy. Wherever possible, *Let's Go* includes vegetarian dining options, but if you have any doubts, check with your waiter to make sure that your food is completely meat-free. For **more information on vegetarianism abroad** contact the **North American Vegetarian Society**, P.O. Box 72, Dolgeville, NY 13329 (☎518-568-7970; www.navs-online.org), which publishes *The Vegetarian Traveler: Where to Stay If You're Vegetarian*, a guide to international vegetarian-friendly restaurants and accomodations(US$16). In Mexico, try the **Asociación Mexicana de Vegetarianos,** c/o Alternative World, Apartado Postal WTC 031 World Trade Center, Mexico City, D.F. 03812 (☎5453 51 21; fax 5398 11 86; mmobarak@nova.net.mx).

Despite the increasing number of Jews in Mexico (especially in Mexico City), keeping **kosher** can be difficult. Many large supermarkets sell kosher foods, but travelers will have less luck in restaurants and smaller towns. Those who keep kosher should contact synagogues for information on kosher restaurants. Your own synagogue or college Hillel should have access to lists of Jewish institutions across Mexico. Another good resource is the *Jewish Travel Guide*, by Michael Zaidner (Vallentine Mitchell, $17).

ALTERNATIVES TO TOURISM

STUDYING ABROAD

Mexico welcomes students of all ages and abilities with open arms. However, keep in mind that foreign study programs vary tremendously in expense, quality, living conditions, and degree of cultural exposure. Small, local schools and universities are generally cheaper, but international organizations may be better able to arrange academic credit at your home institution. As you can see, it's best to do your homework beforehand.

UNIVERSITIES AND UNIVERSITY PROGRAMS

Most undergraduates enroll in programs sponsored by US universities. Those relatively fluent in Spanish may find it cheaper to enroll directly in a local university, though getting credit may be more difficult. Applications to Mexican universities are usually due in early spring and require a transcript and a copy of your passport or birth certificate. Some schools that offer study abroad programs to foreigners are listed below. The first four listings are Mexican universities that accept foreign students for study abroad; the others are foreign schools with campuses or programs in Mexico.

Universidad Nacional Autónoma de México (UNAM), Apdo. 70-391, Ciudad Universitaria, México, D.F. 04510 (☎5622 2470; fax 5616 2672; cepe@servidor.unam.mx; www.cepe.unam.mx), is the largest public university in Mexico with over 100,000 students. It operates the **Centro de Enseñanza para Extranjeros (CEPE),** which provides semester, intensive, and summer programs in Spanish, art, history, and literature. The school also operates a satellite campus in Taxco.

Universidad de las Americas (UDLA), Santa Catarina Mártir, Cholula, Puebla 72820, Mexico (http://info.pue.udlap.mx), is a private university that has the distinction of being the only Mexican university accredited in the US. Write to the Decanatura de Asuntos Internacionales (☎2229 3160; fax 2299 3169; informes@mail.pue.udlap.mx) for information on becoming a visiting student.

Tecnológico de Monterrey (study@itesm.mx; http://dri.sistema.itesm.mx/dial/proyectos/webdpi). One of the most prestigious private universities in the country, specializing in science, mathematics, and engineering. There are seven campuses across the country; each hosts its own international program.

Universidad Iberoamericana, Paseo de la Reforma No. 880, Col. Lomas de Santa Fe, Deleg. Alvaro Obregón, 01210 Mexico, D.F. (international@uia.mx; www.uia.mx), or

Ibero for short, is a private university that offers semesters abroad, summer programs, and intensive Spanish instruction. Its main campus is in Mexico City, but there are satellite campuses.

Augsburg College Center for Global Education, 2211 Riverside Ave., Minneapolis, MN, 55454 (☎800-299-8889; fax 612-330 1695; www.augsburg.edu/global/index.html). Semester-long programs based in Cuernavaca focusing on issues of gender, human rights, and ecology.

Central College Abroad, Office of International Education, 812 University, Pella, IA 50219 (☎800-831-3629 or 641-628-5284; studyabroad.com/central). Offers semester- and year-long programs in Mexico. US$25 application fee.

Council on International Educational Exchange (CIEE), 633 3rd Ave. 20th fl., New York, NY 10017 (☎888-268-6245 or 800-407-8839; www.ciee.org/study) sponsors a semester program at the University of Guadalajara. Contact program assistant Angela Munro (☎212-872 2762; studyinfo@ciee.org).

School for International Training, College Semester Abroad, Admissions, Kipling Rd., P.O. Box 676, Brattleboro, VT 05302 (☎800-336-1616 or 802-258-3267; www.sit.edu). Semester- and year-long programs in Mexico run $10,600-13,700. Also runs the **Experiment in International Living** (☎800-345-2929; fax 802-258-3428; eil@worldlearning.org), 3- to 5-week summer programs that offer high-school students cross-cultural homestays, community service, ecological adventure, and language training in Mexico for $1900-5000.

International Association for the Exchange of Students for Technical Experience (IAESTE), 10400 Little Patuxent Pkwy. #250, Columbia, MD 21044 (☎410-997-2200; www.aipt.org). Operates 8- to 12-week programs in Mexico for college students who have completed 2 years of technical study. $25 application fee.

LANGUAGE SCHOOLS
Geared more toward high school students and older adults, language schools concentrate in colonial cities, such as Cuernavaca, Puebla, and Oaxaca. Visitors to

these cities can easily obtain information directly from the schools. Programs generally cost anywhere from $100 to $500, depending on duration and whether the school is foreign or Mexican-owned.

The Center for Bilingual Multicultural Studies, San Jeronimo 304, Col. San Jeronimo, Cuernavaca, Morelos 62179 Mexico (☎(7) 317 10 87; www.bilingual-center.com). Mailing address: Apdo. postal 1520, Cuernavaca, Morelos 62000 Mexico. Intensive classes for $200 per week. Offers special language programs for executives and nurses.

Instituto Falcon, Callejon de la Mora 158, Guanajuato, 36000 Mexico (☎(4) 731 10 84; fax 731 07 45; www.institutofalcon.com). Offers a 16-week program in Mexican culture and Spanish language for $495. Regular classes $65-120 per week. Dorms and homestays $5-20 per day. Senior discounts.

Instituto Habla Hispana, Calzada de la Luz 25, Apdo. 689, San Miguel de Allende, Gto., C.P. 37700 Mexico (☎(4) 152 07 13; fax 152 15 35). Mail c/o Kima Cargill, 814 E. 4th St., Austin, TX 78751 (kcargill@mail.utexas.edu). Spanish courses $100 per week.

Language Immersion Institute, 75 South Manheim Blvd., The College at New Paltz, New Paltz, NY 12561 (☎914-257-3500; www.newpaltz.edu/lii). 2-week summer language courses and some overseas courses in Spanish. Program fees are about $295 for a weekend or $750 per 2 weeks.

Spanish Institute of Puebla, 15 Poniente #504, Puebla, Puebla 72420 Mexico (☎(2) 240 86 92; www.sipuebla.com). $1550 for four weeks of intensive classes.

FURTHER READING AND RESOURCES

www.studyabroad.com

www.studyabroadlinks.com

Academic Year Abroad 2001/2002. Institute of International Education Books ($47).

Vacation Study Abroad 2001/2002. Institute of International Education Books ($43).

Peterson's Study Abroad 2002. Peterson's ($30).

Peterson's Summer Study Abroad 2002. Peterson's ($30).

WORKING ABROAD

The Mexican government is wary of giving up precious jobs to foreigners when so many Mexicans are unemployed. Previously, only 10% of employees of foreign firms located in Mexico could have non-Mexican citizenship; the limit now varies by sector. If you want to work in Mexico, you must secure a work visa (see **Business Visas,** p. 9).

TEACHING ENGLISH

International Schools Services, Educational Staffing Program, P.O. Box 5910, Princeton, NJ 08543 (☎609-452-0990; www.iss.edu). Recruits teachers and administrators for American and English schools in Mexico. $150 program fee.

Office of Overseas Schools, US Department of State, Room H328, SA-1, Washington, D.C. 20522 (☎202-261-8200; fax 261-8224; www.state.gov/www/about_state/schools). Keeps a comprehensive list of schools abroad and agencies that arrange placement for Americans to teach abroad.

World Teach, Center for International Development, 79 John F. Kennedy St., Cambridge, MA 02138 (☎800-483-2240; www.worldteach.org). Volunteers teach English and environmental education for 6-12 months in Chiapas and the Yucatán. A bachelor's degree is required.

ARCHAEOLOGICAL DIGS

Archaeological Institute of America, 656 Beacon St., Boston, MA 02215 (☎617-353-9361; www.archaeological.org). The *Archaeological Fieldwork Opportunities Bulletin* ($20 for non-members) lists field sites throughout Mexico. Purchase the bulletin from Kendall/Hunt Publishing, 4050 Westmark Dr., Dubuque, Iowa 52002 (☎800-228-0810).

VOLUNTEERING

Volunteer jobs are readily available, and many provide room and board in exchange for labor. You can sometimes avoid high application fees by contacting the individual workcamps directly or save even more money by seeking out local volunteer opportunities after arriving in Mexico.

AmeriSpan, P.O. Box 40007, Philadelphia, PA, 19106 (☎800-879-6640; www.amerispan.com). Internships and placements all over Mexico in the fields of education, public health, the environment, ESL, and social work.

Earthwatch, 3 Clocktower Pl., P.O. Box 75, Maynard, MA 01754 (☎800-776-0188; www.earthwatch.org). Arranges 1-3-week programs in Mexico to promote conservation of natural resources. Programs average $1600.

Global Exchange, 2017 Mission #303, San Francisco, CA 94110 (☎415-255-7296 ext. 239; mexico@globalexchange.org; www.globalexchange.org/campaigns/mexico). Mexico campaigns focus on education, research, and economic and human rights, and aim to put activists in contact with Mexican grassroots movements. Also offers "Reality Tours" of local life and politics. Tours cost $500-1000.

Habitat for Humanity International, 121 Habitat St., Americus, GA 31709 (☎800-422-4828; www.habitat.org). Offers opportunities to live in Mexico and build houses in a host community. Costs range $1200-3500.

Volunteers for Peace, 1034 Tiffany Rd., Belmont, VT 05730 (☎802-259-2759; www.vfp.org). Arranges placement in workcamps in Mexico. Annual *International Workcamp Directory* $20. Registration fee $200. Free newsletter.

FURTHER READING

International Jobs: Where They Are, How to Get Them, Eric Kocher. Perseus Press ($17).

Work Abroad: The Complete Guide to Finding a Job Overseas, Clayton Hubbs. Transitions Abroad ($16).

International Directory of Voluntary Work, Louise Whetter. Vacation Work Publications ($16).

Teaching English Abroad, Susan Griffin. Vacation Work ($18).

OTHER RESOURCES

Let's Go tries to cover all aspects of budget travel, but we can't put *everything* in our guides. Listed below are books and websites that can serve as jumping off points for your own research.

A *MUY* USEFUL PUBLICATION

México Desconocido: These popular monthly travel magazines, in Spanish and English, describe little-known areas and customs of Mexico. Subscriptions in the US cost $50 (mexdesco@compuserve.com.mx); subscriptions in Mexico cost 300 pesos. Online at www.mexdesco.com.

THE WORLD WIDE WEB

Almost every aspect of budget travel (except, of course, experience) is accessible on the Internet; in less than 10 minutes at the keyboard, you can make a reservation at a hotel in the Yucatán, get advice on travel hotspots from travelers who have just returned from Baja California, or find out how much a bus from Ciudad Juárez to Guadalajara costs. Listed here are some budget travel sites to start off your surfing. Because website turnover is high, use search engines to strike out on your own.

ON BUDGET TRAVEL

How to See the World: www.artoftravel.com. A compendium of great travel tips, from cheap flights to self-defense to interacting with local culture.

Rec. Travel Library: www.travel-library.com. A fantastic set of links for general information and personal travelogues.

INFORMATION ON MEXICO

CIA World Factbook: www.odci.gov/cia/publications/factbook/index.html. Tons of vital statistics on Mexican geography, government, economy, and people.

Foreign Language for Travelers: www.travlang.com. Provides free online translating dictionaries and lists of phrases in Spanish.

MyTravelGuide: www.mytravelguide.com. Country overviews, with everything from history to transportation to live web-cam coverage of Mexico.

Geographia: www.geographia.com. Highlights, culture, and people of Mexico.

Atevo Travel: www.atevo.com/guides/destinations. Detailed introductions, travel tips, and suggested itineraries.

TravelPage: www.travelpage.com. Links to official tourist office sites throughout Mexico.

PlanetRider: www.planetrider.com/Travel_Destinations.cfm. A subjective list of links to the "best" websites covering the culture and tourist attractions of Mexico.

Foreign Language for Travelers: www.travlang.com. Helps you brush up your Spanish.

Mexico City Subway System: http://www.century.com.mx/mapa/metro.htm. A good map and guide to Mexico City and its Metro.

Mexico Reference Desk: www.lanic.utexas.edu/la/Mexico. An abundance of links to Mexico-related sites.

Microsoft Expedia: www.expedia.msn.com. This mega-site has everything you'd ever need to make travel plans on the web—compare flight fares, look at maps, and book reservations.

US State Department Travel Advisory for Mexico: http://travel.state.gov/mexico.html. The word from above on travel safety and recommended precautions.

Yahoo! Mexico Links: www.yahoo.com/regional/countries/mexico. Well-indexed and searchable database of over 2000 links related to Mexico.

Zapatista Web Page: www.ezln.org. Provides up-to-the-minute information in English and Spanish about Mexico's most prominent rebel group.

AND OUR PERSONAL FAVORITE...

Let's Go: www.letsgo.com. Our constantly expanding website features photos and streaming video, online ordering of all our titles, info about our books, a travel forum buzzing with stories and tips, and links that will help you find everything you ever wanted to know about Mexico.

LIFE AND TIMES

THE LAND

Mexico curves from north to south, maximizing coast and topical variance to form some two million sq. km of the world's most varied landscape. Containing parched scrub-brush deserts, jungle rainforests, mile-high volcanoes, temperate valleys, low coastal lagoons, and red canyon land, Mexico is one of the most physically and ecologically striking countries in the world.

GEOGRAPHY AND GEOLOGY

Mexico is situated at the eastern extremity of the "Ring of Fire," the region of tectonic activity encircling the Pacific Ocean that causes earthquakes and volcanic activity from Indonesia to Canada. These geologic forces have, over the millennia, shaped Mexico into a landscape of crags, valleys, and high mountain chains that can change drastically over the span of a few kilometers.

BAJA CALIFORNIA AND THE NORTH

Northern Mexico is by and large low, arid, and hot. The *noreste* (northeast) is dryer than the *noroeste* (northwest), and over time, periodically flooded rivers have carved much of the northwest into canyons. The **Barranca del Cobre** (Copper Canyon) is the treasure of the region—five canyons converge to form one, covering an area four times the size of the Grand Canyon in Arizona.

The spur of the **Baja Peninsula** begins in Mexico's northwest corner and descends, dividing the **Gulf of California** (commonly called the **Sea of Cortés**) from the Pacific Ocean. The Peninsula is rocky and scaldingly hot. A spine of mountains runs its dusty 1330km length, sloping gently to the eastern shore, but cutting sharply on the west to create a craggy coast.

THE CENTER

Two great mountain ranges, the **Sierra Madre Occidental** on the west and the **Sierra Madre Oriental** on the east, slice a V-shape through the heart of the country. The Sierra Madre Occidental is volcanic, with peaks nearly 3000m high, and the Sierra Madre Oriental reaches heights of nearly 4000m. Between the two ranges lies the **Altiplano,** a vast network of highlands stretching from the US border more than 2500km southward to the **Isthmus of Tehuantepec,** near the Guatemalan border. The hospitable southern Altiplano, including the Valley of Mexico, is home to Mexico City and more than half of Mexico's entire population. The land just south of Mexico City at the base of the V, the **Cordillera Neovolcánica,** is the most volcanic in all of Mexico. The volcanoes **Citlaltépetl, Popocatépetl,** and **Iztaccíhuatl** all tower over 5000m above sea level, and smaller ones sprinkle the region. Though many of these volcanoes have lain dormant since the 1800s, Popocatépetl ("Smoking Mountain" in Náhuatl) erupted in 1994, spewing ash over the city of Puebla.

Farther south are the **Southern Highlands,** a series of mountain ranges, plateaus, and valleys in the states of Guerrero and Oaxaca. The largest range, the **Sierra Madre del Sur,** runs along the southwest coast of Mexico, dipping into the Pacific, and sheltering resort towns like Acapulco at its base. The eastern side slopes into the verdant **Oaxaca Valley,** the largest and most populous in the area.

The lands directly to the east and west of the area bounded by the Sierra Madre Occidental and the Sierra Madre Oriental are far less mountainous than the interior. Bordering the Sea of Cortés, the **Pacific Coastal Lowland,** east of the Sierra Madre Occidental, is a dry, relatively flat region of *mesas*. On the eastern side of the country, past the Sierra Madre Oriental, is the much wetter **Gulf Coastal Plain.**

This humid and swampy lagoon land runs from the US border to the **Isthmus of Tehuantepec.** The isthmus itself is a low stretch of land with hills rarely reaching higher than 300m. With the **Gulf of Campeche** to its north and the **Gulf of Tehuantepec** to its south, the isthmus narrows to little more than 200km at its slimmest. Northeast of the isthmus is the **Tabasco Plain,** and southeast are the **Chiapas Highlands,** an area of high mountains surrounding a large rift valley. The highlands continue into Guatemala, forming the northern tip of the Central American ranges.

THE YUCATÁN PENINSULA

Northeast of the Highlands juts the **Yucatán Peninsula.** An extremely flat region, the Peninsula is surrounded by the Gulf of Mexico to the west and north, and the Caribbean Sea to the east. The northern part of the peninsula is much drier than the south, and the porous limestone soil absorbs moisture before it can consolidate into rivers. Pockmarking the limestone are caverns and *cenotes,* natural wells that were often part of Maya cities or ceremonial centers. These *cenotes* provide the only source of fresh water on the Yucatán. Some scientists believe the unusually high density of *cenotes* in the Yucatán is the result of the same **meteor impact** that may have killed the dinosaurs 65 million years ago. In the 1940s, an oil company drilling in the Yucatán uncovered evidence of what is now known as the **Chicxulub Crater.** A gigantic bowl 180km across and more than 200km deep, buried half on land and half under the Gulf of Mexico, the crater cannot be seen without intricate instruments. A ring of caves on the perimeter of the crater supports the idea of a link between impact and the formation of *cenotes.*

CLIMATE, FLORA, AND FAUNA

Mexico's climate runs the gambit from desert to rainforest. There are two seasons: wet (May-Aug., though a few regions receive rain year round and others almost never) and dry (Sept.-Apr.). Hurricanes and tropical storms are most likely to hit the coast in August and September. Mexico's patchwork landscape makes for a patchwork ecosystem, dependent more on altitude than latitude. In Mexico you will find cool coniferous forests, humid lagoons, luscious rainforests, icy mountain peaks, and arid cactus-covered big-sky country.

THE NORTH

Baja California and the north most closely resemble the Mexico depicted in Hollywood films: dusty, bone-dry, and oppressively hot. Annual rainfall is often less than 25cm, and summer temperatures may exceed 43°C (110°F). Travelers recognize Baja California as the hottest place in all of Mexico. Though days may be broiling in these regions, be wary; once the scalding sun disappears for the night, cloudless skies allow the day's heat to escape, and temperatures fall dramatically.

The Sonoran and Chihuahuan deserts meet in the north of Mexico, and, together with the Mojave and Great Basin deserts in the US, comprise one of the world's largest desert regions. Over 250 kinds of cactus populate the **Chihuahan Desert.** Not to be outdone, the **Sonoran Desert** is the only place where one can find the huge **cardón** cactus that dominates the barren landscape and the unique **boojum tree,** a columnar succulent that can reach heights of over 15m. Larger **desert animals,** including armadillos, rabbits and other rodents, and lizards, inhabit both deserts.

Baja California and the northern Pacific Coast are home to many large **aquatic mammals.** Those who yearn to swim with the dolphins will finally get their chance, while those who prefer to save the whales can treat themselves to an eyeful of over 15 different species. If your tastes run to the exotic and slightly erotic, Baja California offers ample opportunity to view the mating of elephant seals. The seals mate up and down the coast, but **Bahía de Sebastián Vizcaíno,** near Guerrero Negro (see p. 162), is the best place to view the dirty deed—nearby islands are overrun with elephant seals, most in the process of making more elephant seals.

THE SOUTH

The southern climate varies greatly, mainly due to fluctuations in altitude. People often distinguish between *tierra caliente* (from sea level to an elevation of 1000m), *tierra templada* (1000-2000m), *tierra fria* (2000-3000m), and *tierra helada* (3000m and up). Both the Sierra Madre Occidental and Oriental receive rainfall year round. At lower elevations (300-1000m) the mountainside is covered in deciduous forest. Trees and flowering plants such as orchids and bromeliads flourish during the summer, but most trees lose their leaves during the winter. Higher in altitude (1000-2000m), the forests become coniferous. Pines, junipers, and evergreen oaks are common. At the topmost levels (4000-5000m), trees cannot survive, and snow covers the ground year round. Between the two mountain ranges, the Altiplano is covered in grassland, punctuated by scrub brush and prickly-pear cactus. Many large mammals populate the highlands, among them foxes, mountain lions, and coyotes.

The states of **Tabasco** and **Campeche,** southwest of the Yucatán Peninsula, contain the only true **rainforests** in Mexico. These rainforests are composed of several interlocking ecosystems—each level, from ground to canopy, supports many distinct species. Anteaters, tapirs (floppy-snouted, odd-toed beasties), and monkeys abound, along with an endless variety of birds, lizards, frogs, and insects. At higher elevations, the rainforest becomes a **cloud forest.** Here, moisture reaches the forest directly from standing clouds. Home to the Zapatista rebels, the **Selva Lacandona** is Mexico's most notable tropical forest. The remainder of the Gulf Coast is largely composed of swamp and marshland. Mangrove trees densely line the sweltering shore, as fresh water mixes with salt in the region's many river deltas. Marshes, like rainforests, contain an incredible diversity of plant and animal life, the exact composition of which varies greatly along the Gulf Coast.

A "BRIEF" HISTORY

Over the span of 10,000 years, Mexico has seen the rise and fall of mighty empires, the pain of conquest, three tumultuous revolutions, and the struggle to rebuild in the era of modern capitalism. Such enduring drama can hardly be condensed into a neat 18-page segment. Nonetheless...

PRE-HISPANIC SOCIETIES

Archaeologists generally categorize Mexican Pre-Hispanic societies into five different time periods: **Pre-Agricultural** (or Paleoindian, 40,000-8000 BC), **Archaic** (8000-2000 BC), **Formative** (or Pre-Classic, 2000 BC-AD 200), **Classic** (200-900), and **Post-Classic** (or Historical, 900-1521).

PRE-AGRICULTURAL AND ARCHAIC PERIODS

Archaeologists believe that the first Mexicans arrived by crossing the **Bering Strait,** the stretch of dry land left by the receding ocean during the **Wisconsin (Pleistocene) Ice Age.** From about 50,000 to 9000 BC, a large-scale migration took place as nomadic hunters tracked game across the Bering Strait from Russia into Alaska. Archaeologists know very little about the lives of the early Mexicans; what has been uncovered indicates that they were most likely hunter-gatherers who used primitive tools to hunt large game such as hairy mammoths and giant armadillos. After 7500 BC, the climate became more arid, causing the demise of the game that had long provided the hunter-gather with sustenance. This change led early Mexicans to agriculture and the cultivation of crops such as maize and beans.

THE FORMATIVE PERIOD

The development of agriculture gave rise to the great empires of Mesoamerica. Society during the Formative (or Pre-Classic) Period centered around a dependence on maize and the linkage between religion and agricultural fertility.

THE OLMECS

Olmec culture flourished in the warm, humid areas that today comprise the states of Veracruz (see p. 493) and Tabasco (see p. 522). The Olmec reign began in the farming and fishing village of **San Lorenzo** (see p. 522) around 1700 BC. By 1350 BC, the small town had grown up, boasting large scale public works decorated with intricate artistic motifs including the trademark Olmec stone heads and delicate jade figurines and masks. When San Lorenzo succumbed to invasion around 900 BC, the settlements at **La Venta** (see p. 526), southeast of San Lorenzo, and **Tres Zapotes** (see p. 517) began to take on more power. Perhaps the most important contribution of the Olmec culture was the development of **hieroglyphic writing,** influences of which are evident in the written works of later civilizations, most noticeably that of the Maya. Of particular importance was the **long count system** calendar, which used a system of dots and bars to represent days and months. After the demise of La Venta around 600 BC, the golden age of the Olmecs came to an end; they disappeared just as mysteriously as they had appeared.

THE CLASSIC PERIOD

During the Classic Period, from AD 250 to 900, civilizations comparable to those of the great European empires developed throughout Mesoamerica. Archaeologists recognize **Teotihuacán, Monte Albán,** and the **Maya** as the great civilizations of the era, but other groups—such as those at **El Tajín** (see p. 504), **Cholula** (see p. 356), **Cacaxtla** (see p. 346), and **Xochicalco** (see p. 337)—were also formidable powers.

TEOTIHUACÁN

The city at **Teotihuacán** (see p. 126) was likely the most powerful of the great Classic civilizations. When the Aztecs settled the valley several centuries later, they were so impressed with this magnificent city that they named it Teotihuacán, which means "Place of the Gods" in Náhuatl. Archaeological evidence indicates that Teotihuacán's advanced system of urban design arose around 200 BC—Teotihuacanos developed a complex road system anchored by ceremonial plazas, massive pyramids, and residential quarters. The influence of Teotihuacán spread well beyond the area of the central valley and evidence of trade has been found as far south as Guatemala.

MONTE ALBÁN AND THE ZAPOTEC EMPIRE

While Teotihuacán dominated the Valley of Mexico, **Monte Albán** (see p. 468), the Zapotec capital, controlled the Oaxaca Valley to the south. Between 500 and 100 BC the Zapotecs began settling this hilly region, located just west of modern-day **Oaxaca City.** The city grew rapidly from a small terraced farming community to the greatest power in the region. Home to nearly 20,000, Monte Albán was large enough to support a complex social structure of nobles and priests. Between AD 400 and 700, however, this sophisticated city began to lose its dominance, perhaps due to the rise of neighboring powers, such as the **Mixtec,** who ruled from the holy city of **Mitla** (see p. 465).

THE CLASSIC MAYA

Unlike their contemporaries, the Maya did not concentrate their power in one location. The cities of **Palenque** (see p. 551),

50,000-9000 BC: Intrepid Mexicans-to-be cross the Bering Strait.

1750-1350 BC: Olmecs "invent" Mesoamerican civilization and make lots of large stone heads.

900 BC: Olmecs make the move to La Venta.

600 BC: La Venta is no more; the Olmecs are likewise.

AD 200-900: Classic Period. Good times for all.

500: Mighty Teotihuacán is the most powerful Classic center. It is also very big.

(500-100 BC: Zapotecs made the scene in Monte Albán.)

400-700: Monte Albán is no more.

LIFE AND TIMES

100-900: The Maya are in their prime. They develop arts and sciences to a level never before seen in the Americas, and rarely before in the world.

Tikal, Copán, and others throughout Chiapas and Central America served as regional capitals, each governing over neighboring villages. The Classic Period was a time of tremendous growth and advancement for the Maya, who became proficient in engineering, mathematics, art, architecture, and astronomy. They devised a method to predict the movement of celestial bodies with total precision, and were the first in the world to understand the mathematical concept of zero. The Maya created a highly advanced calendar and displayed their artistic talents in manuscripts, ceramics, murals, and reliefs. Their famous temples, now popular ruins, were tall, steeply terraced pyramids with false fronts. Hardly the peaceful society of popular imagination, Maya history includes evidence of human sacrifice, warfare, and internal revolt. This violence may have hastened the end of the Maya Classic Period around 900.

900: The Maya fall from grace.

A VERY LONG COUNT

Well before they developed a writing system, the Maya already had three sophisticated, interlocking calendar systems. The basis of all three was a ritual count of 20 days, called *k'in*, the Maya word for sun, each of which has a name and a glyph. A period of 20 *k'in* composed a *uinal* (month). From here the three systems diverge: there was the 13-*uinal* (260-day) ceremonial year and the 18-*uinal* and 5-*k'in* (365-day) secular year. These two calendars quickly diverged from one another, but they would realign once every 52 years. The Maya celebrated these convergences with enormous festivals, ceremonies, and, sometimes, massive destruction. The third way of measuring time was the Long Count. Linear rather than cyclical, the Long Count counted all dates from the original 0.0.0.0.0, defined by scholars as August 11th, 3114 BC. Besides the *k'in* and *uinal*, Long Count incorporated the *tun* (18 *uinal*), the *k'atun* (20 *tun*), and the *baktun* (20 *k'atun*). Dates were written in the same manner that odometers display mileage, with the shortest periods, *k'in*, farthest right, and the longest, *baktun*, farthest left. November 11th, 1983 would correspond to 12.18.10.8.7—12 *baktun*, 18 *k'atun*, and so on. After 13 *baktun*, one Great Cycle is completed and the world is reborn. The fourth creation in the entire history of the earth is scheduled for December 23rd, 2012. Mark your calendars!

THE POST-CLASSIC PERIOD

AD 900: Post-Classic Period begins. Everything goes awry.

The Post-Classic Period began with the demise of the great civilizations of Teotihuacán, Monte Albán, and the Maya around 900, continued with the rise of the Toltecs and eventually the Aztecs, and ended with the Spanish conquest of the Aztecs in 1521. The spread of the great Aztec empire facilitated long-distance trade. While architecture and arts suffered considerably, technological innovation also slowed at the expense of centralization and conquest.

THE TOLTECS

The Toltecs, originally known as the **Chichimeca** or the **Toltec-Chichimeca,** established their presence in central Mexico around 800, in the modern-day states of Zacatecas and Hidalgo. The greatest Toltec leader was the benevolent and learned **Ce**

Acatl Topiltzin (later called **Topiltzin-Quetzalcóatl**) who assumed the throne by killing his treacherous uncle. In 968, he founded the city of **Tula** (see p. 325), the splendid Toltec capital renowned for its agriculture and architecture. Tricked by his enemies, Topiltzin-Quetzalcóatl was shamed into exile in 987. However, he vowed to return in the next year of Ce Acatl, the year of **One Reed.** That year, for better or for worse, would eventually correspond with **1519,** the year of the Spanish invasion. The Toltec empire thrived into the 1100s, when drought and famine ravaged their civilization.

THE POST-CLASSIC MAYA

Whereas the Classic Maya civilizations had established strongholds throughout Mexico and Central America, the Post-Classic Maya settled almost exclusively in the Yucatán Peninsula around the **cenotes,** or sinkholes, that provide the only source of fresh water in the flat, limestone peninsula. Unlike the Classic Maya, who had developed a unique artistic tradition, the Post-Classic Maya style drew from many cultures, particularly that of the Toltec, an influence likely due to extensive contact between Tula and the Post-Classic Maya. (Because of this influence, this time period in Maya history is also known as the **Toltec Period.**) The three major city-states, **Chichén Itzá** (see p. 591), **Mayapán** (see p. 579), and **Uxmal** (see p. 575) together formed the **Mayapán League,** which Chichén Itzá dominated until its demise in the mid-1400s. Mayapán then emerged as the most important Post-Classic Maya center. The violent fall of Mayapán in 1441 marked the end of a centralized Maya civilization, and independent city-states assumed control of the region.

THE AZTECS (THE MEXICA)

The last great power of Pre-Hispanic Mexico, the violent and militaristic Aztecs inhabited the central **Valley of Anáhuac** (the modern-day Valley of Mexico) from the late 1200s until the fall of their capital, Tenochtitlán, in 1521.

ORIGINS. The Aztec, then known as the **Mexica,** arrived in the fertile Valley of Anáhuac in the 13th century. From 1270 to 1319, the Aztecs lived at the mercy of the dominant **Tepenec empire.** By trading and forming alliances, the Aztecs slowly accumulated power. Under the rule of **Itzcóatl,** they finally won independence and celebrated by establishing the city of **Tenochtitlán** (modern-day Mexico City, see p. 75). Itzcóatl's successor, **Nazahualcoyótl,** defeated the lesser city-states of the Anáhuac, and cleared the way for centuries of Aztec domination.

EAGLE BITES SERPENT Legend has it that the patron deity of the Mexica, the hummingbird god of sun and war, **Huitzilopochtli,** revealed a vision to his people: they would find an eagle perched upon a cactus with a serpent in its talons, and when they did, they were to settle in that very spot. While wandering south, they discovered this vision near Lago Texcoco, the ancient lake upon which Mexico City now sits. The image was so enduring that the eagle and serpent can still be seen, battling eternally on Mexico's flag.

800-1100: The Toltecs have their day in Tula.

987: Topiltzin-Quetzalcóatl leaves Tula, promising to return in the year One Reed (1519).

1100: The Toltecs succumb.

1050-1450: The Post-Classic Maya diaspora settles in the Yucatán, drinking from *cenotes* and exchanging culture with the similarly down-and-out Toltecs.

1441: The Maya bicker and unceremoniously bite the dust.

1200-1521: The Aztecs, Mexico's bad boys, whip the region into shape.

1350: Tenochtitlán, the Aztec capital, is a model of good urban planning.

LIFE AND TIMES

SOCIETY. As the Aztec empire grew, its social hierarchy became more regimented and complex. Tenochtitlán was at one point the largest and most magnificent city in the world, surpassing cities such as Paris and Rome, not only in population, but also in cleanliness, urban planning, and architecture. The royal family and nobles occupied the highest position in Aztec society, followed closely by the warring class. The Aztecs valued the art of war, and distinction on the battlefield was one of the few ways male citizens could enter the nobility. Traders, known as **pochteca**, were next in line. Their trade networks linked the entirety of Mesoamerica and formed the bedrock of the Aztec empire. Farmers, laborers, and artisans comprised the common class. Women in Aztec society enjoyed more rights than did their European counterparts and were active in religion, agriculture, and politics.

RELIGION. The Aztecs believed in cyclical time. The earth and sun had been recreated four times, and it was during the present time, that of the fifth sun, that the earth would finally be destroyed. Because the Aztecs relied on their patron god Huitzilopochtli to sustain the cycles, they strived to appease him through human sacrifice. Sacrifice was a solemn affair— the palpitating heart of the sacrificial victim was removed with a sharp obsidian knife and then presented to the deity. Such ceremonies took place in Tenochtitlán's main temple, the **Templo Mayor** (see p. 102). The Aztecs worshipped an extensive pantheon of deities, including the rain god **Tlaloc** and the feathered serpent **Quetzalcóatl.**

AZTEC RULE. With over five million people, the Aztec empire was the largest empire in Pre-Hispanic Mexico. They ruled by requiring townships to recognize Aztec sovereignty and contribute goods, land, and sacrificial victims to the empire. By the beginning of the 16th century, the Aztecs had reached the peak of their power in the Valley of Mexico.

CONQUEST & COLONIZATION

With the arrival of the Europeans in the 16th century, the growth of the Aztec empire came to an abrupt end. The course of Mexican history radically changed, and a new hybrid of native and Spanish cultures began to emerge.

ENTER CORTÉS

ARRIVAL

After **Christopher Columbus** discovered the islands of the Caribbean in 1492, waves of Europeans flocked to Mesoamerica to explore and exploit the new territories. In the early 16th century, the governor of Cuba, **Diego Velázquez,** launched numerous expeditions to search for slaves and gold. Having heard rumors of a mighty empire on the Mexican mainland, Velázquez chose a veteran explorer, 34-year-old **Hernán Cortés,** to lead an expedition. In 1519, Cortés landed on the island of **Cozumel** (see p. 623). There he met **Jerónimo de Aguilar,** a Spaniard, and former prisoner of the Maya, who spoke fluent Maya.

Taking Aguilar with him, Cortés made his way up the Gulf Coast, toward Tabasco. There, after defeating the local natives, Cortés received a reward of 20 maidens. One of these was

1350: Aztecs swipe certain notions of time from the Maya and busy themselves with gruesome human sacrifice.

1350-1521: The Aztecs thrive, reproduce, sacrifice, and generally dominate.

1492: Columbus sails the ocean blue.

LIFE AND TIMES

Malintzin (known to the Spanish as **Doña Marina** and to Mexicans by the traitor appellation **La Malinche**), an Aztec who had been enslaved in the southern part of the country. La Malinche could speak both Náhuatl, the Aztec language, and Maya. Using these two interpreters (Náhuatl to Maya by way of La Malinche, Maya to Spanish by Aguilar), Cortés was able to overcome the language barrier. La Malinche later became Cortés's mistress and advisor. Continuing up the coast, Cortés traveled to the Totonac capital of **Zempoala** (see p. 511) and eastward to **Tlaxcala** (see p. 339), persuading both the Totonecs and the Tlaxcalans to join him against the Aztecs. Cortés then marched on **Cholula** (see p. 356), where his army massacred 6000 Aztec allies in a battle known as the **Cholula Massacre**.

FALL OF THE AZTECS

The mighty Aztec emperor **Moctezuma II** nervously awaited Cortés's arrival. According to legend, Quetzalcóatl had foretold his return in the year One Reed, which, by the Toltec calendar, corresponded to 1519. Grappling with rumors that Cortés was the light-skinned Toltec ruler Topiltzin-Quetzalcóatl, Moctezuma had no choice but to greet him, inviting Cortés and his men to stay as royal guests in Tenochtitlán. The initial period of peaceful, though tense, relations quickly soured when Moctezuma was kidnapped by the Spanish. In retaliation, the Aztecs expelled Cortés from Tenochtitlán on July 1, 1520, a night known to the Spanish as **La Noche Triste (the Sad Night)**. Nevertheless, Cortés quickly regrouped and the Aztecs—weakened by plagues and famine and overwhelmed by the Spaniards' technology—were unable to resist the Spanish attack. On August 13, 1521, the Aztecs, and their new emperor **Cuauhtémoc**, were soundly defeated at **Tlatelolco**.

THE COLONIAL PERIOD

Soon after the fall of Tenochtitlán, the Spaniards completely sacked the vestiges of the Aztec empire, building "New Spain" from the ground up.

EXPANSION OF CONTROL

Because the Aztec empire had controlled much of central Mexico, most of the area was immediately brought under Spanish control. *Conquistadores* aplenty dispersed to rein in the rest of Mesoamerica. Many were lured into the northern parts of the country by the search for the mythical cities of gold—the so-called **Northern Mystery**. Explorations led by **Francisco Vázquez de Coronado** and **Juan Rodríguez de Cabrillo** traveled as far north as Kansas and California; however, their search for the fabled cities proved futile.

THE PLAGUES OF MESOAMERICA. As the Spaniards pushed through Mexico, a powerful ally helped to clear the way. The everyday sicknesses carried by Spaniards from the Old World turned into plagues that killed millions of Indians who had no natural immunities to the diseases. **Smallpox, typhoid,** and **dysentery** wiped out whole villages, leaving behind empty tracts of land that settlers grabbed eagerly. Disease is now recognized as the most important contributing factor in the European conquest of the New World.

1519: (The year One Reed) Cortés picks a good time to arrive in Mexico. Rumors spread that he is the returned deity-king Topiltzin-Quetzalcóatl. He is, in fact, not.

LIFE AND TIMES

1521: Cortés overstays his welcome. Tenochtitlán falls and Moctezuma is killed. **Dead Leader Meter: 1.**

1521-1600: The Spanish take over, raping land and people in their quest for gold and power. The trend continues for quite some time.

1521-1600: Millions of indigenous people die from illnesses carried by the Spanish.

THE ENCOMIENDA SYSTEM. As the *conquistadores* realized that their appetite for gold would go unfulfilled, they began to demand labor and land from the conquered natives. Villages had to send a quota of laborers to work on Spanish farms, called **encomiendas,** and in return, the **encomendero** was responsible for Christianizing and educating his workers. The system was less than perfect, and reports of abuse were rampant.

1521-1600: The *encomienda* system provides the Spaniards with cheap labor.

THE RELIGIOUS CONQUEST. As soon as the Spaniards took Tenochtitlán, they razed the Aztecs' central temple and built a cathedral—now Mexico's **National Cathedral** (see p. 101)—with the rubble. Some communities tried to defend their native religions, but, by the mid-1500s, missionaries had converted and baptized millions. Roman Catholicism was interwoven with traditional practices, creating the religious fusion that persists today in many rural areas.

1521-1810: The Spanish convert millions to Catholicism.

RACE AND CLASS. Clear racial boundaries characterized colonial society. **Peninsulares,** whites born in Spain, were at the top of the social hierarchy. **Criollos,** Spaniards born in Mexico, were considered "second-class" citizens and were overlooked for high positions in the Church and government. **Indígenas** (or **Indios**) occupied the lowest social rung. Complete segregation, however, was impossible, and, within a few generations, a huge new racial group had emerged—**mestizos,** children of mixed Spanish and *indígena* parentage. This group now forms nearly the entire racial fabric of Mexican civilization.

A COUNTRY IS BORN

THE STRUGGLE FOR INDEPENDENCE

"My children: a new dispensation comes to us today. Will you receive it? Will you free yourselves? Will you recover the lands stole three hundred years ago from your forefathers by the hated Spaniards? Will you not defend your religion and your rights as true patriots? Long live our Lady of Guadalupe! Death to bad government!"
—Miguel Hidalgo, *El Grito de Dolores*

HIDALGO AND MORELOS

The rumblings of rebellion began with **Father Miguel Hidalgo y Costilla,** a rebellious priest in the small parish of **Dolores** (see p. 316). Along with **Juan de Aldama, Miguel Domínguez,** and the young priest **Ignacio Allende,** Hidalgo formed a "literary club," which soon turned its thoughts from literature to revolution. When Spanish officials got wind of the revolutionary plans, they arrested Allende. Alarmed, the others decided to strike for independence at once.

On the morning of **September 16, 1810,** Hidalgo ran to the church of Dolores and rang the bells to summon the parishioners. He then delivered an electrifying call to arms—**El Grito de Dolores (The Cry of Dolores)**—to end Spanish rule, to promote the equality of races, and to demand a redistribution of the land. **Mexican Independence Day** commemorates this rebellion.

Hidalgo's army quickly grew, capturing several major cities before its march was stopped by a Spanish ambush in March

1811 in the desert town of Monclova in Coahuila. Hildalgo was promptly tried for treason and heresy and executed by a firing squad. However, the quest for independence had begun, and, after Hidalgo's death, another parish priest, **José María Morelos y Pavón**, rose to lead the independence movement. Under his command, the rebels captured Oaxaca, Orizaba, and Acapulco before Morelos was captured and, like his predecessor Hidalgo, tried for treason and heresy and executed by a firing squad.

INDEPENDENCE WON

The Hidalgo and Morelos uprisings begat five years of chaos. In the Mexican countryside, rebels such as **Vicente Guerrero** and **Guadalupe Victoria** kept the Spanish busy with guerilla skirmishes. Meanwhile in Spain, **King Ferdinand VII**, under military pressure, had sworn allegiance to the Spanish Constitution of 1812, which promoted popular sovereignty and other liberal ideals. Alarmed by this new radicalism and by the rural rebels, many Mexican conservatives and clergy decided that the best way to preserve conservative ideals would be to join the revolution, and establish an independent conservative government.

The most important convert was **Agustín de Iturbide**, a *criollo* loyalist who had led Spanish troops in battle against Hidalgo. In 1820, Iturbide was given thousands of men to battle Guerrero in southern Mexico. Rather than fight, however, Iturbide joined forces with the revolutionaries. Over several meetings the rebel and the traitor drafted the **Plan de Iguala.** Issued on February 24, 1821, it is most remembered for three guarantees—the creation of an independent constitutional monarchy, the institution of Roman Catholicism as the state religion, and the establishment of equality before the law. **The Ejército de las Tres Garantías (the Army of the Three Guarantees)** was formed under the direction of Iturbide and grew significantly in both numbers and support, especially from conservative *criollos*. The new Spanish general, **Juan de O'Donoju,** knew Mexico was lost to the popular uprising and on August 24, 1821, Iturbide and O'Donoju signed the **Treaty of Córdoba,** formalizing the principles set forth by the Plan de Iguala and establishing Mexico as an independent country.

THE NEW NATION

ITURBIDE'S EMPIRE

The national congress, intimidated by Iturbide and his supporters, quickly voted to name him Emperor of Mexico, and on July 21, 1822, Iturbide was coronated. The victory was bittersweet: a decade of war had left the economy in shambles, the mining industry in disarray, and commerce at a standstill. These problems worsened as antagonism developed between the emperor and members of congress, many of whom disapproved of Iturbide's *criollo* origins. Rather than address the problems, Iturbide decided to do away with congress altogether, disbanding the assembly on October 31, 1822. Reaction was swift and immediate, and those opposed to Iturbide summoned **Antonio López de Santa Anna** to head the rebel army. On December 1, 1822, Santa Anna officially launched his revolution, persuading many important rebel leaders to join him. After the unification of all anti-imperialist rebels under the **Plan de Casa Mata,** a fearful Iturbide abdicated the throne in February 1823, immediately leaving the country and seeking safe exile in Europe.

1810: Hidalgo and smoking-buddies kick off the revolution with the *Grito de Dolores.*

LIFE AND TIMES

1811: Hidalgo raises an army, is swiftly captured, and has his head removed. Morelos quickly suffers the same. **Dead Leader Meter: 3**

1812-20: People agree: Spain is terrible. Independence movement gains ground.

1821: Iturbide converts from loyalist to revolutionary.

Revolution #1 1821: Sensing defeat, Spain signs the Treaty of Córdoba. Mexico is now independent.

THE ERA OF SANTA ANNA

Santa Anna won the presidential election of 1832 by the largest margin in Mexican history. The great general, however, was a man more interested in the pursuit of power rather than its proper application. He soon tired of the daily minutia of the office and left the presidency in the hands of his vice president, **Valentín Goméz Farías.** Goméz Farías, a true liberal, began his presidency by instituting a series of anti-Church reforms designed to revitalize the country. Outraged, clergy members called for his removal and summoned Santa Anna out of retirement. Santa Anna answered their call and was soon at the helm of another rebellion, this time on the conservative side.

Santa Anna's new regime was conservative rather than liberal. Mexico became a centralized military state, and the ruling class grew rich on graft and bribery. As Santa Anna drained the state treasuries, Mexico was unable to pay off its foreign debt, and tensions with foreign creditors soared. In 1838, one of the infuriated creditor nations, France, attacked Veracruz and its defending fortress, San Juan de Ulúa. The conflict was dubbed the **Pastry War** in honor of a French pastry chef whose wares had been gobbled by rioting Mexican troops. The attacking French ships were driven back to sea and ultimately forced to accept the Mexican offer of 600,000 pesos in reparation.

ALL HAIL...THE LEG? During the Pastry War, Santa Anna's left leg was severely wounded and eventually had to be amputated. Not a man to take a lost limb lightly, Santa Anna had the leg transported to Mexico City where, after an elaborate procession, it was given a formal burial. Entombed in an urn atop a pillar, the decayed limb was serenaded and applauded by cabinet members and diplomats.

THE GRINGO INTERVENTION

TEXAS SECESSION

Throughout the early 1800s, American citizens had settled in the northern Mexican province of Texas. Concerned by this influx, the Mexican government tried to restrict immigration with the **Emancipation Proclamation of 1829** and the **Colonization Law of 1830.** Incensed by these laws and by the under-representation of Texas in Mexican assemblies, Texans began to demand independence.

Never one to turn his back on a good fight, Santa Anna gladly reassumed the role of general and led an army of 6000 to the north. In February of 1836, his troops overwhelmed Texan rebels hidden in a Franciscan monastery at the **Alamo.** The Mexicans triumphed, killing all 150 defenders of the fortress. This defeat further incensed Texans and "Remember the Alamo!" became a universal battle cry. Under the leadership of **Samuel Houston,** the revitalized Texans captured Santa Anna and his army on April 21, 1836. In captivity, Santa Anna was forced to sign a treaty pushing back Mexican control to the Río Grande and granting Texas its independence. The humbled Santa Anna was freed soon thereafter, and, although Mexico made no further attempt to reconquer Texas, Santa Anna's government refused to recognize Texas's newly won independence.

LIFE AND TIMES

1822: In a great show of immodesty, Iturbide crowns himself Emperor of Mexico.

1822: Emperor Iturbide dissolves congress. People think this is a bad idea.

Revolution #2 1822: Santa Anna launches his first rebellion.

1823: Iturbide goes into exile.

1832: Deprived of attention, Santa Anna gets bored and leaves.

Revolution #3 1832-35: Santa Anna gets bored again and comes back, leading yet another rebellion.

1838: Pastry chef is attacked. Angry French people declare war. Mexicans are confused, but win.

WAR WITH THE UNITED STATES

While the US had eyed the Lone Star Republic for some time, it was not until 1845 that the US Congress voted to annex Texas. This move enraged the Mexican government and tensions escalated. After a series of border skirmishes, the US formally declared war in May 1846. At stake was the US-Mexico border: whether it would lie on the Río Nueces as Mexico hoped or the Río Bravo (known to US citizens as the Rio Grande) as the US wanted. US troops quickly made headway in the north, seizing control of New Mexico, California, and Chihuahua. Forces under future US President **Zachary Taylor** moved in a more central direction, capturing Nuevo León and its capital, Monterrey. On February 21 of the following year, Taylor and Santa Anna met head-to-head in the **Battle of Buena Vista.** Santa Anna could not stall Taylor's forces, and his forces were defeated.

The most ambitious of the many invasions was led by general **Winfield Scott,** who, with 10,000 men, landed on March 9, 1847 in Veracruz. For almost a month, the Americans held the city under siege, plundering homes, raping women, and killing civilians. Moving west, Scott defeated another army led by Santa Anna at **Cerro Gordo** and proceeded to Mexico City. Despite valiant fighting, the Mexicans could not hold the Americans back. First to fall were the neighborhoods of **Contreras** and **Churubusco,** and, by September 7, only the **Castle of Chapultepec** (see p. 110) remained. Protected by young cadets from the military academy, the castle stood for several days before succumbing to the unceasing American barrage. Despite the loss, the cadets became known throughout Mexico as the **Niños Héroes (Boy Heroes)** for their bravery and refusal to surrender; particularly impressive was the young **Juan Escutia,** who wrapped himself in the Mexican flag and leapt from the roof of the castle to avoid American capture. The heroic actions of its youth and soldiers notwithstanding, Mexico suffered many losses.

GREEDY GRINGOS

Signed on February 2, 1848, the **Treaty of Guadalupe Hidalgo** officially ended the war. Mexico relinquished to the United States ownership of Texas at the Río Bravo border. In addition, Mexico was forced to sell California and New Mexico to the US for a paltry US$19 million. Already devastating, this was not to be the last of the US land grab. Five years later, in 1853, Santa Anna returned from exile. To raise funds, he sold what are today Arizona and southern New Mexico for US$10 million in the **Gadsden Purchase.** Two thousand Mexicans had died in the battle for Mexico City—only to lose half the nation's territory.

REFORM

The Reform Era paved the way for modern Mexico. However, this was hardly a time of peace and prosperity as the country was bitterly divided between liberal reformers and conservative supporters of the Catholic Church.

JUÁREZ AND THE LIBERALS

Unhappy with the Mexican state of affairs, several intellectual liberals—among them **Melchor Ocampo, Santos Degollado, Guill-**

LIFE AND TIMES

1829-36: Texas itches to secede.

1836: Santa Anna gets back on the horse, attempting one last hurrah.

1836: Santa Anna is soundly defeated.

1836: Texas wins. Mexico pretends not to notice.

1845: US annexes Texas. North Americans are confused. Mexico is furious.

1846: US declares war on Mexico over border disputes. Again, North Americans wonder why.

1847: Winfield Scott leads an ambitious and violent invasion of Mexico. Mexico is the big loser.

1847: Mexican youth hurl themselves off of Chapultepec Castle. People think this is cool.

1848: US ends war and takes a lot of Mexican land.

1853: US takes a lot more Mexican land in Gadsden Purchase, kicking Mexico while it's down.

Revolution #4
1855: Juárez and liberal buddies push for Santa Anna's removal. Santa Anna takes a look around and resigns for good.

1857: Juárez and his cohorts pass complicated liberal policies. Clergy become alarmed.

Revolution #5
1858: Conservative General Félix Zuloaga disbands congress and arrests Juárez.

ermo Prieto, and **Benito Juárez**—had begun tinkering with the possibility of revolution. Choosing **Juan Alvarez** as their leader, the exiles banded together behind the **Plan de Ayutla,** which set forth grievances against Santa Anna and called for his removal. The fledging movement gained support, and in 1855 Santa Anna finally stepped down from office for good.

Under the leadership of new president **Ignacio Comonfort,** the intellectuals began to enact liberal change. As the Minister of Justice, Juárez passed the **Ley Juárez,** which abolished old regulations protecting the military and clergy from prosecution under civil laws. The new constitution, the **Constitution of 1857,** reflected the ideals of the new leadership by declaring Mexico a representative democracy and republican nation and granting greater rights and liberty to its people. Naturally, conservatives and religious authorities were extremely alarmed by the new constitution and set out to extort popular allegiance by withholding sacraments and other Catholic rites from those who swore allegiance to the constitution. And thus the stage was set for yet another divisive confrontation.

WAR OF THE REFORM

Known as the **War of the Reform,** the 1858 revolt of the conservatives against the liberal reformers was Mexico's bloodiest ever. Conservatives banded together behind General **Félix Zuloaga,** rallying against the increasingly secular state. With the support of the clergy, Zuloaga disbanded congress, arrested Juárez, and declared himself president. While Zuloaga busied himself with repealing the liberal *leyes,* Juárez escaped to Querétaro where he established a rival government. The tide turned in favor of the liberals in 1860 when their troops defeated a conservative army at **Silao;** another win shortly before Christmas in the town of San Miguel Calpulalpan foreshadowed liberal victory.

FRENCH INTERVENTION

THE INVASION

The election of 1861 returned liberal reformers to power, and Juárez assumed the presidency. However, civil war had left the country economically exhausted. Convinced that Mexico would be unable to pay its huge foreign debt, Juárez declared a moratorium on payments, once again aggravating creditor nations. At the **Convention of London** in 1861, representatives from Britain, France, and Spain agreed to occupy Veracruz in order to forcibly extract dues. Spanish and British troops soon tired and pulled out, but France's **Napoleon III,** nephew of the great conqueror, had imperialistic ambitions in mind, and he ordered his troops to march on the capital. The first major confrontation occurred on **May 5, 1862** when outnumbered Mexican troops under the command of General Zaragoza successfully repelled French troops from the city of Puebla (see p. 348). Mexicans today celebrate **Cinco de Mayo** to commemorate this triumph. Despite their defeat, the French regrouped and returned a year later to take Puebla. With the fall of this stronghold, Mexico City was doomed, and, on May 31, 1863, Juárez surrendered to the French.

FRENCH RULE

Napoleon chose the Austrian archduke **Ferdinand Maximilian** of the Hapsburg clan, a man of noble birth and naïve ideologies, to rule Mexico. Maximilian's left-leaning, anti-Catholic policies angered conservatives, and what little support he had soon evaporated. Meanwhile, Juárez was seeking help from the US, which was eager to eliminate European imperialism in the western hemisphere. The US gladly donated mercenaries and weapons to the cause, and Juárez's rebel army began to gain strength. Recognizing the futility of his position, Napoleon withdrew his troops in 1867. The abandoned Maximilian surrendered in Querétaro on May 15, 1867 and, like so many Mexican rulers before him, was executed.

CRAZY CARLOTA Maximilian was a sensible fellow, but his wife, Charlotte (Carlota in Spanish) has gone down in Mexican history as a woman a few bolts short of a tool kit. In 1867, with the knowledge that her husband's regime was about to topple, Carlota left Mexico to appeal directly to Napoleon III. Her pleas were ignored, and, guilt-ridden and depressed, the 26-year-old Carlota really lost it. Convinced that Napoleon was trying to poison her, she tied up chickens in her room and refused to eat anything but the eggs they laid or drink anything but water fetched directly from the Trevi Fountain in Rome. Institutionalized soon thereafter, Carlota survived to the ripe old age of 86 and outlived nearly every other person involved in the French Intervention.

RESTORATION

Juárez triumphantly returned to the capital on July 15, 1867 and easily won a third term. As president, he sought to improve social conditions and promote equity; for the first time, education was free and compulsory. Despite his successes, Juárez only narrowly defeated **Sebastían Lerdo de Tejada** and General **Porfirio Díaz** in the 1871 election. Juárez died shortly after, and Lerdo assumed the presidency. On November 16, 1876, Díaz made a grab for power, defeating federal troops at Tecoac in Tlaxcala. After Lerdo fled to the United States, Díaz triumphantly made his way to Mexico City, occupying the capital on November 21, 1876 and refusing to leave for over 30 years.

THE PORFIRIATO

Mexico flourished under the Díaz regime, known as the **Porfiriato** or the **Pax Porfirinana.** Transportation expanded, duties were slashed, the gold standard eliminated, and useless bureaucrats dismissed. Aided by a new railroad system, mining entered a golden age. Profitable ore and copper mines gave rise to the extravagant haciendas that still dot the country. Many, however, grew increasingly discontent with Díaz's dictatorial rule, which was enforced by his personal army corps, the **rurales,** who blanketed and oppressed the countryside. Local governments were merely for show; **jefes politicos,** Díaz's local bosses, held the true power. As industry prospered and land values skyrocketed, the gap between rich and poor widened. *Indígenas* suffered the most. Under a new law, they could be forced to sell their lands if they couldn't provide a legal title. By the turn of

---

**Revolution #6
1860:** Juárez escapes and starts rival government. He eventually regains power.

1861: Juárez becomes Mexico's first *indígena* president. Towns clamor to name their main streets "Juárez."

1862: Angry over unpaid debt, Napoleon III tries to be like his uncle.

1863-67: Maximilian is set up as emperor. He is somewhat inept.

**Revolution #7
1867:** Maximilian surrenders to Juárez. He is executed. **Dead Leader Meter: 4.**

1867-75: With Juárez back in power, times are good.

LIFE AND TIMES

the century, most villages had lost their land—and hence their sustenance—to wealthy individuals and companies. In addition, the **científicos**—as Díaz's advisors were called—denounced the Indians as weak, immoral, and ineducable.

1876: Porfirio Díaz grabs power. He will hold it for a very long time.

REVOLUTION

THE DÍAZ DOWNFALL

Díaz faced a strong opponent in the 1910 presidential election; **Francisco Madero,** a wealthy *hacienda* owner from Coahuila, ran on an anti-re-election platform and openly criticized the Díaz regime. Madero was soon arrested and imprisoned, and Díaz was declared a landslide victor. After his family posted bail, Madero fled to Texas, where he came to the realization that achieving social change would require force. On October 5, 1910, he issued the **Plan de San Luis Potosí,** proclaiming that the time had come for revolution.

1876-1910: Porfiriato. The country prospers, but people are oppressed and cynical.

Madero was not the only one prepared to strike. Two days earlier, the home of a Puebla leader, **Aquiles Serdán,** had been discovered to house a large stash of artillery. Killed in an ambush, Serdán and his family became the revolution's early martyrs. While Díaz's minions cracked down in central Mexico, forces under the control of **Emiliano Zapata, Pascual Orozco,** and **Pancho Villa** employed guerilla tactics to keep the revolutionary movement growing in the south and in the north. After the fall of Ciudad Juárez (see p. 215) on May 10, 1911, Díaz accepted defeat and resigned four days later.

1910: Madero, like many others, is unhappy with Porfy. He calls for another revolution.

> # WHERE THE STREETS HAVE THOSE NAMES
> Do most of these **names** sound familiar? Perhaps you've noticed that nearly every Mexican city has a Calle Madero, a Blvd. Obregón, an Av. Benito Juárez, a Calle Zapata, a Calz. Orozco, and an Av. Lázaro Cárdenas.

REVOLUTIONARY GOVERNMENTS

MADERO

1910: Aquiles Serdán is killed by Díaz's thugs. **Dead Leader Meter: 5.**

The Election of 1911 brought Madero and vice president, **José María Pino Suárez** to power. The government tried to improve education, infrastructure, and labor regulation, but they were undermined by rebel skirmishes and hostile politicians. On November 25, 1911, dissatisfied with the administration's lack of progress, Zapata, the rebel from Morelos, proclaimed his own agrarian program, the **Plan of Ayala,** which disavowed Madero as president and set off a string of similar revolts.

Revolution #8 (*The* Revolution) **1911:** Madero, with the help of Orozco, Villa, and Zapata, forces Díaz out of power. The Porfiriato is through.

On February 9, 1913, the tide changed permanently. **Manuel Mondragón,** a general in Madero's army, released two rebels, **Bernardo Reyes** and **Félix Díaz** (nephew of the former dictator), from prison; Reyes was promptly slain, but Díaz assumed control of the rebel forces. For the next 10 days, known as the **Decena Trágica,** Mexico City was terrorized by fighting between Díaz and the federal general **Victoriano Huerta.** On the 10th day, however, Huerta suddenly switched sides, joining the rebels in the **Pact of the Embassy,** so called because of the US Embassy's role in organizing the agreement. The unified army then marched on the National Palace (see p. 101), where Madero and vice-president Suárez were immediately taken prisoner and shot. Huerta assumed the presidency that day.

THE HUERTA REGIME

The Huerta presidency was characterized by cruelty and intolerance, and opposition rose quickly. Under the **Plan de Guadalupe, Pancho Villa, Alvaro Obregón,** and **Venustiano Carranza** united as **Constitutionalists** to protest the illegal ousting of Madero and Huerta's treachery. To the south, in the state of Morelos, forces under Zapata also defied Huerta; their primary grievance was the administration's refusal to redistribute land to the Indians. Domestic pressures aside, it was foreign intervention that eventually caused Huerta's fall. After an international diplomatic *faux pas* involving American sailors in Veracruz, US President **Woodrow Wilson** ordered an invasion of the city. Huerta was forced to rush troops to Veracruz, leaving a military vacuum in the rest of the country. Seizing advantage of this distraction, Pancho Villa captured the city of Zacatecas. Realizing his precarious position, Huerta resigned on July 8, 1914.

THE CARRANZA REGIME

REBEL CONTROL. Following Huerta's resignation, Mexico was governed by four separate leaders, each clamoring for official recognition. Obregón presided over the capital, Carranza controlled Veracruz, Villa ruled the north, and Zapata held the south. At the **Battle of Celaya,** Villa attempted to wrest control of the capital from Obregón. Obregón was prepared, and 4000 Villistas were impaled or wounded on barbed-wire entrenchments. His reputation tarnished, Villa escaped to the north where, angered by the American decision to recognize the Carranza government, he took his revenge on several US towns. (Some jokingly call these raids the only successful invasion of the US mainland by a foreign power.) In return, the US sent General **John J. Pershing** on a long and fruitless search for Villa.

THE CONSTITUTION OF 1917. Although no clear victor had emerged, Carranza was able to consolidate strength in the east and northeast parts of the country, and in 1917, he called for a new constitution. The remarkably liberal **Constitution of 1917** declared that private ownership of land was a privilege, not a right, and that lands seized from *pueblos* during the Porfiriato should be returned. Workers were guaranteed better conditions and the right to strike. These promises helped Carranza win the special elections held in March 1917, but he failed to implement most of the Constitution's radical provisions.

ZAPATA ASSASSINATED. In order to dispense with his most ardent critic, Carranza cooked up an elaborate scheme to assassinate Emiliano Zapata. On April 10, 1919, an unsuspecting Zapata walked into a presumed surrender only to be shot down in cold blood. Zapata was no more, but Obregón remained, still causing trouble in the northern states. He formed an alliance with **Adolfo de la Huerta** and **Plutarco Elías Calles,** declaring yet another revolt under the banner of yet another plan, this time called the **Plan de Agua Prieta.**

1911: Madero takes power but is ineffective. Rebels cause trouble.

Revolution #8 1913: Madero and his VP are killed. Huerta seizes power. **Dead Leader Meter: 7.**

1913-14: Huerta is not a nice man. Villa, Obregón, and Carranza unite against him.

Revolution #9 1914: Huerta's resources are diverted when the US invades Veracruz. The rebels take over.

1914-16: Four governments vie for control. Things are complicated.

1915-1916: Villa successfully "invades" the US. Americans are not amused.

LIFE AND TIMES

OBREGÓN AND CALLES

1917: Carranza takes the helm.

Alarmed at the turn of events, Carranza fled the capital, but was killed en route. Obregón assumed the presidency and poured his energies into an impressive expansion of the rural school system. His most unprecedented achievement came at the end of his term, when Obregón peacefully ceded power to Calles, in 1924. Calles was succeeded by a line of puppet presidents, completely under his control. Known during this time as the **Jefe Máximo,** Calles founded the **Partido Nacional Revolucionario (PNR),** which in one form or another ran Mexico for 71 years.

CÁRDENAS

1919: Carranza kills Zapata in a sneaky way. **Dead Leader Meter: 8.**

1919: Someone is named "Plutarco."

The Election of 1934 ushered in another great figure in Mexican history, **Lázaro Cárdenas.** Groomed as another of Calles' puppets, Cárdenas broke with tradition and had the *Jefe* deported to the US in 1936. Cárdenas then busied himself with land reform, distributing some 44 million acres—twice as many as all of his predecessors combined—to thousands of Indians. Perhaps his most lasting accomplishment was the creation of a national oil company, **Petróleos Mexicanos (PEMEX),** to regulate the industry and keep it free from foreign pressures. While PEMEX was slow in accomplishing Cárdenas's economic goals, its foundation electrified Mexican national pride. Cárdenas also immeasurably strengthened the ruling party, which he renamed the **Partido de la Revolución Mexicana (PRM).**

1924: In unprecedented fashion, Obregón willfully lets power pass to Calles. **Peacefully Retired Leader Meter: 1.**

POST-WWII

MID-CENTURY

CAMACHO, ALEMÁN, AND CORTINES

1934: Cárdenas, supposedly a puppet of Calles, instead deports him.

1938: Cárdenas creates PEMEX. Foreign oil hawkers are thwarted.

In 1940, an industrialist named **Avila Camacho** succeeded Cárdenas. During World War II, Camacho supported the Allied cause with Mexican natural resources such as copper, lead, zinc, and human labor. He also renamed the ruling party, changing it to the current **Partido Revolucionario Institucional (PRI).** He was followed in 1946 by **Miguel Alemán,** the first civilian president since Carranza. With a passion for public works, Alemán built dams and hydroelectric stations and completed Mexico's segment of the Pan-American highway. He also oversaw the completion of the modern campus of the **Universidad Autónoma Nacional de México, (UNAM,** see p. 117), a marvel of modern art and architecture. Alemán's successor, **Adolfo Ruiz Cortines,** shared a similar ideology. Between 1952 and 1960, he completed many projects begun by Alemán and used his power to expand social services. During his administration women finally won the right to vote.

THOSE TURBULENT 60S

1940-58: A slew of uninteresting presidents are elected.

The Election of 1958 saw the emergence of a different PRI candidate. The young and energetic **Adolfo López Mateos** approached the presidency with an infectious enthusiasm. Stepping up land redistribution and using presidential power to support labor movements, López Mateos nudged government slightly to the left. Elected in 1964, conservative **Gustavo Díaz Ordaz** presided over a troubled time. In the summer of 1968, rioting broke out in several of Mexico City's universities, most prominently at the UNAM. Standoffs between students and the military reached crisis levels in **Tlatelolco Plaza** (or **Plaza de las Tres Culturas,** see p. 111), where police killed an estimated 400 peaceful demonstrators and jailed another 2000 just 10 days before the 1968 Olympics were to open in Mexico City. The 1970 election of **Luis Echeverría** did little to relieve the dissatisfaction many Mexicans felt. Inflation skyrocketed and foreign debt hampered the growth of Mexico's economy.

MEXICO IN MODERN TIMES

The election of 1976 brought in **José López Portillo** to correct Mexico's accumulating heap of economic problems. In an effort to slow the overheated economy, Portillo nationalized 59 banks in 1982. Still, the nation's economic woes spilled over into the presidency of **Miguel de la Madrid,** who also faced mounting political problems. Foreign debt multiplied, and in response Madrid slashed thousands of government jobs. Perhaps the biggest blow to the de la Madrid administration was the **1985 Mexico City earthquake;** the quake, which registered an 8 on the Richter scale, leveled the city, killing thousands, depleting financial reserves, and leaving the country more shaken than the peso.

SALINAS

When Harvard-educated **Carlos Salinas de Gortari** came to office amid rumors of fraud in 1988, the country was faced with high unemployment, a drug crisis, and a US$105 billion foreign debt.

ECONOMIC REFORMS AND NAFTA. Salinas immediately attempted to revive the economy, instituting wage and price controls, privatizing businesses, and halting land redistribution. In 1992, Mexico signed the **North American Free Trade Agreement (NAFTA),** which created a unified free trade zone between the US, Canada, and Mexico. Salinas hoped that the treaty would attract foreign capital and make Mexican industry more competitive by eliminating the tariffs, quotas, and subsidies that had existed since the 1940s. Whether NAFTA will actually succeed in helping Mexican industry or simply flood the Mexican market with cheap US goods remains to be seen.

REBELLION IN CHIAPAS. The economic reforms proposed by Salinas did not please all segments of the population. On January 1, 1994, the day NAFTA went into effect, a coalition of angry Maya rebels captured the city of San Cristóbal de las Casas (see p. 540) and held it in a 12-day siege. Named the **Ejército Zapatista de Liberación Nacional (EZLN),** or the **Zapatista National Liberation Army,** the army was comprised of over 9000 Maya peasants led by the eloquent masked guerilla **Subcomandante Marcos**—later revealed to be **Rafael Sebastián Guillén Vicente,** a university-educated Marxist. The Zapatistas called for a complete government overhaul, land reform, and fair elections. Months of negotiations followed with the Bishop of Chiapas, **Samuel Ruiz,** eventually mediating a tenuous compromise.

ZEDILLO

The Zapatista uprising foreshadowed more problems to come. In March 1994, PRI presidential candidate **Luis Donaldo Colosio** was assassinated as he left a rally in Tijuana; his murder still remains unsolved. To replace Colosio, the PRI chose reform-minded Budget Minister **Ernesto Zedillo Ponce de Léon.**

1958: Young, dashing Adolfo Mateos is elected. A hippie before his time, he pushes government left.

1968: Police kill an estimated 400 student protestors in the Tlatelolco Massacre.

1970: Echeverría lets things get out of hand.

1976-88: López Portillo and de la Madrid try to bail out Mexico. They fail.

1985: An earthquake hits Mexico City, killing thousands.

1988: Salinas elected. He does his very best to save the economy, but people are too preoccupied with his bald head.

1994: NAFTA. Everyone is confused.

LIFE AND TIMES

1994: Displeased with NAFTA, Maya rebels in Chiapas hold San Cristóbal under siege.

1994: Colosio assassinated, Zedillo takes charge. **Dead Leader Meter: 9.**

1994: The peso is in dire straits.

1994-97: Zedillo fights drugs and refuses to pick a successor.

1997: Cuauhté-moc Cárdenas, who has a fun name, becomes an important non-PRI governor.

2000: Vicente Fox, who is very tall, is elected president. The PRI loses power for the first time since 1929. Zedillo retires peacefully. Peacefully Retired Leader Meter: 2.

2002: *Let's Go* ponders the future.

PESO CRISIS. Just months into his presidency, in December 1994, Zedillo was faced with a precipitous drop in the value of the peso. Bailed out by a US$20 billion loan from the US government, Mexico was saved from the depths of economic crisis. Nonetheless, interest rates soared and inflation accelerated, bringing the banking system to near collapse.

REFORM AND CHANGE. Undaunted, Zedillo shifted his focus to political reform. He formally ended the PRI tradition of **degazo,** the practice of the incumbent president choosing his successor. Zedillo arrested several high-level officials on charges of conspiracy and murder, earning US endorsement as a "partner in the war on drugs." The July 1997 elections proved that the reforms were working: **Cuauhtémoc Cárdenas** of the **Partido de la Revolución Democrática (PRD)** won a landslide victory in the race for governorship of the State of Mexico, and the PRI lost its majority in the lower house of congress for the first time in 68 years.

THE CHANGING OF THE GUARD

The momentous reforms enacted by the Zedillo administration foreshadowed the end of the PRI's reign. "A Crowning Defeat—Mexico as the Victor," cried *The New York Times* on July 4, 2000, one day after opposition candidate **Vicente Fox Quesada** soundly defeated the groomed PRI candidate **Francisco Labastida Ochoa.** The tall, outgoing Fox, a former Coca-Cola executive and governor of Guanajuato state, ran as a candidate of the conservative **Partido de Accion Nacional (PAN)** on a platform of free trade, advocating an increase of wages and foreign investments, reduction of bureaucracy, elimination of corruption, revival of agrarian land reform, and a return of the country to its Catholic roots. Declared by many international observers to be the cleanest Mexican election ever, the campaign was hard-fought with mud-slinging galore; Fox questioned his opponent's virility while Labastida ridiculed Fox's divorced status. When the dust settled, Fox emerged as the surprising victor, and the humbled PRI was finally removed from power.

Many problems face Vicente Fox in the early years of his administration; the growing land shortage and sluggish economy await resolution. Millions of Mexicans have pinned their hopes to Fox's cowboy boots, believing fervently that the man who dispensed with the PRI and broke the longest hold one party has ever had on a modern government will lead the nation triumphant into the 21st century.

IT COULD HAVE BEEN TELENOVELA

Sex. Lies. Bad haircuts. Even the best *telenovela* screenwriters would have been hard pressed to come up with a plot as thick and intertwined as the one that enveloped the Salinas family in the mid-90s. In February 1995, it was revealed that **Raul Salinas de Gortari,** Carlos's brother, had been the mastermind behind the murder of their former brother-in-law, **José Francisco Ruiz Massieu.** Further investigations linked Raul with drug cartels on the Gulf Coast, large foreign bank accounts, and presidential kickbacks. His reputation tarnished and his balding head mercilessly mocked, former president Carlos was forced into exile in Ireland. Ah, this is the stuff soaps are made of.

PEOPLE AND CULTURE

ETHNICITY AND LANGUAGE

Mexico's heterogeneity is grounded in history. The Spanish conquest gave rise to the nation's largest ethnic group, the **mestizos**—persons of mixed indigenous and European blood—who now comprise 60% of the population. The term *"mestizo,"* however, has come to have such varied meanings that the Mexican census no longer uses it as a category. Today, **criollos**—light-skinned Mexicans of pure European descent—make up around 9% of the population and concentrate in urban areas and the north. **Indígenas**—sometimes referred to by the politically incorrect appellation **Indios**—comprise 25-30% of the population and to this day are the majority in most rural areas, particularly in the southern half of the country.

Mexico's official language is Castilian (Spanish), spoken smoothly and without the lisp that characterizes speakers from Spain. Many people, mostly *indígenas*, still speak some form of a native language. In the Valley of Mexico, one can often hear the Aztec language, **Náhuatl;** in the Yucatán Peninsula and Chiapas, **Maya** is frequently spoken in villages and markets; **Zapotec** is still spoken in the Oaxaca Valley. The 50 traditional languages, spoken by over 100,000 people in the country, are emblematic of Mexico's unique cultural identity.

FAITH AND RELIGION

Although religion is never explicitly mentioned in the constitution, Mexico's Catholic consciousness permeates the country and unites the population. Walk around village streets, and you'll pass wooden crosses and roadside shrines dedicated to the Virgin Mary. Ride in a Mexico City taxi cab (*sitio*, of course) and you might see a rosary hanging from the rearview mirror. Shop in a supermarket, and you'll see polychrome candles depicting Christ and the saints. Step inside a parish church and discover dozens of devout Mexicans, crossing themselves and whispering. With around 90% of the population Catholic, Mexico is a country devoted to its faith. This faith, however, has fused with native traditions and created a distinct flavor of Catholicism. The best example of this syncretism is the **Virgin of Guadalupe** (see p. 112), the dark-skinned apparition of the Virgin Mary that prompted the conversion of thousands of Indians in the 16th century. Moreover, recent years have seen a developing interest in native faiths, perhaps prompted by new archaeological research and a new embrace of Mexican indigenous identity. Aztec symbols have become synonymous with nationalism and Mexican pride. The famous Aztec **Sun Stone**, for example, adorns everything from belt buckles to soccer jerseys. Recent years have also seen the increasing presence of Protestantism. Although only about 6% of the population is Protestant, the numbers are on the rise, perhaps thanks to missionary activity. Other faiths—while not as well represented in Mexico as in the rest of the world—are increasing in numbers, particularly Judaism and Pentecostalism.

ART AND ARCHITECTURE

Mexican art is generally classified into three periods: **Indigenous** (6000 BC to AD 1525), **Colonial** (1525-1810), and **Modern** (1810-present). Art created before the Spanish invasion is studied by archaeologists; for the most part, no written commentary on artistic expression exists from the time before the Conquest. With the arrival of the Spanish, Mexican art changed dramatically and has continued to do so throughout the Modern period.

THE PRE-HISPANIC ERA

Much of the art and architecture from this period has provided the basis for understanding early Mexican history (see **Pre-Hispanic Societies**, p. 48). Some aspects of

Pre-Hispanic styles were prevalent across Mexico. The use of **stone** is perhaps one of the most noticeable. The Olmecs shaped basalt into the colossal heads for which they are famous. The Maya used limestone and sandstone all over their cities as building blocks for palaces and temples, stelae (upright stone monuments often inscribed with glyphs and reliefs), and altars. Cities such as Teotihuacán, Tula, and Tenochtitlán exhibit the continued use of monumental stone architecture in their buildings, carved reliefs, and statuary.

On a smaller scale, some of the most impressive pieces of Pre-Hispanic art would fit in your hand. **Carved jade** and **ceramic figurines** are plentiful from the very beginnings of Mexican culture through the Colonial period. Maya gods and nobility are often depicted adorned with massive headdresses replete with lengthy feathers, necklaces of beads the size of eggs, and gold and copper bracelets to match the enormous bangles hanging from their earlobes. Much of the information gained from art such as monuments or carvings pertains only to elite society; much less material has been recovered from the other classes of these cultures.

Besides buildings and monuments, another form of creative expression employed by Pre-Hispanic peoples was **narrative depiction. Murals** such as those covering the walls at the Maya site of Bonampak reveal scenes of warfare, sacrifice, and celebration. **Frescoes** on interior walls of buildings at Teotihuacán depict, among other subjects, paradise scenes, floral arrangements, religious rituals, and athletic events. Scenes painted onto the **pottery** of these cultures depict mythological stories. Other reliefs and objects reveal calendrical events and dates—the famous **Aztec Stone of the Sun** is a prime example. This prophetic calender measures nearly 4m in diameter. Within its concentric rings are contained the four symbols of previous suns—rain, jaguar, wind, and fire—the plagues responsible for the destruction of earlier populations. The Aztecs believed that they were living in the period of the fifth sun, and they expected to be obliterated by an earthquake—the symbol for which also ominously appears on the stone.

THE ARCHITECTURE OF NEW SPAIN

Not surprisingly, the first examples of **colonial art** were created specifically to facilitate religious indoctrination of the *indígenas*. Churches were often constructed on top of pre-existing temples and pyramids. Volcanic stone, plentiful in most areas, was the main building material. Colonial architecture, recalling **Romanesque** and **Gothic** traditions, incorporates huge buttresses, arches, and crenelations (indented or embattled moldings). An early architectural development was the open chapel *(capilla abierta)*, a group of arches enclosing an atrium.

Monasteries and churches under the direction of **Franciscan, Dominican,** and **Augustinian** missionaries were built according to climatic and geographic limitations. The Franciscan style tended to be functional and economic, while the Dominican style was more ascetic and harsh, due to earthquake danger and warm weather. Augustinian style was the most free-spirited and grandiose, and architects indulged in gratuitous and excessive decoration whenever possible. Remarkable Augustinian buildings include the **Monastery of St. Augustín of Acolman** near Mexico City and the **Monastery of Actopán** in Hidalgo.

A BLOSSOMING OF THE BAROQUE

The steady growth and spread of the Catholic Church throughout the 17th and 18th centuries necessitated the construction of cathedrals, parochial chapels, and convents. Moreover, this period brought the Baroque style to New Spain. Luxurious **Baroque** facades, teeming with dynamic images of angels and saints, aimed to produce a feeling of awe and respect in the hearts of the recently converted *indígenas*. The narratives set in stone could be understood even by *los analfabetos* (illiterate people) and easily committed to memory. A look at the cathedrals of Zacatecas and Chihuahua reveals the degree of artistry Baroque ideals encouraged. Baroque painting found its quintessential expression in the works of **Alonso López de Herrera** and **Baltazar de Echave Orio** (the elder).

Sumptuousness, frivolity, and ornamentation became more prevalent in the works of the late 18th-century artists and builders who couldn't get too much of a good thing. During this time, the **Churrigueresque** style was born and **Mexican High Baroque** was carried to the extreme. A hallmark of this style is the intricately decorated *estípites* (pilasters), often installed merely for looks, not support.

20TH CENTURY

As the Revolution reduced their land to shambles, Mexican artists began to reject European models in their work, instead developing a national style that reflected native Latin American culture. After the Revolution, Mexican artists found themselves under the rule of a new government, intent on building the concept of Mexico as a nation, and eager to use nationalist art to do so. **José Vasconcelos,** the Minister of Public Education, developed a program that commissioned *muralistas* to create their art on the walls of hospitals, colleges, schools, and ministries, and sent artists into the countryside to teach and participate in rural life.

The Mexican **mural,** unequivocally nationalistic in its current form, dates back to the early days of the Conquest when Catholic evangelists, who could not communicate with the *indígenas*, used allegorical murals to teach them the rudiments of Christian iconography. **Diego Rivera,** the most renowned of the *muralistas*, based his artwork on political themes—land reform, Marxism, and the marginalization of *indígena* life. Rivera used stylized realism to portray the dress, action, and expression of the Mexican people, and natural realism (complete with ugly faces, knotted brows, and angry stances) to represent Spaniards and other oppressors of the *indígenas*. His innovative blend of Mexican history and culture reached a wide audience and embroiled him in international controversy.

Though Rivera is credited as the first to forge the path for *muralistas*, two other artists were vital in defining the art form and achieved national recognition: **David Álfaro Siqueiros,** who brought new materials and dramatic revolutionary themes to his murals; and **José Clemente Orozco,** whose dark, angular shapes captured the brooding nature of his works' racial themes. Murals were also adopted by other artists, including Cubism-influenced **Rufino Tamayo.**

Not all 20th-century Mexican artists have exchanged the traditional canvas for walls. **Juan Soriano,** by combining vanguard and traditional Mexican art, forged a name for himself as a painter and sculptor. Due in part to her incredible talent and **Hayden Herrera**'s landmark biography, **Frida Kahlo** (1907-54) surpasses many Mexican artists in worldwide recognition. Kahlo's paintings and self-portraits are icons of pain, forcing the viewer to confront the artist's self-obsession in its most violent and extreme manifestations.

LITERATURE

PRE-HISPANIC WRITING

As far as linguists and archaeologists have been able to tell, two languages were dominant in Mexico before the arrival of the Spanish: **Náhuatl** and **Maya.** The earliest examples of writing are thought to be the glyphs inscribed at **San José Mogote** and **Monte Albán,** Oaxaca—two sites containing reliefs perhaps dating back to 600 BC. The destructiveness of the Conquest, particularly in its initial years, and the imposition of the Spanish language resulted in the loss of valuable information relating to *indígena* language. Considered a dangerous affront to Christian teachings, Maya and Aztec **codices** (unbound "books" or manuscripts) were fed to the flames. But due to the foresight of some indigenous leaders and a handful of missionaries, a number of Maya and Aztec codices did survive. Other historical works such as the **Books of Chilam Balam** (Books of the Jaguar Priest) and the **Annals of the Cakchiquel** cover a range of topics. They are not exclusively historical works, but are instead narrative and poetic, laden with symbolism and lofty metaphor. The **Rabinal Achi** (Knight of Achi), the story of a sacrificed warrior, is considered to be the only surviving example of Pre-Hispanic drama.

COLONIAL LITERATURE

Surrounded by a new world, the Spanish were eager to send news home about the land they had conquered and the Mexican way of life. These letters home, among them Cortés's *Cartas de Relación* (Letters of Relation), were mainly crown- and church-flattering documents detailing the exhaustive ongoing efforts to educate and Christianize *indígenas*. Other chronicles, such as the *Nuevo Mundo y Conquista* (New World and Conquest), by **Francisco de Terrazas**, and *Grandeza Mexicana* (Mexican Grandeur), by **Bernardo de Balbuena**, were written in rhyme in order to take the edge off the monotonous stream of facts.

Although historical documents dominated literary output throughout much of the 16th and 17th centuries, poets also found their place in Mexican literary culture. **Sor Juana Inés de la Cruz** (1648-1695), a *criolla* of illegitimate birth who joined a convent in order to pursue an education, became a master lyricist known for her wit, as well as an intellectual favorite of Mexico City. Her most famous works are *Respuesta a Sor Filotea* (Response to Sor Filotea) and *Hombres Necios* (Injudicious Men), poems renowned for their passion and portrayal of a feminist sensibility ahead of their time.

STRUGGLING FOR A LITERARY IDENTITY

By the end of the 18th century, the struggle for independence became the singular social fact from which many Mexican texts emerged. In 1816, **José Fernández de Lizardi,** a prominent Mexican journalist, wrote the first Latin American novel: *El Periquillo Sarniento* (The Itching Parrot), a satirical tale indicative of Mexican society's displeasure with the status quo and the social restlessness of the times. Many romantic novels of the period used historical themes to introduce sweeping indictments of the military and clergy as novelists sought to define Mexico's national identity, glorifying strength, secularism, progress, and education. Whereas European Romanticism was an aesthetic challenge to Neoclassicism, Mexican Romanticism was an artistic response to the country's political and social realities. Shortly after the heyday of the Romantic novel came popular novels of manners, most notably *El Fistol del Diablo* by **Manuel Payno,** and *Juanita Sousa* and *Antón Pérez* by **Manuel Sánchez Mármol.**

Literature during the **Porfiriato** (1876-1911) abandoned Romanticism for realism, and most writers expressed little sympathy for the poor. A modernist trend and aesthetic movement, *modernismo*, also developed at the end of the 19th century, emphasizing language and imagery and replacing didactic social themes with psychological topics. *Modernismo* reshaped Spanish literature under the direction of figures like **Manuel Gutierrez Nájera.** Both poet and journalist, Nájera founded *Revista Azul*, a literary periodical, and established himself as a precursor of modernism in his elegant works of poetry and prose. Also at the center of the modernist movement was **Amado Nervo,** the famed "monk of poetry." Nervo abandoned his studies for the priesthood in order to pursue his writing and ultimately produced several collections of his introspective and often mystical poetry, such as *Serinidad* and *Elevación*.

20TH-CENTURY GLOBAL PERSPECTIVES

Mexican literature in the Post-Revolutionary era is marked by a frustrated desire to forge a national tradition from the vestiges of pre-colonial culture. Works produced immediately after the revolution centered predominantly around social themes, particularly the plight of Mexico's *indígenas*. **Mariano Azuela,** who joined **Pancho Villa**'s forces in 1915, relays a first-hand account of the military exploitation of the *indígenas* in *Los de Abajo* (The Underdogs). Similar works such as *El Indio* (The Indian) by **Gregorio López y Fuentes** reinstated the novel as a vehicle of social reform. **Octavio Paz,** the first Mexican writer to win a Nobel Prize, draws on Marxism, Romanticism, and post-Modernism to explore the making and unmaking of a national archetype in such works as *El Laberinto de la Soledad* (The Labyrinth of Solitude). Paz concerns himself with myths and legends in an effort to come to terms with Spanish cultural dominance. The 1960s saw the advent of **magical realism** in Spanish-American literature, a literary movement that blends the ordinary and common with fantasy and wonder, resulting in texts that portray a dreamlike and distorted reality. At the forefront of this movement in Mexico stood **Carlos Fuentes,** an acclaimed contemporary novelist whose many works include *La Región Más Transparente* and *The Death of Artemio Cruz.*

Of late, the work of female writers, such as Hollywood darling **Laura Esquivel** (*Like Water for Chocolate,* see p. 67), has been well received both nationally and internationally. **Elena Poniatowska,** the author of *Tinisma*—a novel recounting the life of another famous Mexican author, **Tina Modotti,** who was a secret agent for the Soviet Union during the Spanish Civil War—is making a name for herself in the world of Latin American writers. In the past two decades, a new literary movement has emerged from Mexico—the **Chicano movement.** Chicano literature describes the experiences of Latinos who come to the US and must overcome numerous barriers to adapt to the new culture. Many Chicano authors are rapidly gaining respect in the international community. **Sandra Cisneros's** *House on Mango Street*—a novel narrated by an 11-year-old girl who talks about her life on both sides of the Mexican border—has made Cisneros one of the most recognized Chicana authors today. Other Chicano writers such as **Américo Paredes** have used their literary status to put traditional Mexican folklore into written form. In *With His Pistol in His Hands,* Paredes immortalized the tale of **Gregorio Cortez,** a Mexican who was persecuted by the US judicial system for shooting a sheriff in self-defense. The ballad of Gregorio Cortez continues to inspire pride in Mexicans to this day.

POPULAR CULTURE

MUSIC

Every aspect of Mexican life is filled with music—it is heard in fine restaurants, at public events, and on street corners where people gather around local *guitarristas.* To understand Mexican music is to understand the heart of the nation, and when you feel moved by the spirit (or the tequila), don't be afraid to throw your head back, and cry "ay, ay, ay..." along with the music.

FOLK MUSIC

On bus rides, in local bars, and on the street, you will hear three major types of traditional Mexican music:

CORRIDOS. *Corridos,* usually sung by guitar-plucking troubadours, remain truest to their folk origins. Grown out of oral storytelling, *corridos* recount the epic deeds of famous, infamous, and occasionally fictional figures from Mexico's past. A *corridista* may additionally function as a walking newspaper, singing songs about the latest natural disaster, political scandal, or any other decisive event.

RANCHERAS. Born in a fit of nationalistic fervor following the 1911 revolution, **rancheras** were originally conceived as "songs of the people," dealing with matters of work, love, and land. Once performed with marimba and flute, *rancheras* are now backed by the guitar and trumpets of *mariachi* bands. The songs are characterized by a passionate, sincere singing style, with final notes dragged out. Like American country western music, today's *rancheras* are sentimental songs about down-and-out towns, faithful dogs, and love gone wrong. **Norteños** are a type of *ranchera* strongly influenced by polka, and *norteño* bands such as **Los Tigres del Norte** kick it accordion style. Some even feature utensil-based percussion.

MARIACHI. The black-and-red-clad men with bells and capes—the same ones that appear in tequila ads around the world—are **mariachis.** The most famous of Mexican musical styles, *mariachi* is lively and light-hearted, with strong guitar and energetic horn sections. Nowadays much of Mexican music, even lonesome *corridos,* are performed with *mariachi* backing. Wandering *mariachis* strike up in front of restaurants and play at traditional *fiestas*. The world-famous tradition of women being serenaded by a group of *mariachis* in Mexican garb is an almost obligatory supplement to a romantic evening. Traditional *mariachi* music may deal with one or several of the following topics: being very drunk, loving a woman, being abandoned by a woman, wanting to get drunk, needing a woman, pondering the fidelity of one's horse, loving one's gun, and marveling at one's own stupefying virility. In their more somber (and sober) moments, *mariachis* have also been known to sing of death, politics, and revolutionary history.

OTHER MUSIC

In addition to the *corridos*, *rancheras*, and *mariachi*, Mexican music along the east-central coast and continuing into the Yucatán, carries a strong dose of Afro-Caribbean **rhumba**. In Veracruz and Quintana Roo, drum-laden bands often strike up irresistible beats in the sea breeze and evening twilight of central plazas. The style has inspired countless **marimba** bands, whose popularized music can be found blasting in markets throughout the republic. Imported from Columbia, **cumbia** has joined **salsa** as the dance music of choice across central and southern Mexico, inspiring young and old alike to cut loose with **merengue** dance steps.

Mexico also knows how to rock. The latest alternative groups like **El Nudo** and **Caifanes** provide stiff competition to Spanish and American bands. Travelers from up north will feel at home, though, as American pop and hip-hop is ubiquitous in bars and *discotecas*. Striving to Mexicanize imports (and exports), Mexican artists often take American pieces and make them their own with altered lyrics or Latin beats.

FILM

A long time ago in the southern highlands of Mexico, the rolling hills and lush forests produced hundreds of films filled with gorgeous *señoritas* and dashing *caballeros*. Today, although much of the romance of Mexican film has vanished, the glamour of Hollywood still finds its way south to make a movie once in a while.

Throughout the book, *Let's Go* notes filming sites of popular movies. For those who'd like to see some scenery on the screen, here is a list of feature films, both new releases and offbeat hits, that will bring a little of Mexico to you:

Tarzan the Ape Man (1932), Acapulco, Guerrero. Johnny Weissmuller starred in 12 Tarzan movies between 1932 and 1948, all filmed on the southern Pacific coast.

Night of the Iguana (1964), Puerto Vallarta, Jalisco. Depicts the turbulent relationships of an ex-clergyman turned tour guide. *Richard Burton, Ava Gardner, Deborah Kerr.*

Planet of the Apes (1968), Cabo San Lucas, Baja California. A sci-fi classic remade by Tim Burton in 2001. *Charlton Heston.*

Catch 22 (1970), San Carlos, Sonora. Based on the famous novel by Joseph Heller, this film follows the struggles of Captain John Yossarian during WWII. *Alan Arkin, Jon Voight, Martin Sheen.*

Close Encounters of the Third Kind (1977), Querétaro and Tesquisquiapan, Estado de México. Another fantasy flick, this time directed by Steven Spielberg. *Richard Dreyfus.*

Romancing the Stone (1984), Xalapa, Veracruz. The awesome jungles and waterfalls of Veracruz stand in for Colombia. *Kathleen Turner, Michael Douglas, Danny DeVito.*

Honey, I Shrunk the Kids (1989), Mexico City. Middle America comes to life on the streets of Mexico's capital. *Rick Moranis.*

Total Recall (1990), Mexico City. This sci-fi thriller set on Mars was also filmed in stately D.F. *Arnold Schwarzenegger, Sharon Stone.*

Free Willy (1993), Mexico City. This family drama, about a kid and an orca, also made use of the capital. *Jason James Richter, Lori Petty.*

Titanic (1997), Rosarito, Baja California. Director James Cameron constructed a life-size ship and ocean tank that remain popular tourist attractions. *Leonardo DiCaprio, Kate Winslet.*

Tomorrow Never Dies (1997), Rosarito, Baja California. James Bond also sailed the seas of this northern Baja town. *Pierce Brosnan, Michelle Yeoh.*

The Game (1997), Mexicali, Baja California. Try to piece together which parts of this thriller were filmed in Baja's capital city. *Michael Douglas, Sean Penn.*

Mask of Zorro (1998). This adventure western set in California was actually filmed all over Mexico, from Guaymas, Sonora, to Tlaxcala, Estado de México. *Antonio Banderas, Catherine Zeta-Jones, Anthony Hopkins.*

Traffic (2000), Nogales (not Tijuana!), Sonora. This Oscar-winner drew international attention to the war on drugs. *Benicio del Toro, Michael Douglas, Catherine Zeta-Jones, Don Cheadle.*

Before Night Falls (2000), Mérida, Campeche. The struggles and accomplishments of exiled Cuban poet Reinaldo Arenas are remembered in this indie hit. *Javier Bardem.*

The Mexican (2001), Real de Catorce, San Luis Potosí. The cast and crew of this romantic blockbuster took over the tiny mountain town. *Brad Pitt, Julia Roberts.*

In the Time of the Butterflies (2001). The adaptation of Julia Alvarez's popular novel was filmed in Veracruz, Morelos, and Mexico City. *Salma Hayek, Edward James Olmos, Marc Anthony.*

Texas Rangers (2002), Durango. This post-Civil War teeny-bopper western was filmed in the barren northeast. *James Van der Beek, Rachel Leigh Cook, Dylan McDermott.*

Frida Kahlo (2002), Barrio del Alto, Puebla and Mexico City. The life of one of Mexico's most revered artists hits the screens this year. *Salma Hayek, Antonio Banderas, Ashley Judd, Edward Norton, Alfred Molina.*

SPORTS

Mexicans are never ones to pass up a good fight. Although perhaps more frequently associated with Spain, **bullfighting**—the epic combat between man and large male cow—is Mexico's national sport. During the summer months, matadors and their entourages perform in packed bullrings all across the country, including Mexico City's **Plaza México,** the largest bullring in the world. James Michener's epic historical novel about the country, aptly titled *Mexico*, provides a detailed account of the history and practice of Mexican bullfighting.

Despite the popularity of publicly slaughtering cows, Mexico's heart belongs to **fútbol,** association soccer. Any unused patch of dirt, grass, or concrete is likely to be swarming with young boys (and the occasional brave girl) playing a rowdy pick-up game. (For your safety, it's best not to take sides; games can get vicious.) In addition to informal street games, Mexico has a popular professional *fútbol* league with teams in most major cities. Guadalajara, for example, has arch-enemy teams—Las Chivas and Atlas—complete with rival fan bases. At the international level, the entire country cheers and jeers the **Mexican National Team,** the gang of green-clad flashy young men who always seem to be the underdogs, and life comes to a standstill during important *fútbol* matches. Mexico played host to the World Cup in 1970 and 1986, and hosts other important matches in the **Olympic Stadium** and the enormous **Estadio Azteca,** both in Mexico City.

Other sports coexist to a lesser degree with these two monoliths. Mexico has had its fair share of world **boxing** champions in the lighter weight divisions, and there have been some notable Mexican **marathon runners** in past years. **Baseball** is starting to attract players and spectators alike at all levels. Perhaps no discussion of sports can be complete without mention of Mexico's illustrious history in the Olympic event of **walking,** one of the only sports in which Mexico has medaled.

FOOD AND DRINK

Leave your preconceived notions of what constitutes "real Mexican food" behind and prepare your taste buds for a culinary treat. With some dedication (and at times, a little courage) the pleasures of Mexican cuisine can be yours.

LIFE AND TIMES

THE STAPLES

Although regional and local cuisine varies widely, **tortillas** are popular throughout the country. This millennia-old staple is a flat, round, thin pancake made from either *harina* (wheat flour) or *maíz* (corn flour). Restaurants almost always serve both. In the north, flour tortillas are the norm while corn rules the south, but request your preference and most places will oblige. *Arroz* (rice) and *frijoles* (beans) round out the triumvirate of Mexican staples. **Rice** is usually yellow Spanish or white Mexican rice and prepared with oil, tomato sauce, onions, and garlic. **Beans** can range from a thick paste to soupy "baked" beans. Expect to see this trio of staples accompany nearly every meal—breakfast, lunch, and dinner.

DESAYUNO (BREAKFAST)

Breakfast can range from a simple continental-style snack to a grand feast, rivaling the midday meal. Eggs are the mainstay of most Mexican breakfasts and are prepared in any and all conceivable combinations and often served with *cafe con leche* (coffee with milk) and *pan dulce* (sweetened bread). **Scrambled eggs** (*huevos revueltos)* are usually prepared with *jamón* (ham), *tocino* (bacon), *machaca* (dried, shredded beef), or *nopales* (cactus). *Huevos rancheros* (fried eggs served on corn tortillas and covered with a chunky tomato salsa), *huevos albañil* (scrambled eggs cooked in a spicy sauce), *huevos motuleños* (eggs served on a fried corn tortilla, topped with green sauce and sour cream), *huevos ahogados* (eggs cooked in simmering red sauce), and *huevos borrachos* (fried eggs cooked in beer and served with beans) are other common ways in which eggs are prepared. In more expensive restaurants omelettes are offered with any of the common meats plus *camarones* (shrimp) or *langosta* (lobster). To round out your *desayuno*, leave room for the tortillas and *frijoles*.

COMIDA (MIDDAY MEAL)

Mexicans eat their biggest meal of the day—*la comida*—between 2 and 4pm. Both children and parents come home for an hour or two, eat, and relax afterwards, perhaps indulging in a little *siesta*. Restaurants often offer *comida corrida* (sometimes called *la comida* or *el menú*), which is a fixed price meal including soup, salad, tea or *agua fresca*, a *plato fuerte* (main dish), and sometimes a dessert.

SOPA

Often a starting dish for the *comida*, Mexican soups come in two varieties: *sopas caldozas* (or *caldos*, water-based soups) and *sopas secas* (dry soups). *Sopas secas* are soups cooked to the point where the rice or pasta has absorbed the broth—hence the name *seca* (dry). *Caldos*, or normal *sopas*, are much more variable. One of the most popular is the *sopa de tortilla* (or *sopa Azteca*), a chicken-broth soup with strips of fried tortilla, chunks of avocado, and *chipotle* peppers. Another favorite is the *caldo tlalpeno*, which is a smoky blend of chicken broth and vegetables. Variety abounds: *sopa de mariscos* features fish and shellfish. One of the most popular dishes in Mexico is **pozole**, a chunky soup with red, white, or green broth. Served with *tostadas* (fried tortillas) and lime wedges, *pozole* is made with large hominy kernels, radishes, lettuce, and meat—usually pork.

PLATO FUERTE

The main dish of any *comida* will usually feature some sort of meat platter (commonly beef, but fish is prevalent along the coasts) with sides of *frijoles*, *tortillas*, and *arroz*. *Platillos* vary throughout the republic, and many regions produce specialties that have earned renown worldwide.

THE NORTH. Happy and well-fed will be the carnivorous northern traveler, as meat dishes abound. One of the most famous is *cabrito*, a young goat roasted over hot embers and basted in *adobo* (a red paste made from a mixture of garlic, cloves, peppers, oregano, and cumin) or its own blood. Dried and shredded beef, called *machaca*, is used to make a variety of dishes, from eggs to *taquitos*. Often served with beef are the popular *frijoles a la charra*, pinto beans cooked with onions, coriander, and tomatoes to the point where they attain a soup-like consistency.

PUEBLA. Anything ending in *"poblano"* originated in this state, rich in culinary history. A shiny, dark green variety of chile, the large *chile poblano* is used in a variety of Mexican dishes, mainly stuffed with ground beef or *queso fresco* (a soft, milky cheese) or smothered in walnut sauce to create another regional specialty, *chiles en nogada*. Perhaps the most famous dish from the area is bittersweet *mole poblano*, a rich chocolatey-brown sauce served with chicken and rice. Making *mole poblano* is not for the lazy chef; made with everything from chiles to raisins to peanuts to cinnamon to chocolate, *mole poblano* is one of the most complicated of Mexican dishes.

OAXACA AND THE PACIFIC COAST. Despite the popularity of *mole poblano*, Oaxaca is known as the land of **seven moles:** black, light red, green, yellow, *chichilo*, *manchamanteles*, and dark red *moles* all odiferously bubble in the region. Of these, the black Oaxacan *mole*—which uses the *chilahuacle chile*—is the most famous and is served over chicken, rice, or turkey. Almost as famous as Oaxaca's *moles* are its *tamales*, which are chicken and beef chunks imbedded in *masa* (corn paste) and steamed in banana-leaf wraps.

VERACRUZ AND THE GULF COAST. In Veracruz and in most coastal areas, *marisco* is the word. Seafood dishes such as *cangrejo* or *jaiba* (crab), *ostiones* (oysters), and *camarones* (shrimp) are available everywhere, from world-class restaurants to beach-side shacks. Try the *huachinango* (wah-chee-NAAN-go) *a la vercrazuzana*, a snapper cooked with olive oil, garlic, tomatoes, and jalapeño peppers, or *filete de pescado al mojo de ajo*, fish cooked or dressed with a garlic puree sauce. Finally, munch on the ubiquitous *tacos de pescado* (fish tacos), available at any self-respecting beach-side shack.

THE YUCATÁN. The most famous dish in the Yucatán Peninsula is the *cochinita pibil*, a pig seasoned with red paste and roasted and wrapped in banana leaves. Second to the *chochinita* are *papadzules*, tortillas dressed with pumpkin seed sauce and rolled with hard-boiled eggs. The *papadzules* are then served with a light tomato sauce. All food in the Yucatán is to a certain extent inspired by the famous *achiote* seasoning, made with annatto seeds and a mixture of other spices and herbs such as garlic, cumin, and oregano and sold in blocks called *recados*.

POSTRES Y DULCES (DESSERTS AND SWEETS)

Mexicans have an incurable sweet tooth. Beyond the ubiquitous junk food—the chocolates and pastries on store shelves—traditional desserts include *flan*, a vanilla custard served over burnt sugar, *nieve* (ice cream), and *arroz con leche* (rice pudding). Puebla, the country's candy capital, is full of sweet shops selling *dulces de leche* (milk sweets) and *camotes* (candied sweet potatoes). Morelia and Michoacán specialize in *ates*, sticky sweet blocks of ground and candied fruit concentrate. San Cristóbal de las Casas and parts of Chiapas are renowned for their *cajetas* (fruit pastes) as well as coconut candies and cookies, and in the Yucatán, you can taste yummy pumpkin marzipan.

HEY, DIDN'T I SEE THAT BACK THERE? Rest assured, it's not déjà vu. Nearly every single Mexican town has a **Sanborn's** or a **VIPS** restaurant. Sanborn's, easily distinguished by its owl logo and pretty waitresses dressed in traditional Mexican garb, is the classier of the two. Sit inside and sip your *chocolate caliente* with business clientele and hip urbanites. VIPS, on the other hand, caters more to Mexican families with its special kids' menu. Especially yummy are the *sopa de fideos* (noodle soup) and the french fries that come in the shape of letters.

CENA (SUPPER)

Mexicans tend to snack lightly before going to sleep, usually around 9 or 10pm. Found on almost any Mexican menu, *antojitos* (little cravings) are equivalent to a large snack or small meal. Tacos are small, grilled pieces of meat placed on an open, warm tortilla topped with a row of condiments. Burritos, popular in northern Mexico, are thin, rolled tortillas filled with meat, beans, and cooked vegetables. *Enchiladas* are rolled corn tortillas filled with meat or chicken and baked with sauce and cheese. *Quesadillas* are flat tortillas with cheese melted between them; *quesadillas sincronizadas* (sometimes called *gringas*) are filled with ham or gyro-style pork. *Tostadas* resemble flat, open tacos, topped with raw vegetables. *Chimichangas* are essentially burritos but are deep-fried, producing a rich crunchy shell. *Flautas* are similar to *chimichangas* but are rolled thinly (like a cigar) before being deep-fried.

BEBIDAS (DRINKS)

BEERS AND LIQUORS

Along with tortillas, beans, and rice, *cerveza* (beer) might as well be the fourth national staple. It is impossible to drive through any Mexican town without coming across numerous Tecate and Corona billboards, painted buildings, and roadside beer stands proudly selling their products. Popular beers in Mexico (listed roughly in order of quality) are **Bohemia** (a world-class lager), **Negra Modelo** (a fine dark beer), **Dos Equis** (a light, smooth lager), **Pacífico, Modelo, Carta Blanca, Superior, Corona Extra,** and **Sol** (watery and light). Mexicans share their love for bargain beer with the world, demonstrated by the Mexican-made Corona Extra's status as a leading export and international chart topper in Canada, Australia, New Zealand, France, Italy, Spain, and many European markets

Tequila is the king of Mexican liquor. A more refined version of *mezcal*, tequila is distilled from the *maguey* cactus, a large, sprawling plant often seen along Mexican highways. **Herradura, Tres Generaciones, Hornitos,** and **Cuervo 1800** are among the more famous, expensive, and quality brands of tequila. **Mezcal,** coarser than tequila, is sometimes served with the worm native to the plant—upon downing the shot, you are expected to ingest the worm. If you get a chance to sample **pulque,** the fermented juice of the *maguey*, don't hesitate—it was the sacred drink of the Aztec nobility. **Ron** (rum), while originally manufactured in the Caribbean, enjoys incredible popularity in Mexico and is manufactured in parts of the Valley of Mexico. Coffee-flavored **Kahlúa** is Mexico's most exported liqueur, but well-made **piña coladas** (pineapple juice, cream of coconut, and light rum), or **coco locos** (coconut milk and tequila served in a coconut) are much less tasty outside Mexico.

NON-ALCOHOLIC BEVERAGES

Plenty of popular beverages are non-alcoholic. Unique Mexican **refrescos** (sodas) out-taste Coke and Pepsi. Try the *sodas de fresa* (strawberry soda), *piña* (pineapple soda), *toronja* (grapefruit soda), *manzanita* (apple soda), and Boing! (mango soda). If carbonation isn't your thing, you may like traditional **aguas frescas,** which come in any imaginable fruit or vegetable flavor. Favorites are *agua de jamaica* (a red juice made from hibiscus) and *agua de horchata* (a sweet rice milk).

For those desiring something warmer, Mexico is the land of plenty. Nearly every meal is capped off with a *taza de cafe* (cup of coffee) or *té* (tea). For a truly unique Mexican experience, try coffee with steamed milk. Another hot favorite is *chocolate caliente* (hot chocolate). Far from the sticky sweet American variety, Mexican hot chocolate is dark and bittersweet with a rich aftertaste. For chocolate lovers, the best place to get this famous chocolate is the area behind Oaxaca city's main market (see p. 456).

MEXICO CITY

The word "city" hardly does justice to this place. Encompassing over 1480 sq. km of sprawling humanity shrouded in a semi-permanent yellow haze, the capital of the republic appears to have no boundaries, no suburbs, no beginning, and no end; modern architecture and aluminum-covered shacks alike coat the drained, saline lake-bed as far as the eye can see. Mexicans call this megalopolis **el D.F.** (deh-EFF-ay), short for **Distrito Federal** (Federal District). Others simply refer to it as **México.** Regardless of what you call it, Mexico City's staggering statistics speak for themselves. Depending on how you measure it, el D.F. is home to between 17 and 30 million people, one quarter of Mexico's entire population, in over 350 *colonias* (neighborhoods). Virtually the entire federal bureaucracy inhabits the D.F., including the Navy, which paradoxically commands the nation's fleet from 2240m above sea level. From the enormous central square to a sprawling governmental palace to the 40-story skyscrapers, everything here is larger than life. First-time visitors stop dead in their tracks when they realize the imposing three-story palace across from Bellas Artes is simply the post office. No one here buries the ruins of the past nor apologizes for the excesses of the present. While torrents of problems have descended upon the city—earthquakes, volcanic eruptions, poverty-induced crime, pollution—the average *chilango*'s (D.F. native) laments are grounded in unconditional love for this apocalyptic metropolis. Mexico City is, after all, not really a city, but life itself, leaping and surpassing every extreme.

HIGHLIGHTS OF MEXICO CITY

MOURN for Frida Kahlo at her former home while perusing the remnants of her shattered life in the **Museo Estudio Diego Rivera y Frida Kahlo** (p. 116).

LOSE yourself in the **Bosque de Chapultepec** (p. 110), the largest urban park in the Americas—it's got everything from panda bears to free concerts to the **Museo Nacional de Antropología** (p. 108), Mexico's biggest and best museum.

RULE over a kingdom of dance floors in the flashy and glamorous **Zona Rosa** (p. 121)

KNEEL with the devout in the **Basílica de Guadalupe** (p. 112).

PICNIC beneath shady poplars in pretty **Parque Alameda Central** (p. 103), before enjoying a dazzling show of **Ballet Folklórico** in the **Palacio de Bellas Artes** (p. 104).

HIT the road; many of Mexico City's most fabulous attractions lie outside the city itself. Check out our **daytrips** (p. 132), including the nearby pyramids at **Teotihuacán** (p. 126), the most visited ruins in all of Mexico. Or, get a workout and climb out of the pollution on a ⬛ **mountain bike** tour of the Valley of Mexico's mountains (p. 86).

A BRIEF HISTORY

Cities like this just don't happen. Centuries upon centuries crafted and shaped Mexico City into the biggest, baddest city in the world.

ORIGINS 101: FACT AND FICTION

The history of the Valley of Mexico begins with the arrival of the **Mexica** (mee-SHI-ka, later known as the **Aztecs**) in the 13th century AD. According to legend, the Aztecs were guided by Huitzilopochtli, their patron god of war, who told his chosen people to settle where they discovered an eagle with a serpent in its beak, perched on a cactus. Lo and behold, the Aztecs saw this very sight next to **Lake Texcoco** in the Valley of Mexico. Initially shunned by neighboring tribes as barbarous and uncouth, the savage Aztecs slowly but surely rose to power through trading and strategic alliances (as well as the occasional back-stabbing). At its height in

Central Mexico City

🏠 ACCOMMODATIONS
Casa de los Amigos, **B**
Hostel Catedral, **F**
Hostel Moneda, **I**
Hotel Antillas, **D**
Hotel Atlanta, **E**
Hotel Buenos Aires, **K**
Hotel Edison, **C**
Hotel Isabel, **M**
Hotel Juárez, **G**

Hotel Manolo Primero, **N**
Hotel Monte Carlo, **L**
Hotel Principal, **J**
Hotel San Antonio, **H**
Hotel Yale, **A**

⭕ SIGHTS
Casa de los Azulejos, **16**
Catedral Metropolitana, **21**
Centro Cultural José Martí, **9**
FONART, **15**
Glorieta Ángel de la Independencia, **33**
Glorieta Cristóbal Colón, **25**
Glorieta Cuauhtémoc, **26**
Iglesia de San Francisco, **18**
La Lagunilla, **2**
Mercado de Artesanías de la Ciudadela, **27**

MEXICO CITY

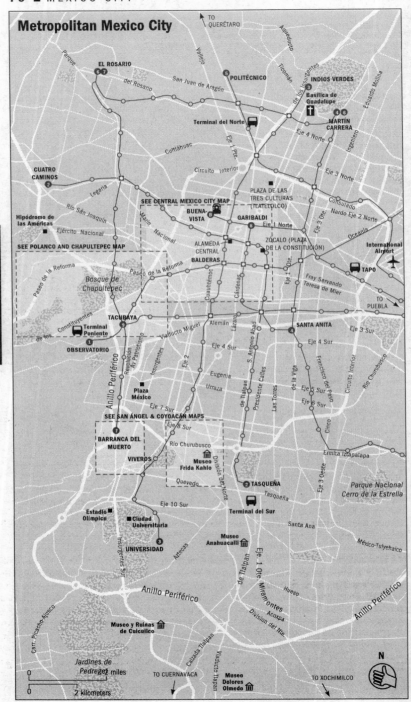

Metropolitan Mexico City

TO QUERÉTARO

EL ROSARIO 6 7

POLITÉCNICO 5

INDIOS VERDES 3

San Juan de Aragón

del Rosario

Vallejo

Aqueducto

Ticomán

de los Insurgentes

Eduardo Molina

Basílica de Guadalupe

MARTÍN CARRERA 4 6

Ingeniero

Terminal del Norte

Eje 4 Norte

Eje 1 Pte.

Cuitláhuac

Circuito Interior

Eje 3 Norte

Consulado

Nardo Eje 2 Norte

Oceanía

CUATRO CAMINOS 2

Legaria

Río San Joaquín

Ejército Nacional

Marín Nacional

PLAZA DE LAS TRES CULTURAS (TLATELOLCO)

Eje 3 Ote.

Hipódromo de las Américas

SEE CENTRAL MEXICO CITY MAP

BUENA-VISTA

GARIBALDI 8

Eje 1 Norte

International Airport

SEE POLANCO AND CHAPULTEPEC MAP

Paseo de la Reforma

Marín Nacional

Paseo de la Reforma

ALAMEDA CENTRAL

ZÓCALO (PLAZA DE LA CONSTITUCIÓN)

TAPO

BALDERAS

Cuauhtémoc

Fray Servando Teresa de Mier

TO PUEBLA

Bosque de Chapultepec

Constituyentes

TACUBAYA

Viaducto Miguel

Alemán

Lázaro

Cárdenas

Eje 1 Pte.

SANTA ANITA 4

Eje 3 Sur

de los

Terminal Poniente 1

Revolución

Av. Patriotismo

Insurgentes

Eje 2

Eje 4 Sur

de Tlalpan

S. Antonio Abad

Presidente Calles

de la viga

Francisco del paso

Eje 3 Sur

Circuito Interior

Río Churubusco

OBSERVATORIO

Anillo Periférico

Eugenia

Urraza

Las Torres

Eje 5 Sur

Eje 6 Sur

Cinco

Plaza México

Eje 7 Sur

SEE SAN ÁNGEL & COYOACÁN MAPS

Eje 8 Sur

Ermita Iztapalapa

BARRANCA DEL MUERTO 7

Río Churubusco

Parque Nacional Cerro de la Estrella

VIVEROS

Museo Frida Kahlo

División del Norte

Quevedo

TASQUEÑA 2

Tasqueña

Eje 3 Oeste

México-Tulyehaico

Eje 10 Sur

Terminal del Sur

Santa Ana

Estadio Olímpico

Ciudad Universitaria

UNIVERSIDAD 3

Aztecas

Museo Anahuacalli

Insurgentes Sur

Eje 1 Ote. Miramontes

Hueso

Anillo Periférico

División del Nte.

Acoxpa

Anillo Periférico

Carr. Picacho-Ajusco

Museo y Ruinas de Cuicuilco

Jardines de Pedregal

Calzada Tlalpan

Viaducto Tlalpan

Museo Dolores Olmedo

0   1 miles

0   2 kilometers

TO CUERNAVACA

TO XOCHIMILCO

N

the 15th century, the central Aztec city, **Tenochtitlán,** was a wonder to behold. Its population (200,000) ranked sixth in the contemporary world, and its complicated canals and drainage system made London seem a filthy pit in comparison.

THE COLONIAL ERA

When **Hernán Cortés** arrived in Tenochtitlán in 1521, the gleaming city spread before him for miles, laid out in an inconceivably meticulous manner. Impressed, the Spaniard reacted in the only way he knew and conquered it. After the fall of Tenochtitlán, the triumphant conquistador busied himself with transforming the Aztec city into a capital for his new empire. Aztec temples were razed and the rubble used to build new *palacios* and cathedrals, including those now in the *zócalo*. The lovely grids of Aztec canals were drained and replaced with roads; some form the backbone of the city's modern infrastructure. Spanish viceroys came and went, and the city, the bureaucratic center of the empire, thrived under Spanish control. By the time of Independence, Mexico City was Latin America's cultural capital, and consecration as a bishopric in 1533 made it the spiritual capital as well. The 18th century especially was a time of great construction and renovation; a new aqueduct linked the city to reservoirs in Chapultepec, and the giant underground lake was finally drained, opening more of the Valley for settlement.

INDEPENDENT MEXICO

During most of the movements for Independence and, later, during Reform, Mexico City became something of a holy grail—the only goal for both revolutionary and foreign armies. No sooner had the *Grito de Dolores* left Hidalgo's lips than construction and sanitation fell by the wayside, and the city became booty traded back and forth between the Mexican people and US soldiers (in 1847), French interventionists (in 1863), and revolutionary armies (in 1821, 1867, and 1876). Not until the dictatorship of Porfirio Díaz did the city regain some stability. Construction resumed, and, around the turn of the century, buildings such as the magnificent Palacio de las Bellas Artes were erected. The bustle and construction attracted countless immigrants seeking work and housing. By the mid-1930s, over one million people identified themselves as *chilango*.

THE 20TH CENTURY

The wartime economic boom of the 1940s and 1950s gave way to stagnation and frustration in the 1960s, and Mexico, along with the rest of the world, fell upon desperate times. Emblematic of the social controversies arising from economic hardship were the student protests of 1968, when, during Olympic celebrations, innocent protestors were gunned down in places like UNAM and Tlateloco. Despite economic frustration, population growth was on the rise. Within a span of fifty years, the capital's population soared—from one million in 1930 to eight million in 1980. City planning abruptly halted, unable to handle the loads of domestic immigrants arriving in search of work. This cessation paved the way for the rise of shanty-towns and slums, which still line the roads to the capital.

MODERN DAY

When it rains it pours. Amidst a stagnant economy and increasing frustration, a mighty earthquake sent both buildings and spirits tumbling to the ground. The June 1985 eruption of Popocatépetl was another lingering reminder of the city's precarious position atop a highly active geological area. To add insult to injury, the 80s and 90s saw air quality in the city deteriorate to dangerous levels; the city renowned for its cleanliness and breathable air had become one of the world's most polluted. Fortunately, all hope was not lost. The creation of a governor of Mexico in 1998 brought newfound hope to the millions who call the city home, and the subsequent election of progressive leftist **Cuauhtémoc Cárdenas** raised many *chilangos'* hopes. Cárdenas's optimistic promises have begun to materialize; crime, made rampant by police abuses and corruption, may be descending from its notoriously high levels. The city has also begun to fight pollution in earnest, through educational campaigns and the use of strict controls. Perhaps most importantly, Mexico City has gained confidence in its complicated identity. The clearing of the Templo Mayor in the early 80s brought indigenous pride to the city, giving *chilangos* a newfound respect for the accomplishments of their Aztec fore-fathers. The city today is a dizzying mix of old and new, foreign and native. Although cynical and street-wise, most *chilangos* are head over heels in love with their city. Huitzilopochtli, wherever he is, is no doubt smiling upon his beloved nomads, pleased with the happy ending of his prophecy.

✈ GETTING THERE AND AWAY

All roads lead to Mexico City. Buses, trains, and planes from every town in the republic haul passengers through the smoggy hyperactivity of the city's many tem-ples of transport—the constantly-expanding Benito Juárez International Airport, four crowded bus stations, desolate train station, and network of freeways. Fortu-nately for frazzled tourists, airports and stations have information booths some-times with English-speaking personnel, official zone-rated taxi service, and nearby Metro stations.

BY AIR

The city's one public international airport, **Benito Juárez International Airport** (☎ 5571 32 95; M: Terminal Aérea, Line 5) lies 6.5km east of the *zócalo*, the formal city cen-ter. **Blv. Capitán Juan Sarabio** heads northeast to the airport from **Blv. Puerto Aéreo,** one of the major roads circling the city.

GETTING TO AND FROM THE AIRPORT

Transportation into the city is uncomplicated. The Metro is the cheapest route to the city. The airport metro station, **Terminal Aérea,** Line 5, at Sarabio and Puerto Aéreo, is just outside Sala A. Signs will point the way. Large bags are officially pro-hibited, but if you avoid rush hour (6-10am and 6-9pm) and can maneuver through the turnstile, a backpack should not pose too much of a problem. If returning to the airport by Metro, get off again at **Terminal Aérea,** Line 5. (Metro open M-F 5am-midnight, Sa-Su 6am-midnight). Special fixed-rate airport **taxis** (also called *trans-porte terrestre,* ☎ 5784 48 11 or 5571 36 00) also run into the city. Ticket windows

GET OFF HERE If traveling to the airport by Metro, **do not get off** at the Aeropuerto stop on Line 1 (also known as Blvd. Aeropuerto). The correct stop is **Terminal Aérea,** on Line 5.

by the exits to both arrival gates sell fare-tickets whose price depend on the zone of your destination. Expect to pay 120-150 pesos to reach hotels in central Mexico City. Give the ticket to one of the cabs waiting outside while avoiding uniformed "taxi supervisors"—porters who will expect a tip for taking your bags to the cabs.

FLIGHT INFORMATION

Flight Info Hotline and General Information: (☎ 5571 36 00 or 5762 67 73). Specify domestic or international flights.

Terminals: Sala A: All AeroMéxico, baby. **Sala B:** Mexicana, Aeromar, and AeroCalifornia. **Sala C:** Aerolineas Internacionales and AVIACSA. **Sala D:** ALLEGRO, TAESA, and charter flights. **Sala E:** International arrivals. **Sala F1:** AeroMéxico (international flights), Amer-ica West, Avianca, Continental, Delta, Ecuatoriana, Lan Chile, and LAB. **Sala F2:** Air France, Aviateca, British Airways, Canadian, Copa, Cubana, ETA, JAL, KLM, Malaysia, Miami Air, Northwest, and Grupo Taca. **Sala F3:** Air Canada, American Airlines, Argentin-ian Airlines, Iberia, Lufthansa, TWA, and United Airlines.

Domestic Carriers: Prices are similar from airline to airline, but flight schedules and prices change frequently. Ask about *tarifas promocionales,* which may save you up to 50%. **AeroCalifornia,** Sala B (☎5207 13 92), tends to be the most competitive. Open daily 7am-7pm. **AeroMéxico,** Paseo de la Reforma 445 (☎5514 97 36), at Mississippi (open M-Sa 9am-8:15pm), and Reforma 80 (☎5566 10 78), at Versailles (open M-Sa 9am-6:15pm). At the airport, Sala A, (☎5726 02 34. Open daily 4:30am-2am). Reservations hotline ☎5133 40 50 or 01 800 021 40 50; www.aeromexico.com. **Mexicana,** Reforma 312, (☎5511 35 79, ext. 4508), at Amberes in the Zona Rosa and other offices throughout the city. Open M-F 9am-5:45pm. At the airport, Sala C, (☎5785 47 63; www.mexicana.com. Open daily 5am-1am).

International Carriers: Air Canada, Reforma 389-14 (☎5208 18 83; www.aircanada.ca). **Air France,** Edgar Allen Poe 90, in Col. Polanco. (☎5627 60 60; www.airfrance.com/mx.) Open M-F 9am-2pm and 3-6pm. **American,** Reforma 314, and at the airport in Sala F (☎5209 14 00; www.aa.com). Open M-F 9am-6pm, Sa 9am-8:30pm. **British Airways,** Balmes 8, Mez. office #6, in Col. Polanco. (☎5387 03 00; www.britishairways.com/regional/mexico. Open M-F 9am-5:30pm, Sa 9am-1pm.) **Continental,** between Salas D and E. Open M-F 7am-7pm, Sa-Su 7am-6pm. Central telephone reservations and information line (☎5283 55 00 or 01 800 900 50 00; www.continental.com. Open M-F 8am-11pm, Sa-Su 8am-6pm. **Delta,** Reforma 381 (☎5202 16 08; www.delta.com.), and at the airport in Sala F (☎5279 09 09). Open daily 6am-6pm. **Lufthansa,** Las Palmas 239, Col. Lomas de Chapultepec (☎5230 00 00; www.lufthansa-mexico.com). Open M-F 9am-6pm. At the airport (☎5571 27 02). Open daily 2:30-9:30pm. **TWA,** Sala F (☎5627 02 22 or toll-free 01 800 007 8000.) **United,** Hamburgo 213 (☎5627 02 22 or 01 800 003 07 77; www.united.com.mx.); at the airport in Sala F. (☎5627 02 22.) Open daily 9am-noon and 3-5pm.

AIRPORT SERVICES

Tourist Office: in Sala A (☎5786 90 02), with the yellow signs. Hotel reservations available. Open daily 8am-8pm. Information kiosks in Salas A and F have flight info.

Buses: The airport runs a convenient bus service that allows direct access to nearby towns from just outside Sala D. Buy tickets at the booth in front of parked buses. Buses go to: **Cuernavaca** (21 per day 6:30am-11pm, 80 pesos); **Pachuca** (15 per day 7:15am-9:15pm, 100 pesos); **Puebla** (42 per day 6am-12:30am, 100 pesos); **Querétaro** (14 per day 8:30am-9:15pm, 160 pesos).

Currency Exchange: Banks exchange currency and traveler's checks in almost all of the *salas.* **ATMs** accepting a number of cards, are available in Sala A, directly under Sala B, and throughout Salas E and F. **Casas de cambio,** every foot or so (open 6am-9pm), have rates comparable to what you'll find throughout the city.

Car Rental: In Sala E. Rates very similar at each company. Open until about 10:30pm.

Luggage Storage: Corner of Sala A and in Sala E. 50 pesos per bag per day. Open 24 hr.

Police: (☎5599 00 53), upstairs from Sala C. Also in Sala E1 (☎5599 00 44).

Pharmacy: In Sala C (open daily 6am-10pm) and Sala F (open daily 6am-11pm).

Medical Assistance: Upstairs from Sala C; follow the Red Cross signs.

Fax: Between Salas D and E. Open 24hr.

Internet: Axon Cyber Cafe, in Sala E (☎5786 93 72). Fast connection 1 peso per min. Web kiosks scattered around the airport operate on LADATEL phone cards.

Post Office: In Sala A. Open M-F 8am-7pm, Sa 9am-5pm.

Postal Code: 15620.

BY TRAIN

Mexico City no longer has passenger train service to or from other cities.

BY BUS

Mexico City's four main bus stations correspond to the cardinal directions and serve corresponding areas of the country.

Central de Autobuses del Norte (North Station): Baja California, northern Veracruz, Jalisco, and all of northern Mexico.

Terminal Central de Autobuses del Sur (Tasqueña; South Station): Guerrero, Morelos, and Oaxaca.

Terminal de Autobuses de Pasajeros de Oriente (TAPO; East Station): Puebla, southern Veracruz, Oaxaca, Chiapas, and the Yucatán Peninsula.

Terminal de Autobuses del Poniente (West Station): Estado de México and Michoacán.

All stations are served by the Metro and have 24hr. fixed rate taxi service. Buy your ticket inside to avoid being ripped off. *Peseros (colectivos)* also serve the four stations. Bus prices change frequently, and listings are incomprehensive.

CENTRAL DE AUTOBUSES DEL NORTE

The vast Central de Autobuses del Norte, commonly referred to as "Cien Metros" or "Mexico Norte," is on Cien Metros. (☎5587 15 52. M: Autobuses del Norte, Line 5.) Services include: **hotel reservations** (open 7am-9pm), **tourist information** booth (open 9am-7pm), and **casa de cambio** (open daily 11am-6pm), all near the main entrance. There are **ATMs** and a **pharmacy** (all open 24hr.), as well as a **post office** (open M-F 8am-7:30pm, Sa 9am-1pm) and **telegram office** (open M-F 9am-7:30pm, Sa 9am-4:30pm). At least one Sendetel office has **Internet.** (15 pesos per hr. Open 6am-10pm.) From the **taxi stand,** rides to the *zócalo* or Revolución are 45 pesos.

ADO (☎5133 24 24) goes to: **Oaxaca** (6hr., 9 per day 7am-noon, 246 pesos); **Papantla** (5hr., 7 per day 9:30am-12:30am, 137 pesos); **Puebla** (2hr., every 30min. 4am-10pm, 77 pesos); **Tuxpan** (6hr., every hr. 6am-midnight, 152 pesos); **Veracruz** (7hr., 8 per day 7am-12:15am, 189 pesos); **Villahermosa** (10hr., 7 per day 8:30am-11:15pm, 424 pesos); **Xalapa** (5hr., 3pm and 12:15am, 147 pesos).

Elite (☎5729 07 07). The name says it all. Posh service to: **Hermosillo** (30hr., every hr. 5:30am-1:15pm, 795 pesos); **Puerto Vallarta** (14hr., 3 per day 5-11:45pm, 600 pesos); **San Luis Potosí** (7hr., every hr., 236 pesos).

Estrella Blanca/Futura (☎5729 07 07) motors to: **Acapulco** (5hr., every 1½hr. 6am-11:30pm, 230 pesos); **Aguascalientes** (6hr., every hr. 7:30am-12:30am, 300 pesos); **Chihuahua** (18hr., every hr. 8:50am-11:30pm, 837 pesos); **Durango** (12hr., 6 per day 5:30am-11:45pm, 515 pesos); **Matamoros** (14hr., 5 per day 2:15-10:30pm, 586 pesos); **Monterrey** (12hr., every hr. 7am-midnight, 530 pesos); **Tampico** (9½hr., every 2hr., 262 pesos); **Zacatecas** (7hr., every hr., 362 pesos).

Flecha Amarilla (☎5587 52 22) runs to: **Guadalajara** (9hr., every hr., 300 pesos); **Guanajuato** (6½hr., 4 per day 11:45am-7:40pm, 187 pesos); **Morelia** (5hr., 16 per day, 145 pesos); **Querétaro** (3½hr., every 15min. 4:50am-12:20am, 120 pesos); **San Miguel de Allende** (4½hr.; 7:10, 11:15am, 5:40pm; 126 pesos).

TERMINAL DE AUTOBUSES DE PASAJEROS DE ORIENTE (TAPO)

The Terminal de Autobuses de Pasajeros de Oriente, General Ignacio Zaragoza 200 (☎5762 59 77. M: San Lázaro, Line 1), is connected to the Metro by an indoor walkway. Services include: **currency exchange** (open daily 7am-11pm), **travel agency** (☎5542 90 92; open M-F 9:30am-6pm, Sa 9:30am-1:30pm), and **pharmacy. Police** booths are scattered throughout. **Taxi** ticket booths are near the Metro entrance (to the *zócalo* 25 pesos, to Monumento a la Revolución 35 pesos).

ADO (☎5542 71 92) sends buses to: **Cancún** (24hr., 4 per day 8:30am-6:45pm, 809 pesos); **Córdoba** (4½hr., 25 per day, 161 pesos); **Mérida** (20hr., 5 per day 12:30-9:30pm, 615 pesos); **Oaxaca** (6hr., 20 per day, 246 pesos); **Palenque** (12hr., 4 and 6pm, 485 pesos); **Veracruz** (5hr., 21 per day, 212 pesos); **Villahermosa** (10½hr., 17 per day, 424 pesos); **Xalapa** (4½hr., 23 per day, 132 pesos).

Autobuses Cristóbal Colón (☎5133 24 33) travels to: **Oaxaca** (6hr., 5 per day 12:30-11:30pm, 246 pesos); **San Cristóbal de las Casas** (18hr.; 2:30, 5:30, and 7:30pm; 502 pesos); **Tonalá** (13hr.; 5 per day noon-10pm; 449 pesos); **Tuxtla Gutiérrez** (15hr., 3 and 8pm, 578 pesos).

Autobuses Unidos (AU; ☎5133 24 24) goes to: **Córdoba** (5hr., 21 per day, 145 pesos); **Oaxaca** (9hr., 11 per day, 198 pesos); **San Andrés Tuxtla** (8hr., noon and 9pm, 247 pesos); **Veracruz** (5hr., every hr. 7am-11pm, 175 pesos); **Xalapa** (5hr., 20 per day, 131 pesos).

Estrella Roja (☎5542 92 20) will take you to: **Puebla** (2hr., 60 pesos).

UNO (☎5522 11 11) services: **Oaxaca** (8 per day 8:30am-11:45pm, 390 pesos); **Veracruz** (10 per day 8:15am-midnight 335 pesos); **Villahermosa** (8 and 9:30pm, 674 pesos); **Xalapa** (7 per day 9am-midnight, 239 pesos).

TERMINAL DE AUTOBUSES DEL PONIENTE

Follow signs to **Central Camionero Pte.**, Av. Sur 122. (☎5271 45 19; M: Observatorio, Line 1), as you exit the Metro—a vendor-lined bridge leads to the terminal. From the terminal to the Metro, walk up the staircase and turn left. The station is built in the shape of a "V" with the most important services at the vertex. Services include: **pharmacy** (open daily 7am-10pm), **Telecomm fax** (open M-F 8am-7pm, Sa-Su 9am-4pm), and **Western Union.** Buy **taxi** tickets from the authorized stand (to the *zócalo* 60 pesos, to the Monumento a la Revolución 50 pesos).

Autobuses del Occidente (☎5271 01 06) goes to: **Guadalajara** (12hr., 4 per day 1:15am-6:10pm, 263 pesos); **Manzanillo** (16hr., 4 per day 7:10am-9:40pm, 410 pesos); **Morelia** (6hr., every hr. 6:15am-4:15pm, 146 pesos).

Caminante drives to **Toluca** (1hr., every 5min. 5:50am-10:30pm, 31 pesos).

Elite (☎5271 05 78) travels to **Chihuahua** (20hr., 2:30pm, 832 pesos) and **Morelia** (4hr., 10:30am and 3:30pm, 170 pesos).

ETN (☎5273 03 05) motors to: **Guadalajara** (7hr., 7 per day, 480 pesos); **Morelia** (4hr., 34 per day, 240 pesos); **Toluca** (1hr., every 30min., 40pesos); **Uruapan** (5½hr., 8 per day, 320 pesos).

Pegasso Plus (☎5277 77 61) sends buses to: **Morelia** (4hr., 36 per day, 185 pesos) and **Pátzcuaro** (5hr., 10 per day 6:30am-midnight, 205 pesos).

Servicios Coordinados rolls to: **Morelia** (5½hr., 11 per day 9:30am-11:15pm, 146 pesos).

CENTRAL DE AUTOBUSES DEL SUR (TASQUEÑA)

To get to the Tasqueña terminal, Tasqueña 1320 (☎5689 97 45; M: Tasqueña, Line 2), from the Metro, go out the "Central" exit on the upper level, then down a staircase on your left. The terminal is on the other side of the market, yellow fence, and row of trees. Services include: mini-**travel agency** for hotel reservations in select cities (open Su-F 9am-9pm, Sa 9am-3pm), **Telecomm** with cash wire transfer (☎5549 80 15; open M-F 8am-7:30pm, Sa-Su 9am-4:30pm), and a **pharmacy** (☎5689 08 83; open 24hr). Get a cab from the **taxi stand** (to the *zócalo* 42 pesos, to the Monumento a la Revolución 32 pesos).

ADO, Cristóbal Colón (☎5544 24 14), and Estrella Roja (☎5549 87 49) go to: **Oaxaca** (6hr.; 7:30am, 4pm, and midnight; 285 pesos); **Puebla** (3hr., every hr. 6:30am-9:30pm, 77 pesos); and places on the **Gulf Coast** and **Yucatán.**

Estrella de Oro (☎5549 85 20) travels to: **Acapulco** (5hr., every hr. 6am-10pm, 230 pesos); **Cuernavaca** (1½hr., 4 per day 12:50-8:40pm, 47 pesos); **Ixtapa/Zihuatanejo** (9hr., 11:20pm, 295 pesos); **Taxco** (2hr., 6 per day 7:40am-8:10pm, 78 pesos).

Futura and Turistar (☎5628 57 39) leave for: **Acapulco** (5hr., 38 per day, 230 pesos); **Ixtapa/Zihuatanejo** (9hr., every 30min., 359 pesos); **Taxco** (2hr. every hr. 7am-10pm, 86 pesos).

Pullman de Morelos (☎5549 35 05) goes to: **Cuernavaca** (1¼hr., every 15min. 5:30am-midnight, 47 pesos); **Tepoztlán** (1hr., every 30 min. 6:30am-9pm, 45 pesos).

BY CAR

Few car-related experiences can match the shock of driving into Mexico City, the heart of the nation's highway arteries. Traffic keeps the city crawling from 9 to 11am and 3 to 7pm. Don't expect anyone to drive defensively—*chilangos* in a hurry dismiss stoplights as optional (see **Getting Around By Car**, p. 86). Several major roads lead into the district and intersect with the **Circuito Interior,** the route that rings the city, at which point they change names. **Mex. 57,** from Querétaro and Tepoztlán, becomes **Manuel Avila Camacho** just outside the Circuito. **Mex. 15,** from Toluca, turns into **Reforma** as it enters the city. **Mex. 95,** from Cuernavaca and Acapulco, becomes **Insurgentes,** which enters the city from the south side. **Mex. 150,** from Puebla and Texcoco, becomes **Ignacio Zaragoza,** which begins on the city's east side. **Mex. 85,** from Pachuca, Teotihuacán, and Texcoco, also becomes **Insurgentes** when you reach the northern city limits.

GETTING AROUND

BY METRO

The Metro never ceases to amaze. The fare is cheap, the crowds enormous, the ride smooth and efficient, the service extensive, and the stations immaculate. Built in the late 1960s, the Metro now transports five million people per day, making the equivalent of two and a half trips around the world.

Metro tickets (1.5 pesos, including transfers) are sold in *taquillas* (booths) at every station. Directions are stated in terms of the station at either end of a given line, and each of the two *andenes* (platforms) has signs indicating the terminus toward which trains are heading. For example, if you are on Line 3 between Indios Verdes and Universidad, you can go either "Dirección Indios Verdes" or "Dirección Universidad." Trains run M-F 5am-midnight, Sa-Su 6am-midnight. During rush hour (M-F 7:30-9:30am, 2-4pm, and 6-9pm) commuters pack the cars like sardines.

Theft is a huge, avoidable, problem of riding the Metro. To avoid hassles, it's a good idea to carry any bags in front of you or on your lap. The safest place in a crowded car is with your back against the wall and your belongings in front of you. Remember that rear pockets are easy to pick, front pockets are safer, and empty pockets are best. Because of overcrowding, large bags or suitcases are sometimes not allowed on the Metro. If you are intent on carrying an overstuffed pack, travel very early or after 10:30pm.

Most transfer stations have information booths, where you can pick up a Metro map, also available at the tourist office. You can also contact **COVITUR** (Comisión de Vialidad y Transporte Urbano del D.F.; Public Relations), Felicia 67 (☎5709 80 36), outside M: Salto de Agua (Lines 1 and 8). Nearly all stations have guards and security offices, and all are required to have a *jefe de la estación* (chief of station) in a marked office to deal with questions, complaints, and panic attacks. Lost belongings can be reported to the **Oficina de Objetos Extraviados** in M: Candelaria (Lines 1 and 4). (☎5542 53 97. Open M-F 9am-8pm.)

WOMEN AND CHILDREN FIRST

Sexual harassment on the Metro is one of the most common complaints among female visitors to the city; women and girls of all ages are subject to mistreatment. Thankfully, the Metro management has started to respond. At the busiest stations, the first two cars of each train are reserved for women and children before 10am; at a few stations, the cars are also set apart during the evening rush hour. Look for signs saying "Mujeres y Ninos," or "Damas." Unfortunately, men do enter the cars at unguarded stations, and this plan fails to address problems outside rush hour. Still, the front two cars are always a good bet as they are slightly less crowded, and tend to contain more women anyway. Additionally some women only wear loose-fitting slacks or jeans on the Metro, and many tie a sweater around their waists; traveling with a man may also help. Despite all your precautions, it may be impossible to completely avoid unwanted attention and sometimes even the horrible experience of being groped. Do not hesitate to call attention to the offender with a loud *"¿No tiene vergüenza?"* (Don't you have any shame?) or, *"¡Déjame!"* (Leave me alone!).

EL METROPOLITAN

Some Metro stops are sights in their own right; nearly every transfer station boasts some kind of exhibit, from elementary school drawings of the subway system to a re-creation of a London theater. Here are some notable stops:

Pino Suárez, Lines 1 and 2: a small Aztec building at mid-transfer.

La Raza, Lines 3 and 5: Tunel de la Ciencia (science tunnel). Marvel at nifty fractals, glow under a black-lit map of the constellations, or visit the science museum (open M-Sa 10am-6pm).

Zócalo, Line 2: models of the *zócalo* as it has appeared throughout history.

Bellas Artes, Lines 2 and 8: Aztec statuettes, replicas from Templo Mayor.

BY BUS

Peseros, autobuses, trolebuses—the variety of buses makes getting around more convenient rather than complicated. *Peseros* date back to the time when riding the green and white minibuses cost only one old peso, which is equivalent to about US$0.01 today. Although not quite the steal they once were, *peseros* are still extremely affordable and—though crowded—excellent ways to make short, direct trips around town. *Autobuses* are the big long buses like those commonly seen on the streets of Western Europe, Canada, and the US. They run on the most popular *pesero* routes, though less often. Fare is 3-4 pesos depending on the destination you tell the driver, and all destinations cost 5 pesos 11pm-6am. Destinations are posted on the front window. If you are unsure, ask the driver: *"¿Se va a...?"* ("Are you going to..."). *Trolebuses* (electric buses or "trackless trolleys") are even rarer than *autobuses*, and charge 1.5 pesos for the smoothest ride in town.

In 1997, a great effort was made to establish set bus stops. Look for the nifty stainless steel bus shelters or a little blue sign with a picture of a *pesero*. If neither is to be found, the nearest big intersection is probably a designated bus stop. Note that buses must be hailed even from designated stops; stick your arm straight out into the street like the locals do. Most *peseros* now only let you on and off at these stops, but some will still slow down at any corner. To get off, ring the bell (if there is one) or simply shout loudly *"¡La parada, por favor!"* (The stop, please!). To prevent a missed stop, tell the driver your destination. Hang on tight—the driver will take off whether you're ready or not.

Most *peseros* run until midnight, but major routes—on Reforma, between Chapultepec and San Ángel, and along Insurgentes—run 24hr. Other frequented *pesero* routes are M: Hidalgo to Ciudad Universitaria (via Reforma, Bucareli, and Cuauhtémoc); La Villa to Chapultepec (via Reforma); Reforma to Auditorio (via Reforma and Juárez); *zócalo* to Chapultepec (via 5 de Mayo and Reforma); San Ángel to Izazaga (via 5 de Mayo and Reforma); Bolívar to Ciudad Universitaria/ Coyoacán (via Bolívar in *centro*); San Ángel to M: Insurgentes (via Av. de la Paz and Insurgentes Sur); and M: Chapultepec to San Ángel, La Merced, and airport.

BY TAXI

Due to increased hijackings, robberies, and rapes, the US State Department has issued a warning against hailing cabs off the street—including those delicious lime-green Volkswagen bugs. If you simply must travel by taxi, call a **sitio taxi** (radio taxi). Late at night when buses no longer run, they're worth the cost (about twice as much as regular taxis). Ask your hotel or check the yellow pages for the best rates; though if push comes to shove, an overpriced cab recommended by a night club or restaurant is better than nothing. Despite their names, *sitio* cab companies often don't operate *sitios* (stands). If you can't locate a *sitio* number or a hotel cab, try **Servi-taxi** (☎5271 25 60). To get to the airport in a pinch, call **Transporte Terrestre al Aeropuerto** (☎5571 41 93). When traveling from the bus station or airport, head straight to the nearest taxi stand, where you can pay a fixed rate. It's appropriate to tip in any type of taxi. If you insist on using cruising *(libre)* cabs, make sure that the picture on the displayed badge matches the driver's face—if it doesn't, or if there isn't one, don't get in. You may want to note the licence plate number and driver's name, and avoid riding alone.

BY BIKE

Sick of the city's pollution and the crowds that plague most transit options in the D.F.? Hop on a bike and get out of town with ◧**Advent Mexico Mountain Biking,** Periférico Sur 2930, Local 14, 2nd fl. Expert adventurer guide Pedro Saad and associates lead travelers on 1- to 15-day all-inclusive English-language mountain bike tours of the mountains, volcanos, forests, and towns (including Taxco and Cuernavaca) surrounding Mexico City. Tours are also available for destinations farther afield, such as Chihuahua. A new package includes guided tours of D.F.'s cultural and historical sites, followed by a trip through the surrounding mountains. (☎5681 47 14; fax 5681 45 74; info@advent.com.mx; www.advent.com.mx. From US$85 per day; inquire about student discounts. Reservations are recommended one month in advance, though last-minute spots may be available.)

BY CAR

Driving is the most complicated and least economical way to get around the city, not to mention the easiest way to get lost. Mexico City's drivers are notoriously reckless and aggressive, which is necessary for survival on the over-trafficked and confusing roads. Yellow lines are frequently absent, pedestrians pounce on any sign of hesitation, and stop signs are planted midstream. Red lights are so routinely defied that police officers often direct traffic. If your car should break down within city boundaries, call the **Asociación Nacional Automovilística** (ANA; ☎5292 1970 through 77) and request assistance. Wait beside your car with the hood raised. If you decide to leave your car alone, give it a goodbye kiss before you go.

Parking within the city is seldom a problem; garages are everywhere (4-8 pesos per hr.). Be wary of valet parking; cars are sometimes given to the wrong person. Street parking is difficult to find, and vandalism is extremely common. Police will put an *inmobilizador* on your wheels if you park illegally; alternatively, they'll just tow your car. If you return to an empty space, locate the nearest police depot (not station) to find out whether your vehicle has been towed—or stolen. If anything is missing from your car and you suspect that the police tampered with it, call the English-speaking **LOCATEL** (☎5658 11 11).

Car rental rates are exorbitant, driving is a hassle, and the entire process is draining. Still interested? To rent a car you must have a valid driver's license (from any country), a passport or tourist card, and be at least 25 years old. Prices for rentals at different agencies tend to be similarly high: a small VW or Nissan with unlimited kilometers, insurance, and tax (known as IVA) costs about 350-450 pesos per day or 3000-3500 pesos per week. Most agencies have offices at the airport or in the Zona Rosa: **Avis,** at the airport (☎5588 88 88 or toll-free 01 800 70 777; open daily 7am-11pm) and at Reforma 308 (☎5533 13 36; open M-F 7am-10:30pm); **Budget,** at the airport (☎5271 43 22; open 24hr.) and at Hamburgo 68; **Dollar,** at the airport (☎5207 38 38) and at Chapultepec 322 (open daily 7am-8pm); **Hertz,** at the airport (☎5592 28 67; open daily 7am-10:30pm).

 AND ON THE SEVENTH DAY... All vehicles, even those of non-Mexican registration, are subject to Mexico City's strict anti-smog regulations. Restrictions apply M-F 5am-10pm, and penalties for violations are stiff. Every vehicle must "rest" one day per week and stay off the streets. The day of the week is determined by the last digit of the license plate. Note that some cars manufactured after 1995 may be exempt from the limitations.
Monday: 5 or 6.
Tuesday: 7 or 8.
Wednesday: 3 or 4.
Thursday: 1 or 2.
Friday: 9 or 0.

THE MOVING MARKET Slumped in your seat on the Metro, you're about to drift off into daydreams of Aztec glory, when a voice calls you back into the 21st century. "Attention señores passengers! Announcing the presentation of an article of great utility in the home, the office, the school, the workshop, perfect for resolving the most difficult problems arising in today's hectic world...for only 5 pesos, yes, the price of 5 pesos each. You are invited today only to take advantage of the special offer of 3 for 10 pesos..." You look on, partly amused, partly pitying, at a lone man or woman carrying a pile of small trinkets (or perhaps even only two or three), talking them up like they were the cure for the cold. But then something happens. Haven't I been looking for something like that? And wasn't that 3 pesos more on the street? Before you know it, you've handed over a few coins in exchange for a paperback Mexican cookbook, a sewing kit, a children's puzzle, a chocolate bar, or a pack of pistachios. Though station entrances display Mexico City's law against commerce on Metro property, no one seems to mind that the subway has become the city's largest market.

✦ ORIENTATION

MEXICO CITY

Mexico City extends outward from the *centro* roughly 20km to the south, 10km to the north, 10km to the west, and 8km to the east. There is much debate about where the city actually begins and ends. Few tourists venture past the Bosque de Chapultepec to the west, La Basílica de Guadalupe to the north, the airport to the east, or San Ángel and the UNAM to the south. A rectangular series of routes (the **Circuito Interior**) and a thorough system of thoroughfares (**Ejes Viales**) help to make cross-city travel manageable. Of these, the **Eje Central**, commonly known as **Lázaro Cárdenas**, is the central north-south route. At a more local level, the city is difficult to know well; even most *chilangos* don't have it all down pat. What's more, many different neighborhoods use the same street names—more than 300 streets are named for Benito Juárez. Still, it is only a matter of cardinal directions and good ol' trial and error before you've mastered the basics of this megalopolis. The most important thing is to know the name of the **colonia** (neighborhood). Mexico City has over 350 such *colonias;* **Col. Polanco, Zona Rosa, Col. Roma,** and **Col. Juárez** are some of the most touristed. Disregard street numbers, orient yourself using nearby monuments, museums, *glorietas* (traffic circles), cathedrals, and skyscrapers. Street names tend to be themed regionally. Streets in the Zona Rosa are named after European cities, those directly across Reforma bear the names of large rivers of the world, and those in Polanco honor famous philosophers. If you are sufficiently insane and driving around the city, a good map of the outer routes is essential. **Guía Roji Ciudad de México** (110 pesos), a comprehensive street atlas, is a valuable aid for anyone planning to stay in the city for some time. You can also pick up its little sibling, the abridged *mini-Guía Roji* (60 pesos).

CIRCUITO INTERIOR AND EJES VIALES
Aside from the large thoroughfares—Insurgentes, Reforma, Chapultepec, and Miguel Alemán—a system of *Ejes Viales* (axis roads) conducts the majority of traffic within the Circuito Interior, a rectangular artery made up of several smaller connected routes. *Ejes* either run north-south or east-west, and together make a sort of super-grid of faster roads laid over the city. *Eje* numbers increase heading away from the *zócalo*. Theoretically, using the *Ejes* together with the Circuito, any general area of the city can be reached without much delay. Realistically, heavy traffic makes zipping around gleefully unusual.

CITY CENTER
As huge as Mexico City is, almost everything of interest to visitors lies within easy reach of the city center. Many attractions are on or just off **Paseo de la Reforma,** the broad concourse that runs southwest-northeast, or **Insurgentes,** which cuts

north-south through the city. These two main arteries intersect at **Glorieta Cuauhté-moc.** From Bosque de Chapultepec, Reforma proceeds northeast, punctuated by *glorietas* (traffic circles), each with a monument in the center. Some of the more famous ones, in southwest-to-northeast order, include: Glorieta Ángel de la Independencia, Glorieta Cuauhtémoc, and Glorieta Cristóbal Colón.

Accommodations and food listings for Mexico City are divided according to the areas of most interest to visitors. Moving northwest on Reforma from Chapultepec, the **Zona Rosa** is followed by the area **near the Monumento a la Revolución,** the **Alameda,** and, east of the Alameda, the **Centro Histórico.**

CENTRO HISTÓRICO. The *centro histórico* contains the *zócalo*, the largest number of historic sights and museums, extensive budget accommodations, and lively inexpensive restaurants. The area is bounded by Cárdenas to the west, El Salvador to the south, Pino Suárez to the east, and Rep. de Perú to the north. **Metro: Allende,** Line 2 (closer to the accommodations and the Alameda), **Zócalo,** Line 2 (literally the center of the city); **Isabel la Catolica,** Line 2; and **Pino Suárez,** Lines 1 and 2, are closer to a few sites on the south side.

THE ALAMEDA. The Alameda, the central city park and its surroundings, contains many restaurants and many of the city's most attractive sights. The area is bounded by Eje 1 Pte. (known as Rosales, Guerrero, and Bucareli) to the west, Arcos de Belén to the south, Lázaro Cárdenas to the east, and Pensador Mexicano to the north. **Plaza Garibaldi** is approximately a ½km northeast of the Alameda. **Metro: Hidalgo,** Lines 2 and 3, **Bellas Artes,** Lines 2 and 8 (closer to the park, Palacio de Bellas Artes, Plaza Garibaldi, and the post office), and **San Juan de Letrán,** Line 8 (closer to most food and accommodations).

NEAR THE MONUMENTO A LA REVOLUCIÓN. The area around Monumento a la Revolución—**Col. Buenavista** and **Col. Tabacalera,** on the north and south sides of Puente de Alvarado, respectively—contains perhaps the most copious supply of inexpensive hotels and eateries, though considerably fewer glitzy attractions than other neighborhoods. It is bounded by Insurgentes Centro to the west, Reforma to the south and east, and Mosqueta to the north. **Metro: Revolución,** Line 2.

ZONA ROSA. The capital's most touristy, commercial district, home to some of the country's most exciting nightlife, is contained by Reforma to the north and west, Chapultepec to the south, and Insurgentes to the east. A few of the area's listings lie just east of Insurgentes, and a string of clubs leaks south past Chapultepec along Insurgentes Sur. The **Bosque de Chapultepec** sits just west of the Zona Rosa. The mostly residential Colonia Roma lies just south of the Zona along Insurgentes; cheaper, laid-back versions of the Zona's entertainment, restaurants, and accommodations spill into here. **Metro: Insurgentes,** Line 1 (right in the middle of the action), and **Sevilla,** Line 1 (farther west toward Ángel de la Independencia).

FARTHER FROM THE CENTER

THE NORTHERN DISTRICTS. Approximately 3km north of the *zócalo* is the district of **Tlatelolco** (**M: Tlatelolco,** Line 3), famous for its pyramid and Plaza de las Tres Culturas. Approximately 4km farther north lies **La Villa Basílica** (**M: La Villa Basílica,** Line 6), home to the Basílica de Guadalupe.

THE SOUTHERN DISTRICTS. Several major southern districts are strung along Insurgentes Sur, 10-15km southwest of *zócalo*. Roughly from southwest to northeast are **Ciudad Universitaria** (M: Universidad, Line 3), the suburb of **San Ángel** (**M. A. Quevedo,** Line 3), and posh **Coyoacán** (**M: Coyoacán,** Line 3). Approximately 20km southeast of *zócalo* is **Xochimilco** (**M: Tasqueña,** Line 2), the Venice of Mexico City.

SAFETY AND HEALTH

Like most bloated metropolitan areas, Mexico City has a fair amount of crime. Before you cancel your visit to D.F., however, keep in mind that most crimes perpetrated against tourists fall under the category of petty street crime—muggings, pick pocketings, and purse-snatchings. A community of con artists concentrates in highly touristed areas, sending teary-eyed children armed with sob stories to extract funds from altruistic tourists. Shake your head, avoid eye contact, and walk to a more crowded area. Some tourists have also been the targets of crime perpetrated by men in uniform. Just because someone is dressed as a figure of authority doesn't mean he won't rob you blind. Foreigners are particularly vulnerable near obvious tourist spots, such as Zona Rosa and the *zócalo*. In general, the downtown area, where most sights and accommodations are located, tends to be safer, but the back streets near Buenavista and the Alameda are significantly less so.

In addition to petty crime, violent crime against tourists is a continuing problem. To avoid becoming the next victim, stay away from untouristed streets and areas, particularly at night or when traveling alone. Refrain from ostentatious displays of wealth and avoid obvious marks of the *extranjero* such as shorts, baseball caps, waistpacks, and cameras. Never display your cash, and visit ATMs discreetly and in well-lit places, preferably at a bank during banking hours. Speaking in Spanish makes would-be attackers far less likely to bother you. Never follow a vendor or shoeshiner out of public view. Car hijackings are on the rise, especially at night—avoid driving at night anywhere in Mexico City, and drive with others if you can. Lock your doors and keep your windows rolled up. For more information about general safety, see **Safety and Security,** p. 15.

Women generally face a higher risk of attack. Mexican culture fosters *machismo*, which mainly manifests itself through insistent stares, provocative smiles, whistling, cat-calling, and vulgar propositions. Having light-colored hair or skin might lead to even more unwanted attention. These displays are usually more annoying than dangerous, and it's best to ignore them. To avoid unwanted attention, dress conservatively and try not to wear shorts, tank tops, or short skirts. For more advice, see **Women Travelers,** p. 35.

Besides the usual slew of health hazards faced by travelers to Mexico, Mexico City poses the additional problem of pollution. The city once known as *la región más transparente del aire* (the region with the most transparent air) is now the most polluted in the world, and the layer of smog that blankets the city can cause problems for contact-lens wearers, those with allergies, the elderly, and small children. Travelers may want to bring eye-drops or throat spray, and asthmatics would be smart to bring along an extra inhaler. Pollution is particularly bad during the winter, due to "thermal inversion," a phenomenon that occurs when warm air passing above the city traps the colder, polluted air in the Valley of Mexico. The summer rainy season, on the other hand, does wonders for air cleanliness, and from May to October the air is quite breathable. Newspapers and news programs often provide daily pollution indices.

 WHEN THE RAIN COMES... If you visit the capital during the summer, keep a light poncho or umbrella handy. The rainy season (May-Oct.) brings daily 1-2hr. rain storms in the late afternoon or early evening. Otherwise, sunny and moderate weather prevails year-round.

⁊ PRACTICAL INFORMATION

TOURIST SERVICES

City Tourist Office: Infotur, Amberes 54 (☎ 5525 93 80), at Londres in the Zona Rosa. (M: Insurgentes, Line 1). Helpful and friendly staff speaks English. Excellent city and

Metro maps available on request. Lists hotels and restaurants grouped by region and price range, as well as upcoming events. Open daily 9am-7pm. The office operates information booths around town; locations were being reorganized at the time of writing.

Tourist Card (FMT) Info: Secretaría de Gobernación, Dirección General de Servicios Migratorios, Homero 1832 (☎5626 72 00), in Col. Palanco. Take the Metro to Chapultepec, then catch a "Migración" *pesero*. The last stop is at the office. Come here to extend your FMT or clear up immigration problems. Arrive early to avoid long lines and prepare yourself for Mexican bureaucracy. Open M-F 9am-12:30pm.

Embassies: Visa processing can take up to 24hr. If you find yourself in an emergency after hours, call anyway—recorded messages provide important information.

Australia, Rubén Darío 55 (☎5531 52 25; www.dfat.gov.au/missions/countries/mx.html), at Campos Eliseos in Col. Polanco. M: Auditorio, Line 7. Open M-Th 8:30am-2pm and 3-5:15pm, F 8:30am-2:15pm.

Belize, Bernardo de Galvez 215 (☎5520 12 74; www.belize.gov.bz/diplomats.html), in Col. Lomas de Chapultepec. M: Observatorio, Line 1. Open M-F 9am-1:30pm.

Canada, Schiller 529 (☎5724 79 00; www.canada.org.mx), in Col. Polanco. M: Polanco or Auditorio, Line 7. Open M-F 8:45am-5:15pm.

Costa Rica, Río Po 113 (☎5525 77 64), between Río Lerma and Río Panuco, behind the US Embassy. Open M-F 9am-5pm.

European Union (☎5540 33 45; www.delmex.cec.eu.int).

Guatemala, Explanada 1025 (☎5540 75 20). M: Auditorio, Line 7. Open M-F 9am-1:30pm.

Honduras, Alfonso Reyes 220 (☎5211 57 47), between Saltillo and Ometusco in Col. Condesa. Open M-F 10am-2pm.

New Zealand, Lagrange 103, 10th fl. (☎5283 94 60; kiwimexico@compuserve.com.mx). M: Polanco, Line 7. Open M-Th 8:30am-2pm and 3-5:30pm, F 8:30am-2pm.

UK, Río Lerma 71 (☎5207 20 89; www.embajadabritanica.com.mx), M: Sevilla Line 1. Open M-F 8:30am-3:30pm. Operators available 24hr.

US, Reforma 305 (☎5080 20 00; for visa inquiries: 01 900 849 4949; citizen services: ccs@usembassy.net.mex; non-citizens: embeuamx@pd.state.gov for non-visa-related matters; www.usaembassy-mexico.gov), at Glorieta Ángel de la Independencia. Open M-F 9am-5pm. Operators available 24hr.

FINANCIAL SERVICES

Currency Exchange: Exchange rates in the city tend to be mediocre at best. *Casas de cambio* keep longer hours than banks, give better exchange rates, exchange non-US currencies, and sometimes stay open Su. Banks offer one exchange rate and usually charge commission. Many *casas de cambio* populate in the *centro,* along Reforma, and in the Zona Rosa. **Casa de Cambio Tíber,** on Río Tíber at Papaloapan, one block from the Ángel. (☎5514 27 60. Open M-F 8:30am-5pm, Sa 8:30am-2pm.) On the south side of the Alameda: **Casa de Cambio Plus,** Juárez 38 (☎5510 89 53. Open M-F 9am-4pm, Sa 10am-2pm). Near the Monumento a la Revolución/Buenavista: **Casa de Cambio Catorce,** Reforma 51, 4th fl., near the Glorieta de Colón. (Open M-F 9am-4pm.)

ATMs: Lost or stolen cards can be reported 24hr. (☎5227 27 77). **Citibank,** Reforma 390 (☎5258 32 00 or 5227 27 27), can also help in an emergency.

American Express: Reforma 350 (☎5207 72 82 or 5208 60 04), in the Torre del Ángel, at Lancaster and the Glorieta del Ángel, in the Zona Rosa. Cashes personal and traveler's checks and accepts customers' mail and money wires. Report lost credit cards and lost traveler's cheques to either office. Open M-F 9am-6pm, Sa 9am-1pm.

LOCAL SERVICES

English Bookstores: American Bookstore, Madero 25, in the *centro,* has extensive fiction, travel, and Latin American history books. (☎5512 03 06. Open M-Sa 9:30am-8pm, Su 10am-3pm.) **Pórtico de la Ciudad de México,** Central 124, at Carranza. English and Spanish books on Mexican history and archaeological sites. (☎5510 96 83. Open M-F 10am-7pm, Sa 10am-5pm.) Also popular is **Librería Gandhi,** on

Juárez along the Alameda. (☎5510 42 31. Open M-Sa 10am-9pm, Su 11am-8pm.) Another at M: M.A. de Quevedo 128 (☎5661 09 11) in San Ángel.

English-Language Library: Biblioteca Benjamin Franklin, Londres 16 (☎5080 20 00, ext. 4089; www.usembassy-mexico.gov/bibliotecaB.htm), at Berlín, 2 blocks southeast of the Cuauhtémoc monument. Books, newspapers, and periodicals. You must be 18 years old to enter. Open M-F 10am-6pm.

Cultural and Arts Info: Palacio Nacional de Bellas Artes (☎5521 92 51, ext. 152 and 159), Juárez and Eje Central. Open M-Sa 11am-7pm, Su 9am-7pm. Check *Tiempo Libre* for city-wide listings.

Gay, Lesbian, and Bisexual Information: Perhaps the best way to find out what's going on in the gay community is through the grapevine. *Tiempo Libre* and the smaller *Ser Gay* (available in gay clubs) provide a little information on gay social and political events along with the nightlife listings. *Ser Gay's* website (www.sergay.com.mx) contains a wealth of information on gay rights issues, gay-friendly businesses, and medical professionals. **Colectivo Sol** has info on upcoming political and social events. (Write to: Apdo. 13-320, Av. México 13, D.F. 03500.) **LesVoz,** the literary and political journal for feminist lesbian and bisexual women, tries to be a springboard for community development. (☎5399 60 19; www.lesvoz.org.mx. Open M-Th 9am-1pm.)

Women's Advocacy: Organización Nacional Pro-Derechos Humanos de las Mujeres y las Lesbianos (☎5399 60 19; proml@laneta.apc.org), gives free legal advice and support to women in cases of sexual discrimination or harassment. Open M-Th 8am-1pm.

LOCATEL: (☎5658 11 11). The city's official hotline for missing persons and cars.

Supermarkets: Most supermarkets are far from the *centro,* at residential Metro stops. Prices are higher than in *mercados* but lower than corner stores. **Mega,** on the way to Tlatelolco from M: Tlatelolco, Line 3. Take the González exit, turn right on González, and walk 3 blocks; it's at the intersection with Cárdenas. Open daily 8am-10pm. **Wal-mart,** 5 blocks north of Puente de Alvarado, on Insurgentes Nte. M: Revolución, Line 2. Also in San Ángel, just outside M: M.A. Quevedo, Line 3. Open daily 7am-11pm. **Superama,** Río Sena and Balsas, in the Zona Rosa, directly outside M: Polanco, Line 7. Open daily 8am-9pm.

EMERGENCY

Emergency: ☎060 or 080.

Information: ☎040.

Police: Secretaría General de Protección y Vialidad (☎5588 51 00). In case of emergency, dial 08 for the Policía Judicial. No English spoken.

Tourist Police: Seguridad y Información Turística (☎5535 40 21), the tourist unit of the metropolitan police, did not have any public offices at the time of writing, though they are often on patrol in the Zona Rosa. English spoken. **Patrullas de Auxilio Turístico** (☎5250 82 21 or 5250 01 23), is an auto service for tourists, which deals primarily with accidents, break-downs, and thefts. Little English spoken. **Procuradura General de Justicia,** Florencia 20 (☎5625 76 92), in the Zona Rosa, is a department of justice catering especially to tourists. File reports on anything—minor robberies, major abuses of power, or lost or stolen tourist cards. Some English spoken. Open 24hr.

Emergency Shelter: Casa de Asistencia Social (☎5744 81 28 for women, 5530 47 62 for men), on Calle Santanita in Col. Viaducto Pietá, near the treasury building.

Rape Crisis: Hospital de Traumatología de Balbuena, Cecilio Robelo 103 (☎5552 16 02 or 5764 03 39; M: Moctezuma, Line 1). Or dial 060.

Legal Advice: Supervisión General de Servicios a la Comunidad, Fray Servando 32 (☎5625 72 08 or 5625 71 84; M: Isabel la Católica, Line 1), south of the *centro* on José Maria Izagaza, 2 blocks south of the Metro stop. Call if you are the victim of a robbery or accident and need legal advice. Little English spoken. Open daily 9am-9pm.

Sexually Transmitted Disease and Innoculation Information: Secretaría de Salud, Benjamin Gil 14 (☎5277 63 11; M: Juanacatlán, Line 1), in Col. Condensa. Open M-F 8am-7pm, Sa 9am-2pm.

AIDS Hotline: TELSIDA/CONASIDA, Florencia 8 Calzada de Tlalpan, 2nd fl. (☎5207 41 43 or 5207 40 77), at Col. Torielo Guerra. From M: General Anaya, Line 2, take a *micro* headed for "Zona de Hospitales." Runs AIDS tests, provides prevention information, and serves as a general help center. Open M-F 9am-9:30pm.

Red Cross: Ejército Nacional 1032 (☎5395 11 11), at Polanco.

Pharmacies: Small *farmacias* abound on almost every street corner. In addition, all **Sanborn's** and supermarkets have well-stocked pharmacies.

Medical Care: The **US Embassy** (see p. 90) has a list of doctors with their specialties, addresses, phone numbers, and English-language abilities. In an emergency, ask for the nearest **IMSS** (Social Security) clinic; there is usually one in every neighborhood.

Dirección General de Servicios Médicos (☎5518 51 00) has information on all city hospitals. Open M-F 9am-5pm.

American British Cowdray (ABC) Hospital, Calle Sur 136 (☎5227 50 00), at Observatorio Col. Las Américas is expensive but trustworthy and excellent. No foreign health plans valid, but major credit cards accepted. Open 24hr.

Torre Médica, José María Iglesias 21 (☎5705 25 77 or 5705 18 20; M: Revolución, Line 2), at Mariscal, has a few doctors who speak English.

COMMUNICATIONS

Fax: Tacuba 8 (☎5521 20 49; fax 5512 18 94), at the Museo Nacional de Arte in the right wing of the building, behind the central post office. Also has **telegram** and **Western Union** service. Open M-F 9am-11:30pm, Sa 9am-10:30pm, Su 9am-4:30pm. Many *papelerías* (stationery shops) also offer fax service.

Internet Access: Mexico City is definitely wired. Internet terminals abound in corner stores and improvised cybercafes. Here are a few special places.

Java Chat, Genova 44K (☎5525 68 53), in the Zona Rosa. Enjoy coffee, soda, and the fast T1 connection. 39 pesos per hr. Also has an Internet international call service charging a fraction of Telmex rates. Open M-F 9am-11:30pm, Sa-Su 10am-midnight.

Lafoel, Donceles 80 (☎5512 58 35), at the corner of Rep. de Brasil in the *centro,* has reasonably fast computers, printer, and scanner. 20 pesos per hr. Open M-Sa 9am-8pm, Su 10am-5pm.

Mac Coffee, Londres 152, upstairs, between Florencia and Amberes, in the Zona Rosa. Ring bell to be let in. Get your Macintosh fix for 15 pesos per hr. Open M-Sa 10am-10pm.

Courier Services: UPS, Reforma 404. (☎5228 79 00. Open M-F 8am-8pm). **Federal Express,** Reforma 308, in Col. Juárez near the Glorieta Ángel de Independencia. (☎551 09 96. Open M-F 8am-7pm, Sa 9am-1:30pm.)

Central Post Office: (☎5521 73 94). On Lázaro Cárdenas at Tacuba, across from the Palacio de Bellas Artes. Open for stamps and *lista de correos* (window 3) M-F 8am-6pm, Sa 9am-4pm, Su 9am-noon. **Mexpost** inside. Open M-F 9am-4pm, Sa 9am-2pm. Postal museum upstairs with turn-of-the-century mailboxes and other old-school gear. Open M-F 8am-10pm, Sa 8am-8pm, Su 8am-4pm.

Postal Code: 06002.

MEXICO CITY PUBLICATIONS

Tiempo Libre: The best resource for getting down and dirty in the city. Available at most corner newsstands. Covers movies, galleries, restaurants, performances, museums, and most cultural events. Every Th. 7 pesos.

El M (the Metro): An informative and professional newspaper featuring both national and international news. Available at most Metro stops. Pick one up early—they tend to go fast. Free.

The Mexico City News: An English-language daily with film and theater listings and extensive international coverage. 7 pesos.

La Jornada: A top national paper, with news and event listings. 6 pesos.

Ser Gay: Available at most gay bars. Contains a complete listing of gay and lesbian nightlife options.

ACCOMMODATIONS

More than 1000 hotels exist within the city's expanse. Rooms abound in *centro histórico* and near Alameda Central. The best budget bargains are near Monumento a la Revolución on Plaza de la República. Avoid the filthier sections around the Alameda and anywhere that makes you feel uncomfortable. Beware of any hotel marked "Hotel Garage." These rooms are frequented by businessfolk "working late at the office" and allow entry directly from garage to room for illicit lovin' on the sly. Rooms priced at 100 to 150 pesos for one bed and 150 to 200 pesos for two beds should be clean and have carpeting, a TV, and a telephone. Some budget hotels charge according to the number of beds, not per person, and beds tend to be large enough for two. If you don't mind snuggling (or simply want an excuse to do so), sharing a bed can save major pesos. Finally, always ask to look at a room before you accept it; this is easier to do after check-out time (noon-3pm).

The shabby neighborhoods around the four bus station stations generally offer expensive rooms. If you arrive late at night, it is not safe to walk even the few blocks to your hotel. For travelers arriving at the **Central de Autobuses del Norte (Cien Metros),** the pricey but comfy **Hotel Brasilia,** Av. de los 100 Mts. 4823, is a fair option, three blocks to the left along the main thoroughfare as you exit the bus station. Rooms are carpeted and clean, with TV, phone, and private safe. (☎5587 85 77. Singles 180 pesos; doubles 240 pesos.) Both the **TAPO** and **Poniente** stations are in especially unsafe neighborhoods. If you arrive at either, take the Metro or a taxi to safer accommodations.

CENTRO HISTÓRICO

The accommodations in the *centro histórico* epitomize one of the great truths of budget travel: you can actually get more by paying less. The older, cheaper hotels here often have beautiful atriums with fountains, unique rooms with high ceilings, and friendly staff. Finding budget accommodations is made even easier by the near-absence of the *hoteles de paso* that dominate elsewhere. While busy during the day, the streets empty out at night—good for a quiet night's sleep, bad if you're walking back after dark. **Metro: Bellas Artes,** Lines 2 and 8, and **Allende,** Line 2. Hotels on 5 de Mayo, Isabel la Católica, and Uruguay are better served by **Zócalo,** Line 2, and **Isabel la Católica,** Line 1.

▨ **Hostel Catedral,** Guatemala 4 (☎5518 17 26; hostellingmexico@remaj.com), directly behind the cathedral, opened to great fanfare in fall 2000. The spacious lobby buzzes with youthful travelers from all over the world snacking at the bar or surfing the web (10 pesos per 30min.). Shared kitchen, washing machine (20 pesos), elevator, pool table, and vending machines. Clean 4- and 6-bed dormitories 110 pesos; triples 220 pesos.

▨ **Hotel Isabel,** Isabel la Católica 63 (☎5518 12 13 or 5518 12 14), at El Salvador. Old-Mexico atmosphere, atrium and outer courtyard, elevator, large rooms with TV, phone, and tidy baths. Many rooms have skyline views. Singles 95 pesos, with bath 150 pesos; doubles 190 pesos; triples 240 pesos; quads 300 pesos.

Hostel Moneda (HI), Moneda 8 (☎5522 58 21; www.hostalmoneda.com.mx), between the Palacio Nacional and the Templo Mayor. Big shared kitchen, washing machine and dryer (35 pesos), internet (10 min. free, 20 pesos per 30min.), elevator, lockers, rooftop bar and cafe, and a friendly international vibe. Breakfast included. Dormitories with 5-6 beds 90 pesos; singles 180 pesos. 10% HI discount.

Hotel Juárez, 1a Cerrada de 5 de Mayo 17 (☎5512 69 29 or 5518 47 18), on a cul-de-sac between Isabel La Católica and Palma. Keep your eyes peeled for the elusive sign. Comfortable, quiet, hotel with a pretty green atrium. Rooms have gleaming bathrooms, TV, and phone, but only half have windows. Singles 120 pesos (1 person), 130 pesos (2 persons max.); doubles 140 pesos; each additional person 10 pesos.

Hotel Principal, Bolívar 29 (☎5521 13 33 or 5521 20 32; reservacion@hotelprincipal.com.mx), between 16 de Septiembre and Madero, by Parilla Leonesa restaurant, which offers room service. Large, bright atrium and elevator. Neat rooms have TV, phone, and clean baths, but many have no windows. Singles 165 pesos; matrimonials 185 pesos; doubles 225 pesos; triples 285 pesos; each additional person 50 pesos.

Hotel Catedral, Donceles 95 (☎ 5518 52 32 or 5521 61 83), 1 block behind the cathedral, between Cinco de Febrero and Seminario. The fountain in the marble lobby sounds like luxury. The elegant bar and restaurant, rooftop terrace, elevators, rooms with phone, cable TV, sparkling baths, and many balconies, really are luxury. Singles 310 pesos; doubles 440 pesos; triples 570 pesos; each additional person 40 pesos.

Hotel Antillas, Domínguez 34 (☎ 5526 56 74 or 5526 56 75), between Allende and República de Chile. The lobby and adjoining bar and restaurant have a colonial feel, while the modern building boasts an elevator. Rooms have private baths, phones, and TV; a few have balconies. Singles 190 pesos; matrimonials 220 pesos; doubles 250 pesos; triples 400 pesos; quads 500 pesos.

Hotel San Antonio, Callejón de 5 de Mayo 2 (☎ 5521 99 06 or 5518 16 25), in the alleyway off 5 de Mayo between Isabel la Católica and Palma. The hotel is #29; knock on the door under the flags to be buzzed in. A small modernized atrium, elevator, clean rooms with TV, phone, private baths (no shower curtains), and unimpressive views await the peace-seeking traveler. Singles and doubles 140 pesos; triples 200 pesos.

Hotel Atlanta, Domínguez 31 (☎ 5518 12 00 or 5518 12 03), at Allende. The color orange pervades the upholstery and carpeting, enhancing the hotel's 1970s feel. An elevator, cable TVs, phones, and clean private bathrooms make this a good deal. Singles 140 pesos; matrimonials 150 pesos; doubles 190 pesos; triples 250 pesos.

Hotel Buenos Aires, Motolinía 21 (☎ 5518 2104 or 5518 2137), between Madero and 5 de Mayo. Scruffy but lovable hotel with a large atrium. TV in most rooms, but no phones, no elevator, and, often, no windows. Ask for a renovated room as others are scruffier and not so lovable. Singles 70 pesos, with bath 95 pesos; doubles with bath 110 pesos; triples with bath 180 pesos with; each additional person 20 pesos.

Hotel Monte Carlo, Uruguay 69 (☎ 5521 25 59), between 5 de Febrero and Isabel la Católica. Large, lovingly mismatched rooms have balconies, red carpets, yellow satin furniture, and clean tiled bathrooms. Relaxing lounge and top-floor skylight. Singles 150 pesos; matrimonials 170 pesos; doubles 170 pesos; each additional person 30 pesos. Reservations recommended.

THE ALAMEDA

The Alameda is a budget traveler's Catch-22. For the most part, the nice hotels aren't cheap, and the cheap hotels aren't nice—especially after dark. If Hotel Manolo I is full, you're better off trying somewhere else; after all, the *centro* and Revolución areas are just next door. **Metro: Balderas,** Line 1; **Salto de Agua,** Line 8; and **San Juan de Letran,** Line 8.

☑ **Hotel Manolo I,** Moya 111 (☎ 5521 37 39 or 5521 77 09), near Arcos de Belén, halfway between M: Balderas, Line 1, and M: Salto del Agua, Line 8. Entering from the dingy street is like going from black and white to vibrant color: pink, blue, and potted-palm green. An elevator, clean rooms with king-size beds, phones, TVs, and large baths greet you on the inside. All rooms (2-person max.) 160 pesos.

NEAR THE MONUMENTO A LA REVOLUCIÓN

Hotels near the Monumento a la Revolución are cheaper and quieter than their counterparts in the *centro* or the Alameda. Backpackers tend to congregate here, particularly in the hotels on Mariscal and Edison. **Metro: Revolución,** Line 2, serves hotels south of Puente de Alvarado/Hidalgo and **Guerrero,** Line 3, serves those to the north, near the train station.

☑ **Casa de Los Amigos,** Mariscal 132 (☎ 5705 05 21 or 5705 06 46), M: Revolución, Line 2. Originally the home of painter José Clemente Orozco, the Casa now houses tourists and social activists. The 4-day minimum stay is designed to promote involvement and understanding. Backpackers, grad students, and eco-warriors from all over the world congregate here. Library, lounge, kitchen, and laundry facilities are all available in this cooperative atmosphere. Quiet hours 10pm-8am. No drugs or alcohol. Breakfast 15 pesos. Dorm rooms 60 pesos; private rooms 65-70 pesos; doubles 110-150 pesos.

Hotel Yale, Mosqueta 200 (☎5591 15 45), M: Buenavista, Line B, between Zaragoza and Guerrero, to the left as you exit the Metro station. Recently remodeled rooms and baths, TVs, phones, and mismatched furniture make for an endearing hotel. Singles and doubles 90 pesos; triples and quads 160 pesos.

Hotel Edison, Edison 106 (☎5566 09 33), at Iglesias. The luxury is worth the splurge. Enormous rooms with full amenities surround a shrubbery-filled courtyard. Singles 170-190 pesos; doubles 210 pesos; triples 240 pesos; quads 260 pesos.

Hotel Ibiza, Arriaga 22 (☎5566 81 55), between Edison and Mariscal, keeps it simple with about 20 identical rooms. Each is small, with 1 bed, phone, and TV. Singles 100 pesos; doubles 150 pesos.

Hotel Oxford, Mariscal 67 (☎5566 05 00), M: Revolución, Line 2, at Alcázar, next to the small park. Large rooms have TVs, phones, and views of the park. Baths with huge sinks are ideal for laundry. At night, the adjoining bar attracts a lively local crowd. Singles 85-105 pesos; doubles 115 pesos; triples 150 pesos; quads 200 pesos.

NEAR THE ZONA ROSA

Generally speaking, accommodations in the glamour district are very expensive. The few exceptions should definitely be reserved far in advance.

Hotel Saratoga, Álvaro Obregón 38 (☎5147 82 33), M: Insurgentes, Line 1. Not actually in the Zona Rosa, but in Roma, about a 15min. walk from the action. Compact but comfortable rooms with cable TVs, phones, clean private baths, and room service from the adjoining restaurant. Singles 200 pesos; doubles 280 pesos.

Hostal las Dos Fridas, Hamburgo 301 (☎5286 38 49 or 5286 38 57), M: Sevilla, Line 1, between Toledo and Burdeos; turn right on Toledo as you exit the Metro, then turn left on Hamburgo. Mexico City's newest hostel is backpacker luxury for the lucky few who snag one of the 15 beds. Shared luxuries include cable TV and VCR, washer/dryer, kitchen, PC with internet (30 min. free, 10 pesos per additional 30min.), and an adorable little dog. No drugs or alcohol allowed inside; smoking only in central hall. Shared rooms 100-140 pesos. 5% ISIC discount.

Hostel Home (HI), Tabasco 303 (☎5511 16 83; www.hostelhome.com.mx), between Valladolid and Medellín. From M: Insurgentes, take Insurgentes Sur and turn right on Tabasco; from M: Sevilla, walk down Salamanca and turn left on Tabasco. The cozy hostel is a 10min. walk from the Zona Rosa. Shared TV room and kitchen with 6 and 8-bed bunk rooms. US$8; US$7 for HI members.

⬛ FOOD

Options for meals fall into six basic categories: the very cheap (and sometimes risky) vendor stalls scattered about the streets; fast, inexpensive, and generally safe *taquerías;* slightly more formal *cafeterías;* more pricey and decorous Mexican restaurants; locally popular US-style eateries; and expensive international fare. In addition, US fast-food chains mass-produce predictable fare for the timid palate. **VIPS** and **Sanborn's,** popular with middle-class Mexicans, run hundreds of restaurants throughout the capital. Vegetarians will have more to eat here than anywhere else in Mexico. When you can't wait for a home-cooked vegetarian meal, there's always **Super Soya,** the bright orange chain with soy-meat versions of all your Mexican and US fast-food favorites. If preparing your own food, local neighborhood markets stock almost anything you need. For fresh produce and meats, try **La Merced** (see p. 125), the mother of all markets.

CENTRO HISTÓRICO

The old-fashioned atmosphere of the *centro*'s numerous restaurants goes well with their tried-and-true cuisine. Locals offset the throngs of tourists, keeping prices lower than in the Zona Rosa, but not as low as those near Revolución. After the Zona Rosa, this is the best place for vegetarian cuisine. **Metro: Zócalo,** Line 2; **Bellas Artes,** Lines 2 and 8; **Allende,** Line 2; and **Isabel la Católica,** Line 1.

🔳 **Cafe Tacuba,** Tacuba 28 (☎5512 84 82 or 5512 20 48), a block from Bellas Artes. Vaulted ceiling, stained glass, *azulejo* tiles—the gorgeous interior speaks to this restaurant's storied history (numerous wedding feasts and movies) and well-prepared Mexican dishes. Be prepared to wait for a table. Menu in English and Spanish. *Antojitos* 18-44 pesos, entrees 41-96 pesos. Open daily 8am-11:30pm.

Restaurantes Vegetarianos del Centro, Madero 56, upstairs (☎5521 68 80); Mata 13 (☎5510 0113), between 5 de Mayo and Madero. Since the 1940s, this popular mini-chain has proven that not all Mexican vegetarian restaurants disappear. Inventive dishes feature vegetables you've never heard of. Open daily 8am-8pm.

Cafe El Popular, 5 de Mayo 10 (☎5510 11 22 or 5510 91 76), between Mata and Condesa, 2 blocks from Bellas Artes. The matching peach waitress uniforms, lunch counter, and booths have a 1950s feel. Breakfast, served all day, includes coffee, juice, eggs, and frijoles (18-33 pesos). Open 24hr.

Comedor Vegetariano, Motolinía 31, upstairs (☎5521 65 15), between Madero and 6 de Septiembre. The *comida corrida*-only menu (28 pesos) features vegetarian variations of Mexican staples and plenty of protein. Open daily 1-6pm.

Vitamex, Tacuba 66 (☎5512 94 60), and other locations. A vitamin shop/vegetarian cafeteria, like Super Soya, only tastier. *Paquetes* (set menus) of juice, dessert, and a light entree, 23-30 pesos. Frozen yogurt, 10 pesos. Open daily 10am-8pm.

Cafe Dayi, Isabela la Católica 9-11 (☎5521 62 03), between Tacuba and Cinco de Mayo. An exemplar of a Mexico City dining institution: the Chinese-Mexican restaurant. In true Chinese-Mexican tradition, there are very few meatless options. *Comida corrida china* 31 pesos, *comida corrida mexicana* 28 pesos. Open daily 8am-11pm.

THE ALAMEDA

The restaurants in Mexico City's Chinatown, located on the streets off Juárez across from the Alameda, offer a break from tortillas, but may leave vegetarians hungry. Prices are similar to those in the neighboring *centro*. **Metro: Hidalgo,** Line 2; **Bellas Artes,** Lines 2 and 8; **Juárez,** Line 3; and **San Juan de Letran,** Line 8.

🔳 **Fonda Santa Anita,** Humboldt 48 (☎5518 46 09), M: Juárez, Line 3. Go a block west on Artículo 120, turn right on Humboldt, and continue a half-block. The restaurant has represented Mexico in five World's Fairs and feels no need to dispel stereotypes—the table-cloths are bright pink and colorful depictions of bullfights and busty women cover the walls. Incredible versions of old standards and specialties from all over the country. *Comida corrida* 40 pesos. Open M-F 1pm-10pm, Sa-Su 1pm-8pm.

Centro Naturista, Dolores 10 (☎5512 65 15), between Juárez and Independencia. Locals and tourists pack this place before 3pm, when the food is freshest. *Comida corrida* with 1, 2 or 3 *guisados* (dishes; 28, 30, and 33 pesos, respectively). Features vegetarian variations of traditional Mexican dishes. Doubles as a natural healing center—try not to bang your head on the crystals on the way in. Open daily 1pm-6pm.

El Moro, Cárdenas 42 (☎5512 08 96), M: San Juan de Letran, Line 3. Indulge in Mexican tradition and finish your night with conversation over chocolate and churros. Delicious *chocolate* available in *mexicano* (light), *español* (thick and sweet), *francés* (medium thickness and sweetness), and *especial* (slightly bitter). Each cup comes with 4 freshly-made cinnamon-sugary pastry strips (24-25 pesos). Open 24hr.

Oriental (☎5521 30 99), on a pedestrian walkway at Dolores and Independencia, on a block of Chinese restaurants. The prices here are slightly lower (*comida corrida* 45 pesos) and there's a huge bronze Buddha at the entrance. Open daily 10am-11pm.

Energía Natural (☎5521 20 15), at the corner of 16 de Septiembre and Dolores. The brightest and most beautiful of the bunch, with healthful touches such as whole wheat bread. Sandwiches and burgers 9-20 pesos. Open daily 8am-7pm.

NEAR THE MONUMENTO A LA REVOLUCIÓN

Without many affluent residents or big tourist draws, this area lacks the snazzy international cuisine of other areas. Instead, homey cafes, *torterías*, and *taquerías* dominate the scene. For hearty portions and low prices, this is the spot. **Metro: Revolución**, Line 2, and **Guerrero**, Line 3.

■ **La Especial de París,** Insurgentes Centro 117 (☎5703 23 16). This *nievería* (ice cream place) has been scooping frozen wonders since 1921. 100% natural treats, from *malteadas* (milkshakes) to *frutas glacé* (fruit ices). Double scoop 16 pesos, triple scoop 23 pesos, quadruple scoop 28 pesos. Open daily noon-9pm.

El Tigre, at Mariscal and Arrispe, is home of the formidable *Super Torta Gigante*. The friendly guys behind the counter will make you a big, big *torta* (13 pesos), such as the *española*, with ham, *chorizo* (spicy sausage), and cheese; or the *milchory*, with *chorizo*, cheese, and *milanesa* (breaded steak). Open daily 10am-8:30pm.

La Taberna (☎5591 11 00), Arriaga at Ignacio Mariscal, below street level next to Hotel Pennsylvania. The service is fast and *comida corrida* (25 pesos) sure to please. Also has a relaxed and friendly bar. Open M-Sa 1pm-late.

Super Cocina Los Arcos, Ignacio Mariscal at Iglesias. Bright orange furnishings and a homey, cozy atmosphere. Service is a little slow, but it's all right—their chicken soups (16 pesos) and *alambres con queso* (22 pesos) are the best around. *Comida corrida* 16 pesos. Most dishes 12-30 pesos. Open M-Sa 8am-10pm.

Restaurant El Paraíso, Orozco y Berra at Gonzales Martínez, across the street from Museo del Chopo. Offers vegetarian *comida corrida* (18 pesos) in a friendly, family atmosphere. Open daily 8am-midnight.

ZONA ROSA

Welcome to ground zero for chic atmosphere, good coffee, and great vegetarian cuisine—all less expensive than expected. Though the Zona's club scene may have gotten a little duller, its restaurants shine as bright as ever. And yes, if you insist, there are also a lot of rock-bottom cheap cafeterias and *taquerías*, catering to the budget-conscious. **Metro: Insurgentes**, Line 1, and **Sevilla**, Line 1.

■ **Vegetariano Yug,** Varsovia 3 (☎5533 32 96 or 5525 53 30), between Reforma and Dresde. Also runs a cafeteria in the less touristy Roma neigborhood. Once past the big neon sign, this place is all taste, from the soft-pastel decor to the creative, internationally-inspired vegetable dishes. *Comida corrida* 42-49 pesos. Lunch buffet upstairs 53 pesos (1-5pm). Open M-F 7am-10:15pm, Sa 8:30am-8pm, Su 1-8pm.

■ **Saint Moritz,** Genova 44, in an alleyway, next to Java Chat. Cheap, basic, lunch (hamburgers, anyone?) in a clean spartan cafeteria—your wallet will thank you for the amazing value. *Comida corrida* 19 pesos. Open M-Sa 1-4:30pm.

El Meson de la Huerta, Río Pánuco 137 (☎5511 48 91), between Río Ebro and Río Guadalquivir. Cheerful, bright-yellow decor and solid vegetarian cuisine attract crowds of office workers, especially 12:30-3pm, when the lunch buffet (40 pesos) is tastiest. Open M-F 8:30am-noon (breakfast; 30 pesos) and 12:30-5pm (buffet only).

MEXICO CITY

LAKE MEXICO It may seem impossible that anyone would ever want to leave Mexico City, but long ago the entire settlement was almost abandoned. In 1629, the Valley of Mexico flooded and—for five whole years—Mexico City was under water, its rooftops like rafts adrift on the ocean. All but 400 Spaniards left the city, and as many as 30,000 *indígenas* died. After four years, serious debate began over whether just to give up and pack up. But defiant property owners vowed to hold on to their assets, and an abandoned drainage project called the *Desagüe General*, the brainchild of engineering visionary Enrico Martínez, restored the city to its present glory. By 1634, the apocalyptic metropolis was once again high and dry and ready to face down Mother Nature another day.

Coffee House, Londres 102 (☎5525 40 34), between Niza and Génova. In a city where most restaurants serve instant coffee, a real latte (19 pesos) can be a life-saver. Good sandwiches (38-47 pesos, includes a meatless option), pastries (11-27 pesos), and people-watching (free). Open daily 9am-8pm.

Las Fuentes, Río Pánuco 127 (☎5207 64 14 or 5525 70 95), at Río Tiber, 3 blocks from the Ángel de Independencia. The greenery overgrowing this vegetarian restaurant is rivaled only by the vegetables and soy meats overflowing the *a la carta* choices (40-90 pesos) and filling *comida corrida* (60 pesos). Open daily 8am-6pm.

Los Murales, Liverpool 152 (☎5726 99 11, ask for the restaurant), at Amberes, on the ground floor of the Hotel Century. Features vegetarian and meat options side-by-side (sandwiches 40 pesos), though a sumptuous vegetarian lunch buffet (59 pesos, M-F 1:30-5:30pm) will tempt even carnivores. Sleek, sparkling dining room has a slightly corporate feel. Menu in English and Spanish. Open daily 7am-11pm.

NEAR CHAPULTEPEC

Inside the Bosque de Chapultepec, sidewalk stands offer an enormous variety of snacks. Should you prefer a sit-down eatery, the area around the Metro station, just outside the park, is cluttered with vendors and small restaurants. **Metro: Chapultepec,** Line 1. A ritzier alternative are the *antojitos* in beautiful Colonia Polanco, north of the Museo de Antropología, accessible by **M: Polanco,** Line 7.

El Kioskito (☎5553 30 55), on Chapultepec at the corner with Sonora, serves succulent *antojitos* (20-30 pesos), and Mexican specialties (45-100 pesos) in a classy, relaxed atmosphere with tiled fountain and old city photos. Or you can eat at the adjoining taco counter (7 pesos each). Open M-W 8-10pm, Th-Sa 8am-12:45am.

Vegetariano, Veracruz 3, at Acapulco, facing M: Chapultepec. One of the city's few restaurants offering both meat and vegetarian dishes. *Comida corrida* 24 pesos. Open daily 10am-8pm.

COYOACÁN

If you crave great coffee, cheesecake, or pesto, spend an afternoon in one of the outdoor cafes and *taquerías* that line the cobbled streets of Coyoacán. For excellent, inexpensive meals, try the **indoor food market** on Hijuera, just south of Plaza Hidalgo. Heavily frequented by locals, these tiny restaurants serve home-cooked food at delicious prices. (Open M-Sa 9am-9pm.) **Metro: Coyoacán,** Line 3.

Cafe El Parnaso, Carrillo Puerto 2 (☎5554 22 25 or 5658 31 95), on Jardín Centenario, diagonally across from the cathedral. A celebrated book and record store with an outdoor cafe, all on the plaza's edge. Though the food is a bit pricey, the people-watching and eavesdropping are unbeatable. Coffee and cheesecake with strawberries 30 pesos. Open Su-Th 8am-midnight, F-Sa 8am-late.

El Guarache (☎5554 45 06), on the south side of Jardín Centenario. Bask in the beauty of the nearby coyote fountain from a *jardín*-side table at this classy cafe. *Comida corrida* (30 pesos), entrees 50-70 pesos, *antojitos* 22-45 pesos. Open daily 9am-10pm.

El Jarocho (☎5554 54 18), on Allende and Cuauhtémoc, 1 block north of Pl. Hidalgo. Follow the smell of freshly ground coffee to this legendary corner stand, or look for the line of customers overflowing into the street. Straight out of Veracruz, Jarocho has been serving some of the best java in the city since 1953. Cappuccino, mocha, and hot chocolate 6-7 pesos each. Open daily 7am-midnight.

VegeTaco, Carrillo Puerto 65 (☎5659 75 17 or 5658 93 11), at Zamora, behind all the other taco joints. Put together a meal of vegetarian tacos (6 pesos each) or enjoy a combination *platillo* (33-59 pesos) from a wooden stool at the counter.

SAN ÁNGEL

Though some restaurants here are too chic (and too expensive) for their own good, quite a few homey establishments sell solid, reasonably-priced food. The very stylish Plaza Jacinto offers great lunch deals. **Metro: M. A. Quevedo,** Line 3.

■ **Casona del Elefante,** Plaza San Jacinto 9, near the Casa de Risco. In case you miss the taste of *samosas* (26 pesos), or are looking for a vegetarian option in San Ángel (1 dish—*thali* 46 pesos), eat in the ornate dining room or people-watch in front of this Indian restaurant. Open Tu-Th 1-11pm, F-Sa noon-midnight, Su 1-6pm.

La Mora, Madero 2 (☎5616 20 80), a few doors down from Plaza San Jacinto. Impressive views of Plaza San Jacinto from the upstairs dining room accompany traditional Mexican *comida corrida* (20 pesos). Open daily 8am-6pm.

Pulp, in the basement of Museo Carrillo Gil; use the entrance around the corner from the main museum entrance. This cool little cafeteria has sandwiches (25 pesos), pastries (8-15 pesos), and delicious fresh apple juice (15 pesos). Open Tu-Su 10am-6pm.

La Finca Cafe Solo Dios (☎5550 33 02), on Madero right off Plaza San Jacinto. This hole-in-the-wall coffee stand only serves 100% Mexican-grown beans. Delicious hot mocha, espresso, and chocolate under 8 pesos; cold versions 11 pesos. Kilos of Chiapan coffee beans start at 60 pesos. Open daily 8:30am-8:30pm.

◉ SIGHTS

Overflowing with history, culture, and entertainment, Mexico City truly has something for everyone. A thorough exploration of its sights will require a week at the very least, and even natives are always discovering something new. Most major museums and sights are open seven days a week, while smaller museums and attractions usually close on Mondays. Admission is almost always free for national students and teachers, and, oftentimes, smooth talking will enable you to enter free with an international student or teacher ID. There is often a fee for those who wish to carry cameras or videocameras. Sights are listed by neigborhood on the following pages; below is a comprehensive, alphabetical list of neighborhoods and sights that will serve as a useful cross-reference.

SIGHTS, ALPHABETIZED

MEXICO CITY

CENTRO HISTÓRICO

*To reach the centro histórico by Metro, take Line 2 to **M: Zócalo**. The station's exit is on the east side of the square, in front of Palacio Nacional. Catedral Metropolitana lies to the north, the Federal District offices to the south, and Suprema Corte de Justicia (Supreme Court) to the southeast. Some sights south of the zócalo can be better accessed by **M: Isabel La Católica**, Line 1, or **M: Pino Suárez**, Line 2.*

Mexico City spans thousands of kilometers and thousands of years, but all is drawn together in the *centro*. On the city's main plaza, known as the **zócalo**, the Aztec **Templo Mayor,** the gargantuan **Catedral Metropolitana,** and **Palacio Nacional** sit serenely side by side. The architecture isn't lonely in its eclecticism; the space is shared by street vendors hawking everything from hand-woven bags to used-looking razors, AK-47-sporting soldiers reading adult comic books, permanent political protestors, homeless people, and hordes of picture-snapping tourists. The tourist masses don't even begin to compare to the number of Mexicans who daily pass through or work in this center of the centers. If you have time to visit only one area in Mexico City, this is the place.

▨ THE ZÓCALO

Officially known as **Plaza de la Constitución,** the *zócalo* is the principal square of Mexico City. Now surrounded by imposing colonial monuments, the plaza was once the nucleus of **Tenochtitlán,** the Aztec island-capital and later the center of the entire Aztec empire. Cortés leveled the city and, atop the ruins, built the capital of New Spain. Southwest of the **Templo Mayor**—the Aztecs' principal place of worship (*Teocalli* in Náhuatl)—was the Aztec marketplace and major square. The space was rebuilt and renamed several times, becoming Plaza de la Constitución in 1812. In 1843, the dictator Santa Anna ordered that a monument to Mexican independence be constructed in the center of the square. Only the monument's *zócalo* (pedestal) was in place when the project was abandoned. The citizens of Mexico City began to refer to the square as the *zócalo*, a term which has since become the generic name for the central plazas that mark most cities and towns in Mexico.

PALACIO NACIONAL. Stretching the entire length of the enormous *zócalo*, the Palacio Nacional is as over-the-top as Mexico City itself. The building occupies the spot of Moctezuma's palace, some of whose ruins are on display near the entrance of the **Recinto de Homenaje a Benito Juárez.** After Tenochtitlán fell in 1521, the King of Spain granted the land to Cortés, who constructed his own home here using stones from the original palace. In 1562, the King bought back the house from Martín Cortés, the illegitimate son of the *conquistador*, to build a palace for the royal viceroys. It was destroyed by a riotous mob in 1692 and rebuilt a year later with the same stones. In the 1930s, the building was restored and a third story added under the direction of architect Augusto Petriccioli. Today the *palacio* houses the headquarters of the president's administration and other federal bureaucracies. Stern security guards will keep you from going into the courtyard to the right of the entrance, where the most important executive business is conducted.

Over the entrance to the *palacio* is the **Bell of Dolores,** which was brought to the capital in 1896 from the village of Dolores Hidalgo (see p. 316). It was this bell that Miguel Hidalgo rang on the morning of September 16, 1810, summoning Mexicans to fight for their independence. Every year on the 16th the bell is rung again as the president repeats Hidalgo's inspiring *Grito de Dolores*.

The *palacio's* biggest attractions are the **Diego Rivera murals** in the main staircase and along the western and northern walls. Rivera spent the years from 1929 to 1951 sketching and painting the frescoes, entitled *Mexico Through the Centuries*. The mural is divided into eight smaller scenes, each of which depicts an event in the social history of Mexico. Although commissioned by the government, the murals are shockingly honest, making no attempt to sugar-coat the atrocities of Mexico's past. On the east side of the *palacio's* second floor is the recently renovated and expanded **Museo del Recinto de Homenaje,** dedicated to revered Mexican president Benito Juárez. The museum occupies the room in which Juárez died and displays a collection of his personal artifacts, described in Spanish.

Don't leave the *palacio* without visiting the newly restored **gardens,** at the far end of the palace, straight ahead from the entrance. Immaculate landscaping highlights flowers and cacti from all over Mexico. *(On the east side of the zócalo. Open daily 9am-5pm. Free. Trade your ID for a big red turista badge at the entrance. Guided tour usually available M-F 10am-4pm. 60-70 pesos. Joining a tour that has already begun is free. Museo del Recinto de Homenaje open Th-Tu 9am-5pm. Free.)*

▨ CATEDRAL METROPOLITANA. The third cathedral built in New Spain was **Catedral Metropolitana,** a mishmash of architectural styles from three different centuries that somehow turned out beautifully. The area was originally part of the main Aztec temple, but it was quickly replaced by a small cathedral, begun by Cortés in

1524 and completed by famous bishop Juan de Zumárraga. This, in turn, was replaced with a larger cathedral, begun in 1577. For the next 200 years the cathedral was under constant construction; it was finally completed in 1813.

The cathedral has a series of altars and *capillas* (chapels) throughout the interior. Greeting the visitor at the entrance is the **Altar de Perdón** (Altar of Forgiveness), a radiant gold-leaf altarpiece replacing one built by Jerónimo de Balbás between 1731 and 1736 and destroyed by fire in 1967. The cedar interior of the choir gallery, constructed over 90 years beginning in 1695 by Juan de Rojas, features intricately carved saints and important figures in the Church. Juan Correa's murals of dragon-slaying and prophet-hailing cover the sacristy walls. The magnificent, gilded **Altar de los Reyes** (Altar of the Kings), constructed between 1718 and 1743, dominates the far end. Around the central paintings of the Three Kings are statues of royal saints such as Louis IX of France. Two chapels near the entrance honor Mexico's patron saint—the Virgin of Guadalupe. Mass takes place almost hourly on weekends; visitors should take extra care to show respect and be silent at these times. The cathedral was built on especially soft soil, and sank lop-sidedly into the ground at an even faster rate than the rest of Mexico City. Several years of work completed at the end of 2000 have ensured the building's integrity, with high-tension wires and green girders running the width of the ceiling. In a pit 20m deep, ballast is added to the soil under the cathedral to firm it up. Note that unauthorized individuals will often try to sell tours outside the entrance, though volunteers guide free tours in Spanish and French. *(On the north side of the zócalo. ☎ 5518 20 43. Information desk open Tu-Su 9:30am-3pm and 4-5:30pm, M 9:30am-4:30pm. Tours of the coro in Spanish, French, and English 10 pesos.)*

■**TEMPLO MAYOR.** When Cortés defeated the Aztecs in 1521, one of the first things he did was to destroy the Aztec's main center of worship, the *teocalli*. He took stones from the plaza and its main temple (the Templo Mayor) to build his magnificent cathedral across the street. The temple and surrounding plaza were eventually paved over and almost forgotten until 1978, when workers unearthed it while laying wires and piping for the Metro. From 1978-1981, the site was extensively excavated, revealing layers of pyramids and artifacts. Today, a catwalk leads through the outdoor ruins, which include the remnants of several pyramids and colonial structures. The tour makes for a surreal escape from the throbbing *zócalo*. Most interesting by far is the Great Pyramid, which houses the remains of a twin temple dedicated to *Tlaloc* (the god of rain) and *Huitzilopochtli* (the god of war and patron of the Aztec). Legend has it that the temple sits on the exact spot where the Aztecs discovered *Huitzilopochtli*'s predicted eagle perched on a cactus eating a snake (see p. 51).

The extraordinary **Museo del Templo Mayor** houses some 7000 artifacts unearthed at the site. The museum is divided into eight rooms that are meant to imitate the layout of the original temple, and the artifacts found in the excavation are accompanied not only by dry museum inscriptions but also by excerpts from the ancient Aztec texts that describe them (both in Spanish). The highlight of the museum is the flat, round sculpture of **Coyolxauhqui**, goddess of the moon and mother of *Huitzilopochtli*. Audio guides are available in Spanish (40 pesos) and English (50 pesos). The English version is worth every *centavo* if you don't read Spanish, but the Spanish version only repeats the detailed written information. *(On the corner of Seminario and República de Guatemala, just east of the cathedral and north of the Palacio Nacional. ☎ 5542 47 84. Open Tu-Su 9am-5pm. 30 pesos.)*

SUPREMA CORTE DE JUSTICIA. Aside from the spectacle of hand-cuffed foreigners pleading ignorance about the cannabis in their socks, the Supreme Court draws tourists mainly for its murals. The four murals painted by José Clemente Orozco in the 1940s cover the second-floor walls of the court, built in 1929 where the southern half of Moctezuma's royal palace once stood. Filled with roaring tigers, masked evildoers, bolts of hellish flame, and a thuggish axe-wielding Señor Justice, the murals will make you think twice about breaking the law. *(On the corner* *of Pino Suárez and Corregidora. ☎ 5522 15 00. Officially, murals only viewable 9am-noon or by appointment. Call M-F 10am-2pm to schedule a free visit; however, visitors can usually sweet talk their way in any time, provided a big case is not being tried. Bring an ID to leave at the entrance.)*

MUSEO NACIONAL DE LAS CULTURAS. Originally built in 1731 by Spanish architect Juan Peinado to house the *Real Casa de la Moneda* (royal mint), the building was turned into an anthropology museum by order of Emperor Maximilian in 1865. In 1964, the vast collection of Pre-Hispanic artifacts was moved to Chapultepec and the museum was redesigned to promote understanding of different world cultures. The European collection consists mostly of copies of famous works of art, but there is an impressive collection of original works of traditional art from sub-Saharan Africa. *(Moneda 13, just behind the Palacio Nacional. ☎ 5521 14 38, ext. 226. Open Tu-Su 10am-6pm. Free.)*

SOUTH OF THE ZÓCALO

MUSEO DE LA CIUDAD DE MÉXICO. This museum, once one of Cortés's homes, is still searching for its place in Mexico City's vast constellation of museums and experimenting with exhibits on graphic arts. A collection of maps and pictures of Mexico City, located to the right of the entrance, features an awe-inspiring artist's conception of the Aztec capital just before the Conquest. On the opposite corner from the museum, a plaque marks the spot where Cortés and Moctezuma had their fateful first meeting. The spacious courtyard is a good place to relax, and the store sells excellent information on the city and the rest of Mexico. *(Pino Suárez 30, at República de El Salvador, 3 blocks south of the zócalo's southeast corner. ☎ 5542 00 83. Open Tu-Su 10am-6pm. Free.)*

MUSEO DE LA CHARRERIA. The small collection of saddles, spurs, and ropes proudly explains—in Spanish, English, and French—the development of *charreria* (rodeo) and its revered status as Mexico's national sport. Learn how quintessentially Mexican the cowboy, his clothes, and his sport are as you marvel at the artifacts. The museum is housed in an old Benedictine monastery, **Nuestra Señora de Monserrate,** dating from the 17th century. *(At the corner of Izagaza and Isabel la Católica. Most easily accessible from M: Isabel la Católica, Line 1. Open M-F 10am-7pm. Free.)*

THE ALAMEDA

*The Alameda is serviced by 4 Metro stations: **M: Hidalgo,** Lines 2 and 3, at the intersection of Hidalgo and Paseo de la Reforma, 1 block west of the park, is best avoided. **M: Bellas Artes,** Lines 2 and 8, 1 block east of the park's northeast corner; **M: San Juan de Letrán,** Line 8, 1 block south of the Torre Latinoamericana; and **M: Juárez,** Line 3, on Balderas 1 block southwest of the southwest corner of the park, are safer.*

The museums, libraries, and historical buildings clustered around the Alameda are worthy of any cultural capital, and you'll face some tough time-budgeting decisions vis-a-vis the attractions and astounding sights in the *centro histórico*, Chapultepec, and elsewhere. Still, serious shoppers cannot afford to miss the best crafts market in the city, **La Ciudadela.** Chess-addicts will be happy to find Mexico City's most popular chess park, in the **Jardín de la Solidaridad,** on the steps near the Museo Mural. Play is at various levels and vendors usually rent sets. The trash talk can get ugly—be prepared for remarks about your nationality, your mother, etc. Sadly, the outskirts of the peaceful Alameda are home to some of Mexico City's most aggressive beggars and trouble-makers.

ALAMEDA CENTRAL

Today's downtown oasis of sanity and photosynthesis, the Alameda was originally an Aztec marketplace, and later the site where heretics were burned during the Inquisition. Don Luis de Velasco II created the park in 1592, intending it to be a place where the city's elite could meander peacefully. Enlarged in 1769 to its current size, the park was repaired after the 1985 earthquake, and in 1997 the sidewalks were restored by the city government. The park takes its name from the rows of shady *alamos* (poplars) that flood it. Snack vendors, lovers, and babbling old fountains give the tranquil park just the right dose of activity.

At the center of the Alameda's southern side is the **Monumento a Juárez,** a semi-circular marble monument constructed in 1910 to honor the beloved president on the 100th anniversary of Mexican Independence. A somber-faced Benito Juárez, about to be crowned with golden laurels by an angel, sits on a central pedestal among 12 doric columns. On July 19 of each year, a civic ceremony commemorates the anniversary of Juárez's death.

EAST OF THE ALAMEDA CENTRAL

■ **PALACIO DE BELLAS ARTES.** This impressive Art Nouveau palace is probably the best thing to come out of Porfirio Díaz's dictatorship (1876-1911). Begun in 1905, work was halted in 1916 when it was noticed that the massive building had started to sink into the city's soft ground. Construction began again in 1919 under Antonio Muñoz, who added the massive dome, and finally completed the building in 1924. Architecture aside, most tourists come here to see the middle two floors, which are covered with murals by the most celebrated Mexican muralists of the 20th century. The best-known of these is on the third floor: John D. Rockefeller commissioned Rivera to paint a mural depicting "Man at Crossroads, Looking with Hope and High Vision to the Choosing of a New and Better Future" in New York City's Rockefeller Center. However, Rivera was dismissed from the project when Rockefeller discovered Lenin's portrait in the foreground. The Mexican government allowed Rivera to recreate the work in this *palacio*. The result was **El Hombre, Controlador del Universo, 1934.** A Marxist vision of revolution, it depicts Rockefeller at the controls of a massive industrial apparatus that will eventually destroy him, with not only Lenin, but Marx as well, lurking in the background.

The second floor holds a permanent collection of pieces by Rivera, Kahlo, Tamayo, and others, as well as space for temporary exhibits. The third floor displays murals by leftist José Clemente Orozco and frescoes by David Alfaro Siqueiros, the 20th-century Mexican muralist, Stalinist, nationalist, and would-be assassin of Leon Trotsky. His **Tormento de Cuauhtémoc** depicts Cortés's attack on the Aztec nation. On the top floor is the **Museo Nacional de Arquitectura** (☎5709 31 11), showcasing temporary exhibits on the city's architecture.

The amazing ■**Ballet Folklórico de México** performs regional dances here and occasionally in the **Teatro Ferrocarrilero** (☎5529 17 01), near **M: Revolución,** Line 2. Their exciting and vivacious performances combine *indígena* dancing with more formal aspects of traditional ballet. Many concerts, especially of orchestral works, are also performed. Attending a Bellas Artes performance is the only way to see the crystal curtain designed by Gerardo Murelli, made of almost one million pieces of multicolored crystal which, when illuminated from behind, represents the Valley of Mexico at twilight. The Bellas Artes **ticket office** sells tickets for these and other performances throughout the city. An **information booth,** up the set of stairs next to the ticket booth, has information on all performances in Mexico City. Travel agencies snatch up a lot of tickets during Christmas, *Semana Santa,* and summer; check first at Bellas Artes, then try along Reforma or in the Zona Rosa. *(Juárez and Eje Central, at the northeast corner of Alameda Central complex; it's hard to miss. Open Tu-Su 10am-6pm. 25 pesos to see the murals and art exhibits on the upper floors, free with student ID. Dance performances and concerts W 8:30pm, Su 9:30am and 8:30pm. Tickets 200-330 pesos. Ticket booth open M-Sa 11am-7pm, Su 9am-7pm. Information booth ☎5521 92 51, ext. 152 and 159. Open daily 11am-7pm. Some English spoken.)*

■ **MUSEO NACIONAL DE ARTE.** Opened in 1982 and thoroughly renovated and expanded in 2000, the museum houses the city's (and perhaps the world's) most comprehensive collection of Mexican fine arts. Paintings and sculptures dating from 1550 through 1954 are organized chronologically and carefully explained in Spanish. A number of *salas de orientación* have fun hands-on multimedia displays to help you understand how art is made, displayed, and interpreted. The elegant building was originally built during the Porfiriato to house the Secretary of

THE MURALISTS. During World War I, a new artistic movement flourished in Mexico, continuing into the 1960s and earning acclaim worldwide. The movement was dominated by three men: **Diego Rivera, José Clemente Orozco,** and **David Alfaro Siqueiros.** Though each had a distinct technique and personality, they shared common aspirations. The three muralists worked during the time of liberation just after the suffocating regime of Porfirio Díaz, embracing the new spirit of nationalism and populism encouraged by the Constitution of 1917. The artists received government commissions to decorate public buildings with themes that glorified the revolution and Pre-Hispanic history of Mexico. The principal messages of the murals were easily understood by any Mexican: Rivera, Orozco, and Siqueiros believed that Europeans had strangled the art of Mexico. They returned to *indígena* themes, shunning the elaborate decorations of colonialism and exaltations of the church. With their grand scope of expression, the murals soon became the silent voice of the Mexican people.

Communications. The architect, Silvio Conti, took particular care with the central staircase; its Baroque handrails were crafted by artists in Florence. In front of the museum is the famous equestrian statue of Carlos IV of Spain, **the Caballito,** sculpted by Manuel Tolsa. A plaque explains, "Mexico preserves it as a monument of art"—not in honor of the king. *(Tacuba 8, half a block from Bellas Artes. ☎5512 32 24. Open Tu-Su 10:30am-5:30pm. 30 pesos, students and teachers free; Su free.)*

TORRE LATINOAMERICANA. One of the tallest buildings in the city at 182m and 44 stories high, the tower's 44th-floor observatory commands a startling view of the sprawling city. At night, the view is positively sexy, with city lights sparkling for miles in every direction. Completed in 1956, this was Mexico City's first quake-resistant building taller than 40 stories. In 1957, the tower successfully survived a minor earthquake. The *torre* repeated its performance in the far more devastating quake of 1985, swaying with the moving earth rather than breaking apart. *(Lázaro Cárdenas and Madero, 1 block east of Alameda Central's southeast corner. Observatory open daily 9:30am-11pm. 35 pesos, children 30 pesos.)*

TEMPLO DE SAN FRANCISCO. Built in 1525, only four years after the fall of Tenochtitlán, the temple was the first church in the Americas. Soon after construction ended, Cortés himself visited the vast Franciscan complex, which included several churches, a school, and a hospital. In 1838, the church hosted the funeral of Emperor Iturbide. After extensive remodeling in 1716, only the temple and the *capilla* (chapel) remain. Two fragments of the original cloisters can be seen at Gante 5, on the east side of the church, and at Lázaro Cárdenas 8, behind a vacant lot. *(Just east of the Torre LatinoAmericana. Open M-F 9am-1pm and 5-7pm, Sa 9am-1pm.)*

CASA DE LOS AZULEJOS. The house was first built in the 1500s and called the Blue Palace. In the following century its exterior and much of the interior were covered in expensive *azulejos* (blue and white tiles). According to legend, the son of the Count of Orizaba ordered the redecoration in order to impress his father, who had told him he'd never amount to much. The Sanborn's restaurant chain now occupies the building with four dining rooms, a miniature department store, and a gift shop. You can view the interior for free from the upstairs balcony by ascending the staircase in the main dining room or the elevator in the gift shop. *(Madero 4, it's the only tile-covered building in the centro. Sanborn's ☎5512 13 31. Open daily 8am-1am.)*

PALACIO ITURBIDE. The grand 18th-century *palacio*, best known for having served as the home of Mexico's short-lived first Emperor, Agustín Iturbide, from his coronation in 1821 to his ousting in 1823, is now occupied by the Fomento Cultural Banamex, which puts on beautiful temporary exhibits on Mexican history. *(Madero 17, between Bolívar and Gante, 1½ blocks east of the Torre Latinoamericana, near the Templo de San Francisco. ☎5225 02 47. Open daily 10am-7pm. Free.)*

WEST OF THE ALAMEDA CENTRAL

■ **MUSEO MURAL DIEGO RIVERA.** Also known as Museo de la Alameda, this fascinating building holds Diego Rivera's masterpiece, **Sueño de una Tarde Dominical en la Alameda Central** (*Sunday Afternoon Dream in the Alameda Central*). The key in front of the mural points out, in English and Spanish, the famous figures woven into the work: Frida Kahlo, Antonio de Santa Anna, and Hernán Cortés (with his hand covered in blood), among others. On the walls of the exhibition space are exhibits on Rivera's life and the cultural climate in which he lived. One exhibit explains the attack on the painting committed by a group of 100 university students the morning of June 4, 1948. The students blotted out the controversial words "God does not exist," held up by Ignacio Ramírez, an excerpt from a speech he had given in 1836. Rivera eventually allowed the phrase to be left out when the mural was repaired. Upstairs you can get a great panoramic view of the mural. *(Colón and Balderas, facing the park at the west end of the Alameda.* ☎ *5512 07 59. Open Tu-Su 10am-6pm. 10 pesos, students free; Su free.)*

PINACOTECA VIRREINAL DE SAN DIEGO. Constructed as a church between 1591 and 1621, the building now holds unique temporary exhibits of contemporary multi-media art. The interior, with walls painted bare white or concealed behind curtains, reveals little of the building's past. *(Dr. Mora 7, next to Centro Cultural José Martí.* ☎ *5510 27 93. Open Tu-Su 9am-5pm. 10 pesos, Su free.)*

CENTRO CULTURAL JOSÉ MARTÍ. The poet José Martí, a leader of the Cuban independence movement in the late 19th century, warned against foreign imperialism and dreamed of a united and free Latin America, led by Mexico. The center features a rainbow-colored mural devoted to Martí's poetry. A tally sheet in the corner of the mural records Spanish, British, French, and US interventions in Latin America from 1800 to 1969; the grand total is a staggering 784. Temporary exhibits on Cuba share the space. A white tarp often covers the mural (to avoid clashing with the temporary exhibits), but nobody minds if you stick your head under and take a look. Movies, concerts, plays, and other cultural events take place in the adjoining theater, and a small library holds books on Latin America. *(Dr. Mora 2 at Hidalgo, on the Alameda's west end.* ☎ *5521 21 15. Open M-F 9am-9pm, Sa 10am-7pm. Free.)*

ALONG AVENIDA HIDALGO

■ **MUSEO FRANZ MAYER.** In the small, sunken Plaza de Santa Veracruz lies the Museo Franz Mayer, in the restored Hospital de San Juan de Dios, which houses a beautiful collection of applied arts: furniture, textiles, ceramics, tiles, and church ornaments, especially from the *virreinal* (colonial or viceroyal) period. This is arguably the art for which Mexico is most famous, though international pieces are also on display. Some landscape paintings and portraits expand the meaning of "applied art." Fliers in English explain parts of the collection (2 pesos). The courtyard of the adjoining cloister is a tranquil refuge from the modern city. The upstairs library, specializing in the arts and rare books, is open to university graduates or students who have a demonstrable interest in the collection. The courtyard cafe alone is worth the price of admission. *(Hidalgo 45.* ☎ *5518 22 65. Open Tu-Su 10am-5pm. Museum 20 pesos, students 10 pesos.)*

MUSEO NACIONAL DE LA ESTAMPA. The museum houses the National Institute of Fine Arts's graphic arts and engraving collection. To the left of the entrance, a permanent display explains the art of printmaking through artifacts and text in Spanish. The rest of the museum holds temporary exhibits from the permanent collection and loans. Highlights have included the work of José Guadalupe Posada, Mexico's foremost engraver and printmaker. His woodcuts depict skeletons dancing, singing, and cavorting in ridiculous costumes—a graphic indictment of the Porfiriato's excesses. *(Hidalgo 39, next to the Museo Franz Mayer, in the pale yellow building.* ☎ *5521 22 44 or 5510 49 05. Open Tu-Su 10am-6pm. 10 pesos; Su free.)*

NEAR THE MONUMENTO A LA REVOLUCIÓN

*To get to the Monumento a la Revolución, take **M: Revolución**, Line 2.*

The area around the Monumento a la Revolución is home to three fine museums: the Museo Nacional de la Revolución, the Museo del Chopo (the Chopo), and the Museo San Carlos.

MONUMENTO A LA REVOLUCIÓN/MUSEO NACIONAL DE LA REVOLUCIÓN. In the early 1900s, president Porfirio Díaz planned this site as the seat of Congress, but progress halted as revolutionary fighting paralyzed the city streets; the dome was left only half-completed. It wasn't until the 1930s that the monument and the space below were finally dedicated to the memory of the Revolution. Today, 32 flag poles representing the Mexican states line the pathway to the dome, which now contains the Museo Nacional de la Revolución. The museum features Revolutionary artifacts (cars, clothing, guns, etc.) and a thorough chronology of the Revolution. Temporary exhibits connect contemporary art with political history. Sunday is the only day you can ascend to the top of the monument. *(At Plaza de la República; the museum is in a park just northeast of the monument. ☎ 5546 21 15. Museum open Tu-Sa 9am-5pm, Su 9am-3pm. 5 pesos; Su free. Call ahead to arrange a tour.)*

MUSEO DEL CHOPO. The modern, relatively tourist-free Chopo (as it's commonly called) displays the works of rising Mexican artists in every medium. Every mid-June to mid-July, for 12 years running, the museum has proudly hosted a show of gay and lesbian photography, sculpture, and painting. The unusual building was built in France and rebuilt at this spot in 1910. *(Dr. Enrique González Martínez 10. Just after Puente de Alvarado turns into San Cosme, turn right on Dr. Enrique González Martínez; it's one block up on the left. Open Tu-Su 10am-7pm. 10 pesos, students 5 pesos; Tu free. Free guided visits Tu-F 10:30am, noon, 4:30, and 6pm.)*

MUSEO SAN CARLOS. The museum is in the old **Palacio Buenavista**, constructed in 1795 for the Count of Buenavista by his mother. The building served as temporary residence for Santa Anna and later belonged to Emperor Maximilian. Today, it is home to the Museo San Carlos, which will make you feel as though you're in Spain not Mexico. Housing the former collection of the Academy San Carlos, founded by the King of Spain in 1783, its impressive holdings span European art from the 14th to 19th centuries. The museum features excellent work by minor artists, as well as standards by artists such as Rubens and Goya. Temporary exhibits often highlight certain themes in post-Renaissance European art. *(At the corner of Puente de Alvarado and Ramos Arizpe, 3 blocks north of the Monumento a la Revolución. ☎ 5566 85 22. Open W-Su 10am-6pm. 20 pesos, students and teachers 10 pesos; Su free.)*

▧ BOSQUE DE CHAPULTEPEC

*To reach the park, get off the Metro at **M: Auditorio**, Line 7, farther west, closer to the zoo, or **M: Chapultepec**, Line 1, farther east, closer to the Niños Héroes monument and most museums. Alternatively, take any pesero on Reforma to Auditorio or Chapultepec.*

Mexico City has to do everything a little bigger and better, and the D.F.'s major park and recreational area are no exception. The Chapultepec area is home not only to the park itself, but to a slew of fabulous museums, including the Museo Nacional de Antropología, the most famous museum in the country.

THE PARK. The 1000-acre expanse of green on the western side of the *centro* is the largest and oldest urban park in all the Americas, established in the 15th century when Aztec emperor Moctezuma I decided to create a recreational area, with streams and aqueducts. Today, Chapultepec (Grasshopper Hill) is filled with museums, hiking paths, zoos, bikes, amusement parks, castles, balloon vendors, and modern sports facilities. Mexico's most famous museum, the **Museo Nacional de Antropología,** sits among the hills of the park. During official visitation hours, it is as safe as anywhere in the city, but the park should be avoided after nightfall. The best time to visit the Bosque is on Sunday, when families flock to open-air concerts and receive free admission to the zoo and museums. To explore the entire park, rent a bike near the corner of Reforma and Gandhi, across Reforma from the anthropology museum. (30 pesos per hr. Open Tu-Su 5am-4:30pm.) Helpful signs point you toward major sites, but the Bosque's myriad paths wind and curve without warning; pay attention to where you're going. All the museums and sights listed are in Old Chapultepec, the eastern half of the park, which fans out to the west of the Zona Rosa. *(Open Tu-Su 5am-5pm.)*

■**MUSEO NACIONAL DE ANTROPOLOGÍA.** Some journey to Mexico simply to view this magnificent and massive mega-museum, considered by many to be the best. Housing 4 sq. km of Mexico's most exquisite archaeological and ethnographic treasures in 23 exhibition halls, this museum is the yardstick for measuring all other Mexican museums. Designed by Pedro Ramírez Vázquez, it was built of volcanic rock, wood, and marble, and opened in 1964. Poems from ancient texts and epics grace the entrances from the main courtyard. In the center of the courtyard, a stout column covered with symbolic carvings supports the tremendous weight of a vast, aluminum pavilion that shields the courtyard from weather.

It would take days to pay proper homage to the entire museum. As you enter on the right side of the ground floor, a general introduction to anthropology precedes a series of chronologically arranged galleries moving from the right to the left wings of the building. These trace the histories of many central Mexican groups, from the first migration to America up to the Spanish Conquest. Among the highlights not to be missed: the **Sala Teotihuacana,** with detailed models of Teotihuacán; the **Sala Toltec,** with huge statues of Quetzalcóatl; the **Sala Golfo de Mexico,** with colossal stone Olmec heads; the **Sala Maya,** where you can descend into a model of the tomb of King Pacal; and the museum's crown jewel, the **Sala Mexica,** which houses the world-famous **Aztec Calendar Stone (Sun Stone),** featuring Tonatiuh, the Aztec god of the sun, and an enormous statue of Coatlicue ("the one with the skirt of snakes"), goddess of life and death. The museum also has a pricey **cafeteria** (open Tu-Su 9am-7pm; entrees 50-90 pesos) and a large **bookshop** that sells English guides to archaeological sites around the country. Across from the museum's entrance, you can see performances by the **voladores,** who, in true Totonac tradition, climb up a wooden mast and slowly swirl to the ground. *(Paseo de la Reforma and Gandhi. Take an "Auditorio" pesero (2 pesos) southwest on Reforma and signal the driver to let you off at the 2nd stop after entering the park. M: Auditorio, Line 7. The museum is just east down Reforma. ☎5553 62 66. Open Tu-Su 9am-7pm. 30 pesos; Su free. Audio guides in Spanish 45 pesos, in English 50 pesos.)*

MUSEO RUFINO TAMAYO (MUSEO ARTE CONTEMPORÁNEO). The government built the nine halls of this museum after Rufino Tamayo and his wife, Olga Flores Rivas, donated their international art collection to the Mexican people. The murals of Rufino Tamayo were much criticized in the first half of the century for not being sufficiently nationalistic, but, since the museum's opening in 1981, Tamayo's reputation has been restored, though his more abstract style has garnered less acclaim than the "Big Three" muralists—Rivera, Orozco, and Siqueiros. The museum houses a permanent collection of Tamayo's work, as well as works by Willem de Kooning, Fernando Botero, surrealists Joan Miró and Max Ernst, and first-rate temporary exhibits. *(East of Museo Nacional de Antropología, on the corner of Reforma and Gandhi. Take the 1st right on Gandhi from M: Chapultepec, Line 1. After a 5min. walk on Gandhi, the museum is to the left down a small, semi-hidden path through trees. Alternatively, walk due east (straight ahead as you exit) from the entrance of the anthropology museum into the woods; Tamayo is 100m straight ahead. ☎5285 65 19. Open Tu-Su 10am-6pm. 15 pesos; Su free.)*

■**MUSEO DE ARTE MODERNO.** This wonderful museum houses a fine collection of paintings by Frida Kahlo, including the exquisitely gory **Las Dos Fridas.** Works by Siqueiros, José Luis Cuevas, Rivera, Orozco, Angelina Beloff (another of Rivera's lovers), and Remedios Varo are also on display. Temporary exhibits feature up-and-coming Mexican artists. The museum is linked to the **Galería Fernando Camboa,**

MEXICO CITY

Polanco and Chapultepec

○ ⑪ SIGHTS

Audiorama, 13
Auditorio Nacional, 4
Castillo Chapultepec
  (Museo Nacional de Historia), 12
Centro Cultural Arte Contemporáneo, 3
Fuente de Petróleos, 2
Monumento a José Real, 17
Monumento a los Niños Héroes, 11
Monumento a Mahatma Gandhi, 7
Museo David Alfaro Siqueiros, 6
Museo de Arte Moderno, 10
Museo del Historia Natural, 18
Museo Nacional de Antropología, 8
Museo Rufino Tamayo, 15
Museo Tecnológico, 9
Pabellón Polanco, 1
Papalote Museo del Niño, 16
Residencia Oficial del Presidente, 14
Zoológico, 5

an outdoor sculpture garden with pieces by Moore, Giacometti, and others. *(On Reforma and Gandhi, north of the Monumento a los Niños Héroes, opposite the anthropology museum on Reforma. ☎ 5553 62 33. Open Tu-Su 10am-6pm. 15 pesos; Su free.)*

MUSEO NACIONAL DE HISTORIA. Housed in the Castle of Chapultepec, once home of the hapless French emperor Maximilian, this museum exhaustively narrates the history of Mexico since the Conquest. An immense portrait of King Ferdinand and Queen Isabella of Spain greets visitors in the first room. Galleries contain displays on Mexican economic and social structure during the War for Independence, the Porfiriato, and Revolution. The upper level exhibits Mexican art and dress from the vice royalty through the 20th century. The walls of **Sala 13** are completely covered by Siqueiros's *Del Porfirismo a la Revolución*, a pictorial cheat-sheet for modern Mexican history. Admission to the museum also allows a peek at some of the castle's interior, and access to the most impressive views of Chapultepec and the surrounding area. *(Walk up the hill directly behind the Niños Héroes monument to the castle. Be prepared to open your bag for the guard. ☎ 5286 99 20. Open Tu-Su 9am-5pm. Tickets sold until 4pm. 20 pesos; Su free. Su only 2nd floor open.)*

MUSEO DEL CARACOL (GALERIA DE HISTORIA). Officially Museo Galería de la Lucha del Pueblo Mexicano por su Libertad (Museum of the Struggle of the Mexican People for Liberty), the museum is more commonly known as Museo del Caracol (Snail Museum) because of its spiral design. The gallery contains 12 halls dedicated to late Mexican history; the downward spiral begins with Hidalgo's *Grito de Dolores* and ends with the establishment of democracy. The exhibitions consist of life-like mini-dioramas, documentary videos, paintings, and historical artifacts. The staircase leads to a beautiful, round, sky lit hall that holds a copy of the Constitution of 1917, handwritten by Venustiano Carranza himself. Visitors unfamiliar with the contours of Mexican history may be bewildered by the Spanish-only explanations next to each piece. *(On the southern side of Chapultepec Hill. On the road to the castle, turn right at the sign just before the castle itself. ☎ 5553 62 85. Open Tu-Su 9am-5:30pm. 25 pesos, under 13, over 60 and Su free.)*

MONUMENTO A LOS NIÑOS HÉROES. At the end of the long walkway inside the park on the east side stand six white pillars capped with monoliths. In 1847, during the Mexican-American War, the US, under the command of general Winfield Scott, invaded Mexico City. The last Mexican stronghold in the capital was the Chapultepec Castle, protected by military academy cadets. Legend has it that as the invaders closed in, the last five boys and their lieutenant wrapped themselves in a Mexican flag and threw themselves from the castle wall, refusing to surrender. This monument—and countless city streets—honors those boy heroes.

TREE OF MOCTEZUMA. The tree has a circumference of 14m and is reputedly as old as the Aztecs. *(On Av. Gran, east of Gandhi, in the south end of the park.)*

■ **MUSEO SALA DE ARTE PÚBLICO DAVID ÁLFARO SIQUEIROS.** Twenty-five days before his death in January 1974, famed muralist, revolutionary soldier, republican, fanatical Stalinist, anti-fascist, and would-be Trotsky assassin David Álfaro Siqueiros donated his house and studio to the people of Mexico. In compliance with his will, the government created this museum. Fifteen thousand murals, lithographs, photographs, drawings, and letters document his fascinating life. *(Tres Picos 29, at Hegel, just outside the park. Walk north from the Museo Nacional de Antropología to Rubén Darío. On the left, Tres Picos forks to the northwest; follow it for 1 block. The museum is on the right. Open Tu-Su 10am-3pm. 10 pesos; Su free. Call to arrange a guided tour.)*

PARQUE ZOOLÓGICO DE CHAPULTEPEC. Although animal lovers might shed a tear or two over some of the humbler habitats, the zoo is surprisingly excellent, mostly shunning the small-cage approach for larger, more amenable tracts of land. *(Accessible from the entrance on Reforma, east of Calzada Chivatitio. From the M: Auditorio exit, head away from the National Auditorium. ☎ 5553 62 63. Open Tu-Su 9am-4:30pm. Free.)*

JARDÍN DE LA TERCERA EDAD. West of the Siqueiros museum, up Reforma past the Auditorio Metro station, is this *jardín*, reserved for visitors over age 50. It contains the **Jardín Escultórico**, a sculpture park full of realist and symbolist statues, and the **Jardín Botánico**, a botanical garden. *(Botanical garden open daily 9am-5pm. Free.)*

LAGO DE CHAPULTEPEC. At the heart of it all, Lago de Chapultepec rents rowboats for up to five people. *(Rentals available daily 8am-5pm. 8 pesos per hr.)*

TLATELOLCO

*Go to **M: Tlatelolco**, Line 3, and take the González exit. Turn right on González, walk 3 blocks east until Cárdenas, then turn right and walk up 1 block. The plaza is on the left.*

Archaeological work has shown that the city of Tlatelolco ("Mound of Sand" in Náhuatl) existed long before the great Aztec capital of Tenochtitlán. By 1473, the Tlatelolco king, Moquíhuix, had built his city into a busy trading center coveted by the Aztec ruler, Axayácatl. Tension mounted over territorial and fishing boundaries, and soon Moquíhuix learned that the Aztecs were preparing to attack his city. The Aztec war machine was too powerful for Moquíhux and Tlatelolco was absorbed into the huge empire.

PLAZA DE LAS TRES CULTURAS. Tlatelolco's central square, at the corner of Lázaro Cárdenas and Ricardo Flores Magón, 13 blocks north of the Palacio de Bellas Artes, is marked by the three cultures that have occupied it—Aztec, colonial Spanish, and modern Mexican. Today, the three cultures are represented by ancient ruins, a mammoth church, and the ultra-modern Ministry of Foreign Affairs. A plaque in the southwest corner of the plaza explains: "On August 13, 1521, heroically defended by Cuauhtémoc, Tlatelolco fell to Hernán Cortés. It was neither a triumph nor a defeat, but the painful birth of the *mestizo* city that is the Mexico of today." That battle marked the last serious armed resistance to the conquest. More than 400 years later, the plaza witnessed another bloody event, for which it is most famous: the **Tlatelolco Massacre** of October 2, 1968.

PIRÁMIDE DE TLATELOLCO. In the plaza, parts of the Pyramid of Tlatelolco (also known as the **Templo Mayor**) and its ceremonial square remain dutifully well-kept. Enter from the southwest corner, in front of the Iglesia de Santiago, and walk down a steel and concrete path that overlooks the eight building stages of the main pyramid. At the time of the conquest, the base of the pyramid extended from Insurgentes to the Iglesia de Santiago. The pyramid was second in importance only to the great Teocalli, and its summit reached nearly as high as the skyscraper just to the south (the Relaciones Exteriores building). During the Spanish blockade of Tenochtitlán, the Aztecs heaved freshly sacrificed bodies of Cortés's forces down the temple steps, within sight of the *conquistadores* camped to the west at Tacuba. Nearby is the **Templo Calendárico "M,"** an M-shaped building used by the Aztecs to keep time. Scores of skeletons were discovered near its base. A male and female pair that were found facing each other upon excavation have been dubbed "The Lovers of Tlatelolco." *(Open daily 8am-6pm. Free.)*

IGLESIA DE SANTIAGO. On the east side of the plaza is the simple, fortress-like church erected in 1609. The stonework and plain masonry of the church were designed to fit in with the surrounding ruins and their stonework.

MASSACRE AT TLATELOLCO On October 2, 1968, after a silent pro-peace sit-in held in the plaza, government troops descended, shooting and killing hundreds of protestors and taking prisoners, who were later tortured to death. In memory of the victims, a simple sandstone was dedicated in 1993, the 25th anniversary of the incident—before then, the government repressed all mention of the event, even removing related articles from all national archives. In 1998, PRD Congressional members proposed a reopening of the investigation on the army's actions that fateful day.

THE DARK VIRGIN The Virgin of Guadalupe, patron saint of Mexico, embodies the religious hybrid that characterizes the nation. She first appeared as a vision on a hill to the *indígena* peasant Juan Diego in December 1531. When Diego told the bishop of his vision, the clergyman was doubtful. Juan Diego returned to the hill and had another vision; this time the Virgin told him that on the hill he would find, in the middle of winter, a great variety of roses that he should gather and bring to the bishop as proof. Juan Diego gathered the roses in his cloak, and when he let them fall at the feet of the bishop, an image of the Virgin remained emblazoned on the cloak. As news of the sighting grew, a temple was erected in her honor and Guadalupe quickly gained in importance, aiding in the conversion of many *indígenas* to Christianity. The Virgin of Guadalupe's prominence arose from her ability to unite native beliefs with the Catholic tradition; her dark skin and knowledge of Náhuatl reassured many *indígenas* that Catholicism looked kindly upon them as well as upon the light-skinned Spaniards.

LA VILLA BASÍLICA

M: La Villa Basílica, Line 6. Pass the vendor stands and turn right on Calzada de Guadalupe. A small raised walkway between the 2 lanes of traffic leads directly to the Basílica.

Ever since the legend of Juan Diego, Our Lady of Guadalupe has been the patron saint of Mexico, an icon of the nation's religious culture. Diego's famous cloak is now housed in the Basílica de Guadalupe, north of the city center.

LA BASÍLICA DE GUADALUPE. Designed by the venerated Pedro Ramírez Vásquez and finished in 1975, the new *basílica* is an immense, aggressively modern structure. Although the flags from different cultures inside of the *basílica* make it feel more like the United Nations than a church, thousands flock daily to observe the Virgin's miraculous likeness emblazoned in Diego's robe. Visitors, crowd around the central altar and impressive organ to step onto the *basílica*'s moving sidewalk—it allows for easier (and faster) viewing of Diego's holy cloak. Perhaps the *basílica*'s most striking feature are the words written in gold Byzantine script across the top of the edifice: *"¿Aqui no estoy yo que soy tu madre?"* ("Am I not here, I who am your mother?"). *(Open daily 5am-9pm.)*

MUSEO DE LA BASÍLICA DE GUADALUPE. Next to the new *basílica* is the old one, built at the end of the 17th century and remodeled in the 1880s. Religious services and quiet prayers are still performed here, amid gawking visitors and a gift shop. These days, the old *basílica* houses the **Museo de la Basílica de Guadalupe**, whose entrance is at the back left side as you face the entrance. Colonial religious paintings and portraits comprise most of the collection, although they pale in comparison to the emotional collection of *ex votos* in the entryway. *(Plaza Hidalgo 1, in the Villa de Guadalupe.* ☎ *5781 68 10. Open Tu-Su 10am-6pm. 10 pesos.)*

TEPEYAC HILL. Behind the *basílica*, winding steps lead up the side of a small hill, past lush gardens, crowds of pilgrims, and cascading waterfalls. A small chapel sits on top of the hill, at the very site Juan Diego indicated as the site of the apparition of the Virgin. Murals inside depict the apparitions witnessed by Juan Diego. From the steps beside the church, you can absorb a panoramic view of the city framed by the hillsides and distant mountains. Descending the other side of the hill, past the spouting gargoyles, statues of Juan Diego and a group of *indígenas* kneel before a gleaming Virgin doused with the spray from a rushing waterfall.

COYOACÁN

*To reach Coyoacán from downtown, take the Metro to **M: Coyoacán**, Line 3.*

The Toltecs founded **Coyoacán** (Place of the Skinny Coyotes, in Náhuatl) between the 10th and 12th centuries. Cortés later established the seat of the colonial government in Coyoacán, and after the fall of Tlatelolco, he tortured the Aztec leader Cuauhtémoc here in hopes that he would reveal the hiding place of the legendary

Aztec treasure. Well-maintained and peaceful, Coyoacán merits a visit for its museums or simply for a stroll in beautiful **Plaza Hidalgo**, neighboring **Jardín Centenario**, or nearby **Placita de la Conchita**. The neighborhood centers around Plaza Hidalgo, which is bounded by the cathedral and the **Casa de Cortés**. Calle Carrillo Puerto splits the two parks, running north-south just west of the church. Obtain **tourist information** (☎5659 22 56, ext. 181) in the Casa de Cortés, the big red building on the north side of the plaza. The office gives free tours of the area in Spanish (Sa every hr. 8am-noon).

MUSEO FRIDA KAHLO. Works by Rivera, Orozco, Duchamp, and Klee hang in this restored colonial house, the birthplace and home of surrealist painter Frida Kahlo (1907-1954). Kahlo's disturbing work and traumatic life story have gained international fame since her death, and she is today regarded as one of Mexico's greatest artists. At 18, Kahlo was impaled by a post during a trolley accident, breaking her spine, rendering her infertile, and confining her to a wheelchair for much of her life. Married twice to the celebrated muralist Diego Rivera, Kahlo was notorious for her numerous affairs with both men and women—most famously with Leon Trotsky. The first two rooms display her early and late work, including her first sketches as a student, and her very last painting, *Viva la Vida* (1954). The third room contains paintings by Rivera and other contemporaries. Wandering through the rest of the house is an emotionally wrenching experience: witness the bed on which Frida suffered her injuries, Rivera's adjoining bedroom, a testament to the volatility of their marriage, the names "Diego" and "Frida" lovingly scrawled on the kitchen wall, and Rivera's painting of his "little girl" Frida hanging alongside sultry portraits of various lovers. Read the excerpts of her diary and letters posted on the walls that intimately describe childhood dreams, Rivera's adultery, and the inspiration that fueled her work. Kahlo's ashes are in a jar in the back of the studio, beneath her desk mask. The house fronts a gorgeous courtyard, a green sanctuary decorated with Pre-Hispanic artifacts from Rivera's collection. Explanatory labels are sparse, so you may want to bring this guide in with you. *(Londres 247. On Allende, 5 blocks north of Plaza Hidalgo's northeast corner. Kahlo had the building painted blue to ward off bad spirits. ☎5554 59 99. Open Tu-Su 10am-6pm. 30 pesos, 15 pesos with student ID. Guided tours in Spanish.)*

MUSEO CASA DE LEON TROTSKY. After Stalin expelled Leon Trotsky from the USSR in 1927, he wandered in exile until Mexico's president Lázaro Cárdenas granted him political asylum at the suggestion of Trotsky's friends, muralist Diego Rivera and painter Frida Kahlo. Trotsky arrived in 1937 with his wife and moved in with Rivera and Kahlo in "Casa Hazel," now the Museo Frida Kahlo (see above). In 1939, however, Rivera became infuriated at the affair Trotsky was having with his wife, and kicked the Trotskys out of his house. The family relocated to this house, on Churubusco. Though bunny rabbits now nibble peacefully in the gardens, bullet holes riddle the interior walls, relics of an attack on Trotsky by the muralist David Alfaro Siqueiros on May 24, 1940. Intending not to kill Trotsky, only to scare him, Siquieros wildly sprayed the inside of the house with machine-gun fire and stole many of Trotsky's documents. Fearing further violence, this self-proclaimed "man of the people" living in a posh house in a posh suburb, installed bullet-proof bathroom doors and hired a team of bodyguards. Despite the precautions, Trotsky was eventually assassinated by a Spanish communist posing as a friend-of-a-friend, who buried an axe in his skull. For more choice details of Trotsky's life, ask Jesús, the English-speaking punk tour guide. *(Río Churubusco 410. From M: Coyoacán, Line 3, turn right on Universidad, then left onto Churubusco. ☎5658 87 32. Open Tu-Su 10am-5pm. 20 pesos, students 10 pesos.)*

CASA DE CORTÉS. Contrary to popular belief, the *casa*, built in the 1750s, never housed Cortés's administration. Instead, the present-day municipal building honors the past by displaying murals by local artist Diego Rosales, a student of Rivera's. The murals depict scenes from the Conquest and relay information about Coyoacán. *(On the north side of the plaza. ☎5659 22 56, ext. 181. Open daily 8am-8pm.)*

IGLESIA DE SAN JUAN BAUTISTA. The church, bordered by Plaza Hidalgo on the north and Jardín Centenario on the west, was begun in 1560 and rebuilt between 1798 and 1804. The interior is elaborately decorated with gold and bronze, and the roof supports five beautifully painted frescoes, depicting scenes from the New Testament. *(Open Tu-Sa 5:30am-8:30pm, M 5:30am-7:30pm.)*

CASA COLORADA. Cortés built this house for La Malinche, his Aztec lover. When Cortés's wife arrived from Spain, she stayed here briefly with her husband, but soon disappeared without a trace. Legend tells that Cortés murdered his spouse for the love of La Malinche, but he later gave the Aztec woman away as booty to another *conquistador*. The *casa* is now a private residence and cannot be visited. *(Higuera 57. A few blocks southeast of Plaza Hidalgo, facing Placita de la Conchita and marked by the gardened plaza at the end of Higuera.)*

MUSEO NACIONAL DE LAS CULTURAS POPULARES. Temporary exhibits of music, video, and little figurines trapped in big glass cases will teach you a lot about contemporary indigenous culture in Mexico. The adjoining courtyard sometimes hosts live performances on weekends. *(On Hidalgo between Allende and Abasolo, 2 blocks east of Plaza Hidalgo. ☎5554 86 10. Open Tu-Th 10am-6pm, F-Su 10am-8pm. Free.)*

CONVENTO DE NUESTRA SEÑORA DE LOS ANGELES DE CHURUBUSCO. The convent once held a pyramid dedicated to the Aztec war god *Huitzilopochtli*, all traces of which vanished after the convent was rebuilt in 1676. On August 20, 1847, 800 citizen-soldiers, led by generals Manuel Rincón and Pedro Anaya, defended the building against 8000 US invaders, surrendering only when the last cartridge had been spent. Today, bullet holes still mark the front wall, where two cannons used in the defense are kept as memorials. Inside is the **Museo Nacional de las Intervenciones**. Artifacts and an extensive written narrative in Spanish tell the sordid history of the attacks on Mexico's sovereignty perpetrated by the Spanish, French, British, and US governments from the late 18th century to 1917. You have to pass through the museum to reach the **Acervo Artístico de Churubusco**, several rooms of Mexican religious art from the 17th and 18th centuries. *(20 de Agosto and General Anaya. From Coyoacán, walk 4 blocks down Hidalgo and then follow Anaya as it branches left; follow this street 4 blocks. M: General Anaya, Line 2, is only 2 blocks east of the convent along 20 de Agosto. The "Gen. Anaya" pesero (2 pesos) goes from Plaza Hidalgo to the museum; take the "Sto. Domingo" back. ☎5604 06 99. Museum open Tu-Su 9am-6pm. 30 pesos; Su free.)*

MUSEO ANAHUACALLI. Designed by Diego Rivera with Aztec and Maya architectural motifs, the formidable stone building is an exhibit in and of itself. The interior exhibits Rivera's huge collection of Pre-Hispanic art. Built atop a hill, Anahuacalli commands an excellent view of the area, including nearby Aztec Stadium. *(Calle Museo 150. To reach the museum from Plaza Hidalgo or Churubusco, take a "Huipulco" or "Huayamilpa" pesero south on División del Nte. and get off at Calle Museo. You might want to ask the driver to point out the stop; it is not immediately visible. Turn right onto Calle Museo and you'll soon be there. ☎5617 43 10. Open Tu-Su 10am-2pm and 3-6pm. 20 pesos.)*

VIVEROS DE COYOACÁN. Wander among rows of skinny saplings and frolicking Mexican squirrels in this botanical garden paradise, whose tranquility is enforced by rules prohibiting bicycles, balls, dogs, cameras, and food—though jogging, strolling, and PDA are welcome. *(Enter on México, between Madrid and Melchor Ocampo, between M: Coyoacán and Plaza Hidalgo. Open daily 6am-5:30pm. Free.)*

SAN ÁNGEL

*To reach San Ángel, 10km south of the centro along Insurgentes, take the Metro to **M: M.A. Quevedo**, Line 3. Head west on Quevedo, away from the big Santo Domingo bakery, for three blocks; when it forks, take a left onto La Paz, and continue along the Parque de la Bombilla. Alternatively, buses traveling Insurgentes with a "San Ángel" sign in the windshield will take you straight to the heart of the neighborhood. To get back from San Ángel to points as far north as Buenavista station, take a bus with an "Indios Verdes" sign.*

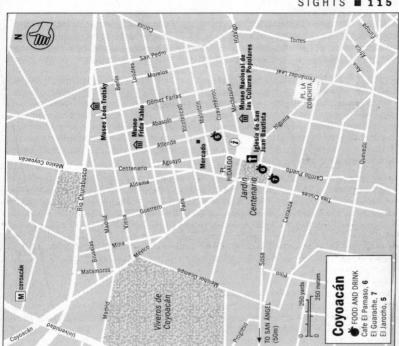

MEXICO CITY

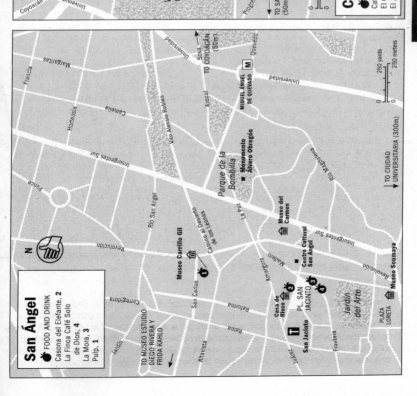

Near Coyoacán is another well-heeled, though less bohemian, section of town, San Ángel. Hidden behind the maddening traffic on Insurgentes and Revolución, narrow cobblestone streets and beautiful colonial buildings, not to mention some outstanding museums, make a great escape from the modern city.

PARQUE DE LA BOMBILLA. The centerpiece of this park is the **Monumento al General Álvaro Obregón,** which honors one of the revolutionaries who united against Victoriano Huerta, the militaristic dictator who executed Francisco Madero and seized power in 1913. The main statue accurately depicts Obregón, who lost an arm during the revolution. A separate statue of the severed limb stands on the lower level of the monument. In 1920, Obregón became the first president of the post-revolutionary era, but he was assassinated by a religious fanatic. The inscription on the sunken lower level reads, "I die blessing the Revolution."

MUSEO DEL CARMEN. Expropriated under the Reform Laws of 1857, this former Carmelite convent was abandoned in 1861 and restored in the 20th century to house a museum of art and history. The collection of colonial art has crucifixes galore, but few labels or explanatory texts. Some of the upstairs rooms have been restored to look as they did when the building was a convent; note the flat wooden beds and oh-so-comfy log pillows. Downstairs is the crypt, where the mummies are displayed. The identities of the bodies, eerily preserved in a water-tight crypt, are still a mystery—they were discovered in 1916 by invading Zapatistas, who thought the crypt held treasures. (In the converted ex-convent next to the Iglesia del Carmen, at Revolución and Monasterio. ☎ 5550 48 96. Open Tu-Su 10am-4:45pm. 30 pesos; children, students, and teachers free; Su free.)

IGLESIA DEL CARMEN. The church adjoining the convent was designed and built between 1615 and 1626 by Fray Andrés de San Miguel of the Carmelite order. Beautiful *azulejo* tiles adorn the inner walls. (Open daily 7am-1pm and 5-9pm.)

CASA DE RISCO. This well-preserved 17th-century house contains an important collection of meticulously-labeled 14th- to 19th-century art. The whitewashed inner courtyard has an amazing fountain made of pieces of *talavera* tile (called *riscos*), plates, cups, and other bits of porcelain from China, Mexico, and Europe. Upstairs, in the last room, are three small paintings by Mexico's landscape master, José María Velasco (1840-1912). A variety of European portraits, religious paintings, and furnishings form the heart of the collection. The ground floor hosts temporary exhibits of contemporary art. (Plaza San Jacinto 15, on the north side of the plaza. ☎ 5550 92 86. Open Tu-Su 10am-5pm. Free.)

MUSEO DE ARTE CARRILLO GIL. Inside the dull grey building is one of the capital's most interesting collections of art. It includes works by the big three muralists—Siqueiros, Orozco, and Rivera—but only their paintings on canvas, and not the famed murals. Siqueiros's renowned **Caín en los Estados Unidos** (*Cain in the United States*, 1947) depicts the lynching of a black man by a crowd of monstrous whites. The Rivera paintings date from the artist's early years, when he was heavily influenced by Picasso. Other 20th-century artists are also represented. The top two floors house rotating exhibits. (Revolución 1608, 3 blocks north on Revolución from the intersection with La Paz, to the right if coming from Parque de la Bombilla. ☎ 5550 39 83. Open Tu-Su 10am-6pm. Free.)

MUSEO ESTUDIO DIEGO RIVERA Y FRIDA KAHLO. These two buildings were the home of Mexican art's royal couple, Diego Rivera and Frida Kahlo, from 1934-40. Rivera lived in the pink house until his death in 1957, and his wife Frida stayed in the blue house until moving back to her home in Coyoacán in the early 1940s. Juan O'Gorman designed the two giant blocks, which were among the first houses built in the functionalist style that inspired the public housing blocks popularized later in the 20th century all over the Americas and Europe. The museum shows a small collection of Rivera's work and photographs and displays on the artists' lives. On the top floor of the Rivera house, you can see where and how he worked—his leftover paints are still lying around. *(5 blocks up Altavista from Revolución. The museum is on the corner of Altavista and Diego Rivera. Look for the 2 pink and blue blocks with a cacti fence. ☎ 5550 15 18. Open Tu-Su 10am-6pm. 10 pesos; Su free.)*

MUSEO SOUMAYA. This museum's pride and joy is its vast collection of Rodin sculpture, promoted as the third most important in the world. International visitors, however, may be more interested in the collection of Mexican portraits from the 18th and 19th centuries, colonial Mexican art, and paintings by Tamayo. *(In Plaza Loreto, a small shopping mall, at Revolución and Río Magdalena. ☎ 5616 37 31 or 5616 37 61; soumaya@prodigy.net.mx; www.soumaya.com.mx. Open W 10:30am-8:30pm, Th-M 10:30am-6:30pm. 10 pesos, students 5 pesos; Su-M free.)*

OTHER SIGHTS. Across the street from the Iglesia del Carmen is the **Centro Cultural,** which borders lovely **Plaza del Carmen.** Besides hosting changing art exhibits and plays, it's a good source of information on local happenings, especially at the numerous small performance venues. *(☎ 5616 12 54 or 5616 20 97. Open Tu-Sa 10am-8pm, Su 10am-7pm.)* One block up Madero is **Plaza San Jacinto,** at San Francisco and Juárez, which fills on Saturdays with shoppers scoping out pricey arts and crafts at the **Bazar del Sábado** (see p. 125). One block past Casa de Risco on Juárez lies the beautiful **Iglesia de San Jacinto,** a 16th-century church with an orange facade, carved wooden doors, and a peaceful courtyard. *(Open daily 8am-8pm.)* The surrounding neighborhood, the oldest in San Ángel, has some jaw-dropping, swank, and impressive mansions. Come see how the rich live, Mexican style.'

CIUDAD UNIVERSITARIA (CU)

*The sheer size of UNAM makes it difficult to navigate by foot. Luckily, **M: Universidad,** Line 3, lets you off (via Salidas D and E) in front of the free shuttle service. The shuttles are limited and irregular over summer vacation (July 22-Aug. 15), but still available to all campus areas. There are 3 principal routes. Route #1 will take you to the green and lively heart of the campus—Jardín Central, to the far north of the station. Walk toward the library (you can't miss it), away from Insurgentes. Alternatively, if you have a good sense of direction, a few pesos, and are willing to walk a bit, buses on Insurgentes run to the edge of driveways leading to both the Jardín Central and the Centro Cultural Universitario. Maps of the CU are available at the photocopy store across the greenery from the library. Open M-F 8am-7pm. 20 pesos. Should you have any serious problems, call **university security** (press the button on any security phone throughout campus).*

The **Universidad Nacional Autónoma de México** (National Autonomous University of Mexico), or **UNAM,** is the largest university in Latin America, with a staggering enrollment of over 100,000. Immediately after the new colonial regime was established, the religious orders that arrived in Mexico built elementary and secondary schools to indoctrinate new converts and to educate young settlers from Spain. The original university, the University of Mexico, was established in 1553 in the building at the corner of Moneda and Seminario, just off the *zócalo*. Modern UNAM was brought into existence by president Justo Sierra at the turn of the century. The Ciudad Universitaria campus was dedicated in 1952, one of the greatest achievements of President Miguel Alemán. Designed by famous architects like Félix Candela and Juan O'Gorman, the campus boasts 26km of paved roads, 430,000 sq. m of greenery, and four million planted trees.

CENTRO CULTURAL UNIVERSITARIO (CCU). Films, plays, concerts, and temporary art shows abound in UNAM's modern, beautifully maintained facilities. The magazine *Tiempo Libre* and the *Cartelera* and *Los Universitarios* leaflets provide comprehensive schedules, and hundreds of other events are posted on kiosks around campus. Most events of interest to tourists take place in the Centro Cultural Universitario (CCU—not to be confused with CU), Insurgentes Sur 3000. This large, modern complex houses the **Teatro Juan Ruíz de Alarcón,** the **Foro Sor Juana Inés de la Cruz** *(☎ 5665 65 83; ticket booth open Tu-F 10am-2pm and 5-9pm; tickets 50 pesos, students 25 pesos),* several other concert halls, the artsy movie theaters **Sala José Revueltas** and **Sala Julio Bracho** *(☎ 5665 28 50; tickets 20 pesos, students 10* *pesos),* and **Sala Netzahualcóyotl** (☎ *5622 71 11; shows Sa 8pm and Su noon; tickets 50-100 pesos, 50% student discount),* which regularly hosts big-name concerts and music festivals. *(Take Line 3 of the UNAM shuttle.)*

LIBRARY. A huge mosaic by Juan O'Gorman wraps around the university library, to the left of the Jardín Central. The breathtaking, nearly windowless building features eagles and Aztec warriors peering out from the side facing the philosophy department. The esplanade side shows the Spaniards' first encounter with the natives; the opposite side depicts a huge atom complete with whirling electrons. Across the *jardín* from the library is the **Museo Universitario de Ciencias y Artes.** Opposite the museum entrance is the university's **administrative building,** distinguished by a 3-D Siqueiros mosaic on the south wall that shows students studying at desks supported by society. *(Library ☎ 5622 16 13. Open daily 8:30am-7pm. Museo de Ciencias ☎ 5622 02 73. Open Sept.-June M-F 10am-7pm, Sa 10am-6pm. Free.)*

ESTADIO OLÍMPICO. The stadium, built in the 1950s, was designed to resemble a volcano with a huge crater, and real lava coats the ground upon which it is built. The impressive mosaic covering the stadium was created by Diego Rivera using large colored rocks. It depicts a man and a woman holding two torches, a symbol of the 1968 Olympics, which were held here. Today, the stadium is home to UNAM's popular professional *fútbol*-playing **Pumas;** you'll see their navy blue and gold logo everywhere around campus. *(On the opposite side of Insurgentes Sur from the Jardín Central cross via the footbridge.)*

ESPACIO ESCULTÓRICO. Just outside the CCU is the impressive Espacio Escultórico, a collection of large sculptures from the 1980s. The largest is *Las Serpientes del Pedregal,* by Federico Silva (1986), a long snake crafted from uneven blocks of stone several meters high and separated by narrow spaces. The Espacio Escultórico should only be visited during the day as its secluded location—and the risk of slipping off the sculptures—makes it dangerous in the dark.

UNIVERSUM (MUSEO DE LAS CIENCIAS). This natural science museum features a special exhibit on light and the *Cueva de Pedregoso,* a fake dinosaur's egg containing hands-on exhibits on the area's ecology. A popular place to bring children. *(In the giant peach-colored building adjacent to the CCU. Open M-F 9am-5pm, Sa-Su and holidays 10am-5pm. 30 pesos, children and students 25 pesos.)*

SENDA ECOLÓGICA. The volcano Xitle erupted 2500 years ago, covering this area in lava which later hardened and was broken apart by a wide variety of new plant life. In 1983, UNAM rescued 1.46 sq. km from the rapidly sprawling city and created the **Reserva Ecologica El Pedregal.** A small nature trail (the *senda*), allows you to enjoy a little of the exquisite rock formations and biodiversity of the reserve. The lack of handrails and secluded location make daytime visits advisable. *(Across from the entrance of the Universum. Free.)*

CUICUILCO ARCHAEOLOGICAL ZONE. A bit south of the CCU is the archaeological zone of Cuicuilco (Place of the Many-Colored Jasper). The centerpiece, the **Pyramid of Cuicuilco,** was built between 600 and 200 BC. The area served as a ceremonial center with a population of around 20,000, making it the largest central settlement in Mesoamerica before the rise of Teotihuacán in the early Classic Period. Measuring 125m across its base and 20m in height, the pyramid consists of five layers, with an altar to the god of fire at its summit. The area was abandoned near the end of the Pre-Classic Period, when the tiny volcano of **Xitle** erupted around AD 100, coating 8 sq. km of surrounding land in a thick layer of lava. The lava rock around the base of the pyramid has been removed, allowing visitors to walk up to the altar. However, very little other restoration has taken place and to the unsuspecting visitor, the pyramid appears to be little more than a quiet green hill in the middle of an urban area. On a clear day, the summit affords a faint view of Xitle to the south and the much larger Popocatépetl to the east. A small museum displays artifacts found at the site, including a tomb, with lengthy descriptions in Spanish of the site and the civilization. *(On the southeast corner at the intersection of*

Insurgentes Sur and Anillo Periférico, south of Ciudad Universitaria. From M: Universidad, Line 3, exit on the side away from campus, toward the small outdoor market, and take any "Cuicuilco" or "Villa Olímpica" pesero (2 pesos) to the entrance on the west side of Insurgentes Sur, just after you pass under the Periférico, the big highway overpass. The entrance to the site is marked by a sign that says "Parque Ecológico Cuicuilco." Peseros will let you off on the other side of Insurgentes, next to the Villa Olímpica housing and business development. To return, take any "CU Metro" pesero. ☎ 5606 97 58. Open daily 9am-4:45pm. Free.)

XOCHIMILCO

M: Tasqueña, Line 2. Ride the tren ligero (trolleybus; 1.5 pesos; follow the "correspondencia" signs) in the "Embarcadero" direction. For the gardens, get off at the "Xochimilco" stop. For the museum, get off at the "La Noria" stop.

In Xochimilco ("so-she-MILK-o"; Place of the Flower Growing), there are two things to do. The first is what everyone does: cruise the **floating gardens** of Xochimilco in a hand-poled *chalupa*. The second is far less known. Beyond the gardens a gorgeous museum, the **Museo Dolores Olmeda,** houses an impressive Rivera collection and largest Kahlo collection in Mexico.

■**THE FLOATING GARDENS.** The floating gardens of Xochimilco were not for pleasure but essential elements of the Aztec agricultural system. Settled since the Pre-Classic times, it was only under the rule of Axayácatl that the city became an Aztec territory. In the Aztec's brilliantly conceived system, *chinampas* (artificial islands) were made by piling soil and mud onto floating rafts. These rafts were held firm by wooden stakes until the crops planted on top sprouted roots, reaching through the base of the canals. They became fertile islands, supporting several crops per year. Though polluted today, the canals still bear the waterborne greenery planted centuries ago.

Multicolored **chalupa** boats crowd the maze of filthy canals, ferrying passengers past a floating market of food, flowers, and music. Families, young people, and couples lounge and listen to the *mariachis* and *marimba* players, while downing goodies and booze from the floating taco stands and bars. Stop at a local store to buy a few beers before the journey to avoid the obscene prices asked at many of the floating stands. For a private boat for up to four people, expect to pay at least 100 pesos per hour with bargaining; consult the official charts for prices, as boat owners may try to charge eight or ten times as much. You may be able to bargain down during the week, but prices are quite reasonable if you can fill a boat. The standard price for *mariachis* is 50 pesos per song, though you can always ask your driver to pull up near the musical fun another boat has paid for.

Xochimilco also offers two enormous land-bound **markets,** one with the usual food and household items, the other filled with live plants and animals. To reach the marketplace from the trolleybus, turn left on any street within three blocks of the station as you walk away from it, then walk until you reach the market, just beyond the Iglesia de San Bernardino de Cera. *(From M: Tasqueña, take the tren ligero to the "Xochimilco" stop. Numerous "Embarcadero" signs and white-shirted boat owners will direct you. Peseros below the station will also take you; ask to be let off at "un embarcadero.")*

■**MUSEO DOLORES OLMEDA.** As a young woman, the beautiful Dolores Olmeda Patino mingled with Mexico's elite. This museum, once her estate, features the art collection she amassed throughout her life. As the long-time lover of Diego Rivera, she is the subject of many of his paintings. The collection holds 144 of his paintings, including a series of 25 sunsets painted from Olmeda's Acapulco home in 1956, the year before Rivera's death. Perhaps even more impressive, the 25 paintings by Frida Kahlo, much of whose work is held abroad or in private collections, make this the best Kahlo collection in all of Mexico. Temporary exhibits support lesser-known but excellent work by current Mexican artists. Those unimpressed by Mexican art will appreciate the museum's gorgeously landscaped grounds; peacocks strut around the green lawns surrounding the mansion and boldly approach visitors. *(From M: Tasqueña, Line 2, take the tren ligero to "La Noria." Av. México 5843. ☎ 5555 12 21 or 5555 08 91. Open Tu-Su 10am-6pm. 30 pesos; Su free.)*

MEXICO CITY

♫ ▐ ENTERTAINMENT AND NIGHTLIFE

Welcome to D.F.—the District of Fun. Bars, clubs, cinemas, theaters, concerts, professional dancers, table dancers, street performers, and streetwalkers all congregate here. From *mariachi* to electronic pop, from drama to comedy, from ultra-chic night clubs to *cantinas*, the options, like the city, are almost limitless.

Cover charges are a necessary evil of the capital's night life. At *discotecas* (dance clubs) they range from 50-200 pesos for men. Women are often admitted free before a certain hour (usually 11pm or midnight) or at half the price of men. Most covers include at least one free drink, while those approaching 200 pesos often translate to *barra libre nacional* (open bar on domestic drinks). Most dance clubs, except for those specializing in *salsa*, *merengue*, and Cuban *son*, have moved to this open-bar system, making club-hopping an expensive pastime. Many bars with live musical acts also charge covers (30-70 pesos). If drink prices are not listed, ask to avoid exorbitant *gringo* prices. *Bebidas nacionales* (Mexican-made drinks, from Kahlúa to *sangría*) are considerably cheaper than imported ones.

The hours, prices, and coolness of entertainment establishments sometimes change faster than even an annually-updated book can track. In the summer of 2001, night-life-seekers were stopped in their tracks by mysterious green seals placed over the doors of dozens of the city's bars and clubs. Reading *CLAUSURADO* (SHUT DOWN), the seals explained that the city government had closed the establishments indefinitely, "for violations of the regulatory statutes in effect." Some of the establishments re-opened within a few weeks, but the future of most remains unclear. The Zona Rosa, the *centro histórico*, and the city's gay nightlife were the hardest hit. For the most current information, consult the publications *Tiempo Libre* (7 pesos) and *Ser Gay* (for gay entertainment; free), or ask locals.

Women venturing out alone will likely be approached by men offering drinks, dances, and much more. In light of Mexico City's sometimes staggering crime statistics, both men and women should go out with a friend.

> **❗ WE CAN'T WARN YOU ENOUGH.** Taxis run all night and are the safest way of getting from bar to disco to breakfast to hotel, but—especially after dark— avoid flagging cabs off the street. Remember to get the number of a *sitio* taxi company from your hotel or hostel before you leave, or ask any respectable-looking bartender, bouncer, or waiter to call one for you.

CENTRO HISTÓRICO

The *centro histórico* has traditionally been home to glamorous, upscale bars and clubs. Sadly, many of the neighborhood's flashiest nightlife jewels have been shut down, and it is not yet clear whether the area will rise again to its former glory. **Metro: Zócalo,** Line 2; **Bellas Artes,** Lines 2 and 8; **Allende,** Line 2; and **Isabel la Católica,** Line 1.

■ **Salon Bar Aima,** Filomena Mata 5 (☎5510 44 88), off 5 de Mayo. The small club is packed on weekend nights with *salsa* and *merengue* dancers, twisting and twirling to the music of talented live musicians. Beer 25 pesos. Cover men 70 pesos, women 35 pesos. Open Th-Sa 8pm-4am.

■ **Oraculo,** Motolinia 23 (☎5510 50 40). Enter this 2nd-floor disco and you might think you've descended into the tomb of a pharoah. Hieroglyphics cover the domed ceilings, while video screens play rock and house. Cover men 200 pesos, women free before midnight, 100 pesos after. Open F-Sa 10pm-4am; doors close at 2am.

NEAR THE MONUMENTO A LA REVOLUCIÓN

True *chilangos* fill the inexpensive bars scattered around the monument's flood-lit dome. The darkened streets are not particularly safe—it's best to visit these places with a group of friends. Sadly, the sweeps of summer 2001 cut short this area's budding club life. **Bar Milan,** Milan 18, set all by itself between the monument and Reforma, is emerging as a place for young beautiful people to be seen, in t-shirt and jeans or designer evening ensemble. You can dance during the week, but with the shoulder-to-shoulder crowd on weekend nights, there's only enough room to sip 25-peso bottles of domestic beer and shout conversation. (☎5592 00 31. No cover. Open Tu-Sun 8pm-2am.) **Bar Rasta,** at the intersection of Reforma and Insurgentes, a 15min. walk from either the Revolución or Insurgentes stations, with its huge, Disney-esque facade, hosts a young, gregarious crowd grooving to reggae, hip-hop, and other pop tunes. (Domestic open bar. Cover men 180 pesos, women 30 pesos. Open daily 9pm-5am.) **Metro: Revolución,** Line 2.

ZONA ROSA

Home to some of the republic's fanciest discos and highest cover charges, on weekend nights the Zona Rosa can feel like the center of the universe. Several smaller, quirkier, and cheaper places were lost in the recent raids—what remains tends to be either sleazy (and outrageously expensive) strip joints, or enormous, hyper-commercialized establishments found in any global metropolis. Exemplars of the second group are three US-sports-bar-themed bars, **Yarda's, Freedom,** and **Yuppie's,** all of which attract the young and moneyed set. At these and other Zona clubs, you're guaranteed a comfortable environment, large crowds, and minimal flack from bouncers. The high covers and open bars at most clubs makes club-hopping prohibitively expensive. Sidewalk recruiters will likely try to lure in groups, especially those with high female-to-male ratios; hold out and you might be offered a deal. Dress codes are relaxed, but sneakers are never a good idea. Steer clear of strip clubs in the area as drink prices are astronomical (upward of 50 pesos). After a wild night, hop in a *pesero* that runs all night long on Reforma or Insurgentes Sur (3 pesos). **Metro: Insurgentes,** Line 1; and **Sevilla,** Line 1.

Caramba!, Génova 44 (☎5208 96 11), near the corner with Hamburgo. Groove with teenagers to the latest Latin American pop. Exhilarating fun at a genuinely popular place that won't keep you waiting outside. Cover men 200 pesos; women free until 11pm, after 11pm 100 pesos; open bar until 3am. Open W-Sa 9pm-4am.

Rock Stock Bar & Disco, Reforma 261 (☎5533 09 07), at Niza. Clubs come and go, but this one is packed year after year. Inside, the pounding beats of irresistibly danceable rock and reggae shake the vast dance floor slathered in fluorescent paint. Cover men 170 pesos, women 70 pesos. Open F-Sa 9pm-4am; doors close at 2:30am.

CANTINFLAS While walking down the streets of the Zona Rosa, or perhaps while admiring the Monumento a la Revolución, you're confronted by a man in a jumpsuit holding a small box. "I can make those really shine, sir," he says, looking down at your feet. "But they're sneakers," you say. "I have something especially for sneakers," he replies. "But I bought them yesterday!" you protest. "I have something especially for *new* sneakers!" he answers. So you submit to a sneaker-shine, overwhelmed by this man's unlimited optimism, and a strange feeling you've seen him somewhere before. And indeed, you have, sort of: it's the spirit of Cantinflas (1911-1993), the most famous Mexican comedian of all time, beloved by Spanish-speakers throughout the Americas. Born Mario Moreno, the actor played essentially the same character in all of his films: a down-and-out man trying to get by, using a combination of good humor and sly fast-talk, a part played by millions of Mexicans in real life then and today. In one of his most famous films, *El bolero de Raquel* (1956), Cantinflas portrayed a Mexico City *bolero* (shoe-shine man) getting the better of *gringo* tourists, rich locals, and the police, and using his earnings to support an adopted son. Today, a statue of Cantinflas stands in front of Hospital Obregón (Obregón 123, between Jalapa and Orizaba) in Colonia Roma. A quotation by the actor inscribed on the base summarizes his life well: "Man's commitment to life is to be happy and to make others happy."

Cantina Las Bohemias, Londres 142 (☎5207 43 84), at Amberes. This is, thankfully, not a true *cantina*: beautiful decor, tables for 2, soft lighting, and romantic music will put you in the mood for love, not a brawl. Beer 15 pesos, tequila 34-55 pesos. *Antojitos* 25-60 pesos, entrees 70-150 pesos. Open M-Sa 1pm-1am.

Yuppie's, Génova 34, at Hamburgo. Loud pop, flashing table lamps, and a big crowd, but no dance floor. Domestic beer 25 pesos. No cover. Open daily 1pm-3am.

Yarda's, Niza 40 (☎5512 21 08). Early in the evening, US and Canadian pro sports dominate the big screen. Later, disco lights bring the all-ages crowd to its feet. Domestic beer 30 pesos. No cover. Open M-Sa 7pm-4am; doors close at 2am.

Freedom, Copenhague 25 (☎5207 84 56), at Hamburgo. 3 floors of throbbing pop and no cover may entice you to put up with the sometimes rude staff and cheesy decor. Beer 25 pesos, mixed drinks 30-60 pesos. Open daily 1pm-2am.

El Chato, Londres 115 (☎5511 17 58). A smoky piano bar with fittingly beat tunes. The lack of glitz and booming beat pleases an older crowd. Beer 25 pesos, tequila 30 pesos. Occasional musicians (cover 30 pesos and up). Open M-Sa 6pm-1am.

Melodika, Florencia 52 (☎5208 01 98), between Londres and Liverpool. Enormous menus of mixed drinks (30-70 pesos) and songs make this karaoke bar a fun place to start the night. Cover 15 pesos. Open M-Sa 7:30pm-3am.

Black Light, Florencia 58 (☎5208 01 61), between Londres and Liverpool. A new club playing electronica, rock, and pop. Domestic drinks 30 pesos. Cover men 70 pesos, women free. *Barra libre* men 200 pesos, women 50. Live Caribbean Th and Sa. Open W-Th and Su 9pm-3am, F-Sa 9pm-4am; doors close at 2:30am.

▓ PLAZA GARIBALDI

Plaza Garibaldi flaunts some of Mexico City's gaudiest and most amusing nightlife. By 5pm, both wandering *mariachis* and roving *ranchero* bands begin to play for a negotiable prices. Fifty pesos for a three-song set (10 pesos for solo performers) is a good deal. Tourists, locals, prostitutes, musicians, vendors, transvestites, children—anybody and everybody mingles here, many reeling, dancing, and screaming in the street, enjoying the alcoholic offerings of the plaza. The big nightclubs surrounding the plaza do their best to lure crowds. Though they advertise no cover, per-drink prices are astoundingly high. Your best bet is to find a table at one of the open-air cafes, where you can order cheap beers (11 pesos) or try *pulque*, an alcoholic drink made from the *maguey* cactus. If you're hungry, don't miss the **Mercado de Alimentos San Camilito,** on the northwest corner of the plaza. This indoor market contains tons of small, inexpensive eateries. Most will feed you quite well for under 30 pesos. Exercise caution and especially avoid wandering beyond the plaza to the back streets, which are considerably less charming. The best time to visit Garibaldi is in the evening, between 8pm and midnight.

The plaza is at the intersection of Lázaro Cárdenas (Eje Central) and Rep. de Honduras, north of the Alameda. **Metro:** get off at **Bellas Artes,** Lines 2 and 8, and walk three blocks north on Cárdenas; Garibaldi will be on your right. **Garibaldi,** Line 8, plants you three blocks north of the plaza. Exit to your left and walk south.

COYOACÁN

Plaza Hidalgo and adjacent Jardín Centenario, Coyoacán's historic heart, never seem to completely empty out. The biggest crowds form on weekend evenings, drawn to free performances by comedians, mimes, and musicians. The buildings nearby often host plays and other performances. Inquire at Casa de Cortés before 8pm for showtimes. **Cineteca Nacional,** México-Coyoacán 389, next to the footbridge, screens classic films and recent flops. Check D.F.'s daily, *La Jornada*, for information on shows. (☎5688 59 26 or 5688 88 64. Open M-Sa; showtimes vary.) Many restaurants host live music, but clubs in the area are sparse, and by midnight everything quiets down considerably. One nightlife option is **El Hijo del Cuervo,** on the north side of Jardín Centenario which draws a diverse crowd with live rock and Latin music. (☎5658 78 24. Open daily 1pm-2am.) **Metro: Coyoacán,** Line 3.

COLONIA ROMA

Located next to the Zona Rosa, this tranquil residential neighborhood has become a great destination for unique nightlife. An increasing number of gay clubs and bars are also opening here. Unfortunately, there's no single nightlife cluster; you'll need to know where you're going before you come. *Tiempo Libre* and *Ser Gay* have especially good listings for this area. The non-profit **Cafe-Bar Las Hormigas,** upstairs in Casa del Poeta, Álvaro Obregón 73, features live performances of music and spoken word in its intimate bar. Domestic beer 18 pesos, free *botanas* many nights. Modest cover for some of the weekend musical acts. (☎5533 5456. Open M-F 11am-10pm, Sa 6-10pm.) **Metro: Insurgentes,** Line 1.

NEAR THE WORLD TRADE CENTER

Lining Insurgentes near the World Trade Center skyscraper are a bunch of themed nightlife hotspots. Although not the most authentic entertainment in the capital, these places are fun and less expensive than their counterparts in the Zona Rosa and *centro histórico*. The area has its share of semi-sleazy strip clubs—in which male performers dance for groups of screaming women. Take any "San Ángel" bus on Insurgentes from points north or from Buenavista. If you're coming from San Ángel or Ciudad Universitaria board an "Indios Verdes" bus.

■ **La Cantina de los Remedios,** Insurgentes Sur 744 (☎5687 10 37). The vast bar will blow you away with 2-for-1 drinks from 6-10pm (domestic beer 26 pesos, cocktails 33 pesos). Live music nightly—usually *mariachi* but also *son* and rock on weekends—make this one of the most fun bars in the city. Food also served; *botanas* 30-70 pesos, main dishes 50-130 pesos. No cover. Open M-Th and Sa 1:30pm-midnight, F 1:30pm-1am.

■ **Polyforum Siqueiros,** Insurgentes Sur 701 (☎5687 10 37), at Filadelfia. An entire building constructed to display the audacious murals of David Alfaro Siqueiros. A multimedia show narrated by the recorded voice of the artist himself plays Sa-Su 11:30am, 12:45, and 5pm. By night, patrons enjoy a theater, restaurant, piano bar, and disco.

Congo, Insurgentes 810 (☎5543 03 09). Live *merengue* and *salsa* every night, live rock F-Sa, and strippers on Th—includes performers from neighboring Chippendale's. F-Sa cover 90 pesos. Open Th-Sa 9pm-4am.

La Taberna de Morsa, Insurgentes 623 (☎5543 04 00), between Belmont and Yosemite. Get in a nostalgia groove with live rock & roll from the 60s, including a Beatles-revival group. Cover 80 pesos. Open Th-Sa 8pm-4am; doors close at 2am.

SAN ÁNGEL

The many upscale bars situated along Insurgentes and Revolución cater to an executive crowd, who often arrive clad in business suits. Cover charges here are low or nonexistent. Although there are no real dance clubs—besides a couple of strip joints on Insurgentes—there's plenty of activity even on a Wednesday night. Jazz bars abound, and a number of small venues host classical concerts and plays. Check in at **Centro Cultural San Ángel** (☎5616 12 54 or 5616 20 97), the big yellow building at the corner of Revolución and Madero, before 8pm, to find out what's on. Take a "San Ángel" bus on Insurgentes to get here from points as far north as Buenavista station.

New Orleans, Revolución 1655 (☎5550 19 08). The self-proclaimed "Cathedral of Jazz in Mexico" features live jazz in a wood-panelled bar and restaurant. Performances are listed in *Tiempo Libre.* Cover 35 pesos, F-Sa 50 pesos. Open daily 8pm-midnight.

La Cantina San Ángel, Insurgentes Sur 2146 (☎5661 22 92). Another upscale bar calling itself a *"cantina,"* San Ángel plays loud pop and rock to entertain the pretty young people filling the small tables. Domestic rum 30-40 pesos. Free 4-course meal when you buy 4 drinks. Open M 1pm-midnight, Tu 1pm-1am, W-Th 1pm-2am, F-Sa 1pm-4am.

La Planta de Luz (☎5616 47 61), in Plaza Loreto at Revolución and Río Magdalena. Features a changing roster of live music, comedy, and drama. Cover for shows. M and W-F shows start at 8:30 or 9pm, Su noon or 6:30pm; call ahead about performances.

GAY AND LESBIAN ENTERTAINMENT

The capital presents a full range of social and cultural activities for gays and lesbians, and a fledgling and active gay rights movement has made its presence known. General tolerance of homosexuality is still very low, and although not illegal, public displays of affection by gay and lesbian couples on the street or on the Metro are sure tickets to harassment, especially by the police. Gay men will have a much easier time finding bars and discos, although more and more venues have begun to welcome lesbians. The free pamphlet *Ser Gay* is a great source of information, with listings for gay entertainment, art events, clubs, and bars in the city. Copies are available at all the clubs listed below. For exclusively lesbian activities, contact one of several Mexico City lesbian groups (see p. 91). In June, Mexico's gay pride month, an inordinate number of parties, rallies, art exhibits, marches, and *fiestas* occur throughout the city.

- **Butterflies,** Izazaga 9 (☎5761 18 61), between Cárdenas and Bolívar, near M: Salto del Agua, Lines 1 and 8. This unmarked, cavernous dance club fills to capacity on weekend nights with a mixed crowd. Great drag shows, irresistibly danceable rock, techno, *salsa* and *merengue,* and an extremely relaxed atmosphere make this one of the most fun clubs in the city for anyone. Snack bar in the back. Domestic beer 25 pesos. Cover F-Sa 60 pesos (includes 2 drinks). Open Tu-Su 9pm-3am.

- **El Antro,** Londres 77 (☎5511 16 13), at Insurgentes in the Zona Rosa. Table dancers in the front room; stage show, dancing, and tables in the main room; and we can't print what goes on upstairs. A fashionable crowd gathers to watch the nightly spectacle Su-F cover 50 pesos, Sa 60 pesos (includes 1 drink). Open W-Sa 7pm-5am, Su 6pm-2am.

- **El Celo,** Londres 104 (☎5514 43 09), in the Zona Rosa. This laid-back bar/club draws one of the city's hippest crowds, with gays and lesbians alike crowding its floors to get down to techno and pop. Su afternoon it becomes a gay-friendly restaurant. Beers 20 pesos. Cover after 11pm 50 pesos; includes 1 drink. Open Th-Sa 9:30pm-late.

- **Cabaré-tito,** Londres 117 (☎5207 25 54), under a stained-glass awning, in the Zona Rosa. A relaxed bar to hang out and meet gay men. Domestic beer 20 pesos, tequila 35-50 pesos. Tu-Su stage shows (usually drag, strippers on Su) start at 10:30pm. Cover for shows. Open daily 1pm-2am.

- **El Almacen,** Florencia 37 (☎5207 07 27). Mediterranean food and pop dance music. Growing numbers of lesbians are joining the men, who throw back beers on their way to the high-octane gay male club in the basement, El Taller. Open daily 4pm-late.

- **El Taller,** Florencia 37A (☎5533 49 84), underground in the Zona Rosa. El Almacen bar upstairs. A well-known blue-collar hangout. Throbbing music, construction-site decorations, and dark, private alcoves create an intense men-only pick-up scene. Private barroom attracts an older crowd. W and Su mostly 20-ish; Sa theme night. Cover Th-Su 40 pesos; includes 1 drink. Open Tu-Su 9pm-late.

- **La Estación,** Hamburgo 234 (☎5207 07 27), in the Zona Rosa. A brand new all-male leather bar. Open daily 4pm-2am.

- **La Cantina del Vaquero,** Algeciras 26 (☎5598 21 95), in Col. Insurgentes, near Parque Hundido, between M: Mixcoac, Line 7, and M: Zapata, Line 3. The first openly gay *cantina* in Mexico has been a favorite for over 25 years. Working-class gay men still flock to the bar to watch XXX videos, sample the darkroom, or simply grab a beer and chat. Videos screened daily 5-11pm. Cover 35 pesos; includes 2 beers. Open M-Su 5pm-late.

🗒 SHOPPING

While most Mexican cities rely on one large, central market, Mexico City seems to have one on every corner. Each *colonia* has its own market, and downtown markets rival the size of small cities. Markets are all relatively cheap, but vary widely in quality and content. Shopping throughout the *centro* and the Alameda proceeds thematically: there is a wedding dress street, a lighting fixtures street, a lingerie street, a windowpane street, even a military surplus street.

■ **Mercado de La Ciudadela,** 2 blocks north of M: Balderas, Lines 1 and 3, off Balderas. A vast array of *artesanía* and traditional clothing at low prices. Non-stop tourist traffic flows through the capital's biggest and best *artesanía* market. Open daily 8am-7pm.

■ **San Juan Artesanías,** Plaza El Buen Tono, 4 blocks south of Alameda Central, 2 blocks west of Lázaro Cárdenas. From M: Salto de Agua, Lines 1 and 8, walk 4 blocks up López and make a left on Ayuntamiento. 3 floors of *artesanía* from all over Mexico, ranging from standard tourist items to exquisite handmade treasures. Prices similar to La Ciudadela, but comparison shopping always helps. Fewer tourists wander here, which gives you more bargaining power. Open M-Sa 9am-7pm, Su 9am-4pm.

■ **La Merced,** Circunvalación at Anaya, east of the *zócalo*. M: Merced, Line 1. Not just a market but a way of life. The largest market in the Americas, has an enormous selection of fresh produce from all over the country, and more raw meat than your nose can handle, all at rock-bottom prices. The nearby **Mercado de Dulces** (candy market) will make you feel like the proverbial kid in a candy store. Between the 2 lies the **Mercado de Flores** (flower market). All 3 markets open daily 8am-7pm.

The Zócalo, along Corregidora, the street between the Palacio Nacional and the Supreme Court, is the unofficial "market," which has been the subject of much controversy through the years. Vendors clog the street with stands, their brightly colored umbrellas stretching as far as the eye can see. The government has long been trying to drive out these non-rent-paying shopkeeps, but to no avail. The persistent vendors have some of the best prices in town on sundries, clothing, toys, CDs, and electronics. If you don't mind insanely crowded streets, come here for your non-*artesanía* needs.

FONART, Patriotismo 691 (☎ 5563 40 60), also at Juárez 89 (☎ 5521 01 71). A national project to protect and market traditional crafts sells *artesanía* from all over the country: giant tapestries, rugs, silver jewelry, pottery, and colorful embroidery. Regulated prices are not quite as low as those in the markets, but crowds and haggling are eliminated. Open M-Sa 9am-8pm, Su 10am-7pm.

La Lagunilla, Comonfort at Rayón, east of the intersection of Lázaro Cárdenas and Reforma. 2 large yellow buildings on either side of the street with stands spilling outside. On Su it becomes a gargantuan flea market, notable for its antique books. The rest of the week, it specializes in party dresses. Open daily 8am-7pm.

Sonora, Teresa de Mier and Cabañ, 2 blocks south of La Merced. This unique market attracts those who enjoy witchcraft, medicinal teas and spices, figurines, and ceremonial images. Search no further for lucky cows' feet, shrunken heads, eagle claws, black salt, and powdered skull (for the domination of one's enemies). Beware, this is a prime spot for pickpockets. Open daily 8am-7pm.

Bazar del Sabado, Plaza San Jacinto, in the center of San Ángel. Overflowing onto the plaza, this market tends to be pricey and touristy, but is one of the few to which contemporary artists bring their work. One of San Ángel's biggest draws. Open Sa 9am-6pm.

Jamaica, Congreso and Morelos (Eje 3 Sur). M: Jamaica, Lines 4 and 9. Immediately outside the exit, a clump of vendor stalls sells cheap eats and some of the juiciest mangos and *piñas* in town. The real pride and joy of the market is the assortment of fragrant and brightly colored flowers, including, of course, the deep-red *jamaica* (hibiscus), source of the lip-smacking *agua de Jamaica* sold at many stands. Live animals and exotic birds (all for sale) squawk and scream in their tiny cages. Open M-Sa 8am-6pm.

SPORTS

Whether consumed by their passion for bullfighting, *fútbol* (soccer), *béisbol* (baseball), or horse racing, Mexican fans share an almost religious devotion to *deportes* (sports). If sweaty discos and endless museums have you craving a change of pace, follow the sports-loving crowds and prepare yourself for a rip-roarin' rowdy good time. *¡Andale!*

■ **Estadio Azteca,** Calz. de Tlalpan 3465 (☎ 5617 80 80). Take a *pesero* or *tren ligero* (trolley bus) from M: Tasqueña, Line 2. Proud home of the *Águilas de America* (Ameri-

MEXICO CITY

GOOOOOOOOOOOOOOOOAAAAAAAAAAAAL!

Although *charretería* (horsemanship, rodeo, bullfighting) may be the official national sport of Mexico, *fútbol* (soccer) is by far the most popular. If you want to check out the *fútbol* phenomenon, you're in luck—matches take place year-round. The Winter League runs July-Dec. and the Summer League Jan.-May. In addition, countless minor and amateur *fútbol* leagues play throughout the year. Every fourth June, the World Cup takes Mexico by storm—even gas and water delivery stops as soccer fans throughout the country pack bars and restaurants to watch the games. Whenever Mexico scores a goal, the entire nation shakes in unison as the word "GOAL!" rings from every bar, boulevard, business, and bus.

can Eagles), Mexico's largest stadium packs in 100,000-person crowds for popular *fútbol* matches. Good luck getting tickets. Season runs Oct.-July. Tickets 50-1200 pesos.

▨ **Plaza México,** (☎5563 39 59), M: San Antonio, Line 7, on Insurgentes Sur, is Mexico's principal bullring, seating 40,000 fans. July-Nov. professional fights; Nov.-Feb. *novillada* (novice) fights. Tickets run 10-100 pesos, depending on proximity to the ring and the *sombra* (shade) or *sol* (sun). Next door is the very big and very blue **Estadio Azul,** home of Mexico City's professional *fútbol* team Cruz Azul. Bullfights take place Su 4pm.

El Foro del Sol, in the Ciudad Deportiva (Ticketmaster☎5325 90 00), M: Ciudad Deportiva, Line 9. This "sports city" complex contains volleyball courts, a boxing ring, an ice-skating rink, many soccer fields, and other assorted facilities. The *Foro*, at the center of the complex, hosts the home games of Mexico City's 2 professional baseball teams, the *Diablos Rojos* (Red Devils) and the *Tigres* (Tigers). Sparks fly when the teams face each other, and local papers have dubbed the matchup the *Guerra Civil* (Civil War). Tickets (10-80 pesos) are easy to come by and can be purchased at the gate.

Hipódromo de las Américas, M: Tacubaya, Lines 1, 7, and 9, houses a horse track and hosts *jai alai* matches, an extremely fast game a bit like raquetball (see **The World's Fastest Game, the World's Strangest Name,** p. 143). Though some may not call it a sport, *lucha libre,* Mexico's version of professional wrestling, takes over the *hipódromo* every F night. Mexico City's main *jai alai* venue, the famous **Frontón México,** facing the north side of the Monumento a la Revolución, is currently closed due to a strike.

▶ DAYTRIPS FROM MEXICO CITY

Even those who've fallen deeply in love with Mexico City need some time away to maintain a healthy relationship. Fortunately, the capital's great location makes for easy and painless escape. From small towns to not-so-small towns, from ruins to volcanoes, all of the following places make convenient daytrips.

TEOTIHUACÁN

Direct bus service from Mexico City is available via Autobuses Teotihuacán *(1hr., every 15min. 7am-3pm, 21 pesos), in the* Terminal de Autobuses del Norte *(☎5587 05 01) at Sala 8. Buy your tickets for the "Pirámides" bus. If you prefer, you can catch the same buses outside M: Indios Verdes, but seats may be hard to come by. The last bus back to Mexico City leaves from the main entrance at 6pm, Puerta 1. ☎5956 00 52. There are 5 entrances to the site. Buses drop visitors off by Puerta 1, the main entrance. Puerta 5, the easternmost entrance, is by the* Pirámide del Sol. *Free guided tours for groups of 5 or more can be arranged at the administration building by Puerta 1 (southwest corner). Site open daily 7am-6pm. 30 pesos; under 13 and Su free. Free parking.*

The massive ruins at Teotihuacán present a perplexing mystery: nobody is quite sure who the Teotihuacanos were. They may have been the Olmeca-Xicalanca, a Mixtec-speaking group, or, as another theory argues, a Totonac tribe. They were most likely a Pre-Toltec or Pre-Aztec, Náhuatl- or Mixtec-speaking people. Regardless of exact origins, the area was settled in the late Pre-Classic period, around 100 BC. Teotihuacán was meticulously planned and split into quadrants, with the Calle

Near Mexico City

N

20 miles

20 kilometers

TO ATLACOMULCO
AND QUERÉTARO

TO ZITÁCUARO

TO TULA

Tepotzotlán

57

MEXICO

TLALNEPANTLA

NAUCALPAN

★ Mexico City

130

85

Parque
Nacional
Desierto de
los Leones

FEDERAL
DISTRICT

CD.
NEZAHUALCÓYOTL

TO PACHUCA

Teotihuacán

Acolman

San Martín
de las
Pirámides

Tepexpan

136

HIDALGO

Apan

Calpulalpan

Santa Rosa

Hueyotlipan

Nanacamilpa

190

Texmelucan

Cacaxtla

★ **Tlaxcala**

Tenancingo

Puebla ★

TO VERACRUZ

Cholula

Huejotzingo

PUEBLA

San N. de
los Ranchos

Parque
Nacional
Ixta Popo

Tlamacas

150

Parque
Nacional
Zoquiapan

Tlalmanalco

115

Amecameca

Ozumba

Chalco

TO CUAUTLA

MORELOS

Parque Nacional El
Tepozteco

Tepoztlán

115

Cuernavaca

950

95

TO XOCHICALCO

Parque
Nacional
Lagunas de
Zempoala

Xonacatlán

15

Metepec

Mexicaltzingo

55

Joquicingo

Malinalco

Tenancingo

TO IXTAPAN
DE LA SAL

Toluca ★

TO VALLE
DE BRAVO

130

134

15

55

Parque Nacional
Nevado de Toluca

de Los Muertos and a now lost road forming the axes of the city. The city sprawled over an area of 20 sq. km from which it controlled the entire Valley of Mexico, with evidence of trade and influence extending as far south as the Maya city of Tikal in Guatemala. The Pirámide del Sol, one of the largest pyramids in the world, was built in the late Pre-Classic period, while the newer Pirámide de la Luna was built during the Classic period. At its height (AD 150-250), Teotihuacán accommodated a population of nearly 200,000, making it the sixth-largest city in the world.

Sometime around AD 700, Teotihuacán began to weaken. While the reasons for its downfall are far from certain, many speculate that the city eventually collapsed under its own weight, having grown so large and crowded that it could no longer produce enough food to properly support its inhabitants. New buildings were built on top of old ones, presumably due to overcrowding, and evidence of a tremendous fire around AD 800 is in the layers of blackened stone. By AD 850, few residents remained in the enormous urban complex. When the Aztecs founded Tenochtitlán in the 14th century, Teotihuacán, 50km northeast of their capital, lay abandoned. The Aztecs were so impressed by the size and scope of the buildings that they adopted the areas as ceremonial grounds, believing its huge structures to be built by gods and those buried there to be of some superhuman order. They christened the area Teotihuacán, meaning "Place Where Men Become Gods." When the Spaniards destroyed Tenochtitlán in the 16th century, they were almost certainly unaware of the pyramid's existence, and this fortunate oversight allowed the site to remain astonishingly intact. Extensive excavation began in 1906 under the orders of Porifirio Díaz, in a project meant to emphasize the cultural wealth of the Mexican people and to celebrate 100 years of Mexican independence in 1910.

CALLE DE LOS MUERTOS (STREET OF THE DEAD). The ceremonial center, a 13 sq. km expanse, was built along a 3km stretch now called Calle de los Muertos, so named because the Aztecs believed ancient kings had been buried alongside it. The Teotihuacanos planned their community around the four cardinal points, and this main road runs in a straight north-south line from the Pirámide de la Luna to the Templo de Quetzalcóatl. The southernmost end of the avenue has still not been fully explored. The main structure, the Pirámide del Sol, lies to the east, aligned with the point on the horizon where the sun sets at the summer solstice. An east-west thoroughfare of equal length and importance is believed to have bisected the Calle at some point in front of the Ciudadela.

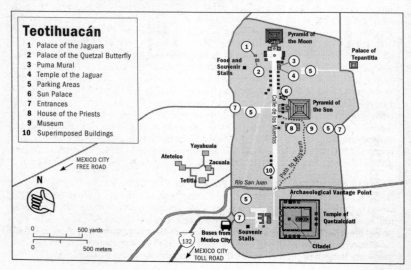

Teotihuacán

1 Palace of the Jaguars
2 Palace of the Quetzal Butterfly
3 Puma Mural
4 Temple of the Jaguar
5 Parking Areas
6 Sun Palace
7 Entrances
8 House of the Priests
9 Museum
10 Superimposed Buildings

CIUDADELA (CITADEL). At the southern end of the site is the expansive Ciudadela, where priests and government officials once lived. The large plaza was so named because of its resemblance to a military complex, though it actually functioned as royal residences. On the northern end of the Ciudadela lie four small pyramids. The top of the second one is an "Archaeological Vantage Point," which gives a wonderful view of the two pyramids in the near distance.

TEMPLO DE QUETZALCÓATL. At the center of the Ciudadela is the Templo de Quetzalcóatl, dedicated to the plumed serpent god. The pyramid was obstructed by another, later pyramid, eventually removed to provide access to the older pyramid inside. Lining the main staircase, enormous carvings of the serpent Quetzalcóatl regularly pop out from the stone flowers. Along the outer surface, images of Quetzalcóatl alternate with those of the rain god Tlaloc, easily identifiable by his google-eyes and fangs. The still-visible red paint that originally decorated these sculptures was made by collecting nopal leaves into which tiny bugs had burrowed, carving out the colorful critters, and smashing them. Note the shell motifs along the sides of the pyramid which may be evidence of trade with coastal areas.

MUSEO DE SITIO (SITE MUSEUM). Southeast of the Pirámide del Sol stands the Museo de Sitio. The elaborate design of this museum imitates the forms and colors used by the site's ancient inhabitants. Displays compare the size of the ancient city to various present-day cities, illustrate the architecture and technology of the pyramids, describe the social, religious, and economic organization of the society, and exhibit *indígena* art. All of the pieces in the museum are replicas; the originals are at the Museo Nacional de Antropología in Mexico City (see p. 108).

EDIFICIOS SUPERPUESTOS. Continuing north along Calle de los Muertos, you will cross what was once the San Juan river. On the west side of the street are the remains of two temples, the Edificios Superpuestos, that were built in two phases (AD 200-400 and AD 400-750) atop older, partially demolished temples. The older buildings were filled in to clear the way for construction, unintentionally preserving the temples, which can now be viewed with the aid of metal catwalks.

PIRÁMIDE DEL SOL (PYRAMID OF THE SUN). Farther north and east towers the Pirámide del Sol, the single most massive structure in the ceremonial area. Second in size only to the pyramid at Cholula, the pyramid's base measures 222m by 225m, and its volume is over one million cubic yards—dimensions comparable to those of Cheops in Egypt. It was built sometime in the late Pre-Classic era, around 100 BC, and completed just before the zenith of Teotihuacano civilization, around AD 150. The inside of the pyramid is filled with rubble and brick, and there is evidence that it was built over the remains of another pyramid, perhaps originally of equal size. In 1971, a natural cave was discovered below the pyramid. Archaeologists now believe that the cave was a sacred site, perhaps the reason the pyramid, and subsequently all of Teotihuacán, was built on this spot. At over 60m in height, the pyramids afford a breathtaking view of the surrounding valley. Smokers and slowpokes: don't quit. A rope railing helps you up the steepest stretch, and the platforms of the multi-tiered pyramid make convenient rest stops. The hard-working vendors never give up, even on the peak of this mammoth pyramid. As soon as you reach the top, weary and awe-struck, be prepared to say, *"No me faltan tortugas de obsidiana, gracias"* (No, I don't need any more obsidian turtles, thank you).

PALACIO DE QUETZALPAPALOTL (PALACE OF THE QUETZAL BUTTERFLY). Between the Pirámide del Sol and the Pirámide de la Luna on the west side of the street is the Palacio de Quetzalpapalotl. This columned palace, next to the ceremonial space and far removed from the residential complex, housed royalty. The gorgeous inner patio features colored frescoes and bird glyphs, which, though faded, have survived years of decay and retain much of their intricate detail. On the columns are images of plumed butterflies, which give the *palacio* its name.

PALACIO DE LOS JAGUARES (PALACE OF THE JAGUARS). Behind the palace and through the short maze of an entrance stands the Palacio de los Jaguares and the now-subterranean **Palacio de las Conchas Emplumadas** (Palace of the Feathered Seashells). The restored jaguar palace comes complete with fluorescent lights and plastic handrails. Some of the original frescoes remain, adorned with red, green, yellow, and white symbols representing birds, corn, and water. The palace was built over a temple, in which patterns of plumed seashells adorned the walls.

PIRÁMIDE DE LA LUNA (PYRAMID OF THE MOON). At the northern end of Calle de los Muertos is the stunning **Pirámide de la Luna.** A sculpture of **Chalchiutlicue,** the revered Aztec water goddess, was discovered here. The pyramid was built later than the Pirámide del Sol, most likely during Teotihuacán's height around AD 300. Though the hike up this pyramid is steeper and rougher than the walk up the Pirámide del Sol, there are fewer vendors and a more magnificent view.

PALACIO DE TEPANTITLA. On the northeast side of the Pirámide del Sol near Puerta 4 sits the **Palacio de Tepantitla,** which has some of the best-preserved frescoes in Teotihuacán, still showing a full range of colors. Priests with elaborate headdresses and representations of Tlaloc exist pictorially within the Teotihuacano ideal of a butterfly-filled paradise.

DESIERTO DE LOS LEONES

Buses for Desierto de Leones leave from the Centro Cultural San Ángel (see p. 98). Whenever 10 people gather, a bus (1hr., 10 pesos per person) will head off. If people are slow to gather (this is especially likely during the week), you can pay for the empty seats. The last stop is in front of the convent. To return to the city, colectivos to San Ángel or M: Tacubaya leave from the entrance approximately every hr., last bus 5pm. Park open daily 6am-5pm. Convent open Tu-Su 10am-5pm. 5 pesos. Tours Sa-Su 11am-3pm. 15 pesos.

Just outside the city, the Desierto de Los Leones (Desert of the Lions) offers solace and clean air among millions of pines. Hundreds of paths wind through the woods, perfect for hiking, picnicking, walking, or jogging. At the heart of the park sits the pristine **Convento Santo Desierto,** for which the park is named. Like all Barefoot Carmelite convents, this one was purposefully placed in a desolate area to facilitate the extreme self-abnegation practiced by its sisters. The lions who lived in this desert-like region were not those of African glory but pumas. The convent was originally built between 1606 and 1611, and exactly 100 years later, it was demolished by an earthquake. The reconstruction was completed in 1723, but between 1780 and 1801, the sisters abandoned it for another convent in the Nixcongo mountains due to weather conditions. Wander through the immense corridors to catch a glimpse of a bedroom as it was left in 1801. Bring a flashlight or buy a candle (5 pesos) to descend into the basements. It is completely dark underneath the convent, and the winding passages are not for the claustrophobic.

On Saturdays and Sundays from noon-3pm, the church hosts free (with admission) **theater,** ranging from passion plays to the more avant-garde work of Federico García Lorca. Shows change weekly. The **cafeteria** serves decent food. Another food option is at **Los Leones** restaurant, just outside the convent, which serves delicious *conejo* (rabbit) and *trucha* (trout) specialties and homemade *mezcal*.

POPOCATÉPETL AND IXTACCÍHUATL

*From TAPO, several bus lines go to **Amecameca**, the best jumping-off point for Ixtaccíhuatl. Volcanos has the most frequent service (1½hr., every 30min. 5:30am-10pm, 16 pesos). Taxis in front of Hotel San Carlos on the Amecameca plaza can take you to the La Joya trailhead. Expect to pay at least 300 pesos for a round-trip fare including waiting time while you hike. A 1-way trip runs 150 pesos, but no return taxi is guaranteed. If you decide to visit Ixtaccíhuatl via **San Rafael**, catch a pesero from Tlalmanalco (5am-7pm, 5 pesos) and get off in front of La Fábrica, a printing press. From there, another pesero (8 pesos) will take you to the San Rafael trailhead. To return to Mexico City, take a Volcanos bus or any bus labeled Metro San Lázaro (the TAPO station). They stop along the plaza in Amecameca or on the road labeled "Mexico" in Tlalmanalco (every 30min. 6am-8pm).*

*From Cuernavaca, you'll want to take Estrella Roja to **Cuautla** (every 15 min. 6am-10pm), then walk to the Cristóbal Colón station. Go right on Ing. Mongoy as you exit the station, walk 1 block and turn left on 5 de Mayo; the station is half a block ahead on your left. Catch a Volcanos bus to **Amecameca** (1hr., every 15min. 5am-7pm, 8 pesos). Buses return to Cuernavaca from Cuautla (1½hr., every 15min. 5am-7pm, 14 pesos).*

Overlooking Morelos and Puebla are two snow-capped volcanoes, Popocatépetl (5452m) and Ixtaccíhuatl (5282m), the second- and third-largest peaks in the country. Aztec legend has it that the warrior Popocatépetl ("Smoking Mountain" in Náhuatl) loved Ixtaccíhuatl ("Sleeping Woman"), the emperor's daughter. Once, when Popocatépetl went off to battle, Ixtaccíhuatl came to believe that he had been killed, and she subsequently died of grief. When Popo (as he was known to friends) learned of his lover's death, he built the two great mountains. On the northern one he placed her body (which you can see by looking at Ixtaccíhuatl from afar, with a little imagination), and on the southern one he stood vigil with a torch. Locals pay their respects to the supine, death-pale Ixtaccíhuatl on the mountain's snowy summit. The passage between the two is called *Paso de Cortés* because it is the route the Spanish conqueror took to the valley of Tenochtitlán.

Due to its volatile status, Popocatépetl has been closed to hikers since 1994; regular explosions have continued to the time of writing, and approaching within 12km of the crater is not recommended. Signs pointing to *Rutas de Evacuación* (escape routes) in all nearby towns are reminders of the omnipresent danger. Parts of Ixtaccíhuatl can be explored on easy daytrips, but only seriously seasoned or those with a tour group should attempt the peak. Federación Mexicana de Alpinismo, all Mexican officials, and *Let's Go* strongly recommend against making even a daytrip when the **Socorro Alpino** (Alpine Assistance ☎ 5531 1401) is not nearby. No season is free from rapid weather change; always bring both warm clothes and rain gear. By taking all the right precautions, you can have a superb adventure hiking the volcano. The Socorro Alpino is at **Paraje la Joya trailhead** every weekend to provide guidance. Although Ixtaccíhuatl is most easily reached from San Rafael via Tlalmanalco, a safe hike is well worth the extra pesos it takes to get to La Joya via Amecameca. Arrangements can be made with Socorro Alpino from Mexico City or at the trailhead on weekends. If you are planning a longer or non-weekend trip, be certain to register with Socorro Alpino before you go. Should you have an accident or **medical emergency** in the mountains, do your best to reach Danton Valle Negrete, Socorro Alpino's medical director in Mexico City (☎ 5740 67 82; beeper 227 79 79, code 553 1773).

MALINALCO

*Take a 2nd-class **bus** to Xalapa that passes through Malinalco, from Terminal Poniente (1-2hr. depending on stops, 25 pesos). To avoid overpaying and to make sure the driver remembers to stop, tell both the ticket-seller and the bus driver your destination. To get to the ruins from the zócalo, follow the blue pyramid signs along Guerrero and go straight. Take a left on Milgar, a right at the next blue arrow, and another right at the blue sign that appears to lead into someone's driveway. Site open Tu-Su 9am-6pm. 30 pesos; Su free. Malinalco's helpful **tourist office** is in a red building located on one corner or the zócalo. ☎ 7147 01 11. Open M-F 9am-3pm, Sa 9am-1pm.*

Malinalco (pop. 20,000) is a peaceful town with one huge attraction—one of the best-preserved Aztec temples in the country. **Templo de la Iniciación** was cut whole from a nearby mountain, and, along with pyramids in India, Jordan, and Egypt, is one of only four monolithic pyramids in the world. Every year on March 21, hundreds of people pour into Malinalco to witness the temple's dazzling spring equinox—a ray of light shines through the doorway and reveals the image of an eagle on the floor. The ruins at Malinalco were the sacred ground for the rituals that officially transformed an Aztec youth into a tiger or eagle warrior. On the open circular stone platform—the first structure on the right as you enter—prisoners were bound to a pole with only their arms left free and made to wrestle the recently initiated warriors. If the prisoner won consecutive bouts with two *águila* and two *tigre* warriors, he was matched against a left-hander. If the prisoner defeated the lefty, he was granted freedom. Defeat, on the other hand, had more unpleasant consequences: the small rectangular basin in front of the entrance to the pyramid was used to hold the prisoner's blood after his ritual sacrifice. Behind the pyramid, the bodies of the sacrificed were burned to ashes on the oval bed of rock. Inside the pyramid, all of the statues, rooms, and facades were originally painted a brilliant crimson. To the right of the pyramid stand the remains of a *temascal*, the ancient predecessor to the sauna.

OTHER DAYTRIPS FROM MEXICO CITY

Cuernavaca: This lovely-colonial-town-turned-chic-upperclass-getaway overflows with expats and language schools. The gaggle of *gringos* and high prices come part and parcel with Cuernavaca's lush greenery, luxurious living, and trendy nightlife. (Morelos; 85km; see p. 332.)

Grutas de Cacahuamilpa: Have you ever wanted to see rock formations shaped like people making out? Of course, we all have. Let your imagination run wild through stalagmites and stalactites, some over 85m high. Hilarious guides lead you through the underground wonderland. (Guerrero; 130km; see p. 438.)

Ixtapan de la Sal: Despite the nearby Disney-ish waterparks and resorts, Ixtapan couldn't be lovelier or more good-natured if it tried. The Mediterranean-style plaza and church are two of a kind. This is a good place to check out rustic life and enjoy long mid-afternoon *siestas*. (Estado de México; 117km; see p. 328.)

Pachuca: An important silver mining and processing center since the 16th century, Pachuca's delightful streets shelter lovely plazas, extremely friendly inhabitants, and invigorating mountain air. (Estado de México; 90km; see p. 323.)

Puebla: Legend has it that Puebla's gridded streets were laid by angels who streaked across the land to shape this elegant city. Modern sophistication complements the city's rich past. (Puebla; 120km; see **p. 348.**)

Taxco: Everyone knows about the silver, but have you heard about the cable cars, stunning vistas, and gorgeous church? Picturesque Taxco sits way up in the hills, and its pink stone Catedral de Santa Prisca ranks among the loveliest in the republic. (Guerrero; 180km; see p. 433.)

Tepoztlán: Surrounded by towering cliffs, this cobbled *indígena* village preserves an ancient feel and the Náhuatl tongue. Bring plenty of spirit (and bottled water and sunscreen) if you plan to scale the town's steep pyramid. (Morelos; 70km; see p. 338.)

Tlaxcala: Known for its calm, colonial Tlaxcala enchants the eye with pretty *talavera* and an abundance of museums and art galleries. Sit in one of the quiet parks and take a breather from the capital (Tlaxcala; 85km; **p. 339**).

Tula: The archaeological site at Tula houses the ruins that once formed the capital of the Toltec civilization. Set in a hilly semi-desert landscape, the ruins are famous for their 10m-tall stone warrior statues, known as the Atlantes. (Hidalgo; 65km; see p. 325.)

Valle De Bravo: Wealthy *chilangos* go play in the beautiful town of Valle de Bravo, where the lake may be man-made, but the white stucco houses, cobblestone streets, and blossoming bougainvillea are irresistible. Grab a picnic basket and loll around the hills. (Estado de México; 140km; see p. 327.)

Xochicalco: Ceremonial center, fortress, and trading post in one, Xochicalco is the most impressive archaeological site in the state. The only sounds to be heard among the rolling green hills are the buzzings of swarms of dragonflies. Budding photographers will find ecstasy here. (Morelos; 120km; see p. 337.)

BAJA CALIFORNIA

Cradled by the warm, tranquil Sea of Cortés on the east and the cold, raging Pacific Ocean on the west, the peninsula of Baja California claims one of the most spectacular and diverse landscapes in the world. Sparse expanses of sandy deserts give way to barren mountains jutting into the cloudless sky. The high-altitude national parks of northern Baja California are home to seemingly out-of-place evergreens and snow during the winter months. And then, of course, there's the unbelievably blue-green water surrounding Baja California's miles of uninhabited shore. This aqua liquid flows past coral reefs, dances around in rocky storybook coves, and laps at the white sandy shores of thousands of miles of paradisiacal beaches lining both coasts. Called "el otro Mexico" (the other Mexico), Baja California is neither here nor there, not at all California, yet nothing like mainland Mexico. Even its history is different—it was permanently settled by the Franciscans and Jesuits in the 1600s. While mainland Mexico has massive Maya and Zapotec temples, Baja has small Jesuit missions. The peninsula's tradition of carefully blending wildness and tranquility, domesticity and simplicity, are emblematized by the Jesuit legacy in sleepy towns like San Ignacio.

Until relatively recently, Baja California was an unknown frontier of sorts; the only way to reach its rugged desert terrain was by plane or boat. However, with the completion of the Transpeninsular Highway (Mex. 1) in 1973, and the addition of better toll roads and ferry service, Baja has become a popular vacation spot, especially among Californians, Arizonans, and Mexicans. Vacationers range in type from hardy campers setting out to tame the savage deserts of central Baja to families living in one of the peninsula's many RV parks. Large resort hotels and condominium complexes are sprouting like grass to house these human torrents in the south. Cabo San Lucas, the mega-resort haven on the southern tip, now has almost as little integrity and authenticity as Tijuana, the bawdy border wasteland of **Baja California** state, wedged in the hilly crevices of the peninsula's northern extreme. The honest Mexican city of La Paz, the capital of **Baja California Sur,** is a southern beacon of beauty for resort-weary port-seekers. But it is Baja's southern midsection—from the tranquility of Mulegé to the palm-laden oasis town of San Ignacio to the thousands of undisturbed beaches beneath sheer cliffs—that is most pristine and mysterious. Most of Baja California is still somewhat of an undiscovered country, prime for the hearty budget traveler to explore.

HIGHLIGHTS OF BAJA CALIFORNIA

DISCOVER the secluded and beautiful beaches of **Bahía de la Concepción** (p. 169), 48km of turquoise water, powdery sand, bubbly springs, and abundant marine life.

SLEEP under a million stars in **San Ignacio** (p. 164), a tiny leafy Northern Baja oasis with a remarkable **mission** (see p. 166).

HIKE through the amazing **Parque Sierra Nacional San Pedro Mártir** (p. 160), home to mountains, valleys, waterfalls, and Mexico's **National Observatory.**

STROLL down the gulf side boardwalk of breezy, beautiful **La Paz** (p. 175), the good-natured capital of Baja Sur, and a favorite Mexican vacation destination.

DROP IN on artsy expatriates in the friendly town of **Todos Santos** (p. 181), and then catch the perfect wave at one of the area's pristine surfing beaches.

GETTING AROUND

BY CAR

Driving in Baja is far from easy. Highways often degrade into pothole ridden, rotting pavement, making speeds in excess of 80km/hr. dangerous. Livestock on the highways and a general lack of guardrails make night driving impossible—if this warning doesn't convince you, check out the huge number of roadside shrines to the deceased. Furthermore, the intense heat pummels cars, and repair service can be hard to find. Still, a car is the only way to get close to the more beautiful and secluded areas of Baja, and the ride is probably one of the most beautiful in Mexico. Though the proposition might make your mother cringe, driving in Baja is reasonably secure if you stay slow, never drive at night, and keep your tank full. If you need roadside assistance, the **Angeles Verdes** (Green Angels) pass along Mex. 1 twice per day. Unleaded gas may be lacking along this highway, so don't pass a **PEMEX station** without filling up. If you are driving in from the US, obtain a **vehicle permit**, which is required south of San Felipe on the Sea of Cortés side and Ensenada on the Pacific side. If you will be driving in Baja for more than 72 hours, show the vehicle's title and proof of registration for a free permit at the border. For more information on driving in Mexico see **Getting Around: By Car,** p. 32.

BY BUS

If you plan to navigate the peninsula by bus, note that almost all buses between Ensenada and La Paz are *de paso* (in passing), which means that buses pass through cities, rather than originate and terminate in them. It is therefore impossible to reserve seats in advance. You'll have to leave at inconvenient times, fight to procure a ticket, and then probably stand the whole way. A much better idea is to buy a reserved seat in Tijuana, Ensenada, La Paz, or Los Cabos, and traverse the peninsula in one trip. Getting around by bus, while certainly possible, will try your patience (for more info, see **Getting Around: By Bus,** p. 32). Some swear by **hitching**—PEMEX stations are thick with rides. *Let's Go* does not recommend hitchhiking, as it is unpredictable and potentially hazardous. (For more information on the evils of hitchhiking, see **Getting Around: By Thumb,** p. 34.)

BY SEA

Ferry service was instituted in the mid-1960s as a means of supplying Baja California with food and supplies. There are three different ferry routes: **Santa Rosalía to Guaymas** (8hr.), **La Paz to Topolobampo/Los Mochis** (9hr.), and **La Paz to Mazatlán** (17hr.). The La Paz to Topolobampo/Los Mochis route provides direct access to the train from Los Mochis through the **Copper Canyon.** Ferry tickets are generally expensive, even for *turista*-class berths, which are two-person cabins with a sink; bathrooms and showers are down the hall. It's extremely difficult to find tickets for *turista* and *cabina* class, and snagging an *especial* berth is as likely as snow in Baja—there are only two such suites on each ferry. This leaves the bottom-of-the-line *salón* ticket, entitling you to a seat in a large room with few communal baths. If you find yourself traveling *salón*-class at night, ditch your seat and stake out a spot on the floor or outside on the deck. Storage is available, but your belongings will be inaccessible until arrival. For those who plan to take their car aboard a ferry, make reservations a month in advance, as passenger vehicles may take up only the space left over by the top-priority commercial vehicles. For further ferry information, contact a **Sematur** office, listed in the **Practical Information** sections of the cities from which the ferry departs. Beware: By the time you finish reading this page prices will have risen dramatically and schedules altered drastically—both favorite practices of Sematur.

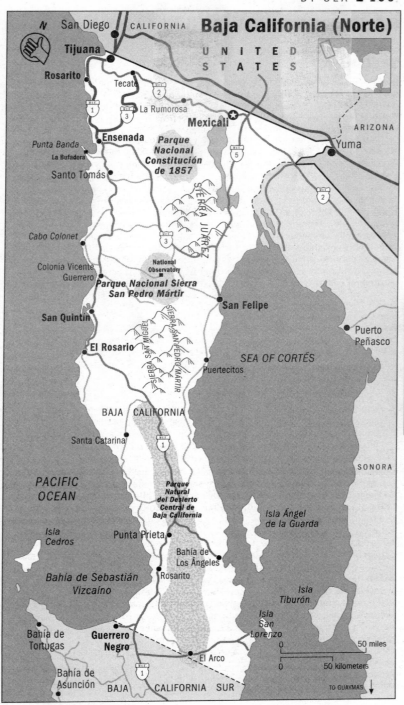

Baja California (Norte)

NORTHERN BAJA CALIFORNIA

TIJUANA ☎ 6

In the shadow of swollen, sulphur-spewing factories lies the most notorious specimen of the peculiar border subculture: Tijuana (pop. 2 million). By day, swarms of tourists cross the US border to haggle with street vendors, pour gallons of tequila down their throats, and get their picture taken with zebra-painted donkeys. By night, Revolución, the city's main drag, becomes a big, bad party with *gringos* stumbling between *mariachi* bands and exploding bottle rockets, doing little to drown out the thumping dance beats blaring from packed nightclubs. In the wake of the Mexican-American War, modest Rancho Tía Juana found itself on the new dividing line between US Alta California and Mexican Baja California. Tijuana suddenly became an important frontier town, and the settlement's population began a meteoric rise. The three-ringed, duty-free extravaganza now attracts more than 30 million eager tourists a year, most of them jaunting across the border to unload wads of cash on everything from *jai alai* gambling to slimy strip shows. In recent years the city has made a conscious effort to clean up its act, nearly successfully eliminating sex shops and prostitution from the center of town. "TJ" also offers an array of cultural attractions to divert your attention if you can drag yourself away from the uniquely entertaining Revolución. Rife with flashy sleaze and border intrigue, it's hard to say whether it's the city's strange charm, its cheap booze, or its sprawling, unapologetic hedonism that attracts tourists to Tijuana like flies.

▐ TRANSPORTATION

GETTING THERE

From San Ysidro: Take the red Mexicoach bus (☎685 14 70 or 619 428 9517 in the US) from its terminal at Border Station Parking next to the Nike factory outlet. It stops right in the middle of all the Revolución madness. (Every 30min., 9am-9pm, US$1.)

From San Diego: Grab a trolley at Kettner and Broadway downtown (25min., US$20) and ride it all the way to the border. From there catch the southbound Mexicoach or walk across the pedestrian footbridge, which continues as a walkway over the Río Tijuana and ends at the corner of Calle 1a and Revolución (10min.). Taxis on the Mexican side of the border charge US$5 for the same 6 blocks.

From Mexicali: If you drive in from Mexicali on Mex. 2, get on to Mex. 2D, the toll road, and follow the *"Aeropuerto"* signs west. The airport road turns into Cuauhtémoc and crosses the river before running into Agua Caliente, and eventually Revolución.

From Rosarito: Homeward-bound beachgoers on Mex. 1 arrive on 16 de Septiembre, head north until the intersection with Agua Caliente and turn left to reach the *centro.* Those who choose scenic 1D drive in on Calle 2A, which continues east to Revolución.

CROSSING THE BORDER

At the world's largest border crossing, northbound lanes often have backups of more than 150 cars. The best time to cross is during weekday mornings. The southbound ride is almost always smoother, but weekends can be rough in both directions. If you're crossing into Tijuana for a day or so, it's easier to leave your car in a lot on the US side and join the throngs of people walking across the border. Remember that a **tourist card** (US$20) is needed if you plan to travel farther south than Ensenada. Regardless of which way you are crossing, bring proper ID—ideally a driver's license or passport—and leave your bushels of fruit, truckloads of livestock, stashes of drugs, and armory of weapons behind.

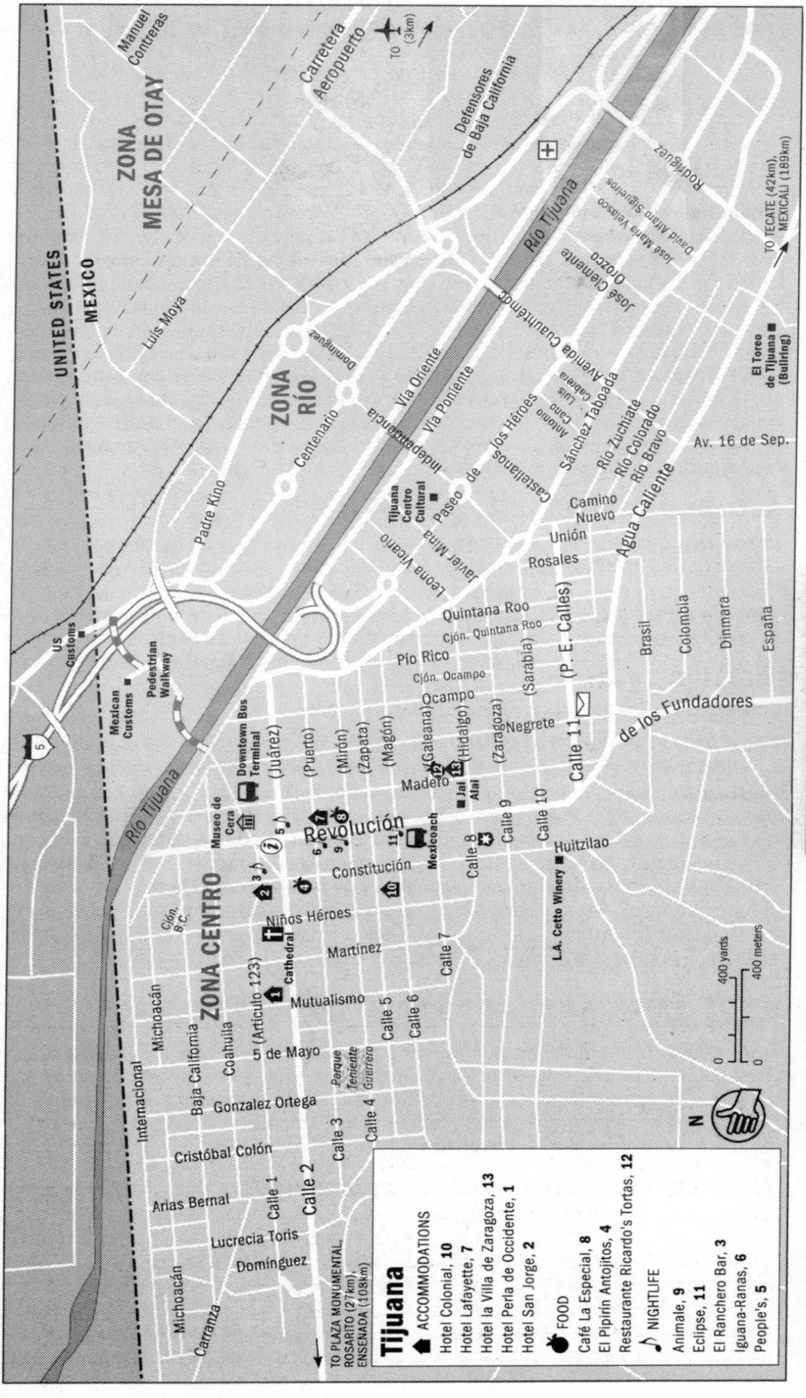
Tijuana
ACCOMMODATIONS
Hotel Colonial, 10
Hotel Lafayette, 7
Hotel la Villa de Zaragoza, 13
Hotel Perla de Occidente, 1
Hotel San Jorge, 2
FOOD
Café La Especial, 8
El Pipirín Antojitos, 4
Restaurante Ricardo's Tortas, 12
NIGHTLIFE
Animale, 9
Eclipse, 11
El Ranchero Bar, 3
Iguana-Ranas, 6
People's, 5
UNITED STATES
MEXICO
ZONA MESA DE OTAY
ZONA RÍO
ZONA CENTRO
Río Tijuana
Carretera Aeropuerto
TO (3km)
Defensores de Baja California
Manuel Contreras
Luis Moya
Padre Kino
Centenario
Domínguez
Vía Oriente
Vía Poniente
Independencia
Paseo de los Héroes
Tijuana Centro Cultural
Javier Mina
Leona Vicario
Castellanos
Sánchez Taboada
Antonio Cano
Luis Cabrera
Avenida Cuauhtémoc
José Clemente Orozco
José María Velasco
David Alfaro Siqueiros
Rodríguez
TO TECATE (42km), MEXICALI (189km)
El Toreo de Tijuana (Bullring)
Av. 16 de Sep.
Río Zuchiate
Río Colorado
Río Bravo
Camino Nuevo
Unión
Agua Caliente
Rosales
Quintana Roo
Cjón. Quintana Roo
Pío Rico
Cjón. Ocampo
Ocampo
(Sarabia)
(P. E. Calles)
Negrete
(Zaragoza)
Calle 11
de los Fundadores
Brasil
Colombia
Dinmara
España
US Customs
Mexican Customs
Pedestrian Walkway
Downtown Bus Terminal
(Juárez)
(Puerto)
(Mirón)
(Zapata)
(Magón)
(Galeana)
(Hidalgo)
Madero
Jai Alai
Museo de Cera
Revolución
Mexicoach
Calle 8
Calle 9
Calle 10
Huitzilac
L.A. Cetto Winery
Constitución
Niños Héroes
Cathedral
Martínez
Mutualismo
5 de Mayo
Gonzalez Ortega
Cristóbal Colón
Arias Bernal
Lucrecia Toris
Domínguez
Carranza
Michoacán
Internacional
Baja California
Coahuila
Cjón. B.C.
(Artículo 123)
Parque Teniente Guerrero
Calle 1
Calle 2
Calle 3
Calle 4
Calle 5
Calle 6
Calle 7
TO PLAZA MONUMENTAL, ROSARITO (27km), ENSENADA (108km)
N
0 400 yards
0 400 meters

By bus: Tijuana has 2 bus stations. To get to the center of town from the **Central Camionera** (☎621 29 82), the more remote bus station, avoid the cab drivers' high rates (up to 80 pesos to downtown) by exiting the terminal, turning left, walking to the end of the building, and hopping on a local bus marked "Centro" (30min., every 5min. 5am-10pm, 4 pesos), which will let you off on Calle 3 and Constitución, 1 block west of Revolución. The **downtown station** is more conveniently located at Calle 1A at Madero, one block east of Revolución.

GETTING AROUND

Traditional **yellow cabs,** which prey almost exclusively on tourists, charge absurd rates; set a price before getting in. **Communal cabs** are a popular option with many locals. Operating as miniature buses, they run circuits of the routes painted above the rear tires and on the windshield, and are much cheaper than the yellow cabs—you can get almost anywhere in the city for 20-30 pesos. Most communal cabs originate on Madero between Calle 1 and Calle 5. Aside from the Central Camionera, colorful station wagons can take you to **Parque Morelos** (5.5 pesos; orange and grey), **Rosarito** (10 pesos, yellow and white), or **El Toreo** (5 pesos) among other destinations. It's a good idea to take cabs at night in the *centro*, and tourist officials recommend avoiding the Zona Norte, downhill from Calle 1a, which is filled with prostitution and drugs at all times.

GETTING AWAY

FROM THE CENTRAL CAMIONERA. To get back to the Central Camionera, board a blue and white "Central Camionera" bus on Calle 2A between Revolución and Constitución (4.5 pesos), or jump in a brown and white communal cab on Madero between Calles 2 and 3 (5.5 pesos). Autotransportes de Baja California (☎621 26 68) runs to: **Ensenada** (1½hr., every hr. 6am-9pm, 78 pesos); **La Paz** (24hr., 4 per day 8am-9pm, 725 pesos); **Loreto** (18hr., 4 per day 8am-9pm, 500 pesos); **Mexicali** (3hr., every hr. 6am-9pm, 117 pesos); **San Felipe** (5hr., 3 per day 8:30am-3:30pm, 213 pesos); **Santa Rosalía** (15hr., 6 per day 8am-9pm, 455 pesos).

FROM THE DOWNTOWN STATION. Elite (☎621 29 49 or 688 19 79) buses stop at the downtown bus station 1 hr. before embarking from the Central Camionera for: **Guadalajara** (36hr., every hr., 1137 pesos); **Hermosillo** (12hr., every 30min., 489 pesos); **Mexico City** (44hr., 5 per day, 945 pesos). Greyhound (☎688 19 79) also picks up passengers downtown before leaving the *Central* for **Los Angeles** (3hr., every hr. 5am-midnight, US$14), and connecting to other North American cities. **Suburbaja** (☎688 00 82), in the downtown terminal, sends buses (every 30min., 5am-9pm) to the neighboring cities of **Rosarito** (10 pesos) and **Tecate** (33 pesos). Mexicoach buses depart from their station on Revolución between Calles 6 and 7 for **Rosarito** (30min., 5 per day 9am-7pm, US$3) and **San Ysidro** (every 30min., US$1).

■※🛈 ORIENTATION AND PRACTICAL INFORMATION

Immediately south of the border, the area surrounding Revolución is known as the **Zona Centro,** a.k.a. the tourist hotspot. Most tourists never even leave Revolución, let alone venture into other areas of the city. East-west *calles*, which are both named and numbered, cross Revolución; perpendicular to the *calles*, *avenidas* run north-south, parallel to Revolución.

TOURIST, FINANCIAL, AND LOCAL SERVICES

Tourist Office: Revolución 711 (☎688 05 55), at Calle 1. English-speaking staff makes up for a lack of useful maps with great advice. Open M-Sa 8am-5pm, Su 10am-5pm.

Customs Office: (☎683 13 90) at the border on the Mexican side, after crossing the San Ysidro bridge. Open 24hr.

Consulates: Canada, German Gedovius 10411-101 (☎684 04 61 or 01 800 706 2900 for after hours emergency assistance), in the Zona Río. Open M-F 9am-1pm. **UK,** Salinas 1500 (☎681 73 23 or 686 53 20 for after hours emergency assistance), in Col. Aviación, La Mesa. Open M-F 9am-3pm. **US,** Tapachula Sur 96 (☎681 74 00), in Col. Hipódromo, adjacent to the racetrack southeast of town. In an emergency, call the San Diego office (☎619-692-2154) and leave a message and phone number; an officer will respond. Open M-F 8am-4:30pm.

Currency Exchange: Banks along Constitución exchange money and traveler's checks at the same rates. **Banamex,** Constitución at Calle 4, has a shorter lines (☎688 00 21; open M-F 9am-5pm) than more central **Bital,** Revolución at Calle 2. (☎685 00 06. Open M-F 8am-7pm, Sa 8am-5:30pm.) Both have 24hr. **ATMs.** *Casas de cambio* offer better rates, but may charge commission, and refuse to exchange traveler's checks.

Supermarket: Calimax (☎688 08 94), Calle 2 at Constitución. Open 6am-midnight.

Car Rental: @West Rent a Car, 1453 Rosecrans St., in San Diego, will rent to drivers aged 18-25 and charges decent rates. (☎619-223-2343. Open daily 8am-8pm.) Before driving into Mexico from the US, get **car insurance** for US$5 per day in San Ysidro. Many drive-through insurance companies have offices just before the border at Sycamore and Primero. **Budget,** Paseo de los Héroes 77 next to the Hotel Camino Real (☎634 33 03; open M-F 8am-7pm, Sa-Su 8am-4pm), and **Hertz,** 16 de Septiembre 213-B, in the Hotel Palacio Azteca, offer similar rates and a wide variety of vehicles. (☎686 12 22. Open M-F 8am-6:30pm, Sa 8am-4pm.)

EMERGENCY AND COMMUNICATIONS

Emergency: ☎060.

Police: (☎638 51 68), Constitución at Calle 8. English spoken. Specialized tourist assistance (☎688 05 55).

Red Cross: (☎621 77 87; emergency 066) Gamboa at Silvestre, across from Price Club. Some English spoken.

Pharmacy: Farmacia Vida (☎685 14 61), Calle 3 at Revolución. Open 24hr.

Hospital: Hospital General, Centenario 10851 (☎684 02 37 or 684 09 22), in the Zona Río. **IMSS** (☎629 63 42), Agua Caliente and Francisco Zarabia. Both have 24hr. emergency service.

Fax: Telecomm (☎684 79 02; fax 684 77 50), to the right of the post office, in the same building. Open M-F 8am-5pm.

Internet: Ciber Tequila, Revolución 1200, just south of Calle 8. 25 pesos per hr. Open daily 9am-5am.

Post Office: (☎684 79 50), on Negrete at Calle 11. Open M-F 8am-5pm.

Postal Code: 22000.

⌔ ACCOMMODATIONS

Budget hotels concentrate on Calle 1, between Revolución and Mutualismo. As a general rule, hotels become sketchier the farther north you go. Avoid any in the area downhill from Calle 1 (the Zona Norte). While crowded during the day, Zona Centro becomes something of a red-light district at night, especially between Revolución and Constitución close to the Zona Norte. Rooms tend to be roachy—ask to see them before paying. Please exercise caution when walking home at night, or take a cab (US$2) from anywhere on Revolución.

Hotel Colonial, Calle 6a 1812 (☎688 16 20), between Constitución and Niños Héroes, in a quieter, residential neighborhood away from Revolución. Large, comfortable rooms have A/C and private baths. Singles and doubles 240 pesos.

Hotel Perla de Occidente, Mutualismo 758 (☎685 13 58), between Calles 1a and 2a, 4 blocks from the bedlam of Revolución. Funky murals of Jesus and a chimp smoking a joint decorate the hallway. Inside the rooms, you'll find private baths, cozy beds, and fans on request. Singles 140 pesos; doubles 280 pesos.

Hotel Lafayette, Revolución 325 (☎685 39 40 or 685 33 39), between Calles 3a and 4a. Remarkably quiet for being in the middle of Revolución's chaos. Large rooms have color TVs, phones, fans, and private baths, but the great (or terrible) location drives up the price. Singles 200 pesos; doubles 260 pesos.

Hotel San Jorge, Constitución 706 (☎685 84 40 or 685 26 01), at Calle 1a. A refreshingly respectable establishment on the edge of the lurid Zona Norte, the San Jorge boasts a friendly young staff, clean rooms with private baths, TV, phones (free local calls), and room service. Singles 180 pesos; doubles 220 pesos; TV 30 pesos extra.

Hotel La Villa de Zaragoza, Madero 1120 (☎685 18 32), between Calles 7a and 8a. Semi-affordable luxury for those too squeamish to handle Tijuana's truly budget offerings. Spacious rooms come with TVs, enormous king-sized beds, and lots of clean towels. Also has laundry, room service, and 24hr. security to keep you and your car very safe. Singles 390 pesos; doubles 475 pesos.

⬛ FOOD

Like most things in Tijuana, restaurants tend to be loud and in-your-face; menu-waving promoters try to drag tourists—and their dollars—into the over-priced restaurants lining **Revolución.** Savvy travelers make tracks to **Constitución,** one block west of the mayhem, for better food, superior service, and a mellower environment. For ultra-cheap, ultra-fast food, taco stands all over the *centro* sell several tacos or a *torta* for 10 pesos.

🍴 **El Pipirín Antojitos,** Constitución 878 (☎688 16 02), between Calles 2 and 3, wows the weary tourist with exceptional food and service. Enjoy delicious burritos (35 pesos) under the gaudy orange arches. Open daily 8:30am-8:30pm.

🍴 **Restaurant Ricardo's Tortas,** Madero and Calle 7 (☎685 40 31). A huge, sparkling restaurant, Ricardo's cooks the best *tortas* in town. Try the *super especial,* with ham, *carne asada,* cheese, avocado, tomato, and mayo (36 pesos). Fills growling tummies 24hr.

Cafe La Especial, Revolución 718 (☎685 66 54), downstairs from Hotel Lafayette. Like the hotel upstairs, La Especial is a refreshing respite from the noise of Revolución. Munch on a 2-enchilada and 1-taco special (49 pesos) amidst crooning *mariachis* and local families. Open daily 9am-10pm.

Los Panchos Taco Shop (☎685 72 77), Revolución at Calle 3. By day, the orange vinyl booths are packed with locals munching fresh tortillas. By night, raucous tourists refuel before tackling the clubs. Steak tacos US$1. Bean and cheese burritos US$2. Open Su-Th 8am-midnight, F-Sa 8am-2am; in summer Su-Th 8am-midnight, F-Sa 8am-4am.

👁 SIGHTS

Many of the most entertaining sights in town are right on Revolución, where zebra-striped donkeys and gaudily-costumed cowboys vie for your attention. Fortunately, while most tourists can't be bothered to move beyond the multi-tiered dance clubs and curio shops that line Revolución, those who do are greeted with a wide array of beautiful parks and dazzling cultural attractions.

PARQUE TENIENTE GUERRERO. Dedicated in 1924 to the memory of Vicente Guerrero, the beautiful and shady park on Calle 3a and 5 de Mayo is a favorite gathering place for local families and an oasis from the noisy circus of Revolución.

CATEDRAL DE NUESTRA SEÑORA DE GUADALUPE. Originally built in 1902 as a modest adobe chapel, modern expansions and reinforcement have resulted in a huge stone cathedral checkered in adobe orange and grey and crowned with a giant image of the Virgin of Guadalupe. Check out the massive and magnificent central chandelier. (*At the intersection of Calle 2a and Niños Héroes.*)

MUSEO DE CERA. One of only three wax museums in Mexico, this Tijuana attraction is home to a motley crew of 81 eerily realistic wax figures, including such strange bedfellows as Eddie Murphy, Gandhi, Gorbachev, and Tía Juana herself. The sculptures are split into four basic categories: cinema, history, politics, and terror. *(Calle 1A and Madero. ☎ 688 24 78. Open daily 10am-7pm. 15 pesos.)*

LA CETTO WINERY. Established in 1926 by Italian immigrants, the family-run winery maintains its vineyards in the Valle de Guadalupe, northeast of Ensenada. Visitors are welcome to tour the facilities and sample the products. Avoid removing anything from the storeroom—the staff still remembers the North American woman who pulled out the wrong bottle and caused a wine avalanche that destroyed more than 30 cases. *(Cañon Johnson 2108. Follow Constitución south to Calle 10a and turn right. ☎ 685 30 31. Tours M-F every 30min. 10am-6:30pm. US$2 including tasting.)*

PARQUE MORELOS. An amazing assortment of exotic birds and picnic tables welcome families to this sprawling state-run park south of the *centro*. Attractions include rides, a miniature golf course, botanical gardens, and an open-air theater. *(Blvd. de los Insurgentes 26000. Take a green and white local bus (5 pesos) from the corner of Calle 5a and Constitución or any of the orange and grey communal cabs (5 pesos) on Madero south of Calle 2a. ☎ 625 24 70. Open Tu-Su 9am-5pm. 5 pesos, children 2 pesos.)*

🎵📷 ENTERTAINMENT AND NIGHTLIFE

In the 1920s, Prohibition drove US citizens south of the border to revel in the forbidden nectars of cacti, grapes, and hops, and the constant flow of North American tourists eager to fill their stomachs with booze still remains strong. Stroll down Revolución after dusk and you'll be bombarded with thumping music, neon lights, and abrasive club (of both the strip and dance varieties) promoters hawking "two-for-one" margaritas at the not-so-low price of US$5. The chaotic mix of pop, reggae, rap, and Latin hits spun by DJs sets the tone for all of Revolución, as the throbbing music is often all that can be heard within a three-block radius of the main street. Those who prefer laid-back nights of bar chat have come to the wrong place—Revolución doesn't know the meaning of quiet.

Animale, Revolución at Calle 4a, is the biggest, glitziest, and loudest hedonistic haven of them all. Less than a year old, Animale has already taken over the Tijuana club scene, attracting kids and adults alike into its colorful lair with special deals (2 beers and a shot of tequila US$4) and deafeningly loud music. Open daily 10am-3am.

Iguanas-Ranas (☎ 685 14 22), Revolución at Calle 3a. A sublimely wacky world of life-size plaster clowns, balloons, and various pieces of kitschy US pop culture paraphernalia, Iguanas-Ranas is one of the most happening places in town. Where else do you get the opportunity to pound beers (US$2.50) in an authentic yellow school bus perched high above Revolución? Lively on weeknights and packed on weekends with US and Mexican 20-somethings. For bargain-basement booze, come on W, when guys pay US$1 per beer, and girls drink free. Open M-Th 10am-2am, F-Su 10am-5am.

Eclipse, Revolución at Calle 6a. Brace yourself for this 3-tiered party palace. Miami-esque decor complete with platforms attracts masses of patrons eager to toss back some of the cheapest booze in town: 2 beers and a shot of tequila are a mere US$3. The 3rd fl. occasionally doubles as a strip club. Open daily 11am-5am.

People's (☎ 685 45 72), Revolución and Calle 2a. Fluorescent constellations and silver-painted sports equipment decorate the purple arches of the open-air terrace, where revelers guzzle 10 beers for US$18. Open M-W 10am-2am, Th-Su 10am-5am.

Tilly's 5th Avenue (☎ 685 90 15), at Revolución and Calle 5a. A small club by Tijuana standards, Tilly's attracts customers with an intimate dance floor, a dance-happy staff that mingles with customers, and half-price beer (US$1) on W nights. Open M-Th 10:30am-2am, F-Sa 10:30am-5am.

GAY AND LESBIAN NIGHTLIFE

Clubs catering to gays and lesbians cluster in the southern part of the *centro* around Calle 6a and 7a or down the hill to the north of Calle 1a.

Mike's Disco (☎ 685 35 34), Revolución south of Calle 6a. A wild bunch, mostly men, gets down on the dance floor, cheering the drag queens who perform every weekend. Straight by day, but gay Th-Tu 10pm-5am.

El Ranchero Bar (☎ 685 28 00), in front of the fountain in Plaza Santa Cecilia. Rainbow-colored parrots and palm trees decorate the long bar where a mellow mixed crowd drinks 10-peso beers. Open M-W 10am-2am, Th-Su 10am-3am.

Los Equipales, Calle 7a between Revolución and Madero. A transvestite cabaret entertains the mixed clientele in this friendly *discoteca*.

CULTURAL EVENTS

The monumental **Tijuana Centro Cultural,** more popular with locals than tourists, is on Paseo de los Héroes at Mina. Inside the strikingly modern complex is **Museo de las Californias,** a series of exhibits exploring the history and culture of Baja California. (☎ 687 96 50. Open daily 10am-8pm. 20 pesos, children 12 pesos). The Centro Cultural hosts a variety of other offerings, including a central gallery of temporary art exhibits. The enormous sphere in the plaza contains **Cine Planetano,** a giant 180-degree screen that shows OmniMax films dubbed in Spanish. (Open daily 2-9pm. 45 pesos, children 23 pesos.) Another theater plays cycles of foreign films and children's movies. (Open Sa-Su 10am-8pm. 25 pesos, children's films free.) **Sala de Ciencia** presents interactive exhibits about health and technology. Performances by visiting dance troupes, musicians, and theater groups occur in **Jardín Caracol.** Ask at the information booth in the lobby for details on upcoming shows.

Several movie theaters screen first-run films. **Multicinemas Río,** in Plaza del Río shopping mall across from the Centro Cultural, is closest to the *centro*. (☎ 684 04 01. Open daily 2pm-midnight. 38 pesos.) Blue and white buses (5 pesos) on Calle 2a at Constitución can take you to the Centro Cultural and the cinema.

SPORTS

Completed in 1947 after 21 years of complications and delays, the grandiose baroque **Frontón Palacio,** on Revolución at Calle 7a, hosts daily competitions of **jai alai.** (☎ 685 16 12. Games take place M-Sa at 8pm. Free.) If you're in town on the right Sunday, you can watch the graceful and savage battle of man versus bull in one of Tijuana's two bullrings. **El Toreo de Tijuana,** southeast of town just off of Agua Caliente, hosts the first round of fights (May-July alternate Su). To get to El Toreo, catch a bus on Calle 2a west of Revolución. The seaside **Plaza Monumental** hosts the second round (Aug.-Oct.). Mexicoach sends buses (US$4 round-trip) to Plaza Monumental on fight days. Alternatively, take the blue and white local buses (5 pesos) on Calle 3a at Constitución all the way down Calle 2a. Tickets to both rings go on sale at the gate the Wednesday before a fight (☎ 685 15 10 or 686 12 19) or at the Mexicoach office (☎ 685 14 70) on Revolución between Calles 6A and 7a (tickets 95-400 pesos).

SHOPPING

As soon as tourists cross the footbridge from the US, they're bombarded with vendors peddling everything a gaudy *gringo* desires. The crazy shopping scene continues most of the way up Revolución, close to the intersection with Calle 7a. Other spots for assorted tourist-oriented wares are the **Mercado de Artesanía,** on Calle 1a right under the pedestrian footbridge, and the vendors on **Plaza Santa Cecilia** behind the tourist office. Bargaining is a must, as quoted prices can be more than twice the bottom line. For a good selection of higher-quality *artesanía*, visit the **Bazar de México** on Revolución at Calle 7a.

TECATE ☎ 6

Free of *burros* and aggressive vendors, Tecate (pop. 100,000) provides a peaceful respite from the frenzy of Tijuana. Perhaps most famous as the birthplace and namesake of Mexico's unofficial national beer, this friendly border town prides

THE WORLD'S FASTEST GAME, THE WORLD'S STRANGEST NAME
If you think the name *jai alai* (pronounced HIE-lie) doesn't sound like Spanish, you're right. The game and the name are imported from the Basque, a race of people living in the Pyrenees mountains between Spain and France, linguistically and culturally distinct from both the Spanish and French. In *jai alai*, two to four players take to the three-sided square court at once (spectators sit behind a barrier on the fourth side), using slender, otherworldly *cestas* (arm-baskets) to catch and throw an extremely hard ball of rubber and nylon encased in goatskin. The handmade balls fly at speeds of up to 300km/hr., earning *jai alai* the Guinness World Record for "World's Fastest Game." Competitions are similar to squash tournaments, with players rotating on and off the court king-of-the-hill style. The game is so fast that it's quite dangerous—30 professional players were killed between 1900 and 1960, when helmets were introduced. Today, *jai alai* is a popular betting sport not only in Mexico, but many parts of the world, including Chile and the Philippines.

itself not on the vats of suds produced each day in its brewery, but on its small-town camaraderie and the safety of its streets. You can't pose with zebra-painted donkeys or buy cheap hammocks in Tecate, but you can kick back and enjoy the serenity of the central Parque Hidalgo, where lively fiestas often spontaneously erupt. Instead of being blanketed by smog and pollution, Tecate's air carries the pleasant smell of barley and hops. A tranquil afternoon spent sipping *cerveza* and tapping your foot to live *mariachi* will relax even the most harried of travelers.

E TRANSPORTATION. Catch **buses** one block east of the park at the station on Juárez at Rodríguez. Autotransportes de Baja California (☎554 12 21) sends buses to: **Ensenada** (2hr., 6 per day 8am-10pm, 87 pesos); **Mexicali** (2hr., every hr. 6:30am-10pm, 87 pesos); **Tijuana** (1 hr., every 20min. 5am-9pm, 33 pesos). Transportes Norte De Sonora (☎554 23 43) offers cushy *de paso* buses every hour beginning at 7:30am to: **Guaymas** (13hr., 520 pesos); **Hermosillo** (12hr., 416 pesos); **Mazatlán** (24hr., 925 pesos); **Sonoita** (5hr., 226 pesos).

⬛🔽 ORIENTATION AND PRACTICAL INFORMATION. Tecate lies 42km east of Tijuana on **Mex. 2.** Driving in from Mexicali or Tijuana you will be on the main street, **Juárez,** which intersects Cárdenas, heading south from the border crossing, at the northwest corner of Parque Hidalgo, the center of social and commercial activity. East-west streets parallel **México,** which runs along the border fence; continuing south, they are Madero, Revolución, Reforma, Juárez, Libertad, and Hidalgo. Streets named for early 20th-century presidents run north-south perpendicular to Juárez and the border. Starting from the east, they are Gil, Rodríguez, Rubio, Cárdenas, Elias Calles, Obregón, de la Huerta, Carranza, and Aldrete.

Extremely undetailed maps are available from the English-speaking folks at the **tourist office,** Libertad 1305, facing Parque Hidalgo. (☎554 10 95. Open M-F 8am-5pm, Sa-Su 10am-3pm.) **Bancomer,** on the corner of Cárdenas and Juárez, exchanges traveler's checks and has a 24hr. **ATM.** (☎554 13 50. Open M-F 8:30am-4pm, Sa 10am-2pm.) **Banamex,** Juárez and Obregón, provides the same services. (☎654 11 88. Open M-F 8:30am-4pm.) Big, yellow **Calimax,** on Juárez between Carranza and Aldrete, sells groceries and more. (☎554 00 39. Open daily 7am-11pm.) **Emergency:** ☎060. **Police:** Paseo Morelos 1978, (☎654 11 76). Walk east on Juárez out of town; it will become México 2. The station is at the traffic circle, a 10min. walk from the *parque.* English spoken. **Red Cross:** Juárez 411 (☎554 13 13, emergency 066). Some English spoken. **Pharmacy: Farmacia Roma** (☎554 18 18), on the corner of Juárez and Aldrete, has got you covered 24hr. The **IMSS Centro de Salud** is south of town at Carranza 220 and Gil. (☎654 58 03. Some English spoken.) **Fax: Telecomm,** next door to the post office. (☎554 13 75. Open M-F 8am-2pm, Sa 8-11am.) **Internet Access: Centro de Enseñanza Computacional** Ortiz Rubio 261-3, upstairs from the stationery store. (☎654 69 71. 30 pesos per hr. Open M-F 8am-8:30pm, Sa 8am-6pm.) **Post office:** Ortiz Rubio 147, two blocks north off Juárez. (☎554 12 45. Open M-F 8am-3pm.) **Postal code:** 21400.

🖪🖵 ACCOMMODATIONS AND FOOD. Tecate has many budget hotel choices scattered throughout the city. The friendly staff at **Hotel Frontera,** in a residential neighborhood on Madero between Obregón and Elias Calles, welcomes visitors to large, cheery rooms complete with private baths. (☎654 13 42. US$5 key deposit. Singles US$18, doubles $35.) Very central **Hotel Tecate,** on Libertad at Cárdenas around the corner from the tourist office, has clean and simple but dark rooms with private baths and fans. (☎554 11 16. Singles and doubles 180 pesos, with TV 220 pesos.) Four blocks away, **Motel Paraíso,** Aldrete 83, one block north of Juárez, welcomes guests with spacious rooms. Some are dark, spartan, and feel like jail cells, while others get plenty of light from big windows. (☎654 17 16. Singles 160 pesos; doubles 225 pesos; each additional person 55 pesos.)

Taquerías lining Juárez east of the park and Obregón serve Tecate's cheapest food, with tacos and burritos starting at 5 pesos. **Restaurant Jardín Tecate,** next to the tourist office on the southern end of Parque Hidalgo, has unbeatable outdoor seating right in the park. Enjoy *burritos de machaca* (dried shredded beef) or a huge club sandwich (30 pesos) under the shady trees. (☎554 34 53. Open daily 7am-10pm.) You'll feel right at home in the cozy dining room/kitchen of family-run **La Escondida,** on Libertad between Rubio and Rodríguez. Fill up on huge *comida corrida* (25 pesos) and even bigger combination meals of soup, salad, *antojitos,* guacamole, beans, rice, and a drink (50 pesos). Vegetarians will enjoy the *ensalada de aguacate* (30 pesos), a huge bowl of veggies, olives, and lots of avocado. (☎554 21 64. Open M-F 8:30am-6pm, Sa 8:30am-5pm.)

◎🎵 SIGHTS AND ENTERTAINMENT. The town's biggest building, the **Tecate Brewery,** on Hidalgo at Obregón, attracts thousands of beer-loving visitors each year. Opened in 1944, the brewery, officially known as the Cervecería Cuauhtémoc Moctezuma, now pumps out 39 million liters of amber-colored pleasure each month. Groups of five or more can arrange free tours. If you forget to call ahead, **🍺Jardín Cerveza Tecate,** just inside the gate, is still a must. Beer is on the house at this outdoor courtyard shaded by huge palms, but drunkenness is frowned on. Next to the Jardín, a "soubeernir" shop hawks Tecate-emblazoned aprons, clocks, briefcases, and bathing suits, as well as a wide selection of goodies adorned with logos from the company's seven other beers: Bohemia, Carta Blanca, Dos Equis, Indio, Sol, Superior, and the Christmastime-only Noche Buena. (☎654 20 11. Garden open M-F 10am-5:45pm, Sa-Su 10am-4pm.)

Other than hanging out in the Jardín, Tecate offers little in the way of entertainment, which is just the way most visitors like it. South of Juárez near Parque Hidalgo, several self-proclaimed "ladies clubs" cater to groups of hormonally-charged tourists and local men. More mainstream is **Ricky's Bar,** at Juárez and Aldrete. A large, loud disco that serves as the gathering spot for the town's young people, Ricky's offers a variety of pop hits and occasional live music. (Open F-Sa 6pm-2am. 80-100 peso cover, depending on night and event.)

ROSARITO   ☎6

Once a little-known playground of the rich and famous, the Pacific beach haven of Rosarito (pop. 120,000) has become a mecca for sun-seekers of all sizes, shapes, and classes. The town's proximity to California drew elite Hollywood stars to the landmark **Rosarito Beach Hotel.** Today, hordes of *gringos* make the trek across the border every weekend for fun in the sun and cheap booze. Baja California's youngest city, Rosarito only gained municipal status in 1995. The city remains a popular Hollywood filming site—the highest-grossing movie of all time, *Titanic,* was filmed just south of Rosarito in 1996, and the still-standing sets and massive fabricated shipwreck at **Fox Studios Baja** attract wannabe celebrities aplenty.

TRANSPORTATION. To get to Rosarito from **Tijuana,** grab a yellow and white *taxi de ruta* (30min., 9 pesos) from Madero, between Calles 5A and 6A. To return to Tijuana, catch a *taxi de ruta* along Juárez or at its start in front of the Rosarito Beach hotel. To go to **Ensenada**, take a "Primo Tapia" taxi from Festival Plaza, north of the Rosarito Beach Hotel, to the toll booth on Mex. 1 (4 pesos). From there, take a bus to Ensenada (every 30min. 6:30am-9:30pm, 30 pesos).

ORIENTATION AND PRACTICAL INFORMATION. Rosarito lies 27km south of Tijuana. **Mex. 1** runs straight through Rosarito, becoming the city's main drag, **Juárez,** before continuing south. Coming from the toll road, the first Rosarito exit takes you to the north end of Juárez, which, with its non-sequential street numbers and almost universal lack of street signs, can be befuddling. Virtually all the businesses in town are on Juárez—mostly between the huge and very fluorescent Hotel Festival Plaza and the pink Ortega's Restaurant in Oceana Plaza.

The **tourist office,** toward the north end of Juárez in gaudy pink and green Plaza Villa Floresta, offers brochures and a decent map. (☎612 02 00. Open M-F 8am-5pm, Sa-Su 10am-3pm.) **Banamex,** on Juárez at Ortiz, exchanges cash and checks and has a 24hr. **ATM.** (☎612 15 56. Open M-F 8:30am-4:30pm.) For weekend pesos, visit a *casa de cambio* on Juárez and pay commission. **Supermarket: Calimax,** at Cárdenas and Juárez, before Hotel Quinta del Mar heading south on Juárez. (☎612 15 69. Open daily 7am-11pm.) **Lavamática Moderna,** on Juárez at Acacias. (Wash 10 pesos, dry 4 pesos. Open M-Sa 8am-8pm, Su 8am-6pm.) **Emergency:** ☎060. **Police:** (☎612 11 10), at Juárez and Acacias. English spoken. **Red Cross:** (☎613 11 20, emergency 066), on Juárez at Ortíz, around the corner from the police. English spoken. **Farmacia Roma,** at Juárez and Roble. (☎612 35 00. Open 24hr.) **El Tunel.com,** Juárez 208 near Cárdenas, offers **Internet access.** (30 pesos per hr.) The **post office** is on Juárez, near Acacias. (☎612 13 55. Open M-F 8am-3pm.) **Postal code:** 22710.

ACCOMMODATIONS AND FOOD. Most budget hotels in Rosarito are cramped or situated on the outskirts of town. Prices soar during spring break, holidays, and summer weekends. Exceptional **Hotel Palmas Quintero** is tucked away on Privada Guadalupe Victoria 26, a tiny road off Cárdenas, three blocks inland from Hotel Quinta del Mar. Huge rooms have cable TV and clean baths. The everpresent pack of exuberant children will brighten anyone's day. (☎612 13 59. Singles US$20; doubles US$40.) Right on Juárez is gaudy **Hotel El Portal de Rosarito,** at Via de las Olas. The ceaseless din from Juárez may prevent rest despite the spacious rooms with cable TV and A/C. (☎612 00 50. Singles US$26; doubles US$45.) **Alamo Campground,** Calle Alamo 15, less than a block from the beach, has six clean beds for rent. If you need more room to stretch out, they also rent small trailers from US$25. (☎613 11 79. Bunks US$10 in winter, US$15 in summer.)

With tons of pricey restaurants serving international cuisine, Rosarito's culinary scene caters mostly to tourists who consider US$10 cheap. Nevertheless, searching yields quality budget eateries with simple, yummy fare. **La Flor de Michoacán,** Juárez 291, at the north end of town, is a carnivorous paradise. Huge *ordenes de carnitas* (60 pesos) come as either "solid" or "mixed" pork—solid comprises the parts of a pig usually eaten, while mixed includes tongues, stomachs, and all sorts of good stuff. Those with gargantuan appetites can order by the kilogram. (☎612 18 58. 190 pesos per kg. Open daily 9am-10pm.) At **Just for the Halibut Fish Tacos,** Juárez 60, across from Hotel Festival Plaza, enjoy the best tacos in town, if your ears can stand thrash-guitar rock blasting from the stereo. The special combination, two tacos, rice, beans, and a soda (US$3), can't be beat. (Open daily 10am-6pm.)

SIGHTS AND ENTERTAINMENT. Rosarito entices with fancy resorts, beautiful shores, and wild nightlife. Spanning the coast two blocks west of Juárez, **Rosarito Beach** has soft sand and gently rolling surf. The **Museo de Historia Wa Kuatay,** on Juárez next to the Rosarito Beach Hotel, showcases local folk art and

> ### SEEKING PETITE, DANGEROUS SCORPIO
>
> "Scorpions?! But this isn't the jungle," you gasp. Tough break. These nasty little pests (*alacranes* in Spanish) frequent Baja, especially around the mid-peninsula. Unless you are allergic, you won't encounter a slow, painful death—these aren't the fatal black scorpions found in Asia and Africa, but beige, desert-and-beach-camouflaged scorpions. The critters like dark, warm, damp places, so shake your shoes and clothing before you put them on. Most bite victims experience intense pain for a day or two. Ice packs help alleviate the pain, while locals swear that garlic is the best relief. If you wake up in the middle of the night and a scorpion is crawling up your chest, don't try to flatten or squash it—it will get angry and sting your hand. Due to their hard protective armor, scorpions are hard to crush. Instead, give the intruder a hard flick from the side and watch it fly far, far away.

history. Admission and informative personal tours from knowledgeable curator Pedro Arias are free, but donations are welcome. (☎613 06 87. Open W-Su 9am-5pm.) The new **Foxploration** at **Fox Studios Baja,** 2km south of town on the free road, holds a number of exhibits, including props from *Titanic*. (☎614 94 44. Open Th-M 10am-5pm. US$12.) Rosarito's nightlife centers around Hotel Festival Plaza. The hotel itself contains nightlife options including **Cha Cha's,** a loud dance club. Live music on weekends. (Beers US$2.75, mixed drinks US$3.75. Open daily 10am-midnight.) The multitude of clubs on the streets behind the hotel are packed with drunken revelers on weekend and summer nights. **Papas and Beer,** a multilevel party palace, includes a great beach volleyball court. (☎612 04 44. Beer US$2.50. Cover Sa US$5. Open daily 11am-3am.)

ENSENADA   ☎ 6

Despite a lack of beaches and big waves, Ensenada (pop. 370,000) is fast becoming a tourist hotspot. Mexico's second-most popular cruise port entertains *gringos* galore and offers an array of cultural attractions. A strong sense of civic pride and responsibility is evident in Ensenada's clean streets, lined with signs asserting that the best quality of life in all of Mexico can be found here . While the *gringo* surplus can be overwhelming, the cool sea breezes and friendly locals will win you over.

⌗ TRANSPORTATION

GETTING THERE

Ensenada is 108km south of Tijuana on **Mex. 1.** The 1½hr. drive offers a continuous view of the Pacific, and the last 20min. on the Ensenada **cuota** (toll road) are especially breathtaking—if traveling by bus, grab a seat on the right-hand side (car toll 21 pesos). The less scenic **libre** (free road) is a poorly maintained two-lane highway that parallels the *cuota* until La Misión, then cuts inland for the remaining 40km. Drive only during the day—there are no streetlights and many tight curves. Most driving is done in the right lane; the left is for passing only.

GETTING AWAY

Buses: Buses from Tijuana arrive at the **Central de Autobuses,** at Calle 11 and Riveroll. To get to the *centro*, turn right as you come out of the station, walk south 10 blocks, and you'll be at Mateos (also called Primera), the main tourist drag. Transportes Norte de Sonora (☎178 66 80) goes to: **Guaymas** (16hr., every 2hr., 582 pesos) and **Los Mochis** (20hr., 6 per day 7am-9:30pm, 779 pesos). Autotransportes de Baja California (☎178 66 80), runs to: **Guerrero Negro** (10hr.; 6 per day 10am-11pm; 315 pesos); **La Paz** (22hr.; 4 per day 10am-11pm; 730 pesos); **Loreto** (16hr.; 4 per day 10am-11pm; 545 pesos); **Mexicali** (4hr.; 8 per day 5:30am-8pm; 185 pesos); **San Felipe** (4hr.; 8am and 6pm, 160 pesos); **Santa Rosalía** (13hr., 7 and 9:30pm, 385 pesos); **Tijuana** (1½hr., every 30min. 5am-11:30pm, 70-78 pesos). Transportes Brisas (☎178 38 88), at Calle 4 #771, runs buses to small towns nearby.

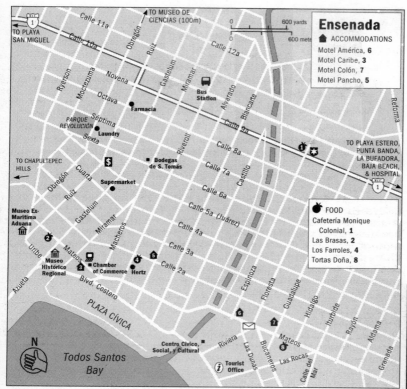

Ensenada
ACCOMMODATIONS
Motel América, **6**
Motel Caribe, **3**
Motel Colón, **7**
Motel Pancho, **5**

FOOD
Cafetería Monique
    Colonial, **1**
Las Brasas, **2**
Los Farroles, **4**
Tortas Doña, **8**

ORIENTATION AND PRACTICAL INFORMATION

Mateos, the main tourist drag, is also known as **Primera** (Calle 1). Numbered *calles*, including **Juárez** (Calle 5) run approximately east-west, and increase to the north. Named *avenidas* run north-south. Street signs are nonexistent more than one block from Mateos. If you're driving, follow signs to downtown Ensenada; these will lead you to **Costero,** one block south of Mateos. Local *urbanos* (☎178 25 94) leave from Juárez at Calle 6, and from Calle 2 at Macheros (7 pesos for most destinations in the city). After sundown, avoid the area near the shore, and use caution while navigating the region bounded by Miramar, Macheros, Mateos, and Calle 4.

Tourist Office, Costero 540 (☎172 30 22; fax 172 30 81), at Azueta. Friendly, English-speaking staff doles out maps and pamphlets in English. Open M-F 8am-5pm, Sa-Su 10am-3pm. The **Chamber of Commerce,** Mateos 693, 2nd fl. (☎178 23 32), at Macheros, is closer to the center of town. Provides brochures and city maps. Open M-F 8:30am-2pm and 4-6:30pm.

Currency Exchange: Banks clutter Juárez at Ruíz. **Bancomer** (☎178 18 01), on Juárez at Ruíz, exchanges dollars and traveler's checks. Open M-F 9am-4pm, Sa 10am-2pm. **ATMs** are everywhere in the bank district.

Supermarket: Supermarket Calimax (☎178 33 97), Gastelum at Calle 4. Open daily 6am-10pm.

Laundry: Lavandería Lavadero (☎178 27 37), on Obregón between Calles 6 and 7, across from Parque Revolución. 16 pesos wash, 3 pesos dry. Open M-Sa 7am-9pm, Su 8am-4pm.

Luggage storage: in the main station. 5 pesos per hour.

Car Rental: Hertz (☎ 178 29 82), Calle 2 at Riveroll. Cars 600 pesos per day with 300km per day limit. Open M-F 8am-6pm, Sa 8-10am.

Emergency: ☎ 060.

Police: (☎ 176 24 21), at Calle 9 at Espinoza. Some English spoken.

Red Cross: (☎ 174 45 85, emergency 066), on Clark at Flores. Some English spoken.

Farmacia San Martín: (☎ 178 35 30 or 178 19 21), at Ruíz and Calle 8. Open 24hr.

Hospital General: (☎ 176 78 00 or 176 77 00), on the Transpeninsular at km 111.

Fax: Telecomm (☎ 177 05 45), on Floresta at Calle 3. Open M-F 8am-6pm, Sa 8-11am.

Internet: Cafe Internet MaxiComm (☎ 175 70 11), on Mateos between Miramar and Gastelum. 15 pesos per 30min., 20 pesos per hr. Open daily 9am-11pm.

Post office: (☎ 176 10 88), on Mateos at Espinoza. Open M-F 8am-3pm, Sa 8am-noon.

Postal code: 22800.

▓ ACCOMMODATIONS

Most of Ensenada's budget hotels line Mateos between Espinoza and Riveroll. Most quote prices in dollars and simply multiply by 10 for those paying in pesos. Lining the beach between Tijuana and Ensenada are RV parks—near Ensenada is **Ramona RV Park,** at km 104 of the Transpeninsular Highway. (☎ 174 60 45. Full hookup for 2 people US$10; each additional person US$2.)

Motel América (☎ 176 13 33), Mateos at Espinoza. Huge, sparkling rooms contain overhead fans, baths, and cable TV; some have kitchens. Singles US$22; doubles US$28.

Motel Caribe, Mateos 627 (☎ 178 34 81). Rooms in the main building are huge, carpeted, and have cable TV, fans, and baths, while those across the street are more modest, and more inexpensive. Ultra-gloomy fluorescent lamps. Singles US$15-30; doubles US$35-45; triples US$55. Rates rise US$5 on weekends.

Motel Colón (☎ 176 19 10), Guadalupe between Mateos and Calle 2. Large, old rooms with cable TV, fans, big baths, and a chance at scoring a kitchenette. Enthusiastic owner Manuel is full of advice and historical lore. Singles US$22; doubles US$30.

Motel Pancho (☎ 178 23 44), on Alvarado at Calle 2, 1 block off Mateos (near the giant flagpole), has large rooms with tiny showers. Singles 140 pesos; doubles 200 pesos.

◖ FOOD

Restaurants on Mateos have pleasant outdoor seating but sky-high prices. Head farther east, to Juárez or Espinoza for more affordable grub. For the best deals in town, visit the fish market on the waterfront west of the huge flag, where a bevy of *loncherías* serve delicious fish tacos for less than US$1 apiece.

Las Brasas, Mateos 486 (☎ 178 11 85), between Ruíz and Gastelum. A budget oasis in the heart of the tourist district. Enjoy a ½-chicken rotisserie grilled before your eyes (49 pesos). Open M-Th noon-8pm, F noon-9pm, Sa-Su noon-9:30pm.

Cafetería Monique Colonial (☎ 176 40 41), Calle 9 at Espinoza. Relax at the diner-style counter amidst packs of chattering locals. A bowl of soup accompanies every meal. Entrees 30-60 pesos. Open M-Sa 6am-10pm, Su 6am-5pm.

Tortas Doñas, Mateos 1478 (☎ 177 36 56), between Guadalupe and Hidalgo. A good option for quick eats. Hefty *tortas* (20-35 pesos) will satiate, and any of the vast selection of *aguas frescas* will wash the meal down nicely. Open daily 9am-10pm.

Los Farroles Villa Mexicana (☎ 178 34 87), Riveroll and Calle 2. Local police crowd this hidden gem. Quick, tasty, and cheap *tortas* (20 pesos) are served at the outdoor counter. Avoid illegal activity during your meal. Open daily 7am-4pm.

SIGHTS

A cosmopolitan dream by Baja California Norte standards, Ensenada is chock full of museums and other cultural attractions for your viewing pleasure.

PLAZA CÍVICA. The second-largest Mexican flag in the country flies in the quiet Plaza Cívica. Eerily large golden busts of Venustiano Carranza, Benito Juárez, and Miguel Hidalgo stare at you as you enjoy the **Ventana al Mar** (Window to the Sea), a pleasant, if unspectacular, view into the city's harbor.

CENTRO CÍVICO, SOCIAL, Y CULTURAL DE ENSENADA. The lovely, Moorish buildings and perfectly maintained grounds of this huge complex once housed a world-famous casino. Today, kids and adults alike paint, sing, and rehearse plays within the center's walls that also contain the **Galeria de Arte de la Ciudad.** *(On Costero, 1 block from the tourist office. ☎177 05 94. Free.)*

MUSEO EX-MARITIMA ADUANA. The oldest building in town, the *museo* holds artifacts and images of early missionary settlements in Baja California, including several church bells. *(Ryerson 99, at Uribe. ☎178 25 31. Open M-F 9am-4pm. Free.)*

BODEGAS DE SANTO TOMÁS. The mild, dry climate of Baja's northern coast has made it Mexico's prime grape-growing area. These *bodegas* have produced wine since 1888. Today, Santo Tomás distills over 500,000 cases of wine and champagne each year. Tours include tasting complete with breads and cheeses. *(Miramar 666, at Calle 7. ☎178 33 33. Tours daily 11am, 1, and 3pm. Open M-F 8am-5pm. 20 pesos.)*

MUSEO HISTÓRICO REGIONAL. The museum houses artifacts and photographs from all over Baja California. Originally built in 1886 as barracks, it is the oldest public building in the state. The building was converted to a jail in 1914 and served as such until 1986. *(Near the Museo Ex-Maritima on Gastelum between Uribe and Mateos. ☎178 25 31. Open Tu-Su 10am-5pm. Free, but donations welcome.)*

MUSEO DE CIENCIAS. Housed in an old wooden boat, the museum displays photographs of and information about the endangered species of Baja California. *(Obregón 1463, at Catorce, a 15min. walk from Mateos. ☎178 71 92. Open M-F 9am-5pm, Sa noon-5pm. 15 pesos, children 12 pesos.)*

CHAPULTEPEC HILLS. A stunning view of the bay and the city from a ritzy residential neigborhood west of town. *(To reach the top, follow Calle 2 up the steep hills until you can't go any higher—about 15-20min.)*

🎵 ENTERTAINMENT

Mateos is packed with popular restaurant/bar/disco establishments, which stuff tourists with overpriced food during the day and overpriced booze at night. To escape the chaos, head to the multitude of pool halls on Calle 2a, which are perpetually jammed by locals. No trip to Ensenada would be complete without a pilgrimage to ◼**Hussong's Cantina,** Ruiz 113, the most famous bar in Baja and possibly Mexico. A venerable 107-year-old watering hole, Hussong's maintains some semblance of Mexican flavor with dusty floors and deer heads on the walls. (☎178 32 10. Beer 20 pesos, margaritas 27 pesos. Open daily 10am-1am.) If you tire of *mariachi*, cross the street to **Papas and Beer,** an ultra-modern bar/dance party. Packed with college students, Papas is loud, rowdy, and serves up good margaritas for a price. (40 pesos. ☎174 01 45. Th live music. F ladies night 8-10pm. Cover US$5. Open Su-Th noon-2am, F-Sa 10am-3am.)

Those looking to stay sober can kick back at **Cinemas Ensenada,** on Juárez at Ruiz, which screens recent American hits, most subtitled and some dubbed into Spanish. (☎178 86 79. Shows daily 4-10pm. 25 pesos.)

BAJA CALIFORNIA

DAYTRIPS FROM ENSENADA

Ensenada is an excellent base for exploring Baja California. Unfortunately, you'll need wheels, ideally with 4-wheel-drive, to reach many of them. The best rental rates can be found in Tijuana or San Diego (see **Tijuana: Car Rental,** p. 139).

BAHÍA DE TODOS SANTOS
Good sand and a nice swim can be found on the beaches along Bahía de Todos Santos, to the west of the city, stretching down to the Punta Banda Peninsula.

PLAYA SAN MIGUEL. Made up of large rocks, the beach isn't of any use to sun-worshippers or swimmers, but the large waves breaking off shore attract a healthy supply of surfer dudes. *(Drive North on Calle 10 to the toll gate and take a left on the road marked "Playa San Miguel." Alternatively, catch a "San Miguel" bus departing Gastelum at Costero (6.5 pesos). Buses back must be flagged down.)*

PLAYA ESTERO. Packed with volleyball courts, banana boats, and people, Playa Estero is a pleasant, if not secluded, place to pass the time. The area can get muddy during low tides, when sea lions come ashore—keep your eyes peeled. Access is available through the **Estero Beach Resort,** which houses the **Estero Beach Museum,** an impressive display of Mexican folk art. *(Take a right at the "Estero Beach" sign on Mex. 1 heading south. Free parking available in the first lot of the hotel. Alternatively, catch a bus marked "Aeropuerto," "Zorrillo," "Maneadero," or "Chapultepec" from Pl. Cívica. Museum ☎ 177 55 20. Open W-M 9am-6pm. Free. Beach open daily 8am-5pm.)*

PLAYA EL FARO. Playa El Faro, 10km south of town, is similarly rife with volleyball courts and *norteamericanos,* but has slightly better sand and allows camping on the beach. Another nearby beach is **Playa Santa María,** which has horse rentals. *(El Faro ☎ 177 46 20. Camp space, parking, and bathroom privileges US$7 per car. Full RV hookup US$12. Rooms for 2 people US$30; for 4 people US$50.)*

PUNTA BANDA
Take a right onto the Transpeninsular Highway off Mateos at the south end of town, and head past exits for the airport, military base, and Playa Estero. Take a right on Mex. 23 after 20min. at the "La Bufadora" sign. This road goes the length of the Punta Banda peninsula. To traverse the peninsula by public transport, take a yellow microbús from Ensenada to the town of Maneadero (7 pesos), at the start of the peninsula, and get a connecting "Nativos" bus to La Bufadora (3 pesos). The driver will let you off anywhere along Mex. 23, but a return trip is not assured.

Punta Banda, the peninsula at the southern end of Bahía de Todos Santos, boasts better hiking and more secluded beaches than the north. The mountains around **La Bufadora,** a geyser near the tip of the peninsula, are laced with beautiful, serene trails. Many parts of the peninsula are equally breathtaking, and warrant exploration. The following sights are listed in order from mainland to peninsular tip.

BAJA BEACH. The clean, soft, and uncrowded sands are buffeted by small waves and provide some of the best swimming in the area. The rolling hills provide a pleasant backdrop for sunbathing, swimming, and relaxing. Horses are often available for rent. The Baja Beach Resort runs a pool of **hot springs** on the left side of Mex. 1, 2km before the Punta Banda road. *(By car, bear right at the 1st fork after turning onto the Punta Banda road. Follow the signs saying "Horses for rent" and "Aguacaliente" that lead to the beach. Beware, the loose packed sand can trap cars.)*

THE TOWN OF PUNTA BANDA. The town of Punta Banda is little more than a roadside **grocery market,** some fruit stands, and a tiny **post office.** *(Open M-F 8am-3pm.)* You can camp or park an RV in town at **Villarino,** adjacent to the plaza, which has modern bathroom facilities and full hookups. *(☎154 20 45; fax 54 20 44. 65 pesos per person, 45 pesos per child. Call for reservations.)*

CERRO DE LA PUNTA. The best spot to enter the hiking trails of Punta Banda is Cerro de la Punta, on the road to La Bufadora near the end of the peninsula. Hike the mountains for views of the surrounding area or descend beautiful trails to the ocean. Bring food for cliffside picnics and a bathing suit to refresh your body in the chilly Pacific. Best of all, the area is essentially undiscovered by tourists. Most of the trails are unmarked footpaths and dirt roads. Be sure to stay on the paths; trail blazing will damage surrounding flora. *(Turn right up a long driveway at the "Cerro de la Punta" sign. You'll see a small clearing and a large house on the cliffs. Parking 10 pesos.)*

LA BUFADORA. The Pacific coast's largest geyser is one of Ensenada's biggest attractions. Souvenir vendors take advantage of "the blowhole's" popularity, cramming the road with curio shops and restaurants. The geyser itself is a natural cave through which seawater is forced by the ebbing waves, causing water to burst up to 40m into the air, accompanied by dramatic snorts. The fabulous view of the Pacific from the parking lot should console those who don't see La Bufadora on a good day. *(Parking US$1 or 10 pesos.)*

PARQUE NACIONAL CONSTITUCIÓN DE 1857

Follow Mex. 3 from Juárez east toward San Felipe and Ojos Negros. At the military checkpoint, stay on Mex. 3 toward San Felipe. Around km 58, turn left onto a marked dirt road leading into the park and continue for 1¼-1½hr. The road is usually passable (with caution) by a passenger car, but be sure to inquire about current conditions in Ensenada before venturing into the wilderness.

Situated 1650m above sea level, the 5009 hectare **Parque Nacional de Constitución** is unlike anyplace else in Baja. The focal point of the park is Laguna Hanson, a small lake frequented by grazing cows. Campsites with fire circles surround the laguna (US$7 for a tent spot). The park's design does not seem to have hikers in mind. The towering pines and granite boulder mountains are enticing, but try to explore them and you'll be stopped short by *"Zona Restringada"* (Restricted Area) signs. Nevertheless, a few excellent hiking trails are accessible. The *Aventura en el bosque* (Adventure in the woods) is a 2km loop beginning west of Laguna Hanson. Signs along the trail point out various plants and animals in the park, including coyotes, rattlesnakes, and pumas, which the sign admits "occasionally attack humans." If planning on camping in the park, bring warm clothes and a good sleeping bag—temperatures drop dramatically at night.

MEXICALI ☎ 6

Capital of Baja California, the sprawling industrial metropolis of Mexicali (pop. 1.2 million) presents a stark contrast to the endless stretches of barren desert surrounding the city. Mexicali straddles both the US and the Mexican mainland in a colorful chaotic maze of liquor stores, auto shops, and Chinese restaurants. Huge industrial plants skirt the southern edges while a constant stream of cars inches across the northern border. Founded in 1903, Mexicali was first settled by cotton pickers and laborers for the Colorado River Land Company, and many, including thousands of Chinese immigrants, stayed on, creating a unique Chino-Mexican culture that is evident in the architecture, cuisine, and even the dialect of Mexicali. Pollution and overwhelming crowds deter most tourists, but Mexicali is not all industrial wasteland. Shady parks, stunning cathedrals, towering monuments, cultural centers, professional sports facilities, and even a forest within city limits offer a wide array of options for dallying visitors.

▐ TRANSPORTATION

To get to the **Central de Autobuses** (☎ 557 24 51) take any bus headed south (away from the *frontera*) on Mateos (every 10min., 4.5 pesos) to the intersection of Mateos and Independencia, two blocks south of the big Plaza de Toros on your right. The station is one block farther west on Independencia. To get to the **border** from the bus station, cross the footbridge just outside the station and hop on the local bus marked "Centro" (every 10 min. 5am-11pm, 4.5 pesos). When the bus goes around the rotary and starts heading the other way on Mateos, it's time to get off. The border is five blocks farther north on Mateos. All buses leaving Mexicali are *de paso*. Autotransportes de Baja California (☎557 24 15) goes to: **Ensenada** (14hr., 6 per day, 185 pesos); **Puerto Peñasco** (5hr., 6 per day, 180 pesos); **San Felipe** (2hr., 6 per day, 118 pesos); **Tijuana** (3hr., every hr., 125 pesos). Elite (☎557 24 50) covers the same routes for slightly higher prices and also heads to: **Chihuahua** (17hr., 10:30am and 2:30pm, 763 pesos); **Ciudad Juárez** (15hr., 4 per day, 629 pesos); **Nogales** (9hr., 11am, 364 pesos). Transportes Nortes de Sonora (☎557 24 10) motors east to **Guaymas** (11hr., every hr., 378 pesos); **Hermosillo** (9hr., every hr., 315 pesos); **Los Mochis** (17hr., every hr., 560 pesos). Golden State (☎553 61 69) can take you to **Los Angeles, CA** (4½hr., 5 per day, US$30) via Coachella, Colton, and Onteria; and **Phoenix, AZ** (6hr., 1 per day, US$40) via Yuma and Tucson.

■ 🕑 ORIENTATION AND PRACTICAL INFORMATION

Mexicali straddles the US border 189km inland from Tijuana, just south of Calexico and California's Imperial Valley. Plagued with zig-zagging, haphazardly numbered streets, Mexicali can be incredibly difficult to navigate. If you drive across the border you'll end up on Mateos, the main boulevard in the *centro*, which heads southeast through **La Chinesca** (Chinatown), past the enormous mall to the civic center, where government and big business coexist with the bulls of the Plaza de Toros. From there continue past the *Central de Autobuses* and the ritzy clubs and restaurants of the **Zona Hotelera** before leaving town, where the road becomes México 2. Both north-south *calles* and east-west *avenidas* intersect Mateos.

Tourist Office: Comité de Turismo y Convenciones (☎557 23 76; fax 552 58 77), the adobe-colored building on Mateos facing the Vicente Guerrero Monument and park, 3km south of the border. Take any bus headed away from the border on Mateos, and get off at the rotary after Plaza Cachanilla. Loads of brochures, huge maps, and knowledgeable English-speaking staff. Open M-F 8am-6pm. For **tourist cards,** visit the Mexican customs office in the immigration office at the border.

Currency Exchange: *Casas de cambio* line Madero, and banks occupy every corner in *La Chinesca.* **Banamex,** at Morelos and Madero, changes currency and has a 24hr. **ATM.** Open M-F 9am-5pm. So does **Bancomer** (☎553 46 10), closer to the border on Madero at Azueta. Open M-F 8:30am-4pm.

Car Rental: Budget (☎556 48 40), Mateos and Los Héroes in the Holiday Inn Crowne Plaza. Call ahead and let them know you're coming. **Hertz,** Juárez 1223 (☎568 19 73), opposite the Hotel Araiza Inn. Open M-F 8am-6pm, Sa 8am-12:30pm. **Optima,** Sierra 901 (☎568 29 19), next to the Siesta Inn. Open M-Sa 8am-8pm, Su 8am-1pm.

Luggage Storage: In the **convenience store** in the bus station, to the right as you enter the station. 6 pesos per hr.

Laundromat: Lavamática Josue, Obregón and Morelos. Wash 10 pesos, dry 10 pesos. Bring your own detergent. Open M-Sa 9am-8pm.

Emergency: ☎060.

Police: (☎060) at Calle Sur and Mateos. Some English spoken.

Red Cross: Cárdenas 1492 (☎552 92 75), Quinta and Durango. Some English spoken.

Pharmacy: Farmacia Patty's, México 305 (☎554 14 06), south of Obregón. Open 24hr.

Hospital: IMSS (☎555 51 50), Lerdo at Calle G. English spoken. **Hospital General** (☎556 11 23, through 28), Calle del Hospital at Libertad. Some English spoken. **Hospital Mexico-Americano** (☎552 23 00), Reforma at Calle B.

Fax: Telecomm (☎552 20 02), next to the post office. Open M-F 8am-6pm, Sa 8am-3pm, Su 8am-1pm.

Internet Access: La Zona Internet and Games Club, Plaza Cachanilla 7B (☎552 40 08), offers blazing fast computers. 38 pesos per hr. Open daily 10am-9:30pm.

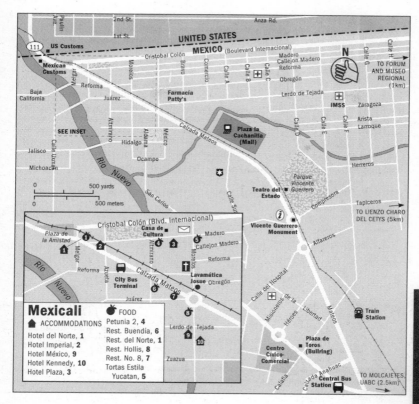

Mexicali

🏠 ACCOMMODATIONS
Hotel del Norte, **1**
Hotel Imperial, **2**
Hotel México, **9**
Hotel Kennedy, **10**
Hotel Plaza, **3**

🍖 FOOD
Petunia 2, **4**
Rest. Buendia, **6**
Rest. del Norte, **1**
Rest. Hollis, **8**
Rest. No. 8, **7**
Tortas Estila
Yucatan, **5**

Post Office: Madero 491 (☎552 25 08), at Morelos. Open M-F 8:30am-6:30pm, Sa 9am-1pm.

Postal Code: 21100.

🏨 ACCOMMODATIONS

La Chinesca overflows with budget hotels. Ask to see a room before you pay—it may be unworthy of your money. Hotels on Madero close to Mateos dig deeper into your wallet but tend to be cleaner and safer for women traveling alone.

Hotel México, Lerdo 476 (☎554 06 69), at Morelos. Clean, cheerful pink rooms with TV and super-cold A/C surround the central gated parking lot. The office doubles as a grocery store. Free parking. Singles and doubles 260 pesos.

Hotel Kennedy, Morelos 415 (☎554 90 62), between Lerdo and Zuazua. Large, slightly dim rooms boast TVs, A/C, phones, and the ugliest carpets known to man. Helpful management and huge baths make it even better. Singles and doubles 200 pesos.

Hotel Plaza, Madero 366 (☎552 97 57), between Altamirano and Morelos, puts distance between you and bustling *la Chinesca* with carpeted floors, soft cushy beds, A/C, TVs, phones, and spacious baths. Singles 290 pesos; doubles 540 pesos.

Hotel Imperial, Madero 222 (☎553 67 90; fax 552 29 01). Rooms come equipped with big, comfy beds, carpeting, A/C, phones, private baths, and even cable TV. Singles and doubles 360 pesos.

Hotel del Norte (☎554 00 24), on Madero at Melgar. Compared to other *frontera* hotels, this bright pink Art Deco building with cheerful carpeted rooms, huge TVs, and attentive staff seems like paradise—for double the price, that is. Singles 410 pesos.

FOOD

Mexicali has more Chinese restaurants per capita than any other city in Mexico, most of them concentrated in the border area cleverly dubbed *La Chinesca*. Restaurants offering lunchtime specialties and veggie combinations line Juárez and Lerdo south of Mateos. For even cheaper fare head to the food court in Plaza la Cachanilla, where huge combination plates of 3-5 entrees cost less than 25 pesos. If soy sauce isn't your thing, you can chow down on hearty *tortas de carne asada* (15 pesos) at any of the sandwich stands on Madero and Reforma west of Mateos.

Petunia 2 (☎552 69 51), Madero between Altamirano and Morelos, dishes out tasty and strictly Mexican *comida corrida* (34 pesos) at a friendly, colorful outdoor counter with bar-style seating and a private parking lot. Open daily 7am-9pm.

Restaurant No. 8, Juárez 150 (☎555 54 35), at Mateos. No. 8 is the perfect stop to placate your growling tummy after a night on the town. Massive combinations of soup, egg rolls, and entrees 40 pesos. Open 24hr.

Restaurant Buendía, Altamirano 263 (☎552 69 25). Despite sharing a name with the illustrious family of Gabriel García Márquez's epic *100 Years of Solitude*, Buendía specializes in Chinese cuisine—but chefs are always happy to whip up some *antojitos*. Heaping plate of beef with broccoli, fried rice, egg roll, and fried chicken 32 pesos; veggie combo 32 pesos. Open daily 7am-9pm.

Restaurant del Norte, Madero 205 at Melgar (☎552 81 01, ext. 42), downstairs in Hotel del Norte. Huge portions of decent Mexican food, and a great place to watch the flow of people to and from the border, only 1 block away. Open daily 7am-10:30pm.

Tortas Estilo Yucatán, at Morelos and Madero (☎552 31 32). Huge, filling *tortas* (30 pesos) served in a chaotic but friendly atomosphere. Open daily 9am-9pm.

Restaurant Hollis (☎552 66 96), Morelos and Mateos near Juárez. Feast on chop suey, *huevos rancheros*, or french fries at the multi-cultural Hollis. Chinese *comida corrida* 40 pesos, sandwiches 20 pesos, Mexican breakfast 20 pesos. Open daily 10am-9pm.

⊙ SIGHTS

A major attraction for kids and grownups alike, Mexicali's **Bosque y Zoológico** is on Alvarado between San Marcos and Cárdenas in the southwestern part of town. To get there, hop on a southbound black and white "Sta. Isabel" bus at the stop on Juárez, near Mateos. Get off when you see the Bosque's entrance in front of you. If you're driving, head south on Azueta over the Río Nuevo. The road becomes Uxmal south of the river; turn left on Independencia, then right on Victoria. Admire birds in the aviary, pedal paddleboats on the lake, or pity the lions, tigers, and bears panting in the hot sun. The grounds contain carousels, bumper cars, tons of jungle gyms and playground equipment, a small water park (15 pesos per hr.), and a **science museum.** (☎558 63 76. Open Tu-Su 9am-5pm. 13 pesos, children 6 pesos.) Take it easy and mingle with young lovers and families enjoying the jungle gyms, picnic spots, and grassy lawns at **Parque Vicente Guerrero,** off Mateos right next door to the mall. (☎554 55 63. Open Tu-Sa 8am-10pm.) Closer to the border on Madero between Azueta and Altamirano is **Parque Niños Héroes de Chapultepec,** a small grassy park full of trees and ice cream vendors.

The bright orange **Catedral de la Virgen de Guadalupe,** on Morelos at Reforma, provides a more sedate experience. The cathedral is part of *La Parroquía de Mexicali*, founded in 1918 by Padre Juan Rossi after he discovered that no official church existed and the sacraments were being administered out of a tiny shack. (Open M-Sa 7am-9pm, Su 7am-6pm.) To learn more about Mexicali's past, visit the **Museo Regional,** on Reforma at Calle L. (☎552 57 15. Open M-F 9am-6pm, Sa-Su 9am-4pm. 6 pesos.)

♫ 🎦 ENTERTAINMENT AND NIGHTLIFE

Unless you're looking for strip clubs, most entertainment options in Mexicali lie in the eastern part of town, away from the budget hotels. Public buses stop running at 11pm, so you'll have to call it an early night, take a cab, or make the trek on foot—which can be dangerous as you get closer to *La Chinesca*. Relatively close to the border are ■**Cafe Olé** and **Olé Patio and Fun** at Reforma 1150, between Calles B and C. The cafe is a bar and restaurant that draws a slightly older, more sedate crowd. (Open Tu-Su 6pm-2am.) **Patio and Fun** is the Cafe's younger, louder, and wilder brother. Offering live music (W and F-Sa) in a large open air venue with thatched roof bars, Patio and Fun is the place to see and be seen for Mexicali's *jovenes*. (☎568 31 11. US$5 cover for Patio). Right next door, **Mandalinos**, Reforma 1070 (☎552 95 44), is a classy Italian restaurant by day and a hopping bar by night. Mandalino's offers occasional live music free of cover, but they'll make you pay with drinks—beers are US$3. **Forum** (☎552 40 91), Reforma and Justo Sierra, is a large and rowdy *discoteca* popular with a younger crowd. If you're looking for dependable *musica en vivo*, head to trendy **Molcayetes** (☎556 07 00), on Montegano south of Independencia. Most clubs get busy around 11pm and keep the music and liquor flowing until 2 or 3am.

The huge **Plaza de Toros Calafia** (☎554 43 73), on Calafia at Independencia, hosts regularly scheduled bullfights (monthly on Sa) and other events. To get there, get on a blue-and-white "Centro Cívico" bus headed away from the border at the *centro* stops at Mateos and Reforma (10min., 4.5 pesos). Tickets for the bullfights range from 50 pesos to 400 pesos, but almost all the seats in the house offer a great view, and the plaza holds up to 10,000 people (9999 when the bull has a good day). Wild and crazy rodeos rampage in the winter and spring at **Lienzo Charro del Cetys**, at Cetys and Ordente. Check with the tourist office for schedules.

Mexicali boasts two major theaters and a very active **Casa de la Cultura**, on Madero and Altamirano, just west of the post office. Hundreds of people, from grade school students to senior citizens, flock to this beautiful Neoclassical building to study sculpture, drawing, painting, theater, dance, and English. The Casa holds rotating displays of student art, and presents plays, concerts, and dance shows. (☎553 40 57 or 557 14 17. Open M-F 9am-9pm.) **UABC**, the university, also presents cultural and theatrical performances in its theatre and has artistic displays in the **Galeria Universitaria** and **Sala de Arte** on campus (☎566 42 76 for more information). If you're looking for a major play, symphony, or musical, visit **Teatro del Estado**, on Mateos at the northern end of Parque Vincente Guerrero. (☎554 64 18 or 554 64 19. Shows approximately 150 pesos.)

SAN FELIPE ☎ 6

San Felipe (pop. 25,000) may put on Mexican airs, but it's a tourist-oriented beach town at heart. From Monday to Thursday, San Felipe has the feel of the idyllic fishing village that it once was, and its roads are almost free from *gringos* and annoying ATV noise pollution. On weekends and in high season, however, the town morphs into a tourist zoo, as hotels fill up with North American families and the streets become lined with souvenir vendors. Surrounded by stunning desert valleys and sparkling sand dunes, San Felipe deserves all the attention it gets. The laid back, scenic town offers a stellar selection of seafood and a beautiful stretch of beach teased by the warm, shallow waters of the gulf. This is the perfect place to relax for a day, but beware—before you know it, a day will become a week.

▐ TRANSPORTATION

San Felipe has two bus stations. The main one is on Mar Caribe, just south of Manzanillo (☎577 15 16). To walk downtown (15min.), head north on Mar Caribe and turn right onto Manzanillo. Walk until you see Hotel Costa Azul, until Mar de Cortés, the main drag, a block from the beach. A smaller station is located closer to the center of town at Mar Blanco and Acapulco. Autotransportes de Baja California stops first at the main station and then at the smaller one on its way to: **Ensenada** (3½hr., 8am and 6pm, 170 pesos); **Mexicali** (2½hr., 5 per day 6am-8pm, 118 pesos); **Tijuana** (5 per day 6am-4pm, 243 pesos).

✦ ⓘ ORIENTATION AND PRACTICAL INFORMATION

San Felipe is 190km south of Mexicali at the end of dip-plagued Mex. 5. The town is also accessible via Mex. 3 from Ensenada, a poorly maintained paved road. Los Arcos (a tall, white double arch) marks the entrance to town. **Chetumal** continues straight from the arch toward the sea. Hotels, restaurants, and curio shops cluster on **Mar de Cortés**, which runs parallel to the beach. The **malecón**, lined with seafood stands, lies just east of Cortés along the beach. Paralleling the *malecón* and Mar de Cortés, *avenidas* are named for international seas. Starting one block west of Mar de Cortés, **Mar Baltico, Mar de Tazmania, Mar Catabrico, Mar Negro, Mar Blanco**, and **Mar Bermejo** all run north-south. Perpendicular to the *avenidas*, *calles* are named for Mexican port cities and run east-west. From north to south they are **Acapulco, Chetumal, Ensenada, Topolobambo, Manzanillo**, and **Isla de los Cedros.**

Tourist Office: Mar de Cortés 300 (☎577 18 65 or 577 11 55), at Manzanillo. Cheerful, English-speaking speaking staffers will load you up with information and maps. Open M-F 8am-5pm, Sa-Su 10am-3pm. For a US perspective, direct questions to Linda at the **People's Gallery,** 2 blocks south of the tourist office on Mar de Cortés. Open daily mid-Sept. to mid-June 9am-4pm.

Currency Exchange: Bancomer (☎/fax 577 10 90), Mar de Cortés Norte at Acapulco, is the only bank in town. It exchanges cash and traveler's checks, and has a 24hr. **ATM.** Open M-F 8:30am-4pm, Sa 10am-2pm.

Emergency: ☎060.

Police: (☎577 11 34), on Isla de los Cedros at Mar Negro. Some English spoken.

Red Cross: (☎577 15 44, emergency 066), at Mar Bermejo and Peñasco. English spoken.

Pharmacy: Farmacia San José, Mazatlán 523 (☎577 13 87). Open 24 hr.

Medical Assistance: Centro de Salud (☎577 15 21), on Mar Bermejo between Chetumal and Ensenada. English spoken.

Fax: Copicentro (☎577 14 02; fax 577 14 66), on Chetumal. Open daily 8am-9pm.

Internet Access: The Net (☎577 16 00), next to the People's Gallery on Mar de Cortes. US$2 per 15min. Open Oct.-May M-Sa 8am-4pm, June-Sept. M-Sa 8am-1pm.

Post office: (☎577 13 30), Mar Blanco at Ensenada. Open M-F 8am-3pm, Sa 9am-1pm.

Postal code: 21850.

⌂ ACCOMMODATIONS

One of the most expensive cities in one of the most expensive parts of the country, San Felipe has limited choices for budget travelers. Most accommodations line Mar de Cortés and Mar Baltico near the beach, and as a general rule, the smaller the hotel, the lower the price. Expect prices to rise US$5-10 during weekends, and more in high season. If you can't afford to sleep in a bed, camping on the federally owned *playas* is, as always, perfectly legal, but tourist officials warn against it. If you must camp, do so within an established RV park. For bargain accomodations, try renting a room in a private home. Look for signs that say *"se rentan cuartos"* (rooms for rent), and enjoy cozy accommodations and good conversation.

☒ **Carmelita's** (☎577 18 31), a 4-room motel across from Motel Chapala, has super powerful A/C, mini refrigerators, *agua purificada,* spacious bathrooms, and cable TV. You'll have to watch whatever the owners choose, though, as there's only 1 cable input that channels to all the rooms. Singles and doubles 300 pesos; 250 pesos per night for stays of 4 or more days.

La Posada de Don Jesús Mini Motel, on Ensenada at Mar Baltico. If you don't have your own trailer, try renting one at La Posada. Each comes equipped with kitchenette, electricity, running water, and a funky smell—you may need to leave the door open. Smaller trailers US$25; larger US$30.

Ruben's (☎577 20 21), toward the end of Golfo de California in Playa Norte, is the best known RV park. At the end of Mar de Cortés, turn left onto Golfo de California. Ruben's is a 10min. walk. Beachfront and other spaces are topped with cool 2-story, open-air bungalows that look like *palapa* tree-forts. Each spot easily accommodates carloads of folks with sleeping bags, and RVs can hook up to electricity, hot water, and sewer connections. There's a restaurant and bar on the premises, so you don't have to walk to town to party. 2 people in summer US$15, US$20 on weekends; in winter US$12; each additional person US$2. Office open daily 7am-7pm.

Campo San Felipe (☎577 10 12), Mar de Cortés, just south of Manzanillo, lures campers with a fabulous beachfront location close to the center of town. A thatched roof shelters each fully loaded trailer spot. Spots US$10-20; each additional person US$2, children under 6 free; tent space US$10.

Casey's Beach Cabins (☎577 14 31), on Mar y Sol, a private road 2 blocks past Campo San Felipe off Mar de Cortés, is among the best deals in town if you're traveling with 2 or more people. Modern condos have 2 bedrooms, kitchenette, A/C, and satellite TV with a mind-blowing 155+ channels. Pristine location on a quiet stretch of beach south of the noisy, littered public beach. Condos US$55 per night, up to 10 people.

FOOD

Mar de Cortés is crammed with restaurants advertising air-conditioned relief, while fish *taquerías* line the *malecón*, offering shrimp, fish, or *carne asada* tacos (8-10 pesos). Locals rave about **Arturo's,** on Mar Baltico between Chetumal and Ensenada. Enjoy yummy tortilla soup, which accompanies big Mexican combination plates (*enchiladas*, taco, burrito, rice, and beans; 50 pesos) while you admire Arturo's own paintings of San Felipe. Try the best (and biggest) margaritas in town (25 pesos) to wash it all down. Unfortunately, Arturo closes shop from June-Aug. (Open daily Sept-May 10am-10pm.) Feast on beef, chicken, or shrimp enchiladas (23 pesos) and a calming view of the sea at **Restaurant El Club,** on the *malecón* at Acapulco. (☎577 11 75. Delicious *carne asada* 35 pesos. Open daily 7am-10:30pm.) **Restaurant los Mandiles (Luis's Corner),** at the corner of Mar de Cortés and Chetumal, is a great spot for a peaceful breakfast. Serves excellent *huevos rancheros* (25 pesos) and real-brewed coffee. (☎577 11 68. Open daily 7am-11pm.)

SIGHTS AND BEACHES

Each year, more than 250,000 people come to San Felipe to swim in the warm, tranquil, and invitingly blue waters of the Sea of Cortés. The beach in town follows the *malecón* and gets very crowded on weekends. South of town, away from the rumbling of shrimping boats and jet skis, clearer water and peaceful beaches provide a better setting for snorkeling. The southern beaches are also a seashell collector's paradise; low tides reveal perfect sand dollars and thousands of colorful shells. Land-lubbers can rent ATVs from any of the setups along Mar de Cortés; friendly local Tito sets up shop every day outside Campo San Felipe and charges US$20 per hr. For extra fun in the water, choose from the jet skis (US$20 per hr.) and the banana boats (30-50 pesos per 20min.) waiting along the beach.

Take time to visit the **Capilla de la Virgen de Guadalupe,** a shrine to the virgin at the top of a small hill north of the town center, off Mar de Cortes. Breathtaking views of the town, the sparkling blue bay, and the surrounding hills await you at the end of a 2min. climb. The world's largest strand of *cardón* cacti makes its home at the foot of the Sierra San Pedro Martir, 20km southeast of San Felipe.

Nicknamed **Valle de los Gigantes,** this hidden valley was the original home of the giant cactus that represented Mexico at the 1992 World's Fair in Seville, Spain. To reach the valley, drive south on Mex. 5 away from town to a small dirt road on the right marked with a sign proclaiming *"Sahuaro, Valle de Los Gigantes,"* and turn right onto the dirt road. Local ranchers don't mind letting visitors in as long as you remember to close the fence behind you (or you'll let the cows out). Passenger vehicles with partially deflated tires should be able to navigate the sandy terrain. In the valley, towering *cardón* (many nearly 15m tall), thorny orange-tipped *ocotillo*, bearded *abuelo* (grandfather), and easily-provoked jumping *cholla* cacti shelter a small community of cows, roadrunners, jackrabbits, coyotes, and other desert dwellers. Local activists are campaigning for designation of the Valle as a national reserve in order to protect the gnarly 200-year-old *cardón*.

For an escape from the tourist zoo of San Felipe, pay a visit to the tiny village of **Puertocitos** (pop. 130), 90km south of town down a treacherous paved road—allow at least 3hr. for the drive. Visitors come to enjoy the refreshing hot springs, but remember to bring nose clips—the sulphur smell can be overpowering. **Casey Hamlin,** on Mar y Sol, a private road two blocks south of Campo San Felipe in town, offers interpretive tours of the San Felipe area, including treks to Valle de los Gigantes, Puertocitos, and a petrified forest. (☎577 14 31. Open daily 8am-8pm. Tours require a minimum of 4 people and cost US$25-55 per person, depending on length. Kayak rental US$20 1st hr., US$15 each additional hr.)

🎵 ENTERTAINMENT

San Felipe courts tourists with beautiful beaches—and an enormous variety of venues to get tipsy or blasted. The biggest parties in town go down at **Rockodile** and **Beach Comber;** both are packed most weekends and overflowing during Spring Break. Rockodile, on the *malecón* at Acapulco, attracts a young crowd with a central volleyball/basketball/soccer court, outdoor terrace, and loud pop music. The relatively low-key daytime crowd gets shoved out at night by a super-sweaty dance party. Try the obscenely-named electric-blue king-sized beverage (US$4) to begin inducing amnesia. (☎577 12 19. Sa cover US$3. Open daily 11am-3am.) A block down the *malecón* lies Beach Comber, Rockodile's marginally less rowdy cousin. Beach Comber spends its days posing as a sports bar, complete with mellow beer-sipping tourists, but changes into a raucous dance party at night. On busy nights, you may be lucky (or unlucky) enough to encounter a *fiesta de espuma*, or suds party. (☎577 21 22. Beer 13 pesos, mixed drinks 30-35 pesos. Open daily 10am-2am.) Seasoned veterans nurse drinks at **Bar Miramar,** at the north end of the *malecón*. The oldest bar in San Felipe may look like a 60s *cantina*, but the patrons come for friendly company and an escape from the debauchery and glitz. Play a round of pool on the open-air patio overlooking the sea. (☎577 11 92. Beer 15 pesos, margaritas 25 pesos. Open M-Th 10am-2am, F-Su 10am-3am.)

YOU SAY TOMATO, I SAY CLAMATO Everyone knows that *mexicanos* prefer to drink their beer with a bit of *limón*, and most tourists quickly embrace the habit, believing themselves to be sophisticated and knowledgeable of Mexican culture. If you don't know what a clamato is, however, you'll never convince a true local, especially not a sea-side dweller, of your cultural savvy. A bottled blend of *almeja* (clam) and tomato juices, and ubiquitous in *mercado* refrigerators, clamato makes a versatile mixer for vodka, tequila, rum...or Tecate, and often appears on drink lists throughout Baja California. The next time you find yourself seated in a restaurant watching neighboring groups of men down salty glasses of a peculiar orange mixture at a table littered with bottles of salsa (the more *picante* the better), order up a clamato and *cerveza*, squeeze in a few *limones* and splash on some salsa to taste.

VALLE DE SAN QUINTÍN   ☎ 6

On the lonely mid-Pacific coast of northern Baja, the unassuming San Quintín Valley is the lifeblood of Baja California agriculture. Nearly every square inch of land enclosed by the huge barren mountains to the east and the Pacific Ocean to the west earns its keep as cropland. The region's three main towns, conveniently located one after the other on Mexico 1, are: **San Quintín, Lázaro Cárdenas** (not to be confused with the other Lázaro Cárdenas, 100km to the northeast), and **El Eje del Papaloto.** The few tourists who visit Valle de San Quintín usually come for the superb fishing and surfing in and around the bay. They may not look like much, but the sleepy towns of the San Quintín Valley are friendly and cool, making them a great rest stop for trips both north and south, and a practical base for exploring the nearby **Parque Nacional Sierra San Pedro Mártir.**

TRANSPORTATION AND PRACTICAL INFORMATION. All three towns border Mex. 1, Mexico's Transpeninsular Highway. Streets off the highway lack street signs and common-use names, and addresses are designated by highway location. Beaches are all located to the west of the highway, accessible by small dirt roads. Coming from the north, San Quintín is the first town, Cárdenas (as it is known in the region) is next in line, and little Eje rounds out the trio.

The Valle de San Quintín **tourist office,** with its friendly English-speaking staff, actually comes before the towns themselves at km 178 in Col. Vicente Guerrero— look for signs. (☎166 27 28. Open M-F 8am-5pm, Sa-Su 10am-3pm.) To exchange currency or traveler's checks, or for 24hr. **ATMs,** head to **BITAL,** with branches in San Quintín just before the bridge at km 194, and in Cárdenas behind the PEMEX station—the **last banks before Guerrero Negro.** (Both open M-F 8am-7pm, Sa 8am-2:30pm.) **Police:** (☎165 20 34, emergency 060), in Cárdenas, by the park. Some English spoken. **Farmacia Baja California:** in Cárdenas, Mex. 1 at km 195. (☎165 24 38. Open M-F 8am-10pm, Sa-Su 8am-2pm.) **Hospital: IMSS** (☎165 22 22), at km 193.5 in San Quintín. Some English spoken. **Internet** cafes dot Mex. 1 in Cárdenas. **Internet Milenio** is at km 195, across from the post office. (☎165 21 38. 30 pesos per hr. Open daily 9am-7pm.) **Post office:** a grey building next to Farmacia Baja California in Cárdenas. (Open M-F 8am-3pm.) **Postal code:** 22930.

ACCOMMODATIONS AND FOOD. Hotel rooms tend to be clean, modern, and very reasonably priced. Don't be fooled by the ramshackle exterior of ◪**Motel Uruapan,** at km 190 in San Quintín. Inside, huge, sparkling rooms come with fans, baths, and blindingly white tile floors. (☎165 21 08. Singles 150 pesos; doubles 200 pesos.) The oh-so-comfortable beds at **Motel Chávez,** in San Quintín next to BITAL, make a night here worthwhile. Rooms come with TV and baths. (☎165 20 05. Singles 195 pesos; doubles 260 pesos.) *Taquerías* line both sides of Mex. 1, and serve excellent tacos *de pescado* or *carne asada* for 7 pesos, and fresh local clams claim a spot on every menu. **El Viejo San Quintín,** opposite the post office in Cárdenas, is fast, cheap, and tasty. The *almejas rancheras* (clams in salsa; 50 pesos) are the house specialty. Carnivores will love the yummy *machaca* (40 pesos; open daily 6am-9pm). **Asadero el Alazán,** next to Motel Chávez in San Quintín, plastered with pictures of John Wayne and other Marlboro-man types serves up *carne asada* (50 pesos) and an all-meat menu. Open daily 7:30am-11pm.

SIGHTS AND ENTERTAINMENT. Tourists who stop in San Quintín for more than a night have come for the fishing—and oh, what fishing it is! The nearby stretch of protected bays (**Bahía San Quintín, Bahía Falsa,** and **Bahía Santa María**) host dizzying numbers of cabrilla, corvina, rock cod, and halibut year-round. The open water beyond the bays supports healthy populations of tuna (yellow and bluefin) and sometimes marlin and other sailfish. Many *pangas* around the Old Mill Hotel, in Cárdenas right off the water, offer fishing tours. Most speak English well enough to show you the fish, but only if you show them the money. **Don**

Eddie's landing is right next to the hotel. (☎ 162 27 22. Trips daily 6am-1pm. US$180 inshore, US$220 to leave the bay. Fishing permits US$10.)

San Quintín boasts exceptional **surfing** and little competition for amazing waves. To get to most surfing spots, you'll need 4-wheel drive and a good map from the tourist office—the roads are terrible and never marked. The best surf is accessible at off-shore breaks only by boat. Capt. Kelly Catian of **El Capitán Sportfishing,** near the Old Mill hotel, transports eager surfers on his fancy fishing cruiser. El Capitán's fishing trips are smoother than those on the *pangas,* complete with fish-finding gadgets and high prices .(Surfing US$120-160 per half-day. Fishing US$320 inshore, US$360 for tuna and sailfish. ☎ 162 17 16.) Bring your own gear.

Those in desperate search of spirits can visit **Bar Romo,** on Mex. 1 in Cárdenas, next to the motel of the same name. *Mariachis* and local singers croon into the wee hours. In San Quintín, grab a chilly beer (18 pesos) or margarita (25 pesos) at the touristy **Restaurant Bar San Quintín,** on Mex. 1 next to Hotel Chavez. The well-stocked bar and weekend *mariachi* will help you strum a buzz in no time.

▨ PARQUE NACIONAL SIERRA SAN PEDRO MÁRTIR

The road leading to the park branches off Mex. 1, 51km north of San Quintín, and runs east of the highway for 100km. The ride to the entrance is approximately 2½hr. on a well-marked dirt road (closed during heavy rainfall). The access road becomes the main road inside the park, passing through Vallecitos and ending at the closed observatory gates. Passenger vehicles will have no problem driving the road, but careful attention is advised as the curves are sharp and cliffs are steep. Watch out for cattle; local vaqueros use the road to herd their cows to greener pastures. The views along the way are stunning—plunging canyons divide yellow and red tinted peaks.

Most travelers bypass breathtaking Parque Nacional Sierra de San Pedro Mártir in their quest for breaks and beaches. Situated between the crashing waves of the Pacific and the calm, turquoise waters of the Sea of Cortés, the park is one of the least visited, and most dazzling, in all of Mexico. Oriented around the **Vallecitos** plateau (2430m), the park receives much more rainfall than the surrounding desert, and the towering forests of pines and junipers stand in stark contrast to the bone-dry land below. While the most abundant wildlife in the park are magnificently lazy cows, deer are also plentiful, puma and eagles make their home in the peaks, and the ice-cold streams support an endemic population of Nelson rainbow trout. A few difficult trails lead to these elusive streams, where anglers are rewarded with excellent **fishing** and tranquil solitude; no permits are required.

The jagged double peak of **Picacho del Diablo** (also known as **Cerro de la Encantada** or **La Providencia**), the highest point in Baja California (3086m), attracts mountaineering enthusiasts. The scramble up "the Devil's" steep slopes should be attempted only by experienced climbers or with a reliable guide. Allow 2-3 days to hike to the base from the main road, summit the mountain, and return to your car. Everyone attempting the climb must register at the ranger station, where detailed maps are provided. The summit rewards successful climbers with fantastic views of the deep-blue Pacific, the Sea of Cortés, and the narrow Baja peninsula in between. Hikers not brave, skilled, or deluded enough to attempt Picacho del Diablo can take in the view at **Mirador el Altar,** a fantastic lookout 2880m above sea level. The 2-2½hr. trail there is a steep double track strewn with loose rocks; look for signs from the main road just east of Vallecitos. Those exploring San Pedro Mártir's trails should carry a compass or GPS and plenty of food and remain well-hydrated. The altitude and thin air may leave even the most experienced hikers sucking wind after a few steps.

Taking advantage of the park's clean air and high altitude, the Mexican government built the **National Observatory** here in 1967. The largest of the observatory's three gigantic telescopes boasts a lens diameter of 2.12m. Friendly scientists are usually willing to lead free tours (especially on Sa), but call ahead—access to the observatory closes during periods of telescope maintenance. (☎ 174 45 80, ext. 315. Open daily 11am-1pm.) To get to the observatory, follow the main road 1½km past

Vallecitos, park and hike uphill for 2km. Even without the assistance of Mexico's biggest telescopes, Parque San Pedro Mártir's nighttime skyscapes are dazzling.

Camping costs US$7 per car; if no one is at the ranger station, set up camp and someone will come to collect your money and give you useless maps. The extensive system of trails is poorly marked, and only knowledgeable guides can help find the best ones. Some trails are closed except to authorized guides—ask around in Ensenada (see p. 146) to find one.

EL ROSARIO

Home to the **last PEMEX station for nearly 100 miles,** tiny El Rosario is accustomed to passers-through. Hardcore Baja enthusiasts stop and enjoy a final taste of civilization before setting off into true backcountry Baja—the Desierto Central and beyond. After filling your tank, walk 50m down the hill to legendary **Mama Espinoza's Place.** Since 1930, Mama Espinoza herself has stuffed generations of Baja trekkers with famous lobster burritos. (☎ 165 87 70. Open daily 7am-10pm.) Less expensive, but not nearly as tasty is **Baja Lym Restaurant,** at km 56 of the highway, down the road and left at the fork. Concrete floors and ceiling fans keep things cool, and the fish tacos are worth a try (40 pesos; open daily 7am-10pm). If you're too gorged to move on, **Motel El Rosario,** next door to Mama Espinoza, will take you in. Slightly shabby, basic rooms have powerful fans, TVs and moderately dingy baths. (☎ 166 88 58. Singles 190 pesos; doubles 220 pesos.)

BAHÍA DE LOS ANGELES ☎ 6

Spectacular, rugged mountains give way to warm ocean in heavenly Bahía de los Angeles (pop. 2000). A diverse array of fish make their homes amidst the barren islands and sheltered coves of this tranquil fisherman's paradise. Isolated Bahía (as it is known to locals) has no dance clubs or *mariachis.* Most visitors come to fish leisurely or swing away the day in oceanside hammocks.

■◪ **ORIENTATION AND PRACTICAL INFORMATION.** A very bumpy, paved road leads from Mex. 1 to Bahía de los Angeles, approximately 1½hr. from the Guerrero Negro junction. The panoramic views of stark islands rising out of Bahía's gentle sapphire waters are thrilling. The access road becomes the town's main drag, home to everything of interest to the tourist. Guillermo, the English-speaking owner of **Guillermo's,** a restaurant/market/RV park/motel, serves as Bahía's tourist liasion. (Open daily 6am-10pm.) The closest banks are in Guerrero Negro, and all local business is conducted in cash. Guillermo's has the only **pay phone** in town (12 pesos per min.), across the park from the **police.**

◪◫ **ACCOMMODATIONS AND FOOD.** If you've got a tent, camping is the cheapest way to stay in Bahía. The best sites are at ◪**Campo Archelón,** an environmentally and all-around friendly campground right on the water. Cool stone-walled *palapas* (US$8) and rustic *cabañas* for up to 8 people (US$15) come with the use of clean bathrooms and hot showers. Just down the road is **Daggett's Campground,** a village of stick *palapa* huts, RVs, spotless bathrooms, and hot showers. (*Palapas* US$8 per couple; each additional person US$2.) To get to the campgrounds, follow the signs down the dirt road off the main road just before the beginning of town. Those looking for an affordable roof will appreciate **Casa Díaz,** at the edge of town where the road curves. Spacious and tidy rooms have baths but no A/C. (Singles US$20; doubles US$25.) Park your RV at **Guillermo's** (US$4 per person for a full hookup). Because of its isolated location, food in Bahía isn't cheap. Your best bet is to grill up your catch of the day. If the fish just aren't biting, head to ◪**Restaurante las Hamacas,** in front of the hotel. The simple, trophy-adorned dining room is cooled by fans and ice-cold *cerveza.* (Warm, buttery *pescado al mojo de ajo* 50 pesos. Open W-M 6am-9pm.) The rooftop patio at **Restaurante las Islas,** across from Las Hamacas, is a great place to watch the bay and munch on yummy fish tacos (45 pesos; theoretically open daily 6am-9pm).

⑤🔄 SIGHTS AND SAND. Small and undeveloped Bahía de los Angeles boasts a rich history. Originally inhabited by the **Cochimi,** an indigenous group prevalent in central Baja, the town later served as the center of Baja's sea turtle industry until the business was outlawed. Check out the bleached whale skeleton and extensive mining gear in front of the **Museo de Historia y Cultura,** a tiny building behind the police office. Inside you'll find natural history exhibits, newspaper articles on the area, and a recreation of a rancher's house. (Open daily 9am-noon and 3-5pm; in winter 9am-noon and 2-4pm. Free, but donations accepted.) The turtle population around Bahía has been recovering slowly but surely since the ban on their capture, and the friendly folks at the **Sea Turtle Project,** next to Cample Archelón, have had a lot to do with the recovery. The project studies the physiology and ecology of the different types of turtles in the bay—mostly loggerhead, hawksbill, and black turtles. The rehabilitiation area provides a chance to get up close and personal with injured turtles, and scientists are a great source of information on Bahía's marine ecosystems. (Open from early morning to evening. Free.)

Bahía's widely touted fishing is excellent year-round, and a constant stream of *gringos* passes through the town. Expect to hook corvina, yellowtail, dorado, grouper, and halibut during late spring/summer and roosterfish, sailfish, cabrilla, and sierra in winter. Triggerfish swallow bait year-round. Smart fishermen bring their own equipment as rentals are both expensive and rare. Guides, on the other hand, are everywhere. **Díaz sportfishing tours** leave from Casa Díaz, coasting in *pangas* among the bay's numerous islands. (6am-1pm, US$120-140.) The islands also provide a great setting for **sea kayaking.** However, experience is advised, as winds in the bay can pick up without warning, and a few kayakers are lost to the almighty ocean each year. Daggett's Campground also rents kayaks. (Single US$20, double US$35 per 5hr.) **Diving** in Bahía has also gained popularity. You won't see as many colorful fish as on the cape, but the warm water makes the depths worth a look. A friendly Italian named **Mauro,** next to Campo Archelón, leads certified divers on tours of the bay. If you can't find him, ask at the Sea Turtle Project. Daggett's also takes divers out in its *pangas.* Fill your tanks (US$7) or get equipment at **Larry and Raquel's,** next to Daggett's. The beaches in town are not exactly sandy, but broken shells give way to fine, gold grey sand farther north, along the **Punta la Gringa** peninsula. To get to La Gringa, follow signs to Daggett's along the dirt road at the edge of town. Instead of turning right into Daggett's, stay straight for 12km. The series of small roads leading off the road to the water are usually passable in a passenger car, but flooding can turn them into gooey mud.

BAJA CALIFORNIA SUR

GUERRERO NEGRO ☎ 1

For most of the year, Guerrero Negro's (pop. 10,000) biggest attractions are the salt plant and two PEMEX gas stations. Everything changes when January comes, and nearby Scammon's Lagoon, **Laguna Ojo de Liebre,** fills with playful grey whales. Gas and salt take a back seat to whale-watching as the town becomes inundated with tourists eager to frolic with the gentle giants. If you miss the whales, fill up on gas, enjoy a refreshing salty breeze or two, and blaze along to the next town.

 IN THE ZONE Baja California Sur is one hour ahead of Baja Norte, so be sure to set your clock forward when you arrive in Guerrero Negro.

🚌 TRANSPORTATION. The **Autotransportes de Baja California terminal** (☎ 157 06 11), on Zapata, is one of the first buildings off the highway. ABC sends buses north (6 per day 6:30am-10pm) to: **El Rosario** (6hr., 165 pesos); **Ensenada** (10hr., 315 pesos); **Lázaro Cárdenas** (7hr., 210 pesos); **San Quintín** (8hr., 210 pesos); **Tijuana**

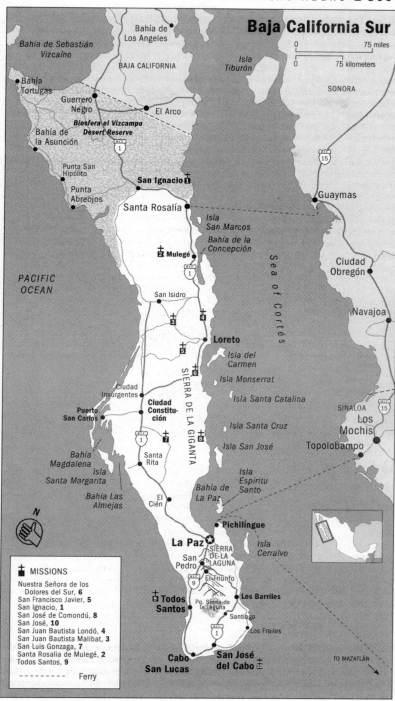

Baja California Sur

Bahía de Los Angeles

Bahía de Sebastián Vizcaíno

Isla Tiburón

0 — 75 miles

0 — 75 kilometers

BAJA CALIFORNIA

SONORA

Bahía Tortugas

Guerrero Negro

El Arco

Biosfera el Vizcampo Desert Reserve

Bahía de la Asunción

[1]

Punta San Hipólito

San Ignacio [+][1]

Punta Abreojos

Santa Rosalía

Isla San Marcos

Guaymas

Bahía de la Concepción

[+][2] Mulegé

[1]

Ciudad Obregón

PACIFIC OCEAN

San Isidro

[+][3]

[+][4]

Navajoa

Loreto

[+][5]

Isla del Carmen

Isla Monserrat

[+][6]

Isla Santa Catalina

S e a   o f   C o r t é s

Ciudad Insurgentes

SINALOA

[15]

Ciudad Constitución

Isla Santa Cruz

Los Mochis

Puerto San Carlos

[+][8]

Isla San José

Topolobampo

[1]

[7]

S I E R R A   D E   L A   G I G A N T A

Santa Rita

Bahía Magdalena

Isla Santa Margarita

Isla Espíritu Santo

Bahía de La Paz

Bahía Las Almejas

El Cién

Pichilingue

La Paz [✪]

Isla Cerralvo

San Pedro

SIERRA DE LA LAGUNA

El Triunfo

[9]

Los Barriles

[+] Todos Santos

Pq. Sierra de la Laguna

Santiago

Los Frailes

[1]

TO MAZATLÁN

Cabo San Lucas

San José del Cabo [+][10]

[+] MISSIONS

Nuestra Señora de los
  Dolores del Sur, **6**
San Francisco Javier, **5**
San Ignacio, **1**
San José de Comondú, **8**
San José, **10**
San Juan Bautista Londó, **4**
San Juan Bautista Malibat, **3**
San Luis Gonzaga, **7**
Santa Rosalia de Mulegé, **2**
Todos Santos, **9**

- - - - - - - - - Ferry

(11hr., 390 pesos); and south to: **La Paz** (11hr., 4 per day 6am-7pm, 430 pesos); **Mulegé** (4hr., 4 per day, 165 pesos); **Santa Rosalía** (3hr., 6 per day, 115 pesos); and points in between. Yellow **minivans** run on Zapata to both ends of town and residential neighborhoods (every 15min. 7am-10pm, 7 pesos).

⚡📶 ORIENTATION AND PRACTICAL INFORMATION. Guerrero Negro lies along a 3km strip west of the Transpeninsular Highway. Most businesses line **Zapata** and **Baja California. Banamex,** Baja California in front of the plant, exchanges currency and has **ATMs.** (☎157 05 55. Open M-F 9am-3pm.) Travelers continuing south should change currency here, as **ATMs** and **bank services** become sparse. **Lavamática Cristy,** 1 block south of Zapata—follow the signs next to Hotel Brisa Salma. (Wash 10 pesos, dry 10 pesos. Open daily 9am-9pm.) **Police:** (☎157 00 22), in the Delegación Municipal, before the salt plant on the left. Little English spoken. **Farmacia San Martín,** the big yellow building on the north side of Zapata. **Fax** machine 16 pesos per min. (☎157 01 11. Open M-Sa 8am-10pm, Su 9am-5:30pm.) **IMSS** (☎157 04 33) on Zapata at Tabasco, past PEMEX. Little English spoken. **Internet: PC Vision,** hidden off Zapata. Go down Sanchez between Motel San Ignacio and Hotel El Morro two blocks, and turn left onto an unnamed street. PC Vision will be on your right. (20 pesos per hr. Open M-Sa 9am-10pm, Su 3-10pm.) **Post office:** on Baja California, two blocks past the church and left onto a dirt road just before the basketball courts. (☎157 03 44. Open M-F 8am-3pm.) **Postal code:** 23940.

🏠🍴 ACCOMMODATIONS AND FOOD. Guerrero Negro has a healthy supply of good budget rooms. During whale season, rooms are at a premium, and reservations are a good idea. **Motel Las Dunas,** on Zapata, below the water tank, looks somewhat rundown, but rooms are huge and shiny with private baths and TV. (☎157 04 55. Singles and doubles 200 pesos.) The bright pink paint job at **Motel Brisa Salma,** on Zapata four blocks beyond the water tank, may hurt your eyes, but the price will heal your wallet. Tidy rooms have TVs and fans. (Singles 100 pesos; doubles 140 pesos; each additional person 60 pesos.) **Motel Las Ballenas,** one block from Zapata, behind Motel el Morro, offers decent re-carpeted rooms. (☎157 01 16. Singles 165 pesos; doubles 200 pesos.)

Street-side taco stands offer the city's cheapest, and perhaps best, food. **Asadero Viva Mexico,** on Zapata, two blocks beyond the water tank, is an overblown *taquería* with outdoor counter seating and indoor tables. Specializes in good, simple *carne asada* tacos. (7 pesos. Open daily 2pm-1am.) **Cocina Económica Edith,** on Tabasco, off Zapata next to the IMSS, has a friendly, family atmosphere. (Tasty *tortas* 15-20 pesos. Open daily 7am-10pm.)

◀ SIGHTS. Conveniently situated 10km from the whale-watching of **Laguna Ojo de Liebre** or **Scammon's Lagoon,** Guerrero Negro welcomes whales and watchers alike. More than 50% of the world's grey whale population is born in the lagoon. **Eco-Tour Malarrimo,** on Zapata, on the right as you come into town, leads tours from January through March. Schedule at least one day in advance, and arrive 30 min. before the tour leaves. (☎157 01 00; fax 157 01 00; www.malarrimo.com. 4hr. tours; 8 and 11am; US$45, children US$35; price includes a light lunch.) If your Spanish is good and you've got a car, the road to the Laguna is 10km south of Guerrero Negro on Mex. 1—watch for a sign with a whale on it. Follow the sandy bumps for 24km until you reach the Laguna. The whales are shy and sensitive, so private boats are prohibited during mating season (Dec.-Apr.). Trained local fishermen can provide you with a closer look. (1½hr.; US$15, children US$10.)

SAN IGNACIO   ☎1

In the deserts of Baja, San Ignacio (pop. 2000) is a welcome oasis. From a distance, the town appears as a cruel illusion—leafy date palms, flowering bushes, and broad swaths of green appear magically in the middle of the blistering desert. Go ahead and pinch yourself—you're not dreaming. The area around San Ignacio is blessed with the most plentiful underground supply of freshwater in Baja California Sur. Of late, it's been pumped up to form a murky lake, which is used for swimming and irrigating local orchards. A prime point of departure for cave painting and whale-watching tours, the town's intimate atmosphere, nighttime starscapes, and historic mission have seduced many a traveler.

TRANSPORTATION. **Buses** pick up and drop off passengers at the sheltered bench across from the PEMEX, 2km from San Ignacio on Mex. 1. Trek north out of Calle Luyando on foot, or grab a **cab** at the *zócalo* (25 pesos). *De paso* buses (6 per day 2am-7pm) head north to: **Ensenada** (13hr., 385 pesos); **Guerrero Negro** (3hr., 110 pesos); **Tijuana** (14hr., 435 pesos); or south (4 per day 8am-9pm) for: **La Paz** (8hr., 360 pesos); **Loreto** (1hr., 138 pesos); and **Mulegé** (1hr., 53 pesos) via **Santa Rosalía.**

ORIENTATION AND PRACTICAL INFORMATION. San Ignacio lies 142km south of Guerrero Negro on Mex. 1. A winding road canopied by swaying date palms leads south from the highway and becomes **Luyando** at the *zócalo*. Most activity revolves around the tranquil *zócalo*, bordered by Luyando, **Morelos** on the south, **Juárez** on the east, and **Hidalgo** on the west.

There is no official tourist office, but for an informative chat visit **Jorge Antonio Fischer,** the owner of the mini-mart next to Restaurant Chalita on Hidalgo at the *zócalo*. (☎ 154 01 50. Open M-Sa 7am-6pm, Su 7am-1pm.) He also leads whale expeditions and tours to the cave paintings (see **Sights** below). **Nuevos Almacenes Meza,** on the corner of Juárez and Luyando, facing the *zócalo*, sells general goods. (☎ 154 01 22. Open M-Sa 8am-noon and 2-6pm, Su 8am-noon.) **Police:** (☎ 154 01 47), in the Delegación Municipal on Ocampo and Zaragoza, a 5-10min. walk out Hidalgo to the south. Little English spoken. **Pharmacy: Boticas Ceseña,** Madero 24A, parallel to and east of Juárez and Hidalgo. (☎ 154 00 76, emergency 154 00 75. Open daily 8am-2pm and 4-11pm.) To reach the **Centro de Salud,** walk down Hidalgo away from the mission and turn right on Cipris, a tiny dirt road; when you reach the auto parts shop, turn right, then left just past the tin-roofed warehouse. Continue straight for two blocks; it's the white building surrounded by flowers on the right side. English spoken. Place calls or send **faxes** at a pricey **caseta,** Hidalgo 24. (☎ 154 02 50. Open M-Sa 8am-1pm and 3-6pm.) Mail can be sent from the **Delegacion Municipal.**

ACCOMMODATIONS. San Ignacio's few hotels don't come cheap. Reservations are necessary during *Semana Santa* or *El Día de San Ignacio* (July 31). The family living in **Restaurant Chalita,** Hidalgo 9, rents three rooms with two beds, fans, TV, and tiny baths. (☎ 154 00 82. Doubles 150 pesos.) **Hotel Posada,** a 5min. walk down Cipris from Hidalgo, has clean rooms with baths, fans, and nifty colorful windows in a family atmosphere. (☎ 154 03 13. Singles and doubles 200 pesos.) **El Padrino RV Park** is 500m from the *zócalo* on the road connecting San Ignacio to the highway. (☎ 154 00 89. Full hookup 100 pesos, without electricity 80 pesos. Tent camping US$3; cars 100 pesos.)

FOOD. San Ignacio's few restaurants are within a stone's throw of the *zócalo*, and serve delectable, affordable cuisine. Seafood receives top billing on most menus. Eat under a starry sky at **Restaurant-Bar Rene's,** just outside the *zócalo*, off Hidalgo. If you'd prefer a roof, head into their stone-floored thatched hut, complete with ceiling fan and 80s tunes. Wash down the *calamar empanizado* (breaded squid; 70 pesos), with a 12-peso beer. (Open daily 7am-10pm.) You'll be sourrounded by children playing and birds singing as you dine in the house that is **Restaurant Chalita,** on Hidalgo at the *zócalo*. Watch and smell the cook prepare your tasty *enchiladas* (35 pesos) or *chiles rellenos*. (40 pesos. ☎ 154 00 82. Open daily 7:30am-11pm.) **Flojo's Restaurant/Bar** is a round *palapa*-roofed hut at El Padrino RV Park, 5min. out of town on Luyando, with a reputation for good, cheap seafood (40-60 pesos). Unfortunately, staff shortages sometimes keep them from feeding the hungering public. (☎ 154 00 89. Theoretically open daily 7am-9pm.)

◙◙ **SIGHTS AND ENTERTAINMENT.** The area's main tourist draw are **painted caves,** 75km away in the Sierra de San Francisco mountains. 500 paintings, probably more than 10,000 years old, are contained within a 12 sq. km area. Anthropologists are unsure who created these paintings or why, but unassuming central Baja boasts more rock art than more famous sites in Spain and France. Most of the paintings are found high (around 10m) above ground, leading local Cochimí to believe a race of giants made them. All cave trips require quick local authorization from the INAH office in San Ignacio next to the mission. (☎154 02 22. Open Tu-Sa 8am-3pm; Oct.-Apr. daily 8am-6pm.) Guides are available all over town to take you to any of the sites in the Sierra. Most popular are **Cueva El Ratón,** a short hike from a parking area, and **Cueva La Pintada,** the most spectacular site. Prices are around US$120 for 1-6 people or US$20 per person for 7 or more. Oscar and Dagoberto Fischer of **Hotel Posada** (☎ 154 03 13) will bring you to any of the sites, as will Jorge Fischer of Fischer's mini-mart (☎ 154 03 13). For a more professional tour, contact **Eco-tour Malarrimo** in Guerrero Negro (US$75 per person).

San Ignacio has become a popular launch point for whale-watching trips. **Laguna de San Ignacio** fills with literally tons of grey whales from Jan.-Mar., offering visitors a great chance to get up close and personal with the animals—whales in San Ignacio have a reputation for being especially friendly. Contact **El Padrino RV Park** (☎154 00 89) for tours (4-6hrs., US$120).

A colonial colossus towering over wild, leafy vegetation, the **Mission of San Ignacio,** on the north side of the *zócalo,* was founded in 1728 by Jesuit missionary Juan Bautista Luyando. The construction of the mission proved a logistical nightmare; wood had to be hauled from the Guadalupe mission in the Sierras, furniture brought from Mulegé on a four-day mule ride through the desert, and paintings carried by boat from the mainland. Its walls, over 9m thick, are made from blocks of volcanic rock. The mission is a beautiful achievement—magnificent on the outside, cool on the inside, and heavenly at night when illuminated by spotlights. The **Mission Museum,** next door, is a great source of facts on the cave paintings around San Ignacio, with captions in Spanish only. There's even a huge faux cave painting for those who can't make it into the Sierra. (☎154 02 22. Open Tu-Sa 8am-3pm; Oct.-Apr. daily 8am-6pm. Free.) For extra fun, hit town during the week-long celebration of **El Día de San Ignacio,** beginning on July 28th, which celebrates the day of the town's patron saint (July 31st) and coincides with the harvest celebration (July 30th). San Ignacio blossoms into a huge *fiesta* complete with singing, dancing, horse races, fireworks, and plenty of eating.

SANTA ROSALÍA ☎ 1

Not merely a transportation hub, Santa Rosalía (pop. 10,500) is heir to a colorful history. After rich copper ore was discovered here in 1868, a French mining company settled the area, building the town on the sides of the mountain according to rank: the wealthier, higher-ranking officials lived at the top and the poorer classes below. They even brought with them their own church, the Iglesia Santa Bárbara. Closed in 1986, the mines, abandoned and rusting, now guard the eclectic city.

▐ **TRANSPORTATION.** Most buses depart from the **ABC station** (☎152 01 50), across from the ferry office. Buses travel north (4 per day, 3pm-5am) to: **El Rosario** (9hr., 300 pesos); **Ensenada** (13½hr., 450 pesos); **Guerrero Negro** (3½hr., 190 pesos); **Mexicali** (18½hr., 660 pesos); **San Ignacio** (1hr., 50 pesos); **San Quintín** (9½hr., 340 pesos); **Tijuana** (15hr., 530 pesos). Heading south (6 per day 9am-3am), all buses go to: **Ciudad Constitución** (4½hr., 200 pesos); **La Paz** (8hr., 310 pesos); **Loreto** (3hr., 120 pesos); **Mulegé** (1hr., 50 pesos).

From Santa Rosalía, you can catch the **ferry** connecting Baja California to **Guaymas** on the mainland (8hr.; Tu and Th 9am; *salón* 460 pesos, *turista* 1040 pesos, *cabina* 1270 pesos, *especial* 1500 pesos). The boat leaves from the blue and green **Sematur** office on Mex. 1, south of town (☎152 00 13. Open M, W, and F-Sa

8am-3pm; Tu and Th 8am-1pm and 3-6pm). Those with cars must purchase tickets in advance and show a tourist card, registration, vehicle permit (get one at the border—they don't have them in Santa Rosalía), and proof of their Mexican insurance. *Salón* class is first come, first served, but *turista* and *cabina* reservations should be made three days to a week in advance. Departure days and times, prices, and office hours constantly vary, so call the office to confirm the schedule. To get from the ferry or bus station to downtown, turn right as you leave the ferry compound (left from the bus station) and walk along the water to the old train engine.

⑦ ORIENTATION AND PRACTICAL INFORMATION. Santa Rosalía lies 555km north of La Paz. Almost all services are on the two main streets, **Obregón** and **Constitución,** which run approximately east-west. Crossing these, running north-south is a series of named and numbered streets. Attractive and historic **Mesa Francesa** lies up the hill via **Alta Mirano,** parallel to and north of Obregón.

Banamex, on Obregón and Calle 5, changes traveler's checks and has a 24hr. **ATM.** (☎ 152 09 84. Open M-F 9am-3pm.) **Police:** (☎ 152 23 80), at Carranza and Plaza. Little English spoken. **Farmacia Central,** on Obregón at Plaza, is owned by English-speaking Dr. Chang Tam (☎ 152 20 70. Open M-Sa 9am-2pm and 4-10pm, Su 9am-1pm). **Centro de Salud:** (☎ 152 07 89), at Costeau next to the museum in Mesa Francesa. Little English spoken. **Red Cross:** (☎ 152 06 40, emergency 060), on Calle 2 and Carranza, right off Constitución. Nelson Romero speaks English. **Telecomm:** On Constitucíon, across from the post office. (Open M-F 8am-3pm.) For 15 min. of free **Internet access,** visit the Telmex office at the west end of town. (☎ 152 00 00. Open M-F 8am-3pm.) **Post office:** on Constitución, between Calle 2 and Altamirano. (☎ 152 03 44. Open M-F 8am-3pm.) **Postal code:** 23920.

⌂⌂ ACCOMMODATIONS AND FOOD. If you're going to stay overnight in sweltering Santa Rosalía, seriously consider forking over the extra pesos for A/C. The budget standout is **Hotel Olvera,** Calle Plaza 14, three blocks from shore on Constitución, right of the foot bridge. Enjoy spacious bathrooms, large double beds, lukewarm *agua purificada,* and an airy porch. (☎ 152 02 67. Singles 150 pesos, with A/C 200 pesos; doubles 180 pesos, with A/C 250 pesos.) **RV Park Las Palmas,** 3½km south of town, has full hookups, laundry, and a restaurant, but closes for much of the boiling-hot summer. (2 people US$10.) Constitución is lined with cheap and good *taquerías* and *comida corrida* joints. The town's best-known eatery, **◪El Boleo Bakery,** on Obregón at Calle 4, has excellent baked goods. (☎ 152 03 10. Fabulous French bread 2 pesos, *pan dulce* 2 pesos, turnovers 3 pesos. Open M-Sa 8am-9pm.) For a heavier meal, head to **Terco's Pollito,** at Obregón and Playa, where powerful A/C offers relief from the heat. (☎ 152 00 75. Exceptional half-chicken 45 pesos, *enchiladas suizas* 40 pesos. Open daily 8am-11pm.)

◧ SIGHTS. The wooden houses, general stores, and saloons in Santa Rosalía recall the town's mining-boom days. Startling specimens of 19th century French architecture include the many-windowed **Palacio Municipal,** on Plaza Juárez between Carranza and Constitución, **Hotel Francés,** at the top of the Mesa Francesa on Cousteau, and **El Boleo Bakery,** on Constitución, with pure colors, simple forms, and modern use of glass and steel. The pre-fabricated, white, cast-iron **Iglesia Santa Bárbara,** at Obregón and Calle 1, designed by Gustave Eiffel for a mission in Africa, was never picked up by the company that had commissioned it. French mining moguls spotted the church at the 1889 Exhibition Universale de Paris and decided Santa Rosalía couldn't do without it. For a great view of the town, climb the decrepit stone steps just off the beginning of Obregón, which lead to the new **Museo Histórico Minero de Santa Rosalía,** housed in an old French mining office building. The offices give the impression that the employees just went home for *siesta*—the mining and office equipment is arranged as if the mines were still running. (Open M-F 9am-3pm. 10 pesos, children 5 pesos.)

MULEGÉ ☎ 1

Mulegé (pop. 3000), on the banks of palmy Rio Mulegé, has long been a favorite stop for travelers. Narrow one-way streets disguise one of Baja's true gems—an authentic and friendly Mexican *pueblo* with its character intact in the face of an ever-increasing tourist onslaught. Best of all, it is the ideal place for exploring the glistening beaches and cobalt sea of **Bahía de la Concepción**.

⊡ TRANSPORTATION. The **Igriega bus station** is a sheltered blue bench at the turn-off to Mulegé from Mex. 1. All buses are *de paso*. Tickets and bus info are available at the restaurant overlooking the bench. Northbound buses stop daily at 4:30, 6:30, and 7:30pm. The 4:30 goes all the way to **Tijuana**, the 6:30 motors to **Santa Rosalía**, and the 7:30 to **Mexicali** via **El Rosario** (10hr., 340 pesos); **Ensenada** (14½hr., 480 pesos); **Lázaro Cárdenas** (11hr., 400 pesos); **Mexicali** (19½hr., 710 pesos); **Santa Rosalía** (1hr., 50 pesos); **San Ignacio** (2hr., 90 pesos); **San Quintín** (10½hr., 400 pesos); **Tecate** (17hr., 610 pesos); **Tijuana** (16hr., 520 pesos). Southbound buses stop daily at 11am and 12:30pm, and go to: **Ciudad Constitución** (3½hr., 160 pesos); **Insurgentes** (3hr., 140 pesos); **La Paz** (6hr., 225 pesos); **Loreto** (2hr., 70 pesos). Arrive 30min. early for all buses.

▰▱ ORIENTATION AND PRACTICAL INFORMATION. Soon after leaving the Transpeninsular Highway, the road into Mulegé forks. To the left is **Moctezuma**; to the right is **Martínez**. Both are crossed by **Zaragoza**. Take a right onto Zaragoza to get to the *zócalo*, which is one block away. **Madero** heads east from the *zócalo* (away from the highway) and, follows the Mulegé River for about 3km, ending at the town beach, **Playa de Mulegé**.

Mulegé has no official tourist office, internet cafes, or even banks, but the town has plenty of other tourist services. **Kerry "El Vikingo" Otterstrom** has plenty of town history and information—buy him a few drinks and he can talk for hours. Look for Kerry at **El Candil** restaurant; the staff will point you toward him. **Hotel Las Casitas**, Madero 50 (☎ 153 00 19), also has tourist info. Ask for Javier—besides leading tours, he has info on beaches, camping, and fishing. You can pick up a sketch **map** of the town from **Cortez Explorers** on Moctezuma, just past the entrance to town (☎/fax 153 05 00. Open M-Sa 10am-1pm and 4-7pm.) **Lavamática Claudia**, on Zaragoza near Hotel Terrazas. (☎153 00 57. Wash 17 pesos, dry 6 pesos. Open daily 8am-7pm.) **Police**: (☎ 153 00 49), in the old Pinatel de Educación building on Martínez, next to the PEMEX station **Red Cross**: (☎ 153 01 10), on Madero, 20m past the turn-off into town on Mex. 1. Little English spoken. **Farmacia Moderna** at Madero on the plaza. (☎ 153 00 42. Open daily 8am-1pm and 4-10pm.) **Centro de Salud B (ISSTE)**, Madero 28. (☎153 02 98. Open daily 8am-2:30pm.) **Minisúper Padilla** (☎ 153 01 99; fax 153 01 90), on Zaragoza at Martínez, one block north of plaza, has many **phones** for international calls and now offers **fax** service. **Post office**: in the same building as the police. (☎ 153 02 05. Open M-F 8am-3pm.) **Postal code**: 23900.

▰ ACCOMMODATIONS. Mulegé has a fair number of cheap rooms. **Hotel Mulegé**, near the bus station, on the left heading into town, is the best. Big, white-tiled rooms come with spotless baths and cable TV. (☎ 153 00 90. Singles 252 pesos; doubles 280 pesos.) **Casa de Huéspedes Manuelita**, on Moctezuma, next to Restaurant Los Equipales, has smallish, tidy rooms with private baths, but no A/C. Campers can use baths and showers for 15 pesos. (☎ 153 01 75. Singles 120 pesos; doubles 150 pesos.) **Orchard RV Park** is south of town at km 133 on Mex. 1. Right on Rio Mulegé, the immaculate park boasts great palm-shaded spots. Paddleboats and canoes for exploring the river US$3 per hr. (☎ 153 03 00. Tent sites US$4; full hookup US$19.95.) Farther along at km 132, **Villa María Isabel RV Park** isn't as tidy or shady as the Orchard, but it has a great bakery and laundromat on site. (Tent sites US$5; full hookup 150 pesos. Outside campers can use showers for US$2.50.)

◘ **FOOD.** For something informal and delicious, **Taquería Doney** is across from Hotel Mulegé, past the bus station coming into town. Locals cram indoor tables and outdoor stools, wolfing down stupendeous steak tacos. (8 pesos. Open W-M 8am-10pm.) **El Candil Restaurant**, on Zaragoza near Martínez, is filled with loud, red-faced, white-bearded *gringos* by day, but the scene mellows and locals out by evening. The *combinacion mexicana* (60 pesos) is billed as the biggest in Baja. (☎ 153 04 03. Open daily 7am-10pm.) **La Almeja** has the best location in town, at the end of Madero right on the beach, about 3km from town. Old driver's licenses and the remains of what appear to be endangered species line the flimsy walls. Try the house specialty—steamed chocolate clams (named for the color, not the taste; 10 pesos a piece. ☎ 153 02 84. Open daily 8:30am-11pm.)

◙◘ **SIGHTS AND ENTERTAINMENT.** Mulegé is a great spot for exploration of cave paintings at nearby **La Trinidad** and **Cuevas San Borjita**. Both **Salvador Castro** of Castro Tours at Hotel Las Casitas and **Kerry Otterstrom** (see above) lead hiking tours to the caves. Trips last from 8am-4 or 5pm and include stops at nearby *ranchos*, as well as descriptions and lectures on native plants and wildlife. (Castro Tours ☎ 153 02 32. Tours US$40-60 per person; include food and permit.) If you want to bring a camera, get a permit at the INAH office (guides will direct you). Mulegé offers great sport-fishing, mostly confined to outside the Bahia Concepción. Talk to Javier at **Hotel Las Casitas**. (☎ 153 00 19. Trips US$120 for 3-4 people.)

The lovely 18th-century **Misión Santa Rosalía de Mulegé** sits on a hill to the west of town. To get there, walk down Zaragoza away from the *zócalo*, go under the bridge, and turn right on the calm-shaded lane. The church's massive and imposing stone facade hide a lovely and quiet interior. The small *mirador* behind the mission affords a great view of the town, river, and palms. The **Museo Comunitario Mulegé** is housed in the town's old prison, once known as the "prison without doors." Walk down Moctezuma away from the highway until you reach a steep set of stairs on your left. Exhibits include artifacts of the indigenous Cochimí, displays of local marine life, and a piece of the spaceship that fell to earth on a *rancho* near Mulegé. (Open M-F 9am-3pm, Sa 9am-1pm. 10 pesos.)

The seas and river around Mulegé offer a great variety of aquatic activities. To explore the river, rent a canoe or paddleboat from **Orchard RV Park** (☎ 153 03 00; canoes and paddleboats US$3 per hr.), and paddle leisurely among the river's palms and birds. For snorkeling or diving tours of Mulegé or the Bahía, head to **Cortez Explorers**, Montezuma 75A, the only dive shop in town. Experienced Swiss divers will take you to Bahía de la Concepción or the Santa Inéz Islands, another great dive spot. (☎ 153 05 00. Dive tours US$60 with 2 tanks, US$70 with full equipment. Snorkeling tours US$30 with full equipment. Make reservations at least 1 day in advance. Open M-Sa 10am-1pm and 4-7pm.)

◪ **BEACHES.** Though located a convenient 3km from town, Mulegé's beaches can't hold a candle to those 18km south in Bahía de la Concepción (see below). The town beach lies at the end of Madero, where the river meets the Sea of Cortés. The sand is rocky, and usually deserted, as most beachgoers prefer Bahía. Keep an eye out for stinging jellyfish and sting rays, especially from June-September.

BAHÍA DE LA CONCEPCIÓN

Heaven on earth may just be the 48km arc of rocky outcrops, shimmering beaches, and bright-blue sea of Bahía de la Concepción. Cactus-studded hills and stark cliffs drop straight to white sand and translucent waters, creating the most breath-taking beaches in Baja California. Sport-fishers and shell collectors weep for joy at the variety and sheer size of the specimens caught here, and divers fall under the spell of underwater sights. As if this weren't enough, Bahía is blissfully noiseless, with serious tourist traffic occuring only during Christmas and *Semana Santa*.

TRANSPORTATION

To get there from Mulegé (or from anywhere to the north), go to the bus station and take *de paso* bus south. Wait to pay the fare until the bus arrives, and check with the driver to ensure that he will stop at one of the beaches. Don't count on a return bus—service to beaches is infrequent, and drivers may not stop along the busy highway. Beach-hoppers should consider renting a car for the day, as access to and from beaches farther south is limited. Many nomadic travelers hitch from Mulegé to the beaches, catching one of the RVs or produce trucks barreling down the highway toward the bay. While *Let's Go* does not recommend hitchiking, those who do thumbride are most successful across from the bus stop or at the PEMEX Station south of town. Hitching back to Mulegé is reputedly even easier, since many people drive in that direction. Never attempt to hitchhike at night.

> **BEASTS OF THE BEACH** "During summer months, sting rays mate close to shore, hidden from view underneath the sand. So as not to interrupt and get stung, shuffle your feet as you walk into the water. If they nab you, find the hottest water you can stand, immerse the stung area, and wait out the pain. Or, find a *garumbillo* ("old man") cactus, cut a chunk and squeeze a few drops of juice onto the sting. Locals swear it will get rid of the pain in seconds, but be sure to cut off all the cactus spines first, or you'll have even more pain on your hands.

BEACHES

Illuminated by millions of stars, the beaches of Bahía are otherworldly after dark. Come at night only if you plan to camp out or are equipped with wheels; it's impossible to hitch back and no buses run. Almost all the beaches have *palapa* shelter for campers (20-60 pesos). Camping is safe, but stick to well-populated beaches, and always be on guard. Those traveling alone should head to one of the larger camping complexes (like EcoMundo on Playa la Posada).

When choosing a beach in the Bahía, you can't go wrong. While some attract more of a crowd, none are packed or loud. The Bahía is completely sheltered and calm as a lake, so don't come here to catch great waves. Every beach listed offers fine white sand, mind-boggling turquoise water, and stunning views.

PLAYA EL BURRO. A peaceful little beach popular with US snowbirds and RVers, El Burro has soft sands and a quiet atmosphere that draws plenty of campers and sunbathers, as well. *(Close to the road at km 119.)*

PLAYA EL COYOTE. One of the less attractive beaches in Bahía, El Coyote is still one of the most popular. Rocky sand and dirty outhouses litter the area, but better sands and *palapas* await on the southern end. *(A short dirt road off Mex. 1 at km 108.)*

PLAYA LA PERLA. La Perla is a thin, heavenly strip of sand tucked between two rocky outcroppings. Excellent *palapas* make the lonely beach a perfect place to achieve zen-like tranquility. Check out the neighboring rock formations outlined in white paint by University of Tijuana students. *(Close to the road at km 91.)*

PLAYA LA POSADA. Dominated by an RV village, La Posada is also home to **Eco-Mundo,** a camping village for nature lovers. Huge, well-kept *palapas* are equipped with hammocks, fans, and lights. After a day of kayaking, unwind at the "Thirst Aid Station"—Jimmy Buffet himself couldn't imagine a better place to sip a *cerveza* (15 pesos. ☎ 153 04 09. *Palapas* US$2-15; showers 10 pesos; tent camping US$6; kayak rentals US$20-25 per day.) The dirt road (next to EcoMundo) leads to **Playa la Escondida,** a short, beautiful beach completely devoid of facilities. Great views and snorkeling, but camping is not recommended due to its isolatation.

PLAYA PUNTA ARENA. Surprisingly isolated considering its proximity to Mulegé, Punta Arena offers spectacular views but poor camping facilities—*palapas* are sparse and rickety. The sand tends toward foot-searingly hard packed, but gets better toward the water. *(3km down a washboard dirt road at km 119.)*

PLAYA REQUESÓN. Shimmering water lines both sides of stunning Requesón, a thin strip of white sand connected to tiny Isla Requesón. Adventurous souls sometimes camp on the strip, but the rising tide may leave you and your gear soaking wet. The Bahías best sands make their home here. *(On a short dirt road at km 92.)*Playa Santispac. The immensely popular Santispac draws crowds with its location, right off Mex. 1 at km 114. Much of the beach feels like a parking lot—the hard-packed sand behind the motor homes is rougher than asphalt, but it improves closer to the ocean. Showers are US$2.50 at **Ana's Restaurant**, on the northern end of the beach. Santispac's biggest highlight, **Ray's Place,** serves phenomenal, cheap, and fresh seafood. (Catch of the day 60 pesos. Open M-Sa 2-10 or 11pm.)

LORETO   ☎ 1

Founded by Jesuit missionaries in 1697, lovely Loreto (pop. 9500) was the first capital of the Californias and the first in a chain of Jesuit missions along the west coast of Baja California. The Jesuits were no dummies: they sandwiched their capital between the calm blue waters of the Sea of Cortés and golden mountains. It's hard to believe this town would be abandoned for any reason, but after a combination of hurricanes and earthquakes in the 1800s, Loreto stood empty for almost a century. Today, thanks to its cobblestone streets, gorgeous mission, well-tended public gardens, and tranquil palm-shaded *malecón*, the compact city center is doubtlessly the most beautiful in Baja California Sur.

Loreto

ACCOMMODATIONS
Motel Brenda, 6
Motel Davis, 3
Motel Salvatierra, 7
El Moro RV Park, 1

FOOD
Café Olé, 2
McLulu's, 4
Mexico Lindo, 5

▬ TRANSPORTATION

Aguila buses stop by **Terminal E,** on Salvatierra two blocks west of Allende near the highway, about 1km from Madero. (☎135 07 67. Ticket office open 24hr.) To get to the *centro* from the **bus station,** walk down Salvatierra (15min.) or indulge in a taxi (30 pesos). Northbound buses leave at 2, 6pm, 1 and 2am for **Guerrero Negro** (7½hr., 260 pesos); and at 5pm for **Santa Rosalía** (4hr., 120 pesos). All buses stop at **Mulegé** (2½ hr., 70 pesos). Guerrero Negro buses stop in **San Ignacio** (5hr., 170 pesos). Southbound buses go to: **La Paz** (5hr., 5 per day 8am-midnight, 190 pesos).

✴ ❼ ORIENTATION AND PRACTICAL INFORMATION

Loreto is easy to navigate. Most points of interest lie on **Salvatierra,** which runs east-west, connecting the Transpeninsular Highway to the Gulf. **Allende, León,** and

Ayuntamiento run roughly north-south and cross Salvatierra on their way to the sea. **Hidalgo** branches off Salvatierra and curves to parallel it farther south, while **Juárez** parallels it to the north. **Independencia** crosses Salvatierra at Hidalgo, and **Madero** crosses both, closer to the water. The *malecón* hugs the coast, running the width of the city. The *zócalo* is at Salvatierra and Madero, just past the mission.

The **Palacio Municipal,** on Madero, between Salvatierra and Comercio, holds the helpful **tourist info center,** stocked with maps, brochures, and English-speaking staff. (☎ 135 04 11. Open M-F 8:30am-3pm.) The only bank, **Bancomer,** on Madero across from the *zócalo*, changes dollars and checks and boasts a 24hr. **ATM.** (☎ 135 03 15. Open M-F 9am-3:30pm.) **Car Rental: Budget** on Hidalgo a block from the water, rents cars with unlimited kilometers for US$70 per day. (☎ 135 10 90. Open M-Sa 8am-1pm and 3-6pm, Su 8am-1pm.) **Supermarket: El Pescador** is on Salvatierra and Independencia. (☎ 135 00 60. Open daily 7:30am-10:30pm.) **Police:** (☎ 135 00 35). **Red Cross:** on Salvatierra at Deportiva. Little English spoken. (☎ 135 11 11; emergency 135 00 35. Open daily 10am-noon and 3-8pm.) **Pharmacy:** Every night, a different pharmacy is open 24hr. Check the door of **Farmacia Flores,** on Salvatierra, between Ayuntamiento and Independencia, for the schedule. (☎ 135 03 21. Open 8am-10pm.) **Hospital: Centro de Salud** on Salvatierra, one block from the bus terminal. English spoken. (☎ 135 00 39.) **Fax: Telecomm,** next to the post office (☎ 135 03 87. Open M-F 8am-2pm, Sa 8-11am.) **Internet access: Internet C@fé,** on Madero by the *zócalo*. (☎ 135 00 84. 30 pesos per 30min. Open M-F 9am-2pm and 4-7pm, Sa 10am-1:30pm.) **Post office:** on Salvatierra and Deportiva, behind the Red Cross. (☎ 135 06 47. Open M-F 8am-3pm.) **Postal code:** 23880.

ACCOMMODATIONS

Loreto caters to a more affluent crowd; good cheap rooms can be tough to find. But fear not—a bit of searching rewards the diligent.

Motel Brenda (☎ 135 07 07), on Juárez near Marquez de Leon. Immaculate rooms with powerful A/C and cable TV. Free parking. Singles 200 pesos; doubles 230 pesos.

Motel Salvatierra (☎ 135 00 21), on Salvatierra, across from PEMEX and near the bus station. Small, yellow rooms with loud but effective A/C and private baths. The busy road out front can be noisy in the morning. Singles 200 pesos; doubles 220 pesos.

Motel Davis, on Davis about 4 blocks north of the *zócalo*. Hand-painted sign marks the door. The cheapest rooms in town, if you can tolerate a muddy yard and slightly run-down conditions. Simple, very small rooms with tiny baths and fans. Rooms 100 pesos.

El Moro RV Park, Robles 8 (☎/fax 135 05 42), a couple of blocks inland off Salvatierra. A big dusty parking lot. Minimal shade, but the friendly staff makes up for it. Pitch a tent anywhere. Office open daily 7am-midnight. Trailer US$14; camping US$6 per person.

FOOD

Good, cheap food is plentiful. Most spots in the *centro* offer at least a few budget options, and a variety of eateries surround the bus station on Salvatierra.

▨ **Mexico Lindo,** on Hidalgo just past the intersection with Salvatierra. Unknown to most tourists, this tiny 1-room restaurant serves the best food in town. Grab a few cold *cervezas* to cool you down—the room gets swelteringly hot. Try the *alambres* (a mixture of beef, cheese, peppers, onion, and bacon; 50 pesos). Open daily 7:30am-10:30pm.

McLulu's, on Hidalgo between Independencia and Militar, offers up 8 different types of tacos and claims the largest selection in Baja. Tasty *carne asada, carne con chile, chorizo, fish,* or shrimp tacos (9 pesos). Open daily 10am-8pm.

Cafe Olé, Madero 14 (☎ 135 04 96), just off the *zócalo*. The local breakfast spot. Tourists and locals alike lounge at outdoor tables, chatting over *chilaquiles con huevos* (30 pesos) and *huevos rancheros* (27 pesos). Open M-Sa 7am-10pm, Su 7am-2pm.

👁 🎵 SIGHTS AND ENTERTAINMENT

Lined with shady waterfront benches, Loreto's *malecón* is a popular place for an evening stroll. The **public beach,** at the south end of the *malecón* has fine grey sand and stunning views, but slightly murky waves. **Nopoló,** 7km south, has better beaches and excellent snorkeling. FONATUR, the Mexican tourist promotion board, had planned to make this little port a mega-resort like Los Cabos, but the project was stalled by investor skepticism. Now, lonely hotels are surrounded by manicured gardens and eerily vacant lots overlook sandy beaches and crystal clear water. Walk boldly through the "hotels" to reach the beach.

Three desert islands and a few rocky points jut from the water like sentinels guard the port of Loreto. **Isla del Carmen,** the largest island in the Sea of Cortés, is home to several animal and plant species unique to the island, including a rattle-less rattlesnake and a species of gigantic barrel cacti. Unfortunately, access to the privately-owned island has been seriously restricted. Nearby **Isla Coronado** is easier to access, and its wide white sand beaches host a herd of friendly sea lions.

Las Parras Tours, Madero 16, takes small groups on boat trips around the island. The 4-5hr. trip includes plenty of time to snorkel or relax on the beautiful beach. (☎ 135 10 10; fax 135 09 00; www.tourbaja.com. US$35 per person; min. 2 persons. Diving trips US$70. Mountain bike rentals US$5 per hr.; 4-5hr. tours US$45. Kayaks US$5 per hr.) **Arturo's Sports Fishing Fleet,** on Hidalgo half a block from the beach, offers fishing trips in the waters around Loreto. Summer anglers (May-Sept.) hook mostly dorado, marlin, and tuna; from December-June, look for yellowtail, cabrilla, and red snapper. (☎ 135 07 66. Open M-Sa 9am-1pm and 4-7pm, Su 9am-1pm. 7hr. fishing US$170 for 2 people aboard a *panga;* US$195 for 3 people on a super *panga.*) If you prefer to go it alone, sizable red snapper and grouper hide among the large rocks at the end on the left side of the pier, toward the north end of the *malecón.*

Museo de las Misiones, one block west of the plaza, is built in a monastic complex reconstructed in the 1940s. Sculptures and paintings accompany displays on Jesuit mission life. The museum also provides information on missions throughout Baja. (☎ 135 04 41. Open Tu-Su 9am-1pm and 1:45-6pm. 27 pesos.) The **Misión de Nuestra Señora de Loreto,** as the plaque above the door proclaims, is the mother of all California missions. The church was consecrated in 1697 in a small tent, made permanent in 1699, and enlarged to its present form by 1752. It mirrors the simple lines and plain walls of early Renaissance churches, with semicircular stone arches in perfect proportion to the height of the whitewashed nave. The earthquakes that prompted the town's abandonment did surprisingly little damage to the church, which has been almost completely restored.

Loreto is not the place to go for rip-roaring nightlife. For a quiet evening of beer and traditional guitar, head to **Mike's Bar,** on Hidalgo a few blocks from the water. (☎ 135 11 26. Beer 20 pesos. Open daily 11am-3am.)

CIUDAD CONSTITUCIÓN ☎ 1

Though there is nothing wrong with the clean and safe transportation hub of Ciudad Constitución (pop. 35,000), it lacks charm, sophistication, and sights. A few inexpensive hotels, banks (the last until La Paz), and gas (the last before El Cien) are the only reasons to stop here. Autotransportes Águila (☎ 132 03 70), at Suárez and Juárez goes to **La Paz** (3hr., every hr. 1am-7pm, 105 pesos); **Loreto** (2hr., 6 per day 11:45am-11:45pm, 84 pesos); **Puerto San Carlos** (1hr., 10:45am and 5:15pm, 40 pesos); **Tijuana** (20hr., 11:45am and 10:45pm, 730 pesos); and points in between. From the bus station, walk two blocks to the corner of Olachea, the main street. There's a **Banamex** with a 24hr. **ATM** a few blocks farther on, at Olachea and Francisco Mina. (Open M-F 8:30am-4:30pm.) **Police:** (☎ 132 11 12) on Olachea, at the turn off for Puerto San Carlos. **Red Cross:** (☎ 132 11 11) 5 blocks off Olachea at Ramirez and Degollado. No English spoken. **Farmacia San Martín,** Suárez at

BAJA CALIFORNIA

Olachea, has a list of nearby pharmacies open on any given night. (☎ 132 14 28. Open daily 8am-10pm.) **IMSS** (☎ 132 03 88) at Olachea and Independencia. No English spoken. **Supermercado El Mar,** Olachea and Morelos. (☎ 132 10 21. Open daily 7am-10pm.)

On Olachea at Hidalgo, two blocks before the bank is olive-colored **Hotel Conchita.** Rooms vary in size, and are furnished simply and practically, with TV. (Singles 170 pesos; doubles 230 pesos.) **Carnitas Selva** is a local favorite on Olachea between Niños Héroes and Domínguez. (☎ 132 55 51. Big orders of *carnitas* and other exotic pig parts 30 pesos. Open daily 9:30am-when they run out of meat.)

JUST SAY NO. At the 11km marker north of Ciudad Insurgentes, the Mexican military maintains a semi-permanent checkpoint where all vehicles must stop to be searched for illegal arms and drugs. The check will go faster if you are not carrying sealed boxes, tied bags, or locked chests (or drugs and weapons). Keep everything available for quick inspection, and soldiers may wave you through with a cursory glance. Then again, they may thump your car hood, probe your upholstery, and pick apart the fibers of your floor mats. Buses are not spared this treatment. **Let's Go does not recommend smuggling contraband.**

PUERTO SAN CARLOS ☎ 1

Every year at whale-watching time, tiny Puerto San Carlos (pop. 3000) undergoes a magical transformation. Beginning in November, hotels dust off their bedposts, tent encampments blossom, and local pilots commandeer every available fishing boat to transport tourists to see the estimated 18,000 grey whales that migrate from the Bering Sea through the Pacific to Bahías Magdalena and Almejas. During peak mating season (mid-Jan. to mid-Mar.), the lovestruck creatures wow crowds with aquatic acrobatics. When they leave in April, the town once again becomes a sleepy village of boarded-up restaurants and nearly vacant sand roads.

⊟ TRANSPORTATION. Puerto San Carlos is easily accessible by car and bus. **Autotransportes Águila** buses, leaving from the small white terminal on La Paz and Morelos, head to: **Cabo San Lucas** (7hr., 1:45pm, 235 pesos); **Constitución** (1hr., 7:30am and 1:45pm, 40 pesos); **La Paz** (4hr., 7:30am and 1:45pm, 150 pesos).

⊟⊟ ORIENTATION AND PRACTICAL INFORMATION. Almost all services are along the main street, **La Paz,** or near the docks of the bay. All streets here are sand (be wary of parking on the side of the road—you may get trapped), and marked by illegibly bleached street signs. Most streets don't have names. The new, well-marked **tourist office** near the docks is open August-April. If you come during low season, ask at **Hotel Alcatraz** for information—the staff's patience and friendliness compensate for their limited English. Be forewarned: San Carlos has **no banks, ATMs, casas de cambios, or credit card connections.** Everything here operates using cash. The nearest bank is in Ciudad Constitución (see p. 173). **Police:** (☎ 136 03 96) on La Paz and Callejon Baja California near the park. No English spoken. **Farmacia Isaac** is on La Paz near IMSS. Open daily 8am-1pm and 4-7pm. The **IMSS** is at La Paz and México. No English spoken. (☎ 136 03 96.) **Post office:** on La Paz between México and Juárez, near the park. (Open M-F 9am-3pm.) **Postal Code:** 23740.

⊟⊟ ACCOMMODATIONS AND FOOD. Finding budget rooms in San Carlos isn't easy. This town has only 100 simple rooms among its few hotels, and come whale-watching season they are at a premium. The best deal in town is **Motel Las Brisas.** From the bus station, take a right onto La Paz, then make a right and a quick left on Madero; the hotel will be on your left. Clean, yellow rooms with large fans surround a parking lot decorated with murals and exotic plants. (☎ 136 01 52 or 136 01 59. Singles and doubles 135 pesos.) **Hotel Palmar,** on Acapulco and Puerto Vallarta, has slightly older but tidy rooms. (☎ 136 00 35. Singles 230 pesos; doubles

280 pesos.) **Nancy's RV park,** near the port (☎ 136 01 95) offers full hookups for 100 pesos. Camping on the barrier islands is free, but only accessible by boat.

Dining in San Carlos is homey: a string of restaurant/living rooms along La Paz and Morelos allow you to meet locals, while enjoying remarkably fresh delicacies from the sea. **Lonchería La Pasadita,** on La Paz and México, is a town favorite, and is the epitome of informal dining with concrete floors and counter seating. Platters of *machaca* (grilled shredded beef with peppers and onions) or *pollo con mole* run 30-35 pesos. (☎ 136 01 29. Open daily 7am-10pm.) **Mariscos los Arcos** on La Paz near IMSS is known for its seafood. (☎ 136 03 47. *Sopa de mariscos* jammed with every kind of seafood available 50 pesos. Open daily 8am-11pm.)

⌨⌨ SIGHTS AND BEACHES. Both **Bahía Magdalena** and **Bahía Almeja** lie just south of Puerto San Carlos and are home to some of the best whale-watching in the world. Grey whales migrate south from feeding grounds in Alaska to visit Baja California every winter. The warm, shallow waters of Bahía Magdalena make it one of the most important calving areas, and hundreds of whales stop over here in November and December for this purpose. Fertile soon after calving, the whales spend their days from January to March mating, and dazzling tourists, in the bay.

Lying at the intersection of temperate and tropical currents, Bahía Magdalena is rich in both temperate and tropical species of fish, shellfish, and birds, making it a worthwhile visit even in whale-less summer months. The **barrier islands** appear to be mostly sand and dunes, but extensive mangroves, intertidal sand and mud flats, and sea grass beds make these ecosystems as biologically diverse as the bay itself. Among the animals calling the islands home are two colonies of sea lions. The **Center for Coastal Studies** outside of town studies animal activity in the bay. The cheapest way to explore the islands is to make an ad-hoc deal with one of the fishermen departing from **Playa la Curva** in front of the PEMEX station. Unless you plan to camp on the islands, be sure to make pick-up plans before you embark. The tourist office will help you find a secure boat (licensed and insured), or you can rent one directly at **Hotel Alcatraz,** a member of the local boating consortium. (US$40 per hr. or US$80 per half-day for up to 6 people.)

Feisty Pacific waves at **Cabo San Lázaro** and **Point Hughes,** both on the western tip of **Isla Magdalena,** will keep even veteran surfers on their toes. A surf encampment (☎ 136 00 04) operates July through December. Reed huts scattered along the beach offer protection from the oppressive sun. Fifteen species of clam and starfish inhabit the sparkling water. A large colony of *lobos marinos* (sea lions) lives near the island's southern tip. Most tourists are oblivious to the fact that **Bahía Magdalena** has some of Baja's best **windsurfing.** Breezes blow between barrier islands and the main shore, carrying surfers for miles. If you plan to pursue the winds in San Carlos, bring your own gear—its impossible to find rentals in town.

LA PAZ ☎ 1

John Steinbeck's novel *The Pearl* depicted La Paz (pop. 200,000) as a tiny, unworldly treasure chest. However, the town's pearl industry was wiped out in the 1940s when the oysters died from illness, and the tiny capital of Baja California Sur was forced to depend on fish and tourists to pay the rent. While the city has grown and prospered, it still maintains the small-town friendliness and grace that have enchanted visitors for generations. Contemporary La Paz is part port, part partytown, and part idyllic paradise. Ten tranquil beaches hug the bathwater-warm **Bahía de La Paz,** and breezes ruffle the hair of the Mexican families, skateboarders, glammed-up teens, and scruffy backpackers who turn out to meander along the serene boardwalk every evening.

▮ TRANSPORTATION

As the capital and largest city of Baja California Sur, La Paz is also the region's main transportation hub. In addition, it's possible to reach the Mexican mainland via the ferry connecting La Paz to Mazatlán and Los Mochis.

HAVING A WHALE OF A TIME! In 1970 the grey whale, long preyed upon by Pacific coast whalers, was thought to be extinct. Today, with a total population of around 18,000, the species has become a poster child for the effectiveness of wildlife preservation laws. Their breeding grounds along the coast of Baja California Sur are among the most important protected coastlines in North America. The entire world population of grey whales gives birth and mates in three sections of Baja California's coast: the lagoons of Ojo de Liebre, the lagoons of San Ignacio, and Bahía Magdalena. The whales are generally friendly, curious, and playful, and some may approach your boat and let you touch them. Watch for the following kinds of behavior:

Sounding: Arching the back above water before beginning a deep dive.

Breaching: A whale will jump out of the water, flip over, and enter the water nose-first. They often slap the water with their flukes (tails) on reentry.

Blowing: As a whale exhales, it will often "spit" water droplets into the air.

Eating: Although whales generally fast during the winter months, they have occasionally been observed eating in the bay late in the season. They will scoop up a large mouthful of sediment from the bottom of the bay and, lying on one side, let the mud and water filter through a series of baleen plates which trap small crustaceans and edible particles.

Dozzing: A whale may noisily slap water with a fins while it lies on its side.

Spyhopping: A whale will pop its head out of the water, fix an enormous eye on whatever strikes its fancy, and stare for minutes on end, like a submarine periscope. They often pivot to survey the area before slipping back into the water.

GETTING AROUND

The **municipal bus system** serves the city irregularly (every 30-45min., 6am-10pm, 4 pesos). Flag down buses anywhere, or wait by the main stop on Revolución and Degollado, next to the market. The city center is easily navigable on foot.

GETTING AWAY

Airport: West of La Paz, easily accessible by taxi (120 pesos). The airport is served by **AeroMéxico,** on Obregón between Hidalgo and Morelos (☎ 122 00 91; open M-Sa 9am-7pm, Su 9am-5:30pm), and **AeroCalifornia,** Obregón between Ocampo and Bravo (☎ 125 10 23; open daily 8am-8:45pm).

Buses: La Paz has 3 bus stations.

Main station: on Jalisco and Independencia, about 25 blocks southeast of downtown (open for tickets daily 6am-9:30pm). 2 municipal buses, "Central Camionera" and "Urbano," head to the terminal; catch them near the public market at Degollado and Revolución. **Taxis** 30 pesos. Águila Autotransportes (☎ 122 30 63, ext. 113) serves points north (6 per day 9am-8pm): **Ciudad Constitución** (3hr., 104 pesos); **Loreto** (5hr., 188 pesos); **Mulegé** (7hr., 260 pesos). The 9am, noon, and 8pm buses continue to **Ensenada** (18hr., 760 pesos); **San Ignacio** (10hr., 350 pesos); **Santa Rosalía** (8hr., 300 pesos). The 8pm goes all the way to Tijuana (22hr., 840 pesos). Buses head south to **Los Cabos** every hour 6am-8pm (2½hr., 100 pesos).

La Paz Autotransportes: (☎ 122 21 57), Degollado at Prieto, sends buses south to: **Todos Santos** (1½hr., 9 per day 6am-7pm, 45 pesos) continuing to **Cabo San Lucas** (2½hr., 85 pesos).

Águila Malecón: (☎ 122 78 98), on Independencia at Obregón, runs south along the East Cape (7:30, 11:30am, 1:30, and 3:30pm) to: **Cabo San Lucas** (2½hr., 8 per day 9:30-7:30pm, 100 pesos); **Los Barriles** (2hr., 70 pesos); **San José del Cabo** (3hr., 100 pesos); **Santiago** (2½hr., 80 pesos). The same station has buses to nearby beaches: **Playas El Caimancito, El Coromuel, Palmira, Tesoro,** and **Pichilingue** (every hr., 15 pesos), and to **Playas Balandras** and **Tecolote** (45min.; 11am, noon, 2, and 5pm; 25 pesos). The last bus back to La Paz leaves Tecolote 5:30pm and Pichilingue 7pm; be sure to confirm schedules with the driver.

Ferries: Ferries leave from the suburb of **Pichilingue** to the mainland. **Autotransportes Aguila** buses run between the dock and the downtown terminal on Obregón, between Independencia and 5 de Mayo (M-F 9:30am and every hr. 11:30am-5:30pm; 20

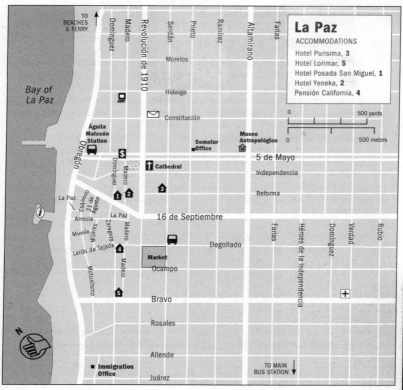

La Paz

ACCOMMODATIONS

Hotel Purisima, 3
Hotel Lorimar, 5
Hotel Posada San Miguel, 1
Hotel Yeneka, 2
Pensión California, 4

pesos). Taxis from the dock to downtown cost 100 pesos. Buy ferry tickets at the **Sematur Company** office, on 5 de Mayo at Prieto. (☎ 125 88 99 or toll-free 01 800 696 96 00. Open M-F 8am-6pm, Sa-Su 8am-noon. Dock office open daily 8am-10pm.) Ferries go to **Mazatlán** (15hr.; daily at 3pm; 460-1500 pesos, cars 3550 pesos, motorcycles 850 pesos) and **Topolobampo,** a suburb of **Los Mochis** (9hr.; M, W, F, 8 and 9pm; Tu, Th, Sa at 10pm; 360-1270 pesos, cars 2200 pesos, motorcycles 720 pesos). To get a vehicle on the ferry, you will need **three photocopies** of proof of Mexican insurance (or a major credit card with the car owner's name on it), car registration showing it is registered to the driver, permission for the importation of a car into Mexico, and a tourist card. You can get permits at **Banjército,** at the ferry stop in Pichilingue (☎ 122 11 16; permits US$16.50; open daily 9am-2pm), or through **AAA** in the US. Whether or not you have a car, you will need a **tourist card (FMT)** if you entered Mexico via Baja California and are bound for the mainland (see p. 177). Clear all paperwork before purchasing the ticket; otherwise, Sematur will deny you a spot whether or not you have reservations.

TICKET TO RIDE. Getting a ferry ticket isn't as easy as it seems—it requires persistence and determination. To secure a ticket, make reservations days in advance. Go to the Sematur office first thing after arriving into town, preferably right after it opens, and get the ticket in hand as soon as possible. During holidays, competition for tickets is fierce. *Clase salón* (3rd class) is cheapest, and usually most in demand. In addition, Sematur has a reputation for raising prices without prior announcement.

▼ PRACTICAL INFORMATION

TOURIST, FINANCIAL, AND LOCAL SERVICES

Tourist Office: (☎ 122 59 39), Obregón at 16 de Septiembre, in a pavilion on the water. Excellent maps and information. Helpful English-speaking staff. Weekends and evenings staffed by the tourist police. Open M-F 8am-10pm, Sa-Su noon-midnight.

Tourist Police: Fabulous folks easily recognized by their starched white uniforms and big grins. Their job is "protection and orientation," but they will also give recommendations about hiking, beaches, hotels, restaurants, and barbers.

Immigration Office: Servicios Migratorios, Obregón 2140 (☎ 125 34 93; fax 122 04 29), between Juárez and Allende. You must stop here to obtain a tourist card if you entered Mexico via Baja California and are bound for the mainland. Open M-F 9am-6pm. After hours, visit the airport outpost (☎ 124 63 49). Open daily 8am-8:30pm.

Currency Exchange: Banks line 16 de Septiembre within a few blocks of the bay. **Bancomer** (☎ 125 42 48), on 16 de Septiembre, half a block from the waterfront, is open for exchange M-F 8:30am-4pm. **BITAL** (☎ 122 22 89) 5 de Mayo, at Madero, has talking doors. Open for exchange M-F 8am-7pm, Sa 8am-3pm. Both banks have 24hr. **ATMs** and exchange traveler's checks and foreign currencies.

American Express: (☎ 122 86 66), 5 de Mayo at Domínguez. Open daily 8am-8pm.

Laundry: La Paz Lava, Mutualismo 260 (☎ 123 40 37), on Ocampo a block down from Mijares. 20 pesos; full service 36 pesos. Open daily 8am-midnight.

EMERGENCY AND COMMUNICATIONS

Emergency: ☎ 066.

Police: (☎ 122 13 99; emergency 060), on Colima at México. Little English spoken.

Red Cross: Reforma 1091 (☎ 122 12 22), between Católica and Ortega. Little English spoken.

Pharmacy: Farmacia Bravo (☎ 122 69 33), Bravo at Verdad, next to the hospital. Open 24hr. In the *centro*, one of the pharmacies on Plaza Constitución is always open.

Hospital: Salvatierra (☎ 122 14 96 or 122 14 97), on Bravo at Verdad, between Domínguez and the Oncological Institute. Little English spoken.

Fax: TELECOM (☎ 125 90 71; fax 125 08 09), upstairs from the post office. Open M-Sa 8am-7:30pm, Su 8-11:30am.

Internet: Baja Net Cafe Internet, Madero 430 (☎ 125 93 80), between Hidalgo and Constitución. 1 peso per min., 10min. minimum. Open M-Sa 8am-8pm, Su 10am-8pm.

Post Office: (☎ 122 03 88), on Revolución at Constitución. Open M-F 8am-3pm, Sa 9am-1pm.

Postal Code: 23000.

▼ ACCOMMODATIONS

Budget hotels are common in the downtown area. Most are simple, no-nonsense rooms for travelers waiting for a ferry.

Hotel Yeneka, Madero 1520 (☎ 125 46 88), between 16 de Septiembre and Independencia. Legendary among backpackers. Whale skeletons and a stuffed monkey driving a bright blue Model-T Ford decorate the lush courtyard. Very firm beds in very clean rooms. Laundry, fax, bike rentals, and restaurant. Reservations recommended. Singles 199 pesos; doubles 259 pesos; triples 331 pesos.

Hotel Purisima, 16 de Septiembre 408 (☎ 122 34 44). La Paz's most luxurious budget hotel. Large, sparkling rooms with A/C and TV fill the huge, retina-burning, bright orange building. Singles 250 pesos; doubles 300 pesos; triples 350 pesos.

Hotel Posada San Miguel, Domínguez 1510 (☎ 125 88 88), off 16 de Septiembre. Photographs, painted tiles, and wrought-iron scrollwork recall La Paz's early days. Too bad the charm hasn't seeped into the spartan rooms. Fans and large, comfortable beds. Singles 110 pesos; doubles 130 pesos; triples 150 pesos; quads 170 pesos.

Hotel Lorimar (☎/fax 125 38 22), on Bravo between Madero and Mutualismo. Half of this family-run hotel has been renovated. Newer rooms are freshly painted, with new baths. Old singles 200 pesos; old doubles 270 pesos. New singles and doubles 360 pesos; new triples 415 pesos; each additional person 50 pesos.

Pensión California Casa de Huéspedes, Degollado 209 (☎ 122 28 96), at Madero—look for the bright blue and yellow building. Another famous, funky backpacker hangout. Windowless small rooms come with concrete furniture, air vents, and ceiling fans. Private baths, but the toilet is in the shower, and you may have to bathe with a few bugs from the drain. Singles 120 pesos; doubles 160 pesos; triples 200 pesos.

▣ FOOD

On the waterfront you'll find decor, menus, and prices geared toward peso-spewing tourists. Move inland a few blocks and watch prices plunge, as sit-down restaurants disappear amid the abundant *taquerías*. Seafood meals are generally fresh and *tacos de pescado* delicious (and cheap). Grab fruits, veggies, and fresh fish at the **public market,** Degollado and Revolución. La Paz loves its ice cream and *paletas;* Revolución alone has five **La Michoacana** ice cream shops.

▣ **La Fonda** (☎ 125 47 00), Revolución and Bravo. Undiscovered by tourists, La Fonda serves the cheapest and best food in the *centro. Comida corrida* or delectable *pescado a la plancha* 30 pesos. Open M-Sa 8am-8pm, Su 8am-5pm.

▣ **Restaurant Palapa Adriana** (☎ 122 83 29), on the beach off Obregón at Constitución. Practically in the water. Great view, with complimentary sea breeze and lollipop. Red snapper 60 pesos. *Pollo con mole* 40 pesos. Open M-F 8am-10pm, Sa-Su 1pm-9pm.

Restaurante El Quinto Sol (☎ 122 16 92), on Domínguez at Independencia. One of the few strictly vegetarian joints in Baja California, the menu includes excellent *licuados* (20 pesos) and a tasty veggie combo (40 pesos). Generous *comida corrida* 50 pesos. Open M-Sa 7am-10pm, Su 8am-3pm.

Cafe El Callejón, on de La Paz just off Obregón. Be serenaded by guitar-wielding musicians as you enjoy the salty air and munch on traditional Mexican dishes. Generous *antojitos* 21-38 pesos. Try the *milanesa* (breaded carne asada; 50 pesos). Open Tu-Su 8am-10pm, but get there before 9pm if you want to snag a table.

◉ SIGHTS

The **Museo Regional de Antropología e Historia,** at 5 de Mayo and Altamirano, has four floors of fascinating, well kept exhibits on the history of the southern peninsula from Pre-Hispanic to modern times. All descriptions are in Spanish. (☎ 122 01 62; fax 125 64 24. Open M-F 8am-6pm, Sa 9am-2pm. Free.) Fans of handicrafts will appreciate the **pottery factory,** at Iglesias between Revolución and Serdán. Artisans will gladly show you around, though their English ranges from limited to nonexistent. (Open M-Sa 9am-noon and 4-8pm.)

≋ BEACHES

The beaches of La Paz snuggle into small coves, between cactus-studded hills and calm, transparent water. This is prime windsurfing territory. Be careful—lifeguards make appearances only on weekends and at popular beaches. If you're looking to sunbathe, some of the smaller beaches along the *malecón* have fine sand, but don't expect tranquility—the city's main road runs 20 ft. from the water—or cleanliness.

NEAR PLAYA TECOLOTE. The best and most popular beach is **Playa Tecolote** (Owl Beach), 25km northeast of town on Rte 1. A quiet extension of the Sea of Cortés laps against this gorgeous stretch of gleaming white sand near tall mountains. Unfortunately, the beach is lined with restaurants. Tecolote is terrific for **camping.** Spots on the east side of the beach, along the road to the more secluded but rockier **Playa El Coyote,** come equipped with a stone barbecue pit. The road to El Coyote itself is only passable by high clearance vehicles. **Actividades Aquatica** (☎ 122 16 07), on Tecolote, run by Hotel Miramar, rents snorkeling gear (80 pesos per day) and organizes trips to **Isla Espíritu Santo** (300 pesos per person, 4 person minimum). **Playa Balandra,** just south of Tecolote, is the answer for those looking to escape from the restaurants and crowds. A stunning ring of white sand surrounds the shallow cove. Snorkeling at Balandra is excellent. Because facilities are sparse and sporadically open, it is best to rent equipment either in the city or at nearby Pichilingue or Tecolote. *(Take an Autotransportes Águila bus (45min., noon and 2pm, 20 pesos; return bus at 5:30pm) from the mini-station on Obregón and Independencia.)*

NEAR PLAYA PICHILINGUE. Beaches near Playa Pichilingue are out of walking distance from the city center, but within a 30min. bus ride. From the stop at the ferry dock, an additional ½km walk leads to **Playa Pichilingue,** a favorite among teens, who splash in the shallow waters and ride paddleboats (30 pesos per hr.). The bus route loops, passing many beaches near the city. Although **Playa El Coromuel** is closest to La Paz, its the last bus stop. The powdery sands are often dirty and packed with raucous partiers, but small rock outcroppings at the north end of the beach hide a relatively tranquil stretch. **Playa Caimancito,** a little past Coromuel, is cleaner and more scenic, but just as busy. Most beaches between La Paz and Tecolote have *palapa* shelters and some kind of food and drink available. *(Take the "Pichilingue" bus up the coast (up to 30min., every hr., 15 pesos). You'll see the beaches from the bus before you reach them, so if you like what you see, let the driver know.)*

DIVING AND SNORKELING. The fun doesn't stop at the shoreline—magnificent offshore opportunities await snorkelers and certified divers. North of La Paz is **Salvatierra Wreck,** a dive spot where a 91m ferry boat sank in 1976. Decked with sponges and sea fans, the wreck attracts hordes of colorful fish, but strong currents may deter inexperienced divers. Also popular is the huge **Cerralvo Island,** east of La Paz, which promises reefs, large fish, and untouched wilderness. **Isla Espíritu Santo** has hidden caves, pristine beaches, good diving reefs, and excellent snorkeling; the shallow reef at **Bahía San Gabriel** here is appropriate for both snorkeling and diving. Due to strong currents, fluctuating weather conditions, and inaccessibility, diving in the La Paz area requires guides, but unguided snorkeling is possible if you stay close to shore and check conditions before heading out. **Baja Diving and Service,** Obregón 1665, between 16 de Septiembre and Callejón La Paz, organizes daily scuba and snorkeling trips to nearby reefs, wrecks, and islands. (☎ 122 18 26; fax 122 86 44. Trips leave at 7am and return between 3 and 5pm. Scuba trips 870 pesos per day without equipment, US$20 extra for equipment; snorkeling trips 400 pesos per person per day. All include lunch; diving trips include 2-3 tanks. Open daily 9am-1pm and 4-8pm.) They also rent kayaks for exploring the calm waters of Bahía de La Paz (Singles US$18 half day, US$30 full-day; doubles US$30 half-day, US$50 full-day.) For excellent snorkeling easily accessible by car, head to **San Juan de la Costa** just past Centenario, 13km north of La Paz on the Transpeninsular. Nearby on the same road is the beachcomber's paradise of **El Comitán,** with sand and mud flats where, particularly after a storm, the tides deposit shells, amethyst, and other semi-precious stones.

▓ NIGHTLIFE

For a small city, La Paz has a lot to offer night owls. The *malecón* becomes an intense cruise scene, and, around midnight, revelers pack the many waterfront clubs. Guys, let her get this one—women are often charged less for drinks.

Las Varitas (☎ 125 20 25), Independencia and Domínguez. A large stage and live bands dominate one side of the club, and a young crowd packs the multi-level platforms. The central dance floor never seems to have enough room—dancers gradually take over tabletops. Lively and fun, even on weeknights. Open Tu-Su 10pm-3am.

La Cantina, at Obregón and Bunado, across from the dock. A pool hall occupies the front, behind it is a usually mellow sports bar, and a loud disco-ball lit dance party breaks it down in back. 2-for-1 drinks 7-9pm. Open Tu-Su 7pm-3am.

Carlos 'n' Charlie's/La Paz-Lapa (☎ 122 92 90), Obregón and 16 de Septiembre, the most noticeable structure in town. Savor huge margaritas (34 pesos), or go buck-wild at the outdoor booze and rockfest. US and Mexican teens get down to everything from hard rock to rap to house under giant palm trees. Tu ladies' night before midnight (free drinks and no cover). W open bar, cover 120 pesos for men, 60 pesos for women. Cover 30 pesos other nights. Restaurant open daily; club open Tu and F-Sa 10pm-4am.

Bling Bling, Arreola 270C (☎ 122 35 26 or 122 75 86), 2 blocks from the water. Walls jammed with gaudy glow in the dark palm trees and monkeys. Vast floor leaves plenty of elbow room to dance to house, disco, and early 80s favorites. Th ladies' night, complete with male dancers 9-11pm. W and Sa open bar 9pm-2am, cover 120 pesos for men, 60 pesos for women. Other nights no cover. Open Tu-Sa 9pm-4am.

Paradise Found (☎ 125 73 40), Obregón and Allende. Inexpensive drinks draw crowds for Happy Hour 3-9pm. Quieter later in the evening, though the seashore view and free pool table serve as decent incentives to stay. Happy Hour beer 8 pesos, margaritas 11 pesos; prices double after 9pm. Open M-Sa 11pm-late.

TODOS SANTOS ☎ 1

Halfway between La Paz and Cabo San Lucas on Baja's Pacific coast, the sophisticated town of Todos Santos (pop. 4000) has become known in recent years for its community of English-speaking expats who have fallen in love with the area's rolling cactus hills and laid-back demeanor. However, the local Mexican population and culture—from the popular daily *siesta* to the abundance of excellent *taquerías*—still influence the lifestyle. Still, the town is rapidly filling up with gourmet shops, classy restaurants, and art galleries. Real estate developers have had their eye on idyllic Todos Santos for several years, but locals steadfastly fight off the resort plague. Many a visiting tourist has fallen under the spell of the lively village and spectacular beaches, and some have decided to become expats themselves.

▟ TRANSPORTATION

The **bus stop** (☎ 145 01 70) is in front of Pilar's taco stand, on the corner of Zaragoza and Colegio Militar. Buy tickets inside from Pilar; if you have questions about bus times or anything else, she is an excellent person to talk to. *De paso* buses run north to **La Paz** (1hr., every hr. 6:30am-8pm, 45 pesos) and south to **San José del Cabo** (1½hr., 8 per day 7am-9pm, 70 pesos) via **Cabo San Lucas** (1hr., 45 pesos). Arriving buses may drop you off near Degollado and Militar, where the Transpeninsular Highway turns to head toward Los Cabos from La Paz.

▓ ▟ ORIENTATION AND PRACTICAL INFORMATION

Most services are located in the *centro*. **Legaspi** begins next to the church and runs north-south through town, paralleling **Centenario** on the other side of the church. Next come the two main streets, **Juárez** and **Militar,** which continue south to the *parque* and bus station. Be sure to grab the monthly *Calendario de Todos Santos,* which is available for free around town (try El Tecolote Libros) and has a small map in the center.

Todos Santos has no tourist office, but the American-owned **El Tecolote Libros,** on Juárez and Hidalgo, sells English-language magazines, maps, and a comprehensive book on the town. (☎ 145 02 95. Open Nov.-July daily 9am-5pm; Aug.-Oct. M-F

BAJA CALIFORNIA

9am-5pm.) **BanCrecer,** on the corner of Obregón and Juárez, the only bank in town, exchanges currency and traveler's checks and has a 24hr. **ATM.** (Open M-F 9am-1pm.) **Mercado Guluarte,** Morelos between Militar and Juárez. (☎ 145 00 06. Open M-Sa 7:30am-9pm, Su 7:30am-2pm.) Buy fruit at the small markets on Degollado and Juárez. **Police:** (☎ 145 08 85), in the Delegación Municipal complex at the plaza. Little English spoken. **Farmacia de Todos Santos,** on Juárez near León. (☎ 146 04 09. Open 24hr; knock at night.) **Hospital:** (☎ 145 00 95), on Juárez at Degollado. English spoken. **Internet Cafe,** across the street from the Message Center. (15 pesos per 10min. Open M-Sa 9am-5pm.) **Post office:** on Militar at León. (☎ 145 03 30. Open M-F 8am-3pm.) **Postal code:** 23300.

▓▟▓ ACCOMMODATIONS AND CAMPING

The best way to sleep on the cheap is to camp out. If you have the equipment, Todos Santos has plenty of gorgeous beaches, rolling hills, and pot-smoking, Kerouac-reading, boogie-boarding bodies. For those who prefer a roof, ▓**Motel Guluarte,** on Juárez at Morelos has clean, cozy rooms, fans or A/C, refrigerators, and TV. The motel also has a pool, which may or may not contain water. (☎ 145 00 06. Singles 170 pesos; doubles 250 pesos.) A step down is **Hotel Miramar,** three blocks off Degollado at Pedrajo and Mutualismo. Cheerful green-tiled rooms complement the green, algae-filled pool water. (☎ 145 03 41. Singles and doubles 175 pesos; triples 225 pesos.) Pleasant, shady **Las Casitas Bed and Breakfast,** on Rangel near Hidalgo, has a small space for tents. Bathroom and shower access included. (☎ 145 02 55. Camping US$6 for 1 person, US$10 for 2; discount in summer.) Mellow surfers wander the sprawling sands of **Pescadero Surf Camp,** south of Todos Santos on Mex. 9 at km 164. The camp is run by enthusiastic Americans, and offers a sweet pool with a swim-up *palapa* bar. (☎ 145 02 29. Camping US$7.)

▐ FOOD

Loncherías line Militar near the bus station, offering tacos for 10-14 pesos. ▓**Pilar's Taco Stand,** on the corner of Zaragoza and Militar, is not only the town's *de facto* bus station but also makes glorious fish tacos, with huge, golden-fried chunks of fresh fish. (8 pesos. ☎ 145 00 72. Open daily 8am-7pm.) Locals are understandably addicted to **Barajas Tacos,** an outdoor stand on Degollado and Cuauhtémoc uphill from the PEMEX, with excellent meat tacos (9 pesos). **Caffé Todos Santos,** on Centenario at the plaza, serves non-traditional Mexican food with vegetarian options. (Generous *quesadillas* with squash blossoms and mushrooms 60 pesos. Entrees 50-90 pesos.) The oldest eatery in town, **Restaurant Santa Monica,** on Degollado and Militar, has been open for 26 years. Try their *pescado a la veracruzana* (50 pesos) and you'll know why. (☎ 145 02 04. Open daily 7am-10pm.)

▥ ART GALLERIES

Modern art lovers are sure to be wowed by the high quality of galleries in Todos Santos. The town's new pride and joy, the **Galería de Todos Santos,** on Legaspi and Topete, displays the work of local artists, both Mexican and expat. (☎ 145 05 00. Open June-Sept. M-Sa 11am-4pm; Oct.-May M-Sa 10am-5pm.) A branch of the gallery is dedicated solely to abstract art recently opened on Centenario at Hidalgo. **Galería Logan,** at Juárez and Morelos, is devoted to the surreal landscapes and bold, swirling colors of Todos Santos resident Jill Logan. (☎ 145 01 51. Open M-Sa 10am-5pm.) Futuristic bronze and clay sculptures, off-the-wall clocks, and ornate mirrors are on parade at the **Santa Fe Art Gallery,** Centario 4, between Hidalgo and Márquez de León. (Open W-M 10am-5pm.) Take a peek into the **Charles Stewart Gallery and Studio,** on Obregón at Centenario, which is both Mr. Stewart's home and studio. Stewart helped found the Todos Santos artists' community by moving from Taos, New Mexico in 1983. His work ranges from realistic watercolors of nearby towns to abstract oil paintings. (☎ 145 02 65. Usually open M-Sa 10am-4pm.)

BEACHES

Todos Santos is surrounded by some of the region's most unspoiled beaches. Unfortunately, powerful Pacific currents make many of them unsafe for swimming. If you find yourself swept out to sea, do not immediately thrash toward shore—instead, swim parallel to the beach for a few hundred yards, and then calmly swim for land. The isolation of these pristine beaches may unsettle travelers; always bring a friend and return to town before dark. To get to romantic **La Posa**, go up Juárez and turn left on Topete. Follow the signs toward Hotel La Posa along a bumpy dirt road (2km). Leave your car next to the orange building and scramble up the rocky hill around the lagoon to the fabulous, and deserted, beach. Vicious undercurrents and powerful waves make La Posa unsuitable for swimming. To reach **Punta Lobos,** the stomping ground of the local sea lion population, turn left onto Degollado as you walk away from town. Roughly six blocks later, the city ends as the road becomes Mex. 19. Around km 54, turn right and follow the washboard road until you come to the rocky beach.

The only nearby beaches suitable for swimming are **Playa de las Palmas** and **Playa los Cerritos.** Scuffle your feet when you walk in to let the stingrays, who mate near the shore in June, know you're there. Los Cerritos, a popular family beach, lies approximately 14km south of Todos Santos. Look for a turn-off on the right side of the highway around km 65. The current is tamer here than elsewhere, but the waves are just as big—and great for surfing. Although relatively well-populated, the endless sands are anything but crowded. To rent boards and get the day's surf report, head to **Pescadero Surf Camp,** at km 64. All boards are ding-free and less than a year old. (☎ 145 02 29. Open daily 8am-1pm and 4-8pm. Surfboards US$3 per hr., US$12 per day; boogie boards US$2 per hr., US$7 per day. 1hr. surfing lesson US$20, includes board.) To reach **Playa de las Palmas (Playa San Pedrito),** drive 5km south from town on the highway, and turn right when you see the white Campo Experimental buildings on the left. Travel another 2½km, past verdant palm trees, to the beach. The serene and deserted shore is excellent for swimming and body surfing, and the fine sand is considered some of the best in the area.

A quiet and lovely surfing beach by the highway is **Playa San Pedro,** 8km south of town. To get there, turn off at the sign for San Pedrito RV Park. It's easy to find a sunbathing spot on these bohemian beaches, and nobody cares if you bare all. Head south for the best sands. Again, strong waves and currents deter swimmers.

DAYTRIPS FROM TODOS SANTOS

SIERRA DE LA LAGUNA

To get to the trailhead, drive south out of Todos Santos. After passing the marker for km 53 and climbing a small hill, you will see the turn-off on the left at the top of the hill. Drive down this dirt road through a fenced-off cattle ranch and bear right at the 1st unmarked major fork in the road. Follow signs for 40min. until you reach a locked gate and the end of the road. There is a small dirt lot to park your car.

Sierra de la Laguna, the mountain range that lines the cape, is visible from virtually any beach around Los Cabos and Todos Santos. The dark rain clouds hovering above the mountains are responsible for some of the most exotic flora and fauna in Baja California. The climate of the mountains is completely different from the surrounding coastal areas and can, in the winter, drop below freezing. **La Laguna,** the Sierra's most popular hiking destination, is a meadow of about four sq. km perched at an altitude of 1700m amid the rocky peaks of **Picacho la Laguna** and **Cerro las Casitas,** the range's tallest points. Once a lake, erosion from excessive rainfall destroyed the laguna's edges in the late 19th century, transforming La Laguna into a grassy meadow. The climb to the meadow is a grueling 8hr., with steep inclines toward the top. Successful hikers are rewarded with many beautiful vistas and rest-stops along the way, one of which (3hr. into the hike) offers a view of the entire width of the peninsula. The trail is well-marked with several campsites along the way, and at La Laguna as well.

LOS CABOS

The towns of Cabo San Lucas and San José del Cabo have undergone a dramatic transformation from the sad, sleepy towns described by John Steinbeck in his *Log from the Sea of Cortez*, into an elite, luxurious vacation destination. Along the beach leading from San José to San Lucas, luxury hotels form a glittering border between the desert and the ocean, and sparkling emerald golf courses attract a never-ending stream of moneyed tourists. Although Los Cabos are filled with margarita-guzzling, gift-buying, jet-skiing *norteamericanos* year-round, it's still possible to escape the crowds and enjoy the southern coast's stunning natural beauty—spectacular rock formations, unique underwater sandfalls, surf that rivals that of Hawaii, and glistening white beaches, arguably the most beautiful in all of Baja.

CABO SAN LUCAS ☎ 1

Cabo San Lucas, or simply "Cabo," stands majestically at the confluence of the Pacific Ocean and the Sea of Cortés. Dramatic golden cliffs plunge into warm azure waters, while rowdy *norteamericanos*, and the resort hotels that house them, occupy the glistening sands. As tourists pour more and more money into Cabo's restaurants and clubs, the town can't help but grow and prosper—at last count the population had swelled to 50,000 residents, including some 5,000 expatriates. Despite the influx of fast food and neon, Cabo has remained a friendly town, particularly as you move beyond the *centro*, where aggressive time share vendors and club promoters prowl day and night. Cabo's guilty pleasures merit the occasional splurge, and even budget travelers can delight in fabulous fish tacos, entertaining and gloriously tacky nightlife, and the requisite nonstop flow of margaritas beginning at breakfast and lasting until the next day's sunrise.

▐ TRANSPORTATION

Local Subur Cabos buses run to San José del Cabo (30min., every 15min., 16 pesos). Hop on the bus at the stop on Cárdenas between Vicario and Mendoza. ABC Autotransportes and Aguila (☎ 143 04 00) are north of town, by the PEMEX station—follow signs to Todos Santos; the bus station is right after you get on the highway. To get into town from the bus stop, take a local yellow bus (4 pesos) to Blvd. Marina. **Buses** go to **La Paz** (3hr., every hr. 6am-8pm, 100 pesos) via **Todos Santos** (1hr., 50 pesos) and **San José del Cabo** (30min., every 20min. 5am-10pm, 20 pesos). One *de paso* bus per day leaves at 4:30pm and heads north, stopping at: **Ciudad Constitución** (6hr., 200 pesos); **Ensenada** (23hr., 860 pesos); **Guerrero Negro** (14½hr., 540 pesos); **La Paz** (3hr., 100 pesos); **Loreto** (8½hr., 290 pesos); **Mulegé** (10½hr., 360 pesos); **San Ignacio** (12½hr., 450 pesos); **Santa Rosalía** (11½hr., 410 pesos); **San Quintín** (19hr., 750 pesos); **Tijuana** (26½hr., 940 pesos).

▐ ORIENTATION AND PRACTICAL INFORMATION

Restaurants, bars, and most tourist services concentrate on **Cárdenas**, between Morelos and the western edge of town, and along **Blvd. Marina**. Plazas are concrete malls or tight conglomerations of shops and follow the curve of the marina.

Tourist information: No official tourist office exists, but free, biased information and bad maps are dispensed by time-share hawkers all over the *centro*, from "tourist information" booths. Most car rental agencies have better maps (and often better advice).

Currency Exchange: Many hotels and restaurants prefer US dollars, and exchange them at 10 pesos to US$1 regardless of the going rate. **BITAL**, in Plaza Bonita (☎ 143 38 88), has a 24hr. **ATM.** and exchanges traveler's checks and foreign currencies. Open M-F 8am-7pm, Sa 8am-3pm. Another branch at Plaza de las Glorias has the same hours.

American Express: (☎ 143 57 88), in Plaza Bonita. Open M-F 9am-6pm, Sa 9am-1pm.

Supermarket: Almacenes Grupo Castro, Morelos at Revolución. Open daily 7am-11pm.

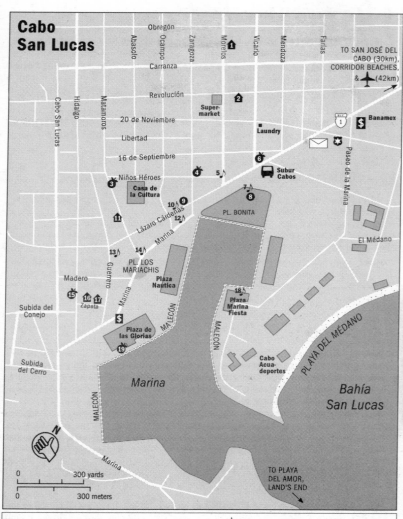

Cabo San Lucas

♦ ACCOMMODATIONS
Hotel Casa Blanca, **2**
Hotel Dos Mares, **16**
Hotel El Dorado, **1**
Hotel Maria Elena, **11**
Siesta Suites Hotel, **17**

🍎 FOOD
The Crazy Lobster Bar and Grill, **15**
El Pescador, **4**
Restaurant Doña Lolita, **3**
Restaurant Rey Sol, **6**
Solomon's Bar and Grill, **19**

♪ MUSIC AND CLUBS
Cabo Wabo, **13**
Giggling Marlin, **14**
Kokomo's, **12**
The Love Shack, **5**
The Rainbow Bar, **18**
Squid Roe, **10**
The Wave, **7**

● SERVICES
American Express, **8**
Farmacia Aramburo, **9**

BAJA CALIFORNIA

Car Rental: Budget (☎ 143 51 51), on Cárdenas between Guerrero and Hidalgo. Old school Volkswagens with unlimited km US$35 per day. Open daily 8am-6pm.

Police: (☎ 143 39 77), on Cárdenas, 2 blocks north of Morelos. No English spoken.

Red Cross: (☎ 143 33 00), at km 121 on the *carretera* to Todos Santos, near the PEMEX. No English spoken.

Pharmacy: Farmacia Aramburo (☎ 143 14 89), on Zaragoza and Cárdenas, at Plaza Aramburo. Open 8-11pm.

Hospital: IMSS (☎ 143 15 89), uphill from the bus station, near the Red Cross and PEMEX. Some English spoken.

Faxes: Telecomm (☎ 143 19 68; fax 143 02 31), next to the post office. Open M-F 8am-7:30pm, Sa 8am-3pm, Su 8am-11am.

Internet access: C@fé Europa, on Blvd. Marina in Plaza Nautica. 1 peso per min. Open M-Sa 9am-9pm.

Post office: (☎ 143 00 48) on Cárdenas, next to the police station. Open M-F 9am-4pm, Sa 9am-noon.

Postal code: 23451.

▚ ACCOMMODATIONS

Multi-million-dollar resorts dominate the coast of Cabo San Lucas, and even the cheapest hotels will take a bite out of your wallet. If you decide not to camp or sleep in San José, a few mid-range hotels will can meet your needs. During the winter high season, call ahead and be prepared to shell out 25% more than during the slower summer months. Most hotels base rates on US dollars and not pesos.

Hotel Maria Elena (☎ 143 32 96), on Matamoros between Cárdenas and Niños Héroes. Sparkling rooms have A/C and TVs. May-Oct singles 300 pesos; doubles 350 pesos. Nov.-Apr. singles 400 pesos; doubles 450 pesos; each additional person 50 pesos.

Hotel El Dorado (☎ 143 67 37), on Morelos near Carranza. Gigantic tiled rooms are spotless and simply furnished. A big swimming pool for grown-ups and a separate little one for the kiddies. Singles and doubles 275 pesos, with A/C 325 pesos; each additional person 50 pesos.

Siesta Suites Hotel (☎ 143 27 73 or 602 331 1354 in the US; fax 143 64 94; siesta@cabonet.net.mx), on Zapata near Guerrero. Colorful tiles, bright prints, and painted light fixtures. Most rooms have full kitchens (with utensils) and a separate bedroom off a fully-furnished living/eating area. A/C and satellite TV. Singles US$40; doubles US$50; each additional person US$10.

Hotel Dos Mares (☎ 143 03 30; hoteldosmares@cabo.com.mx), on Zapata. An incredibly tacky lobby fronts the slightly worn, institutional hotel. Basic yellow rooms come with refrigerator, phone, TV, and A/C. Outdoor swimming pool with a tiny but entertaining slide. Singles and doubles 350-400 pesos; each additional person 50 pesos.

Hotel Casa Blanca (☎ 143 53 60), on Revolución at Morelos. One of the cheapest places in town and probably an option only for the truly broke. Singles and doubles 200-240 pesos. Towel deposit 50 pesos.

Club Cabo Hotel Resort and Campground (☎ 143 33 48). Head out Cárdenas to the intersection with Mex. 19; continue to the beach, and turn left down a dirt road. Club Cabo is about 1km down on the right. A small, tidy campground with a wacky owner. The ping-pong table, hammock area, and pool are all pluses, and most sites are shaded. A short walk to the beach. US$7.50 per person for full hookup or tent site.

▟ FOOD

Fancy *palapa*-shaded waterfront meals are not for the budget traveler; for better deals, head inland along Morelos and its side streets or to the abundant *taquerías*.

▨ **Restaurant Doña Lolita,** at Niños Héroes and Matamoros, is a tiny open air shack filled with chattering locals. Roll the sand between your toes as you chill alongside trees sticking up through the roof and a deer head on the wall. Rotating menu of traditional Mexican food is written on a blackboard every day. Everything is cheap (30-50 pesos), tasty, and fresh from the grill or huge black pots. Open M-Sa 8am-10pm, Su 8am-4pm.

San José del Cabo

🏠 ACCOMMODATIONS

Hotel Ceci, **3**
Hotel Colli, **4**
Hotel Diana, **2**
San José Inn, **1**
Trailer Park Brisa del Mar, **5**

ACCOMMODATIONS

Thanks to the ever-encroaching mega-resorts of Cabo San Lucas and the corridor, room prices in the center of San José del Cabo are on a constant rise. Compared to Cabo San Lucas, however, San José del Cabo is still a virtual heaven for budget accommodations, most of which are on or near Zaragoza.

Hotel Diana (☎ 142 04 90), on Zaragoza near the *centro*. Friendly staff keep the Diana spotless and pleasant. Bright woven bedspreads add color to otherwise bland rooms, each with satellite TV and A/C. Singles or doubles 250 pesos; triples 300 pesos.

Hotel Ceci, Zaragoza 22, 1½ blocks from Mijares. Basic rooms with comfortable beds. Singles and doubles 160 pesos, with A/C 190 pesos; triples with A/C 210 pesos.

San José Inn (☎ 142 24 64), on Obregón and Guerrero. Worn pink rooms with fans, old mattresses, and lukewarm water. Many rooms have open windows on central hallways and roaches milling in the shower. Singles, doubles, and triples 120-200 pesos; key deposit 20-50 pesos. More expensive rooms are upstairs, quieter, and more secure.

Hotel Colli (☎ 142 07 25), on Hidalgo, between Doblado and Zaragoza. Sizable, air-conditioned rooms are a decent value. Enjoy the evening breeze blowing across the large terrace and garden. Singles and doubles 350 pesos; triples and quads 400 pesos.

Trailer Park Brisa del Mar (☎ 142 39 99), just off the highway to San Lucas near km 29, where it reaches the coast. Offers sweet beachfront *palapas,* sparkling bathrooms and showers, a good sized pool, and a restaurant/bar. Beachfront hookup US$25 (US$5 more in the winter), back row spots US$18.50; tents US$10.

FOOD

The constant influx of fancy tourist eateries has left few options between taco stand and filet mignon. A healthy suspicion of anglophone restaurants will save you money: be wary of any menu printed in flawless English.

Cafetería Rosy, on Zaragoza and Green. The food is exquisite for the price, the service is spectacularly friendly, and a good bowl of soup and unlimited lemonade come with your meal. Delectable *bistec pipian* (45 pesos). Open M-Sa 8am-5pm.

Taquería Erika, on Doblado near Mex. 1. No place in the *centro* offers light fare as superb or as inexpensive as the tacos, *quesadillas,* baked potatoes, and other *antojitos* served at Erika's. It's well worth the 10min. walk, especially to satisfy an early afternoon or late-night craving. Tacos 9-10 pesos. Open daily 1pm-5am.

El Descanso, Castro near the *mercado.* Tasty *barbacoa* (stringy meat soup) and *menudo* (stomach stew) from huge black vats on the pungent fire (30-40 pesos). Open 24hr.

Baja Natural (☎ 142 31 05), Doblado between Morelos and Hidalgo. A health food joint specializing in huge, tasty *licuados* and *eskimos* (ice cream shakes, 36 pesos). Vegetarian fare includes salads (35-50 pesos), sandwiches (40 pesos), and veggie burgers (45 pesos). Free delivery to your hotel. Open M-Sa 7am-8pm.

👁 SIGHTS AND BEACHES

A 20min. walk down Mijares will lead to good, uncrowded local beaches. Hurry—even as you read this, new hotel complexes are springing up. Long, empty **Playa California** is great for sunbathing, but like many beaches in this area of Los Cabos, undertow makes swimming potentially hazardous. To get to the best surfing waters, flag down a local bus on Mex. 1 (every 15min.) where it meets Doblado, and ask the driver to drop you at **Costa Azul** or **Playa de Palmilla** (see **The Corridor,** above). **Killer Hook Surf Shop** (☎ 142 24 30), in town on Guerrero between Castro and Doblado, has the latest surf conditions. For more solitude, head 4-5km down Juárez to **Pueblo La Playa,** and bear right at the fork before town. The Pueblo is lined with a vast expanse of unpopulated beach. *Pangeros* will take tourists out fishing for reasonable prices (5-6hr., US$150 for 3 people). Your catch may be limited to tuna and dorado—local fishermen rarely go out far enough for marlin. Information booths scattered along Mijares are more than happy to "inform" you about the glass-bottom boat tours, fishing trips, and snorkeling expeditions that they sell along with condos and time shares. Prices are often not bad, and perhaps even worth the annoying sales pitch. Just outside of town, at km 31 on Mex. 1, **Baja Salvaje** (☎/fax 142 53 00; www.bajasalvaje.com), offers high-end equipment rentals, tours, and classes for diving, kayaking, surfing, and even rock climbing.

A few attractions occupy time between trips to the beach. **Huichol Gallery,** on Zaragoza and Mijares, features brilliantly colored beadwork and embroidery made by the Huichol people. (☎ 142 37 99. Open daily 9am-10pm.) **Misión Estero de las Palmas de San José del Cabo,** on Hidalgo between Obregón and Zaragoza, is one of the most noticeable structures in town. Founded in 1730, the mission could never quite find enough indigenous people to convert. Annoyed locals revolted in 1734, and a vivid mosaic above the mission's entrance depicts them dragging Father Nicolás Tamaral to be burned alive. The huge yellow and white mission is pleasantly imposing from the outside but a bit of a let-down inside. Nature lovers should visit the **Estero de San José,** which is home to over 200 species of birds. A pleasant, shaded path meanders among huge palm trees and chirping birds to an unceremonious end on Blvd. Mijares, near the post office.

🌙 NIGHTLIFE

San José del Cabo can't compete with wild Lucas, but a good time isn't hard to find—just kick back, relax, and don't expect conga lines or table dancing. **Iguana**

Bar, under the giant iguana on Mijares, is the main party spot, with large weekend crowds drinking, playing pool, and dancing to pop music. (☎142 02 66. Beer 25 pesos, margaritas 30 pesos. Open Tu-Su 6pm-3am.) **Piso #1** and **#2,** Zaragoza 71, two blocks from the church, form a mellow bar. Red chairs, palm trees, pool tables, and neon lights help wash down Dos Equis beer (20 pesos) or mixed drinks (20 pesos. F 9-11pm free, open bar for women; W 9pm-2am men 120 pesos, women free. Open in summer daily 6pm-3am; in winter noon-3am.)

EAST CAPE

LOS BARRILES ☎1

Aficionados insist that windsurfing at the small town of Los Barriles, where brisk breezes can carry you for several kilometers along the inside of Bahía de Palmas, is the best in Baja California, if not all Mexico. While a number of new, cutely decorated bungalow houses and "for sale" signs around Los Barriles broadcast the resident *gringo* presence, foreign investment and development stops there.

◢ PRACTICAL INFORMATION. From the highway, the *entrada principal* runs into the center of Los Barriles, where a left turn (at the giant EXIT sign) puts you on **Calle 20 Noviembre,** To get to the **Delegacion Municipal,** which houses the **police** and **post office,** head left on the dirt road next to Tio Pablo's, and go uphill for 1km. No English spoken. (☎141 05 25. Post office open M-F 8am-3pm.) **IMSS** is at the *entrada* and 20 de Noviembre. Little English spoken. (☎141 03 22. Open M-F 9am-2pm, 4-8pm). After hours find the **doctor** at Baja Propiedades, across from Tio Pablo's on 20 de Noviembre. The town **laundromat** is two blocks beyond Tio Pablo's on 20 de Noviembre. (Full service 45 pesos. Open M-Sa 8am-4pm.) **Supermercado Chapitos,** on the *entrada.* (☎141 02 02. Open daily 7:30am-10pm.)

◖◗ ACCOMMODATIONS AND FOOD. Most of the town's accommodations are all-inclusive resorts, but camping on the town's vast stretch of beach is free and safe north of the PEMEX station. **Martín Verdugo's Beach Resort Motel** (☎141 00 54), a block before the laundromat, is a tidy and extensive campground/hotel/restaurant. Full RV hookups (US$13) and tent sites (US$11) include *palapa* shelter, baths, electricity, and pool access. Offers reasonable game fishing packages. **Little Martín** (no relation), off the *entrada* past the little mall, rents basic rooms with washing machines and kitchenettes. Most have A/C. (☎141 01 84. 230 pesos; reduced rates for longer stays.) Budget meals in Los Barriles are found exclusively at Tío Pablo's. **Tio Pablo's Bar and Grill** specializes in American fare: massive, tasty burgers US$4-6. The adjoining **Taquería de Tío Pablo** serves a variety of delicious tacos (7-11 pesos), but doesn't provide seats. (Open daily 11am-10pm.)

◗ SIGHTS. Baja Dive Adventures and **Mr. Bill's Boardsurfing,** both based at Casa Miramar (☎141 02 71), opposite the PEMEX station, provide equipment, tours, and lessons for scuba, snorkeling, and windsurfing. The most popular dive spots in the area are around **Cabo Pulmo** and **Los Frailes,** south of Los Barriles, and separated by secluded beaches and coves. Off Cabo Pulmo, eight fingers of a living coral reef—thought to be 25,000 years old and one of only three in North America—host hundreds of species of tropical fish, crustaceans, and other critters.

SANTIAGO ☎1

Little Santiago (pop. 4500) boasts the only **zoo** in Baja California. The small zoo houses a surprisingly diverse collection of well-cared-for animals. (Open daily 6am-6pm. Free, but donations gladly accepted.) To get there, follow the main road and make a left at the far side of the *zócalo.* Follow this road toward Palomar's restaurant until it ends, turn right, and continue until the Parque Zoológico appears on the right. Hourly Autotransportes Águila buses from La Paz and San José del Cabo drop visitors 2km outside Santiago.

Most people come to Santiago for the nearby **hotsprings** in **Chorro.** Tepid sulfur pools await wearied travelers' aching feet, and in high season, the springs are diverted into more luxurious artificial tubs. To get to the pools, continue past the zoo for 7km until you arrive in the town of **Agua Caliente.** Bear right at the Casa de Salud and follow this road, keeping to the right at the forks. After 5km, the road ends at a dam, and the sulfur smell indicates your arrival. Depending on the level of recent rainfall, you may have to hike up the stream for about 40min. to find larger pools; the tranquility and beauty is well worth the effort.

IF YOU PLAN ON GOING FARTHER. If you plan to travel beyond Nogales, obtain a **tourist card** (see **Tourist Cards,** p. 9) at the border and have your passport on hand. It's much simpler to get the card here than farther south. When you cross the border through the arched crossing complex, turn right into the **immigration center,** the last door in the first building on the right.

TRANSPORTATION

The **bus terminal** and **train station** are directly across from each other on Carretera Internacional, 4.5km south of town (not to be confused with the border street of the same name). A taxi from the bus station to the center of town will cost an exorbitant 55 pesos; instead cross the street and walk north to the plaza at the end of the block, where you can catch one of the local white buses (3.5 pesos) marked "Central Camionera." Downtown Nogales is the last stop. To return to the bus terminal and train station, catch the "Central Camionera" at the bus stop by the plaza on López between Ochoa and Campillo. A supermarket called *Ley* will be on your right when you reach the correct stop on the corner of Carretera International.

At the main station, Elite (☎313 16 03) offers luxurious bus service to: **Guadalajara** (25hr., every hr. 7:30am-6pm, 1070 pesos), with stops in **Los Mochis** (11hr., 365 pesos) and **Mazatlán** (17hr., 747 pesos); **Hermosillo** (3½hr, every hr. 7:30am-11:30pm, 133 pesos); **Tepic** (22hr., every hr. 8:30am-9pm, 918 pesos); **Mexico City** (32hr., 6 per day, 1386 pesos). Transportes del Pacífico (☎313 16 06) has buses *de paso* that leave every hour from 8am-8:30pm. Transportes Golden State buses (in Nogales, AZ, ☎520-287-5628) leave for **Tucson** (1½hr., every hr., US$10) from the Greyhound Station half a block from the US side of the border.

ORIENTATION AND PRACTICAL INFORMATION

The *primer cuadro* is relatively small, making Nogales easy to navigate. If you're crossing the border by foot, you'll be on **Pesqueira;** by car, you'll drive in on **López Mateos.** From east to west, **Pesqueira, Juárez** (which merges with **López Mateos** several blocks south), **Morelos** (a walkway), **Obregón** (the main tourist drag), **Hidalgo,** and **Ingenieros** run parallel to each other and perpendicular to the border. **Internacional** runs parallel to the tall chain-link fence that marks the border. Moving south away from the border, **Campillo, Ochoa, Pierson, Aguirre, Vázquez, Díaz,** and **González** all run parallel to each other and to Internacional.

Tourist Office: (☎312 06 66) next to the immigration center, to your right coming in from the US. Helpful and friendly staff. Maps available. Open daily 9am-7pm.

Currency Exchange: The *primer cuadro* contains a number of **banks** and **Casas de Cambio,** most of which line López Mateos and Obregón. Your best bet is to stick to the major banks. **Banamex** is at Obregón and Ochoa (☎312 07 80 or 312 55 05). Open M-Th 8:30am-4:30pm, F 8:30am-5:30pm. Also farther south on Obregón at Elías Calles (☎312 12 51 or 312 10 65). Open M-F 8:30am-4:30pm, Sa 9am-3:30pm. All exchange dollars and traveler's checks and have 24-hr. **ATMs.**

Luggage Storage: At the bus terminal. 5 pesos per hr.

Emergency: ☎060.

Police: (☎312 01 04 or 312 11 04) at González and Leal. Some English spoken.

Red Cross: (☎313 58 08) on Elías Calles and Providencia. Open 24hr.

Medical Assistance: Hospital Básico (☎ 313 07 94), about 3km south of the border on Obregón. English spoken. Open 24hr.

Pharmacy: Comercial 3 en 1 Farmacia (☎312 55 03) Campillo 73, between Obregon and Morelos. Doubles as a liquor store. Open 24 hr.

Fax: Copy Xpress 401 López Mateos (☎312 15 84, or 312 60 06), 1 block south of the Hotel Granada. Also offers internet access (25 pesos per hr.). Open M-Sa 9am-8:30pm, Su 10am-5pm.

Post Office: Juárez 52 (☎312 12 47). Open M-F 8:30am-2:30pm. Shares a roof with **Telecomm.**

Postal code: 84001.

⌐ ACCOMMODATIONS

Relative to towns farther south in Mexico, rates in Nogales are steep, and steadily rising. High prices mean high quality, and most hotels in Nogales are clean and friendly. The cheapest budget hotels can be found on the block behind the tourist office on Juárez.

Hotel San Carlos, Juárez 22 (☎312 13 46 or 312 14 09; fax 312 15 57), between Internacional and Campillo. Spacious, clean rooms have A/C, cable TV, high-pressure showers, and phones. Mingle with the ever-present locals watching TV in the lobby. Reservations recommended. Singles 250 pesos; doubles 290 pesos. MC/V.

Hotel Regis, (☎312 51 81 or 312 55 35), one door down from the San Carlos. Clean rooms with A/C, phone, and TV. Sink into the comfy leather couches in the lobby and relax. Reservations necessary. Singles 326 pesos; doubles 360 pesos. MC/V.

Motel San Luis, Ingenieros 138 (☎312 41 70, 312 42 19, or 312 40 35). The floors are carpeted and clean, the beds comfortable, the bathrooms large, and the TVs complete with cable. Reservations recommended. Singles 320 pesos. MC/V.

Hotel Olga, Juárez 17 (☎312 35 60), across the street from the San Carlos. This is as close as you're going to come to a true budget hotel in Nogales. Most of their rooms have seen better days, and the floors don't exactly sparkle, but the rooms do have decent beds, phones, TV, and bathrooms. Singles 200 pesos; doubles 250.

◖ FOOD

Nogales is home to oodles of high-priced restaurants that cater to daytrippers from the US. If tourist pricing is driving you crazy, head for the **plaza** on Mateos at Ochoa, where vendors entice your tastebuds with an array of fruits and *tortas* for rock-bottom prices. For a truly economical meal, look no further than the tiny makeshift counters a few steps off of Obregón, where local families offer up excellent traditional *antojitos* (5-20 pesos) prepared while you wait.

Restaurante Elviras, Obregón 1 (☎312 47 43). Elviras's peaceful courtyard is a great place to enjoy their delicious, award winning *pescado elvira* (US$12), but it becomes much less serene by 8pm, when neighboring club Kookaracha's opens its doors. Open daily 9am-11pm. MC/V.

La Posada Restaurante, Pierson 116 (☎312 04 39), west of Obregón. Chow down on big breakfasts (20-40 pesos) and delicious *carnes* (meats) amidst local families and chirping birds. *Burritos de machaca* (dried beef flavored with onions, tomatoes, and *chile verde*) 12 pesos, *chimichangas* 15 pesos. Open daily 7:30am-10pm.

Cafe Ajijic, Obregón 182 (☎312 50 74). Features a picturesque fountain and roving *mariachis* belting out popular Mexican tunes. The tiled tables, shaded by umbrellas, provide the perfect setting for sipping from the huge selection of espresso drinks (15-22 pesos). Entrees 25-40 pesos. Open daily 9:30am-12:30pm. MC/V.

Restaurante El Oasis Los Equipales, Pierson 89. The mix of aging American pop hits and Mexican favorites blaring detract a bit from the otherwise peaceful atmosphere, but few of the predominately Mexican clientele seem to mind. Delicious, authentic entrees ranging from fried steak to *enchiladas* (30-45 pesos). Open daily 8am-noon.

Cafeteria Leo's, Obregon and Campillo (☎313 60 03). Leo's has all the ambience of a college dining hall, but it serves up decent *enchiladas, quesadillas,* and even hamburgers (25-50 pesos). Open daily 7:30am-10:30pm.

🎵 NIGHTLIFE AND ENTERTAINMENT

There isn't much in the way of museums or other cultural attractions to entice you in Nogales, but the curio and craft shops lining Obregón and Campillo are a mecca for bargain hunters. Merchandise is priced in anticipation of haggling, so confidence and knowledge of the goods can get you great deals. Right after lunch, the bars on Obregón open their doors to a mixture of locals and tourists, and by 10pm on a Friday or Saturday night, walking is all but impossible.

Coco Loco, Obregón 62 (☎ 312 41 05), The huge dance floor and remarkable cleanliness draw a young crowd that fights its way to the bar for tequila shots (US$2) and mixed drinks (US$2-3). Before the evening rush you can relax on the balcony with a bucket of eight beers (US$10), but after dark the DJ-mixed American pop hits will call you to your dancing feet. Open Tu-Su 1pm-3am. F-Sa cover US$5.

Bora Bora, Obregón 38, a large, dark, room between Campillo and Internacional offers live music nightly, after 9pm. Enjoy one free drink on Sundays; beer and mixed drinks are 10 pesos. Open W-Su noon-3am.

Kookaracha's, Obregón 1 (☎ 312 47 73). Dance the night away and down tequila shots (US$1.50), or just chill with a *cerveza* by the fountain in the "roach's" techno-colored courtyard. For open bar, go on ladies night (Wednesdays), when girls pay US$9 and guys US$18. US$5-8 cover other nights. Open W and F-Sa 8pm-3am.

Catooche Cafe Bar (☎ 312 31 44). Lively *salsa* and *norteño* tunes sound even better when belted out by tipsy locals on karaoke nights. Open Tu-Sa 1pm-3:30am. F-Sa cover US$5, includes 3 beers.

Fray Marcos de Niza Cocktail Lounge, at Obregón and Campillo (☎ 312 11 12). Comfy leather couches and chairs and big screen TVs create a chill atmosphere, and the drinks are surprisingly cheap-US$1.75 for tequila or beer. Open daily 11:30am-1am.

Not in the mood for tequila? **Cinemas Gemelos,** Obregón 368 (☎ 312 50 02), between González and Torres, shows recent American films dubbed or subtitled in Spanish (40 pesos). For those seeking a bit of culture, the new **Teatro Auditorio de Nogales,** Obregón 286, between Vásquez and González (☎ 312 41 80), brings live performances from Mexico City. Call or visit for showtimes and prices .

PUERTO PEÑASCO   ☎ 6

Puerto Peñasco (pop. 40,000) is home to incredible stretches of rocky coastline broken by spotless sandy beaches and pastel condominiums full of US retirees. Just 105km south of the Arizona border and known to its northern neighbors as "Rocky Point," Puerto Peñasco attracts spring break revelers, vacationing families, and aging beach bums by the thousands. Once a launching pad for shrimp boats, the town dried up when overfishing decimated the shrimp population in the Sea of Cortés and now depends heavily on tourism. Holiday weekends bring hordes of *gringos* who eagerly purchase heaps of gaudy pottery and plastic sunglasses. Despite the throngs of Americans, the magnificent Sea of Cortés, the swaying palms, and the pristine beaches make for a beautiful—if not exactly tranquil— retreat. Budget travelers beware of "tourist pricing." To get the best deals, always ask for prices in pesos instead of in dollars, even if the seller is reluctant.

▐ TRANSPORTATION

The bus station is at Juárez and Calle 24, nine blocks north of Calle 13. To get downtown, turn left as you exit and take an immediate left on Juárez. Continue south and turn right at Calle 13 for budget lodgings and Playa Hermosa or continue to Fremont. A cab anywhere in town will cost you 20-35 pesos; the bus station is pretty far, so it may be worth the extra money. Autotransportes de Baja California (☎ 383 20 19) goes to: **Ensenada** (10hr., 320 pesos); **Mexicali** (5hr., 180 pesos); **Tecate**

(6hr., 250 pesos); **Tijuana** (8hr., 272 pesos); **La Paz** (27hr., 1008 pesos). All buses are *de paso* and there are only four departures per day. The 1am bus goes as far as Tijuana (via Mexicali and Tecate), the 8am heads to every destination listed above, and the 1pm and 5pm buses go only to Mexicali. For travel within Sonora, Transportes Norte de Sonora (☎383 36 40) can luxuriously transport you to **Guaymas** (9hr., 3 per day, 285 pesos) and **Hermosillo** (7hr., 5 per day, 245 pesos).

⚡🧭 ORIENTATION AND PRACTICAL INFORMATION

No official *centro* exists. This is a small town, but fear not—it's not nearly as confining as it sounds. Banks and markets cluster around the intersection of **Fremont** and **Juárez,** the main drag, which runs north-south through the entire town, while other services surround Juárez farther north at **Constitución.** Hotels, motels, and many restaurants tend to be nearer the beach and concentrate on the *malecón* (at the southern end of Juárez, a 10 min. walk from the intersection with Fremont) or just west of Juárez on Calle 13. At its northern end, Juárez runs diagonal to most of the other streets, and at its southern end the ubiquitous boulevard splits into Paseo de los Pescadores, west of the *malecón*, and Campeche, which continues south to the Playa Miramar.

The **tourist office,** Juárez 320, on the northern outskirts of town, is a tiny green shack where English may be spoken, depending on what day you're there. (☎383 61 22. Open M-F 9am-4pm, Sa 9am-1pm.) If you're too lazy to make the trek, stop in at any hotel or shop for one of the many free **tourist guides,** such as *The Rocky Point Times* or *Join Us*, most of which contain decent maps. **Bancomer,** just past Jim Bur Plaza heading south on Juárez (at the intersection with Estrella), exchanges currency and traveler's checks. (☎383 24 30. Open M-F 8:30am-4pm, Sa 10am-2pm.) **Banamex,** on Juárez, just south of Fremont, provides the same services. (☎383 25 82. Open M-F 8:30am-4:30pm.) Both have 24hr. **ATMs.** Stock up on snacks and bottled water at **Supermarket Jim Bur,** on Juárez in the Jim Bur Plaza. (☎383 25 61. Open M-Sa 8am-9pm, Su 8am-4pm.) **Lavamática Peñasco,** on Constitución across from Hotel Paraíso del Desierto. Wash 12 pesos, dry 15 pesos. (Open M-Sa 8am-7pm.) **Police:** at Fremont and Juárez. Little English spoken. (☎383 20 56. Open 24hr.) **Red Cross,** on Fremont at Chiapas. (☎383 22 66.) **Farmacia Botica Lux,** Ocampo 146, is two blocks east of Juárez. (☎383 28 81. Open daily 8am-midnight.) **Hospital Municipal,** Morúa and Juárez. Little English spoken. (☎383 21 10.) **Fax:** in the same building as the post office. (☎383 27 82. Open M-F 8am-6pm, Sa 9am-noon.) **Internet** service is available at **Infotech,** on Juárez at Ocampo. Look for the white building on the corner, across the street from the Corona building (☎383 64 60. 30 pesos per hr. Open M-F 8am-8pm.) **Post office:** on Chiapas, two blocks east of Juárez on Fremont. (☎383 23 50. Open M-F 8am-2:30pm.) **Postal code:** 83550.

🛏 ACCOMMODATIONS AND CAMPING

Budget rooms in Puerto Peñasco are a rare commodity these days, as small establishments are being replaced by expensive resorts, condos, and time-shares. Expect rates to rise US$10-15 during spring break. The cheapest way to spend the night is to camp at one of the multitude of trailer parks that abound around Playa Miramar. **Playa Miramar RV Park,** at the southern end of Campeche, rents scenic spots year-round with cable TV, full hookup, and spectacular views. Washers, dryers, and showers available. (☎383 25 87. 1-2 people US$13, each additional person US$2; weekly US$80; beachfront spaces slightly higher.) Public camping is permitted northwest of the Playa Boruta Resort on Sandy Beach all the way down to La Choya. Camping at trailer parks is always safe; sleeping on the beach is only wise if you're with a large group.

The cheapest beds in town surround a small patio and hot tub behind **Margaritavilla,** a slightly run-down US-run bar and restaurant on Campeche, one block south of Banamex in what used to be the town brothel. Each of the five rooms,

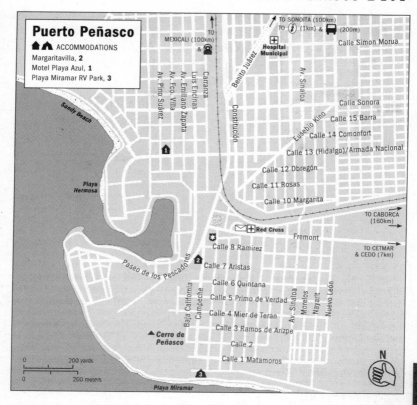

Puerto Peñasco

🏠🏕 ACCOMMODATIONS

Margaritavilla, **2**
Motel Playa Azul, **1**
Playa Miramar RV Park, **3**

TO
MEXICALI (100km)
& 🏧

TO SONOITA (100km)
TO ℹ (1km) & 🚌 (200km)

Calle Simon Morua

Hospital
Municipal

Calle Sonora

Calle 15 Barra

Eusebio Kino

Calle 14 Comonfort

Calle 13 (Hidalgo)/Armada Nacional

Calle 12 Obregón

Calle 11 Rosas

Calle 10 Margarita

TO CABORCA
(160km)

Red Cross

Fremont

Calle 8 Ramirez

TO CETMAR
& CEDO (7km)

Paseo de los Pescadores

Calle 7 Aristas

Calle 6 Quintana

Calle 5 Primo de Verdad

Calle 4 Mier de Teran

Calle 3 Ramos de Arizpe

Calle 2

Calle 1 Matamoros

▲ Cerro de
Peñasco

Baja California
Campeche
Av. Sinaloa
Morelos
Nayarit
Nuevo León

Benito Juárez
Construción
Av. Pino Suárez
Av. Fco. Villa
Av. Emiliano Zapata
Luis Encinas
Carranza
Av. Sinaloa

Sandy Beach

Playa
Hermosa

0   200 yards
0   200 meters

Playa Miramar

N

NORTHWEST MEXICO

named for Jimmy Buffet songs, contains two clean and comfortable beds and not much else. Communal baths and showers are in good shape. (☎383 53 44. 1-3 people US$20.) If you're willing to stay farther from the center of town, deals can be found at the **Hotel Villa Granada,** Av. Imadero 47 (☎383 27 75). Heading south on Juárez, take a left at the Comision Federal de Electricidad, 3 blocks before Calle 13. US$25 will get you a room with two double beds, private bath, hyperactive A/C, access to the hotel pool, and some of the friendliest management around. The more centrally-located **Motel Playa Azul,** Calle 13 and Suárez, is about two blocks from Playa Hermosa and offers nicely furnished, clean rooms with ancient one-channel TVs, generous A/C, and, yes, private baths. Bargain with the manager. (☎383 62 96. Singles US$25; doubles US$35.)

🍴 FOOD

Food stands line Calle 13 and Juárez, offering everything from mangoes to *mariscos*; while busy on most weekends, many close due to lack of customers during the week. For traditional Mexican cuisine, head east on Calle 13 and turn left onto Kino to **La Curva.** Grab a Tecate and chill with the locals as they cheer on their favorite *fútbol* teams. The aptly named *combinación grande* (45 pesos) includes nachos with cheese, salsa, sour cream, rice, beans, and your choice of entree. (☎383 34 70. Open daily 7:30am-10pm.) **Cocina Economica,** Campeche 44 , is a simple, inexpensive eatery down the street from Playa Miramar. *Camarones rancheros* (Mexican style shrimp) US$7. (☎383 48 74 or 383 20 86. Open M-Th 7am-10:30pm, F-Su 7am-11pm.)

👁 🖋 SIGHTS AND BEACHES

Puerto Peñasco's beaches are full of warm turquoise water and plenty of tourists. **Sandy Beach** and **Playa Hermosa** are the best choices for swimming; both have curio shops, restaurants, and hotels galore. To reach Sandy Beach, head north on Encinas or Juárez until the intersection with Camino a Bahía Choya, 2 km. north of Fremont. Turn left and follow the souvenir shops and bars until you see signs that say "To Sandy Beach." To get to Playa Hermosa, turn right on Calle 13 when heading south on Juárez; the beach is straight ahead five or six blocks down, but you'll have to veer right around the wall of luxury hotels. The beaches around **Las Conchas** and **Playa Miramar**, at the southern end of town, are less crowded but also rockier, rougher, and less suited to swimming. To reach Playa Miramar, head south on Juárez, and take a left onto Campeche near the Benito Juárez monument. Continue uphill for three blocks; Playa Miramar is straight ahead. To reach Playa Las Conchas, head south on Juárez, turn left on Fremont after Bancomer, take a right onto Camino a las Conchas, and follow the rock-slab road for 3km. **Jeff Reeco** (☎383 62 09), who lives across the street from Thrifty Ice Cream on Victor Estrella in the old port, rents sea kayaks (single US$35; double US$45 per day) and boogie boards (US$10 per day). Multi-day and group discounts can be negotiated. **Sun 'n Fun**, a respected dive shop on Juárez at the entrance to the old port, will arrange fishing trips (half-day or full day all-inclusive, US$35-70), whale-watching (3hr., US$30, in season), sunset cruises (2hr., US$25), and guided dives (5hr., US$50). (☎383 54 50). The **Intercultural Center for the Study of Deserts and Oceans (CEDO)**, at Playa Las Conchas 9km from town (taxi 60 pesos), gives free guided tours of its wet lab and museum—including a 55 ft. whale skeleton. They also run kayak tours of Estero Morua and nature walks. (☎382 01 13. Tours Tu 2pm, Sa 4pm. Visitor center and gift shop open M-Sa 9am-5pm, Su 10am-2pm.) The **Center for Technological Sea Studies (CETMAR)**, 2km before CEDO on the Las Conchas road, operates a small aquarium stocked with local marine species. A large tank in the rear contains a family of sea turtles. (☎382 00 10. Open M-F 10am-2pm, Sa-Su 10am-5pm. Adults US$2, children US$1.)

🎵 ENTERTAINMENT

Nightlife in Puerto Peñasco all depends on when you come. Calle 13, Campeche, and the *malecón* all host a ridiculous number of bars, pool halls, discotecas, and some raunchier establishments, most of which are full and lively during spring break and on weekends. During the week, you may have to settle for exchanging fishing stories with US retirees. **Margaritavilla** holds on to its "most popular" status by offering live music and/or karaoke nightly, shots US$1, free Cuervo Gold from 11am-noon and 11pm-midnight, and cheap bar food. (Open daily 8am-1am.)

📽 DAYTRIPS FROM PUERTO PEÑASCO

EL PINACATE

Guides are necessary. For information about tours, ask at the tourist office or talk to Peggy Turk Boyer at CEDO (☎382 01 13). If you do decide to go it alone, 4WD high-clearance vehicles with partially deflated tires are a must, as are tons of water, a shovel, spare tire, compass, and firewood. Camping is permitted, but please don't leave anything behind and don't remove any souvenirs. The ideal time to visit is Nov.-Mar., when temperatures range 15 to 32°C, as opposed to summer months, when the daytime temperatures can often exceed 47°C.

Forty-eight kilometers north of Puerto Peñasco on Mex. 8 lies the El Pinacate volcanic preserve, one of the largest and most spectacular biospheres in the world. Created in June 1992 to limit volcanic rock excavation and protect endangered species, El Pinacate encompasses more than 4 million acres and extends between the Arizona border and the Sea of Cortés. Over 600 craters and 400 cinder cones pockmark the 30,000-year-old lava shards and sea of sand that once served as an important food source for the people of the Tohono O'odham Nation, for whom this landscape had great significance. Guided by shamans, adolescent men would cross the barren expanse surviving on water retained in natural rock tanks. Weary and tired from the exertion and heat, they were made to run across the beaches, inducing a light-headed semiconsciousness perceived as spiritual nirvana. If they completed the rite successfully, the men were allowed to marry. Those who passed out from exhaustion failed and were left to die. To this day, members of the Tohono O'odham Nation cross the desert on foot from Arizona to bathe in the waters of the Sea of Cortés, which they believe to be sacred and healing.

The preserve's amazing emptiness and endless kilometers of igneous rock are reminiscent of the moon's rough surface; so much so that NASA trained astronauts for the Apollo mission in El Pinacate. Technical climbs and challenging hikes await around every corner, and excellent physical condition (plus a whole lot of water!) are essential to survive in this strikingly beautiful environment.

CABORCA ☎ 6

About halfway between Hermosillo and Puerto Peñasco rises the sprawling agricultural city of Caborca (pop. 200,000). Surrounded by desert and cattle pastures, Caborca lacks both the beautiful beaches of seaside towns and the excitement of more urban areas. The few tourists who come to Caborca usually stop only for a quick meal at one of the many *asaderos* before moving on to more glamorous destinations. However, the city lays claim to a few enticing attractions, especially for those needing to indulge their carnivorous instincts.

▛ TRANSPORTATION. From the **Transportes del Pacífico** bus station, on Calle 8 and Av. A, walk to your left as you exit the station and turn left onto (unmarked) Av. B; three more blocks will bring you to Obregón, Caborca's main street. *De Paso* buses leave Transportes del Pacífico (☎372 35 59) every hour for: **Guadalajara** (24hr., 1010 pesos); **Guaymas** (6hr., 220 pesos); **Hermosillo** (3hr., 148 pesos); **Mexicali** (7½hr., 240 pesos); **Mexico City** (32hr., 1400 pesos); **Tijuana** (9hr., 370 pesos). The **Transportes Norte de Sonora** bus station is on La Carretera and Calle 8 next to Motel Los Arcos. To get downtown, take a right onto Calle 6 at Motel Los Arcos, walk one block into town, and turn left. A few blocks later you'll find yourself on Obregón with the *centro* on your right. Transportes Norte de Sonora (☎372 12 32) offers almost identical service as Transportes del Pacífico.

▦▟ ORIENTATION AND PRACTICAL INFORMATION. Caborca lies 269km northwest of Hermosillo on Mex. 2. The main drag, **Obregón,** runs east-west, beginning in the east at the carretera (Mex. 2) and becoming Highway 37 heading out of town to the west. Running parallel to Obregón are Calle 1, Calle 2, etc. Bounding the downtown area are Calle 1 to the south and Calle 8 to the north. Perpendicular to the *calles* run the *avenidas*, which are lettered A-Z. Most businesses are concentrated on Obregón between Av. A, two blocks north of the carretera, and Av. M, 12 blocks to the west. Although the *calles* and *avenidas* intersect nicely at right angles, navigating them is difficult, as many of the letters and numbers have been replaced by proper street names and street signs are rare. The most important names to know are Obregón (Calle 5), Juárez (Av. B), 6 de Abril (Av. D), Quiroz y Mora (Av. E), Sotelo (Av. F), and Luis Barredo (Av. G).

Bancomer, at Obregón and Av. F, exchanges cash and American Express Traveler's Cheques and has a 24hr. **ATM. (**☎372 06 16 or 372 06 17. Open M-F 8:30am-3pm). Another Bancomer, one block up at Obregón and Av. E, has identical services and hours. **Lavamatic,** Av. E between Calles 6 and 7, provides self or full-service laundry. (Open M-Sa 9am-9pm, Su 9am-3pm.) **Emergency:** ☎ 060. **Police:** ☎372 08 69. No English spoken. **Red Cross:** Av. K between Calle 7 and 8 (☎372 16 57 or 372 11 77). Some English spoken. **Farmacia Principal,** at Obregón and Av. M, has the best hours. (☎372 25 79. Open daily 8am-midnight.) **Hospital:** Calle 1 and Av. K. (☎372 09 98. Open daily 8:30am-7pm.) **Fax: Telecomm,** at Av. E, one block north of

Obregón. (☎372 03 55. Open M-F 8am-6pm, Sa-Su 9am-noon.) **Internet: Sistemas Modernos de Caborca,** Calle 8 between Av. P and Q. (☎372 34 34. 20 pesos per 30min., 25 pesos per hr. Open M-F 9am-1pm and 3-7pm.) **Post Office:** on Av. H between Calle 4 and 5. (☎372 01 16. Open M-F 8am-3pm.) **Postal Code:** 83600.

◪◩ ACCOMMODATIONS AND FOOD. Caborca isn't oriented toward tourism, and as a result, hotel rates remain low throughout the year. **Motel Jesusita,** Av. B at Calle 4, offers clean, spacious rooms with A/C, cable TV, and super high pressure showers. (☎372 13 70. Key deposit 50 pesos. Singles 180 pesos; doubles 230 pesos; triples 280 pesos.) The more central but shabbier **Hotel La Rivera,** on Av. H between Obregón and Calle 6, has pink rooms with A/C, private baths, and, if you're lucky, a TV. (☎372 13 90. Singles 180 pesos; doubles 250 pesos.) Caborca is not a town for vegetarians, and you'll have a tough time finding restaurants other than the *asaderos* that line Obregón. The airy, clean **Asadero Bífalo,** Obregón and Av. K serves up all sorts of carnivorous treats. Try the fresh tacos (8 pesos) or indulge in an *order de carne* (75 pesos), with broiled meat, ribs, veggies, *quesadillas*, beans, tortilla chips, and fresh guacamole. (☎372 27 35. Open daily 10am-midnight.) **El Asadero OK Arizona,** Obregón 237, between P and Q, sells tacos for 7-15 pesos and huge portions of *carne asada* for 125 pesos in an environment straight out of an old western. (☎372 65 88. Open Th-T noon-midnight.)

◪◩ SIGHTS AND ENTERTAINMENT. *Carne asada* aside, Caborca's main attraction is **La Concepción de Nuestra Señora de Caborca** on Av. D, less than 2km south of Obregón. The church, constructed in 1809, served as a defense outpost against invading Americans in 1857. Every year on April 6, the locals commemorate their victory with a *fiesta.*

While the locals claim there is little to do in Caborca at night except sleep, and weekend entertainment consists largely of heading to Puerto Peñasco, **Dunas Discoteca Bar,** Av. E at the corner of Calle 10 serves as the town's main nighttime hot spot with live music Th-Sa after 11pm. Beer 15 pesos. (☎372 70 00, ext. 173. Cover F-Sa 40 pesos after 11pm. Open Th-Su 9pm-2am.)

HERMOSILLO ☎6

A sprawling metropolitan center of commerce and education, the capital of Sonora state entices visitors with imposing government palaces, beautiful murals, huge manicured parks, a glorious cathedral, and an ecological research center and zoo. Not all of Hermosillo (pop. 700,000) is, however, so alluring. The crowded, dusty roads of the *centro* scream with the frenzied activity of urban life, and, by sundown, little more than garbage lines the streets. Many visitors breeze through on their way to the more glamorous towns and beaches to the south, giving Hermosillo only a passing glance. Although parts of the city can be unsavory, those who choose to spend a day are in for a pleasant surprise.

◪ TRANSPORTATION

Airport: (☎261 00 08), 10km west of town on Transversal toward Bahía Kino. To get there, take a small red bus from the bus station (3 pesos) or catch a taxi (70 pesos). AeroMéxico (☎218 06 12) goes to: **Guadalajara** (2hr., 4 per day); **Mexico City** (2½hr., 8 per day); **Tijuana** (1hr., 2 per day). Aero California (☎260 25 55) will take you to **La Paz** (1hr., 1 per day) or **Los Angeles, CA** (1½ hr., 1 per day).

Buses: 2km east of the city center on Encinas. To get from the station to town, catch a "Centro" bus (every 10min. 5am-10:30pm, 3 pesos). Taxis cost 45 pesos. To get back to the station from the *centro,* wait for a bus at Elías Calles and Matamoros, across from Óptica Morfín. Transportes Norte de Sonora (☎213 06 10) goes to: **Chihuahua** (12hr., 536 pesos); **Ciudad Juárez** (11hr., 6:30pm, 489 pesos); **Mazatlán** (12hr., 649 pesos); **Mexico City** (31hr., 795 pesos). Elite (☎213 40 50) sends buses every hr. to nearby cities including: **Caborca** (4hr.); **Guaymas** (2hr.); **Nogales** (3½hr.).

ORIENTATION AND PRACTICAL INFORMATION

Hermosillo lies 271km south of the border on **Mex. 15**, the main highway connecting the western US and central Mexico. Most of the activity in Hermosillo occurs inside the *centro*, the area bordered by **Rosales** on the west, **Juárez** on the east, **Serdán** on the south, and **Encinas** on the north. If you get lost in the center, remember that the antenna-capped mountain **Cerro de la Campana** is always to the south.

TOURIST AND FINANCIAL SERVICES

Tourist Office: (☎217 29 64; fax 217 00 60), on the 3rd fl. of **Centro de Gobierno de Sonora** at Cultura and Comonfort. Walk south on Rosales over the highway, turn right, and walk 1 block west to the 1st big pink building on the right. Open M-F 8am-3pm.

Banks: Banks line Encinas and Serdán. **Banamex** (☎214 76 15), on Serdán at Matamoros, has a 24hr. **ATM.** Open M-F 8:30am-4:30pm, Sa 9am-3:30pm.

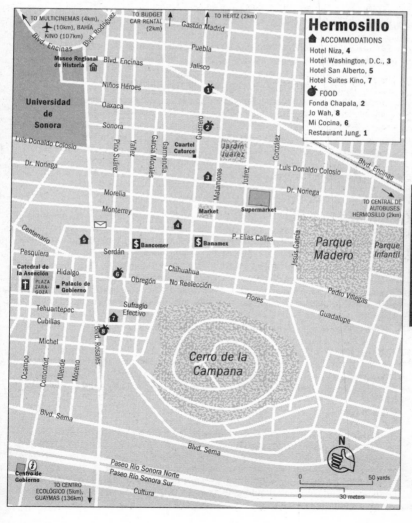

Hermosillo

🏠 ACCOMMODATIONS
Hotel Niza, **4**
Hotel Washington, D.C., **3**
Hotel San Alberto, **5**
Hotel Suites Kino, **7**

🍴 FOOD
Fonda Chapala, **2**
Jo Wah, **8**
Mi Cocina, **6**
Restaurant Jung, **1**

NORTHWEST MEXICO

American Express: Hermex Travel (☎ 213 93 71), on Rosales at Monterrey. Open M-F 8:30am-1pm and 3-6:30pm, Sa 9am-1pm.

LOCAL SERVICES

Supermarket: Ley Centro (☎ 217 32 94), Juárez at Morelia. Open daily 6:30am-10pm.

Laundry: Lavanderia Lavarama (☎ 217 55 01), on Sonora at Yañez. Wash 20 pesos per 3.5kg, dry 10 pesos. Open M-Sa 8am-8pm, Su 8am-2pm.

Car Rental: Budget (☎ 214 30 33), Garmendia 46 and Tamaulipas. Open M-F 8am-6pm, Sa-Su 8am-3pm. **Hertz** (☎ 212 16 95), Rodríguez and Guerrero. Open M-F 8am-6pm, Sa-Su 8am-3pm.

EMERGENCY AND COMMUNICATIONS

Emergency: ☎ 080.

Police: (☎ 218 55 64), at Periférico Nte. and Solidaridad. Some English spoken.

Red Cross: (☎ 214 00 10), on Encinas at 14 de Abril. English-speaking staff on hand 9am-5pm.

Pharmacy: Farmacia Margarita, Morelia 93 (☎ 213 15 90), at Guerrero. Open 24hr.

Hospital: (☎ 213 25 56), on Transversal at Reyes. English spoken.

Fax: Telecomm (☎ 217 21 50), in the same building as the post office on the Rosales side. Open M-F 8am-7pm, Sa 8:30am-4pm, Su 9am-12:30pm.

Internet Access: VirtualCafe Internet, Rosales 97 (☎ 212 79 00), between Morelia and Monterrey. 25 pesos per hr. Open M-Sa 8:30am-10pm, Su noon-8pm.

Post Office: (☎ 212 00 11), on Elías Calles at Rosales. Open M-F 9am-3pm, Sa 9am-1pm.

Postal Code: 83000.

![] ACCOMMODATIONS

With one exception, Hermosillo is a budget traveler's nightmare.

Hotel Washington, D.C., Dr. Noriega 68 Pte. (☎ 213 11 83), between Matamoros and Guerrero. Almost too good to be true, the D.C boasts comfortable beds, sparkling rooms, warm showers, English-language advice, free coffee, a communal refrigerator, ironing board, and microwave. Singles 165 pesos; doubles 180 pesos.

Hotel Niza, Elías Calles 66 (☎ 217 20 28), between Guerrero and Garmendia. Rooms have A/C, TV, and comfortable beds (but uncomfortably dim lights). Private baths are small and not always the cleanest, but Niza's central location makes it a decent choice for those just looking for a place to sleep. A lobby restaurant serves *comida corrida* (21 pesos). Singles 150 pesos; doubles 200 pesos.

Hotel Suites Kino, Suárez 151 Sur (www.hotelsuiteskino.com). A step above budget. Hang out with business travelers around the pool table and restaurant/bar. All rooms have cable TV, powerful A/C, phones, and nice bathrooms. Free parking and swimming pool. Reservations recommended. Singles 325 pesos; doubles 340 pesos.

Hotel San Alberto (☎ 213 18 40), at Rosales and Serdán. An oasis complete with A/C, rustic furniture, magazines, TVs, and phones. Singles 324 pesos; doubles 344 pesos.

![] FOOD

Everything from the typical *sonorense* staple of *carne asada* to authentic Chinese food and veggie burgers can be found within the *centro*. For cheap refueling, head for the taco and *torta* places around Serdán and Guerrero, where *taquitos* and *quesadillas* cost 7-8 pesos and *comida corrida* goes for 15-20 pesos. If you feel brave, the food counters lining **Mercado Municipal** on Elías Calles, between Matamoros and Guerrero, cook up tasty and very cheap *antojitos*. Most are sufficiently sanitary, but avoid eating any uncooked vegetables.

▓ **Mi Cocina,** Obregón 84 (☎217 55 38), between Suárez and Yañez. Omar opens his cocina (kitchen) to budget travelers, serving up a mean 2-course meal (35 pesos) and making great conversation all the while. Open M-F 7:30am-6pm.

Fonda Chapala (☎212 39 92), on Guerrero between Sonora and Oaxaca. Mexican oldies blare while middle-aged men drown their sorrows in 40oz. bottles of Tecate. Chicken, fish, or meat comes fried to crispy perfection and served with french fries, frijoles, tortillas, salad, and a drink (42 pesos). Open M-Sa 8am-10pm, Su 8am-2pm.

Restaurant Jung, Niños Héroes 75 (☎213 28 81), at Encinas. Relax to soothing music and the faint smell of incense as you savor the rejuvenating comida corrida, which comes with wheat rolls, soup, freshly-squeezed juice, an entree, veggies, french fries, queso fresco, yogurt, and dessert (70 pesos). Whole grain cereals with fruit 25 pesos, Belgian waffles 36 pesos. Open M-Sa 7:30am-8pm, Su 9am-5pm.

Jo Wah, Pino Suárez 180 (☎213 13 99). Enjoy huge portions of authentic Chinese food and chat with the kindly Cantonese owner. Comida corrida, including egg rolls, veggies, rice, chop suey, and more (45 pesos). Vegetarians can savor pan-fried tofu and veggie chop suey for 27 pesos. Open daily noon-2am.

👁🎵 SIGHTS AND ENTERTAINMENT

Look for the cross-capped spires of the pale yellow **Catedral de la Asunción** as you walk south on Rosales. Turn right on Hidalgo and walk two blocks west. Fugitives from the relentless sun will enjoy the shady trees of peaceful and well-kept **Plaza Zaragoza,** which separates the cathedral from the grey-and-white **Palacio de Gobierno.** The palacio, from which the state of Sonora is governed, should not be confused with the pink brick **Palacio Municipal** next door, where city government functions are carried out. Both are worth investigating for their architecture. The Palacio de Gobierno contains four historical murals surrounding its tree-laden inner courtyard, where statues immortalize Sonoran patriots and senators.

Museo Regional de Historia, on Rosales at Encinas across from the **University of Sonora,** contains exhibits on Pre-Hispanic and colonial history. The building also houses a **university art display.** (Open M-F 9am-1pm and 4-6pm, Sa 9am-1pm. Free.) **Cuartel Catorce** is a rough structure with walls of brown brick on Guerrero and Colosio. The room in the back of the colonnaded inner courtyard once housed the army's cavalry. (☎217 12 41. Open M-F 8am-3pm.)

Hermosillo has gained a reputation not only for great nightlife, but also for its student population that lives up to the city's "beautiful" name. To hang with locals, head to the bars on Rosales south of Colosio. Shoot pool, watch sports or surf the Internet at **La Biblioteca,** on Rosales at Dr. Noriega. (☎212 47 50. Beer 18 pesos, tequila 25 pesos. Open M-Sa 10am-2am.) Also popular are **La Verbena** and **El Grito del Callejón** ("the Cry of the Alley"), both at Obregón and Pino Suárez—La Verbena is to the south and El Grito to the north. Adjacent to La Verbena is **Extasis Night Club,** in a beautiful colonial building with a neon green glow. Although not exactly dangerous, the area around these bars is less than desirable. If you are staying in the centro, conveniently located **Napy's,** Matamoros 109, between Dr. Noriega and Morelia, is a good pick. After 9pm food service stops, the speakers are pumped up to maximum volume as couples hit the dance floor, and friends cheer them on with pitchers of Tecate (50 pesos). (☎213 28 70. F-Sa live salsa. Open daily 10am-2am.) Those in need of a little levity can head to **Multicinemas,** Encinas 227, a 5min. bus ride from the center of town. (☎214 09 70. Open daily 3-9pm. 38 pesos.)

🔼 DAYTRIPS FROM HERMOSILLO

CENTRO ECOLÓGICO DE SONORA

Take a white "Luis Orci" bus from the Guerrero and Dr. Noriega at "Ruta 20" stop (20min., 3 pesos). ☎ 250 12 25. Open Tu-Su 8am-6pm; winter Tu-Su 8am-5pm. 15 pesos.

More than your token neighborhood **zoo**; the *Centro* is host to an impressive array of animal life, a mini-aquarium (complete with outdoor sea lions), hundreds of plant species, and ground breaking biological research. A clearly marked walkway dotted with water fountains, shady benches, restrooms, and a wading pool guides visitors through the exhibits and affords a spectacular view of Hermosillo and its surrounding mountains. The most spectacular feature of Centro Ecológico is its incredible collection of cacti—over 340 species are labeled and displayed throughout the animal exhibits and just outside the main pavilion. Keep your eyes peeled for the rare and beautiful *cina* and *biznaga*, from which candy is made, and the *maguey bacanora*, the fanned-out, spiked cactus that is the source of all those tequilas you've been downing. Children delight at clowns and animated films in the air-conditioned movie theater (Sa-Su noon-6pm; free).

BAHÍA KINO   ☎ 6

Bahía Kino, a 20km stretch of glistening sand, brilliant blue water, and radiant sun, is comprised of a pair of beach towns on the beautiful Sea of Cortés. **Kino Viejo**, a dusty, quiet fishing village, lies down the road from **Kino Nuevo**, a 4km strip of posh, secluded homes and condos. Diving, fishing, and sailing entertain the more adventurous traveler, while soft sandy beaches and gentle waves beckon those looking to relax. As weekend daytrippers from Hermosillo will tell you, Kino provides an ideal destination for an escape from raucous urban desert to *palapa*-shaded tranquility. Soothing breezes, warm waters, and vast expanses of sand make the rickety ride from the city more than worthwhile.

█ TRANSPORTATION. Bahía Kino is 107km west of Hermosillo, at the end of a dusty two-lane highway. **Buses** in Hermosillo leave from the old blue and red-striped **Transportes Norte de Sonora** station on Sonora between Jesús García and González, near Jardín Juárez (2hr., 10 per day 5:40am-5:30pm, 42 pesos). The bus stops in **Kino Viejo** before going on **Kino Nuevo**. Look for water on your left and get off where you'd like. Early birds can make it a daytrip—get an early bus from Hermosillo and sleep (if you can) during the ride. Missing the 5:30pm bus back to Hermosillo means spending the night in Kino. To get from one Kino to the other or back to Hermosillo, flag down the bus (every hr., 5 pesos) on Nuevo's only road, **Mar de Cortés**, or on **Blvd. Kino** in Kino Viejo. If you choose to walk the couple of kilometers between towns, be sure to keep plenty of water and sun protection on hand. Hitching is a popular mode of transportation in Kino.

▨ PRACTICAL INFORMATION. **Public bathrooms** can be found in Nuevo toward the beginning of the beach in front of La Palapa Restaurant. In Viejo, **pleasant potties** are available at the **Centro de Salud** at Tampico and Blvd. Kino; bring your own toilet paper. In an **emergency**, your best bet might be to look for the American-run **Club Deportivo**, on the right side of Monaco toward the end of Mar De Cortés. Knock on the door; the friendly expatriate community takes good care of visitors. **Emergency:** ☎ 080. **Police:** Santa Catalina and Mar de Cortés (☎ 242 00 67) in Viejo or Blvd. Kino and Cruz (☎ 242 00 32) in Nuevo. **Farmacia San Francisco**, at Blvd. Kino and Toplobambo serves the needs of both towns. (☎ 242 02 30. Open daily 9am-1pm and 2-9pm.) **Red Cross:** Blvd. Kino and Manzanillo in Viejo, near the post office and police. There is no phone, but it can be contacted via the emergency number. For English-speaking **medical attention**, call Dr. José Luis (☎ 242 03 95). **Long-distance phones** are available at the clothing shop at Blvd. Kino and Tampico in Kino Viejo; **LADATELs** dot Mar de Cortés in Nuevo and can be found across from the *farmacia* in Viejo. **Post Office:** Next to the police in Viejo. (Open M-F 9am-3pm.)

▛◨ ACCOMMODATIONS AND FOOD. Safe and comfortable lodgings are plentiful on the beachfront—just find a free *palapa* and set up camp. For those who prefer mattresses to sand, Kino's version of "budget" awaits at **Hotel Posada del Mar**, Mar de Cortés at the beginning of Kino Nuevo. Rooms have A/C, baths, and use of the pool. (☎242 01 55. Singles 360 pesos; each additional person 70 pesos.) If you've got big wheels you're in luck—more than 10 RV parks offer beachfront hook-ups (about US$15 per day). **Islandia Marina** is right on the beach in Viejo. Take Blvd. Kino and follow the road to the end. It has one of the better locations and also rents cabins complete with four beds, a refrigerator, a kitchen, a bathroom, and two powerful fans. (Quads 360 pesos; each additional person 60 pesos.)

Restaurants in Kino tend to be expensive; for a meal that's as economical as you want it to be, do as the *hermosillanos* do and pack a lunch to enjoy under a beach *palapa*. Otherwise, a decent budget meal can be found in Viejo at the family-run **Dorita**, Blvd. Kino and Sabina Cruz, which is eclectically decorated with "Spice Girls" paraphernalia and paintings of Christ. Plastic-topped tables and kitschy animal-shaped vases crowd this little restaurant, known for its moderately-priced breakfasts (about 30 pesos), delicious *carnes asadas* (45 pesos), and all-you-can-drink *agua purificada*. (Open daily 7am-8pm.) In Nuevo, **Restaurante la Palapa**, toward the beginning of the beach, cooks up fresh *pescado* any way you like it (55 pesos). Homesick *gringos* will like the juicy *hamburguesas* (30 pesos). Relax under the *palapa*-covered balcony and watch the sunset. (Open daily 8am-8pm.)

◙ ◿ **SIGHTS AND BEACHES.** Kino's **beaches** are peacefully deserted early in the week, but as the weekend approaches, so does the crowd. Fortunately, the masses in Kino are nothing compared to the masses at other beach towns, and it is possible to find an unoccupied and garbage-free *palapa*. *Gringos* with homes in Kino tend to populate the beaches in winter, making for some long, lonely stretches of sand during the summer months. In general, beaches are better in Kino Nuevo. To rent **diving** equipment or a guide, call **Carlos Montes** (☎246 89 01) or find him at Islandía on weekends. **Fishing** trips can be arranged with **Ernesto Hínojosa** (☎242 03 20), or ask a local fisherman if you can come along for a ride.

For non-beach entertainment, **Museo de los Seris,** on Mar de Cortés at Progreso near the end of Kino Nuevo, offers an air-conditioned refuge and teaches you more than you ever thought you'd learn about the Seris, an indigenous fishing tribe. (Open W-Su 9am-4pm. 3 pesos, children 2 pesos.) In Kino Nuevo, 300 yards past Museo de los Seris, you'll see a giant image of the virgin painted on the face of a hill. The short pilgrimage to her perch affords a breathtaking sea view.

GUAYMAS ☎6

Splattered across a backdrop of jagged sandstone mountains, Guayamas (pop. 150,000) looks like it was made by a meteor shower of falling buildings, stray dogs, and above all, trash. The most popular places in town are those with A/C, and as a result, the city has three gigantic supermarkets within blocks of one another. The icy cool aisles offer a pleasant contrast to the treacherously pot-holed sidewalks and freeway-like traffic of the *centro*. In spite of their infernal environs, locals are super friendly, and take a break from grocery-shopping once a year in order to throw a lavish carnaval. This hospitality, combined with the city's budget-friendliness, make it a functional base for the traveler who wants to kick it in San Carlos (10min. away) without stubbing toes on hefty beachside prices.

▐ **TRANSPORTATION**

Airport: To reach the airport, catch a "San José" bus along Serdán (10min., every hr., 3 pesos). AeroMéxico (☎222 01 23), Serdán at Calle 16, flies to: **La Paz** (1½hr., Sa-Su 4:20pm); **Los Angeles** (2hr.; Th, Su 9:25am); **Mexico City** (3½hr., via **La Paz**); **Phoenix, Arizona** (1½hr., Sa-Su 10:55am). Office open M-F 8:30am-6pm, Sa 9am-2pm.

Buses: Buses arrive at Calle 14. To get to the main street, Serdán, turn left if you're coming out of the Transportes del Norte station, and turn right if you're coming out of the Transportes del Pacífico or the Transportes Baldomero Corral stations. Transportes del Pacífico (☎222 12 71) buses leave every 45min. for: **Guadalajara** (20hr., 700 pesos);

Hermosillo (1½hr., 36 pesos); **Los Mochis** (5hr., 183 pesos); **Mazatlán** (12hr., 528 pesos); **Mexicali** (12hr., 506 pesos); **Nogales** (6hr., 170 pesos); **Puerto Peñasco** (9hr., 310 pesos); **Tepic** (18hr., 698 pesos); **Tijuana** (13hr., 654 pesos). Transportes Norte de Sonora (☎222 12 71) offers similar service. Across the street, Transportes Baldomero Corral can take you to **Navojoa** (4hr., every hr., 56 pesos).

Ferries: (☎222 23 24). Ferries leave from a small dock on Serdán, about 2km east of the *centro*. To get to the dock, take any local bus headed east on Serdán and ask the driver to let you off at the ferry. A blue and white "Sematur Transboradores" sign will be on your right. Ferries go to **Santa Rosalía** (6hr.; Tu, Th 9am; *salón* 270 pesos, *turista* 540 pesos) and **La Paz** (18hr.; F 3pm; *salón* 680 pesos, *turista* 1360 pesos).

■✦🛈 ORIENTATION AND PRACTICAL INFORMATION

Guaymas is 407km south of Nogales on **Mex. 15**. The *centro* is the area surrounding the chaotic main strip, **Serdán**, beginning at **Calle 10** and ending at **Calle 29**. Running perpendicular to Serdán are Calle 1, Calle 2, Calle 3, etc. The waterfront begins at **Calle 20**, two blocks south of Serdán at **Av. 11** (the *malecón*), and Serdán itself continues along the sea after **Calle 24**. Women should avoid walking alone more than two blocks south of Serdán after dark. Note that upon leaving the city, northbound vehicles are often stopped by narcotics police. Have your identification ready and be prepared to have your belongings searched.

Tourist Office: Av. 19 and Calle 6 (☎224 41 14). Open M-F 8am-2pm.

Currency Exchange: Banamex (☎224 18 70), Serdán at Calle 20, exchanges currency and traveler's checks and has 24hr. **ATMs.** Open M-F 8:30am-4:30pm.

Luggage Storage: Lockers are available at the Transportes Norte de Sonora bus terminal. 12 pesos for the 1st 8hr.; each additional hr. 5 pesos. Open 24hr.

Car Rental: Hertz, Calzada García López 625 (☎222 30 28). Open M-F 8am-6pm, Sa-Su 8am-3pm. **Budget** (☎222 55 00), Serdán and Calle 4. Open M-F 8am-6pm, Sa-Su 8am-3pm.

Market: VH Supermarket (☎224 19 49), on Serdán, between Calles 19 and 20. Open M-Sa 7am-11:30pm, Su 7am-8:30pm.

Police: (☎224 01 04 or 224 01 05), on Calle 11 at Av. 9. Some English spoken.

Red Cross: (☎222 55 55 or 224 08 76), on México 15, about 1½km north of the *centro*. Also has **ambulances.**

Pharmacy: Farmacia Sonora (☎222 11 00), Serdán at Calle 15. Open 24hr. **Pabellon Guadalupe** Av. 6 at Calle 11 (☎222 04 85). Some English spoken. Open 24hr.

Fax: Telecomm (☎222 02 92), next to the post office. Open M-F 8am-7:30pm, Sa-Su 9am-noon.

Internet Access: The Web@.com (☎222 66 40), on Serdán just past Calle 14. 15 pesos per hr. Open M-Sa 9am-9pm, Su 2-7pm.

Post Office: (☎222 07 57), Av. 10 between Calle 19 and 20, next to the pink Luis G. Davila School. Open M-F 9am-3pm, Sa 9am-1pm.

Postal Code: 85400.

▐ ACCOMMODATIONS

Heat and humidity conspire to create the perfect micro climate for the proliferation of roaches, fleas, gnats, and other vermin who make otherwise adequate budget hotels somewhat uncomfortable. It may be worth your while to pay for A/C, sterility, and frequent fumigation.

Motel Santa Rita, Serdán 590 (☎224 19 19), at Calle 9. Large sparkling rooms with A/C, TV, and phone. A good pick for a quiet, bug-free night of shut-eye. Boasts a huge parking lot. Singles 200 pesos; doubles 250 pesos; triples 300 pesos.

Motel del Puerto, Yañez 92 (☎224 34 08), 2 blocks south of Serdán on Calle 19. Reminiscent of a beachfront motel (without the beach). Rooms have soft beds, satellite TVs, and A/C. Singles 170 pesos; doubles 230 pesos; triples 300 pesos.

Casa de Huéspedes Lupita, Calle 15 #125 (☎222 84 09), 2 blocks south of Serdán and across from the jail. Tidy, small rooms come equipped with fans, and an *agua purificada* dispenser awaits downstairs in the office. Singles 60 pesos, with bath 80 pesos, with A/C 100 pesos; doubles with bath 100 pesos, with A/C 150 pesos.

Hotel Impala, Calle 21 #40 (☎224 09 22), 1 block south of Serdán. A somewhat scuzzy option; A/C and TV make the "death by peach" color scheme and tawdry lobby more palatable. Singles 200 pesos; doubles 275 pesos; triples 320 pesos.

🗲 FOOD

Seafood is Guaymas's specialty. Local favorites include *ancas de rana* (frog's legs), *cahuna* (endangered turtle steaks), and *ostiones* (oysters) in a garlic and chile sauce. Unfortunately, if you want to sample these local delicacies, you will pay dearly. For those on a tighter budget, **Mercado Municipal,** on Calle 20, one block from Serdán, sells fresh produce, and an abundance of *comida corrida* joints dots Serdán.

Restaurant Bar La Barca de Guaymas (☎224 30 77), on Calle 9 just north of Serdán. A genuine boat crowns the roof and a huge thatched *palapa* decorates the dining area. Savor *tacos de pescado* (35 pesos) and *ceviche* (15 pesos). Open daily 10am-2am.

Las 1000 Tortas, Serdán 188, between Calles 17 and 18. Not just for *torta*-lovers. Serves up delicious *burritos de machaca* (3 for 33 pesos), *bistec ranchero* (40 pesos), and *quesadillas* (3 for 33 pesos). Open daily 8am-11pm.

Restaurant Santa Rita, Serdán 590 (☎224 19 19). The only place with passable coffee. Breakfast 30-50 pesos, club sandwich 47 pesos. Open daily 7am-10pm.

Cafeteria Deli (☎224 17 84), in the VH supermarket complex at Serdán. Guaymas' version of Denny's; slurp chicken noodle soup in this *paper-mache* decorated, nursing-home like cafeteria. Salads are one of Guaymas' few veggie options (15-28 pesos). *Tortas* 25 pesos, breakfast around 30 pesos.

S. E. Pizza Buffet (☎222 24 46), Serdán at Calle 20. Disney images and framed posters of American cars and athletes decorate the walls. Satisfy your appetite with the all-you-can-eat buffet of pizza, spaghetti, and salad (25 pesos). Open daily 11am-11pm.

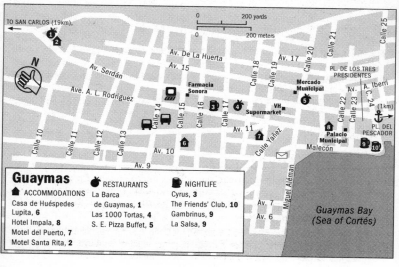

Guaymas

🏠 ACCOMMODATIONS
Casa de Huéspedes
 Lupita, **6**
Hotel Impala, **8**
Motel del Puerto, **7**
Motel Santa Rita, **2**

🍅 RESTAURANTS
La Barca
 de Guaymas, **1**
Las 1000 Tortas, **4**
S. E. Pizza Buffet, **5**

🍸 NIGHTLIFE
Cyrus, **3**
The Friends' Club, **10**
Gambrinus, **9**
La Salsa, **9**

Guaymas Bay
(Sea of Cortés)

♪ BEACH AND ENTERTAINMENT

Guaymas's **beaches,** popular with both tourists and locals and accessible via a short bus ride from Serdán, are located to the north in **San Carlos** (see p. 212) and **Miramar** (10 min., 6 pesos). The nicer (but smaller) beaches in Miramar are back along the bus route in front of the fancy villas.

Huge signs advertising **travesty shows**—transvestite acts imitating popular Latin singers—are everywhere in Guaymas. **Cyrus,** the club with the concrete wolf façade on Serdán, between Calles 16 and 17, has the most frequent shows. (M, W, Th, and Su. Half-price beer 9-11pm. No cover.) On Serdán at Calle 14 is **Todos Carmen,** which has a show on Th. (Live *banda* on F. Cover 30 pesos, Sa women free.). If you're looking for drinks and dancing without the frills, **Sahuaro Piano Bar** and **Zodiakos,** next to Charles Baby Disco Video, serve beers (10 pesos). Also near the waterfront, on Rodríguez, just behind the statue of Adolfo de la Huerta, many locals dance the night away at **Gambrinus** or **La Salsa,** while their uncles shoot pool at **The Friends' Club** two doors down.

SAN CARLOS   ☎ 6

Thirty-five years ago, San Carlos (pop. 2500) was just a dusty road in the desert north of Guaymas; now, condos, hotels, and malls sprout like wildflowers to accommodate the growing tourist influx. San Carlos greets visitors with a lush country club, Sonora's only five-star hotel, and the largest, shallowest artificial shipwreck in the world. With a population that swells to 8000 come winter, when sunseeking *norteamericano* retirees return to their pastel-colored beachfront homes, San Carlos knows exactly how to pamper its guests.

▄ TRANSPORTATION. White striped buses come from downtown Guaymas and run down the main road to the Marina Real and Plaza Las Glorias, but don't make it all the way to the El Mirador Escénico or Playa Los Algodones. (Approx. every 10min. 6am-11pm; to Guaymas 10 pesos, within San Carlos 5 pesos.)

▄✚▊ ORIENTATION AND PRACTICAL INFORMATION. The main road in San Carlos, **Manlio F. Beltrones,** runs east-west. Most shops, restaurants, and accommodations lie on Beltrones between Hacienda Tetakawi Hotel and Trailer Park to the east and the small road to Plaza Las Glorias to the west. The **tourist office** is in **Hacienda Tours,** on Beltrones just before El Mar Diving Center. (☎226 13 14. Open M-F 9am-5pm, Sa 9am-2pm.) **Banamex,** on Beltrones next to the PEMEX station, exchanges dollars and traveler's checks and has a 24hr. **ATM.** (☎226 12 40. Open M-F 8:30am-4:30pm.) Buy your groceries at **San Carlos Super Mercado** in front of the church at the end of the road to Plaza Las Glorias. (☎226 00 43. Open daily 7am-9pm.) **Lavandería Automática,** next to Piccolo Restaurant, offers full or self-service and hand-washing. (☎226 00 13. Wash 18 pesos, dry 22 pesos. Open daily 9am-5pm.) **Emergency:** Call **Rescate** (☎226 01 01), which is funded entirely by donations from San Carlos residents. English spoken. **Police:** (☎226 13 10), up the hill on the road to Plaza Las Glorias. English spoken. **Farmacia Bahía San Carlos,** across the street from Motel Creston. (☎226 00 97. Open M-Sa 8am-7pm.) **Post office:** (☎226 05 06), next to Ana Maria's Beauty Shop. **Postal Code:** 85504.

▐▛ ACCOMMODATIONS AND FOOD. San Carlos is full of hotels, none of which suit budget travelers. For those wise enough to pack a tent or an RV, **El Mirador RV Park,** on the road to El Mirador Escénico, provides full hookups in RV paradise—scenic views, a glistening pool, abundant free modem access, many table games, plentiful pristine showers, and two new tennis courts. (US$15 per day, US$120 per week.) **Hacienda Tetakawi,** on Beltrones, km 8.5 at the beginning of the main strip, has full hookups and tent spaces. (☎226 02 20. RV hookups US$20 per day, US$130 per week; tent space 1-2 people US$10, each additional person US$3.)

Motel Creston, across the street from Jax Snax, and an easy walk to the beach, is the cheapest hotel you'll find. Sparkling rooms have two beds, A/C, and bath. The patio faces a clean pool. (☎226 00 20. Singles and doubles 450 pesos.)

While most restaurants are on the expensive side, a few places here and there cater to the budget traveler. Peso-pinchers can satisfy cravings with *burritos de carne asada* or fresh *almejas* (clams) eaten raw with salsa, *limón*, or chocolate from vendors toward the western end of Beltrones. Local expatriates enjoy starting the day with breakfast (34-37 pesos) and fabulous milkshakes (28 pesos) at **Jax Snax** (☎226 02 70), on Beltrones. **Mamacita's Cafe,** also on Beltrones, serves "healthy food." (☎229 50 21. Salads 25-40 pesos, juices 10-15 pesos, big fruit and yogurt plates 35 pesos. Open M-Sa 7am-2pm.) Similar fare and the best coffee in town can be found at **Evie's Simply Coffee,** Estrada 137, at Plaza Las Glorias. (☎226 06 04. Coffee 10 pesos, *quesadillas* and hamburgers 35-40 pesos, yummy cinnamon rolls and pastries 15-25 pesos.)

⬛⬛ SIGHTS AND BEACHES. A colorful array of marine flora and fauna make their home in the Sea of Cortés, attracting divers eager to catch a glimpse of the underwater brilliance and fishermen eager to catch dinner. Near the town is **San Pedro Nolasco Island,** a popular dive site where sea lions and marine birds coexist in harmony. The state of Sonora recently spent a large sum of money to sink a 120ft. tuna boat and 300ft. passenger liner to create an artificial reef for scuba divers. **El Mar Diving Center,** off Beltrones, rents scuba gear and sea kayaks and leads guided dives for a pretty penny (US$65 for an 8hr. trip to the island). For those who prefer *terra firma*, El Mar also rents bikes. (☎226 04 04. Open daily in summer 7:30am-6:30pm; in winter 7:30am-5:30pm.) If fishing is your thing, pick up a license (58 pesos per day) at the **Secretaria de Pesca** on Beltrones just before the turn-off to Plaza Las Glorias. (Open 9am-3pm.) It's illegal to fish without one.

Playa San Francisco, which extends parallel to the freeway from Guaymas, is the most easily accessible beach. The sands are rocky, but the water is pleasant. If you have access to a car, **El Mirador Escénico,** a vista atop a steep road, affords views of Tetakawi and the secluded coves of **Playa Piedras Pintas.** A dirt road near the gate to Costa Del Mar about 8km past the end of the bus route leads to ⬛**Playa Los Algodones** (Cotton Beach), so named because the soft sand is often compared to cotton. Taxis can take you on a tour of the area, including El Mirador, Piedras Pintas and Los Algodones (200 pesos per 1½hr.)

ALAMOS   ☎6

The sleepy town of Alamos (pop. 8000), in the scenic foothills of the Sierra Madre Occidental, is a rambling collection of handsome colonial *haciendas*. Founded in 1531, Alamos was relatively ignored until silver was discovered in 1683. For nearly a hundred years, Alamos produced more silver than any area in the world, but when the silver veins ran dry at the turn of the century, the former boomtown shrank to ghost-town proportions. Over the last 50 years, however, wealthy Americans and Canadians have taken an interest in the town, particularly in the rambling mansions left behind by the silver tycoons. Thanks to their funds, Alamos has returned to its glory days—the refurbished *haciendas* and cobblestone streets give the city a bygone feel unlike any in northwest Mexico.

⬛ TRANSPORTATION. To reach Alamos by bus, you must change buses in **Navojoa,** 53km southwest of Alamos. From the Transportes Norte de Sonora and Elite bus stations in Navojoa, stand at the corner of Allende and Ferrocarril, looking down Ferrocarril as you face the bus stations. Walk one block to the Transportes del Pacífico station and turn left (toward the center of town) onto Guerrero. Six blocks along Guerrero (passing the Transportes de Baja California bus station after 3 blocks) is the Los Mayitos bus station at Rincón, where you can catch a bus to **Alamos** (1hr., every hr. 6am-6:30pm, 22 pesos). From the other stations, ask directions for buses to Alamos. The return trip from Alamos starts from the station at Plaza Alameda.

NORTHWEST MEXICO

> **LIKE WATER FOR CHICHARRONES** When in Mexico, there's no escaping the *chicharrones* (pork rinds). In some towns the popular snack has even become an ice cream flavor. On sweltering hot days, vendors push long carts loaded with rows of metal casks and scoop out ice cold salvation in a crazy variety of flavors including *elote* (cornmeal), *cerveza* (beer), *aguacate* (avocado), tequila, and *chicharrones*. Hand a vendor 5 pesos and he'll cram a mammoth portion into a cone or plastic cup. Mexican ice cream is known to harbor more than a few nasty amoebas, so check the stand before placing the spoon in your mouth.

◪ ▮ ORIENTATION AND PRACTICAL INFORMATION. Small and compact, Alamos is easily explored on foot. As you come into town on **Madero**, you'll reach a fork in the road at the bronze statue of Benito Juárez; the left branch leads to **Plaza Alameda**, the commercial center (where the bus stops), and the right branch to **Plaza de Armas** in the historic district. A small alley known as **Callejón del Beso** connects Plaza de Armas with the market behind Plaza Alameda. The cathedral south of Plaza de Armas marks the entrance to **Barrio La Colorada,** where the expats have concentrated their *hacienda*-restoring efforts.

The Alamos **tourist office,** Juárez 6, under Hotel Los Portales on the west side of Plaza de Armas, has maps and historical information. Local tour guides, an older group of men, can usually be found lounging in Plaza de Armas. Ask a tourist official to point them out. (☎428 04 50. Open M-F 9am-3pm and 4-8pm, Sa 9am-2pm). **Currency exchange: Bancrecer,** on Madero before the fork in the road. (☎428 03 57. Open M-F 8:30am-3pm, Sa 10am-2pm.) A 24hr. **ATM** is next door. **English Bookstore: Los Amigos,** Victoria at Obregón. (☎428 10 14. **Internet access** 25 pesos per hr.) **Supermarket: SuperTito's,** at the fork of Madero, operates as a 24hr. **pharmacy,** grocery store, and liquor store. (☎428 05 12. Open daily 7:30am-10:30pm.) **Commandencia Policia** (☎428 02 09), just off Plaza de Armas on Comercia. Some English spoken. **Medical Assistance:** farther from the center on Madero is **Hospital Básico** (☎428 00 25 or 428 00 26). **Internet: Compulmages** on Morelos 39. Walk down Callejón de Beso from Plaza de Armas, continue straight one block and turn right on Morelos. (10 pesos per hr. Open daily 8am-9 or 10pm.) **Post office:** in the Palacio Municipal. (Open M-F 8am-3pm.) **Postal code:** 85763.

▮ ACCOMMODATIONS. Unless you re-discover silver on your way into town, you'll probably have to pass on the *hacienda* hotels. Luckily for budget travelers, there is *one* slightly scuzzy, bargain option left in the *centro*. **Hotel Enrique,** next to Hotel Los Portales on Juárez, on the west side of Plaza de Armas, has rooms with fans in a beautiful old building. (☎428 03 10. Singles 100 pesos; doubles 150 pesos.) **Motel Somar,** Madero 110, on the way out of town, has clean rooms in good repair, as well as a list of hotel regulations. (☎428 01 95. Singles and doubles 300 pesos, with A/C 340 pesos.) **Hotel Dolisa,** Madero 72, next to Motel Somar, offers *agua purificada,* A/C, and baths in every room. (Singles and Doubles 300 pesos; each additional person 80 pesos.)

▢ FOOD. Peso-pinchers patronize taco stands, such as **Taquería Blanquita,** in the Mercado Municipal by Plaza Alameda. (Open daily 7am-10:30pm.) In the market, you can buy fruits and vegetables within walking distance of where they were grown. For a good view of Plaza de Armas and the distant foothills, eat under the arches at **Restaurant Las Palmeras,** Cárdenas 9, northeast of Plaza de Armas. (☎428 00 65. Breakfasts 25-40 pesos, *antojitos* 20-35 pesos. Open daily 7am-10pm). To work up an appetite before dinner, hike to **Restaurant el Mirador** (see below), on top of the hill overlooking Alamos. (Sonoran *chimichangas* (flour tortilla tacos) 26 pesos, hamburgers 26 pesos, *chiles rellenos* 40 pesos. Open W-M 3-10pm.)

◪ SIGHTS. The best reason to visit Alamos is to glimpse the glory days of the *hacienda*. One of the grandest homes in town was constructed in 1720 and refinished in the 19th century, when it became the home of José María Almada, owner of one of the world's richest silver mines. **Hotel Las Portales** now occupies most of the building, including Don Almada's foyer and courtyard. Other impressive restored homes can be found around the cathedral, including **Casa de los Tesoros** (a former convent), **Hotel La Mansión, Casa Encantada,** and **Las Delicias.** For 10 pesos you can tour the incredibly swanky **Hacienda de los Santos,** a series of colonial homes that have been turned into a five-star hotel. Tours start daily at 1pm from the main entrance on the corner of Molina and Gutierrez.

The town's cathedral, **La Parroquia de la Purísima Concepción,** was completed in 1786 and occupies a commanding position on Plaza de Armas. The town jail and the Mirador offer excellent views. To get to the jail, walk along Madero west of the center of town and follow the signs. **Museo Costumbrista,** the yellow and white building across from Las Palmeras in Plaza de Armas, has exhibits of Alamos' history. (☎428 00 53. Open July-Aug. W-Su 9am-6pm; Sept.-June W-Su 9am-3pm. 10 pesos, students and children 5 pesos.) Brand new **Museo Casa de Maria Felix,** at Galeana 41, in the Barrio la Colorada, occupies the birthplace of Mexico's much-idolized screen queen, who was born in Alamos. (☎428 0929. 10 pesos.)

CHIHUAHUA

CROSSING THE BORDER. The easiest way to cross the border is to walk. Take the north-south #8 or #10 green trolley operated by Sun Metro to the Santa Fe Bridge, the last stop before the trolley turns around (every 20min.; M-F 6:15am-8:15pm, Sa 7:45am-8:15pm, Su 8:45am-7:15pm; US$0.25). Do not confuse the green trolley with the more expensive Border Jumper Trolley. Two pedestrian and motor roads cross the Rio Grande: **El Paso Ave.,** a crowded one-way street, and **Stanton Ave.,** a parallel road lined with stores and restaurants. Walk to the right side of the Stanton Bridge and pay the US$0.25 fee to cross. Daytrippers, including foreign travelers with multi-entry visas, should be prepared to flash their documents of citizenship. US citizens need proof of citizenship, or a driver's licence. Non-US citizens must have either an I-94 form, a visa, or a passport. If you are planning to venture more than 22km into Mexico's interior, you need a **tourist card.** Get one at the Mexican immigration office, directly to your right as you enter into Ciudad Juárez.

To enter the United States, cross over the Santa Fe Bridge near the large *"Feliz Viaje"* sign. Be ready to answer questions posed by US border guards and to show a valid visa or proof of citizenship. You must also pay a US$0.30 fee. Once in El Paso, wait at the bus stop on the right-hand sidewalk just across from the bridge. The north-south bus runs M-F 6:15am-8:15pm, Sa 7:42am-8:15pm, Su 8:42am-7:22pm. Either the #8 or the #10 bus will return you to downtown El Paso. If **driving** into or out of Mexico, note that vehicles are charged US$1.25 each way, and may require a permit.

CIUDAD JUÁREZ   ☎ 1

Ciudad Juárez is more business-oriented than it may at first seem. While wild nights of drunken debauchery are easy to come by, the majority of the city's 1.2 million residents live and work away from the bar-studded main drag in a labyrinth of *maquiladoras*, auto shops, "yonke" yards, and piecemeal residences. Though obscured by this chaotic day-to-day scramble, the city possesses an illustrious history. Originally known, along with El Paso, Texas, as the Paso del Norte, Juárez got its modern name in 1860 when President **Benito Juárez** fled here to escape the French intervention and seek US aid in the overthrow of Emperor Maximilian (see **History,** p. 59). The city was later occupied by Pancho Villa several times during the Mexican Revolution. Today, Juárez is a phenomenon worth experiencing, whether in a drunken haze while bar-hopping or in the similarly dizzying rush of traffic through the central market.

▐ TRANSPORTATION

It's a good idea to grab a map from the **tourist office**. The streets get convoluted outside of Old Juárez in the area adjoining the Santa Fe and Stanton bridges.

GETTING AROUND

Most of Old Juárez can be covered on foot. Street numbers start in the 800s near the two border bridges and descend to zero at **16 de Septiembre,** where **Av. Juárez** (the main street) ends. Most city buses leave from the intersection of **V. Guerrero** and **Francisco Villa** or thereabouts; ask the driver whether your bus will take you to your destination. To reach ProNaf and the Rio Grande Mall, catch the "Juárez/Aeropuerto" bus heading east from Av. Juárez on 16 de Septiembre. **Taxis** are always downtown, but fees are steep. Negotiate before getting in, and don't pay more than 50 pesos to get from Old Juárez to ProNaf. To get from the central bus terminal to downtown, walk out the door to the left of where you entered and up the parking lot to the main road. Do not cross, but wait for an old converted school bus labeled "Ruta 1A" or "Ruta 6," both of which go to Av. Juárez. Again, ask the driver if he or she is going to Av. Juárez as Ruta 6 will take you to the shantytowns on the outskirts of town if you travel in the wrong direction.

During the day, Juárez is relatively safe. Yet as darkness increases, so does the ratio of alcohol to blood. Use common sense, and don't stray more than two blocks west of Av. Juárez at night. The **police station** is on the corner of 16 de Septiembre and Av. Juárez, and several police officers usually patrol downtown.

GETTING AWAY

Airport: (☎ 633 07 34), about 17km out on Mex. 45 *(Carretera Panorámica)*. Catch the "Juárez/Aeropuerto" bus near the train tracks on Francisco Villa (3.5 pesos). **AeroMéxico** (☎ 623 23 94 or 623 23 95) flies to Chihuahua, Mexico City, Monterrey, and a few nearby US locations.

Buses: Central Camionera, Blvd. Oscar Flores 4010, (☎ 613 20 83), north of the ProNaf Center. To get there, take the "Omnibus de México" bus from the El Paso terminal to Juárez (US$5), or cram into a bus with "Central Camionera" or "Futuras" written on the front window from the area around F. Vila and V. Guerrero (4-5 pesos). Chihuahuenses (☎ 629 22 29), Estrella Blanca (☎ 629 22 29), Omnibus de México (☎ 610 72 97), and others offer service to: **Chihuahua** (7hr., every 30min., 207 pesos); **Guadalajara** (24hr., 8 per day, 886 pesos); **Hermosillo** (10hr., 5 per day, 489 pesos); **Mazatlán** (24hr., 1 per day, 12:45pm, 719 pesos); **Mexico City** (26hr., 6 per day, 1043 pesos); **Dallas** (US$57); **El Paso** (50min., every hr., US$5); **Los Angeles** (US$40).

▐ PRACTICAL INFORMATION

TOURIST AND FINANCIAL SERVICES

US Consulate: López Mateos Nte. 924 (☎ 613 40 48 or 613 40 50), at Hermanos Escobar. From Av. Juárez, turn left on 16 de Septiembre, right on López Mateos, and then walk for 15-20min. Open M-F 8am-4:45pm. In an emergency, call the El Paso tourist office in the US (☎ 915-544-0062).

Tourist Office: While the main office at Eje Vial and Juan Gabriel Asernados is a hassle to find, it operates an information booth 3 blocks down Juárez from the border on the right-hand side that provides maps and English-language advice. (US toll free: ☎ 800-221-0660; Open daily 9am-4pm.)

Currency Exchange: Both pesos and dollars are accepted throughout Juárez. Pesos can give the competitive edge when driving a hard bargain, and money is easily exchanged at any of the *casas de cambio* downtown. Banks line 16 de Septiembre on either side of Juárez, and most have 24hr. **ATMs.**

LOCAL SERVICES

Luggage Storage: At the bus station. 3 pesos per hr.

Supermarket: The **Río Grande Mall,** Ruta 8 at Guerrero and López Mateos, sells groceries, clothes, and more. **Soriana Market,** also along Ruta 8, sells groceries. Open Tu-Sa 7am-11pm, Su-M 8am-11pm. For both, catch the blue and white "Juárez/Aeropuerto" buses going east on 16 de Septiembre.

Laundry: Lavasolas (☎612 54 61), Tlaxcala and 5 de Mayo. 12 other locations in town. Washers 8-9 pesos; dryers 6 pesos. Open M-Sa 9am-9pm, Su 8am-4pm.

EMERGENCY AND COMMUNICATIONS

Emergency: ☎060.

Police: (☎615 15 51), Oro and 16 de Septiembre, near Juárez. English spoken. You can also contact the **Federal Highway Police** (☎633 01 95).

Red Cross: (☎611 43 30 or 611 43 21; fax 616 50 89), in the ProNaf Center next to the OK Corral. English spoken. Open 24hr.

Pharmacy: Pharmacies abound along Juárez, but for late night needs, try **Superfarmacias El Félix** (☎615 80 54), at Av. Juárez and Tlaxcala. Open daily 24hr.

Hospital: Hospital Latinoamericano, 250 N. López Mateos (☎616 14 67 or 616 14 15; fax 616 13 75), in the ProNaf area. English spoken. Open 24hr. Take "Ruta 8A."

Fax: Secrefax (☎615 15 10 or 615 20 49; fax 615 16 11), on Juárez near the Santa Fe Bridge, partially obscured under a white awning. Open 24hr.

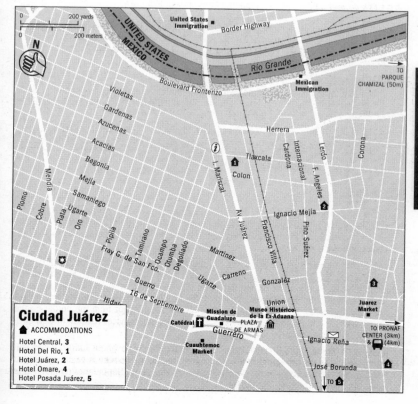

Ciudad Juárez

🔺 ACCOMMODATIONS

Hotel Central, **3**
Hotel Del Rio, **1**
Hotel Juárez, **2**
Hotel Omare, **4**
Hotel Posada Juárez, **5**

Telephones: **LADATEL** phones are plentiful on Av. Juárez and 16 de Septiembre.

Internet: Instituto de Computación, Corona 171 Nte. (☎612 36 61). 20 pesos per hr. Open M-Sa 9am-7:30pm, Su 7:30pm-2pm. For reasonably fast service in the ProNaf area try **Interclick,** Paseo Triunfo de la República 4407-3 (☎616 09 06). 20 pesos per hr. Open daily 10am-10pm.

Post Office: Lerdo at Ignacio Peña. Open M-F 8am-5pm, Sa 9am-1pm.

Postal Code: 32000.

▌ ACCOMMODATIONS

In Ciudad Juárez, budget hotels meet minimal standards—a place to sleep, maybe a fan—and charge some of the highest "budget" rates in Mexico. Moreover, a modest increase in quality can translate into a significant hike in price. Hotels on Calle Juárez are sketchy. Better budget options can be found on Lerdo and Corona, which run parallel to Juárez. From Juárez, turn left on 16 de Septiembre and walk several blocks. Hotels are one to two blocks off 16 de Septiembre.

▨ Hotel Juárez, Lerdo 143 Nte. (☎615 02 98, 615 03 58, or 615 04 18), at Mejía. This 1940s hotel makes up in cleanliness and safety—and TVs and A/C—for what it lacks in repairs. For each floor you ascend, prices descend 10 pesos. The English-speaking owner and downstairs cafe (8am-8pm) make the hotel cozy and convenient. Singles start at 117 pesos; doubles 136 pesos.

Hotel Omare, 12 Corona 213 Sur (☎612 06 18), 2 blocks south of 16 de Septiembre on the right. Don't be detracted by the shabby downstairs entryway; the rooms upstairs are clean and painted in eye-popping bright colors. 100 pesos for a single/double M-Th. 120/150 pesos respectively F-Sa.

Hotel Posada Juárez, Internacional 26, Plaza Cervantina (☎615 60 03 or 615 60 63), at the end of Lerdo, across Ignacio de la Peña on the left of the courtyard. Spartan rooms with heat and TV, located off a quiet alleyway. Hosts a Mexican budget crowd. Shared rooms available at 60 pesos per bed. Singles 100 pesos; doubles 120 pesos.

Hotel Central, Corona 151 Nte. (☎615 01 17), 1½ blocks up from 16 de Septiembre. Caters to a loyal crowd of Mexicans who return frequently to Juárez on business. Rooms are shabby and in chaotic disrepair, but the congenial family atmosphere is fun. Singles 81 pesos; doubles 100 pesos; triples 117 pesos.

Hotel del Rio, Juárez 488 Nte. (☎615 55 25). Pricey, but if you need to crash in Juárez, this is the place to do it. Clean, white rooms, vigilant staff and good A/C distinguish this hotel from its neighbors, as does the "No Guests in Rooms" sign on the front desk window. Singles 250 pesos; doubles 300 pesos.

◖ FOOD

Eateries in Ciudad Juárez vary from tourist traps in the **ProNaf** area to roadside shacks and open pit grills. For cheap eats head to the open-air Mercado behind the cathedral where taco stands abound. Vegetarians be warned: tacos are made with everything but the squeal.

Cafetería El Coyote Inválido, Juárez 615 (☎614 27 27), is *the* place to dilute the tequila during a night of revelry on Calle Juárez. Open all night, this authentic holdover from the 1950s is kind of pricey, but worth it for the great staff and high-power A/C. Burritos 25 pesos; hamburgers 35 pesos; Mexican plates 40 pesos. Open 24hr.

Lonchería Imperial, Mejía 170 Ote. (☎125 04 32), 1½ blocks off Juárez. Homey little diner where you can sit at the counter and watch your food being grilled while sipping a cup of fresh-brewed coffee. *Comida corrida* 35 pesos. Open M-Sa 8am-7pm.

Restaurant Madrid, Plaza Continental building (☎612 42 14), on Ignacio de la Reña between Corona and Lerdo. Offers calm, air-conditioned dining off the main street. Cheap Mexican breakfast (20-25 pesos) served all day in addition to the usual Juárez fare and the occasional Spanish dish.

Tacos Lucas, Av. Juárez and Mejia (☎ 612 55 31). A good place to sit and watch Juárez stumble by. A hearty breakfast of *chilaquiles*, french fries, beans, steak, 2 eggs, and salad can be had for a mere 34 pesos. Open Su-Th 8am-2am, Sa 8am-3pm.

🞉 SIGHTS

The Siberia of Mexico, Juárez historically functioned as a place of escape and exile. By the 20th century, it began to assume a similar role for US citizens fleeing everything from Prohibition to divorce laws. For a pocketable tour guide and a bit of Juárez history, grab a "Downtown Historic Walking Tour Juárez" pamphlet from the tourist office info booth.

Down Calle Juárez is the Victorian **Aduana Fronteriza**, or customs house, finished in 1889 as the official point of entry for import goods. In 1911 Porifirio Díaz signed away his dictatorship here, granting the revolutionaries victory after a bloody battle. Today the Aduana Fronteriza is open as the **Museo Histórico de Ciudad Juárez,** which chronicles the region's history from the beginning of civilization up to the 20th century. (☎ 612 47 07. Open Tu-Sa 10am-6pm. Free.)

Turn right at the customs house and down 16 de Septiembre to Mariscal to find a bust and commemorative plaque in honor of the city's most famous exile and namesake, **Benito Juárez,** who hid here during the French Coup under Maximilian in 1865-66. Across the street is **Plaza de Armas,** the **Catedral,** and the beautiful white adobe 🞉**Mission de Guadalupe,** built in 1662. The church boasts an impressive wooden Moorish-style ceiling, whose mixture of Spanish heritage and Indian influences is evident in the carvings of serpents on the rafters.

The **Museo de Arte e Historia,** at the **ProNaf Center,** exhibits Mexican art of the past and present. (☎ 616 74 14. Open Tu-Su 11am-7pm. Admission 10 pesos, students free.) To escape from the clamor and commotion of downtown Ciudad Juárez, head to **Parque Chamizal,** down Av. Presidencia east of the Stanton Bridge. There you'll see a Mexican flag rumored to be as large as an American football field. The **Museo Arqueológico,** Av. Pellicer in Parque Chamizal, houses plastic facsimiles of Pre-Hispanic sculptures as well as prehistoric fossils, rocks, and bones. (☎611 10 48 or 613 69 83. Open Tu-F 11am-6pm, Sa-Su 10am-5:30pm.)

🎜 ENTERTAINMENT

On weekends, *gringos* swarm downtown Juárez in a 24hr. quest for fun, fights, and *fiestas*. Every establishment along Av. Juárez that isn't selling Viagra or pulling teeth is likely to be a club or a bar, but although these watering holes are easiest to get to, the best nightlife is found in the ProNaf area in Mejía. Take the "Juárez/Aeropuerto" or "Ruta 8" bus (3 pesos) or a cab (50 pesos) to get there.

Vertigo, Mejía and Montes de Oca (☎611 00 30). The house DJ spins "pure house" Th (cover US$3) "Spanish" F (US$2) and "Top 40" S (US$4). Beers at US$1 will keep you dancing and dizzy all night. Open W-Su till 1 or 2am.

Charmucas, Mejía and Franklin (☎ 616 89 37). Home to a slightly older, more down-home crowd. From M-W you can challenge the talented house pool team to a game.

Dalí, Mejía 3118 (☎611 48 98). A pseudo-intellectual nightlife escape for sophisticates-in-training. Surrealist posters, quiet music and a variety of coffee drinks (with and without alcohol, 28/25 pesos respectively) promote conversation and completely un-Juárez ambience. Open daily 5pm-1am.

Sinaloa, Juárez 142. If you must party downtown, this is the place to do it. Cowboys sit at a long bar looking sultry whilst their women-folk get down on the large dance floor. Cumbia and Norteño bands play on alternate nights. Beer 15 pesos, tequila 15-18 pesos. Open M-Th till 1:30am, F-Sa till 2:30am.

Once you are sufficiently partied-out, remember that Juárez offers more than just bars and clubs. If you enjoy bullfights, you can find them at **Plaza Monumental de Toros,** Paseo Triunfo de la República at López Mateos (☎613 16 56). They usually occur at 5:30pm on Sundays from April to September. **Lienzo Charro** (☎627 05 55), on Charro off República, also hosts bullfights and a *charreada* (rodeo) on Sunday afternoons during the summer. Prices range from 70 pesos in the sun to 95 pesos for nice seats in the shade. At the western edge of town, **Galgódromo** (also known as the Juárez Racetrack, ☎625 53 94) rises from Vicente Guerrero. Dogs run Wednesday through Sunday at 7:30pm, with a Sunday matinee at 2:30pm.

NUEVO CASAS GRANDES ("NCG")   ☎1

Nuevo Casas Grandes (pop. 80,000) belongs to a time when cowboys ruled the land. A quiet town in the expansive Chihuahuan desert, NCG arose at the beginning of this century after a group of pioneering families from the old Casas Grandes decided to move to the newly constructed railroad station. Nuevo (New) Casas Grandes is still an agricultural center and a good place to pick up *vaquero* (Mexican cowboy) wear. Travelers use the city as a base for exploring **Casas Grandes**, the ruins of **Paquimé** (pah-kee-MEH)—one of the most important cities in Pre-Hispanic northern Mexico, and the pottery-making town of **Mata Ortiz**.

TRANSPORTATION. Nuevo Casas Grandes is most easily reached by bus. To get from the bus stations, on Obregón and **16 de Septiembre**, to the center of town, walk one block down 16 de Septiembre to **Constitución**, which runs along the railroad tracks that form the backbone of the city. Constitución, along with **Calle Juárez** (one block over), **5 de Mayo**, and 16 de Septiembre form the grid that is the city center. Taxis loiter near the corner of 16 de Septiembre and Constitución.

Estrella Blanca and **Omnibus de México** (☎694 07 80) run buses to **Chihuahua** (4hr., every hr., 163 pesos); **Ciudad Juárez** (3½hr., every hr., 128 pesos); and **Cuauhtémoc** (6½hr., 3 per day, 150 pesos); **Hermosillo** (8hr., 6 per day, 612 pesos); **Monterrey** (16 hr., 6 per day, 612 pesos); **Tijuana** (16hr., 3 per day, 695 pesos).

PRACTICAL INFORMATION. The tourist office is no longer, but the receptionists at all the hotels listed are experienced in helping travelers. Change money at **Casa de Cambio California**, Constitución 207, at 5 de Mayo (☎694 32 32 or 694 45 45. Open M-F 9am-2pm and 3:30-7pm, Sa 9am-2pm and 3:30-6pm.) Banks line 5 de Mayo, and most have 24hr. ATMs. **Police** (☎694 09 73) are located on Blanco and Obregón. No English spoken. **Red Cross** (☎694 20 20) on Carranza at Constitución. **LADATELs** can be found throughout the town. Do laundry at **Lavandería** on Madera between Madero and Obregón. **Internet** access is available at **La Playa**, Juárez 105, 1½ blocks up from the church on the right. (☎694 12 12. Open M-Sa 10am-8pm; 20 pesos per hr. for slow service.) The **post office** is at 16 de Septiembre and Madero (☎694 20 16. Open M-F 9am-4pm). **Postal code:** 31700.

ACCOMMODATIONS AND FOOD. Nuevo Casas Grandes' numerous hotels and restaurants cluster on Constitución and Juárez between 5 de Mayo and Urueta. The only true budget accommodation, **Hotel Juárez**, Obregón 110, is an easy 36 ft. stumble down Obregón from the bus station. It is cheap for a reason—the stuffy and windowless rooms give one the feeling of being incarcerated. Mario, the owner, speaks flawless English and is a great source of information about the region. The lobby is a late-night hangout for travelers and locals, and a good place to restock your supply of stories and dirty jokes. (☎694 02 33. Singles 90 pesos; doubles 100 pesos.) For something more sterile, head to **Hotel California**, Constitución 209, whose spacious white stucco rooms have A/C and TV. (☎694 11 10. Singles 280 pesos; doubles 330 pesos.) Nicer still is the **Hotel Piñon**, Juárez 605, complete with adjoining bar and swimming pool, and whose newly remodeled rooms have A/C and TV. The front desk staff has good advice for visiting the surrounding areas. (☎694 06 55 or 694 01 66. Singles 340 pesos; doubles 410 pesos.)

NCG's restaurants may not be steeped in ambience, but they do offer a welcome break from the elements. American fast-food style charm and prices can be found at **Piñones**, on Juárez at the corner of Urueta, across from Hotel Paquimé. Giant

TRAFFIC Don't be fooled by the small-town atmosphere of NCG—there may be more than meets the eye. This small agrarian community is rumored to be an important stop in the narcotics industry, as illegal substances are moved from southern Mexico to Chihuahua and into NCG, then north to Nogales and finally Tucson. Incidentally, when traveling between Juárez and NCG, your vehicle may be stopped by military officials toting AK-47s and looking for hidden stashes. The Mexican Government is currently undergoing efforts to stop drug trafficking from Colombia and Guatemala to the United States. NCG is said to be home to several *federales* and dealers, who maintain a fairly stable relationship with each other as their cargo is shipped through. Keep that in mind as you pass the shiny new American-made pickup trucks and fancy homes; only so much of that money came from growing apples and peaches.

burritos (8 pesos), sandwiches (17 pesos), and double cheeseburgers (25 pesos) comprise the menu. (☎694 13 80. Open daily 9am-10pm.) For a fancier sit-down meal, try **Restaurant Constantino,** on Juárez at Minerva which has all the Mexican specialties your heart may desire. Try the chicken tacos (31 pesos) or steaks (70-80 pesos), the house specialty. (☎694 10 05. Open daily 7am-midnight.) Still more steaks can be found just up Juárez at **Denni's Restaurant,** Juárez 412 (☎694 10 75), where the ranching set comes to drink coffee and read the paper. Chow down on a big breakfast (35 pesos) or any kind of drippy red meat you can imagine (55-145 pesos). Vegetarians can escape to the three **Dinno's Pizzas** in town. Before devouring an individual pizza (30 pesos), check with the staff to make sure it is meat-free. Norteños have a hereditary desire to put a little animal in everything. (☎694 02 40. Open daily 7am-11:30pm.)

ENTERTAINMENT. Although there is a small movie theater at Constitución and Minerva, **Cinema Vaviedades** (☎669 35 35), the main activity in NCG seems to be drinking one's troubles away. **El Badito Pub,** at Juárez and Prado (☎694 65 53) is a good place to do this. The big pickup trucks parked outside may be intimidating, but the interior has a clean-cut western friendliness. Live "romantic" music on weekends. Beer 18 pesos; tequila 20 pesos and up. Of course, they also serve steaks—something's got to fuel all that *machismo*. While the *banditos* succumb to "romantic" music, the real men head to the bars on Juárez, including the bars at **Hotel Piñon, Hotel Paquimé,** and especially **Hotel Hacienda.** Practice your swagger before walking into that last one! If the wild west is making your saddle sore, you can vacation in Medieval England at **Camelot,** *the discoteca* in NCG, located all the way down Juárez at the entrance to town. Typical Latin dance mix plays for a young crowd. (Open weekends only, 9pm-1 or 2am.)

NEAR NUEVO CASAS GRANDES

Surrounding Nuevo Casas Grandes are many points of archaeological interest, including the **Cueva de Olla** (75km southwest), the **Arroyo de los Monos** (35km southeast), and **Mata Ortiz** (40km south). About 254km southeast of Nuevo Casas Grandes is **Madera,** from which the **Cuarenta Casas** site can be reached (54km north). Ask at the tourist office for more info.

PAQUIMÉ (CASAS GRANDES)

Paquimé is an easy 10min. walk from the town of Casas Grandes. From NCG, catch a bus labeled "Pueblo" from the intersection of Constitución and 16 de Septiembre (10 min., 1-2 per hr., 3.5 pesos). Get off at the main plaza of Casas Grandes and walk back in the direction the bus just came on Constitución. This road quickly turns into dirt, rounds a bend, and goes straight to Paquimé (a 10min. walk). ☎692 41 40. Ruins open Tu-Su 10am-5pm, 30 pesos.

The huge network of earthen walls rising out of the desert plain just beyond Casas Grandes isn't some figment of George Lucas' imagination—it's the astoundingly intact remnant of Mexico's northernmost Pre-Hispanic civilization. Built by a people culturally related to the Anasazi of the American Southwest, Paquimé is an 11th to 14th-century city that thrived on mining and corn. A sophisticated system of aqueducts and channels carried precious rainfall from the distant mountains and made it possible to farm the arid valley. Minerals were traded for shells from the coast and brightly feathered macaws from the south, which were kept in bird-size adobe houses and later used in religious ceremonies. Paquimé has filled its museum with an amazing collection of artifacts found on-site, including exquisite pottery, with explanations in Spanish and English. The museum also houses extensive scale recreations of the city to help explain the partially eroded site.

If you are traveling by car or have a generous budget, there are many areas around NCG worth visiting. A bus leaves daily around 4pm from the corner of Constitución and 16 de Septiembre for **Mata Ortiz,** a town famous for its revival Paquimé-style pottery. Be sure to ask around locally for the most accurate departure time, as it varies. The beautiful town is home to artists who have followed in the footsteps of **Juan Quezada,** who recreated the Navajo-looking Paquimé style, but be forewarned that hotels in the area are expensive. On the way to Mata Ortiz, the dirt road passes **Colonia Juárez,** 23km. southwest of NCG, which was founded by Mormons escaping the 19th-century prosecution of polygamy in the US. 19th-century buildings and apple-growing **Mennonite colonists** abound here. Discover more archeological sites at **Arroyo de los Monos** (35km south), which has ancient cave paintings, and 55km southwest at **Cueva de la Olla,** which is a series of adobe structures built into a cave. To see these sights without a car, it is best to hire a guide who has a truck. Mauricio Guzman, bartender at Hotel Piñon (☎694 01 66) runs tours for US$60-70 which include Mata Ortiz, San Dijo, Colonia Juárez, and Paquimé. Tours must be arranged a day or two in advance.

CHIHUAHUA ☎1

The capital of Mexico's largest state, Chihuahua (pop. 800,000) is a historically rich outpost in the northern desert. The city has seen its share of bloody conflict in the 300 years since its founding in 1709. It was here in 1811 that Miguel Hidalgo's quest for independence ended in his execution, and here that Pancho Villa established his revolutionary headquarters during the Porfiriato. Revolutionary skirmishes aside, modern-day Chihuahua is a peace-loving city with a bustling downtown and pastoral surroundings. A major transportation hub for the northwest, Chihuahua's culture has been shaped by a diverse array of influences, from Mennonites to backpackers bound for the Copper Canyon, to the indigenous Tarahumara who arrive on market days to sell their crafts.

⌐ TRANSPORTATION

Airport: (☎420 06 76), 14km from town. The "Aeropuerto" bus stops near Niños Héroes and Independencia; look for the sign. **AeroCalifornia** (☎437 10 22), **AeroMéxico** (☎414 61 67 or 414 67 68), and **Continental** (☎420 47 51; fax 435 26 97).

Buses: From the **bus station,** a municipal bus (3 pesos) will take you to the cathedral. Taxis cost 40 pesos. Omnibus de México (☎420 15 80) sends luxurious buses to: **Aguascalientes** (7 per day, 584 pesos); **Casas Grandes** (6 per day, 162 pesos); **Cuauhtémoc** (7 per day, 55 pesos); **Durango** (9 per day, 333 pesos); **Guadalajara** (3 per day, 677 pesos); **Mexico City** (6 per day, 832 pesos); **Monterrey** (4 per day, 454 pesos); **Torreón** (250 pesos); **Zacatecas** (472 pesos). Estrella Blanca (☎429 02 40) has a slightly older fleet that chugs to nearly all the same locations. Rapidos Cuauhtémoc (☎410 52 08) runs to Cuauhtémoc (1½hr., every 30min. 5am-noon, 55 pesos). Autotransportes Rapidas Relicias (☎120 07 51) goes to **Hidalgo de Parral** (90 pesos).

Trains: Chihuahua has 2 major rail stations. The **Chihuahua al Pacífico** train station, Méndez at Calle 24, is south of the city center off Ocampo and 2 blocks from 20 de Noviembre. To shorten the 20min. walk to the *centro,* hop on one of the public buses (3 pesos) that run up and down Ocampo to Libertad. The station is popular with backpackers for its daily trip between Chihuahua and **Los Mochis,** which cuts through the breathtaking **Barranca del Cobre** (13hr., 7am, 500 pesos). The train stops at various points along the way, including **Creel, Divisadero, Posada Barraces, Bahuichivo, Temoris,** and **El Fuerte.** A 2nd station, **Estación Central de los FFNN,** features the night Division del Norte train, with service between **Ciudad Juárez** and **Mexico City.**

ORIENTATION AND PRACTICAL INFORMATION

Don't let the sheer size of Chihuahua intimidate you—most sights are within walking distance of the cathedral. With the exception of Victoria, streets in Chihuahua are poorly lit and may be dangerous at night. Avoid walking alone.

Tourist Office: (☎410 10 77; fax 416 00 32), on Aldama between Carranza and Guerrero, in the Palacio del Gobierno. Helpful staff and tourist guides. Open daily 9am-7pm.

Currency Exchange: Casas de cambio cluster along Victoria. **Banorte,** Victoria 104 (☎410 15 93). Open M-F 9am-3pm. **Hotel San Francisco** (☎416 75 50), across the street, has 24hr. exchange. **ATMs** crowd the streets near the cathedrals.

Car Rental: Alamo, Borunda #2500 (☎416 50 31) before Revolución. **Avis** (airport ☎420 19 19; *centro* ☎414 19 19). **Hertz,** Revolución 514 (☎416 64 73), at Santos.

Emergency: ☎060.

Police: Homero 540 (☎481 19 00), across from the Ford plant. No English spoken.

Red Cross: (☎411 22 11 or 411 14 84), Calle 24 and Revolución. No English spoken.

Pharmacy: Farmacia Hidalgo (☎410 65 08), at Guerrero and Aldama.

Chihuahua

■ ACCOMMODATIONS

Casa de Huespedes
Posada Aida, **4**
Hotel del Pacífico, **1**
Hotel San Juan, **5**
Hotel Turista, **2**
Nuevo Hotel Reforma, **3**

NORTHWEST MEXICO

Hospital: Hospital General (☎416 00 22 or 415 60 84), Revolución and Colón, in Colonia Centro. **Clínica del Centro,** Ojinaga 816 (☎416 00 22).

Internet: La Red, Ojinaga 511-B (☎415 56 15). 20 pesos for 1hr. of speedy air-conditioned service. You may wish to spend the night. Open M-Sa 9am-9pm, Su 10am-4pm.

Post Office: (☎437 12 00), on Libertad in the Palacio Federal. Open M-F 8am-7pm, Sa 9am-1pm.

Postal Code: 31000.

ACCOMMODATIONS

Budget hotels in Chihuahua resemble the city itself—charm smiling through grit. Cheap hotels of questionable moral fiber can be found around the market, uphill from Niños Héroes before Ocampo. American chains dot the roads into town.

■ **Casa de Huespedes Posada Aida,** Calle 10 #106 (☎415 38 30), between Niños Héroes and Juárez. Should be listed as the last stop for the *Barranca* train. Backpackers love it, and with its courtyard garden and clean, simple rooms its easy to see why. Aida herself cooks breakfast for those who ask. Singles 80 pesos; doubles 100 pesos.

Hotel San Juan, Victoria 823 (☎410 00 36). A 1930s gem, with a beautiful (if decaying) tile courtyard and great views from the 3rd fl. Most rooms have A/C and TV, and the hotel is connected to a popular *cantina* and a small restaurant. Towel deposit 10 pesos. Singles 95 pesos; doubles 105 pesos.

Nuevo Hotel Reforma, Victoria 823 (☎410 39 98), has high ceilings and swishing fans. Some rooms have balconies, all have TV. Singles 100 pesos; doubles 122 pesos.

Hotel Turista, Juárez 813 (☎410 04 00), near the cathedral. Lobby sells toiletries. Rooms have A/C. Singles 130 pesos; doubles 130-160 pesos.

Hotel del Pacífico, Aldama 1911 (☎410 59 13), at Calle 21, a few blocks from the Palacio de Gobierno. A/C, fans, and baths in every room. Kind of worn-out looking, but free coffee, eggs, and toast are provided to backpackers catching the early morning train during winter months. Singles 175 pesos; doubles 230 pesos; TV 10 pesos extra.

FOOD

Chihuahua's eateries favor function over form, with an abundance of cheap, hearty meals being served at the city's many 1960s style diners. Good meals can be found in the small *cantinas,* where bands serenade drunken, rowdy men. Women should avoid entering *cantinas* alone. Though eating in the *mercado,* which starts at Calle 69 and Ángel Trias, qualifies as a contact sport, crowds flock there for a reason. Revel in greasy bargain splendor at **Taqueria Anita,** 4a and Ángel Trias.

Antojitos "Pam-Pam," Carranza 1204-A at Calle 11. Follow Carranza as it branches off to the right from the Palacio del Gobierno. Locals come to this small vintage diner to read the paper, chat, and eat cheap, good food. Indulgent *tostadas* with guacamole 25 pesos, *tortas* 13 pesos, steak 55 pesos. Open daily from 8:30am-11pm.

Degá Restuarante-Bar, Victoria 409 (☎416 75 50), at Hotel San Francisco just south of the cathedral. If you're willing to act swank and pay a bit more, Degá offers a rare chance at a vegetarian meal. *Plato vegetariano* 52 pesos, *plato de verduras mixtos* 40 pesos. Serves a great weekend brunch. Open daily 7am-10pm.

Mi Cafe, Victoria 1000 (☎410 12 38), at Calle 10, across from Hotel San Juan. Generous portions at 1970s prices in a fabulously orange crêpe-paper-decorated restaurant. Breakfast 40 pesos, amazing chicken burritos 18 pesos, friendly staff priceless.

Ostioneria Galleon del Pirata (☎410 29 27), at Calle 6a and Ángel Trias. This pioneering restaurant charges seaside prices for the magical fish-beer combo. Fillets 35 pesos, *tostadas de ceviche* 35 pesos, *carta blanca* 12 pesos. Open daily 8am-9pm.

SIGHTS

After you buy your cowboy hat and boots, an even more eye-opening shopping experience awaits at **Botanica Meza,** Juárez 523, which sells a wide selection of herbs, talismans, *milagros*, magic powders, and charms to a serious clientele of *curanderas* (traditional healers) and the occasional witch. Even if you think it's moonshine don't say so—*botanica* is not a good place to make enemies. (Open M-Sa 9am-2pm and 3pm-8pm, less predictably Su.)

■ **MUSEO DE LA REVOLUCIÓN.** Also known as **Quinta Luz,** this 50-room mansion was the home of Villa's (legal) widow, Luz Corral, who lived here, maintained the museum, and led tours until her death in 1981. Items on display include Villa's personal effects, photographs, and the revolutionary's gun collection. The star of the show is the bullet-ridden Dodge in which the unsuspecting Villa was assassinated. *(Hike 1½km south on Ocampo, turn left on 20 de Noviembre, and go 2 blocks to Calle 10 and Méndez. Turn right; the house is 2 blocks down. ☎416 29 58. Open Tu-Su 9am-1pm and 3-7pm, Su 9am-5pm. 10 pesos, children 5 pesos.)*

■ **QUINTA GAMEROS CENTRO CULTURAL UNIVERSITARIO (MUSEO REGIONAL DE CHIHUAHUA).** One of the more stunning mansions in Mexico, this building is a prime example of the French Art Nouveau style. Mining engineer Manuel Gameros, the aristocrat who contracted the building (1907-1911), never had a chance to live here before the Revolution drove him to Texas. The house was seized by revolutionaries, and at one point served as Pancho Villa's barracks and Venustasio Carranza's home. Upstairs is an impressive collection of modern Mexican art, while the downstairs houses rotating exhibits. Don't miss the extravagant lily-pond bathroom or elaborate wooden dining room. *(On the corner of Calle 4 and Paseo Bolívar, a 10min. walk from the cathedral. ☎416 66 84. Open Tu-Su 11am-2pm and 4-7pm. 22 pesos, children 12 pesos; W half-price.)*

PALACIO FEDERAL AND POST OFFICE. Constructed on the foundation of a much older Jesuit College that comprised the center of Spanish colonial Chihuahua, this Neoclassical building was finished in 1910. Walk down the stairs and to the back of the building to find the ■**Calaboso de Miguel Hidalgo,** visible as a small entrance several steps below street level. Here you can visit the building's 17th-century foundation, where revolutionary priest **Miguel Hidalgo** was held until his execution by the Spanish government in 1811. The chilling museum displays his writings, crucifix, and the wall of his jail cell on which he scrawled a few parting words to his captors with a piece of charcoal. *(☎424 29 03, ext. 1056. Open Tu-F 9am-7pm, Sa-Su 9am-3pm and 4-7pm. 5 pesos, children 2 pesos.)*

PALACIO DE GOBIERNO. A 19th-century testament to Chihuahuan history, the palace holds Aarón Piña Mora murals, with flames marking the spots of Hidalgo's and Allende's executions, and a nude statue of Emiliano Zapata, whose modesty is maintained by a well-placed rifle. *(At the center of Chihuahua on Aldama and Victoria.)*

MUSEO DE LA LEALTAD REPUBLICANA. An appropriately sober museum chronicling the years the Mexican government spent in exile during the Maximilian-Hapsburg reign. Writings in Spanish of Benito Juárez and timelines elaborate the renovated rooms of Juárez's Chihuahuan home, where he lived from 1864 to 1866, when the Republican government was restored. *(On Juárez between Independencia and Carranza. Open Tu-Su 9am-7pm. 5 pesos, children 2 pesos.)*

CATHEDRAL. Due to Apache raids and the unpredictable nature of mining money, it took 100 years to construct Chihuahua's **Nuestra Señora de Regla y San Francisco de Asís.** Finally finished in 1826, the cathedral was well worth the wait. The beautiful Churrigueresque facade features the 12 apostles and a humongous pipe-organ. In the southeast corner of the Cathedral is the small **Museo de Arte Sacro,** housing pastoral 18th-century religious paintings and pictures from the Pope's last visit. *(Open M-F 10am-2pm and 4-6pm. 12 pesos.)*

CENTRO CULTURAL DE CHIHUAHUA. Once the home of a former governor of Chihuahua, Luis Terrazas, this 1889 mansion houses a small cultural and educational institution. The center hosts cultural events, artwork, and displays on Paquimé pottery. Posters for events and a classical concert series are posted throughout the *centro*. (On Aldama at Ocampo. Open Tu-Su 10am-2pm and 4-7pm. Free.)

🎵 ENTERTAINMENT

In Chihuahua, plenty of folks just home from the range like to cut loose in the many *cantinas* surrounding the market southwest of the cathedral. The darkened taverns are saturated with enough tequila and heartbroken accordion riffs to soften even the most leathery *vaquero*.

Two blocks east but worlds away, sophisticates young and old enjoy coffee, wine, *antojitos*, and pastries at **Cafe Calcicanto**, Aldama 411, across from the Casa de Cultura. Live "romantic" and Bolivian music fills the open-air courtyard. (After 9pm on weekends, *tortas* 25 pesos, beer 16 pesos, tequila starts at 25 pesos. ☎410 44 52. Open Su-Th 4pm-midnight, F-Sa 4pm-2am.) Beautiful people rub elbows at **La Casa de los Milagros**, 1½ blocks south of the cathedral on Victoria. An impressive selection of beer (18 pesos) and wine are served in the tiled courtyard to the sounds of live guitar music. (☎437 06 93. Open Su-Th 5pm-midnight, F-Sa till 1am.)

Blissfully free of the aforementioned pretense, a multi-generational crowd shimmies on the dance floor at **Sports Champ Club** at the corner of Juárez and Calle 2. (Beer or tequila 12 pesos. Live bands every night. No cover.) If that isn't steamy enough, **Ole Bar**, on Pablado across the bridge from the corner of Pablado and Independencia, doesn't provide a dance floor—they say it encourages patrons to get up and dance on the tables. You may break a sweat just waiting to get in—a substantial line of well-dressed Chihuahuanecos usually forms by 10:30pm. Patrons pay 40 pesos to hear live bands Thursday through Saturday.

If all this is too intense, escape to the movie theater on Santos and Pablado, or **Cinema 2001** on Guerrero 618 at Escorza. (☎416 50 00. 20 pesos.)

🔼 DAYTRIPS FROM CHIHUAHUA

CUAUHTÉMOC

Cuauhtémoc lies half-way between Creel and Chihuahua, a 1½hr. bus ride from each. Ómnibus de México (☎420 15 80) leaves Chihuahua's train station for Cuauhtémoc (7 per day, 54 pesos), as does Estrella Blanca (☎429 02 40. 8 per day, 35 pesos). Public **buses** *run all over the city and stop at the blue bus stop signs—the main stop is on Calle 3 between Allende and Guerrero (3 pesos). To leave town, the Estrella Blanca bus station, Allende at Calle 9, (☎582 10 18), runs buses to:* **Casas Grandes** *(5hr., 2 per day, 140 pesos);* **Chihuahua** *(1½hr., every 30min. 8:30am-9:30pm, 35 pesos);* **Ciudad Juárez** *(9hr., 11pm, 259 pesos);* **Creel** *(3½hr., every hr. 7:30am-7:30pm, 92 pesos).*

Though the city's Aztec namesake may be immortalized in a statue in the center of town, only two blocks away hundreds of indigenous Rarámuri live in a giant warehouse on bunks stacked five high, without adequate sanitation or employment. Cuauhtémoc seems to thrive on this sort of contradiction, serving as both a modern center for agricultural production and as a supply station for the extremely traditional societies of the Mennonites and the Rarámuri. Residents don't look when they pass the oddly dressed, Germanic Mennonites on the street, but instead busily occupy themselves with their own cowboy boots and souped-up lowriders.

For visitors passing through Cuauhtémoc on their way to or from **La Barranca**, the Mennonites and their tidy *campos* in the surrounding valley are the city's main attraction. Founded in the 15th century, this German pacifist religious group moved from Europe to Russia to Canada trying to escape persecution and forced military service. After the British government impressed Mennonites into WWI, many migrated to Mexico with the stipulation that they would not fight any wars.

Since the 1920s, they have become the most important agricultural producers in the state, enjoying traditional agrarian lifestyles in numbered *campos*.

Most *campos* are reachable by **Omnibus de México** (☎582 12 01) buses, which will stop along the freeway about 1km from the camp's houses. (7 per day, 5:30am-9pm, 27 pesos to *campos* 26, 15, 21, and 101.) The station is on Calle 7a at Morelos.

If you're not ready to convert just yet, Cuauhtémoc has many cheap places to stay while you think it over. Sleeping at **Hotel Cuauhtémoc**, Morelos 306 between Calles 3 and 5, is a bit like lying in a swimming pool—though very blue and somewhat shabby, the price helps keep things afloat. (☎852 00 06. Singles 70 pesos; doubles 80 pesos.) One step up is **Hotel San Francisco**, around the corner on Calle 3. (☎582 31 52. Free breakfast 8-9:30am. 95-105 pesos.)

Late risers can eat at **El Den**, across from the *zócalo*, which has real coffee, breakfasts, reasonably priced dinner fare, and a tranquil ambience that refreshes you after the frenzy of Cuauhtémoc's streets. (☎582 38 43. Open daily 7am-10:30pm.) True budget food is available 24hr. at **Cafe de la Esquina**, around the corner on Varezcoello, home of the 8-peso burrito.

HIDALGO DEL PARRAL ☎1

For the first 300 years of its history Parral was as close as Mexico ever came to living the legend of *El Dorado*. In 1640, when silver from local mines began pouring into Spain, the King himself dubbed Parral "The Silver Capital of the World." So it was until the mines became unprofitable in the 1950s. Locals remained unabashed by this turn of fate, simply dropping the silver bit to become "capital of the world." Today they continue to act the part. Proud and unaccommodating, residents can be as difficult to navigate as the city's winding streets, but efforts to do so will be rewarded. The mining days left behind a trove of beautiful buildings dating from the 17th century to the 1970s. Local disregard for timetables and technology distinguish Parral from the more developed north.

TRANSPORTATION. To go downtown from the bus station, exit left out of the front door and walk two blocks down Pedro de Sille. Turn left onto Independencia and follow it as it careens downhill to the *centro*. The 15min. walk can be avoided with a 20- to 25-peso taxi ride.

Estrella Blanca (☎523 00 75) runs buses to: **Chihuahua** (4hr., 7 per day, 118 pesos); **Ciudad Juárez** (7hr., 8 per day, 309 pesos); **Guadalajara** (1 per day, 589 pesos); **Mexico City** (20hr., 3:30pm, 748 pesos). Cheaper 2nd-class buses (no A/C or TV) are also available to: **Durango** (173 pesos) and **Chihuahua** (80 pesos).

ORIENTATION AND PRACTICAL INFORMATION. Parral's center consists of a compact, confusing tangle of streets. It helps to get a map (30 pesos) at a downtown **bookstore** or the **Museo de Pancho Villa**. In general, you're never too far from the city center if you're near the river(bed). Taxis can be hailed at **Plaza Principal**, and buses to the outskirts stop along **Mercaderes**, which parallels the river.

None of this 9-5 business for Parral. This city takes *siesta* seriously. Everything but the *cantinas* and restaurants closes from 1-3:30pm, and they won't help you, even if you beg. Parral has no official tourist office, but the staff of history-freaks at the **Museo de Pancho Villa** will be happy to point out sights. Like most northern cities Parral has many competing **casas de cambio**—the most centrally located **ATM** is **Banamex**'s on Mercaderes just before Ojinaga. **Pharmacy:** next to El Camino Market on the corner of Madrazo and Independencia. (☎523 06 63. Open daily 8am-midnight.) **Supermarket: El Camino** (☎523 06 63), on Independencia just outside downtown, next to Hotel Margarita's. **Post office:** on the corner of Rago and Libertad, a few blocks from the cathedral. (Open M-F 8am-3pm.) **Postal code:** 33800.

ACCOMMODATIONS AND FOOD. Parral is home to what may very well be the cheapest hotel in Northwestern Mexico. **Hotel Zaragoza**, Zaragoza 115, a 10min. walk up Calle Rangel Baisma from the *centro*, has polyester sheets, styrofoam pillows and a communal bathroom whose prominent feature is a "don't pee in the shower" sign. While this may not be endearing, the prices are. (☎ 522 65 90. Singles 46 pesos; doubles 61 pesos; triples 81 pesos.)

Those with standards should avoid Zaragoza and stay in one of the slightly pricier hotels in the *centro*. The most central budget option is **Hotel Chihuahua,** Colón #1 (☎ 522 15 13). To get there from Plaza Baca, walk on Mercaderes heading back toward the center, but turn left on Garcia. Keep left on Garcia until Colón. The hotel is kitty-corner from Club Viet-Nam. Clean rooms with good ventilation are available for 100-150 pesos. (Keep an eye out for the 85-year-old owner, who is something of a neighborhood celebrity.) At **Restaurante el Aseradero,** on the left side of Independencia after Primavera heading toward the *centro*, you can watch your food cook over a wood fire. Good chicken, beef, and *cabrito* (roasted young goat) for 35-45 pesos. (Open daily 10am-10pm.)

◎ ♫ SIGHTS AND ENTERTAINMENT. Parral's mining days may be over, but the city has just begun to capitalize on the history left behind. A good place to get a sense of Parral's former wealth is the **Palacio Alvaro** at the corner of Riva and Palacio. Constructed from 1899-1903 by a man so wealthy he once offered to pay off Mexico's entire national debt, the building is currently being restored as a museum (scheduled to open in 2003). Though you won't get inside until then, the edifice is interesting in its own right. Look for two windows to the left of the main entrance—through the one on the right, Don Pedro Alvaro paid the miners every eighth day (the building's decorative moulding has a caricature of one of their ago-nized, overworked faces), while through the holes in the bar of the other, he gave money to the sick and farmers whose crops had failed. It is said that a young Pan-cho Villa once came to the window with a wounded leg, and seeing his promise, Don Alvaro took him in and had his leg treated by a personal physician. The two became fast friends, as Alvaro eventually gave Villa the building to the left of Catédral Guadalupe, and Villa invaded Texas to rescue Alvaro's son from an Amer-ican jail where he was being held for manslaughter.

Villa spent the last years of his life on Mercaderes across the river until he was killed by assassins who perforated his car with 150 bullets. Right next to the scene of the crime is the newly opened **Museo de Francisco Villa,** which indulges his cult-like followers with a downstairs shrine, and an upstairs exhibit focusing on Villa's martyrdom, complete with pictures of his gory end. (☎ 525 37 92. Open Tu-Su 9am-1pm and 3-7pm. 5 pesos, children 3 pesos.) Mystery shrouds Villa's grave at the **Panteón Municipal,** on the outskirts of town. According to the government, Villa is interred in Mexico City, but Parral residents believe a government conspiracy moved a decoy body instead of the real body, which still resides in Parral.

The violence of the city's mining history is slightly less evident, though a visit to the **Templo de la Virgen de Fátima** gives a sense of the local devotion to the patron saint of miners. The walls are constructed from thousands of small glittering chunks of local ore, and the square pews replicate those in the mine's under-ground shrines. Many of the city's other churches are also elaborately decorated. The oldest is the **Templo de San José,** which was finished in 1684. Slightly newer but also worth a look is the **Templo de Nuestra Señora del Ruyo,** also in the *centro*.

Outside of the usual *cantinas*, a good time can be had at **J. Quísseme,** a lounge and dance club on Independencia near the bus station. Things start hopping after 10pm. (Beer 25 pesos. Cover 30 pesos. Open Th-F 8pm-1am, Sa 9pm-2am.) The **Lone Star** club, by the stadium, is another local favorite. (Open W-Sa 9pm-3am.) You can take in a **bullfight** two weekends each summer, usually in mid-July and late-Aug. To get to the stadium, follow the noise; walk a few blocks left of Indepen-dencia, and turn left near Pedro de Lille as you head out of town.

CREEL ☎ 1

A western boom town whose railway drags in tourists rather than gold, Creel's high altitude and dramatic, rocky surroundings help it stay cool and collected in the midst of backpacker bombardment. While the steady flow of foreign visitors has turned Creel's main street into a row of hotels, restaurants, and gift shops, it hasn't diluted the town's rugged ambience. Frigid winter temperatures, a hospital and school for indigenous Tarahumara children and the town's position as a base for the local lumber industries help keep things real. As the most popular base for excursions into the Sierra, the town's incongruous mix of budget travelers, *indígenas*, and small-business entrepreneurs make it a worthy stop in its own right.

▐ TRANSPORTATION

Creel is one of the few towns in the Copper Canyon accessible both by bus and train and a good starting point for trips into the Copper Canyon.

Trains: CHEPE trains (☎456 00 15) leave daily for **Chihuahua** (1st class 6hr., 3pm, 463 pesos; 2nd class 6hr., 4pm, 227 pesos), and **Los Mochis** through the Copper Canyon (1st class 10hr., 11:30am, 557 pesos; 2nd class 11hr., 1pm, 275 pesos). You can get off anywhere along the way to avoid paying full price. Tickets aren't sold in advance from the Creel station, so scramble on quickly when the train pulls up and elbow for a seat.

Buses: The Estrella Blanca station (☎456 00 73), is a small white-and-green building uphill across the tracks from town. Buses to **Chihuahua** (5hr., 8 per day 7am-5:30pm, 150 pesos), pass through **Cuauhtémoc** (4hr., 98 pesos). To travel to **Hidalgo de Parral,** take a bus to **Guachochi** (noon and 7:30pm, 43 pesos) and transfer to **Parral.** Buses also go to **Ciudad Juárez** (8:30am, 358 pesos). Buses to **Batopilas** (6hr.; Tu, Th, and Sa between 6am and 7:15am, depending on when the bus fills) leave across from Hotel Los Piños. Check in town to verify times, as service is dependent on weather and road conditions.

✴ ⁊ ORIENTATION AND PRACTICAL INFORMATION

The railroad tracks function as a rough compass: toward Chihuahua is north and toward Los Mochis is south. The *zócalo* is the best place from which to get your bearings. The main street, **Mateos,** runs parallel to the trains on the opposite side of the *zócalo*, and is the only street near the *zócalo* that extends any distance. Everything you need can be found on or near Mateos. **Caro,** farther south, runs perpendicular to Mateos and up to the tracks. **Villa** parallels the tracks on the opposite side of Mateos. A helpful map is posted next to Banco Serfín.

Tourist Information: Artesanías Misión (☎456 00 97), on the north side of the *zócalo*. Not an official tourist office, but the best source of information. Sells maps and Tarahumaran books and crafts. Proceeds are donated to the Tarahumaran Children's hospital fund. English spoken. Open M-Sa 9:30am-1pm and 3-6pm, Su 9:30am-1pm.

Currency Exchange: Banco Serfín, Plaza 201 (☎456 02 50), next door to the Misión has a 24hr. **ATM.** Exchanges US dollars M-F 9am-1:30pm. Open M-F 9am-3pm.

Market: Comercial de Creel, Mateos 55. Open M-Sa 9:30am-7pm.

Bike Rental: Margaritas Plaza Hotel, Bautista SIN (☎456 6054). 100 pesos per day.

Police: (☎456 04 50), in the Presidencia Seccional, on the south side of the *zócalo*.

Pharmacy: Farmacia Rodríguez, Mateos 43 (☎456 00 52). Open M-Sa 9am-2pm and 3:30-9pm, Su 10am-1pm.

Medical Services: Clínica Santa Teresita, (☎456 01 05), on Parroquia, at the end of the street, 2 blocks from Mateos. Little English spoken. Open M-F 10am-1pm and 3-5pm, Sa 10am-1pm.

Fax: Papelería de Todo, Mateos 30 (☎/fax 456 01 22). Open M-Sa 9am-8:30pm, Su 9am-2pm.

Post Office: (☎456 02 58), in the Presidencia Seccional, on the south side of the *zócalo*. Open M-F 9am-3pm.

Postal Code: 33200.

ACCOMMODATIONS AND CAMPING

Due to Creel's popularity with Canyon-seeking tourists, a large number of establishments compete for tourist pesos. The result: budget rooms are plentiful and prices may be negotiable during low season. Many budget accommodations are within a couple of blocks of the *zócalo*. For the adventurous, the local **KOA** campground offers safe and affordable camping, as does the area around **Lake Arareco.**

■ **Casa de Huéspedes Perez,** Flores 25 (☎456 00 47). Follow Mateos away from the train station, make a left at the "Cafe Luli" sign, walk down the street, cross the green bridge and walk directly uphill to the first house. The comfortably rustic accomodations are located behind the family's house. Prices and arrangements are negotiable, but always include heaters and meticulously clean baths. Kitchen and laundry facilities available. English language tours offered by Luli's sons. Dorm style housing 80 pesos in high season; 70 pesos in low season. Private rooms from 70-100 pesos.

■ **Margarita's Casa de Huéspedes,** Flores 257 (☎456 00 47). This hostel maintains a mafia-like grip on Creel's tourist industry. Squadrons of Margarita's young emissaries meet every train at the station, leading new arrivals both to the hostel and her more upscale hotel down the street. Breakfast and dinner included. Dorms 70 pesos.

Departamentos Confortables Casa de Huéspedes (☎456 02 15), on Batista off Mateos. On the right, 100m down Batista, just after the brick complex. The *casa* with the long name is a good place for large groups; up to 8 people can stay in the *cabañas*, which come with kitchenette and an outdoor BBQ. Quads 150 pesos.

Hotel Posada de Creel (☎456 01 42), the grey building near Telas Gloria across the train tracks from the *zócalo*, is a cheap option for nice private rooms. Spacious rooms with wood paneling have gas heating and 24hr. hot water. Singles 70 pesos, with private bath 130 pesos; doubles with private bath 160 pesos.

Hotel Los Pinos, Mateos 39 (☎456 02 79) is a slightly nicer choice for private rooms. Great service and clean rooms and baths. Singles and doubles 200 pesos.

KOA Campground (☎456 0665; koacreel@infosell.net.mx), at the end of Mateos about 1.5km from the *zócalo* on the left. The suburban location would be a nice retreat if it weren't for the kitschy KOA touches (playground, restaurant, gift shop). Tent camping 5 pesos per day, 50 pesos per week. Full RV hookups with electricity and plumbing 20 pesos per day. 10% discount for KOA, AAA, and Passport America members.

FOOD

It is almost impossible to distinguish one restaurant from another; all are slightly overpriced and have "rustic" furniture with bright tablecloths. Because there is no cheap market fare, true bargain hunters are advised to stay at Margarita's.

■ **Restaurant El Tungar,** on the train tracks to the left when facing away from the station. A "Hospital para crudos" (hangover hospital), El Tungar is *the* place in Creel for *menudo* (Mexico's gastronomic solution to a night of hard drinking). Locals eat here, curled up on stools while cooks prepare *pozole, birria,* and excellent Chihuahua-style burritos (12 pesos per piece). Open M-Sa 8am-5pm, Su 8am-1pm.

Tío Molcas, Mateos 35 (☎456 00 33). The cheerful banter of the waitresses entertains customers during commercial breaks. Filling beef dishes 43 pesos, fried chicken 35 pesos, burritos 12 pesos. Open daily 8am-11pm.

Cafeteria Gaby, Mateos 50 (look for the "Cafe Combate" illustration). Serves up basic foods like toast (10 pesos), cheese omelettes (22 pesos), and orange juice (12 pesos). For lunch, try the excellent *tortas* or burritos (10 pesos). If you're confused by the door, just pull the string. Open daily 7am-10pm.

👁 🎵 SIGHTS AND ENTERTAINMENT

Tourists come to Creel to visit the breathtaking Copper Canyon, which lies south of the town. To explore the surroundings, you'll need a car, a tour guide, or a brave heart and strong legs (see **Barranca del Cobre**, p. 232). Still, the town has some sights closer to home. **Casa de las Artesanías del Estado de Chihuahua**, on Ferrocarril 17, in the old railroad station across from the *zócalo*, displays local and Tarahumara arts, crafts, and an assortment of historical relics. (☎456 00 80. Open Tu-Sa 9am-2pm and 4-6pm, Su 9am-1pm. 5 pesos.)

While most establishments in Creel close before 9pm, a few stay open late, and tourists roam the streets or people strum guitars until midnight. At night, **Laylo's Lounge and Bar**, Mateos 25, inside El Caballo Bayo restaurant and hotel, is a local *cantina* with a touch of class. The comfy lounge chairs and charming decor outdo most watering holes. (☎456 01 36. Beer 15 pesos. Open daily 3pm-1am.) **Tío Molcas**, Mateos 35, at Caro, also breaks *cantina* stereotypes with its relaxed atmosphere. Doubles as a restaurant during the day. (Open daily 11am-1am.) A happening place for foreigners is the bar at **Margarita's Plaza Hotel**. Turn left on Caro heading away from the *zócalo*, and then right into the hotel courtyard. (Beer 15 pesos, tequila 30 pesos. Happy Hour 7-10pm. Open daily 6:30-11:30pm.)

TOURS

One of the safest and surest ways to get to the surrounding Copper Canyon sights is with a tour. This of course, will cost a little more than doing it on your own, but it is usually worthwhile. Day tours should be arranged a day in advance, while overnight treks must be planned 2-3 days in advance. Band together with as many other interested travelers as possible to keep costs down. Most tours head to **Aguas Termales de Rekowata, El Divisadero, La Bufa, Basihuare, Rio Urique, Basaseachi Falls,** and sometimes **Batopilas**. Most companies also run tours to **Lago de Arareko, Cueva de Sabástian, Valle de las Ranas,** and **Valle de los Hongos,** but these destinations are all easy day hikes from Creel.

Casa Margarita: Margarita offers reasonably priced van tours to all the standard Canyon locations with sack lunches included. The most popular tour is down into the canyon to the hot springs in the Rio de Rekowata (8hr., 120 pesos per person). General guide services 100 pesos per day (not including transportation). Visit either the Casa de Huespedes or the Plaza Hotel (☎456 60 50) to arrange a tour.

Taruhamara Tours: Reasonably priced treks go to all major destinations, as well as to Batopilas (400 pesos per person not including lodging). Office located in the *zócalo* across from Banco Serfín (☎456 00 65 or 456 01 65).

Casa Perez: The Perez brothers run tours from their family's hotel, on Flores 257 off Mateos. A good pick for long tours. Make arrangements at the hotel (☎456 00 47).

Cabanas Bertis: (☎592 08 10) guides wait along Mateos near the video arcade. Has the lowest rates in town, but only if you find enough people to defect from Margarita's to get the tour to go. With 8 people, the trip to the Rekowata hot springs is 80 pesos per person, and the 2-day trip to Batopilas is 250 pesos. The principal guide, Oscar Aguirre Gonzalez, speaks Tarahumara, making this a good choice for anyone interested in cultural tourism.

KOA Campground: A pricey fleet of cute yellow minivans conveys you to the usual array of destinations. Call or visit the campground **(See Accommodations).**

⮞ DAYTRIPS FROM CREEL

The rocky, alpine valleys surrounding Creel shelter plenty of worthwhile sights, and are one of the few areas in the Barranca where it is safe to explore without navigational equipment or a guide. Most sights are en route to **Laguna Arareco.** To get to the Laguna "trailhead" from town, head south on Mateos. Keep left at the first fork in the road. When the road forks again, take the left path uphill to the gate, where you'll have to pay 10 pesos for admission and a rough map of the area. This is a good place to ask more specific instructions to your destination. The first sight on the way to the Laguna is **San Ignacio Mission** which stands in a valley surrounded by Tarahumara farms. Constructed by Jesuits in 1744, San Ignacio's Sunday mass is celebrated in Raramuri, the native language of the Tarahumara. After the mission, the trail passes through **Valle de los Hongos,** whose strange rock formations are said to resemble mushrooms. The map at the entrance also locates nearby **Valle de las Ranas** (Valley of the Frogs) and **Valle de las Chichis** (Valley of the Breasts). A more ambitious 9km walk out of Creel is the **Valle de las Monjas** (Valley of the Nuns). Ask at the trailhead for directions.

About 7km southeast of the "trailhead" lies the man-made **Laguna Arareco,** 3km long and 8 acres in area. The lake's cold water is not ideal for swimming—to take a dip, head to the nearby **Recowata Hot Springs** (admission 10 pesos). Though the thermal waters are one of the most popular tour stops, they remain unspoiled. The round-trip hike to Laguna Arareco from Creel takes at least 6hr., though it would be wise to factor in extra time for getting lost.

BASASEACHI FALLS

If you have a car, pick up a map in Creel and enjoy a drive on the newly paved road. Otherwise take a tour or a bus. The latter is cheaper and just as safe. Take an Estrella Blanca bus from either Cuauhtémoc (2 per day, 80 pesos) or Creel (5hr., 3 per day, 91 pesos). The bus from Creel stops at a pair of tiny crossroads called San Pedro. Change buses there to get to Basaseachi.

With water cascading from a height of 246m, Basaseachi (Rarámuri for "place of the cascade" or "place of the coyotes") is the highest waterfall in Mexico and the fourth-highest in North America. Tucked into a corner of Canyon Candameña, the falls don't get many visitors, but those who do make the trip are rewarded with scenery from a postcard photographer's wildest dreams. Walk 3km down the paved road that runs through town to the trailhead to see the falls. The path is clearly marked and reaches the top of the falls after 30min. Hike down the steep path to the natural *ventana* (window), which affords a breathtaking view of the falls and surrounding canyon (45min. each way). Adventurous spirits can trek to the base of the falls by following the path. The hike is difficult and takes another hour from the *ventana*, but the end reveals a sub-tropical paradise.

Along the way to Basaseachi, you'll pass through some of the most sparsely populated areas of the Sierra Tarahumara. **San Juanito** is the only town along the road with gasoline, reliable phones, and decent restaurants and hotels.

BARRANCA DEL COBRE

Fast becoming the most popular travel destination in Northern Mexico, rumors of the Copper Canyon's tremendous size, remoteness, and beauty have lured thousands of backpackers north from the well-trodden Maya Riviera. Also known as the **Sierra Tarahumara,** the **Copper Canyon** is actually just one of six huge, interlocking canyons that traverse the Sierra Madre Occidental, covering an area four times the size of the United States' Grand Canyon and encompassing micro climates ranging from tropical rainforest (in the Canyon's depths) to rocky Alpine heights that resemble California's Sierra Nevada.

Though there can be no doubt about the Canyon's stunning natural beauty, travelers often find that visits to the Sierra are by turns rewarding and terribly frustrating. While the **Chihuahua al Pacífico (Chepe)** train that winds through the canyons en route to the coast makes passengers long to get out and hike through the spectacular sights passing by their windows, actually doing so often proves very difficult. The area lacks trails, transportation, adequate topographical maps, administrative infrastructure, and even decent roads, so hiking much of the canyon requires extremely advanced outdoorsmanship or the aid of a knowledgeable and dedicated guide. Infrastructure problems are exacerbated by the fact that most people visit during the rainy season (July-Aug.), when storms routinely wash out the roads and the train tracks, stranding visitors for days on end. In the end most resort to being shuttled to the sights by a Creel-based tour company. Anyone interested in hiking extensively in the canyons should plan carefully, allow extra time for complications and be prepared to pay dearly for a guide.

Those who spend the time will be amply rewarded. The Sierra's back country is laced with a uniquely picturesque human history visible in the traditions of the indigenous **Tarahumara** people and the beautiful colonial missions that tend to pop up unexpectedly in the rugged landscape.

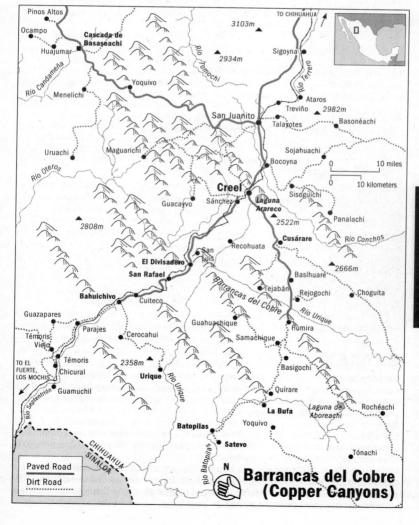

THE TRAIN ROUTE

Two types of trains make the daily journey between Mochis and Chihuahua. The **first-class train** has large tilt-o-matic seats, big picture windows, a dining car, and sometimes an open-air viewing car. The bad news is that it is **twice as expensive** as the **second-class train,** which has been recently upgraded with bigger seats, bathrooms, and air conditioning.

In order to see the most spectacular scenery (which lies between Temoris and Creel), take the train from Mochis to Chihuahua. Going the other way, the train usually sails by these sights in the dark. Grab a seat on the right side of the train if you're on the way to Chihuahua, and the left side if Mochis-bound.

Trains go from Los Mochis to Chihuahua (1st-class 13hr., 6am, 1020 pesos; 2nd-class 14hr., 7am, 501 pesos) and from Chihuahua to Mochis (1st-class 7am, 2nd-class 8am). Stops, listed for second-class trains from Mochis, are: **Sufragio, El Fuerte, Loreto, Temoris, Bahuachivo, Cuiteco, San Rafael, El Divisadero, Creel, San Juanito, La Junta, Cuauhtémoc** and **Chihuahua.** It is possible to get off and on at any one of these stops, but keep in mind that since the train only comes through any town twice a day, disembarkation is the beginning of a 12hr. commitment. All schedules are imprecise and subject to lengthy delays.

ALONG THE WAY, MOCHIS TO CREEL

Leaving Mochis, the train passes flat farmlands and well-watered Sinaloan thorn forest, cruising through **Sufragio** and the colonial town of **El Fuerte.** After crossing **Rio Fuerte,** the train enters the foothills of the Sierra around the Loreto stop. Look out for nail-biting when crossing over the **Rio Chinipas.** From here, the train climbs 1km through **El Descanso** to the **Temoris** station. Make sure to be awake at this point, since the route pulls a famous engineering stunt in which the train loops back on itself before passing though a tunnel. In a surreal Wizard of Oz moment, the terrain makes an abrupt switch from pre-tunnel tropical jungle to post-tunnel alpine forest. From here, the tracks climb another 1km, passing through the towns of **Bahuiuchivo, Cuiteco,** and **San Rafael** before arriving at **El Divisadero** (2400m). Cuiteco has a beautiful 300-year-old church, but no lodgings. Getting off to see the church probably isn't worth the wait for the next train.

BAHUICHIVO. Bahuichivo, in a forest clearing 97km south of Creel, is a convenient train stop for access to the towns of **Cerocahui** and **Urique,** which lie farther south in the canyon. The trip from Bahuichivo to Urique is best made by car, and is difficult without 4-wheel-drive. You're better off going with a tour if you're not familiar with the road. There is always a slew of Urique-bound passengers waiting at the train station (60-80 pesos). If a man with a brown van offers to take you for 20 pesos, don't get in.

CEROCAHUI. The mountain village of Cerocahui (pop. 600, elevation 1525m) is 17km southeast of Bahuichivo. The main attraction is the **Jesuit Mission,** founded in 1681 by the priest Juan María de Salvatierra. The gold and silver mines of **Sangre de Cristo,** the **Gallego Mountain** (38km away), the **Misión Churo,** and the **Yeparavo Waterfall** (4km south) are among the possible excursions from Cerocahui. The grocery store at the fork in the road has all the information you need about these excursions. Several locals offer tours for steep prices, and unless you know the way yourself, they are your best bet.

URIQUE. The village of Urique, 154 km from Creel, rests at the bottom of the **Barranca de Urique,** the deepest of the six canyons. About halfway to Urique from Cerocahui, the canyon opens to reveal magnificent cliffs and the village of Urique far below. The lookout point rivals Divisadero as the best place to take in the Copper Canyon. The limited services available in Urique are all along **Principal,** the main street, parallel to the river. Accommodations are fairly cheap; options include the **campgrounds** on Principal and one or two hotels in town.

SAN RAFAEL. Eleven kilometers down the tracks from El Divisadero is the dusty village of **San Rafael.** The town sprung up on the hillsides around the saw mill, now outside town, and offers a peek into an older way of life. San Rafael has just a handful of phones and all cooking is still done on wood-burning stoves—running water is a luxury few people have. The town itself, situated in the crook of two intersecting ridges, offers less than spectacular views. The surrounding high ground provides much better vistas.

EL DIVISADERO. At **El Divisadero** station, the jagged mountain edges overlap to create a maze of gorges and an amazing view of the canyons. Eight hours out of Mochis and two hours out of Creel, both trains stop here for sightseeing (15min.). As you get off, you'll be bombarded by people selling local Tarahumara crafts as well as *gorditas* and burritos (10 pesos). Spending a day in Divisadero is well worth the time. In general, hiking around Divisadero is more varied and more accessible than it is from Creel. Only the costliness of the area's hotels makes this an impractical base. Three resort hotels near the train station offer tours (about 350 pesos per person) and are the best source of information for hikes in the area.

Several trails of varying difficulty start in town. A reasonably easy day hike descends to **Las Cuevas,** traditional Tarahumara cave dwellings with an incongruous view of the luxury hotel on the rim above. The trail is relatively well-worn, but leave plenty of time to make the trip down and back (about 8hr.). Divisadero is home to **La Piedra Volada,** a large rock precariously balanced on the canyon rim.

It is technically possible (though quite difficult) to attempt a full-day hike between **Divisadero** and **Cusarare,** but an expert guide is a must. A far more manageable and popular hike leads down into the canyons. A 4km round-trip hike meanders to the Tarahumara village of **Bacajipare** (6hr.). The 27km descent to **Rio Urique,** at the bottom of the canyon consumes 8hr. each way. Guides are recommended for all overnight hikes, and can be found hanging around the hotels. Don't be afraid to haggle over prices and plans—it's a good way to get to know the person who will be walking beside you down the steep and winding trails.

CREEL TO BATOPILAS

The best way to get to this end of the Canyon is to hire a guide. If you want to rough it, catch the red and white striped converted schoolbus from Creel to Batopilas in front of the train station. (6-8hr.; Tu, Th, and Sa 6-7:15am, depending on when bus fills; 50 pesos). If you go as far as Cusárare, getting around is difficult—not having a car limits options.

Heading south from Creel, a road winds through the more scenic parts of the Copper Canyon. Buses rumble around nail-biting hairpin turns along the edges of steep cliffs. The first 75km section of road is happily paved, but the rest is not.

TARAHUMARA CAVES. On the right side heading south, the still-inhabited Tarahumara caves are within view of the road if you search very hard. On tours, it's possible to go in and visit traditional homes for a small donation.

CUSÁRARE. The town of Cusárare, 22km from Creel, features its very own 18th-century Jesuit mission. Check out the mission's Tarahumara interior, with wood floors and indigenous designs. There are no pews—when it is used on Sunday, people sit on the floor. **Cusárare Falls** is a 3km hike uphill through a pine forest.

BASÍHUARE. Another 20km beyond Cusárare on the road to Batopilas is Basíhuare, an old overnight stop for silver carriers en route to Batopilas. Farther south, the road weaves through the narrowing canyon in perhaps its most frightening stretch, offering spectacular vistas as it crawls by the **Cerro de Siete Pisos** (Seven-Story Hill), so named for the seven distinct layers of earth that lead up along the rocky inner walls of the canyon.

LA BUFA. The seven steps can best be seen from **La Bufa,** 60km from Basíhuare, a scenic lookout with a magnificent view. You can make out the Río Urique far, far below and the yellow wooden bridge that runs across it. A left at the fork in the road before La Bufa, will bring you to **Norogachi,** a Tarahumara mission near the river with beautiful *Semana Santa* services, and **Guachochi,** a rocky, frontier-like village with both colonial and Tarahumara influences. The right fork will take you to the more impressive town of **Batopilas.** On the way, you'll pass the bridge that spans the Urique and offers a smashing view of the waterfall below. Keep your eyes peeled for **tescalama** trees, which have yellow flowers and grow out of the sheer rock. The last quarter of the ride to Batopilas has plenty of **piedra cobriza** (copper rock), which gives the canyon its distinctive color.

BATOPILAS. Batopilas (pop. 2000), a small village on the river in the depths of the canyon, is a rough 35km from La Bufa, 140km from Creel, and almost 2km below the rest of civilization. A rich silver town founded in 1708, tiny Batopilas was the second city in all of Mexico (after Mexico City) to receive electricity, though iron-ically, its availability today is anything but a sure thing. Everything in Batopilas centers around the old stone **plaza,** referred to as the **parque.** Streets have names, but even the locals don't know them. The main street (which connects Batopilas to Creel) splits off into two; one branch becomes Juárez, the other dead ends. As you drive into town, take a left both times the road forks to get to the main *parque.* The magnificent ruined *haciendas* along the river recall the excesses of the mining days. Look for the *tescalama* trees with their masses of yellow roots growing directly from the *hacienda* walls. Guided hikes leave daily for the **Porfirio Díaz mine** and the more interesting **Peñasquito** (both hikes 1hr.), for **Cerro Colorado,** a section of the old Camino Real (12hr.), and for the lost mission of **Satevó** (see below). The best source of information about tours is the **Riverside Lodge,** in town diagonally across from the plaza on the bench side. A restored *hacienda,* the lodge is now an incredibly posh package-tour inn, with a luxurious piano room, historical photo exhibits, and a great rooftop view. **Artesanías Monse,** on the south side of the plaza next to Hotel Juanita, sells Tarahumara handicrafts.

SATEVÓ. The most fascinating excursion from Batopilas is to Satevó, a miniscule town with an eerie and beautiful mission. It's a 40min. drive (you'll need 4WD) or a 2hr. walk. In the middle of a valley straddled by the towering canyon, rises a lonesome, round mission. No one knows why this site was chosen, when it was built, or how the Taramuhara gathered the materials and energy to build the mis-sion. To take a peek inside, you'll have to tip the family living next door—they have the key. The inside of the mission is even more mysterious than the outside, with ancient tombs below and darkness above.

SINALOA

EL FUERTE ☎ 6

El Fuerte's colonial history sets it apart from the modern and unsightly Mochis. Founded in 1564 by conquistador Don Francisco de Ibarra, El Fuerte (pop. 30,000) became the capital of an area including present-day Sinaloa, Sonora, and part of Arizona. Unfortunately, the city's distance from the train station and sporadic bus service make it an impractical base for travelers visiting the Copper Canyon.

◪◪ TRANSPORTATION AND PRACTICAL INFORMATION. From the train station, 7km outside of town, you'll have a hard time getting to El Fuerte without a taxi. In town, **Juárez** is the main street. Walk west from Juárez and turn left onto **5 de Mayo,** which puts you in the *zócalo,* in front of the Palacio Municipal. **Trains** leave daily for **Chiuhuahua** (1st-class 6am, 2nd-class 7am) and **Los Mochis** (1½hr., 6:30pm). **Taxis** gather on Juárez. **Buses** to **Los Mochis** (every 1½hr., 45 pesos) leave from Juárez and 16 de Septiembre.

The **tourist office** is inside Palacio Municipal, Room 27. (Theoretically open daily 9am-3pm.) You can get information at **Hotel Posada,** 5 de Mayo and Hidalgo. **Ban-amex,** at Juárez and 16 de Septiembre, has a 24hr. **ATM.** (Open M-F 8:30am-2:30pm.)

SOTOL, FROM THE HEART Since the hearty *agave* plant is strong enough to survive the harsh desert—it seems only proper to make it into a strong drink. Mexicans in the present-day state of Jalisco believed this, and the drink they created is known far and wide as tequila. Yet the same *agave*, processed a slightly different way, has also been made into *sotol*, the state drink of Chihuahua, for the last 800 years. In *sotol* production, the heart of the plant is roasted and squeezed, releasing a sweet juice which is collected and naturally fermented. Tequila production mixes the heart with water, making it more bitter. After being distilled in copper containers, *sotol* is distilled for six months in white oak casks. Today, the number one brand of *sotol* is Hacienda. Go to your local Chihuahuan bar and give it a shot.

Caseta: at Mariela, Juárez and 16 de Septiembre. (Open M-Sa 8am-1pm and 4-6pm, Su 8am-1pm.) **Post office:** in the Palacio Gobierno in the Playuela. (Open M-F irregularly.) **Postal code:** 81820.

ACCOMMODATIONS AND FOOD. El Fuerte's budget accomodations lie along Juárez. **Hotel San José,** Juárez 108 (☎893 08 45), has large rooms and high ceilings. (Cots without bath 30 pesos; singles with bath 60 pesos; doubles 90 pesos.) **Hotel Guerrero,** Juárez 210, has rooms with baths, coolers (like A/C but less strong), and comfy beds. (Singles in summer 120 pesos, in winter 170 pesos; doubles 220-270 pesos.) **La Fogata,** Rosales 103, has good food (20-40 pesos) and a semi-outdoor patio connected to Rosa's kitchen. **Cocina Economica,** Juárez 57, lives up to its name with cheap *antojitos*, *quesadillas*, and burritos (5-6 pesos). At **Restaurante El Meson General,** Juárez 202, food is served around an open courtyard, and live music is occasionally played on weekends. (☎893 02 06. *Pulpo* (octopus) 70 pesos, good drinks 12 pesos.)

SIGHTS. El Fuerte has a few pleasant attractions. Follow 5 de Mayo west over the hill to stroll along **Río Fuerte.** Keep your eyes peeled for native birds such as the Crested Caracara, the Mexican Blue-Rumped Parrotelet, and the Plain-Capped Starthroat. Also keep your eyes on the path ahead of you: it's a frequently used cow path. A beautiful view of the river and city can be found at the hilltop **Hotel Río Vista;** follow 5 de Mayo to the river and walk up the hill.

LOS MOCHIS ☎6

For visitors to the Copper Canyon, Los Mochis is a necessary evil. Founded and developed by Americans first as a utopian experiment and later as part of a sugar-growing money-making scheme, the US colonial roots are visible in the city's monotonous grid of wide streets and modern buildings. The sugar days are over, but Mochis continues to be an important link between the coast and the interior, funneling goods and backpackers into the mountains efficiently.

TRANSPORTATION

GETTING AROUND
Municipal buses run throughout the city (2.6 pesos). The main stop is on Zaragoza at Obregón; ask the driver if he goes to your destination. Taxis (☎812 02 83) can be found waiting on the corner of every major intersection.

GETTING AWAY
Buses: Though the city is serviced by many bus carriers, finding the individual stations can be a challenge. The most obvious is the modern station run by Elite (☎815 00 62), at the corner of Juárez and Degollado. The cheaper carrier, Transportes Norte de Sonora, goes to: **Guaymas** (5hr., every hr., 85 pesos); **Mazatlán** (5½hr., every hr. 5am-5pm, 148 pesos); **Mexicali** (18hr., 7 and 8:15am, 705 pesos); **Mexico City** (24hr.,

6pm, 550 pesos) via **Culiacán** (3hr., 68 pesos); **Navajoa** (2hr., every 2hr., 36 pesos); **Tijuana** (22hr.; 4, 7, 8:15pm; 600 pesos) via **Hermosillo** (7hr., 113 pesos). Transportes del Pacífico, on Morelos between Leyva and Zaragoza (☎812 03 47), sends *de paso* buses south to **Mazatlán** and north through **Guaymas, Hermosillo,** and **Mexicali** to **Tijuana.** Buses to **El Fuerte** and nearby destinations leave from Zaragoza, between Ordonez and Cuauhtémoc. Norte de Sinaloa (☎818 03 57) sends buses every 15min. to **Culiacán** (3½hr., 68 pesos); **Guamuchil** (2hr., 35 pesos); **Guasave** (1hr., 27 pesos). Buses to **Topolobampo** (every 20min., 1 peso), leave from a stop on Cuauhtémoc between Prieta and Zaragoza, 1 block north of Obregón. **Tufisa** (☎818 22 22) at Zapata and Moreles sends buses to **Ciudad Obregón** (107 pesos), **Guaymas** (158 pesos), and **Hermosillo** (215 pesos) at 12:30, 5, 7:30 and 9:30pm. Mochis also has a Pacífico station (coastal destinations to the south) and an Azteca de Oro station.

Ferry: The ferry to **La Paz** leaves from the nearby coastal town of **Topolobampo** daily at 10pm. Ticket prices change frequently, and are sold at the **Sematur** office by the ferry until 6pm the day of departure (☎862 01 41; fax 862 00 35). Office open daily 8am-10pm. Tickets are brokered through the travel agency **Viajes Ahome,** Morelos 392 Pte. (☎815 61 20). Open M-Sa 9am-2pm and 3-7pm, Sa 9am-2pm.

Train: The **Chihuahua al Pacífico Train** or **"Chepe"** (☎824 11 51) runs between Los Mochis and Chihuahua with stops throughout the **Copper Canyon.** The posh 1st-class train leaves daily at 6am for Creel (557 pesos) and Chihuahua (1030 pesos). The equally comfortable 2nd-class train lacks dining cars, but is a better deal overall. (274 pesos to Creel, 501 pesos to Chihuahua.) Tickets can be purchased in the station or on the train. During peak backpacker season (July-Aug.) you may wish to purchase tickets in advance. **Viajes Flamingo,** Hidalgo 419 Pte. (☎812 16 13), in Hotel Santa Anita sells tickets.

✦♒ ORIENTATION AND PRACTICAL INFORMATION

The city is laid out in a grid. Downtown, the principal north-south avenues are (east to west) Degollado, Zaragoza, Leyva, Guerrero, and Rosales. Perpendicular to these from north to south are Juan de Batiz, Cárdenas, Morelos, Independencia, Castro, and Ordoñez. The **tourist office,** on Ordoñez and Allende, is next to the Palacio de Gobierno in the Unidad Administrativa; use the entrance off Ordoñez and turn right. (☎815 10 90. Open M-F 9am-4pm.) **Travel Agencies: Viajes Anome** sells ferry tickets. Morelos 392 Pte. (☎815 6120. Open M-F 9am-2pm and 3-7pm, Sa 9am-2pm.) **Viajes Flamingo,** Hidalgo 419 Pte. (☎812 19 29), sells plane and train tickets. **Currency exchange: Bancomer,** on Leyva and Juárez, has four 24hr. **ATMs.** (☎812 23 23. Open M-F 8:30am-4pm and 3:30-7pm, Sa 9am-1:30pm.) **American Express,** on Obregón between Flores and Morelos cashes traveler's checks. (☎612 05 90. Open M-F 9am-2pm and 4-6pm, Sa 9am-1pm.) There is a **market** near Zaragoza, between Castro and Ordoñez. Most stands close around 7pm. **Lavanderia,** Juárez 225 Pte. (Open M-Sa 8am-7pm. Wash 14 pesos per kilo.) **Emergency:** ☎060. **Police:** (☎812 00 33), Degollado at Cuauhtémoc in the Presidencia Municipal. No English spoken. **Red Cross:** (☎815 08 08 or 812 02 92) Tenochtitlán and Prieto, one block off Castro. **Pharmacy: Farmacia Cosmos** at the corner of Castro and Prieta (☎612 15 61. Open 24hr.) **Hospital Fátima,** Jiquilpán Pte. 639 (☎812 33 12). No English spoken. **Medical Assistance: Centro de Salud** (☎812 09 13). **WebSurf** in the mall at Obregon and Rosales. (15 pesos per hr. Open M-Sa 9am-9pm, Su 9am-7pm.) **Post office:** Ordoñez 226, two blocks off Castro, between Prieta and Zaragoza. (☎812 08 23. Open M-F 9am-3pm.) **Postal code:** 81200.

♠♣ ACCOMMODATIONS AND FOOD

Most decent hotel rooms in Mochis hover around 200 pesos. **Hotel Lorena,** Obregon 186, comes furnished with everything but a butler. Rooms come with views, A/C, TV, purified water, and clean baths. (Singles 210 pesos; doubles 230 pesos; triples 260 pesos.) **Hotel Hidalgo,** Hidalgo 260 Pte. between Prieta and Zaragoza, is a step down. Ceiling fans take the heat out of small rooms. (☎812 34 56. Singles 160

Old Mazatlán

Av. del Mat
Mexico
Flores
16 de Septiembre
Bolívar
Quijano **1**
2
Zúñiga
Juan Carrasco

Paseo Claussen
Zaragoza
Schehiena
Uribe
Domínguez
5 de Mayo
Guillermo Nelson
Zuñiga
Zaragoza
Morelos
Hidalgo

Paseo de
las 3 Islas

Cerro
de Nevería
(Ice Box Hill)
Estrada
Ocampo
Ámula
Mercado
El Estrada
Ocampo

High Divers
■ **of Mazatlán**
Canizales
3
Canizales
Valle

Pedregoso
21 de Marzo
Serdán
21 de Marzo

PLAZA
REVOLUCIÓN
Ángel Flores

Olas Altas
Domínguez
5
Escobedo

N
Machado
6 **Museo-Casa**
Juárez
Serdán
Guerrero

Venus
PLAZA Constitución
MACHADO
Carnaval
Galeana

7
Ozuna
Trías
Hidalgo

Museo de
Arqueología
Roosevelt
Avenida Miguel Alemán

Isla de los
Pájaros
Playa
Brujas

Marina
Mazatlán

Estero del
Sábalo

Playa
Sábalo
Tiburón
(i)

Calz. Camarón Sábalo

EL CID
RESORT

de la Marina

ZONA
DORADA

Las Garzas
Laguna
Loaiza

Lomas de Mazatlán
Bugambilia

Calz. Rafael Buelna

Playa las
Gaviotas

Laguna del
Camarón

Insurgentes

Mazatlán

▲ ACCOMMODATIONS

Hotel Belmar, 7
Hotel Central, 5
Hotel del Centro, 4
Hotel del Rio, 2
Hotel Emperador, 9
Hotel Fiesta and
  Hotel Los Arcos, 8
Hotel La Siesta, 6
Hotel Lerma, 1
Hotel Milán, 3

Isla de los
Lobos

Isla de los
Venados

Bahía de Puerto Viejo

del Mar

Universidad
Carretera Internacional

Ferrusquilla
9

Beltrán
Pánuco
San Lorenzo

Estero
del
Infiernillo

| 0 | | 2 miles |
| 0 | | 2 kilometers |

N
OLD
MAZATLÁN
(See Inset)

Paseo Claussen

Zaragoza
5 de Mayo
16 de Sept.
Juárez
Serdán
Fuente
Baluarte
Pánuco
Benemérito de las Américas
Piaxtla
Gaviotas
Pesquería

Bahía de
Olas Altas

Playa
Norte

Carrasco
G. Nájera

Canaval
Juárez
Serdán
Villa Iturbide
Germán Evers
A. Flores Constitución
Miguel Alemán
Aseres
Serdán
Emilio Barragán
Potrero del Llano
Calz. Gabriel Leyva Solano

Playas
del Sur

Mazatlán

Canal de Navegación

Isla de la
Piedra

Isla de
Ocón

beaches and clubs in a herdlike manner. Mazatlán was not always so. In 1531, the city's harbor was chosen as the launching pad for Spanish galleons. Three centuries later, the town weathered both a US blockade (1847) and a French bombardment (1864). In 1859, the city was named the capital of Sinaloa, a distinction rudely snatched away 14 years later. During the Mexican Revolution, Mazatlán became the second city in the world to be shelled from air, a dubious distinction to be sure. Despite its eventful past, Mazatlán offers little of historical or cultural interest to travelers. Far from picky, the *Bronzus norteamericanus* contents itself with the city's great assets—beautiful sunsets, glittering ocean, and wide beaches. The animal is a rarer sight in Mazatlán's downtown, which, with its shady *zócalo*, is more traditionally Mexican. The sage budget traveler will wisely stay and eat in this part of the town, saving the Zona Dorada for occasional excursions into the realm of the *Bronzus*. Be careful—they are known to bite.

⌐ TRANSPORTATION

GETTING AROUND

An efficient **bus system** makes navigating the city a breeze. At some point, all municipal buses pass the public market on Juárez, three blocks north of the *zócalo* at Ocampo. The "Sábalo-Centro" bus runs from the downtown market, with stops a few blocks from the *malecón* in Olas Altas and at Playa Sábalo in the Zona Dorada. "Cerritos-Juárez" continues up to Playa Bruja at Puerta Cerritos. The "Insurgentes" route services bus and train stations, and "Playa Sur" goes to the ferry dock and lighthouse (every 15min. 5am-10pm, 3 pesos). For late night disco hopping, take a taxi or *pulmonía* (like a large golf cart). Standard fare between Old Mazatlán and the Zona Dorada is 35-40 pesos, depending on time of night (later is more expensive), and the walk is more than an hour. Don't be afraid to haggle with *pulmonía* drivers—there are plenty to choose from.

GETTING AWAY

Airport: Rafael Buelna International Airport (☎982 23 99), 18km south of the city. The "Central Camionera" bus goes to the *centro* but you must return by taxi (150 pesos). Served by **AeroCalifornia** (☎913 20 42), El Cid Resort; **AeroMéxico,** Sábalo 310A (☎914 11 11 or 01 800 021 40 00); **Alaska Airlines** (☎001 800 252 75 22; fax 85 27 30); **Mexicana,** Pasco Claussen 101-B (☎982 77 22 or 01 800 502 20 00).

Buses: The bus station is 3 blocks from the *malecón* and about 2km north of Old Mazatlán, between downtown and the Zona Dorada. To get downtown, catch any of the red buses with "Centro" or "Mercado" on their windshields 1 block west of the station and about 1 block south, to your right along Benemérito de las Américas (3 pesos; after 9pm 3.5 pesos; buses stop running at 10pm). Avoid the "Sabado-coco" bus, as it goes downtown only after an enormous loop around the city. Cabs also make the trip (35 pesos and up). Estrella Blanca Group (☎981 38 11) sends buses to: **Chihuahua** (16hr., 2 and 6pm, 506 pesos); **Ciudad Juárez** (21hr., 2 and 6pm, 719 pesos); **Durango** (7hr., 4 per day, 214 pesos); **Mexico City** (18hr., every hr., 443 pesos); **Monterrey** (17hr., 3 per day, 498 pesos); **Torreón** (12 hr., 3 per day, 275 pesos). Transportes de Pacífico (☎981 51 56) travels to: **Culiacán** (every hr., 154 pesos); **Mochis** (6hr., every hr., 290 pesos); **Puerto Vallarta** (7½hr., 297 pesos); **Tepic** (4½hr., every hr., 180 pesos). Elite (☎982 19 49) is the best pick for Central Pacific locations, going to: **Guadalajara** (4 per day, 374 pesos); **Mexico City** (15hr., 4 per day, 510 pesos); **Manzanillo,** (4pm, 633 pesos); **Morelia** (14hr., 4 per day, 522 pesos).

Ferry: Sematur (☎981 70 20), at the end of Carnaval, south of Flores and the *centro*. It's a grueling 20min. walk from the *centro* to the ferry docks, or a quick ride on the blue "Playa Sur" bus (3 pesos). Taxis 30-35 pesos. Tickets sold only on the day of departure. Arrive at least 2hr. early to procure a spot. Ticket office open Su-F 8am-3pm, Sa 9am-1pm. Advance ticket purchases are available at a local travel agency. During high season (Dec. and July-Aug.), make reservations at least 2 weeks ahead. 1 ferry every day to **La Paz,** arrives around 8am (call for fares).

⚡🛈 ORIENTATION AND PRACTICAL INFORMATION

Mazatlán is divided into Old Mazatlán, home to the *zócalo* and budget hotels and restaurants, and the Zona Dorada, home to the *gringo* tourist. The boardwalk follows the beachy shoreline and connects the two sides of the town. Since Mazatlán is very spread out, the easiest way to traverse the city is by bus.

TOURIST, FINANCIAL, AND LOCAL SERVICES

Tourist Office: (☎916 51 60; fax 916 51 66) on Sábalo at Tiburón, on the 4th fl. of the pinkish Banrural building past El Cid resort on the "Sábalo-Centro" bus line. Helpful staff doles out good maps. Open M-F 9am-5pm; reachable by phone Sa 9am-1pm.

Tourist Police: (☎01 800 903 92 00), on Ruíz and Santa Mónica in the Zona Dorada.

Consulates: Canada (☎913 73 20), and **US** (☎916 58 89), Loaiza at Bugambilia in Hotel Playa Mazatlán in the Zona Dorada. Both open daily 9am-1pm.

Currency Exchange: *Casas de cambio* are open all day in the northern downtown area, but have poor rates. Stick to banks in the *centro* and the *zócalo*. **Banca Serfín** (☎982 66 66), 21 de Marzo and Nelson, across from the *zócalo*, has a 24hr. **ATM.** Open M-F 8:30am-5pm, Sa 10am-2pm.

American Express: (☎913 06 00; fax 916 59 08), in Centro Comercial Plaza Balboa on Sábalo. Open daily 9am-5pm.

Car Rental: Hertz, Sábalo 314 (☎985 05 45 airport office; fax 14 25 23). **Budget,** Camarón Sábolo 402 (☎913 20 25), and **National,** Camarón Sábado 7000 (☎913 60 00). Cars start at 487 pesos per day.

Laundry: Lavanderia Acalá, Azueta 1817 in the *centro*. Wash and dry 12 pesos per kg. Open M-Sa 8:30am-7pm, Su 8:30am-1pm.

EMERGENCY AND COMMUNICATIONS

Emergency: ☎060.

Police: (☎983 45 10), on Buelna in Colonia Juárez. Some English spoken.

Red Cross: (☎985 14 51), on Zaragoza and Corona. Some English spoken.

Pharmacy: Farmacia Ibael (☎982 62 49), on Ángel Flores and Campana. Open daily 8:30am-10:30pm.

Hospital: Sharp Hospital (☎986 56 76), on Kumate and Buelna, near Zaragoza park. English spoken. **Hospital General de Zona #3** (☎984 78 65; emergency ext. 270 and 271), on Mateos.

Internet Access: Telefona Automatica de Pacífico, Flores 810 (☎981 71 59), in the *centro*. 15 pesos per hr. Open daily 8:30am-9:30pm. Also **fax** service and **caseta.**

Post Office: (☎981 21 21), on Flores at Juárez, across from the *zócalo*. Open M-F 8am-6pm, Sa 9am-1pm.

Postal Code: 82000.

🏠 ACCOMMODATIONS

Whiles it's most fun to stay in the mid-range waterfront hotels of Olas Altas, more budget hotels line Juárez and Serdán in Old Mazatlán, and for the truly self-denying, in the area around the bus station. One cheap option is a trailer park near the Zona Dorada, **La Posta,** on Buelna. (☎983 53 10. Hook-up 85 pesos.)

OLAS ALTAS

Back in the 1950s, Olas Altas was the focal point of Mazatlán's fledgling resort scene. Although newer restaurants have sprung up, the area remains mostly unchanged since its glory days, perched on the cliffs in a state of rusting glamour. A 10min. walk from the *centro*, Olas Altas connects to the rest of Mazatlán by the "Sábalo-Centro" and other bus lines.

NORTHWEST MEXICO

▨ **Hotel Belmar,** Olas Altas 166 (☎985 11 12), at Osuna. Marble floors, wood paneling, and colorful arches accompany spacious rooms with baths, TV, and A/C. Dip in the pool, or curl up with a book from their library. Singles 224 pesos, with ocean view 255 pesos; doubles 265 pesos, with ocean view 306 pesos.

▨ **Hotel La Siesta,** Olas Altas Sur 11 (☎981 26 40 or 01 800 71 15 2 29), at Escobedo. Swiss Family Robinson meets the Ewok Village at La Siesta, where creaky rampways lead through a courtyard of overgrown trees and nautically-inspired rooms with A/C, TV, phones, and hot water. Singles 246 pesos, with ocean view 304 pesos; doubles 281 pesos, with ocean view 374 pesos.

OLD MAZATLÁN
Downtown offers easy access to most points in the city.

Hotel Lerma, Bolívar 622 (☎981 24 36), at Serdán. Spacious rooms and ceiling fans make the heat bearable. Singles 50 pesos, with bath 80 pesos; doubles 60 pesos, with bath 80 pesos.

Hotel del Centro, Canizales 705 (☎981 26 73), between Serdán and Juárez. Rooms have A/C, TV, and baths. Singles 163 pesos; doubles 187 pesos; triples 210 pesos.

Hotel Central, Domínguez 2 Sur (☎982 18 88), at Escobedo. Spotless rooms decorated with funky wood carvings, phones, TV, A/C, and private baths. Singles 250 pesos; doubles 280 pesos; triples 310 pesos.

Hotel del Rio, Juárez 2410 Nte. Clean white halls and rooms hung with antique cowboy propaganda are a welcome relief from Mazatlán's relentless nautical decor. Pleasant furniture, management, and central location. Singles and doubles 120 pesos.

Hotel Milán, Canizales 717 (☎985 34 99) across from the Telmex building in the business district. A/C, TVs, and excellent service make up for the brown color scheme. Singles 143 pesos; doubles 163 pesos. Prices rise 20 pesos July-Aug.

NEAR THE BUS STATION
Noisy buses detract from the convenient location.

Hotel Los Arcos, Río Panoco 1006 (☎981 33 70), around the block to the left from the station's main exit. Newly constructed with basic rooms. Singles and doubles 120 pesos, with A/C 140 pesos.

Hotel Fiesta, Ferrosquila 306 (☎981 78 88), in front of the bus station. Clean rooms have baths and purified water. Enjoy "hot kakes" (20 pesos) or an "homlet" (18 pesos) at the hotel's cafe. Singles and doubles 160 pesos, with A/C and TV 200 pesos.

Hotel Emperador, Río Panoco 1000 (☎982 67 24), next to Hotel Los Arcos. High-rise hotel has a top-notch cleaning crew, tile floors, and fans. Rooms have powerful A/C and TVs. Singles 150 pesos; doubles 200 pesos. 30-peso discount for not using the A/C.

◗ FOOD

Restaurant prices escalate closer to the tourist glam of the Zona Dorada. The *centro*, however, is just the place for quality meals on a budget. The busy **public market,** between Juárez and Serdán, three blocks north of the *zócalo,* serves the best and cheapest food in the area. If you need a headless pig (or a pig's head), look no further. For something more formal, try one of the *centro's* many inexpensive restaurants or, for the view, an establishment along the *malecón* in Olas Altas. Enjoy your meal with **Pacífico** beer, the pride of Mazatlán.

OLAS ALTAS
A string of solid local eateries helps subsidize the Olas Altas art of doing nothing. Breakfasts can be had well into the afternoon at **Copa de Leche Cafe,** 1220 A Sur, on the *malecón.* (☎982 57 53. Eggs and pancakes 28 pesos, classic *cafe con leche* 13 pesos. Open daily 7:30am-11pm.) Head to **Meson Marisquero** on Puerto Viejo at the *malecón* for small doses of *ceviche* (10-13 pesos). (☎982 82 26. Tostada plates 28 pesos, beer 10 pesos. Open Su-Th 11am-11pm, F-Sa 11am-1am.)

OLD MAZATLÁN

▨ **El Tunnel,** in a tunnel that starts at Carnaval 1207, in the *centro*, across from the theater. The incredible ambience is only upstaged by the amazing food. Dedicated to (pre)serving classic Sinaloense cuisine, this place has dished out delicious *gorditas* since 1945. Full meals 35 pesos. Open daily noon-midnight.

▨ **Restaurante Karica Vegetariano,** Flores 601 (☎981 79 52), at Frías. A fine place for even the carnivore. The enormous *comida corrida* includes salad, soup, a main course, bread, juice, and dessert (42 pesos). Mexican fruit masterpieces 12-17 pesos. A vegetarian bakery sells organic coffees and herbal products. Open M-Sa 8am-4:30pm.

▨ **Panamá Cafe and Restaurant,** Juárez and Canizales, also at Serdán and Morelos. Gusty A/C will whip up your appetite for amazing pastries or authentic *sinaloense antojitos* (33 pesos). Salads 25-35 pesos, breakfasts 25 pesos, all served quickly. Open daily 7am-10pm.

Restaurant la Cocina de Esther, Serdán 1605B (☎982 81 72) at Canizales, tucked back from the street. Crawl into this cool little *loncheria* and devour *ricas gorditas* (3 for 24 pesos) or *comida corrida* (30 pesos). Open M-Sa 7am-9pm, Su 7am-3pm.

PLAZUELA MACHADO

When it's cool enough, a mixed crowd of locals and tourists eat outdoors at the restaurants bordering Plazuela Machado. For hardcore *gringo* fare, stop into **Thorny's Surf Burger,** Sixto Osuna No. 510-B, on the plaza. Roast beef and meatloaf draw expatriates, who languish around satellite TV in the fan-cooled interior. Gigantic hamburgers 28 pesos. Next door at Osuna 34, **Machado Fish Taco** offers imported Baja fish taco taste, but not the dirt-cheap prices. Seafood tacos 40 pesos. Coffee addicts should try **El Tempo de Cafe** on Carnaval across from the theater. Coffee 12 pesos. (Open daily 7am-11pm.) Also try **Altrazador Ars Cafe** on Constitución 519, which is somewhere between a cheap restaurant, bar, cafe, and music club. (Music nightly at 8:30pm. Open daily 9am-midnight.)

👁 📷 SIGHTS AND BEACHES

BEACHES. Mazatlán's famous beach stretches 16km from Olas Altas to well past the Zona Dorada. North of Old Mazatlán and along del Mar is **Playa Norte,** a decent stretch of sand if you don't mind small waves and a general lack of activity. As you approach on the Zona Dorada, the beach gets cleaner, the waves larger, and Playa Norte eases into **Playa Las Gaviotas.** Past Punta Sábalo, in the lee of the islands, is **Playa Sábalo,** whose great waves and golden sand enthral crowds of norteamericanos. "Sábalo-Centro" buses pass all these beaches. As Playa Sábalo recedes to the north, crowds thin rapidly and you can frolic alone. In most places, boogie boards (40 pesos) and sailboats (500 pesos per hr.) are available. Take the "Cerritos-Juárez" bus to the last stop and walk left (if you walk straight ahead you'll end up at a rocky outcropping with restaurants but little sand) to nearly deserted **Playa Bruja** (Witch Beach), with beautiful sand and 1-2m waves. Camping is permitted, but exercise caution after dark, and camp in groups whenever possible.

EL FARO. For a 360-degree view of Mazatlán and the sea, climb to the top of El Faro, at the end of the "Playa Sur" bus route, the second-tallest lighthouse in the world. The 30min. hike is almost unbearable in the summer; ascend in the early morning or late evening to avoid the heat.

TOWER DIVERS. Mazatlán's tower divers perform acrobatic and dangerous plunges into rocky surf from an 18m high ledge. Dives take place during the day, but be warned that divers will not perform unless they pull in a sufficient amount of money beforehand. The best time to watch is 10-11am and 4:30-6:30pm, when tour buses arrive and tourists fork over their pesos, allowing you—the savvy budget traveler—to see dives for free. Great viewing just south of the towers. *(On Claussen, south of Zaragoza and north of La Siesta Hotel.)*

ISLAS VENADOS (DEER ISLAND). For those itching to escape the beaches, the island is a relatively deserted scrap of land with fine diving; catamaran boats leave from the Agua Sports Center at El Cid Resort in the Zona Dorada. (☎913 33 33, ext. 341. Boats depart daily 10am, noon, and 2pm. 100 pesos round-trip.)

MAZAGUA. Waterpark mania hit Mazatlán with Mazagua, north of the Zona Dorada near Puerta Cerritos. Go bonkers in the wave pool or shoot down slippery slides. (Take a "Cerritos-Juárez" bus (3 pesos). ☎988 00 41. Open Mar.-Oct. daily 10am-6pm. 60 pesos, children under 4 free.)

ACUARIO MAZATLÁN. The largest aquarium in Latin America keeps piranhas and other fiesty fish (up to 250 breeds in all) in a slew of cloudy tanks, and also hosts performing sea lions and birds. (Av. de los Deportes 111, off Av. del Mar, 1 block back from the beach; the turn-off is marked with a blue sign. ☎981 78 15. Open daily 9:30am-6:30pm. 40 pesos, children ages 5-10 20 pesos.)

TEATRO ANGELA PERALTA. The newly restored and luxurious theater, at Carnaval and Libertad near Plazuela Machado, hosts an impressive variety of cultural programs. (Information ☎982 44 47. 5 pesos.)

MACHADO MUSEO CASA. This 19th-century mansion is filled with relics from Mazatlán's glory days as the state capital. The museum's collection of spectacularly gaudy old *carnaval* costumes makes it worth a visit. (Constitución 79 just off Plazuela Machado. Open 10am-6pm. 20 pesos, children 10 pesos.)

MUSEO DE ARQUEOLOGÍA. This mildly interesting museum offers the standard fare of clay figurines, rocks, and dioramas. (Osuna 72 between the centro and Olas Altas. Open M-F 10am-3pm. Free.)

🎵🎭 ENTERTAINMENT AND NIGHTLIFE

Masses of *norteamericano* high schoolers hit Mazatlán each year to twist, shout, and drink. More than a dozen discos and bars clamor for *gringo* dollars, with only the occasional Mexican rock tune reminding that this is not the US. Most of the hot clubs are in an area known as **Fiesta Land**, in the Zona Dorada, a block from Paseo del Mar. Prices for transportation and cover are steep, and because most nightclubs cut deals with package-tour companies, the unpackaged tourist is often charged more. Mellower amusements entertain locals in and around the *centro*.

THE CENTRO AND OLAS ATLAS

🗺 Club Muralla, at the corner of Venus and Sixto Osuna, just uphill from the Museo Arqueología. A bland yellow wall labeled "Club Deportiva" disguises the coolest scene in Mazatlán. Enjoy a courtyard full of low-stakes gambling and sports TV. Locals sip 9 peso beers, nosh on *ceviche*, and occasionally dance to live bands that play on weekends until 1am. Don your *guayabera*, channel your cool, and kick it with the best of them.

Cafe Pacífico, Constitución 501 (☎981 39 72), across from Plazuela Machado. A "classic pub" with an odd assortment of animal skins, rifles, and stained glass windows. The cool interior and 12 peso beers attract a fun crowd of amiable locals seeking respite from the Mazatlán sun. Marlin burritos 50 pesos. Open daily 9am-2am.

Altrazor Ars Cafe, Constitutión 519, across from Plazuela Machado. Cafe Pacífico for the younger generation. Local Gen-Xers come for the 12-peso beer and live music that kicks off at 8:30pm nightly. Snacks (*quesadillas* 15 pesos, sandwiches 18 pesos) also served. Open Su-W 9am-midnight, Th-Sa 9pm-2am.

Mesón Marisqueto, Puerto Viejo (☎982 82 26), on the Olas Altas *malecón*. Locals congregate at sunset, inhaling the foamy breeze and 10-peso Pacíficos. Tequila 18-29 pesos, excellent *ceviche* 10-38 pesos. Open Th-Su 11am-11pm, F-Sa 11am-1am.

ZONA DORADA

Home to the big, the bad, and the ugly—knock yourself out.

Bora-Bora (☎986 49 49), on Paseo del Mar at the southern end of the Zona Dorada. Scantily-clad teens frolic on "swimming" pools, foot bridges, and a sweaty beach volley-ball court. Those so inclined may dance in cages. Beer 30 pesos. Cover varies; expect to pay at least 60 pesos. Open daily 9pm-4am.

Valentino's (☎984 16 66), in the same complex as Bora-Bora. Attracts a slightly more sophisticated crowd of locals who dress to be seen. Standard American music, with more variety in the 2nd floor karaoke booths. Beer and mixed drinks 30 pesos. Cover F-Su 50 pesos; open bar men 120 pesos, women 240 pesos. Open daily 9pm-4am.

El Caracol (☎985 32 38), in El Cid Hotel on Camarón Sábado. A 4-level premier dance club, with insane lights rising from the floor. Beer and mixed drinks 30 pesos. Cover men 30-125 pesos, women 75 pesos during open bar. Open daily 9pm-4am.

Señor Frog's (☎985 11 10), on Paseo del Mar. The beach resort restaurant whose empire extends from Tijuana to Cancún was born 30 years ago in Mazatlán. A place of pilgrimage for locals and foreigners alike, who check their thrift at the door and enjoy obscenely expensive food, 25-peso beers and 30-peso mixed drinks. Cover is the price of your 1st drink on busy nights. Open daily 9pm-4am.

NEX'US Av. del Mar 2500 (☎984 00 90). Halfway between the Zona Dorada and the *centro*, Nex'us spurns gimmicky attractions in favor of music and pool tables. Live *mariachis* most nights, "romantic" on W. Sa open bar; men 150 pesos, women 90 pesos.

Joe's Oyster Bar, Louiza 100 (☎983 53 53), next to Los Sábados Hotel. A good place to put away a few beers before hitting the club scene (2 beers for 20 pesos 5-7pm and 10pm-2am). Cover 30 pesos, includes a beer. Open daily 11am-2am.

FESTIVALS

As if the nightly scene weren't garish enough, the city comes out in force each year to celebrate a particularly debaucherous **carnaval.** More than just a money-making scheme hatched by local hoteliers, Mazatlán's carnaval has a history dating back to the 17th century. Hotel reservations should be made several weeks in advance for this party during the week before Lent.

◤ DAYTIPS FROM MAZATLÁN

ISLA DE LA PIEDRA

Take a green "Independencia" bus (3 pesos) from the market at Serdán to the Embarcad-ero de la Isla de la Piedra. From there, take a boat to the island (5min., every 10min., last return 5pm; 10 pesos round-trip) to the island. Pulmonías (15 pesos) and taxis (10 pesos) take passengers to the beach from the ferry landing. If walking, go straight from the boat landing and follow the concrete path across the island for about 15min.

A short boat ride from the mainland, Isla de la Piedra boasts 10km of glistening sand, crashing waves, and rustling palm trees. Less crowded and not as shame-lessly developed as mainland beaches, the island is an unspoiled haven of sun-shine and ocean popular with Mexican families, and according to local families, "American Hippies." Take a trip on a banana boat (80 pesos), rent snorkeling equipment (120 pesos per hr.), or borrow a body board (30 pesos per hr.). Aging horses can be hired (85 pesos per hr.) up the beach. If you want to stay longer than a day, **Carmelita's,** a few steps from shore, has free space for tents, sturdy trees for hammock slinging, baths, and grills. Clean rooms with electricity, private baths, and kitchenette. (☎987 50 50. Single 200 pesos; doubles 250 pesos.) **Lety's,** adjacent to Carmelita's, offers similar camping space and spacious rooms with modern baths and desks. (Rooms with A/C and TV 200 pesos.) Nothing's nicer than camp-ing on a secluded beach, but be careful and don't stray too far from the center.

DURANGO

DURANGO   ☎ 1

State capital and commercial center, Durango (pop. 490,000) is a city caught in the heavy traffic of Mexico's push toward industrialization. The *centro* is cacophonous with the sounds of hammers and drills renovating any building old enough to celebrate a centennial, while the blocks behind the cathedral have sprouted a crop of cafes, health food stores, and museums. The many factories and textile mills lining the way into town contrast with the historic buildings in the town center that contributed to the government's decision to declare Durango a national monument. Hollywood decided to immortalize the city as well—using Durango's outskirts as the backdrop for many classic and modern Western films. While it's far from a thriving tourist mecca, the city's collection of colonial architecture and its worthwhile museums give more than just the John Wayne set a run for its money.

▐ TRANSPORTATION

Durango's bus station is located on the eastern outskirts of town. To reach the *centro*, walk past the taxis and under the highway overpass, where you can catch a "Ruta 2" bus (3.2 pesos); **taxis** are also available, thankfully with meters to avoid the usual tourist rip-off (22 pesos). After dark, a taxi is the only way to travel. Omnibus México (☎ 818 33 61; www.omnibusdemexico.com.mx) goes to **Aguascalientes** (6hr., 9 per day, 230 pesos); **Ciudad Juárez** (18hr., 7 per day, 546 pesos); **Chihuahua** (8hr., 4 per day, 336 pesos); **Mexico City** (11hr., 8 per day, 515 pesos); **Guadalajara** (10hr., 6 per day, 376 pesos). Estrella Blanca (☎ 818 30 61) goes to: **Parral** (6hr., 2 per day, 203 pesos); **Torreón** (3hr., 144 pesos); **Zacatecas** (3 per day, 160 pesos); **Aguascalientes** (6-7hr., 3 per day, 230 pesos). Transportes de Durango sends buses to the smaller cities throughout the state.

✳▐ ORIENTATION AND PRACTICAL INFORMATION

The suburbs and outskirts of Durango are full of tractor-trailers and warehouses; to find fun, culture, and amenities, you'll have to head downtown. Most sites of interest lie within a few blocks of **Plaza de Armas** and the cathedral. **20 de Noviembre,** which passes in front of the cathedral, and **5 de Febrero,** running parallel just across the plaza, are the major east-west thoroughfares. Juárez runs north-south. Downtown is fairly simple; streets are in a grid and rarely change names.

Information is available at the **Tourist Office: Dirección de Turisma y Cinematografía** Florida 1106, upstairs from the Museo de Cine at the intersection of 20 de Noviembre and Independencia. Maps and useful information in English. (☎811 21 39. Open M-F 8am-8pm.) **Banco Serfín,** Constitución 312 Sur, near the plaza, has great exchange rates and a 24hr. **ATM.** (☎812 80 33. Open M-F 9am-5pm; exchange 9am-3pm.) **Laundry Service: Lavandería "La Cenicienta,"** Zarceo 212-2 Sur between 20 Noviembre and Negrete. (Wash and dry 30 pesos per 3kg. Open M-Sa 9am-7:30pm.) **Emergency:** ☎060. **Police:** (☎817 54 06), at Felipe Pescador and Independencia. **Hospital General,** on 5 de Febrero and Norman Fuentes. (☎811 91 15.) Cruz Roja (☎ 817 34 44 or 817 35 35). **Fax: Telecomm,** Felipe Pescada and Zaragoza, eight blocks from the plaza. (Open M-F 8am-8pm, Sa 9am-4pm.) **Cybercom,** 5 de Febrero 1302, has **Internet** access. (☎811 37 01. 16 pesos per hr. Open M-F 9am-9pm, Sa 9am-8pm, Su 9am-5pm.) **Post office:** at 20 de Noviembre and Roncal, 12 long blocks from Plaza de Armas. (☎811 41 05. Open M-F 8am-7pm, Sa 9am-1pm.) **Postal code:** 34000.

▐ ACCOMMODATIONS

Inexpensive accommodations can be found along 5 de Febrero near the market, a few blocks west of Plaza de Armas.

Hotel Gallo, 5 de Febrero 117 (☎811 52 90). The Mexican Canterbury Tales start here. Chat with the gregarious parrot Francisco (aka Chanticleer) and his roost of parakeets, or weep over the *telenovelas* with travelers from all walks of life who gather around the lobby TV (the Wife of Bath gets a word in during commercials). Rooms are clean and spartan, centered around an airy courtyard. Singles 70 pesos; doubles 90 pesos. Cable TV available in some rooms for an extra 20 pesos.

Hotel Reforma, Madero 303 Sur (☎813 16 22 or 813 16 23). Hard to say if Reforma's decor is at the avant- or rear-guard of interior design, but it's definitely at an extreme. The halls have enough foliage to be centerfolds for Potted Plant Digest. A red refrigerator-looking elevator whisks you up to rooms with color TVs, fans, and windows. 3pm check-out allows you to see some more sights before packing. Adjacent cafe is open 8am-8pm. Singles 154 pesos; doubles 213 pesos.

Hotel Ana Isabel, 5 de Febrero 219 Ote. (☎ 813 45 00). Looks like the interior of a Mormon Temple, with a sterile, white hallway that makes one expect to meet St. Peter at the door to your room. Nice rooms with clean, tiled bathrooms, all in good repair. Singles 150 pesos; doubles 200 pesos.

Hotel Las Palmas, Progresso 322 (☎ 813 00 30) is a standard upstairs budget hotel. Clean, worn-out rooms and mediocre bathrooms. Only some rooms have windows. Singles or matrimonials 70 pesos; doubles 80 pesos.

Hotel Plaza Catedral, Constitución 216 Sur (☎813 26 60), off 20 de Noviembre in a convent next to the cathedral, has a dark, mysterious charm. Well-maintained rooms have phones and cable TV. Singles 170 pesos; doubles 200 pesos; triples 220 pesos.

🍎 FOOD

Inexpensive meals aren't hard to rustle up in Durango. While tacos and hot dogs battle for the title of supreme late-night fast food, the day is ruled by the prickly pear-fruit of the local cacti. Vendors negotiate the spines and sell them peeled and ready to eat, seeds and all. Look for bags of the green, kiwi shaped fruit off 5 de Febrero. Other local favorites are *gorditas*, *quesadillas* with *chincharron*, and a meaty local stew called *caldillo durangueño*.

Los Farolitos (☎812 79 87), on Martínez, 1 block up from *teatro*, focuses on the concept of "taco" with Zen-like clarity, and the result tastes like enlightenment. Though they dabble in *quesadillas*, take the hint and go for one of the big, 6.5-peso tacos (with a variety of *típica* fillings). Drinks 6 pesos. Open daily 8am-6pm.

NORTHWEST MEXICO

Durango

🏠 ACCOMMODATIONS
Hotel Ana Isabel, **8**
Hotel Gallo, **9**
Hotel Las Palmas, **1**
Hotel Plaza Catedral, **6**
Hotel Reforma, **7**

🍎 FOOD
Al Grano, **4**
Las Flores, **3**
Los Farolitos, **5**
Samadhi, **2**

Samadhi, Negrete 403 Pte. Healthful, 100% vegetarian fare that pleases foreigners but leaves most *durangueños* staring longingly at the plump, succulent goldfish in the restaurant's aquarium. Breakfast bargains (30 pesos for granola, eggs, french fries, and beans), and all the usual suspects done vegetarian-style. Open daily 8am-10pm.

Cafe Al Grano, at Negrete and Zaragoza, a few blocks west of the cathedral, somehow manages to cram giant feline masks, a blow-up of a tarot magician, a ceramic clown, a wooden Don Quixote, and countless plants into its small space. Specialties include breakfast plates with fresh squeezed orange juice (20 pesos) along with vegetarian plate such as soy *chorizo* (36 pesos). Open M-Sa 8am-8pm.

Las Flores, Zaragoza 101 at Negrete. This small restaurant serves homestyle *Durangueño* cuisine, and gives you an idea of what you missed out on by growing up somewhere else. A good pick for midday meal. *Gorditas* 4.5 pesos, burritos 5 pesos; drink included. Open M-Sa 9am-6pm.

◉ SIGHTS

Durango's sights seem to be slightly off-beat variations on the prototypical Mexican Colonial theme. Begun in 1691 and finished in 1770, the impressively brooding **cathedral** comes complete with unnerving colonial ghosts. In addition to a phantasmal nun, who can be seen at sunset on the middle balcony of the west tower awaiting her murdered lover, the cathedral's east nave contains a must-see **confessional** for all those considering a pact with the devil. In 1738, after a lifetime of benefitting from the dark lord's patronage, a dying Spanish don was trying to get out of his bargain by way of confession when he was suddenly struck down by a sulfurous beam of light. Locals have stayed away since, and it is recommend that all persons of questionable moral fiber follow suit.

Durango's huge **Palacio de Gobierno,** on 5 de Febrero between Martínez and Zaragoza, was built as a residence by a Spanish mining tycoon, Juan José Zambrano, and expropriated by the government after Mexico gained independence. The inside walls and stairwell are decorated with the typical murals depicting the state's history. At the top of the stairs awaits an unnerving surprise—the golden death mask of Benito Juárez, made from a post-mortem mold of the famous president's face. Just west of the cathedral, on 20 de Noviembre, stands the white brick **Teatro Ricardo Castro,** which hosts theatrical productions and film screenings and is considered to be one of the best theaters in northern Mexico. Built around the turn of the century, this elegant, French-styled building is named for the famous Durango musician Ricardo Castro, who contributed his skills to several movie soundtracks. For a listing of cultural events, buy a copy of *Sol de Durango*.

For the museum-lover, intelligently-curated exhibitions of contemporary Mexican art can be seen at the **Museo de Arte Contemporanea,** in one of the colonial buildings on Negrete 301. (Open Tu-F 9am-6pm, Sa-Su 11am-6pm. Free.) The **Museo Regional de Durango,** at Serdán and Victoria (behind the cathedral), houses paintings by Miguel Cabrera and exhibits on the state's history, indigenous groups, and paleontology. (☎ 12 56 05. Open Tu-Su 9am-4pm. 1 peso; Su free.) Designed to make archaeology exciting for the masses, the **Museo de Arqueologia Durango** at Zaragoza 315 is an interesting feat of museumology in which the rather tame history of Durango's desert cultures is dramatized with cinematic tricks. (☎ 13 10 47. Open Tu-F 10am-6:30pm, Sa-Su 11am-5pm. 5 pesos, children 3 pesos.)

By far the most hyped attraction in Durango is its cinematic history. Over 200 films, including several John Wayne classics, have been filmed in the dusty desert outskirts of Durango, and the city has recently opened a **Museo del Cine,** Florida 1106 at the corner of Independencia and 20 de Noviembre, to commemorate its golden age of Westerns. The old sound-recording equipment, camera, and Victoria 8 projector give some insight into how cumbersome earlier productions must have been. (Open Tu-Su 9am-6pm. 5 pesos, children 3 pesos.) Some of the original **movie sets** have been left standing and are now popular tourist attractions. One of the most impressive sets is at **Chupaderos,** 10km north of Durango. More Westerns have been filmed in this dusty village than anywhere else in the state. To get there, take a Chihuahuenses bus to "Chupaderos" (30min., every 25min., 12 pesos), and ask the driver to let you off the route near the sets. On the same bus, you may be able to reach **Villa del Oeste,** a movie set that, in an interesting reversal, was eventually turned into a village. **Los Alamos,** 29km south of Durango, was the set for *Fat Man and Little Boy* (1989), a film about the development of the atomic bomb in Durango, New Mexico. It may be difficult to get to these sets without a car; ask the tourist office for advice if you are interested in seeing the latter two.

🎵📷 ENTERTAINMENT AND SHOPPING

Come sundown, throw your hands in the air at **La Covacha,** Pino Suárez 500 Pte., at Madero, where locals dance to international and Latin hits. (☎812 39 69. Cover 25 pesos. Open Th-Su 9pm-4am.) A variety of courtyard bars featuring live music have sprouted off **Negrete** behind the **cathedral.** Try **La Casa de la Monja** at Negrete and Madero. (Open F-Su noon-midnight.) Live mariachi music and ballads sound better with 12-peso tequila and 15-peso sangría. Slightly more upscale is **El Alebrije** on Serdán 309 Pte. Th-Su live romantic music in the brightly-painted courtyard from 9pm-midnight. Wine 15 pesos, beer 15 pesos, tequila from 30 pesos.

Though most farmers are kept busy raising cattle (to feed the *campesinos'* endless appetite for beef), a select few have scorpion ranches instead. **Mercado Gómez Palacio** on 20 Noviembre, three blocks east of the cathedral, is full of the poisonous bugs. Thankfully, most are entombed in transparent plastic bubbles adorning belt buckles, keychains, and fabulously kitschy Durango souvenir clocks. Vendors keep aquariums full of the state arachnid on-site, lending the market a certain edge. You never know what you'll find in your new cowboy boots.

On Sundays, head to **Parque Guadiana** to celebrate *Domingo Familiar,* where vendors hawk treats and street performers play to the crowds. For 10 days during the second week of July, Durango commemorates the city's founding with the **Feria Nacional.** Parades, fireworks, auctions, and carnival rides liven things up and reservations are a must. Most of the festivities take place at the **Parque Guardiana,** quite a distance from downtown—you may have to take a taxi (20 pesos).

TORREÓN ☎1

The completion of international railways running through the area gave rise to Torreón in 1888. The settlement flourished as an important crossroads for trade and commerce, and today, a century after its founding, the modest train stopover has blossomed into a large metropolis. Although the city is relatively untouristed, most visitors traveling across the north will find themselves near Torreón for a night or two. The city's clean streets and quality museums merit a closer look.

🚍 TRANSPORTATION

Airport: Aeropuerto Internacional Francisco Sarabia, 2km northeast of downtown. Serviced by **AeroCalifornia,** Independencia 15 Ote. (☎722 18 88), and **AeroMéxico,** Independencia 1890 Ote. (toll-free in Mexico ☎01 800 021 4000).

Bus Station: The **Central de Autobuses de Torreón,** Juárez 4700 (☎720 31 24), about 4½km east of downtown, is most easily accessible by taxi (22 pesos). Estrella Blanca (☎20 08 08) provides service to: **Durango** (9 per day, 129 pesos); **Guadalajara** (4 per day, 400 pesos); **Matamoros** (4 per day, 325 pesos); **Mexico City** (1 per day, 578 pesos); **Parral** (1 per day, 157 pesos); **Zacatecas** (every hr., 189 pesos).

✳️🛈 ORIENTATION AND PRACTICAL INFORMATION

All hotels and restaurants and most services listed are located in the area immediately surrounding **Plaza de Armas,** which is bordered on the north by palm-tree divided **Morelos** and on the south by **Juárez.** Running between the city center and the sprawling periphery is **Independencia,** which, along with **Colón,** forms the city's other major intersection. **Buses** and *carritos* (collective taxis) going to almost any part of Torreón and the adjacent cities of Gómez Palacio and Lerdo can be caught on Juárez by the plaza. Torreón is saturated with **taxis,** which honk at everyone and everything they pass on the street, giving the city a ringing, cacophonous edge.

TOURIST, FINANCIAL, AND LOCAL SERVICES

Tourist Office: While the tourist office, on **Pasco de La Rosita** 308 (☎ 732 22 44), is inconvenient from the city center and only mildly helpful, they post wonderful maps in front of the **Palacio de Gobierno** and **Plaza de Armas,** and provide a toll-free line (☎ 01 800 718 42 20) manned by a somewhat English-proficient staff.

Currency Exchange: Dolares La Merced (☎ 716 43 84 and 716 43 91), Matamoros 344 Pte. Open daily 9am-6:30pm. **Dolares** (☎ 712 98 50), Colón 525 Sur.

ATM: Banks with 24hr. **ATMs** cluster near Plaza de Armas. You may be able to use an ATM card with no fee at **Citibank** on the corner of Colón and Matamoros.

American Express: Garcia 95 Sur (☎ 718 36 20), at Matamoros. Open M-F 9am-2pm.

Car Rental: Airways Rent-a-car, located at the airport (☎ 716 02 79), rents cars from 516 pesos per day within Torreón (747 pesos if you wish to go farther afield). **Hertz** (☎ 712 66 16) is also located at the airport, and has toll-free national (☎ 01 800 709 5000) and international (☎ 001 800 654 3030) reservations. Rentals from 778 pesos per day. **Budget** has locations in the *centro* (☎ 721 90 91) and airport (☎ 716 86 02; budgettr@halcon.laguna.ual.mex). Cars from 727 pesos per day.

Market: Soriana, located on an entire city block defined by Mina, Hidalgo, Jiménez, and Juárez, is the place to stock up on all your grocery needs. "Ruta Centro" *colectivos* and buses leave from Juárez at the plaza. Open daily 8am-10pm.

Laundry: Lavandería Los Angeles (☎ 713 44 59), Independencia 37 Ote. at Colón. Walk to Independencia and then catch a bus going to Colón (2.5 pesos). Laundry washed and dried (50 pesos). Open M-F 10am-2pm and 4-8pm, Sa 10am-5pm.

EMERGENCY AND COMMUNICATIONS

Emergency: ☎ 060.

Police: (☎ 712 13 15), Colón and Revolución.

Red Cross: Cuauhtémoc 462 (☎ 713 00 88 or 713 01 92).

Pharmacy: Farmacia Santander (☎ 712 87 38), Morelos and Carillo. Open 24hr.

Hospital: Hospital Los Angeles, Paseo del Tecnológico 909 (☎ 730 02 02 or 730 03 36). Little English spoken.

Fax: Telecomm/Western Union (☎/fax 716 68 48) in the Palacio de Gobierno. Open M-F 8am-6pm, Sa 9am-midnight.

Internet Access: Meganet Internet Cafe, Juárez and Fuentes. 20 pesos per hr. Open M-Sa 8am-11pm, Su 10am-10pm.

Post Office: (☎ 712 02 64), Juárez and Galeana, on the 1st fl. of the Palacio Federal. Open M-F 9am-5pm, Sa 9am-1pm. **MexPost** available next door.

Postal Code: 27000.

▓ ACCOMMODATIONS

Torreón's budget accommodations cluster around **Plaza de Armas** and tend to be large, dilapidated hotels from the 1930s and 40s. If decaying elegance isn't your style, plenty of functional options can be found along **Morelos** for 300-400 pesos.

Hotel Princesa, Morelos 1360 (☎ 712 11 65). A kerosene lamp burns in Princesa's lobby shrine to the Virgin of Guadalupe, and it is probably by her good graces alone that the hotel is still standing. Though the 2nd floor rooms look ready to fall at any moment, they are large and clean with high ceilings. Rooms with bath 80-100 pesos.

Hotel Galicia, Cepeda 273 Sur (☎716 11 11), between Juárez and Morelos. This landmark building from the 1930s has beautiful stained glass windows, carved wood detailing, and funky rooms. Forgive the disrepair and live the dream on the Grand Balcony overlooking Plaza de Armas. Rooms 118-153 pesos.

Hotel Naves Hidalgo 1249 Pte. (☎716 15 68), 1 block from Plaza de Armas. Large, clean rooms with windows and baths. Singles 106 pesos; doubles 118 pesos.

FOOD

The number of good, affordable restaurants in Torreón guarantees that you won't be washing dishes to pay for your meal. The cheapest *torta* stands and *gordita* vendors can be found in and around the city's *mercado* southeast of Plaza de Armas. Torreón also specializes in ice cream and frozen yogurt. Look for both on **Morelos** going toward Colón. The homesick can seek refuge on Independencia or Colón, which are stocked with American and Mexican fast food chains.

■ **De Granero,** Morelos 444 Pte. (☎712 71 44), is a vegetarian restaurant extraordinaire, popular with Torreón's health-conscious bourgeois. Fruit salads with granola and yogurt 35 pesos. Soy *chorizo* burritos 8 pesos, and a wide selection of *licuados* 9-18 pesos. Health food store and bakery attached. Other locations at Estadio and Carranza (☎717 84 41) and Constitución 712 (☎718 76 61). Open daily 9am-9pm.

Restaurant La Cope de Leche, Valdes Carrillo 359 Sur (☎716 88 81), gets its name from the 50s-style glasses it uses to serve great milkshakes (19.5 pesos). Clean, cozy place to start your day with a large breakfast (37-50 pesos) and juice (9-15 pesos).

Loncheria Coahuila, Juárez 544 Pte. (☎712 47 45), is sure to please those who came to Mexico in search of Mexican food. A local favorite, the basics are excellent. *Enchiladas* 34 pesos, 5 tacos with beans and guacamole 25-35 pesos. Open F-W 9am-8pm.

SIGHTS

Sights in Torreón revolve around the dozens of parks and museums that dot the downtown area, including centrally located **Plaza de Armas, Parque de los Fundadores** on Muzquiz and Constitución, the large **Alameda Zaragoza Juárez and Donato Guerra,** and the enormous 30-block **Bosque Venustiano Carranza** on Cuauhtémoc between Juárez and Bravo. The *bosque* (forest) is home to the **Museo Regional de la Laguna,** Juárez 1300 Ote., which in addition to a display on the nomadic desert cultures indigenous to the region, holds Licio Lago's wonderful collection of Pre-Hispanic art and artifacts. The collection is made especially interesting by a number of brilliantly executed fakes, which have managed to fool even the collector, and still confound some archaeologists. (☎713 95 45. Open Tu-Su 10am-6:30pm. 27 pesos, children free.) The most exciting secret of the *bosque* however, is that it is a center for the **International Break Dancing Revival.** If you thought headspins went out with the 80s, think again. A group of 30 or so teenage boys meet in the park almost every afternoon to practice the ancient art of "Break," executing acrobatics to the delight of girls in the bleachers. This is not to be missed. To get to the *Bosque* catch a collective taxi labeled "*Ruta Centro*" on Juárez near Plaza de Armas which will drop you off 2 blocks from the park entrance (3 pesos). Return cabs can be found on Matamoros.

The ■**Museo de la Revolución,** Muzquiz and Constitución, has displays on Mexican history and Independence. (Open Tu-Sa 10am-2pm, Su 10am-1pm. Free.) The **Museo del Ferrocarril,** (☎712 23 12), Revolución and Carrillo, displays some of the large trains that shaped the city's growth. Torreón is also home to the third-largest statue of Jesus Christ in the world, which stands on a nearby mountain with arms spread over the city. Stairs lead up the mountain to **Cristo de las Noas,** as does a road. The summit provides an amazing view of Torreón, nearby Gómez Palacio, and a church built with locally-mined marble.

🎵 📻 ENTERTAINMENT AND NIGHTLIFE

Lounging in the park is by far the most popular type of entertainment in Torreón. On Saturday and Sunday evenings, speakers are rolled onto Plaza de Armas and the whole city comes out to polka, *salsa*, and tango under the trees. Alternately, look for a game of pick-up soccer on weekends at Morelos and Treviño.

Bars and clubs congregate downtown near Plaza de Armas and along Paseo de la Rosita. Across from the plaza, inside Hotel Palacio Real is **El Greco,** Morelos 1280 Pte., a "Ladies Bar" that has live music. Check the schedule posted outside for a listing of events. (☎ 716 00 00. Happy Hour 7-9pm. Open Tu-Sa 6pm-2am.) For more live music, check out **Jazz Boozz,** Paseo de la Rosita 513A. Gentlemen, don't forget your ties—this is a classy joint. (☎ 721 22 89. Open daily 9pm-2am.)

Torreón has two main festivals: **Feria del Algodón** (mid-Aug. to mid-Sept.) and **Feria Laguna** (early to mid-Oct.). The **Gran Reguta del Río Nazas** (early July), is a boat race which involves much fanfare.

NORTHEAST MEXICO

Historic colonial settlements, deserted mines, congested urban centers, and dust-swept border towns dot the expansive deserts and occasional forests of Northeast Mexico. The disparate towns and cities of the Northeast, home to parched white missions and wide streets, exude a sense of calm fostered by small town hospitality and a lack of tourists. Eager for the industry, but not yet inundated with tourists, Northeastern Mexicans welcome the few travelers who trickle through with intense heat, *norteño* tunes, platters of *cabrito*, and old-fashioned friendliness.

Yet, in such a vast landscape, there are exceptions to every rule, and travelers in the border towns of **Tamaulipas, Nuevo León,** and **Coahuila** states may not encounter quite as friendly a reception. Not for the faint of heart, the cities that line the Texan border are replete with booze-guzzling day-trippers, boundless urban sprawl, industrious Mexicans and Central Americans seeking access to better work, and US border police determined to keep them away.

Farther south, the *gringo* influence and grubbiness fade. In Monterrey, a metropolis of millions, lovely cathedrals and inviting parks peek out from behind a sea of grey skyscrapers. The city has become chic without catering to tacky tourists and has some of the best nightlife outside the capital. If it's beach you crave, the *noreste* offers little more than a taste. Fresh, salty Tampico has never drawn flocks of tourists: you can swim, tan on the sand, and munch on fresh seafood, but it's far from picturesque. Named for its soothing hot springs, **Aguascalientes** boasts bustling streets and a festive annual fair. The capital city of **Zacatecas** was blessed with a location smack in the middle of Mexico's legendary silver store. As a result, the classically colonial and cosmopolitan city stands out in the barren Northeast.

Perhaps the Northeast's most attractive region is within the state of **San Luis Potosí.** The town of Real de Catorce, a favorite stop for peyote-hungry backpackers, is largely untouched by modernity, with one phone, hundreds of *burros*, and panoramic mountain views. Xilitla offers the eco-warrior caves, waterfalls, rivers, wild parrots, semi-tropical rainforests, and ruins an hour or two from congested city centers. The capital city of San Luis Potosí is a jewel—a playground of regional culture, awesome architecture, and colonial appeal. While the *noreste* may not feature prominently in the plans of most tourists, the quiet charm of its towns and cities may pleasantly surprise you.

HIGHLIGHTS OF NORTHEAST MEXICO

DELIGHT in the glorious architecture, raging nightlife, and the enormous Gran Plaza of eclectic, fast-paced **Monterrey** (see p. 265).

JUMP down a rabbit hole to **Las Pozas** (see p. 298), and bathe in the waterfalls and pretty pools of a kooky Englishman's tropical homage to surrealism. Spend another day in the nearby town of **Xilitla** (see p. 298), the **noreste**'s very own Eden.

HONEYMOON in tiny **Real de Catorce** (see p. 296), an ex-mining town high in the Sierra Madres that now specializes in peyote and gorgeous mountain views.

DAYDREAM in lovely **San Luis Potosí** (see p. 288), dubbed "the city of plazas," and enjoy *musica en vivo* while soaking up the brilliant northeast sun.

SAVOR traditional *pan de pulque* in **Saltillo** (see p. 273), and wrap yourself in a beautiful handmade *sarape.*

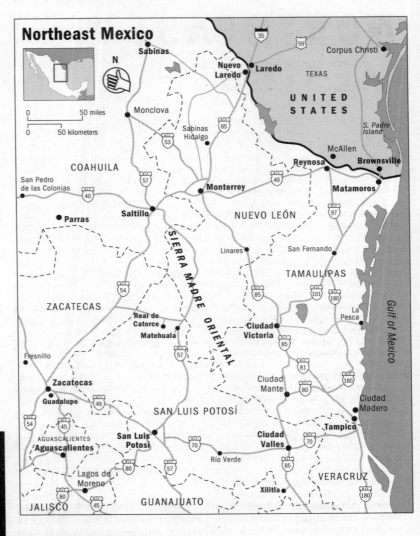

Northeast Mexico

Sabinas

Corpus Christi

Nuevo
Laredo
Laredo

TEXAS

UNITED
STATES

S. Padre
Island

Monclova

Sabinas
Hidalgo

McAllen

Reynosa

Brownsville

COAHUILA

Matamoros

San Pedro
de las Colonias

Monterrey

NUEVO LEÓN

Parras

Saltillo

Linares

San Fernando

TAMAULIPAS

SIERRA MADRE ORIENTAL

ZACATECAS

La
Pesca

Real de
Catorce

Matehuala

Ciudad
Victoria

Gulf of Mexico

Fresnillo

Zacatecas

Ciudad
Mante

Guadalupe

Ciudad
Madero

AGUASCALIENTES

SAN LUIS POTOSÍ

Tampico

Aguascalientes

San Luis
Potosi

Ciudad
Valles

Lagos de
Moreno

Río Verde

VERACRUZ

JALISCO

GUANAJUATO

Xilitla

0 — 50 miles

0 — 50 kilometers

N

NORTHEAST MEXICO

TAMAULIPAS

MATAMOROS ☎ 8

Though big and brash, Matamoros retains a measure of small-town appeal. The city remains vibrant with Mexican culture, stores aplenty even for the most exuberant shopper, and enough booze and brawls to urge travelers to exercise caution after dark. And, like any self-respecting border town, the streets of Matamoros are packed with young people partying to their hearts' content.

TRANSPORTATION. From the border crossing, the city extends out in a V-shape following the bend in the Río Grande. To reach the center of town from the

CROSSING THE BORDER. To reach Matamoros from Brownsville, Texas, walk or drive across the **International Bridge.** Pedestrians pay a budget-busting US35¢ (or 2 pesos) to cross from either side. Cars pay US$1.25. At this point, the **Río Grande** might not look so big—since much of its water has been diverted for irrigation, it's only a 2min. walk over the bridge. If you're traveling farther south than the border zone, pick up your tourist card (US$18) and vehicle permit (US$12). See p. 11 for more information on border crossings.

border area, take one of the yellow minibuses labeled "Centro" (4 pesos). "Central" minibuses go to the bus station, the Central de Autobuses. Take care not to confuse the two. Returning to the border, catch a minibus marked "Puente." These converted school buses (called *peseros*) make continuous stops; just wave your hand at them and they'll stop almost anywhere (local transport info ☎817 88 80). Don't be shy about asking where your stop is—the bus name (e.g. "Centro") might not be indicative of the final stop.

   Bus traffic to out-of-town destinations flows through the **Central de Autobuses,** on Canales at Aguilar, off Calle 1. (Open M-Sa.) **ADO** (☎812 01 81) goes to: **Tampico** (7hr., 5 per day 2:50pm-11:30pm, 285 pesos); **Tuxpan** (11hr., 4 per day 2:50pm-11:30pm, 360 pesos); **Veracruz** (16 hr., 3 per day 4pm-10pm, 500 pesos), with numerous stops in between. **Noreste/Sendor** (☎813 27 68) services: **Monterrey** (6hr., 18 per day 1:20pm-11pm, 198 pesos); **Reynosa** (2hr., 18 per day 6am-10pm, 51 pesos); **San Luis Potosí** (10 hr., 11 per day, 377 pesos). **Transportes del Norte** (☎816 65 80) runs to: **Mexico City** (14hr.; *ejecutivo* at 7pm, 700 pesos; 1st-class buses 6 per day, 575 pesos); **Saltillo** (7hr., 6 per day, 251 pesos); **San Luis Potosí** (10hr., 11 per day, 377 pesos). **Omnibus de México** (☎813 76 93) sends 18 buses per day to **Reynosa** (51 pesos), **Saltillo** (251 pesos), and **Monterrey** (198 pesos). Travelers to Noreste destinations may find it more convenient to depart from the **Noreste station** downtown (☎813 40 50), at the corner of Calle 12 and Abasolo, where it's possible to catch buses coming from the Central de Autobuses en route to their destinations.

🛂 ORIENTATION AND PRACTICAL INFORMATION. The center of town is dominated by Abasolo, which hosts a pedestrian shopping mall and Plaza Hidalgo. The **tourist office** (☎812 36 30), past the turnstile marking entry into Mexico on the right, offers pamphlets and lots of friendly advice in Spanish. Matamoros maps are also available at the Brownsville Chamber of Commerce. **Casas de cambio** dot the *centro*, particularly along Calles 5 and 6. The best exchange rates are in the bus station or at banks such as **Bancrecer** (☎812 34 22), Calle 7 between González and Abasolo, or **Bancomer,** Matamoros and Calle 6, which also exchanges **traveler's checks.** (☎816 30 67. Open M-F 8:30am-4pm, Sa 10am-2pm.) **ATMs** are available at most major banks. **Luggage storage:** at the bus station. (2 pesos per hr., 1 peso each additional hr.) **Market: La Estrella,** Abasolo between Calle 10 and Calle 11. Although there is no **Laundromat,** all hotels listed have laundry services. **Emergency:** ☎060. **Police** (☎816 20 21 or 817 22 05) are always stationed around International Bridge and the border. **Red Cross:** (☎812 00 44). **Pharmacy: Super Farmacia El Fenix,** Abasolo between Calle 8 and Calle 7. (☎812 29 09. Open daily 8am-10pm.) **Hospital Guadalupe** 72 Calle 6 (☎812 16 55). **Internet Access: Libros y Revistas Proceso** (☎816 23 10) at the corner of Calle 6 and González. You can browse the Internet or the store's wide selection of sexually explicit comic books and magazines. (20 pesos per hr.) **Post office:** in the bus station. (Open M-Sa 9am-3:30pm.) **Postal code:** 87370.

🛏 ACCOMMODATIONS. Although prices in Matamoros are reasonable, expect little more than the basics. The market area, where most of the budget accommodations are located, quickly becomes deserted after nightfall—be careful. **Hotel Majestic,** on the pedestrian mall on Abasolo between Calles 8 and 9, offers simple, clean, bright rooms with private bath and fan. (☎813 36 80. Singles 120 pesos; doubles 150 pesos; each additional person 20 pesos.) **Hotel Mexico,** a few doors down on the same block, offers rooms of similar quality and price. (☎812 08 56. Singles

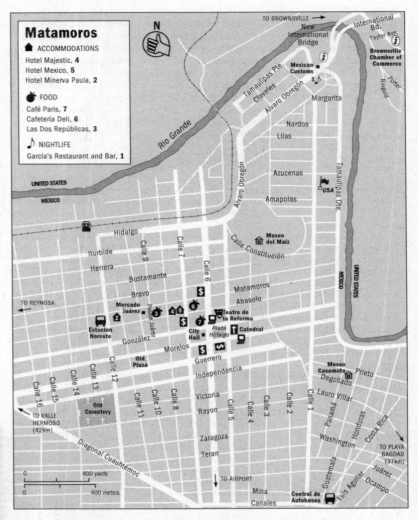

Matamoros

🏠 **ACCOMMODATIONS**
Hotel Majestic, **4**
Hotel Mexico, **5**
Hotel Minerva Paula, **2**

🍎 **FOOD**
Café Paris, **7**
Cafetería Deli, **6**
Las Dos Repúblicas, **3**

♪ **NIGHTLIFE**
García's Restaurant and Bar, **1**

120 pesos; doubles 160 pesos; each additional person 40 pesos.) Those willing to spend more may prefer the relative luxury of **Hotel Minerva Paula** on Matamoros #125 near Calle 11. Every room has cable TV, A/C, and carpeting. (☎816 39 70. Singles or doubles 300 pesos; each additional person 50 pesos.)

🍴 **FOOD.** While the food in Matamoros is often overpriced and border-town bland, good deals can be found in the small *taquerías* and stands surrounding the pedestrian mall. ◼**Las Dos Repúblicas** (☎816 68 94), on Calle 9 between Abasolo and Matamoros, the restaurant where the margarita originated (see **The Original Margaritaville,** below), soothes tourists with its beautiful interior and relaxed atmosphere. Enjoy drinks (beers US$1.50, mixed drinks US$3) and *antojitos* (US$4) from a cushioned chair, next to a fountain and three-story fresco. Slip into a booth and sway to the sounds of an old-fashioned jukebox in **Cafetería Deli,** 1307 Calle 7, between Abasolo and Matamoros, to escape the bright sun and to savor a range of

> **THE ORIGINAL MARGARITAVILLE.** To be a true margarita connoisseur requires a visit to **Las Dos Repúblicas,** the self-proclaimed "birthplace" of the famous drink. According to legend, a lovely young lady from Brownsville, Marguerite Henri, was a restaurant regular in the 1930s. One day in 1935, the bartender mixed her that first magical drink. She immediately fell in love. Unfortunately for him, it was the drink she was enamored of and, in her honor, the smitten bartender named the drink the "Marguerita." Whether fact or fiction, the legend makes a good excuse to stop in and order a couple of 18oz. margaritas.

antojitos for 15-25 pesos. (☎813 93 87. Open daily 6am-9pm.) **Cafe Paris,** Calle 6 and González, couples a delicious bakery (entrees 20-25 pesos) with a gorgeous interior. (☎816 36 80. Open daily 7am-10pm.)

🎭🎨 **SIGHTS AND ENTERTAINMENT.** Matamoros and Abasolo, pedestrian streets between Calles 6 and 11, are lined with shops and vendors. Immerse yourself in the streets' tourist kitsch while bargaining with the craft vendors. Try **Pasaje Juárez** on Calle 9 between Matamoros and González for everything from colored glasses and silver jewelry to the ubiquitous cowboy belt. Abasolo is known for its shoes, and every other shop seems to be a *zapatería* (shoe store).

Discover the history of Matamoros in **Museo Casamata** at the corner of Panamá and Degollado. Casamata itself was constructed in 1830 as a fortress to defend the city against the invading Americans. Turned into a museum in 1970, it is now filled with photos of revolutionaries and antique guns. The city's history is inscribed in Spanish on the walls of the museum. (Open M-F 8am-8pm, Sa-Su 9am-6pm. Free.) Matamoros's **cathedral** on Calle 5 across from Plaza Hidalgo is home to a full-sized replica of Christ in a glass coffin. The candles are always lit and visitors are always welcome.

For a cultural evening, stop by the **Teatro de la Reforma** (☎812 51 21), on Calle 6 between González and Abasolo. Renovated in 1992, the colonial brick building is home to everything from classical drama to *ballet folklóric.* Tickets vary by event (150 pesos and up, students and seniors half-price). If you're in the mood to bar-hop, boogie, and booze, think twice. Most reasonably priced **bars** and **discos** near the border are very unsafe at night. If you insist, **Garcia's** (☎812 39 29), straight ahead after you cross the International Bridge, on the left side of Obregón, has everything a border-hopping tourist could want, day or night. Feast on filet mignon in the classy restaurant (lunch specials US$8, dinner US$11), relax with a Mexican beer at the bar (beers US$2, mixed drinks US$3-4), or search for bargains in the gift shop and pharmacy. Live music ranges from *mariachi* to rock.

REYNOSA   ☎8

Expect to see lots of brilliant smiles around Reynosa (pop. 600,000). Loads of dental offices advertising low prices draw North Americans across the border to perfect their grins. Despite its increasing size and industrialization, Reynosa still manages to exude a small town atmosphere. With its clean streets, charming shops, and packs of street performers competing for attention, Reynosa is a gem by border town standards.

📧 **TRANSPORTATION.** The **bus station** is on Colón in the southwest corner of town. To reach the *centro* from the bus station, take any "Centro" bus or turn left on Colón, walk five blocks, and take a right onto Juárez; the plaza is six blocks down. **ADO** (☎922 87 13) goes to: **Tampico** (7hr., 6 per day 4:30-11pm, 260 pesos); **Veracruz** (16hr., 6:50 and 8:30pm, 510 pesos); **Villahermosa** (24hr., 6:50 and 11pm, 675 pesos). **Futurama** (☎922 14 52) offers *ejecutivo* service to: **Monterrey** (3hr., 7 and 8pm, 200 pesos); **Mexico City** (15hr., 5:20pm, 760 pesos); **Guadalajara** (15hr., 7 and 8pm, 710 pesos). **Omnibus de México** (☎922 33 07) runs to: **Chihuahua** (15hr., 9am and 10:30pm, 570 pesos); **Monterrey** (3hr., 6 per day 4am-7pm, 140 pesos); **Saltillo** (5hr., 6 per day 4am-7pm, 171 pesos). **Noreste/Sendor** (☎922 02 06) has the most extensive service including: **Matamoros** (2hr., every 45min., 54 pesos); **Nuevo Laredo** (4hr., every 2hr. 5:15am-9:40pm, 144 pesos); **San Luis Potosí** (11½hr., 8 per day 7am-10:45pm, 377 pesos).

■ **ORIENTATION AND PRACTICAL INFORMATION.** Reynosa is 90km from Brownsville and 150km from Monterrey. It can be reached from McAllen, Texas, by taking 23rd St. 12km south onto Hidalgo and then crossing the **International Bridge.** Routes 2 and 40, from Matamoros and Monterrey respectively, lead straight into town. Reynosa is square, with the international bridge border crossing at the northeast corner. The central plaza, known as **Plaza Principal,** is bounded by Zaragoza on the north, Hidalgo on the west, Morelos on the south, and Juárez on the east. Minibuses *(peseros)* run in nearly all directions (4 pesos). **Taxis** are known to overcharge, so try to set a price before getting in.

Though there is no tourist office, the **Cámara de Comercio,** on the corner of Chapa and Allende, one block north of Zaragoza and one block east of Juárez, has free maps with listings of restaurants, bars, and hotels. (Open M-F 9am-5pm.) **Casas de cambio** are scattered along Hidalgo and the plaza, but none accept traveler's checks. **Banorte,** on Morelos at Hidalgo (☎922 46 90; open M-F 9am-3pm) and **Bancomer,** opposite Banorte on Zaragoza (☎922 81 01; open M-F 8:30am-4pm, Sa 10am-2pm), have competitive rates, change traveler's checks, and offer 24hr. **ATMs. Police:** ☎060. **Red Cross:** ☎060. **FAX: Telecomm,** in the building connected to the post office. (☎922 01 65. Open M-F 8am-7:30pm, Sa-Su 9am-12:30pm) **Internet: Internet Cafe,** Matamoros No. 735. Rows of new computers will greet your eyes at this technology center. (☎922 19 81. 20 pesos per hr.) **Post office:** on the corner of Díaz and Colón. (☎922 01 10. Open M-F 8am-4pm, Sa 9am-1pm.) **Postal code:** 88500.

■ **ACCOMMODATIONS.** Hotels near the plaza are pricey with the cheapest located to the southeast around **Díaz, Hidalgo,** and **Zaragoza.** Though boisterous and congested during the day, these areas become desolate and a little scary at night. *Cuídate.* (Be careful.) **Hotel Avenida,** Zaragoza 885 Ote., sets its sparkling clean, carpeted rooms around a beautiful leafy patio. With its proximity to the main plaza and A/C and cable TV, you can't lose. (☎922 05 92. Singles 250 pesos; each additional person 50 pesos.) For lodging close to the shopping area, try the **Hotel Riviera,** 615 Mendez. Walking south from the plaza, take a left out of the Hidalgo market area. Large, sunny suites come with cable TV and A/C. (☎922 13 79. Singles 340 pesos; each additional person 50 pesos.) A bit farther off the main plaza, **Hotel Rey,** on Díaz between Mendez and Madero, has six floors of cable TV and A/C glory fit for a budget king. (☎922 26 32. Singles 272 pesos; doubles 320 pesos.) If you're looking to splurge, **Hotel San Carlos,** Hidalgo in front of Plaza Principal has a friendly English-speaking staff, A/C, and cable TV. (☎922 12 80. Singles 450 pesos; each additional person 50 pesos.)

¡ÁNDALE! *¡Ándale, ándale!* (loosely translated: "Hurry up! Hurry up!") Cartoon fans the world over will recognize this catchphrase, often uttered by Speedy González, the fleet-footed, sombrero-toting Mexican mouse of Warner Brothers fame. Speedy's slogan is essential vocabulary for any visitor to Mexico. The word can have a number of meanings, depending on context. There's the standard *¡ándale!* ("hurry the hell up!"), the *¡ándale!* shouted by impatient drivers leaning on their horns ("move it, buddy!"), the more amiable *¡ándale!* exchanged between friends ("I agree"), and the even more congenial *¡ándale!* ("hey, no problem!"). And there's always the "hey, let's go" *ándale* (*Ándale Mexico: 2002,* perhaps?). The uses are varied and subtle; to command them all is key to speaking like a real Mexican.

🔅 **FOOD.** Locals will tell you that outdoor stands and open-air cafeterias near the bus station and plaza are the places to enjoy delicious, super-cheap fare. If you want to sit down and escape the heat, try clean, simple **Cafe Sánchez,** on Morelos off Hidalgo at the southwest corner of the plaza, which is often crowded with patrons enjoying the fajitas and *enchiladas poblanas.* Very tasty entrees run 26-60 pesos. (☎922 16 65. Open daily 7am-8pm.) For affordable dining in an elegant setting, try **Cafe La Villa,** on the plaza at the corner of Hidalgo and Zaragoza. Sit in the fancy *salon comedor* while you sample a variety of *antojitos* and desserts (30 pesos and up; breakfast specials 30-40 pesos). **Cafe Paris,** Hidalgo 815, just past Morelos on the pedestrian mall, is not only beautiful, but bakes possibly the best pastries in town. In the corner window, passing bread lovers can buy *pan* to go. Breakfast 17 pesos, entrees 20-55 pesos. (☎922 55 35. Open daily 7am-10pm.) The east meets the south in **Santa Fe Restaurant,** at Plaza Principal on Zaragoza 690, a Chinese restaurant for those desiring a break from Tex-Mex cuisine. Wonton fries 32 pesos, entrees 60 pesos. (☎922 85 16. Open daily 10am-11pm.)

🎭 **SIGHTS AND ENTERTAINMENT.** In the evening, locals of all ages crowd the main plaza to enjoy street performers and chill after the day's heat. The **Hidalgo Marketplace,** open to pedestrians from the plaza to Colón, is a good spot for people-watching. For an abridged history lesson, check out the beautiful storefront **mural** on the corner of Zaragoza, one block east of Canales, and a few blocks south of the border crossing. It was paid for by Bacardi, the rum company, and their billboard forms the last scene of the mural.

Clustered along Ocampo near the border, most nightspots in Reynosa have on- and off-seasons. For one month during US spring break (Mar.-Apr.), the town turns into a miniature Cancún—all the booze, but (alas!) none of the beaches. The off-season (most of the time) is more mellow. Deserted a good chunk of the week, it is only on weekend and Wednesday nights that this "Zona Rosa" comes to life with *mariachis* and enthusiastic Texans. Young people head to the **Alaskan Bar and Disco,** on Ocampo between Allende and Zaragosa, a dark, cold *discoteca* with two levels and an enormous dance floor. Beer US$1, mixed drinks US$1.50. (Open bar F. US$10 cover; W and Sa no cover.) The brand-new **Neptune's Shell Disco** is another option for party-goers, featuring an under-the-sea decor and a young crowd from both sides of the border. It really *is* better down where it's wetter. (F-Sa open bar. Cover men US$10, women US$8. Open W and F-Sa until 2am.) Underage visitors to Reynosa beware—clubs have recently started to enforce the Mexican drinking age of 18. Be sure to bring your ID.

Check out Reynosa's community theater for free at **La Casa de la Cultura,** next door to the Cámara de Comercio on Chapa and Allende. The Casa regularly hosts plays, painting exhibits, concerts, and dances; drop in to see the schedule of upcoming events. (☎922 99 89. Open M-F 9am-2pm and 3-7pm.) Reynosa's **Museo de la Ciudad,** at Ortega and Allende, houses a collection of masks, dolls, antique guns, old coins, and other historical artifacts. Most impressive are the historical photos of Reynosa and biography of the man responsible for the museum—Sr. Donato Palacios Saenz. The rotating art exhibit now features paintings of bull fighters and ballerinas. (Open Tu-Sa 9am-2pm and 4-8pm, Su 10am-2pm. Free.)

NUEVO LAREDO ☎8

Nuevo Laredo (pop. 420,000) pulses with commerce. From small souvenir shops to enormous trucks laden with NAFTA-spurred trade, pesos and dollars pour in and out of Nuevo Laredo at such a dizzying pace that many residents are left without any for themselves. The city's cheap liquor, abundant crafts, and many plazas attract lots of afternoon tourists, making Nuevo Laredo a good place to visit for a day or evening, though probably not for an extended vacation.

🚍 **TRANSPORTATION.** From **International Bridge #1,** the main pedestrian crossing, **Guerrero** emerges as the main thoroughfare running south. Three plazas along

Guerrero, **Plaza Juárez, Plaza Hidalgo,** and **Palacio Federal,** define the downtown. The bus station lies at the far south of town. To get from there to the border, take any blue-and-white or green-and-white bus marked "Puente." To get to the bus station from the border, take a bus labeled "Central."

The **airport** (☎714 07 05), is southwest of the city, off Mex. 2. Purchase tickets at **Viajes Furesa,** Guerrero 830, to Mexico City or to US destinations leaving via the Laredo airport. (☎712 96 68. Office open M-F 9am-7pm.)

The **bus station,** Refugio Romo 3800, is southwest of the city and quite a trek from the *centro.* **Omnibus de México** (☎714 06 17) goes to: **Aguascalientes** (8hr., 3 per day, 461 pesos); **León** (12hr., 3 per day, 590 pesos); **Saltillo** (3½hr., 195 pesos); **Zacatecas** (8hr., 2 per day, 393 pesos). **Noreste/Sendor** (☎714 21 00) travels to: **Matamoros** (6hr., 8 per day 7am-midnight, 198 pesos) and **Reynosa** (4hr., 10 per day, 144 pesos). **Turistar, Futura,** and **Transportes del Norte** share an information line (☎714 06 70) and a counter, but they maintain separate routes and services. Transportes del Norte runs a bus to **Monterrey** (3hr., every 30min., 140 pesos).

🛈 ORIENTATION AND PRACTICAL INFORMATION. Plaza Hidalgo and **Av. Guerrero** make up Nuevo Laredo's center. The **tourist office,** at Juárez and Maclovio Herrera, 8 blocks south of Hidalgo Plaza, provides many brochures in Spanish and English. (☎712 73 97. Open M-F 8am-8pm.) Major banks line Guerrero near Plaza Hidalgo. **Banorte** (open M-F 9am-4pm) and **Serfin** (open M-F 9am-3pm), on the corner of Canales and Guerrero, both have 24hr. **ATMs. Luggage storage** is available at the bus station. (3 pesos per hr. Open 24hr.) **Supermarket: Los Super Fruteria Primes,** at Ocampo and Arteaga, is closest to the center of town. (Open daily 6am-9pm.) **Laundromat: Wash Fast,** 3017 Canales. Wash 14 pesos, dry 18 pesos. (☎722 79 06. Open daily 9am-9pm.) **Emergency:** ☎060. **Police:** ☎060. **Pharmacy: Farmacia Calderón,** on Guerrero west of Plaza Hidalgo. (☎712 55 63. Open 24hr.) **Medical Services: ISSTE** (☎712 34 91), on Victoria and Reynosa east of Plaza Juárez, has a limited English-speaking staff. **Internet: Cyber Cafe,** 3112 Canales and Morelos. (☎713 00 85. 20 pesos per hr. Open M-F 10am-9pm, Sa 11am-7pm.) **Post office:** in the back of the Palacio Federal, on the corner of Dr. Mier and Camargo, has **fax** and **telegram** service. (☎712 21 00. Open M-F 8am-6pm, Sa 9am-noon.) **Mexpost** is located on the opposite side of the *palacio.* (☎713 47 17. Open M-F 9am-6pm, Sa 9am-1pm.)

🛏 ACCOMMODATIONS. Hotels of all prices are found within a few blocks of the main plazas. There are good bargains if you're willing to look around. With just six rooms, 🢰**Hotel Mina Maeva,** Mina 3521, six blocks west of Guerrero, has better-than-US lodgings at less-than-US prices. Individually decorated rooms have carpet, cable TV, A/C, and phone. The staff provides superb service and conversation. Chat with the two parrots who really run the place. (☎713 14 73. Singles 350 pesos; doubles 448 pesos; each additional person 60 pesos.) **Hotel La Finca,** Reynosa 811, just off González in the southeast corner of Plaza Hidalgo, sits on a quiet street just a few steps from the *centro.* Spacious, clean rooms rise above a red-tile patio and have A/C, cable TV, and phone. (☎712 88 83. Singles 230 pesos; doubles 300 pesos; each additional person 50 pesos.) **Hotel Alameda,** González 2715, offers clean, comfortable rooms. (☎712 50 50. Singles 230 pesos; doubles 315 pesos.)

🍴 FOOD. Pricey tourist border joints aside, most eateries are similar in quality and price, with plenty of tacos, *enchiladas,* and *carne asada* (grilled meat). *Fajitas* and *cabrito* (roasted goat that tastes similar to lamb) are often sold by the kilogram. Most of the good stuff is right on Guerrero, not far from the plazas. At **Restaurant Principal,** on Guerrero just north of Hidalgo Plaza, you can order chicken or *cabrito* (110 pesos), then watch through glass windows as they roast and cut it. Ambitious meat-loving groups can even devour the whole animal (700 pesos), while standard entrees (40-60 pesos) are available for the less carnivorous. (☎712 13 10. Open daily 9am-1am.) At the corner of Peru and Reynosa, health food and vegetarian restaurant **El Quinto Sol** awaits to delight the senses. Vitamins, all-natural cookies, and soy hamburgers (16 pesos) are just a few of the healthy treats. For dessert, *nieve* (shaved ice) with granola cereal or sweet sauce (14 pesos) is a must. (☎715 52 75. Open M-Sa 7am-10:30pm, Su 10am-10:30pm.) For sweet bread served fresh from the oven (3 pesos), visit **Panadería** at González 2705. (Open daily 7am-9pm.)

⌖♫ SIGHTS AND ENTERTAINMENT. The largest (and most expensive) *mercados* are concentrated around **Guerrero** near the border. Though they offer an ample selection of sturdy wooden furniture, pottery, and *sombreros*, better prices (and higher-quality goods) can be found farther south. Those in search of cultural titillation can head to the **Teatro de la Ciudad** on Guatemala near Aguirre in the southeast corner of town, accessible via the "Viveros" buses.

The **Archivo Histórico Municipal,** Calle Herrera 3030, presents rotating shows on the history of the city, displaying photographs from the official archives. (☎712 34 85. Open M-F 9am-5pm, Sa 9am-1pm. Free.) The **Casa de la Cultura** (House of Arts), Herrera 3440, shows a rotating art exhibit in its beautiful courtyard. You can also watch the various art, dance, and music classes that start around 4pm.

Strolling up and down Guerrero can be relaxing in the evening, when the three plazas fill with people gaily chatting and passing time; the fountain on Nacatez and Guerrero is a favorite resting spot. If ambling about is not your style, head to **Señor Frog's,** just blocks south of the border on Belden at the corner of Ocampo. Though beers and tequila shooters are steeply priced (US$2 or 20 pesos), Frog's patrons come for the expert bartending and wonderfully campy cartoons papering every inch of this chain restaurant/bar. (☎713 30 11. No cover.)

TAMPICO   ☎1

It's no accident that sun-loving tourists bypass the northeast coast of Mexico. Littered with oil tankers and devoid of swimmers, the shores are more suitable for refineries than sunbathers. Though it's a little grimy, pretty crowded, and incredibly hot, Tampico (pop. 565,000) is the region's best seaside getaway and a refreshing break for land-locked travelers. The pleasant beach is often deserted on weekdays, and Tampico's two main plazas are full of intriguing architecture and greenery. Founded in the 16th century on the ruins of an Aztec village, the original Tampico was destroyed by booty-hungry pirates in 1623. Two hundred years later, Santa Anna ordered the city resettled, and it soon grew into one of the most important oil ports in the world. Despite the ominous tankers and loads of litter, Tampico today is trying to carve out a new identity. *Tampiqueños* built the first beach resort in all of Tamaulipas, and their seafood is amazingly fresh. Tampico may not be a great vacation destination yet, but it's definitely trying.

⌕ TRANSPORTATION. The **bus station** is on Zapotal, north of the city. Take a taxi (35 pesos), minibus (4 pesos), or *colectivo* (5 pesos, with luggage 7 pesos) to the *centro*. To return to the bus station, hop on any *colectivo* marked "Perimetral" (4 pesos). Omnibus de México (☎213 43 49) goes to: **Ciudad Valles** (2½hr., 3 per day 7:45am-7:30pm, 87 pesos); **Monterrey** (7hr., 3 per day 7:45am-11:30pm, 296 pesos); **Saltillo** (8½hr., 9 and 11pm, 324 pesos); **Tuxpan** (3½hr., 5 per day 6am-3:30pm, 110 pesos). ADO (☎213 55 12) heads to: **Matamoros** (7hr., 7 per day, 241 pesos); **Puebla** (10hr., 4 per day, 257 pesos); **Xalapa** (9hr., 2 per day, 251 pesos). Futura and Frontera (☎213 42 55) go to: **Guadalajara** (12hr., 4 per day, 463 pesos) and **Reynosa** (7½hr., 8 per day, 244 pesos). Estrella Blanca, Del Norte, Oriente, and Turistar (☎213 46 55) share service to **Mexico City** (9-12hr., 8 per day, 226 pesos).

⌖▌ ORIENTATION AND PRACTICAL INFORMATION. The town centers around **Plaza de Armas,** bordered by Carranza to the north, Olmos to the east, and Mirón to the south. One block south of Mirón, Madero marks the northern border of **Plaza de la Libertad,** marked by Juárez on the west. Continuing east and parallel to Olmos you'll find Aduana and López de Lara; to the west and parallel to Olmos are Colón, 20 de Noviembre, and Sor Juana Inés de la Cruz.

NORTHEAST MEXICO

The **tourist office,** 20 de Noviembre 218 Nte., one block west and two blocks north of Plaza de Armas, between Altamira and Obregón, has helpful maps and city guides. (☎212 26 68 or 212 00 07. Open M-F 8am-7pm, Sa 9am-1pm.) **Exchange currency** or checks at **Central de Divisa,** Juárez 215 Sur. (☎212 90 00. Open M-F 9am-6pm, Sa 9am-1:30pm.) **Bancrecer,** on Díaz Mirón next door to Sixpack, also exchanges traveler's checks and has a 24hr. **ATM.** (☎212 20 32. Open M-F 9am-5pm, Sa 10am-2pm.) **Luggage storage** is available at the bus station. (5 pesos per hr., 35 pesos per day.) **Sixpack,** Díaz Mirón 405 Ote., 3 blocks east of the southeast corner of Plaza de Armas, sells beer and food. (☎212 24 15. Open daily 8am-10pm.) A **lavandería** is next door to Hotel Posada Don Francisco on Díaz Mirón. (9 pesos wash, 10 pesos dry. Open M-Sa 8am-8pm.) **Emergency:** ☎060. **Police:** (☎212 10 32 or 212 11 57), on Tamaulipas at Sor Juana de la Cruz. **Red Cross:** has ambulance service. (☎212 13 33. Open 24hr.) **Pharmacy: Benavides,** Carranza 102, in Plaza de Armas. (☎219 25 25. Open daily 8am-11pm.) **Hospital General de Tampico,** Ejército Nacional 1403 (☎215 22 20 or 213 20 35), near the bus station, has English-speaking doctors. **Fax: Telecomm,** Madero 311, next to the post office. (☎214 11 21. Open M-F 8am-7pm, Sa 9am-noon.) **LADATELs** are clustered around the corners of Plaza de Armas. **Internet access: CNCI,** Obregón 210, off Juárez. (☎219 06 01. 20 pesos per hr. Open M-Sa 7am-9pm, Su 10am-3pm.) **Post office:** Madero 309 Ote., in the yellow building on Plaza de la Libertad (☎212 19 27. Open M-F 8am-7pm, Sa 9am-1pm) has a **MexPost** office (☎212 34 81) inside. **Postal code:** 89000.

⌂ ACCOMMODATIONS. Quality budget hotels are rare in Tampico. Those willing to pay 400 pesos or more can get an excellent room in one of the many larger hotels on Madero and Díaz Mirón near the plazas. ☗**Hotel Posada del Rey,** Madero 218, in the northwest corner of Plaza de la Libertad, warrants its expense. Each room includes A/C, phone, TV, and breakfast at the delicious hotel restaurant, **La Troya.** (☎214 10 24. Singles 280 pesos; doubles 330 pesos.) Slightly cheaper accommodations are a few blocks from the main plaza, primarily on Díaz Mirón. **Hotel Posada Don Francisco,** Díaz Mirón 710, furnishes its pink rooms with carpets, TV, A/C, and phones. (☎219 28 35. Singles 260 pesos; doubles 360 pesos. Hotel restaurant and bar open 7am-11pm.) **Hotel Copacabana,** Díaz Mirón 819, houses small, dark, relatively clean rooms with A/C, cable TV, and carpeting. (☎212 99 58. Singles 165 pesos; doubles 270 pesos.) **Hotel Buena Vista,** Héroes de Canonero 112, one block from Plaza de la Libertad, offers a great view of docked oil tankers. The cheapest rooms in the downtown area, these small, bare quarters have fans and hot water—only in winter. (☎212 29 46. Singles 60 pesos; doubles 100 pesos.)

▣ FOOD. Seafood is standard fare in Tampico, where specialties include *jaiba* (blue crab), but the city's best known dish is *carne asada a la tampiqueña* (seasoned grilled steak served with guacamole, refried beans, and red enchiladas). Chow down at a seaside stand or in the covered food court, the **Centro Gastronómico de Tampico,** on the Canonero side of Plaza de la Libertad. Upstairs, you will be accosted by small "restaurant" (moving counter top) owners pushing their fresh food at low prices. The most crowded counters generally serve the tastiest and cleanest food. **Naturaleza,** Aduana 107 Nte., one of Tampico's only vegetarian restaurants, offers excellent *tamales, licuados,* and vegetarian soups (15-25 pesos. ☎212 85 56. Open daily 9am-9pm.) Locals don't mind the wait at **Restaurant Lucy,** on Altamira, half a block past López de Lara. (*Comida corrida* 16 pesos, *antojitos* 10-20 pesos. Open F-W 11am-11pm.) Serious seafood fans shell out the extra money to eat at **Salón Palacio,** Aduana 315, in the corner of Plaza de la Libertad. Delectable regional entrees include shrimp, crab (50-80 pesos), and *carne asada a la tampiqueña* (80 pesos). Outside, check out the small photo gallery of yesteryear's Tampico, featuring facts about *The Treasure of the Sierra Madre,* the 1948 Humphrey Bogart movie filmed in the city. Live music on weekends. (☎212 43 21. Open Su-Th noon-midnight, F-Sa noon-2am.)

◙◨ SIGHTS AND ENTERTAINMENT. For a seaside getaway, **Playa Miramar** is the northeast's best beach, home to gentle waves and stretches of white sand. The beach is accessible by the "Tampico Playa" bus (½hr., 4 pesos), a shared "Tampico Playa" taxi (4 pesos), or a private taxi (15min., 35 pesos). Once there, stake out a spot under a palm-front umbrella on the beach's 10km of sand, and expect an endless stream of vendors to disrupt your relaxation.

In the *centro*, nightlife consists of upscale hotel bars or borderline seedy local hangouts. If you really want to party, take a taxi (20 pesos) to ◪**Byblos**, a large black pyramid adorned with Versace art, three fountains, and a black marble bar. The adjoining club hosts the biggest names in Latin music, and on Saturdays, Byblos pulsates with lasers and video screens. (☎217 00 42. Cover 70 pesos. Open W-Sa 10pm-2am.) A host of bars populated by sailors stationed at the nearby naval base surrounds Byblos. **Papa Cuerva,** Aduana 401, on Plaza de la Libertad, looks like a pirate ship, sails and all, with octopi and deep-sea divers decorating the walls. Papa's "poop deck" has additional seating and pool tables. (☎219 32 14. W open bar, cover men 80 pesos, women 50 pesos. Th-Sa cover 30 pesos, Sa free for women if accompanied by a man. Beer 25 pesos. Open W-Sa noon-2am, Su-Tu noon-1am.) For more authentic local flavor, head to the intimate **Boys and Girls,** 316 Olmos, for live music, black lights, and beer (15 pesos). Be there late Saturday night for a lively *norteño* show. (Cover 20 pesos. Open W-Su 9pm-late.)

NUEVO LEÓN

MONTERREY   ☎ 8

At three million people and growing, Monterrey is the third-largest city in Mexico, yet it remains overlooked by most foreign tourists. Founded in 1596 by Diego de Monemayor at the foot of Cerro de la Silla (Saddle Mountain), the small trading outpost grew as Monterrey's position between central Mexico and the US made it important center of business and commerce. Today, the city is home to many of the country's wealthiest businesspeople and known for its shrewd capitalism. The city's wealth has created a unique blend of the old and the new: across the street from the ancient yellow cathedral, a 30-story modern lighthouse shoots fluorescent blue laser beams into the mountainous night. Restricted to the opulence of the Zaragoza district, most tourists never see the dark side of Monterrey's commerce. But across from the bus station, cheap bars, prostitutes, and drug dealers await the adventurous traveler. An eclectic mix of European cobblestone streets, American capitalism, and Mexican spirit, Monterrey serves as a reminder of where Mexico has been, and of where it can't help but go.

▐ TRANSPORTATION

GETTING AROUND

Buses: Local buses usually move in only one direction on any given street, except for on Constitución and Juárez (6am-midnight, 3 pesos). Popular routes include stops at the Gran Plaza (#18 or 42), points along Padre Mier and Hidalgo (#15), and along the perimeter of the downtown area (#69). To get from the budget hotel area to the city center, take the #1 Central or #17 Pío X bus, both of which run the lengths of Pino Suárez and Cuauhtémoc. For more detailed route information, ask locals or the English-speaking staff at the tourist office.

Subway: Monterrey's amazing **subway** system, the **Metrorrey,** has all but replaced the large and confusing bus system. Although buses are useful in providing transportation to points far from the *centro* and near the city's periphery, the subway system is clean, and efficient—only 7 min. from the bus station to the Gran Plaza. The system runs on 2 lines. Line 1 (the yellow line) extends from the western station of **San Barnabe** to

Monterrey

(LEGEND REFERS TO MAPS ON FACING PAGE)

🛏 ACCOMMODATIONS

Hotel Amada Nervo, **3**
Hotel Casino, **7**
Hotel Mundo, **4**
Hotel Nuevo León, **5**
Hotel Paraíso Reforma, **2**
Hotel Posada, **1**
Hotel Virreyes, **6**

🍴 FOOD AND DRINKS

Cafe Paraíso, **18**
El Rey de Cabrito, **21**
El Siciliano, **19**
Restaurant Mi Tierra, **16**
Taquería Las Monjitas, **15**

🍸 ♪ BARS AND CLUBS

Barreiros, **13**
Cafe El Infinito, **20**
Cafe Iguana, **17**
El Reloj, **12**
Nueva Luna, **11**

● SHOPPING AND SERVICES

Plaza México Shopping
Center, **10**
Benavides Pharmacy, **14**

NORTHEAST MEXICO

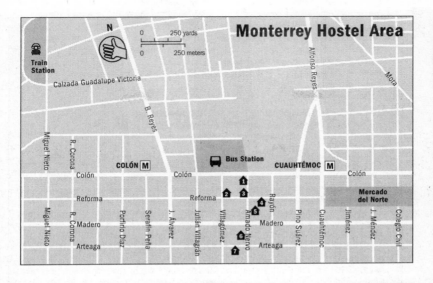

Monterrey Hostel Area

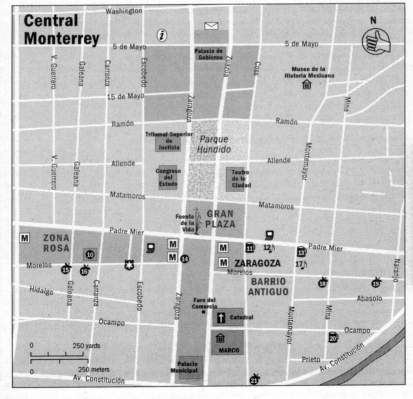

Exposición in the east. Line 2 (the green line) runs from the north, at **Anaya** station, to Gran Plaza **Zaragoza**. Line 2 brings passengers to the downtown Zona Rosa and close to the Barrio Antiguo. The 2 lines intersect at **Cuauhtémoc**, which is right next to the bus station and many budget hotels. Signs point to the final station to which the train is headed. Buy passes from a machine in quantities of 1 (4 pesos), 2 (7.8 pesos), 4 (15 pesos), 6 (21 pesos), or 7 (24 pesos). Subway runs daily 6:30am-midnight.

GETTING AWAY

Airport: Far northwest corner of town, off Mex. 54. **Taxis** charge 80-130 pesos for the 4km trip (20-30min.) to the center. **AeroMéxico** (☎343 55 60) or **Mexicana** (☎340 55 11) require 2-3 day advance reservations, more for weekend flights.

Buses: All buses in and out of the city pass through Monterrey's huge **Central de Autobuses** at Colón and Villagrán. To reach the city center from the bus station, take any bus going south on Pino Suárez, the thoroughfare to the left as you exit the station (#18 lets you off at the central Gran Plaza), or walk 2 blocks east to the grey subway station at Cuauhtémoc and Colón and take the metro (Line 2; 3.50 pesos) to Padre Mier or Zaragoza. Ómnibus de México (☎374 07 16) departs for: **Aguascalientes** (8hr., 4 per day 12:30-11:35pm, 310 pesos); **Chihuahua** (12hr., 3 per day 5am-9:45pm, 445 pesos); **Guadalajara** (12hr., 3 per day 12:30-9:30pm, 433 pesos); **Mexico City** (12hr., 3 per day 7:15am-10:30pm, 510 pesos); **Querétaro** (8hr., 9 and 10:30pm, 338 pesos); **Zacatecas** (6hr., 5 per day 11am-11:15pm, 243 pesos); and more. Sendor, Tamaulipas, and Noreste share offices (☎375 00 14) near Sala 5. Noreste heads to **Nuevo Laredo** (3hr., 12 per day, 150 pesos) and **Matehuala** (4hr., every hr., 177 pesos). Frontera (☎375 09 87) rolls to **Saltillo** (1½hr., every 20min., 51 pesos) and **León** (10 hr., 5 per day, 393 pesos). Similar service is provided by Estrella Blanca (☎318 37 37), Líneas Americanas, and luxurious Futura and Turistar.

🛈 ORIENTATION AND PRACTICAL INFORMATION

Budget travelers will spend most of their time in one of two areas. Hostels cluster across from the bus station, near the Cuauhtémoc stop of the Metrorrey. The Monterrey's *centro* forms a cross with Zona Rosa on the left, the Barrio Antiguo on the right, and the Gran Plaza down the center.

TOURIST AND FINANCIAL SERVICES

Tourist Office: Paez building, 3rd fl. (☎345 67 45 or 345 68 05; www.monterrey-mexico.com), on 5 de Mayo between Escobedo and Zaragoza. Helpful staff with an abundance of maps and bilingual brochures. Open daily 8am-6pm.

Consulates: Canada, 1300 Zaragoza (☎344 32 00). Open M-F 9am-5:30pm. **UK,** Priv. Tamazunchale 104 (☎333 75 98). Open M-F 8am-5pm. **US,** Constitución Pte. 411 (☎344 52 61; emergency ☎362 91 26), downtown. Open M-F 8am-1pm for passports and citizens' concerns, 9am-5pm for telephone information. 24hr. guard and emergency service.

Currency Exchange: Banks dot Madero near the budget hotels and flood the Zona Rosa, especially along Padre Mier. Many refuse to cash traveler's checks and most of those who do charge high service fees (10%). All have 24hr. **ATMs.** Most open M-F 9am-4pm. **Mexdollar Internacional,** 1136 Suárez (☎374 43 11), right by the bus station and the Cuauhtémoc subway stop, offers 24hr. currency and traveler's check exchange at good rates. **Eurodivisas** (☎340 16 83) in Plaza Mexico on Morelos at Galeana, exchanges checks at poorer rates but charges no commission. Open M-F 10:30am-8:30pm, Sa 10am-9pm, Su 11am-8pm. **Western Union:** Omnibus de México Office at the Central de Autobuses (☎374 07 16), or pick up money transactions from any Bital.

American Express: San Pedro 215 Nte. (☎318 33 04). Catch bus #214 headed for "San Pedro" on Pino Suárez at the stop just past Ocampo. Get off before Calzada de Valle and cross the street. Open M-F 9am-5pm, Sa 9am-1pm.

LOCAL SERVICES

Luggage storage: At the bus station. 4 pesos per hr. up to 30 days.

Supermarket: Gigante (☎374 40 24), on Colón across from the bus station. Clothes, groceries, baked goods, and an adjoining **pharmacy.** Open daily 8am-10pm.

Laundry: Hotel Royalty, on the corner of Hidalgo and Carranza, is happy to wash clothes. (☎340 28 00, not available Su.) Laundry services available at most *centro* hotels for about 40 pesos per load.

EMERGENCY AND COMMUNICATIONS

Emergency: ☎060.

Police: (☎345 54 19), on the corner of Carranza and Espinosa or at the 24hr. stand on Morelos at Paras in the Zona Rosa.

Pharmacy: In the bus station, in the Gigante Supermarket on Colón (☎374 40 24), or **Benavides,** on Morelos past Zaragoza (☎345 02 57). Open daily 8am-10pm. Pharmacy attached to VIPS restaurant (☎343 01 55), on the corner of Hidalgo and Carranza. Open Su-Th 7am-2am, F-Sa 24 hr.

Medical Assistance: Red Cross, Alfonso Reyes 2503 Nte. (☎375 11 77 or 375 12 12), at Henry. **Cruz Verde** (☎371 50 50 or 371 52 06), at Ciudad Madero and Ciudad Victoria. English spoken.

Fax: Telecomm, in the bus station next to the post office. Open M-F 8am-7pm, Sa-Su 9am-4pm.

Internet Access: La Tumba Cafe/Bar, Padre Mier 827 (☎333 88 43), in the Barrio Antiguo. 4 computers. 25 pesos per hr. Open M 11am-9pm, Tu-W 11am-1am, Th-F 11am-3am. **Ships 2000,** Escobedo 819 (☎343 25 68), between Padre Mier and Morelos in the Zona Rosa. 14 computers, high speed fiber-optic connection. 20 pesos per 30min., 35 pesos per hr. Scanning, laser printing, and CD burning also available. 2-story arcade downstairs features the latest video games. Open daily 10am-10pm.

Post Office: (☎342 40 03) on Zaragoza at Washington, inside the Palacio Federal. Open M-F 8am-7pm, Sa 9am-1pm. Also on the 2nd fl. of the bus station. Stairs near Sala 5. Open M-F 8am-4pm, Sa 9am-1pm. **Mexpost:** (☎344 94 23), next to the post office inside the Palacio Federal. Open M-F 9am-6pm, Sa 9am-1pm.

Postal Code: 64000.

⌨ ACCOMMODATIONS

Hotels located near the Zona Rosa tend to be of four- or five-star quality, and even three-star accommodations inflate their rates to gouge tourists and business travelers. If you feel like spending 600 pesos, a hotel downtown will reward you with luxury: restaurants, room service, and elegantly decorated rooms. But fear not—cheaper accommodations are sprinkled generously in the less glamorous area near the bus station, with easy access to the metro and the city's main points of interest. Be very careful in this area; prostitutes and drug dealers reign supreme, especially after nightfall. Also, many hotels are full by early afternoon, so act fast.

Hotel Mundo, Reforma 736 (☎374 68 50), off Nervo. More luxurious than bus station hotels: the A/C works well, the TVs are newer, the floors shine brighter. Singles or doubles 220 pesos, with A/C 280 pesos; triples or quads 250 pesos, with A/C 330 pesos.

Hotel Casino (☎372 02 19), on Arteaga just off Amado Nervo. Despite its name, staying here is no gamble. Guests are guaranteed clean rooms with bright marble floors. Some rooms are equipped with a *tina de hidromasaje* (jacuzzi). Rooms are 200 pesos, with TV and A/C 250 pesos, with cable TV and jacuzzi 600 pesos.

Hotel Nuevo Leon, Nervo 1007 (☎374 19 00 or 374 07 13), 1½ blocks from the Central de Autobuses. A large statue of Buddha welcomes you to a maze of dark but spacious rooms. Many rooms come with a dresser and a table. Singles 160 pesos, with TV and A/C 250 pesos; doubles 250 pesos, with TV and A/C 400 pesos.

Hotel Virreyes (☎374 66 10), on Nervo 2 blocks from the bus station. The rooms are basic and sterile, but low prices make this an ideal resting place for wallet-conscious travelers. Singles or doubles 100 pesos, with A/C 140 pesos; triples 120 pesos, with A/C 160 pesos; quads 150 pesos, with A/C 200 pesos.

Hotel Posada, Nervo 1138 (☎372 39 08), across from the bus station. Cross the overhead walkway on Colón. Clean but small rooms. The tiny restaurant in the lobby serves breakfast and sandwiches (15-25 pesos). Singles 180 pesos, with A/C 210 pesos; doubles 210 pesos, with A/C 240 pesos.

Hotel Amado Nervo, Nervo 1110 (☎375 46 32), across from the bus station. Somewhat run-down, small rooms come with TV and phone. The balconies on the 3rd and 4th floors provide views of the neighborhood and the mountains that surround the city. Singles 220 pesos; doubles 340 pesos; triples 370 pesos.

Hotel Paraíso Reforma (☎374 67 27), on Reforma between Nervo and Villagomez. Not quite paradise, but hardly hell either. Small, dark, colorfully decorated rooms. Singles 120 pesos, with A/C and TV 180 pesos.

■ FOOD

Roasted meat is king in Monterrey. Make sure to indulge your carnivorous tooth by eating plenty of *bistecs* (steaks), a regional speciality. Other popular dishes include *frijoles a la charra* (beans cooked with pork skin, coriander, tomato, peppers, and onions) and *machacado con huevos* (scrambled eggs mixed with salsa and dried, shredded beef). For dessert, you'll love *piloncillo con nuez*, a hardened brown sugar candy with pecans, and the heavenly *glorias*, candy balls of nuts and goat's milk. The Zona Rosa, home to some of Monterrey's most expensive shopping, can't be beat for its selection of food. Catering mainly to hungry businesspeople and shoppers, the service is good, the food succulent, and the prices reasonable. *Buen Provecho.*

Restaurant Mi Tierra (☎340 56 11), on Morelos across from Plaza México, offers the value of the best *taquerías* in an intimate open-air setting. If you can't find a seat, get it to go. Tacos, *enchiladas, tostadas,* and more (25 pesos). Open daily 9am-10pm.

Taquería Las Monjitas (☎342 85 37), on Morelos at Galeana in the Zona Rosa; 2 more on Escobedo and on Galeana. Stained-glass and paintings of angels decorate this open-air restaurant, where you will be served by waitresses dressed as nuns. Heavenly specialty tacos (40-60 pesos) have names like *El Papa* (the pope) and *La Pecadora* (the sinner). Open daily 8am-11pm.

Cafe Paraíso (☎344 66 16 or 344 66 17), on Morelos at Mina. A great place to take a break from sightseeing in the heart of the *Barrio Antiguo*. The flavored cappuccinos will reaffirm your caffeine addiction (30 pesos). This hip spot also serves drinks and good French and Mexican cuisine. Try a sweet crepe for 45 pesos. M-W 9am-midnight, Th-Sa 9am-2am, Su 4:30am-midnight.

El Rey de Cabrito (☎345 33 52), on Constitución and Gonzalitos, behind MARCO, reigns supreme for roasted meat, with plenty of *cabrito* and steak dishes (95-110 pesos). Mounted deer and dueling mountain lions add to the elite hunting-lodge atmosphere. Open daily 11:30am-midnight.

El Siciliano, Morelos #1076 (☎375 57 84), between Mina and Naranjo in the *Barrio Antiguo*. Delve into a thin-crust pizza or lasagna (40-60 pesos), but save room for the tantalizing Italian desserts. Open Tu-Su 12:30-5pm, Th-Sa 12:30pm-midnight.

■ SIGHTS

Monterrey's architects were kind to tourists. Despite the city's size, most sights are packed into the 40-acre **Gran Plaza** and nearby **Barrio Antiguo.** A visitor could easily spend the day strolling through the Gran Plaza and admiring the statues, architecture, and greenery, all surrounded by beautiful mountains on the horizon. Though the Barrio Antiguo is relatively calm during the day, numerous art galleries and antique stores make a visit worthwhile.

GRAN PLAZA. Bounded by Washington to the north, Constitución to the south, Zaragoza to the west, and Coss to the east, the Grand Plaza displays all elements of Monterrey: government, religion, commerce, romance, and art. It hosts three government palaces: the **Palacio Federal,** the **Palacio de Gobierno,** and the **Palacio Municipal.** Beyond these immense structures lies the resplendent **Catedral de Monterrey,** its spiritual grandeur rivaling the governmental mammoths. Towering above all, however, is the bright orange **Faro del Comercio** (Commerce Lighthouse). Built in 1983 to commemorate the 100th anniversary of Monterrey's Chamber of Commerce, it represents Monterrey's lifeblood—business. Topped with a laser beacon that circles the skies at night, the lighthouse is a testament to the economic ambitions of Monterrey's leaders. The laser begins to pulse after 10pm on weekend nights, when hundreds pack the adjoining *Barrio Antiguo* in search of some late-night fun. Stoic, dazzling institutions are not all the plaza holds. Beneath these towers and spires, the cool garden of the **Parque Hundido** (Sunken Park) draws slews of young lovers. Farther along, to help cool off after the park's passionate heat, is the **Fuente de La Vida** (Fountain of Life). Built in 1984 by the government of Nuevo Leon, it contains a gaggle of cavorting Nymphs who douse the centerpiece, an imposing statue of Neptune. With so many attractions, the plaza fulfills the promise of its nickname *"Macroplaza."*

▨ MUSEO DE HISTORIA MEXICANA. This state-of-the-art museum uses movies and interactive computer displays to illuminate thousands of years of Mexican history. The enormous climate display room upstairs includes realistic reproductions of forests, deserts, and jungles, complete with plastic animals and chirping bird sounds. *(Dr. Coss 445 Sur, at the far end of the plaza 400 Años. ☎ 345 98 98; www.museohistoriamexicana.org.mx. Open Tu-F 11am-7pm, Sa-Su 11am-8pm. W-F 10 pesos, students 5 pesos; Sa-Su 5 pesos; Tu free.)*

MUSEO DE ARTE CONTEMPORÁNEO (MARCO). This wonderfully odd orange building proves its mantra, "Por amor el arte," repeatedly. MARCO exhibits the best of Mexico's innovative modern artists, including Juan Soriano and Enrique Canales. If art's not your thing, just recline by the enormous decorative pool in the center of the museum and enjoy the periodic water shows. *(At the southern end of Dr. Coss across from the Cathedral. ☎ 342 48 20. Open Tu and Th-Su 10am-6pm, W 10am-8pm. 25 pesos, students and children 15 pesos; W free.)*

TEATRO DE LA CIUDAD. For a calm night away from the city's busy bars and clubs, stop by the Gran Plaza's enormous theater, which regularly hosts plays, operas, and dance performances. Amateur actors occasionally perform outside. *(On the plaza across from the Fuente de la Vida. ☎ 343 89 74. Opens 1hr. before evening performances. Information and tickets available at the office on Zuazúa between Matamoros and Allende, below the theater. Open M-F 9am-7pm. Prices vary by show.)*

LIKE A RHINESTONE COWBOY One cannot visit

Monterrey without hearing *norteño*, the signature music of northeast Mexico, absolutely everywhere: at markets, in bars, and on the street. Sung by such popular bands as Intocable, La Mafia, and Los Tigres del Norte, this unique musical genre—devoted to Mexico's *vaqueros* (cowboys)—is Mexico's answer to American country-western. Groups nearly always consist of five or six men, sporting matching cowboys hats and garish outfits, and swaying in unison to *cumbios* (upbeat rhythms good for dancing) or *rancheros* (slightly slower rhythm). The distinguishing characteristic of this music is the accordion; without its trademark polka sound, it just wouldn't be *norteño*. Love it or hate it, after a few days in Monterrey you'll find yourself unconsciously humming the hit songs of the moment...and maybe even singing along.

CERVECERIA CUAUHTÉMOC MOCTEZUMA. Beer and sports go hand in hand. With this in mind, Monterrey's leading beer manufacturer built a complex, which, in addition to a brewery, contains the Mexican Baseball Hall of Fame and Museum. The brewery tours take you through the production of Carta Blanca, Tecate, and Dos Equis beers, and conclude in the Beer Garden, where adults can sample a glass or two under the shade of trees and fermentation tanks. Afterward, head to the **Salon de la Fama,** a museum that chronicles the birth of baseball in the mid-1800s and its arrival in Mexico shortly thereafter. Interactive exhibits allow kids of all ages to try their luck at batting, pitching, and catching. (On Alfonso Reyes, 1½ blocks south of the Anaya metro station on Line 2. ☎328 53 55. Brewery open M-F 9am-5pm, Sa 9am-2pm. Museum open M-F 9am-5pm, Sa-Su 10:30am-6pm. Tours given throughout the day in both Spanish and English. Free.)

OBISPADO. The former palace of the bishop of Monterrey is now a state museum displaying artifacts from the colonial era. The museum itself may not be worth the half-hour bus ride from the *centro*, but the view and cool breeze compensate. Bring a picnic and enjoy a break from the city on the wandering terraces. (Take bus #1 from Coss along the Macroplaza. Ask the driver to point out the stop, and hike up to the top of the hill. ☎346 04 04. Open Tu-Su 10am-5pm. 20 pesos, students and children free; Su free.)

PLANETARIO ALFA. This large complex (also called the **Centro Cultural Alfa**) houses interactive science exhibits and shows, as well as gardens and halls honoring Mexico's Pre-Hispanic cultures with sculpture and art. The centerpiece of the Alfa is its IMAX theater, which provides an intense movie experience on its 79 ft. screen. (Garza Sada 1000, 25min. southwest of the city. Free round-trip transportation available on the hr. from the Alfa stop on the Alameda, at the corner of Villagrán and Álvarez. Open M-F 3-8:30pm, Sa 2-8:30pm, Su noon-8:30pm. 30 pesos, with IMAX ticket 60 pesos.)

⚡ NIGHTLIFE

The **Barrio Antiguo** is quiet during the day, but after sundown police cordon it off to cars, and the streets come alive with party-goers. The action usually doesn't get started until 10:30pm or so, but note that early birds get in free at many places.

BARS AND CAFES

Nueva Luna (☎344 12 17), on the corner of Padre Mier and Dr. Coss, boasts the best margaritas in town (available in 5 flavors; 40 pesos) and nightly live music. The 2-for-1 deal on beers (25 pesos) and margaritas (40 pesos) until 9pm makes the relaxed Nueva Luna all the more attractive. Open Su-Th noon-midnight, F-Sa noon-2am.

Barreiros, Padre Mier 1032 (☎301 23 82). The decor of this live-music bar will make you feel like you're relaxing in the *zócalo* of a small Mexican town, surrounded by colonial facades. The loud, live Mexican rock, however, serves as a constant reminder that you're here to party. Beer 25 pesos, mixed drinks 50-70 pesos. F-Sa cover 30 pesos for men. Women get their 1st drink free. Open daily 9pm-late.

Cafe El Infinito, Jardón 904 Ote. (☎340 36 34). This cafe/bar/used-bookstore/art-house movie theater promises radical politics and challenging conversation. Sip international wine (starting at 30 pesos a glass) or get a free cup of coffee with the donation of a book. Art films (50 pesos) are shown Th-Sa at 9pm. Open M-Tu 7pm-1am, W-Th 10am-3pm and 7pm-1am, F-Sa 10am-3pm and 7pm-2am, Su 5pm-midnight.

CLUBS

El Reloj, Padre Mier 860 (☎343 42 32). Reloj always has long lines of youth and reverberating US and Mexican rock. Sa night is the time to see and be seen at this fashionable club. Cover 60 pesos. Open daily 9pm-whenever the crowd dwindles.

Cafe Iguana, Montemayor 927 (☎343 08 22). The young, eclectic crowd fits in with the funky, colorful decor. Big, cushy couches line the stone walls and party-goers revel on the open-air patio. Beer 20 pesos, mixed drinks 25 pesos. Cover on some weekend nights, depending on whether there's live music. Open daily 8pm-late.

La Casa Immortal, Benito Juavez #735. With a name like that, you know this disco keeps jumping till early morning. A little rowdier than the *Barrio Antiguo,* this one is only for the most hard-core clubbers. No cover before 11pm. Open Th-Su.

GAY AND LESBIAN NIGHTLIFE

After its first-ever Pride March in the summer of 1997, Monterrey has quickly become one of the most gay- and lesbian-friendly cities in Mexico. Young same-sex couples walk the streets of the Zona Rosa and the *Barrio Antiguo.* Although most nightspots cater primarily to men, women are more than welcome. For more listings, ask for a copy of the free gay and lesbian monthly magazine, *Rola Gay,* at either of these bars.

Club Vongole, Pedreras 300 (☎315 72 59), east of *Barrio Antiguo.* The most hip-hop, happening gay and lesbian night spot in town, with over 1000 people W, F, and Sa.

Charao's (☎374 18 72), at the corner of Garza and Zaragoza, 7 blocks north of the Gran Plaza. An exciting, young crowd of men and women stay late every night. Drinks 15 pesos. F-Sa cover 15 pesos for men, no cover for women.

■ ♫ SHOPPING AND ENTERTAINMENT

The **Zona Rosa,** particularly along Morelos, is the city's true commercial center, with a variety of stores and boutiques ranging from mid-priced to expensive. The new **Plaza Mexico** mall, in the center of the Zona Rosa, has the most organized display for easy spending, with two floors of upscale stores and a food court. Bargain-hunters may prefer the **Mercado del Norte** (also known as **La Pulga**), a seemingly endless maze of vendor stalls covering Reforma, just south of Colón. The clothing vendors, *taquerías,* and music stores stretch from Cuauhtémoc all the way to Juárez; enter on Cuauhtémoc, directly across from the metro station. (Open daily 9am-7pm.)

Monterrey celebrates **Mexican Independence Day** in style, with partying and parades September 15 and 16. In late November, the **Festival Del Barrio Antiguo** shuts down the streets around the Old Neighborhood for a week of cultural events, including open-air theater, music festivals, dance, and painting exhibitions.

COAHUILA

SALTILLO ☎8

Saltillo (pop. 900,000) is a wonderful but often overlooked retreat from Monterrey. Founded in 1577, the city was named for the small *salto de agua* (spring) that sprung miraculously from the desert. Today, Saltillo is famous for its hand-woven sarapes, *pan de pulque,* abundant silver, and the calming oasis of its *centro* which holds three relaxing plazas and a gorgeous cathedral.

▐ TRANSPORTATION

The **bus station** is 3km southwest of the city center on Echeverría Sur. To get to the *centro,* exit the terminal, cross the pedestrian overpass, and catch minibus #10 (20min., 6:30am-11pm, 3 pesos), from the small street perpendicular to Echeverría across the street from Restaurant Jaslo. To return to the station, catch bus #9 at the corner of Aldama and Hidalgo, a block down the street from the cathedral, in front of the furniture store's entrance. A taxi from the bus station to the *centro* costs 30 pesos. From the station, **Frontera** (☎417 00 76) runs buses to **Matehuala** (3hr., 7 per day 6:15am-11pm, 150 pesos) and **Monterrey** (every 20 min., 46 pesos).

Omnibus de México (☎417 03 15) serves **Aguascalientes** (7hr., 10 per day 4am-11pm, 267 pesos) and **Reynosa** (5hr., every hr. noon-9pm, 171 pesos). **Transportes del Norte** (☎417 09 02) goes to: **Guadalajara** (10hr., 5 per day, 398 pesos); **Mexico City** (10hr., 5 per day 6am-9pm, 478 pesos); **San Luis Potosí** (5hr., 7 per day 6am-11pm, 235 pesos); **Zacatecas** (5hr., 5 per day 3:30am-9pm, 200 pesos).

✴ ⁷ ORIENTATION AND PRACTICAL INFORMATION

Located in a valley between the jagged peaks of the Sierra Madre, Saltillo lies 87km southwest of Monterrey along desolate **Mex. 40.** Saltillo's two main streets run perpendicular to each other. **Victoria** (which becomes Benito Juárez in the east) is parallel to Allende (which becomes Carranza in the north). Walking east on Victoria, you will find **Plaza de la Nueva Tlaxcala,** the **Palacio de Gobierno,** and **Plaza de Armas,** home to the awe-inspiring Cathedral of Saltillo. Facing the cathedral, walk left for a block until Aldama. Take another left and walk until you reach Allende; here you will find **Plaza Acuña** and the adjoining **Mercado Juárez.** North on Allende (right when facing Plaza Acuña), you will discover Saltillo's more upscale hotels, bars, and restaurants.

Tourist Information: A small stand in the bus station offers maps and answers. For more guidance, try the **tourist office** (☎412 51 22) at the corner of Acuña and Coss, 5 long blocks north of Plaza Acuña. Little English spoken. Open M-F 9am-5pm, Sa 9am-2pm.

Banks: Banamex, Allende at Ocampo, behind the Palacio de Gobierno has a 24hr. **ATM.**

Market: Soriana, on Coss across from the tourist office.

Laundry: Juárez # 615. (☎412 63 05) Read about Mexican soaps and chat with strangers while cleaning your clothes. 30 pesos to wash and dry a load. M-F 9am-1pm and 3-8pm, Sa 9am-8pm, Su 10am-2pm.

Police: (☎414 45 50) at Treviño and Echeverría Ote.

Emergency: ☎060.

Red Cross: (☎414 33 33), at the corner of Cárdenas and Rayon.

Pharmacy: El Fenix, Juárez 360 (☎412 49 10), across from Mercado Juárez.

Fax: Telecomm (☎414 25 85), by the post office. Open M-Sa 9am-4pm, Su 9am-noon.

Internet access: CNCI, Victoria 444 (☎414 83 44), across from Hotel Urdiñola. 6 computers, 20 pesos per hr. Open daily 9am-6pm.

Post office: Victoria 453 (☎414 90 97) next to Hotel Urdiñola. Open M-F 9am-4pm, Sa 9am-1pm. **MexPost:** (☎414 18 90) inside. Open M-F 9am-4pm, Sa 9am-2pm.

Postal code: 25000.

▐ ACCOMMODATIONS

Echeverría, which runs along the bus station, has several cheap, low-quality places to rest your head. While on Carranza four-star hotels do not cater to budget tourists, the *centro* includes clean, comfortable lodging at reasonable prices.

▨ Hotel Urdiñola, Victoria 251 (☎414 09 40), behind the Palacio de Gobierno. Visually exquisite with a marble staircase, beautiful stained-glass windows, and a sunny, tiled courtyard, this retreat is equipped with fans, cable TV, phones, and room service. However, the elegance translates into extravagant prices. Singles 260 pesos; doubles 285 pesos; triples 310 pesos; quads 340 pesos—plus 47 pesos for tax.

Hotel Saade, Aldama Pte. 397 (☎412 91 20), 1 block west of Plaza Acuña, has clean, well-furnished, quiet rooms near the heart of the city. Top-floor rooms offer a panorama of Saltillo and the Sierra. Rooms come in 3 styles, from *económico* with twin bed and bath, to *ejecutivo* with bed, bath, cable TV, and phone. Single *económico* 265 pesos; standard 230 pesos; *ejecutivo* 320 pesos; each additional person 55 pesos.

Hotel de Auila (☎412 59 16), on Padre Flóres across from the Mercado Juárez. Small, clean, dark rooms. Singles 110 pesos; each additional person 30 pesos.

FOOD

Be sure to sample Saltillo's specialty, *pan de pulque* (bread made with *pulque*, an unrefined cactus drink). This sweet bread, full of pecans and brown sugar, is available at ◼**Mena Donas,** Madero #1350, the absolute best bakery in Saltillo. Half the fun is competing with old women for fresh bread. (☎412 16 71. 4 buns for 24 pesos.) For upscale dining and adventurous dishes, head to the **Restaurant Principal,** Allende Nte. 702, seven blocks north of the Palacio de Gobierno. Their *cabecito* (steamed goat's head; 35 pesos) will leave you with that invigorating post-hunt feel, as will a splurge on grilled ram (100 pesos). Squeamish diners shouldn't worry; traditional *antojitos* are just 40 pesos. Goat and steak dishes (75-100 pesos) are also served. (☎414 33 84. Open daily 8am-midnight.) **Cafe and Restaurant Arcasa,** Victoria 263, is a family-run cafe with delicious food and fast breakfasts (19-29 pesos). Three-course *menú del día* (30 pesos) draws in locals. (☎412 64 24. Open daily 7:30am-midnight.) Browse the silver store at **La Penumbra,** on Juárez opposite Plaza de Armas, before scarfing down traditional *antojitos* (30 pesos) at this family-run establishment (☎414 02 21. Open daily 9am-8pm).

SIGHTS

Weary travelers rest assured: Saltillo is not sight-intensive. Until recently, the most alluring sight in town has been the **Museo de las Aves,** on Hidalgo 3 blocks up from the cathedral. The museum is home to hundreds of birds, the majority of which are dead and stuffed. (☎414 01 68. Open Tu-Sa 10am-6pm, Su 11am-6pm. 10 pesos, children and students 5 pesos.) Saltillo's new pride and joy is the recently opened **Museo del Desierto,** Pérez Treuiño 3745, in Parque Las Marauillas. The state-of-the-art museum includes exhibits on geology, ecology, paleontology, and the desert. The #6 bus takes you there (35min.) from the corner of Aldama and Ocampo; ask the driver to point out the stop. (☎410 66 33. Open Tu-Su, 10am-6pm. 20 pesos.)

To explore Saltillo's history and panoramic view, hike up Miguel Hidalgo and turn left after the Museo de las Aves. The **Iglesia del Ojo de Agua** was built on the spot where the "saltillo" was first discovered in 1577. Continue past the church up to the small pink-painted plaza. Known as Plaza México or El Mirado, this is where Zachary Taylor's North American army camped before their battle with Santa Anna's troops. The site offers a breathtaking view of Saltillo.

NIGHTLIFE AND ENTERTAINMENT

What there is of the city's nightlife lies well beyond *el centro*, and not much happens during the week. On weekend nights, however, many head to **Frug's Clubhouse,** Acuña 1212, across from the tourist office, for live music, beer (15 pesos), and billiards. (☎412 77 83. Cover Th men 30 pesos, F-Sa everyone 40 pesos. Open M-Sa 4pm-2am.) Another option for nightlife is **Carlos 'N Charlies,** Carranza 3070 (☎416 48 42 or 416 64 28), a bar and grill that plays live music on weekends.

To fill your day, the downtown **Centro Cultural (Teatro Garcia Carrillo),** on Aldama in Plaza Acuña, presents regular sculpture and art exhibitions, films, and concerts, all free of charge. Drop by to check the list of weekly events. (Open Tu-Su 10am-2pm and 4-7pm. Children's theater Sa 11am.)

SHOPPING AND ENTERTAINMENT

Since the 17th century, Saltillo has enjoyed a long tradition of weaving. Famed throughout Mexico for its colorful wool *sarapes* (shawls), the city has spawned its own style, called the "saltillo." The best place to buy sarapes (and watch them made) is ◼**El Sarape de Saltillo,** before Museo de las Aves, which is famous for its quality Mexican crafts (☎412 48 89. Open M-Sa 9am-1pm and 3-7pm). For less expensive *sarapes*, crafts, and silver, visit Mercado Juárez behind Plaza Acuña.

Saltillo's streets bustle with artistry and cultural pride during the **Feria de Saltillo** in mid-August. This two-week fair, featuring agricultural and art exhibitions, performances, and *sarapes*, dates back to the town's first years in the 16th century.

ZACATECAS

ZACATECAS   ☎ 4

A beautiful colonial city is perhaps the last thing a weary traveler would expect to find rising out of the prickly Central Mexican desert. Yet, almost miraculously, the city of Zacatecas overcomes its arid surroundings, perched between, on, and over the mineral-laden hills that serve as the city's lifeblood. A silver trinket, given to early Spanish colonists by an indigenous Cascane in the mid-1500s, triggered the mining frenzy that led to the founding of the town in 1585 and eventually stripped the surrounding hills of 6000 tons of silver. Although the silver mines have since gone dry, Zacatecas managed to survive, and even thrive, without the mine's economic crutch. Under the patronage of the affluent silver barons, the arts flourished, and the rows of grand colonial mansions, beautiful parks, and nationally renowned museums testify to an era of lavish consumption—an era in which the great barons swore they would coat the streets with silver. Today, happy and silver-free are the city's residents, enjoying their busy university town, a center of commerce and tourism. And, of course, they enjoy plenty of Corona beer, homebrewed in the state of Zacatecas.

▐ TRANSPORTATION

Airport: (☎928 03 38), accessible by *combis* (☎922 59 46) from the Mexicana office (20min., departs 1¼hr. before flight, 50 pesos). **Mexicana,** Hidalgo 406 (☎922 74 29). Open M-F 9am-7pm. **Taesa,** Hidalgo 306 (☎922 00 50 or 922 02 12). Open M-F 9am-7pm, Sa 10am-6pm. **Aero California,** Juan de Montoro 203 (☎925 24 00).

Buses: Central de Autobuses (☎922 11 12), Lomas de la Isabélica, at Tránsito Pesado on the outskirts of town. City buses (2 pesos; "Ruta 8" to the *centro)* and taxis (20 pesos to the *centro*) wait outside. After dark, a taxi is the only option. To get to the station from the *centro*, take the "Ruta 7" or "8" bus on González Ortega, 1 block from Juárez. Omnibuses de Mexico (☎922 54 95) provides the broadest range of service, including: **Mexico City** (8hr., 10 per day, 338 pesos); **Guadalajara** (5hr., 14 per day, 192 pesos); **Ciudad Juárez** (26hr., 13 per day, 642 pesos); (6hr., 11 per day, 150 pesos); **Matamoros** (11hr., 7 per day, 386 pesos); **Aguascalientes** (3hr., 3 per day, 66 pesos); and most other major Mexican cities. Transportes del Norte (☎922 00 42), Rojos de los Altos (☎922 06 84), Chihuahuenses (☎922 00 42), and Estrella Blanca (☎922 06 84) also service the area.

▐ PRACTICAL INFORMATION

Tourist Office: Hidalgo 403 (☎ 922-3426), on the 2nd fl. Helpful staff answers questions in both Spanish and English and provides a variety of maps and pamphlets. Open daily 9am-8pm. Coffee addicts take note: the best coffee in Zacatecas is located downstairs in the same building. Office operates an equally-helpful module farther up the street, just across from the *teatro*. Open Tu-Su 10am-6pm.

Currency Exchange: Banca Promex, González Ortega 122 (☎922 93 69), has good rates and a 24hr. **ATM.** Open M-F 8:30am-5:30pm, Sa 10am-2pm. The 1st blocks of González Ortega and Hidalgo away from Juárez are inundated with banks.

Zacatecas

⌂ ACCOMMODATIONS
Hostel Villa Colonial, **3**
Hotel del Parque, **8**
Hotel María Conchita, **6**
Hotel Rio Grande, **7**
Zamora de Zacatecas, **5**

🍎 FOOD
El Pueblito, **2**
Gorditas Doña Julia, **1**
La Unica Cabaña, **4**

Car Rental: Autos Último Modelo, Alcatraces 147 (☎/fax 924 55 09), is among the cheapest in town, with prices starting at 400 pesos per day with the 1st 200km free; **Avis,** López Mateos 615 (☎922 30 03). Open M-Sa 8:30am-3pm and 5-7:30pm. **Alamo** (☎01 800 849 80 01) has an airport location (☎01 57 86 92 14). **Mazzocco,** Fátima 115 Sierra de Alicia (☎/fax 922 77 02), rents everything from car to buses. **Budget,** López Mateos 104 (☎922 94 58), rents cars from 450 pesos.

Luggage Storage: At the bus station. 1.5 pesos per hr.

Laundry: Lavamatic Plus, Rosadela 18 (☎923 47 06), at México. Open M-Sa 9am-5:30pm. 30 pesos per 3kg.

Market: The wonderful open-air that follows the twisty Arroyo de la Plata from Independencia to the small bus station at López Mateos, spilling into adjacent streets.

Emergency: ☎060.

Police: Héroes de Chapultepec 1000 (☎922 01 80 or 922 05 07). No English spoken.

Red Cross: Calzada de la Cruz Roja 100 (☎922 30 05 or 922 33 23), off Héroes de Chapultepec, near the exit to Fresnillo. Some English spoken.

Pharmacy: Farmacia Guadalajara, López Mateos 305 (☎ 922 3862), across the street from the Howard Johnson next to KFC, is the most visible pharmacy. Open 24 hr.

Hospital: Hospital General, García Salinas 707 (☎923 30 04 or 923 30 05). **Dr. José Cruz de la Torre González** (☎924 07 03) speaks English.

Fax: Telecomm (☎922 00 60; fax 922 17 96), on Hidalgo at Juárez. Open M-F 8:30am-7pm, Sa-Su 9am-noon.

Internet Access: The **public library,** at the end of Juárez across from Jardín Independencia, provides free service (30min. limit if someone's waiting). Open daily 9am-9pm. If you need more time, go to **Optimus Prime** at Tacuba 118 (☎ 922 0423), right across from the fountain. Fast service and competent assistance. (Open M-Sa 9am-9pm.)

Post Office: Allende 111 (☎922 01 96), off Hidalgo. Open M-F 9am-4pm, Sa 9am-1pm. **Mexpost** service next door. Open M-F 9am-6pm, Sa 9am-1pm.

Postal Code: 98000.

▚ ACCOMMODATIONS

While most budget accommodations have been priced out of the *centro*, they linger at its fringe on **López Mateos,** the main thoroughfare bordering the historic core. Reservations are a good idea at the cheapest hotels.

▨ Hostal Villa Colonial, 1 de Mayo (☎ 922 19 80; hostalvillacolonial@hotmail.com), up Callejón Mono Prieto behind the cathedral. The island of budget hospitality in the overpriced city center, this family-run hostel has a kitchen, dining room, internet service (15 pesos per hr.), luggage storage, mini-pool table, book exchange, and washing machine (25 pesos per 10kg). Comfortable dorm-style rooms with 4 beds (60 pesos with ISIC discount; 80 pesos without). Private rooms (140 pesos) have spectacular views of the cathedral. Pickup service from the bus station from 6-8am and 2-4pm.

Hotel Zamora de Zacatecas, Plazuela de Zamora 303 (☎ 922 1200), which is the continuation of Independencia just downhill from the Jardín. WIth a lobby that lingers in the external twilight of *telenovelas* and bathroom drains that seem predestined to clog, Hotel Zamora is recommended only for those who value convenience above all else. Singles 82 pesos; doubles 92 pesos.

Hotel Río Grande, Calzada de la Paz 513 (☎ 922 98 76). From the *centro*, cross Mateos at the bus station and walk uphill, turn left at La Paz and follow it uphill; the hotel is on the left. The climb is rewarded by beautiful views, clean, functional rooms, and excellent prices. Singles 70 pesos; doubles 100 pesos; 2 beds 120 pesos.

Hotel del Parque, González Ortega 302 (☎922 04 79), near the aqueduct. With the Hotel Quinta Real in the backyard, you can dream of the day you return to Zacatecas a millionaire and reminisce about the days you stayed at del Parque. Until that day arrives, del Parque has a nice location, clean rooms and bathrooms, and TVs. Singles 105 pesos; doubles 120 pesos; triples 150 pesos; quads 170 pesos.

Hotel María Conchita, López Mateos 401 (☎922 14 94 or 922 14 96), just across Mateos from the *centro*. Rooms are well-maintained and pleasant and come equipped with phones and TVs. Recently remodeled 4th- and 5th-floor rooms aren't worth the price (or stair) hike. The late-night restaurant next door offers cheap breakfasts (30 pesos) and other Mexican standards. Singles 130 pesos; doubles 150 pesos.

Hotel Gami, López Mateos 309 (☎922 08 05), has simple rooms with desks, TVs, and tiled baths, but no fan or A/C. Singles 140 pesos; doubles 250 pesos.

▛ FOOD

Zacatecas is famous for its sweets. For good coffee and an opportunity to meet all of the city's politicians and businessmen, head to **Acropolis** on Hidalgo next door to the cathedral. (Open 8am-10pm.) Also try the fashionable new **Tacuba Cafe,** Tacuba 164, across from the mall. (Open daily 4-11pm.) Get that sugar rush with a chunk of *dulce con leche, camote, coco* (coconut), or *batata* (sweet potato)—all 5 pesos, peddled by vendors throughout the *centro*.

▨ La Unica Cabaña, on Independencia at Juáraz. Easily the most popular restaurant in town, this *taqueria* does everything right. Fast, hot, and served with excellent salsas. Extraordinarily good *quesadillas* 7 pesos, tacos 3.6 pesos, ½-roasted chicken meal 37 pesos. Open daily 7am-noon.

El Pueblito, Hidalgo 403 (☎924 38 18), downstairs from the tourist office. Offers the best prices for regional specialties. Try the Zacatecan *enchiladas* (36 pesos) or the regional sampler (45 pesos). Classy enough to impress your date. Open daily 1-11pm.

Gorditas Doña Julia, Hidalgo 409 (☎923 79 55), additional locations on Tacuba (across from the fountain) on Obregón, and on the freeway out of town. If Doña Julia keeps up the present rate of colonization she'll have to hire a chihuahua to advertise her delicious *gorditas* (6 pesos). All sorts of fillings are stuffed into these fat little tortilla sandwiches, which are Zacatecans' favorite takeout. Open daily 8am-11pm.

👁 SIGHTS

Zacatecas's entire city center is a declared UNESCO World Heritage Site. Strict building codes and prohibitions against gaudy advertisement make it hard to tell where the city ends and the museums begin—but it hardly matters since both are spectacular. Not to be missed are the two Coronel museums and the vista of the city from **La Buta.** Also be sure to leave time for the neighboring town of **Guadalupe** and the ruins of **La Quemada.**

▨**CATHEDRAL.** The pride of Zacatecas, the pink sandstone cathedral, officially called **Nuestra Señora de Asunción,** was begun in 1729, completed in 1752, and consecrated as a cathedral 1862. The magnificent building is undoubtedly one of the most beautiful cathedrals in all the Americas. The intricate three-story facade is perhaps the best example of Mexican Baroque and depicts, among a myriad of figures, Christ blessing the Apostles and images of the Eucharist. The northern facade bears a representation of Christ on the cross, and the European Baroque southern facade pays homage to *Nuestra Señora de las Zacatecas.* The interior of the cathedral, in contrast to its lavish exterior, is surprisingly plain, although legend has it that prior to the War of Reform it was as splendid as the outside. *(4 blocks northeast of Juárez, on Hidalgo. Open daily 7am-1pm and 3-9pm.)*

▨**MUSEO DE PEDRO CORONEL.** Housed in the former *Colegio de San Luis Gonzaga,* a Jesuit college established in 1616, the museum is now home to the tomb, sculptures, and paintings of Zacatecan artist Pedro Coronel. In addition, it has one of the best modern art collections in Latin America, with works by such varied artists as Picasso, Braque, Chagall, Miró, Goya, and Hogarth. *(On Villapando at Serdán. Facing away from the Cathedral entrance, cross Hidalgo going right, turn left into the 1st alleyway, turn left as it ends on Dondina, and right at your 1st opportunity, following Villapando to museum.☎922 80 21. Open F-W 10am-5pm. 15 pesos, students and seniors 7.5 pesos, children free.)*

PALACIO DE GOBIERNO. The Palacio de Gobierno was built in 1727 as the residence of Joseph de Rivera Bernández, a count. The building distinguishes itself with the mural that surrounds its interior stairwell. Painted in 1970 by Antonio Rodríguez, the work traces the history of Zacatecas from the Pre-Hispanic era until the present. *(Next to the cathedral. Open M-F 9am-8pm.)*

LA MICHELADA The favorite beer of Zacatecanas is undoubtedly world-famous Corona, *"La cerveza mas fina,"* and the *Michelada* is one of the most popular ways to enjoy the great brew. This interesting drink is made with 2oz. of tequila (Casa Noble Crystal), the juice of two lemons, a quarter-teaspoon of *sal de gusano* (from Oaxaca; toasted agave worms, chili, and salt), and Corona poured over ice. The taste is similar to *tamarindo* (a popular component of Mexican candies) and packs quite a punch, both in terms of alcohol and taste. *La Michelada* may be more of an acquired taste, but locals swear it's the best way to enjoy your Corona.

TEMPLO DE SANTO DOMINGO. Built by the Jesuits in 1746, the Temple contains nine impressive Baroque wooden altars and a rare 18th-century German pipe organ. *(Right next to Museo Pedro Coronel at the end of Villapando. Open daily 7am-1pm and 5-8pm. Masses held frequently on weekends.)*

MUSEO ZACATECANA. Has a permanent exhibit on the art of the region's Huichol people as well as a collection of 19th-century *retablos* (or icons), which provide something of a crash-course in Mexican Catholicism. (☎ 922 65 80. *At Dr. Itievro Zol 2 blocks down from Santo Domingo. Open W-M 9:30am-5pm. 12 pesos.)*

MUSEO RAFAEL CORONEL. This museum is housed in the dramatic **Ex-Convento de San Francisco,** built by Franciscans in the 17th century and then occupied by the Jesuits until the late 18th century. The building is worth a close look, as is the museum inside, which showcases an enormous collection of masks, figurines, pottery, and puppets donated by Rafael Coronel, brother of Pedro. Though the masks are artfully arranged, the frustrating lack of explanatory labels leaves visitors with more questions than answers. Photographs of such events as *Semana Santa* and *Cristianos y Morros* help somewhat, but not enough, to contextualize these strange artworks. *(To reach the museum from the cathedral, follow Hidalgo, bearing left at the fountain at the 1st fork, and right at the 2nd. Open Tu-Th 10am-5pm. 15 pesos, students and seniors 7.5 pesos, children free.)*

MINA DE EDÉN. Discovered in 1583, the Mina de Eden was one of Zacatecas's most productive silver mines until the 1960's, when continual flooding made mineral extraction futile. Now re-opened as a tourist attraction, the interior lacks the beauty of natural caves—its cramped depths make it easy to see why it was sarcastically called "The Mine of Eden" in reference to the miserable conditions suffered by its workers. The tour includes some fairly tame treks across rope bridges and auto-pilot descriptions by Spanish-speaking guides. The mine has two entrances. Tours start from the west entrance, which can be reached by following Dr. Hierro from Santo Domingo as it turns into Codina and climbing the ridiculously steep Callejón de Garcia that branches off to the left. From there, follow signs pointing left. If you begin at the eastern entrance, you can take the old mine train half-way in and walk through the caves to where tours begin. (☎ 922 56 94. *Open daily 10am-6pm. 20 pesos, children 15 pesos.)*

CERRO DE LA BUFA. Named in Basque for its resemblance to a Spanish wineskin, and surrounded by both myth and history, the *cerro* peers down on Zacatecas from the city's highest crag. **Museo de la Toma de Zacatecas,** adjacent to the *cerro*, was built to commemorate Pancho Villa's decisive victory over federal troops in the summer of 1914. The museum displays an array of revolutionary memorabilia, including photographs, a cannon, and small arms. (☎ 922 80 66. *Open Tu-Su 10am-4pm. 10 pesos.)* On one side of the museum lies the 18th-century **Capilla del Patrocinio,** whose graceful facade and cloistered courtyards are carved from deep red stone. Nearby shops sell arts, crafts, and loads of geodes. A short but steep walk up the hill leads to the Moorish **Mausoleo de los Hombres Ilustres de Zacatecas** (Tomb of the Famous Men of Zacatecas), worth the hike if only for the view of the city. There's yet another vista behind the museum, from the castle where the **Meteorological Observatory** is housed. *(The most appealing way to make the trip is by the teleférico, an enclosed ski-lift that runs between the peak of El Grillo and La Bufa. To get to the teleférico stop, follow García Rojas northwest up a steep incline to its end. The teleférico doesn't run in rain or high winds. Or, take the lengthy and convoluted Ruta 7 bus from González Ortega. To get there, follow instructions to La Mina, but then turn right rather than left at the top of Callejon Garcia Rojas. Every 10 min. 10am-6pm, 20 pesos. ☎ 922 01 70. From the top, you can either take the costly teleférico back, or make the short walk downhill into the centro. The most cost-effective (if strenuous) way to see both attractions is to climb la Bufa on foot, then take the teleférico down to the west entrance of the Mina de Edén, and then take the train to the east entrance and walk down the hill.)*

PARQUE ENRIQUE ESTRADA. Southeast of the downtown area, 39 pink stone arches mark the end of Zacatecas's famous colonial aqueduct, **El Cubo.** Beside the aqueduct is the manicured **Parque Enrique Estrada.** To one side of the park is the former governor's mansion, now the **Museo de Francisco Goitia,** Enrique Estrada 101. The museum displays regional historical artifacts and gives a good account of Mexican history. (☎922 02 11. *Open Tu-Su 10am-5pm. 20 pesos, students 10 pesos.*)

🎵 📷 ENTERTAINMENT AND NIGHTLIFE

Zacatecas's nights can be as classy and as expensive as its days. Though the city comes with the full complement of cheap cantinas and pool halls, those wishing to mingle with fashionable university-types will have to pay. Night spots listed are in the *centro*, where well-lit, relatively safe streets eliminate the need for cabs.

Chat and sip drinks to live music on Tacuba below Mercado González Ortega next door to the cathedral. The hippest place to chill is the pricey **Rincón de las Troubadores** or *"Rincón Bohemia,"* Calzadores de Zacatecas 104 (follow Hidalgo into Codina; it is visible at the end of street) where romantic ballads and *salsa* play to a roomful of nicely dressed 20- and 30-somethings. Tequila from 32 pesos, beer 18 pesos. (Open F-Sa 7pm-2:30am, closes at 11pm or midnight during the week.)

If it's dancing you want, varying degrees of boogie are available. Certainly the most unique place to get down is 📷**El Malacate,** 600m in from the side entrance of the Mina de Edén. You've never experienced a bass beat until you hear it reverberating off the solid stone walls of this former mine shaft. (☎492 82 30 02. Beer 18 pesos, mixed drinks 25 pesos. Cover 50 pesos. Open Th-Sa 9pm-2:30am.) Newer and less-tarnished by tourist riff-raff is **Malaga,** Guerrero 106, across from the fountain. Techno/electronica plays on the dance floor—more secluded balcony tables above cradle young couples. (☎ 446 56 05. Cover men 100 pesos, women 40 pesos. Open Th-Sa 10pm-3am.) **El Claustro,** Calle Aguascalientes 10, is a two-story converted mansion built for partying. Pool and quieter tables upstairs provide a break from dancing to the pop/trance/electronic mix. On Saturday, cover buys 1L of wine per table; men 80 pesos, women 30 pesos. Open Th-Sa 9pm-3am.) **Cactus,** Hidalgo 111, at the Juárez intersection, is suitable for lounging with a beer (18 pesos), dancing on the faux-cathedral floor, or shooting some pool upstairs. (☎922 05 09. Happy Hour is 2-for-1; 8-10pm. Cover F-Sa 30 pesos. Open M-Sa 8pm-3am.)

The yearly cultural highlight is **Zacatecas en la Cultura,** a festival during *Semana Santa,* in which concerts and artistic activities are held in the elegant Teatro Calderón, on Hidalgo near the cathedral, and throughout the city. Zacatecas is also reputed to have Mexico's best **Morismo,** a mock re-creation of the battle of the Moors and the Spanish enacted with masks and costumes in mid-August. Call the tourist office for specific details. From September 8-22, the city celebrates the **Feria Nacional de Zacatecas** with musical and theatrical events, bullfights, agricultural and crafts shows, and sporting events.

📷 DAYTRIPS FROM ZACATECAS

📷 LA QUEMADA

Take a Camiones de los Altos bus from the main bus station in Zacatecas (or from a smaller station on López Mateos near the Howard Johnson) to La Quemada (30min., every 30min. 6am-10pm, 20 pesos). Be sure to specify that you want to get off at the ruins, not the city itself. The road to the ruins is on the left of the main route, right after the white, yellow, and blue restaurant with the Corona sign. Walk about 3km along this road to reach the entrance. Site open daily 10am-5pm. 25 pesos. Museum open daily 10am-4pm. 7 pesos, children 2 pesos; Su free. To get to Jerez from here, walk back to the main route and hop on a bus heading back to Zacatecas. You'll have to get off in Malpaso and change buses to get to Jerez. Ask the bus driver where to get off to wait for the Jerez bus.

About 50km south of Zacatecas lie some very cool ruins that very few people have ever heard of. **La Quemada** (AD 500-800) hasn't yielded any spectacular golden artifacts, nor is it attributable to any major Mesoamerican civilization, and for these reasons the visually stunning ruins have been left more or less untouristed. The temples, dwellings, fortresses, and ball-court of La Quemada are impressively built into a mountain with a 360-degree view of the surrounding countryside and, if anything, seeing the ruins is a great excuse for a hike. The site's museum explains the mystery surrounding Quemada's origins. Some postulate that it was the site of the legendary Aztec city Chicomostoc, Tenochtitlán's precursor and the capital of the region north of the Río San Antonio. It also offers a scale model of the ruins that are a helpful guide to those interested in the more remote sections.

GUADALUPE

Catch a Transportes Guadalupe bus from the bus station or the smaller station behind the Howard Johnson on López Mateos (30 min., 3 pesos). It's difficult to discern when Zacatecas ends and Guadalupe begins, so be sure to tell the bus driver you want to get off in Guadalupe's centro. From the bus station in Guadalupe, walk a short distance to your left along Mateos and turn right on Constitución at the monument in the center of the street. The cathedral is a couple of blocks in front of you. Catch a return bus to Zacatecas from the same bus station. Cathedral open daily 10am-4:30pm. 20 pesos.

The village, named after the town church, was founded in 1707 as a training site for Franciscan missionaries. The **Ex-Convento de Guadalupe,** located on the main plaza, is known not only for having produced over 3000 missionaries, but for its famous statue of the **Virgin of Guadalupe,** located above the altar. Next to the cathedral is the **Museo de Guadalupe,** which contains paintings depicting scenes from the life of St. Francis, as well as nearly every known incident in the life of Christ. Those yearning for medieval misadventure can walk into the museum courtyard, around the side of the stone block, and down into the dank, dark cistern.

JEREZ

Camiones de los Altos buses go to Juárez (1hr., every 30min. 5:15am-10pm, 25 pesos). To get to the centro from the Jerez bus station, turn right on the street directly ahead. It's a good 25min. walk, so consider taking a cab or a bus (if you can find one).

About an hour's bus ride from Zacatecas lies the rapidly expanding colonial town of Jerez (pop. 12,500). If Zacatecas isn't sedate enough, both beautiful colonial buildings and an old-fashioned pace of life can be found here. Among the buildings is the **Edificio de la Torre,** built by architect Dámaso Muñetón in 1896. The **Casa-Museo Ramon López Velarde** celebrates the life of the native poet. The **Santuario de Soledad** is a beautiful mid-19th-century church. Also visit the **Iglesia Parroquia.** The impressive **Teatro Hinojosa,** a replica of New York City's Lincoln Center, was built in 1878, and will give you some idea of the town's past mining wealth.

AGUASCALIENTES

AGUASCALIENTES   ☎ 4

The city of Aguascalientes (pop. 520,000), named for the hot springs that once filled the region, is a town that history has passed by. Run your finger down the index of any Mexican history textbook and you'll likely find just one uninspiring entry, which probably would read, "The Convention of Aguascalientes was held in Aguascalientes in 1914." Today, Aguascalientes is a city of modern buildings and noisy streets, dotted with Blockbuster Videos, liquor stores, and pizzerias. The city has rallied around what little history it has; to its credit, it has accomplished several feats—its central square, Plaza de la Patria, is marvelous. Residents claim that the city's annual fair, the *Feria de San Marcos,* it is the biggest, best, and wildest festival in all Mexico. A large city with small-town ambience, Aguascalientes is a good place to stay for a day or two.

TO BALNEARIO OJO CALIENTE (92m)

TO PLAZA KRISTAL (250m)

TO PLAZA (250m)

TO MUSEO DE GUADALUPE POSADA (25m)

Museo de Aguascalientes

Templo de San Antonio

Zaragoza

Madero

Wasco

5 de Febrero

Prima Verdad

Sarcho

Paraga

Hidalgo

16 de Septiembre

Montoro

Hotnedo

Mina

Museo de Arte Contemporaneo

Hospitalidad

Díaz de León

Del Sol

Morelos

Palmira

Colón

Mercado Morelos

Juárez

Colón

Central Parian

Obregón

PLAZA DE LA PATRIA

Basílica de la Asunción

José María Chávez

Riviera y Gutiérrez

Hotnedo

Héroes de Chapultepec

5 de Mayo

Mercado Jesús Terán

Unión

Guadalupe Victoria

Montezuma

Galeana N.

Galeana Sur

Casa de Cultura

López Mateos

Allende

Guadalupe

Gorostiza

Alarcon

Museo Regional de Historia

Insurgentes

Guerrero Norte

Guerrero Sur

Macías

Liberad

Zapata

Carranza

Matamoros Norte

Matamoros Sur

Bernal

Nieto

Rayón

Pocitos

Correa

Elizondo Norte

Las Américas

Los Laureles

Contreras

Jardín de San Marcos

SAN MARCOS FAIRGROUND AREA

Pani

Templo de San Marcos

Area de la Feria

Ponce

Ego Plaza

Plaza de Toros

N

250 yards

250 meters

Aguascalientes

ACCOMMODATIONS
Hotel Brasil, 1
Hotel Rosales, 8
Hotel San Antonio, 2
Hotel San José, 6
Hotel Señorial, 11
Posada San Rafael, 7

FOOD
Restaurant Vegetariano de Venad, 3
El Zodiaco, 12
Gorditas Victoria, 5
La Fogata, 9
Sanfer Restaurant, 4

NIGHTLIFE
Merendero San Marcos, 10

NORTHEAST MEXICO

▐▄ TRANSPORTATION

Buses: The bus station is on Convención Sur and Av. 5a, a few blocks west of José Marí Chávez. Green and white city buses with numbers in the 20s or 30s (3 pesos) run from outside the bus station to the Mercado Morelos, 2 blocks north of Plaza de la Patria, the center of town. To get back to the station, take a "Central Camionera" bus or a taxi (20 pesos). Omnibus de Mexico (☎978 27 70) and Chihuahenses (☎918 27 58) go to: **Ciudad Juárez** (15hr., 6 per day, 752 pesos); **Durango** (7hr., 6 per day, 214 pesos); **Torreón** (6hr., 5 per day, 273 pesos); **Zacatecas** (2½hr., 8 per day, 71 pesos), and other major cities. Futura goes to: **Acapulco** (11hr., several per day, 450 pesos); **Cuernavaca** (7hr., 11pm, 305 pesos); **Monterrey** (9hr., 2 per day, 312 pesos); **Durango** (6hr., 7 per day, 230 pesos); **Guadalajara** (3hr., every hr. 5am-9pm, 144 pesos); **Mexico City** (6hr., 10 per day, 307 pesos); and most other major cities. Primera Plus (☎918 26 71) and ETN (☎918 24 29) also go to major cities.

▄▲▐ ORIENTATION AND PRACTICAL INFORMATION

Aguascalientes is 168km west of San Luis Potosí, 128km south of Zacatecas, and 252km northeast of Guadalajara. **Circunvalación** encircles the city, while **López Mateos** cuts through town east to west. From **Plaza de la Patria**, the center of town, most sights are within walking distance on either **Montoro**, which runs east from the southeast corner of the plaza, or **Carranza**, which begins to the west of the plaza behind the *basílica*. The city takes its *siestas* quite seriously; many sights and businesses close from 2-4pm.

Tourist Office: (☎915 95 04 or 916 00 51), off Plaza de la Patria, in the Palacio de Gobierno. 1st door on the right on the 1st fl. Decent maps and a plethora of brochures, some in English. Open M-F 8am-7:30pm, Sa-Su 9am-6pm.

Currency Exchange: Moneytron, Montoro 120 (☎915 79 79), 1 block from the *zócalo*, has excellent rates and charges no commission. You can also pawn precious metals. Open M-F 9am-5pm. **Bancomer,** 5 de Mayo 120 (☎915 51 15), 1 block from the plaza, also offers good rates. Open M-F 8:30am-4pm, Sa 10am-1pm.

Emergency: ☎060.

Police: (☎914 20 50), at the corner of Libertad and Gómez Orozco. English spoken.

Pharmacy: Farmacia Sánchez, Madero 213 (☎915 35 50), 1 block from the plaza. Open 24hr.

Hospital: Hospital Hidalgo, Galeana 465 (☎916 57 77 or 917 29 83).

Fax: Telecomm (☎916 14 27), Galeana at Nieto. Open M-F 8am-7pm, Sa 9am-1pm, Su 9am-noon. Another office in the bus station. Open M-F 8am-7:30pm, Sa 9am-noon.

Telephones: LADATELs are along the plaza and throughout town; there is a **caseta** (with a good cigar selection) at the Tabaquería Plaza, Colón 102, on the corner of the plaza. Open daily 9am-9pm.

Internet Access: @ Internet, Calle Colon 401, 1 block across López Mateos from the plaza. Open M-F 9:30am-9pm, Sa 10:30pm-8pm. 15 pesos per hr. **Cybercafe 2000,** Allende 105 Internal #1 (☎916 94 15). 25 pesos per hr., students 20 pesos per hr. Open M-Sa 10am-8pm.

Post Office: Hospitalidad 108 (☎915 21 18). Open M-F 8am-3pm, Sa 9am-1pm.

Postal Code: 20000.

▐▌ ACCOMMODATIONS

Budget hotels in **Aguascalientes** are all tucked away on side streets extending from the plaza. As a general rule, the *centro* is much nicer than the area near the bus station; the hotels are better and the prices are about the same. During the **Feria de San Marcos** (mid-April-early May), reservations are a must.

Hotel Brasil, Guadalupe Victoria 110 (☎915 11 06), 3 blocks up Victoria from the plaza, and another 1½ blocks to the left down Guadalupe. It takes a while for the hot water to get flowing in Brasil, but that is the Achilles heel of this very clean, friendly hotel. Optical illusions provided by eclectic tiling make every day a trip. Singles 70 pesos; matrimonials 100; doubles 120 pesos.

Hotel Rosales, Victoria 104 (☎915 21 65), off Madero, right across from the basilica and Plaza Patria. Simple, clean rooms, phones, TV, and a nice courtyard. Singles 70 pesos; matrimonials 120; doubles 140 pesos; triples 170 pesos.

Hotel San Antonio, Zaragoza 305 (☎915 93 41), 3 blocks east of the plaza and 2 blocks up. This hotel is paved with beautiful grey marble, from front stairs to bathrooms. Plenty of parking in motel-style courtyard, and all rooms have TVs. Singles 135 pesos; matrimonials 175 pesos; doubles 210 pesos.

Hotel Señorial, Colón 104 (☎915 16 30 or 915 14 73), at the corner of Montoro, on Plaza de la Patria; the location couldn't be better. Nice rooms with cable TV, phones, and a supply of purified water. Singles 150 pesos; doubles 200 pesos; triples 200 pesos; quads 300 pesos.

Posada San Rafael, Hidalgo 205 (☎915 77 61), at Madero, 3 blocks from the plaza. Ceiling fans, cable TV, free parking, and complimentary coffee or tea in the morning. Singles 135 pesos; doubles 165 pesos; triples 185 pesos; quads 225 pesos.

Hotel San José, Hidalgo 207 (☎915 51 30 or 915 14 31), next to Posada San Rafael. Somewhat institutional rooms with TVs, phones, and ceiling fans. Ask about the laundry service. Singles 135 pesos; doubles 165 pesos; triples 185 pesos; quads 210 pesos.

⚡ FOOD

You don't need to be loaded to get your grub on in Aguas. Check out the **San Marcos Plaza,** the shopping area north of Plaza de la Patria, and Madero. Although a chain, it would be neglectful to omit the fact that there is a **Tepozuieves** in Aguascalientes, Centro Parián at Juárez and Primo Verdad. If you are uninitiated, go and enjoy this unique and delicious *nieve.*

El Zodiaco, Galeana Sur 113 (☎915 31 81). The eye-opening decor combines an open kitchen, orange chairs, formica tables, live canaries, and a painted shrine to the Virgin. Order a sandwich (15 pesos) or a hamburger (15 pesos) from among the many tasty items in this popular local hangout. Open daily 8:30am-10pm.

Gorditas Victoria, Victoria 108 (☎91 8 17 92), next to the Hotel Rosales. The ever-popular restaurant serves up every kind of *gordita* (10.5 pesos) imaginable. Grab your food *para llevar* (to go) and enjoy it in the plaza. Open daily 8am-8pm.

Sanfer Restaurant, Victoria 204 (☎915 45 88). A cozy little place with unbeatable prices. Breakfasts (10-20 pesos), chicken tacos (24 pesos), and *milanesas* (36 pesos). *Comida corrida* is a 26-peso steal. Open daily 8:30am-9:30pm.

La Fogata, Moctezuma 111, across the street from the cathedral, in Plaza de la Patria. Those with a late-night craving for red meat should make tracks to La Fogata. Savor mammoth homemade tortillas—the preferred method (as opposed to forks) for eating your steak (28 pesos). Eclectic decor, with a copy of Da Vinci's *Last Supper* hanging next to a shot of a '69 Corvette. Open daily 5:30pm-2am.

Restaurant Vegetariano "de Venad," (☎918 27 21), at the corner of Zapata and Libertad, just north of Jardín San Marcos, is well worth the walk. Veggies and rice 35 pesos. *Quesadillas* 15 pesos. Open M-Sa 11am-7:30pm.

Rincón Maya, Abasolo 113 (☎916 75 74), across the park from Museo Guadalupe Posada. If the north is getting you down, get your fill of *tacos conchita, tamales yucantecos,* and *panuchosat* at this airy, southern-style restaurant. The *cafe de olla* is especially spicy and delicious. Prices aren't like they are down south, but this restaurant makes a lovely meal. Open daily 2pm-midnight.

SIGHTS

Aguascalientes is not famous for its sights, but many, particularly the art museums, are actually quite good.

MUSEO JOSÉ GUADALUPE POSADA. The museum displays morbidly witty turn-of-the-century political cartoons drawn by Posada, an ardent critic of the Porfiriato who perhaps inspired the scathing social commentary of later Mexican muralists such as Diego Rivera and José Clemente Orozco. The collection includes 220 of his original works and images, the most famous of which is of La Catrina, a society lady-*calavera* (skull) wearing an outlandish hat. Rivera used her figure in *Sueño de Una Tarde Dominical en la Alameda*, now on display in Mexico City (see **Mexico City: Sights,** p. 106). The museum also displays 100 works by Posada's mentor, Manuel Manilla, and has rotating exhibits of contemporary art. *(On León, next to the Templo del Encino, 4 blocks south of López Mateos.☎915 45 56. Open Tu-Su 11am-6pm. 10 pesos, students 5 pesos, children free; Su free.)*

PLAZA DE LA PATRIA. The part of the newly remodeled plaza that isn't a shopping mall is shaded by trees and made inviting by numerous benches. To the north, the plaza is bordered by the **Palacio de Gobierno,** constructed in the 1660s as a residence for the Marqués de Guadalupe. The interior of the Palacio houses several murals by Oswaldo Barra, a Chilean artist whose mentor was the famed Diego Rivera. To the south of the plaza is the **Teatro Morelos,** site of the 1914 Convention of Aguascalientes, in which rival factions led by Zapata, Carranza, and Villa grappled over the course of the Mexican Revolution.

BASÍLICA DE LA ASUNCIÓN DE LAS AGUASCALIENTES. The soft greys and rose-colored Solomonic Baroque facade of the 18th-century basilica make it the city's most remarkable structure and a center of daily activity. Look for the sculptures of church patrons San Gregorio, San Jerónimo, and San Agustín. The cathedral's interior, restored in the 18th and 19th centuries, is graced with high ceilings, gold trimmings, and ornate icons, along with 17th- and 18th-century paintings by José de Alcíbar, Andrés López, and Miguel Cabrera. *(In the center of Plaza de la Patria. Open daily approx. 7am-2pm and 4-9pm.)*

TEMPLO DE SAN ANTONIO. Take a walk down Zaragoza to get an appreciation of this large, unusual church which rises up at the end of the street. Construction of the church began in 1895 and was completed in 1908 under self-taught architect José Refugio Reyes. The mix of patterns on the interior murals, frescoes, oil paintings, and delicate stained-glass windows matches the eclectic exterior, which is a blend of many styles, including Baroque, Classical, and Oriental. *(On Pedro Parga and Zaragoza. From the plaza, walk 3 blocks down Madero, then 3 blocks left on Zaragoza. ☎915 28 98. Open M-Sa 6:30-10am, 11:30am-12:30pm, and 6-9pm, Su 6:30am-noon and 5:30-9pm.)*

CASA DE CULTURA. The institute hosts temporary sculpture, painting, and photography exhibits in a beautiful 17th-century *hacienda*. Kiosks in the courtyard are cluttered with listings of cultural events; you can also check Casa's monthly bulletin. *(Carranza 101 at Galeana.☎915 00 81 or 915 00 97 for monthly events. Open M-F 10am-2pm and 5-9pm, Sa-Su 10am-2pm and 5-8pm. Free.)*

CENTRO CULTURAL LOS ARQUITOS. Serving as a public bathroom from 1821 until 1973, the building became a beautiful cultural center in 1994 after a magnificent restoration process. It now houses a bookshop, a video room that shows children's movies (F 5pm), and a small museum. *(On the Alameda at Héroes de Nacozari.☎917 00 23. Open M-F 9am-1pm and 3-8pm, Sa 9am-1pm and 3-6pm, Su 9am-1pm.)*

MUSEO DE AGUASCALIENTES. Built in the 1900s, this museum was designed by José Refugio Reyes, who also designed the Templo de San Antonio. The bright orange museum showcases local and national art, highlighting the works of Aguascalientes native Saturnino Herrán. A strange collection of classical busts is tucked away in a corner of the building. *(On Parga and Zaragoza, across from Templo de San Antonio. Open Tu-Su 11am-6pm. 10 pesos, students and seniors 5 pesos; Su free.)*

JARDÍN DE SAN MARCOS. The area around the *jardín* was originally an Indian settlement, but around 1600, *indígenas* erected the **Templo Evangelista San Marcos** on the site. The small church still has services today and is the center of a crowded pedestrian thoroughfare popular with Mexican families in the evenings. The adjacent arcade is lined with bars and vendors and remains active late into the night. *(The jardín is a 5-10min. walk on Carranza from Plaza de la Patria. Church open daily 7am-2pm and 4-9pm.)*

HOT SPRINGS. Aguascalientes does, after all, mean "hot waters," and sure enough, there are several thermal *Balnearios* at the edge of town. The most accessible is **Baños Thermales de Ojo Caliente.** However, anyone who comes expecting a Roman spa may be disappointed. The turn-of-the-century building consists of many private thermal showers, and an outdoor swimming pool. The waters are reputed to have cured many cases of rheumatism. *(Balneario located across the Parque Urbano La Pona at the fork of Revolución and San Luis Potosí. To get there from the center take an east-bound bus from Maderoz and ask the driver if its bound for the Balneario. Open daily 7am-7pm. 70-180 pesos per hr., depending on size.)*

OTHER SIGHTS. Clustering around the *centro* are other museums worth a look. The **Museo de Arte Contemporaneo,** at the corner of Morelos and Verdad, houses a collection of contemporary art. (☎915 7953. Open Tu-W and F-Su 10am-6pm, Th 10am-8:30pm. 5 pesos, students and teachers 2.5 pesos.) The **Museo Regional de Historia,** Carranza 118, occupies yet another building designed by Refugio Reyes. The collection explores the area's history, from Pre-Hispanic to Revolutionary. (☎ 916 5228. Open Tu-Su 10am-7pm. 27 pesos.)

🎵 ENTERTAINMENT

Aguascalientes is not a beacon of wild nightlife, but the intrepid partier will find a good time. By city ordinance, *discotecas* in Aguascalientes are not allowed in the *centro histórico* around Plaza de la Patria and can only open their doors Thursday to Saturday. Bars, on the other hand, are open every night of the week and exist in particular concentration on Pani, between Ponce and Nieto, in the area of the San Marcos Fairgrounds just south of the Jardín. Buses stop running around 10pm, making taxis the best way to get around.

Merendero San Marcos, Arturo Pani 144. This bar and grill is one of the most happening places in town. Beer (16 pesos), tequila (30 pesos), and heart-felt live *mariachi* music are served to a mix of tourists and locals. Open daily 1pm-2am.

Disco El Cabús, (☎913 04 32), Zacatecas at Colosia in the Hotel Las Trojes. Shake your caboose amid the usual flashing lights and bass-heavy dance beats. Don't wear shorts, though—you may be apprehended by the fashion police. Cover Th-F 40 pesos, Sa 50 pesos. Open Th-Sa 9pm-3am.

Jubilee, Laureles 602-101 (☎917 05 07 or 918 04 94). The place to go if you value drinking over dancing. Drinks are about half as much as at other *discotecas,* and the lounging areas are more happening than the dance floor. Live music Th-Sa until 3am. Cover 30 pesos for men, women free. W no cover.

For dancing, also try **Metro,** Aguascalientes 507 (☎908 07 72) or **The Station,** Donaldo Colosio 129 (☎ 912-0990), which spin the usual electronic pop Mexican club mix Th-Sa after 10pm. Those not into the club scene may be able to find mellower diversions. Be part of Mexican *beisbol* by cheering on the hometown **Rieleros** (www.rieleros.com.mx). To get to the stadium, catch a #12, 24, or 25 bus heading east on López Mateos. Snag a bleacher seat in the sun (9 pesos) and compete with local kids in chasing down home run balls. (Games Apr.-Sept.)

During the ▉**Feria de San Marcos** (mid-Apr. to early May), one of Mexico's largest celebrations, everything from cockfights to milking contests takes place in the

Jardín de San Marcos. To reach the Expo Plaza, filled with shops and restaurants, walk two blocks to the left down the pedestrian route as you face the *templo* in the *jardín*. The expansive plaza has everything: a 10-screen movie theater, upscale dining and accommodations, great shopping, cheap snacks, and a rose garden. The festival of the patron saint of Aguascalientes, **La Romería de la Asunción** (Aug. 1-15), takes place with dances, processions, and fireworks. The **Festival de las Calaveras** (last week in Oct. and the 1st week in Nov.) is another occasion for the city to cut loose and celebrate.

SAN LUIS POTOSÍ

SAN LUIS POTOSÍ ☎ 4

With spacious plazas, plenty of pedestrian walkways, and cathedrals dotting the landscape like overgrown trees, San Luis Potosí (pop. 830,000) is a lesson in good urban planning. Founded in 1592, after Franciscan missionaries began to convert local Guachichil and Tlaxcaltec tribes, and prospectors discovered silver and gold, San Luis has twice served as the capital of Mexico. The tranquility of the city belies a tumultuous history—it was here in 1910 that Francisco Madero was incarcerated and wrote his dramatic *Plan de San Luis Potosí*, proclaiming the beginning of the Revolutionary War. Today, lanterns glow in the cathedrals and fountains at dusk, while bands, magicians, and soap-bubble blowers gather in the town plazas to entertain assembled crowds of young and old. On a warm evening, it's hard to ignore the feeling that San Luis Potosí is the quiet capital of some magical world.

◩ TRANSPORTATION

San Luis Potosí is at the center of a triangle formed by Mexico's three largest cities—Monterrey, Guadalajara, and Mexico City. Five main routes (**Rtes. 57, 85, 70, 49,** and **80**) snake their way into the city. Once in the city, the streets have a nasty habit of changing names as they pass through the main plazas, so keep that in mind (and a map in hand).

Airport: (☎822 00 95) 25min. north of the city. Tickets can be purchased at **2001 Viajes,** Obregón 604 (☎812 29 53). Open M-F 9am-2pm and 4-8pm, Sa 9:30am-2pm. **AeroCalifornia** (☎811 80 50), **AeroLiteral** (☎818 73 71), and **Mexicana** (☎813 33 99) fly to various destinations.

Buses: To get downtown from the **Central de Transportes Terrestres,** catch an "Alameda" or "Centro" bus (5:30am-10:30pm, 2 pesos) and hop off at Parque Alameda, the 1st big stretch of green. Continue walking in the direction the bus was going, up Othón, past Plaza del Carmen, until the city's center, Plaza de Armas (also called Jardín Hidalgo). A taxi costs 20 pesos. Del Norte (☎816 55 43) goes to **Chihuahua** (14hr., 10 per day, 572 pesos). Estrella Blanca (☎816 54 77) sends buses to: **Aguascalientes** (3hr., 7 per day, 87 pesos); **Monterrey** (7hr., every hr., 253 pesos); **Ciudad Valles** (4 hr., 10 per day, 166 pesos); **Guadalajara** (6 hr., 5 per day, 182 pesos); **Zacatecas** (3hr., every hr., 87 pesos). Omnibus de México (☎816 81 61) runs to: **Mexico City** (6 hr., 9 per day 12:45am-10:30am, 236 pesos); **Reynosa** (9hr., 2pm and 8pm, 377 pesos); **Saltillo** (5hr., 2 per day, 231 pesos); **Tampico** (7hr., 3 per day, 251 pesos). Transportes Tamaulipas and Noreste (☎816 69 64) jointly serve: **Matehuala** (2hr., 14 per day, 100 pesos) and **Matamoros** (10 hr., 2 per day, 377 pesos).

◪ PRACTICAL INFORMATION

TOURIST, FINANCIAL, AND LOCAL SERVICES

Tourist Office: Visitors to San Luis have the luxury of two excellent offices. **Turismo Municipal** (☎812 27 70) is on the 1st fl. of the Palacio Municipal, at the northeast cor-

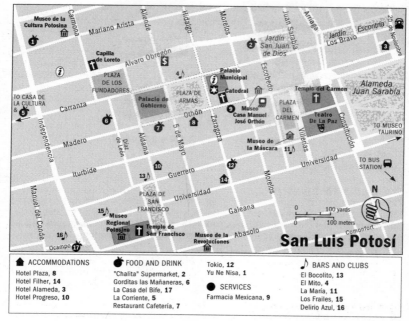

San Luis Potosí

ACCOMMODATIONS	FOOD AND DRINK		BARS AND CLUBS
Hotel Plaza, **8**	"Chalita" Supermarket, **2**	Tokio, **12**	El Bocolito, **13**
Hotel Filher, **14**	Gorditas las Mañaneras, **6**	Yu Ne Nisa, **1**	El Mito, **4**
Hotel Alameda, **3**	La Casa del Bife, **17**	SERVICES	La María, **11**
Hotel Progreso, **10**	La Corriente, **5**	Farmacia Mexicana, **9**	Los Frailes, **15**
	Restaurant Cafetería, **7**		Delirio Azul, **16**

ner of Plaza de Armas. Friendly, English-speaking staff and excellent information. Open M-F 8am-7pm, Sa-Su 10am-2pm. The **state tourist office**, Obregón 520 (☎812 99 39) is 1 block west of Plaza de los Fundadores. Information on attractions in the rest of the state. Open M-F 8am-9pm, Sa-Su 8am-2pm.

Consulate: US, Mariel 103 (☎812 15 28). Take a "Morales" bus. Open M-F 8:30am-1:30pm. In case of an emergency, the police and the tourist office have consulate employees' home numbers.

Currency Exchange: Casas de cambio can be found along Morelos, north of Plaza de Armas. **San Luis Divisas** (☎812 66 06), at the corner of Morelos and Bocanegra, usually accepts traveler's checks. Open M-Sa 9am-8pm. Many banks lie near Plaza de Armas and are open M-F 9am-3pm. **Banamex,** at Allende and Obregón, 1 block east of Plaza de Armas, has a 24hr. **ATM** and exchanges traveler's checks with no commission.

American Express: Grandes Viajes, Carranza 1077 (☎811 11 27), will help you out with lost or stolen checks or cards but does not cash traveler's checks. Open M-F 9am-2pm and 4-6pm.

Luggage Storage: At the bus station. 4 pesos per hr., 40 pesos per day.

Supermarket: Chalita, on the corner of Bravo and Escobedo, 3 blocks north of Plaza de Armas. Open daily 9am-9pm.

Laundry: Lavandería La Gotita, on 5 de Mayo and Comonfort. 20 pesos for a medium load. Open M-Sa 10am-8pm.

Car Rental: Hertz, Obregón 670 (☎812 95 00). 280 pesos per day plus insurance and mileage. Must be 25. Open M-F 9am-2pm and 4-8pm, Sa 9am-2pm.

EMERGENCY AND COMMUNICATIONS

Emergency: ☎060 or 072.

Police: (☎812 54 76 or 812 25 82) can always be found in the Palacio Municipal. Keep your eyes out for the special female division of the police. Formed in 1998, "Minerva" aims to protect citizens and help tourists.

Red Cross: (☎815 36 35 or 820 39 02), on Juárez at Díaz Gutiérrez.

Pharmacy: Farmacia Mexicana, Othón 180 (☎812 38 80), by the cathedral. Open 24hr.

Hospital: Hospital Central, Carranza 2395 (☎813 03 43 or 817 01 64), 20 blocks west of the *centro*. Some English spoken.

Fax: Computel, Carranza 360 (☎812 01 89; fax 812 01 86), opposite Hotel Panorama. Open M-Sa 7:30am-9pm.

Internet Access: CNCI, Othon 150 between Plaza de Armas and Plaza del Carmen. (☎812 01 06). Open M-F 7am-9pm, Sa 9am-7pm.

Post Office: Morelos 235 (☎812 27 40), 1 block east and 3 blocks north of Plaza de Armas. Open M-F 8am-3pm, Sa 9am-1pm. Contains a **MexPost.** Open M-F 9am-3pm, Sa 9am-1pm.

Postal Code: 78000.

ACCOMMODATIONS

The cheapest hotels are located near the bus station or at Los Bravos and 20 de Noviembre. If you dislike small, dark rooms, head to the *centro*, where old hotels relive their glory days with large rooms, plaza views, and surprisingly low prices.

■ **Hotel Filher,** Universidad 335 (☎812 15 62), at the corner of Zaragoza, 3 blocks south of Plaza de Armas. By far the most gorgeous rooms in San Luis Potosí. Bright paintings, beautiful wool bedspreads and wooden furniture adorn each room. Amenities include bottled water, TVs, phones, and A/C. Singles 270 pesos; doubles 320 pesos.

Hotel Plaza, Jardín Hidalgo 22 (☎812 46 31), on the south side of Plaza de Armas. This hotel, the city's 1st, has seen better days, but the clean rooms have old-fashioned charm. Ask for a balcony so you can watch and hear the action all night long. Singles 200 pesos; doubles 220 pesos; triples 230 peso.

Hotel Progreso, Aldama 415 (☎812 03 66), off Guerrero, near Plaza de San Francisco. Tall, dark hallways lead to clean dark rooms. Squint your eyes and you can imagine its former beauty. Fans and hot water in all rooms. Singles 165 pesos; doubles 180 pesos; triples 195 pesos; quads 215 pesos.

Hotel Alameda, Callejón La Perla 3 (☎814 89 01), next to the PEMEX station on the northwest corner of the Alameda, is the cheapest option in San Luis Potosí. Rooms are small, dark, and in minor disrepair, but the water is hot and the manager is friendly. Singles 90 pesos; doubles 100 pesos; triples 150 pesos.

Motel Potosino, Carretera Mexico, km 426 (☎818 25 56), on the left after you exit the bus station. A good choice if you're unable to get into the more scenic downtown. Spacious, carpeted rooms with TV and phone. Singles 220 pesos; doubles 280-400 pesos.

FOOD

San Luis Potosí boasts some of the best food in Northeast Mexico. The mango and cantaloupe sold on the street (with chile and lime) is always fresh and ice-cold. *Gorditas* and *sopas*, sold at ridiculously low prices, are made in front of you. *Enchiladas potosinos*, a regional favorite, are stuffed with cheese and then fried. Cactus is used to make such diverse dishes as *melcocha* (molasses candy) and *nopalitos* (cactus slices cooked in a salty mixture of garlic, onion, and tomato sauce). The sheer number and range of restaurants near the *centro* will satisfy even vegetarians and those looking for international cuisine.

■ **La Corriente,** Carranza 700 (☎812 93 04 or 812 19 65). The decor is a cross between your grandfather's ranch house and the garden of Eden; red tile floors and stucco walls meet a skylight and hanging vines. The traditional Mexican food manages to surpass the relaxing ambience. Try the divine *enchilados potosinos* (36 pesos) or a juicy steak with guacamole and black beans (75 pesos).

Yu Ne Nisa, Arista 360 (☎814 36 31). Even carnivores will be delighted with this vegetarian restaurant and health food store. The lime green counter-top and chairs are reminiscent of a 50s diner. Delicious veggie burgers smothered in guacamole and served with carrot salad are only 20 pesos. A variety of fruit juices and yogurt concoctions are created behind the counter. Open M-Sa 9:30am-8:30pm.

Restaurant Cafetería (☎812 29 57), with the orange doors on Madero, just west of Plaza de Armas. It may not look like much, but at one of the 3 tiny tables, you can get a lip-smacking breakfast, lunch, or dinner (*tortas* and *gorditas* 15-25 pesos, meals 20-60 pesos), and rare and scrumptious desserts (10-15 pesos). Open M-F 8am-9pm.

La Guëra, Tata Nacho 799 (☎811 87 28), on the left as you approach the Parque Tangamanga, on the block before the entrance. This traditionally decorated treasure offers some of the best meals in all of Northeast Mexico. Specializes in breakfast (35 pesos; 8:30am-noon) and *comida corrida* (45 pesos; 1-6pm). From the pickled *nopalito* garnish to the homemade *mole*, everything here is excellent. Open Tu-Su 8:30am-6pm.

Tokio, Zaragoza 305 (☎814 61 89). Only the jade-colored decor fits the quasi-Japanese name. Tokio serves tasty Mexican dishes in a cool, modern atmosphere. *Comida corrida* (30 pesos) starts at 1:30pm. Open daily 7:30am-11pm.

Churrasqueria, La Casa del Bife, Ocampo #135 (☎812 36 83), behind Plaza de San Francisco. This Argentinean restaurant is the chic choice of upper-class *potosinos*. Start with cheese or meat *empanadas* (25 pesos) and splurge on the house specialty beef roasted in front of your eyes; thin cut (95 pesos) or thick cut (130 pesos). Open Tu-Th noon-6pm, F-Sa 1pm-midnight, Su 1-6pm.

Gorditas las Mañaneras, on Díaz de León between Madero and Carranza. In this speedy joint, division of labor is the name of the game. While one woman pats tortillas into shape, another minds the griddle and adds cactus, eggs, beans, and cheese to your *sopa* (4 pesos) or *gordita* (3 pesos). Still another packages your food, handles the money and hands you an unforgettable eating sensation. Open daily 6am-2pm.

◎ SIGHTS

As the former center of the state's booming silver and gold trade, prosperous San Luis Potosí had the money and the stature to build some of the country's finest museums, cathedrals, and plazas. The sheer number of beautiful sights can be almost intimidating; fortunately, the majority have historical markers in English and Spanish and are within easy walking distance of each other. When exploring churches, please avoid interrupting mass.

PLAZA DE ARMAS. Called the "City of Plazas," San Luis Potosí has four main town squares. The most central of these is Plaza de Armas, filled with trees and lounging *potosinos*. At the start of the 17th century, residents watched bullfights from the balconies of the surrounding buildings. Since 1848, a red sandstone gazebo bearing the names of famous Mexican musicians has graced the plaza, which hosts local bands. Today, loudspeakers hooked up to the gazebo blare popular music, political announcements, and soccer games. *(Concerts Th and Sa evenings.)*

PALACIO DE GOBIERNO. The west side of Plaza de Armas is marked by the Neoclassical facade of the Palacio de Gobierno, constructed in 1798. Briefly serving as the capital of the country in 1863, the structure was renovated in 1950 and now functions as San Luis Potosí's administrative center. Displays on the second floor feature murals, statues, plaques, and legends. It was in this building that President Benito Juárez signed former emperor Maximilian's death sentence in 1867. *(Open M-F 9am-2:30pm. Free.)*

CATEDRAL SANTA IGLESIA. Opposite the Palacio de Gobierno stands the cathedral, with two bell towers that play a different melody every 15min. The cathedral was completed in 1710, and "upgraded" when San Luis Potosí became a diocese in 1855. Miners donated gold and silver to glorify the interior, and marble statues of the apostles (copies of those at the Basilica of San Juan de Letrán in Rome) stand between the Solomonic columns of the Baroque facade. *(Open daily 8am-7pm.)*

MUSEO CASA MANUEL JOSÉ OTHÓN. This small museum was once the house of one of Mexico's greatest poets. Manuel José Othón (1858-1906). The museum preserves the house's appearance at Othón's death and displays some of his manuscripts and photographs. (Othón 225 between Escobedo and Movelos. Open Tu-F 10am-2pm and 4-6pm. 2 pesos.)

PLAZA DEL CARMEN. The bright, lively Plaza del Carmen, two blocks east of Plaza de Armas, hosts Sunday festivals, and during the week street performers, vendor stands, and a young crowd mill around at night.

TEMPLO DEL CARMEN. This serene church was constructed from 1749-1764 and is regarded by many *potosinos* to be the most beautiful religious building in the city. It features hanging chandeliers, golden altars, and a huge mural of the Crucifixion. During the Mexican Revolution, the government used the convent to jail local rebels. Once released, the prisoners went on to lead the revolt of San Luis Potosí. *(In the northeast corner of Plaza del Carmen. Open daily 7am-1:30pm and 4-9pm.)*

TEATRO DE LA PAZ. This theater is one of the four most famous and acoustically well-constructed in Mexico—most performers don't need microphones. The *salón* holds a collection of modern art, the foyer is filled with sculptures and murals, and the theater hosts everything from international dance festivals to "Sesame Street Live." The best news? Prices are cheap. *(Behind Templo del Carmen. ☎ 812 26 98. Pick up a schedule at the tourist office or look for posters outside the theater. 40 pesos and up.)*

MUSEO NACIONAL DE LA MÁSCARA. The museum displays ancient and modern masks from all over Mexico, from devils to dancing cows. Most masks have ceremonial origins, and many were used in elaborate dances. Check out the oversized *mojigangas* in the hall—these enormous, eccentric representations are paraded in the streets during seasonal festivals. *(Villerías 2, in Plaza de Carmen across from Teatro de la Paz. ☎812 30 25. Open Tu-F 10am-2pm and 5-7pm, Sa-Su 10am-2pm. 3 pesos.)*.

MUSEO TAURINO. By 1895, San Luis Potosí had an active bullring that housed up to 7500 spectators. Today, the abandoned "Plaza de Toros" contains statues of bull fighters. Across the street, the Museo Taurino shows off an impressive collection of posters and suits of famous bullfighters. Experience the romance and the violence of the bullfighting culture. *(On Universidad east of Alameda. Walk up the stairs and over the freeway to get there. Open Tu-Sa 11am-2pm and 5:30-8pm. Free.)*

JARDÍN DE SAN FRANCISCO. San Luis Potosí has at least one garden for each of its seven districts. This one, on Plaza de San Francisco, is distinguished by its bronze fountain, cobblestone streets, and red sandstone buildings. Recently, the west side of the garden on Universidad has become a nightlife hotspot. Enjoy the many bars, cafes, and artisan sellers that crowd the street.

IGLESIA DE SAN FRANCISCO. Construction began on the Iglesia de San Francisco, on the west side of the garden by the same name, in the 1860s. Less ornate than its counterparts, the orange stucco facade displays a Baroque interior beautifully accentuated by flickering votives. *(Open daily 6:30am-1:30pm and 4:30-9pm.)*

MUSEO REGIONAL POTOSINO. The museum occupies the grounds of a former Franciscan convent. The first floor contains artifacts from all over Mexico, including a collection of Pre-Hispanic Huasteca relics. On the second floor, the marvelous **Baroque Capilla a la Virgen de Aranzazu** is displayed. According to legend, a local 18th-century shepherd found the altar's wooden image of the Virgin Mary in a prickly thicket. The name *aranzazu* means "from within the thorns." *(On Independencia near the corner of Galeana, behind Iglesia de San Francisco. ☎814 35 72. Open Tu-Su 10am-7pm, Su 10am-5pm. 10 pesos; Su free.)*

MUSEO DE LAS REVOLUCIONES (MUSEO MARIANO JIMENEZ). This museum is the birthplace of revolutionary Mariano Jimenez. Guides will gladly explain the significance of the richly painted murals, and a rotating gallery shows some of the best artwork in San Luis Potosí. *(On 5 de Mayo between Abasolo and Comonfort. ☎814 73 93. Open Tu-F 10am-2pm and 4-6pm, Sa 9am-3pm, Su 10am-2pm. Free.)*

MUSEO DE LA CULTURA POTOSINA. This museum, geared to children, uses interactive displays to teach the history of San Luis Potosí, beginning with man's arrival in Mexico in 22,000 BC. *(On Arista 340 to the west of Plaza de los Fundadores. ☎812 18 33. Open Tu-F 10am-2pm and 4-6pm, Sa-Su 10am-2pm. 3 pesos.)*

CASA DE LA CULTURA. This beautiful mansion, complete with immaculate gardens and marble sculptures, was built in 1919 and became a museum in 1970. Lose yourself among the dazzling antiques and paintings. *(Carranza 1825. ☎813 22 47. Open Tu-F 10am-2pm and 4-6pm, Sa 10am-2pm and 6-8pm, Su 10am-2pm. 6 pesos.)*

PARQUE TANGAMANGA. With lakes for paddle-boating and fishing, a baseball field, electric cars, and bike paths, this *parque* is an ideal place to picnic and spend the day lounging. The tree- and lawn-filled park is huge, but you can rent a bike to explore it all. *(Catch a Route #10 "Perimetral" bus on Constitución across from the Alameda (20 min., 2 pesos). Get off at Monumento a la Revolución, a statue of soldiers firing rifles, in the middle of a rotary. Facing the soldiers' backs, take a left and go 3 blocks. Open Tu-Su 9am-6pm. Bike rental 20 pesos per hr.)*

MUSEO DE LAS CULTURAS POPULARES. Parque Tangamanga houses this museum of indigenous crafts and rare photo exhibitions of indigenous communities and ceremonies. *(☎817 29 76. Open Tu-Su 9am-4pm. 2 pesos.)*

🔲 NIGHTLIFE

Much of San Luis Potosí's nightlife revolves around upscale bars and live music. Recently, the area around Plaza de San Francisco has become very popular, including the upstairs of **El Bocolito,** a restaurant on Guerrero in the north corner of the plaza. A rowdy crowd of all ages congregates here for music and food. (☎812 76 94 or 812 73 97. Live music W-Sa 9pm-2am.) You are sure to find students from the university mingling upstairs at **Cafe Los Frailes,** Universidad 165. (☎812 58 26. Live music F-Sa 9pm-midnight.) For serious dancing, head to Independencia and Ocampo, where patrons of **Delirio Azul** shake their hips (among other things) to the rhythms of *salsa.* Closer to *el centro,* **El Mito,** on Plaza de Armas, is *the* place to be on a weekend night. An exclusive young crowd packs the dance floor and adjoining balcony as DJs spin the latest Latin dance and pop. (☎814 41 57. Cover F-Sa 50 pesos. Open W-Sa 9pm-2:30am.) **La María,** at the corner of Escobedo and Guerrero, pumps electronica in a small former home near Plaza del Carmen. Check out the 5m-deep well in the middle of the dance floor, a vestige of the city's past. Fortunately, a grate keeps tipsy patrons from stumbling in. (☎812 36 44. Cover F-Sa men 25 pesos, women 15 pesos. Open Th-Sa 9pm-2am.) Also close to the *centro* is **Staff,** Carranza 423, where a young, gay-friendly crowd grooves to Latin dance music. (☎814 30 74. Cover 25 pesos. Open F-Su.)

🔲 SHOPPING

While the city's quiet plazas and fountains of the *centro* are usually devoid of frantic shoppers and crowded stores, shops line Morelos north of Plaza de Armas, and vendors sell silver and crafts on Universidad east of Plaza de San Francisco. The best shopping can be found along Hidalgo, called Zaragoza south of the plaza. This pedestrian street has blocks and blocks of small stores, coffee shops, and *heladerías* (ice cream stands). If you are looking for a change from all the usual tourist buys, drop into **Puros,** Carranza 325. This gorgeous shop sells Mexican, Cuban, Jamaican, and Dominican cigars. Buy a "Te Amo" Mexican cigar and send it home to the one you love. (☎810 43 00. Open daily 10am-9pm.)

FESTIVALS

The last two weeks of August mark the **Fiesta Nacional Potosina,** often called FaNaPo. With concerts, bullfights, fireworks, and a parade, a splendid time is guaranteed. However, the festival pales in comparison with the city's celebration of Semana Santa. The powerful culmination of this festival is the **Procesión del Silencio** on the evening of Good Friday. This silent procession involves 25 *cofradías* (local groups), who bear life-like statues portraying the events leading to Christ's death. The **Festival Internatcional de Danza Contemporaneo** invades San Luis Potosí the last week of July and the first week of August, as dance groups from around the world come to participate in Mexico's most important dance festival.

MATEHUALA   ☎ 4

Although Matehuala (pop. 100,000) derives its name from a Náhuatl phrase meaning "don't come," this former mining town is anything but unfriendly. The few tourists who do trickle in are mostly adventure-seeking backpackers en route to Real de Catorce, who are often surprised to find the town so relaxing and pleasant.

▐ TRANSPORTATION

Matehuala is 261km from Saltillo and 191km from San Luis Potosí. The **Central de Autobuses** is located on 5 de Mayo, just south of the city and near the large, red *Arco de Bienvenida.* Across the street from the station, a *pesera* labeled "Centro" will take you downtown (2 pesos)—ask the driver to let you off near the cathedral, or get off at Hidalgo, next to the Chalita market. **Taxis** charge 20 pesos for the trip. The bus station provides the consolidated services of Transportes del Norte, Frontera, Estrella Blanca, and El Águila to: **Mexico City** (7hr., 9 per day, 345 pesos); **Monterrey** (4hr., every hr., 177 pesos); **Nuevo Laredo** (7hr., 10 per day, 148 pesos); **Querétaro** (6hr., 3 per day, 212 pesos); **Saltillo** (3hr., every hr., 148 pesos); **San Luis Potosí** (2hr., every hr., 100 pesos). Noreste (☎882 09 97) serves **Monterrey** (4hr., every hr., 177 pesos) and **Reynosa** (7hr., 8 per day, 273.5 pesos). Tamaulipas (☎882 27 77) goes to **Real de Catorce** (5 per day, 34 pesos) and **San Luis Potosí** (2 hr., 18 per day, 100 pesos). A smaller bus station (☎822 08 40), at Guerrero and Mendez, travels to Real de Catorce (34 pesos) and will take you to the Central de Autobuses to reach all other destinations.

✳🛈 ORIENTATION AND PRACTICAL INFORMATION

Constantly forking or changing names, the streets of Matehuala are confusing, but so short and close together that you'll never be lost for long. **Hidalgo** runs north-south through most of the city; **Juárez** runs parallel to the west. Most points of interest lie somewhere on or not far from the intersection of **Hidalgo** and **Morelos.**

Tourist Information: Cámara de Comercio (☎882 01 10), Morelos 427, 1 block east of Hidalgo. These friendly people will even let you use their computer for **internet access** (15 pesos per hr.). Open M-F 9am-1:30pm and 4-7:30pm. **Maps** are for sale (15-20 pesos) at the blue **Papelería Corias,** Morelos 512, across the street and ½ block from the Cámara de Comercio. Open daily 9am-8:30pm.

Currency Exchange: Casas de cambio dot the *centro,* all offering good rates. **Bital,** 111 Reyes (☎882 48 18), exchanges cash and traveler's checks and has a 24hr. **ATM.** Open M-Sa 8am-7pm.

Markets: Chalita, on Hidalgo 2 blocks from the cathedral, sells groceries and clothing. Open daily 8am-8pm. The **indoor market** next to the Templo de la Inmaculada Concepción sells crafts and produce. Open daily 9am-6pm.

Laundry: Lavandería Acuario (☎882 70 88), Betancourt and Madero, offers self-service wash and dry for 40 pesos per 5kg. Open daily 8:30am-2pm and 4-8pm.

Emergency: ☎060.

Police station: (☎882 06 47), next to the bus station.

Red Cross: (☎882 07 26), at Ignacio y Ramírez and Betancourt, about 8 blocks east of the fork from Morelos.

Pharmacy: Farmacia del Centro, Morelos 623 (☎882 05 92). Open daily 9am-midnight.

Hospital: Hospital General (☎882 04 45), on Hidalgo a few blocks north of the *centro*. Little English spoken.

Fax: Telecomm, 5 de Febrero at Juárez (☎882 00 08), a few blocks east of the *centro*. Also houses a **Western Union** office. Open M-F 9am-7pm.

Post office: (☎882 00 71), at Valle and Negrete. Walk up Constitución, turn right on Independencia 1 block before Iglesia Santo Niño, turn right again on Negrete, and it's on your left at the corner. Open M-F 8am-3pm, Sa 9am-1pm.

Postal code: 78700.

ACCOMMODATIONS

Budget accommodations populate the *centro*. Starting at around 50 pesos, the *casas de huéspedes* on Bocanegra are the cheapest options, but spending slightly more will get you considerably nicer rooms.

Hotel y Casino Del Valle, Morelos 621 (☎882 37 70), right off Plaza de Armas. Comfort and fun reasonable prices. Balconies on each floor, ceiling fans, *agua purificada*, TVs, and an attached dance hall make this hotel as swank as a Las Vegas casino. 200 pesos per person; each additional person 25 pesos. Maximum 4 per room.

Hotel del Parque (☎882 55 10), on the corner of Rayon and Bocanegra. Luxury digs close to the *centro* and next to Parque Vincente Guerrero. Beautiful carpeted rooms with A/C, cable TV, and telephone. Singles 350 pesos; doubles 390 pesos; triples 430 pesos; each additional person 30 pesos.

Hotel Matehuala, Bustamante 134 (☎882 06 80), just north of Plaza de Armas. A huge (empty) tiled courtyard is monasticly reflective. Though the rooms are as dark as confessional booths, the soaring ceilings with wooden rafters, white walls, and rust-colored bureaus are decidedly appealing. Ask for a room with a balcony and windows to the outside. Singles 150 pesos; each additional person 25 pesos.

Hotel Blanca Estela, Morelos 406 (☎882 23 00), next to the video store. Fans cool small, clean, colorful rooms with TVs. Beautiful wooden furnishings give a classy feel to the rooms in this narrow hotel. Check in early; this may well be the most crowded place in town. Singles 130 pesos; doubles 150 pesos.

Hotel Álamo, Guerrero 116 (☎882 00 17). Small tiled rooms surround a bright courtyard. Each room comes with its own TV and bathroom. Singles 100 pesos; doubles 140 pesos; each additional person 60 pesos.

FOOD

The few restaurants in Matehuala are family-owned cafeterias, clustered around Plaza de Armas, with good food at low prices. **Restaurant Fontella,** Morelos 618, between hotels Casino and Matehuala, serves some of the best food in town. Charcoal-roasted specialties 27-34 pesos. (☎882 02 93. Open daily 7:30am-4am.) **Pizza Italia y Giovanni,** on Guerrero across from Plaza de Armas, offers delicious, cheap pizza. Dig into 12 slices of hot cheese and thick-crust heaven for only 60 pesos. Beer 12 pesos. (☎882 29 55. Open daily 11am-midnight.) **La Cava,** Callejón del Arte 1, between Hidalgo and Morelos, is a pleasant escape from the merciless sun. The sleek dining room serves a mix of Mexican, French, and American cuisine (33-50 pesos). Cocktails here are especially smooth. (☎882 28 88. Open M-Sa 2-10:30pm)

👁 SIGHTS

Standing solemnly at the center of Matehuala between Juárez and Hidalgo is the recently completed **Templo de la Inmaculada Concepción,** a copy of Saint Joseph's Cathedral in Lyon, France. Construction began in 1905, but poor funding slowed progress. In front of the main cathedral is **Plaza Juárez,** now permanently occupied by vendor stalls and makeshift cafes. Sprawling onto adjoining streets, the bazaar is collectively known as **Mercado Arista,** selling leather and ceramic goods and slews of cheap plastic trinkets. Relax amidst the limited greenery and street vendors that define **Parque Vicente Guerrero.** For a larger expanse of grass and a pick-up game of basketball, head to **Parque Álvaro Obregón,** just south of Insurgentes.

REAL DE CATORCE   ☎ 4

Once a thriving mining town with 30,000 inhabitants, Real de Catorce now looms mysteriously on the side of a mountain, a veritable ghost town with barely 1500 residents. Once one of the largest silver producers in the country, the early 20th century brought on flooding, destruction, and desertion, leaving behind the empty mine shafts and carts that give Real de Catorce its eerie feel. Today, backpackers and travelers trek to see this town's *burro*-trodden paths and brick ruins and to pay respect to the town's patron saint, Saint Francis. Huichol Indians make springtime pilgrimages to Real de Catorce to gather peyote, which they consider sacred.

⬅ TRANSPORTATION

To get to Real de Catorce, you must go through Matehuala. From Matehuala's cathedral, walk one block up Hidalgo, take a left onto Guerrero, and walk down two blocks to Mendez. Buses leave from the station at the corner of Guerrero and Mendez. The bus also stops at the Matehuala bus station. Autobuses Tamaulipas (☎ 882 08 40) will bring you to Real de Catorce (1½hr.; M-Su 7, 8, 10am, and noon; 36 pesos). Confirm schedules with the bus driver and arrive early if possible.

The ride to "Real de 14" is guaranteed to whiten the knuckles of the timid traveler; the bus rambles along a winding path chiseled into the mountain, and riders change to a smaller bus for the tunnel at the end of the ride. This bus trip, complete with loud *norteño* is the true beginning to the Real de Catorce experience.

✦🛈 ORIENTATION AND PRACTICAL INFORMATION

The town's main road is **Lanzagorta,** which runs from the bus stop past the famed cathedral and a few hotels and restaurants to a town square. Constitución runs parallel to Lanzagorta up the hill, through **Plaza Principal.**

There are no financial services in Real de Catorce, and hotels do not accept credit cards. Tourist brochures and helpful information can be found in a small room past Hotel Mesón de Abundancia on Lanzagorta. **Police:** at the **Presidencia Municipal,** next to Plaza Principal. **Caseta:** on a side street running perpendicular to Constitución, next to the Presidencia Municipal. (☎ 882 37 33. Open M-Sa 9:15am-3pm and 5-8pm, Su 10am-3pm.) **Post office:** on Constitución to the right of the Presidencia Municipal as you are facing it, on the right side of the street. (Open M-F 9am-1pm and 3-6pm.) **Postal Code:** 78550.

🏠🍴 ACCOMMODATIONS AND FOOD

For so tiny a town, Real de Catorce has a number of good budget accommodations. Hotel prices vary drastically according to season and day of the week (weekends are the most expensive). Those traveling to Real de Catorce during *Semana Santa,* December, or in July and August should book in advance and be prepared for steeper prices. The *casas de huéspedes,* on the streets off of Lanzagorta, offer the cheapest lodging. Most hotels are beautiful and richly decorated. For lower price without lower quality, try **Hotel San Francisco,** on Terán right off Constitución. The family-run hotel has only a few rooms, but it is clean and comfortable. (90 pesos, with bath 120 pesos.) A more luxurious option is **El Mesón de la Abundancia,** Langazorta 11. This former town treasury is the oldest building in town and houses rooms adorned with private terraces and sitting rooms. (☎887 50 44. Singles 250-450 pesos; matrimonials 550 pesos; triples and quads 650 pesos.). The adjoining restaurant/bar serves superb Mexican and Italian entrees (50 pesos). At **Hotel El Real,** the antique furniture, tiled bathrooms, and personal balconies will make you feel like you're on a honeymoon. (☎887 5058. Singles 300-500 pesos; each additional person 100 pesos.) The Hotel's Restaurant **El Real,** with its dim, intimate atmosphere, proves that Mexico really can do Italian. Pizzas and pasta dishes 50-90 pesos. **Hotel Providencia,** Lanzagorta 29, offers a few bare-bones rooms (singles 150 pesos; doubles 200 pesos) and a few more expensive and modern rooms with bathtubs and impressive views (singles 250 pesos; doubles 300 pesos). The restaurant downstairs serves *comida corrida* (25 pesos). At the corner of Zaragoza and Iturbide lies the newly-opened **El Ángel y El Corazon,** a vegetarian restaurant and holistic center. The ever-changing menu features Mexican, Arab, and Italian vegetarian specials (50 pesos).

👁 SIGHTS

Real de Catorce is home to the most beautiful church in northeast Mexico: **Templo de la Purísima Concepción,** down Lanzgorta on the right. The altar retains its original stucco and painting of the Virgin of Guadalupe and houses a life-size image of St. Francis, whose miracles have created a devoted following. The rectangular blocks of wood on the floor are doors to subterranean tombs, and side rooms are filled with letters to St. Francis giving thanks for everything from miraculous cures to visa waivers. Across from the cathedral, the **Casa de Moneda,** formerly a mint, houses a small photography exhibit of the town. (Open daily noon-2pm. Free.) At the corner of Morelos and Constitución is **Cine Club.** From Hitchcock to Disney cartoons to recent box office hits, this independent movie house is a gold mine. (F 9am, Sa 9am, Su 11am. "Voluntary donation" 15 pesos, children 12 pesos.)

Much of the action in Real revolves around the gazebo at **Jardín Hidalgo,** beyond the cathedral between Lanzagorta and Constitución. *Norteño* and *mariachi* bands occasionally play there. On Xicotencatl off Zaragoza, the terraced steps of the **Palenque de Gallos** (cock-fight ring) replicate the layout of a classic Athenian theater. At the top of Zaragoza stands the white **Capilla de Guadalupe** (also called the **Panteón**). At the high end of Constitución lies **El Mirador,** an area full of ruined miners' homes that offers a vista of the city. The surrounding cliff, known as **El Voladero,** grants breathtaking views of mountains and valleys, dry riverbeds, and herds of cows on distant hilltops.

For a **horseback tour** of the region, walk from the bus stop down Lanzagorta until you reach Plaza Hidalgo. To the left across Lanzagorta is a stable that rents out horses (40 pesos per hr.). Try a 2hr. trip to **Ciudad de las Fantasmas** (Ghost City), an abandoned mining town nearby, or a descent into desert valley. If you're feeling really adventurous, make a two-day trip to a nearby ranch. The guides expect a tip of 50 to 70 pesos; try to arrange a fixed price before the trip.

FESTIVALS

La Semana Santa is the most celebrated festival in Real de Catorce. Nightly parades and glittering candles light up the usually peaceful mountain evenings. October 4 is the feast day of St. Francis of Asisi, Real de Catorce's beloved patron saint. From the end of September through October, the normally quiet town explodes with activity as visitors come from all over Mexico to pray at the cathedral. This **Feria de San Francisco** packs the streets with daily and nightly *fiestas* outside of the cathedral. Local hotels double their rates, but buses run in and out of town every 20min., ensuring that everyone can enjoy the festivities.

NORTHEAST MEXICO

CIUDAD VALLES ☎ 1

Ciudad Valles (pop. 350,000) is a major crossroads between northeast and central Mexico, and provides the easiest access to the state's Huastecan region, including Xilitla. Commonly known as Valles, the hot and dirty city lacks the charm and culture of San Luis Potosí.

The **Central de Autobuses** lies on the outskirts of town, on Luis Venegas. To get into town, exit the station and take any "Mercado" bus (3 pesos); this will take you to the station for municipal buses. Tickets for **taxis** are available from the **ServiBus** stand in the middle of the station (15 pesos to the *centro*).

From the station, Oriente (☎382 39 02) serves: **Ciudad Victoria** (4hr., 20 per day, 113 pesos); **Guadalajara** (10hr., 5 per day, 332 pesos); **Matamoros** (8hr., 8 per day, 285 pesos); **Monterrey** (7½hr., 10 per day, 292 pesos). Vencedor goes to: **San Luis Potosí** (5hr., 1 per hr., 156 pesos); **Tampico** (2½hr., 1 per hr., 87 pesos); **Xilitla** (1½hr., 1 per hr. 4am-7pm, 37 pesos).

Banorte, on the corner of Hidalgo and Carranza, has a 24hr. **ATM. Red Cross:** (☎382 00 56). **Police:** (☎382 21 85 or 382 27 38). **Post office:** Juárez 520. (☎382 01 04. Open M-F 8am-3pm, Sa 9am-1pm.) **Postal code:** 79000.

If you find yourself stuck in Valles for a night, the area around the bus station has several good, inexpensive hotels. **Hotel San Carlos,** Venegas 140, across the street from the bus station, offers bright, clean rooms with TV and much-needed A/C. (Singles 150 pesos; doubles 200 pesos.) For an easy meal, **Restaurant Don Felix,** also across from the station, serves *comida corrida* for 20 pesos and cheap *antojitos*. (Open daily 7:30am-11:30pm.)

XILITLA ☎ 1

A narrow road snakes through the rocky *huasteca* highlands to the lush hamlet of Xilitla (hee-LEET-la; pop. 10,000). Only 1½ hr. from and 1000m above Ciudad Valles, the jungle-like wilds of Xilitla are a completely different world. Sixty small communities, surviving mainly on coffee production, surround the main town. Due to dropping coffee prices, efforts have mounted to develop eco-tourism in the area. Xilitla serves as the gateway to over 150 caves (including the 450m-deep, six-acre **El Sótano de las Golondrinas**), dozens of waterfalls, wild orchid sanctuaries, rare animals, horseback trails, and rivers ripe for rafting. The most notable attraction, however, is the beautiful and bizarre architectural feat of **Las Pozas** (the pools). Built by English millionaire Edward James, this tribute to surrealism includes three waterfalls, nine pools, and over 36 fantastic and whimsical structures. Be forewarned: rainy season in Xilitla takes place from 5-7pm every day.

■ TRANSPORTATION AND PRACTICAL INFORMATION. The bus station sits on the hillside just below town. Vencedor runs to: **Ciudad Valles** (1½hr., 1 per hr. 5:30am-7:30pm, 37 pesos); **San Luis Potosí** (6½hr.; 5am, 12:30, 1:30pm; 172 pesos); **Tampico** (4½hr., 7 per day, 119 pesos). To get to **Plaza Central,** officially **Jardín Hidalgo,** on foot, go up the stairs to the right of the bus station and turn right on Zaragoza. The plaza is a 5min. uphill walk away. **Taxis** to Las Pozas wait up the stairs to the left of the station (60 pesos).

THROUGH THE LOOKING GLASS Friend and patron to an entire generation of artists, Edward James's own artistic dreams were only realized after he discovered the jungle paradise of Las Pozas. Here, he expressed his dedication to fantasy and surrealism by creating a jungle labyrinth of nature and concrete and earning recognition from the same surrealist innovators that he once championed: "Look we move among a bunch of 'pseudo-realists,' who...produce nothing but junk. So, they try to act like madmen to justify themselves. On the other hand, you who are really mad, labor to act sane."—Salvador Dalí to Edward James.

Tourist information about Xilitla can be found at **www.junglegossip.com**, the website of **El Castillo**, a lovely resort down the hill from Xilitla's main plaza. Exchange currency or traveler's checks at **Centro de Cambio**, on the right-hand side of Zaragoza as you walk toward the plaza. (☎365 02 81. Open daily 8am-8pm.) **Banorte**, on the Zaragoza side of the plaza, also exchanges currency and checks and has a 24hr. **ATM.** (☎365 00 29. Open M-F 9am-2:30pm.) **Police:** in the Palacio Municipal (☎365 00 85; no English spoken). **Emergency:** call police station—Xilitla has neither a hospital nor a Red Cross. **Pharmacy: Farmacia San Agustín**, on Hidalgo, at the northwest corner of Plaza Principal. (☎365 01 25. Open daily 8:30am-9pm.) No **LADATELs**, but there is a long-distance public phone in the Hotel Ziyaquetzas, on the Zaragoza side of the plaza. **Post office:** in the back of the Palacio on Zaragoza, 2nd fl. (Open M-F 9am-3pm.) **Postal code:** 79902.

▐▐ ACCOMMODATIONS AND FOOD. In mid-summer and during *Semana Santa*, Xilitla's few but wonderful hotels fill up fast and require reservations. Down the hill from Jardín Hidalgo is gorgeous **Posada El Castillo** (The Castle), Ocampo 105. El Castillo was the former home of Plutarco Gastelum, close friend of Edward James and foreman of the Las Pozas Project. Each of the nine rooms have high ceilings, huge windows, and a balcony or veranda. The swimming pool offers an extraordinary view of the surrounding jungle. (☎365 00 38. Rooms 300-600 pesos.) Six cabins are available for rent in **Las Pozas**. The bare rooms come with hot water and sturdy wooden beds. The experience of sleeping in the jungle, in complete solitude next to concrete structures and rushing waterfalls is unforgettable. (☎365 02 03. Reception 9am-8pm at the entrance of Las Pozas. Singles 140 pesos; doubles 280 pesos; triples and quads 380 pesos.) **Hotel Ziyaquetzas**, Zaragoza 110 opposite Jardín Hidalgo, offers small, clean rooms with fans and astounding views. (☎365 00 81. Rooms 150-180 pesos.)

The open-air **restaurant at Las Pozas** is an attraction unto itself. Tourists from the world over gather to devour traditional cuisine—the thick corn tortillas and *huevos a la mexicana* (25 pesos) are superb. (Open daily 9am-6pm, subject to the whims of the cook.) In town, tiny restaurants line the plaza, offering meals at rock-bottom prices. Try **La Flor de Cafe**, Calle Hidalgo 215, left of the church. Behind the bright mural, a group of women from surrounding communities rotates chef duties. (Tamales 2 pesos, enchiladas 3 pesos, chicken with rice and beans 16 pesos.)

◙ SIGHTS. ◙Las Pozas (The Pools), formally called the **Enchanted Garden of Edward James**, are Xilitla's main attraction. Head downhill on Ocampo; continue as it veers right and turns into a path after the northwest corner of the plaza. This path lets you out onto the main road at a white bridge. Cross the bridge and take your first left, following the upward dirt path until you get to a gravel road; make a left and walk about 2km. After 40min., Las Pozas will be on your right. Those with sore feet can take a *combi* (5 pesos) from the top of the stairs near the bus station to the white bridge, or find a taxi to take you right to the gate (60 pesos). The son of a wealthy nobleman, Edward James was an old-fashioned English eccentric. An aspiring artist and friend of Salvador Dalí, his early experiments in poetry and art were largely unsuccessful. In the early 1950s, James visited Xilitla and, enchanted by its natural beauty, decided to build his home as a living surrealist monument. The result is a universe of concrete, steel, and stone in wild colors and even wilder shapes. The melange of bridges, arches, and artistic relics recalls *Alice in Wonderland*, with doors that open into nothing, winding staircases that lead nowhere, a library without books, and other touches of madness. James channeled the waterfall running through Las Pozas's 36 structures into nine pools—don't forget your bathing suit. (Open daily 9am-8pm. 15 pesos.)

If a day of exploring Las Pozas hasn't exhausted you, the nearby **Cueva del Salitre** (Parrot Cave) makes a good early evening excursion. To reach the cave, head down Ocampo, take a left at Morelos, and follow the road to its end. There, take a left and walk past the PEMEX station. A few hundred meters later, you will come to a mechanic's shop. The cave is a 5min. walk down the hill behind the shop; you may want to ask the mechanics to help find you a guide (a 10-peso tip is appreciated). Each night at dusk, over 200 green and yellow parakeets gather outside the cave, squawking and creating an impressive spectacle.

In town, Xilitla's historical draw is the quietly greying **Templo de San Agustín,** on the west side of the plaza. Built between 1550 and 1557, the ex-convent is the oldest colonial building in the state. Though the exterior could use a good whitewashing, the interior is beautifully preserved, and the large, quiet courtyard is surrounded by altars and childrens' creations.

For the commercially inclined, shops selling fruit, shoes, crafts, and trinkets line either side of the plaza on Zaragoza and Escobedo. Each August 28, the plaza comes alive for the **Feast Day of San Agustín,** with fireworks and regional dances.

CIUDAD VICTORIA   ☎ 1

Ciudad Victoria (pop. 230,000) may be the sleepiest state capital in Mexico. On the edge of the Sierra Gorda, Victoria makes an ideal stopover near the US border. The city also serves as a good starting point for exploring the great outdoors. Among the sights a short ride from the city are **Cañón del Novillo,** a glorious spot for hiking and camping, and **Boca de San Juan Capitán,** a beautiful stream. Ardent naturalists or those simply looking for escape may enjoy a visit to the **Reserva de la Biosfera El Cielo,** approximately 100km from the city. Though unexciting, Ciudad Victoria offers a relaxed, welcoming environment for the weary traveler.

⊏ TRANSPORTATION. From the **Central de Autobuses,** a "Boulevard" minibus can take you to the *centro* (3 pesos). From there, walk two blocks up Calle 8 or 9 to Plaza Hidalgo, the home of most of Ciudad Victoria's attractions. A taxi will cost about 30 pesos. From the station, Transpaís (☎316 77 99) runs to: **Ciudad Valles** (4hr., every hr., 110 pesos); **Matamoros** (4hr., every hr., 149 pesos); **Reynosa** (4hr., every hr., 152 pesos); **Tampico** (3½hr., every hr, 113 pesos). Transporte del Norte (☎316 01 38) runs to **Monterrey** (4hr., 7 per day 9:15am-10:45pm, 144 pesos) and **San Luis Potosí** (10hr., every hr., 166 pesos).

⊒⊓ ORIENTATION AND PRACTICAL INFORMATION. The **tourist office,** Calle 8 #1278, between Anaya and Ramírez, seven long blocks past the cathedral, will be happy to tell you everything you need to know about Victoria and the state of Tamaulipas. (☎314 05 21. Open daily 9am-9pm.) Exchange currency or traveler's checks at **BanCrecer,** on Hidalgo in the main plaza, which also has a 24hr. **ATM. Luggage storage** is available at the bus station. (3.5 pesos per hr. Open daily 7am-10:30pm.) **Market: Tienda ISSSTE,** on Calle 13 between Matamoros and Guerrero. (Open daily 9am-8pm.) **Laundry: Lavandería Virues,** Matamoros 939, between Calles 8 and 9. (Wash 10 pesos, dry 30 pesos. Open M-Sa 9am-8pm.) **Emergency:** ☎066. **Police:** ☎312 01 95 or 312 42 43. **Red Cross:** ☎316 20 77. **Hospital General Libramiento Fidel:** 1845 Velázquez Ote. 1845 (☎316 21 97). **Pharmacy: Benavides,** on the corner of Hidalgo and Calle 9. (Open 24hr.) **Internet Access: Tel.Net Cyber Cafe,** Calle 8 between Hidalgo and Juárez, off of Plaza Hidalgo, also provides **fax** service. (☎315 39 26. 18 pesos per hr. Open daily 8am-11pm.) **Post Office:** on Calle 8 between Morelos and Matamoros, in the Palacio Municipal. (Open M-F 8am-7pm, Sa 8am-noon.) **Postal Code:** 87000.

⌐⊏ ACCOMMODATIONS AND FOOD. While expensive luxury hotels surround Plaza Hidalgo, quality budget lodging can be found a few steps away, hiding in the nearby streets. **Hotel de Escandon,** Calle 8 143, just off the plaza, provides comfortable rooms and three square meals a day. The rooms face a small courtyard, protected from the brutal sun by a sky-blue dome. (☎312 90 04. Singles 132 pesos, with bath, A/C, and TV 230 pesos; doubles 162 pesos, 240 pesos.)

If you get an urge to lose the backpack and don the bow tie, try some of the fancy restaurants in the hotels around the *centro*. On the other end of the spectrum, street-side vendors line the shopping area on Hidalgo by Calle 7 until about 6pm. The filling *comida corrida* (30 pesos) at **Cafe Canton,** Colón 114, just south of the plaza, soothes the palate and helps beat the empty-wallet blues. (Entrees, from *antojitos* to hamburgers, 20-40 pesos. Open daily 6am-10pm.) **Restaurant Carolina,** next to the Posada Don Diego, is an even better value. (Breakfasts 20 pesos, entrees 15-35 pesos, *comida corrida* 25 pesos. Open daily 6am-10pm.)

⌾ 🗐 SIGHTS AND ENTERTAINMENT. As the state capital, Ciudad Victoria's **Palacio de Gobierno,** on the corner of Hidalgo and Calle 17, is appropriately grandiose and harbors large, impressive murals. The **mercados** north of Hidalgo between Calle 6 and 7 offer everything from crafts to goat liver. For those craving knowledge, **Museo de Antropología e Historia,** on the north side of Plaza Hidalgo, is supposedly open M-F 9am-7pm, but often closes unexpectedly. The collection displays indigenous art and artifacts, historical photographs, and assorted fossils.

Victoria provides relatively easy access to **El Cielo Reserva de la Biosfera,** the state's most impressive nature reserve. Often referred to as simply "La Reserva," it encompasses more than 300,000 acres of lush vegetation, mountains, and wildlife. The area supports hundreds of species of birds, reptiles, and mammals; including bears, armadillos, pumas, and jaguars. To reach the reserve by bus, go to the Transpaís booth at the bus station and ask for a ticket to la "griega" (the "Y") of Gómez Farías. You'll get on a bus to Ciudad Mante, but make sure to have the driver let you off at the "Y," about two hours from Victoria (112km). After disembarking, wait for a blue minibus that takes you to downtown Gómez Farías (every hr., 5 pesos). There, register at the **caseta de vigilancia** in order to enter the reserve. Further information and accommodations are available in town. Take a 7km hike or rent the services of a 4-wheel-drive taxi (up to 1000 pesos per day). The friendly staff at Ciudad Victoria's office of **Dirección General de Recursos Naturales y Medio Ambiente** (☎312 60 18), on Calle 13 between Guerrero and Bravo, can help the ecotourist plan the perfect adventure.

If you come to Ciudad Victoria in the second week of October, be sure not to miss the **Ciudad Victoria Expo,** featuring music, dancing, and artisanry from the area.

CENTRAL MEXICO

The states of **Guanajuato** and **Querétaro** form a vast, bowl-shaped plateau of fertile soil, rolling farms, and verdant hillsides, that shelters some of Mexico's most alluring colonial cities. For more than 500 years, their silver-rich land has brought the region prosperity and shaped its history. In the 18th century, the city of Guanajuato supplied most of Mexico's minting silver, later becoming the commercial and banking center of this thriving region. Today, the area is home to a growing expatriate population in and around San Miguel de Allende, one of the most lively and culturally charged cities in the republic. Nearby relatively untouristed and mountainous **Hidalgo** attracts tourists to the stunning archaeological site of Tula and numerous hiking opportunities in the Sierra Madre Oriental.

After docking in Veracruz in 1919, Cortés worked his way inland, making his mark on **Puebla** and **Tlaxcala,** where many local tribes joined his entourage. A glimpse into one of the region's 16th-century temples, where images from *indígena* mythology mingle with Catholic icons, illustrates the pervasive strength of these indigenous cultures in the face of attempts at complete destruction.

Contrary to popular belief, the **Estado de México** has more to offer than chaotically overpopulated Mexico City. Outside of the giant smog cloud that contains the *Distrito Federal*, wide green plains creep up snowy volcanoes and bustling towns expand against their natural barriers. The state is speckled with impressive archaeological sites, solemn convents, and vestiges of the colonial era.

After Emperor Maximilian built his summer home in Cuernavaca, thousands of Mexicans eagerly followed him and made the state of **Morelos** a prime vacation destination. Mexicans and foreigners alike come to take advantage of Cuernavaca's "eternal spring," Xochicalco's beautifully desolate ruins, and Tepoztlán's striking landscape. Unlike the frenetic capital, parts of surrounding Morelos remain undeveloped, with plentiful tree-covered vistas and unspoiled streams.

HIGHLIGHTS OF CENTRAL MEXICO

DAYDREAM the day away in the perfect colonial town of **Valle de Bravo** (see p. 327).

BURROW underground and wander through the narrow and dimly lit tunnels of the **great pyramid of Cholula** (see p. 356), one of the largest in the world.

DRINK a round or two with your new language-school friends in artsy and intelligent **San Miguel de Allende** (see p. 310).

SHOW OFF your historical knowledge by reciting the *Grito de Dolores,* in little **Dolores Hidalgo** (see p. 316), where Miguel Hidalgo first proclaimed Mexican independence.

FLIRT shamelessly with the brawny and massive statues of warriors at the archaeological site of **Tula** (see p. 325), once the capital of the Toltec Empire.

SALSA your way through the dizzying array of posh nightclubs in sophisticated **Cuernavaca** (see p. 332).

STARE into the wizened, dried-out eye sockets of naturally mummified bodies at **Guanajuato**'s creepy **Museo de las Momias** (see p. 308).

FATTEN UP on the delicious mole dishes and the million and one types of sweets created by centuries of cloistered **Puebla** cooks (see p. 348).

Central Mexico

N

75 miles

75 kilometers

Gulf of Mexico

San Andrés
Tuxtla
Catemaco
145

Santiago
Tuxtla

Tuxtepec

Veracruz

150

OAXACA

VERACRUZ

Córdoba

Huautla

Xalapa

Tehuacán
125

Huajuapan
de León

Papantla

150

Tuxpan

El Tajín

PUEBLA

190

SIERRA MADRE ORIENTAL

Pachuca

TLAXCALA

Tlaxcala

Puebla

Cholula

105

HIDALGO

Netzahualcóyotl

MORELOS

SAN LUIS POTOSÍ

Tula

Mexico
City

Popocatépetl

Cuernavaca

57

Tequisquiapan

Teotihuacán

95

Querétaro

15

Toluca

Taxco

Iguala

Cacahuamilpa

QUERÉTARO

MEXICO

GUERRERO

GUANAJUATO

57

Zitácuaro

Valle de
Bravo

Dolores
Hidalgo

Guanajuato

San Miguel
de Allende

Salamanca

45

Morelia

León

Pátzcuaro

Lagos de
Moreno

La Piedad

Uruapan

AGUASCALIENTES

45

15

Zamora

MICHOACÁN

Lázaro
Cárdenas

Aguascalientes

80

JALISCO

COLIMA

PACIFIC OCEAN

GUANAJUATO

GUANAJUATO ☎ 4

The contours of Guanajuato's (pop. 110,000) future—the peaks of economic realization and the pits of horrific repression—were mapped out in 1558, when massive veins of silver were discovered in the area. Over the next 200 years, the city would become one of Mexico's wealthiest, supplying much of the world's silver. Wealth without liberty, however, meant little to the *guanajuatense* men and women; after getting fat under Spanish rule, Guanajuato bit the hand that had fed it. It was during Hidago's stop here in 1810 that the wealthy and poor united, helping to defeat the Spanish at Alhóndiga de Granaditas. Though the electrifying spirit of the War for Independence is long gone, Guanajuato is livelier than ever. The city's serpentine streets overflow with monuments honoring silver barons and revolutionary luminaries, while *callejones* sneak through Spanish archways and courtyards, leading to myriad museums, theaters, and cathedrals.

▛ TRANSPORTATION

GETTING AROUND

Guanajuato's **bus station** is 3km west of town. An "El Centro" bus will take you to the heart of the city, while "Mercado" buses go to the market. Buses cross the city running westward above ground and eastward underground (every 5 min. 6am-10:30pm, 2.5 pesos). Drivers shout locations rapidly and incoherently—ask if you're unsure. Taxis cost about 15 pesos in town.

GETTING AWAY

Buses: To get back to the Central de Autobuses, take a "Central de Autobuses" bus from Plaza de la Paz. A taxi will make the trip for 30 pesos. Primera Plus/Flecha Amarilla (☎ 733 13 33) offers 1st-class service to: **Celaya** (2hr., 2:45pm, 64 pesos); **Guadalajara** (4hr., 8 per day 9am-11pm, 193 pesos); **León** (50min., 7 per day 9am-11:30pm, 30 pesos); **Mexico City** (4½hr., 10 per day 5:30am-midnight, 227 pesos); **Salamanca** (1hr.; 5:30, 8am, 12:30, and 3:30pm; 37 pesos); **San Miguel de Allende** (1½hr.; 3, 5:15, and 7:15pm; 62 pesos). 2nd-class service is only to **Aguascalientes** (3hr., 5 per day 6:20am-4:10pm, 90 pesos); **Dolores Hidalgo** (1½hr., every 20min. 5:20am-10:20pm, 30 pesos); **San Luis Potosí** (5hr.; 7:20am, 1, 4:40, and 7:40pm; 114 pesos). Omnibus de México (☎ 733 26 07) offers similar service, while Futura/Estrella Blanca (☎ 733 13 44) travels to more distant locations.

✳❼ ORIENTATION AND PRACTICAL INFORMATION

Guanajuato lies 380km northwest of Mexico City. The city's tangled maze of streets and *callejones* can leave even the best navigator dizzy. **Plaza de la Paz**, the **basílica**, and **Jardín Unión** mark the center of town. **Juárez** climbs eastward past the *mercado* and Plaza de la Paz, becoming Obregón just past the *basílica*, and turning into **Sopeña** after Teatro Juárez.

Tourist Office: Coordinación de Turismo, Plaza de la Paz 14 (☎ 732 15 74; fax 732 42 51; turismo@quijote.ugto.mx.), on your right as you head up Juárez from the market. Good free maps and expensive historical pamplets. English spoken. Open M-W 9am-7pm, Th-F 9am-8pm, Sa 10am-4pm, Su 10am-2pm.

Currency Exchange: Banks line Juárez and Plaza de la Paz. **BITAL**, Plaza de la Paz 59 (☎ 732 00 18). Open for exchange M-Sa 8am-7pm. **Banco Bilbao Vizcaya**, Plaza de la Paz 69 (☎ 732 94 78). Open for exchange M-F 8:30am-4pm.

Laundry: Lavandería Automática, Manuel Doblado 28 (☎ 732 67 18). Self- and full-service. Wash and dry 38 pesos. Open M-Sa 9am-2pm and 5-8pm.

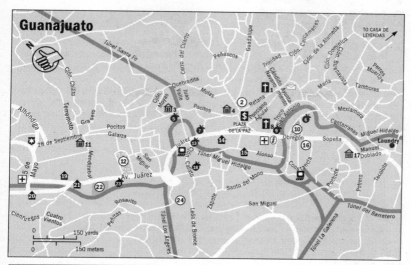

Guanajuato

📛 ACCOMMODATIONS
Casa Kloster, 15
Hotel La Condesa, 14
Hotel Posada del Carmen, 19
Hotel Posada San Francisco, 21
Posada Hidalgo, 20

🚹 🏛 ○ SIGHTS
Basílica de Nuestra Señora
de Guanajuato, 8

Callejón del Beso, 24
Jardín de la Reforma, 12
Jardín Unión, 10
Mercado Hidalgo, 22
Museo de la Alhóndiga
de Granaditas, 11
Museo del Pueblo de Guanajuato, 4
Museo Iconográfico del Quijote, 17
Museo y Casa de Diego Rivera, 3

Teatro Juárez, 16
Templo de la Compañia, 1
Universidad de Guanajuato, 2

🍎 FOOD
Carnitas Sam, 13
La Loca Rana, 5
Panaderia Purisima, 23
Picasso's Cafe, 7
Restaurant Crisalida, 18
Restaurant Pengüis, 6
Truco No. 7, 9

Emergency: ☎060.

Police: Alhóndiga 10 (☎732 02 66 or 732 27 17). Some English spoken.

Red Cross: Juárez 131 (☎732 04 87), 2 blocks past the *mercado*. No English spoken.

Pharmacy: San Francisco de Asis, Aguilar 15 (☎732 89 16), just off Plaza de la Paz. Open daily 7am-10:30pm.

Hospital: Clínica Hospital de Especialidades (☎732 23 05 or 732 13 38), in Plaza de la Paz. No English spoken.

Supermarket: Comercial Mexicana (☎732 96 28), 2 blocks past the market on Juárez. Open M-Sa 8am-10pm, Su 8am-9pm.

Fax: Telecomm, Sopeña 1 (☎732 27 47), to your left facing Teatro Juárez. Open M-F 8am-7pm, Sa-Su 9am-2pm.

Internet Access: Redes Internet Guanajuato, Alonso 70 (☎732 06 11; root@redes.int.com.mx). 10 pesos per hr. Open M-F 9am-8pm, Sa-Su 24hr. **Servicom,** Constancia 9. 8 pesos per hour. Open M-Sa 9am-11pm.

Post Office: Ayuntamiento 25 (☎732 03 85), across from the Templo de la Compañia. Follow Truco, the street running behind the *basilica*, for 1 block and turn left. Open M-F 9am-5pm, Sa 9am-1pm.

Postal Code: 36000.

🚩 ACCOMMODATIONS

A few inexpensive hotels populate the area around the *basílica*. More economic lodgings surround the *mercado*. Those visiting on weekends or during *Festival*

Cervantino in October should make reservations in advance and expect higher prices. The tourist office has a list of families who rent rooms during the festival.

☒ **Casa Kloster,** Alonso 32 (☎ 732 00 88). Clean, airy dorms overlook an open courtyard filled with flowers and birds. Sparkling communal bathrooms. Friendly international students lounge in the upstairs sitting room. Extremely helpful management. Reservations recommended. 80-90 pesos per person.

Hotel Posada San Francisco, Juárez 178 (☎ 732 24 67), the big brown hotel next to the market. Bright rooms with shiny baths, bottled water, and TVs. Be aware of the street noise, and make reservations for weekends. Singles 180 pesos; doubles 225 pesos.

Posada Hidalgo, Juárez 220 (☎ 732 31 45), 1 block past the *mercado*. Rooms have faux wood paneling and tiny baths. The restaurant inside serves breakfast and lunch (all-you-can-eat 40 pesos). Singles 100 pesos; doubles 170 pesos; triples 225 pesos.

Hotel La Condesa, Plaza de la Paz 60 (☎ 732 14 62). Neon signs and suits of armor brighten up the spooky lobby. Rooms with baths are old but clean. Expect noise from the *discoteca* downstairs. Students can sometimes get a discount. Singles 100 pesos; doubles 130-200 pesos; triples and quads 250 pesos. Ask about student discounts.

Hotel Posada del Carmen, Juárez 111-A (☎ 732 93 30) near the market. Spiral-carved stone columns decorate the courtyard, and small rooms have tiled baths, TVs, double beds, and a slightly rank smell. 100 pesos per person.

▶ FOOD

An abundance of inexpensive restaurants inhabit Guanajuato's plazas. Prices near **Jardín Unión** rise proportionally with the ratio of *gringos*-per-square-inch. Several open-air bargains exist at Mercado Gavira, to the left of Mercado Hildalgo.

☒ **Truco No. 7,** Truco 7 (☎ 732 83 74), the 1st left beyond the *basílica* heading toward the *jardín*. Artsy, funky, dark, and popular with locals. Fruit salad 16 pesos, sandwiches 10 pesos, espresso 8 pesos, cappuccino 16 pesos. Open daily 8:30am-11:30pm.

Picasso's Cafe, Juárez 5B (☎ 732 38 25), houses dozens of replications of Pablo Picasso's works painted by the owner, who has also constructed all the furniture and created 20 different cappuccinos (18 pesos). Delicious *chilaquiles* (30 pesos) and *antojitos* (20-25 pesos). *Sincronizadas* and sandwiches (15 pesos) and a stocked bar may keep you here late into the night. Open Tu-Su 10am-10pm.

Carnitas Sam, Juárez 6 (☎ 732 03 55). Savory *carnitas* (cut and marinated pork) draw customers late. Good-sized tacos 4 pesos. Open M-Sa 8:30am-3am, Su 8:30am-6pm.

Restaurant Pingüis, Allende 1 (☎ 732 14 14), at the northern tip of the *jardín*. Enormous breakfasts and rock-bottom prices attract hordes of Mexicans (and bargain-seeking travelers) to this diner-style restaurant. The service is about as fast as the senior citizen waitresses can manage, but *molletes a la mexicana* (10 pesos) and *pan frances* (14 pesos) are worth the wait. Coffee 7 pesos. Open daily 8:30am-9:30pm.

Restaurant Crisalida, Calixto 20, up the hill from Plazuela de los Angeles. This vegetarian restaurant serves a mountain-like *comida corrida* (35 pesos). For the less ravenous, chomp on a soy burger (12 pesos) on the outdoor patio. Open M-Sa 2-6pm.

Panaderia Purisima, Juárez 138 (☎ 732 01 14), on the right side, 1 block past the *mercado*. Follow the wafting scents of fresh-baked rolls, *galletas* (cookies), and pastries (1-4 pesos). Open daily 6am-10pm.

La Loca Rana, Pozitos 32 (☎ 732 13 25), across the street from Diego Rivera's house. Catch a *fútbol* game while filling up on the tasty 3-course *menú del día* (30 pesos). Breakfast 17-20 pesos. Open M-Sa 8am-8pm.

◉ SIGHTS

Guanajuato's many attractions range from the historically fascinating to the mind-numbingly grotesque. Most sights are located in the *centro*.

JARDÍN UNIÓN. One block east of the *basílica*, the triangular *jardín* is the town's social center, boasting enough shops, cafes, and guitar-strumming locals to satisfy any tourist. During afternoons and evenings, crowds gather on shady benches and listen to the state band perform. *(Th 6pm, Su noon and 6pm.)*

TEATRO JUÁREZ. Completed in 1903 for dictator Porfirio Díaz, the theater has an unabashedly ornate Doric-Roman facade—columns, lampposts, statues, bronze lions, and eight staring muses. In addition to housing government offices, the Teatro hosts plays, operas, ballets, classical music concerts, and the main events of *Festival Cervantino*. *(☎ 732 01 83. Faces the corner of Jardín Unión. Open Tu-Su 9am-1:45pm and 5-7:45pm, except performance days. 10 pesos, students 5 pesos. Performances Sa 8pm; tickets 50-80 pesos.)*

▨ MUSEO ICONOGRÁFICO DEL QUIJOTE. This gorgeous example of 18th-century Spanish architecture contains 10 large galleries displaying over 600 works of art inspired by Cervantes's anti-hero Don Quijote, including paintings, sculptures, stained-glass windows, clocks, and chess pieces created by artists such as Dalí, Picasso, Daumier, Ocampo, and Coronel. *(Manuel Doblado 1. East of Jardín Unión following Sopeña. ☎ 732 33 76 or 732 67 21. Open Tu-Sa 9am-6:30pm, Su 9am-2pm. Free.)*

BASÍLICA DE NUESTRA SEÑORA DE GUANAJUATO. This elegant 17th-century Baroque structure took 25 years to construct. Dozens of candelabra illuminate the Doric interior, decorated with fine ornamental frescoes and paintings of the Madonna by Miguel Cabrera. A wooden image of the city's protectress, Nuestra Señora de Guanajuato, rests on a pure silver base and is believed to be the oldest piece of Christian art in Mexico. *(On Plaza de la Paz. Basílica open daily 8am-9pm.)*

TEMPLO DE LA COMPAÑÍA. Completed in 1765, this Jesuit temple and college was shut down in 1785; just two years later, the Jesuits were expelled from Spanish America altogether. In 1828, the building hosted the Colegio del Estado, which spawned the city's modern university. The ornate stone exterior remains striking, with four Churrigueresque facades still intact. Left of the altar is the entrance to a small art museum, which includes a 17th-century painting of San Ignacio de Loyola and an 18th-century representation of San Francisco de Asis. Ending the exhibit is a spooky *relicario*, a wooden shelf enveloped in gold leaf and holding human bones. *(Next to the university and 1 block north of the basílica. ☎ 732 18 27. Open daily 7:30am-9:30pm. Museum open M-Sa 10am-4pm. 5 peso donation requested.)*

MUSEO DEL PUEBLO DE GUANAJUATO. This 18th-century colonial mansion houses a permanent collection of 18th- and 19th-century works by Mexican artists and rotating exhibits of contemporary art. A 7ft. tall red paper-maché devil-man glares down from the ceiling. *(Positos 7. ☎ 732 29 90. Open Tu-Sa 10am-6:30pm, Su 10am-2:30pm. 15 pesos, students 5 pesos.)*

▨ MUSEO Y CASA DE DIEGO RIVERA. The museum chronicles the life of Guanajuato's most famous native son, born in 1886 in this house. Visitors can admire the many beds from his childhood home and then move upstairs to study chronologically arranged works representing his artistic periods. Don't miss the watercolor illustrations for the *Popol Vuh* (the sacred book of the Maya), which imitate Maya iconography, nor Rivera's preliminary sketch for a section of the mural commissioned in 1933 by New York's Rockefeller Center, which was later destroyed. The museum also holds photos of Rivera and his wife, Frida Kahlo. *(Positos 47. ☎ 732 11 97. Open Tu-Sa 10am-6:30pm, Su 10am-3pm. 10 pesos, students 5 pesos.)*

CALLEJÓN DEL BESO. According to local lore, a Spanish aristocrat living on one side of the "Alley of the Kiss" became so upset upon discovering his daughter kissing her forbidden lover across the alleyway, that he flew into a rage and stabbed her to death. *(From Juárez, walk south along Plaza de los Angeles and turn left into the alley.)*

MERCADO HIDALGO. Established in 1910 in honor of the 100th anniversary of the struggle for independence, the *mercado* sells everything from meat to hand-crafted woolen dolls. Most of the fun is haggling over the price. The market is also home to some of the best and cheapest meals and candies in town. *(One block down Juárez from the Callejón del Beso. Most stalls open daily 9am-9pm.)*

MUSEO DE LA ALHÓNDIGA DE GRANADITAS. Originally built in 1809 to guard the city's grain supply, this neo-classical building witnessed the victory of Mexican hero "El Pípila," who massacred over 300 Spaniards holed up here on September 28, 1810. After Hidalgo's rebellion was squelched, the angry Spanish displayed the severed heads of the executed leaders—Hidalgo, Allende, Aldama, and Jiménez—from the corners of the building. Today, the Alhóndiga is an ethnographic, archaeological, and historical museum. Captivating murals covering the ceiling and sides of the stairwells are often mistaken for those of José Clemente Orozco or Diego Rivera; the true painter, José Chávez Morado, was a contemporary of both artists. One of the most striking murals features his interpretation of the display of Hidalgo's head—lit by unearthly fire and stuck in a bird cage. *(At the west end of Pozitos on the corner of Mendizabal. Open Tu-Sa 10am-1:30pm and 4-5:30pm, Su 10am-2:30pm. ☎ 732 11 12. 30 pesos; students, seniors and children under 13 free; Su free.)*

■ **MUSEO DE LAS MOMIAS.** The high mineral content of Guanajuato's soil naturally mummified the 122 corpses now on display in the museum. Cautiously tread through catacombs like the *Salón de Culto a la Muerte*, and view morbid holograms, a mummified fetus, and torture weapons of the colonial era, including a fierce-toothed chastity belt. Gag at the purplish, inflated body of a drowning victim; a woman buried alive, frozen in her attempt to scratch her way out of the coffin; two fashionable Frenchmen; a man who died by hanging; and another who was stabbed. The museum's oldest mummy has been here for around 135 years, while its youngest has been on display for less than 15 years. The most popular sight in Guanajuato, the mummies draw a larger crowd than less gory museums downtown. At the exit, vendors offer visitors candy figurines of the more memorable mummies, some wearing little *sombreros*. *(Next to the city cemetery west of town. Take a "Las Momias" bus (2 pesos) from in front of the basílica or the market. From where it lets you off, walk up the street to the left, and follow signs. To return, catch a bus in the same spot across the street. ☎ 732 06 39. Open daily 9am-6pm. Museo de las Momias 20 pesos, students and seniors 14 pesos, children 12 pesos. Museo del Culto de la Muerte 8 pesos.)*

MONUMENTO AL PÍPILA. Looking down on the *jardín* from a nearby hill, the Monumento al Pípila commemorates the miner who torched the Alhóndiga's front door and opened the way for a riotous massacre of the Spanish. The titanic Pípila looks best at night when he is illuminated by spotlights. While the view from the base is striking, the top of the monument affords a magnificent vista of the city and the surrounding mountains. Pay a peso to climb the narrow staircase inside the monument to a small platform behind the back of the infamous miner. For a panoramic view of the city while descending the hill, follow the steeper path down the west side, which ends near the *Tunel de los Angeles*. If you're planning to walk up at night, take a friend. *(Follow Sopeña to the east and take the steep but manageable Callejón del Calvario to your right (5min.) before Sopeña starts to curve, or hop on a "Pípila" bus from Plaza de la Paz (2 pesos). Open daily 8am-8pm.)*

CASA DE LEYENDAS. The museum aims to preserve *Guanajuatense* legends, with dioramas and moving figures retelling many of the city's tragic and humorous myths. Cringe as you watch the father of the famous lover from *Callejón del Beso* violently stab his daughter, then enter an elevator and "descend" into a mine filled with snakes, skeletons, and miners' unrealized dreams. *(Catch a "La Presa" bus (2.5 pesos) down in the subterranean tunnels and ask the driver to let you off at Escuela Normal. From the Escuela, walk up the unmarked street to your left for 2 blocks. Veer left at the fork; the museum will be in front of you at Súbida del Molino and Panorámica. ☎ 731 01 92. Displays and guides in Spanish. Open daily 11am-6pm. 40 pesos.)*

EX-HACIENDA DE SAN GABRIEL DE BARRERA. These 17 glorious gardens, covering about three acres, are perhaps the most beautiful of Guanajuato's many natural attractions. Cobbled paths, well-groomed flora, and whistling birds create the perfect atmosphere for a stroll. The *ex-hacienda* itself borders the gardens; its rooms contain 16th-century furniture, silverware, and paintings. *(Catch a "Noria Alta/ Marfil" bus across from the mercado (2.5 pesos), and tell the driver you're headed to San Gabriel de la Barrera. ☎732 06 19. Open daily 9am-6pm. Closed from Christmas to New Year's. 16 pesos, children and students 10 pesos.)*

MONUMENTO A CRISTO REY. This mountain, called the **Cerro del Cubilete**, 2850m above sea level and 20km from Guanajuato, is considered the geographical center of Mexico. The dark, bronze statue of Jesus by local *indígenas* at the summit measures 16m tall and weighs more than 80 tons. Though the statue is striking, so are the stretches of blue hills visible from the summit. *(From the station, take a "Cristo Rey" bus in the last parking spot to the left. Round-trip 3½hr., 15 pesos. ☎732 82 46.)*

🎵 ENTERTAINMENT

Theater, dance, and musical performances abound. Ask at the tourist office for listings or consult posters around town. On Thursday and Sunday nights in Jardín Unión, the state band performs around 6pm. *Callejonadas (*sing-alongs) happen on Friday and Saturday nights at 8:30pm and depart from Teatro Juárez. Student groups present films almost every day of the week. Check out Teatro Principal, Hidalgo 18 (☎732 15 26; 20 pesos, students and seniors 10 pesos) or Teatro Cervantes, on Plaza Cervantes (☎732 11 69; 15 pesos, students and seniors 13 pesos).

Guanajuato explodes for the first two weeks in October during the **Festival Internacional Cervantino.** The city invites repertory groups from all over the world to make merry with the *estudiantinas* (strolling student minstrels). Festivities take place mostly at local theaters, but also at museums and churches. Tickets are sold by TicketMaster a month in advance and sell rapidly. The **Office of the Festival Internacional Cervantino** (☎732 11 69; fax 732 67 75) can provide more information. Guanajuato also celebrates the **Feria de San Juan** (June 24), at Presa de la Olla, with dancing, cultural events, fireworks, and sports, and **Día de la Cueva** (July 31), when residents walk to a cave's entrance to honor San Ignacio de Loyola, first patron saint of Guanajuato and founder of the *Compañía de Jesús*.

🎵 NIGHTLIFE

Many bars and clubs concentrate around Jardín Unión and Plaza de la Paz.

Damas de las Camelias es Él, Sopeña 32 (☎732 75 87). A sophisticated crowd of professionals and 30-something tourists groove to late-night Latin rhythms and down *cerveza* (15 pesos) and mixed drinks (30 pesos). A wide selection of flamenco, jazz, *salsa*, Cuban, Peruvian, and Portuguese music. No cover. Open daily 8pm-5am.

Cafe Dada, Baratillo 16. Follow Truco until it meets Nuevo, then head down Nuevo until you reach Baratillo, a small avenue extending to the left. Play chess or chat over espresso (5 pesos) while admiring the work of local artists. Open daily 8:30am-11pm.

Guanajuato Grill, Alonso 4 (☎732 02 87), 1 block behind Jardín Unión. Fake stars in the covered courtyard, gilt-framed pictures on maroon walls, and pounding Latin and American pop music set the mood, while chairs, tables, and booths serve as the dance floor. Beer 20 pesos, drinks from 30 pesos. Tu 2-for-1 beers. W-F cover 30 pesos (2 beers included), Sa cover 50 pesos (1 drink included). Open Tu-Sa 9:30pm-3:30am.

The Bar, Sopeña 10 (☎732 25 66). Mexicans and foreigners show off their moves on the packed dance floor, while those without partners (or skills) throw back beers (15 pesos) at the surrounding tables. Drinks from 30 pesos. Open daily 8pm-4am.

Bar 8, (☎ 732 71 79), at Constancia and Santo del Mono, behind Teatro Juárez. With a more laid-back atmosphere and cheap drinks, Bar 8 fills with a student crowd on weeknights. Toast your friends at the bar or play pool. Beer from 15 pesos, drinks from 30 pesos. Tu 2-for-1 beers. No cover. Open M-Sa noon-3am, Su 6pm-3am.

El Capitolio (☎ 732 08 10) on Plaza de la Paz, next door to Hotel La Condesa. Similar to the Grill but with more tables and a younger crowd. Don't show up in sneakers and shorts or the bouncer will turn nasty. Beer 15 pesos, mixed drinks 30 pesos; min. consumption 30 pesos. Sa cover 50 pesos. Open Tu-Sa 9pm-3am.

SAN MIGUEL DE ALLENDE   ☎ 4

San Miguel (pop. 80,000) has been dually shaped by its reign as a bustling commercial center in the 18th century and by its pivotal role in the struggle for independence. On September 16, 1810, when Hidalgo, the priest of nearby Dolores, led his rebel army into the city, the town rallied in opposition to Spanish rule under the leadership of Ignacio Allende. In 1826, the infant republic recognized Allende's role in the drive for independence by joining his name to San Miguel's. These days, San Miguel de Allende is overrun by North Americans rather than revolutionaries, and bloated with Reuben sandwiches, Haagen Daäz ice cream, and yuppies looking to painlessly inject their children with some Spanish skills. Still, although nearly swallowed by US culture, Mexican life marches on. The lively *mercado* refuses to yield to air-conditioned malls, and the city's shady plazas, colonial churches, and quiet green gardens retain their appeal.

▐ TRANSPORTATION

Buses: To get from the bus station to the center (known as Jardín Allende or Plaza de Allende), take a "Centro" bus to the corner of Colegio and Mesones, near the statue of Allende on horseback (every 15min. 7am-10pm, 2.5 pesos). Walk 2 blocks down Mesones, then left 1 block on Reloj to v Plaza Allende. Alternatively, take a taxi (20 pesos). Flecha Amarilla (☎ 152 73 23) goes to: **Aguascalientes** (4½hr., 12:30pm and 2:30pm, 112 pesos); **Dolores Hidalgo** (45min.; every 15min. 4:30am-9:15pm, and 11:45pm; 19 pesos); **Guadalajara** (5hr.; 7:30, 9:45am, and 5:30pm; 268 pesos); **Guanajuato** (1½hr.; 7:30, 9:45am, noon, 5:30pm; 62 pesos); **León** (2½hr.; 7:30, 9:45am, noon, and 5:30pm; 98 pesos); **Mexico City** (3½hr., 9:40am and 4pm; 158 pesos); **Querétaro** (1½hr.; 12:30, 2:30am, and every 40min. 5:20am-8pm; 32 pesos); **San Luis Potosí** (4hr., every 2hr. 7:30am-6:50pm, 98 pesos). Herradura de Plata/Pegasso Plus (☎ 152 07 25) and ETN (☎ 152 64 07) provide similar service to fewer locations. The Estrella Blanca group (☎ 152 22 37) travels to more distant locations.

✳ ▐ ORIENTATION AND PRACTICAL INFORMATION

San Miguel is 94km southeast of Guanajuato and 428km northwest of Mexico City. Most attractions are within walking distance of the town center, **Jardín Allende** (or **Plaza Allende**), and the streets form a near-grid. **San Francisco, Reloj, Correo,** and **Hidalgo** border the *jardín*. East-west streets south of the *jardín* change their names every few blocks. The always-visible, towering *basílica* in Jardín Allende can orient even the most frustrated of travelers.

TOURIST AND FINANCIAL SERVICES

Tourist Office: Delegación Regional de Turismo (☎/fax 152 65 65), on Pl. de Allende, to your left as you face the Parroquia. Knowledgeable staff distributes maps. Some English, French, and Italian spoken. Open M-F 10am-5pm, Sa 10am-2pm, Su 10am-2pm. During high season, groups gather in front of the church in the *jardín* for **tours** of the city (1½hr., 30 pesos per person). Departure times vary; call for more information.

San Miguel de Allende

🏠 ACCOMMODATIONS

Casa de Huéspedes, **6**
Hostal Internacional San Miguel, **1**
Hostal Alcatraz, **2**
Hotel La Huerta, **8**
Hotel Parador San Sebastián, **7**

🍅 FOOD

The Bagel Cafe, **18**
El Capri, **14**
El Tomato, **11**
La Piñata, **16**
La Villa de Pancho, **3**
Los Burritos, **5**

🎵 NIGHTLIFE

100 Angeles, **10**
Agave Azul, **15**
Char Rock, **17**
El Ring, **13**
La Cucaracha, **19**
Le Petit, **4**
Mama Mía, **12**
Pancho & Lefty's, **9**

Consulates: US, Macías 72 Interior 6 (☎ 152 23 57, after-hours emergencies ☎ 152 00 68 or 152 06 53), across the street from Bellas Artes. Open M-F 9am-1pm or by appointment. For other countries, or to extend visas or visitors' permits, contact the **Delegación Regional de Servicios Migratorios,** Plaza Real del Conde Shopping Center, 2nd fl. (☎ 152 25 42 or 152 28 35). Catch the "Gigante" bus from Colegio and Mesones or from Juárez. Documents may be dropped off 9am-12:30pm and picked up 1:30-3pm. Processing takes at least 1 day. Open M-F 8am-8pm.

Currency Exchange: Intercam, Correo 15, San Francisco 4, and Juárez 27 (☎ 154 66 60), has great rates. Open M-F 9am-6pm, Sa 9am-2pm. **Banamex** (☎ 152 10 40) on the west side of the *jardín*, has 24hr. ATMs. Open M-F 9am-5pm, Sa 10am-2pm. So does **Bancomer** (☎ 152 21 24), Juárez 11. Open M-F 8:30am-4pm.

American Express: Hidalgo 1 (☎ 152 18 56; fax 152 04 99). Full financial and travel services. Open M-F 9am-2pm and 4-6:30pm.

LOCAL SERVICES

English Bookstore: El Colibrí, Sollano 30 (☎ 152 07 51), near Cuadrante. Paperback fiction, some in French and German. Open M-Sa 10am-2pm and 4-6pm. **Lagundi,** Umarán 17 (☎ 152 08 30), at Macíashas. Large selection of art supplies and magazines in several languages. Open M-Sa 10am-2pm and 4-8pm, Su 11am-3pm.

▨ Library: Insurgentes 25 (☎ 152 02 93), between Reloj and Hidalgo. Art-filled courtyard serves as a gathering place for expats and students. Wide selection in English and Spanish. Old paperbacks (6-8 pesos) sold Th 10am-1pm. Library and gift shop open M-F 10am-2pm and 4-7pm, Sa 10am-2pm.

Supermarket: Bonanza, Mesones 43A (☎ 152 12 60). Open M-Sa 8am-3pm and 4-8pm, Su 8am-5pm. **Gigante** is even bigger. Take a "Gigante" bus (2.5 pesos).

Laundry: Lavandería El Reloj, Reloj 34 (☎ 152 38 43), between Mesones and Insurgentes. Full-service wash and dry 40 pesos per 4kg. Open M-Sa 8am-8pm.

EMERGENCY AND COMMUNICATIONS

Emergency: (☎ 152 09 11). Direct contact with Red Cross, fire department, and police. A few dispatchers speak English.

Red Cross: (☎ 152 16 16), 1km outside of town Carretera Celaya. English spoken.

Pharmacy: Botica Agundis, Canal 26 (☎ 152 11 98), at Macías. Helpful staff. Open daily 10am-midnight. Call police to find out which pharmacy is on-call 24hr.

Hospital: Hospital de la Fe San Miguel, Libramiento Mex. 43 (☎ 152 22 33 or 152 23 20, emergency 152 25 45), to Dolores Hidalgo, near the bus station. English spoken. In case of emergency, you may also call **Hospital Civil** (☎ 152 09 11). English spoken.

Fax: Telecomm, Correo 16-B (☎ 152 32 15; fax 152 00 81), next to the post office. Open M-F 9am-7pm, Sa-Su 9am-noon.

Internet Access: Cyberc@fe, upstairs at Zacateros 29. 20 pesos per hour. Open M-F 9am-10pm, Sa 9am-8pm, Su 9am-5pm.

Post Office: Correo 16 (☎ 152 00 89), 1 block east of the *jardín*. **MexPost** available. Open M-F 9am-5pm, Sa 9am-1pm.

Postal Code: 37700.

▌ ACCOMMODATIONS

As is the case in many hot spots on the *gringo* trail, budget accommodations can be hard to find in San Miguel. In general, prices drop as you move away from the *jardín*. Rooms fill up fast, particularly during the winter, *Semana Santa*, and September, when the city throws a month-long *fiesta* in honor of Independence Day and the city's founding. Reservations are recommended during these times.

▨ Hostal Internacional San Miguel de Allende (HI), Jaime Nuno 28 (☎ 152 31 75). Walk north on Macías until Calzada de la Luz. Go left 2 blocks and turn right on Jaime Nuno; the red hostel is 3½ blocks up on the left. Backpackers engage in afternoon discussions around the courtyard. Kitchen use, clean communal bathrooms, laundry machines, Internet access (20 pesos per hr.), and book swap. Includes breakfast. Key deposit 50 pesos. No lockout, but lights out at 11pm. Reservations not accepted. Quick morning chores required. 60 pesos, with ISIC or HI card 50 pesos.

Hostal Alcatraz, Relox 54 (☎ 152 85 43; info@hostal-alcatraz.com). Another popular hostel, with a hotel feel. Dorms house males and females separately, but everyone mingles in the TV room and kitchen. Internet access 30 pesos per hr. No curfew. Office open 9am-9pm. 100 pesos, with ISIC or HI card 90 pesos.

Hotel La Huerta, Callejon de Atascarero 9 (☎ 154 44 65). Walk up Mesones 3 blocks past Colegio; when you see a stream to your left, turn right onto Atascadero. Follow the stone path about 1 block uphill—the hotel is the large blue building on your left. Rooms have great city views, *agua purificada*, and large baths. The fountain-filled patios and sitting rooms with wood floors will make you feel like you're in a *hacienda*. Singles and doubles 250 pesos, each additional person 50 pesos. TV 50 pesos extra. Student discount: singles 200 pesos, meals included.

Casa de Huéspedes, Mesones 27 (☎ 152 13 78). Good sized-rooms with *talavera* baths branch off the 2nd-floor plant-filled courtyard. The top-floor terrace has spectacular views of the city's churches. Singles 150 pesos; doubles 200 pesos.

Hotel Parador San Sebastián, Mesones 7 (☎ 152 70 84). Take Relox away from the *jardín* and turn right onto Mesones. The hotel is on the left. Friendly and family-owned. Pleasant rooms with tiled baths, some with kitchenettes. Sitting room off the courtyard is filled with books and a TV. Singles and doubles 150-200 pesos; triples 220 pesos.

🍴 FOOD

The sweet aroma of international cuisine wafts through the cobbled streets of San Miguel, and restaurants and cafes occupy almost every corner. Unfortunately, prices can be as *norteamericano* as their clientele. For the best value, visit **Calle Insurgentes** and the streets around the *mercado* on **Colegio.**

La Villa de Pancho, Quebrada 12 (☎ 152 12 47). From the corner of Hidalgo and Insurgentes, follow Insurgentes 3 blocks west until it meets Quebrada and walk half a block to your left. Welcome to the kitchen of Cristina, the bubbly owner, who is very popular among backpackers. *Comida corrida* 25-40 pesos, breakfast 15-25 pesos, *cerveza* 10 pesos. Open daily 9am-9pm. A **Casa de Huespedes** is on the 2nd floor with 3 spacious rooms connected by a communal bathroom. 80 pesos.

La Piñata (☎ 152 20 60), on the corner of Jesús and Umarán, 1 block from the *jardín*. Join the mellow mix of artists, students, backpackers, and families feasting upon vegetarian-friendly *tostadas* (7 pesos), *tacos de guisado* (5 pesos), and sandwiches (12-16 pesos). *Comida corrida* 35 pesos, breakfast 20-25 pesos. Open W-M 9am-8pm.

El Capri, Hidalgo 10 (☎ 152 05 26). After the clubs close, sample out-of-this-world *pozole* (22 pesos), *tortas* (10 pesos), and *taquitos* (20 pesos). Open daily 1pm-7am.

Los Burritos, Mesones 69-A (☎ 152 32 22), between Hidalgo and Reloj. Tasty and economical *comida rápida*. *Burritacos* (3 pesos) or *burriquesos* (4.5 pesos) have vegetarian options too. Ravenous travelers will like the *burrito maxi* (7.5 pesos) and the hot and cheesy *burriqueso maxi* (12 pesos). Open M-Sa 10:30am-6pm.

El Tomato, Mesones 62B. This all-organic restaurant serves fruit juices (13 pesos) and scrumptious salads (40 pesos). Meal of the day 55 pesos. Open M-Sa noon-9pm.

The Bagel Cafe, 19 Correo, across from the post office. Serves excellent sandwiches, freshly baked bagels, and sourdough bread (about 40 pesos). Homemade cookies and soups are excellently prepared in an ultra-clean environment. Open M-Sa 8:30am-3pm.

👁 SIGHTS

The cheapest and most effective way to experience San Miguel is on your own two feet—nearly all sites of interest lie within walking distance of the *jardín*.

LA PARROQUIA. The neo-Gothic facade and tower were designed in 1890 by *indígena* mason Zeferino Gutiérrez, who is said to have learned the style from postcards of French cathedrals. Pointed arches and flute-like towers enclose glittering chandeliers and gold trim sunlight from the tower windows. At the front is a tremendous gold-leaf altar. The basement holds the tomb of former president Anastasio Bustamante. *(Next to the jardín. ☎ 152 41 97. Open daily 5:30am-9:30pm. Mass M-Sa 6, 7, 9am, noon, and 8:15pm; all day Su.)*

MUSEO HISTÓRICO DE SAN MIGUEL DE ALLENDE. The birthplace of Ignacio Allende houses a respectable collection of ancient ceramics, Pre-Classical artifacts, historical exhibits, and, of course, a tribute to the man himself. *(Cuna de Allende 1 at Umarán, across the street from La Parroquia. ☎ 152 24 99. Open Tu-Su 10am-3pm. 30 pesos, children and students 27 pesos. Mini-guide 6 pesos.)*

TEMPLO DEL ORATORIO DE SAN FELIPE NERI. Founded in 1712 and rebuilt many times, the church is an amalgamation of styles; its interior is mainly Neoclassical but the engraved Baroque facade belies *indígena* influences. On the west side, the towers and dome belong to *Santa Casa de Loreto*, a reproduction of the building by the same name in Italy. Enter through the doorway west of San Felipe Neri. The floors and lower wall are covered with glazed tiles from China, Spain, and Puebla. (*At the corner of Insurgentes and Loreto, 2 blocks east of the library.* ☎ *152 05 21. Open daily 6:30am-1pm and 6:30-8:30pm. Santa Casa open M-Su 8am-2pm.*)

IGLESIA DE LA CONCEPCIÓN. Construction on the enormous church began in 1755 and lasted until 1891. A representation of the Immaculate Conception graces the two-story dome, and the ornate gold altar features a likeness of the *Virgen* in blue metallic robes. (*At the corner of Canal and Macías, 1 block west of the jardín.* ☎ *152 01 48. Open daily 7:30am-7pm. Mass M-F 7:30am and 7pm; Su 9:30, 11:30am, and 7pm.*)

BELLAS ARTES. Housed in an 18th-century former convent, this cultural center and art school has a concert hall and galleries with rotating exhibits. The stunning murals echo the impressive talent of the students and enliven the walls surrounding the peaceful, manicured courtyard. Look for *campesina* L. R. Santos lassoing a dreaded purple *chupacabras* (a monster that sucks the blood of goats). The school offers classes in ceramics, dance, art, guitar, and more (a few are even in English). European and US films are occasionally screened. (*Macías 75, next door to Iglesia de la Concepción.* ☎ *152 02 89. Open M-Sa 9am-8pm, Su 10am-2pm.*)

OTHER SIGHTS NEAR THE CENTRO. The **Instituto de Allende,** Ancha de San Antonio 20, a hike up Zacateros from Iglesia de la Concepción, houses several galleries with exhibits by local artists and offers art, Spanish, and social studies classes. (☎ *152 01 90. Open M-F 8am-5:30pm.*) Every Tu, vendors converge upon the **Tianguis del Martes** (Tuesday market) near the municipal stadium to sell their wares (*open 7am-4pm*). Clothing, groceries, old doorknobs, and assorted odds and ends await the adventurous shopper. (*To get there, take a (1.8 pesos) "Gigante" bus from Juárez or a 15-peso taxi ride.*) Reverberating with the calls of tropical birds, **Parque Juárez** is a large, lush garden just south of the *centro*. (*From the jardín, head down Luna de Allende until it meets Cuadrante. Follow Cuadrante for one short block to your left, and take your first right on Hermanos Aldama.*)

OTHER SIGHTS AWAY FROM THE CENTRO. Jardín Botánico Cante is home to a dazzling array of cacti and succulents. About 1,300 species grow along the *jardín's* 8km of walking paths. (*Mesones 71. Walk past Mercado Ignacio Ramírez, turn right at Homobono, and continue up the incline until it flattens (10min.). Keep going (20min.) and follow the signs; the jardín will be on the left. Or, take a taxi (12 pesos) from Jardín Allende. Open daily sunrise-sunset. 8 pesos, children 5 pesos.*)

Take in a breathtaking view of San Miguel and the surrounding mountains from the **mirador** above the city. (*From the jardín, go 2 blocks up Correo to Recreo. Take a right and walk for 10min. 1 block past Plaza de Toros, take a left and continue uphill 3 blocks until the street ends at the main road, with a sign that says "Salida a Querétaro." The mirador is a few minutes to your right. Or, take a "Gigante" bus (2 pesos) from Colegio and Mesones or Juárez.*)

Hot springs fans will find their paradise at **La Gruta,** just outside of town. (*Take a Dolores Hidalgo bus (10min., 8 pesos) and ask to be let off at the hotel near the billboard. Walk toward the billboard and turn left on the dirt road directly ahead. To reach the springs, veer left. When returning to San Miguel, flag down a bus along the road. Open daily 8am-5pm. 50 pesos.*) The **Centro de Crecimiento** organizes trips to San Miguel's surroundings, and profits benefit children's health care. (*Zamora Ríos 6.* ☎ *152 03 18. Tours leave from the jardín, Sa 10am. 150 pesos.*)

🎵 🎭 ENTERTAINMENT AND NIGHTLIFE

There are as many clubs as churches in San Miguel, and music pumps through the city's veins daily. The magazine *Atención*, available every Monday in the tourist office and at local newsstands, is the best source of information on upcoming concerts, theatrical productions, and lectures. **Bellas Artes** and the **Instituto Allende** post advertisements for art exhibits, openings, and other events. Expect cover charges at clubs to skyrocket during *fiestas*, especially *Semana Santa*.

BARS

La Cucaracha, Zacatecas 22A (☎ 152 01 95). The former hangout of Jack Kerouac, Bob Dylan, and Alan Ginsburg remains a mecca for artists and writers. *Gringos* and Mexicans are everywhere, but the only *cucaracha* in sight is the large decoration on the wall. Have a beer (10 pesos) or a mixed drink (about 20 pesos) as you listen to US, British, or Mexican tunes on the jukebox. Free bar snacks on Th. Open daily 9pm-3am.

Le Petit, Macías 95 (☎ 152 32 29). This restaurant-by-day, bar-by-night is dripping with atmosphere—wine racks, watercolor paintings, colonial architecture—but the young, international student crowd packing it full every night couldn't care less. They come for the cheap drinks: beer 10-12 pesos, mixed drinks from 15 pesos. Open daily 6pm-3am.

Char Rock, Correo 7, 2nd fl. (☎ 152 73 73), right off the *jardín*. It's hard to know what's the bigger draw at this relaxed and casual bar—the great live music on the 2nd fl., or the fabulous view from the top-floor terrace. Beer 20 pesos, drinks from 30 pesos. Live music after 8pm. No cover. Open Su-W 6pm-1am, Th-Sa noon-3am.

Agave Azul, Mesones 80 (☎ 152 51 51). By the time evening rolls around, live jazz, reggae, or Latin music will be playing in this bar/restaurant. During Happy Hour (5-8pm), which precedes the daily music fest, drinks are 15 pesos. Beer 20 pesos.

CLUBS

Mama Mía, Umarán 8 (☎ 152 20 63), just off the *jardín*, is a favorite destination of foreigners and *gringita*-friendly locals. Restaurant, bar, and *discoteca* in one, this enormous building is divided into several smaller establishments. **Mama Mía Bar,** to your right as you enter, attracts a 20-something crowd and features live *salsa*, jazz, reggae and funk. 50 peso cover. Open Th-Sa 9pm-3am. **Leonardo's,** across the entryway, scores points for its big-screen TV. Techno music blares and college-age customers crowd the bar. Open M-W 7pm-2am, Th-Sa 7pm-3am. In front of the entrance is a pricey **restaurant** appealing mostly to tourists and hosting nightly *música folklórica*. Open M-W 8am-midnight, Th-F 8am-1am. The **terrace** upstairs pulsates with live, loud rock F-Sa. When there is no live music, a young crowd enjoys the view of the city and makes conversation over beers (16-19 pesos; drinks from 28 pesos). Open F-Sa 9pm-2am.

El Ring, Hidalgo 25 (☎ 152 19 98), features standard *discoteca* fare and a very young Mexican crowd. Latin and US dance hits will keep even the weariest club-hopper bouncing until the wee hours. Drinks 25-80 pesos. Cover W-Th 20 pesos, F 40 pesos, Sa 60 pesos. Open W 8pm-3am, Th-Sa 10pm-4:30am, Su 5:30-10:30pm; nightly in July.

Pancho and Lefty's, Mesones 99 (☎ 152 19 58), provides hours of entertainment for students craving a pounding beat and a big drink. Loud rock and cover bands or DJs spinning techno, disco, and Mexican pop songs thrill a tightly packed crowd every night. W 2-for-1 beers. Sa cover 30-50 pesos. Open W and F-Sa 8pm-3am.

100 Angeles, Mesones 97 (☎ 152 59 37), next door to Panchos, is a private club that caters to a primarily gay and lesbian clientele. Disco balls illuminate the otherwise dark dance floor as the all-ages crowd gets down to tunes from the 70s and 90s. Cover F 30 pesos, Sa 50 pesos with 1 drink. Open F-Sa 10pm-4am.

FESTIVALS

San Miguel boasts more *fiestas* than any other town in Mexico, and a celebration of some sort takes place nearly every weekend. In September, the city celebrates its independence and founding on the third Saturday of the month with **San Miguelada,** a running of the bulls in the *jardín*. The impressive **International Chamber Music Festival** is held in August at Bellas Artes. Ticket packages start at 1000 pesos and go on sale in February. Other festivals include the **Jazz Festival** in November and **El Día de San Antonio** and **El Festival de Locos** on June 13. San Miguel celebrates the birthday of **Ignacio Allende** (January 21) with parades and fireworks.

DOLORES HIDALGO   ☎ 4

"Mexicanos, viva México!"
—Miguel Hidalgo, Grito de Dolores

Nearly 200 years later, Miguel Hidalgo's rousing words still echo through Mexico's dusty "Cradle of Independence." Dolores Hidalgo (pop. 40,000) has little more to offer than hot, dirty streets, a thriving ceramics industry and an amazing story. On Sunday, September 16, 1810, Miguel Hidalgo y Costilla, the town's priest, learned that his independence conspiracy had been discovered by the Spanish. Deciding to take immediate action, Hidalgo woke the entire town at 5am by tolling the parish church bell. The town's residents tumbled out of bed and gathered at the church, where Hidalgo delivered an electrifying speech, the *Grito de Dolores*, proclaiming Mexico's independence. Then, calling his flock to arms, Hidalgo rallied an army to march to Mexico City. With this brazen move, Hidalgo not only signed his own death warrant (he was executed a year later), but he single-handedly began the movement that led to Mexican independence.

⊏ TRANSPORTATION. To get downtown from the **Flecha Amarilla bus station,** walk straight out the door and left on Hidalgo. Three blocks down the street are the *Jardín*, the tourist office, Plaza Principal, and the *Parroquia*. Flecha Amarilla (☎182 06 39) goes to **Aguascalientes** (3½hr., 1:30 and 3:30pm, 107 pesos); **Guadalajara** (8hr., every hr. 5:20am-12:45pm, 203 pesos); **Guanajuato** (1½hr., every 20min. 5:20am-9pm, 30 pesos) en route to **León** (3hr., 56 pesos); **Mexico City** (5hr., every 40min. 5am-7pm, 147 pesos) via **Querétaro** (2½hr., 48 pesos); **San Luis Potosí** (3hr., every 2hr. 5:30am-8pm, 75 pesos); **San Miguel de Allende** (1hr., every 30min. 5:10am-8:50pm, 19 pesos). To get to Plaza Principal from the **Herradura de Plata bus station,** go out the door on your left as you face Yucatán. Walk down Chiapas, which turns into Tabasco, take a left on Hidalgo, and follow it to the plaza. Herradura de Plata (☎182 29 37) goes to many of the same destinations.

⊅ PRACTICAL INFORMATION. Streets change names as they cross the plaza, and the town's points of interest all lie within a few blocks of the center. The **tourist office** is the large yellow building on your right as you exit the Parroquia. Handy maps, but no English spoken. (☎/fax 182 11 64. Open M-F 10am-7pm, Sa-Su 10am-3pm.) **Centro Cambiar Paisano,** Plaza Principal 22, has good exchange rates. (☎182 45 35. Open M-Sa 9am-5pm, Su 9am-3pm.) **Bancomer,** Hidalgo 29, will exchange traveler's checks and currency during the week, and has 24hr. **ATMs.** (☎182 05 90. Open M-F 8:30am-4pm, Sa 10am-2pm.) **Emergency:** ☎182 09 11. **Police:** Mexico 2 (☎192 00 21), 11 blocks north of the plaza. No English spoken. **Pharmacy: Botica de San Vicente,** Potosí and Zacatecas. (☎182 24 17. Open daily 9am-10pm.) **Hospital General,** Hidalgo 12 (☎182 00 13). Some English spoken. **Internet Access: Cybercafe.com,** Zacatecas 3. (☎182 00 87. 15 pesos per hr. Open M-Sa 10am-9pm, Su 10am-4pm.) **Post office:** Puebla 22 between Jalisco and Veracruz, one block from Plaza Principal. (☎182 08 07. Open M-F 9am-3pm.) **Postal code:** 37800.

⌂⌂ ACCOMMODATIONS AND FOOD. Quality budget rooms are scarce in Dolores Hidalgo. Prices rise and vacancies fall dramatically during *Semana Santa*, and between September 8 and 17 when the town is overrun by Independence Day celebrants. Reservations are advised. **Posada Dolores,** Yucatán 8, one block east of the plaza, has simple peach-painted concrete cube rooms, but they're very clean, and the family atmosphere is welcoming. Communal baths are spotless. Cheap *comida corrida* (22 pesos) is available in the adjoining restaurant. (☎182 06 42. Singles 60 pesos, with bath 120 pesos; doubles 100 pesos, 150 pesos.) Nicer, pricier, and farther away, is **Hostal de Insurgentes,** Calz. de los Héroes 13. Follow Nayarit (2 blocks north of the plaza) until it intersects Tamaulipas. Take Renovación, the street that angles off that intersection for 10min., until you come to the Red Cross. Take a left onto Calz. de los Héroes and walk one block—the hotel is on your right. Large rooms have Indian print bedspreads and curtains, bright yellow tiled baths, and purified water. (☎182 24 97. Singles 210 pesos; doubles 240 pesos; triples 280 pesos.)

Around the *jardín*, most restaurants are reasonably priced. **Torticlán**, Plaza Principal 28, at the west end, serves tasty food in a cafeteria-style setting. Join families and fellow tourists as you munch on *tortas* (9 pesos) with juice (6 pesos) or beer (9 pesos). Soyburgers (12.5 pesos) mean vegetarians can have their fill too. (☎182 26 76. Open daily 9am-5:30pm.) For a substantial meal, try **D'Jardín**, Plaza Principal 30, at the corner of Zacatecas. Cool off under fans and enjoy Mexican favorites like *chilaquiles* or *flautas* for 25 pesos. (☎182 02 52. Open daily 9am-7pm.)

◪ **SIGHTS.** Most of Dolores's sights lie within four blocks of the bus station, and revolve around the beautiful **Parroquia de Nuestra Señora de los Dolores**, where the *Grito de Dolores* was sounded. Constructed between 1712 and 1778, the church's lavish interior features a main altar surrounded by beautifully ornamented gold leaf columns and two side altars, one Churrigueresque and the other Ultrabaroque. Dress appropriately—no shorts or tight dresses are allowed. The original bell, is now positioned atop Mexico City's Palacio de Gobierno. (Open daily 9am-2pm and 4-8pm.) On the west side of the plaza is **Casa de Visitas**, built in 1786 to house Spanish officials. The building hosts each Mexican president when he reissues the *Grito* during his last year in office. In the center of the plaza is a huge bronze statue of Hidalgo, the man who made Dolores Hidalgo *la cuna de la independencia nacional* (the cradle of national independence; open M-Sa 10am-6pm, Su 11am-3pm). **Museo de la Independencia**, Zacatecas 6, lies less than one block northwest of the Parroquia. Gory technicolor paintings detail the physical and spiritual costs of Spanish rule and the fight for independence. Relive Hidalgo's *Grito* in an eerie life-sized diorama with wooden statues of an inspired Hidalgo and anxious Mexicans. The museum also includes Mexican *artesanía* and a shrine to Dolores Hidalgo's favorite musical son, *mariachi* legend José Alfredo Jiménez. (Open daily 9am-5pm. 10 pesos; Su free.) Hidalgo's home from 1804 until 1810, the **Museo Casa Hidalgo**, at Morelos and Hidalgo, one block from Plaza Principal, is less than thrilling. The collection contains contemporary religious paraphernalia, documents, and artwork relating to the independence movement. (☎182 01 71. Open Tu-Su 10am-6pm. 30 pesos; Su free.)

Seasonal activities include the **Fiestas de Septiembre** (Sept. 15), Dolores Hidalgo's biggest shin-dig. The President himself makes an appearance in election years, re-issuing the *Grito de Dolores*. **Purísima Concepción** (Nov. 30-Dec. 8), is a fair that includes massive *artesanía* sales and pyrotechnic displays.

QUERÉTARO

QUERÉTARO ☎4

Between Mexico City and Guadalajara on the republic's busiest stretch of road, Querétaro (pop. 870,000) has witnessed some of the most decisive moments in Mexican history. The city's many museums recreate Emperor Maximilian's last days, as does a hike up *Cerro de las Campanas* (Hill of the Bells), where the ill-fated ruler spoke his famous last words: "Mexicans, I am going to die for a just cause: the liberty and independence of Mexico." Querétaro again displayed patriotism 50 years later, when victorious Venustiano Carranza drafted 1917 constitution here, establishing modern Mexico. Contemporary Querétaro is a prosperous agricultural and industrial center. Whining grain elevators, monstrous warehouses, and truckloads of squealing pigs assault the senses. Enclosed within the commercial ring, Querétaro is a colonial wonder, with lantern-lit squares and an 18th-century aqueduct of graceful arches. In the city's heart, students and entrepreneurs traverse centuries-old brick streets and *andadores* (pedestrian walkways). Often overlooked by foreigners, the city is a popular destination for Mexicans.

⌐ TRANSPORTATION

GETTING AROUND

Querétaro lies between Mexico City and Guadalajara on **Mex. 57**. The modern **bus station** (☎ 229 00 61) is on the south side of town, not within walking distance of the *centro*. Take the "Ruta 25" bus on Allende and Zaragoza; "Ruta 8" on Ocampo and Constituyentes; "Ruta 19" at the corner of Madero and Guerrero; or "Ruta 72" on Universidad—all are labeled "Central" (every 5-10min. 6am-10:30pm, 3.5 pesos). To catch a bus to the *centro* (3.5 pesos), walk toward the highway, veering to the right, toward the sign that says "Paradero de Micros." Taxis to most destinations are 22 pesos—tickets are sold inside the station and handed to the driver.

GETTING AWAY

Querétaro's bus station is divided into two terminals: Terminal A offers first-class service and Terminal B offers second-class service.

Terminal A: Elite (☎ 229 00 22) drives to: **Acapulco** (9hr.; 11am, 7:45, and 10pm; 356 pesos); **Cuernavaca** (5hr., 11am and 7:45pm, 150 pesos); **Mexico City** (3hr., every hr. 7:30am-8pm, 126 pesos); **Monterrey** (10hr., 8 per day 9am-11pm, 400 pesos); **Tampico** (8½hr., 9:25pm, 287 pesos). Primera Plus/Servicios Coordinados (☎ 211 40 01) travels to: **Aguascalientes** (4½hr., 8 per day 6:45am-7:45pm, 187 pesos); **Guadalajara** (5hr., 9 per day, 225 pesos); **Guanajuato** (2½hr., 13 per day 5am-11:15pm, 86 pesos); **León** (2½hr., every hr. 6:45am-1:30am, 110 pesos); **Morelia** (3hr., 6 per day 11:30am-11:15pm, 105 pesos); **Pátzcuaro** (4½hr., 6:30am, 133 pesos); **San Luis Potosí** (2½hr., 6 per day, 126 pesos). Omnibus de México (☎ 229 00 29) has similar service. Autobuses Americanos (☎ 229 00 03) goes to the US.

Terminal B: Flecha Amarilla (☎ 211 02 45) sends buses to: **Aguascalientes** (6hr., 6 per day 4:50am-3:35pm, 143 pesos); **Colima** (12hr., 4 per day, 242 pesos); **Guadalajara** (8hr., 3 per day, 207 pesos); **Guanajuato** (3½hr., 5 per day 11:05am-8:05pm, 73 pesos); **León** (4hr., every hr., 90 pesos); **Manzanillo** (13hr., 7:05am and 7:30pm, 335 pesos); **Mexico City** (3hr., every 10min., 107 pesos); **Morelia** (4hr., 12 per day 5:05am-11:35pm, 90 pesos); **San Miguel de Allende** (1½hr., every 40min. 6:20am-10:20pm, 32 pesos); **Tula** (6½hr., every hr. 6:40am-9:30pm, 70 pesos); **Uruapan** (7hr., 1:10pm, 160 pesos); **Zamora** (6hr.; 1:45, 3:20am, and 7:30pm; 133 pesos). Flecha Roja/Herradura de Plata (☎ 224 02 45) provide similar service. The Estrella Blanca group (☎ 229 00 22) travels farther north.

⌐ PRACTICAL INFORMATION

Tourist Office: Pasteur Nte. 4 (☎ 238 50 00, ext. 5067; turismo@queretaro.com.mx). From Jardín Zenea, take 5 de Mayo to the end of Plaza de Armas. Maps and events schedules available. City tours in English or Spanish depart Tu-F (1hr., 6 per day, 15 pesos). Open daily 9am-8pm.

Currency Exchange: Banks can be found all over the *centro*. **Banamex** (☎ 225 30 00), on the corner of Juárez and 16 de Septiembre, has a 24hr. **ATM** and changes currency and traveler's checks. Open M-F 9am-5pm, Sa 10am-2pm; open for exchange M-F 9am-3pm, Sa 10am-2pm. **Casa de Cambio,** Corregidora Sur 108 (☎ 212 80 86), 2 long blocks south of Jardín Zenea, just past Reforma. Open M-F 9am-5pm, Sa 9am-2pm.

Laundry: Speed Wash, Montes Nte. 42 (☎ 214 14 45), go 4 blocks west of the *jardín* down Hidalgo, then turn left. Full service 14 pesos per kg, 3kg minimum. Dry cleaning available. Open M-F 9am-3pm and 4-8pm, Sa 9am-3pm.

Luggage Storage: in the bus station. 3 pesos per hr. Open daily 6:30am-midnight.

Supermarket: Comercial Mexicana, Zaragoza Pte. 150 (☎ 216 33 57), 7½ blocks west on Corregidora. Take any westbound "Zaragoza" *micro* or walk 20min. Open M-Sa 8am-10pm, Su 8am-9pm.

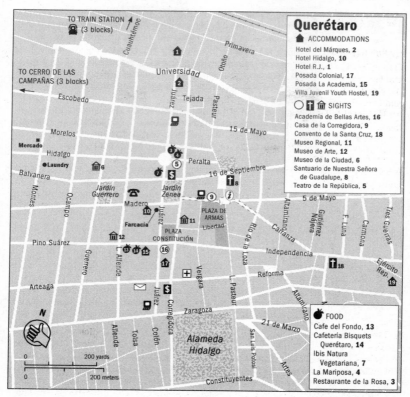

Querétaro

🛏 ACCOMMODATIONS

Hotel del Márques, **2**
Hotel Hidalgo, **10**
Hotel R.J., **1**
Posada Colonial, **17**
Posada La Academia, **15**
Villa Juvenil Youth Hostel, **19**

⊙ 🍴 🏛 SIGHTS

Academia de Bellas Artes, **16**
Casa de la Corregidora, **9**
Convento de la Santa Cruz, **18**
Museo Regional, **11**
Museo de Arte, **12**
Museo de la Ciudad, **6**
Santuario de Nuestra Señora
 de Guadalupe, **8**
Teatro de la República, **5**

🍎 FOOD
Cafe del Fondo, **13**
Cafetería Bisquets
 Querétaro, **14**
Ibis Natura
 Vegetariana, **7**
La Mariposa, **4**
Restaurante de la Rosa, **3**

Mercado: Mercado Hidalgo, on Montes between Hidalgo and Morelos. Small, but offers fresh produce and meat, as well as inexpensive taco stands. Open daily 7am-6pm.

Emergency: ☎066. **LOCATEL** finds lost people (☎214 33 11).

Police: Pie de la Cuesta 112 (☎220 91 91), in Colonia Desarrollo San Pablo. No English spoken. The **Angeles Verdes** (☎213 84 24) rescue stranded motorists.

Red Cross: (☎229 05 45), at Balaustradas and Circuito Estadio, near the bus station. **Ambulances** (☎229 05 05). No English spoken at either.

Pharmacy: Farmacias del Ahorro, Juárez 2 (☎216 17 60). Open 24hr.

Hospital: Sanatorio Alcocer Poza, Reforma 23 (☎214 19 20), near Corregidora.

Fax: Telecomm, Allende Nte. 4 (☎212 07 02; fax 214 39 48), 1 block west of the *jardín*. **Telegrams** and **Western Union.** Open M-F 8am-7:30pm, Sa-Su 9am-1pm.

Internet: CNCI, Juárez Sur 68 (☎214 45 84). Follow the narrow hallway between the cubicles to get to the *caja* to pay. 20 pesos per hr. Open M-Sa 7am-9pm.

Post Office: Arteaga Pte. 5 (☎212 01 12), between Juárez and Allende, 2 blocks south of the *jardín.* Open M-F 8am-5pm, Sa 9am-1pm.

Postal Code: 76000.

🏠 ACCOMMODATIONS

There are a handful of colorful places to lay your head near Querétaro's *jardín.* The cheapest are a hike from the *centro.* Call ahead on summer weekends, as Querétaro is a favorite for weekend warriors from Mexico City.

🏨 **Hotel Hidalgo,** Madero Pte. 11 (☎212 81 02), half a block from the *jardín*. A huge court-yard leads to comfy rooms with small baths and cable TV. Parking available. Attached restaurant serves tasty, inexpensive food. Singles 135 pesos; doubles 170 pesos.

Hotel del Márques, Juárez Nte. 104 (☎212 04 14 or 212 05 54), 4 blocks north of the *jardín*. An enormous stained-glass depiction of Querétaro's aqueduct and *agua purificada* welcome guests. Carpeted rooms have cable TV, phones, and sparkling tiled bathrooms. Some 2nd-fl. rooms with balconies. Parking lot. Singles 130 pesos; doubles 160 pesos; triples 180 pesos; quads 200 pesos.

Villa Juvenil Youth Hostel (☎223 31 42), on Ejército Republicano. From the *jardín*, walk 1 block south on Corregidora, then left on Independencia for 8 blocks. Veer right onto Ejército Republicano, just past Convento de Santa Cruz. Follow the stone wall on the right until you reach the sports and recreation complex; hostel is next to the swimming pool. While a bit remote, it's a bargain—large groups of athletes fill the rooms quickly so be sure to call ahead. No drinking or smoking. Reception 7am-10pm; call if arriving or staying out later. 20-peso linen deposit. Dorms with 8 bunks per room 30 pesos.

Posada Colonial, Juárez 9 (☎212 02 39), 2 blocks south of the *jardín*. Shabby rooms sport naked light bulbs and lack windows. Hope for quiet neighbors—some room partitions don't quite reach the rafters. Communal baths recently remodeled and have clean showers. Reception 24hr. Singles 60 pesos, with bath 72 pesos; doubles 102 pesos, with bath and TV 150 pesos; triples and quads with bath and TV 250 pesos.

Posada La Academia, Suárez 3 (☎224 27 39), 1 block southwest of the *jardín*. Rooms are a little dingy, but have private baths and TVs. Great location for the price. Singles 75 pesos; doubles from 100 pesos; up to 5 people 250 pesos.

Hotel R.J., Invierno 21 (☎212 04 88). Walk 5 long blocks north of the *jardín* to Universidad, cross the bridge to Invierno and continue half a block; RJ is on the left. Not the lap of luxury, but acceptable and easy on the wallet. Non-smokers may want to sniff their room first. Singles and doubles 80 pesos; triples 120 pesos; quads 145 pesos.

🍴 FOOD

Inexpensive restaurants face Jardín Zenea; pricier *loncherías* and outdoor cafes surround nearby Plaza Corregidora. Taco, *torta*, and other fast-food stands line 5 de Mayo and Juárez. Many restaurants stop serving the *menú del día* at 5 or 6pm.

🍴 **La Mariposa,** Peralta 7 (☎212 11 66), a block north of the *jardín*. This cafeteria and *pastelería* has been a local favorite for 60 years. Enjoy a variety of salads (9-32 pesos), *tortas* (13.5 pesos), or *comida típica* (34-38 pesos), served by blue-uniformed, apron-clad waitresses straight out of the 1940s. Open daily 8am-9:30pm.

Cafetería Bisquets Querétaro, Suárez 7. This popular family restaurant is packed from dawn until closing. Plain biscuits 4 pesos, with *pollo en mole* 12 pesos. *Antojitos* (16-30 pesos) and salads (23-32 pesos) are also tasty. Open daily 7am-11pm.

Ibis Natura Vegetariana, Juárez Nte. 47 (☎214 22 12), half a block north of the *jardín*. Sells vitamins and supplements to rescue your meat-weary metabolism. Lip-smacking veggie cheeseburgers (10 pesos), hearty *menú del día* (25 pesos), and an enormous selection of flavored yogurt (10 pesos). Open Su-F 8am-9:30pm.

Restaurante de la Rosa, Juárez Nte. 24 (☎212 87 84), at Peralta, across from Teatro Republicano. Mexican cuisine seasoned to perfection. *Enchiladas queretanas* 25 pesos, 4-course *menú del día* (27 pesos). Open M-Sa 9am-7:30pm, Su 9am-1pm.

Cafe del Fondo, Suárez 9 (☎212 09 05), between Juárez and Allende. This local hang-out boasts an enormous coffee grinder, constantly producing strong, exotic coffee drinks (15-35 pesos). Chess played all day. *Quesadillas* 10.5 pesos, sandwiches 8.5 pesos, breakfast specials 19-23 pesos. Open M-Sa 7am-10pm, Su 7:30am-9:30pm.

🔆 SIGHTS

If you've tired of art exhibits and Churrigueresque churches, Querétaro offers plazas, parks, and walkways perfect for a post-meal, pre-siesta stroll.

MUSEO REGIONAL. In the **Ex-Convento Franciscano de Santiago,** this modern museum highlights Mexican history with *indígena* artifacts, including a reproduction of a Nanho/Nonho (a modern indigenous group) chapel—enter through the 4-ft. door to come face-to-face with an enormous altar. The second floor is dedicated to the ex-convent's history; eerie holy music and mammoth audiovisuals set the stage for proper religious awe. *(At Corregidora and Madero, on the east side of the jardín.* ☎ *212 20 31. Open Tu-Su 10am-6pm. 25 pesos; seniors, children under 12, and Su free.)*

TEATRO DE LA REPÚBLICA. The *teatro* has borne witness to many historic events: the 1867 decision on Emperor Maximilian's fate, the 1917 drafting of the constitution in the **Sala de Constituyentes** upstairs, and the 1929 founding of the Partido Nacional de la Revolución (PNR), the precursor to today's Partido Revolucionario Institucional (PRI). The theater resembles a European opera house, with four levels of red velvet seating. *Tesoro Turístico,* available in the lobby, details upcoming events. *(At Peralta and Juárez, 1 block up from the jardín.* ☎ *212 03 39. Open Tu-Su 10am-3pm and 5-8pm. Free.)*

CONVENTO DE LA SANTA CRUZ. Built on the spot where the Spaniards defeated the Chichimeca Indians, this convent was an integral part of the evangelistic movement in Mexico and lower California. Nearly everything inside Santa Cruz (founded in 1683) is original—the clay pipes and rain-catching system date from the city's aqueduct days. The cell where Maximilian spent his last moments, on the second floor, has been left exactly as it was on the day of his execution. In one courtyard, trees grow thorns in the shape of crucifixes. A type of mimosa, they are known simply as **Árbol de la Cruz** (Tree of the Cross). It is said that these are the only trees of this kind in the world; attempts to plant seedlings elsewhere have failed. *(South of Jardín Zenea, follow Corregidora to Independencia; you'll reach the convent after 5 blocks.* ☎ *212 02 35. Open Tu-Su 9am-2pm and 4-6pm. Free, but small donation requested. Monks still inhabit the convent, so there is only access to the courtyard during 20min. guided tours, in Spanish or English. Tours leave every 5-10min.)*

SANTUARIO DE NUESTRA SEÑORA DE GUADALUPE. The church's white towers and central dome rise above their surroundings. The stained-glass windows toward the top let in dim light, and delicate chandeliers hang against a backdrop of pillars and frescoes. The image of *La Guadalupana* is by Miguel Cabrera. *(1 block north of Casa de la Corregidora, at Pasteur and 16 de Septiembre.* ☎ *212 07 32. Open daily 7am-9pm. Mass M-F at 8, 10am, and 8pm. Sa-Su at 2 and 7pm.)*

LA ALAMEDA HIDALGO. Built in 1790, the Alameda is a huge park perfect for a morning jog, romantic rendezvous, or afternoon stroll. *(3 blocks south on Corregidora from the jardín, entrance on Zaragoza. Open Th-Tu 8am-7pm.)*

MUSEO DE ARTE DE QUERÉTARO. Housed in an 18th-century Augustinian monastery with a beautiful courtyard, the museum's columns are topped with grimacing heads. An exhibit on local architecture supplements the many Baroque paintings. European canvasses, modern Mexican art, and Cristóbal de Villa Pando's 19th-century depictions of the apostles round out the formidable collection. *(Allende Sur 14, between Madero and Pino Suárez, 2 blocks south of the jardín.* ☎ *212 23 57. Open Tu-Su 10am-6pm. 12 pesos, seniors and children under 12 free; Tu free.)*

MUSEO DE LA CIUDAD. A well-organized display of religious art shares space with revolving exhibits of contemporary art. *(Guerrero 27, near Hidalgo.* ☎ *212 47 02 or 224 37 56. Open Tu-Su 11am-7pm. 5 pesos, students and children free; Su free.)*

CERRO DE LAS CAMPANAS (HILL OF THE BELLS). Named for the peculiar sound its rocks make as they collide, this hill is where Maximilian first established his military headquarters and later surrendered his sword in 1867. Directly ahead of the park entrance is the small **chapel** Maximilian's family built over the ground where the emperor and two of his generals were shot. Flowering trees and quiet paths lead the way to an impressive panoramic view of Querétaro and a large stone statue of Benito Juárez, the man responsible for Maximilian's execution. Behind the statue is **Museo del Sitio de Querétaro,** home to a small collection of maps and pictures detailing Maximilian's involvement in Mexico. *(Walk north of the jardín on Corregidora and turn left onto Escobedo. Proceed until Escobedo ends at Tecnológico (30min.), take a right and then your 1st left at the park entrance. Or, catch a "Ruta R" bus (3.5 pesos) on Allende anywhere south of Morelos; enter in front of the statue of Escobedo. Park open daily 7am-6pm. Museum open Tu-F 8am-6pm, Sa-Su 10am-6pm. Free.)*

OTHER SIGHTS. Querétaro's **Acueducto** stretches along de los Arcos, west of the *centro.* This distinctive structure, with its 74 arches of pink sandstone, was constructed in 1735 as a gift to perpetually parched Querétaro from the Marqués de Villas del Águila. A *mirador* overlooking all 1280m of the aqueduct is on Républicano, about three blocks past the Convento de la Santa Cruz. Up 5 de Mayo to the east of the *jardín* is **Plaza de la Independencia (Plaza de Armas),** a monument to Marqués. Faithful stone dogs surround his statue, drooling respectfully into a fountain. The plaza is bordered by trees, colorful cafes, shaded benches, and beautiful colonial buildings, including the **Casa de la Corregidora,** which housed government officials during colonial times. Today, the *casa* serves as the seat of the state government. **Andador Libertad,** two blocks from the *jardín,* connects Plaza de la Independencia and Corregidora. It is host to a slew of mellow vendors and *artesanía* shops. *(Open Th-M approximately 10am-9pm.)*

🎵 ENTERTAINMENT

Local entertainment, like almost everything else in Querétaro, revolves around Jardín Zenea. Brass-band concerts are given in the gazebo Sunday evenings 6-8pm, and myriad jugglers, *mariachis,* and magicians perform sporadically. **Jardín de los Platitos,** where Juárez meets Universidad north of the *zócalo,* dances to *mariachi* music. Things heat up around 11pm on Fridays and Saturdays.

NIGHTLIFE

Querétaro has many night clubs popular with locals and visiting 20-somethings from Mexico City. Leave your flip-flops, jeans, and t-shirts at home.

- ◼ **Quadros,** 5 de Mayo 16 (☎212 63 86). Look for the blinking light on the walkway to the left of Ex-Convento de San Francisco. Each night at 8pm musicians start 1hr. sets of anything from blues to *trova.* At this intimate cafe/bar, would-be Selenas compete for drinks and prizes during amateur hour (Sa 10pm). A small menu served. Beer 20 pesos, drinks from 35 pesos. Cover F and Sa 30 pesos. Open Tu-Su from 5pm.

- ◼ **Vazzo,** Juárez 30 (☎214 30 33), on the west side of Pl. de la Constitución. The hip place to be for young locals. Huge metal light fixtures and candles the size of cannons light up the covered courtyard, sprinkled with black couches and tall tables. Dancing starts late, and people writhe to techno and top 40 anywhere they find space. Beer 18 pesos, drinks from 30 pesos. Cover 50 pesos. Open Th-Sa 9pm-3am.

- **Jota B Jota Club and Bar,** Quintana 109 (☎213 43 07), a 25-peso cab ride from the *centro.* Groove to booming rhythms and a merciless strobe light. For a more relaxed environment, the bar next door has pool tables (free). Sip a strong margarita while gazing at vintage coke signs and the ornately carved bar. Live music starts at midnight. Bar cover 10 pesos, disco cover 20 pesos. Open F-Sa 9pm-3am.

FESTIVALS

The annual **Feria de Querétaro** usually takes place during the second week of December. The **Feria de Santa Anna,** complete with bulls running through the congested streets, happens on July 26. The whole town dances during the **Celebración de la Santa Cruz de los Milagros** and the **Fiestas Patrias,** which take place during the second or third week of September. Other festivals include the **Feria International** del **Queso y del Vino** in May or July, a festival commemorating the founding of the city on July 25, and, of course, *Semana Santa* in March and April.

For information about cultural events, stop by the **Casa de la Cultura,** on your right after Carranza splits off from 5 de Mayo. There you can pick up *ACONSE-Jarte,* a comprehensive monthly bulletin including listings on art, dance, theater, literature, music, and workshops. Or visit **Querétaro 2000,** on Quintana, a huge stretch of parks and athletic facilities. *(Take a "Ruta 15" bus from Ocampo or "Ruta B" from Allende.☎ 220 68 14. Open daily 6am-8pm.)*

HIDALGO

PACHUCA   ☎7

An easy hour from Mexico City, Pachuca (pop. 220,000), Hidalgo's capital city, appears on the tourist map like a breath of fresh mountain air. The busy but untouristed town draws its delectable flavor from the combination of original Spanish settlers and English miners, who arrived in hordes in the 19th century. From Pachuca, visitors can explore the breathtaking mountains nearby or stay within the city for a good lesson in silver mining and processing.

⬛ TRANSPORTATION. Pachuca is approximately 90km northeast of Mexico City on **Mex. 85.** The bus station is a fair distance from downtown. Frequent *combis* run from the station to Plaza de la Constitución (6am-10pm, 2.5 pesos). To get from there to the *zócalo* (Plaza de la Independencia), make a left on Hidalgo and a right on Ocampo. From the bus station, ADO (☎713 29 10) goes to: Mexico City's **Cién Metros** (1¼hr., every 15min. 24hr., 42 pesos); **Poza Rica** (4½hr.; 8:20am, noon, 3, 8:45pm; 85 pesos); **Tuxpan** (6hr., 8:45pm, 110 pesos). Flecha Roja (☎713 24 71) goes to: **Mexico City** (1¼hr., every 10min. 4am-10:30pm, 38 pesos). Estrella Blanca (☎713 27 47) goes to **Mexico City Airport** (2hr., every hr. 4:15am-6:15pm, 70 pesos) and **Querétaro** (4½hr., every hr. 5:15am-6:15pm, 97 pesos).

⬛⬛ ORIENTATION AND PRACTICAL INFORMATION. Finding one's way can be difficult, as many streets curve and change names. Be prepared to ask for directions. Pachuca's *zócalo* is **Plaza de la Independencia,** bordered by **Matamoros** on the east and **Allende** on the west. **Guerrero** is parallel to Allende, one block to the west. Matamoros and Allende converge a few blocks south at **Plaza Juárez,** which has two parts: an open cement space with a statue of the man himself and a small park. **Av. Juárez** juts from the statue's base, while **Revolución** extends from the park.

Pachuca's **tourist office** is at the bottom of the clock tower in the *zócalo.* The friendly staff speaks English and offers road maps to surrounding sights. (☎715 14 11. Open M-F 9am-7pm, Sa-Su 10am-6pm.) **Bancomer,** on Allende at the west side of the *zócalo,* has a 24hr. **ATM.** (☎718 00 22. Open M-F 8:30am-4:30pm, Sa 10am-2pm. Open for exchange M-F 8:30am-3pm.) **Mercado Juárez** lies on the north side of Plaza de la Constitución. **Emergency:** ☎060. **Police:** (☎711 18 80), in Plaza Juárez. **Red Cross** (☎714 17 20). **Farmacia Similares,** Revolución 702, seven blocks south of Plaza Juárez. (☎714 43 61. Open 24hr.) **Medical Assistance: IMSS** (☎713 78 33), off Maderos, far from downtown. **Internet Access: Compu Renta,** Revolución 303, a block past the rotary on the left side of the street. (☎714 56 54. 20 pesos per hr. Open M-F 10am-9pm, Sa 10am-6pm.) **Post office:** Juárez at Iglesias, two blocks south of Plaza Juárez. (☎713 25 92. Open M-F 8am-5pm.) **Postal code:** 42070.

⬛⬛ ACCOMMODATIONS AND FOOD. Fewer than two blocks south of the *zócalo* is **Hotel Noriega,** Matamoros 305. Spacious rooms with tiled floors and wooden furniture include private baths. (☎715 15 55. Singles 175 pesos; doubles 205 pesos; triples 250 pesos; quads 300 pesos. TV 10 pesos extra.) A few blocks farther south is **Hotel Hidalgo,** Matamoros 503. Carpeted rooms have clean private baths. (☎715 17 35. Singles 140 pesos; doubles 160 pesos; triples 200 pesos; quads 280 pesos. TV 20 pesos extra.)

An influx of Cornish miners came to Pachuca in the 19th century. Their two lasting legacies are *fútbol* and *pastes* (pastry shells full of meat, potatoes, and onions, with a dash of *chile*). The filling snacks are sold all over town (3 pesos), stuffed with anything from beans to tuna. Try **Pastes Kikos,** across from Plaza Juárez in the *portal* facing the statue's back. (*Pastes* 3.5 pesos.) ◪**Lisú Vegetariano,** Revolución 401, four blocks south of Plaza Juárez, is *the* place to go for delicious food in Pachuca. The hearty *menú del día* (30 pesos) is a full-course vegetarian feast. You're likely to find entrees such as veggie pizza with avocados, peppers, and jalapeños, or eggplant lasagna. (☎714 78 73. Open M-Sa 9am-6pm.) **La Luz Roja,** at the corner of Guerrero, in the *portal* next to Plaza Juárez facing the statue's left shoulder, is a bit cramped due to immense popularity. Try the delicious *pozole* or *morelianos* (15 pesos each; open M-Sa 8am-9pm).

◪ **SIGHTS.** The *zócalo* is dominated by the imposing **Reloj Monumental,** built in England by Big Ben's manufacturers to celebrate 100 years of Mexican independence. This huge clock tower is an example of the French architecture popular during Porfirio Díaz's regime. The female statues represent Independence, Liberation, Constitution, and Reform. Funded by local mining companies, the clock was fashioned of white stone from nearby Mineral del Monte. To reach **Archivo Histórico** and **Museo de Minería,** Mina 110, walk one block past the *zócalo* on Matamoros and take the first left onto Mina (the street across from the Bital). Follow it for 1½ blocks. A former mining company office, it holds a notable collection of rocks, minerals, mining tools, and heavy machinery. (☎715 09 76. Open Tu-Su 10am-2pm and 3-6pm. 6 pesos. Video in English and Spanish at 11am, noon, 1, 4, 5pm.)

The **Centro Cultural Hidalgo** is in the **Ex-Convento de San Francisco.** To get there from the *zócalo,* take Matamoros south of the square for one block, turn left on Mina, take it for two blocks, and turn right on Hidalgo (not to be confused with Viaducto Hidalgo). After three blocks you'll be in front of the *centro.* The cultural center contains the **Museo Nacional de la Fotografía,** an impressive survey of the technological history of photography. The museum holds a fascinating collection of Mexican photographs, one showing Pancho Villa and Emiliano Zapata as they marched into Mexico City in 1914. (☎714 36 53. Open Tu-Su 10am-6pm. Free.) Adjoining the cultural center is the **Church of San Francisco.** One block past the Ex-Convento is **Parque Hidalgo,** a favorite hangout for local teens.

NEAR PACHUCA: MINERAL DEL CHICO

Combis run to Mineral el Chico (40min., every 30min. 7:30am-7:30pm, 6.5 pesos). They leave from Galeana; follow Guerrero north of the zócalo and make a left on Galeana, then head uphill about 2 blocks. The stop is in front of Bazarcito, a blue shop.

Forty minutes of breathtaking scenery separate Pachuca from the tiny town of Mineral del Chico (pop. 500). Nestled in **Parque Nacional el Chico,** the town has a couple of restaurants, a small church, and a few houses. Numerous hikes and striking views of nearby rock formations make it a great escape from urban congestion. Follow the road that runs uphill to the right from the *combi* stop to reach the spectacular vista point, **Peña del Cuervo** (6km). If the trek is too long for your tastes, ask the driver; he may agree to take you there. Walking past the church and heading downhill to the left will take you through old silver mines, and lead to the rock formation dubbed **Tres Monjas** (3km) for its resemblance to nuns bowed in prayer. Locals are very friendly and will happily suggest other trails to explore.

NEAR PACHUCA: REAL DEL MONTE

Catch a colectivo in front of the Iglesia de la Asunción, on the corner of Carranza and Villigran, near the east side of Plaza de la Constitución (4 pesos).

The streets used to reverberate with the sounds of nearby mines, but now, Real del Monte is a colorful, idyllic little town 9km north of Pachuca. **Mina Acosta,** on Guerrero north of Plaza Principal (20min.), is a relic of Real's mining history. This mine passed through the hands of Spanish, English, Mexican, and US owners before finally coming under government control. The building on your left as you enter housed mine managers. The obsidian shards that line the tops of the walls surrounding the mine kept silver-robbers out. (Open M-F 9am-3pm.)

Real del Monte offers good hiking and climbing opportunities. *Combis* depart from La Madre in front of Deportivo de la Ciudad, a.k.a the Escuela Primaria, for **Peñas Cargadas** (every hr. 6am-5pm; 5 pesos), a massive rock formation 3km away. You can hike there, mostly uphill, by following the signs. At the site, **Cargada Mayor,** on your left, is 100m. To its right is **Cargada Menor,** a mere 80m. Next to Menor stands **El Pilón** (70m tall), and on the far right, **Cerrote** (30m). Many hiking paths weave through **Peñas Cargadas.** Only very experienced rock climbers should attempt to scale the rocks (crosses at the bottom mark spots where several have met their deaths). Interested climbers should contact **Lucio Ramírez** (Club Alpino, Lerdo de Tejada 4 in Mineral del Monte) or stop by **Club Alpino**'s headquarters in Deportivo de la Ciudad. (Climbing excursions Su 7am. Open Su 7am-7:30pm.)

TULA
☎ 7

Travelers come to Tula (pop. 90,000) for one reason only: to see her famous ruins. The archaeological site of Tula, is, without a doubt, one of the most historically significant in Mesoamerica. Ruins aside, the city of Tula is unexciting at best, with little to distinguish it from other Mexican towns. Daytrippers from Mexico City (80km) and Pachuca (75km) are lured here by glossy pamphlets and the myth of Quetzalcóatl, but usually leave quickly when the day and ruin-stomping is done.

TRANSPORTATION AND PRACTICAL INFORMATION

From Mexico City to Tula, take an AVM (☎737 96 91) bus from Central de Autobuses del Norte, Sala 8 (1½hr., every 40min. 7am-9pm, 39 pesos). Once in Tula, to reach the *zócalo* from the **bus station** (☎732 02 25), head toward the cathedral, visible from most of the city. AVM (☎732 01 18) runs to **Mexico City** (2hr., every 20min. 6am-8pm, 30 pesos) and **Pachuca** (2hr., every hr. 5:30am-6:30pm, 35 pesos). Flecha Amarilla (☎732 02 25) goes to: **Guanajuato** (5hr., 10:20am, 140 pesos); **Morelia** (6hr., 8am, 157 pesos); **Querétaro** (2½hr., 4am-7:30pm, 58 pesos).

Banamex, at Valle and Juárez, exchanges currency and traveler's checks and has a 24hr. **ATM.** (☎732 37 72. Open M-F 9am-5pm, Sa 10am-2pm.) **Farmacia Central,** is on the corner of Hidalgo and Zaragoza. (☎732 01 04. Open daily 8am-10pm.) **Market:** behind the cathedral. (Open daily 6am-8pm.) **Police** (☎733 20 49) are at 5 de Mayo 408. **Red Cross:** ☎732 00 18 or 732 12 50. **LADATELs** are near the bus station and on Zaragoza and Hidalgo. **V-Link 86,** Plaza de la Constitución 17, at the back of the ground floor, behind the ice cream stand, has **Internet** access. (☎732 7359. 15 pesos per hr. Open M-Sa 9am-8pm.)

ACCOMMODATIONS AND FOOD

Budget rooms don't come easy in Tula. The best deal in town is the **Auto Hotel Cuéllar,** 5 de Mayo 23. Rooms with phone, cable TV, carpet, and slightly worn baths surround a quiet courtyard of flowering plants. (☎732 04 42. Singles 133 pesos; doubles 183 pesos.) Good, cheap food is cooked right in front of your eyes in the market behind the cathedral. (*Comida corrida* 20 pesos.) **Restaurante Casa Blanca,** Hidalgo 114, serves a tasty five-course *comida corrida* (42 pesos) in a bright, traditional setting. (☎732 22 74. Open M-Sa 8am-8:45pm, Su 8am-7pm.) Family-run **Pizza In-Out,** Plaza de la Constitución 17, upstairs, has pizzas (from 50 pesos) and delicious *tortas* (25 pesos). Meatless options are available.

CORTÉS AS GOD One of the most legendary stories of the Spanish conquest is set in Tula. Though accounts diverge, the most widely accepted version tells that: following the assassination of Ce Técpatl Mixcóatl, the leader of a Tolteca-Chichimeca tribe, his son, Ce Acatl Topiltzin, who was born in the year 1 Reed (AD 947), avenged his father and led his people to establish the new capital of Tollán (later known as Tula). The benevolent and beloved Ce Acatl Topiltzin identified himself with and worshipped Quetzalcóatl, the peaceful feathered-serpent god and sponsor of the arts. After many years, a rival faction favoring Quetzalcóatl's rivals, worshippers of the war god Tezcatlipoca, tricked Ce Acatl into neglecting his religious duties (or, by other accounts, into sleeping with his mother). Horribly disgraced, Ce Acatl left Tula in self-imposed exile and boarded a raft of serpents, promising to return in the year 1 Reed. Hundreds of years after Ce Acatl's departure, the *conquistador* Hernán Cortés landed on Mexico's shores in the year 1 Reed. The rest, as they say, is history.

👁 THE ARCHAEOLOGICAL SITE OF TULA

Taxis will take you from the sitio stand on Zaragoza at Hidalgo in town. ☎ 732 05 65. (20 pesos.) Frequent peseros return to the bus station or centro (3 pesos). You can also walk (30min.). From the bus station, turn right on Ocampo and follow signs to the archaeological zone. Open daily 9am-5pm. 25 pesos; Su free. Museum free.

Tula's importance in Pre-Hispanic Mexico cannot be overstated. Settled and occupied by various small nomadic tribes during the Pre-Classic and Classic Periods, control of the city is thought to have been concentrated in the hands of powerful Teotihuacán. In the late Classic Period, however, the area was abandoned and then resettled by a different group—the Tolteca-Chichimeca (more commonly, the Toltec). By the early Post-Classic Period (AD 900-1000), the Toltec capital entered a period known as the Tollán phase, marked by construction and expansion. New pyramids arose, the city was carefully realigned, and the population peaked at around 40,000. A close resemblance in architecture between Tula and the Post-Classic Maya center at Chichén Itzá (see p. 591) has led archaeologists to hypothesize on some sort of relationship between the two, perhaps through trade or conquest. The Toltecs, whose name means "builders" in Náhuatl, relied on irrigation, and modeled their architecture after the style of Teotihuacán. During the 200-year-long Toltec heyday, the once-peaceful kingdom turned violent and vicious. When crop failures and droughts weakened the capital in 1165, neighboring Chichimecas sacked the city, burning temples and destroying much of what the Toltecs had built. The devastated city was further ravaged when the Aztecs subsequently occupied and looted it. Today, among the Toltec remains, the Aztecs' temporary stay is evident—bits of scattered Aztec ceramics and pottery. Unfortunately, the ruins as they stand provide little testament to the Toltec's power—only 17 sq. km of the ruins have been excavated and many buildings have eroded due to poor rock quality, lack of maintenance, and the destructive practices of the original excavators.

JUEGO DE PELOTA #1 (BALLCOURT #1). From the entrance area, a 600m dirt path zigzags past cacti through two sets of vendor stalls before arriving at the main plaza. The first structure to the right as you reach the main plaza is Ballcourt #1, just north of the large Edificio de los Atlantes. This court, nearly 70m long, once held a depiction of a ball player in ritual dress, which is now located in the Museo Nacional de Antropología in Mexico City (see p. 108).

EDIFICIO DE LOS ATLANTES (PYRAMID B). To the left lies the monumental Edificio de los Atlantes, Tula's signature edifice. In front of the pyramid stand three rows of 14 columns, which presumably supported some sort of walkway leading to the pyramid. Close inspection of the statues (each a whopping 9.6m tall) at the top of the pyramid reveals traces of red pigment. These statues of warriors originally supported a temple and altar dedicated to Quetzalcóatl. The sides of the pyramid were decorated with reliefs of jaguars, coyotes, eagles, and feathered serpents, each symbolizing different classes of warriors.

EL COATEPANTLI (THE WALL OF SNAKES). Along the pyramid's northern side is El Coatepantli. This wall, which depicts jaguars and serpents in procession, so impressed the Aztecs that they built copies around the plazas of their own cities. Reliefs of serpents feasting on humans adorn the adjacent wall.

PALACIO QUEMADO (BURNT PALACE). Immediately west of Edificio de los Atlantes is Palacio Quemado, so named because it was originally thought to have been burned during the Chichimecas' sacking of Tula. The building was once an administrative center. A *chac-mool* (reclining model of the rain god Tlaloc) found in the central patio now reclines near Edificio de los Atlantes, under the awning.

TEMPLO PRINCIPAL (PYRAMID C). The Toltecs built their largest building, Templo (or Edificio) Principal, on the eastern boundary of the plaza facing sunrise. The object of deliberate destruction by the Chichimecas and others following Tula's abandonment at the end of the 12th century, Templo Principal now pales in comparison to Edificio de los Atlantes. Not fully excavated and overgrown with weeds, Templo Principal cannot be climbed from the front—you must scramble up a steep path in its southeast corner. The temple was likely adorned with a massive sculptural slab found nearby, covered with images of Quetzalcóatl in his manifestation as Tlahuizcaltec Uhtli, "the morning star."

OTHER SIGHTS. Adjoining **Ballcourt #2** on the interior of the plaza is **El Tzompantli**, a small platform built by the Aztecs. Tzompantli means "place of skulls"; the platform was used to display the victims of sacrifice. Ballcourt #2 is smaller than Ballcourt #1, and associated more with the sacrificial uses of the game.

ESTADO DE MÉXICO

VALLE DE BRAVO   ☎ 7

From the mountain views at the end of every cobblestone street to the luscious fruit sold in the market by traditionally-clad *indígenas*, everything about this 16th-century town is perfect. Even the stray dogs look well-fed. Wealthy Mexico City residents keep vacation homes on the edges of Valle, and though new business has made the town wealthy, it retains a cozy, traditional feel. This is not accidental; in 1972 Valle was declared a "typical town," and among other restrictions, construction on new buildings was strictly curtailed. You don't come to Valle to "do," rather to wander and marvel at the beauty of it all.

TRANSPORTATION. To get to the *centro* from Valle's bus station, turn right as you exit, walk downhill one block, and make a right on Zaragoza. Continue for two blocks until you see Centro Comercial Isseymym, and turn left. You will see the church at the end of the street. The **market** is one block before the church on the right. To the right of the church, as you face it, is **Plaza Independencia. 5 de Mayo** runs in front of the church, and **Toluca** is the street on the opposite side of the plaza, becoming **Bocanegra** as it continues uphill. Intersecting Toluca and 5 de Mayo is **Pagaza.** Second-class buses leave for **Mexico City** (3hr., every 20min. 6am-6pm, 62 pesos) via **Toluca** (2hr., 35 pesos). Tickets are sold in the booth out front.

PRACTICAL INFORMATION. **Bancomer,** across from the church, changes currency or checks, and has a 24hr. **ATM.** (☎262 02 08. Open M-F 8:30am-4pm.) **Emergency:** ☎060. **Police:** Díaz 200 (☎262 01 26). **Red Cross:** (☎262 03 91) on the corner of Jiménez and de la Cuenca. Some English spoken. **Farmacia Paty,** on the right of the plaza, facing the church. (☎262 01 62. Open daily 8am-9pm.) **Fax: Telecomm,** 16 de

Septiembre 415B, near the bus station. (☎262 01 71. Open M-F 9am-3pm, Sa 9am-1pm.) **Internet Access: Tiempo en Línea.** Walk one block down Pagaza and take a left—the cafe is on your left. (☎262 15 48. 20 pesos per hr., free coffee with Internet use. Open M-Sa 10am-9pm, Su 2-9pm.) **Post office:** Pagaza 200. (☎262 03 73. Open M-F 9am-4pm, Sa 9am-1pm.) **Postal Code:** 51200.

▐▊ ACCOMMODATIONS AND FOOD. Posada Mary, Pl. Independencia 1, has a prime location, with affordable prices, and clean, simple, comfortable rooms with mismatched decorations. Try to get one with a plaza view. (☎262 42 61. Singles 150 pesos; doubles 200 pesos; cable TV 20 pesos extra.) **Posada Familiar,** 16 de Septiembre 417, is down the street from the bus station. Look for the "Hotel Interior" sign on the left. Peach-colored rooms have low ceilings, and baths have a touch of mildew, but the courtyard is pleasant. (☎262 12 22. Singles 120 pesos; doubles 130 pesos; triples 160 pesos.)

If you're hungry for something little, cheap, and quick, try any of the holes-in-the-wall between the bus station and the *centro*. For something a bit nicer, duck into **Restaurant Bar Los Torres,** across from Centro Vocacional Isseymym, en route from the bus station to the *centro*. The friendly patrons have been known to bust out guitars and sing. (☎262 27 24. Breakfast and *comida corrida* 25 pesos, beer 10 pesos. Open daily 8am-8pm.) At **Cafe Herencia,** Pagoza 100, beaming staff serve delectable *tortas* (8-10 pesos), including a deliciously mushroomy vegetarian one. (☎262 27 90. Coffee 8-13 pesos, beer 10 pesos. Open Th-Tu 10:30am-8pm.)

IXTAPAN DE LA SAL   ☎7

Life is good in Ixtapan de la Sal (pop. 40,000). A short walk from the mass-produced water park, upscale spas, and fancy resorts is a uniquely beautiful, clean town that seems entirely made of shiny, white stones. Surrounding the lively plaza are a refreshingly simple rust-and-white church and quiet streets. Tranquil Ixtapan de la Sal may be forgotten by history books, but pleasant memories last forever.

▐ TRANSPORTATION. The **bus station** is actually in Tonatico, a small town just to the south of Ixtapan. Buses usually stop in front of Ixtapan's water park before proceeding to the station. Only a 15min. walk from the center of town, this is a much more convenient place to disembark, provided you haven't stowed anything under the bus. If you get off at the bus station, take an "Ixtapan" *combi* (2 pesos). To leave town, you'll have to go to the bus terminal (taxis 20 pesos). Tres Estrellas de Centro (☎141 10 05) sends second-class buses to: **Mexico City** (2hr., every hr. 6am-8pm, 65 pesos); **Taxco** (1hr., every 40min. 6:10am-7:35pm, 40 pesos); **Toluca** (1hr., every 20min. 6am-8pm, 37 pesos). Flecha Roja (☎141 10 05) goes second-class to: **Acapulco** (6hr., 3 per day, 160 pesos) via **Taxco** (1¼hr., 33 pesos) and **Cuernavaca** (3hr., 7 per day 8am-6pm, 40 pesos).

▐▊ ORIENTATION AND PRACTICAL INFORMATION. Ixtapan's main street is **Juárez,** which ends after 500m at the spa, water park, and resorts. Running parallel to Juárez, to the right while looking toward the resorts, is **Allende.** Some of the main streets perpendicular to Juárez, listed in order from the south end of town to the resorts, are **20 de Noviembre, Independencia, 16 de Septiembre, Aldama,** and **Constitución.** There is no tourist office, but an **information booth** stands at the end of Juárez, on the north side of the market in front of the resorts. **Banco Santander,** Allende Sur 20, exchanges currency. (☎143 07 77. Open M-F 9am-4pm.) **Farmacia El Fénix,** Pl. de Mártires 1, on the *zócalo*. (Open M-F 8am-10pm, Sa-Su 9am-3pm and 5-9pm.) **Luggage storage:** in the bus station. (3.5 pesos per day. Open daily 7am-8pm.) **Police:** ☎143 02 44. **Red Cross:** (☎143 19 39), Carretera Federal at Deportiva. English spoken. **Fax: Computel,** Juárez 7. (☎143 25 37. Open daily 7am-9pm.) **Internet: Inter Coffee,** 16 de Septiembre 208. (☎143 10 10. 20 pesos per hr. Open M-Sa 9am-8pm, Su 9am-noon.) **Post Office:** on 16 de Septiembre, two blocks from the church. (☎143 02 23. Open M-F 9am-4pm, Sa 9am-1pm.) **Postal code:** 51900.

⌐⌐ ACCOMMODATIONS AND FOOD. If you avoid obscenely priced resorts and spas, Ixtapan has some great deals. ◪**Hotel María Isabel,** Kiss 11, is the best bargain. To get there from Júarez facing the resorts, turn right on 20 de Noviembre, take the first right onto Matamoros, and then the first left. The hotel is in the middle of the block on the right and has impeccable rooms, baths, cable TVs with remotes, and a top-floor sun deck. (☎143 01 02. 90 pesos per person; 150 pesos with 3 meals.) **Casa de Huéspedes Sofía,** 20 de Noviembre 4, off Juárez, down one block on 20 de Noviembre. Pink walls, cable TV, fluffy floral bedspreads, and large baths with purple fixtures reward guests. (☎143 18 51. 100 pesos per person.) Pleasant **Casa de Huéspedes Francis,** Obregón 6, near the church, has a large, fern-filled lobby and a friendly dog. (☎143 04 03. 70 pesos per person.)

A good meal in Ixtapan's *centro* isn't cheap; *comida corrida* prices hover around 50 pesos. The stands directly before the water park are more reasonably-priced (*comida corrida* 30 pesos). Still, a leisurely meal in the gorgeous *centro* is worth it. **La Puga,** off the *zócalo* on Guerrero, is a favorite local hangout. (☎143 38 10. Tacos 6 pesos, *tostadas* 7 pesos. Open daily 4pm-11:30pm.) **Pepe's Pizza and Pasta,** on the corner of Juárez and Aldama, is a Mexican-style pizzeria. Pizzas start at 19 pesos, pastas at 14 pesos. (☎143 11 15. Open daily July-Aug. 9am-10pm; Sept.-June noon-10:30pm.) **Panificadora Ixtapan,** Obregón 101, near Allende, sells hot bread fresh from the oven. (1 peso per roll. ☎143 06 54. Open daily 7am-9:30pm.)

◪ SIGHTS. Most people visit Ixtapan to enjoy the massive water park/spa/thermal springs complex aptly named **Ixtapan,** at the end of Juárez. (☎143 22 00. Open daily 7am-7pm. Water park open M-F 11am-5pm, Sa-Su 10am-5:30pm. 110 pesos, children 50 pesos.) For a less expensive dip in soothing thermal waters, go to the **balneario** in town at the corner of Allende and 20 de Noviembre. Splurge on a massage (70 pesos per 25min.) or mud mask. (☎143 06 00. 15 pesos, children 10 pesos. Open daily 7am-6pm.) To reach **Plaza de los Mártires,** turn right off Juárez, facing the water park, onto Independencia and continue straight three or four blocks. The plaza is a bright, beautiful combination of old and new architecture. An obelisk-like monument dedicated to the martyrs of the Revolution stands in front of the **Santuario de la Asunción de Maria,** an astonishing white church with burgundy and rust trim. Inlaid mosaic benches surround the garden, while gold ornamentation, stained-glass windows, and murals adorn the interior. A glass case holds a silver Christ in adjoining **Capilla del Santísima y del Perdón.** (Open daily 6am-8pm.)

TOLUCA ☎7

Toluca ("Those who bow their heads" in Náhuatl) was a thriving Pre-Hispanic center until its conquest by Hernán Cortés. Officially declared a city in 1799, Toluca became the capital of the Estado de México in 1846. Today, old-timers wistfully recall the old Toluca, before industry rapidly expanded, traffic congestion and pollution became serious problems, and the overt hand of US capitalism slapped the town with ungainly billboards. Despite these changes, a lingering small-town atmosphere and incredible cultural attractions still charm visitors.

⌐ TRANSPORTATION

The **bus terminal** is tucked between Paseo Tollocan and Berriozabal, southeast of the *centro.* Buses run back and forth from the *centro* to the terminal. To return, board a "Terminal" bus (3 pesos) on Juárez north of Independencia. Taxis make the jaunt for 20-30 pesos. Flecha Roja serves **Mexico City** (1 hr., every 5min. 4:40am-8:30pm, 33 pesos) and **Querétaro** (3½hr., every 20min. 4:40am-7:20pm, 80 pesos). Naucalpan goes to Mexico City's Metro stop Torero (1½hr, every 7 min. 5am-9pm, 28 pesos). Herradura de Plata (☎217 00 24) heads for **Morelia** (4hr., every 45 min. 6:15am-7pm, 85 pesos) and other destinations. Tres Estrellas serves: **Cuernavaca** (2½hr., every 30min. 5am-7:45pm, 41 pesos); **Ixtapan** (1hr., every 20min. 3am-8:15pm, 33 pesos); **Taxco** (2½hr., every 40min. 6:20am-8:20pm, 68 pesos).

■ ⓘ ORIENTATION AND PRACTICAL INFORMATION

Paseo Tollocan connects Toluca to Mexico City. The *zócalo*, cathedral, and *portales* constitute the *centro* and are bounded by **Hidalgo** on the south, **Lerdo de Tejada** on the north, **Juárez** on the east, and **Bravo** on the west. **Independencia** parallels Hidalgo one block to the north and forms the south side of the *zócalo*. **Morelos** runs parallel to Hidalgo one block to the south. A word of warning: address numbers on Hidalgo increase in either direction from the center of the *portales*. Most of Toluca's attractions are a short walk from the *portales;* big blue signs marked "M" for museum point the way.

Tourist Office: Urawa 100, Ste. 110 (☎212 60 48 or 01 800 849 13 33), at Paseo Tollocan, 6 blocks northeast of the bus station in the large yellow municipal government building behind Wal-Mart. Take any "Wal-Mart" bus. Open M-F 9am-6pm.

Currency Exchange: Bancomer (☎214 37 00), on the corner of Juárez and Hidalgo, has a 24hr. **ATM.** Open M-F 8:30am-4pm.

Luggage Storage: In the bus terminal. 5 pesos per hr. Open daily 7am-9pm.

Markets: Mercado 16 de Septiembre, Manuel Gómez Pedraza between Ignacio Rayón and Sor Juana Inés de la Cruz, 2 blocks north of the Cosmovitral. Open M-Sa 8am-7:30pm, Su 8am-6:30pm. **Mercado Juárez,** behind the bus station on Fabela. When vendors pour in from the countryside, is the best time. Open daily 8am-6:30pm. Artisans sell crafts in the square west of the Cosmovitral. Usually open daily 9am-7pm.

Supermarket: Gigante (☎215 94 00), Juárez at Instituto Literario. Open daily 8:30am-10pm.

Emergency:☎060 or call **LOCATEL** (☎213 31 83).

Police: Morelos 1300 (☎214 93 52).

Red Cross: (☎217 25 40), Jesús Carranza, southwest of the *centro*, 1 block south of Paseo Tollocan and 1 block west of Paseo Colón. No English spoken.

Pharmacy: Farmacia Regis, Morelos 110 (☎213 28 80), a block south of Hidalgo at Aldama. Open M-F 8am-10pm, Sa-Su 9am-9pm; knock after hours.

Medical care: IMSS, Paseo Tollocan 620 (☎217 07 33), 5 blocks from the bus station. Some English spoken.

Internet Access: Punto Imagen (☎215 95 30), Hidalgo Pte. 205. Stationery store, bookstore, and Internet cafe all in one. 20 pesos per hr. Open daily 8am-8pm.

Fax: Telecomm (☎217 07 74), in bus station. Open M-F 9am-2:45pm, Sa-Su 9am-12:30pm.

Post office: Hidalgo 300 (☎214 90 68), 2 blocks east of Juárez. Open M-F 8am-4pm, Sa 9am-1pm.

Postal code: 50141.

▐ ACCOMMODATIONS

Inexpensive hotels occupy prime real estate, amid the museums and restaurants of the *centro*. Toluca's budget accommodations have little else to offer besides location. Thanks to business travelers and their expense accounts, prices are higher than those in more touristed towns. Meanwhile, budget hotels earn a substantial portion of their income from couples looking for a bit of privacy.

Hotel La Casa del Abuelo, Hidalgo 404 (☎213 36 42). If you crave luxury, or just a TV and seat on the toilet in your bath, this pretty pink hotel will come to your rescue. Singles 190-225 pesos; matrimonials 250 pesos; doubles 350 pesos.

Hotel La Hacienda, Hidalgo 508 (☎214 36 34), between Ascension and Ocampo. Sparkling halls and lobby lead to rooms with TVs and private baths. Not as nice as you may expect for the price. Singles 200 pesos; doubles 350 pesos.

Hotel Maya, Hidalgo 413 (☎214 48 00), a few blocks west of the *centro*, is small and homey. Quirky homespun quilts, clean communal bathrooms, and a flower-laden courtyard. Singles 70-80 pesos; doubles 100 pesos.

Hotel Alpez, Ascencio 200 (☎214 86 19), 2 blocks north of Hidalgo, across the street from Museo de la Acuarela. If you can't get in somewhere else, this busy little hotel will do. Private baths are clean but small. Not overflowing with niceties, but the price is right. Singles 95 pesos, with TV 110 pesos; doubles with TV 185 pesos.

█ FOOD

Restaurants and cheap stalls clutter the storefronts of the *portales*. *Chorizo* (spicy sausage), a local specialty, is served with everything—from *queso fundido* (melted cheese) to *tortas*. Traditional candies including *palanquetas* (peanut brittle), candied fruits, and *dulces de leche* (milk sweets) are popular. *Panaderías* on Hidalgo make delicious sweet breads, good for breakfasts or light snacks.

Cafe Zodiac, Hidalgo 232. Relax with a sandwich (24-45 pesos) and coffee (23 pesos) in this intimate bar-cafe. Around 9pm, live shows incorporating audience participation entertain an all ages crowd, including families. Open Tu-Sa 6:30pm-11pm.

Cafe Dalí, Villada 108A, less than a block south of the *portales*. This cozy cafe is a great place to sip coffee (6-15 pesos) or beer (12 pesos). Breakfast 15-24 pesos. Pie, *tortas*, donuts, and *cuernitos* (8-18 pesos) are on hand to satisfy any late-night cravings. A neon jukebox plays latin tunes. Open Tu-Su 9am-midnight.

Cafe Hidalgo, Hidalgo 231-A, (☎215 27 93). A full menu with great breakfast (pancakes and juice, 25 pesos) and filling *comida corrida* (28 pesos) makes this old-fashioned cafe a great place to eat. Open Tu-Sa 6:30pm-11pm.

◉ SIGHTS

Toluca hosts a number of museums which, though small, are excellent and unique. All are organized and maintained by the **Centro Cultural Mexiquense,** which has outdone itself in presenting the artifacts in easily digestible forms.

COMOVITRAL AND JARDÍN BOTÁNICO. For sheer dazzle, few buildings can match this. Built in 1909, this steel Art-Nouveau structure housed a market until 1975. In 1980, after a year of design by the artist Leopoldo Flores, and four years of work by a team of 60 artisans, the building was re-inaugurated as the **Cosmovitral.** Half a million tiny pieces of colored glass convey the struggle among the forces of the universe. If you can take your eyes off the walls, the building holds a **botanical garden** of plants from all over the world thoroughly labeled in Spanish. *(☎214 67 85. Open daily 10am-6pm. 10 pesos, children 5 pesos.)*

CENTRO CULTURAL MEXIQUENSE. This complex outside town houses three separate museums. The **Museo de Culturas Populares** is a beautifully restored *hacienda* with a large collection of Mexican folk art, including an impressive Metepec Tree of Life, a large tree-like figure composed of clay figurines. The **Museo de Antropología e Historia** displays Mexican artifacts. Don't miss the hair-raising collection of preserved animals, including a pig with two snouts. The **Museo de Arte Moderno**'s exhibits include paintings by Diego Rivera and Rufino Tamayo. *(8km out of town. Accessible by "C. Cultural" buses running along Lerdo de Tejada (30min., 3.5 pesos). All museums open Tu-Su 10am-6pm. 5 pesos each, all 3 museums for 10 pesos; W and Su free.)*

MUSEO JOSÉ MARIA VELASCO AND MUSEO FELIPE S. GUTIÉRREZ. Hidalgo 400 and Bravo 303, on the *zócalo*'s northwest corner. Housed in adjacent colonial buildings, these museums hold permanent works by Velasco and Gutiérrez, two 19th-century naturalist painters. The museums also host visiting collections. *(☎213 28 14 and 213 26 47, respectively. Both open Tu-Sa 10am-6pm, Su 10am-3pm. Free.)*

MUSEO DE LA ACUARELA. Striking canvases by Mexican watercolor masters like **Vicente Mendiola** and **Ignacio Barrios** fill the upstairs of this peaceful Neoclassical building. The hallways and downstairs display temporary shows. *(Pedro Asencio 13, 2 blocks west of the portales.* ☎214 73 04. *Open Tu-Sa 10am-6pm, Su 10am-3pm. Free.)*

MUSEO NUMISMATICA. If you love money, this museum is for you. Mexican coins glut the upstairs rooms, while the last two rooms exhibit foreign money. *(Hidalgo 506, a few blocks west of the portales.* ☎213 29 27. *Open Tu-Su 10am-6pm. Free.)*

MORELOS

CUERNAVACA   ☎7

It seems everyone, eventually, comes to Cuernavaca. First were the Tlahuicans, who founded the city of "Cuauhna'huac" ("Place on the Outskirts of the Grove"). In 1520, Cortés arrived with an army of Tlaxcaltecans, conquering the city as a stepping stone to Tenochtitlán. Later, generations of *criollos* corrupted the indigenous name to "Cuernavaca." Today, a constant stream of students floods the city's innumerable Spanish-language schools, "living the language," in the company of thousands of other international travelers. Locals aid learning by shouting English at anyone who looks vaguely non-Mexican, and restaurants in the *centro* do their part translating their menus into the language of Shakespeare and Spears. Meanwhile, *chilangos* rush here en masse on weekends, inhaling the relatively clean air. The famous and infamous have also been drawn, from Gabriel García Márquez to the Shah of Iran, to Cuernavaca. They come to experience a small city with the amenities of a metropolis. These visitors have helped to spawn an amazing wealth of restaurants, nightlife, museums and a stylish international scene. Even as Cuernavaca becomes ever bigger and more expensive, the city's history, from its Tlahuican pyramid to grand 20th-century mansions, continues to entice.

▐ TRANSPORTATION

GETTING AROUND

Taxis go almost anywhere in the *centro* for under 30 pesos. Make sure to only take **Radio Taxis** (☎322 12 00, 322 06 41, or 317 37 66). They are the safest, and least likely to swindle you. Always set prices before hopping in. Frequent local buses (3.5 pesos) called *rutas* run along Morelos and Álvaro Obregón; the final destination of the bus is painted on the windshield, and the route numbers are painted on the hood or over the windshield.

GETTING AWAY

Buses: The **Estrella Blanca station,** Morelos 503 (☎312 81 90), is four long blocks north of Jardín Borda. To get to the *centro* from the bus station, take a right at the exit and head south on Morelos. Turn left onto Rayón or Hidalgo. Flecha Roja travels to: **Acapulco** (4hr., every 2hr. 8am-midnight, 200 pesos); **Guadalajara** (9hr., every hr. 6:15am-10pm, 400 pesos); **Mexico City** (1¼hr., every hr. 7am-7pm, 45 pesos); **Taxco** (1¾hr., every hr. 7am-10:35pm, 42 pesos). Tres Estrellas serves **Toluca** (2½hr., every 30min. 5am-7:45pm, 40 pesos). Those arriving via Estrella de Oro should cross the street and flag down any northbound minibus on Morelos (3.5 pesos)—they all run past the center of town. Estrella Roja goes to: **Matamoros** (3hr., every hr. 5am-8pm, 50 pesos) and **Puebla** (3½hr., every hr. 5am-8pm, 80 pesos).

✦ ▐ ORIENTATION AND PRACTICAL INFORMATION

Route 95 from Mexico City intersects Cuernavaca's main avenues. To reach the *centro* exit onto **Domingo Díaz** or **Emiliano Zapata,** which splits into **José María More-**

TO PYRAMIDS OF TEOPANZOLCO (1km)

Pericon

Parque
Melchor
Ocampo

Melchor Ocampo

Chamilpa

Leandro Valle

Madera

Cuaglia

Vicente

Guerrero

Balsas

Train
Station

Plan de Ayala

Fabregas

Morelos

Linares Guemez

Linares

Guemes

Ayuntamiento

Victoria

No Reelección

Estrella Blanca

Arista

Matamoros

Guerrero

Clavijero

López
Mateos
Market

López Mateos

Popocatépetl

Degollado

Aragón y León

Salinas

Morrow

Arteaga

F. Zarco

Tejada

Jardín
Borda

Rayón

Jardín
Juárez

Gutenberg

Callejón Borda

Alarcón

Hidalgo

PLAZA
CONSTITUCIÓN

20 de Nov.

Catedral de
la Asunción

Fray Bartoleme de Las Casas

Palacio de Cortés

Abasolo

Autobuses Pullman de Morelos
& Autobuses Zacatepec

Blvd. Juárez

Motolinia

Humbolt Palmira

Cuauhtémoc

Atlacomulco

Álvaro Obregón

Netzahualcóyotl

Estrella Roja

Cuauhtémotzin

González Bocanegra

Amates

Morelos

Galeana

Leyva

Tamayo

Chulavista

Laurel

Himno Nacional

Monte Albán

Plan de Ayutla

N

0 yards 550

0 meters 500

Autobuses
Estrellas de Oro

San Juan

Jallsco

Cuernavaca

🏠 ACCOMMODATIONS

Hotel América, 5
Hotel Colonial, 6
Los Canarios, 3
Mesón Las Hortensias, 11
Villa Calmecac, 1

🍴 FOOD

Gin Gen, 9
La Cueva, 13
La India Bonita, 7
Restaurante Los
 Arcos, 14
Trattoria Marco Polo
 Pizzería, 10

♪ ENTERTAINMENT

Harry's, 8
Kaova, 15
La Casa del Dictador, 2

● SERVICES

Explora Internet, 4
Farmacia del Ahorro, 12

los to the north and **Obregón** to the south. Cuernavaca is not easily navigated—expect random turns and abrupt name changes, especially near the plaza. Even and odd numbers usually stay on different sides of the street but, because of two different numbering systems, buildings opposite each other may have addresses several hundred numbers apart. As if this isn't headache enough, by some strange governmental decree, the official address system has changed. On Morelos and nearby streets, it's not uncommon to see two addresses on each building. "400/antes 17" means that the old address was 17 and the new "official" one is 400.

Tourist Offices: Municipal Office, Morelos 278 (☎318 75 61), a 10min. walk north Hidalgo. Open daily 10am-6pm. Information booths in all bus stations. **State Office,** Morelos Sur 187 (☎314 38 72), a 15min. walk south from Hidalgo and Morelos. Look for a yellow wall on the right side of the street. Dispenses information on the entire state of Morelos. Open M-F 8am-5pm.

Currency Exchange: Banca Serfín (☎314 00 67), on the corner of Galeana and No Reelección, has a 24hr. **ATM.** Open for exchange M-F 9am-3pm, Sa 9am-2pm. Only changes US currency. *Casas de cambio,* along Morrow, handle a wider variety of currencies and are open later.

American Express: Marín Agencia de Viajes Gutenberg 3 #13 (☎314 22 66), in Las Plazas shopping mall on the *zócalo.* Open M-F 9am-2pm and 4-6pm, Sa 10am-1pm.

Luggage Storage: At the Estrella Blanca bus terminal. 3 pesos per hr. Open 24hr.

Market: Mercado López Mateos. Head east on Degollado, up the pedestrian bridge, and past the vendor stands. Open daily 9am-8pm.

Supermarket: Superama (or **Wal-Mart**), Morelos 249 (☎314 01 19), south of the Estrella Blanca bus station. Open daily 7am-11pm.

Laundry: La Burbuja, Morelos 395. Up Morelos, less than a block north of Hotel Canarios. 30 pesos per 3kg. Open M-F 8am-7pm, Sa 8am-2pm.

Emergency: ☎08 or 060.

Police: Members of **Agrupamento Turístico,** a special tourist unit of **Policía Metropolitana,** (☎311 24 48), wear white polo shirts and black or grey slacks. Open daily 10am-6pm. Morelos also operates a Tourist Security hotline (☎01 800 903 92 00).

Red Cross: (☎315 35 05), on Ixtaccíhuatl at Río Amatzmac. Open M-F 8am-5pm.

Pharmacy: Farmacia del Ahorro, Hidalgo 7 at Galeana. Open 24hr.

Medical Assistance: IMSS (☎315 50 00 or 315 52 65), on Plan de Ayala. **Hospital General C.P.R.** (☎311 22 10 or 311 22 37), on the corner of Díaz and Gómez Ascarrate. Some English spoken.

Fax: Telecomm, Plaza de la Constitución 3 (☎314 31 81; fax 318 00 77), to the right of the post office. Open M-F 8am-7:30pm, Sa 9am-4:30pm, Su 9am-12:30pm.

Internet Access: Explora, Morelos 266A (☎318 55 28), north of the bus station on the right. 12 pesos per hr. Open M-Sa 8am-9pm, Su 1-9pm.

Post Office: Plaza de la Constitución 3 (☎312 43 79), on the southwest corner of the *zócalo.* Open M-F 9am-3pm, Sa 9am-1pm. **Mexpost** inside.

Postal Code: 62001.

ACCOMMODATIONS

Numerous hotels in every price range are located within walking distance of Cuernavaca's center. Some less glamorous, but cheap, *casas de huespedes* are on Aragón y León between Matamoros and Morelos. On weekends, you're competing for a room with half of Mexico City's middle class; it's best to make a reservation, but ask to see the room before you check in.

Villa Calmecac, Zacatecas 114 (☎313 21 46; www.turismoalternativo.org), at Tanque. From the *centro,* hop on a Ruta 12 bus and head north up Morelos. Get off just past the statue of Zapata and continue on, taking your 1st left on Zacatecas. Billing itself as an "ecotourist hostel," the hotel offers an art gallery, high-tech recycling system, and clean communal baths. Breakfast included. Reception 9am-2pm and 4-7pm; call before arrival. Doubles 470 pesos; dorms 180 pesos. 10% discount with HI or ISIC.

Hotel Colonial, Aragón y León 19 (☎318 64 14), uphill between Matamoros and Morelos. Despite the low quality of neighboring hotels, this one is a gem. Orange colonial home with a central courtyard and hospitable staff. Front door closes 11pm but a bell summons the person at the desk. Singles 200 pesos; doubles 250 pesos.

Los Canarios, Morelos 369 (☎313 00 00 or 313 44 44), 5 long blocks north of the *centro.* Run-down but comfortable 1950s-era motel, with 2 pools, tennis court, and rooms with private bath, all in glorious yellow and red. Singles 130 pesos; doubles 250 pesos; triples 290 pesos; quads 350 pesos.

Hotel América, Aragón y León 14 (☎318 61 27), between Morelos and Matamoros. A rose-tiled courtyard livens this modest hotel. The great location, well-kept rooms, TVs, and private baths appeal to connoisseurs of convenience. Singles and matrimonials 200 pesos, with TV 220 pesos; doubles 260 pesos; each additional person 20 pesos.

Mesón Las Hortensias, Hidalgo 13 (☎318 52 65), across from the plaza. This charming hotel has a green courtyard and clean rooms with private bath, and TV, though you may want more for the price. Singles 175 pesos; doubles 235 pesos; triples 330 pesos.

⬛ FOOD

If you have any money left over after paying your hotel bill, there's no better place to spend it than Cuernavaca's restaurants. Plenty of decent, cheap places to eat populate the *centro,* especially around Galeana and Juárez.

La India Bonita, Morrow 15 (☎318 69 67), less than a block east of Morelos. One of the most beautiful buildings in Cuernavaca, especially after dark, when the city quiets. If not springing for the filling regional dishes (45-95 pesos), share *antojitos* with someone special (18-28 pesos). Open Tu-F 8am-10pm, Sa 9am-11pm, Su 9am-6pm.

Trattoria Marco Polo Pizzería, Hidalgo 30, 2nd fl. (☎312 34 84). Delicious food stands out even amid the balconies, attentive service, and neat candlelit tables. Pizzas smothered in thick cheese come in 4 sizes (31 pesos and up). Reservations accepted. Open M-Th 1:30-10:30pm, F-Sa 1pm-midnight, Su 1-10pm.

Restaurante Los Arcos, Jardín de Los Héroes 4 (☎312 15 10), on the *zócalo*'s south side. Flanked by plants and a bubbling fountain, the outdoor tables are ideal for watching the day slip by. Los Arcos doubles as an evening watering hole. *Comida corrida* 55 pesos, breakfast 20-35 pesos, *antojitos* 25-33 pesos. Open daily 8am-midnight.

Naturiza, Álvaro Obregón 327-1 (☎312 46 26), a block downhill from Hospital ISSSTE. Vegetarian versions of Mexican standards may be slow coming, but for vegetarians, this is one of your only options. *Comida Corrida 35 pesos.* Open M-Sa 8:30am to 6pm.

La Cueva, Galeana 4 (☎312 40 02), across from the south side of the *zócalo.* A wide range of food—from seafood to sandwiches to soup, all with tasty fresh tortillas. Friendly service and the well-stocked bar attract local youth, who pour in around 9pm. *Comida Corrida* 25 pesos. Open daily 8am-midnight.

Gin Gen, Rayón 13 (☎318 60 46), 2 blocks east of the *zócalo* at the corner of Alarcón. Fans, lanterns, and pictures of Chinese pop stars adorn the walls. From 1-5pm, the filling *guisados del día* (soup, rice, 2 entrees, and dessert) go for only 46 pesos. Plenty of meatless vegetable dishes (38-48 pesos). Open M-Sa 8am-8pm, Su 8am-6pm.

◉ SIGHTS

Cuernavaca's popularity has little to do with its scintillating sights, but the City of Eternal Spring has a lot to show, including striking historical sites and museums.

PLAZA DE LA CONSTITUCIÓN AND JARDÍN JUÁREZ. Extending east from the Palacio de Gobierno is **Plaza de la Constitución,** the heart and soul of the city. Food vendors, *mariachis,* and shoe-shiners tempt passersby. A bandstand designed by

THESE AIN'T NO SUNDAY FUNNIES While waiting for the bus, you notice the teenage boys standing next to you are completely absorbed in the pocket-sized comic books in their hands. Your curiosity wins out and you take a closer look and see pictures of scantily clad couples doing things impossible for two-dimensional characters. Surprised, but amused, you shrug it off (after all, boys will be boys), but then you spot an elderly woman reading the very same comic. These little comics (called *revistas*) are all the rage in Mexico. Each book graphically weaves tales of romance, passion, and lust, leaving little to the imagination. You'll find someone selling them or someone reading them on virtually every street corner and at every bus stop in Mexico. Although they may seem a little strange at first glance, the comics are harmless and often even amusing. If nothing else, they're a good source of new slang.

Gustave Eiffel, commissioned by Cuernavaca's Viennese community, stands in **Jardín Juárez,** at the northwest corner of the plaza. A local band belts out polkas, classical music, and Mexican folk music *(Th and Su 6pm).*

MUSEO CUAUHNAHUAC (PALACIO DE CORTÉS). The Palacio de Cortés stands as a reminder of the city's grim history. The *conquistador* Hernán Cortés set Cuernavaca on fire in 1521, and built this two-story fortress atop the remains of a ruined pyramid. Cortés occasionally lived here until his return to Spain in 1540, and his widow remained here until her death. The building functioned as a prison during the 18th century, becoming the city's Palacio de Gobierno during the dictatorship of Porfirio Díaz. A grant from the former British ambassador to Mexico (pilot Charles Lindbergh's father-in-law) transformed the Palacio into the Museo Cuauhnahuac. The first floor features exhibits on Pre-Hispanic cultures, including a collection of indigenous depictions of the conquest. A Diego Rivera mural decorates the western balcony of the second floor. *(At the southeast corner of Plaza de la Constitución, east of Juárez. ☎ 312 81 71. Open Tu-Su 9am-5pm. 20 pesos; Su free.)*

CATEDRAL DE LA ASUNCIÓN. Begun in 1525 and completed by the 1550s—mainly through the labor of indigenous craftsmen—this former Franciscan convent is one of the oldest churches in the Americas. Age notwithstanding, only 20 years ago the removal of aisle altars revealed **Japanese frescoes** depicting the persecution and martyrdom of Christian missionaries in Sokori, Japan. Historians speculate that these startling frescoes were painted in the early 17th century by a converted Japanese artist who settled in Cuernavaca. Two smaller chapels flank the main entrance. To the right is the 17th-century **Capilla de la Tercera Orden;** to the left is the late 19th-century **Capilla del Carmen.** *(3 blocks down Hidalgo from the zócalo, at Morelos. Open daily 7am-2pm and 4-7pm. Masses daily at 11am.)*

JARDÍN BORDA. In 1783, Fr. Manuel de la Borda built this garden of magnificent pools and fountains as an annex to the home of his father, wealthy silver tycoon José de la Borda. In 1864, Emperor Maximilian and his wife Charlotte established a summer residence here. Today, the garden has a faded splendor. Modern additions include the art collection near the entrance, small theater, cafe, and museum near the emperor's summer home. **Rowboats** are available on the small duck pond. *(Enter through a stone building on Morelos, across from the cathedral. ☎ 312 92 37. Open Tu-Su 10am-5:30pm. 10 pesos, students 5 pesos; Su free. Rowboats 20 pesos per hr.)*

PYRAMIDS OF TEOPANZOLCO. This small archaeological site contains the ruins of a pyramid and two temples built by the Tlahuicans. The pyramid resembles the Templo Mayor in Mexico City, and indeed, the Tlahuicans kept close ties with the Aztecs. Little remains of the temples, dedicated to the God of War, Huitzilopochtli, and the God of Rain, Tlaloc, which are located atop the pyramid. The remains of a monument to Quetzalcóatl and the God of Wind, Ehe'catl. *(Farther up Balsas from the train station. To get to the site from the marketplace or Morelos, take a taxi (12 pesos) or the ruta #10 at the corner of Degollado and No Reelección (3.5 pesos) and ask the driver to let you off at the pirámide. Open daily 9am-6pm. 17 pesos; Su free.)*

 ENTERTAINMENT

Cuernavaca's popularity as a vacation spot fuels a glitzy nightlife. **Discos** are typically open from 9 or 10pm to 5am on Friday and Saturday, while a few signs of life brighten the week. The more popular discos lie beyond walking distance from the *zócalo* in the outlying *colonias*, and are best reached by *ruta* or taxi after 9pm. (Most *rutas* stop running around 10:30pm.) All the spots listed are familiar to cab drivers. Only Harry's and Kaova are within walking distance of the *zócalo*.

Kaova, Av. Morelos Sur 241 (☎318 43 80), 3 blocks south of the cathedral. The epitome of Cuernavaca's slick night life, with a young, stylish crowd moving to electronic pop or lounging elegantly at one of the little tables above the dance floor. Beer 25 pesos, domestic drinks 35 pesos. Open W-Sa 9pm-late.

La Casa del Dictador, Jacarandas 4 (☎317 31 86), a few blocks south of the Zapata statue, on the corner of Zapata in Col. Buenavista. Raging music welcomes a strictly gay clientele (mostly men). Beer 20 pesos. Cover 30 pesos. Open F-Sa 10:30-late.

Barbazul, Prado 10 (☎313 19 76). This club would make even Bluebeard shake his "booty." Popular with the early-20s, hard-hitting techno crowd. Drinks 20 pesos and up. Sa cover men 100 pesos, women free. Open W and F-Sa 10pm-late.

Zúmbale, Chapultepec 51 (☎322 53 43), next to Ta'izz. If you make the trek out here and then deal with the attitude of the guys at the entrance, you'll be rewarded with a crowded theme-park feel: 4 floors of *salsa, merengue,* and pop complete with a fake waterfall. Beer 25 pesos. Open bar Th 9-10pm. Th no cover. F-Sa cover men 100 pesos, women free. Open Th 9pm-4:30am, F-Sa 9pm-5am.

Harry's, Gutenberg 5 (☎312 76 69), at Guerrero, southeast corner of Jardín Juárez. Harry's caters to the local 20-something crowd, who dismiss the lack of dance floor and whirl between the tables. The place starts to swing after 10:30pm when the fashion-conscious clientele arrives—fashionably late, of course. Th karaoke. F open bar, cover men 120 pesos, women 30 pesos. No cover on other nights. Open Tu and Th-Sa.

UP Barra Bar, Cuauhtémoc 93, (☎312 63 05), inside Plaza Vendome. Soft rock kept at reasonable decibel levels, because that's how the older crowd likes it. Beer 28 pesos, drinks 30-40 pesos. 2-for-1 before 9pm. Open Tu-Sa from 7pm; doors close at 1am, though you can stay a couple more hours to finish your conversation.

DAYTRIPS FROM CUERNAVACA

XOCHICALCO

From Cuernavaca, Pullman de Morelos buses go to the Crucero de Xochicalco (30 min., every 30 min., 19 pesos). Ask the driver to announce the stop. Either take a taxi to the site (25 pesos) or attempt the 4km uphill climb yourself (1hr). Bring a hat, sunblock, and some water. Returning home is easier; small buses pass by the site every hr. en route to Cuernavaca (7 pesos; last bus 6pm, but it may run late.) Site open daily 9am-5pm. Museum open daily 9am-5pm. 30 pesos; Su free. Guides give tours in Spanish and English starting in the museum as soon as a group has assembled.

Perched atop a steep plateau amid the beautiful rolling hills that surround the village, Xochicalco (zoh-chee-CAL-co, "house of flowers" in Náhuatl), is one of Mexico's most fascinating—and mysterious—archaeological sites. More of a religious and trading center than city, Xochicalco was first settled during the early Classic Period, around the time neighboring Teotihuacán was reaching its zenith in the 7th century. It was not until Teotihuacán's demise around AD 700-900 that Xochicalco truly flourished, becoming an important trading and cultural center and maintaining diplomatic and trading relations with the Maya, Zapotec, and Toltec civilizations, traces of which are visible in the architecture of the site. Indeed, among the several construction projects initiated in AD 700 is a ball court almost identical to those built by the Classic Maya. Its presence has led archaeologists to speculate that Xochicalco may have been a Maya outpost. Others believe that Xochicalco was the mythical city of **Tamoanchan,** the place where Maya, Zapotec and Toltec sages met every 52 years to synchronize calendars and renew the cult of Quetzalcóatl. Xochicalco fell around AD 1200, probably due to internal insurrection.

Before entering the ruins, visit the **Museo del Sitio de Xochicalco,** to the right of the entrance. Comprehensive exhibits, invaluable brochures (5 pesos), and the ticket office make the museum a necessary stop. From there, a rocky path leads to the ruins, which are best explored in a circular manner. Start at the elevated plaza to the left of the first patch of greenery. On the right side of the first plain is the **Pirámide de las Estelas (Structure A),** which forms the northern boundary of **Plaza Central.** Because of the convergence of roads, this area was most likely a trading center. Twin pyramids on the east and west sides of the plaza, **Structure C** and **Structure D,** were used in the worship of the sun. One is oriented toward sunrise, the other toward sunset. At the center of the plaza is a carved obelisk that bears two glyphs relating to the god Quetzalcóatl. It is believed that priests plotted the sun's trajectory over the pyramids by tracing the obelisk's shadow.

The southwest corner of plaza offers a good view of the **Juego de Pelota** (ballcourt) below. Many archaeologists believe that this ballcourt was one of the earliest built in Mesoamerica; ballcourts as far south as Honduras show signs of a heavy Xochicalco influence. After heading up the hill to the central plaza, make your way to the base of the **Gran Pirámide (Structure E),** atop which rest the remains of an even more ancient structure. To the left is the stairway/portico section, used to protect the city in case of invasion. Past the portico and up two sets of impressive stairways, rebuilt in 1994, is **Plaza Ceremonial,** which served as the ceremonial center of the city. The top of Pirámide de las Estelas is accessible from here, enclosing a huge central pit that was the burial site for high priests and a place for ritual offerings. In the center of the plaza is the renowned **Pirámide de la Serpiente Emplumada** (Pyramid of the Plumed Serpent). Haphazardly reconstructed in 1910, it bears carved reliefs of Quetzalcóatl.

At the rear of the plaza is the tremendous **Montículo 2,** the highest area of the site and supposedly the spot where the rulers of Xochicalco lived. The east side was intended for daily activities, while the west end was exclusively ceremonial. Down the slope to the west is the **Hall of the Polichrome Altar,** where a colored altar rests beneath a reconstruction of Toltec roofing. Farther down is a cistern, a sauna used for pre-ballgame initiation rites, and **Teotlachtli,** the northern ballcourt. Two massive rings of rock are attached in the middle—most ballcourts in Mesoamerica have only one ring. Teams competed for the privilege of being sacrificed atop the Pyramid of Quetzalcóatl, a true honor and a sign of good sportsmanship. Nearby remain the foundations of the **Calmecac,** the palace in which Toltec and Aztec priests underwent training and initiation.

To the west along a weed-ridden path, around the back of the base of Montículo 2, is the entrance to the underground **Observatorio.** On summer solstices, Aztec sages and stargazers adjusted their calendar by peering through a shaft in the ceiling to trace the path of the sun. It is said that you can see the aura of a person who stands in the middle of the shaft of light.

TEPOZTLÁN ☎ 7

Tepoztlán is a village of cobblestone streets hidden among sheer cliffs of mythical beauty, and crowned by a mysterious, ancient pyramid. Villagers cling to their heritage: many still speak Náhuatl, and massive commercial development is kept out. The town has remained friendly to small-scale settlement, attracting throngs of tourists and resident expatria. However, the struggle to preserve has made prices extraordinarily high. Pack a picnic lunch, spend the night in a town with cheaper hotels, buy your crafts elsewhere, and live the fairy tale if only for a day.

▐ TRANSPORTATION. The *centro,* consisting of the *zócalo,* several government buildings, and the church, is bounded by **5 de Mayo** on the west, **La Conchita** on the east, **Revolución** on the south, and **Zaragoza** on the north. 5 de Mayo turns into **Tepoz-**

teco, which leads straight to the pyramid. "Ometochtli" buses go to and from **Cuernavaca** (40min.; every 15min. 5:45am-8pm; 12 pesos, students 9 pesos). In Tepoztlán they leave from the office at Teposteco 1; in Cuernavaca, from the east side of Mercado López Mateos. To go to or from **Mexico City,** take a Pullman de Morelos or Cristobal Colon bus (75 min., every 40 min. 5:15am-7:50pm, 45 pesos). Catch one in Tepoztlán at 5 de Mayo 35, in Mexico City at the Terminal Sur (Taxquena). Try to get a bus that will take you straight to the *centro* (one that terminates in Tepoztlán). If you get dropped off at the toll booth, you can take a cab (20 pesos), or walk down the road away from the toll booth for about 10min., and wait for a *combi* (4 pesos) in front of the first gas station, to the *centro.*

ⅠⅠⅠ ACCOMMODATIONS AND FOOD. If you find yourself stranded, your best bet is to stay at **Casa Iccemanyan,** Calle de Olvido 26. Situated on a beautiful hacienda are several immaculate bungalows for guests, a wading pool, and a common kitchen, all attached to the home of a charming family. Go through the gate and knock on the door marked, "Bienvenidos." (☎395 08 99; fax 395 21 59. Singles 240 pesos; doubles 400 pesos. Group rates available.) Dozens of restaurants offering both trendy and traditional Mexican food line 5 de Mayo and Revolución. Prices hover around 40-90 pesos for main dishes. Right in front of the *zócalo* and the intersection of 5 de Mayo and Revolución is **El Encuentro.** The international menu at this chic little restaurant, which doubles as an *artesanía* shop, includes meatless dishes. At night, it becomes a bar (*Comida corrida* 50 pesos. Open Th-M 1pm-1am, occasionally open on Tu or W). The cheapest meal in town is one you put together at the market under the sea of tarpaulines behind the *zócalo.*

ⅠⅠⅠ SIGHTS AND ENTERTAINMENT. Tepoztlán's crowning attraction is the **Pirámide del Tepozteco,** on the northern ridge of the cliffs 3km from the valley. Some say the 10m-tall pyramid was once a Tlahuica observatory and defense post (it is inscribed with barely discernible Tlahuica glyphs), while others swear it served as a sacrificial Aztec temple. To reach the pyramid, follow 5 de Mayo north out of town (passing the *zócalo* on your right) until the road ends. From there, you'll have to climb uphill for at least an hour. The steep, rough trail is especially treacherous when wet—which is almost always the case in the summer. Equip yourself with appropriate footwear, water, a fresh coat of insect repellent, and spirit. Watch your step and don't rush, especially on the way down. Be especially careful on the pyramid itself; unfortunate travelers have fallen to their deaths. If you can't make it all the way up, don't worry—there are numerous vistas to reward you along the way. (Open daily 10am-5:30pm. 30 pesos; Su free.)

The **Museo de Arte Prehispánico** (commonly known as the **Museo Carlos Pellicer**), is at the rear of Capilla Asunción, way behind the *zócalo.* The collection is one large room of beautifully-preserved pieces of Tlahuican, Olmec, Maya, Aztec, and *Teotihuacano* applied and religious art—regrettably, the pieces are neither individually labeled nor explained. (☎395 10 98. Open Tu-Su 10am-6pm. 5 pesos.)

Celebrations every September 8 honor **Tepozécatl,** also known as Quetzalcóatl, who was thought to have been born in this magical valley over 1200 years ago. *Chinelos*—colorfully attired folk dancers—invite visitors to join in their traditional dance, *el salto,* while musicians play age-old tunes. The night before, participants ascend to the top of the mountain to parade down the next day.

TLAXCALA

TLAXCALA ☎2

There is no better place to sit in all of Mexico than the colonial city of Tlaxcala (pop. 100,000), where *talavera* architecture fills a small valley just beyond the last remains of Poblano sprawl. Despite a growing population and increasing modernization, Tlaxcala retains its small town charm. However, Tlaxcalans were not always so peaceful; unable to withstand the Spanish onslaught during the 16th century, they made a pact with Cortés and sent 6000 warriors to raid and plunder the city of Cholula, ultimately helping Cortés to take Tenochtítlan in 1521. In return, Tlaxcala was granted Spanish protection and recognized as *"muy noble y muy leal"* (very noble and very loyal). Today few traces of Tlaxcala's mercenary history remain, and its tranquil beauty draws refugees from Mexico City and Puebla on weekends. Tlaxcala may be peaceful, but it's hardly a dead-end. A great base from which to explore the state's now-deserted convents, untouristed *indígena* communities, and well-preserved ruins, Tlaxcala's museums, art galleries, and cultural center provide an authentic taste of Mexico's heartland.

◧ TRANSPORTATION

GETTING AROUND

Tlaxcala is approximately 85km east of Mexico City and is most easily reached by **Mexico 150.** Don't be fooled by the large number of *colectivos* leaving from the market; Tlaxcala is a very walkable city. Distances are manageable, and it's cheaper and often more direct to chug up the hills yourself than to ride in the VW vans whose 1600cc engines can't handle the steep grades and force drivers to take longer routes. Most services are in and around **Plaza de la Constitución** (the *zócalo*) and diagonally adjacent **Plaza Xicoténcatl.** To get from the *zócalo* to Revolución, the city's main commercial street, catch a "Santa Ana" *colectivo* by the *mercado* at 20 de Noviembre and Alonso y Escalona, or behind the Parroquía de San José (3.5 pesos). Or take a 40min. walk to save pesos and enjoy the air.

GETTING AWAY

To get to the *centro* from the **bus station,** exit through the glass doors to a swarm of idling *colectivos.* Those facing the right go to the downtown area, the market, and the hotel district along Revolución (3.5 pesos). To return to the bus station, take a "Central" *colectivo* from the *mercado* or flag one down behind San José at 20 de Noviembre and 1 de Mayo. Autotransportes Tlaxcala (☎462 00 87) runs to **Mexico City** (2hr., every 20min. 6am-9pm, 67 pesos) and **Veracruz** (6hr, 10:30am and 3:30pm, 120 pesos). Autotransportes México-Texcoco (☎462 03 62) has similar service to **Mexico City.** Flecha Azul (☎462 33 92) serves **Puebla** (55min., every 10min. 5:30am-9:30pm, 11 pesos).

◪ PRACTICAL INFORMATION

TOURIST, LOCAL, AND FINANCIAL SERVICES

▨ **Tourist Office:** Juárez 18 (☎465 09 60 or 465 09 61, www.tlaxcala.gob/turismo.com), in the lovely turn-of-the-century building at Juárez and Lardizábal. The office sponsors cheap and comprehensive tours of Tlaxcala and its *señoríos* (Pre-Hispanic warrior-cities) every Sa and Cacaxtla and Xochitécatl every Su. The tours leave at 10:15am from the Hotel Posada San Francisco on the south side of the *zócalo* (15 pesos). A gold mine of information, pamphlets (10 pesos), and fancy computer presentations (also available online) from a friendly staff. Open M-F 9am-7pm, Sa-Su 10am-6pm.

Currency Exchange: Banamex, Plaza Xicoténcatl 8 (☎462 20 55), and **Bancrecer,** Portal Hidalgo 10 (☎462 67 41), under the *portales,* offer 24hr. **ATMs,** as do several banks on Juárez past the tourist office. The **Centro de Cambio Tlaxcala,** Guerrero 3 (☎462 90 85), at the corner of Independencia, exchanges cash, money orders, and traveler's checks. Open M-F 9am-4pm, Sa 10am-2pm.

Supermarket: Everything from underwear and refrigerators to bottled water and gum can be found at **Gigante,** Valle 66 (☎462 58 46), the city's behemoth supermarket, in the shopping center on the corner of Vera. Open daily 8am-9pm.

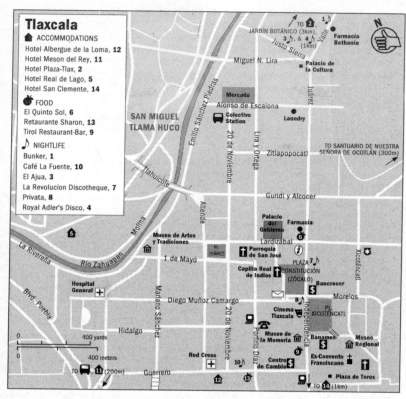

Tlaxcala

🏠 ACCOMMODATIONS
Hotel Albergue de la Loma, 12
Hotel Meson del Rey, 11
Hotel Plaza-Tlax, 2
Hotel Real de Lago, 5
Hotel San Clemente, 14

🍖 FOOD
El Quinto Sol, 6
Retaurante Sharon, 13
Tirol Restaurant-Bar, 9

🎵 NIGHTLIFE
Bunker, 1
Café La Fuente, 10
El Ajua, 3
La Revolucion Discotheque, 7
Privata, 8
Royal Adler's Disco, 4

Markets: Get your fresh avocados or freshly blended lard at the fresh market on the corner of Alonso Escalona and Lira y Ortega. Open M-Sa 8am-8pm, Su 8am-5pm. On weekends, vendors sell *artesanía* in **Plaza Xicoténcatl.**

Laundry: Lavandería de Autoservicio Acuario, Alonso Escalona 13A (☎462 62 92). Full-service 11 pesos per kg.; self-service 8 pesos per 10min.; 1hr. service may be available, if they're not too busy. Open M-Sa 8am-8pm, Su 8am-2pm.

EMERGENCY AND COMMUNICATIONS
Emergency: call police station or hospital directly.

Police: (☎462 07 35 or 462 10 79) at the corner of Lardizábal and Xicoténcatl. Open 24hr. No English spoken.

Red Cross: Allende Nte. 48 (☎462 09 20), at the corner where Allende dead-ends into Guerrero. 24hr. walk-in emergency service. Staff may speak English—just ask.

Pharmacy: Farmacía Bethanía, Valle 17A (☎462 11 55). Take Juárez from the *zócalo* until it turns into Valle; the pharmacy is on the right just before the stadium appears on the left. Open daily 8am-8pm; after 8pm, ring the bell on the outside wall. **Unión de Farmacías de Descuento,** Juárez 14A (☎462 34 30), between Lardizábal and Guridi y Alcocer. Open daily 9am-9pm.

Hospital: Hospital General, Jardín de la Corregidora 1 (☎462 00 30 or 462 35 55), 5 blocks from the *zócalo* at the corner of Camargo and Josefa Castelar. No English spoken. **IMSS** (☎462 34 00), on Valle, across the street from the stadium, past the Nestlé factory. Take Juárez from the *zócalo* until it turns into Valle. The clinic is the building on the left once you enter the IMSS compound. No English spoken.

Fax: Telecomm, Díaz 6 (☎462 00 47). Also offers Western Union services. Open M-F 8am-6pm, Sa-Su 8am-noon.

Internet Access: Internet cafes abound on the streets surrounding the *zócalo*. A fast connection and open terminal can be found at the 2-story **Internet Cafe**, Independencia 21 (☎462 44 64). 15 pesos per hr. Open M-S 9am-9pm.

Post Office: Plaza de la Constitución 20 (☎462 00 04), on the corner of Camargo. Open M-F 9am-4pm, Sa 9am-1pm.

Postal Code: 90000.

▞ ACCOMMODATIONS

While dirt cheap accommodations aren't exactly plentiful in Tlaxcala, 150 pesos for a single and 200 pesos for a double pays for some very comfortable rooms. Be sure to make reservations on weekends and holidays, as low-cost hotels, especially those near the *zócalo*, tend to fill up quickly.

Hotel Albergue de la Loma, Guerrero 58 (☎462 04 24). Although exhausted travelers may find the 62 steps leading up to the *Albergue*'s hill-top perch daunting, immaculate rooms with TV, private baths, and large windows that display Tlaxcala and the surrounding countryside reward those who make the trek. Spacious rooms with 2 to 3 beds each are perfect for family stays. The downstairs restaurant serves inexpensive food daily 8am-10pm. Singles 150 pesos; doubles 190 pesos; triples 220 pesos.

Hotel San Clemente, Independencia 58 (☎462 19 89). Follow Independencia south past Plaza Xicoténcatl for about 10min. The bright yellow hotel is on the left 4min. after Independencia starts to curve to the right. Warm pastel rooms, tiled baths, and a fountain-bedecked courtyard more than compensate for San Clemente's distance from the *zócalo*. All rooms have TV and phone. 10% discount for ISIC card holders or stays of more than 3 days. Singles 170 pesos; doubles 240 pesos.

Hotel Meson del Rey, Calle 3 #1009 (☎462 90 55), across the intersection to the left after exiting the bus station doors. The modern, if unglamorous and somewhat gloomy, rooms, complete with TV, phone, and private baths, front a flowered courtyard and are the cheapest singles in town. Singles 95 pesos; doubles 175 pesos.

Hotel Plaza-Tlax, Revolución 6 (☎462 78 52). From the *zócalo*, head north on Juárez, which changes into Valle; the hotel will be on your left soon after Valle becomes Revolución. Alternately, take a "Santa Ana" or "Gigante" *colectivo* from behind San José, and get off near the large Hotel Jeroc complex. If your priority list ranks discos higher than historic sights, Plaza-Tlax's location—smack-dab in the middle of Revolución's club scene, but far from the *zócalo*—isn't much of a drawback. Clean rooms come with TV and colorfully-tiled baths. Singles 153 pesos; doubles 224 pesos.

Posada Mary, Xicoheténcatl 19 (☎462 96 55), is a rare breed in Tlaxcala—a cheap hotel near the *zócalo*. What you save in money and transport time you lose in decor. All rooms have private baths with peeling paint and mildew, and open onto a cement parking lot. If the reception is not open, just inquire at any of the open rooms to the left after entering the main gate. Rooms for 1 or 2 persons (double bed) 100 pesos.

Hotel Real de Lago, Av. de los Deportes 15 (☎462 03 99). Take Primero de Mayo from Plaza Juárez, cross the foot bridge and follow Av. Joaquin Cisneros Molina to the left. At the 1st intersection, veer right on Col. Aldolfo López Mateos until it turns; the hotel is on the corner. The accommodating staff will be happy to show you to a recently refurbished room with TV, tiled bath, fresh towels, and carpeting. Singles 190 pesos; doubles 260 pesos. Ask for a discount if you're staying for 3 or more days.

▟ FOOD

Tlaxcalteca specialties include *pollo en xoma* (chicken stuffed with fruits and other meats), *barbacoa en mixiote* (meat cooked in *maguey* leaves), and *pulque* (an unrefined alcoholic drink made from the *maguey* cactus), which is popular both straight and as *pulque verde*, a drink made with honey water, *yerba buena* (spearmint), and lemon juice. With all these yummy treats, it's hard to go wrong when picking a place to eat. For delicious midday meals, duck into one of the small family-run restaurants on **Juárez** between **Zitlalpopocatl** and **Alonso de Escalona**, where *comida corrida* is usually 25 pesos or less. Around the *zócalo*, meal prices rise to 50-80 pesos.

Restaurante Sharon, Guerrero 14 (☎462 20 18), between Independencia and Díaz. Watch the soaps on TV or the cooks in the tiled, open kitchen while tasting the 8 *quesos fundidos* (35 pesos), or make a meal out of 3 stuffed-to-the-brim tacos (29 pesos). Meat dishes come with salad and beans (37-40 pesos). Open Su-F 1:30-9:30pm.

El Quinto Sol, Juárez 12 (☎466 18 57). The bright and cheery garden setting will lift your spirits as the vitamins flood your veins. Sprinkled with grains and smothered with fruit, their yogurt will leave your taste buds begging for more. Breakfasts include coffee, juice, yogurt, eggs, and fresh bread (20-22 pesos). Salads and *antojitos* 25 pesos. Specialty cure-all juices 15 pesos. Open M-Sa 8am-7pm.

Restaurant Tirol, Independencia 7A (☎462 37 54), along Plaza Xicoténcatl. Catering to weekday business lunchers and a hip evening crowd, Tirol offers *zócalo* quality service and food at more reasonable prices. *Sopa Tlaxcalteca* 25 pesos, *especialidades regionales* 40 pesos, *comida corrida* 35 pesos. Open M-Sa 7am-2am, Su 9am-6pm.

Restaurant Albergue de la Loma, Guerrero 58 (☎462 04 24). Large helpings complement beautiful views. Patrons peer at Tlaxcala through floor-to-ceiling windows as they eat hearty breakfasts (12-27 pesos) and *antojitos* (20 pesos), or enjoy local specialties at bargain prices (from 30 pesos). Open daily 8am-10pm.

👁 SIGHTS

Most of Tlaxcala's attractions center around peaceful streets off **Plaza de la Constitución,** but easy-to-find *colectivos* make the trek to farther sights manageable. Visitors should make sure to see **Cacaxtla** and **Xicoténcatl,** two well-preserved archaeological sites nearby. The tourist office provides cheap, well-structured tours of Tlaxcala City and the archaeological sites.

PLAZA DE LA CONSTITUCIÓN. The serene Plaza de la Constitución is the heart of Tlaxcala. Look for the octagonal fountain of Santa Cruz in the center by the bandstand. Built in Europe during the 14th century, it was given to the city by King Phillip IV in 1646—no small token considering the distance those stones were hauled—to symbolize Spanish gratitude toward *La Ciudad Leal* (The Loyal City) and its instrumental role in Mexico's colonization.

PLAZA XICOTÉNCATL. Southeast of the *zócalo* is Plaza Xicoténcatl, dedicated to the young Tlaxcalan warrior **Xicoténcatl Axayacatzin** who battled against Cortés before the forces became allies. Xicoténcatl is a hero today, and his statue commands a center spot in the plaza. Normally a tranquil area, the plaza livens up on weekends as a carousel and small artisan market occupy the grounds.

MUSEO DE LA MEMORIA. A great first stop for anyone on the museum route, *La Memoria* guides visitors through Tlaxcalan history from 1521 to the end of the 18th century, providing essential background information that will make other sites more meaningful. The museum occupies a 16th-century building that once housed the sisterhood of Santa Cruz of Jerusalem; today, interactive computer programs and videos located throughout help explain the various exhibits. Highlights include the enormous diorama of the *Ex-Convento Franciscano* as it appeared during colonial times, the room of the *Virgen de Ocotlán,* where thunderous holy music plays while visitors examine paintings and read about the legend of the virgin, and a passageway of closely grouped metal shafts that commemorates the diaspora of Tlaxcalans after the alliance with Cortés. *(Independencia 3, across from Plaza Xicoténcatl. ☎466 07 92. Open Tu-Su 10am-5pm. 10 pesos, students 5 pesos. Tu free. Guided tours 30 pesos; in English or French, US$5.)*

EX-CONVENTO FRANCISCANO DE LA ASUNCIÓN. Built sometime between 1537 and 1540, this was one of the first convents in the Americas. The thick, wooden door of the cathedral opens into a beautiful Romanesque nave and a ceiling of intricate Muslim-influenced *(mudéjar)* woodwork. The main altar contains, among other artifacts, *la conquistadora*, the canvas of the Virgin that Cortés is said to have kept between his armor and his breast. In the first of four chapels is a corn paste sculpture dating back to the 16th century. The side chapel closest to the altar, **La Capilla de la Tercer Orden**, holds the basin used to baptize the four Tlaxcalteca lords at the time of the alliance. *(On the southeast side of Plaza Xicoténcatl a 400-year-old cobblestone way leads about 200m up to the ex-convent. Open M-F 6:30am-2pm and 4-6:30pm, Sa 6am-6:30pm, Su 6am-8:30pm.)*

MUSEO REGIONAL DE TLAXCALA. Meandering through the cloister of the ex-convent, the museum presents artifacts from nearby archaeological zones, examples of colonial art, and a library with works on Tlaxcalan history. Take a peek through the fence at one of Tlaxcala's pride and joys, the **Plaza de Toros.** Named for famed *torero* Jorge "El Ranchero" Aguilar, the plaza has been used since 1788 and comes to life in the last week of October and first week of November, when Tlaxcala celebrates its annual fair. *(Next door to the ex-convent, on the side closest to the entrance. ☎ 462 02 62. Open Tu-Su 10am-5pm. 30 pesos, students; Su free.)*

PALACIO DE GOBIERNO. The former palace of the viceroys, where Cortés stayed when he was in Tlaxcala, now commemorates the entire history of man in the region. Covering the interior walls of the 16th-century palace are immense murals by Desiderio Hernández Xochitiotzin, depicting everything from early inhabitants of the Valley of Mexico to the Wars of Independence. Having dedicated 30 years to painting, Xochitiotzin has begun researching Tlaxcala's reform and revolutionary history in order to continue his work. *(Open daily 8am-8pm. Free. Guides loiter inside, offering to explain the murals for 50 pesos in Spanish, 150 pesos in English.)*

PARROQUIA DE SAN JOSÉ. With its immense yellow bulk visible from afar, the old parish church, formerly the Cathedral of Tlaxcala, was originally built atop a hermitage dating from 1526. At its entrance stand two stone founts of holy water, on which weary pedestrians often sit and relax for a moment. The *talavera* tile and brick now covering the exterior of the church were laid over the original mortar facade in the 17th and 18th centuries. *(Northwest of the zócalo. Open daily 6am-8pm.)*

MUSEO DE ARTES Y TRADICIONES POPULARES DE TLAXCALA. The museum features seven exhibition halls in which artisans demonstrate their crafts. Presentations include a tour of a traditional indigenous kitchen, an explanation of textile production, and a discourse on how *pulque* is made—including a taste of the fiery drink. *(Mariano Sánchez 1, on the corner of Lardizábal. A short walk west on Lardizábal from the Parroquia. ☎ 462 23 37. Open Tu-Su 10am-6pm. 6 pesos, students 4 pesos.)*

SANTUARIO DE NUESTRA SEÑORA DE OCOTLÁN. While San José is Tlaxcala's main place of worship, Ocotlán boasts greater religious, symbolic, and historical significance and is a prime example of the Churringueresque style. Tlaxcala's own Virgin of Guadalupe, Nuestra Señora de Ocotlán, appeared in 1541 to an ailing Indian named Juan Diego Bernardino, curing him and ordering him to build the church. The modern-day *santuario* holds the 16th-century wooden image of the Virgin, which is carried through the city streets every year on the first Monday of May. In the interior, a shell motif tops the pilasters and frames the end of the nave. The star of the show, is the *camarín*, a small octagonal room located behind the altar where the Virgin is "dressed" for important festivals. *(Head 1 block past the tourist office on Juárez, and hang a right on Guridi y Alcocer. When the road forks, follow it up the hill to the left. The road climbs to a small Capilla del Pocito de Agua Santa, where it becomes a cobblestone street with a staircase alongside and leads directly to the church.)*

JARDÍN BOTÁNICO TIZATLÁN. For indigenous beauty without tourist packaging, this garden displays native plants in an otherworldly setting. No bikes, balls, radios, or beer are allowed in the pastoral paradise. Rocky paths meander across a creek to reveal a hidden greenhouse. *(Take a "Camino Real" colectivo from the market and tell the driver where you want to go. On foot, follow Juárez past the tourist office until it turns into Valle and then Revolución. From the hotel district on Revolución, turn left at Camino Real before the brick bridge passes over the road. ☎ 462 65 46. Open daily 9am-3pm and 4-6 pm. Free.)*

THE RUINS OF TIZATLÁN. These tiny ruins 4km outside of Tlaxcala are all that remains of one of the four *señoríos* (warrior city-states). While the ruins aren't impressive, the view from the site is magnificent. A plaque points to the locations in the surrounding hills where the other three *señoríos* once stood. In front of the site is the golden-domed **Templo de San Estéban,** and access to the original 16th-century *capilla* of the church is included in admission. *(To reach the ruins, take a 3-peso colectivo from the corner of Sanchez and 1 de Mayo labeled "Tizatlán." Tell your driver where you want to go, and he or she will drop you off in front of a small, yellow building. Walk left on the stone path, then up several flights of stairs until you reach the ruins at the top behind the Templo de San Estéban. Open daily 10am-5pm. 12 pesos, students; Su free.)*

🎵 ENTERTAINMENT

On weeknights in Tlaxcala, lights go out early. However, discos on Valle and Revolución and a cluster of bars near the *zócalo* make for raucous weekends. Many of the restaurants and bars under the *portales* feature live music and outdoor seating that attract swarms of hip, coffee-sipping sophisticates.

BARS AND CLUBS

In Tlaxcala, many of the bars also function as discos on weekends—hence the term "disco-bar." Early in the evening, patrons sit calmly at their tables. Later on, around 11:30pm, a sort of universal twitch sinks in, and the crowd surges to its feet, grinding and undulating in sweaty, drunken bliss.

El Ajua, Valle 113 (☎ 462 35 44). Pounding rock, pop, and electronica keep the crowd dancing, as music videos flash on the enormous front screen and psychedelic images swirl overhead. Down a pitcher of beer with your friends at a table (150 pesos) or snuggle with that special someone in the theater-style seats on the top level (it doubles as a movie theater by day). Cover 40 pesos. Open Th 9pm-3am, F-Sa 9pm-5am.

Bunker, Valle 73 (☎ 462 38 88). 20-something locals boogie on the large dance floor to all types of tunes, played live on Fr. An ISIC discount and no cover on Th makes Bunker great for those on a tight budget. Cover 40 pesos. Open Th-Sa from 10pm-late.

Privata, (☎ 462 56 83), at the corner of Independencia and Camargo, above the Antiguo Mesón. The enormous video screens and tabletop dancing provide plenty to watch. Rock and pop music, occasionally live. Cover 40 pesos. Open F-S from 9pm.

La Revolución Discotheque, Portal Hidalgo 9 (☎ 462 60 52), under the *portales*. Dirty dancing a bit closer to home. Young clubbers get down to a variety of music, including pop, techno, reggae, and *salsa*. Live rock F-Sa. Cover 20 pesos. Open Tu-Su 5pm-5am.

Royal Adler's Disco, Revolución 4 (☎ 462 15 77), at the Hotel Jeroc. Ritzy hotel patrons drift here for high-class clubbing. Spring for the cab ride over, the 40 peso cover, and the pricey drinks, and you, too, can be part of the elite. Open F-Sa 10pm-3am.

THE CHILL SCENE

Cafe La Fuente, Guerrero 29 (☎ 462 97 22), at the corner of 20 de Noviembre. If the bar scene along the *zócalo* is too chaotic, this cafe offers the opposite: couples sipping typical coffeehouse fare and sharing tiny private balconies. The dim lights throw the artesanía-hung ceiling into shadows as slow jazz plays and the strongly spiked *cafes* work their magic (10-22 pesos). Open daily 10am-1am.

Cinema Tlaxcala, Plaza de la Constitución 18, on the south side of the *zócalo* across the street from the post office. Shows 1st-run American movies (20 pesos, Th 10 pesos). Open daily 3:30pm-10pm.

FESTIVALS

For information on cultural events in Tlaxcala, head to the **Palacio de la Cultura,** Juárez 62, four blocks from the *zócalo* at the corner of Justo Sierra. To the right as you enter are monthly schedules and announcements of theater productions, dances, and art expositions. The *Palacio* also stages concerts, exhibits, and performances all over town and in its own courtyard. **Teatro Universitario** and **Teatro Xicoténcatl** host most of the events. The bookstore offers some books in English on Tlaxcalan culture. (☎ 462 60 69. Open M-F 9am-8m, offices open 9am-6pm.)

Tlaxcala's state fair, the **Feria de Tlaxcala,** is held from October 16 to November 15. During the month-long *feria*, exhibitions of *artesanía* and *ganaderos* (livestock) dot the town, while Tlaxcalans from across the state participate in cultural and sporting events. If you have a taste for religious events, stop by Tlaxcala on the first Monday in May to see the sacred pine image of the **Virgin of Ocotlán** paraded through the streets. If that doesn't suit your schedule, visit the Church of Christ the Good Neighbor (to the right of the ex-convent) on July 1 for the celebration of the **Día de la Purísima Sangre de Cristo** (Day of the Purest Blood of Christ).

⚡ DAYTRIPS FROM TLAXCALA

▨ CACAXTLA

In Tlaxcala, take a bus marked "Nativitas" or "San Miguel del Milagros" from 20 de Noviembre next to the market or behind San José. Tell the driver where you want to go, and he or she will drop you off at the main entrance (40 min., 7 pesos). If you happen to be dropped in San Miguel del Milagros, walk up the windy road, following the signs. If driving, take Mex. 119. ☎ 416 00 00. Open daily 9am-5:30pm. 35 pesos, students; Su free.

One of the best-preserved and best-presented archaeological sites in the country is the hilltop ruin of Cacaxtla (kah-KASH-tla), 19km southwest of Tlaxcala. The Olmec-Xicalancas, who once dominated the southwest corner of Tlaxcala state and most of the Puebla Valley, built and expanded the city during the Classic Period, between 700 and 900 AD. Cacaxtla was abandoned by 1000, and its inhabitants were driven from the area by Toltec-Chichimec invaders in 1168. Excavation began here in 1975; since then 4000 sq. m of ruins have been unearthed.

The small museum on the right by the entrance contains artifacts and bones collected from the site. From the museum, a paved road leads toward the ruins which, to prevent erosion, are covered by the world's second largest archaeological roof. Once upstairs, visitors move clockwise around ceremonial courtyards, temples, tombs, and palatial remains. Location markers provide historical information in Spanish, English and Náhuatl. The remains of many small rooms within the palace are thought to have been priests' quarters.

Several features distinguish this site from others. One is a latticework window, **La Celosia,** on the west side, opposite the entrance. The free-standing window, made by surrounding a latticework of twigs and branches with mud and stucco, is the only one of its kind in Mesoamerica. Another attraction is the series of murals throughout the site, considered to be among the best-preserved Pre-Hispanic paintings in Mesoamerica. The largest, the **Battle Mural,** depicts a historical-mytho-logical battle of two armies, one dressed in jaguar skins defeating another dressed in eagle feathers. The still-visible original mineral-based colors show a distinct Maya influence, which may indicate the existence of a trading network between the Maya and the Olmec-Xicalancas.

XOCHITÉNCATL

From Cacaxtla, walk down from the entrance of the Cacaxtla archeological site to the main highway, Mex. 119, and flag down any colectivo headed right (3.5 pesos). Ask the driver to drop you close to Xochiténcatl site. From there, take a right off the main highway, and another right at the well-marked site entrance. 1km up the hill is the ticket booth. To return to Tlaxcala, walk back down the hill to the town of San Miguel Xochitecatilla and take a "Tlaxcala" colectivo (3.5 pesos). Open Tu-Su 10am-4:30pm. 17 pesos, students; Su free.

The civilization at Xochiténcatl (so-chee-TEN-cahtł) predates Cacaxtla by several hundred years, and its ruins are located on a hill just opposite Cacaxtla. Before they were conquered in AD 300 by the Olmec-Xicalancas, the inhabitants of Xochiténcatl constructed the temple to honor Xochiqueteali, the goddess of fertility. For this reason, archaeologists think many of the artifacts at the site are figures of women or babies, which were sacrificed with some regularity at the site. There are four pyramids, the largest of which, **The Pyramid of Flowers,** is actually a pyramid on top of a pyramid. The columns on top are thought to have been constructed to bring great fertility to all women who passed through them. To the left of the pyramid is the **Pyramid of the Snake.** The basin on top of the pyramid caught water and served as a mirror in which to observe the stars. Behind the Pyramid of the Snake is a small, flat pyramid, the **Basement of the Volcanoes.** At the far left of the site is the **Spiral Pyramid.** Dedicated to the wind god Ehecatl, it is the only such spiral pyramid known to exist. The site offers a spectacular view of nearby volcanoes **Popocatépetel, Ixtaccihuatl,** and **La Malinche (Malintzin).** On your way to the site, peek into the small museum near the entrance and view some of the many artifacts found atop the Pyramid of Flowers.

HUAMANTLA

From Tlaxcala, take an ATAH bus from the station to Huamantla (every 10 min., 12 pesos). Ask to be let off near Parque Juárez. To return, continue past Museo Taurino to Absolo and hang a right. Buses marked "Tlaxcala" return to the city from the corner of Absalo and Bravo Nte. By car, take Mex. 119 to Mex. 126.

Though most visitors come to Huamantla, 45km east of Tlaxcala, for its renowned bull-runnings, other sights attract plenty of daytrippers from the capital city. Sights are centered around the *zócalo*, **Parque Juárez.** Northeast of the *zócalo*, the **Museo Taurino,** Allende Nte. 200, commemorates Huamantla's famous bullfighting history. Posters, bullfighting attire, and photographs dating from the early 1900s are displayed. Before leaving the museum, peek through the fence in the hallway to the left of the courtyard for a glimpse of Huamantla's famous bull ring. (Open M-F 9am-3pm and 5-7pm, Sa-Su 9:30am-2pm. Free.) Not all in Huamantla is bull-related. The **Museo Nacional del Títere,** Parque Juárez 15, is on the west side of the *zócalo*, along De La Reforma. In the year 1835, Huamantla became famous for its *títeres* (puppets) when Rosete Aranada, a *títere* company located in the city, began putting on shows involving more than 5000 puppets. Today, the museum contains the third largest collection of original Rosete Aranada puppets in Mexico. Trace the history of puppets all over the world, examine the elaborate Aranada puppets, and sign your name and comments on the wall of graffiti in the last *sala*. The friendly staff offers guided tours, included in the cost of admission. (☎472 10 33. 10 pesos, students 5 pesos. Open T-Sa 10am-2pm and 4-6pm, Su 10am-3pm.)

From the museum, walk to the yellow church, the **Parroquia de San Luís,** Parque Juárez 3, located half a block to the left. Constructed in 1641, the parish church's plain exterior belies a respectable collection of artifacts within. The altars are beautiful examples of Baroque artwork and feature a depiction of the Virgin Mary and Christ by the noted artist Miguel Cabrera. (☎472 03 10. Open daily 7am-8pm. Free.) On the east of the *zócalo* opposite the museum and parroquia, the **Ex-Convento de San Luis Obispo de Tolosa** bears witness to the centuries of tackiness it has endured since it was built by the Franciscians, sometime before 1569. The cloister now functions as a school. (☎472 10 00. Open daily 9am-7pm. Free.) On the south side of the *zócalo* is the **Palacio Municipal.** If you enjoyed his murals in Tlaxcala, you can check out Desiderio Hernández Xochitiotzin's work in the entrance of the Palacio. A small tourist office operates out of this building, with English-speaking staff and maps of Huamantla. (M-F 9am-5pm. Free.)

Huamantla fills with visitors, carpets of flowers and sawdust, and newly-free bulls in a spectacular early August festival. It all begins on ▧**La Noche que Nadie Duerme** (The Night No One Sleeps), August 14, when flower and sawdust designs are crafted over 2km of the city streets, and the image of the Virgin is paraded down the carpeted path. Later in the week, on August 19th, the streets close for the traditional *Huamantlada*, the running of the bulls.

PUEBLA

PUEBLA ☎ 2

Puebla (pop. 2 million) was a great social experiment—Renaissance met ruffian, Enlightenment met real world. Conceived by a group of humanist Spaniards, Puebla was to be a crossroads of faith and education, with libraries, schools, and administrative buildings designed to civilize and Christianize. Surprisingly enough, Puebla was completed as planned, and to this day is a mix of 17th- and 18th-century European art and ideals and colorful Mexican energy. Built on solid, empty ground, Puebla's streets are said to have been laid by angels who streaked ribbons across the land, forming the grid that makes the city so simple to navigate. Angels notwithstanding, the city has been shaped by pious visitors. Franciscans built hospitals, libraries, and orphanages for illegitimate children, while nuns from a variety of orders set up cloisters and kitchens, where they invented some of Mexico's most famous dishes and the sugar-candy sweets which the city is known for. Today, Puebla is one of the largest and most important cities in the country. Gilded churches elegantly blend with trendy clothing stores, while in the shady *zócalo*, teen hipsters and older locals relax side by side.

⊏ TRANSPORTATION

GETTING AROUND

Most sights and accommodations are located within walking distance of the *zócalo*. If traveling farther in an independent **taxi,** set a price before getting in and don't be shy about haggling. Municipal **buses** and **micros** (also known as *combis*), white Volkswagen vans that operate like buses, cost 3 pesos. Anything labeled "Centro" will take you close to the *zócalo*.

GETTING AWAY

Airport: There is an **airport** (☎232 00 32) in nearby Huejotzingo, 22km northwest of Puebla on Mex. 150. Regional airline **Aeromar** (☎232 96 33) flies to Monterrey and Guadalajara; **AeroCalifornia** (☎230 48 55) will take you to Tijuana and Guadalajara.

Bus: CAPU (Central de Autobuses Puebla; ☎249 72 11), at Norte and Tlaxcala, is one of the largest bus stations in the country. To get to the *zócalo* from the station, exit to the street, take one of the walking bridges over the nearby highway, and flag down a "Centro" bus. To get back to the bus station, take a northbound bus labeled "CAPU" on Héroes de 5 de Mayo. Official yellow **taxis** labeled *taxis controlados* will make the trip for 26 pesos. From the station, ADO (☎230 40 00 or 230 40 14; www.adogl.com.mx) goes to: **Cancún** (20hr., 11:45am, 740 pesos); **Mexico City** (2½hr., every 40 min. 6:20am-10pm, 83 pesos); **Oaxaca** (4½hr., 7 per day, 183 pesos); **Veracruz** (3½hr., 7 per day, 149 pesos). Estrella Roja (☎249 70 99) offers similiar service to **Mexico City** and serves **Cholula** (30min., every 40 min. 5am-9pm, 5 pesos). Cristóbal Colón (☎225 90 07) goes to: **Puerto Escondido** (14hr.; 7:30pm, 411 pesos, 10:45pm, 349 pesos) and other resort cities. Estrella Blanca (located under the "Futura" sign; ☎249 75 61) goes to: **Acapulco** (7hr., 5 per day, 345 pesos); **Cuernavaca** (3.5hr., 4 per day, 78 pesos); **Taxco** (5hr., 8am, 116 pesos); and most points north. Flecha Azul (under "PTC"; ☎249 76 40) goes to **Tlaxcala** (1hr., every 8 min. 5:30am-6pm, 11 pesos). Smaller buses also serve the CAPU station.

◢ ⁊ ORIENTATION AND PRACTICAL INFORMATION

Puebla, capital of the state of Puebla, is connected through an extensive route network to **Mexico City** (120km northwest along Mex. 150), **Oaxaca** (Mex. 190, 125, or 131), **Tlaxcala** (Mex. 119), **Veracruz** (Mex. 150), and countless other cities. Street names change as they pass the *zócalo*. Numerical addresses follow a rigid pattern:

Puebla

▲ ACCOMMODATIONS
Hotel Avenida, **14**
Hotel Catedral, **8**
Hotel Imperial, **2**
Hotel Real del Parián, **7**
Hotel Ritz, **3**
Hotel Teresita, **12**
Hotel Victoria, **9**

🍴 FOOD
Antojitos la Concordia, **18**
Barra Vegetariano
La Vanahoria, **15**
Fonda La Mexicana, **19**
La Mesa Poblano, **13**
Restaurant El Vegetariano, **11**
Restaurante La Princesa, **10**

🍺 BARS
El Alebrije, **17**
La Batalla, **16**
Teorema, **5**

⚙ SERVICES
Farmacias del Ahorro, **6**
Lavandería Roly, **1**
Ultramarinos el Puerto de
Vercruz, **4**

TO CAPU BUS
STATION (4km)

TO MUSEO DE LA NO
INTERVENCIÓN, MUSEO DE
HISTORIA NATURAL, PLANETARIUM,
FUENTE DE GUADALUPE, Y MUSEO
REGIONAL DE ANTROPOLOGÍA

Red
Cross

Av. 20 Oriente
Av. 18 Oriente
Av. 16 Oriente
Av. 14 Oriente
Av. 12 Oriente
Av. 8 Oriente
Av. 4 Oriente
Av. 2 Oriente
Av. 5 Oriente
Av. 7 Oriente

Calle 14 Norte
Calle 12 Norte

Mercado
el Alto

Iglesia de
San Francisco

Blvd. Héroes del 5 de Mayo

TO AFRICAM
SAFARI (16km)

Calle 6 Norte

Teatro
Principal

Barrio
del Artista

Mercado
el Parián

Calle 4 Norte

Av. 18 Ote.
Av. 16 Oriente
Av. 14 Oriente
Av. 12 Oriente
Av. 10 Oriente
Av. 8 Oriente

Casa de
Aquiles Serdán

La Casa de
los Muñecos

Av. 6 Oriente
Av. 4 Oriente
Av. 2 Oriente

Palafox y Mendoza

ZÓCALO

Casa de
Cultura and
Biblioteca
Palafoxiana

Museo
Amparo

Calle 2 Sur
Calle 3 Oriente
Calle 5 Oriente
Calle 7 Oriente
Calle 9 Oriente

Catedral
Basílica
de Puebla

Av. 5 de Mayo

Av. 16 de Septiembre

Ex-convento de
Santa Mónica

Mercado 5
de Mayo

Ex-convento
de Santa Rosa

COMMERCIAL
CENTER

Santo
Domingo

Portal
Juárez

Museo
Bello

Calle 3 Norte
Calle 5 Norte

Av. 16 Poniente
Av. 14 Poniente
Av. 12 Poniente
Av. 10 Poniente
Av. 8 Poniente
Av. 6 Poniente
Av. 4 Poniente
Av. 2 Poniente
Av. Reforma

Calle 3 Sur
Calle 5 Sur
Calle 7 Sur

Calle 7 Norte
Calle 9 Norte

Calle 16 Poniente
Calle 14 Poniente
Calle 12 Poniente

Av. 3 Poniente
Av. 5 Poniente
Av. 7 Poniente
Av. 9 Poniente

Calle 9 Sur

PASEO
BRAVO

Calle 11 Sur
Calle 13 Sur

Juárez

TO ZONA ESMERELDA (1km),
CHOLULA (12km)

300 yards
300 meters

they correspond to the number of the lowest cross-street. For example, Av. 4 Ote.
237 would be bounded by Calle 2 Nte. and Calle 4 Nte. One block farther down,
between Calles 4 Nte. and 6 Nte., addresses are in the 400s. Note that there are two
major streets in Puebla celebrating the date of Mexico's victory over the French:
Av. 5 de Mayo and **Blvd. Héroes 5 de Mayo.** Take care not to confuse them.

TOURIST AND FINANCIAL SERVICES

Tourist Office: Av. 5 Ote. 3 (☎246 12 85 or 246 20 44), in the same building as the
Casa de la Cultura and the post office. Offers free maps and pamphlets and a very efficient, English-speaking staff. Open M-Sa 9am-8:30pm, Su 9am-2pm.

Currency Exchange: Banks line Reforma and 16 de Septiembre around the *centro*. Most
have 24hr. **ATMs. Bital,** Reforma 316 (☎246 30 50), changes money. Open M-Sa
8am-7pm. **Casas de cambio** offer slightly better rates and cluster in the Zona Esmeralda along Juárez, far from the *zócalo*. Try **Casa de Cambio Puebla,** Juárez 1706
(☎248 01 99). Open M-Sa 9am-6pm, Su 9am-1pm.

American Express: Calle 10 Sur #3715 2nd fl. (☎243 97 83). Cashes and replaces
AmEx checks. Open M-F 9am-6pm.

LOCAL SERVICES

Luggage Storage: At the bus station. 3 pesos per bag per hour. Open 24 hr.

Markets: Puebla's squawking **Mercado 5 de Mayo,** on Av. 18 Ote. between Calles 3 and
5 Nte., spills into 5 de Mayo and adjoining streets, selling everything from fresh veggies
to raw meat. Open daily 8:30am-6pm. For your processed and packaged needs, try
Ultramarinos el Puerto de Veracruz, Av. 2 Ote. 402 (☎232 90 52). Open M-Sa 8am-
9:30pm, Su 8am-4pm.

Laundry: Lavandería Roly, Calle 7 Nte. 404 (☎232 93 07). 30 pesos for 3kg self-service. Open M-Sa 8am-9pm, Su 8am-3pm.

Car Rental: The many agencies in town include **Avis** (☎/fax 249 61 99) and **Budget**
(☎230 50 08).

EMERGENCY AND COMMUNICATIONS

Emergency: ☎060.

Police: Policía Auxiliar (☎288 18 64). No English spoken.

Red Cross: Av. 20 Ote. 1002 at Calle 10 Nte. (☎243 82 44, 235 86 31, or 234 00 00).
24hr. ambulance service. Some English spoken.

Pharmacy: Farmacías del Ahorro Av. 2 Ote. #15A (☎231 33 83). Open daily 7am-
11pm.

Hospital: Hospital UPAEP, Av. 5 Pte. 715 at Calle 39 Sur (☎232 32 21 or 246 69 99).
24hr. service. Some English spoken. **Hospital Universitario** (☎246 64 64 or 243 13
77), Calle 13 Sur at Av. 25 Pte. 24hr. emergency service. No English spoken.

Fax: Telecomm, 16 de Septiembre 504 (☎232 77 19), just south of the post office.
Western Union, telegrams, fax. Open M-F 8am-7:30pm, Sa-Su 9am-noon.

Internet Access: Internet Cyber-Byte, Calle 2 Sur 505B, has lots of computers, fast connections, and free coffee. 15 pesos per hr. Open daily 10am-9pm. **Cyber-Cafe,** Calle 2
Sur 907C (☎232 42 42), 2 blocks farther south. Computer screens embedded in rustic
wooden tables. Reasonably quick connections. 20 pesos per hr., 10 pesos with ISIC
card. All-you-can-drink coffee 8 pesos. Open M-Sa 9am-9pm, Su 11am-5pm.

Post Office: (☎232 66 30) 16 de Septiembre at Av. 5 Ote., 1 block south of the zócalo,
just around the corner from the state tourist office. Open M-F 8:30am-5pm, Sa
9am-1pm. **Administración 1,** Av. 2 Ote. 411 (☎242 62 30). Open M-F 9am-5pm, Sa
9am-1pm. The branches have separate Listas de Correos, for mail pick-up.

Postal Code: 72000 or 72001.

ACCOMMODATIONS

Puebla is well stocked with budget hotels with most of them within a five or six block radius of the *zócalo*. When walking around the *zócalo*, be on the lookout for large, red "H" signs jutting from tightly-packed buildings. These signs, friends of the weary traveler, indicate that a hotel—most often a cheap one—is near.

Hotel Imperial, Av. 4 Ote. 212 (☎/fax 242 49 80). On the expensive side, but oh, the amenities! Phone and TV in all rooms, Internet access, a mini-golf course, a workout area, purified water, laundry service, pool and ping-pong tables, and a Hershey's Kiss on your pillow. Breakfast in the downstairs cafe (7:30-10:30am) and *cena del patrón*—snacks and drinks (8-9:30pm)—included. A **30% discount** for proud *Let's Go* readers makes the Imperial's luxury more affordable. Singles 264 pesos; doubles 378 pesos.

Hotel Teresita, Av. 3 Pte. 309 (☎232 70 72). The small rooms are models of modernity, with stuccoed walls, TVs, impeccably clean and attractively tiled baths, coordinating bedspreads and soft lighting. The staff speaks some English. Check-out 2pm. Singles 160 pesos; doubles 250 pesos.

Hotel Victoria, Av. 3 Pte. 306 (☎232 89 92). Brave the suspended concrete walkways connecting upper-level rooms to take advantage of a convenient location, accommodating staff, and affordable prices. Though a little dark, rooms and bathrooms are tidy and spacious. Singles (or 1-bed doubles) 100 pesos; doubles with 2 beds 150 pesos.

Hotel Ritz, Calle 2 Nte. 207 (232 44 57). While offering many of the same amenities as Hotel Teresita (TV, tiled private baths, the same new bedspreads), the Ritz has not been as thoroughly renovated, nor is the staff as charming. Still, the location is good, as is the free coffee. Singles 160 pesos; doubles 210 pesos.

Hotel Real del Parián, Av. 2 Ote. 601 (☎246 19 68), across the street from the *mercado* and upstairs from some of Puebla's best bargain restaurants. In a confusing priority of amenities, the Parián offers laundry facilities but dingy towels, private baths without toilet seats, and brightly painted but tiny rooms. Some rooms with balconies available. Singles 130 pesos; doubles 150 pesos; triples 210 pesos.

Hotel Catedral, Av. 3 Pte. 310 (☎232 23 60). The decayed glamour will make you sigh and long for the days when the intricate hardwood floors and soaring ceilings were not counterbalanced by dangling bare lightbulbs, dingy sheets, and finicky communal showers. Check-out 1pm. Singles 85 pesos; doubles 120 pesos. A 2nd location, at Av. 3 Pte. 724, has private bathrooms (15 pesos more).

Hotel Avenida, Av. 5 Pte 336 (☎232 21 04). Arguably the cheapest hotel in Puebla, and it shows. Discolored toilets lack seats. Beds have saggy mattresses and lumpy pillows. Still, the price and location make Hotel Avenida an option for (hard-core) budget travelers. Singles 60 pesos, with bath 90 pesos; doubles 110 pesos, with bath 140 pesos.

FOOD

Puebla is most famous for its *mole poblano*, a dark chocolate chile sauce that can be found slathered on chicken, rice, and just about everything else. *Mole poblano* just might be the national dish of Mexico, but don't leave Puebla without tasting other regional specialities. Taste *mole pipian*, containing pumpkin seeds and chiles, and *mole adobo*, a spicier blend with cumin powder. Leaving *mole* behind, try *chiles en nogada*, green peppers stuffed with beef and fruit fillings and smothered in white walnut sauce. The patriotic green, red, and white recipe was devised by the nuns of Santa Monica as a birthday present for Mexican Emperor Augustín de Iturbide when he visited the city in 1821 and is now eaten throughout August—Iturbide's birth month. Puebla's famous cooking nuns are perhaps best known for their *dulces* (sweets). Sample their centuries-old recipes and creative genius in the *dulcerías* along **Av. 6 Ote.**, just east of 5 de Mayo, which are filled with delicate, colorful candies, some of which are named after the convents of their origin.

Puebla is also home to a multitude of taco stands, many of them on **Calle 5 Nte.** between Avs. 10 and 12 Pte., on **Av. 5 de Mayo** at Av. 14 Ote., and at the **Mercado El Alto,** on the far side of La Iglesia de San Francisco. In addition to the taco-stand staples of *tortas* and tacos, these cheap joints feature *cemitas*, sandwiches made with a special long-lasting bread. In colonial times, Puebla exported the sandwiches to Veracruz, where they were subsequently consumed on trans-Atlantic ships. While Puebla has a number of fine restaurants, visit these stands for a more authentic (and cheaper) sampling of *poblano* cuisine.

🔳 **Fonda La Mexicana,** 16 de Septiembre 707 (☎232 67 47), 3 blocks south of the *zócalo*. On the wall hangs the 1st-place certificate that says it all: the best *chiles en nogada* in the state of Puebla. Fonda also serves excellent *mole* and *pipian* dishes—although at prices that may stretch your wallet (*mole* dishes 55 pesos). If you're pinching pesos, you can order the *menu económico* (soup, a main dish, and dessert or coffee, M-F 35 pesos, Sa-Su 38 pesos). Speedy, no-frills service. Open daily 10am-8pm.

🔳 **Barra Vegetariano La Zanahoria,** Av. 5 Ote. 206 (☎232 48 13). A high ceiling, bubbling fountain, and winding cast-iron stair give this veggie hangout the most agreeable ambience around. The real attraction, however, is the trendy but inexpensive food. Order dishes from the menu or go with the plate of the day, which includes 5 different vegetarian dishes and a fruit beverage (35 pesos; Su buffet 52 pesos). Top it all off with a fruit-flavored *licuado* made from yogurt, milk, or soy, served in a tall, old-fashioned milkshake glass (12 pesos). Open daily 7:30am-8:30pm.

Restaurante La Princesa, Portal Juárez 101 (☎232 1195), under the *portales* on the west side of the *zócalo*. Mingle with locals as you enjoy *platillos mexicanos* (5-35 pesos, with meat 30-75 pesos). A convenient location, casual and unpretentious atmosphere, and friendly staff add to its appeal. Open daily 7am-10:30pm.

La Mesa Poblana, Av. 3 Pte. 301 (☎242 00 41). The cheap *comida corrida* (27 pesos) and great atmosphere draw crowds of locals and travelers. Enjoy a pitcher of guyabana *agua fresca* (generous *media jarra* 10 pesos) as you relax. Open daily 7:30am-10pm.

Restaurant El Vegetariano, Av. 3 Pte. 525 (☎246 54 62). While the Vege's cafeteria-style 1950s decor may make you think you've come to the wrong place, stay cool—the *chorizo* and *jamón* (sausage and ham) on this menu are made of spiced soy. Fruit drinks (9-15 pesos) and gigantic salads (24 pesos). For take-out, bring your own container for a 5% ecologically-minded discount. Their *energética* (28 pesos), tropical fruits topped with yogurt and granola, will make you wish for a franchise in your neighborhood. *Comida corrida* 34 pesos. Open daily 7:30am-9pm.

Antojitos la Concordia, Av. 2 Sur 509 (☎232 13 73). For cheap and generous *antojitos* (20 pesos), or an ice cream float or banana split (25 pesos), this is the place to be. Surrounded by religious memorabilia and mushy Mexican couples, you'll be charmed by the speedy service and the fresh flowers on the tables. Open daily 8:30am-9:30pm.

👁 SIGHTS

Historic Puebla is a sightseer's paradise. Perhaps this is why bus loads of Mexican students and North Americans from nearby language schools file into the *zócalo* every weekend, cameras and maps in hand. Most sights are clustered around the *zócalo*, but some are located a few minutes away in the **Centro Cívico 5 de Mayo.**

SIGHTS NEAR THE ZÓCALO
The 1999 Puebla earthquake damaged several of the major sights near the *zócalo*. Most damaged sights are scheduled to reopen in 2002.

CATEDRAL BASÍLICA DE PUEBLA. Visible from all directions, the massive cathedral is the obvious starting point for any tour of the city. Constructed between 1575 and 1649 by an indigenous labor force working under Spanish direction, the cathedral's dark Baroque facade is enlivened by bright *talavera* domes. No less impressive is its interior, with ornate, inlaid choir stalls behind the freestanding octagonal Altar of the Kings, and a statue of the Virgin, known as *la conquistadora* because she arrived with the first Spaniards. (*Guided tours start at 30 pesos, 100 pesos for a group. Open M-Sa 10:30am-12:30pm, and 4-6pm.*)

¡HOLY *MOLE*! In 17th-century Puebla, nuns of the Santa Rosa order lived lives of extreme devotion. They slept without covers on beds of wooden slats, wore crowns of thorns to ward off bad thoughts, and installed 4 ft. doors throughout their convent so that they had to bow their heads in prayer each time they entered a room. The one area in which the nuns didn't skimp was food. Sor Andrea de la Asunción is said to have concocted the first ever *mole poblano* inside the convent. As the story goes, her sisters gathered around her as she rolled four different types of chiles together, commenting on her skill in grinding the peppers. *"¡Que bien muele!"* ("how well she grinds") became *"¡que bien mole!"* and thus the famed *mole* earned its name. To balance the spicy peppers, the sisters added chocolate, sugar, and 21 other ingredients before they were satisfied with the final product. Today, the nuns' culinary expertise is celebrated during the month of June by the *Festival del Mole Poblano* where chefs submit samples of their own family recipes, hoping to win best *mole* honors. The cooking nun phenomenon seems to have been widespread in Puebla; nuns of Santa Rosa, Santa Monica, and other orders are credited with the invention of Puebla's unique *dulces, chiles en nogada,* and other regional specialties.

MUSEO AMPARO. Three blocks south of the *zócalo*, the Museo Amparo traces the social history of Mesoamerica through art and architecture. The *salas* of *arte virreinal* have been stunningly restored. Skip the 10 peso headphones—the audio presentations offer only the most basic and obvious of information. Much more is available in the written guides (in Spanish, English and French) available for free in each room. *(Calle 2 Sur 708. ☎ 246 46 46. Open W-M 10am-6pm. 16 pesos, students 8 pesos; M free. Guided tour Su at noon, 76 pesos. Headphones 10 pesos plus 10 peso deposit.)*

CASA DE LOS MUÑECAS. The 1999 earthquake badly damaged the *casa*, and it is expected to be closed until summer 2002. If it's open, the museum, one of Puebla's most entertaining buildings, is worth a visit. This "House of the Dolls" is decorated on the outside with *talavera* renditions of the labors of Hercules. Some say the sculptures on the outside are the architect's rivals, while others say they are meant to be the city aldermen who protested when the *casa* was built higher than the municipal palace was. Inside, the **University Museum** displays exhibits on regional history and portraits of over 200 martyrs. *(Calle 2 Nte. 4 at the zócalo's northeast corner. ☎ 246 28 99. Open Tu-Su 10am-5pm. 11 pesos, students 5 pesos; W free.)*

MUSEO BELLO Y GONZÁLEZ. The Museo Bello, like the Casa de los Muñecos, was badly damaged in the 1999 earthquake. Because the stairs and part of the second floor caved in, the museum is expected to be closed until the summer of 2002. The museum displays the art collection of late textile magnate José Luis Bello, including a diverse selection of ivory, iron, porcelain, earthenware, and talavera artifacts. Guided tours are offered in Spanish and English, but English tours may be indecipherable. *(Av. 3 Pte. 302 at Calle 3 Sur, 1 block west of the southwest corner of the zócalo. ☎ 232 94 75. Open Tu-Su 10am-4:30pm. 10 pesos, students 5 pesos; Tu free.)*

IGLESIA DE SANTO DOMINGO. Puebla's first great religious foundation, this extravagant, gilded church is an important example of Spanish and international Baroque. The building was constructed between 1571 and 1611 by Dominican rural converts. Statues of saints and angels adorn the altar, but the church's real attraction is the **Capilla del Rosario,** a chapel, to the left of the altar, laden with enough 22-karat gold to make the King of Spain jealous. Masks depicting an Indian, a *conquistador* in armor, and a *mestizo* hang above three doors on the side of the chapel. On the ceiling, three statues represent Faith, Hope, and Charity. The 12 pillars represent the 12 apostles; the six on the upper level are each made from a single onyx stone. Since there was no room for a real choir, designers painted a chorus of angels with guitars and woodwinds on the wall over the door. *(Between Av. 4 and 6 Pte. on 16 de Septiembre. Open daily 10am-2pm and 4-8pm. Free.)*

CASA DE AQUILES SERDÁN. Originally the home of Aquiles Serdán, printer, patriot, and martyr of the 1910 Revolution, the house is today the **Museo Regional de la Revolución Mexicana.** Hundreds of bullet holes, both inside and out, bear witness to Serdán's assassination. The museum also includes photos of Serdán and other revolutionary faces and names and newspaper clippings and correspondence that narrate the development of the revolution. One room is dedicated to Carmen Serdán and other female revolutionaries. *(Av. 6 Ote. 206. ☎ 242 10 76. Open Tu-Su 10am-4:30pm. 10 pesos, children and students 4 pesos; Tu free.)*

■ **EX-CONVENTO DE SANTA MÓNICA.** When Benito Juárez's Reform Laws went into effect in 1857, they not only weakened the Church's power, but forced the nuns at the *convento* into hiding. The convent operated in secrecy for 77 years before it was accidentally rediscovered. Today, the *ex-convento* serves as a museum of curious and sporadically-labeled religious art, much of which was produced by the nuns themselves. Particularly eerie is a life-sized re-enactment of the Last Supper, in which plaster apostles in real robes sit around a colonial dinner table. Even more unnerving is the nun's crypt, where those who died during the period of hiding were quietly plastered into the walls. Also open to visitors is the beautiful kitchen (doubling as a laboratory) where the nuns first made *chiles en nogada.(Av 18 Pte. 103. ☎ 232 50 01. Open Tu-Su 9am-6pm. 22 pesos; Su free.)*

EX-CONVENTO DE SANTA ROSA. The birthplace of the original *mole*, from 1683 to 1861, this building housed the nuns of the order of Santa Rosa. Today, the ex-convent is a museum of *artesanía poblano*, offering examples of arts and crafts from different areas of the state. The kitchen and a nun's cell have been preserved in their original condition, and provide a glimpse into the combination of piety and joyous cooking that was cloistered life. On Sunday afternoons, the courtyard doubles as a theater for free concerts. *(Ave. 14 Pte. between Calles 3 and 5 Nte. Open Tu-Su 10am-5pm. 10 pesos, includes a guided tour.)*

IGLESIA DE SAN FRANCISCO. Across Blvd. Héroes de 5 de Mayo from El Parián, Puebla's oldest neighborhood contains the city's oldest church. Built by the Franciscans between 1535 and 1585, it features an incredible *talavera* and orange-red tile facade that contrasts sharply with the ominous bell tower. On your way out, experience the legacy of the city's nuns in the delectable *dulces típicos* being sold in the surrounding plaza. *(Av. 14 Ote. and Blvd. Héroes del 5 de Mayo. Open 24 hr.)*

CASA DE LA CULTURA. A base for exploring cultural events in the city, the *Casa* houses the **Biblioteca Palafoxiana,** an impressive 43,000 volume library that began with Juan de Palafoxiana's 6000-book collection, donated to the city in 1646. His original library includes an illuminated copy of the Nuremberg Chronicle from 1493. Although it, too, sustained extensive damage in the 1999 earthquake, the library is expected to reopen by summer 2002. Ask for a monthly calendar of cultural events at the information desk in the back of the courtyard. *(Av. 5 Ote. 5.☎ 246 13 01. Open Tu-Su 10am-5pm. 10 pesos, students 5 pesos.)*

CENTRO CÍVICO AND OTHER SIGHTS

With the exception of **Africam Safari,** the following sights are located in the **Centro Cívico 5 de Mayo.** A short trip from the *centro,* the Centro Cívico was the location of the May 5, 1862 **Battle of Puebla,** in which general Ignacio Zaragoza defeated the French in their advance toward Mexico City. The former battleground is now a large, unkempt park, where austere patriotic signs compete for attention with frolicking young lovers. *(To get to the Centro Cívico, Catch a #72 bus or #8 colectivo (both 3 pesos) on Blvd. Héroes de 5 de Mayo, 3 blocks east of the zócalo. Get off when you see a large, multi-armed cement monument to Zaragoza that sits on an empty glorieta. Facing away from the monument, cross the street and walk uphill toward the park.)*

MUSEO DE LA NO INTERVENCIÓN. This oddly-named museum houses artifacts, paintings, and documents dealing with the Battle of Puebla and General Zaragoza. The museum also features a panoramic recreation of the battlefield as it might

THE INFESTATION Where have all the Beetles gone? They're all in Mexico—more than a million of them. One in every eight passenger vehicles in Mexico is a classic VW Beetle, and Puebla is the only remaining place on Earth to manufacture them. The VW factory on the outskirts of town employs more than 16,000 workers and churns out 1,000 cars each day. Many of these are the chic, New Beetle (US$20,000), but almost all are shipped north. Mexican drivers still overwhelmingly prefer the classic model (US$6,700), affectionately known as "Vochos." Souped-up Beetles, including the majority of Mexico City's 35,000 taxis, are meticulously customized, often sporting chrome fenders, oversized tires, and mini steering wheels.

have looked in 1862 and exhibits on French rule in Mexico. *(From the Zaragoza monument, follow the road as it curves past a defunct information center. A large concrete Mexican flag marks a fork in the road. To the right is the Fuerte de Loreto, which now houses the museum. Open Tu-Su 10am-4:30pm. 25 pesos; Su free. Guided tours from 30-40 pesos for a group.)*

FUERTE DE GUADALUPE. This semi-ruined fort, honoring *Cinco de Mayo* offers stunning views of Puebla and the surrounding mountains. Beware of amorous couples lurking behind walls. *(Follow the road to the left of the Museo de la No Intervención and take a right at the 2nd intersection. The fort is all the way at the end of the road. Free.)*

■ **MUSEO REGIONAL DE ANTROPOLOGÍA.** With lots of visual exhibits, the museum narrates the social history of Puebla state, from man's arrival until today. The model of an indigenous dwelling will make you appreciate your hotel room. *(Once you leave the fort, retrace your steps up the road. The yellow museum is on the right before the intersection. ☎ 235 87 13 or 235 67 00. Open Tu-Su 10am-4:30 pm. 30 pesos; Su free.)*

PLANETARIUM. Next to the Museo de Historia Natural, the planetarium—in the shape of a giant, glittering, silver pyramid—features the typical slew of space exhibits and an **Omnimax** theater. Across from the museum is the **Recinto Ferial,** an exposition center and fairground. *(Next to the Museo Regional de Antropología. ☎ 235 20 99. Open Tu-F 4-6pm, Sa-Su noon-6pm. At 2pm on weekends, there is a free movie (regular format). 25 pesos, students 20 pesos.)*

MUSEO DE HISTORIA NATURAL. This museum teems with fossils, live snakes, and well-behaved school kids. Life-sized (but out of date) dinosaur models hold court in the foyer, while a spectacular butterfly collection lights up the left exhibition wing. The museum also boasts the largest collection of stuffed deer heads you'll ever see under one roof. *(Next to the Planetarium. ☎ 235 34 19. Open Tu-Su 10am-5pm. 20 pesos, students and children 10 pesos; Tu free.)*

AFRICAM SAFARI. A longer trip takes you to this ecological zoo dedicated to conservation and recreation. The park holds over 3000 live animals, representing approximately 250 species. The geographically organized theme areas span Asia, the Americas, and Antarctica. What sets the Africam Safari apart from your average zoo is that the animals roam freely. Visitors drive through the park, stopping at designated locations to take photos and mingle with the quadrupedal residents. *(16km southeast of Puebla, the Africam Safari is best reached by bus. Estrella Roja offers packages that include roundtrip fare from CAPU or the zócalo and park admission From CAPU: M-F 11am, Sa-Su 10am. From the zócalo: Tu-Su 11am and 2pm. 110 pesos, children 100 pesos. If driving, head to the south of the city and then east, following the signs to Valsequillo. Africam ☎ 235 88 29 or 235 87 18. Open daily 10am-5pm. 75 pesos, children 70 pesos.)*

🎵 **ENTERTAINMENT**

Bars and theaters pile up in the *zócalo*, while a younger local crowd heads for the bars in **Plazuela de los Sapos,** creating a loud and social weekend scene. Farther from the *zócalo*, between Calles 21 and 29 Sur on Juárez, is the **Zona Esmeralda,** lined with even more bars and discos. If you're prepared to spring for a cab, however, you may as well continue on to the clubs and bars on the **Recta Cholula**, the highway connecting Puebla and Cholula. The true center of the area's thriving nightlife, the *Recta* is jam-packed with college and language school students all night, every night. Since buses stop running early, it's best to take a taxi (50 pesos). Ask to be let off by the clubs near UDLA (Universidad de las Américas).

■ **Teorema,** Reforma 540 (☎242 10 14), 3 blocks west of the *zócalo*. A bookstore/cafe by day, Teorema is a trendy alternative to the bar scene by night. After 9pm, a varied young clientele crowds in to hear nightly live music, chat with friends, and drink *cafe con licor* (25 pesos) in this literary lair. Cover M 11 pesos, Tu-W 15 pesos, Th-Sa 20 pesos, Su 15 pesos. Open 9:30am-2:30pm and 4:30pm-2am; music starts at 9:30pm.

El Alebrije, Recta Cholula km 2 (☎249 42 95). If you're young, beautiful, and rich, El Alebrije welcomes you. Talk to the capitán to get a table, or mingle with friends on one of the zebra-striped dance floors while the pop and electronica thumps and the 42 disco balls twinkle. Drinks from 40 pesos. Cover 50 pesos. Open Th-Sa 10:30pm-4am.

La Batalla, Calle 6 Sur 504A (☎246 35 65), in Plazuela de los Sapos. Spiffy young socialites and stout, middle-aged men shake it under low lights to a pounding beat. Beer from 13 pesos, mixed drinks 22 pesos. Cover Th 15 pesos, F-Sa 25 pesos. Open M-W 6pm-2am, Th 5pm-2am, F-Sa noon-3am, Su noon-1am.

▟ SHOPPING

Home to embroidered textiles, clay ornaments, woven palms, and a 450-year tradition of *talavera*, Puebla offers numerous and diverse shopping opportunities. At **Mercado El Parián,** with entrances on both Av. 2 Ote. and 4 Ote. at Calle 6 Nte., tourists gather to buy hand-painted *talavera* ceramics and tiles, as well as leather purses, beads, and other trinkets. For less expensive *talavera* purchases, head to **Av. 18 Pte.**, west of Av. 5 de Mayo. North of El Parián, at Calle 8 Nte. 410, is the **Barrio del Artista**, where *poblano* artists paint and sell their works in the street. Sundays from 10am-6pm, the **Plazuela de los Sapos,** south of the *zócalo* on Calle del Sapo, fills with antique bazaars selling bronze figures, old coins, and *talavera*.

▟ FESTIVALS

The **Casa de la Cultura,** Av. 5 Ote. 5, is the place to go for information about Puebla's cultural events. Pick up a monthly calendar and check the board at the rear of the courtyard for the latest schedules. (☎246 13 01. Folk dances Sa and Su. Films Th-Su. Open 24hr.) Also be sure to check the schedule posted inside the **Teatro Principal,** which lists weekly performances. A new program at **Centro Cultural Santa Rosa** (☎232 92 40), located in the **Ex-Convento de Santa Rosa,** includes performances of popular and traditional music and experimental theater. On Sunday afternoons, the courtyard at the ex-convent hosts free concerts and dance exhibitions.

In addition to June's *mole* cook-off and August's *festival de chiles en nogada*, the city of Puebla celebrates several secular events throughout the year. The end of April kicks off a month-long *fiesta* celebrating May. Each day the streets fill with various types of expositions. Special events include *corridas de toros* and cock fights. In the **Festival Palafoxiana,** Juan de Palafox is remembered for his religious influence and the generous donation of his namesake library to the city. The celebration runs F-Su, from the last Friday in September until November 19, and features dances, concerts, theater performances, and art.

CHOLULA   ☎2

The energy and exuberance of the student population from the Universidad de las Américas, (UDLA for short) unite with small-town hospitality to make Cholula (pop. 95,000) a welcome alternative to the big-city anonymity of nearby Puebla. Olmecs, Zapotecs, Toltecs, and Aztecs all had their moments of glory here, and each left their mark by adding another tier or temple to the city's Great Pyramid.

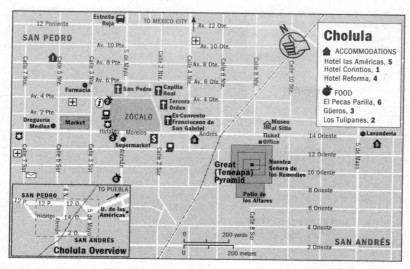

Cholula

🏠 ACCOMMODATIONS
Hotel las Américas, 5
Hotel Corintios, 1
Hotel Reforma, 4

🍴 FOOD
El Pecas Parilla, 6
Güeros, 3
Los Tulipanes, 2

Cholula's ceremonial importance had waned by 1520, when Cortés and his men slaughtered 6000 Cholutecos in what is now known as the Cholula Massacre—punishment for a supposed alliance between the Cholutecos and the Aztecs. To further punish the city, Cortés vowed to erect 365 churches—one for every day of the year—on top of the city's native temples. While he never completed his goal, the 37 churches in Cholula today have ensured the city's continued role as a place of pilgrimage, both for the faithful and for the curious. An easy daytrip from Puebla or Mexico City, Cholula draws urban escapists with its churches, balmy weather, and lively *portales*. Just don't expect much sleep—bells from the 37 church towers start ringing early on Sunday morning.

▐ TRANSPORTATION

GETTING AROUND

Colectivos to Puebla and destinations within Cholula can be flagged down at a variety of locations in the city center, including the corner of **Av. 4 Pte.** and **Calle 3 Nte.**, as well as at **Morelos** and **Calle 2 Sur** (30min. to Puebla's CAPU, 5 pesos). After the *colectivos* stop running at 10pm, you'll have to negotiate a price with a local taxi (40 pesos or more). *Sitios*, available throughout the city, can be found at the southeast corner of the *zócalo*.

GETTING AWAY

To get to the *zócalo* from the Estrella Roja **bus station**, Av. 12 Pte. 108 (☎247 19 20), between 5 de Mayo and Calle 3 Nte., walk east to the intersection of Av. 12 Pte. and 5 de Mayo, turning right on 5 de Mayo. Walk four blocks downhill toward the large yellow church of San Pedro. Estrella Roja runs buses to: **Mexico City** via Puebla (2½hr., 2 per hr. 4:25am-8pm, 39 pesos) and **Puebla** (30min., 2 per hr. 4:25am-9pm, 5 pesos). For more destinations, try Puebla's CAPU (see p. 348).

☀ ☑ ORIENTATION AND PRACTICAL INFORMATION

Cholula is on Mex. 150, 122km east of Mexico City and 8km west of Puebla. The municipality encompasses two small towns—**San Pedro Cholula** and **San Andrés Cholula**. The *zócalo*, tourist office, and most restaurants are located in San Pedro.

San Andrés, on the other hand, is mostly residential and contains everything to the east of the Great Pyramid. The walk between the two can be lonely at night; taxis travel the distance for 20 pesos.

TOURIST AND LOCAL SERVICES

Tourist Office: Av. 4 Pte. 103 (☎247 31 16). From the *zócalo*, walk north past the *portales* and turn left at the northwest corner. The tourist office is the second building on the left. A nearly illegible map, a historical pamphlet that you can make copies of next door (at exorbitant prices), and a preoccupied staff is all that you will find here. No English spoken. Open M-Su 10am-6:30pm.

Currency Exchange: Casa de Cambio Azteca, Calle 2 Sur 104 (☎247 21 90). Open M-F 9am-7pm, Sa 9am-2pm. Banks on Morelos at the *zócalo* have more limited hours but offer comparable rates and have **ATMs. Bancomer,** Morelos 10 (247 03 10), on the south side of the *zócalo*, is open M-F 8:30am-4pm and changes American Express traveler's checks.

Market: Cosme del Razo, with entrances on Calles 3 and 5 Nte., between Hidalgo and Av. 4 Pte., also in the *zócalo*. Open 8am-8pm. On W and Su, the already crowded market swells with even more merchants.

Supermarket: For pre-packaged food and toiletries, try **Tienda Sindical de Consumo Crom,** Alemán 116, a supermarket near the corner of Av. 3 Ote.

Laundry: Lavandería Aquiahuac, on Av. 14 Ote. 2D, 4 blocks east of the pyramid, just after 5 de Mayo. 7 pesos per kg. Open M-F 9am-8pm, Sa 9am-6pm.

EMERGENCY AND COMMUNICATIONS

Emergency:☎ 060.

Police: At the Presidencia Municipal, Portal Guerrero 1 (☎247 05 62), in the arcade under the arches. Little English spoken.

Red Cross: Calle 7 Sur 301 (☎247 85 01), on the corner of Av. 3 Pte., a bit of a hike from the *centro*. Walk-in service. No English spoken.

Pharmacy: Droguería Medina, Hidalgo 502 (☎247 16 44), on the corner of Calle 5 Nte. Open 24hr. **Farmacía San Juan Bautista,** Calle 3 Nte. 405 (☎247 34 45), on the corner of Av. 6 Pte. Open daily 8am-10:30pm.

Hospital: Clínica de IMSS (☎247 51 55), at Calle 4 Nte. and Av. 10 Ote. No English spoken. **Hospital San Gabriel,** Av. 4 Pte. 503 (☎247 00 14). No English spoken.

Fax: Telecomm, Portal Guerrero 9 (☎247 01 30). Telegrams, fax, Western Union. Open M-F 8am-7:30pm, Sa-Su 9am-noon. **Papelería Toño,** Morelos 8 (☎/fax 247 11 49), on the south side of the *zócalo*. Open daily 8am-8pm.

Telephones: LADATELs, line Morelos and Hidalgo on the south side of the *zócalo*.

Internet: Cafe Internet La Gioconda, Av. 3 Ote. 203 at Calle 2 Sur (☎247 77 01). Relatively quick connection is a bargain at 10 pesos per hr. Open M-Sa 9:30am-8:30pm, Su 10am-4pm. **Cafe Internet,** Portal Guerrero 11 (☎247 41 98), on the west side of the *zócalo*. Fast connection, 16 pesos per hr. Open M-Sa 10am-8pm, Su 9am-2pm.

Post Office: Calle 7 Sur 505 (247 59 17), just past Av. 5 Pte. Open M-F 8am-3pm.

Postal Code: 72761.

⌂ ACCOMMODATIONS

Near the *zócalo* and the pyramid, budget hotels are scarce. While several moderately priced hotels are located north of Cholula on **Carretera Federal México-Puebla,** visitors willing to make the trek should consider staying just 30min. away in Puebla, where they will hit the cheap hotel jackpot.

Hotel Reforma, Calle 4 Sur 101 (☎247 01 49), near Morelos. A short stumble from the *portales*. Private baths, extremely helpful, and friendly staff compensate for street noise and somewhat flimsy doors. Duck into the connected **Bar Reforma** to examine wall murals and photographs of all 128 churches in and around Cholula. Ring to enter after 10:30pm. Singles/doubles 160 pesos.

Corintios, Calle 5 Nte. 801 (☎247 94 40). Walk up the winding stairway in the light-filled interior to get to your spacious, bright blue and white room. Private baths have separate compartments for shower, toilet, and lavatory. Discounts for 3-day and week-long stays. Night-owls beware—you can ring to enter after the front door locks at 6pm, but the staff will only stay awake to let you in until 11:30pm. Singles 120 pesos; doubles 180 pesos.

Hotel Las Américas, Av. 14 Ote. 6 (☎247 09 91). From the *zócalo*, take Morelos and walk past the pyramid approximately 4 blocks. The hotel is on the right after 5 de Mayo. The bright flowers and uncut grass surrounding the empty courtyard pool hardly disguise the 70s architecture. Comfortable rooms have TVs and phones; curtain-less private bathrooms are one giant shower. Visitors should be wary of walking the long, desolate path past the pyramid at night. Singles 100 pesos; doubles 130 pesos.

▶ FOOD

Influenced in part by Puebla's culinary traditions, most of Cholula's restaurants feature several variations of *mole poblano*. For a good variety of cheap local food, wander through the **Cosme del Razo** market and the food stands in the *zócalo*. Cholula's most affordable establishments are located on **Hidalgo,** perpendicular to the *portales*. Toward the bus station, family-owned *torta* shops and market stands offer even better prices, but eating in the *zócalo* is a great way to meet locals, and the *charla* (chat) is worth the few extra pesos.

▩ Güeros, Hidalgo 101 (☎247 21 88). Select your favorite North American or Mexican tunes from the jukebox to hum as you munch on reasonably priced regional specialties (20-40 pesos) or *antojitos* (12-18 pesos). Local families and couples populate the modern, spacious eating area, while the bar is an informal meeting place for solo diners. Tacos start at 7 pesos, sandwiches and *tortas* 12-26 pesos, and main dishes 40 pesos. Open daily 9am-midnight.

Los Tulipanes, Portal Guerrero 13 (☎247 17 07), on the west side of the *zócalo*. The scenic views of the *zócalo*, piped-in Mexican melodies, and delicious *comida corrida* (35 pesos; Su 38 pesos) draw locals and visitors to relax in the shade of *portales*. The moderately priced menu features breakfast (starting at 24 pesos), *antojitos* (15-25 pesos), *comida típica* (40 pesos), and meat and fish entrees (27-50 pesos). Open daily 8am-9pm.

El Pecas Parrilla, Alemán 512A (☎247 16 18), at the corner of Calle 7 Pte., offers all the quality service, savory meat dishes, and colorful ambience of tourist restaurants at lower prices. Tacos from 5 pesos; tender *arracheras* complete with excellent guacamole 48 pesos. Open daily 2pm-2am.

◉ SIGHTS

Cholula's chief attractions are also its most visible: the **Great Pyramid** looms over the town's center, while the brightly colored towers of Cholula's 37 churches just above the cityscape. The June 1999 earthquake that devastated so many of Puebla's sights impacted Cholula as well: many churches sustained extensive damage. Fortunately, the combined efforts of the government, churches, and community enabled the reconstruction of many churches. Although a few churches, such as the *Santuario de Nuestra Señora de los Remedios*, are still being repaired, others near the *zócalo* are resplendent in their newly restored beauty.

THE GREAT PYRAMID AND ENVIRONS

TENEAPA PYRAMID. When Cortés destroyed the Toltec temple atop the mis-shapen hill that dominates Cholula, he was unaware that the hump of earth was actually a giant pyramid. Tunneling into the "hill" in the twentieth century, archaeologists discovered three other pyramids built one on top of the other, indicating successive enlargement of a smaller original pyramid. Archaeologists believe that the original pyramid, dating from roughly 200 BC, was built by the Olmecs or a related group. When the Toltec-Chichimec groups settled in Cholula in the 12th century, they named the pyramid Tlachiaualtepetl, or "man-made hill," and may have practiced human sacrifice atop it. Sophisticated drainage systems kept the structure, by volume the largest pyramid in the world, intact. Today, the tunnels and some excavations on the south and west sides of the pyramid are open to visitors. A joint conservation-excavation program is currently under development, with plans to resume excavation in 2005. (*Entrance is on Morelos, across from the railroad.* ☎ *247 90 81. Ruins and tunnels open daily 9am-6pm. 30 pesos, Su free.*)

MUSEO AL SITIO. Before entering the Indiana-Jones-style tunnels at the pyramid's base, visit the museum across the street from the ticket booth. Centered around a helpful diorama of the pyramid (guaranteed to convince skeptics that it is not, in fact, a hill), the museum features area artifacts, tracing Cholula's rise as a ceremonial center. A reproduction of "Los Bebedores," one of the site's famous frescoes and one of the largest murals in Pre-Hispanic Mesoamerica, graces the spooky back room. Exhibits are narrated in both Spanish and English. (☎ *247 90 81. Open daily 9am-6pm. Free with tickets to the pyramid.*)

TUNNELS AND PATIOS. To reach the open-air excavations on the side of the pyramid opposite the entrance, most visitors walk through the labyrinthine archaeological tunnels that riddle the pyramid's base. Deeper, darker, slightly scary side tunnels can be explored with a guide or by yourself. Look for a particularly stunning section of one of the interior pyramid's main staircases, which has been excavated from bottom to top. The underground adventure ends at the south side of the pyramid in the **Patio de los Altares,** a mostly unexcavated grassy area dotted with pyramid chunks in various renovated states. English language pamphlets can be purchased at the bookstore near the end of the outdoor excavations, though the bare essentials can be gleaned from the explanatory markers, written in Spanish and English. Guides help greatly. (*Guides in Spanish or English, 70 pesos.*)

SANTUARIO DE NUESTRA SEÑORA DE LOS REMEDIOS. No ticket is required to reach the Santuario, a church built atop the pyramid in 1594, but the trek is more taxing than a Stairmaster workout. When the Spanish built the sanctuary, they dedicated it to La Virgen de los Remedios to safeguard against the gods from whose ruined temple the sanctuary walls were constructed. After collapsing in a 1864 earthquake, the structure was rebuilt using much of the original material. Nature seems to repeat herself, for once again Cholulans are repairing the small, flower-filled sanctuary after the 1999 earthquake. Fortunately, the virgin figure, set in her fabergé jewelry box, remained unharmed, and celebrations in her honor continue each June and September. On a clear day, the snow-capped volcanoes **Popocatépetl** and **Ixtaccíhuatl** are visible from the church site, as well as the rest of Cholula and its many churches. (*From the patio, follow the path as it takes you back to the railroad tracks. Make an immediate right where the fence ends and begin climbing. Free.*)

CHURCHES OF THE ZÓCALO

If you don't have the energy to hike to every single one of Cholula's 37 churches, don't despair: four of the most spectacular border the *zócalo* itself.

EX-CONVENTO FRANCISCANO DE SAN GABRIEL. Hoping to use the church for a great conversion, the 16th century Franciscans used Indian labor to construct San Gabriel on top of the Templo de Quetzalcóatl. Despite San Gabriel's imposing size, the Franciscans found it too small for their epic conversion campaign, and in 1575 began work on the Capilla Real, two doors down. The altar in today's chapel was built in 1897, utilizing a Neoclassical style designed to emphasize the mass of the already weighty church. (*At the southeast corner of the zócalo.*)

CAPILLA REAL. Possibly the most striking of the city's churches, the 49-domed structure was finished in the early 17th century, filling its role as the long-awaited auditorium for thousands of Indians to hear mass at once. The wall behind the splendid altar is covered with three famous paintings depicting the story of the Virgin of Guadalupe. The Capilla Real lacks the ornate gold filigree of the surrounding churches; its simplicity is defined by the ever-changing panorama of whitewashed arches, soaring domes, and uniquely decorated side-chapels. *(The northernmost church on the east side of the zócalo. Open daily, except 1-3:30pm.)*

CAPILLA DE LA TERCERA ORDEN. Gold ornamentation and seven large 18th and 19th century paintings decorate the interior, while the church's small dome s balances Capilla Real's vastness. *(Between San Gabriel and Capilla Real.)*

PARROQUIA DE SAN PEDRO. As a 17th-century construction, San Pedro displays an architectural style unique to its age: Baroque meets Renaissance in ornate fashion. The interior has been spectacularly restored, and features a *Churringueresque* cupola. Eighteenth century paintings adorn the walls, including one of Diego de Borgraf's most powerful depictions of Christ. *(In the northwest corner of the zócalo, entrance on 5 de Mayo. Open daily 6:30am-1:30pm, 4-6pm.)*

ON THE OUTSKIRTS OF CHOLULA

SANTA MARÍA TONANTZINTLA. Almost as famous as Cholula itself are several churches in the surrounding villages, particularly Santa María Tonantzinla. Built in the 10th century on top of a Pre-Hispanic temple, the church's bright saffron facade hides a startling interior, with over 450 stucco faces staring from the walls and ceiling. Saints, musicians, and chiefs congregate with animals and flowers in an explosion of iconography, the handiwork of the same indigenous artisan who executed the plans of European artists in Puebla's Capilla del Rosario (see p. 353). *(To get to Tonantzintla, take a colectivo marked "Chipilo" at Ave. 6 Ote. and 5 de Mayo. 3-4 pesos. Get off when you see a yellow church on your left; Tonantzintla is a short walk down the pedestrian-only street to your right.)*

SAN FRANCISCO ACATEPEC. A 15min. walk away (or an even shorter 3-peso bus ride) lies the town and church of San Francisco Acatepec. Built in 1588, the facade of the church is almost as ornate as Tonantzintla's walls. Entirely covered in brilliant *talavera* tile set into an overgrown graveyard, this is perhaps the most exquisite application the famous tiles yet found. *(To go directly from Cholula to Actapec, simply ride a few km farther on the same "Chipilo" bus that you would take for Tonantzintla.)*

UNIVERSIDAD DE LAS AMÉRICAS. The elite, private university UDLA (pronounced OOHD-lah), is an example of the universality of university culture. The verdant, bench-filled campus serves as a respite from the city's dusty mayhem. Students, locals, and visitors find cheap diversion watching UDLA's *beisbol* and *fútbol* teams face neighboring colleges during the fall and spring semesters. **Cafetería Santa Catarina** serves Mexican institutionalized food. Souvenirs are available in the nearby social center kiosk. *(Take an eastbound colectivo anywhere on Av. 14 Ote. 3 pesos. Cafeteria open M-F 7am-9:30pm, Sa-Su 7:30am-8pm.)*

♫ ▓ ENTERTAINMENT AND NIGHTLIFE

Although dingy and dusty by day, Cholula is at it's best by night. Most of the cafes and bars on and near the *zócalo* are open daily, and fill up with a lively, yet low-key student crowd from UDLA. For more high-powered and high-cost social activity, venture out of Cholula to the Recta Cholula on the way to Puebla.

BARS

Bars in Cholula center around the lively *zócalo* and Av. 14 Ote., west of Hotel Las Américas in San Andrés. The bars in San Andrés serve local, slightly older clientele, but those in the *centro* cater to a more diverse, younger crowd. The coolest place in Cholula is the ▨**Casa de la Luna,** Morelos 203, a student-owned-and-operated cafe-bar that features live bongo and Afrocuban music every night. For more lively conversation, check out the back rooms and the courtyard, where the line between experimental art gallery and cafe blurs. The limited menu is a budget traveler's dream—nothing over 12 pesos. (Open daily 11am-3am.) **Bar-Restaurant Enamorada,** Portal Guerrero 1, under the *portales,* feeds and inebriates a social, varied crowd. While patrons visit Enamorada earlier in the day for its affordable *comida típica,* the young crowd flocks to its doors around 10:30pm for the live *trova* music until midnight. (Beers 13 pesos, mixed drinks 30 pesos, and *cafe con licor* 28 pesos. ☎ 247 02 92 or 247 70 22. Open Tu-Su 8am-2am.) **Cafe Tal,** Porral Guerrero 7, also under the *portales,* provides coffee lovers with a cheap, relaxing place to caffeinate. Start the night right with one of the liquored-up cafes. (Coffees start at 8 pesos. Open daily 9am-2am.)

CLUBS

Undoubtedly, the **Recta Cholula** is *the* place to be. Littering the highway between Puebla and Cholula, warehouse-sized *discotecas* are fueled by both cities' youthful energy. Bars and discos in this area frequently reinvent themselves, attempting to get an edge on the market, but you'll find the same student-filled scene regardless of the packaging. Those wanting a wild night of clubbing should dress well and fill their wallets with cash; this is no place for amateurs. To get to the Recta, take a Puebla-bound bus from Av. 14 Ote. past UDLA. Buses stop running around 10pm, so the return trip is best made in a taxi—a pricey finish to a pricey evening. **El Alebrije,** Recta Cholula Km. 2, is the top choice of the UDLA crowd. Drinks from 40 pesos, cover 50 pesos. (☎ 249 42 95. Open Th-Sa 10:30pm-4am.)

GAY AND LESBIAN NIGHTLIFE

In Cholula, the young, mostly gay and bisexual clientele of **Keops,** on the corner of Av. 14 Ote. and 5 de Mayo, keep it jamming to a techno beat. Don't miss *Travesty,* the midnight drag show. (Cover F 40 pesos, Sa 50 pesos. Open F-Sa 9pm-4am.)

FESTIVALS

A deeply religious town, Cholula celebrates religious festivals with flair. Two different celebrations honor the Virgen de Remedios. Since 1640, Cholula has celebrated the **Bajada de la Virgen** for two weeks in June, when the Virgin descends from her celestial sanctuary to visit the city and surrounding towns. Cholulans carry the figurine through the streets by motorcycle every morning at 7am during the week of the festival. In the evenings, locals revel under the elaborate gateways of flowers, seeds, and glitter decorating the Virgin's route. An even bigger festival takes place from the first day in September to the 8th, the Virgin's **Día Santa.** Celebrations for *Carnaval, Semana Santa,* and Christmas are also big events, when Cholula fills with visitors from Puebla, Mexico City, and surrounding villages.

CENTRAL PACIFIC COAST

Stretching from the quiet fishing hamlets near San Blas to the busy port of Manzanillo, the central Pacific coast boasts kilometer after kilometer of smooth sand massaged by the ebb and flow of the tide. Hot but not overly humid, the region's climate easily pleases, and the sun rarely fails to illuminate the azure skies.

A state of varied terrain, **Nayarit** is marked by volcanic highlands, tropical jungles, and a network of lakes and rivers. The republic's oldest indigenous group, the Huichol, make their home here, brightening village streets with their colorful dress. This verdant region grows the lion's share of the nation's marijuana and served as the setting for *Journey to Ixtlán*, Carlos Castañeda's renowned book describing experiences with hallucinogens in a small town between Tepic and Guadalajara. Hallucinogen use has long been part of Cora and Huichol *indígena* traditions and is still common practice among shamans in their incantations.

South of Nayarit lies **Jalisco,** the most touristed state along the central Pacific coast. Much of the world's perception of Mexican pop culture could be stamped *"Hecho en Jalisco"* (Made in Jalisco). The *jarabe tapatío* (hat dance), *mariachis, charreria* (cowboy culture), and tequila all originated in this state. For much of its history, however, the province remained isolated from the rest of the republic, possessing neither silver nor gold, jewels nor water, fertile land nor agricultural climate. It wasn't until the 1920s, when railroad tracks extended to Guadalajara, that this Sierran town (elevation 1552m) grew into a metropolis; today, it is Mexico's second-largest city. On the coast, Puerta Vallarta—full of discos, English-language bookstores, cafes, and, of course, tourists—further exemplifies Jalisco's boom. Only an hour and a half away, tiny Perula offers a stark contrast with its undeveloped, unspoiled, and almost uninhabited beaches.

Tiny **Colima** is home to spectacular black-sand beaches and pleasant mountain towns where tourists can escape the resort scene and breathe in cool, crisp air. The state is also home to the city of Colima, a sparkling, untouristed gem full of gardens, and Manzanillo, the workhorse of Mexico's Pacific coast. This port has not paused once in 700 years of commerce to wipe its sweaty brow, and only recently has it begun to polish its image for the benefit of visitors.

HIGHLIGHTS OF THE CENTRAL PACIFIC COAST

REVEL in **Guadalajara** (see p. 369), Mexico's 2nd-largest city; home to *jarabe tapatío, la avenida de zapatos,* and many *mariachis.*

GO GAUDY in **Puerto Vallarta** (see p. 385), which is no longer the quiet, secluded paradise of the 1960s. The thriving tourist industry has transformed the city with glitzy nightlife, luxury hotels, shop-stuffed streets, and a very happening **gay scene** (see p. 379). The **best beaches** lie south of the city (see p. 390).

SCORCH your feet on the dazzling black-sand beaches of **Cuyutlán** (see p. 400), which accompany a wondrous lagoon, and quiet solitude.

TRAVEL to **Tequila** (see p. 383), the kitschy and fun birthplace of your favorite liquor.

SNEAK AWAY from it all in **Bahía de Navidad** (see p. 392), where you can swim, surf, and sunbathe on your choice of beautiful beaches. Both **Bahía de Navidad** and **Melaque** (see p. 393) offer budget accomodations and gorgeous beaches on the bay.

CONQUER El Nevado (see p. 407), Colima's own snow-capped volcanic peak.

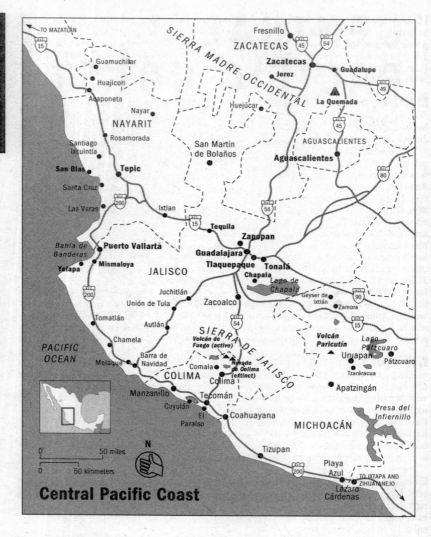

Central Pacific Coast

NAYARIT

SAN BLAS

☎ 3

San Blas's corner of the Nayarit Coast is a benevolent Bermuda Triangle. Travelers who run aground here glance at the scruffy *zócalo* and start to wonder why they came, but before giving it much thought, a hot drowsy haze descends, transporting them to a dreamy *siesta* land embedded in the sounds of crashing surf and humming jungle. Some get stranded permanently, drawn by the mythological mile-long wave, the surrounding jungle estuaries, and the Nayarit mountains, full of waterfalls and coffee plantations.

TRANSPORTATION. The **bus station** is in the *zócalo*, but has limited departure schedules. Estrella Blanca (☎ 285 00 43) goes to: **Guadalajara** (5hr., 7am, 172 pesos); **Puerto Vallarta** (3hr., 7 and 10am, 100 pesos); **Tepic** (1¾hr., every hr. 6am-7pm, 39 pesos). Transporte Noreste y Nayarit sends its rickety fleet to: **Culiacán** (8hr., 300 pesos); **Mazatlán** (5hr., 177 pesos); **Santiago** (9am, 11am, 1pm; 39 pesos); and other local destinations.

■⁊ ORIENTATION AND PRACTICAL INFORMATION. San Blas is 69km northeast of Tepic by Mex. 15 and 54. **Juárez,** the town's main street, runs parallel to the bus station on the south side of the *zócalo*. **Batallón** runs perpendicular to Juárez from the *zócalo*'s center and leads to the closest beach, **Playa Borrego.**
    The **tourist office** on Mercado, one street west of Juárez, provides maps and information. (Open M-F 9am-5pm.) For a more detailed guide to the area's estuary wildlife, pick up *Where to Find Birds in San Blas Nayarit* at the tourist office. **Banamex,** on Juárez east of the *zócalo*, changes money and has a 24hr. **ATM.** (☎ 285 00 30. Open M-F 8am-3pm.) **Police:** (☎ 285 00 28) on Sinaloa opposite the bus station, through the last door in the Palacio Municipal, as you walk away from the *zócalo*. **Farmacia Económica,** Batallón 49. (☎/fax 285 01 11. Open daily 8:30am-2pm and 4:30-9pm.) **Centro de Salud:** (☎ 285 02 32) on Batallón and Campeche, five blocks south of the *zócalo*, at the turnoff for Hotel Garza Canela. No English spoken. **Clínica IMSS:** at Batallón and Guerrero. (☎ 285 02 27. Open daily 7am-6pm; at other times, enter on Canalizo.) **Phones:** Make long-distance calls from the **caseta,** Juárez 4, which also has **fax** service. (Open daily 8am-10pm.) **Internet: Quinta California Bungalows,** about seven blocks south of the *zócalo*, marked by a sign directing you to their off-road location, offers fax, scanner, and video-conferencing as well. (30 pesos per hr. Open M-Sa 9am-2pm and 4-8:30pm.) **Post office:** at Sonora and Echeverría, one block north and one block east of the northeast corner of the *zócalo*. (☎ 285 02 95. Open M-F 8am-2pm.) **Postal code:** 63740.

▐ ⬦ ACCOMMODATIONS AND FOOD. Run by the same family, **Hotel Morels** and **Hotel Ranchero** are immaculately clean, friendly, and filled with birds and flowers. Hotel Morels, Batallón 108, three blocks south of the plaza, has a courtyard with washing facilities, a communal kitchen, and the company of a large, tame pelican named "Pinocho." (Singles 100 pesos; doubles 150 pesos.) Across the street, **Hotel Ranchero** remains orderly despite the chatty parrots and canaries inhabiting its garden. Communal kitchen also available. (Singles and doubles 120 pesos, with bath 150 pesos.) For beach access, try **Bungalows California,** which adjoin an Internet cafe. (www.sanblasmexico.com. Bungalows 200 pesos in the low season.)
    Perhaps the truest incarnation of the *palapa* mentality can be found at **▐Stoner's Cafe,** the last of the row of *palapas* on the left as you enter Playa Borrego from the street. A mean all-day vegetarian breakfast features their incredible rice recipe (30 pesos). Camp under the *palapa* for 15 pesos per night, or use a house hammock for 20 pesos. Veggie *tostadas* 12 pesos, breaded zucchini and salsa 25 pesos, beer 9 pesos. Costly *mariscos* can be found at the seashell-plastered **La Isla,** on Mercado and Parades. (☎ 285 04 07. Shrimp 70 pesos, fried fish 60 pesos. Open Tu-Su 2-10pm.) In town, try **La Familia,** Battalón 18, a family joint with wall-mounted shark's teeth, old drums, sea bottles, and a provocative cow statue. Try the fried fish (47 pesos) and tacos (28 pesos) while wondering how the framed Mike Tyson boxing glove got here. (☎ 285 02 58. Open daily 8am-10pm.) Sandwiches (8 pesos) and *tortas* (15 pesos) await customers at **Loncheria Paz** on Canalizo, one block up from the plaza. (Open daily 7am-4pm and 6:30-11pm.)

▟ BEACHES. Known for its symmetrical waves and safe, sandy bottom, San Blas has churned out many a surfing champ. The president of San Blas's surfing club, Juan García, gives lessons and rents equipment at **La Tumba de Yako,** Batallón 219, about six blocks from the *zócalo*. (☎ 285 04 62. Lessons 150 pesos per hr., surfboard *(tabla)* rental 150 pesos per day.) San Blas's main attraction is the smooth water, packed sand, and long waves of **Playa Las Islitas.** During the stormy months of September and October, surfers flock to San Blas in hopes of catching the famous, yearly mile-long wave from Las Islitas all the way to **Playa Matanchén.** To reach Las Islitas, take a bus from the station (every hr. 6am-5pm, returning 7:30am-4pm; 8 pesos) or from the corner of Sinaloa and Paredes in front of the green-trimmed building (15min., 4 per day 8:30am-2:30pm, 6 pesos). The latter bus continues to other beaches, passing Las Islitas on its return to town an hour later. A taxi to Las Islitas costs 60 pesos. The first few stretches of sand that greet you are lovely, but more seclusion and prettier coves await farther along. At the southern end of Batallón, **Playa Borrego,** an easily accessible grey sand beach, offers a relaxing view of the coast. Borrego's mosquitos feast on those who dare venture out at sunrise or sunset. Quiet, pretty **Playa del Rey,** off the coast of Borrego, has stronger currents. A *lancha* will take you there from the pier at the west end of Juárez (approx. 7am-4pm, round-trip 20 pesos).

◙ SIGHTS. Locals hype San Blas's jungle estuaries—not its beaches—as the town's best attraction. The easiest way to explore the area's ecological wealth is from a *lancha* to the springs of **La Tovara.** The trip is best made in the morning, when the still waters and matted foliage are filled with birds, turtles, iguanas, and if you look hard, crocodiles. Farther upriver you have the option of swimming or continuing on to the **crocodile farm,** where biologists are attempting (with apparent success) to re-introduce crocodiles to the estuary. Trips can be arranged directly with the boat owners who sit around the small wharf on Juárez's eastern end. (1½-2½hr., daily 7am-4pm, 300-400 pesos, depending on tour.)

For do-it-yourself exploration, stroll to the old 17th-century fort and 18th-century church on top of **La Contaduría** overlooking town. Head east on Juárez as if leaving town, and turn right before the "Cape Victoria 7" sign onto the dirt road behind the restaurants. Veer right off that road onto a stone path that winds uphill. The hill affords a great view of San Blas and the estuaries. Other hikes in the region include trips to waterfalls, coffee plantations, and the "Aztec" island of Mexicalitan. Most require a taxi or car to get to the "trailheads." For information, ask at the tourist office, Bungalows California, or Garza Canela Hotel.

▣ ENTERTAINMENT. Except for bands of youths crowded in the *zócalo* on weekends, nights in San Blas are as tranquil as its days. **Mike's CantaBar** rarely gets wild or crazy as dance music rolls and Mike performs vintage rock in what looks like an antique airport lounge. (☎285 04 32. Beer 5 pesos, mixed drinks 36 pesos. Live music Th-Su starting around 10pm. No cover. Open daily 8pm-midnight.) If you are in the mood for something upbeat and raucous, join the town's teen population at **Disco Voga,** Juárez 75, next to Hotel El Bucanero. (☎285 01 01. Beer 12 pesos. Cover up to 30 pesos. Open F-Su 9pm-2am.)

NEAR SAN BLAS: EL CUSTODIO DE LAS TORTUGAS

Transportes Norte de Sonora leaves from Puerto Vallarta (2hr., noon and 2:30pm, 56 pesos) or San Blas (1½hr., 6 per day 6am-2pm, 20 pesos). Ask the bus driver to let you off at Platanitos, then walk down the road and up the hill on the right. ☎292 29 54.

El Custodio de las Tortugas (The Guardian of the Turtles) is an eco-resort in the tiny village of **Platanitos,** between San Blas and Puerto Vallarta. The villa perches on a precipice, overlooking 20km of virgin beach and the longest stretch of turtle camp in Nayarit. Between July and August, the Mexican government and ecological organizations collect turtle eggs to protect them from thieves and predators. Two elegant three-bedroom villas and one two-bedroom villa have TV, A/C, and huge breezy terraces for whale-watching and sunset-worshipping. The gorgeous pool is a respite from salty water. Rooms at the resort are too expensive for budget travelers, but those who volunteer in the turtle camp receive cheap lodging. Don't miss the town specialty, *pescado sarandeado* (mesquite grilled fish, which usually goes for 80 pesos per kg).

RINCON DE GUAYABITOS ☎3

Named for the "little guavas" that fell in local orchards in days of yore, the only thing falling from trees in Rincon de Guayabitos (pop. 3000) today are 8-year-olds diving into the town's swimming pools. A vacation spot for middle-class Mexican families during July, August, December, and *Semana Santa*, parents kick back in the jungle heat as beaches and pools fill with children. In the off-season, the extremely swimmable beaches are deserted, except for a few Canadian snow-birds. Anyone willing to haggle over prices will find Guayabitos's beautifully ver-dant hillsides and calm waters a worthy stop on the path to *tranquilidad*.

TRANSPORTATION. Buses: Transportes del Pacífico (☎274 00 01) in La Peñita at the end of La Avenida on the *carretera* heads to: **Guadalajara** (4hr., every hr. 6am-noon, 200 pesos); **Mexico City** (6 and 8pm, 530 pesos); **Tepic** (2hr., every 30min., 55 pesos). If going north, take a Transportes Norte Sonora bus from the station on the *carretera*, to **San Blas** (3hr.; 8am, 12:15, and 3pm; 55 pesos).

ORIENTATION AND PRACTICAL INFORMATION. Guayabitos snuggles into the southern Nayarit Coast, 100km north of Puerto Vallarta. The town's main street, **Sol Nuevo**, runs from the entrance of town at the *carretera* south along the curve of the beach. Most goods and services, including the bus stations, are in the neighboring town of **La Peñita**. To get there, take a white *colectivo* from the church (3.5 pesos), or walk north on the beach, crossing over the rock headland and con-tinuing inland into town.

The **tourist office** at the entrance to town from the highway has pamphlets and information on less-accessible beaches. (☎274 06 93. Open M-F 9am-6pm.) **Ban-amex**, in La Peñita on La Avenida just before the *carretera*, has a 24hr. **ATM**. (Open for exchange M-F 9am-5pm.) La Peñita has an open-air **market** every Thursday. **Lavanderia**, on Sol Nuevo before the large Los Cocos resort at the south end of the street. (Open M-Sa 7am-8pm. 10 pesos per kg.) **Clinica Rentevía** (☎274 01 40) is in La Peñita on Acapulco. **Police** in La Peñita on the central plaza. **CMG Farmacia**, on La Avenida in La Peñita at the *carretera*. (☎274 12 77. Open 24hr.) **Post Office** at the entrance to town. (☎274 07 17. Open M-F 9am-2:30pm.) **Telegrams and Fax** are available in the same complex. (☎274 03 54. Open M-F 8am-2pm.) **Internet Nivel Zero** halfway down Sol Nuevo, has Internet access. (☎274 12 54. 30 pesos per hr. Open M-Th 8am-9pm.)

ACCOMMODATIONS AND FOOD. Accommodations in Guayabitos are "bungalows," which sleep four to eight people and include a kitchen. Prices are designed for families, so if you aren't traveling with at least four people, you'll have to drive a hard bargain to save pesos. The best option lies up the beach in **La Peñita**, at **Hotel San Juanito** on Valle Punto de Mita #4 just off La Avenida. Relax with fellow travelers and your friendly hosts in the lobby and kitchen area. (☎327 40 036. 70 pesos per person.) **Bungalows Livio**, Livio 28 (☎274 09 95) has low prices for the area at 190 pesos for 4 people in the low season, 250 pesos during high sea-son. **Bungalows Mexico** Sol Nuevo #44 (☎327 40 390) has sparkling red tile floors and a garden-enveloped mosaic pool for 350 pesos.

Most families that visit Guayanitos cook their own meals in the bungalow kitch-ens. Still, lots of informal eateries post their prices outside, allowing you to win-dow-shop for lunch. **Akel's Restaurant,** a *palapa* structure on Nuevo Sol just before Coco's resort, serves up *enchiladas* (20 pesos) or *carne asada* (35 pesos). La Peñita's Avenida is also lined with eateries.

BEACHES. The waters of Guayabitos's main beach are calm enough for float-ing. When visibility is good, you can rent snorkeling gear from **Los Cocos,** the resort on the beach's south side (30 pesos per day) and see fish. Hiring a glass-bottomed boat from the same area (150-200 pesos per hr.) may be a better option for those wishing to glimpse the aquatic fauna. Boats take you to the inshore volcanic-rock reef around **Isla Islote**.

Guayabitos is surrounded by rich mountain jungle. For a pleasant coastal vista, climb the path to the cross that leads up from Sol Nuevo before Los Cocos. Ask boat owners on the beach for directions to **Playa de los Muertos,** the nearby beachside cemetery, and **Playa de los Ayala,** a distant, less touristed beach.

TEPIC ☎ 3

Untouristed Tepic (pop. 600,000) is a budget traveler's delight, filled with bargain hotels, *loncherias,* and a market overflowing with *mariscos* from the state's coastal jungles. Once called *Tepique* (the Place Between the Hills) by Pre-Hispanic inhabitants, Tepic became a center for trade and commerce under the Spanish in the 16th and 17th centuries. Now home to the Nayarit state government, the city is still a crossroads, and a haven of slow-paced cafes and shady green parks.

⌸ TRANSPORTATION. Buses leave from the newer station east of the *centro.* To reach the *centro,* cross the street and catch a yellow bus (6am-10pm, 3 pesos), or a taxi (15 pesos). To return, take a "Central" or "Mololoa Llanitos" bus from the corner of México Sur and Hidalgo. Transportes del Pacífico (☎213 23 20) travels to: **Culiacán** (6hr., every hr., 170 pesos); **Guadalajara** (3hr., 10 per day, 88 pesos); **Mexico City** (10hr., every hr. 3pm-7am, 424 pesos); **Puerto Vallarta** (3½hr., 4 and 5pm, 104 pesos); **San Blas** (2hr., every hr. 6am-7pm, 39 pesos).

▟�🗾 ORIENTATION AND PRACTICAL INFORMATION. Situated 170km north of Puerto Vallarta and 280km south of Mazatlán, Tepic links Guadalajara (230km to the southeast) with the Nayarit beaches. The main drag, **Mexico,** runs north-south six blocks west of the bus station. Addresses on this street change from Nte. to Sur about four blocks north of **Insurgentes,** the largest east-west street. Yellow minivan *combis* run back and forth daily along México and Insurgentes (6am-midnight, 3 pesos). At its northern terminus, **Plaza Principal** (officially called the *centro histórico*) is dominated by the cathedral on one end and the Palacio Municipal on the other. Most tourist services lie on or near México.

Dirección de Turismo Municipal, Puebla at the corner of Nervo, one block from the cathedral, hands out maps and brochures. (☎216 56 61. Open M-F 9am-3pm and 6-8pm.) **Casas de cambio** (most open M-Sa 9am-2pm and 4-7pm) clutter Mexico Nte. **Bancomer,** Mexico Nte. 123 (open M-F 8:30am-5:30pm, Sa 10am-2pm), and **Bancapromex,** Mexico Nte. 103 (open M-F 8:30am-5:30pm), a few blocks south of the plaza, have **ATMs. Luggage storage,** in the new bus station (1.5 pesos per hr.). **Police station:** Tecnológica Ote. 3200 (☎211 58 51), accessible by cab only (10 pesos). Little English spoken. **Farmacia CMQ,** Insurgentes at Mexico. (Open 24hr.) **Hospital General** (☎213 79 37), on Paseo de la Loma next to La Loma Park. **Fax: Telecomm,** Mexico Nte. 50, about one block from the cathedral. (☎212 96 55. Open M-F 8am-7pm, Sa-Su 8am-4pm.) Surf the **Internet** at **Cafeteria La Parroquia,** Nervo 18. (15 pesos per hr.) **Post office,** Durango Nte. 33, between Allende and Morelos. (☎212 01 30. Open M-F 8am-7pm, Sa 8am-noon.) **Postal code:** 63000.

▟🛏 ACCOMMODATIONS AND FOOD. ▧**Hotel Morelia,** Morelia 215, has a lush courtyard and private baths for all. (☎216 60 85. Singles 60 pesos; doubles 70 pesos; each additional person 10 pesos.) Next door, **Hotel Pasadena California,** Morelia 215, is "Morelia's" slightly cheaper twin with clean, basic rooms. (☎212 91 40. Singles and doubles 40 pesos, with private baths 50 pesos.) Family-run **Hotel las Americas,** Puebla 317 at Zaragoza, has spotless rooms with TV, fans, and baths. (☎216 32 85. Singles 80 pesos; doubles 100 pesos.)

Tepic's tons of fruits, fish, and coffee flow through the capital (and into most restaurants). **Cafe La Parroquia,** upstairs at Nervo 18, across from Plaza Principal, serves delicious sandwiches (8 pesos), *tostadas* (8 pesos), and *quesadillas* (16 pesos; open M-F 8am-9:30pm). **Restaurant Vegetariano Quetzalcóatl,** on León Nte. at Lerdo, four blocks west of Plaza Principal, hosts a popular buffet (45 pesos, Tu-Sa 1pm) in its leafy courtyard. (☎212 99 66. Open M-Sa 8:30am-5:30pm.) **Girasol Loma,**

Paseo de la Loma 201 near the plaza, serves fast vegetarian fare to office worker-types. (☎214 39 59. Fruit, yogurt and granola creations 18-25 pesos, guacamole *tostadas* 22 pesos. Open daily 8am-9pm.) To sit with the *campesinos* and shovel cheap, authentic eats, go to **Restaurant Tirayan,** Zaragoza 20, half a block down from the intersection with Veracruz. (Egg breakfasts 18 pesos, fish filets 31 pesos, *tostadas* 10 pesos. Open daily 8am-9pm.)

◨ ♫ SIGHTS AND ENTERTAINMENT. Lounging amounts to a major civic pastime in Tepic. When not playing checkers at **Cafe la Parroquia,** play dominos at **Cafetales de Cordoba,** Lerdo 197. (Open daily 8:30am-9pm.) Across the street is **Museo Emelia Ortiz,** named for the Tepic native and dedicated to promoting local contemporary art. (Open M-F 9am-7pm, free.) The **Museo Regional de Antropologia e Historia,** México Nte. 91 south of the plaza at Zapata, offers an extensive exhibit on Juichol embroidery, accompanied by sparse explanations of the group's other crafts, including their dreamlike, peyote-inspired yarn paintings. (☎215 19 00. Open M-F 9am-7pm, Sa 9am-3pm. 30 pesos.) The **Museo de los Cuatro Pueblos** Hidalgo Ote. 60, also showcases local indigenous groups, with the work of Juichols, Náhuatls, Coras, and Tepehuanos on display. (☎212 17 05. Open M-F 9am-2pm and 4-7pm.) The **state capital** lies at México and Abasolo, a gracefully domed structure dating from the 1870s. At México's southern end, turn west (uphill) on Insurgentes to get to **La Loma,** a large park with several playgrounds.

Tepic's nightlife is pretty tame. Head to **Pat Pac's Restaurant/Bar,** upstairs at Morelos 7, for expensive food (hamburgers 28 pesos) and drinks served in a chill, dimly lit setting. (☎216 70 43 Open daily 7am-1am.) On weekends, a **disco** opens in the downstairs corner of the same building.

JALISCO

GUADALAJARA   ☎ 3

More Mexican than Mexico itself, Guadalajara (pop. 8 million) is the crossroads of the republic. Here, in the capital of Jalisco state and the second-largest city in the country, north meets south, colonial meets modern, and traditional meets cutting-edge. The city has spawned many of Mexico's most marketable icons: bittersweet *mariachi* music, *jarabe tapatío* (Mexican hat dance), and tequila. Founded in 1532 by Nuño de Guzmán, the most brutal of the *conquistadores*, Guadalajara was born in bloodbath; most of the region's *indígenas* were slaughtered, and few Pre-Hispanic traditions survived. In the years following, the city served as the capital of Mexico and a key battle ground in the Revolution. Today, Guadalajara entices natives and tourists with parks galore, a bounty of fine museums, four large plazas, and stately colonial architecture. Its markets overflow with local *artesanía*, and painters, thespians, dancers (including the renowned *Ballet Folklórico*), and street performers continue the city's fine artistic traditions. Meanwhile, the Universidad de Guadalajara, the second oldest in Mexico, keeps Guadalajara young and shades it with a measure of intellectual sophistication. Though not built specifically for tourists, Guadalajara nevertheless fulfills their hopes entirely. One can understand why—the city's *tapatío* (as the city's residents call themselves) heritage epitomizes all that was, is, and will be Mexican.

▐ TRANSPORTATION

GETTING AROUND

Local Buses: Though usually crowded, always noisy, and sometimes uncomfortable, **minibuses** and **regular buses** (3 pesos) and big blue **TUR** buses (6 pesos) are an excellent way to get around. Be sure to check the line (A, B, C, or D) of your bus. Generally,

A and B run almost the same route along the main thoroughfares (with the same numbers), and C and D buses have different routes into the residential neighborhoods. Always check with the driver to confirm the bus's destination. Buses **#60** and **#62** run the length of Calzada Independencia, from the train station past the zoo and Plaza de Toros. The wired **"Par Vial"** bus runs west on Calzada Independencia, then Hidalgo, before turning onto Vallarta, just short of Mateos. Returning eastward, it cruises Hidalgo 3 blocks north of Juárez. Bus **#258** from San Felipe, 3 blocks north of Hidalgo, runs from near Plaza Tapatía down Mateos to Plaza del Sol, nightclub central. Bus **#52** and **#54** are direct links to downtown along 16 de Septiembre from locations north and south of the city. Bus **#24A** runs the length of Mateos, from Zapopan to beyond Plaza del Sol, in both directions. TUR bus **#707A** circles from the *centro* on Juárez west to Mateos, down to Otero at Plaza del Sol, and north on 16 de Septiembre and Corona to the start of the route. The big red **Cardenal** bus runs west on Madero to Chapultepec along the Zona Rosa, the upscale shopping district west of the *centro*. Bus **#45** returns east on Cotilla. Bus **#51** motors up and down La Paz. Buses run 6:30am-10pm; TUR buses run slightly later.

Subway: (☎853 75 70). The 2 subway lines run smoothly (every 5-10min. 6am-10:30pm, 3 pesos) and offer a great alternative to the bus system for anyone tired of breathing exhaust. A very good map is posted in the stations. **Line 1** runs from the northern boundary of the city, Periférico Nte., more or less along Federalismo to Periférico Sur, with a central stop at Federalismo and Juárez. **Line 2** runs from Juárez and Alcalde/16 de Septiembre, conveniently passing Mina, to Patria in the east. Limited coverage makes the subway more practical than buses for only a few destinations.

GETTING AWAY

Airport: Aeropuerto Internacional Miguel Hidalgo (☎688 53 83 or 688 50 11), 17km south of town on the road to Chapala. *Combis* (☎812 42 78 or 812 43 08) run 24hr. and will pick you up from your hotel (40min., 80 pesos). A yellow and white "Aeropuerto" bus passes through the *centro* on Independencia at Los Angeles (every hr. 5:45am-8:45pm, 10 pesos) and makes the trip back from outside "Sala Nacional." Get off at 16 de Septiembre and Constituyentes. Some cabs are metered, and some are not; when making a trip to the airport, negotiate a price around 80 pesos. This can be done even if the cab has a meter (on the meter, a trip to the airport runs 120 pesos). Served by **AeroCalifornia** (☎616 25 25); **AeroMéxico** (☎669 02 09), office on Corona at Madero (open M-Sa 9am-6pm); **American** (☎01 800 834 03 00); **Continental** (☎01 800 900 50 00); **Delta** (☎688 5243 or 01 800 902 21 00); **Mexicana** (☎678 76 76 or 01 800 366 54 00); **Taesa** (☎688 50 90); **United** (☎616 94 89).

Buses: The station, **Nueva Central Camionera**, is in nearby Tlaquepaque. The gargantuan station consists of a failed shopping mall and 7 terminals. Fixed-fare buses and taxis (30-60 pesos, depending on time of day) head downtown frequently, as do "Centro" buses (3 pesos). From downtown, catch a #275, #275A, or "Nueva Central" bus on Revolución or 16 de Septiembre, across from the cathedral. In a taxi, be sure to specify the *new* bus station. Only partial listings provided; call for more info. **Terminal 1:** expensive *ejecutivo* carriers like Primera Plus and Flecha Amarilla (☎600 07 70) go to all major destinations. **Terminal 2:** overflow from Ómnibus de Mexico (Terminal 6) and local carriers. **Terminal 3:** more posh carriers, like Futura (☎679 04 04) and Elite (☎679 04 85, reservations 679 04 04). **Terminal 4:** Transportes del Pacífico (☎600 09 79 or 600 08 54), sends 1st- and 2nd-class buses to lots of coastal destinations. Also home to Transportes Norte de Sonora (☎679 04 63), which offers cheap 2nd class service to distant northern destinations like **Guaymas** (19hr., 760 pesos). **Terminal 5:** Línea Azul (☎679 04 04) goes to many destinations in northeast Mexico. **Terminal 6:** Ómnibus de México (☎600 02 91 or 600 04 69) provides comprehensive service including: **Aguascalientes** (every hr. 6:30am-midnight, 199 pesos); **Ciudad Juárez** (24hr., 10 per day, 886 pesos) via **Chihuahua** (677 pesos); **Durango** (6 per day, 376 pesos); **La Piedad** (3 per day, 94 pesos); **Matamoros** (7 per day, 595 pesos); **Mexico City** (7hr., every 2hr. 7am-midnight, 340 pesos); **Monterrey** (9 per day, 447 pesos); **Querétaro** (5hr., 3 per day, 214 pesos); **Reynosa** (13hr., 7 per day, 580 pesos); **Tampico** (12hr., 5 per day, 381 pesos); **Tepic**

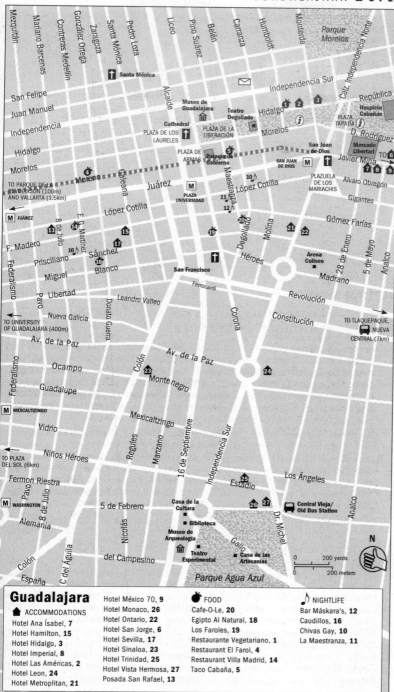

Guadalajara

ACCOMMODATIONS

Hotel Ana Ísabel, **7**
Hotel Hamilton, **15**
Hotel Hidalgo, **3**
Hotel Imperial, **8**
Hotel Las Américas, **2**
Hotel Leon, **24**
Hotel Metropolitan, **21**

Hotel México 70, **9**
Hotel Monaco, **26**
Hotel Ontario, **22**
Hotel San Jorge, **6**
Hotel Sevilla, **17**
Hotel Sinaloa, **23**
Hotel Trinidad, **25**
Hotel Vista Hermosa, **27**
Posada San Rafael, **13**

FOOD

Cafe-O-Le, **20**
Egipto Al Natural, **18**
Los Faroles, **19**
Restaurante Vegetariano, **1**
Restaurant El Farol, **4**
Restaurant Villa Madrid, **14**
Taco Cabaña, **5**

NIGHTLIFE

Bar Máskara's, **12**
Caudillos, **16**
Chivas Gay, **10**
La Maestranza, **11**

(3hr., every 30min., 210 pesos); **Torreón** (9-10hr., 8 per day, 428 pesos); **Tuxpan** (6 per day, 86 pesos); **Zacatecas** (every hr. 5:30am-12:15am, 207 pesos). **Terminal 7:** Estrella Blanca (☎679 04 04) is the parent company of numerous smaller lines, including Rojo de los Altos and Transportes del Norte. This is the biggest terminal and will take you to almost every major city in the republic for competitive prices. Many nearby destinations (up to 2-3hr. away) are serviced by the more convenient **Central Vieja** (Old Bus Station), at Dr. Michel across from Parque Agua Azul.

✦ 🛈 ORIENTATION AND PRACTICAL INFORMATION

The heart of the city is the *centro histórico* around **Plaza Tapatía** and **Plaza de la Liberación**. The two major streets **Calzada Independencia Norte/Calzada Independencia Sur** and **Hidalgo/República** (known as República east of Calzada Independencia, and Hidalgo in the west), divide Guadalajara into quadrants. Streets change names at the borders of these quadrants. Note that in addition to Calzada Independencia, Guadalajara has a Calle Independencia, crossing the city east-west just north of the *centro*. The cities of **Tlaquepaque, Zapopan,** and **Tonalá** are all seamlessly joined to the Guadalajara metropolitan area. When taking a bus to the *centro*, make sure you're going to the correct *centro*. The poorer *colonias* (suburbs) of Guadalajara can be dangerous any time of day; check with the tourist office before blazing new trails. Throughout Guadalajara, travelers should keep to lighted streets and take taxis after 10pm. Solo women travelers may wish to avoid Calzada Independencia after hours, as the street attracts raucous, drunken men and supports a thriving prostitution trade at all hours of the day and night. Neighborhoods tend to be significantly worse to the east of Calzada Independencia.

TOURIST AND FINANCIAL SERVICES

Tourist Office: State Office, Morelos 102 (☎668 16 00, toll-free in Mexico 01 800 363 22 00; vista.jalisco.gob.mx or www.jaliscotour.com), in Plaza Tapatía. Friendly staff with helpful maps. Pick up *Guadalajara Weekly* (a free, English-language tourist paper) or *Mexico Living and Travel Update.* Open M-F 9am-7:30pm, Sa-Su 9am-1pm. Another office in the Palacio de Gobierno. Open daily 9:30am-3pm. Guadalajara, Tlaquepaque, and Zapopan each maintain separate offices. Look for Guadalajara's tourist information booths on Plaza Tapatia just before Hospicio Cabañas.

Consulates: Australia, Cotilla 2030 (☎615 74 18; fax 818 33 90), between Vega and Bara. Open M-F 8am-1:30pm and 3-6pm. **Canada,** Local 30 (☎615 62 70; emergency 01 800 706 29 00; fax 615 86 65), at Hotel Fiesta Americana, on the Minerva traffic circle. Catch a "Par Vial" bus. Open M-F 8:30am-5pm. **UK,** Parra 2539 (☎616 06 29; fax 615 01 97). Open M-F 9am-2pm and 5-8pm. **US,** Progreso 175 (☎825 27 00 and 825 29 98; fax 826 65 49). Open M-F 8am-4:30pm. The **Oficina de la Asociación Consular,** at the UK consulate, can provide listings for other consulates.

Currency Exchange: The block of Cotilla between Corona and Molina is a *mercado* with only one product: money. Rates don't vary much. For banking services, head to **Bancapromex,** on Corona at Juárez. Open M-F 8:30am-5:30pm, Sa 10am-2pm.

LOCAL SERVICES

English Bookstores: Sandi Bookstore, Tepeyac 718 (☎121 08 63), near the corner of Rosas in Colonia Chapalita. Take bus #50 from Garibaldi or the green "Plus" bus from Juárez. New books and newspapers. Open M-F 9:30am-2:30pm and 3:30-7pm, Sa 9:30am-2pm. The **Hyatt,** at Mateos and México, has issues of the *New York Times*.

Cultural Information: Dirección de Educación y Cultura (☎668 16 44), 5 de Febrero and Analco. **Instituto Cultural Cabañas,** Cabañas 8 (☎617 43 22), in Plaza Tapatía. Open M-F 9am-3pm and 6-9pm. Blue and yellow "Ayuntamiento" stands in the major plazas field cultural and tourist queries. Open daily 8am-8pm. Also check out *Pasiones y Sazones,* the Friday supplement of Guadalajara's *Público* for special events.

Market: Mercado Libertad, Calle Independencia, next to the plaza. This enormous market dedicates an entire wing to family-run restaurants. Open daily 8am-8pm.

Supermarket: Gigante, Juárez 573 (☎613 86 38), between Martínez and 8 de Julio. Sells just about everything. Open daily 8am-11pm.

Laundry: Lavanderia Aldama, Aldama 125 (☎617 64 27), 2½ blocks off Independencia on the left. (Open M-Sa 9am-6:30pm.) Full service up to 7 kg, (35 pesos). Self service wash (3 pesos), and dry (12 pesos).

Car Rental: Euro Rent-A-Car, Patria 236 (☎673 54 08). Open M-Sa 10am-9pm. **Auto-Rent,** Federalismo Sur 480 (☎825 15 15), at La Paz. Open M-F 9:30am-8pm, Sa 10:30am-6pm. **Vega's Rent-A-Car,** González 175 (☎613 19 20). Open M-Sa 9am-9pm.

EMERGENCY AND COMMUNICATIONS

Emergency: ☎060 or 080.

Police: Calzada Independencia Nte. 840 (☎617 60 60, ext. 126 or 143), just before the Olympic fountain. For help in English, call 688 08 00.

Red Cross: (☎613 15 50 or 614 27 07, emergency 085), at Manuel and San Felipe behind Parque Morelos. Some English spoken.

Pharmacy: Farmacia Guadalajara, Mina 221 (☎617 85 55), at Cabañas. Open 24hr.

Hospitals: México Americano (☎641 31 41), at Colones and América. English spoken. **Green Cross Hospital** (☎614 52 52), at Barcenas and Veracruz. English spoken.

Fax: Palacio Federal (☎614 26 64; fax 613 99 15), at Alcalde and Álvarez. Open M-F 8am-6pm, Sa 9am-noon.

Internet Access: Cafe Internet, 8 de Julio 73 (☎614 57 36), brews yummy coffee and serves palatable food. Open daily 7am-11pm. Internet access providers are located around the intersection of Juárez and Calzada Independencia.

Post Office: (☎614 74 25), on Carranza between Manuel and Calle Independencia. Open M-F 8am-6:30pm, Sa 9am-1pm.

Postal Code: 44100.

ACCOMMODATIONS

Guadalajara is full of cheap places to stay, with budget hotels most common in the *centro histórico*, and east of downtown along Mina. Unfortunately, most bargain accommodations are plagued by typical big city problems—24hr. traffic, poor room quality, and prostitution. The best values can be found around the old bus station. A 10-15min. walk from Plaza Tapatia, this area's advantages include proximity to Agua Azul and easy access to buses going to Guadalajara's appealing *alrededores*, Tlaquepaque, Tonalá, Lake Chapala, and Tequila. Regardless of where you stay, call ahead; many places fill up early in the day.

AROUND THE BUS STATION

Hotel Sinaloa, Colón 547 (☎614 55 22), halfway between the *viejo central* and Plaza Universidad, is much cleaner and friendlier than its namesake, and amazingly free of *narcotraficantes*. Clean, recently renovated rooms arranged around a courtyard. Singles and doubles 80 pesos, with TV 100 pesos; triples 190 pesos. Parking available.

Hotel Vista Hermosa, Dr. R. Michel 270 (☎586 72 58), across from the old bus station. A still-life paradise, the front lobby exhibits a show-worthy junk collection. Tidy and clean rooms have private baths and hot water. Singles 70 pesos; doubles 80 pesos.

Hotel Monaco, 5 de Febrero 152 (☎619 00 18). Slightly pricier, but also slightly nicer, Hotel Monaco offers a vacation from the civic grime. Singles 110 pesos; doubles 120 pesos; triples 130 pesos.

Hotel Trinidad, Estadio 21 (☎619 13 00). Standard budget hotel, halfway down Estadio from the *viejo central*. Less likely to be booked than hotels near the plaza. Singles and doubles 65 pesos, with TV 85 pesos.

ALONG CALZADA INDEPENDENCIA SUR

Hotels in this area are cheap and safe, but can be extremely noisy at night due to the numerous neighboring 24hr. diners and cantinas.

Hotel Metropolitan, Calz. Independencia Sur 278 (☎613 24 58). A paradise of bland sterility. Rooms with comfortable beds and neatly-tiled bathrooms open to a pleasant, sky-lit courtyard lobby. Beware of windows facing the street as it is a major bus route. Singles 110 pesos; doubles 130-180 pesos.

Hotel Ontario, Calz. Independencia Sur 137 (☎617 80 99). Across from Hotel Metropolitan, Ontario pleases the traveler who wants to embrace chaos; not escape it. Call a week in advance. Singles 80 pesos; doubles 110 pesos.

Hotel Leon, Calz. Independencia Sur 557 (☎619 61 41), at Dr. Michel. Not too terrible rooms are a fine option if all the other budget hotels are booked. Private baths with hot water. Singles 80 pesos; doubles 90 pesos.

WEST OF CONSTITUCIÓN

Prices in this conveniently located area have risen, while the quality of accommodations has not. The multitudes of surrounding bookstores and vegetarian eateries may justify the extra pesos.

Posada San Rafael, Cotilla 619 (☎614 91 46). Newly renovated with an eye to the building's 19th-century charms, this former monastery is a cut above standard Guadalajara fare. Big stone walls keep the city at bay. Singles 160 pesos; doubles 230 pesos.

Hotel Hamilton, Madero 381 (☎614 67 26). Cheap, decent rooms in a good area. The only real problem is getting one. Though Hamilton supposedly takes reservations, showing up at 2 or 3pm with money in hand is a much better guarantee. Singles and doubles with 1 bed 70 pesos, with 2 beds 90 pesos, with 2 beds and TV 110 pesos.

Hotel Sevilla, Sánchez 413 (☎614 91 72 or 614 93 54), between Ocampo and Guerra. Old but clean. Rooms have TVs, phones, fans, and baths, and are graced by landscape photos. Singles 140 pesos; doubles 150 pesos.

AROUND PLAZA TAPATIA

Hotel defects become more exaggerated the closer you get to Guadalajara's ground zero. Swarms of market vendors in need of beds drive up prices and allow hotels to charge more than their rooms are worth. Truly cheap hotels tend to be centers of prostitution, while those southeast of Mina should be avoided.

Hotel Las Américas, Hidalgo 76 (☎613 96 22 or 614 16 41), at Humboldt, gets high marks for cleanliness and the amiable staff. Carpeted rooms with TVs, phones, fans, and purified water. Singles 150 pesos; doubles 170 pesos; triples 200 pesos.

Hotel Hidalgo, Hidalgo 14 (☎613 50 67). At 2pm, eager would be guests line up to get a piece of this hotel's nationally-famous square footage. No reservations. Bare-bones cubicles go far for 35 pesos. Doubles with bath 70 pesos.

Hotel Imperial, Mina 180 (☎586 57 19). Good upkeep and the protected lobby/courtyard arrangement make the Imperial worthwhile. "Family environment" means no prostitution. Coffee 5 pesos. Singles 160 pesos; doubles 190 pesos.

Hotel Ana Ísabel, Mina 164 (☎617 79 20 or 617 48 59), at Cabañas. Small, somewhat dark rooms with ceiling fans and TVs overlook a green courtyard. If you tire of *birria*, make use of the quasi-kitchen area. Singles 135 pesos; doubles 170 pesos.

Hotel México 70, Mina 230 (☎617 99 78), at Cabañas. México 70 is as antiseptic and uninspired as its name. Singles 130 pesos; doubles 150 pesos; triples 180 pesos; TV 20 pesos extra.

Hotel San Jorge, Mina 284 (☎617 79 97). Dark hallways lead to simple rooms with baths and desks for writing, though there is little to write home about. Singles 120 pesos; doubles 140 pesos.

ZONA ROSA

Hotels in Guadalajara's ritziest neigborhood are predictably pricey. If you have pesos to burn, classy lodgings are everywhere. One fairly economical option is **Hotel La Paz**, La Paz 1091, between Guerra and 8 de Julio, accessible via bus #51 or #321. Smart blue rooms have lovely faux marble countertops and phones. (☎613 30 07. Singles 120 pesos; doubles 160 pesos; triples 185 pesos.)

🞖 FOOD

Guadalajara has plenty of budget eateries as well as many expensive, upscale restaurants serving international cuisine. *Birria* is the hearty local specialty of stewed meat (usually pork) in tomato broth, thickened with cornmeal and spiced with garlic, onions, and chiles. *Tortas anogadas*, another local specialty, differ from the standard *torta* in their pork filling and special sauce slathered on top, soaking slightly stale bread. After your meal, quench your thirst with an Estrella beer, brewed *clara dorada* (golden clear) right in Guadalajara.

THE CENTRO

Ice cream and fast food make the scene everywhere, while *panaderías* (bakeries) crowd southwest of the plaza, primarily on the blocks enclosed by Pavo, Sánchez, Galeana, and Juárez. A feast for both tastebuds and eyes is the **Mercado Libertad**, on Calle Independencia, next to the plaza. You can find anything here, from *birria* to fried chicken to live animals, all at prices that will leave you with plenty of pesos for shopping (huge meals average 26 pesos).

- 🞖 **Restaurant Villa Madrid,** Cotilla 553 (☎613 42 50). One wall consists of a heaping pile of fruit that employees convert into delicious smoothies, huge *licuados* (24 pesos), and fruit bowls (18-32 pesos). Lunch special, a choice of sandwich with every vegetable imaginable (24 pesos). Open M-F 12:30-9pm, Sa 12:30-8pm.

- **Egipto Al Natural,** Sanchez 416 (☎613 62 77). Formerly Restaurant Acuarius, the new owner assures loyal customers that nothing has changed, and 24 years of past budget vegetarian cuisine will continue into the glorious future. He appears to be telling the truth. Vegetarian *comida corrida* 40 pesos, juice 9 pesos. Open M-Sa 10am-6pm.

- **Restaurante Vegetariano,** Hidalgo 112 (☎614 54 47), to the left of the black painted window. A wide array of vegetarian foods, including salads (13-15 pesos). Sandwiches (7-10 pesos), *quesadillas* (6-8 pesos). Open M-Sa 9am-7pm, Su 9am-5pm.

- **El Farol,** Moreno 466, 2nd fl. (☎613 63 49), at Galeana. *Comida típica* at rock bottom prices. The friendly owner makes a mean *chile relleno*. Complimentary *buñuelos*, a fried dough dessert doused with syrup. Entrees 20-40 pesos, tacos 5 pesos, beer 12-16 pesos. Open daily 10am-8pm.

- **Los Faroles,** Corona 250 (☎613 47 23), at Sanchez. Though not the cheapest in town, Los Faroles tempts hordes of locals and visitors alike to return for more. Tacos made from various cow parts 4-5 pesos. Excellent *quesadillas* with homemade tortillas 10 pesos. The famous *torta ahogada* is a 15-peso meal. Open daily 7am-midnight.

- **Taco Cabaña,** at Moreno and Maestranza near the Palacio de Gobierno. Celebrate cheap beer (2 for 17 pesos) and tacos (3 pesos) with the *mariachi*-filled jukebox and panel of TVs tuned to *fútbol*. After the game, down one of the many varieties of tequila (13-22 pesos). Open daily 10am-9pm.

- **Cafe-O-Le,** on the corner of Sanchez and Maestranza, a block down and over from San Francisco, sells great coffee—a mix of beans from Veracruz and Chiapas roasted in-house. Cafe americano 10 pesos, cappucino 14 pesos. Open M-Sa 8:30am-9:30pm.

ZONA ROSA

Most of the places listed below are near the intersection of Vallarta and Chapultepec, on the "Par Vial" and bus #321, where extra pesos buy excellent food and a measure of elegance. Past Chapultepec, Vallarta supports both a 24hr. Sanborns and a 24hr. VIPs for those seeking late-night refuge from their budget hotels.

■ **Restaurant Samurai,** Vidrio 1929 (☎826 35 54), a ¼-block north and to the right of the Niños Héroes monument on Chapultepec. Authentic Japanese-Mexican cuisine served among a fish pond, rock garden, and hummingbirds. Many vegetarian options. Japanese *comida corrida* with rice, soup, and main course 26 pesos. Samurai *especial* of teriyaki steak, fish, and shrimp 68 pesos. Open M-Sa noon-10pm, Su 12:30-8pm.

Naló Cafe, Sierra 2046 (☎615 27 15), just off Chapultepec Nte. Outdoor seating under a big umbrella. Delicious breakfast and lunch specials 25-35 pesos. Menu changes daily, but friendly servers and relaxing atmosphere don't. *Fettucine alfredo* 35 pesos, salads 17 pesos, carrot cake 15 pesos. Open daily 8am-9pm.

Cafe Don Luis, Chapultepec 215 (☎625 65 99), at La Paz. When the elite aren't jetting around the world, they're relaxing in this friendly cafe. The patio area is a preserve of social butterflies sampling a huge coffee selection. Cafe americano 10 pesos, cappucino 15 pesos. Open M-Sa 8:30am-midnight, Su 9pm-midnight.

👁 SIGHTS

More a town of promenades and monuments museums, Guadalajara has perfected the concept of "the plaza." The city's many shopping malls spill over into wide public spaces, which are packed with *mariachis*, tourists, vendors, and street performers. That said, many of the city's finer sights can be found in its less chaotic *alrededores*—Zapopan's cathedral, Tonalá's market, Tequila's blue agave, and the picturesque towns around Lake Chapala.

THE CENTRO

PLAZA DE LA LIBERACIÓN. Abuzz with activity, the plaza is the center of historic Guadalajara. Horse-drawn carriages line up near the Museo Regional, waiting to whisk you around the city (45min., 120 pesos). The spacious plaza, with its bubbling fountain and large Mexican flag, is surrounded by the cathedral, Museo Regional, Palacio de Gobierno, and Teatro Degollado. Military personnel ceremonially retire the colors daily at 7pm. An enormous sculpture depicts Hidalgo breaking the chains of servitude, in commemoration of his 1810 decree abolishing the slave trade, which was signed in the Palacio de Gobierno.

PALACIO DE GOBIERNO. The palace, built in 1751, served as the headquarters of the Hildago government from 1810-11 and as the base for the Juárez administration in 1858. Today, the Palacio is graced by several José Clemente Orozco murals. Climb to the roof for a great view. *(Open M-F 9am-8pm. Guided tours available in English.)*

CATEDRAL METROPOLITANA. Facing Teatro Degollado across Plaza de la Liberación, the church was begun in 1561 and completed 60 years later. After an 1848 earthquake destroyed its original towers, ambitious architects replaced them with much taller ones. Fernando VII of Spain donated the cathedral's 11 richly ornamented altars in appreciation of Guadalajara's aid during the Napoleonic Wars. One is dedicated to Our Lady of the Roses and gave Guadalajara its nickname, "City of Roses." Inside the sacristy is the *Assumption of the Virgin*, by 17th-century painter Bartolomé Murillo. The towers, known as the *cornucopías*, can be climbed with the permission of the cathedral's administrators, who are holed up in the side of the building facing Teatro Degollado. Descend underneath the altar (take the steps on the right-hand side) where the remains of three cardinals and two bishops keep good company. The 60m jaunt to the tower tops affords the best view in town. *(Open daily 7:30am-7:30pm.)*

HOSPICIO CABAÑAS. Also known as the Casa de Cultura Cabañas, the Hospicio was constructed in 1801 to house an orphanage. The huge building served as an art school and a military barracks before its present use as an exhibition/performance/office space. The building's chapel, built in the 1840s, is decorated with murals by Orozco. The striking *El Hombre de Fuego* (the Man of Fire)—a dramatic reversal of heaven and hell that tops off Orozco's disturbing portrait of Mexican history—peers down from the dome. *(Hospicio and Cabañas, 3 blocks east of Independencia. Open Tu-Sa 10am-6pm, Su 10am-3pm. 8 pesos, students 4 pesos, children under 12 free; Su free. 10 pesos for camera rights—no flash.)*

MUSEO REGIONAL DE GUADALAJARA. This popular museum, housed in the old San José seminary, chronicles the history of western Mexico starting with the Big Bang. Collections of colonial and modern art are displayed as well. Artsy and educational movie screenings, plays, and lectures take place in the museum's auditorium—inquire within or at the tourist office. *(Liceo 60 at Hidalgo, on the north side of Plaza de la Liberación. ☎ 614 99 57. Open Tu-Sa 9am-5:45pm, Su 9am-4:30pm. 30 pesos, seniors and children under 12 free; Su free.)*

TEATRO DEGOLLADO. Attend the *ballet folklórico* for a good look at breathtaking Teatro Degollado, named for former governor Santos Degollado. Built in 1856, the Neoclassical structure has gold arches, a sculpted allegory of the seven muses, and Gerardo Suárez's interpretation of Dante's *Paradiso* on the ceiling. In addition to ballet, the theater plays host to the Guadalajara Philharmonic and amateur acts. *(On the east end of Plaza de la Liberación. ☎ 614 47 73. Ballet Folklórico performed by the University of Guadalajara Su 10am. Open M-F noon-3pm for non-ticket holders. Tickets available at the theater box office. Open daily 10am-1pm and 4-7pm. Tickets start at 25 pesos.)*

PLAZUELA DE LOS MARIACHIS. Immediately after you sit down in this crowded plaza, roving *mariachis* will pounce, using every trick in their bag to separate you from your pesos. Prices for songs vary from 20-35 pesos. *Mariachis* play deep into the night, but beware: later on the Plazuela becomes a stage for roving unsavories, who may employ other methods to acquire your pesos. *(On the south side of San Juan de Dios, the church with the blue neon cross on Independencia at Mina.)*

PARQUE AGUA AZUL. If tired of the congested city streets, take a stroll in this 168,000 sq. m park, with tropical aviaries, an orchid greenhouse, a butterfly house, and a sports complex. *(South of the centro on Calzada Independencia; take bus #60 or 62 heading south. Open Tu-Su 10am-8:30pm. 6 pesos, children 4 pesos.)*

ZONA ROSA

Cultural activity in the city's wealthier area focuses on **Plaza del Arte,** on Chapultepec, one block south of Niños Héroes.

GALERÍA DE ARTE MODERNO. National artists bare their souls on a rotating basis in the plaza's gallery. Displays vary in quality, but worth a stop if you're in the area. *(On Mariano Ote. at España. ☎ 616 32 66. Open Tu-F 10am-7pm, Sa-Su 10am-2pm. Free.)*

TEATRO JAIME TORRES BODET. The theater hosts everything: book expositions, concerts, theatrical productions, stand-up comedy, and performance art. *(In Plaza del Arte. ☎ 615 12 69. Open M-F 9am-8pm, depending on performance times.)*

NORTH OF THE CENTRO

To reach the following sights, take Ruta #60 or 62 north on Calz. Independencia.

ZOOLÓGICO GUADALAJARA. You wouldn't know it by hanging around Plaza Tapatiá, but Guadalajara is surrounded by ecological wealth. The zoo boasts an extensive collection of species from around the world, including 320 species of tropical birds. At the far end of the zoo is a spectacular view of the deep Barranca de Huentitan ravine. *(Continue north on Calzada Independencia past Plaza de Toros, and walk 1½km to the entrance of the zoo from the bus stop on Independencia. ☎ 674 44 88 or 674 43 60. Open W-Su 10am-7pm. 25 pesos, children 15 pesos.)*

CENTRO DE CIENCIA Y TECNOLOGÍA. The center houses a planetarium, exhibits on astronomy and geology, and a sculpted plant garden. *(A 20min. walk from the zoo. Open Tu-Su 9am-7pm. ☎ 674 41 06 or 674 39 78. Museum 4 pesos, planetarium 6 pesos.)*

♪ 🎭 ENTERTAINMENT AND NIGHTLIFE

Guadalajara is known for its cultural sophistication and dizzying variety of entertainment options. To keep abreast of all the happenings—from avant-garde film festivals to bullfights—check the listings in *The Guadalajara Weekly*, *Vuelo Libre* (a monthly calendar of events), and the kiosks and bulletin boards in places like Hospicio Cabañas. Be prepared to take a taxi after buses stop running (10pm).

BARS AND CAFES

Cheaper, chiller, and closer to the *centro*, Guadalajara's bars are often a much more palatable entertainment option than its pressure-cooker dance halls. The area around Mercado Independencia is packed with *cantinas*, while more gimmicky, glitzy options congregate around Chapultepec.

La Maestranza, Maestranza 179 (☎ 613 20 85), at Cortilla. If you think you've seen bullfighting regalia before, wait 'til you swing open the saloon doors. Food (*enchiladas* 32 pesos) and beer (14 pesos) are also good. Live trio 3-5pm. Open daily 10am-3am.

La Cripta, Tepeyac 4038 (☎ 647 62 07), at Niño Obrero. Cool locals, mostly university types, down beers (16 pesos) and bop to alternative tunes. The small dance floor fills after midnight. Cover 30-60 pesos. Open daily 8pm-3am.

Copenhagen, upstairs at Castellanos 120-2 (☎ 825 28 03), between Juárez and Cortilla. A jazz haven. Live music M-Sa 9pm-12:30am. Open M-Sa 2pm-1am, Su 1-7pm.

Bananas Cafe, Chapultepec 330 (☎ 615 41 91), at Tejada. Images of US and British pop stars deck the walls. Unique drinks 16-18 pesos. Outdoor seating. Open M-Th noon-midnight, F-Sa 4:30pm-1:30am, Su 4:30pm-midnight.

Casa Bariachi, 2 locations on Vallarta, the larger at 2221. Local pride in Mexican staples like tequila and *mariachi* are celebrated in grand style by an all-ages crowd. The 2nd location opened to handle overflow from the 1st. Open M-Sa 1:30pm-3am.

Although they close earlier than bars, cafes still provide a popular nighttime option. **Cafe La Paloma,** López Cortilla 1855, at Cervantes, is a rendezvous point for the hip university crowd. Local artwork sparks the imagination, while desserts stimulate the body. (☎ 630 00 91. *Cafe de olla* 16 pesos, chocolate cheesecake 22 pesos. Open M-Sa 8:30am-11pm, Su 9am-10pm.) For a strange mix of elderly chess players and young net surfers, stop by **Cafe Internet,** 8 de Julio 73. (☎ 614 57 36. Cafe americano 12 pesos, *quesadillas* 15 pesos, *comida corrida* 28 pesos. Internet 15 pesos per hr. Open daily 7am-11pm.)

CLUBS

Elegantly dressed partygoers line up outside classy joints along **Vallarta.** An easy daytime bus ride or walk down La Paz from the *centro* becomes a more expensive cab ride (40-50 pesos) after 10:30pm. To save money, arrive early and eat on **Chapultapec** before hitting the clubs. Newly-opened shopping mall **Centro Magnum** at Vallarta 2455, has become a nightlife mecca. In addition to a very posh disco, the Centro has a multiplex cinema, **Cinepolis** (☎ 122 56 57), a **Hard Rock Cafe** (☎ 616 45 60), and its own **Chili's** franchise—which bravely forges forward where even Taco Bell fears to tread. Needless to say, the mall is busy with window shoppers late into the night, offering a surreal vision of the sanitized Mexican Plaza of the future. More traditional discos with complex track lighting and elevated dance floors surround the older **Plaza Sol,** accessible by cab for about 60 pesos.

La Marcha, Vallarta 2648 (☎ 615 89 99), at Los Arcos. Fancy art, fountains, and pretension galore. Dress to impress and pulse to electronic beats in this converted 2-story 19th-century mansion. Cover men 140 pesos, women 90 pesos.

Cavacruz, Vallarta 2503 (☎ 615 76 21), is much more down-to-earth. Patrons hop to *banda* in a friendly environment. Cover 30-100 pesos. Open W and F-Sa 8pm-3am.

Lado B, Vallarta 2451 (☎ 616 20 96), at Queredo at Los Arcos. Creepy murals with images of the sphinx and phoenix hover over the metal and wire furniture. The dance floor twitches to techno until 3am, and some stay later. Open bar. Cover men 120 pesos, women 100 pesos; 35 pesos before 6pm. Open W and F-Sa 9pm-4am.

El Mito Disco, on the 3rd fl. of Centro Magnum (☎615 20 55). Slightly older crowd, dressed to the nines, grooves to a mix of house, electronic, and salsa. W cover men 130 pesos, women free. Th no cover. F-Sa cover 60 pesos. 25+.

GAY AND LESBIAN NIGHTLIFE

There is more gay nightlife in Guadalajara than anywhere else in Mexico outside of D.F. For event listings, check *Amadeus News*, which covers events in both Guadalajara and Puerto Vallarta, or *Odisea*, both of which are at **Chivas Gay.**

Chivas Gay, Cotilla 150 (☎613 16 17), near the corner of Delgollado. With 35 years in the business, Chivas serves as home base for the Guadalajara scene. The bar's many small tables are usually occupied with patrons nursing drinks as they gaze at the TV. Page through one of the monthly publications and bring any questions up to the bar. Beer 12 pesos, tequila 30 pesos. Lesbian friendly. Open daily 5am-3am.

Sahara, Otero 3445 (☎621 88 40), 2 blocks from Pasaje in Plaza del Sol. The latest in lights, glitz, and racy drag shows. Consistently packs a full house. Cover 35 pesos. Drag shows 10:30pm and 1:30am. Open W-Su 9pm-4am.

Caudillos, Sánchez 407 (☎613 54 45), near Hotel Cervantes, 3 blocks from the *centro*. This small bar and disco draws regulars who enjoy the 2-for-1 beer (18 pesos), spirited dance floor, and occasional live "sensual performances." Cover 20 pesos. Music starts at 8:30pm. Open Th-Su 3pm-3am.

Bar Máskara's, Maestranza 238 (☎614 81 03), at Madero. A popular gay bar with 2-for-1 beers (18 pesos). Don your favorite mask (very optional) and step into the fun. Packed on weekends. Open daily 9am-midnight.

SPORTS

Bullfights take place most Sundays (Oct.-Mar.) at **Plaza de Toros,** on Nuevo Progreso at the north end of Independencia. (Take Ruta #60 or 62 north. ☎637 99 82 or 651 85 06. Tickets 40-250 pesos. Open M-Sa 10am-2pm and 4-6pm.)

Fútbol is enormous in Guadalajara and **Chivas,** the local professional team, are perennial contenders for the national championship. Matches take place (Sept.-May) in **Jalisco Stadium** on Calz. Independencia Nte. in front of Plaza de Toros (☎637 05 63; open daily 8am-4pm) and in **Estadio 3 de Marzo,** at the university. Ticket office at Colomos Pte. 2339. (☎641 50 51. Open M-Sa 8am-5pm.)

ENTERTAINMENT

The ■**Ballet Folklórico** dazzles the world with precise dance, intricate garb, and amusing antics. There are two troupes in Guadalajara. The University of Guadalajara troupe, reputedly better, performs in **Teatro Degollado.** Tickets can be purchased on the day of performance or one day in advance. (☎614 47 73. Performances every Su 10am. Box office open daily 10am-1pm and 4-7pm. Tickets 50-150 pesos.) **Ballet Folklórico de Cabañas,** the Jalisco state troupe, performs in Hospicio Cabañas. (Every W 8:30pm. Tickets 60 pesos.) Early arrivals can take a tour of some of the murals inside the Hospicio, which also premiers Mexican films. (Shows daily noon, 3:50, 6:50, and 9pm. 20 pesos.) The **Instituto Cultural Cabañas** presents live music on an open-air stage in Hospicio Cabañas at least once a week. For schedules, drop by the ticket counter or look for the fliers with the Cabañas insignia (a building with a dome and pillars) for schedules.

University facilities, scattered throughout the city, provide high culture for low budgets. The **Departamento de Bellas Artes,** García 720, coordinates activities at many venues throughout the city. A blackboard in the lobby lists each day's attractions. (Open M-Sa 9am-5pm.)

For both big-budget and art-house films, head to **Cinematógrafo,** Vallarta 1102, just west of the university. A different film is presented each week. (☎825 05 14. Screenings at 6, 8, and 10pm. 35 pesos.) Guadalajara has dozens of other cinemas (about 30 pesos); check the newspapers for listings.

FESTIVALS

Finding a bench in Plaza de Armas, across from the Palacio de Gobierno, can be a tricky task—several nights a week, the **Jalisco State Band** draws crowds of locals. (Performances Tu, Th and Su 6:30pm; seat-seekers should arrive before 6pm. Free.) **Plaza de los Fundadores,** behind Teatro Degollado, serves as a stage every afternoon and evening for clown-mimes. Watch and give tips, but unless you like being the butt of jokes, keep out of the mime's view. Every October, Guadalajara explodes with the **Fiestas de Octubre,** a surreal, month-long bacchanal of parades, dancing, bullfights, fireworks, food, and fun. Each day of the month is dedicated to a different one of Mexico's 29 states and two territories.

■ SHOPPING

The cavernous **Mercado Libertad,** at Mina and Independencia, is touted as the largest covered market in the Americas. Though its size may be exaggerated, there are still oodles of sandals, *sarapes*, jewelry, guitars, dried iguanas, and other witchcraft supplies filling tier after tier of booths. Don't be afraid to bargain. (Open daily 6am-8pm.) The Sunday market **El Baratillo,** on Mina approximately 15 blocks east of Mercado Libertad, is even more tempting. From Mercado Libertad, walk two blocks north to Hidalgo and catch bus #40 heading east or a "Par Vial" bus on Morelos. If you thought Mercado Libertad was huge, check out the real big daddy, which sometimes sprawls over 30 or 40 blocks. Vendors sell everything imaginable, from *tamales* to houses. (Open all day Su.)

■ DAYTRIPS FROM GUADALAJARA

TLAQUEPAQUE

Take a local #275 or 275A bus or the "Tlaquepaque" TUR bus (10 pesos, 30min.) from 16 de Septiembre on the southbound side. For the main markets, get off at Independencia by the Pollo-Chicken joint on the left; if the driver turns left off Niños Héroes, you've gone too far. To get back to Guadalajara, hop back on a #275 or TUR bus at the corner of Niños Héroes and Constitución, 2 blocks north of Independencia.

While all but the most obvious fragments of Guadalajara's colonial past are obscured by the city's commercial bustle, adjacent Tlaquepaque has learned to preserve and profit from its quaintness. Tlaquepaque's downtown streets are lined with brightly colored 17th- and 18th-century homes; most have been converted into shops selling *artesanía* and home decor. Products tend to be of higher quality than similar goods piled high in market trinket shops. **Museo Regional de las Cerámicas y los Artes Populares de Jalisco,** Independencia 237, at Alfareros, set in a beautiful 19th-century residence, sells an interesting collection of regional crafts. (☎635 54 04. Open Tu-Su 10am-6pm.) Another fun, if touristy, spot is **La Rosa de Cristal,** Independencia 232, at Alfareros, where artisans blow glass by hand and sell their work at inflated prices. (☎639 71 80. Glass-blowing M-F 10:30am-1pm, Sa 10:30am-noon. Open M-Sa 10am-6pm, Su 10am-2pm.) Just off Tlaquepaque's main square is the *mercado*, where goods are cheaper and of lower quality than in the shops. A small **tourist information** booth, (☎635 57 56), is on Independencia at Parque Hidalgo. Expensive restaurants dot Independencia, offering menus in English, outdoor seating, and delicious food. More affordable meals can be had near the *mercado*. Forget about accommodations: come to Tlaquepaque by day, but spend your nights in far more economical Guadalajara.

ZAPOPAN

Catch a local #275A bus northbound on 16 de Septiembre (40min., 3 pesos). Ask the driver when to get off; Zapopan is fairly non-descript. Last bus back 10pm.

Once a small town, Zapopan would now blend easily into the Guadalajara metropolitan area if it weren't for its stunning plaza and famous ■**Basílica de la Virgen de**

Zapopan. This giant edifice was erected after a local peasant's vision of the virgin. The altar holds **Our Lady of Zapopan,** a small cornstalk figure made by *indígenas* in the 16th century. Her healing powers are commemorated by decades worth of *ex votos*, small paintings on sheet metal offering a visual testimony of the cured. During the early fall, the figure of Our Lady of Zapopan is frequently moved from church to church throughout Jalisco—each move is occasion for serious partying. One of the most major transfers occurs on **Día de la Raza** (Oct. 12, the day Columbus landed in America), when the figure makes her way from Guadalajara's cathedral to Zapopan in a large procession. Pope John Paul II visited the *basílica* in 1979, and a statue of the pontiff holding hands with a beaming village boy now stands in the courtyard in front of the church. The **Sala de Arte Huichal,** on one side of the cathedral, displays indigenous art and handicrafts. (Open daily 9am-2pm and 4-7pm.) Both the *basílica* and *sala* are situated around **Plaza de las Américas,** whose 28 lances represent the nations of the Americas. The market adjacent to the fountain and tree-rich plaza is the best place to grab a cheap taco or roast chicken.

TONALÁ

Local bus #275 and TUR bus #706, which run southbound along 16 de Septiembre, motor to Tonalá (30min., 2 pesos). Get off at the corner of Av. Tonalá and Tonaltecas. Rows of pottery stores let you know you've arrived. Bear right on Tonaltecas to reach the plaza.

The town of Tonalá is famous for its delicately painted earth-toned pottery. Oddly enough, this pottery can be difficult to find in the *grande dame* of Guadalajaran shopping experiences. The huge number of shops surrounding the *plaza principal* multiply into an endless expanse of stands on ▨market days (Th and Su), sprawling west down Tonaltecas. Vendors sell local products (glassware, silver dishware, basketry, miniature pottery sets), as well as *artesanía* from throughout Mexico. If it's famed pottery you're after, start at the **tourist office,** Zapata 275A (☎683 60 47 or 683 17 40; open M-F 9am-3pm), one block off the plaza, and ask for information on local pottery factories such as **Concotzin, Erandi Copez Cotilla,** and **Kent Edwards Morelos.** Most factories offer tours, which often include the opportunity to buy slightly-imperfect "seconds" at discount prices. Because of its high quality and price of manufacture, Tonalá pottery is made almost exclusively for export, bypassing the local market of bargain hunters and going straight to upscale department stores and boutiques.

NORTH SHORE OF LAKE CHAPALA

Guadalajara straddles the line between Mexico's arid North-Central plain and the lush overgrown hillsides of the Central Pacific Coast. For a taste of the latter, head south from the city to the pretty villages on the north shore of Lake Chapala, Mexico's largest lake. The cooling effect of its waters combined with the mountain barrier conspire to keep the air 22°C year-round. Such temperate weather has attracted everyone from D.H. Lawrence to Porfirio Díaz to thousands of retired Americans and Canadians. Although Guadalajara's vast water consumption and agricultural runoff have diminished the lake's size and made swimming inadvisable, the temperate climate, relaxed atmosphere, and natural beauty are good reasons to pay the north shore a visit.

CHAPALA ☎ 3

Chapala (pop. 20,000) is the first stop along the road from Guadalajara. Founded by Tecuexe Indian chief Capalac in 1510, it was here that D.H. Lawrence began writing *The Plumed Serpent* during the 1920s. Today Chapala keeps its cool and serves as both the transportation and economic hub of Lake Chapala. Chapala's peaceful streets host the North Shore's most affordable accommodations, and are great place to enjoy the mountains without too much of a tourist veneer.

⬛ TRANSPORTATION. From the old bus station in Guadalajara, take a "Guadalajara-Chapala" bus (45min., every 30min. 6am-9pm, 26 pesos). The new bus station also serves **Chapala** (1¼hr., every hr. 7:45am-5:45pm, 16 pesos). From Ajijic, take any bus—all roads lead through **Chapala** (20min., every 20min., 3.50 pesos). In Chapala, the entrance of the **bus station** is on Madero at Martínez. Turn left on Madero as you exit the station to reach the lake. "Guadalajara-Chapala" buses back to Guadalajara leave the station on roughly the same schedule as they arrive.

⬛⬛ ORIENTATION AND PRACTICAL INFORMATION. The lake forms the town's southern and eastern boundaries. **Hidalgo** (called **Morelos** east of Madero) runs west to Ajijic from two blocks north of the lake. **Banamex**, Madero 222, has an **ATM.** (☎765 22 71. Open M-F 9am-4pm.) The **mercado de artesanías**, on the waterfront, extends 4 blocks east of Madero's end, on Corona. **Police:** ☎765 44 44. **Red Cross:** (☎765 23 08), on Fallo across from the seafood restaurants on the *malecón*. Some English spoken. **Farmacia Morelos,** Madero 423. (Some English spoken.) (☎765 40 02. Open daily 8:30am-8:30pm). **Post Office:** Hidalgo 242b, on the *carretera* to Ajijic. (Open M-F 8:30am-3pm, Sa 8:30am-1pm.) **Postal Code:** 45900.

⬛⬛ ACCOMMODATIONS AND FOOD. If you want to stay on the shores of Lake Chapala, an outstanding choice is ⬛**Hotel Cardilejas**, Cotilla 363, something of a *gringo* hideaway run by a cordial elderly gentleman whose well-kept rooms and garden lure the accidental tourist into month—or, in one case, 7 year—long stays. Conveniently located one block off Madero near the bus station (look for the red and white sign), the hotel furnishes a great view of the lake and Chapala's charming rooftops. (☎765 22 79. Singles 120 pesos; doubles 160 pesos; triples 240 pesos.)

Although locals seem to survive on a diet of ice cream, Chapala boasts plenty of dining options. The many coffee/pastry shops have relaxed outdoor seating, making diners feel like moneyed retirees regardless of age or financial status. **Chemaiy,** at Madero 2, is one of the cheaper places to lounge and eat. (Open daily 8am-10pm.) Also visit **Restaurant Superior,** Madero 415 at Hidalgo. (Steaks 45 pesos, hamburgers 18 pesos, breakfast about 20 pesos. Open daily 8am-8pm.)

⬛ ⬛ SIGHTS AND ENTERTAINMENT. While brave weekenders from Guadalajara occasionally rev up their jet skis and tear through the calm waters of the lake, pollution and receding shoreline prevent most water sports. Despite the grime, the lake remains beautiful. For a nice vista, climb up the stone stairway that extends from Manzanillo four blocks up Madero. Though the trails aren't clear, even the most aimless walking won't take you far enough away to be really lost, and the mist-covered green hillsides are gorgeous from all angles. As a general rule, aim for the crosses west of 1a del Cerrito, which serve as a good landmark. Try asking in town for advice on more ambitious hikes.

Though a number of *artesanía* vendors set up shop along the *malecón*, more enticing wares await in Ajijic. By night, young locals and a peppering of older folks hang at **Los Caballos Locos,** on 5 de Mayo at Corona across from the lakeside park. The jukebox incites foot-stomping Norteño romps, and beer and tequila are fairly priced at 13 and 20 pesos, respectively. (Open M-Sa noon-midnight.)

AJIJIC   ☎3

With little to do and many expatriates, Ajijic has all the makings of a tourist trap. However, the pretty rows of white, tile-roofed houses, wedged between the azure lake and emerald mountains legitimately attract visitors seeking a glance at "quintessential Mexico" and its stunning vistas. Ajijic's beauty has attracted a bevy of artists and writers, whose prolific efforts fill the lakeside galleries. The town's modern amenities and natural charm merit the tourist hype and encourage even the most miserly budget traveler to loosen his purse-strings.

TRANSPORTATION. From the old bus station in Guadalajara, take a "Guadalajara-Chapala" **bus** (45min., every 30min. 6am-9:40pm, 20 pesos), which, after stopping in Chapala, will continue along the lake to Ajijic and points beyond. From Chapala, take a bus to Ajijic via San Antonio from the bus station on Madero and Martínez (20min., every 15min. 6am-8pm, 3.5 pesos). Buses back to Chapala or Guadalajara can be caught along Carretera Chapala, the same route the bus arrived on (45min., every hr. 6am-8pm, 20 pesos).

ORIENTATION AND PRACTICAL INFORMATION. The only paved street in Ajijic is **Carretera Chapala,** which divides the town into north and south. The cobbled north-south strip is **Colón.** The **plaza** lies toward the lake, and is accessable via Colón. Tourist information can be had at **Mexico's Travelers Information,** on Guadalupe Victoria just before the plaza, which publishes an expat-oriented guide to the region. (☎766 31 63; www.chapalaguide.com. Open M-F 9am-3pm.) For more information, and an English book and video exchange, head to the **Lake Chapala Society's** outpost in a former silkworm nursery at 16 de Septiembre 16a. (Open M-F 10am-1pm.) **Bancomer,** Parroquia 2 on the plaza, has a 24hr. **ATM. Laundry: Lavandería Real,** just off the plaza. (☎766 10 44. 15 pesos wash, 15 pesos dry. Open M-F 9am-6pm, Sa 9am-3:30pm.) The **police** are also on the plaza at the corner of Colón and Hidalgo. They, as well as Chapala's **Red Cross,** can be reached in an **emergency** by dialing 080. Less urgent medical problems should be taken to English-speaking **Hospital Ajijic,** Carretera Chapala 33 (☎766 06 62). **Farmacia Jessica,** Parroquia 18 on the plaza. (☎766 11 91. Open daily 9am-9pm.) **Internet Service: Aqui Hay,** Castellanos 2. (☎138 54 29. 20 pesos per hr., 20% student discount. Open daily 10am-10pm.) **Post office:** Colón 23, at Constitución. (☎766 18 88. Open M-F 8am-3pm, Sa 9am-1pm.) **Postal Code:** 75920.

ACCOMMODATIONS. Ajijic has no budget hotels, but don't let that stop you—try asking around, and make it clear that you're prepared to stay in places that choosier expats might turn down. With any luck, someone will offer you a cheap room. **Las Casitas,** Carretera Chapala 10, is one of the best hotel options, with red tile floors, a kitchen, and a cozy living room with fold-out couch and chimney. (☎766 11 45. Bungalows for 2 people 220 pesos.) **Posada Las Calandrías,** Carretera Chapala 8, has a flower-filled garden, barbecue space, and a great view of the *laguna* from the terraces. (☎766 10 52. June-Oct. small bungalow with 2 beds 260 pesos, 360 pesos in high season; large bungalow with 4 beds also available.) Both establishments have pools.

FOOD AND NIGHTLIFE. Although expensive restaurants dominate the scene, Ajijic will not disappoint the budget traveler. For breakfast, coffee, and *antojitos,* try **Cafe In Acálli.** (Veggie burgers 13 pesos, *quesadillas* 16 pesos, coffee 7 pesos. Open Th-Tu 8am-6pm.) Another cheap local favorite is **Tepalo Restaurant** on Parroquia at the plaza. Specialties include deep-fried shrimp sandwiches (28 pesos), fish filets (38 pesos), and 24-peso *enchilada* plates. (☎766 07 27. Open M-F 8am-4pm, Sa-Su 8am-6pm.)

At night, people of all ages head to the bar at **Posada Ajijic,** 16 de Septiembre 2, on the *laguna* at Colón, which has live music on weekends—usually *cumbia.* (Beer 15 pesos, tequila 30 pesos. Cover 15 pesos. Open daily 9pm-1:30am.)

TEQUILA ☎3

Surrounded by gentle mountains and prickly, blue-green *agave* plants stretching as far as the eye can see, Tequila has been dedicated solely to the production and sale of its namesake liquor since the 17th century. The town is home to 16 tequila distilleries, and nearly every business in town is linked to alcohol in some way. Tourism sustains a slew of t-shirt and souvenir shops, as well as numerous liquor stores in the *centro* and along the route just outside of town. Although touristy, Tequila is lots of fun and makes a great daytrip from Guadalajara.

TEQUILA TIME! The best tequila, as the tour guides will tell you, bears a label boasting its content: 100% *agave*. Around 1600 varieties of this cactus exist in Mexico, but only the blue *agave* is used to make tequila. Plants take 8 to 12 years to mature, at which point their huge, dense centers (called *piñas*—pineapples—for their appearance) attain a weight of 35-45kg. Once harvested, each plant yields around 5L of tequila. From the field, the *piñas* are taken to the factory where they are cooked for 36 hours in enormous traditional ovens, or for 12 hours in the modern and speedy autoclave. A slightly different cooking process will produce *sotol*, the famous Chihuahuan alcohol (see **Sotol from the Heart,** p. 237). You can sample a bite of cooked *piña* on the factory tour—it's similar to a sweet potato. *Piñas* are then chopped and mixed with water, and the stringy pulp that's strained off is used for rugs, animal food, and stuffing furniture. The remaining mixture is poured into huge tubs where it ferments, attracting bees, flies, ants, and other bugs that inevitably join this not-so-appetizing concoction. Only 10% of this mixture will actually become tequila. Be thankful for modern yeast fermentation—in the past, fermentation options included naked, sweaty workers sitting in the vats, or throwing in a piece of animal dung wrapped in cloth. The tequila then goes through two distillations to remove the methanol and lower the alcohol content. In the factory, you can take a sip of tequila after its first distillation, with an alcohol content as high as 80%. Afterwards it is aged in white oak barrels—the longer the process, the smoother the taste. All of this can only happen here: it's against the law to produce tequila anywhere but Jalisco and a few surrounding areas.

◪ TRANSPORTATION. Rojos de Los Altos **buses** (☎ 619 23 09) leave for Tequila from Guadalajara's old station (2hr., every 15min. 5:40am-9:15pm, 20 pesos). In Tequila, exit to the left of the station and head down the street into town. Turn right when the street ends, and then left at the church to get to **Plaza Principal.**

◪◪ ORIENTATION AND PRACTICAL INFORMATION. All the distilleries are surprisingly close to the town's **Plaza Principal.** The giant José Cuervo and Sauza plants are right next to each other two blocks north of the plaza on a street that starts off as **Corona.** This and several other streets in town tend to change names. Though it's hard to get lost in a town so small, **maps** are available at the **Museo de Tequila,** Corona 34 (☎ 742 24 11), one block off the plaza, which doubles as the tourist office. The tourism board's **module** is located in a corner of the plaza across from the Palacio Municipal. (Open M-Su 10am-4pm.) **Banamex,** on Gorjón at Juárez, has a 24hr. **ATM.** (Open M-F 9am-4pm, Sa 9am-1pm). The **police** (☎ 742 00 56) are located right next door at Cuervo 33. In a **medical emergency,** call 080 for an ambulance. Little English spoken.

◪◪◪ ACCOMMODATIONS, FOOD, AND ENTERTAINMENT. If you must spend the night, **Hotel San Francisco,** next to the cathedral, offers a clean, comfortable sanctuary. (☎ 742 17 57. Singles 150 pesos; doubles 200 pesos.) Cheap restaurants pack the area around the bus station; roast chicken is a local favorite. Dine at **Avicola,** Gorjón 20, where 30 pesos will buy you half a bird, tortillas, and salsa. (Open daily 7:30am-4pm.) For more ambience, try **Resturant Bar El Sauzal,** Juaréz 45, between Gorjón and Cuervo, right by the plaza. (Steak 40 pesos, *quesadillas* 18 pesos, beer 13 pesos. Open daily 11am-2am.)

For 15 days, beginning with a huge parade on the last Saturday of November, Tequila celebrates its **Feria Nacional del Tequila.** Each of the town's factories claims one day on which it holds rodeos, concerts, cockfights, fireworks, and other festivities. And of course, there are always plenty of drinks to go around.

◪ DRINK. There's not much to do here other than drink or take a **tequila factory tour.** But hey, why else did you come to a town called Tequila? The tourist office runs tours every hour from 11am-3pm from their module on the plaza, for 25 pesos. A better option may be to head straight to the **Sauza** factory tour, rumored to be the best. Join in at the factory or trek to the tour's official start: 50m down the highway past the entrance to Tequila at Rancho Indio, where a demonstration of blue *agave* cultivation precedes a visit to the factory. (☎742 00 13. Tours run hourly M-Sa 10am-4pm, Su 10am-2pm. 30 pesos.) To see the factory in action, try to arrive early, and avoid *siesta* (2-4pm). One block back toward the plaza is the less impressive **José Cuervo** factory. (Tours daily every hr. 9am-4pm. 30 pesos.) For the price of a few shots, you'll learn more than you ever wanted to know about *agave* (the plant from which tequila is distilled), the distillation and aging processes, and the history of the famous liquor. Private tours end in the factories' very own bars, where the first three shots of tequila are free; subsequent doses cost 10-30 pesos. The **Museo de Tequila,** Corona 34, teaches more tequila history with bilingual signs and a gift shop. (☎742 24 10. Open Tu-Su 10am-5pm. 10 pesos, children and students 5 pesos.) The **Museo Familia Sauza** in the old Sauza family mansion at Rojas 22 can be visited via guided tour. (Tours approx. every 30min. Open M-F 10am-1:30pm, Sa-Su 10am-4:30pm. Donations suggested.)

PUERTO VALLARTA ☎3

In 1956, tabloid headlines had the world fantasizing about Puerto Vallarta (pop. 150,000). The torrid affair that took place here between Richard Burton and Elizabeth Taylor on the set of *Night of the Iguana* painted the city, at that time a remote and mysterious *pueblo* without highways or phone lines, as the world headquarters of sensuality. Forty-odd years later, Vallarta has become a world-class resort town rife with showy mansions, groomed beaches, and upscale clubs and restaurants—a pleasure-dome designed for those living out their fantasies.

TRANSPORTATION

GETTING AROUND
Taxis leave the *centro* for the bus station, Marina Vallarta, or the airport (60 pesos). **Buses** enter the city on México, which becomes Díaz Ordaz. All *combis* and any municipal bus operating south of the Sheraton or labeled "Centro" pass the main plaza, where those labeled "Hoteles" pass the hotel strip. Buses stop at the clearly marked *parada* signs and at the covered benches. Most buses and *combis* travel Insurgentes between Madero and Cárdenas at some point on their route. (Buses and *combis* operate daily 6am-10pm. 3.5 pesos.)

GETTING AWAY
Airport: 8km north of town. To get downtown from the airport, take a "Centro" or "Olas Altas" bus or a taxi. To get back from town, catch a "Novia Alta," "Marfil," or "Aeropuerto" bus on Cárdenas, Insurgentes, or Juárez. Served by **Alaska** (☎221 13 50), **American** (☎221 17 99 or toll-free ☎01 800 904 6000), **Continental** (☎221 10 25), and **Mexicana** (☎224 89 00).

Buses: The modern, mammoth bus station is north of the *centro*, just beyond the airport. To get downtown, take a "Centro" or "Olas Altas" bus or taxi. To get to the bus station from downtown, take an "Ixtapa" bus (3 pesos) northbound at the plaza. Primera Plus/Autocamiones Chihuatlán (☎221 00 95) offers service to: **Mexico City** (12hr., 7pm, 650 pesos); **Aquascalientes** (8hr., 2:30 and 3:45pm, 435 pesos); **Guadalajara** (5hr., about 1 per hr. 1am-11:59pm, 287 pesos); **León** (8hr.; 4:15, 5, 5:30, 10:15pm; 458 pesos); **Manzanillo** (5hr., 4 and 11:30pm, 170 pesos) with stops in **Barra de Navidad** (4.5hr, 135 pesos) and **Melaque** (4hr., 130 pesos); **Morelia** (8hr., 11:15pm, 405 pesos); **Querétaro** (12hr., 9am, 490 pesos). Futura (☎221 08 49), ETN (☎221 04 50), and Pacífico (☎221 08 69) offer similar services.

⚡📍 ORIENTATION AND PRACTICAL INFORMATION

Running roughly east-west, the not-so-mighty **Río Cuale** bisects Puerto Vallarta before hitting the ocean. **Mex. 200** from Manzanillo runs into town south of the river, becoming **Insurgentes**. The ritzy waterfront between Plaza Mayor and 31 de Octubre, called the **malecón**, contains overpriced restaurants, hotels, clubs, and tacky shirt shops. North of the *malecón*, Morelos becomes Perú before joining the coastal route. North along this route lie the **airport, marina, and bus station**. The south end has almost all the cheap hotels, best beaches, and budget restaurants.

Tourist Office: (☎223 25 00, ext. 230 or 231), on Juárez in the Presidencia Municipal, and at Ascencio 1712 (☎223 07 44; ☎/fax 222 02 43). Free maps, brochures, and *Passport*, a publication that lists discounts at bars and restaurants. English spoken. Open M-F 8am-4pm.

Consulates: Canada (☎222 53 98; emergencies: 01 800 706 29 00. Open M-F 9am-4pm) and **US** (☎222 00 69, emergencies 013 826 55 53; fax 223 00 74. Open M-F 10am-2pm), both at Zaragoza 160 in Vallarta Plaza, on Plaza Mayor.

Currency Exchange: Banamex (☎226 61 10), at Juárez and Zaragoza, in front of the Presidencia Municipal. Open M-F 9am-5pm, Sa 9am-2pm. **Bancrecer,** Olas Altas 246 (☎223 04 84), between Carranza and Badillo. Open M-F 9am-5pm, Sa 10am-2pm. Both have 24hr. **ATMs.** *Casas de cambio* are everywhere, especially near the *malecón*. Their rates differ, but are lower than banks. Usually open daily 9am-7pm.

American Express: Morelos 660 (☎223 29 55; fax 223 29 26), at Abasolo. Open M-F 9am-6pm, Sa 9am-1pm.

Luggage storage: at the bus station. 3 pesos per hr. Open 24hr.

Laundry: Laundry Aguamatic, Constitución 279 (☎222 59 78), between Cárdenas and Carranza. 10 pesos per kg. Open M-Sa 9am-8pm.

Bookstore: Starbooks, Olas Altas 490 (☎222 03 24), at Gómez. 2-for-1 book exchange. Used books 20-40 pesos, new books 60-600 pesos. Coffee 9-16 pesos. Open daily 8am-midnight. **Una Página en el Sol,** Olas Alta 339 at Diéguez. English-language books 5-70 pesos, book exchanges also welcome. Open daily 7:30am-midnight.

Supermarket: Gutiérrez Rico (☎222 02 22), at Constitución and Serdán. Open daily 6:30am-11pm.

Car Rental: Almost all rental companies have offices on Ascencio, the hotel strip. **National,** Ascencio km 1.5 (☎221 12 26 at the airport). VW with tax, insurance, and 200km US$50 per day. **Thrifty,** Ascencio km 5.5 (☎224 07 76 or 224 92 80). VWs with tax, insurance, and unlimited km US$60 per day. The cheapest rentals can be found at **Cafe.com** (☎222 00 92), see **Internet Access,** below.

Emergency: ☎060.

Police: (☎222 01 06) Iturbide 1586, at Morelos. Some English spoken.

Red Cross: (☎222 15 33) on Río de la Plata at Río Balsas. Take a "Cruz Roja" bus from Cárdenas and Insurgentes. English spoken.

Pharmacy: Farmacia CMQ, Badillo 365 (☎222 13 30), at Insurgentes. Open 24hr.

Hospital: CMQ Hospital, Badillo 365 (☎223 19 19), at Insurgentes. **Hospital Medasist,** Diéguez 360 (☎223 04 44), at Insurgentes. Some English spoken at both.

Internet Access: Cafe.com, Olas Altas 250 (☎/fax 222 00 92), at Rodríguez. Offers internet service (35 pesos per hr.), cafe, small bar, fax and copy service, and cheap car rental. Open daily 8am-2am. **The Net House,** Vallarta 232 (☎222 69 53), at Cárdenas. 25 pesos per hr. Open daily 8am-3am.

Post Office: Mina 188 (☎222 18 88), left off Juárez past Plaza Mayor. Open M-F 8am-6pm, Sa 9am-1pm.

Postal Code: 48300.

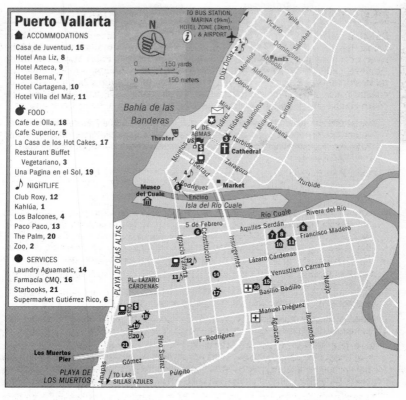

Puerto Vallarta

🏠 ACCOMMODATIONS
Casa de Juventud, 15
Hotel Ana Liz, 8
Hotel Azteca, 9
Hotel Bernal, 7
Hotel Cartagena, 10
Hotel Villa del Mar, 11

🍴 FOOD
Cafe de Olla, 18
Cafe Superior, 5
La Casa de los Hot Cakes, 17
Restaurant Buffet
  Vegetariano, 3
Una Pagina en el Sol, 19

🎵 NIGHTLIFE
Club Roxy, 12
Kahlúa, 1
Los Balcones, 4
Paco Paco, 13
The Palm, 20
Zoo, 2

⬤ SERVICES
Laundry Aguamatic, 14
Farmacia CMQ, 16
Starbooks, 21
Supermarket Gutiérrez Rico, 6

ACCOMMODATIONS AND CAMPING

The best budget hotels in Puerto Vallarta are south of Río Cuale, on or near Madero. Prices vary by season: June is the least expensive month, while December is the most. From November-January, reservations should be made two months in advance. Vallarta officially frowns on beach bums, but most travelers who choose to camp encounter few problems. Some beachfront clubs have night guards who may keep an eye on those who ask before bedding down—a tip is appropriate. Many people sleep on the sand behind Hotel Los Arcos or Castle Pelícanos, or in the open space between the J. Newcombe tennis courts and the Sheraton. Exercise caution when selecting any camping site.

Hotel Azteca, Madero 473 (☎222 27 50), between Jacarandas and Naranjo. Serious *telenovela*-watchers congregate in the hotel lobby. Long-term *huéspedes* and personable staff create a friendly atmosphere. Fans and *agua purificada* make cushy beds and fluffy pillows even more comfortable. Towel deposit 30 pesos. Singles 150 pesos; doubles 190 pesos; small suites with kitchen 250-300 pesos.

Hotel Villa del Mar, Madero 440 (☎222 07 85), 2 blocks east of Insurgentes. Brick detailing, wooden doors, and lanterns give the well-scrubbed rooms a rustic feel. Rooftop terrace has a fabulous view of the *centro*. Towel deposit 50 pesos. Singles 140 pesos, with balcony 175 pesos; doubles 175 pesos; triples 210 pesos.

Casa de Juventud, Aguacate 302A (☎222 21 08). Show ID at the door to be admitted to the immaculate, single-sex, dormitory-style rooms grouped around a courtyard, where students mix around the TV and card table. Bring your own toilet paper. Lock out from 2am-6am, Sa-Su noon-4pm daily. Beds 75 pesos, with discounts for longer stays. 1-time fee of 5 pesos each for sheets, towels, or lockers.

Hotel Ana Liz, Madero 429 (☎222 17 57), has basic, dim rooms with tiny baths. Tasteful landscape photos and less tasteful 70s disco-style curtains do their best to brighten the place. Singles 160 pesos; doubles 190 pesos; triples 220 pesos.

Hotel Bernal, Madero 423 (☎222 36 05), has an inviting covered courtyard, clean but old rooms, fans, and purified water. Beds are extremely firm, and pillows may be lumpy. Towel deposit 30 pesos. Singles 150 pesos; doubles 190 pesos.

Hotel Cartegena de Indios, Madero 428 (☎222 69 14). The warm terra cotta floors give rooms a homey feel, and some have good-sized balconies. The small baths may sport a few permanent stains. A/C 60 pesos. Singles 150 pesos; doubles 190 pesos.

🍴 FOOD

Puerto Vallarta's *malecón* specializes in tourist-oriented, North American cuisine, but excellent, decently-priced restaurants can be found elsewhere on the north side. Near the beach on the south side, many upscale restaurants exist especially for *gringos*, particularly on the blocks enclosed by Badillo, Olas Altas, Cárdenas, and Constitución. Cheaper eateries cluster along Madero, in the *mercado* (open M-Sa 9am-8pm) on the north side, where Insurgentes crosses Río Cuale, and along México to the north. All-night taco and *quesadilla* stands thrive south of the river

🍴 **Una Pagina en El Sol,** Morelos 950 (☎222 36 08), also at Olas Altas 399, is a combination cafe, vegetarian restaurant, and used English bookstore. Coffee 8-20 pesos, veggie sandwiches 25 pesos. Open M-Sa 7:30am-midnight.

🍴 **La Casa de los Hot Cakes,** Badillo 289 (☎222 62 72), at Constitución. Stupendously good breakfasts. Indulge in the specialty pancake or waffle platters (25-38 pesos) or delectable cheese blintzes (35 pesos). Open Tu-Su 8am-2pm. At night, the name changes to **Memo's,** but the rich, inventive food remains. The pistachio *pipian* (55 pesos) and *albondigas al chipotle* (meatballs stuffed with hard-boiled quail eggs and chipotle; 45 pesos) will send your taste buds soaring. Open Tu-Su 5-11pm.

🍴 **Restaurant Buffet Vegetariano,** Iturbide 270 (☎222 30 73), at Hidalgo, a few blocks inland from Plaza Mayor. 100% vegetarian cuisine, with an Indian influence. Join international travelers in the mural-decorated, fan-cooled interior. Buffet includes 5 main dishes (non-dairy options available), soup, salad bar with inventive dressings, *agua fresca*, coffee, tea, and dessert (45 pesos). Open M-Sa 11:30am-10pm.

Cafe Superior, Juárez 155 (☎222 44 23), at Encino. The brain-child of a Mexican mother and an American father, the cafe serves a tasty mix of national dishes and international cuisine in a casual setting. Tangy but sweet tuna salad-stuffed avocado halves 25 pesos. Breakfast 22-28 pesos, *tortas* 20-25 pesos. Open Su-M 8:30am-3:30pm, Tu-Sa 8:30am-8pm.

Cafe de Olla, Badillo 168 (☎223 16 26), 1 block from the beach. A tourist joint with attentive waiters and exceptional food. *Mariachis* weave between tables to serenade vacationers. Burgers and Mexican staples from 45 pesos. Open W-M 9am-11pm.

📷 SIGHTS AND BEACHES

Although the veneer of tourism detracts somewhat from Puerto Vallarta's natural beauty, the panorama of the city's 40km coastline and surrounding palm-tree-covered mountains is still enchanting. Water sport enthusiasts will play happily in Vallarta—aquatic activities are extremely popular, especially during the morning hours. This is your chance to go **parasailing** (US$20). **Wave runners** (doubles 350 pesos per ½hr.), **banana boat** rides (150 pesos per person), **kayaks** (100 pesos per hr.), and **waterskis** (400 pesos per ½hr.) are also available—ask around at the beach. **Chico's Dive Shop,** 772 Díaz Ordaz, offers scuba diving courses and certification classes. (☎222 18 95 or 222 18 75; US$18 for 1hr. US$290 for certification classes. English-speaking staff will gladly lower rates for return customers, groups, or payment in cash. Open daily 8am-10pm.) Equestrian fanatics can take to the hills on **horseback;** rentals are available from the stand in the plaza on Olas Altas at Carranza (☎222 03 86. 100 pesos per hr.). Another horse stand, on the corner of the plaza at Carranza and Suárez, has similar rates (☎222 03 76).

Some of the least crowded and most gorgeous beaches stretch south of town on the road to Mismaloya (see p. 390) and north into Nayarit (see p. 364). The most popular within Vallarta is **Playa de los Muertos** (Beach of the Dead), a strip in front of the south side's costliest hotels. The south end begins at a rocky cliff and stretches north to the small dock that separates it from **Playa de Olas Altas** (High Waves Beach). The clear water at Playa de los Muertos is its primary advantage over its neighbor; Río Cuale empties into the ocean at Playa de Olas Altas, sullying it's waters with sediment. To get there, walk all the way west on Cárdenas and then south along Playa de Olas Altas, which continues to Río Cuale before becoming the rocky *malecón.* Near the southern end of Playa de los Muertos is **Las Sillas Azules** (The Blue Chairs), one of Mexico's only gay (male) beaches.

Isla Río Cuale is accessible by short stairways from both bridges spanning the *cafe con leche*-colored **Río Cuale.** A tree-shaded pathway runs the length of the verdant island, full of small stores selling postcards, jewelry, and souvenirs. The **Museo del Cuale,** at the seaward end of the island, houses interesting displays on Mesoamerican culture and regional history. (Open Tu-Sa 12:30pm-7pm. Free.) During the day the walk along Río Cuale is pleasant, but it can be dangerous at night. Stairs, beginning behind the Church of Guadalupe, lead up the mini-mountain amid bougainvillea and hibiscus into the wealthy Zaragoza neighborhood known locally as Gringo Gulch. The prominent bridge spanning the apex of the street once connected Elizabeth Taylor's humble pad with Richard Burton's.

🎵 NIGHTLIFE

After dark, the *malecón* swarms with hundreds of tanned young Mexicans and Americans batting their eyelashes at each other. Vallarta has sprouted a thriving **gay scene,** and boasts several clubs catering to gay men and, occasionally, gay women. The action centers along **Díaz Ordaz** on the northern waterfront. Late night transportation is greatly aided by the "Marina Vallarta" bus, which goes to the marina, and the "Pitillal" bus, which travels past the hotel strip. After 11pm, you'll be stuck with taxis (60 pesos to the *centro*).

BARS AND CLUBS

Discos are aimed at those who don't mind dropping 50-70 pesos or more for cover charges and 20-50 pesos for a drink. Most don't get going until 11pm or midnight; avoid covers and save a small fortune by collecting free passes (which may not be honored during high season) from the condo-hawkers lurking on the *malecón.* You need not buy a condo, just pretend you might.

Carlos O'Brian's Bar & Grill & Clothesline, Díaz Ordaz 542 (☎222 14 44), at Pípila. The only things hanging out to dry are the totally trashed high-school students. Beer 29 pesos, national drinks 35 pesos. Open daily noon-3am.

Kahlúa, Díaz Ordaz 644 (☎222 24 86), on the waterfront. 20-somethings chug 2-for-1 beers (50 pesos) and national drinks (40-55 pesos). Open daily 11am-3am.

Zoo, Díaz Ordaz 630 (☎222 49 45). The iron-bar dance cages keep with the animal theme. It's the biggest party in town—block-long lines wrap around the building all night.

Club Roxy, Ignacio Vallarta 217, between Madero and Carranza. An international all-ages clientele jams to live reggae, blues, and rock. Beer 25 pesos. No cover. Open M-Sa 7am-3:30am. Live music starts at 10:30pm.

Collage (☎221 08 61), next to Marina Vallarta, is big enough to house all of Vallarta. The dance floor resembles an ice-skating rink, complete with spectators in the stands.

Free pool in the back. Almost every night is a special event—foam party, rave with glow-sticks, Mardi Gras, wet t-shirt contest. Beer 25 pesos, national drinks 30-35 pesos. Cover generally men 100 pesos, women 50 pesos. Open daily 10pm-5am.

J & B, Ascencio 2043 (☎224 46 16), toward the hotel zone. An older crowd dances to live *salsa, merengue,* and the occasional Michael Jackson tune. Those determined not to dance can play pool instead. Beer 29 pesos, national drinks 32 pesos. Live music daily 12:30am-3am. W-Su cover 50 pesos, 2nd drink free. Open daily 10pm-4am.

GAY NIGHTLIFE

A **gay cruise,** departing daily at noon from the Los Muertos pier, takes partners Noah's ark-style to a private beach (around US$50; includes drinks, snorkeling, and table dancing). Tickets are available from travel agents or time-share hawkers; for more info, ask at Paco Paco (below).

Anthropology, Morelos 101 on Plaza Río next to the Vallarta Bridge. Racy fun for every-one. The ground-floor disco hosts strip shows Tu, F, Sa at 1:30am; women's night M (gender of stripper alternates—call ahead if you're picky); and amateur transvestite and stripper nights. Men clad only in the slimmest of thongs gyrate all night long on top of the 2nd-fl. bar. Beer 21 pesos, national drinks 35 pesos. Cover 20 pesos; M, F, Sa 50 pesos—includes 1 beer. Open daily 9pm-4am.

Paco Paco Ignacio Vallarta 278 (☎223 18 99), at Cárdenas. Vallarta's hottest gay disco, with great music, lots of floor space, mirrors, strobe lights, and aquariums. Non-dancing options include pool and video games or enjoying the sunset from the rooftop bar. Beer 22 pesos, national drinks 30 pesos. Cover W-Su 50 pesos. Open daily noon-6am.

Los Balcones, Juárez 182 (☎222 46 71), at Libertad. International gay crowd practices looking languid on the balconies. A giant Frida Kahlo reproduction smiles down on scantily-clad patrons packing a neon-lit dance floor. During high season (Oct.-May), the 50-peso cover includes 1 drink. Beer 23 pesos, drinks 30 pesos. Open daily 9pm-5am.

The Palm, Olas Altas 508 (☎223 48 18). Vallarta's lesbian bar provides a laid-back alternative to the wilder side of the city's gay nightlife. The fiery red interior more often sets the stage for a pool game or conversation. Th is ladies night. Beer 20 pesos, national drinks 30 pesos, 2-for-1 drinks daily 8-10pm. Occasional cover 10 pesos for live music or comedy shows. Open daily 6pm-2am.

▶ DAYTRIPS FROM PUERTO VALLARTA

The **Bahía de Banderas** (Bay of Flags) that shelters Puerto Vallarta owes its name to a blunder: when Nuño Beltrán de Guzmán landed here in 1532, he mistook the col-orful headdresses of the thousands of natives awaiting him for flags. Today, the Bay offers miles of beautiful and often untouristed beaches. Using Puerto Vallarta as a base, it is possible to reach all points around the Bay.

SOUTHERN COAST

Buses go to Mismaloya from Constitución and Badillo in Vallarta (every 10min. 5:30am-11pm, 3.5 pesos). Taxis cost 80 pesos. "Tuito" buses run to Chico's Paradise from Car-ranza and Aguacate (every ½hr. 5am-9pm, 10 pesos). Taxis Acuáticos are the cheapest way to get to the boats-only beaches. They leave from Muelle de los Muertos and stop at Las Ánimas, Quimixto, and Yelapa (45min.; departs at 11am, returns at 4pm; 90 pesos). Cruises to points south of Vallarta leave from the marina (9am, returning 4pm; US$25 and up). Information available in the tourist office, at any large hotel, or at the marina.

Vallarta's most popular beaches lie a few kilometers south of the city itself. The first few are monopolized by resorts, and access is usually only through the hotels.

LOS ARCOS. Farther down the coast lies Los Arcos, a group of pretty rock islands shaped by pounding waves. The coast lacks sand but serves as a platform from which to start the 150m swim to the islands. Bring a mask or goggles or risk miss-ing the tropical fish that flit through the underwater reefscape. Mind your step—

the coral is sharp enough to draw blood; use caution and swim with a friend. *(Take the bus to Mismaloya and ask the driver to stop at Hotel de los Arcos.)*

MISMALOYA. The beautiful crescent beach of Mismaloya lies just around the bend to the south. Best known as the site of *Night of the Iguana* and Arnold Schwarzenegger's *cinéma vérité* classic, *Predator*, Mismaloya has recently been taken over by large hotels and is only slightly less crowded than beaches in town.

BOCA DE TOMATLÁN. Farther down, the road veers away from the coast just beyond Boca de Tomatlán, a narrow cove with a small, relatively untouristed beach. The last place to see on the southern road is **Chico's Paradise,** 5km inland from Boca de Tomatlán. Wash down the view of nearby **Tomatlán Falls** with a beer (20 pesos) at Chico's huge *palapas* or splash in the river and admire the surrounding hills. *(To get to Chico's from Boca de Tomatlán, take a "Tuito" bus from the main highway (5 pesos). ☎222 07 47. Open daily 10am-6pm.)*

LAS ÁNIMAS AND QUIMIXTO. Farther south lie the beaches of Las Ánimas and Quimixto, which are only accessible by boat. The twin beaches have long stretches of unoccupied sand backed by small villages and a few *palapas*.

YELAPA. Highly touted by locals, Yelepa is a bit of a fake. Supposedly a secluded peasant fishing village, its "simple" *palapa* huts were designed by a North American architect whose definition of "rustic" included interior plumbing and hot water. Many of these *palapas* are occupied for only part of the year, and short- and long-term rentals can be arranged easily for sometimes surprisingly low prices. The beach fills with vendors and parasailers by day, but the town, a 15min. walk from the beach, remains tranquil, with waterfalls and nude bathing upstream and poetry readings downstream. Don't miss the secluded swimming hole at the top of the stream that runs through town. Follow the path uphill and duck under the water pipes to the right of the trail just before the restaurant. About 15m before it rejoins the stream, a trail leads left to a deep pool overlooking the bay.

NORTHERN COAST

From Puerto Vallarta, flag down a "Punta de Mita" bus on Cárdenas, Insurgentes, Juárez, or Ascencio (every 20min. 9:15am-5pm); to Piedra Blanca (40min., 17 pesos); Destiladeras (1hr., 20 pesos); or Punta de Mita (1¼hr. plus a 4km walk, 25 pesos).

The northern edge of the bay hosts some of the prettiest and least-developed beaches on Mexico's central Pacific coast. **Nuevo Vallarta,** the largest and southern-most of nine small towns on the north bay, is 150km south of Tepic and 20km north of Puerto Vallarta. Protected by a sandy cove, **Playa Piedra Blanca** has wonderfully calm waters. Farther north along the bay is **Playa las Destiladeras,** named for the water that trickles through the rocky cliff. Although the sandy bottom is colored with occasional rocks, rougher waves make the beach perfect for body-surfers and boogie boarders. **Punta de Mita,** the northernmost point along the bay, is a lagoon sheltered by two rock islets. It is marked by **Corral de Riscos,** a living reef. Freshwater showers in Destiladeras make the bus ride home more comfortable. Bring a bag lunch to avoid inflated prices at the beachside *palapas*.

BAHÍA DE CHAMELA ☎3

Tranquil and secluded Bahía de Chamela, 60km northwest of Melaque, marks the northern point of Jalisco's "Ecological Tourism Corridor." A chain of small rocky islands breaks the horizon, and 11km of golden-brown sand, dotted with gnarled driftwood and the occasional *palapa*, beckon to the beachcomber. The largest village in Chamela is **Perula** (pop. 600), which lacks most services beyond a few hotels and seafood *palapas*, but keeps visitors content with a charming beach. Though Chamela receives its share of tourism, especially in December and April, the Midas touch has yet to spoil the natural beauty and seclusion of the bay. Although crime is virtually nonexistent in Perula (the nearest police station is 3km away), lone travelers should exercise caution on the deserted beaches.

▐ **TRANSPORTATION.** Second-class buses from **Puerto Vallarta** to **Manzanillo** (3½hr., 40 pesos) pass through Perula; buses going from **Melaque** or **Barra de Navidad** to **Puerto Vallarta** (1½hr., 29 pesos) or **Manzanillo** (3hr., 53 pesos) also stop in Perula. Always tell the bus driver where you're going in advance so you don't miss the stop. To get to Playa Perula, get off by the big white "Playa Dorada" sign and walk 30min. down a winding dirt road—don't be surprised if friendly locals offer you a ride. To get to Playa Chamela, get off farther south at "El Súper," marked by the colorful figure directing passersby to Villa Polinesia. Walk 15min. down the country road until you hit the beach. Perula is a 30min. walk along the shore. Hotels in Perula will pick you up or send a taxi. To return, catch a Primera Plus bus from the bus stop on the main highway. They head to: **Guadalajara** (3hr.; 8, 10:30am, and 4pm; 67 pesos); **Manzanillo** (2½-5hr., every hr. 7:30am-10:30pm, 65 pesos) via **Melaque** (1½hr., 35 pesos); **Puerto Vallarta** (6hr., every hr. 7:30am-10:30pm, 75 pesos).

▐ **PRACTICAL INFORMATION.** Centro de Salud (☎333 98 04), at the corner of Juárez and Pargo, one block from the Hotel Punta Perula. (No English spoken. 24hr. emergency service.) There is one **LADATEL** phone outside the Primera Plus Station; your best bet for placing a long-distance call is cajoling one of the hotel or restaurant owners into letting you call collect.

▐▐ **ACCOMMODATIONS AND FOOD.** ▨**Hotel Punta Perula,** on the corner of Juárez and Tiburón, two blocks from the beach, features a massive courtyard laden with trees and overhanging hammocks, eclipsing the comfortable, floral rooms. (☎333 97 82. Singles 200 pesos; doubles 300 pesos. Low season 150 pesos and 250 pesos.) In Perula, **Tejamar Restaurante y Cuartos,** on Independencia, one block south of Hotel Punta Perula near the beach, is a small, family-run taco restaurant and *posada*. Bright and clean basic rooms have ceiling fans and open onto a small courtyard. Friendly owners are eager to accommodate guests with bargain meals, trips to nearby islands, and weekly discounts. (Singles 200 pesos; doubles 350 pesos; low season singles 80 pesos; doubles 200 pesos.) The adjoining restaurant offers cheap and yummy *carne asada* tacos. (3.5 pesos; open daily from 7:30pm.) Feast on the catch of the day as you relax under palm frond umbrellas at **Mariscos La Sirena,** the northernmost of several *palapas* along the shore, which serves shrimp and fish (60 pesos). A cold beer there is 10 pesos well-spent. (☎333 97 16. Open daily 8:30am-7pm.)

▐ **BEACHES.** **Punta de Perula,** the bay's northernmost point, shelters **Playa Perula,** making it perfect for swimming. A 30min. walk down the virgin beach will bring you to the **Villa Polinesia Motel and Campsite,** marking **Playa Chamela.** Here and farther south, rougher waves invite body surfing and boogie-boarding—watch out for the frequent and powerful undertow. Continuing south brings you to **Playa Rosada** and even more secluded beaches. Occasional *palapas* refresh the parched and weary body-surfer, and *lanchas* from Playa Perula transport wanna-be Robinson Crusoes to the nearby islands or on fishing trips (round-trip 300 pesos.) Inquire of the fishermen at the point about 1km north of Perula.

BAHÍA DE NAVIDAD ☎3

Along with Guadalajara and Puerto Vallarta, Bahía de Navidad forms Jalisco's "Tourist Triangle." However, power is not shared equally within the triumvirate. With the exception of December and *Semana Santa*, few tourists are spotted on the placid shores of Bahía de Navidad. The *bahía*, a sheltered cove of powdery sand and shimmering water, is home to the towns of **Melaque** and **Barra de Navidad.** It seems a wonder that more vacationers don't come here year-round—the water is clear and gentle, the beach long and empty, and the entire bay enclosed by scenic, rocky cliffs. During high season the beach between the towns is transformed into a river of bronzed bodies, and hotels in both towns overflow with tourists.

Although restaurants, hotels, and clubs are beginning to invade, the pace of life here is still sleepy, with days spent dreaming on the beach, and nights whiled away in beachside or thatched-roof pool halls and bars.

Melaque and Barra de Navidad lie 55km northwest of Manzanillo on Mex. 200, and 240km southwest of Guadalajara on Mex. 54. Melaque is the northernmost of the two. They're well-connected by **municipal buses** that shuttle between the two towns (20min., every 15min. 6am-8:30pm, 3 pesos). Of course, the 40min. walk along the beach would be the hard-core budget option. **Don't walk after sunset;** some dangerous encounters have been reported. **Taxis** cost 40 pesos.

MELAQUE   ☎ 3

Visitors amble through Melaque's (pop. 7,000) placid *zócalo*, splash in the waves, and nibble on fresh fish while watching the sunset from beachside restaurants. There's not much action in beautiful Melaque, which suits the place just fine.

■ TRANSPORTATION. Melaque's **bus stations** are side-by-side on **Farías,** the main drag that runs parallel to the beach . From the bus station, turn left on Farías and walk two blocks to reach **Mateos.** Another left turn takes you to the plaza, a few blocks inland. Mateos and **Hidalgo** are the main cross-streets toward the ocean.

Autocamiones Cihuatlán (☎355 50 03) offers second-class service; Primera Plus/ Flecha Amarilla (☎355 61 10), offers first- and executive-class service. The two are side-by-side at Farías 34. First class service to: **Guadalajara** (5 hr., 7 per day 9:15am-1:15am, 190 pesos); **Manzanillo** (1½hr., 5 per day 3am-8pm, 39 pesos); **Puerto Vallarta** (3½hr., 3:30am and 9:30am, 130 pesos); **Tomatlán** (2hr., 5 and 9pm, 86 pesos). Second-class service to: **Guadalajara** (6½hr., every 2hr. 4am-12:30am, 159 pesos); **Manzanillo** (1hr. 40min., every hr. 3am-11:30pm, 32 pesos); **Puerto Vallarta** (5hr., every 2hr. 3am-11:30pm, 110 pesos).

⋒ PRACTICAL INFORMATION. Banamex, on Farías, across from the bus station, has a 24hr. **ATM.** (☎355 52 77 or 355 53 42. Open M-F 9am-3pm.) Change money or traveler's checks at **Casa de Cambio,** Farías 27A, inside the commercial center across from the bus station. (☎355 53 43. Open M-Sa 9am-5pm.) **Police:** upstairs at Mateos 52 (☎355 50 80), north of the plaza. No English spoken. **Red Cross:** (☎355 23 00), 15km away in Cihuatlán, accessible by buses that leave from the plaza. Ask the driver for "Cruz Roja." (every 15min. 6am-8pm, 6 pesos) or take a taxi (100 pesos). **Súperfarmacia Plaza,** Mateos 48, on the south side of the plaza. (☎355 51 67. Open daily 7am-8pm). **Clínica de Urgencias,** Carranza 22, two blocks from the bus station. (☎355 56 08. Open M-Sa 8am-2pm, ring the bell outside for 24hr. emergency service.) The **public telephones** by the bus station can be used for long-distance collect calls. **LADATELs** are on both Farías and Mateos. **Casetas:** next to the bus station is **Yimmi's,** Farías 34. (☎355 63 10; fax 355 54 52. Open M-Sa 8:30am-8:30pm, Su 8:30am-1pm.) **Internet Access: Ciber@net,** in the commercial center, Farías 27A. (☎355 55 19; melaque@ciber.net.mx. 45 pesos per hr. Open M-F 10am-2:30pm and 4pm-7:30pm, Sa 9:30am-2:30pm.) **Post office:** Orozco 56, near the corner of Corona, one block from the pool hall with the brown fence. (☎355 52 30. Open M-F 9am-3pm.) **Postal code:** 48980.

■⊡ ACCOMMODATIONS AND FOOD. Melaque boasts a crop of snazzy hotels, but few could be termed budget. Expect rates to rise during high season. Camping is feasible in Melaque if you arrange to stay next to one of the beachside restaurants; expect to pay a small fee. **Hotel Emanuel,** Bugambilias 89, is half a block from the beach. Turn right on Farías from the bus station and walk five blocks, turning left after the teal mansion. Look for the "Abarrotes Emanuel" sign on your left. The spacious rooms and bungalows have floral decor and clean, white-tile bathrooms. Bungalows have very modern kitchens—the huge rooftop bungalow has six double beds in three bedrooms, making it a great place for a large group. (☎355 61 07.

Singles 100 pesos; doubles 130 pesos; triples 180 pesos. Bungalows: 1 person 130 pesos; 2 people 170 pesos; 3 people 230 pesos; rooftop bungalow 900 pesos. No charge for up to 2 children. Discounts available for longer stays.) You can also try slightly more expensive **Bungalows Los Arcos,** Farías 2. Take a right at the bus station and walk to the end of the street; it's on the right. If you can ignore the musty smell, rooms are clean with powerful ceiling fans. Private baths have hot water. (☎355 51 84. 1-3 people 250 pesos; quads 290 pesos.) **Casa de Huéspedes San Juán,** Farías 24, is on the right leaving the bus station, across from the bank. Rooms are a bit old and worn, but they're the best deal in town. Kitchen units have very basic equipment. (☎355 52 70. 1-3 people 150 pesos; quads 200 pesos.)

During the summer, restaurants ship shrimp in from the north, but, come high season, local fishing boats catch everything served in Melaque. Cheaper, more authentic places are located near the central plaza. Cheaper still are the sidewalk food stands that materialize after sunset and the unnamed, dirt-floored eateries in the *mercado.* Locals hail **Restaurant Ayala.** Turn left on the street before Mateos and walk a block; it's on the left. Tasty fish (27 pesos) and burgers with fries (12-15 pesos) are served in an open-air environment. The *tortas* (13-18 pesos) are delicious and the *comida corrida* (17 pesos) is unbelievably cheap. (☎355 66 80. Open daily 7am-5pm.) On López Mateos next to the *zócalo,* sits **Cafetería Siete Estrellas,** a small joint offering terrific food at low prices. Try the filling *comida corrida* (20 pesos) or house favorite hot *tortas.* (12-18 pesos. ☎355 64 21. Open daily 7am-midnight.) A happening place to grab dinner is **Caxcan Restaurant,** on the corner of the *zócalo* above the pharmacy as you enter from Mateos. The bar hands out cheap two-for-one drinks to wash down the fishies. (Open daily 6pm-1am.)

◢◣ BEACHES AND ENTERTAINMENT. The main attraction in Melaque is its beach. Waves get smaller and the beach more crowded toward the western end of the sandy strip. Rent **jet skis** at **Restaurant Moyo,** the last restaurant on the far west end of the beach. (☎355 61 04. 2-person 700 pesos per hr.; 3-person 800 pesos per hr. Available daily 10am-7pm.) Be prepared to get wet if you go for a spin in a **banana boat** (40 pesos per person); ocean currents regularly dump unsuspecting riders into the waves. Nightlife in Melaque concentrates on the beach until 9:30 or 10pm, as people swim and stroll along the shore, enjoying the glorious sunsets. The after-hours oasis of Melaque's under-30 tourist crowd is **Disco Tanga,** at the end of Farías to the right of the bus station. Multicolored walls and stairs lined by strip lights create a game show effect. (☎355 54 75. Cover 30 pesos. Open daily 9pm-2am; low season F-Sa 9pm-2am.) For something more on the mellow and smoky side, twirl cues with middle-aged men at **Billiard San Patricio,** on Orozco and Juárez, up the street from the post office, three blocks from the *zócalo.* (Pool and *carambola* 12 pesos per hr., dominoes 4 pesos per hr. Open daily 10am-11pm.) Women may want to avoid this place. In general, don't get your partying hopes up during the low season; nightlife doesn't awake until the tourists start knocking.

BARRA DE NAVIDAD ☎3

Barra (pop. 6000) is smaller, with less crowded beaches (due to the stronger undertow) than its sister Melaque. However, its shaded streets, numerous sidewalk eateries and popular seaside bars provide a vitality lacking in Melaque. The saltwater *laguna* at the end of town is a great place to swim, play volleyball, or sunbathe. Like Melaque, Barra doesn't offer much in the way of sights, museums, or high-tech entertainment, instead reveling in its own tranquil beauty.

▐ TRANSPORTATION. Veracruz, the main street, runs southeast, angling off at its end to meet **Legazpi,** which runs north-south, along the beach. The **bus stop** is at Veracruz 226, on the corner of Nayarit. Turn left on Veracruz from the bus station to get to the *centro.* Primera Plus/Costa Alegre, Veracruz 269 (☎355 61 11), at Filipinas, has first-class service to: **Guadalajara** (5hr.; 7:45am, 3, 5, and 6pm; 192

pesos); **León** (9hr., 7:45am, 35 pesos); **Manzanillo** (1½hr., 4am, 39 pesos); **Mexico City** (13hr., 5pm, 1555 pesos); **Puerto Vallarta** (4hr., 1:45 and 4am, 135 pesos). Second-class buses go to **Guadalajara** (6hr.; 8:15, 11:15am, 2:15, and 8:15pm; 160 pesos); **León** (10hr., 8:15pm, 295 pesos); **Manzanillo** (1½hr.; 9 per day 7:15am-7:45pm; 32 pesos); **Puerto Vallarta** (5hr.; 7:45, 10:45am, and 2:45pm; 112 pesos).

🛈 PRACTICAL INFORMATION. The **tourist office**, at Jalisco 67, offers brochures and illegible maps. No English spoken. (☎355 51 00. Open M-F 9am-5pm.) Friendly Texans at **Crazy Cactus** (☎355 60 99), next to the church on Jalisco, between Legazpi and Veracruz, offer insider advice. The **travel agency**, Veracruz 204A, sells tickets for ETN buses departing from Manzanillo. (☎355 56 65 or 335 56 66; fax 355 56 67. Open M-Sa 10am-2pm and 4pm-7pm.) Barra has no bank, but a *casa de cambio*, **Cyber@Money,** Veracruz 212C, changes money and traveler's checks at high rates without commission (☎355 61 77. Open M-F 9:30am-2:30pm and 4-7pm, Sa 9:30am-2:30pm.) **Emergency:** ☎060. **Police:** Veracruz 179 (☎355 53 99). **Centro de Salud:** (☎355 62 20), on Puerto de la Navidad down Veracruz, just out of town. Take a right just before Veracruz is divided by a traffic island; it is the peach-colored building on the right. (24hr. emergency service. No English spoken.) No *casetas*, but **LADATEL** calling cards can be used at the phones that line the main streets. **Internet: Cyber@Money** sports aqua keyboards and a speedy connection. Also serves as the *casa de cambio* and a book exchange. (45 pesos per hr. Open M-F 9:30am-2:30pm and 4pm-7pm, Sa 9:30am-2:30pm.) **Post Office:** Mazatlán 11, behind Veracruz. (Open M-F 8am-3pm, Sa 8am-noon.) **Postal code:** 48987.

🛏🍴 ACCOMMODATIONS AND FOOD. Budget accommodations in Barra will be found only by the keen-eyed traveler. Reasonable rooms are occasionally available in private residences—ask around and look for signs in restaurants. All prices are subject to high-season hikes. **Posada Pacífico,** Mazatlán 136, has clean, spacious rooms, most with balcony, centered around a tree-filled courtyard. Couches and chairs in the open hallways provide a cool place to sit and meet your neighbors. The friendly staff offers all sorts of rentals: coolers (10 pesos), boogie boards (20 pesos), beach chairs (15 pesos), and bicycles (40 pesos. ☎355 53 59, fax 355 53 49. Singles 130 pesos; doubles 180 pesos.) **Hotel Caribe,** Sonora 15, has passable pastel rooms with fans and fluorescent-lit desks. The large lobby is enlivened by socializing elderly ladies. (☎355 59 52. Singles 135 pesos; doubles 210 pesos; triples 250 pesos; TV 40 pesos extra.) **Mama Laya,** Veracruz 69, is the cheapest place to sleep. Turn left at the bus station and walk all the way down the road. Dusty rooms are spacious but dark. Communal bathrooms are adequate and have hot water, although the toilets look like they haven't been cleaned since 1980 and lack toilet paper. (Singles 100 pesos; doubles 140 pesos.) It's no longer possible to camp in Barra de Navidad; try Melaque.

For delicious, inexpensive Mexican food in a pleasant atmosphere, try **Restaurant Paty,** Jalisco 52 at Veracruz. Neon plaid tablecloths are even brighter in the outdoor sunshine and they offer a few vegetarian options. (Grilled chicken 35 pesos, enchiladas 20 pesos. Open daily 8am-11pm.) **Tacos Pitufos** (Smurf Tacos), Veracruz 130, is right outside the bus station. Join locals for tacos (5 pesos) and filling *quesadillas con carne* (10 pesos) under the fake greenery and Christmas decorations. (☎355 5808. Open daily 5pm-2am.) For a cheaper way to eat seafood than the beachfront restaurants, try **El Villano,** two blocks from the beach at Veracruz 153. (Fish tacos 6 pesos, fish soup 30 pesos. Open daily 9am-8pm.)

📷💃 SIGHTS AND ENTERTAINMENT. Crazy Cactus, at the corner of Jalisco and Veracruz, is closed during the summer but rents equipment the rest of the year. (☎355 60 99. Snorkeling gear and boogie boards 50 pesos per ½-day, 80 pesos per day; surfboards 70 pesos per ½-day, 120 pesos per day; bikes 100 pesos per day.)

The short trip across the lagoon to the village of **Colimilla** is pleasant; a *lancha* will deposit up to 10 passengers at the far end of the lagoon or amid Colimilla's

TELENOVELA, ANYONE? Every evening, grown men and women across Mexico can be found glued to their TV sets, clutching boxes of tissues, oblivious to the outside world. Why? They are watching *telenovelas*, the strange hybrid of soap opera and mini-series that monopolizes Mexico's airwaves from afternoon to late night. Each *telenovela* lasts between six months and a year and contains enough gooey love stories, heart-wrenching tragedies, and finger-gnawing cliff-hangers to put other series to shame. Characters and story lines are added and removed according to ratings; as a result, each show's plot is guided, in part, by audience response. For example, the protagonist of a show with poor ratings might suddenly get hit by a truck, allowing his younger, sexier brother to assume the leading role.

palms, pigs, cows, and open-air restaurants (150 pesos, from the cooperative stand on the left after Veracruz turns). Deserted **Playa de los Cocos**, 1km away, has larger breakers than those in Barra. If you don't want to swim back, remember to set a time to be picked up. Another option is to tour the **lagoon** behind Barra (up to 8 people, 150 pesos) or take a fully-equipped *lancha* (up to 4 people, 250 pesos per hr.) and go tuna or marlin **fishing**. Operators have formed a cooperative, so prices are fixed. Their office and docks lie at the end of Veracruz. (Open daily 7am-7pm.) Bibliophiles should not miss **Beer Bob's Book Exchange**, Mazatlán 61, a few blocks to the right as you face the Posada Pacífico. It's purely a book exchange—no cash involved. They have quite a collection. In the back room sit Bob and company, watching TV, playing cards, or engaging in "some serious beer-drinking." (Usually open M-F 1-4pm.)

Everyone out past midnight parties at **El Galeón Disco**, Morelos 24, in Hotel Sand's. Sit on cushioned, horseshoe-shaped benches and drink the night away. (☎355 50 18. Beer 15 pesos, mixed drinks 35 pesos. Cover 30 pesos. Open daily 9:30pm-3am, low season F-Sa only.) Those who prefer singing can chill at **Terraza Bar Jardín**, Jalisco 70, a **karaoke** bar above Mango Bay. (☎355 61 35. Beer 15 pesos. Open daily 6pm-2am.) Another popular rooftop hangout is **La Azotea**, upstairs at Legzapi 152. The thatched roof shelters an animal-themed patio, free pool table, and a great view of the sea. (☎355 50 29. Open daily 6pm-2am.) If you want to concentrate your efforts on drinking, make your way to **Piper Lovers**, Legazpi 154A, where the live music is good, drinks are cheap, and pool and ping-pong are free for customers. Piper himself embodies the spirit of the place—shirtless and barefoot, in cut-off camos, he'll drink you under the table, then fall asleep on it. (☎355 64 34. Beer 15-20 pesos, mixed drinks start at 25 pesos. Open M-Th noon-midnight, F-Sa noon-2am.) If you tire of Lovers, the many two-for-one happy hours along Legazpi make the giddy trip toward inebriation that much cheaper. At **Sunset**, on Legazpi across from the church, play pool or hit the dance floor while watching the waves nuzzle the coast. (☎355 54 64. Pool table deposit 20 pesos; 10 pesos all night. Beer 15 pesos, drinks 30 pesos. 2-for-1 happy hour 2-10pm. Open daily 2pm-2am.)

COLIMA

MANZANILLO   ☎3

With its golden sands, green waters, and bountiful sailfish, Manzanillo (pop. 124,000) has been touted as the emerald of the Pacific. However, eager resort builders have one strike against them—Manzanillo is the workhorse port of Mexico's Pacific coast, attracting ships from as far away as Russia, and conventional wisdom holds that a working port can never become a truly world-class resort. Indeed, Manzanillo's best beaches lie west of the dynamic, sweaty *centro*, beyond a huge stretch of barges and cranes. Those seeking only sand and surf would do better to retreat to a secluded village such as Cuyutlán, but for those excited by lively, crowded beaches—and the nightlife of a real city—Manzanillo delivers.

⌐ TRANSPORTATION

White and blue "Miramar" and "Centro" buses run back and forth between the *centro* and the resort strip at the west of town (½hr., every 15min. 5am-11pm, about 4.5 pesos from the *centro* to the beaches).

Airport: (☎333 25 25), Playa de Oro, between Barra de Navidad and Manzanillo. Airlines include: **AeroCalifornia** (☎334 14 14; Open M-F 8am-8pm, Sa-Su 9am-5pm), and **Mexicana,** (☎333 23 23. Open M-F 9am-6:45pm and Sa 9am-6pm). Both airlines have offices in the Comerical Mexicana shopping center, along the "Miramar" bus route. **Taxis** (☎333 19 99) from the airport to the *zócalo* 250 pesos.

Buses: station on Hidalgo, southeast of Jardín Obregón in the *centro*. You can take a taxi (13 pesos) or bus (3 pesos) to the *centro*. From the station, take a "Colomo" bus and get off near the PEMEX gas station. From there, follow the coastline 6min. to get to the Jardín. Estrella Blanca (☎322 04 32) goes to: **Acapulco** (12hr., 4pm, 360 pesos); **Lázaro Cárdenas** (6½hr., 4pm, 180 pesos); **Mazatlán** (12hr., 4pm, 430 pesos); **Mexico City** (14hr., 4pm, 474 pesos); **Puerto Vallarta** (6hr., 4pm, 170 pesos); **Tepic** (7hr., 4pm, 258 pesos); **Zijuatenejo** (9hr., 4pm, 235 pesos). Autobuses del Sur (☎322 10 03), La Línea/Autobuses de Occidente (☎322 01 23), Transportes Cihuatlán (☎322 05 15), and Primera Plus (☎322 02 10) offer similar services. Autobuses Nuevo Horizonte (☎322 39 00) runs to **Colima** (2½hr., 5 per day 8am-9:40pm, 39 pesos).

✳7 ORIENTATION AND PRACTICAL INFORMATION

Tourist Office: Costera Miguel de la Madrid 1033 (☎333 22 64; fax 333 14 26; sectur@bay.net.mx), 2 blocks past Fiesta Mexicana. Catch a "Miramar" bus (4.5 pesos) on México or near the Jardín and tell the driver where you're headed. Provides great maps. Open M-F 9am-3pm and 6-8:30pm, Sa 10am-2pm. **Information booths** in front of the *palacio*, around town, and along the beaches offer many of the same maps. Open daily 8am-10pm. Helpful **tourist police** (☎332 10 02) in the Palacio Municipal on the *zócalo* distribute maps and brochures.

Currency Exchange: Bital, México 99 (☎332 09 50), at 10 de Mayo. Changes traveler's checks before 6pm. Open M-Sa 8am-7pm. 24hr. **ATM.**

Market: Mercado 5 de Mayo, on 5 de Mayo at Guerrero, 5 blocks down México and 4 blocks left on Guerrero. Open daily 5am-5pm.

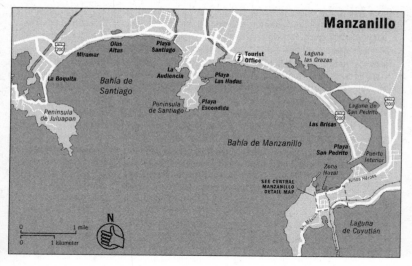

Supermarket: Comercial Mexicana, Costera de la Madrid km 11.5 (☎333 13 75). Take a "Miramar" bus from the *zócalo* (4 pesos). Open daily 8am-10pm.

Laundry: Lavi-Matic, Calle 1 #1 (☎332 08 44), 8 blocks down México, across the small plaza, to the left. Wash and dry 10 pesos per kg., 3kg minimum. Open daily 9am-5pm.

Emergency: ☎060.

Police: (☎332 10 02 or 332 10 04), in the Palacio Municipal. Little English spoken.

Red Cross: (☎336 57 70), on Barotes. No English spoken.

Pharmacy: Farmacia Guadalajara, México 301 (☎332 29 22), at Galindo, 4 blocks from the *zócalo.* Also sells food and has a small deli. Open 24hr.

Hospital: Centro Médico Quirurgico, Costero 1215 (☎334 04 44 or 334 16 66). Some English spoken.

Fax: Telecomm (☎332 30 30), in the Palacio Municipal, to the left of the stairs as you enter. Offers **Western Union,** telegraph, and fax services. Open M-F 8am-7:30pm, Sa-Su 9am-12:30pm.

Internet Access: Internet La Luna, México 69 (☎332 48 03), half a block from the *zócalo.* 25 pesos per hr., students 20 pesos per hr. Open daily 9am-9pm.

Car Rental: Hertz (☎333 31 41), on de la Madrid. Small VWs from 500 pesos a day. Open M-Sa 9am-1pm and 3-7pm, Su 9am-5pm. Airport office (☎333 31 91).

Post Office: Galindo 30 (☎332 00 22), 4 blocks down Av. México from the *zócalo,* on the right. Open M-F 9am-5pm, Sa 9am-1pm.

Postal Code: 28200.

ACCOMMODATIONS

Manzanillo's budget accommodations tend to be basic. In general, the area around the *zócalo* is safer than the bus station. **Camping** is permitted on Playa Miramar, but is only recommended during *Semana Santa* and in December, when bathroom facilities are available and security is heightened.

Hotel Flamingos, Madero 72 (☎332 10 37), 1 block south of the *zócalo.* Carved ceiling beams in lobby, red-tiled hallways, and woven bedspreads come at an incredibly low price. Rooms and baths are spacious and clean. Singles 90 pesos; doubles 120 pesos.

Hotel Emperador, Dávalos 69 (☎332 23 74), 1 block west of the plaza. The blank tile walls give this hotel a somewhat institutional feel. Small rooms with rustic wooden furniture are hot, but fans help cool things off. Baths are cramped but neat. Singles 100 pesos; doubles 120 pesos; triples 190 pesos.

Hotel Costa Manzanillo, Madero 333 (☎332 27 40), 4 blocks down México; go left on Galindo and right on Madero. Plants and bright bedspreads make the hotel cheery. Medium-sized rooms with baths and TVs. Singles 150 pesos; doubles 180 pesos.

Hotel San José, Cuauhtémoc 138 (☎332 51 05), 4 blocks down México, take a right at Galindo, which becomes Cuauhtémoc. The bright lime green courtyard opens onto clean, small rooms with firm beds. The tiny private baths are spotless, but so small that the lavatory is in the shower. Rooms for 1-2 people 150 pesos.

Casa de Huéspedes Doña Juanita, Allende 24 (☎332 67 70), near the corner of México. If you're pressed for cash and aren't picky about looks or amenities, this is the hotel for you. Small rooms have mismatched sheets and floor fans, and some lack windows. Bring your own toilet paper. Singles and doubles 70-90 pesos.

FOOD

Since tourists stake their claims closer to the beach, food at the market and downtown is simple and cheap. During the many festivities enlivening the *zócalo,* food vendors pop up at every corner offering homemade goodies. The obvious local specialty is fresh seafood—whether you prefer it in a spicy *diablo* sauce, sizzled up with lots of garlic, or as a greasy soup, good shrimp and fish dishes are easy to come by and inexpensive near the *jardín*.

🍽 **Mercado de Comida,** at Cuauhtémoc and Madero. Small, open-air eateries offer every imaginable type of seafood and *comida típica*. Squeeze yourself onto a bench and eat to your heart's content. Most dishes 18-40 pesos. Open daily 7am-10pm.

Restaurante Chantilly, Madero 60 (☎332 01 94), at Juárez on the plaza. Professionals and families feast on good staples in a diner-like setting. *Enchiladas* 32 pesos, tuna or chicken salad 32 pesos, meat 32-55 pesos. Open Su-F 7:30am-10:30pm.

Restaurant Emperador, Dávalos 69 (☎332 23 74), below Hotel Emperador. Packed with locals at all hours. Gargantuan *comida corrida* 27 pesos, delicious *enchiladas* 15 pesos; filling hot cakes 13 pesos. Open daily 8:30am-11pm.

Restaurant del Río, México 330 (☎332 25 25). A small, inexpensive place that will fill you up in no time with *comida corrida* (27 pesos) or Mexican specialties (13-28 pesos). Try a barbecue taco (4 pesos) and wash it down with a chilly beer (10 pesos) or *licuado* (9 pesos). Open M-Sa 8am-6pm.

🌊 BEACHES

Manzanillo's beaches stretch along two bays, **Bahía de Manzanillo** and **Bahía de Santiago,** formed by the Santiago and Juluapan peninsulas. Bahía de Manzanillo has more expensive hotels and cleaner, golden sand, but its beach slopes steeply, creating a strong and sometimes dangerous undertow. The beaches at Bahía Santiago are better protected and ideal for swimming, water sports, and sun worshipping.

PLAYA LAS BRISAS. The beach most accessible from the *centro* is Playa Las Brisas, on Bahía de Manzanillo. A few secluded spots remain, but it is for the most part crowded with luxurious hotels and bungalows. *(Take a taxi (25 pesos), the "Las Brisas" bus (4.5 pesos), or a "Miramar" bus and ask to be let off at the crucero (crossroads). Go left for more populated beaches or stake out a private spot nearer the junction.)*

OLAS ALTAS. Cleaner water and excellent beaches occupy the rest of the bay, west of Peninsula Santiago. Beyond **Olas Altas** lies **Miramar Beach,** popular with

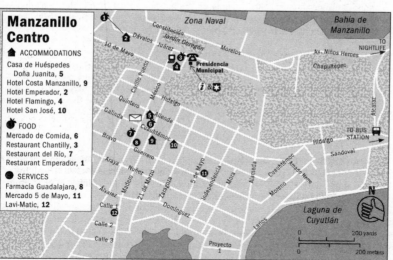

Manzanillo Centro

🏠 ACCOMMODATIONS
Casa de Huéspedes Doña Juanita, **5**
Hotel Costa Manzanillo, **9**
Hotel Emperador, **2**
Hotel Flamingo, **4**
Hotel San José, **10**

🍴 FOOD
Mercado de Comida, **6**
Restaurant Chantilly, **3**
Restaurant del Río, **7**
Restaurant Emperador, **1**

⬤ SERVICES
Farmacía Guadalajara, **8**
Mercado 5 de Mayo, **11**
Lavi-Matic, **12**

experienced surfers and infamous for its powerful waves and undertow. *(Get off where the footbridge crosses the route. Though crowded, here you'll find top-notch restaurants where you can rent bodyboards and surfboards for 20 pesos per hr.)*

PLAYA LA BOQUITA. The calmer waters of *palapa*-lined **Playa la Boquita,** the westernmost point on the Juluapan Peninsula, make it a popular spot for children and water sport enthusiasts. Be sure to make reservations for snorkeling (2hr., 10am, 200 pesos), scuba diving excursions (2hr., 10am, 500 pesos), and deep sea fishing (7 or 8am, 350 pesos per hr.). If you're not much of an underwater enthusiast, try taking a horse for a sandy jaunt (available for rent near the last of the palapa restaurants; 150 pesos per hr.), or riding in a banana boat (30 pesos). *(Take a "Miramar" bus to Club Santiago (40min., 4 pesos). Walk through the white gate along the cobblestone street that becomes a dirt road (25min.). Taxis 20 pesos.)*

PLAYA AUDIENCIA. This small but magnificent cove has calm waters, light brown sand, and a gorgeous, rocky vista. *(Take a "Las Hadas" bus (4.5 pesos) from Niños Héroes or anywhere on Miramar Rte. to the Sierra Radison and follow the path to the beach.)*

🎵 NIGHTLIFE

Manzanillo doesn't sleep when the sun sets, and trendy, tourist-oriented clubs along the resort strip play the latest music all night long. "Miramar" buses run along the strip until 9pm. Taxis back to the *centro* cost 30-50 pesos.

- 🎵 **Vog and Bar de Félix,** Costera de la Madrid km 9.2 (☎333 18 75), on the beach side. Both discos offer unadulterated, steamy, gyrating bliss. The 20s and 30s crowd at Bar de Félix greet every new Latin song with roaring applause while the US and Mexican tunes at more upscale Vog inspire dancing in every possible inch of space. Vog also offers a game area, with pool tables, foosball, and tall booths. Beer 20 pesos, national drinks from 30 pesos. Vog: cover 50 pesos. Open W-Sa 10:30pm-4am. Bar de Félix: 70-peso drink minimum F-Sa. Open Su-F, and Sa 6pm-6am, Su 9pm-4am.

- **Colima Bay Cafe,** Costera de la Madrid km 6.5 (☎333 11 50), on the beach side. Two bars, a sizable dance floor, and a terrace overlooking the Pacific provide plenty of space for dancing. The young, well-dressed crowd knows how to party. Beer 25 pesos, national drinks from 35 pesos. Cover 50 pesos. Open M-F 1pm-2am, Sa 1pm-4am.

- **Tropigala** (☎333 24 74), Costera de la Madrid near Santiago Beach. A crowd of all ages dances up an appetite, only to gorge on the all-you-can eat taco buffet (included in cover). Beer 25 pesos, national drinks from 35 pesos. Live tropical music 11pm-3:30am. Cover 40 pesos, Sa-Su 50 pesos. Open W-Su 9pm-4am.

CUYUTLÁN ☎3

The lush vegetation, black-sand beach, and mysterious lagoon of quiet Cuyutlán (pop. 1650) offer the traveler a few days of solitary paradise. In low season, darkened buildings and silent streets give it a ghost-town feel, and the huge golden head of Benito Juárez amidst the palm trees of Cuyutlán's *zócalo* is often the only face visible. Summer weekends are slightly busier, but it is only during high season (Dec. and *Semana Santa*) that Cuyutlán truly comes alive.

📋 **TRANSPORTATION.** Cuyutlán is an hour's ride down the coast from Manzanillo, off Mexico 200. The only way to get there is through **Armería,** on the highway about 15km inland. From Manzanillo, take a "Colima" bus (45min., every 15min. 5am-10:30pm, 22 pesos) from the station entrance and ask to get off at Armería. To reach the Terminal Sub-Urbana in Armería, exit at the blue "Paraíso" sign and follow the street to the left. If you get dropped off at the other terminal, walk one block left, go right and walk one more block to reach the Terminal Sub-Urbana. Buses to Cuyutlán leave from here (20min., every ½hr. 6:45am-7:30pm, 6.5 pesos). Buses return to Armería on the same schedule and pick up near the *zócalo*.

🔡🔢 ORIENTATION AND PRACTICAL INFORMATION. The road from Armería parallels the coast and becomes **Yavaros** as it enters town. It intersects **Hidalgo**, which marks the eastern border of the *zócalo;* a left at this intersection takes you to the beach. **Veracruz,** Cuyutlán's other mighty boulevard, parallels Yavaros, one block off the beach. Most of Cuyutlán's municipal services are within one block of the *zócalo.* To get to the beach from the *zócalo,* take a right on Hidalgo. **Currency Exchange:** the English-speaking owners of **Hotel Fenix** will change money if they have the cash. **Police:** (☎ 326 40 14) 2 blocks from the *zócalo* on Hidalgo. The friendly, non-English-speaking officers also provide what little tourist information is available in town. To get to the **Centro de Salud,** take a right onto Yavaros from the *zócalo* and walk 1½ blocks—the center will be on your left.

🔠🔣 ACCOMMODATIONS AND FOOD. Hotels are well-maintained, affordable, and comfortable. During high season, rates skyrocket to 200 pesos per person, and meals are included to help justify the price. Make reservations a month in advance during this time. The rooms at **Hotel Fenix,** Hidalgo 201, at Veracruz, may be taller than they are wide, but the second story is encircled by a breezy porch with hammocks, windchimes, and a great view of the ocean. The friendly owners run a popular bar that serves as the town watering hole. (☎ 326 40 82. 70 pesos per person. Make reservations 2 months in advance for high season stays.) **Hotel Morelos,** Hidalgo 185, at Veracruz, has spacious rooms with clean baths and wooden furniture. Tiled floors, festive colors, a restaurant, a small pool, and all the artificial flowers in Cuyutlán give the place pizazz. (☎ 326 40 13. 200 pesos per person including 3 meals, 100 pesos without meals. During high season, 230 pesos per person including 3 meals, 130 pesos without meals.) **Hotel Casa Grande,** Hidalgo 139, offers the cheapest beds in town, as well as showerhead-less showers, crumbling cement walls, and mildewy tile. (40 pesos per person.) Unofficial camping sites lie 200m from Cuyutlán's hotels. Some travelers string hammocks among the *palapas* near the hotels. Campers and daytrippers can use the pool (15 pesos), showers (10 pesos), and bathrooms (5 pesos) at Hotel Morelos. Almost all of the food in Cuyutlán is served up in **hotel restaurants;** seafood (40-70 pesos) is the obvious specialty. During the day, cheaper fare can be found in *loncherías* around the *zócalo.*

🔳🔲 SIGHTS AND ENTERTAINMENT. Cuyutlán's ◼black sand beaches are well patrolled by life guards, who post flags indicating surf conditions. Although the shore is packed with families near the Hidalgo entrance, the crowd thins out rapidly at either end, making it easy for you to stake out your own space. Aside from its gorgeous beach, Cuyutlán's biggest claim to fame is the **green wave,** a phenomenon that occurs regularly April through June. Quirky currents and phosphorescent marine life combine to produce 10m swells that glow an unearthly green. The town itself reaches high tide during the **Festival de la Virgen de Guadalupe,** the first 12 days of December when twice a day men, women, and children clad in traditional dress walk 5km to the town's blue church. The celebrations peak on the 12th day, when *mariachis* accompany the procession, and the marchers sing tributes to the Virgin. To get your historic-cultural fix, check out the **Museo de Sal,** one block right from the *zócalo* on Juárez. This dirt-floor museum depicts the history of Cuyutlán, and features a huge model of the salt-making process that aided in the town's development. If you must have a souvenir, 5kg bags of locally-made salt are available at the entrance for 8 pesos. (Open daily 8am-6pm. Voluntary donation.) Cuyutlán's **Tortugario,** 3.5km east of town along Veracruz, is a combination wildlife preserve and zoo. Home to turtles, iguanas, and crocodiles, the Tortugario also has saltwater pools for (human) swimming. Taxis will take you there (40 pesos from Armería, 60 pesos from Cuyutlán), or you can ask the bus driver to let you off by the Tortugario sign between Armería and Cuyutlán, then follow the dirt road 3 km. (Open daily 8:30am-5:30pm. 10 pesos, children 5 pesos.)

PARAÍSO ☎3

Paraíso outclasses nearby **Armería**, but not by much. Pretty black-sand beaches make for good swimming, but the lack of amenities make it a less desirable getaway than Cuyutlán. Nevertheless, Paraíso is popular among Mexicans for day-trips and weekend vacations.

⊡ TRANSPORTATION. A well-paved road connects Armería and Paraíso, cutting through 7km of banana and coconut plantations before ending at the black sands surrounding Paraíso's few hotels and beachfront restaurants. Follow directions to Cuyutlán, but instead take a "Paraíso" bus (15min., every ½hr. 6:45am-7:30pm, 5 pesos) from Armería's Terminal Sub-Urbano. Buses return on the same schedule.

⬛⬛ ORIENTATION AND PRACTICAL INFORMATION. Besides the main road from Armería, Paraíso's other street is the dirt **Juventud** (also called **Adán y Eva**), which runs behind the beachfront restaurants. The **police station** (☎322 09 90) is two blocks up from Juventud on the main road. No English spoken. Basic medical attention can be found at the **Centro de Salud**, next to the police station. Long-distance **phone calls** can be made from **Abarrotes Valdovinos**, next to the bus stop. (☎322 00 25. Open daily 9am-2pm and 4-9pm.)

⬛⬛ ACCOMMODATIONS AND FOOD. At the far right end of the strip lies **Hotel Valencia.** Bright bedspreads and artificial flowers keep the neat rooms upbeat. (☎322 04 57. Singles and doubles 120 pesos; triples and quads 140 pesos.) At the other end of the strip you'll find **Hotel Paraíso,** whose run-down exterior belies the comfortable, clean rooms within. Beach-front rooms are cheery with yellow tile and pictures, but lack hot water. For more amenities, ask for one of the rooms across the street, with hot water, TVs, and balconies. A jungle-theme mural adds a splash of color to the popular pool. (☎317 18 25. Singles and doubles 225 pesos, with hot water 255 pesos.) The first building to the left at the beach entrance is **Hotel Equipales,** where you'll find no-frills rooms with a view of the shore. The cramped bathrooms leave much to be desired, especially since there is no hot water. (☎332 09 90. Singles and doubles 120 pesos; triples and quads 180 pesos.) Paraíso's extensive beach makes a soft pillow for campers, and Hotel Paraíso provides free access to showers and bathrooms. (Pool access 10 pesos.) Some beachside restaurant owners let you hang hammocks under their thatched roofs. During high season, rooms may be available in **private houses;** ask in stores.

Restaurants run the slim gamut from rustic *enramadas* to cement-floored *comedores*, with seafood-dominated menus. **Restaurant Paraíso**, in Hotel Paraíso at the east end of Juventud, provides snappy service, and string quartets and *mariachis* sometimes appear in the afternoon. (Breakfast 18-28 pesos, tasty shrimp dishes 65 pesos. Open daily 8am-6pm.) The restaurant at **Hotel Valencia** also offers a pleasant atmosphere and seafood dishes (35-70 pesos; Open daily 8am-6pm.)

COLIMA ☎3

Stately Colima (pop. 130,000) maintains a measure of small-town benevolence and informality. On Sundays, slews of stores close shop as families attend mass, walk in the park, or sit and listen to *mariachi* bands in the gazebo of Plaza Principal. In the shadows of El Volcán de Fuego and El Nevado, Colima has experienced its fair share of natural disasters—many of its colonial buildings have suffered the wrath of the volcanoes. Still, despite the looming giants, under-touristed Colima is blessed with cool mountain air, a string of museums, beautiful plazas, and the Universidad de Colima, making it a rewarding place to stop en route to the coast.

☞ TRANSPORTATION

Airport: Aeropuerto Nacional Miguel de la Madrid (☎314 41 60), 2hr. from town. Served by **AeroCalifornia** (☎314 48 50) and **AeroMéxico** (☎313 80 57). **Taxis** (☎313 05 24) from the airport cost 90 pesos.

Bus: Estación Nueva is on the northeast side of town, about 2km from the *centro*. To get there, pick up a "Ruta 5" on Bravo, or "Ruta 4" on Zaragoza (every 5min. 6am-8:30pm, 3.5 pesos), or take a taxi (40 pesos). From the station, Primera Plus (☎314 80 67) sends 1st-class buses to: **Aguascalientes** (6hr., 4pm, 295 pesos); **Guadalajara** (2¾hr., every hr. 5:15am-7:30pm, 128 pesos); **León** (6½hr., 12:30pm, 287 pesos); **Manzanillo** (1hr., every 2hr. 2am-11:40pm, 45 pesos); **Mexico City** (10hr., 9 and 11:30pm, 464 pesos); **Melaque** (3hr., 10:40pm, 75 pesos) via **Puerto Vallarta** (6½hr., 10:40pm, 193 pesos); **Tecomán** (45min., 6:40 and 9pm, 25 pesos). Autobuses de Occidente/La Línea (☎314 87 81), Estrella Blanca (☎312 84 99), Omnibus de México (☎312 16 30) and Autotransportes Galeana (☎313 47 85) have similar service. ETN (☎312 58 99), goes to the **Guadalajara airport, Manzanillo, Mexico City**, and **Morelia. Terminal Suburbana**, known to locals as **Central los Rojos**, is southwest of the *centro*, and offers 2nd-class regional service. The fastest way to get there is to take a "Ruta 2 bus" from Morelos, near Jardín Quintero.

⁊ PRACTICAL INFORMATION

Tourist Office: Hidalgo 96 (☎312 43 60; fax 312 83 60; turiscol@palmera.colimanet.com), at Ocampo, between Plaza Principal and Jardín Núñez. Helpful staff, pamphlets, and maps. English spoken. Open M-F 8:30am-8:30pm, Sa 10am-2pm.

Currency Exchange: Banamex, Hidalgo 90 (☎312 02 85), 1 block east of Plaza Principal, has a 24hr. **ATM.** Open M-F 9am-5pm, Sa 9am-2pm. **Multicambios de Colima** (☎330 12 20), Juárez at the corner of Jardín Nuñez, offers check and currency exchange at slightly better rates. Open M-Sa 9am-7:30pm.

Luggage Storage: At the bus station. 3 pesos for the 1st 6hr., 0.5 pesos per hr. after that. Open daily 9am-8pm. Restaurants offer assistance after hours.

Laundry: Lavandería Automática Amana, Domínguez 147 (☎314 48 41), behind Hospedajes del Rey. 9 pesos per kg, 3kg minimum. Open daily 8am-9pm.

Car Rental: SuperAutos, Sevilla del Río 690-L (☎313 26 26). **National,** Camino Real 399A (☎333 06 11).

Emergency: ☎066.

Police: (☎312 09 67 or 312 25 66). Across from the bus station on Carretera Guadalajara. No English spoken.

Red Cross: (☎313 87 87) Aldama at Obregón. No English spoken.

Pharmacy: Farmacia Guadalajara, Madero 16 (☎314 64 64), at de la Vega. Also has a **supermarket** section. Open 24hr. 2nd location at Hidalgo, on Plaza Principal.

Medical Assistance: Hospital Civil (☎312 02 27), San Fernando at Zandoval. No English spoken. **Centro de Salud** (☎312 00 64 or 312 32 38), Juárez at 20 de Noviembre. No English spoken. Open daily 7am-8pm.

Fax: Telecomm, Madero 243 (☎312 60 64), in the same building as the post office. Open M-F 8am-7:30pm, Sa-Su 9am-noon.

Internet: Colegio Nacional de Capacitación Intensiva, Hidalgo 83 (☎312 01 50), off the southeast corner of Jardín Quintero. 20 pesos per hr. Open daily 8am-10pm. **Ciber-Cafe,** Sevilla del Rio 80, 2nd fl. of Plaza Country Mall. Follow Sandoval past Fernando and turn left on Sevilla del Rio. 25 pesos per hr., students 20 pesos per hr. Open daily 9am-10pm.

Post Office: Madero 247 (☎312 00 33), on the northeast corner of Jardín Núñez. Open M-F 9am-5pm, Sa 9am-1pm.

Postal Code: 28001.

█ ACCOMMODATIONS

Cheap lodging may be found near Jardín Núñez, while higher-priced hotels surround the university. Rooms are generally well-kept and come with TVs.

Hotel La Merced, Juárez 82 (☎312 69 69), on the west side of Jardín Nuñez. Immaculate, decent-sized rooms with TV, fans, cozy wooden furniture, and a citrus scent. White-painted walls with cool green trim, warm tiles, and overhead beams give La Merced charm. Private parking lot. Singles 120 pesos; doubles 150 pesos, triples 210 pesos.

Hotel Colonial, Medellín 142F (☎313 08 77), between Morelos and Bravo, 2 blocks south of Jardín Quintero. Friendly staff. Rooms have fans, wicker chairs, wrought-iron beds, and spotless baths. Singles 100 pesos; doubles 120-150 pesos.

Hospedajes del Rey, Rey Colimán 125 (☎313 36 83), half a block from the southeast corner of Jardín Núñez. Enormous, plush rooms have fans, TVs, and wall-to-wall windows. You could eat off the bathroom floors. Singles 220 pesos; doubles 260 pesos.

Casa de Huéspedes Miramar, Morelos 265 (☎312 34 67), off the southeast corner of Jardín Núñez. A friendly family-run *posada* with breezy but decaying rooms. Bathrooms could use a good scrub and the smell downstairs will make you wonder where the dog pound is. Singles 80 pesos; doubles 120 pesos. Prices may be negotiable.

█ FOOD

Inexpensive meals with traditional favorites like *pozole blanco* and *sopitos*, made Colima-style with thinner tortillas, are easy to come by. Other local treats include the sweet, sometimes chocolatey *enchiladas colimenses*, and *entomatadas*, a spicy *picadillo* (ground beef) dish made with *tomatillos* (little green tomatoes). A jaunt down the side streets of Plaza Principal will lead to budget meals aplenty.

Samadhi, Medina 125 (☎313 24 98), 2½ blocks north of Jardín Núñez, next to the church. Delicious vegetarian cuisine served in a leafy courtyard. Slow service, but the food is worth it. Breakfast buffet 31 pesos, soy burger 21 pesos. Open M-Sa 8am-6pm.

Comedor Familiar El Trébol, 16 de Septiembre 59 (☎312 29 00), at Degollado on Plaza Principal. The Irish clover motif complements an enormous mural of Colima's twin volcanoes. A popular family spot. Modest *comida corrida* 18 pesos. Open Su-F 8am-11pm.

Los Naranjos, Barreda 34 (☎312 00 29), north of Jardín Quintero. Classy but affordable. Magazine-perusing baby-boomers sip coffee over orange tablecloths. Breakfast 15-35 pesos, *pollo a la mexicana* 33 pesos. Open daily 8am-11:30pm.

Cenaduría Selecta de Morelos, Morelos 292 (☎312 93 32), at Domínguez, 1 block off the southeast corner of Jardín Núñez. Delicious and cheap. Both *pozole* (pork stew) and *enchiladas dulces* (sweet enchiladas) come with a mountain of diced onions and fiery sauce (15 pesos). Speedy service. Open Tu-F 5-11pm, Sa 1-11pm, Su 1:30-11pm.

█ SIGHTS

While most visitors come to Colima primarily to explore the natural wonders nearby, the sage traveler will take advantage of Colima's quiet, untouristed Plaza Principal and discover the beauty within the city itself.

PLAZA PRINCIPAL. The gazebo and fountains of the plaza (officially **Jardín Libertad**) are bordered on the north by the **Palacio de Gobierno,** which contains historical murals. The double arcade around the plaza holds the **Museo Regional de Historia de Colima,** the city's newest museum and home to a collection of Pre-Hispanic ceramics and a creepy replica of a western Mesoamerican burial site. An eclectic art gallery shares the courtyard. *(Portal Morelos 1 at 16 de Septiembre and Reforma, on the south side of the plaza. Museum ☎312 92 28. Open Tu-Sa 9am-6pm, Su 5-8pm. 27 pesos; Su free.)*

SANTA IGLESIA CATHEDRAL. The Spanish first built a church on this spot in 1527, but an earthquake destroyed the original wood and palm structure, and a fire

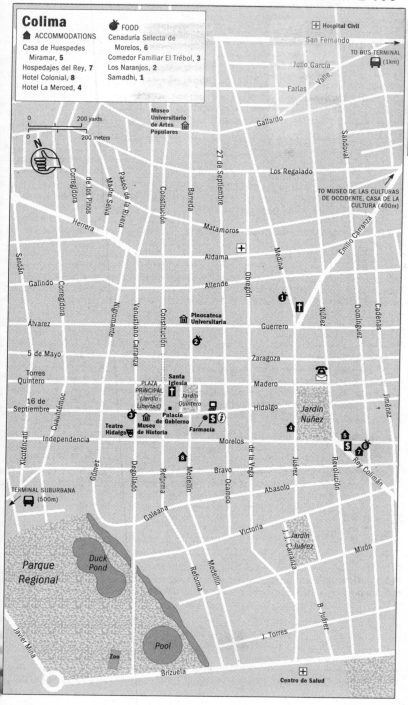

Colima

ACCOMMODATIONS
Casa de Huespedes Miramar, **5**
Hospedajes del Rey, **7**
Hotel Colonial, **8**
Hotel La Merced, **4**

FOOD
Cenaduría Selecta de Morelos, **6**
Comedor Familiar El Trébol, **3**
Los Naranjos, **2**
Samadhi, **1**

consumed its replacement. Undeterred, the Spanish built the current church, whose Neoclassical interior sparkles with gilt paint, chandeliers, polished marble, and statues. A statue of San Felipe de Jesús, the city's patron saint, resides in the pulpit designed by Othón Bustos. (*Adjoining Colima's Palacio de Gobierno on the east side of the plaza. ☎312 02 00. Open daily 6am-2pm and 4:30-8:30pm.*)

PINOCATECA UNIVERSITARIA. The center displays artwork of students and local painters and hosts performances and poetry readings. Call for a schedule of events. (*Guerrero 35 between Barreda and Constitución. ☎312 22 28. Open Tu-Sa 10am-2pm and 5-8pm, Su 10am-1pm. 10 pesos, students and children 5 pesos.*)

MUSEO UNIVERSITARIO DE ARTES POPULARES. The permanent collection includes stunning traditional dresses and masks, figurines recovered from nearby tombs, and descriptions of the Pre-Aztec western coast. 12ft. puppets decorate the central courtyard. A gift shop sells handmade reproductions of local ceramics. (*At Barreda and Gallardo. Catch the "Ruta 7" bus (3.5 pesos) on Barreda between Zaragoza and Guerrero, or walk 15min. north on 16 de Septiembre from the plaza. ☎312 68 69. Open Tu-Sa 10am-2pm and 5-8pm, Su 10am-1pm. 10 pesos, children and students 5 pesos; Su free.*)

MUSEO DE LAS CULTURAS DE OCCIDENTE. The museum features Colima's trademark ceramic figures, rarely seen outside the state, and provides an excellent Spanish narrative of the artifacts' significance to indigenous culture. The **Casa de la Cultura,** at the same site, is the best source of information on cultural events in Colima. (*Galván at Ejército Nacional, an easy ride from the centro. Take the yellow "Ruta #3 Sur" bus (3.5 pesos) on Colimán at Jardín Núñez, or a taxi (10 pesos). ☎313 06 08. Museum open Tu-Su 9am-7pm. 15 pesos. Casa de la Cultura open daily 8:30am-9pm.*)

LA CAMPANA. Named for its pre-excavation bell shape, La Campana's currently excavated area comprises only 1% of the estimated 125 acres this ceremonial center once occupied (1500 BC-AD1500). The discovery of these structures destroyed the myth that the west coast had no organized Pre-Hispanic civilizations or cultural centers. The site offers examples of the naturally-rounded stone and clay mortar architecture used in AD900 and of the technology of their drainage systems and burial practices. Site markers in Spanish and English. (*Flag down a "Ruta 7" bus on Constitución, between Jardín Libertad and Jardín Quintero (3.5 pesos) and get off just past the Comercial Mexicana, or take a taxi (13 pesos). Open Tu-Su 9am-5pm.*)

PARQUE REGIONAL METROPOLITANO. This park offers afternoon strolls or faster-paced buggy-cycles rides (15-17 pesos per 30min.) along a man-made duck pond, home to two large, brazen pelicans. Rent a *lancha* (8.5 pesos per hr.) for a closer view. A miniature **zoo** houses monkeys, crocodiles, and boars in disturbingly small cages while the pool across the street holds most of Colima's under-14 population. (*On Degollado, 4 blocks south of the plaza. ☎314 16 76. Open daily 7am-7pm. 1.5 pesos. Pool open W-Su 10:30am-4:30pm. Pool admission 7.5 pesos, children 7 pesos.*)

▶ NIGHTLIFE

Erupting volcanoes aren't the only things shaking in Colima. Hot nightclubs pull in locals and students with cheap beer and fast music. For something more relaxing, try a movie at **Plaza Country** (☎312 01 73; open daily 1pm-10pm; 28 pesos) or **Cine Soriana** (☎311 32 13; 33 pesos, W 20 pesos), both on Tecnológico/Sevilla del Río.

▨ **Argenta,** Sevilla del Río 615 (☎313 80 12), a 15-peso cab ride from the *centro*. The place to be if you know you're cool and know how to dance. Huge TV screen, lofty balcony, alternative crowd, and good ambience. Beer 15 pesos, national drinks 25-28 pesos. 2-for-1 beers. F cover men 30 pesos, women free. Open W-Sa 10pm-3am.

▨ **Dalí,** the Casa de la Cultura's cafe. Melancholy tunes pierce the air and wrench the heart, as prints of famous works compete with randomly shaped and placed windows to complete the "artistic" scene. Food isn't cheap, but it's worth it just to drink beer while a *tocador* wails from the cafe's small platform (9pm-midnight). *Muy romántico.* Beer 10-12 pesos, national drinks 30 pesos and up. Open daily 5:30pm-midnight.

La Belisaria, Domínguez 479 (☎312 86 88), a 10-peso cab ride from the plaza. Though there is no dance floor to speak of, the young crowd has no qualms about dancing between the tables. With the music blaring, don't expect to have meaningful conversation. Cover W men 100 pesos, women 30 pesos; F men 80 pesos, women 30 pesos; Sa men 50 pesos, women 25 pesos. Open bar W and Sa. Open W-Sa 10pm-3am.

Danza, Colón 113 (☎312 08 14). Colima's only gay night club is actually in the next town over, Villa de Álvarez, a 25-peso cab ride from the plaza. Though on the small side, the pool table, Madonna posters, and great dance music will leave you entertained. Transvestite shows F-Sa 2am. Cover F-Sa 25 pesos. Open Th-Su 9pm-4am.

Aha, Béjar 903 (☎313 77 08), in the southeast end of town, a 15-peso cab ride from the *centro.* Glowing eyes greet you at the entrance to this smoke-filled, dark club. Loud music will have you vibrating on the spacious dance floor. Beer 15 pesos, national drinks 30 pesos. Th open bar; cover men 80 pesos, women 20 pesos. F-Sa cover 30 pesos. Open Th-Sa 10:30pm-3am.

▶ DAYTRIPS FROM COLIMA

If you want to commune with nature, feel the heat of the nearby volcanoes, or relax by serene lakes and quiet towns, Colima serves as an ideal base.

VOLCÁN DE FUEGO AND LAGUNA MARÍA

Take a "Zapotitlán" bus from the Terminal Suburbana (1½hr.; 7am, 2:40, 5pm; 12.5 pesos. Returns at 8am, 3, 4:30pm) and tell the driver that you're visiting the lake/volcano. From the bus drop-off, it's a 10min. walk up a steep road. Since service is infrequent, locals may offer you rides to Comala or Colima if they see you waiting at the intersection.

In Náhuatl, Colima means "place where the old god is dominant." The old god is **El Volcán de Fuego** (3960m), 25km from Colima City. Puffs of white smoke continuously billow from the volcano, and lava was visible in 1994, when El Fuego reasserted its status as an active volcano. (Fear not—the tourist office assures visitors that the volcano is not a threat to the city.) Due to its unpredictable, temperamental volcanic nature, access to El Fuego is strictly controlled by an army outpost stationed in Yerbabuena, the last accessible town at the base of the mountain. The **Laguna María** lies right along the path up to the volcano. The still green water of the lagoon acts as a mirror, perfectly reflecting the natural beauty of Colima. The park offers hiking trails (some which lead up to spectacular views of the nearby volcano), fishing (15 pesos per hr. for equipment, 30 pesos per hr. for *lanchas*), and horseback riding (☎320 88 91; 50 pesos per hr.). Horses are permitted to leave the park, so your best bet for tackling El Volcán may be to ride your horse 4km up the cobblestone path to Yerbabuena, and from there determine the mood of the volcano—and of the *militares.* If you can't tear yourself away from the serenity of the lagoon, you can pitch your tent there (15 pesos per person) or stay in one of the *cabañas* (180 pesos for up to 6 people).

▨ EL NEVADO DE COLIMA

El Nevado is accessible by car or bus, but the last leg of the trip is only recommended for 4x4 vehicles. Autobuses Sur de Jalisco (☎312 03 16) runs buses to Ciudad Guzmán (1hr., every hr. 4:30am-8:30pm, 46 pesos), at the base of the volcano. From there, cranky 2nd-class buses (at the far right end of the bus station) limp up to El Fresnito, a village at the base of the mountain and home to several guides (8 per day 7am-8pm; 7 pesos, last return at 5:45pm). Guides with vans will transport you to La Joya, the highest point on the mountain accessible by automobile and the starting point for your epic mountain assault.

The nearby and slightly taller **El Nevado de Colima** (4335m) earned its name from the blanket of snow draping it in the winter. Although this volcano offers great opportunities for challenging mountain hiking, the park is open sporadically; if you're planning a trip to the top, call the Dirección de Pública (☎312 02 01; open

24hr.) or the police (☎312 18 01) for information. Augustín Ibarra (☎414 70 03) is a reputable guide who leads groups up to the summit. The "El Fresnito" bus drops you off in front of his house, where he'll cart you to La Joya in his 10-person van. The ascent should not be attempted solo or by those without sufficent hiking experience, especially during the rainy season.

LAGUNA CARRIZALILLO

Take an "El Naranjal" bus from the Terminal Suburbana (6 per day 7:05am-6:05pm; 12 pesos, last return at 7pm) and tell the driver you want to visit the lagoon. ☎315 57 89. Open 24hr. 5 pesos per person.

The waters and banks of **Laguna Carrizalillo** are full of life. Birds maintain a constant twitter in the trees, and lizards and frogs leap underfoot. Camping and horseback riding are available at this peaceful retreat 27km north of Colima, but Carrizalillo's biggest attraction is its incredible view of the volcano.

COMALA

Green buses head to Comala from Colima's Terminal Suburbano (45min., every 10min. 6am-10:30pm, 4.5 pesos). Taxis charge 45 pesos.

South of the lagoons and just 9km north of Colima is the picturesque town of Comala (pop. 19,000), known as "El Pueblo Blanco de America" (The White Town of America) for the original white facade of its buildings. The town's lovely *zócalo* is full of white benches, fountains, and orange trees and is bordered by cobblestone streets and lively restaurants serving *ponche* (a punch made from a variety of fruits, and liquor), one of the region's traditional drinks. The city's main claim to fame is its colony of indigenous artisans who craft wooden furniture and bamboo baskets. The **Cooperativa Artesenal Pueblo Blanco,** a small *tianguis* (market), stands just outside Comala's *centro*. To get there, follow Carranza from the southeast corner of the *zócalo*, continue across the bridge, and turn right into the compound just past the orange and green "Residential Campestre Comala" sign. You can browse through the exhibition gallery, or enter the workshops and glimpse the artisans in action. (☎315 56 00. Open M-F 9am-3pm, Sa 9am-2pm.) You can also find *artesanía* at the southeast corner of the *zócalo*.

To the east of the *zócalo* lies the **Iglesia San Miguel del Espíritu Santo** with its beautiful, sky-blue vaulted ceiling and dozens of pigeons. On the other side of the *zócalo* are the city offices, with a four-wall **mural** commemorating Comala's 130-year history and celebrating the "richness of its soil." Unfortunately, the birds who now control the church have graciously added their own splotchy art to the mural. For more information, contact Pedro Venegas, Director of Education, Culture, and Tourism, in the building south of the *zócalo*, next to Los Portales restaurant. (☎315 55 47. Available M-F 9am-2:30pm.)

Ask a taxi driver to take you to Comala's famous Zona Mágica—a segment of road where cars can have their engines turned off but still appear to run uphill. Optical illusion or freak of science, it's buckets o' fun.

SOUTHERN PACIFIC COAST

The glamorous oceanside resorts of the Southern Pacific Coast attract vacationing families by the thousands. Inland, lovely colonial cities and quiet mountain towns offer Spanish immersion courses, exquisite silver work, dazzling vistas, and a relaxing retreat from the frenzied streets and brilliant sun.

Because many of the region's indigenous Purépecha lived by rod and net, the Aztecs called the lands surrounding Lake Pátzcuaro **Michoacán** (Country of Fishermen). The distinctive Purépecha language and terraced agricultural plots have convinced scholars that the Purépecha were not originally indigenous, but immigrants from what is today Peru. Purépecha rule lasted from around AD 800, when they first settled Michoacán, to 1522, when the Spanish arrived. Michoacán's red, fertile soil, abundant rain, and mild weather make for bountiful crops, and agriculture swells the state's coffers. The gorgeous beaches and forested mountains attract wildlife enthusiasts and tourists aplenty.

The state of **Guerrero** has been blessed with good fortune. During the colonial period, the rich mining town of Taxco kept the state and most of New Spain swimming in silver. More recently, the state's riches have been earned along the rugged shores of the Pacific coast. In the 1950s, Acapulco became the darling of the international resort scene, and almost four decades later, neighboring Ixtapa and Zihuatanejo now accommodate their own packs of sun loving vacationers.

Oaxaca has been fractured into a crazy quilt by the rugged heights of the Sierra Madre del Sur. Despite its difficult terrain, the land has inspired a violent possessiveness in the many different peoples—Zapotecs, Mixtecs, Aztecs, and Spaniards—who have fought and died for the region. More than 200 indigenous tribes have occupied the valley over the past two millennia, and over one million *oaxaqueños* still speak *indígena* languages—over 20% of the state's population speaks no Spanish whatsoever. The rich cultural legacies and stunning ruins of Oaxaca's indigenous tribes delight the masses of travelers who come to revel in its diverse beauty. At first intimidating, the confusing network of mountain towns, tiny weaving villages, and pristine Pacific beaches soon begin to enchant.

HIGHLIGHTS OF THE SOUTHERN PACIFIC COAST

HIDE OUT in the gorgeous beaches of the stormy **Michoacán coast** (see p. 431), which boast powerful waves, privacy, and rugged terrain.

SKINNY DIP in a secluded waterfall pool at **Tzararecuita** (see p. 414).

ADORN yourself with pretty silver jewelry in **Taxco** (see p. 433), and enjoy magnificent mountain views from the narrow, hillside streets.

GAZE at your toes through the crystal clear waters of **Barra de Potosí** (see p. 444) and other pristine beaches along the northern **Guerrero coast** (see **Costa Grande**, p. 444), while munching on fresh *pescadillas* (fish tacos) and working on your tan.

BARGAIN for a good price on devil masks, copper vases, woven shawls, guitars, and whatever else tickles your fancy in **Pátzcuaro** (see p. 416).

KICK BACK in **Puerto Escondido** (see p. 481) and nearby **Zipolite** (see p. 478), which draw legions of backpackers ready to sun, surf, and smoke on the beach.

EXPLORE the the ruins at **Monte Albán** (see p. 468), the most important Pre-Hispanic historical site in the region and one of the best preserved in Mexico.

Michoacán de Ocampo

MICHOACÁN DE OCAMPO

URUAPAN ☎ 4

Engulfed in red soil, rolling hills, and rows of avocado trees, Uruapan (ur-oo-AH-pan; pop. 300,000) sits on a checkerboard of farmland wrested from the surrounding jungle. Mountain air and plenty of rain keep the city lush and green year-round. While Uruapan is developing into an important center of commerce, the surrounding countryside remains a naturalist's dream. Tourists come in droves to explore the nearby waterfall, national park, and **Paricutín Volcano.**

▐ TRANSPORTATION

Uruapan lies 120km west of Morelia and 320km southeast of Guadalajara. To reach the *centro* from the **bus station** on Juárez in the northeast corner of town, hail a taxi (18 pesos) or hop on a "Centro" bus. Later in the day, you may have to wait at the bus stop on the street in front of the station (3.5 pesos). Most services are clumped near the *zócalo*, where two separate streets—**Vicente Carranza** and **Emilio Carranza**—honor the Carranza clan.

From the station, La Línea/Autobuses de Occidente (☎523 18 71) sends first-class buses to **Colima** (9:45pm, 165 pesos); **Guadalajara** (4½hr., 8 per day, 138 pesos); **Lázaro Cárdenas** (8:30pm and 11:45pm, 160 pesos); **Manzanillo** (9:45pm, 205 pesos); **Mexico City** (7hr.; 11pm, midnight, and 1am; 226 pesos); **Morelia** (2hr.; 10pm, midnight, 1am; 75 pesos); **Zamora** (2hr.; 3, 4:45am, and 3:15pm; 55 pesos); and **Zitcuaro** (3:45 and 10:30pm, 118 pesos). Second-class buses service the same destinations at slightly lower prices. Primera Plus/Flecha Amarilla (☎524 39 82) and ETN (☎523 86 08) have similar service at higher prices. Autotransportes Galeana/Ruta Paraíso (☎524 41 54) and Parhikini (☎523 87 54) offer regional services.

☑ PRACTICAL INFORMATION

Tourist Office: Casa Regional del Turista, E. Carranza 36 (☎524 30 91), about 3 blocks from the *zócalo*. The friendly folks here provide good maps. Some English spoken. Open daily 9am-7:30pm. If you arrive in Uruapan on a weekend, you can go to the **information booth** in the bus station for the same maps (Open Sa-Su 9:30am-6pm).

Currency Exchange: Bancomer, Carranza 7 (☎524 14 60), offers good exchange rates and a 24hr. **ATM.** Open M-F 8:30am-4pm. A block south of the *zócalo* on Cupatitzio, many other banks have competitive exchange rates and ATMs.

Luggage Storage: At the bus station. 5 pesos per bag per day. Open daily 7am-11pm.

Laundry: Autoservicio de Lavandería, Carranza 47 (☎520 99 38), at García. Full service wash and dry 35 pesos per 3kg. Open M-Sa 9am-2pm and 4-8pm.

Emergency: ☎060.

Police: (☎523 27 33 or 524 06 20), at Eucaliptos and Naranjo. Some English spoken.

Red Cross: Del Lago 1 (☎524 15 88), a block from the hospital. No English spoken.

Pharmacy: Farmacia Guadalajara, Carranza 3 (☎524 27 11). Open 24hr.

Medical Services: Hospital Civil, San Miguel 6 (☎524 80 40 or 524 80 96), 7 blocks west of the northern edge of the *zócalo*. No English spoken.

Fax: Caseta Telefónica, 15 de Febrero 12A (☎523 62 11). Open M-F 7am-9pm, Sa 9am-2pm.

Internet Access: Júparakua, Independencia 33 (519 04 32). 15 pesos per hour. Open daily 10am-10pm. **Caseta Telefónica** also has Internet access for 15 pesos per hr.

Post Office: Reforma 13 (☎523 56 30), 3 blocks south of the *zócalo* on Cupatitzio and 1 block left. Open M-F 8:30am-3:30pm, Sa 9am-1pm.

Postal Code: 60000.

♖ ACCOMMODATIONS

The ritzy and affordable coexist on or near the *zócalo* in Uruapan. Straying too far could be hazardous to your health: cheaper hotels, oozing east of the *zócalo*, tend to be filthy, sleazy, and infested.

Hotel del Parque, Independencia 124 (☎524 38 45), 5½ blocks from the plaza and half a block from Parque Nacional. Far and away the best place to stay. Large rooms circle an airy patio, and squeaky clean baths are beloved by backpackers. Make reservations in advance for weekends. Singles 100 pesos; doubles 140 pesos; triples 160 pesos.

Hotel Los Tres Caballeros, Constitución 50 (☎524 71 70). Go north up Degollado, the eastern border of the *zócalo,* then plunge into the market for about 2 blocks; the hotel is on the right before you emerge at 16 de Septiembre. Red tile floors and stone stairways lend subtle charm. Rooms are very clean, but tiny baths may cramp your style and legs. Singles 75 pesos; doubles 130 pesos; triples 160 pesos.

Hotel Moderno, Degollado 4 (☎524 02 12), next door to Hotel Oseguera on the east side of the *zócalo*. A semi-shabby place, but peach-colored rooms with dark wood furniture are pleasant. Birds, both live and stuffed, keep watch over the lobby TV. Get used to the jingle of the electric pony ride at the front door. 60 pesos per person.

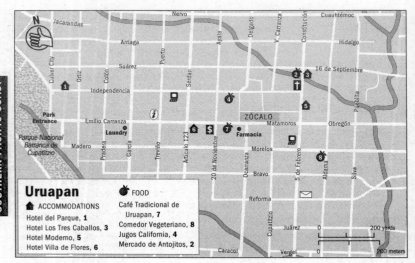

Uruapan

🏠 ACCOMMODATIONS

Hotel del Parque, **1**
Hotel Los Tres Caballos, **3**
Hotel Moderno, **5**
Hotel Villa de Flores, **6**

🍎 FOOD

Café Tradicional de
    Uruapan, **7**
Comedor Vegeteriano, **8**
Jugos California, **4**
Mercado de Antojitos, **2**

Hotel Villa de Flores, E. Carranza 15 (☎ 524 28 00), less than 2 blocks west of the *zócalo*. A reasonably priced nice hotel, Flores lives up to its name with a beautiful flower-dappled courtyard and glowing lavender walls. Spacious rooms have big windows, high wood-beamed ceilings, and attractive tiled baths. Singles 250 pesos; doubles 330 pesos; triples 360 pesos.

🍴 FOOD

Near the *zócalo*, the surrounding farmland means delicious avocado, tomato, and mango dishes are available for next to nothing. Coffee is a local specialty, and most places serve it strong and hot. For the cheapest meals in town, try the food stands and small restaurants inside the *mercado*.

🍎 **Mercado de Antojitos,** between Constitución and V. Carranza, on the north side of the *zócalo*. An outdoor square where dozens of eager restaurateurs vie for your taste buds with unique house specialties and standard Mexican favorites (15-25 pesos). Local musicians wander through to serenade families. Open daily 8am-midnight.

Comedor Vegetariano, Morelos 14 at Aldama, 1 block south of Carranza, serves a variety of *licuados,* including concoctions for stomach problems and colds (7-10 pesos); soy *milanesa tortas* (13 pesos). Open M-F 9am-8pm, Sa 9am-5pm, Su 1-5pm.

Jugos California, Independencia 9, just off the *zócalo*. Get your health food kicks under artificial palms. Huge *licuados* served in giant bowl-glasses 8-16 pesos, freshly made fruit-flavored yogurt in banana split dishes 9 pesos, *tortas* 13-16 pesos. *Nutri-jugos* (16 pesos) specially blended to cure what ails you. Open daily 7:30am-10pm.

Cafe Tradicional de Uruapan, E. Carranza 5B, (☎ 523 56 80), west of the *zócalo*. Follow your nose here, where locals sip their *cafe* so slowly they might lose a race with a 2nd-class Mexican train. Dining here is like sitting inside a cigar box—the entire cafe is covered in richly stained wood. Enjoy a sandwich (15-27 pesos) and a wide variety of coffee (9-24 pesos). Breakfast 24-45 pesos. Open daily 8am-10pm.

🎵 📷 ENTERTAINMENT AND NIGHTLIFE

Most of Uruapan's dazzling sights are located outside the city. For more local entertainment, visit **Parque Nacional Barranca del Cupatitzio,** on San Miguel at the western end of Independencia. A stunning bit of jungle right on the edge of town, the park brims with waterfalls, dense vegetation, shaded cobblestone walkways, and a fishing pond. (☎524 01 97. Open daily 8am-6pm. 8 pesos; children under 10 and adults over 70, 4 pesos.) Though it may be tempting to get lost in the jungle, worthwhile art exhibits, occasional movie screenings, and an archaeological and historical museum await at the **Casa de Cultura**, Ortiz 1, off the north side of the *zócalo*. (☎524 76 13. Open daily 10am-8pm.)

Much of the after-hours scene is in cafes. **Cafe Sol y Luna**, Independencia 15A, about two blocks west of the *zócalo*, has live music and a relaxed atmosphere. (☎524 06 294. Coffee 9-17 pesos, beer 15-18 pesos, national drinks from 33 pesos. Occasional cover 10-20 pesos. Live music F-Sa night. Open M-Th 11am-9:30pm, F-Su 11am-midnight.) The main *discotecas*, **La Scala** and **Euforias**, both at Puertas de Capitzio 12 in Colonia Huerta del Cupatitzio, are outside of town on the road to Tzaráracua, a 20-peso cab ride from the *centro*. A young, local crowd grooves amidst dense fog at La Scala. (☎524 26 09. Beer 20 pesos, drinks from 25 pesos. Cover 30 pesos Tu-Th and Su; 50 pesos F-Sa. Open Tu-Su 6pm-2am.) Gilt angels smile down onto techno, fog, video screens, and hair gel at Euforias. (☎523 93 32. Beer 20 pesos, drinks from 25 pesos. Cover, with open bar, Th men 100 pesos, women 40 pesos; F no cover; Sa cover 50 pesos. Open Th-Sa 9pm-3am.)

🔀 DAYTRIPS FROM URUAPAN

Uruapan is a convenient place for exploring the interior of Michoacán. The checkered landscape encompasses everything from ill-tempered volcanoes to picture-perfect waterfalls. If you're saturated with natural beauty, check out the revered image of Christ in **San Juan Nuevo** that was rescued by the village after a volcano eruption. In nearby **Paracho**, a world-famous guitar competition rages for two weeks in August.

PARICUTÍN VOLCANO

From the station, Autotransportes Galeana/Ruta Paraíso provides service to Angahuán, headed for Los Reyes (☎524 41 54; 30min, every ½hr. 5am-8pm, 12 pesos). From your stop, walk 3km to the Centro Turístico on the other side of the village. Go straight down the main road, right at the market, and left at the sign for the Centro Turístico. To return, wait for buses on the other side of the stop (every half hr., last bus 8:30pm.)

A visit to the still-active Paricutín Volcano makes a great daytrip from Uruapan. In 1943 the volcano began erupting, and by the time it quit spewing lava eight years later, the surrounding land was coated in thick porous lava. Entire towns had been consumed and a 700m mountain had sprung up. The lava covered the entire village of San Juan, save part of the church, which now sticks out of a field of cold, black stone. Horse rentals are available at Angahuán's **Centro Turístico.** (180 pesos. Open daily 9am-7pm). Plan to get an early start to avoid the frequent afternoon thunderstorms, and bring warm clothing; the trip is long but worth the time (4.5km to the church and 13km to the volcano). If you decide to tackle the volcano on your own, take care and ask directions first—trails are poorly marked. The Centro Turistico has a small museum (8 pesos) and restaurant. Cabins are available for rent from the tourist center (1-6 people 400 pesos; bunks 70 pesos).

SAN JUAN NUEVO PARANGARICUTIRIMICUARO

From the Uruapan bus station, take an Autotransportes Galeana/Ruta Paraíso bus (☎524 41 54) to San Juan Nuevo (40min., every 10min. 5am-8pm, 6 pesos). To get back, wait for the same bus on the corner of Cárdenas and Iturbe 2 blocks from the cathedral.

Ten kilometers west of Uruapan is San Juan Nuevo, founded after the destruction of the old village by the Paricutín Volcano in 1943. Many devotees visit the village—to see the **Lord of Miracles,** an image of Christ dating back to the late 16th century. When the volcano erupted, San Juan's 2000 inhabitants abandoned the village and began a three-day, 33km pilgrimage carrying their beloved icon. A beautiful rose brick sanctuary with pastel tiles was eventually built to house the image. The interior's white walls and vaulted ceilings are adorned with gold leaf, delicate stained-glass windows, and sparkling chandeliers. Not quite as refined is the gaudy blue neon sign above the statue that reads "*Sí de los Milagros, en ti confío*" ("Lord of Miracles, I trust in you." Open daily 6am-8pm; mass held Su about every hr. 6:30am-1:30pm and 5-7pm.) The **museum,** Av. 20 de Noviembre, a block past the cathedral down the street to the right once you exit the church, has photos of the eruption. (Open M-F 10am-6:30pm, Sa-Su 8am-6:30pm. Free.)

Besides its church and icon, San Juan Nuevo contains little, but a **mercado** in front of the cathedral sells *artesanía* at good prices. By following the market as it wraps behind the cathedral, you'll stumble across the cheapest and tastiest food in town. Plop down on a bench before *rebozo*-clad women stirring giant vats of *mole* and patting distinctive blue corn tortillas. If stranded, **Hotel Victoria,** Cárdenas 26, on the left as you exit the cathedral, will lodge you. Some of the large rooms with spotless mint green baths have cathedral views. (☎594 00 10. Rooms 140 pesos.)

▨ TZARÁRACUA AND TZARARECUITA

"Zapata-Tzaráracua" buses leave from the south side of the zócalo (25min., every hr. 7am-5pm, 5 pesos). Return bus meets in the parking lot (on the hr. till 6pm). Taxis 40 pesos.

The waterfalls at **Tzaráracua** (sah-RA-ra-kwa), 10km from Uruapan, cascade 20m into small pools surrounded by lush vegetation. The first waterfall, Tzaráracua, is about 1km from the parking lot. Walk down the steps to the right or ride a horse (40 pesos round-trip, from the parking lot), down the rocky path to the left. At the main waterfall look but don't swim—there's a dangerous undercurrent. Walk over the water on the bridge or ask a worker to bring you in a suspended boxcar. (Open daily 9am-6pm. 5 pesos, children 2 pesos; parking 5 pesos; cable car 2 pesos.)

Tzararecuita, a waterfall with two smaller pools perfect for swimming, is 1.5km beyond Tzaráracua. Swim naked if you like. The aid of a guide is necessary to find the falls since there are many confusing trails. Ask one of the boys hanging around at the bridge or the horse handlers in the parking lot. Most ask 40 pesos.

PARACHO

From the Uruapan bus station, take an Autotransportes Galeana/Ruta Paraíso bus (☎524 41 54) bound for Paracho (45min., every 30 min. 4am-8:30pm, 9 pesos).

Thirty kilometers north of Uruapan, Paracho gives aspiring *guitarristas* a chance to strum their hearts out and unleash the *mariachi* within. Carefully crafted six-strings pack just about every store, and fantastic bargains are available for all varieties of guitar. The **Casa de Arte y Cultura,** on the corner of the plaza, also has displays on guitars. (Open daily 10am-8pm.) For two weeks in August, the town holds an internationally renowned **guitar festival.** Musicians and craftspeople partake in a musical dervish of classical concerts, fireworks, dancing, and strumming competitions. A smaller, one-day music fest honors Santa Ursula on October 22.

ZAMORA ☎ 3

Zamora (pop. 156,000) is affectionately known as *"la cuna de hombres ilustres"* (cradle of illustrious men). The city has nurtured such greats as Manuel Martínez de Navarrete and Nobel Peace Prize winner Alfonso García Robles. The intellect of these eminent citizens surely made the valley of Zamora the leading producer of potatoes in all of Mexico. Besides potatoes, Zamora grows strawberries and manufactures renowned *dulces* (candy). While not exactly bursting at the seams with tourist offerings, Zamora is a quiet, pleasant place to pass a day and is a convenient stop between Guadalajara and Morelia.

E **TRANSPORTATION.** The **bus station** is on Juárez, at the edge of town. To get there from the *centro*, take a "Central" bus (3 pesos) from Colón and Hidalgo or take a taxi (13 pesos). Autobuses de Occidente/La Linea (☎515 11 19) go to: **Guadalajara** (3hr., every hour 5:20am-8:10pm, 74 pesos); **Manzanillo** (7hr., 8 per day 3:15am-11:30pm, 160 pesos) via **Colima** (5hr., 122 pesos); **Mexico City** (9hr., every hr. 2:30am-11pm, 207 pesos) via **Morelia** (3hr., 66 pesos) and **Toluca** (7hr., 157 pesos); **Uruapan** (2½hr., every hr. 7:30am-6pm, 45 pesos). ETN (☎515 61 81), La Línea (☎515 11 19), Estrella Blanca (☎515 11 33), and Primera Plus (☎515 13 16) provide similar services. Transportes del Pacífico (☎515 11 25) motors to the north.

■■ **ORIENTATION AND PRACTICAL INFORMATION.** Most activity centers in or around the *centro*, bordered by **Nervo** to the north, **Guerrero** to the south, **Morelos** to the west, and **Allende** to the east. **Hidalgo** curves north behind the cathedral, intersected by **Ocampo** running east-west one block north of the *centro*.

The **tourist office,** Morelos Sur 76, a few blocks from the *centro*, provides good maps. Some English spoken. (☎512 40 15. Open M-F 9am-2pm and 4-7pm, Sa 10am-2pm and 4-6pm, Su 10am-2pm.) **Bancomer,** Morelos 250, has a 24hr. **ATM.** (☎512 26 00. Open M-F 8:30am-4pm, Sa 10am-2pm; open for exchange M-F 8:30am-3:30pm.) **Emergency:** ☎060. **Police:** (☎512 00 22.) No English spoken. **Red Cross:** (☎512 05 34), on Calle Mendoza. No English spoken. **Farmacia Guadalajara,** in the plaza. (☎515 70 55. Open 24hr.) **Hospital: Hospital Civil,** Serdán 251 (☎512 12 02). Some English spoken. **Internet Access: Oficom 2000,** Hidalgo 99, at Colón. Turn left on Hidalgo and walk four blocks. (☎512 17 13. 5 pesos per hr. Open M-Sa 9am-9pm.) **Post Office:** in the Palacio Federal. (☎512 02 05. Open M-F 9am-3pm, Sa 9am-1pm.)

■■ **ACCOMMODATIONS AND FOOD.** The hourly traffic of couples in and out of many of Zamora's cheaper hotels may inspire you to look elsewhere. Try family-oriented **Hotel Nacional,** Corregidora 106, just off the *centro*, which has cramped, comfy rooms, tidy baths, and a 4th-floor balcony. (☎512 42 24. Singles 110 pesos; doubles 180 pesos.) Zamora's many small restaurants close around 6 or 7pm; candy shops are open until about 9pm. Try **Centro Comercial (Mercado) Morelos,** just off the *centro* across from the cathedral, for local sweets or super-cheap eats. **La Pantera Rosa** (The Pink Panther), Hidalgo Sur 234, offers *carnes asadas en su jugo* (grilled beef with beans in a beefy broth, served with freshly-made tortillas; 30-34 pesos) and *quesadillas* for 18 pesos. (☎512 18 66. Open daily 10am-10pm.)

NEAR ZAMORA: ZARAGOZA ARCHAEOLOGICAL ZONE

From the station in Zamora, take a bus to La Piedad (1hr., every 20 min. 5:15am-8:45pm, 22 pesos). In La Piedad, take the road that branches left off the pointy tip of Jardín Principal (near Bancomer) 1 block to Cárdenas, and catch a "Zaragoza" bus (30min., every hr. 6am-8pm, 6 pesos) at the station on your right. In Zaragoza, follow the cobblestone road up the hill, and turn left at Calle Flor de Michoacán, across from the green store. Follow the road as it curves to the left. On your right, just past the corner with the spray-painted "Calle Archeológica" sign, is Joel's house. Ask there about guides—it is virtually impossible to find the ruins without one. Site open M-F 10am-7pm. Free.

The archaeological zone lies along the legendary route of the Aztecs during their migration from Atzlán to Lake Texcoco. The site was a trading zone for the Purépecha empire that named Zaragoza ("The Place Where Stone Was Worked"). Many stones found among the ruins are engraved with *caracoles*, spiral shapes mimicking seashells or snails, or with flag shapes. One large, elaborate rock is thought to depict a map of the city. The ruins include the foundations of residential buildings and a **ballcourt,** an unusual feature in western Mexico. For hundreds of years, the ruins have slowly been diminished by locals carrying off stones for construction; nowadays university-bound archeologists tote away the stones for further study. The site also features **caves,** located high in the cliffs, along with a rock depicting the Virgin of Guadalupe. According to local lore, the Virgin appeared here in the 1930s, and the rock marks the spot of the miracle. Trails are unmarked, so explorations require a good guide. Joel (see above) may be willing to offer his services, and is a fountain of historical information.

Before visiting, try to find Fernando Tejera in **Museo Zaragoza,** next to the library in La Piedad. He may show you around the site, or at the very least, point you in the right direction. The museum offers scant historical background on the Purépecha empire and a small collection of local artifacts.

NEAR ZAMORA: LAGO CAMECUARO

Take a "Camecuaro" bus from the Sala de Servicios Regionales at the station in Zamora. Autotransportes Zamora-La Luz-Santiago leaves often (15 min., every 30min. 6:30am-9pm, 8 pesos). Tell the driver you want to go to the lake, not the village. Walk up a road on the right after you pass a cemetery on the left (1km). Open daily 8am-7pm. 5 pesos.

Peaceful Lake Camecuaro is a haven for outdoor recreation. Enormous cypresses surround crystal-clear waters, and swimming is permitted. The lake offers rowboats (70 pesos per hr.), shady picnic tables, grill pits, volleyball courts, soccer fields, and a few restaurants. Packs of *mariachis* serenade you and the hundreds of local families who visit and swim. The docile duck population is unfortunately dwarfed by the aggressive mosquito population, so remember insect repellent.

NEAR ZAMORA: GEYSER DE IXTLAN

From the Sala de Servicios Regionales in the Zamora station, board an "Ixtlan" bus. Autotransportes Zamora-La Luz-Santiago has frequent service (45min., every 30min. 7am-8pm, 13 pesos). Ask the driver to let you off at the geyser. The stop is before the village of Ixtlan, on the left.☎512 40 15. Open daily from 7am. 5 pesos, children 3 pesos.

Near the village of Ixtlan lies an impressive geyser that erupts sporadically, shooting a fountain up to 60m in the air. Unfortunately, the geyser doesn't erupt on a predictable schedule, so you may have to make do with listening to it boil underground. The subterranean hot water also fuels several concrete-encased pools, which provide a relaxing swim. Local families come to bathe and picnic.

PÁTZCUARO ☎ 4

Michoacán's earthy jewel, Pátzcuaro (pop. 70,000), has become a travelers' favorite. Set high in the mountains, the city is surrounded by rolling hills and forests, extending to the shores of expansive and polluted Lake Pátzcuaro. The compact and busy center is almost as spectacular as the surrounding landscape—tolling cathedral bells resonate through cobblestone streets and white stucco colonial buildings. Pátzcuaro's biggest selling point is its *artesanía*. To increase economic development in the 1530s, Spanish Bishop Vasco de Quiroga encouraged residents of each Purépecha village around the lake to specialize in a different craft. Today Pátzcuaro's plazas overflow with stacks of handmade woolen sweaters, meticulously carved wooden toys, and decorative masks.

▐ TRANSPORTATION

Pátzcuaro lies 56km southwest of Morelia and 62km northeast of Uruapan. To reach the *centro* from the **bus station** off Circunvalación, eight blocks south of the *centro*, catch a *combi* (7am-9:30pm, 3.5 pesos) or a city bus (6:30am-10pm, 3.5 pesos) from the lot to the right while leaving the station. **Taxis** cost 15 pesos.

Primera Plus/Flecha Amarilla (☎342 09 60) sends first-class buses to: **Guadalajara** (4½hr., 9:25am and 11:30pm, 126 pesos); **Mexico City** (6hr., 12:15am and 11:45pm, 205 pesos); **Morelia** (1hr.; 6:45, 7:30, and 9:30am, 8pm; 25 pesos); **Puerto Vallarta** (8hr., 8:10pm, 465 pesos); and 2nd-class buses to: **Guanajuato** (5hr., 8pm, 128 pesos); **León** (5hr.; 6, 6:15, 9:05, 10:30am, and 6:55pm; 135 pesos); **Manzanillo** (9hr., 8am, 220 pesos); **Mexico City** (8hr., 7 per day 7am-midnight, 180 pesos);

Pátzcuaro

🏠 ACCOMMODATIONS

Hotel Concordia, **4**
Hotel Valmen, **1**
Mandala, **10**
Posada de la Rosa, **3**
Posada de la Salud, **5**

🍴 FOOD

Hamburguesas El Viejo
Sam, **6**
Restaurant Los Escudos, **8**
Restaurant Yunuhen, **2**

♪ NIGHTLIFE

El Campanario, **9**
El Viejo Gaucho, **7**

Querétaro (5hr., 11:30pm, 118 pesos); and **Zamora** (3hr., 7 per day 6am-10:30am, 54 pesos) via **Morelia** (1hr., 25 pesos). Herradura de Plata/Pegaso Plus (☎342 10 45) and Autobuses de Occidente (☎342 12 43) offer more limited service. Elite (☎342 40 60) travels north, via Morelia. Autotransportes Galeana/Ruta Paraíso (☎342 08 08) motors to **Uruapan** (1hr., every 10 min. 5:30am-9:30pm, 25 pesos).

⚡🛈 ORIENTATION AND PRACTICAL INFORMATION

Pátzcuaro centers around two principal plazas, **Plaza Quiroga** and **Plaza Bocanegra.** Each of these is also, rather confusingly, called by a nickname. Plaza Quiroga is commonly known as **Plaza Grande**, while Plaza Bocanegra often masquerades as **Plaza Chica.** Avoid making the mistake of thinking there are four plazas.

Tourist Office: The **Delegación Municipal de Turismo,** Plaza Quiroga 50A (☎342 12 14), is on the northern side of Plaza Grande. Open daily 9am-3pm and 5-7pm. The **Delegación Regional** (☎243 17 05), Buenavista 7, has more maps and information about all of Michoacán State. Open M-F 9am-3pm, Sa 9am-2pm, Su 9am-2pm.

Currency Exchange: Banks with competitive rates can be found in both Pl. Grande and Pl. Chica. **Banamex,** Portal Juárez 32 (☎342 15 50), on the west side of Pl. Chica, has a 24hr. **ATM,** and check and currency exchange. Open M-F 9am-5pm, Sa 10am-2pm.

Luggage Storage: At the bus station. 4-10 pesos per day, by size. Open 7am-10pm.

Market: along Lloreda, between Codallos and Obregón. Open daily 8am-6pm.

Supermarket: Merzapack, Mendoza 24 (☎342 52 55), between Pl. Chica and Pl. Grande. Open daily 7am-10pm.

Emergency: Protección Civil (☎342 56 56). Some English spoken.

Police: (☎342 00 04), on Ibarra, between Espejo and Tangara, inside the Agencia del Ministero Público. Some English spoken.

Pharmacy: Farmacia Popular (☎342 32 42), Ibarra at Codallos, 1 block west of Pl. Grande. Open daily 8am-11pm.

Hospital: Hospital Civil, Romero 10 (☎342 02 85), next to San Juan de Díos church. No English spoken.

Telephone/Fax: Computel, (☎342 27 56), on Lloreda next to the Teatro. Offers fax and long distance services, plus a **caseta.** Open daily 6am-midnight.

Internet: Meg@Net, Mendoza 8 (☎342 33 33), between Pl. Chica and Pl. Grande, closer to Pl. Grande. 15 pesos per hr., students 12 pesos per hr. Open daily 9am-9pm.

Post Office: Obregón 13 (☎342 01 28), half a block north of Pl. Chica. Open M-F 8am-3pm, Sa 9am-1pm.

Postal Code: 61600.

⚑ ACCOMMODATIONS

Budget hotels are everywhere, but those in **Plaza Chica** usually have clean and comfy rooms. If you're lucky, you can score a balcony on the plaza and a private bath. Unfortunately, Pátzcuaro isn't the safest town at night, especially for women. Hotels tend to close their doors around 11pm.

Mandala, Lerin 14 (☎342 41 76), just past Casa de los Once Patios. Beautiful rooms ooze rustic charm and have sparkling baths in a friendly environment. Delicious adjacent restaurant (see **Food,** below). The cheapest rooms are downstairs. Singles 160 pesos; doubles 280 pesos; triples 375 pesos. Upstairs rooms with private bathrooms are 70 pesos more. Prices vary during *Semana Santa* and *Día de Muertos.*

Hotel Concordia, Portal Juárez 31 (☎342 00 03), on the west side of Pl. Chica. Rooms are spacious and neat, with soaring wood-beam ceilings and balconies. Communal baths decorated with colored tiles are spotless. Singles 92 pesos, with bath 184 pesos; doubles 196 pesos, with bath 322 pesos; triples 277 pesos, with bath 380 pesos.

Hotel Valmen, Lloreda 34 (☎342 11 61), 1 block east of Pl. Chica. Aztec tiles fill the green courtyards, and some of the well-lit rooms have balconies. Doors lock at 10pm. Popular with international travelers. 75 pesos per person; 85 pesos in high season.

Posada de la Salud, Serrato 9 (☎342 00 58), 3 blocks east of the plazas and half a block past the *basílica* on the right. Tropical flowers are surrounded by clean chambers with baths. Curfew 10pm. Singles 150 pesos; each additional person 50 pesos.

Posada de la Rosa, Portal Juárez 29, 2nd fl. (☎342 08 11), on the west side of Pl. Chica. Red-tiled rooms have a lone lightbulb and comfy beds. Large communal baths are clean, but smell, and toilets lack seats and paper. Curfew 11pm. Singles and doubles 80 pesos, with bath 150 pesos; triples and quads 100 pesos, with bath 200 pesos. Prices double during *Semana Santa.*

⬥ FOOD

Economical restaurants surround Plaza Chica and the accompanying market, while fancier joints group around hotels on Plaza Grande. *Pescado blanco* (whitefish), *charales* (small fish eaten fried and whole), and *caldo de pescado* (a fish soup) are regional specialties—head near the lake for good prices. Within the city you can slurp down *sopa tarasca,* a creamy tortilla soup.

▨ Restaurant Yunuhen, Portal Juárez 24 (☎342 08 94), on the west side of Pl. Chica. This tiny gem, adorned with murals of local history, serves filling *comida corrida* (35 pesos). Regional specialties 30 pesos, *antojitos* 17-19 pesos. Open daily 8am-8pm.

Mandala (see **Accommodations**), has vegetarian food delicious enough to convert even the most blood-hungry. Home-made wheat spaghetti (38 pesos) with a choice of sauce—mushroomy *del bosque* is amazing. Huge *menú del día* with soup and dessert (40 pesos) and many breakfast options (25 pesos). Open W-M 9am-9pm.

Hamburguesas El Viejo Sam, Mendoza 8 (☎342 36 55), behind Meg@Net. Burgers (8-14 pesos) made to order. Try the *sopa tarasca* (15 pesos). Open daily 10am-10pm.

Restaurant Los Escudos, Portal Hidalgo 74 (☎342 01 38), on the west side of Pl. Grande, inside Hotel Los Escudos. The ambience is set by bow-tied waiters and attractive wood furniture. *Sopa tarasca* 20 pesos, *comida corrida* 40 pesos. See *danza de los viejitos*, a dance ridiculing the Spanish (Sa 8:30pm). Live organ music daily 1-4pm and 7-10pm. Open daily 8am-10pm.

👁 SIGHTS

The following are within earshot of the *basílica*, but some of the most notable sights are a short trip from downtown (see **Daytrips**, p. 421).

BASÍLICA DE NUESTRA SEÑORA DE LA SALUD. When Bishop Vasco de Quiroga came to Pátzcuaro, he initiated social change and bold architectural projects. Quiroga conceived the lavender-and-gold Basílica, a colossal structure with five chapels branching off the main nave. Conflicting tales explain their significance: some claim that they represent five major body parts (the head, two arms and two legs), others believe they portray Christ's five wounds, and the historic-minded cite Quiroga's ideals for Christian society—wisdom, justice, honesty, work, and love. An enormous glass booth with gilded Corinthian columns protects the potentially edible *Virgen de la Salud*, crafted out of *tatzingue* paste—corn cobs and orchid honey, typical 16th-century statue material—by Tarascan artists in 1546. *(At Lerín and Serrato. Open daily 7am-7:30pm; mass Su every hr. 7am-1pm, 7, and 8pm.)*

PLAZAS. Statues of Pátzcuaro's two most honored citizens stand in the town's principal plazas. A resplendent, staff-bearing Vasco de Quiroga inhabits **Plaza Quiroga**, a vast and green space, while a massive, bare-chested Gertrudis Bocanegra peers out from the center of smaller **Plaza Bocanegra**. A martyr for Mexican independence, Bocanegra was executed by a Spanish squadron in Plaza Quiroga in October, 1817. Locals claim that bullet holes still mark the ash tree where she was tied, whose stump is in the southwest corner of Plaza Quiroga.

MUSEO REGIONAL DE ARTES POPULARES. Built in 1540 to house the Colegio de San Nicolas de Obispo, the fort-like walls of the museum enclose a flower-filled courtyard, regional pottery, copperware, textiles, and an arresting collection of *maque* (sumac lacquer). The rear courtyard holds a small set of Purépecha ruins and the remains of a 16th-century jail cell with a calendar of thousands of tick marks carved in the walls. *(☎342 10 29. Enseñanza 20, at Alcanterilla, 1 block south of the basílica. Open Tu-Sa 9am-7pm, Su 9am-3pm. Admission and tour 30 pesos, Su free.)*

TEATRO CALTZONTZÍN. Once part of an Augustine convent, this building on Pl. Chica became a theater in 1936. A prophecy was uttered at the theater's ground breaking: one Holy Thursday, it will crumble as punishment for the sin of projecting movies in a sacred place. In the last few years, the scared proprietors have stopped screening films, but the theater continues to host live performances. Other cultural events take place at the **Ex-Colegio Jesuita de Pátzcuaro** (☎342 44 77). Ask at the library next to the theater for a schedule of events at both locations.

BIBLIOTECA GERTRUDIS BOCANEGRA. Constructed as a church in 1576, the building next to the theater now houses a library. The former altar displays a giant mural by Juan O'Gorman, illustrating the history of Purépecha civilization from Pre-Hispanic times to the Revolution. *(☎342 54 95. Open M-Sa 9am-8pm.)*

THE LAST DON By the early 1500s, the Spanish administration in the future state of Michoacán had become so despicable, the don Vasco Quiroga was summoned to make amends. His predecessor, Guzman, had had management problems—he took the system of labor tribute (essentially a feudal system under which the indigenous were vassals to an *encomienda*) to such a brutal extreme that the mounting death toll was making the Church uncomfortable. However, under Quiroga, a bishopric was established, churches were built (most notably in Patzcuaro, Morelia, and Tzintzuntzan), and Indians were converted and given a profitable occupation, craftsmanship. All slept well under the protection of Quiroga.

🏷 SHOPPING

Pátzcuaro's unique crafts—hairy Tócuaro masks, elegant Sierra dinnerware, and thick wool textiles—are sold in Plaza Chica's **market** and in the shops along the passage next to Biblioteca Gertrudis Bocanegra. Bargaining is easier in the market or when you buy more than one item. Don't expect much of a discount on the stunningly handsome wool articles. Thick sweaters, brilliantly colored *saltillos* and *ruanas* (stylized ponchos), vibrant *sarapes*, and dark *rebozos* are Pátzcuaro's specialties. (Most shops open daily 8am-8pm.) For many of the same items at cheaper prices, trek out to Pátzcuaro's surrounding villages.

Higher quality and expensive items can be found at **La Casa de los Once Patios,** so named for the 18th-century building's 11 patios, on Lerín near Navarrete. Originally a convent, the complex now houses craft shops and a mural depicting Vasco de Quiroga's accomplishments. The *casa* sells cotton textiles, wood and copper crafts, and superb musical instruments such as flutes and student, concert, and classical guitars (250-8000 pesos). Dance performances occur sporadically in the main courtyard, usually on weekends. (Open daily 10am-8pm; some shops close in the afternoon.)

🎵 ENTERTAINMENT

Pátzcuaro's nightlife is confined mainly to restaurants and a few bars. At **El Campanario,** Portales Aldama 12 (☎324 13 13), on the south side of Pl. Grande, the masks and toreador's costume on the walls are almost as loud as the live music. (Beer 15 pesos, drinks from 35 pesos. Open Su-Th 3pm-11pm, F-Sa 1pm-3am.) Off-beat **El Viejo Gaucho,** Iturbe 10, a colorful Argentine bar and restaurant with art exhibits, features live music every night, from rock and blues to *cumbias* and *salsa.* Candlelit tables make this place cozy. (☎342 03 68. Cover 15 pesos. Music starts at 9pm. Beer 10-18 pesos, drinks from 28 pesos. Open M-Sa 6pm-midnight.)

Outside of town lies **El Estribo,** a lookout point near the top of a hill 4km from town. The walk takes about an hour, but you are rewarded with a magnificent view of **Lago de Pátzcuaro.** The pilgrimage is only recommended on Saturday and Sunday mornings when other families are making the climb. Otherwise, the hill should be avoided since incidents of foul-play have been reported.

FESTIVALS

Pátzcuaro parties year-round, but the biggest celebration is spectacular **Noche de Muertos** (Oct. 31-Nov. 2). Tourists from around the globe come to watch candle-lit fishing boats proceed to the tiny island of Janitzio. There, families and neighbors keep a two-night vigil in the cemetary, feasting at the graves of loved ones. The first night commemorates lost children; the second remembers deceased adults. Soon after Christmas celebrations end, the town is electrified by **Pastorelas,** religious dances performed on January 6 to commemorate the Adoration of the Magi and on January 17 to honor St. Anthony of Abad, the patron saint of animals. On both occasions, citizens dress their domestic animals in bizarre costumes, ribbons, and floral crowns. A few months later, *Semana Santa* attracts devotees from all over the republic. On Holy Thursday, all the churches in town are visited, and the **Procesión de Imágenes de Cristo** is held on Good Friday, when images of a crucified Christ are carried around town. The faithful also flock here on Saturday for Pátzcuaro's **Procesión del Silencio,** celebrated elsewhere the day before. A crowd marches around town silently mourning Jesus's death.

◢ DAYTRIPS FROM PÁTZCUARO

The area around Pátzcuaro is blessed with diverse landscapes. Surrounding villages sell beautiful handicrafts, usually at better prices than in the cities.

JANITZIO

In Pátzcuaro, hop on a "Lago" combi or bus (3.5 pesos) at the corner of Portal Regules and Portal Juárez. At the docks, buy a ferry ticket at the Muelle General (1hr, ferries leave when full 8am-8pm, 24 pesos round-trip; 28 pesos round-trip to the smaller, less-developed islands of Yunuen and Pacanda). Janitzio does not accommodate the stranded, so make sure you catch the last boat at 8pm.

The tiny island of Janitzio, inhabited exclusively by *indígenas* who still speak their Purépecha and Tarasco, subsists on tourist trade and local fishing. The boat ride to Janitzio provides a peek at local fisherman, who use butterfly nets more for show than function. The town's steep main street is lined with stores selling wool goods, hand-carved wooden chess sets, and masks. Among the shops, the bulk of which are quite pricey, restaurants offer meals of fresh whitefish (45-50 pesos) and *charales* (crispy sardine-like fish; 20-25 pesos), as well as *jarros locos* (a strange concoction of fruit juices, wine, and chile powder; 35-45 pesos). Janitzio is known for the enormous **statue of Morelos** that towers over the island. Inside the statue, a mural traces the principal events in Morelos's life and struggle for independence. Endless steps lead you to a fantastic lookout point, around the height of Morelos' sleeve. Really only two directions exist in Janitzio—up and down. Keep walking up and you'll reach the statue. (Open daily 9am-7:30pm. 5 pesos.) For information, go to the **tourist booth** as you get off the docks in front of the shops (☎ 431 3 61 52. Open daily 8am-8:30pm). One of the best times to visit Janitzio may be on **Noche de los Muertos**, when islanders and tourists alike pour into the tiny mountainside cemetary for an all-night party.

TZINTZUNTZÁN

Tzintzuntzán is perched on the northeastern edge of the Lago de Pátzcuaro, 15km from Pátzcuaro, on the road to Quiroga and Morelia. 2nd-class Ruta Paraíso/Galeana buses (☎ 342 08 08) leave the Pátzcuaro bus station for Tzintzuntzán (30min., every 15min. 6am-7:30pm, 6 pesos) en route to Quiroga. Return buses, on the same schedule, stop near the ferry dock to Janitzio. Last bus leaves at 8pm.

The word Tzintzuntzán (seen-soon-SAHN; "Place of the Hummingbirds") is believed to be an imitation of the sound of the **hummingbirds** that flit through the sky here in the spring. Tzintzuntzán was the last great city of the Purépecha empire. Before his death in the 15th century, the Purépecha lord Tariácuri divided his empire among his son and two nephews. When the separated empire was reunited years later, Tzintzuntzán was declared the capital. Today, its claims to fame are the delicate, multicolored **ceramics** for sale along Principal. Also of interest are the atrium and 16th-century Franciscan **convent** (open W-M 9am-4pm), entered from the gate at the back of the market. The olive shrubs that now cover the extensive, tree-filled atrium were planted under Vasco de Quiroga's instruction over 450 years ago. If you need guidance, head for the **tourist office,** conveniently located next to the bus stop. (Open Th-Tu 10am-2pm and 4-6pm.)

Yácatas, the ruins of several Pre-Hispanic temples, sits on a hill outside the city. Walk up the street in front of the market and convent, and follow the pyramid signs all the way around the hill until you reach the small museum/ticket booth (15min.). The remaining structual bases are standard rectangular pyramids—the missing parts, however, were very unique. Each was originally crowned with an elliptical pyramid constructed of shingles and volcanic rock. The site was named for the Purépecha *yácata*, which describes this combined circular-rectangular plan. At the edge of the hill overlooking the lake is a sacrificial block from which victims were hurled; the bones of thousands are said to lie at the base. Another structure was used to stockpile enemy heads. The museum has Mesoamerican pottery, jewelry, and a narrative of Purépecha history. (Open daily 10am-5pm. 27 pesos, children under 13 free; Su free.)

SANTA CLARA DEL COBRE

From the Pátzcuaro bus station, Ruta Paraíso/Galeana offers service to Santa Clara (20min., every 30min. 6am-8pm, 6 pesos; last return 8pm).

Santa Clara shines with *cobre* (copper), 16km south of Pátzcuaro. Long ago rich mines filled the area, but hidden from the Spanish, they remain undiscovered. However, the townspeople's passion for copper remains unrivaled. When electricity was brought to the town, artisans hammered the wires into pots and pans, causing widespread blackouts. Nearly every store in town sells decorative copper plates, pans, bowls, and bells. Prices here are only slightly better than elsewhere in Mexico, but the quality and variety are unbeatable. For a quick look at some imaginative pieces, step into the **Museo del Cobre,** 263 Morelos Ote., one block from the plaza. (Open Tu-Su 10am-3pm and 4-7pm. 2 pesos, children and students 1 peso.) Santa Clara celebrates the **Feria del Cobre** in early August

LAGO DE ZIRAHUÉN

From Pátzcuaro, take an Occidente (☎ 342 12 43) bus to Lago de Zirahuén (45min.; 7:15, 9:30, 11:50am 1, 2, 4, 6:30pm; last return 4:30pm). Taxis 90 pesos.

The Lago de Zirahuén ("Where Smoke Rose") is a fun trip for those who enjoy a crawling pace of life. You could pull a Rip van Winkle and probably not miss a thing here. Smaller than Lake Pátzcuaro and much cleaner, Zirahuén is bordered by farmland and sloping hills. Camping here is very safe; hike one of the ridges that border the lake and set up a spot overlooking the water, but make sure to bring a tarp and wet-weather gear. If the land is privately owned (usually fenced off), you may have to pay a few pesos—ask before you pitch your tent. A choice spot is the sizeable piece of lakefront on the west end of town (to the left, as you face the lake). The strip, about 15m wide, is covered in grass grazed short by horses. The *cabañas*, to the right along the dirt road bordering the lake (5min.), allow campers to use their bathrooms (1 peso). Be forewarned; heavy rains mid-June to early October can turn your camping soggy.

After roughing it in the great outdoors, head to the *lancha* dock for a smooth ride around the lake (1hr.; "yacht" 35 pesos, *lancha* 20 pesos), then relax at one of the casual lakefront restaurants (tortillas, rice, salad, and fresh fish 25 pesos). Although there is no formal canoe rental, ask around and a local fisherman might rent you his (50-100 pesos), depending on how long you want to use it. Many restaurants will pack a meal for a picnic, but establish the price beforehand.

MORELIA   ☎ 4

The state capital Morelia (pop. 575,000) anchors the proud traditions of Michoacán culture and history. Museums, art exhibits, theater, dance productions, and concerts create a vibrant cultural scene, fueled by the city's sizeable student population. Morelia of late has been caught in a whirl of development; sophisticated department stores and fast food joints press in from the outskirts of town, while in the *centro*, vendors sell traditional textiles and wooden crafts alongside bootleg cassettes and spare blender parts. Nearby stand rose-colored stone arcades and grand, white-washed houses, relics of Morelia's colonial magnificence. Its eclectic art and lively downtown make Morelia one of the most vital cities in Mexico.

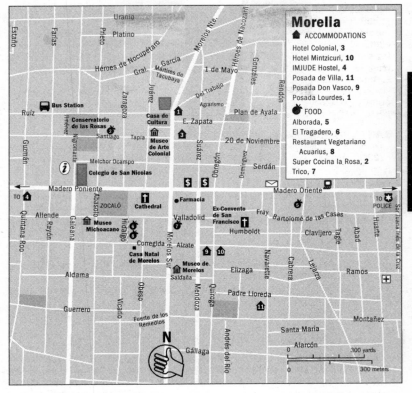

Morelia

🏠 **ACCOMMODATIONS**
Hotel Colonial, **3**
Hotel Mintzicuri, **10**
IMJUDE Hostel, **4**
Posada de Villa, **11**
Posada Don Vasco, **9**
Posada Lourdes, **1**

🍎 **FOOD**
Alborada, **5**
El Tragadero, **6**
Restaurant Vegetariano
  Acuarius, **8**
Super Cocina la Rosa, **2**
Trico, **7**

TRANSPORTATION

GETTING AROUND

Morelia lies 230km west of Mexico City on **Mex. 15.** Buses and *combis* traverse the city (6am-10pm, 3.5 pesos); catch them on **Nigromante** and **Galeana,** one block west of the *zócalo,* and on **Allende,** south of the *zócalo.* **Taxis** wait at the bus station.

GETTING AWAY

Flights: Aeropuerto Francisco J. Múgica, Carretera Morelia-Cinapécuaro km 27 (☎313 67 80). There is no longer bus service to the airport; a taxi costs 145 pesos. **Aeromar** (☎313 68 86). **Aeroméxico** (☎313 01 40). **Mexicana** (☎312 47 25).

Buses: The **Central** (☎313 55 89), is on Ruíz at Farías. Getting downtown from the bus station is a 10min. walk, a short taxi ride (15 pesos), or a quick bus ride (3.5 pesos) on any *combi* that says "Centro." Walk left as you exit the station, take the 1st right onto Farías, walk 3 blocks, then take a left on Madero; the *zócalo* is 2 blocks ahead. Morelia is a transportation hub for Michoacán, and buses head almost everywhere in the country. Primera Plus/Flecha Amarilla (☎313 55 89) provides 1st-class service to: **Aguas-calientes** (5½hr.; 2:30, 8:05am, 12:05, 4:05, and 5:05pm; 210 pesos); **Guadalajara** (3½hr., 10 per day 6:15am-11:59pm, 180 pesos); **León** (3hr., 16 per day, 120 pesos); **Mexico City** (5hr.; every hr. 7:15am-4:15pm and 6, 11:30pm, and midnight; 185 pesos); **Patzcuaro** (1hr., 5:40am and 4pm, 34 pesos); **Puerto Vallarta** (9hr., 8:10pm, 465 pesos); **Querétaro** (3hr., 11 per day, 105 pesos); **San Luis Potosí** (6hr.,

9 per day, 225 pesos); **Uruapan** (2hr.; 1, 2:30, 5:40am, 2:45, 3:45, 4:40, and 9:45pm; 75 pesos); **Zamora** (2½hr., 9am, 1, and 3:30pm, 85 pesos). Also offers 2nd-class service to the same destinations. ETN (☎313 74 40) provides similar, but more expensive, services. Ruta Paraíso (☎312 56 58) offers 2nd-class local services. Elite (☎312 29 89) goes to destinations farther north.

Luggage storage: Most bus lines have their own luggage storage, so prices vary. Usually 5 pesos per day.

▶ PRACTICAL INFORMATION

Tourist Office: Galeria de Turismo, Nigromante 79 (☎312 80 82), at Madero Pte., 2 blocks west of the *zócalo* in the castle-like building on the right. Staff distributes maps and a monthly list of cultural events. Free walking tours of the city leave Sa-Su 10am and 12:30pm. Some English spoken. Open M-F 9am-8pm, Sa 9am-7pm, Su 9am-3pm.

Currency Exchange: Banks cluster on Madero near the cathedral. **Bancomer,** Madero Ote. 21 (☎312 29 90), has a 24hr. **ATM.** Open M-F 8:30am-4pm, Sa 10am-2pm, as does **Banamex,** Madero Ote. 63 (☎322 03 38). Open M-F 9am-5pm, Sa 9am-3pm.

Laundry: Lavandería Cuautla, Cuautla 152 (☎312 48 06), south of Madero. 26 pesos per 3kg. Open M-F 9am-2pm and 4-8pm, Sa 9:30am-1:30pm.

Emergency: ☎066 or 070.

Police: (☎320 19 31), on 20 de Noviembre, 1 block northwest of the Fuente de las Tarascas, at the end of the aqueduct. No English spoken.

Red Cross: Ventura 27 (☎314 51 51 or 314 50 25), next to Parque Cuauhtémoc. Some English spoken.

Pharmacy: Farmacia Guadalajara, Maderos Sur. 117 (☎312 13 60), near the cathedral. Also a mini-supermarket.

Hospital: Hospital Civil (☎313 90 72), at Ramos and Huarte. Open 24hr.

Fax: Computel, Portal Galeana 157 (☎/fax 313 62 56), across from the cathedral. Has a **caseta.** Open daily 7am-10pm. **Telecomm,** Madero Ote. 369 (☎312 03 45), in the Palacio Federal next to the post office. Open M-F 8am-7:30pm, Sa-Su 9am-12:30pm.

Internet Access: Internet cafes abound near the *centro*. **ShareWeb Cyber Cafe,** Madero Ote. 573C (☎312 33 12). 12 pesos per hr. Open M-Sa 10am-10pm, Su 2-10pm.

Post Office: Madero Ote. 369 (☎312 05 17), in the Palacio Federal, 5 blocks east of the cathedral. Open M-F 8am-4pm, Sa 9am-1pm.

Postal Code: 58000.

▶ ACCOMMODATIONS

Unfortunately, budget hotels with vacancies are about as rare as jackrabbits in Morelia. Moderately priced hotels can be found all over, but for a real bargain (and a better chance at an empty bed), the IMJUDE hostel is worth the walk.

▣ IMJUDE Villa Juvenil Youth Hostel, Chiapas 180 (☎313 31 77; villaju@prodigi.net.mx), at Oaxaca, 20min. from the *zócalo*. Walk west on Madero Pte., turn left on Cuautla for 6 blocks, then turn right on Oaxaca and continue 4 blocks to Chiapas. Alternatively, take an *amarilla* (yellow stripe) *combi* from the *centro* (3.4 pesos). Exceptionally well-maintained 4-person single-sex dormitories, bathrooms, and red-tiled lobby. Sports facilities and pool can be used with permission. Linen deposit 50 pesos. Reception 7am-11pm; call ahead if arriving after 11pm, and make arrangements to be let in if staying out late. 15 pesos per meal in the adjoining cafeteria. Dorms 48 pesos.

Posada Don Vasco, Vasco de Quiroga 232 (☎312 14 84), 2 blocks east and 1½ blocks south of the cathedral. Spacious rooms off a beautiful, stone-arched courtyard have cable TV, phones, wood furniture, carpeting, purified water, and clean green baths. Singles 161 pesos; doubles 184 pesos; triples 207 pesos; quads 230 pesos.

Hotel Mintzicuri, Vasco de Quiroga 227 (☎312 06 64). Railings overflowing with flowers enclose sparkling, cozy, wood-paneled rooms equipped with phones and cable TV. Very popular with Mexican tourist families—come early or call ahead. Singles 161 pesos; doubles 184 pesos; triples 207 pesos; quads 230 pesos.

Hotel Colonial, 20 de Noviembre 15 (☎312 18 97), at Morelos Nte. Most rooms have high ceilings, large windows, private baths, and *agua purificada;* some even have balconies. All rooms are not equal, so you may want to take a look. Singles 110 pesos, with TV 160 pesos; doubles 140 pesos, with TV 180 pesos; triples 250 pesos.

Posada de Villa, Lloreda 166 (☎312 69 95), 3 blocks south of Museo de las Artesanías. The comfy rooms have tasteful bedspreads, TVs, and pretty bathrooms with just the tiniest touch of mildew. Try to get a room at the rear; the street can be loud. Singles 143 pesos; doubles 172 pesos; triples 200 pesos.

Posada Lourdes, Morelos Nte. 340, at del Trabajo near the Casa de Cultura. Unattractive exterior, but the rooms are pleasant and clean. Purified water available in the courtyard. Singles 45 pesos, with bath 75 pesos; doubles 75 pesos, with bath 95 pesos.

🍴 FOOD

Budget hotels may be scarce, but it's a breeze to find good, cheap food in Morelia. Almost every street has a family-run restaurant that dishes out delicious, inexpensive *comida corrida* (usually around 20 pesos) in the afternoon. The best deals are around the bus station. Restaurants on the *zócalo* are pricier but tend to stay open later. For local specialties, try *sopa tarasca* (a creamy soup made with beans, cheese, and bits of crispy tortilla, flavored by a bitter black chile) or *sopa tlalpeño* (a chicken-based soup with vegetables and *chipotle*), legacies of the Purépecha and Tarasco indigenous groups that once controlled this region.

■ Trico, Valladolid 8, 2nd fl. (☎313 42 32), at Madero Sur just east of the cathedral. Elegant but economical, Trico is home to businessmen in suits and families in jeans. Vegetarian options available. Offers huge breakfasts (30-45 pesos), baguette sandwiches (22-40 pesos), and regional specialties. Open daily 7am-9pm.

■ Alborada, Lejarza 36 (☎313 01 71), right off Madero near the Palacio Federal. A bakery in front and kitchen in back. The *comida corrida* (37 pesos) makes mouths water: soup, choice of main dish, dessert, and as many trips to the salad bar as your heart desires. Breakfasts 20-25 pesos, *energéticos* (yogurt, fruit, and honey) 12-15 pesos, licuados 7 pesos. Open M-Sa 8am-4:30pm; bakery open M-Sa 8am-9pm.

Super Cocina la Rosa, Tapía 270 (☎313 08 52), at Prieto next to the Conservatorio. This family-run place draws patrons in droves—go at an off time to guarantee a seat. Great food (and lots of it). *Comida corrida* 30 pesos. Open daily 8:30am-4:30pm.

El Tragadero, Hidalgo 63 (☎313 00 92). Packed with artificial flowers and old pictures of Morelia, this open-front restaurant provides a great view of the marketplace. Very filling *comida corrida* 32 pesos, large helpings of local specialties like *caldo tlalpeño* or *sopa tarasco* 23 pesos. Open M-Sa 7:30am-11pm, Su 7:30am-8pm.

Restaurant Vegetariano Acuarius, Hidalgo 75, south of the *zócalo.* Set in a huge inner courtyard with a non-working fountain. Mammoth *comida corrida* (28 pesos) and typical Mexican fare at low prices. Unfortunately, when the chefs took the meat out of these vegetarian dishes, most of the flavor went, too. Open M-W 9am-5pm, Th-Su 9am-9pm.

👁 SIGHTS

Packed with museums and cultural centers spanning all aspects of Michoacán's heritage, Morelia is a history buff's dream. Many of its famous buildings are ornamented in a style peculiar to the city—imitation Baroque, the identifying feature of which is a flat decorative motif on pilasters and columns. Check out the Cathedral for a stunning (and easy to recognize) example.

CASA DE CULTURA. A gathering place for artists, musicians, and backpackers, the *casa* houses a bookstore, art gallery, theater, palatial inner courtyard, and lovely cafe. Offers dance, voice, theater, guitar, piano, and sculpture classes, and hosts book signings, art festivals, and literature workshops. Ask for the weekly schedule of cultural events. The on-site **Museo de la Máscara** exhibits a small collection of masks from all over the republic—the wall of devil masks may scare you onto the path of righteousness. (*Morelos Nte. 485, 4 blocks north of Madero. Museum ☎312 41 51. Casa de Cultura ☎313 12 15 or 313 13 20. Center open M-F 9am-3pm and 5-8pm, Sa-Su and holidays 10am-2pm and 4-8pm. Museum open M-F 10am-3pm and 3:30-8pm, Sa-Su 10am-6pm. Free. 3-month classes 150 pesos.*)

CONSERVATORIO DE LAS ROSAS. Built in the 18th century to protect and educate widows and poor or orphaned Spanish girls, the building and its rose-filled courtyard now houses Morelia's premiere music school, the oldest in the Americas. Check with the conservatory's Public Relations office or with the Casa de Cultura for performance schedules. (*Tapía 334, 2 blocks north of the tourist office. ☎312 14 69. Open M-F 8am-8pm, Sa 8am-2pm. Public Relations office open M-F 9am-4pm.*)

CATHEDRAL. Overlooking the *zócalo*, the massive cathedral has a stunning interior graced by vaulted ceilings, chandeliers, tapestries, stained-glass windows, and a stunning dark wood pipe organ. The church's oldest treasure is the *Señor de la Sacristía*, an image of Christ sculpted by *indígenas* out of dry corn cobs and orchid nectar. Phillip II of Spain donated a gold crown to top off the masterpiece. (*Open daily 5:30am-8:30pm. Masses held Su, ever hr. 6am-noon and 6-8pm.*)

MUSEO MICHOACANO. This museum houses exhibits on the ecology, archaeology, anthropology, history, and art of Michoacán. Here, learn more about why parts of Michoacán tried to secede from Mexico after the Revolution, during the Cristero Rebellion. (*Allende 305, 1 block west of the zócalo at Abasolo. ☎312 04 07. Open Tu-Sa 9am-7pm, Su 9am-2pm. 30 pesos, seniors and children under 14 free; Su free.*)

CASA NATAL DE MORELOS. More of a civic building than a museum, the "Birthplace of Morelos" holds glass cases that preserve Morelos's wartime cartography, communiqués, and letters. Also notable is the shady courtyard and the murals by Alfredo Zalce. Morelos's birthplace—apparently in the middle of a stone courtyard—is commemorated by an eternal flame. (*113 Corregidora, at Obeso, 1 block south of the cathedral. ☎312 27 93. Open M-F 9am-8pm, Sa-Su 9am-7pm. Free.*)

MUSEO DE MORELOS. Originally bought by José María Morelos, the parish priest who led the Independence movement after Hidalgo's death, this 19th-century building now houses a museum detailing Morelos's primary school education, his stint in the clergy, and his glorious ascent to Mexican hero. Maps with zig-zagging arrows trace Morelos's four successful military campaigns and his fatal fifth campaign. (*323 Morelos Sur, 1 block east and 2 blocks south of the cathedral. ☎313 85 06. Open daily 9am-7pm. 22 pesos, seniors and children under 13 free; Su free.*)

CASA DE LAS ARTESANÍAS. This *casa*, occupying part of the **Ex-Convento de San Francisco,** is a huge crafts museum and retail store, selling colorful macramé *huipiles*, straw airplanes, pottery, carved wooden furniture, and guitars. Along the upstairs hallway, rooms stuffed with crafts are labeled with their town of origin. For better bargains, visit the towns themselves, or nearby Pátzcuaro. (*Humboldt at Fray Bartolome de las Casas, 3 blocks east of the zócalo. ☎312 12 48. Open M-Sa 10am-3pm and 5-8pm, Su 10am-4:30pm. Free.*)

BOSQUE CUAUHTÉMOC. More a park than an actual forest, the *bosque* lets you lose yourself among trees and fountains. A **mini amusement park** with bumper cars and a train entertains the young at heart. The **Museo de Historia Natural,** in the southeast corner of the *bosque*, is a tiny museum offering rotating exhibits on the flora and fauna of Michoacán, past and present. On the eastern side of the *bosque* is the **Museo de Arte Contemporaneo Alfredo Zalce,** which displays works in all mediums by that artist—one of Michoacán's most celebrated—as well as temporary exhibits of contemporary art. *(To get to the bosque, take a "Ruta Rojo" combi (3.5 pesos) from behind the cathedral on Allende. Amusement park open daily 11:30am-7:30pm. Entrance free, rides 3 pesos, bumper cars 10 pesos. Museo de Historia ☎312 00 44. Open daily 10am-6pm. 5 pesos. Museo de Arte ☎312 54 04. Open Tu-Su 10am-2pm and 4-8pm. Free.)*

PARQUE ZOOLÓGICO BENITO JUÁREZ. One of the larger and more pleasant zoos in Mexico, the Parque Zoológico keeps most of its animals in natural settings rather than tiny cages. *(Take a maroon combi south on Nigromante or a pink "Santa María" combi from in front of the tourist office (3.5 pesos), or walk south on Nigromante until it becomes Juárez (3km). Entrance on the west side of zoo. ☎314 04 88. Open M-F 10am-5pm, Sa-Su 10am-5:30pm. 12 pesos, children 6 pesos.)*

OTHER SIGHTS. At the eastern end of Madero is the statue of **Las Tarascas,** the most recognizable landmark in Morelia. The statue shows three indigenous women making an offering to the heavens. Nearby is **El Acueducto,** built in the 18th century to meet the city's growing water needs. Though no longer functional, it is a magnificent sight at night. Av. Acueducto runs right along it, to the university. Across from the cathedral is the **Palacio de Gobierno,** Madero 63. Inside, murals by Alfredo Zalce depict the history of Morelia. The **Museo de Arte Colonial,** three blocks north at Juárez 240, proves that colonial artists were solely preoccupied with the crucifixion. *(Palacio de Gobierno open M-F 8am-10pm, Sa-Su 8am-9pm. Museo de Arte ☎313 92 60. Open M-F 10am-2pm and 5-8pm, Sa-Su 10am-2pm and 4:30-7pm. Free.)*

🎵📷 ENTERTAINMENT AND NIGHTLIFE

Morelia overflows with culture. Listings of events can be found at the Casa de Cultura and the tourist office. Lights, music, and theater draw crowds to **Teatro Morelos** (☎314 62 02), on Camelina at Ventura Pte., and to **Teatro Ocampo** (☎312 37 34), on the corner of Ocampo and Prieto (tickets 20-80 pesos). **Corral de la Comedia,** Ocampo 239 (☎312 00 01), at Prieto one block north of Madero, presents comedies written and performed by local artists (Th-Sa 8:30pm, Su 7:30pm; 60 pesos). **La Casona del Teatro,** Serdán 35, at Morelos one block north of Madero, hosts comic dramas in Spanish. (☎317 33 53. Shows generally Th-Sa 8:30pm, Su 7:30pm. 70 pesos.) The **Conservatorio de las Rosas** (see **Sights** above) holds concerts during all but the summer; visit for calendars. The **Casa Natal de Morelos** (see **Sights,** above) shows family movies and holds cultural events (events F 8pm; films Tu-W 5 and 7pm, 5 pesos). **Multicinema Morelia,** on Tapía at Jiménez, next to the conservatory, screens Hollywood's latest. (☎312 12 88. Open daily 1:30-10:30pm. 25 pesos before 6pm, 30 pesos after; Spanish subtitles.) The **Planetario** (☎314 24 65), on Ventura Pte. at Ticateme, in the Centro de Convenciones, has standard planetarium fare (Tu-Sa 7pm, Su 6:30pm; 20 pesos). Take the "Ruta Rojo #3" *combi* from Allende/Valladolid, and watch for the convention center on the right.

If you prefer scantily clad bodies to heavenly ones, writhe with packs of students at Morelia's nightclubs. Most clubs are a 15- to 20-peso cab ride away. Twenty-somethings bounce to the latest Spanish and English pop tunes at **XO Club,** Campestre 100. (Open bar F. Cover men 100 pesos, women 50 pesos; Sa 50 pesos. Open W-Sa 10pm-3am.) For real multi-level, block-rocking club madness, head to either **DV8** or **Metro** (cab drivers know the way). At DV8, join the insanity on the dance floor, or watch it on two huge video screens. Ladies, come early Thursday nights to join the local crowd in their quest for sexual arousal, complete with male strippers and mock sex acts. (☎324 74 45. Beer 20 pesos, drinks from 35 pesos. Cover W men 40 pesos, women free 10-11pm; 2-for-1 drinks. F open bar 10pm-1am men 130 pesos, women 80 pesos. Sa 40 pesos. Open W, F-Sa 10pm-3am.) Metro is a "private club" for Mexican clients, but well-dressed foreigners have automatic membership. Very thin girls and casually cool guys gyrate to techno and top 40 under the millions of star-like lights. (☎315 99 90. Beer 21 pesos, drinks from 30 pesos. W and F open bar, men 100 pesos, women free. Th and Sa cover 70 pesos. Open W-Sa 10pm-3am.) Clubs here have short lives, so ask around for the latest.

CIUDAD HIDALGO   ☎ 1

Hidalgo (pop. 100,000) is a good base for exploring Michoacán's natural beauty at nearby **Laguna Larga** and the spas of **Los Azufres.**

🖰🗹 TRANSPORTATION AND PRACTICAL INFORMATION. The City is a 2hr. bus ride from Morelia. From the **bus station,** Flecha Amarilla/Servicios Coordinados motors to: **León** (11pm, 170 pesos); **Mexico City** (6 per day 1:45am-4:30pm, 98 pesos) via **Toluca** (67 pesos) and **Zitácuaro** (17 pesos); **Morelia** (5 per day, 48 pesos); **Pátzcuaro** (6pm and 12:30am, 85 pesos); **Uruapan** (6pm, 110 pesos). Autobuses México-Toluca (☎ 154 07 22) and Autobuses del Occidente/La Línea (☎ 154 70 73) have more limited service. To get to the *centro*, take a bus headed right on the road in front of the bus station and tell the driver where you want to get off (3 pesos). **Taxis** 15 pesos. The *zócalo* is bordered on the north by **Valle**, on the west by **Cuauhtémoc**, on the south by **Juárez**, and on the west by **Hidalgo. Morelos**, the main commercial drag, is one block south of Juárez.

Tourist office: in the Palacio Municipal. (☎ 154 11 79. Open M-F 9am-3pm and 5-7pm.) **Currency Exchange: Banamex**, in the northeast corner of the *zócalo*, at the intersection of Cuauhtémoc and Valle, has a 24hr. **ATM** and check and currency exchange. (Open M-F 9am-5pm, Sa 10am-2pm.) **Police:** (☎ 154 00 29) in the Palacio Municipal. **Farmacia Morelos**, Morelos Ote. 26, one block past the Centro de Salud. (☎ 154 18 59. Open 24hr.) **Centro de Salud:** at the corner of Morelos and Zapata. Take Cuauhtémoc from the *zócalo* to Morelos, turn left and walk two blocks. The Centro is on the right. (☎ 154 02 63. No English spoken.) **Internet: Evonet**, Hidalgo 20 (☎ 154 60 81. 15 pesos per hr. Open M-Sa 9am-9pm.)

🖰🖸 ACCOMMODATIONS AND FOOD. Your best bet in Ciudad Hidalgo is **Hotel Central**, Abasolo 12. From in front of the Palacio Gobierno, walk right for one block, then left on Abasolo for 1½ blocks. Large, clean rooms have TVs and phones. (☎ 154 00 55. Singles 130 pesos; doubles 150 pesos; triples 180 pesos; quads 210 pesos.) A less attractive option is **Hotel San Carlos**, Cuauhtémoc Sur 22. The peach walls are covered in grime, and you'll have to fight the mildew for space in the bathroom. (☎ 154 56 47. Singles 70 pesos, with TV 100 pesos; each additional person 60 pesos.) Hidalgo is not the place for fine dining. Food vendors can be found around the *zócalo* and *mercado*. If wary of these, try **Güero's Pizza**, Hidalgo 8, near the *centro*. (Sesame seed crust slice 10 pesos, whole pizzas with 3-4 toppings from 60 pesos. ☎ 154 57 66. Open daily 9am-10:30pm.)

🖾 OUTDOOR ACTIVITIES. Los Azufres, 23km northwest of Morelia, are perfect for a nice, relaxing bath (20 pesos). Nearby **Laguna Larga** is a series of man-made lakes or *presos*, perfect for hiking, fishing, or camping. Buses to both leave from the suburban terminal (1hr.; 7am and 2pm, return 8:30am and 3:30pm; 15 pesos). To get to the terminal from the *centro*, take Hidalgo south one block, turn right on Morelos and walk three blocks. Take a left onto Matamoros—the terminal will be on your left. Stop by the **tourist office** for more information on these sites.

ZITÁCUARO   ☎ 7

Zitácuaro (pop. 200,000) would be a much larger city had it not been destroyed three times during the 19th century—once during the War for Independence (1812), again by Santa Anna's troops (1855), and finally during the French Intervention (1865). The city's long tradition of defiance and survival led Benito Juárez to ordain it *Ciudad de la Independencia* (City of Independence). Today, Zitácuaro has safe streets, large markets, and a population that rises with the sun. Tucked into the eastern edge of the Sierra Madre Occidental, the city seems to have mountains looming at the end of every street. Outdoors-enthusiasts will find endless opportunities for camping and hiking nearby, but city-folk may not find much to suit them. Despite its growing population and increasing urbanization, Zitácuaro's cultural traditions have remained as immutable as the mountains.

⌨ TRANSPORTATION. Zitácuaro sits 165km west of Mexico City on **Mex. 15.** The **bus station** is at Pueblita Nte. 17 (☎ 153 72 65), at the end of Cuauhtémoc Nte., two blocks north of Hidalgo and six blocks east of Revolución Nte. Tickets for taxis to the *centro* are sold at a booth inside (15 pesos). "Centro" *combis* are outside the station (6am-9pm, 3 pesos). Flecha Amarilla (☎ 153 14 88) provides second-class service to: **León** (6½hr., 10pm, 182 pesos); **Mexico City** (3hr., 6 per day, 80 pesos) via **Toluca** (1hr., 45min., 48 pesos); **Morelia** (3hr., 9 per day 6am-11:45pm, 67 pesos) via **Ciudad Hidalgo** (45min., 17 pesos); **Pátzcuaro** (4½hr., 4:40 and 11:40pm, 98 pesos); **Uruapan** (5hr., 4:40pm, 124 pesos). Autobuses de Occidente/La Línea (☎ 153 08 66) offers similar service, and goes to: **Lázaro Cárdenas** (12hr., 6:25pm, 230 pesos); **Manzanillo** (13½hr., 4 per day, 264 pesos); **Zamora** (6hr., 7 per day 1:45am- 5:30pm, 184 pesos). Estrella Blanca (☎ 153 71 73) drives to points north and sends buses to **Querétaro** (6hr., 1 and 3pm, 148 pesos). Autobuses México-Toluca (☎ 153 71 63) has similar, but more limited, local service.

◪☷ ORIENTATION AND PRACTICAL INFORMATION. Plaza Principal, the city center, consists of Plaza Cívica de Benito Juárez, Plaza Municipal, and Mercado Juárez. Plaza Municipal is bordered by **Tejada** (south), **García** (west), **5 de Mayo** (east), and **Ocampo** (north). **Hidalgo** runs parallel to Ocampo on the other side of the market. The main avenue, **Revolución,** is one block east of 5 de Mayo. Streets end in "Nte." or "Sur," indicating their relation to Hidalgo.

The **tourist office,** Carretera Zitácuaro km 4, is far away, but provides helpful maps and brochures. To get there, take an orange *combi* (3 pesos) heading south on Revolución and tell the driver where to let you off. (☎ 153 06 75. Open M-F 9am-3pm and 5-7pm, Sa 9am-2pm.) **Banamex,** Tejada 30, exchanges cash and checks and has a 24hr. **ATM.** (☎ 153 04 07. Open M-F 9am-5pm, Sa 9am-2pm.) **Luggage storage:** in the bus station. (2.5 pesos per 6hr. Open daily 6am-10pm.) **Emergency: ☎** 060. **Police:** (☎ 153 11 37), at the north end of Plaza Municipal. **Red Cross:** Prieto 11 (☎ 153 11 05). Pharmacies surround the plaza, including **Farmacia Guadalajara,** 5 de Mayo Sur 12A. (☎ 153 86 33. Open 24hr.) **Hospital: Sanitorio Memorial,** Valle Nte. 10 (☎ 153 11 08), take a left on Valle from Hidalgo, the hospital is on your left. **Telecomm,** Ocampo 7, offers **fax, Western Union,** and **telegraph** services. (☎ 153 12 81. Open M-F 8am-6pm, Sa 9am-2pm.) **Internet: Evonet,** Revolución Sur 8, next to Hotel América. (☎ 153 64 54. 12 pesos per hr. Open M-Sa 9am-9pm, Su 9am-3pm.) **Post office:** Valle Sur 2, walk up Ocampo, cross Revolución and turn left onto Valle—it is half a block down, on the right. (☎ 151 38 73. Open M-F 9am-3pm, Sa 9am-1pm.) **Postal code:** 61500.

▐▐ ACCOMMODATIONS AND FOOD. Illuminated signs all over Revolución and the plaza advertise conveniently located (and sometimes inconveniently priced) hotels and *posadas*. The pesos pay off at the **Hotel América,** Revolución Sur 8. Parking, newly-renovated, very modern private baths, and TVs. Rooms are clean with hardwood floors. (☎ 153 11 16. Singles 120 pesos; doubles 170 pesos; triples 220 pesos.) Another good, inexpensive option is **Hotel Lorenz,** Hidalgo Ote. 14. The accommodating staff will put you up in fresh pink and white rooms with TV and tasteful baths. (☎ 153 09 91. Singles 130 pesos; doubles 150 pesos.)

Zitácuaro's best dining options are on-the-go: fresh market fruits and vegetables, hot *quesadillas*, and ice cream stands line 5 de Mayo. A few sit-down restaurants can be found on Revolución. Converse with the friendly waitstaff at inexpensive **Cafe Chips,** Hidalgo Ote. 22, east of Revolución past Hotel Conquistador. (☎ 153 11 95. Savory *tortas* 6-8 pesos, *comida corrida* 25 pesos. Open M-Sa 9:30am-7pm.)

HOLDING COURT Eastern Michoacán is home not only to vast coniferous forests and rolling hills peppered with small farming communities, but also, during November and December, to over 20 million monarch butterflies. Each October, monarchs from all over the US and Canada begin their journeys in unison, flying at a regal 20km/hr., and gather just north of Zitácuaro. Some scientists say the mass migration instinct is a relic of the ice ages, when southward travel was necessary for reproduction; others insist that even now monarch reproduction is impossible in all but the warmest of climates. Whatever the reason, the sight is stupendous. The butterflies blanket trees, forming orange masses, without a patch of bark visible. To visit the annual convergence, take a green bus labeled "Angangueo" from the station in Zitácuaro to the sanctuary at El Rosario.

◙ **SIGHTS.** Afternoons in Zitácuaro swirl and fade in **Plaza Cívica de Benito Juárez,** where vendors gather, uniformed school children play *fútbol*, and the elderly escape the sun on shaded benches. The **Palacio Municipal,** guarding the north end of the plaza, holds a stunning mural telling Zitácuaro's history, from its settling by the Mazahuas, through independence, to the present day. The small **Jardín de la Constitución,** on Ojeda Sur, three blocks west of the plaza, provides flowers, fountains, and shady seats for starry-eyed lovebirds.

From Zitácuaro's **Cerrito de la Independencia** one can see not only the city itself, but miles of lush valleys, forested hills, and spectacular distant blue peaks. To reach the lookout, follow Tejada as it crosses Revolución Sur until it reaches Altamirano, then turn right and follow the paved path climbing through the woods. (Park open daily 6am-7pm.) You can also take an orange *combi* (3 pesos) south on Revolución to Cañonaso and walk the four blocks uphill. Ten kilometers south of town on the Huetamo Rte., **Presa del Bosque** also provides spectacular views of the countryside. The dirt road to the right of the main road leads to a lake where adventurous souls swim, camp, fish, and hike. Unfortunately, there is no public transportation, so you'll have to flag down a taxi (70 pesos).

LÁZARO CÁRDENAS ☎ 7

Named after the *michoacano* president whose socialist reforms included nationalizing oil in 1938, the hot, noisy city of Lázaro Cárdenas (pop. 150,000) is Mexico's most important Pacific port. The city offers all the services that you'll be unable to find in smaller beach towns along Michoacán's rugged and beautiful 260km coast. However, its noisy, crowded streets and lack of swimmable beaches make Cárdenas more suited for a pit stop or departure point than for a prolonged visit.

▐ **TRANSPORTATION.** Lázaro Cárdenas lies 382km southwest of Morelia and 122km northwest of Ixtapa. The town's principal thoroughfare is **Av. Lázaro Cárdenas.** The main *zócalo*, **Plaza de la Reforma,** is three blocks east of the *avenida*'s intersection with Prieto. *Combis* and buses run up and down Cárdenas and whisk passengers to nearby beaches.

The **airport** (☎532 19 20) hosts carriers **Transporte Aeromar** (☎537 10 84) and **Aerolínea Cuahonte** (☎532 36 35 and 532 00 04). **Buses** run out of independent stations on or close to the main drag. Autotransportes Cuauhtémoc and Estrella Blanca, Villa 65 (☎532 11 71), four blocks west of Corregidora, send buses to: **Acapulco** (6hr., every 2hr. 4:15am-midnight, 138 pesos); **Morelia** (6 hr., 2:30 and 10pm, 310 pesos); **Puerto Vallarta** (12hr.; 1:05, 2:02am, and 2:30pm; 356 pesos); **Zihuatanejo** (2hr., every 2hr., 4:15am-midnight, 49 pesos). Estrella Blanca also provides second-class service to: **Mexico City** (10hr.; 4:30, 8, and 9:45pm; 393 pesos); **Acapulco** (6.½hr., every hr. 2:30am-9pm, 138 pesos); **Manzanillo** (6hr., 2:30 and 4:20pm, 195 pesos); **Zihuatanejo** (2½ hr., every hr. 2:30am-9pm, 49 pesos). Autotransportes Galeana, Cárdenas 1810 (☎532 02 62), Estrella de Oro, Corregidora 318 (☎532 17 98), and La Linea, Cárdenas 171 (☎537 18 50), provide similar service.

🔋 PRACTICAL INFORMATION. Get the maps and info you need to conquer the coast from the **Delegación Regional de Turismo,** Bravo 475, one block east of Cárdenas and two blocks north of Corregidora, in the big white Hotel Casa Blanca. No English spoken. (☎/fax 532 15 47. Open M-Sa 9am-6pm.) **Banamex,** Cárdenas 1646, exchanges currency and has an **ATM.** (☎532 20 20. Open M-F 8:30am-4:30pm, Sa 10am-2pm.) So does **BITAL,** Cárdenas 1940. (☎532 26 33 or 532 26 34. Open M-Sa 8am-7pm.) **Luggage storage** in the Estrella Blanca bus station. (2-6 pesos per bag per hr.) **Police:** (☎532 18 55), Palacio Municipal, on Cárdenas at Río Balsas. **Red Cross:** Aldama 327 (☎532 05 75). **Farmacia Paris,** Cárdenas 2002. (☎532 14 35. Open 24hr.) **Hospital General** (☎532 08 21 5 or 532 05 97), on Cárdenas. **Car Rental: Hertz,** Bravo 475, inside Hotel Casa Blanca. Small VW 500 pesos per day. (☎532 25 70. Open daily 7am-8pm.) Make long-distance **phone calls** and send **faxes** from **Caseta Goretti,** Corregidora 79. (☎537 31 55. Open daily 7:30am-midnight.) **Internet: Sin Límite,** Cárdenas 1745, at the corner of Corregidora. (☎532 14 80. Open daily 9am-9pm.) **Post office:** Bravo 1307. (☎532 05 47. Open M-F 8am-4pm, Sa 9am-1pm.) **Postal Code:** 60950.

🔳 ACCOMMODATIONS AND FOOD. The rent-by-the-hour atmosphere of most budget accommodations in town will make you happy to find **Hotel Reyna Pio,** Corregidora 78, at Cárdenas. Snuggle down in your coffee-colored bed to watch *telenovelas* on TV with the A/C on full-blast. They have phones, too. (☎532 06 20. Singles 145 pesos; doubles 160 pesos.) **El Paraíso,** Cárdenas 1862 (☎532 32 33), near the Galeana bus station, offers traditional fare amid orange, green, and yellow decor straight out of the 70s. The *sopa de tortilla* (15 pesos) and chicken (25 pesos) are both worth a try. *Comida corrida* 20 pesos. At night, El Paraíso doubles as a low-key bar. For even cheaper eats, the street beside the Galeana bus station is full of *torta* and taco stands, most open late.

MICHOACÁN COAST

Michoacán's temperamental, wildly beautiful coastline offers solace and tranquility one moment, and ripping, turbulent surf the next. Hills are pushed against each other; rocks are defaced by crashing white waves spraying into blue skies. Lush tropical vegetation lends a loving touch of green to the state's 260km of virgin beach. Mex. 200, the solitary coastal route, twists up, down, and around the angry terrain. Michoacán's coast is dangerous, and should be treated with caution. Powerful waves make the beaches better suited for surfing than splashing around, and the currents are strong even in designated swimming areas. There are no lifeguards, so use extreme caution. Mex. 200 tends to be deserted and dangerous at night; *Let's Go* does not recommend traveling after dark.

PLAYA AZUL ☎7

Playa Azul (pop. 5000), a small town bordering the Pacific 26km west of Lázaro Cárdenas, is renowned for its soft, golden sands and majestic rose-colored sunsets. The tempting waves attract surfers and boogie boarders, but the strong undercurrent makes swimming treacherous. Crowded with Mexican tourists during December and *Semana Santa*, the beach is very quiet during the rest of the year. Far from being a polished tourist town, Playa Azul is typically *michoacano*: unmarked dirt roads lined with thatched-roof houses and open-air markets crisscross the town, while chickens and tanned locals in bathing suits walk the streets. The village is so small that street names are seldom used (or known) by locals.

🔳 TRANSPORTATION AND PRACTICAL INFORMATION. The *malecón* runs along the beach; it is called **Serdán** to the west of the plaza and **Zapata** to the east. The other streets bordering the plaza are **Montes de Oca** to the west, and **Filomena Mata** to the east. **Lázaro Cárdenas** runs into Playa Azul, then perpendicular to the beach, intersecting Carranza, Madero, and Independencia, which parallel the beach. From Lázaro Cárdenas, take a "Playa Azul" *combi* straight to the beach (45min., every 2min. 5am-9pm, 8 pesos). To get to Caleta de Campos from Playa Azul, take a *combi* across from the PEMEX station (5min., every 10 min., 4.5 pesos) and ask the driver to be let off at **Acalpican**, a marked intersection. From there, hail a bus labeled "Caleta" (1hr., every 20 min., 5:45am-8:30pm, 23 pesos).

Playa Azul has no bank or *casa de cambio*, but does offer most other services. **Market: Flores Magón**, two blocks east of the plaza. (Open daily 8am-5pm.) **Surf board** and boogie board rental is available from several beach front shops. **Police:** (☎536 01 47), across from the PEMEX station. No English spoken. **Farmacia Playa Azul**, Av. Lázaro Cárdenas at Madero. (Open daily 9am-midnight.) **Centro de Salud:** next door to the post office. No English spoken. For **long-distance calls,** use one of the **LADATELs** that can be found on the *malecón* or along Independencia. **Post office:** on Madero at Montes de Oca, just behind Hotel María Teresa. (☎536 01 09. Open M-F 9am-3pm.) **Postal Code:** 60986.

◖◗ ACCOMMODATIONS AND FOOD. Bucolic Playa Azul offers several adequate budget hotels. Reservations are recommended in August, December, and during *Semana Santa.* **Hotel Costa de Oro,** on Madero, three blocks from Lázaro Cárdenas, is the best deal in town. An elegantly scalloped banister looks out over a dirt courtyard, but leads to clean, comfortable rooms with funky tiled floors, fans, and mismatched bedspreads. Bathrooms are clean and have hot water. (☎536 02 51. Doubles 150 pesos; triples 200 pesos). **Bungalows de la Curva,** on Madero at Lázaro Cárdenas, is a good deal for groups, with kitchenettes and basic furniture. A swimming pool is surrounded by a patio with tables for pool-side relaxing or dining. (Singles 160 pesos; bungalows 230-345 pesos.)

Palapa restaurants are so close to the shore that the waves will tickle your toes. The bubbly owners of **Coco's Pizza** will make you feel right at home and their *camarones al diablo* (shrimp with chile; 48 pesos) are a spicy taste of heaven. (Open daily 8am-9pm, low season 8am-6pm.) Inland, **Restaurante Familiar Martita,** on Magón at Madero, is a cozy family-run restaurant that serves just about everything. (☎536 01 11. *Comida corrida* 25-30 pesos, breakfast combos 28-35 pesos. Open daily 7am-11pm.) Another cheap in-town eatery is **Restaurant Galdy,** on Flores, one block from Lázaro Cárdenas. With a good selection of *platillos económicos* (15-30 pesos) and a location right by the market, Galdy fills up with hungry townspeople during the evenings. (Open daily 7:30am-11pm.)

PLAYA AZUL TO CALETA DE CAMPOS

Beautiful beaches cover 43km of coastline between Playa Azul and Caleta de Campos. **Las Peñas**, 13km west of Playa Azul, is a beach better appreciated from the shore: it's terribly turbulent but great for surfing. **El Bejuco**, only 2km west, has a sandy cove with tamer waves and fewer rocks. Go west another 12km and you'll find **Chuquiapan**, a long sandy beach with tall green palms and reasonable waves. **La Soledad,** enclosed by rocky formations 4km farther west, at the base of a hill covered with dense vegetation, is cozier. Its grey sands are strewn with rocks and driftwood. Unfortunately, typically rough waters make for dangerous swimming. **Mexcalhuacán,** 2km west, offers a fantastic view from a bluff overlooking a rocky coast. **Caleta de Campos** comes 7km later. **Nexpa**, a sandy beach with powerful waves, is a surfer's heaven 5km west of Caleta. *Palapa* restaurants, known as *enramadas*, line most of the beaches. **Buses** running from Lázaro Cárdenas to Caleta de Campos leave from Galeana bus station and pass by each of the beaches, listed above, except Nexpa (every 20min., 6:20am-8:10pm). From the highway, you can see signs labeling each beach—keep an eye out for them, because bus drivers don't always drop you off accurately. The beaches are a short walk from the highway (5-10min.). To return to Playa Azul or Lázaro Cárdenas, wave down a bus going in the opposite direction (last return at 7:40pm). To get to Nexpa, take a white *combi* from the bus depot at the beginning of Principal in Caleta de Campos (10min., every 40min., 7am-7pm).

CALETA DE CAMPOS   ☎ 7

A tiny fishing village 47km west of Playa Azul, Caleta de Campos has a pleasant beach but little else for the traveler. The entire town is laid out along one main street; blink and you'll miss it. A dirt path climbs along the hills, offering a spectacular view of the coast. Because the water is somewhat sheltered, the surf is calmer than at Playa Azul, and the rolling waves make for good boogie boarding and body surfing. For most of the year, Caleta's two hotels are empty, but they fill up during *Semana Santa* and Christmas.

⮒ TRANSPORTATION. From Lázaro Cárdenas, Rutas de Transportación Colectiva (☎ 532 02 62) buses run from the **Galeana bus station** to **Caleta** (1½hr., every 20 min. 5am-8:10pm, 30 pesos). To return to Lázaro Cárdenas from Caleta, pick up a bus at the stop near the end of Principal (5:30am-7:40pm). From Playa Azul, get on any bus leaving town, across from the PEMEX gas station (5min., every 10min., 4.5 pesos). Get off at **Acalpican**, a marked city just a few kilometers north of Playa Azul (be sure to tell the driver where you want to go in advance) and catch a bus labeled "Caleta" at the intersection (every 30min., 5:45am-8:45pm, 23 pesos).

⯃ PRACTICAL INFORMATION. Caleta de Campos has one paved main street, **Melchor Ocampo**, locally known as **Principal**. Across from Farmacia Morelia, **Ferretería** will sometimes change dollars. The **police station** is the yellow building on the left as you turn off of the main highway onto Principal. (☎ 532 1855 or 532 2030. No English spoken.) **Farmacia Morelia** is farther along Principal. (Open daily 8am-10pm.) **Centro de Salud:** turn right before Principal turns left and walk three blocks up a dirt road. (No English spoken. 24hr. emergency service.) **LADATELs** line Principal. **Casetas** are on the left, a little past the police station. (Open daily 8am-9pm.) **Post office:** on Principal. (☎ 531 50 06; fax 531 51 29. Open M-F 8am-3pm.)

⯃⯂ ACCOMMODATIONS AND FOOD. Caleta has two hotels, both of which are nice and affordable. The **Hotel Los Arcos**, next to the church as Principal turns left, has very clean rooms with golden doors, tiled floors and bathrooms, and fans. Arch-shaped windows provide a spectacular view of the coast. Some rooms have balconies.(☎ 531 50 38. Singles 150 pesos; doubles 200 pesos, with A/C 350 pesos, with TV 50 pesos more.) **Hotel Yuritzi**, off Principal after the church to the left, offers even greater comforts, with a well-tended courtyard, pool, and rooms available with A/C and TV. The small, sunny rooms have striped bedspreads and tiled baths but no hot water. (☎ 531 50 10. Singles 170 pesos, with TV and A/C 290 pesos; doubles 200 pesos, 400 pesos.) To get to the beach from the hotels, walk to the end of Principal. Pass the church and Lonchería Bahía on your right, and follow the dirt road as it bends to the right; the beach lies at the bottom of the hill (10min.).

Across the street from Hotel Yuritzi is one of Caleta's only restaurants, **Lonchería Bahía** (☎ 531 50 75). The laid-back cafe serves hamburgers (18-27 pesos), *tortas* (17-20 pesos), and 13- to 15-peso fruit drinks. (Open daily 9am-10pm.) For seafood in an even more casual setting, sample the catch of the day (40-50 pesos) at any of the *palapa* restaurants lining the cove. (Most open daily 7am-9pm.)

GUERRERO

TAXCO   ☎ 7

White buildings capped with red roofs, windy cobblestone streets, and sparkling *platerías* (silver shops) make the old mining town of Taxco (pop. 150,000) an antique gem set in the mountains. Cobblestone alleys coil around colonial churches, and streets are so narrow that pedestrians must flatten themselves against walls to let cars pass. Beneath the old-fashioned beauty flow the veins of silver that shaped Taxco's history. When silver was discovered in 1524, Taxco

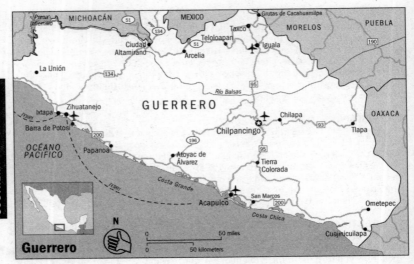

Guerrero

became the continent's first mining town, luring craftsmen and treasure-seekers from all over the world. The town's fortune ebbed with the supply of silver, and it was not until the 1930s, when the tourist industry took hold, that Taxco exploded with *platerías*. Today, the streets are aflutter with tourists buzzing through labyrinthine alleys, drawn like flies to the sweet honey of exquisite jewelry.

TRANSPORTATION

Taxco has two main bus stations. **Estrella de Oro station,** Kennedy 126 (☎ 622 06 48). Estrella de Oro has first-class service to: **Acapulco** (4hr., 6 per day 7:10am-6:45pm, 120 pesos); **Cuernavaca** (1½hr., 6:15pm, 38 pesos); **Mexico City** (2½hr., 7 per day 6am-7pm, 78 pesos). To get to the *zócalo* cross the street and walk up the steep hill known as Pilita. When you reach Plazuela San Juan, with a small fountain, veer left and you will emerge facing Santa Prisca in the *zócalo*. A "Zócalo" *combi* will make the trip (3 pesos), as will a taxi (12 pesos almost anywhere in the city).

   Flecha Roja station, Plateros 104 (☎ 622 01 31), goes to: **Acapulco** (4½hr. 4 per day 12:10pm-6pm, 120 pesos); **Cuernavaca** (1½hr., every hr. 6am-10pm, 37 pesos); and **Toluca** (3hr.; 1am, 11:40 and 2pm; 62 pesos). To reach the *zócalo*, turn right out of the station on to Plateros and turn left on Juan Ruíz de Alarcón. Turn left on Agostín de Tolsa to get to the *zócalo*.

ORIENTATION AND PRACTICAL INFORMATION

Taxco lies 185km southwest of Mexico City. The town is built atop a hillside, making walking a little tiresome but orientation quite simple. The *zócalo*, **Plaza Borda,** is marked by **Catedral de Santa Prisca,** which is visible from anywhere in town.

   Tourist Office: Subsecretaría de Fomento Turístico (☎ 622 22 74), at the entrance to town. "Los Arcos" *combis* end in front of the office, on the 2nd fl. Open daily 8am-8pm. Tourist information is also available at the Flecha Roja station, and most hotels on Plaza Borda have maps.

   Currency Exchange: Citibank, on the *zócalo*, has an **ATM**. Open M-F 9am-4pm. **Banco Santander Mexicano,** Cuauhtémoc 4 (☎ 622 35 35), off the *zócalo*, changes money until 4:30pm. Open M-F 9am-5pm, Sa 10am-2pm.

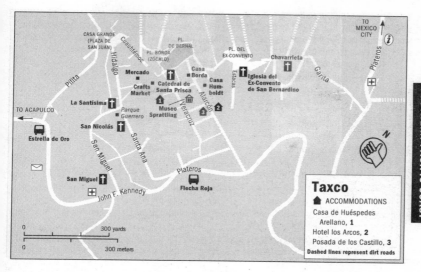

Taxco

ACCOMMODATIONS
Casa de Huéspedes
Arellano, 1
Hotel los Arcos, 2
Posada de los Castillo, 3
Dashed lines represent dirt roads

Market: Mercado Tetitlán, on the street to the right of Santa Prisca or off Hidalgo. Sells everything from meat to jewelry. Open daily 8:30am-8pm.

Police: (☎ 622 00 07). Some English spoken.

Emergency: Procuraduría del Turista (☎ 622 22 74 or 622 66 16). Open M-F 9am-7pm.

Red Cross: (☎ 622 32 32), on Plateros, next door to the tourist information *caseta*. No English spoken. Open daily 9am-2pm and 5-7pm.

Pharmacy: Farmacia Guadalupana, Hidalgo 8 (☎ 622 03 95), near Plaza San Juan. Open daily 8:30am-10pm.

Hospital: IMSS (☎ 622 35 10), on Plateros.

Fax: Alarcón 1 (☎ 622 48 85; fax 622 00 01). Open M-F 9am-3pm, Sa 9am-noon.

Internet Access: XNet, Delicias 4 (☎ 622 17 21), inside Bora Bora Pizza. 20 pesos per hr. Open daily 10:30am-11pm.

Post Office: Plateros 382 (☎ 622 05 01), near the Estrella de Oro station. Open M-F 9am-3pm.

Postal Code: 40200.

ACCOMMODATIONS

A good night's sleep does not come cheaply in Taxco, but the few budget accommodations are sleaze-free and situated in beautiful old buildings with reliably clean rooms. Reservations are recommended.

Casa de Huéspedes Arellano, Pajaritos 23 (☎ 622 02 15). From the zócalo, walk down the street to the right of the cathedral and descend the 1st stairs to the right; the hotel is 3 levels down through the vendor stands. Three charming terraces on which to sunbathe, hang laundry, and relax. Communal baths might be the biggest in Taxco. Rooms for 3 or 4 people (250 and 380 pesos, respectively) are great for families. Dorms 110 pesos; singles 150 pesos.

Hotel Los Arcos, Alarcón 4 (☎ 622 18 36), follow Agostín de Tolsa from the north end of the *zócalo* and turn right on the 1st street. From the shady courtyard to the expansive rooftop terrace, this hotel begs to be explored. Carved wooden furniture and wrought iron window bars create a medieval atmosphere. Private bathrooms are clean but small. Singles 250 pesos; doubles 300 pesos; triples 350 pesos; quads 400 pesos.

Casa Grande, Plaza de San Juan 7 (☎622 09 69), on the *zócalo*. Enter to the left of the building up the street. Don't expect to fall asleep before 1am, when the adjacent bar turns out its lights. Rooms are clean, small, and dark, with adequate communal baths. Singles 100 pesos, with bath 120 pesos; doubles 180 pesos, with bath 200 pesos. TV 40-50 pesos extra.

Posada de Los Castillo, Alarcón 7 (☎622 13 96), across the street from Hotel Los Arcos. Firm beds have fluffy pillows, and a small but scenic terrace occupies the 5th fl. Singles 200 pesos; doubles 290 pesos; triples 305 pesos.

▣ FOOD

Taquerías and *torterías* are virtually extinct around Plaza Borda, but abundant in the market areas. Many of Taxco's restaurants have balconies with lovely views of the busy streets—watch the sunset slip by while you sip *sangría* or *mezcal*.

Sotavento, Juárez 2, down the hill from the Iglesia del Ex-Convento toward the *zócalo*. Delicious food at reasonable prices. Chic clientele devours everything from pasta (40 pesos) to traditional Mexican dishes (32-50 pesos). Log on to the Internet for 15 pesos per hr. Open daily 1pm-midnight.

La Concha Nostra, Plaza de San Juan 7 (☎622 79 44), 2nd fl. of Hotel Casa Grande. While waiting for your *quesadillas* (21 pesos), lasagna (32 pesos), or pizza (19 pesos), watch angsty students blow smoke rings and scribble tormented poetry in their note-books. Live music Sa night. Open daily 7:45am-1am.

Pizzas Bora Bora, Delicias 4 (☎622 17 21), on the unmarked street that slopes to the right from Cuauhtémoc, just off the *zócalo*. Fishing nets and basket lamps dangle from the ceiling. Pizzas 40 pesos, spaghetti from 30 pesos. Open daily 1:30pm-midnight.

La Herradura, Alarcon 3 (☎622 85 24). Refreshingly down-to-earth with solid Mexican dishes (*comida corrida* 30 pesos) and absolutely no pizza. Open daily 9am-7pm.

La Hamburguesa, Plaza de San Juan 5 (☎622 09 41), down from Casa Grande. Satisfying burgers from 12 pesos. Traditional fare 12-30 pesos. Open daily 8am-midnight.

◉ SIGHTS

CATEDRAL DE SANTA PRISCA. Constructed in 1751-1758 with funds donated by silver tycoon José de la Borda, the church's striking Baroque facade is made of faded rose stone and decorated with inverted Corinthian columns. Inside are paintings done by the indigenous artist Miguel Cabrerra, whose racy subjects include a pregnant Virgin Mary and the circumcision of baby Jesus. (*Open daily 8am-8pm, mass held every hr. on Su 6am-2pm.*)

CASA BORDA. Once the 18th-century home of José de la Borda. The house now functions as the **Instituto Guerrerense de Cultura.** In addition to a library, a dance studio, and several exhibition galleries, the center organizes book readings and concerts. Ask for a schedule. (*☎622 66 17. Enter through the bookstore on the zócalo. Open Tu-Sa 10:30am-9pm, Su 9am-4pm.*)

CASA HUMBOLDT. Bas-reliefs in Moorish *mudéjar* style decorate this 18th-century colonial home, a rest stop for explorer Alexander Von Humboldt one night in 1803. The house now holds the collection of **Museo de Arte Virreinal,** including exhibits on 18th-century Catholic rituals and dress. (*Alarcón 12, past Hotel Los Arcos. ☎622 55 01. Open Tu-Sa 10am-6pm, Su 9am-3pm. 15 pesos, students 10 pesos.*)

EX-CONVENTO DE SAN BERNANDINO. Built in 1592 as a Franciscan monastery and later destroyed in a fire, the *ex-convento* was reconstructed in Neoclassical style in 1823. The struggle for independence from Spain officially ended when the Plan de Iguala was signed here in 1821. Today, a school convenes under the roof. (*In Plaza del Convento. Follow Juárez past city offices. Open daily 8am-1pm and 2-6:30pm. Free.*)

ALL THAT GLITTERS IS NOT...SILVER Although unscrupulous sellers and cheating craftspeople occasionally pass off *alpaca* (fool's silver) or *plateados* (silver-plated metals) to unsuspecting tourists, buying silver in Taxco is usually a sure thing. Many proprietors speak English and accept US currency, but if you stick with Spanish and talk in pesos while bargaining, you lower the risk of being charged tourist prices. While it's fun to ogle glamorous silver in the shops around Plaza Borda, the silver gets less expensive and the employees more amenable to bargaining farther from the *centro*. Bargain at stores with silver workshops by faking out the clerk and heading straight for the artisan. Remember that only the official ".925" stamp on the object's side guarantees that your shiny new charm is indeed silver.

MUSEO GUILLERMO SPRATLING. Named for American silversmith William Spratling, who helped jolt the silver industry in the 1930s, this museum holds his collection of Pre-Historic indigenous artifacts. *(Delgado 1. Follow the road downhill; left of the cathedral; the museum is on the left. Open M-Sa 10am-5pm, Su 9am-3pm. 25 pesos.)*

VIEWS OF TAXCO. The vistas of the city and surrounding hills from the hilly streets are superb, but especially at the **Church of Guadalupe.** From the *zócalo*, take Ojeda, to the right of Cuauhtémoc, to Guadalupe, and veer right until you reach the plaza before the church. For a more sweeping view, take a **cable car** to Hotel Monte Taxco. *(Take a "Los Arcos" combi to the white arches at the city's entrance (2 pesos). Before passing through the arches, turn left up a hill, and bear left into the parking lot. ☎ 622 14 68. Cable car runs daily 7:40am-7pm. Round-trip 26 pesos, children 14 pesos, hotel guests free.)*

🎵 🎭 ENTERTAINMENT AND NIGHTLIFE

As shops shut their doors and vendors pack their wares, people head to **Plaza Borda,** in front of the illuminated cathedral. Those with enough energy to dance after hiking Taxco's hills will get their chance at **Windows,** in Hotel Monte Taxco. Accessible only by cable car or taxi, this bar/dance club offers an unparalleled view with a party atmosphere. (☎ 622 13 00. Cover 50 pesos. Open F-Su 10pm-late.) For a more relaxed evening, try **La Concha Nostra** in Hotel Casa Grande, Plaza de San Juan 7, for beer (15 pesos) and great conversation. (Open daily 8am-1am.)

Taxco's crowded streets somehow manage to accommodate the tsunami of tourists that descend on the town during its two major festivals: **Feria Nacional de la Plata,** a national contest during the first week of November that celebrates silver artisanship, and the more popular *Semana Santa* festivities. On Good Friday, hooded *penitentes* carry logs made out of cactus trunks on their shoulders, or subject themselves to flagellation to eradicate their sins. During the annual **Día del Jumil,** on the first Monday of November, Taxco residents make a pilgrimage to the *Huizteco* hill, where they collect and eat insects known as *jumil*. The brown bugs contain more protein per gram than beef, and only appear during this time of year. In December, the **Church of Guadalupe,** from which you can see all of Taxco, comes alive with celebrations in honor of the Virgin.

🛍 SHOPPING

More than 300 *platerías* cater to the steady stream of tourists drawn to Taxco by its silver sheen. If you're dipping uncomfortably deep into your pockets, browse the shops that sell *artesanías* as well as silver, and stop by **Mercado Tetitlán,** behind the cathedral. Here, produce stands are interspersed with standard *platerías*. (Open daily 8:30am-8pm.) **Mercado de Plata,** just behind the Flecha Roja station, is where locals buy the work of silversmiths from the countryside, who often sell their wares at cheaper prices. (Open Sa 10am-6pm.)

▶ DAYTRIPS FROM TAXCO

GRUTAS DE CACAHUAMILPA. Some of the most beautiful natural wonders in Taxco lie underground in an extensive network of *grutas* (caves). According to lore, the **Grutas de Cacahuamilpa** were once a hideaway for runaway Indians. Twenty huge *salones* (halls) are filled with stalactites, stalagmites, and rock formations. The columns and ceilings—some as high as 85m—are the work of a subterranean stream that developed into the **Río San Jerónimo.** A guide will point out funny rock shapes complete with fabricated anecdotes. *("Grutas" combis leave from Taxco's Flecha Roja station, stopping at the parking lot (every hr., 13 pesos). Taxis cost 80-100 pesos. Flecha Roja buses make the trip (30min., every hr. 6:30am-3:30am, 16 pesos), but will drop you off a short jaunt away. To get to the parking lot, take a right, then another right after the curve. Open daily 10am-5pm. 30 pesos, children 20 pesos. Tours leave from the visitors center (2hr., every hr.). You can only enter the caves with a tour guide.)*

LAS GRANADAS. 26km from Taxco, this ecological reserve is little more than a hike in the woods. This 5km rock trail curls around mountain tops and dips into the valley, bringing hikers to a stunning waterfall. The path is both hilly and sunny, so wear comfortable shoes and sunblock. *(Grab a combi heading to Acuitlapan (40min., every 25min. 7am-8pm, 13 pesos). Once there, follow the one road into town. As you enter the main square, look to the far end where the path starts as a dirt road. No set hours. Free.)*

IXCATEOPAN. Lying 42km from Taxco, Ixcateopan is known for its beauty and history. The marble and stone streets supply the beauty, while **Museo de la Resistencia Indígena** tells the history. *(Open daily 9am-5pm. Free.)* The alleged remains of Cuauhtémoc, the last Aztec emperor, are kept in a display case in **Templo de Santa María de la Asunción.** *(Take an "Ixcateopan" combi (1¼hr., every 30min. 6am-9pm, 13 pesos), in front of Seguro Social on J.F. Kennedy.)*

ZIHUATANEJO AND IXTAPA   ☎ 7

Before resort engineers got their hands on Ixtapa (eeks-TAH-pa), it was a wild landscape filled with coconut palms, rocky cliffs, and mangrove swamps. Not until the 1970s, when development began on "the place of the white sands," did both Ixtapa and its counterpart, Zihuatanejo (see-wah-tah-NEH-ho), find themselves on the tourist map. Today, the towns' combined population of about 80,000 thrives almost exclusively on the tourist trade. Ixtapa has been meticulously constructed by Mexican pleasure engineers to cater to moneyed foreigners. Budget accomodations are non-existent amid the sprawling resorts, and budget restaurants are carefully hidden. Meanwhile Zihuatanejo, just a 15min. bus ride away, has yet to shake off the net of its fishing town past. Here, budget hotels are steps from the glittering beach. The differences between Ixtapa and Zihuatanejo make a trip here feel like two vacations in one. If you stay in Zihuatanejo and play in Ixtapa, these twins will supply tourist-town glitz at fishing-village prices.

▌ TRANSPORTATION

GETTING AROUND

Ixtapa's main road, **Blvd. Ixtapa,** lies past a bundle of waterfront luxury hotels on the left and overpriced stores to the right. **Buses** shuttling between the two cities leave Zihuatanejo from Juárez and Morelos, across from the yellow Elektra store; they leave Ixtapa from various stops on Blvd. Ixtapa (15-25min., 6am-10pm, 4 pesos). **Taxis** scuttle between the towns (30 pesos by day, 40 pesos by night). Taxis in Zihuatanejo can be found on Juárez, in front of the market.

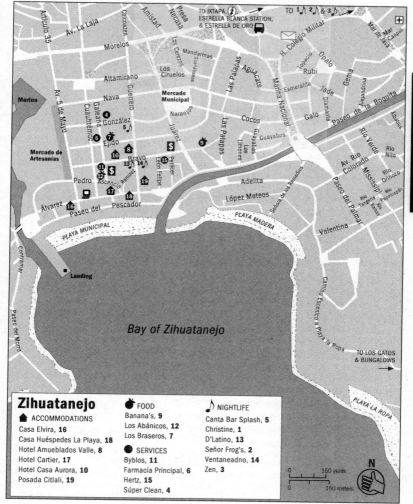

Zihuatanejo

🏠 **ACCOMMODATIONS**
Casa Elvira, **16**
Casa Huéspedes La Playa, **18**
Hotel Amueblados Valle, **8**
Hotel Cartier, **17**
Hotel Casa Aurora, **10**
Posada Citlali, **19**

🍴 **FOOD**
Banana's, **9**
Los Abánicos, **12**
Los Braseros, **7**

⚫ **SERVICES**
Byblos, **11**
Farmacía Principal, **6**
Hertz, **15**
Súper Clean, **4**

🎵 **NIGHTLIFE**
Canta Bar Splash, **5**
Christine, **1**
D'Latino, **13**
Señor Frog's, **2**
Ventaneadno, **14**
Zen, **3**

GETTING AWAY

Airport: (☎554 20 70), 15km outside of town. Taxis leave from the airport for Zihuatanejo (125 pesos) and Ixtapa (160 pesos). *Combis* depart from the left side of the airport parking lot to the intersection of Morelos and Juárez in Zihuatanejo (6am-11pm, 4 pesos). You can catch *combis* to the airport from the intersection of González and Juárez in Zihuatanejo. They are marked with a picture of a plane (6:30am-10:30pm, 4 pesos). Served by: **America West** (☎554 86 34), open M-Sa 9am-5pm, Su noon-4pm; **Continental** (☎554 25 49 or 554 42 17), open daily 9am-5pm; and **Mexicana** (☎554 22 27), open daily 8am-8pm. Mexicana also has a branch office in Zihuatanejo (☎554 22 08 or 554 22 09), Guerrero at Bravo. Open M-Sa 9am-7pm.

Buses: arrive in Zihuatanejo at the **Estrella Blanca** and **Estrella de Oro stations,** side-by-side on the outskirts of the *centro*. *Combis* (3 pesos), across the street as you leave the station, or taxis (15 pesos) bring you to the center of town. To reach the bus station from the *centro*, hop on a *combi* labeled "Coacoyul" (7am-8:30pm, 3 pesos) across from the market on Juárez. Estrella de Oro (☎ 554 21 75) sends buses to: **Acapulco** (5hr., every hr. 5:50am-5pm, 70 pesos); **Cuernavaca** (7hr., 6:40pm, 251 pesos); **Mexico City** (9hr., 8am and 10pm, 305 pesos); and **Papanoa** (1½hr., every hr. 3:45am-7:49pm, 23 pesos). Estrella Blanca (☎ 554 34 77) goes to: **Acapulco** (4hr., every hr. 7am-9:35pm, 94 pesos); **Lázaro Cárdenas** (2½hr., every 3hr. 1am-7:30pm, 49 pesos); **Puerto Escondido** (12hr., 7:30pm, 276 pesos).

🛂 PRACTICAL INFORMATION

TOURIST, FINANCIAL, AND LOCAL SERVICES

Tourist Office: SEFOTUR (☎ 553 19 67), on Blvd. Ixtapa, in Ixtapa across from Hotel Presidente, offers a comprehensive *Guía Turística Urbana* to beaches and services. Some English spoken. Open M-F 8am-8pm, Sa 8am-2pm. For complaints or emergencies call the **Agencia de Ministerio Público en Atención al Turista** in Ixtapa (☎ 554 19 67) or Zihuatanejo (☎ 354 56 41), or **Profeco** (☎ 554 52 36) in Zihuatanejo.

Currency Exchange: Bancomer (☎ 554 74 93), in Zihuatanejo on the corner of Juárez and Bravo. Open M-F 8:30am-4pm, Sa 10am-2pm. Also has a 24hr. **ATM. Money Exchange,** Galeana 6 (☎ 554 28 00), has worse rates but no commission. From the beach, walk a block on Cuauhtémoc, take a right on Ascencio and make the 1st left onto Galeana. Offers **fax** and **long-distance** service. Open M-Sa 8am-9pm, Su 9am-9pm.

American Express, Blvd. Ixtapa, in the Area Comercial Hotel Krystal (☎ 553 0853, fax 553 12 06). Open M-F 9am-6pm, Sa 9am-2pm.

Bookstore: Byblos, Galeana 2 (☎ 554 22 81), in Zihuatanejo, has English magazines, paperbacks, and the handy *Owen's English Language Guide to Ixtapa and Zihuatanejo,* written by a member of Cousteau's team (150 pesos). Open-air cafe (coffee from 10 pesos) is a great place to read or meet friends. Open M-Sa 9am-9pm, daily in summer.

Market: The **mercado municipal** in Zihuatanejo on Juárez, 4 blocks from the water, sells fresh produce and has several small eateries. Open daily 6am-7pm. The **Mercado de Artesanías** in Zihuatanejo offers jewelry and souvenirs. Open daily 9am-8:30pm.

Supermarket: Comercial Mexicana (☎ 483 21 84), behind the Estrella Blanca bus station. Take a "Coacoyul" bus. Open daily 8am-10pm.

Laundry: Súper Clean, González 82 (☎ 554 23 47), in Zihuatanejo at Galeana. 12 pesos per kg., 36 peso min. Open M-Sa 8am-8pm.

Luggage Storage: Estrella Blanca station in Zihuatanejo. 3 pesos per hr.

Car Rental: Hertz, Bravo 13 (☎ 554 22 55; fax 554 30 50), in Zihuatanejo, rents small VWs for 500 pesos per day including insurance and unlimited mileage. Open daily 8am-6pm. Also has an office in the airport (☎ 554 25 90). **Alamo** (☎ 553 02 06), in the Centro Comercial de los Patios in Ixtapa and at the airport. Open daily 9am-9pm.

EMERGENCY AND COMMUNICATIONS

Emergency: ☎ 060.

Tourist Police: (☎ 553 20 08), Police Module in Ixtapa, across from Hotel Presidente. Some English spoken.

Red Cross: (☎ 554 20 09), on Huertas as you leave Zihuatanejo. 24hr. emergency and ambulance service. Some English spoken.

Pharmacy: Farmacia Principal (☎ 554 42 17), Cuauhtémoc 29 at the corner of Ejido in Zihuatanejo. Open M-Sa 9am-9pm.

Medical Services: Centro de Salud (☎ 554 20 88), Boquita at Palmar, in Zihuatanejo. No English spoken. **IMSS** (☎ 554 48 24), across from the Estrella Blanca station. No English spoken.

Internet Access: Net World 2000, Álvarez 34 (☎554 29 56), in Zihuatanejo across from Casa Elvira. 30 pesos per hr., half-price between 9am-1pm. Open M-F 9am-2pm and 5-9pm, Sa 9am-2pm and 6-9pm, Su 5-9pm. In Ixtapa: **Xtapa Connexión** (☎553 22 53), Ixtapa Plaza on the walkway to the left of Señor Frog's. 85 pesos per hr., 20 pesos to check email. Open daily 10:30am-10pm.

Fax: Telecomm (☎553 06 80, fax 554 33 81), beside the post office. Fax, telegraph, Western Union. Also next to Señor Frog's in Ixtapa. Open M-F 9am-7pm, Sa-Su 9am-noon.

Post Office: (☎554 21 92), off Palmar in Zihuatanejo. From Juárez, turn right on Morelos. At the Pollo Feliz, turn right and walk 2 blocks. Open M-F 8am-3pm, Sa 9am-1pm.

Postal Code: 40880.

ACCOMMODATIONS

Zihuatanejo has plenty of budget accommodations within a few blocks of the **Playa Municipal.** Prices rise substantially during high season (Dec.-Apr.), along with the number of *gringos* per square foot. If you visit during low season, with a large group, or plan to stay several days, you will have excellent leverage for negotiating discounts. The tourist office discourages unofficial camping, partly for safety reasons, but if you insist on pitching a tent, **Playa Quieta,** near Club Med in Ixtapa, is the most sensible place. All of the following listings are in Zihuatanejo.

Casa Elvira, Álvarez 8 (☎554 20 61), 1 block from the Playa Municipal, was the 1st guest house in Zihuatanejo. Rooms are cozy and clean, if a bit small, and have private cold-water baths and strong ceiling fans. The courtyard is filled with plants, birds, and gregarious family members; step out back and you're on the beach. Rooms between 100 and 200 pesos, depending on the room and the season. Prices often negotiable.

Hotel Cartier, Acensio 7 (☎554 50 84). The sign in front says it all: "Canadian spoken here, poco español, eh." International students and young people from all corners of the globe can be found here, relaxing in hammocks on the top-floor patio, cooking in the well-supplied common kitchen, or making their mark on the walls of the courtyard. Rooms have private cold-water baths, but communal hot showers are also available. Beds 80 pesos; prices negotiable for longer stays.

Hotel Amueblados Valle, Guerrero 14 (☎/fax 554 32 20, 554 20 84), between Ejido and Bravo. 8 fully-equipped apartments come with a stocked kitchen/eating area, couches, ceiling fan, balcony, and daily towel service. Rooms are spacious and packed with amenities. 1-3 people 300-350 pesos; Dec.-Apr. 400 pesos. 2 bedroom apartment 600 pesos. Prices drop for longer stays. For high-season visits, make reservations up to a year in advance.

Hotel Casa Aurora, Bravo 60 (☎554 30 46), between Guerrero and Galeana. This budget mainstay has a friendly staff, neat, good-sized rooms, and 70s bedspreads. Baths are clean and have hot water. Singles 150 pesos; doubles 220 pesos, with A/C 250 pesos; triples 300 pesos. Each additional person 50 pesos. Beachside bungalow at Playa de la Ropa with kitchen and no A/C holds 2 people for 300 pesos.

Casa de Huéspedes La Playa, Álvarez 6 (☎554 24 47), at Guerrero. The best part is the location. Built like attached houses, the rooms at the Casa are right on the beach, where the waves of the Pacific will lull you to sleep in your hammock on the porch. Basic and reasonably clean, with fans and no hot water. No fixed prices, but rooms with 2 single beds usually cost 160 pesos.

Posada Citlali, Guerrero 3 (☎554 20 43), near Álvarez. A bit pricey, but charming. Vines droop lazily in the courtyard; wooden rockers on the terrace encourage you to do the same. All rooms with overhead fans. Singles 200 pesos; doubles 300 pesos.

FOOD

Like the neighboring hotels, restaurants in Ixtapa are pricey. However, they are spotless and offer an array of authentic-tasting international cuisine. Your meal may be more reasonably priced (50-70 pesos) if you eat at a cafe before they switch to the main menu (around 2pm). Restaurants in Zihuatanejo serve freshly caught fish from the bay at consistent budget prices.

Los Abánicos (☎554 20 20), on the corner of Ascencio and Galeana. Though this open-air restaurant may look like all the rest in Zihuatanejo, the food here is cheaper and delicious—try their *comida corrida* (35 pesos) with a choice of 3 rotating entrees, rice or soup, tortillas, and *agua fresca*. Great *ceviche* 40 pesos. Open M-Sa 8am-5pm.

Los Braseros, Ejido 64 (☎554 87 36), between Galeana and Guerrero. This exuberant open-air eatery specializes in heavenly stir-fried combinations of meat, vegetables, and cheese (46 pesos), with a sprinkling of veggie options. Large portions served with hot tortillas by an attentive staff. Open daily 9am-1am.

Banana's, Bravo 4 (☎556 10 80 or 556 51 03). Locals flock here for the great break-fast combos. Eggs any style with fruit juice or coffee 15 pesos (with meat 18 pesos). The *comida corrida* (25 pesos) offers lots of main course options. Chicken and beef 25-50 pesos, seafood 35-55 pesos. Open daily 8am-4pm.

Taquería Chai (☎559 09 31), in the Centro Comercial in Ixtapa. Walk around the right side of the Centro until you get to a small unattached building in the righthand corner labeled "La Hacienda." One of the only places in Ixtapa for good, cheap food. Friendly staff serves hot tacos (3 pesos) with a smile. Open daily 9:30am-midnight.

▓◉ BEACHES AND SIGHTS

Neither Zihuatanejo's self-conscious charm nor Ixtapa's resorts can eclipse the area's natural beauty. In Zihuatanejo, four patches of sand make excellent beaches. They are, clockwise from the municipal pier: **Playa Principal, Playa La Madera, Playa la Ropa,** and **Playa Las Gatas.** The latter two are the best beaches in Zihuatanejo. Ixtapa overlooks the unbroken stretch of **Playa del Palmar** on the Bahía del Palmar, but less heavily touristed beaches lie beyond Laguna de Ixtapa: **Playa Quieta, Playa Linda,** and, at the bay's west edge, **Isla Ixtapa.**

ZIHUATANEJO

PLAYA PRINCIPAL. Playa Principal is downtown Zihuatanejo's beach, in front of the Paseo del Pescador. This beach is more suited to seashell collectors and fishing boats than swimmers. The attractions here are the basketball court, the pier, and the fish being unloaded onto the dock.

PLAYA MADERA. About 200m long, Playa Madera (Wood Beach) was named for its role as a loading site for local hardwood export. The fine sand and moderate waves show no trace of the beach's lumberyard past, offering a great place to body surf or play in the waves. A number of restaurants and bungalows have sprung up along the shore. *(To get there, follow the cement pathway at the end of Playa Principal.)*

PLAYA LA ROPA. Protected from the rough Pacific by the bay, Playa La Ropa's crescent of sumptuous, white, often-uncrowded sand attracts tourists from the hotels on the surrounding cliffs. *(Take a "Ropa" bus from along Juárez (6am-7pm, 4 pesos). You can also make the 4km trip by foot: follow Paseo de la Boquita along the canal over the bridge and turn left, passing Playa Madera. The road curves to the right and passes Hotel Casa que Canta; follow the stone road to the left down to the beach. If you're planning on leaving late, you may want to arrange a taxi pick-up beforehand. 20 pesos.)*

PLAYA LAS GATAS. According to local tales, Purepecha king Calzontzin ordered the construction of the stone wall in Playa Las Gatas as protection from the sharks while he bathed. Since then, coral and marine life have overtaken the stone barricade. Equally colorful but not nearly as pleasant, lawn chairs and umbrellas, available from local restaurants (free if you order food—farther from the dock, some restaurants may waive this condition), have taken over the beach. The calm, clear waters welcome snorkelers (equipment rental 40 pesos per day) and kayakers (single-person kayaks 100 pesos per hr.). Escape the shops and restaurants by taking the path (2km) behind the last restaurant to the **Garrobo Lighthouse,** which offers a panoramic view. Since it's well hidden, ask any of the waiters for specific directions to the lighthouse. (*To reach Las Gatas, take a lancha from the pier in downtown Zihuatanejo (10min.; every 15min. 9am-4pm, last boat returns 5pm; round-trip 30 pesos). It is possible to walk over the rocks to Las Gatas from La Ropa, but not easy. Alternatively, you may walk on the road that brought you to La Ropa for another 45min., keeping to the left as it splits.*)

IXTAPA

PLAYA DE PALMER. Well guarded from Blvd. Ixtapa by a line of posh hotels, Playa de Palmer is an active, spacious, and beautiful beach. Walk a few kilometers on the soft golden sand or join in one of the casual volleyball or soccer games played near the hotel pools. Without the protection of a bay, the beach is besieged by sizeable waves, attracting para-sailers, scuba divers, and jet skiers. (*The beach can be reached by public access paths at either end, near the Sheraton Hotel, or Carlos 'n' Charlie's. Otherwise, clutch your Let's Go confidently, wear your swimsuit proudly, and cut right through the fancy hotel lobbies.*)

PLAYA QUIETA AND PLAYA LINDA. About 6km northwest of downtown lie Playas Quieta and Linda. The calm waves of these twin beaches, separated by a pier, attract both ritzy hotel patrons and pick-up trucks of Mexican families. One or two restaurants near the pier rent horses (140 pesos per hr). (*From Ixtapa, follow Blvd. Ixtapa northwest beyond most of the hotels, and turn right at the "Playa Linda" sign. From Zihuatanejo, it is more convenient to use the access road from Mex. 200; go past the exit for Ixtapa in the direction of Puerto Vallarta and take the next left, marked Playa Linda. The road skirts Laguna de Ixtapa and hits the beach farther northwest. Taxis from Ixtapa 40 pesos, from Zihuatanejo 70 pesos. A "Playa Linda" bus begins in Zihuatanejo and passes through Ixtapa on its way to playas Quieta and Linda (5 pesos). Buses return to Ixtapa and Zihuatanejo approx. every 15 min. (4-5 pesos). You can also walk along the road 4km on the bicycle path.*)

ISLA IXTAPA. Some claim that of all the area's beaches, the most picturesque lie on **Isla Ixtapa,** 2km off-shore from Playa Quieta. The island is a must-visit for snorkeling enthusiasts. The main beach is **Playa Cuachalalate,** frequented by fishermen and waterskiers. **Playa Varadero** is a small beach with calm waters and *palapa* restaurants. On the ocean side of the island, **Playa Coral** is the least-visited of the three. It has no services and poor swimming, but the coral makes for excellent scuba diving. (*To get there, take a boat from the pier at Zihuatanejo (1hr.; boats leave at noon, return at 5pm; 60 pesos round-trip). A cheaper alternative is the microbus from Zihuatanejo or Ixtapa to the pier at Playa Linda (4-5 pesos). From there, catch a lancha. Every 15min. 9am-5pm, round-trip 30 pesos.*)

◾ NIGHTLIFE

Although beaches in both towns promise spectacular sun, sand, and waves, the only place to go for rip-roarin' nightlife is Ixtapa. **Blvd. Ixtapa,** like most resort strips, is littered with fancy clubs and relaxed bars that rock to the beat of young people. Karaoke is the most popular pastime in Zihuatanejo—if you're more in the mood to sample local vocal talent than to grind to the pounding of house techno, Zihuatanejo may fill the bill.

IXTAPA

Christine (☎ 553 04 56), Ixtapa in front of Hotel Krystal. Ixtapa's premiere club; with stadium-like seats around the dance floor, hanging vines, and a light show. As artificially beautiful as Ixtapa itself. Beer 30 pesos, *bebidas nacionales* 45 pesos. M, W no cover;

Su, Tu 100 pesos; Th men 200 pesos, women free; F-Sa men 200 pesos, women 100 pesos. July and Aug. M no cover; Tu, W open bar, men 200 pesos, women 100 pesos; Th men 200 pesos, women free; F-Sa men 200 pesos, women 100 pesos; Su open bar, men 250 pesos, women 200 pesos. Open daily from 10pm. No shorts on weekends.

Señor Frog's (☎ 553 22 82), may be a restaurant until midnight, but when the clock strikes twelve, drunk Americans climb on tables to begin the party. Spiral fans whirring at top speed and beers (30 pesos) keep it cool. *Bebidas nacionales* 35 pesos. No cover. Open daily 6pm-3am.

La Valentina (☎ 553 11 90 or 552 12 50), on Blvd. Ixtapa after the Radisson. The beautiful and scantily clad gather here to pretend they are vacationing in Europe. The villa-style interior looks onto a faux landscape, complete with flashing electric stars and ringed with columns. Open bar encourages drunken revelry. Cover: *Semana Santa* men 220 pesos, women 200 pesos; July-Aug. and Dec. men 180 pesos, women 160 pesos; other times, men 140 pesos, women 120 pesos. Open daily 10pm-5am.

Zen (☎ 553 00 03, 553 3124), on the Blvd. Ixtapa next to the Radisson. Young, rich, and self-consciously urbane hipsters lounge amidst couches and modern art. Psychedelic projections swirl on the ceiling as techno pounds in the background. Drinks 30-35 pesos. Cover 130 pesos in July and Aug., with open bar; during *Semana Santa* 100 pesos. Open Tu-Su 10pm-3am.

ZIHUATANEJO

D'Latino (☎ 554 22 30), on the corner of Bravo and Guerrero. A spicy Latin dance club featuring *salsa* and reggae, with occasional live music. Short skirted dancers get down under the black lights while others sip drinks (28 pesos) from the fully stocked bar. 2-for-1 beers M and Th. No cover M-Th, F-Sa cover 40 pesos. Open daily 10pm-6am.

Ventaneando, Bravo 23 (☎ 55453 90), across from D'Latino. This dark, smoky bar is the natural departure point for exploration of Zihuatanejo's thriving karaoke scene. Listen to cheesy Mexican ballads while watching cheesier early 90s music videos on TV. Things pick up after midnight when amateur singers strut their stuff. Beer 22 pesos, national drinks 36 pesos. No cover. Open daily 9pm-4am.

Canta Bar Splash, Guerrero between Ejido and González. This pint-sized place feels like an aquarium with cool blue lights washing over the 20-something crowd seated at the bar or up in the balconies. Sip a beer (25 pesos) or a mixed drink (35 pesos) as you croon the sappy Mexican ballad of your choice. Open daily 7pm-3am.

COSTA GRANDE

The Guerrero coast north of Acapulco is often called the Costa Grande to distinguish it from its smaller counterpart, Costa Chica, to the south. Though the stretch from Acapulco to Zihuatanejo/Ixtapa has few inviting beaches, ■**Barra de Potosí,** 20km southeast of Zihuatanejo, and **Papanoa,** 60km farther along Mex. 200, are hidden treasures ideal for wasting the day in the waves.

BARRA DE POTOSÍ   ☎ 7

For the traveler whose head is spinning from ruins, cathedrals, and kitsch, no better tonic exists than a spell on the seemingly infinite stretch of sand known as **Playa Barra de Potosí.** This small town, consisting of a shallow lagoon, a forest of palm trees, and waterfront huts, appears caught in perpetual *siesta*. Water babies can take a dip in the lagoon or stroll over to the beach. Don't be deceived by the crashing waves. Once you're past the breaking point, the water is peaceful and crystal clear. Eat until you're full, walk on the beach, snooze on a hammock in the shade, and slow down to properly enjoy the surrounding beauty.

▐ **TRANSPORTATION.** From Zihuatanejo, "Petatlán" buses leave for Potosí from a station on Las Palmas, around the corner from Restaurante La Jaiba on Juárez (30min., every 15min. 6am-9pm, 6 pesos). Ask to be let off at **Achotes,** an unmarked intersection. A pick-up truck will be waiting (or arriving soon) on the side road to collect passengers for the bumpy trip to the *enramadas* (30min., 7 pesos). Trucks return to the intersection from the same spot (7am-6pm). The bus to Zihuatanejo leaves from the other side of the route.

▐▗▐▖ ACCOMODATIONS AND FOOD. Those unskilled in the art of beachside hammock-napping can splurge at **Hotel Barra de Potosí**, a small-scale resort hotel and recent addition to the pristine beach. From the *enramadas* (open-air seaside restaurants), walk away from the lagoon—you can't miss the large white building with blue balconies. Not all rooms have the same amenities, but all have access to the beachside swimming pool and restaurant. (☎554 82 90. Doubles 300 pesos.)

There are 10 or so *enramadas*, which serve simple seafood dishes at reasonable prices. Enjoy home-cooked food while relaxing in one of the hammocks swinging in the shaded restaurants. In keeping with the casual spirit, restaurants do not have set menus. Instead, they ask you what type of seafood you'd like to eat (expect to spend 40-50 pesos per person). *Enramadas* that face the lagoon offer slightly lower prices, but beware: the lagoon is smelly. (Open daily 7am-6pm.)

◨◪ SIGHTS AND BEACHES. If you insist on exerting yourself while in Barra de Potosí (something the locals may not understand), the only option is to hike up the dirt road to the lighthouse atop **Cerro Guamiule** (200m), the peak near the restaurants that guards the southern entrance to the bay. After a 30min. walk, you will be rewarded with a view of the bay and its 20km of beaches. However, beware of creepy, crawly critters on the path. After gaping, walk north along the shore of **Playa Potosí**, the southernmost beach on the bay, to aptly named **Playa Blanca** ("white beach," 3km). You will pass **Playa Coacoyul** (8km), **Playa Riscaliyo** (19km), and pebbly **Playa Manzanillo** (24km) before reaching another lighthouse (26km) that overlooks the northern edge of the bay. All beaches are free of tourists in the summer months but fill with hundreds of domestic visitors during Christmas.

PAPANOA   ☎ 7

Much like Barra de Potosí, **Papanoa** is a tiny, delectable town with rolling waves. Pigs and roosters scuttle along a road that ends in waterfront *enramadas*. **Cayaquitos**, 2km from town, is a more accessible (and more crowded) than **Playa Vicente Guerrero**, 5km away. While a scarcity of eateries exists on Cayaquitos, numerous restaurants in Vicente Guerrero battle to fill your belly with the day's catch. Sample cheap and savory *pescadillas* (20 pesos for 4) at Restaurante Chiro's, near the beach entrance. (Fish 40-50 pesos. Open daily 7am-6pm.)

▐ TRANSPORTATION. Buses leave from the Estrella Blanca station in Zihuatanejo (1½hr, every hr. 3:45am-7:49pm, 23 pesos). In Papanoa, white trucks pick up passengers under the large, spreading tree across the street on the left from the bus drop-off (6am-7pm, 6 pesos). Taxis run to **Cayaquitos** (6 pesos) and to **Vicente Guerrero** (10 pesos). If you plan to leave the beach later than 7pm, arrange for a taxi to come for you ahead of time.

ACAPULCO   ☎ 7

Once upon a time, Acapulco (pop. 2 million) was a stunningly beautiful playground for the rich and famous. Hollywood legends celebrated their successes here, dancing the nights away in chic clubs, and the privileged few spent their honeymoons lounging on the seductive shores. But times change and fairy tales fade; today, Acapulco is a mere shadow of the luxurious retreat it once was. The city now consists of a crowded beach flanked by tightly packed 14-story hotels, and the slum that starts behind them stretches up the hill. This grimmer Acapulco was born when the flow of vacationers slowed, and the hotel job market could no longer keep pace with the waves of immigrants drawn seaward by the prospect of plentiful pesos. Money still controls Acapulco, but now the focus is on pursuit, not spending. Persistent cabbies and peddlers of everything from bubble gum to "free information" run at tourists like eager bulls. Though the high-rise hotels crowding the waterfront have lost their flush of youth, a full roster of festivals and beautification projects promises a revamped Acapulco. Perhaps it's best to visit the city at night, when darkness shrouds the grime and street lamps evoke its fairy tale past.

⊟ TRANSPORTATION

Airport: Mex. 200, 26km south of the city. Taxis make the run to the airport for 90 pesos; shared cabs (☎462 10 95) will do it for 70 pesos. Served by **Aerolines Internacionales** (☎486 56 30), **Aeroméxico** (☎485 16 25), **American** (☎466 92 32), **America West** (☎800 235 92 92), **Continental** (☎466 90 63), and **Mexicana** (☎486 75 85).

Buses: Acapulco has 3 bus stations. To get from the **Estrella de Oro station** (☎485 87 05), on Cuauhtémoc at Massiu, to the *zócalo* (40min.), cross the street and catch any bus labeled "Zócalo" (3.5 pesos). Taxis charge 30-40 pesos. Estrella de Oro sends buses to: **Cuernavaca** (4hr., every hr. 6am-8pm, 190 pesos); **Mexico City** (5hr., every hr. 6am-2am, 230 pesos); **Taxco** (4hr., every 4hr. 7am-9pm, 120 pesos); and **Zihuatanejo** (4hr., every hr. 4:15am-5:30pm, 70 pesos). **Estrella Blanca** has 2 stations: **Centro Papagayo** (☎469 20 80), Cuauhtémoc behind Parque Papagayo, and **Centro Ejido** (☎469 20 28), on Ejido north of the *zócalo*. The *ejecutivo* class buses leave from Papagayo and travel to: **Cuernavaca** (4hr., 11:30am and 5pm, 197 pesos); **Mexico City** (5hr., every hr. on the half hr., 230 pesos); and **Puebla** (7hr.; 3, 10pm, and midnight; 345 pesos). To get to Centro Papagayo from the *zócalo*, take a "CICI" bus (3.5 pesos) to Parque Papagayo. Cross the park—the bus station is on Cuauhtémoc behind the park. All other buses leave from Ejido—just an "Ejido" bus ride (3.5 pesos) away from the *zócalo*. To get to the *zócalo* from either station, take a "Zócalo" bus.

✴🛈 ORIENTATION AND PRACTICAL INFORMATION

Acapulco Bay lies 400km south of Mexico City and 239km southeast of Ixtapa and Zihuatanejo. Mex. 200 becomes **La Costera** (Costera Miguel Alemán), the main drag that crosses all of Acapulco. **Acapulco Dorado,** full of restaurants, malls, and hotels, stretches from **Parque Papagayo** to the naval base. The ultra-chic resorts are found on **Acapulco Diamante,** farther east. Budget accommodations and restaurants lie between the *zócalo* and **La Quebrada,** the famous cliff-diving spot. Trying to walk the main drag will suck hours away from your beach time, so become acquainted with the basics of public transportation. Buses run along Costera from Playa "Hornos" or Playa "Caleta" in the west to "CICI" or "Base" in the east and back (3.5 pesos, 4 pesos for a yellow bus with air-conditioning). Along Cuauhtémoc, buses run from "Cine Río" in the west to "La Base" in the east and back (3.5 pesos).

TOURIST AND FINANCIAL SERVICES

Tourist Offices: SEFOTUR Costera 4455 (☎484 45 83 or 484 44 16), in the Centro Cultural de Acapulco, west of the CICI water park across the street. Helpful staff will happily overload you with brochures and maps. English spoken. Open daily 9am-11pm. In an emergency, contact the **Procuraduría del Turista** in the same office.

INTERIOR DECORATORS
Though you may think that Acapulco's bus drivers are skilled only in the art of frustrating passengers—idling at the curb for half an hour when you're in a hurry, or careening off on two wheels before you've had a chance to sit down, their talent for decoration may convince you otherwise. Each unique bus interior functions as an altar of self-expression and faith. Everything from fringed drapes, icons of patron saints, favorite CDs, and cartoon characters offer a bewildering glimpse into the persona of the person gripping the gear shift. *Let's Go's* must unusual ride? In a bus ornamented with autographed, unopened maxi-pads.

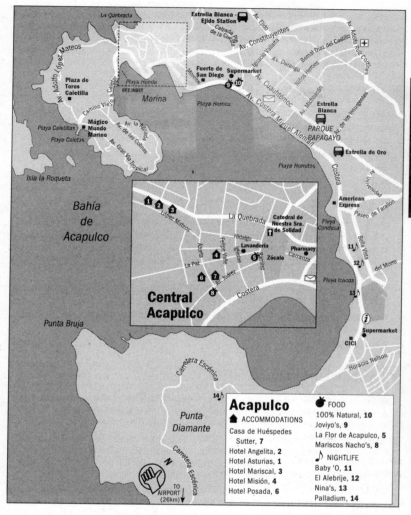

Acapulco

🍎 FOOD

🏠 ACCOMMODATIONS

100% Natural, **10**
Joviyo's, **9**
La Flor de Acapulco, **5**
Mariscos Nacho's, **8**

Casa de Huéspedes
  Sutter, **7**
Hotel Angelita, **2**
Hotel Asturias, **1**
Hotel Mariscal, **3**
Hotel Misión, **4**
Hotel Posada, **6**

♪ NIGHTLIFE

Baby 'O, **11**
El Alebrije, **12**
Nina's, **13**
Palladium, **14**

Consulates: Canada (☎ 484 13 05), Costera at Juan Pérez, in the Continental Plaza Hotel. Open M-F 9am-5pm. **UK** (☎ 481 13 49; fax 484 13 06), in the Centro Comercial Maravilla, Locale 34. Open M-F 1-3pm and 4-8pm. **US,** Costera 121 #14 (☎ 469 05 56), in the Continental Hotel. Open M-F 10am-2pm.

Currency Exchange: Banks on Costera have good rates. Open M-F 9am-4pm, most with 24hr. **ATMs. Casas de cambio** line Costera and often stay open until 8pm.

American Express: Costera 1628 (☎ 469 11 00; fax 469 11 88), on the bottom floor of the Gran Plaza shopping center. Open M-F 10am-7pm, Sa 10am-3pm.

LOCAL SERVICES

Car Rental: Hertz, Costera 137 (☎ 485 68 89), across from Universidad Americana. Small VW with insurance 500 pesos per day. Open daily 8am-8pm. 2nd location at the airport is open daily 6am-10pm.

Market: Constituyentes at Hurtado. Open daily 6am-6pm.

Supermarket: Comercial Mexicana, (☎484 33 73), has 2 locations on Costera: one east of the tourist office and the other 4 blocks east of the *zócalo*. Open daily 8am-11pm.

Laundry: Super Lavandería, José Maria Iglesias 9 (☎480 01 46), between Paz and Hidalgo. 38 pesos per 4kg. Open M-Sa 8:30am-8:30pm.

EMERGENCY AND COMMUNICATIONS

Emergency: ☎060.

Police: LOCATEL (☎481 11 00) No English spoken. **Tourist Police** (☎485 04 90) wander the *zócalo*. Some English spoken.

Red Cross: Cortínez 126 (☎445 59 12), north of the *zócalo*. Take a "Hospital" bus. Some English spoken.

Pharmacy: Botica de Acapulco, Carranza 3 (☎783 84 29), a block from the *zócalo*. Open daily 6am-10pm.

Hospital: IMSS, Ruiz Cortínez 128 (☎445 53 77), north of the *zócalo* along Madero. Take a "Hospital" bus. No English spoken. **Sociedad de Asistencia Médica Turística** (☎485 58 00), in the condominiums across from Plaza Bahía. English spoken.

Internet: Cybercafe IKER NET (ikernet@hotmail.com), upstairs at the corner of Carranza and Escudero, 1 block east of the *zócalo*. Faster and cheaper connection than most in Acapulco. 15 pesos per hr. Open daily 8am-11pm.

Telephones: LADATELs line the Costera. **Caseta Carranza,** Carranza 9, 1 block from the *zócalo* also has a **fax.** Open M-F 9am-7pm, Sa 9am-3pm.

Post Office: Costera 215 (☎482 63 21), 2 blocks east of the *zócalo*. Open M-F 9am-3pm and 4-6pm, Sa 9am-2pm.

Postal Code: 39300.

▗ ACCOMMODATIONS

Camping on Acapulco's beaches is relatively unsafe. Fortunately, although a far cry from the posh hotels, cheap, no-frills places are easily found near the *zócalo*. Rates double during *Semana Santa*, and it's a good idea to make reservations.

▨ **Hotel Asturias,** Quebrada 45 (☎483 65 48), behind the *zócalo*, up the hill to the left. The powerful ceiling fans, firm mattresses, and clean private baths provide an oasis from the frenzied city. A well-tended courtyard and pool set the stage for drinking, relaxation, and conversation. Singles 130 pesos; doubles 180 pesos.

Hotel Misión, Felipe Valle 12 (☎482 36 43), at La Paz, 2 blocks left of the *zócalo* as you face the church. Guests chatting or relaxing in hammocks in the vine-hung courtyard and lazy cats napping on the stairway give Misión a homey feel. Rooms have fans and pretty tiled baths; some have desks and sofas. Singles 150 pesos; doubles 300 pesos.

Hotel Angelita, Quebrada 37 (☎483 57 34), up the street behind the cathedral, 2 doors down from Hotel Asturias. The hallways are packed with birds and flowers (both live and artificial) and the rooms are packed with perks. Multiple fans, brightly painted walls, tiled baths, purified water (and a container and cups), top sheets, and fresh soap make your life easier. Singles 100 pesos; doubles 150 pesos.

Hotel Mariscal, Quebrada 35 (482 00 15), beside Hotel Austurias. With huge balconies off each and every room, you can catch whatever breeze there is in stifling Acapulco. The springy mattresses and table and chairs in the rooms offer a comfortable environment, even if the seat-free toilets don't. Singles 100 pesos; doubles 150 pesos.

Hotel Posada, Azueta 8 (☎483 19 30). No hot water, but the firm beds and pleasant hospitality welcome the sun-weary. Flowered curtains brighten up the locker-room-esque hallways. Towel deposit 15 pesos. Singles 100 pesos; doubles 140 pesos.

Casa de Huéspedes Sutter, Juárez 12 (482 23 96). Although Sutter probably offers the cheapest singles in Acapulco, it does not offer hot water, shower curtains, or toilet seats. The high-powered, high-volume fans will keep you cool in the colorfully sponge-painted rooms with private baths. Singles 70 pesos; doubles 140 pesos.

FOOD

Acapulco's international restaurants cater to tourists' palates, and the chic restaurants between Playa Condesa and the naval base are meant for travelers who don't fret about money. However, interspersed along Costera are many local eateries ready to satisfy any craving without the high prices. For the cheapest eats, grab a barstool in one of the many *torta* shops on the streets surrounding the *zócalo*.

La Flor de Acapulco, Juárez 1 (☎484 75 97), overlooking the *zócalo*. 2nd location at Costera 711, west of the Kentucky Fried Chicken. Observe crowds mingling below in the *zócalo* while enjoying some of Acapulco's cheapest eats. Filling *platillos mexicanos* start at 20 pesos, and tacos and *quesos* range from 35-40 pesos. If you must have seafood, be prepared to pay upwards of 50 pesos. Open daily 8am-midnight.

Mariscos Nacho's, Azueta 7 (☎482 28 91), at Juárez, 1 block west of the *zócalo*. This open-air *marisquería* serves everything from octopus (40 pesos) to baby shark *quesadillas* (18 pesos), and bustles with sunburned families straggling in from the beach and party-kids dolled up for a night on the town. Open daily 9am-9:30pm.

100% Natural, Costera 248 (☎486 20 33), at the corner of Vizcaíno. Other branches line the Costera. A health food restaurant serving sandwiches (38-44 pesos), fruit salads (18-24 pesos), and *licuados* (20-24 pesos). Vegetarian options include soy burgers (28-38 pesos). Open daily 8am-11pm.

Jovito's, Costera 116 (☎484 84 33), across from Fiesta Americana. Indistinguishable from the rest of the restaurants lining Acapulco's main strip, Jovito's offers fresh seafood and satisfying Mexican favorites. Try the *tacos de mariscos* (39.5-49.5 pesos) or the vegetarian tacos (34.5 pesos). Open M-Th 2-11pm, F-Su 2pm-1am.

El Fogón (☎484 36 07), Costera and Yañez, across from the Continental Plaza Hotel. Offers tacos (40 pesos), sandwiches (22-48 pesos), and filling breakfast combos (15-30 pesos). Try the *chilaquiles* (50 pesos). Open daily 7am-11pm.

SIGHTS AND BEACHES

If you're in Acapulco, chances are you seek two things: beaches and booze. Have no fear, intrepid traveler—Acapulco delivers. Just keep in mind that you aren't the only one seeking these pleasures as the beaches here are hardly quiet or virginal. Vendors will harass you incessantly, and you will have to fight back the crowds for a stretch of sand. Those in the mood for unadulterated people-watching will be satisfied. Just don't be surprised if people watch you back.

PENÍNSULA DE LAS PLAYAS. At the westernmost tip of Acapulco Bay, on the seaward side of the peninsula, lie **Playas Caleta** and **Caletilla.** If you don't mind sharing the sea with small fishing boats and rubbish, swimming is good in the calm brownish water, though the hundreds of frolicking families make it hard to find empty beachside turf. A narrow causeway separating the two beaches leads to the island occupied by **Mágico Mundo Marino,** a water park with slides, pools, and a small zoo. (☎483 12 15. *Open daily 9am-6pm. 30 pesos, children 15 pesos.*) You can also take boats to **La Roqueta,** a little island with a zoo across the bay. (*Boats from Mágico Mundo daily 9am-6pm. 35 pesos. Zoo open W-M 10am-5pm. 5 pesos.*)

FROM HOTEL LAS HAMACAS TO PARQUE PAPAGAYO. The stretch of sand along the **Costera,** away from Old Acapulco, is blessed with fewer high-rises and smaller crowds than other beaches. **Playas Tamarindo, Hornos,** and **Hornitos,**

between Las Hamacas Hotel and the Radisson, are called the "afternoon beaches" because fishermen haul in their midday catches here. The waves are moderate, and the sand is ideal for beach sports. Still, you can't escape urban Acapulco— only a thin line of palm trees blocks the traffic on Costera.

Those needing a break from the relentless sun should head to **Parque Papagayo,** sprawling from Costera to Cuauhtémoc. Entering on Costera by the Gigante super-market, you'll find a roller skating rink, shaded paths for bikers and walkers, and artificial lake in the center surrounds an aviary. Children will enjoy the wading pool, exotic birds, and zillion spots for playing hide-and-seek. An amusement park with an assortment of kiddie rides occupies the southeast corner. *(☎ 485 24 90. Park open daily 5am-8pm; rink open daily 4-10:30pm. 13 pesos; with skate rental 15 pesos. Amusement park ☎ 485 96 23. Rides 8 pesos. Open daily 4-11pm.)*

FROM LA DIANA TO THE NAVAL BASE. A trip to **Playa Condesa,** at the center of the bay, is worth the 2km-plus trek from the *zócalo,* despite strong waves and a rapidly dropping sea floor that make the swimming conditions less than ideal. These poor conditions don't bother the throngs of sun worshippers lounging under their blue umbrellas (20-30 pesos) or hordes of vendors offering everything from mangoes-on-a-stick to bathing suits. Farther down, between the golf course and naval base, is **Playa Icacos.** As you move toward the base, the waves become gentler, but are populated by miniature jellyfish.

The **CICI,** a fun water park, lets you hurl yourself head-first down winding water slides, or watch trained dolphins perform. For big-spending dolphin-lovers, the CICI now offers the chance to swim with flippered friends. *(Costera at Colón. Follow Costera until you see the orange walls painted with large green waves; otherwise take a "CICI" or "Base" bus. ☎ 484 19 70. Open daily 10am-6pm. 60 pesos. Dolphin shows M-F 2pm, Sa-Su 2pm and 4pm. Swimming with dolphins 480 pesos.)*

PUERTO MARQUÉS. Lacking the prepackaged polish of the strip, the beach town of **Puerto Marqués** encompasses a ribbon of sand lined with restaurants. The bus ride is the real attraction; views from the top of the hill are magnificent. As the bus rambles along, the Bahía de Puerto Marqués and the pounding surf of **Playa Revolcadero** come into view. Catch a colectivo from Puerto Marqués (6 pesos) to get to quieter and less crowded **Playa Bonville.** *(From the bus station across from Comercial Mexicana at Playa Hornitos, on the beach side of the street, take a "Glorieta" bus to La Glorieta. From there, catch a "Puerto Marques" bus.)*

🎵🎭 ENTERTAINMENT AND NIGHTLIFE

In Acapulco, every night is Saturday night. Luring young party-seekers from the capital, the town transforms at night into one continuous strip of partying with the best clubs clustering on the beach side near the CICI. Most clubs thump from 11pm to dawn, and charge over 100 pesos for cover, which usually includes open bar. It's always easier and cheaper for women to get in and many clubs offer reduced cover (and open bar) to women on weeknights. For further discounts (albeit small ones), grab some of the cards the solicitors hand as you walk down Costera—the guy gets a commission from the club, you get 20 pesos off the cover price, and everybody goes home a little happier.

CLUBS AND BARS

- 🎵 **Baby'O,** Costera 22 (☎ 484 74 74). The *Fraggle Rock*-style cave interior houses a fun-loving staff and a slightly less frenetic and more sophisticated atmosphere than its rambunctious neighbors. M-Th cover 100 pesos for men; M-W 50 pesos for women, Th no cover for women and 2 free drinks. F-Su men 250 pesos, women 150 pesos. Drinks 40 pesos. Open daily 10:30pm-late.

- 🎵 **Palladium** (☎ 446 54 86), on the Carretera Escénica Las Brisas. Accessible only by taxi (40 pesos). This space-age structure is on a cliff with a fabulous view of the harbor and downtown. The club reverberates with pop music and dancing begins at midnight when lights descend from the ceiling. Cover men 280 pesos, women 210 pesos; Tu and Th women 50 pesos until 12:30am. Open bar. Open Tu and Th-Su 10:30pm-5am.

Nina's, Costera 2909 (☎ 484 24 00), on the beach side near CICI. A mature clientele grooves to live tropical music, peppered with impersonations of famous Latin dancers and singers. Open bar. Cover 220 pesos; Th women 50 pesos. Open daily 10pm-4am.

El Alebrije, Costera 12 (484 59 04). A well-dressed, young crowd swings back and forth between downing mixed drinks at the open bar and shimmying to pop and techno on the raised dance floors. The amphitheater set-up is perfect for scoping out the opposite sex—and the competition. Cover men 280 pesos, women 210 pesos. After 4am, cover 100 pesos. Open daily from 11pm.

GAY AND LESBIAN NIGHTLIFE

Savage Disco, Av. de los Deportes 10B (☎ 484 18 00). This large club features leopard-print chairs and a zebra-striped bar. Choose between the flashing lights and booming music of the dance floor, the dimly lit upstairs movie room, or the spicy transvestite shows at midnight and 2am. Mixed. Cover 50 pesos. Open daily from 10pm.

Picante, Privada Piedra Picuda 16 (☎ 484 23 42), behind Carlos 'n' Charlie's. Young, lithe, and predominantly male clientele enjoy late-night racy entertainment. Conservative dress code does not permit cross-dressing. No cover. 2-drink min. Beer 25 pesos, *bebidas nacionales* 30 pesos. Strip show from midnight on. Open daily 10pm-4am.

Relax, Lomas del Mar 4 (☎ 484 04 21), 1 block east of Carlos 'n' Charlie's. Mixed, but mostly male customers frequent this above-average bar, and fine service makes it more "relaxed" than most. Su-Th no cover; F-Sa cover 50 pesos, 1 drink included. Open daily from 9pm. Transvestite shows F-Sa 3am.

Demas, Av. de los Deportes 10A (☎ 484 18 00), next to Savage. The construction worker theme is reinforced by bare-chested, suspended waiters in hard hats, and a steel rod dance floor, completed by rowdy Chippendale shows from 11:30pm on weekends. Beer 25 pesos, *bebidas nacionales* 30 pesos. Cover 50 pesos. Open daily 10pm-5am.

SPORTS AND FESTIVALS

Corridas take place at **Plaza de Toros Caletilla,** 200m west of Playa Caletela near the abandoned yellow *jai alai* auditoriums. (☎ 483 95 61. Dec.-Apr. Su 5pm.) Tickets are sold at the plaza at 4:30pm on the day of the fight.

The Acapulco tourist office organizes a variety of festivals to lighten tourists' wallets. **Festival Acapulco** in May is a celebration of music and the **Black Film Festival** takes places during the first week of June. On December 9, men and women from around the globe journey to Acapulco to test their cliff diving skills during the **Torneo Internacional de Clavados en La Quebrada.**

CLIFF DIVERS OF ACAPULCO Hurling oneself half-naked off jagged cliffs is not a coming of age ritual in Acapulco, but a serious occupation for trained professionals. It is also one of Acapulco's biggest attractions. At La Quebrada cliffs around the north side of the bay, *clavadistas* perform daily, diving 25-35m off a cliff and slipping effortlessly into the frothing surf. Although spectators congregate at the bottom level to see the splash, the view of the dive is better from the area to the right of the ticket booth. To get to La Quebrada, follow López Mateos, the road on your left when facing the cathedral's entrance. The walk takes about 15min. and ends at the top of a very steep hill. As if the dives weren't enough of a show, divers pray rather theatrically (who can blame them?) at a small shrine before the plunge. It's all part of the everyday business of challenging death and impressing the tourists. Shows at 7:30, 8:30, 9:30, and 10:30pm (with torches!). 15 pesos.

OTHER ENTERTAINMENT

Those too tired for yet more clubbing will find milder forms of entertainment at **Plaza Bahía,** a large shopping mall on Costera, 4 blocks east of La Gran Plaza on the beach side. Speed around a tiny race course at **Go-Karts,** on the third floor. (☎440 52 04. 25 pesos for 1 or 30 pesos for 2 per 5min. Open daily 10am-midnight.) Bowl away at **Bol Bahía** on the fourth floor. (☎485 09 70. 30 pesos per person per game or 180 pesos per hr. for a group; shoes 9 pesos. Open M-Sa noon-1am, Su noon-midnight.) Catch a first-run North American movie at **Cinema 5** on the third floor. (☎486 42 55 or 485 98 92. Tickets 34 pesos. Movies shown daily 3-10pm.)

▶ DAYTRIPS FROM ACAPULCO

PIE DE LA CUESTA

*Buses leave from Costera, across the street from Woolworth's next to the zócalo. Buses marked "Pie de la Cuesta Playa" stop on the road along the beach; those labeled "Pie de la Cuesta Centro" stop on a parallel street in a marketplace (40min., 3.5 pesos). From there, turn left down a dirt road; you should see the ocean in the distance. At the end of the road, turn right toward the base. Buses shuttle between the base and the centro (3.5 pesos). A combi will take you as far as **La Barra**, where the lagoon water flows into the ocean (3.5 pesos). To return to Acapulco, go back to the market and hail a bus in the opposite direction.*

A single-lane runs through Acapulco's hills to Pie de la Cuesta—a small town known for its truly magnificent sunsets—ending at the narrow road that separates the rough-and-tumble Pacific from the placid waters of **Laguna de Coyuca.** Swimming is not the best option in Pie de la Cuesta: the pounding surf and strong currents make the ocean a dangerous choice, and the still, green water of the lagoon suggests pollution. Still, the calm fresh water of the lagoon is the site of the area's best waterskiing. Many restaurants and clubs near the air base offer **ski rental** at similar prices. Try the friendly staff at **Chuy** (☎460 11 04; 400 pesos per hr.) or **Tres Marias** (☎460 01 78). Food is available at both places, with breakfasts and *antojitos* from 25 pesos and seafood from 70 pesos. Sample delectable *tacos de camarón* (35 pesos). Unfortunately, rest and relaxation are all too often interrupted by aggressive *lancha* agents offering tours of the lagoon (3 hr.; about 50 pesos per person). If you need a place to stay, **Villa Roxana,** a blue-and-white building a few blocks from the bus stop, defines its own utopia with hammocks, a swimming pool, and rooms with fans and private baths. Some rooms have TV and kitchen. (☎460 32 52. 150 pesos per person.) Beyond the pharmacy toward the base is **Acapulco Trailer Park,** with campgrounds, trailer hook-ups, bathrooms, and a pet raccoon named Charlie. (☎460 00 10; fax 460 24 57. 80-120 pesos, prices negotiable.)

OAXACA

OAXACA   ☎9

Perched on a giant plateau that gracefully interrupts the Sierra Madre del Sur's descent into the Oaxaca valley, the city of Oaxaca de Juárez (wa-HAH-ka dey WA-rez; pop. 300,000) shines with eclectic grace. The city's surname honors native son Benito Juárez, a Oaxacan Zapotec and Mexico's only *indígena* president. Oaxaca was also the birthplace of the much less-loved dictator Porfirio Díaz, who got nothing but a lone street name to commemorate his iron reign. Although selective in its presidential honors, there is not much order to Oaxaca. It is a collision of tombs, temples, churches, rugs, jars, chocolate, diesel fumes, tiny storefront shops, language schools, foreigners, students, *indígenas*, hostels, hotels, apartments, and houses. History and political tension abound, and hand-made crafts are produced in machine-made quantities. Most of the sights—and blights—found scattered about Mexico can be found in some form here. As visitors become smitten with Oaxaca's superb food, culture, highland setting, and delicious contradictions, days spill into weeks, months, and, on occasion, years.

Oaxaca State

TRANSPORTATION

INTERCITY TRANSPORTATION

Airport: Aeropuerto Juárez (☎511 50 40 for the tourist info booth), on Mex. 175, 8km south of the city. You can hire a private **taxi** from the airport, but it is much cheaper and just as easy to share one of the **Transportes Aeropuerto** vans with other travelers. Buy a ticket at the airport exit (to the *centro* 19 pesos). Vans will take you from your hotel to the airport, with prices varying depending on the hotel. Arrangements should be made a day in advance by phone or at the office several doors down from the post office on Plaza Alameda. (☎514 43 50. Open M-Sa 9am-2pm and 5-8pm.) Airlines served by the airport include: **AeroCaribe,** Fiallo 102 (☎516 02 29 or 511 52 47); **Aeroméxico,** Hidalgo 513 (☎516 32 29 or 516 37 65); **Mexicana,** Independencia 102 (☎516 84 14 or 516 73 52), at Fiallo; **AeroCalifornia,** Morelos 1207 (☎241 85 70); and **Aviacsa** (☎518 45 55, airport office ☎511 50 39).

Buses: Oaxaca is served by two bus stations. The first-class bus station, Niños Héroes de Chapultepec 1036 (☎513 33 50), is 11 blocks north of the *centro*. To get to the *centro*, cross the street and take a westbound "Centro" *urbano* (2.5 pesos) or a taxi (25 pesos). ADO (☎515 17 03) heads to: **Mexico City** (6hr., 17 per day, 244 pesos); **Puebla** (4½hr., 7 per day, 184 pesos); **Tuxtepec** (6½hr.; 3, 9:30, 11:30pm; 159 pesos); **Veracruz** (8hr.; 8:30am, 11, 11:30pm; 241 pesos). Cristóbal Colón goes to: **Bahías de Huatulco** (8hr.; 9:30am, 10:40, 11:30pm, midnight; 163 pesos); **San Cristóbal de las Casas** (12hr.; 7:30, 9pm; 242 pesos); **Tehuantepec** (4hr., 14 per day, 92 pesos); **Tuxtla**

EXCEPTIONS TO THE RULE. Under most circumstances it's better (not to mention safer) to take 1st-class buses rather than 2nd-class buses. An exception to the rule is the ride from **Oaxaca** to **Puerto Escondido**. First-class buses tend to take a route through Salina Cruz that is about 5hr. longer than the 2nd-class bus route, which goes directly. Measure the increased efficiency and lower costs against the increased discomfort.

Gutiérrez (10hr.; 7:30, 9, 10:15pm; 212 pesos). Pacífico runs to **Puerto Escondido** (6hr.; 10am, 2:30, 11:30pm; 85-90 pesos). Tickets for ADO and Cristóbal Colón available at 20 de Noviembre #204, "Ticket Bus," as well as at the numerous travel agencies around the *zócalo*. The second-class bus station houses regional bus lines and is 7 blocks southwest of the *zócalo*, just north of the Central de Abastos market. To get to the *centro*, take a "Centro" *urbano* in front of the main terminal. If walking, exit left out of the terminal, cross busy Periférico, and follow the street as it turns into Trujano. After 7 blocks, Trujano reaches the *zócalo*. A taxi will cost 20 pesos. It's a good idea to buy tickets early. On their market days, buses to surrounding towns leave every 10 min.

GETTING AROUND

Most parts of the city are easily accessible by foot. **Local buses** *(urbanos)* cost 2.5 pesos. Ask around for the correct line. **Taxis** run anywhere in the city for 25 pesos. Walk along a major street or look for a "*sitio*" sign to find an unoccupied cab.

✸❔ ORIENTATION AND PRACTICAL INFORMATION

Oaxaca de Juárez sits in the Oaxaca Valley, between the towering Sierra Madre del Sur and the Puebla-Oaxaca range, 523km southeast of Mexico City. Principal access to Oaxaca from the north and east is via **Mex. 190** as well as the brand-new "super-carretera," Mex. 135 from Puebla. The city's ground zero is the *zócalo*, comprised of the square and the block-long Plaza Alameda de León, just north of the square. The five-block stretch of Alcalá between the *zócalo* and the Iglesia de Santo Domingo to the north features a high concentration of museums, restaurants, craft shops, and tourists. Many of Oaxaca's streets change names as they pass the *zócalo*. It is also common for two or more streets to share the same name, so it helps to specify neighborhood as well as street when directing cabbies.

TOURIST AND FINANCIAL SERVICES

Tourist Offices: SEDETUR, Independencia 607 (☎ 516 01 23; info@oaxaca.gob.mx; http://oaxaca.gob.mx/sedetur), across the street from Plaza Alameda. Maps, brochures, and an English-speaking staff. Open daily 8am-8pm. **CEPROTUR,** also at Independencia 607 (☎ 514 21 55; fax 516 09 84), handles all matters of tourist safety. Open daily 8am-8pm. **Info Booth** at the airport (☎ 511 07 40). Also check the *Oaxaca Times* (www.oaxacatimes.com), a free English newspaper available at SEDETUR.

Consulates: In an emergency, CEPROTUR (see above) will obtain consular assistance. **Canada,** Suárez 700 (☎513 37 77 or 513 37 77). Open M-F 11am-2pm. **US,** Alcalá 407 #20 (☎514 30 54 or 516 28 53), at Morelos, hidden under an arched doorway. Open M-F 9am-3pm.

Currency Exchange: Banamex, Valdivieso 116, east of the cathedral, changes currency and has 24hr. **ATMs.** Open M-F 11am-7pm, Su 10am-2pm. **Inverlat,** at the corner of Independencia and Alcalá, offers similar rates and 24hr. **ATMs.** Open M-F 9am-5pm, Sa 10am-3pm. Numerous smaller currency exchanges surround the *zócalo*.

American Express: Valdivieso 2 (☎516 27 00), at Hidalgo across from the *zócalo*. A **travel agency** inside sells plane tickets and bus tickets. Financial services open M-F 9am-2pm and 4-6pm, Sa 9am-1pm; travel agency open M-F 9am-8pm, Sa 9am-7pm.

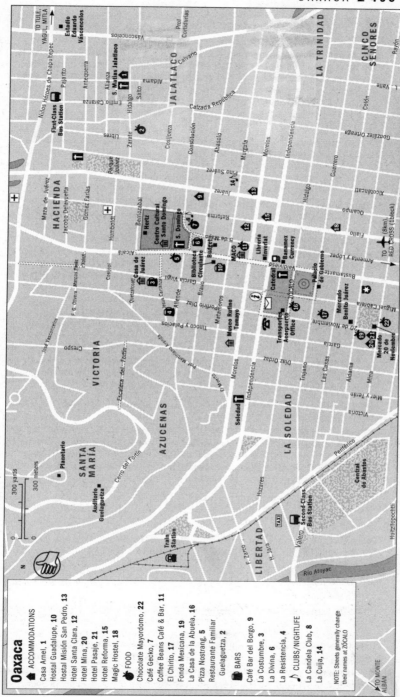

Oaxaca

⌂ ACCOMMODATIONS

Casa Arnel, **1**
Hostal Guadalupe, **10**
Hostal Misión San Pedro, **13**
Hotel Santa Clara, **12**
Hotel Mina, **20**
Hotel Pasaje, **21**
Hotel Reforma, **15**
Magic Hostel, **18**

◆ FOOD

Chocolate Mayordomo, **22**
Café Gecko, **7**
Coffee Beans Café & Bar, **11**
El Chirto, **17**
Fonda Mexicana, **19**
La Casa de la Abuela, **16**
Pizza Nostrang, **5**
Restaurante Familiar
    Guelaguetza, **2**

🍷 BARS

Café Bar Bar del Borgo, **9**
La Costumbre, **3**
La Divina, **6**
La Resistencía, **4**

♪ CLUBS/NIGHTLIFE

La Candela Club, **8**
La Cuíja, **14**

NOTE: Streets generally change
their names at ZÓCALO

LOCAL SERVICES

Luggage Storage: At the 1st-class bus station. 5 pesos per day.

Bookstores: Librería Grañen Porrúa, Alcalá 104 (☎516 99 01), is known for its collection of art and architecture books and offers a small number of books in English. The cafe in back serves *comida corrida* (35 pesos). Open daily 10am-9pm. **Librería Universitaria,** on Guerrero between Armenta y López and Valdivieso, buys and sells English paperbacks. Open M-Sa 9am-2pm and 4-9:30pm. **Amate Books,** Alcalá 307 (☎516 69 60), in Plaza Alcalá. Sells North American magazines and books about Mexico in several languages.

Libraries: Biblioteca Circulante, Alcalá 305. Everything from the *New Yorker* to *Sports Illustrated* for 1 peso. Open M-F 10am-1pm and 4-7pm, Sa 10am-1pm. The **Instituto de Artes Gráficos de Oaxaca,** Alcalá 507 (☎516 69 80), across from Santo Domingo, has a library with works in various languages, as well as a museum of changing art exhibits. Open daily 9:30am-9pm; museum open W-M 9:30am-8pm. Free.

Cultural Centers: Centro Cultural Ricardo Flores Magon, Alcalá 302 (☎514 03 95), at Independencia. Hosts free plays, dance performances, concerts, and gallery openings (daily during high season). Monthly listings can be found on the *Programación Cultural* at the front desk. **Casa de la Cultura,** Ortega 403 (☎516 24 83), at Colón. Hosts theater productions, concerts, summer music and art classes, and art exhibits. Open M-F 9am-6pm, Sa 9am-3pm and 4-6:30pm. **Instituto Oaxaqueño de las Culturas** (☎516 34 34), at the corner of Madera and Tecnológica, has similar programming. To get there, take a westbound "Sta. Rosa" *urbano* from the corner of Independencia and Tinoco y Palacios (2.5 pesos). Listings in the monthly *Guía Cultura* (free at SEDETUR).

Markets: Oaxaca's enormous **Central de Abastos** is the ultimate shopping experience. Walk 8 blocks west of the *zócalo* on Trujano. Open daily 8am-8pm. **Mercado Benito Juárez,** at the corner of 20 de Noviembre and Aldama, 2 blocks from the *zócalo*, sells crafts, produce, flowers, and clothing. Its annex, **Mercado 20 de Noviembre,** on the next block, has lots of food. Both open daily 6am-9pm. **Mercado de Artesanías,** at the corner of García and Zaragoza, offers artisan wares. Prices and quality are often better in nearby villages where the crafts originate. Open daily 8am-8pm.

Laundromats: Lavandería, 20 de Noviembre 605B (☎516 23 42). Open M-Sa 9am-8pm. 45 pesos per 3.5kg of clothes.

Car Rental: Budget, 5 de Mayo 315 (☎516 44 45). Also at the airport (☎511 52 52). VWs 600 pesos per day, less off-season. Open daily 8am-1pm and 4-7pm. **Hertz,** Labastida 115 (☎516 24 34), between 5 de Mayo and Alcalá, charges 550 pesos for a VW sedan. Open M-Sa 8am-7pm. **Alamo,** 5 de Mayo 205 (☎514 85 34), offers Chevy sedans without A/C *(sin aire)* for 650 pesos per day. Open daily 8am-8pm.

EMERGENCY AND COMMUNICATIONS

Emergency: ☎060.

Police: Aldama 108 (☎516 27 26), south of the *zócalo*, between Cabrera and Bustamante. Little English spoken. Open 24hr. Between 8am-8pm, go first to Leprotur at Independencia 607.

Red Cross: Armenta y López 700 (☎516 48 03), between Pardo and Burgoa. Some English spoken. 24hr. ambulance service.

Pharmacy: Farmacias del Ahorro, Niños Héroes de Chapultepec 1102, next to ADO. Open 24hr. Also Hidalgo 603, at 20 de Noviembre. Open daily 7am-11pm with many other loctions throughout the city.

Hospitals: Hospital Civil, Díaz 400 (☎515 13 00), 1.5km north of town. No English spoken. **Hospital Reforma,** Reforma 603 (☎516 61 00), at Humboldt. English spoken.

Fax: Telecomm (☎516 49 02), Independencia at 20 de Noviembre, around the corner from the post office. Open M-F 8am-6pm, Sa 9am-4pm.

Telephones: LADATELs are everywhere, with an especially large concentration in front of the post office in the *zócalo*. *Casetas* available at **Computel**, Independencia 601 (☎514 80 84), across from the Telecomm office. Open daily 7am-10pm.

Internet Access: Cafe Internet, on Valdivieso at Independencia, 2nd fl. Has a central location and speedy connection. 12 pesos per hr. Open M-Sa 8am-11pm, Su 10am-10pm. Internet access is the only thing getting cheaper in Oaxaca. Storefront shops are everywhere, offering connections for as little as 8 pesos per hr.

Post Office: (☎516 26 61), on the west side of Plaza Alameda de León. Open M-F 8am-7pm, Sa 9am-1pm.

Postal Code: 68000.

ACCOMMODATIONS AND CAMPING

Cheap beds are everywhere in Oaxaca—one more commodity in the tourist-generated seller's market. Hotels south of the *zócalo* stick to the same formula: singles for around 100 pesos (more for a private bathroom) with rooms stacked around bland concrete courtyards. Accommodations farther north are better deals: they're just as cheap, but friendlier with aesthetic appeal, escapes from the streets' frenzied capitalism rather than extensions of it. Reservations are advised on *fiesta* weekends: especially during the *Guelaguetza* in July, *Semana Santa* before Easter, and *El Día de Los Muertos* in early November. For longer stays in the city, reasonably priced rooms are available for rent. Check the tourist office and *Oaxaca Times* for listings. **Departmentos del Cuento,** Quintana Roo 107, off Berriozabal past La Iglesia Santo Domingo, rents six one- or two-person rooms with kitchen and bath. (☎514 22 88. 2000-2500 pesos per month, utilities included.)

NORTHEAST OF THE CENTRO: JALATLACO
Jalatlaco is about a 10-block walk northeast of the *zócalo*. Unlike other hotel areas, it is not located near Oaxaca's numerous Calles de "Huge Trucks Without Mufflers or Catalytic Convertors," ensuring you the rarity of peace and quiet.

Casa Arnel, Aldama 404 (☎515 28 56; casa.arnel@spersaoaxaca.com.mex), at Hidalgo, across from the Iglesia San Matias Jalatlaco. Arnel's courtyard houses a mini-jungle that's tremendously attractive by day, if terrifying during nighttime bathroom trips. The hotel offers a bar, internet service (20 pesos per hr.), a travel agency, spotless rooms, laundry service, and helpful staff. Entertainment provided by the social breakfasts (7:30-9:45am) and talking parrots in the courtyard. Tours of the surrounding areas leave from the hotel. Singles 100 pesos, with bath 200 pesos; doubles 180 pesos, with bath 230 pesos. Prices rise in high season.

Hostal Guadalupe (HI), Juárez 409 (☎516 63 65), between Abasolo and Constitución. Ideally situated between the buzz of the *zócalo* and the peace of Jalatlaco, Guadalupe is also home to some of Oaxaca's finest, cleanest bathrooms. Amenities include TV, courtyard seating, kitchen access, and new laundry facilities. 50 pesos, less with HI card; private bedroom 120 pesos.

NORTH OF THE ZÓCALO: THE CENTRO
For the aesthetically discerning traveler, this part of town not only offers the best architecture (many of the hotels are in old colonial buildings), but also the best location for those looking to stay close to Oaxaca's artifacts and galleries.

Hotel Reforma, Reforma 102 (☎516 09 39), between Independencia and Morelos, 3 blocks past the left side of the cathedral. Features hand-carved wood furniture, and a nice view of the city. Singles 130 pesos; doubles 180 pesos; triples 250 pesos; quads 400 pesos.

Hostal Misión San Pedro, Juárez 200 (☎516 46 26), on the corner of Morelos. Though San Pedro lacks the ambience and services of many of the other hostels in town, bathrooms and dorm-style bedrooms are clean, bright, and perhaps the cheapest in town. 40 pesos; singles 120 pesos; doubles 160 pesos.

Hotel Sta. Clara, Morelos 1004 (☎ 516 11 38). Clean rooms and a bright and quiet red-tiled courtyard. Singles 130 pesos; doubles 200 pesos; triples 295 pesos, includes private bath.

SOUTH OF THE ZÓCALO

Filled with budget hotels—four or five on the same block, particularly along **Díaz Ordaz** and **Mina**—discriminating tastes can be obliged on a budget. As many hotels face noisy streets, ask for a room in the back or on an upper floor.

Magic Hostel, Fiallo 305 (☎ 516 76 67), between Guerrero and Colón. Once you get here you may never want to leave. Lively but not overcrowded or intrusively loud, this hostel boasts a courtyard and 2nd-floor terrace/bar/eating area, patio, daily movies, laundry service, cheap coffee and soda, paperback exchange, internet access, plentiful couches, and more. 50 pesos for a bed, 120 for a private room.

Hotel Mina, Mina 304 (☎ 516 49 66), at 20 Noviembre, is one of the cheapest options for those who prefer a private room. Plain rooms have sturdy beds. Communal baths are tidy and convenient. Singles 100 pesos; doubles 120 pesos; triples 140 pesos.

Plata/Gelatina Youth Hostel, Independencia 504 (☎ 514 93 91), 1 block west of the *zócalo.* Outfitted with typical hostel decorations such as flags and eclectic art as well as foosball and ping-pong tables, a cafe/bar, and internet access. Beds 50 pesos.

Hotel Pasaje, Mina 302 (☎ 516 42 13), 3 blocks south of the *zócalo.* Well-scrubbed, tiled rooms open onto a plant-filled courtyard. Bathrooms are large and clean. Location provides convenient access to markets, restaurants, and chocolate shops but also car horns and diesel exhaust. Singles 120 pesos; doubles 150 pesos; triples 210 pesos.

🍴 FOOD

The theme of Oaxacan cooking is preposterously large amounts of food for a very low price. Locals turn to watch as uninitiated tourists are served *hayadas* (enormous tortillas piled high with toppings), giggling in disbelief. Oaxacan cooking features seven kinds of the heavy chile-and-chocolate sauce, *mole,* served in a variety of ways. Other staples include *quesillo* (boiled string cheese), *chorizo* (spicy sausage), *guacamole, tasajo* (thinly cut steak), and *chapulines* (tiny cooked grasshoppers doused in chile—truly yummy). Another specialty, made of ground corn stuffed with beans, chicken, or beef and wrapped in banana leaves before baking or boiling, *tamales* are now found in all parts of the republic. Oaxaca's trademark drink, sold everywhere, is cactus-based tequila cousin *mezcal.*

Oaxaca's cheaper restaurants cluster south of the *zócalo.* The square itself is besieged by middle-priced, middling-quality restaurant/bars. The *Alcalá* features pricier and more international food. The fastest and cheapest regional meals are at the markets and taco stands on Trujano Las Casas, southeast of the *zócalo.*

La Casa de la Abuela, Hidalgo 616, 2nd fl. (☎ 516 35 44), at the corner of the *zócalo* and Plaza Alameda. A large menu of Oaxacan cuisine. Savor delicious renditions of Oaxaca's famous *sopa de guias* (squash flower soup; 22.5 pesos) and *chapulines* (45 pesos) while marveling at the restaurant's postcard-perfect views of the cathedral and *zócalo.* Finish with a cup of *té de poelo* (a regional herbal brew; 10 pesos) or *cafe de olla* (spiced coffee; 10 pesos). Entrees 55-60 pesos. Open daily 1-10pm.

Pizza Nostrang (☎ 514 07 78), at the corner of Alcalá and Allende. Looks more expensive than it is: wood furniture, real table cloths, sophisticatedly dim lighting, sharply dressed waiters. Still, a meal can be had for less than 60 pesos. Pizza starts at 45 pesos, large portions of spaghetti at 40 pesos. Open daily 1-11pm.

El Chirito, 20 de Noviembre 209. One of many *rosticerías* south of the *zócalo* roasting countless chickens, which for the low price of 56 pesos will be pulled dripping from the oven and dropped into a pile of rice on your plate. A whole chicken serves 2. Halves and quarters are also available (28 and 16 pesos, respectively). Oaxacan plates 28 pesos and up. Open daily 8am-9pm.

EAT THE WORM! As the *mezcal* capital of the world, Oaxaca is justifiably proud of itself. Production of *mezcal*, the potent liquor made from the maguey plant and usually containing a *gusano de maguey* (maguey worm), began soon after the Spanish arrived and has been going strong ever since. During the yearly **Fiesta Nacional del Mezcal,** July 17-24, Oaxacans and foreigners alike gather in Parque Juárez to drink themselves numb. Countless vendors crowd the park, and everyone stumbles from booth to booth, giddy with unlimited free shots. Try *mezcal* with the traditional worm at the bottom, but don't miss exotic *mezcal* variations, flavored with nut, blackberry, coconut, chicken breast, and strawberry, among other things. *Mezcal*-filled chocolates are a hit as well. If you've exceeded your taste-test tolerance, take a seat and enjoy the festival's live music, traditional dances, fireworks show, giant paper parade, and the crowning of the *Mezcal* Queen.

Restorán Cafe Alex, Díaz Ordaz 218 (☎514 07 15). Amazing menu runs the gamut of Mexican cuisine. Garden seating available. Breakfasts (27 pesos), *comida corrida* (36 pesos), and vegetarian dishes (22 pesos). Open M-Sa 7am-9pm, Su 7am-noon.

Fonda Mexicana, 20 de Noviembre 408 (☎514 31 21). One of the most popular lunch spots south of the *zócalo*. Always packed with non-*gringos* seeking gigantic *hayudas*, which start at 15 pesos. *Carae* entrees start at 20 pesos. Cheap beer 8 pesos. Open daily 8-11:30am and 2-5pm.

Restaurante Familiar Guelaguetza, Zanate 160 (☎513 32 49). Cheap and fresh food for those in the Jalatco neighborhood. *Jugo de naranja* made before your eyes. *Desayunos* of eggs, fruta, and enchiladas for under 20 pesos; burritos 3 for 10 pesos. Open daily 7am-9pm.

Restaurant Morelos, Morelos 1003 (☎516 05 58). Start your day off right with a high-quality breakfast at possibly the cheapest place in the city. A friendly staff serves full breakfast plates (14 pesos) to the flocks of gossiping earlybirds. *Antojitos* and *tostadas* 10 pesos. Open daily 7am-6pm.

Antojitos Regionales Los Olmos, Morelos 403, at Crespo. For those still unaccustomed to Oaxaca's big breakfast and diminutive dinner lifestyle, Antojitos is the right place. Perfect for filling the stomach after dinner or dancing, they whip up cheap eats: the *patitas en vinagre* is the most expensive item on the menu (12 pesos). *Tomate de mole*, *quesadillas*, and *tortas* 8 pesos. Open daily 7pm-midnight.

Las Quince Letras, Abasolo 300 (☎514 37 69). 50 pesos will buy soup, salad, a main dish, and coffee or dessert. Delicious breakfasts start at 20 pesos. For dinner, try the *sopa oaxaqueña* (28 pesos), a powerful Oaxacan super-stew. Open daily 8am-9pm.

Mariscos Los Jorges, Suárez 806 (☎513 43 08), across the street from Parque Juárez, toward the north end of the park. After their huge, bargain breakfasts (20 pesos), Los Jorges serves delicious Veracruz-style seafood baked in the restaurant's *indígena* oven, excellent both on its own or wrapped up in tacos (39 pesos). Open daily 8am-6:30pm.

Flor de Loto, Morelos 509 (☎514 39 44). Though the fluorescent lighting and quiet clientele leave this restaurant low on ambience, vegetarians in this blood-thirsty town can find a haven here. "Regional" (i.e., meaty) food also served. Veggie soups 15 pesos, *enchiladas de soya* 30 pesos, mushroom tacos 30 pesos. Open daily 8am-10pm.

CAFES AND CHOCOLATE

Chocolate shops produce Oaxaca's favorite confection at the corner of **Mina** and **20 de Noviembre.** Follow your nose to see the chocolate-making process and grab lots of free samples. If you don't make it to the area, don't worry—nearly every restaurant in the city serves *chocolate caliente* (hot chocolate). Also keep an eye out for *cafe de olla*, a sweet, spicy coffee, and *tejate*, a cold, corn-based drink. Many cafes sit on Alcalá and Abasolo between 5 de Mayo and Reforma.

■ **Chocolate Mayordomo,** (☎516 16 19), at the corner of Mina and 20 de Noviembre, with a 2nd shop across the street. The undisputed king of Oaxaca's sweets market, Mayordomo churns out the chocolate and assaults onlookers with free samples. Buy some solid chocolate for the road (20-30 pesos per 500g) or sit with a cup of the city's cheapest hot chocolate (small 5 pesos). Open daily 7am-9pm.

Cafe Gecko, 5 de Mayo 412-3 (☎516 22 85), half a block south of Iglesia de Santo Domingo. Breakfasts (20 pesos) and sandwiches served in the vine-covered courtyard. Convenient internet access (15 pesos per hr.) and *chocolate caliente* (15 pesos) draws a crowd of museum-hoppers. Open daily 8:30am-8pm.

Coffee Beans Cafe and Bar, 5 de Mayo 205. Typical coffeehouse fare is supplemented by drinks from the over-priced bar. Decorations include a pool table and fake concert fliers ("Beatles at Shea Stadium! Tonight!"). *Cafe americano* 12 pesos, *chocolate caliente* 15 pesos, refreshing limeade 20 pesos. Open daily 8am-midnight.

⊙ SIGHTS

Oaxaca's attractions are mostly highbrow. Examine them individually as architecturally notable churches or important anthropological collections, but also as relics of the Spanish/Catholic philosophy that combined violence and religion to produce the kind of impossibly arrogant ostentatiousness which has long since gone out of fashion in the Western world. Said ostentation is mostly found between the *zócalo* and Santo Domingo along the Alcalá and surounding areas.

■ **IGLESIA DE SANTO DOMINGO.** Higher, mightier, and in better shape than the *catedral*, Santo Domingo is the city's tallest building. One of the best examples of Mexican Baroque, the church was begun in 1575, but was not consecrated until 1611. Since then, Santo Domingo has functioned as a place of worship, a museum, and even a military barracks for both sides of the Reform Wars and the Revolution. With waves of gilded stucco covering the ceiling and walls, the spectacular interior fills the massive structure. Built in 1959 by Oaxacan artists and workers, the massive gilded altar is one of the most elaborate (and expensive) of its kind and a treat even for the most jaded, seen-every-church tourists. The **Capilla de la Virgen del Rosario,** to the right as you walk in, was built in 1724 with funds given by Dionisio Levanto. It features relatively new altar works, some of them inaugurated as late as the 1960s. *(3 blocks past MACO, on the Andador Turístico. Open daily 7am-1pm and 4-8pm. Capilla open daily 7am-1pm and 4-7pm.)*

■ **CENTRO CULTURAL SANTO DOMINGO.** The ex-convent next door to the Iglesia de Santo Domingo was converted into the prestigious **Museo de las Culturas de Oaxaca** and underwent a four-year-long renovation finished in 1998. The stellar museum houses rooms and rooms of Mixtec, Zapotec, Spanish conquest-era, and more recent Mexican artifacts, but the prime attraction is the treasure extracted from Tomb 7 in Monte Albán; the gold, silver, turquoise, bone, and obsidian jewelry and artifacts are some of the grandest Zapotec material ever found. The *Centro* also houses the new **Jardín Etnobotánico** and the 17th-century **Fray Francisco de Burgoa** library collection. *(☎516 29 91. Open Tu-Su 10am-8pm. 35 pesos; Su free.)*

CATEDRAL DE OAXACA. Originally constructed in 1553 and reconstructed in 1702-33 after earthquake damage, the cathedral dates from a time when the Mexican church and state were unified. The building is governmental and imposing, if somewhat rundown, with the structural focus provided by the ornate bishop's seat. The facade is Baroque-style bas-relief. The interior contains 14 side chapels. The exterior is alive with dawdlers, children playing with strange balloons, and young girls waiting to ambush the unexpecting with their wares. *(In the northeast corner of the zócalo. Open daily 7am-9pm.)*

PALACIO DE GOBIERNO. Oaxaca's Palacio de Gobierno was constructed in the mid-19th century. Contemporary art expositions decorate the pleasant open-roofed *palacio*. At the top of the stairs, a mural by Arturo García Bustos acts as a pictorial pop-quiz on state history. That culminates with Benito Juárez's oft-repeated phrase *"El respeto al derecho ajeno es la paz"* ("Respect for the rights of others is peace"). *(On the south side of the zócalo. Open 24hr.)*

BASÍLICA DE LA SOLEDAD. A minor but absorbing attraction is the funky museum of religious art located next to the 17th-century church. The museum houses an astonishing array of objects—such as model ships, shell-and-pasta figurines, homemade cassette tapes, and a stuffed cat—sent from around the world as gifts to the Virgin, who is said to have appeared here in 1620. *(Independencia 107, 4 blocks behind the post office. ☎516 50 76. Open daily 10am-2pm and 4-6pm. 2 pesos.)*

CASA DE BENITO JUÁREZ. Mexico's most beloved president lived here for ten years as a child (1818-28). With living room, bedrooms, kitchen, and a "bookbinding/weaving shop," the house has been reconstructed in 19th-century, upper-class *oaxaqueña* style and features informational displays on Mexican culture and politics during Juárez's time. *(García Vigil 609, 1 block west of Alcalá. ☎516 18 60. Open Tu-Sa 10am-7pm, Su 10am-5pm. 27 pesos; Su free.)*

MUSEO DE ARTE CONTEMPORÁNEO DE OAXACA (MACO). This colonial building is known as the Casa de Cortés, although historians insist that it was not, in fact, Cortés's estate. Nevertheless, the 18th-century upper-class home is an example of vice-regal architecture, a style used by *conquistadores* and their heirs. The 15-room museum features three-month rotating exhibitions of mostly abstract art and in the past has showcased *oaxaqueños* Rufino Tamayo, Francisco Toledo, and Rodolfo Morales. *(Alcalá 202, a block down Andador Turístico on the right. ☎514 10 55. Open W-M 10:30am-8pm. 10 pesos; Su free.)*

MUSEO DE ARTE PREHISPÁNICO DE MÉXICO RUFINO TAMAYO. This museum features the artist's personal collection of pre-Hispanic objects. The figurines, ceramics, and masks that Tamayo collected are meant to be appreciated as works of art rather than artifacts, resulting in a hybrid art gallery and archaeological museum. *(Morelos 503, between Díaz Ordaz and Tinoco y Palacios. ☎516 47 50. Open M and W-Sa 10am-2pm and 4-7pm, Su 10am-3pm. 20 pesos, students 14 pesos.)*

TEATRO MACEDONIO ALCALÁ. A Oaxacan beauty, the theater, constructed at the turn of the 20th century, exemplifies the style fostered by dictator Porfirio Díaz, who had a taste for French art and intellectual formulas. *(5 de Mayo at Independencia, 2 blocks behind the cathedral. ☎516 33 87. Weekly shows 6 and 8pm. 20 pesos.)*

OTHER SIGHTS. If you're looking for a beautiful view of the city and surrounding hills, head to the **Cerro de Fortín** (The Hill with the Beautiful View). The *Escalera de Fortín* begins on Crespo, leading past the Guelaguetza amphitheater to the **Planetarium Nundehui.** Balance the splendor of the vista against the cardiological trauma inflicted by the grueling climb. (Planetarium ☎514 75 00. Open Th-Su 10am-1pm and 5-8pm. 30 pesos.) Also worth a visit is the **Centro Fotográfico Álvarez Bravo,** Murguía 302, between Reforma and Juárez, which displays rotating photography exhibits. (☎516 28 80. Open W-M 9:30am-6pm. Free.)

🎵📷 ENTERTAINMENT AND NIGHTLIFE

Every day tourists take over Oaxaca and every night the youth take it back. At night, the *zócalo* itself is open until 9 or 10pm, as both outsiders and locals drink beer and calmly stare at the green trees, fountains, and playing children. A walk up the Alcalá past the closed museums and craft shops will guarantee encounters with roving and loitering bands of youth. There's always something happening inside the city's bars and discos, and sometimes outside as well, where borderline sacrilegious activities take place on the steps of the Iglesia de Santo Domingo.

Those debilitated by the previous night's activity can catch a recent flick in English with Spanish subtitles at **Ariel 2000** (☎516 52 41), at the corner of Juárez and Berriozabal. The Guerreros, Oaxaca's professional baseball team, play just northwest of the complex at the **Estadio Eduardo Vásconcelos**, on the corner of Vásconcelos and Niños Héroes de Chapultepec (tickets 10-50 pesos). **Sala Versailles**, Ocampo 105 (☎516 23 35), three blocks east of the *zócalo*, hosts live shows. Most nightlife can be reached by foot, and taxis go everywhere (25 pesos).

BARS

Centered in the **Alcalá** and two blocks west near **Díaz** and **Allende,** most bars are within safe walking distance of the *zócalo*.

La Costumbre, Alcalá 501, opposite the entrance to Santo Domingo. A little too tight for dancing. Beer 15 pesos, cocktails 27 pesos. Open M-Sa 8pm-2:30am.

La Divina, Gurion 104, across from the south side of Santo Domingo, continues to be popular among the city's younger student bourgeoisie. Trippy ceramic artwork and nooks for close conversation. No cover. Open Tu-Su 9pm-1:30am.

Cafe Bar del Borgo, Alcalá 303. A bit closer to the *zócalo*, del Borgo has a chill coffeehouse atmosphere, with couples and groups sipping cappuccino (13 pesos) and beer (12 pesos) around small tables. Open daily 9am-11pm.

Cafe-Bar La Resistencia, Díaz 503 (☎514 95 84), at Allende. The name and interior design (posters of figures like Che Guevara and Malcolm X) clash with the yuppie/student clientele. The only revolution here is against sobriety. Beer 15 pesos. No cover. Open M-Sa 8pm-2am.

CLUBS

Several hard-core discos lie near the first-class bus station on **Díaz Ordaz** at **Niños Héroes de Chapultepec,** 11 blocks north of the *zócalo*. A taxi is the best way to reach these clubs (20 pesos).

◙ **La Candela,** Murguía 413 at Pino Suárez (☎514 20 10). The dance floor situated in an elegant, well-lit courtyard, surrounded by tables and rocked by a tight *salsa* band, draws a crowd diverse in age, skill, and nationality. Cover 25-35 pesos depending on the band. Live music Tu-Sa from 10pm. Open daily 2pm-1:30am.

NRG, Díaz 102-B (☎515 04 77), down 1 block from Héroes de Chapultepec, is simply a great place to dance. Spanish music W, pop mix other nights. Beer 15 pesos. No cover W; cover Th 30 pesos men, women free; cover F-Sa 40 pesos. Open W-Sa 9pm-3am.

La Cuija, 5 de Mayo (☎412-413), takes over Cafe Gecko on F-Sa. Those yearning for hard-core techno can weigh their desire against the relative unhipness of La Cuija's sparse, young student crowd. F-Sa 8pm-2am.

GAY AND LESBIAN NIGHTLIFE

In typical *machisimo* fashion, Oaxaca's gay and lesbian nightlife is a well-kept secret. The city's one gay club is, however, popular, well managed, and safe.

502, at Díaz 502, across from La Resistencia. As the city's only gay and lesbian nightclub, 502 can afford to be selective. The club is private; ring the bell outside the door and they'll decide whether you're fit to enter. No drugs, heavy drinking, or transvestism allowed. Cover 35 pesos. Open F-Sa 11pm-5am.

FESTIVALS

On the two Mondays following July 16, known as **Los Lunes del Cerro** (Hill Mondays), representatives from all seven regions of Oaxaca state converge on the Cerro del Fortín for the festival of ◙**Guelaguetza.** Guelaguetza refers to the Zapotec custom of reciprocal gift-giving, and at the end of the day's traditional dances, performers throw goods typical from their regions into the outstretched arms of the crowd gathered in the 12,000-seat stadium. In between the gatherings are festive food and handicraft exhibits, art shows, and concerts. (Front-section seats 300 pesos, back-section seats free, but you must come very early to get a seat. Call tourist office for reservations.)

Oaxaca's exquisitely beautiful **Día de los Muertos** (Nov. 1-2) celebrations have become a huge tourist draw in recent years. Most travel agencies offer expeditions to the candlelit, marigold-filled village graveyards. Shops fill with molded sugar *calaveras* (skulls) and dancing skeletons, while altars to memorialize the deceased are erected throughout the city. Because these celebrations occur for very personal reasons, locals might not appreciate being photographed as they remember their deceased.

On December 23, Oaxacans celebrate the unique **Noche de los Rábanos** (Night of the Radishes). The small tuber is so honored for its frequent use in Oaxacan cuisine and its extremely carvable form. Masterpieces of historic or biblical themes made entirely in radish fill the *zócalo*, where they are judged. Hundreds of people admire the creations and eat sweet *buñuelos*, tortillas with honey. Upon finishing the treat, make a wish and throw the ceramic plate on the ground; if the plate smashes into pieces, your wish will come true.

DAYTRIPS FROM OAXACA

The villages surrounding Oaxaca attract travelers by taking once-functional items, be they rugs, jars, or decaying temples, and displaying them as authentic representations of ways of life vanished or vanishing. Villages often specialize in particular products: **Arrazola** and **San Martín Tilcajate** make wooden animals; **San Bartolo Coyotepec,** black clay pottery; **Atzompa,** green clay pottery; **Ocotlán,** natural clay pottery; **Teotitlán del Valle,** wool *sarapes;* and **Villa Díaz Ordaz** and **Santo Tomás Jalietza,** textiles and weavings. Likewise, many villages hold *mercados* on specific days to attract visitors: Miahuatlán (M), Atzompa (Tu), San Pablo Etla (W), Zaachila (Th), Ocotlán (F), and Tlacolula (Su).

The "Tourist Yu'u" program operated by SEDETUR rents out guest houses in Abasolo, Papalutla, Teotitlán del Valle, Benito Juárez, Tlacolula, Quialana, Tlapazola, Santa Ana del Valle, and Hierve el Agua. Accommodations include five beds, a kitchen, and clean bedding; proceeds benefit the community. (☎516 01 23. Open daily 9am-2pm. 70 pesos per person, 25 peso discount for students in some vil-

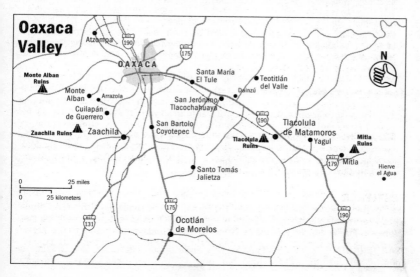

Oaxaca Valley

BUS A MOVE Riding the bus in Mexico is more exciting than in parts of the world with uniformly enforced traffic laws; here it is more terrifying and dangerous. Some tips for success when riding: keep in mind that there is no word in Spanish for "seat belt." This is an exaggeration. *Cinturón de seguridad* means "security belt," but the term will probably fade from use in Mexico like the second-person plural informal conjugation and the concept of lane-changing signals. *Colectivo* drivers often fit five adult passengers in a sedan, which leaves one person, the *gringo* if one is available, splayed awkwardly on top of the emergency brake, legs twisted painfully to avoid the stick shift. If you are this passenger, abandon the notion that a stranger's hand rubbing repeatedly against your thigh constitutes a sexual advance, and do your part to allow the cabdriver to downshift while he passes a semi-truck on a blind uphill curve. If you are patronizing a local bus, know that drivers are much more concerned with maintaining forward motion than with your safety. If you are getting off, move to the front of the bus as your stop approaches. As the bus slows, descend the steps. When the door opens, leap clear and hit the ground running. If you are boarding, first make sure that the bus driver is aware of your presence and prepared to stop. Once this is assured, gather your backpacks/luggage/children and prepare for the door to open; when it does, leap aboard and assume a crouching position: legs apart, knees bent, hands up and ready to grab whatever railings, passengers, sacks of fruit, or loose livestock that will stabilize you as the bus accelerates and you make your way to your seat.

lages; camping in the garden 25-30 pesos.) Additionally, you can try one of the *paseos culturales*, which introduce visitors to the traditional medicinal, agricultural, and artistic practices of the 13 villages in the area.

All the villages can be reached by the *taxi colectivos* that leave the Central de Abastos (3-10 pesos depending on distance). At the intersection of Periférico and Las Casas is an Inverlat bank. Destinations are labeled on taxi windows and on signs along the road. Buses are easy to find on the Mitla route (Mex. 190), but may be more difficult to locate on other routes. Some companies offer bike tours to outlying towns; contact the tourist office for more information.

OAXACA TO MITLA (MEX. 190)

All the following destinations are accessible via a Mitla-bound bus, leaving the 2nd-class station in Oaxaca (1hr., every 10min. 8am-8pm, 10 pesos). Most people visit these sites as daytrips, but the tourist office in Oaxaca can arrange for overnight stays in Teotitlán del Valle, Tlacolula, or Hierve el Agua (see p. 466). Given the time needed for the trip to Hierve el Agua, it's probably impossible to visit all these towns before dark. Saving Mitla and Hierve al Agua for a separate trip might be a good idea.

SANTA MARÍA EL TULE. This friendly little town (pop. 7000), just 14km outside Oaxaca, houses one of Mexico's great roadside attractions: the **Tule Tree.** The 2000-year-old, 42m sabino tree has an astounding circumference of 58m—the largest girth of any tree on earth. Ask the bus driver to drop you off at El Tule; then ask for *el árbol* (the tree). Don't be deceived into thinking the first tree you see is the big one—it's just the 1000-year-old baby. There is a fee (2 pesos) to approach the fence closest to the tree, but the glory of this botanical behemoth can be appreciated within a 100m radius. In fact, farther may be better, as pictures taken too close will look like nothing more than a big piece of bark.

DAINZÚ. The Dainzú ruins, 22km from Oaxaca, date from the first Pre-Classic phase at Monte Albán. This site is only for the ruins completest: Dainzú's pyramids are the smallest and least excavated in the Oaxaca area, and lie 1km from the main road. *(Open daily 8am-6pm. 22 pesos.)*

SAN JERÓNIMO TLACOCHAHUAYA. The walls of the **Iglesia de San Jerónimo** in nearby San Jerónimo Tlacochahuaya (pop. 4700), 23km from Oaxaca, illustrate

Zapotec decorative techniques applied to Catholic motifs. It was built at the end of the 16th century by Dominicans seeking to escape worldly temptation. *(Open daily 7am-2pm and 4-6pm.)*

TEOTITLÁN DEL VALLE. Twenty-eight kilometers from Oaxaca, Teotitlán (pop. 5600) is the oldest community in the state, settled about 2000 years ago. The source of many beautiful woolen *sarapes* and rugs, Teotitlán is home to 200-300 families who earn their livelihood by spinning and weaving. Many allow tourists to visit their workshops. Teotitlán is not as accessible as many of the other stops on the road; it's 4km from where the bus drops you off, but *taxi colectivos* run sporadically from the main road to town, and a few workshops are scattered within walking distance of the main road. Many vendors accept credit cards and some will deliver large *sarapes* to hotels in Oaxaca City.

TLACOLULA DE MATAMOROS. Tlacolula (pop. 13,500), 33km from Oaxaca, is one of the largest towns in the area. It hosts a lively market (Su 6am-2pm, officially 6am-7pm), which features *mezcal.* Slightly more interesting than the town itself are the small Zapotec ruins of **Lambityeco,** several kilometers before the town. Occupied from AD 600 to 1000 by the Zapotecs after they abandoned Monte Albán, the village reached its peak from 700 to 775. The ruins consist of one main pyramid and several houses, with some visible murals. The site also features the only known portraits in the Oaxaca ruins area, unsettling carvings of Zapotecs buried in the site's tombs. *(Open daily 8am-6pm. 17 pesos; Su free.)*

▨ YAGUL. Thirty-six kilometers from Oaxaca, Yagul was a Zapotec city inhabited primarily from 700 BC to AD 1521, though there is evidence of human presence as early as 3000 BC. Less archaeologically impressive than Mitla, Yagul's isolation and disarray—the ruins are scattered about a small mountain whose rocky paths lead to outcroppings with spectacular 360-degree views—make it a more entertaining and aesthetically striking site, albeit a more tiring and slightly more dangerous one. A gorgeous 1.5km jaunt through cornfields and up a hill preps the visitor for the wide green view of a mountain-ringed valley that awaits at the top. If you go on a weekday, you'll be able to act out your long-held fantasies of Zapotec kingship with lizards as your only audience. The more famous buildings and tombs are in the **Acrópolis,** the area closest to the parking lot, 2km north of the road. If you bring some friends you can start a pick-up game in the restored ball court, the largest of its kind in the Oaxaca Valley, though archaeologists have only a vague idea about how the game was played. The **Court of the Triple Tomb** is to the left of the ball court. Carved with an image that resembles a jaguar, the tomb is divided in three sections, with stone faces covering the largest section. Beyond the ball court rises the **Council Hall;** behind that is the **Palace of the Six Patios,** believed to have been home to the city's ruler. Heading back to the parking lot, take the left-hand trail that climbs uphill to the rocky outcropping to catch a great view of the cactus-covered hills. Continue on by heading back to the fork in the path and taking the other trail. It leads to a Zapotec fortress built as a fallback in case the town was attacked. Even farther up is the mountaintop. Turn right and walk through brush for a while to find the unmarked basins carved out of the mountaintop which, it is speculated, were Zapotec bathtubs. There is a picturesque *palapa*-style restaurant before the hill on the way to the ruins, which serves inexpensive regional specialties. *(Site open daily 8am-5pm. 27 pesos; Su free.)*

MITLA

After arriving in Mitla, find the huge highway welcome sign. Walk under the sign; this is the town's main road. Following the green signs, continue on the road for 20min. until you reach the church in front of the ruins. Site open daily 8am-5pm. 27 pesos; Su free.

Mitla: City of death! Bring your camera. Enveloped by a Zapotec-speaking village, this archaeological site, 44km east of Oaxaca, has a bloody history: until the 16th century, it was a place of worship for the gods of the underworld and witnessed

SOUTHERN PACIFIC COAST

both animal and human sacrifice. Although Mitla began as a small village around 1000 BC, the Zapotecs only came to occupy it when the Mixtecs forced them out of Monte Albán. It was later appropriated by the Mixtecs and became the largest and most important of the late Mixtec cities. When the Spaniards arrived in the valley, Mitla was the only ceremonial center of the Mesoamerican Classic Period still in use, and they put a stop to the pagan nonsense by subjugating the Mixtecs, destroying their buildings, and building a church on top of the ruins. Interestingly, the Catholic archbishop of Oaxaca built his home to echo the horizontal lines of the Zapotec priest's residence in Mitla, in what was either an architectural tribute to or an expression of dominance over an indigenous religion virtually exterminated by Catholicism.

Walking to the ruins from the town's main road you will first come upon the **Grupo del Arroyo**, possibly the least interesting archaelogical site in Mexico: a flat stone patio from AD 1100. Continuing on the main road, the ticket booth is in the yellow building on the far side of the red-domed church; it contains a few artifacts and several dioramas of the site. To the left, and symbolically in the shadow of the church are the three patios known as the **North Group** or **Catholic Establishment.** One of them has been almost completely buried by the church. The central patio is on the other side; here, and in the surrounding rooms, you can see pieces of Mixtec paintings, supposedly telling Mixtec history, done in red on stone. The more impressive ruins are across the road in the **Grupo de las Columnas (Group of the Columns),** decorated inside and out with intricate geometric designs. Beyond the entrance are two patios joined at one corner. In the first, which features the **Hall of the Columns,** the tombs of the pyramids form a cross; for years, Spaniards thought this proved that the Mixtecs somehow knew the story of Jesus. On the second patio behind and to the right of the first, two tombs are open to visitors. The easternmost tomb has large stones covered with mosaic patterns. The roof of the northernmost tomb rests on a single huge column known as the **Column of Life.** Pilgrims travel here each year to embrace the column. In exchange for the hug, the column supposedly tells them how much longer they have to live. The two other groups, **Grupo del Sur (South Group)** and **Grupo de Adobe,** are farther from the site, southeast and across the river from the main ruins. Use the diagrams at the site to find these two ruins if you wish to see them, though neither is well preserved.

▧ HIERVE EL AGUA

The site is 13km east of Mitla and 57km east of Oaxaca. Buses from Oaxaca take at least 2hr. From Mitla, take a camioneta (covered pick-up truck) from the terminal (45min., every hr. 8am-6pm, 20 pesos), and ask if the camioneta is headed to Agua Dulce, as they are unmarked. Open daily 8am-6pm. 10 pesos.

The road to Hierve el Agua (Boil the Water) goes up a mountain and through a village whose dirt road is only wide enough for one car. Isolated from the Oaxaca commercial zone, the site seems perched on the edge of civilization. It takes its name from two springs of carbonated water that look like they are boiling. The high concentration of mineral salts in the water resulted in the strange petrification of several giant waterfalls, or, more properly, rockfalls. A path to the top of the largest rock form offers an impressive view and also leads downward, offering a view from below. Be careful when climbing, as rocks are often wet and slippery. The site includes three pools for bathing—two of sulfur water near the petrified waterfall and one of *agua dulce* on the left-hand side of the path.

ARRAZOLA, CUILÁPAM, ZAACHILA, AND ATZOMPA (MEX. 131)

Arrazola, Cuilápam, and Zaachila can all be reached by taking a taxi colectivo from Oaxaca's Central de Abastos. It's easy to hop from one town to the next; go back to Mex. 131 and flag down another colectivo (to get back to Mex. 131 from Arrazola, take a Oaxaca-bound colectivo; otherwise, it's a long walk to the highway). Though close to the other three, Atzonpa does not lie on Mex. 131. From Oaxaca, it can be reached via a separate colectivo (40min., 8 pesos).

ARRAZOLA. This small, hilly village is the hometown of Manuel Jiménez, one of Mexico's most famous artisans. Jiménez is the creator of **alebrijes**, brightly colored figurines of demons and zoo animals. While success has made his pieces unaffordable to most (small pieces go for US$170), his workshop is worth visiting. To get there, walk up Arrazola's main road, passing the plaza and turning left at the first intersection onto Obregón. Continue past the end of the pavement, following as it turns right. The home is on the right-hand side, opposite a corn field. A glimpse of the Jiménez family's kinetic cedar wood sculptures and the possibility of a conversation with the man himself make the substantial trek from Mex. 131 worth the effort. Nearly all the households in town make figurines to supplement their incomes. A medium-sized iguana *alebrije* will cost about 120 pesos. *(20min. from Oaxaca on Mex. 131.)*

CUILÁPAM DE GUERRERO. Cuilápam (pop. 12,800) has an isolated and hauntingly lovely 17th-century **Dominican monastery.** The highlight of the site—aside from the breathtaking vistas—is the cell that was once occupied by the Revolutionary hero Vicente Guerrero in 1831 before his death by firing squad on the patio outside. Today, all that remains is a portrait of him in his cell and a monument where he fell. Built as a retreat for Spanish monks wishing to exile themselves as far as possible from civilization, the upper floor now cloisters archaeologists laboring to reconstruct the region's history in the monk's old stone cells. *(25min. from Oaxaca on Mex. 131. Open daily 10am-6pm. 17 pesos.)*

ZAACHILA. Zaachila (pop. 25,700), the stronghold of the Zapotecs before they fell to the Spanish in 1521, hosts a fascinating market each Thursday. Spend your pesos on preserved bananas and squealing pigs. A yellow and orange cathedral dominates the center of town. To the right and behind the church, a street heads uphill to a partially uncovered archaeological site. Until 1962, locals prohibited excavations to prevent the intrusion of outsiders. Exploration since has been limited, but two Mixtec tombs with well-preserved jewelry have been uncovered. The town's gold, turquoise, jade, and bone artifacts (as well as the tourist dollars they would have attracted) have been spirited away to the national museum in Mexico City (see p. 108). The eerie tombs—the only decorated ones in Oaxaca—are worth a visit. Wide-eyed owls (messengers of the Zapotec underworld) stare from the damp stone walls, while portrayals of the Gods of Death lurk in the dimmer recess of the tomb. *(30min. from Oaxaca on Mex. 131. Open daily 9am-6pm. 17 pesos; Su free.)*

ATZOMPA. Atzompa (pop. 11,000), where that magnificent blend of clay and sprouts, the **Chia Pet®**, was born. Natural, green-glazed pottery can be found here at better prices than in Oaxaca. The **Mercado de Artesanías** is a publicly funded forum that brings together the work of the town's artisans. While the selection is good, no bargaining is allowed. Ask around for Delores, an artisan who will demonstrate the Atzompa method for a price. *(Though close to the other villages, Aztompa does not lie on Mex. 131. Take a taxi colectivo marked "Aztompa" (40min., 8 pesos) from the street north of the bus station.)*

SAN BARTOLO COYOTEPEC AND THE ROAD SOUTH (MEX. 175)

For all three towns, take an "Ocotlán" taxi colectivo from the market (San Bartolo 15min., Santo Tomás 20min., Ocotlán 40min.; all three towns 10 pesos by colectivo).

SAN BARTOLO COYOTEPEC. San Bartolo, 12km south of Oaxaca, is the only place in Mexico that creates the ink-black pottery that populates souvenir shops throughout the state. The dark color comes from the local mud. Though the town had been making the pottery for centuries, it wasn't until 1953, when the diminutive Doña Rosa accidentally discovered that it could be polished, that it became an art form. Doña Rosa kept the polishing technique a family secret for 12 years, then gave it to the town, which has been supported by the craft ever since. In the market, on the west side of Mex. 175, villagers sell jet-black vases, luminaires, figurines, you name it. Many substantial pieces go for under 20 pesos. The polished pottery will only hold water for 20min. or so before soaking it up—don't buy anything you plan to drink out of. Doña Rosa's son carries on the family tradition and gives free demonstrations to groups in the Nieto workshop, several blocks up the town's main street, Juárez, on the east side of Mex. 175. *(Market open daily 9am-7pm. Nieto workshop open daily 9am-7pm.)*

SANTO TOMÁS JALIETZA. Four kilometers farther south and slightly left of the main road, Santo Tomás's artisans specialize in weaving "cotton garments" on back-strap looms, by sitting on the ground and tying the looms to a tree. The items produced here are more practically useful than most Oaxacan crafts—purses, shirts, vests, dresses, etc.

OCOTLÁN DE MORELOS. Above the valley in the foothills of the Sierra Madre del Sur, 33km south of the Oaxaca, Ocotlán offers a fairy-tale powder blue church and what is undoubtedly Oaxaca's finest shoe-flower-bread-taco-rug-shirt-fruit-chili-backpack-knife-hat-belt-spoon-bucket-tupperware-china-birdcage-pliers-extension cord-bra-saddle-Japanese handheld game-80s picture of Demi Moore market, held Fridays 10am-8pm. It's less tourist-oriented than other towns, so visitors willing to be the market's sole and very conspicuous non-Mexican buyer will be rewarded with authentic prices.

⬛ NEAR OAXACA: MONTE ALBÁN

Autobuses Turísticos buses to Monte Albán leave the Hotel Rivera del Ángel, Mina 518 (☎516 53 27), between Mier y Terán and Díaz Ordaz, several blocks southwest of the zócalo (30min; every 30min. 8:30am-4pm, later buses leave little time at site; round-trip ticket with fixed return 2½-3hr. after arrival 20 pesos, 10 pesos extra to come back later.) Site open daily 8am-6pm. 35 pesos, 30 pesos more with video camera; Su and holidays free. Though many travel agencies can set you up with hassle-free transportation and excellent guides, it is usually cheaper to transport yourself and, if you want one, find a guide once you reach the mountain. English-language guides charge 150-300 pesos for a 1½hr. tour, depending on the size and negotiating skills of your group.

High above Oaxaca de Juárez, Monte Albán, the ancient mecca of the Zapotec "cloud people," now watches over the surrounding mountains in utter stillness. Visitors to Oaxaca should not leave without seeing the ruins, some of the most important and spectacular in Mexico. Mysteriously abandoned by both the Zapotecs and Mixtecs over 1000 years ago, the sacred capital of Monte Albán *feels* ancient. Unless you're an expert on Pre-Hispanic civilizations (or the type that likes her ruins unexplained) a good guide to Monte Albán can really make the visit.

HISTORY. The monolithic, geometric stone structures are all that remain of the vast Zapotec capital that once sprawled 20km over three mountaintops. First constructed circa 700 BC, Monte Albán flourished during the Classic Period (AD 300-750), when it shared the spotlight with Teotihuacán and Tikal as the major cultural and ceremonial centers of Mesoamerica. This was the greatest Zapotec capital—the people cultivated maize, built complex drainage systems for water, and engaged in extensive exchange networks, especially with Teotihuacán (see p. 126). As Monte Albán grew, daily life was carefully constructed to harmonize with supernatural elements: architecture adhered to the orientation of the four cardinal points and the proportions of the 260-day sacred calendar, and residences were organized in families of five to 10 people in four-sided houses with open central courtyards. To emphasize the congruence between household and cosmos, families buried their ancestors beneath their houses to symbolize their transmigration to the underworld below. Excavations of burials in Monte Albán have yielded not only dazzling artifacts, but also valuable information on social stratification.

The history of Monte Albán can be divided into five parts, spanning the years from 500 BC until the Spanish conquest in the 16th century. During **periods I** and **II**, Monte Albán rose as the Maya and Zapotec cultures intermingled. The Zapotecs adopted the Maya *juego de pelota* (ball game) and steep pyramid structure, while the Maya appropriated the Zapotec calendar and writing system. Almost all of the extant buildings and tombs, as well as several urns and murals of *colanijes* (richly adorned priests), come from **Period III** (AD 350-700). Burial arrangements of varying size and richness show the social divisions of the period: priests, clerks, and laborers lived and died apart. For reasons that remain unknown, Monte Albán began to fade around 750. Construction ceased, and control of the Zapotec empire shifted to other cities such as Zaachila, Yagul, and, later, Mitla. Possible explanations for the abandonment include drought, over-exploitation of resources, and unrest. As with other Zapotec strongholds during the subsequent **periods IV** and **V**, the Mixtecs took over. The Mixtecs used Monte Albán as a fortress and a sacred metropolis, reclaiming the tombs left by the Zapotecs. When Dr. Alfonso Caso discovered **Tomb 7** in 1932; the treasure found within more than quadrupled the number of previously identified gold Mixtec objects. The treasures from Tomb 7 are now on display at the Museo de las Culturas de Oaxaca (see p. 461).

BALLCOURT. After passing through the ticketing station just beyond the museum, walk left up the inclined path leading diagonally toward the ruins. Before reaching the Main Plaza, you will see the remains of several small buildings on your left and the ballcourt in front of you. The sides of the court, which now look like bleachers, were once covered in stucco and plaster, and served as bouncing boards for the ball toward the goal. In contrast to the Aztecs' more gory use of the game to determine sacrificial victims, the Zapotecs used it to solve all kinds of conflicts and as a means of predicting future events.

MAIN PLAZA. Passing the ballcourt on your left, you will enter the huge Main Plaza, with the mountain-like **North Platform** on the right, and smaller structures lined up on your left. The Main Plaza is flat, remarkable when one considers that the mountain from which is was cut was originally peaked. On your left, look for **The Palace (Building II).** Like other Pre-Hispanic ruins, the structures at Monte Albán were civic and residential as well as religious; this pyramid served as the home of one of Monte Albán's important dignitaries.

MOUND Q. Past the palace sits Mound Q, the ugly red-headed stepchild of Monte Albán, notable for its banality. Even the archaeologists normally willing to claim "great religious and administrative importance" for any pile of rocks suggest only half-heartedly that Mound Q "may be a temple."

SOUTH PLATFORM. Kitty-corner with the palace and forming the plaza's south end is the South Platform, one of the site's highest structures. Another contains a message roughly translated as "North Platform Sux, South Platform Rulz!" believed to be North America's first recorded Zapotec graffiti. The top affords a commanding view of the ruins, valley, and mountains beyond. On both sides of the staircase on the plaza level are stelae carved with priests and tigers. One stela is believed to depict a former Monte Albán king.

BUILDING OF DANCERS. Walking left of the platform to the plaza's west side, you will first come across **System M** and then the Building of Dancers. The reliefs on the center building are known as "dancers," though they more likely depict chieftans conquered by Monte Albán. The over 400 figures date from the 5th century BC and are nearly identical to contemporary Olmec sculptures on the Gulf Coast. Many of the figures show evidence of genital mutilation.

BUILDINGS G, H, I, AND J. Crossing back to the center of the platform, the first structure you hit is Building J, formed in the shape of an arrowhead. Unlike any other ancient edifice in Mexico, it is asymmetrical and built at a 45-degree angle to nearby structures. Its broad, carved slabs suggest that the building is one of the oldest on the site, dating from 100 BC to AD 200. Many of the glyphs depict an upside-down head below a stylized hill. Archeologists speculate that these images represent conquests, the head indicating the tribe defeated and the glyph identifying the region conquered. The next group of buildings moving north, dominating the center of the plaza, are buildings G, H, and I—likely comprising the principal altar of Monte Albán.

THE NORTH PLATFORM. Finish off the Main Plaza by visiting the North Platform near the entrance, a structure almost as large as the plaza itself. The platform contains the **Sunken Patio** as well as the site's highest altar, which you can climb for yet another *buena vista.*

TOMBS AND MUSEUM. Continue straight on the path, exiting the site to **Tomb 104.** Duck underground, look above the entrance, and gaze at the urn, which is covered with interwoven images of the maize and rain gods. On your way out of the site, be sure to stop by the museum, which gives a chronological survey of Monte Albán's history and displays sculpted stones from the site's earlier periods. Although the collection is still impressive, some of the more spectacular artifacts have unfortunately been hauled off to museums in Oaxaca and Mexico City. Near the parking lot is the entrance to **Tomb 7,** where the spectacular cache of Mixtec ornaments mentioned above was found.

BAHÍAS DE HUATULCO   ☎ 9

Huatulco's promotional literature proclaims it "Paradise Found," as if a band of hardy adventurers hacked their way through the jungle and came upon a vast series of huge beach resorts connected by a freshly-paved network of highways. A better name might be "Prefabricated Paradise." This is not necessarily a bad thing; authenticity never cleaned anyone's bathroom. Huatulco is well-designed, very clean, and devoid of the slummy neighborhoods that surround most Mexican tourist areas. It is useful as a sort of decompression chamber for those coming from places like Zipolite back to civilization. Huatulco is still a low-key beach town, but clearly in touch with the most current methods of attracting people with money and taking that money from them. Transportation is expensive, as are all hotels inside La Crucecita, which of course is a good ways from the beach. The high costs mean that the clientele is almost exclusively middle-and upper-class families, with few backpackers. Watch for neighborhoods with charming names like "Sector F."

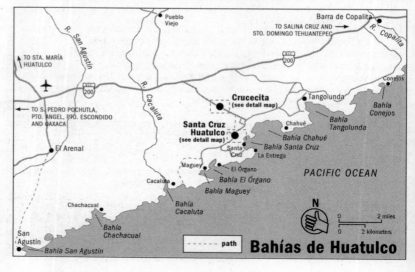

Bahías de Huatulco

▣ TRANSPORTATION

Airport: The airport (☎581 90 07), 19km from the town of Santa Cruz, is served by **Aerocaribe** (☎587 12 20) and **Mexicana** (☎587 02 43). To get to the airport, take a taxi (25min., 100 pesos) or a "Sta. Maria" microbus from the corner of Guamuchil and Carrizal in Santa Cruz (8 pesos). Ask to be let off at the airport, and walk approximately 500m to the right of where the driver drops you.

Buses: The Cristóbal Colón station (☎587 02 61) is at the corner of Gardenia and Ocotillo in La Crucecita. To get to the *zócalo*, exit left and walk 4 blocks down Gardenia. Cristóbal Colón goes to: **Mexico City** (12½hr., 6pm, 433 pesos); **Oaxaca** (8hr., 11pm, 161 pesos); **Puerto Escondido** (2hr.; 7 per day 3am-7pm, 47 pesos); **San Cristóbal** (10hr., 10:45am and 11:30pm, 197 pesos); **Tuxtla Gutiérrez** (9hr., 11:00am and 11:45pm, 184 pesos). Estrella Blanca (☎587 01 03), farther down Gardenia at Palma

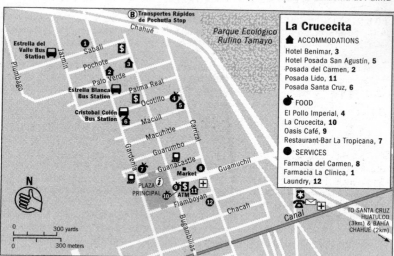

La Crucecita

🔺 ACCOMMODATIONS

Hotel Benimar, **3**
Hotel Posada San Agustín, **5**
Posada del Carmen, **2**
Posada Lido, **11**
Posada Santa Cruz, **6**

🍎 FOOD

El Pollo Imperial, **4**
La Crucecita, **10**
Oasis Café, **9**
Restaurant-Bar La Tropicana, **7**

● SERVICES

Farmacia del Carmen, **8**
Farmacia La Clinica, **1**
Laundry, **12**

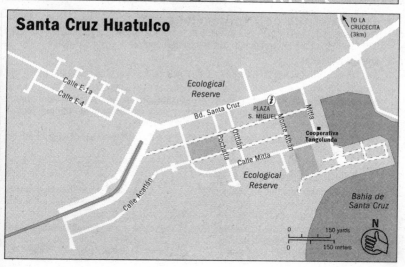

Santa Cruz Huatulco

Real, travels to: **Acapulco** (9hr.; 5, 9am, 6:15, 9pm; 217 pesos). The best way to get to **Pochutla,** gateway to Puerto Ángel, Zipolite, and Puerto Escondido, is a Transportes Rápidos de Pochutla microbus; they leave from Carrizal after it curves into an east-west road on the north end of town (1hr., every 15min. 5:30am-9pm, 12 pesos).

✦ ᘔ ORIENTATION AND PRACTICAL INFORMATION

Huatulco and its *bahías* (bays) consist of 35km of beach and cove on the southern Oaxacan coast between the Coyula and Copalita rivers, about 295km south of Oaxaca de Juárez. The most practical place to stay is **La Crucecita,** in the middle of a string of nine bays, which are, from east to west: Conejos, Tangolunda, Chahué, Santa Cruz, El Órgano, Maguey, Cacaluta, Chachacual, and San Agustín. La Crucecita houses the bus stations and the few existing budget accommodations. **Santa Cruz,** the bay closest to La Crucecita, offers the best access to the airport.

TOURIST, FINANCIAL, AND LOCAL INFORMATION

Tourist Office: SEDETUR (☎581 01 76 or 581 01 77), inconveniently across from the commercial center in Tangolunda on Juárez; cross to the left side of Juárez at the Argentina Restaurant. Open M-F 8am-3pm, Sa 9am-1pm. Help is more accessible at the **Módulo de Información,** in the *zócalo* toward the east side. Helpful maps and advice. Be sure to check the **official taxi tariffs,** posted on the side of the Módulo; many tourists pay more than they should. Open M-F 9am-2pm and 4-7pm during high seasons.

Currency Exchange: Bital, on the corner of Sabali & Bugambilla, has a money exchange and ATM. Open 8am-7pm M-Sa. Half a block from the park on Guamuchil is a 24hr. **ATM. Bancrecer,** Bugambilia 1104, before Macuil and Ocotillo in La Crucecita, exchanges currency and has a 24hr. **ATM.** Open M-F 9am-5pm, Sa 10am-2pm. Large hotels exchange money at slightly less favorable rates.

Market: 3 de Mayo, on Guamuchil off the *zócalo,* sells trinkets, produce, and meat. Open daily 7am-8pm.

Laundry: Lavandería Estrella, on Flamboyan at the corner of Carrizal, offers same-day service. 27 pesos per 3kg. Open M-Sa 8am-9pm.

Car Rental: Budget, Ocotillo 404 (☎587 00 10), 1 block from the 1st-class bus station. VW sedans 480 pesos per day. Also at the airport (☎581 90 00). Open daily 8am-8pm.

Bike Rental: The owner of Restaurant Bar La Tropicana at the NW corner of the *zócalo* rents out serviceable bikes. 15 pesos per hr., 75 pesos per day.

EMERGENCY AND COMMUNICATIONS

Police: At Blvd. Chahué 100 (☎587 02 10), in back of the peach government building, 200m south of the intersection of Guamuchil and Chahué. No English spoken.

Emergency: ☎060

Red Cross: Blvd. Chahué 110 (☎587 11 88), next door to the post office and police. No English spoken.

Pharmacy: Farmacia La Clínica (☎587 05 91), at Gardenia and Sabali, 4 blocks to the right when exiting the bus station. Closer to the *zócalo* is **Farmacia del Carmen** (☎587 20 12), on Guamuchil at Carrizal. Open daily 8am-10pm.

Hospital: Centro de Salud, Carrizal 202 (☎587 14 21) at the corner of Guamuchil. No English spoken.

Fax: Telecomm (☎587 08 94; fax 587 08 85), next to the post office. Open M-F 8am-7:30pm, Sa-Su 9am-12:30pm.

Internet Access: Internet access is hard to find in La Crucecita. **Informática MARE,** Guanacaste 203 (☎587 08 41), across from the market, on the 2nd fl., has quick connections. 30 pesos per hr. Open M-F 10am-9pm, Sa 10am-4pm.

Post Office: Blvd. Chahué 100 (☎587 05 51), in the peach government building. Open M-F 8am-3pm, Sa 9am-1pm.

Postal Code: 70989.

ACCOMMODATIONS AND CAMPING

Camping is a way to escape Huatulco's high-priced hotel scene, but it is allowed only on Chahué, Cacaluta, and Conejos bays. Even in these locations, camping is a risky affair; there is little security, and Cacaluta and Conejos have in the past been sites of confrontation between police and illegal Central American immigrants. Under no circumstances should you attempt to camp on Santa Cruz or Tangolunda; hotel security will not be kind. If camping isn't your thing, prepare yourself for slim pickings. All affordable hotels are in La Crucecita, and even those tend be overpriced. Some families rent out rooms, and those willing to search around and negotiate will be rewarded for the effort. Rates rise 20-50% during high season (July-Aug.); listings below are low-high season ranges.

Hotel Posada San Agustín (☎587 03 68), on Macuil at Carrizal. From the bus station, walk 1 block to the left, turn left on Macuil, and walk 2 blocks to the blue and white building. Spotlessly clean, bright, and run by a young family, San Agustín has fans, balconies, and an upbeat, homey air. Singles 100-150 pesos; doubles 150-250 pesos.

Posada Santa Cruz (☎587 00 41), on Gardenia, just south of the Cristóbal Colón bus station. 5 large, clean rooms with TV, fans, double beds. 150-300 pesos.

Posada Lido, Flamboyan 209 (☎587 08 10), ½ block east of the *zócalo*. 5 very clean rooms, with double beds, fans, and TV. A family shares the building. Just like living at home, if you grew up in a Mexican resort town. Communal baths. Singles 100 pesos; doubles with private bath 200 pesos.

Hotel Benimar, Bugambilias 1404 (☎587 04 47), at Pochote, 3 blocks to the right from the station on Gardenia, and then another block right on Pochote. Dusky interior harbors fans and full baths. Folks congregate in the lobby to watch TV. Singles and doubles 160-260 pesos; triples 200-300 pesos; quads 300-400 pesos.

Posada del Carmen, Palo Verde 307 (☎580 19 58 or 587 05 93), 2 blocks north of the Cristóbal Colón station. This small hotel has new, clean rooms with tile floors that, unlike in most Mexican budget hotels, look like they were designed by someone who was not color blind. Singles 150-180 pesos; doubles 100-150 pesos.

FOOD

In Huatulco, pricey tourist restaurants experiment in Italian pastas and poorly rendered sushi, while restaurants near the *zócalo* charge handsomely for Mexican dishes. A few cheap options are available on most menus. The best bargains are tacos and barbecued chicken found on **Buganbillas** and **Carrizal.**

El Pollo Imperial (☎587 04 98), on Carrizal, just north of Macuil. El Pollo's popular and surprisingly tasty barbecued chicken comes with beans and pasta salad (¼ chicken 20 pesos, entire chicken 60 pesos). Open daily 9am-8pm.

La Crucecita (☎587 09 06), 1 block past the *zócalo* at Bugambillas and Chacah. Upgrade from the plastic tables of taco shops to the plant-rich courtyard of La Crucecita, which manages pleasant dining without exorbitant prices. *Tlayuda*s 35 pesos, *tortas* and sandwiches 15-20 pesos. Open daily 7am-10pm.

Restaurant Bar La Tropicana (☎587 06 61), Guanacastle at Gardenia, across from Hotel Flamboyant. So-so food comes 2nd to location, popularity, and hours. Fish filet 38 pesos. *Antojitos* (23 pesos) are the best bet. Open 24hr.

Oasis Cafe (☎587 00 45), at Bugambillas and Flamboyan. Crowded at all hours, this *zócalo* restaurant has entrees at all prices (from 35 pesos). Open daily 10am-midnight.

BEACHES

As might be expected in a town meticulously designed to rake in tourist dollars, Huatulco's nine bays and 36 beaches, spread over 35km, pose a transportation challenge. It's hard to get off the beaten track without handing over pesos for a taxi or *lancha*. Fortunately, three of the bays are accessible by *colectivos* that leave from the intersection of Guamuchil and Carrizal (4 pesos to Tangolunda, 3 pesos to Santa Cruz). If you plan to take a tour, the tourist bureau recommends going through an official agency in town rather than one of the "guides" vending their services in the street; many tourists have been ripped off in the past. Storefronts such as the **Módulo de Información** next to the Cristóbal Colón station are not official; only the *módulo* in the *zócalo* offers solid advice. If you plan on indulging in water sports, consider going through the company itself to save pesos, rather than dealing with a travel agency. **Hurricane Divers**, at Bahía Chahué, offers reliable diving expertise. (☎587 11 07. Open daily 9am-7pm.) **Piraguas** (☎587 13 33), in La Crucecita, guides white water rafting trips down nearby Río Capolita.

BAHÍA CHAHUÉ. Closest to La Crucecita is Bahía Chahué, which remains relatively unpopulated save the beachside camp of Hotel Castillo, whose facilities are available for a 20-peso charge. Due to economic recession, Chahué is a resort ghost town. Hotels stand half-finished and finely landscaped brick paths lead nowhere. Though the weedy construction zone before the beach is ugly, the beach itself offers a fine stretch of sand perfect for quiet sunbathing. The water is generally safe for swimming, but sometimes rough. *(Take a "Tangolunda" or "Santa Cruz" colectivo. Ask to be let off at Chahué. Alternatively, walk 2 blocks east on Guamuchil to Blvd. Chahué and take a right, then walk 10min. until you come to a T-intersection. The left branch leads to Tangolunda, the right to Santa Cruz. Go straight; Chahué is 5min. down the road.)*

BAHÍA SANTA CRUZ. Bahía Santa Cruz harbors *lanchas*, a profusion of *palapa* restaurants, and a huge, overpriced commercial district. Of its two beaches, **Playa Santa Cruz** and **Playa La Entrega**, Entrega is the better, offering good snorkeling, swimming, and a lesser chance of colliding with a banana boat, but it is a 36-peso taxi ride away. Equipment can be rented at Entrega toward the left end of the beach facing the water. Playa Santa Cruz, just past the *lanchas* at the entrance to town, is easier to reach, but smaller and more crowded. Equipment can be rented past the *lanchas*. **Restaurant Ve el Mar,** on the side of the beach nearest the *lanchas*, reputedly has the best seafood in the area. Fish and shrimp cocktails start at 45 pesos. At high tide, waiters carrying towering plates of *mariscos* are forced to leap onto chairs to avoid drenching their white patent shoes. *(A taxi (36 pesos) or lancha (150 pesos per 10 people) will take you from Santa Cruz to Playa Entrega. Equipment 40 pesos per day. To get to Santa Cruz, continue down the right branch of Blvd. Chahué, a 10min. walk or 5min. ride past Bahía Chahué. Restaurant☎ 587 03 64. Open daily 8am-10pm.)*

BAHÍA MAGUEY. Also 2km from Playa Santa Cruz and less crowded then Entrega, Bahía Maguey is another hot spot for snorkeling and swimming. *(Taxis (45 pesos) and lanchas (up to 500 pesos per 10 people).)*

BAHÍA TANGOLUNDA. Another affordable accessible beach, Tangolunda, in the town of Tangolunda, is home to the Zona Hotelera and the Bahía's swankest resorts. The beach is steep and the surf occasionally rough but it's worth the trip just to look at the huge, opulent hotels. *(Take a 4-peso colectivo; alternately, walk to the right from the hotels when facing the sea.)*

OTHER BAHÍAS. If you don't mind splurging on transportation, **La India, San Agustín,** and **Cacaluta** are best for snorkeling and diving. Cacaluta is also known for its lush plant life and breezes. San Agustín is the most crowded while Cacaluta, La India, Conejos, and El Órgano are the best shots at solitude. The only other beaches accessible by land are **La Bocana, Bahía Cacaluta** (4WD only), and **Bahía San Agustín**; taxis charge hefty rates to travel this far. Another option is renting a bike or car for the day (see **Practical Information**, p. 471). *Lanchas* from the **Cooperativa Tangolunda** in Santa Cruz travel to other beaches (prices vary by beach and size of boat, but are guaranteed to be high—over 400 pesos). If you go in the morning you may find people to share the ride, and during the off-season you can bar-

A NIGHT ON THE PUEBLO. You've spent endless hours conjugating verbs and rolling your "r"s, but you still don't fit in. What you need is something that no 7th-grade Spanish teacher could (or would) teach—a brief review of all the slang necessary for a night out on the town. Luckily, *Let's Go* has compiled a list of the basics. Incorporate these into your vocab, and watch as your *gabacho* (*gringo*) status fades away. The night begins when you greet your friends, *"¿Qué onda?"* (What's up?), and head out *al antro* (to the disco). Once there, grab a *chupe* (drink) or a *chela* (beer) and comment on how *chido* or *padre* (cool) the place is—*Fresas* (snobs) prefer the phrase *de pelos*. Of course, keep your eyes peeled for *papasitos* (studs) and women that are *buenísima* (very fine). Perhaps you'll flirt a bit, *ligar* (hook-up), and—if you are *cachondo* (horny)—maybe you'll *fajar* (make out/get down) with a fellow discotechie. The next day be sure to review the events of the previous night with your friends, exclaiming *"¡Qué peda la de ayer!"* (I was so wasted yesterday!).

gain for lower rates. The *cooperativa* offers the most economical all-day tour of the bays, stopping at Maguey and San Augustín, where you can snorkel with an English-speaking guide and eat lunch. (☎587 00 81. *Open daily 8am-6pm. Tours 10 and 11am in high season; 11am in low season. 250 pesos. Call 1 day in advance.*)

♫ ENTERTAINMENT

The abundance of family vacationers in Huatulco means nightlife isn't quite as wild as in other beach towns. The *zócalo*, though, tends to be fairly crowded and there are a few rockin' joints in Santa Cruz, a 13-peso taxi ride from La Crucecita.

LA CRUCECITA

 Restaurant Bar La Crema (☎587 07 02), at Guanacaste and Gardenia, on the 2nd fl. overlooking the *zócalo*. Wicker chairs, a pool table, a large, mixed crowd, loud Mexican and American music, and kitsch. Beer 14 pesos. Open daily 8pm-4am.

Cafe Internet Choco Latte (☎587 01 65), across from La Crema, on the bottom floor of Hotel Misión Los Arcos. Outdoorsy European ambience and relatively cheap access make the concept of travelling thousands of miles to a beautiful country and then sitting in front of a computer screen slightly less ridiculous. Astoundingly clean bathrooms. Cafe americano 10 pesos. Internet 30 pesos per hour. Open daily 8am-11:30pm.

Iguana Bar, at the northwest corner of the *zócalo*, features a live iguana and sports on TV. Next to the Portales restaurant. Tacos 35 pesos. Beer 12 pesos.

SANTA CRUZ

El Dexkite (☎587 09 71), past the *lancha* docks on the left. Torches light a strip of private beach, while partiers dance in the sand and consume economical drinks. 40 pesos for ½L of beer, 50 pesos for 1L. The action starts at midnight. Cover 60 pesos. Open daily 10pm-5am in high season; closed in low season.

La Aqua (☎587 00 17), past the public beach entrance, down Mitla to where it curves, is a standard disco experience. Cover 60 pesos. Open daily 10pm-late in high season, Th-Sa in low season.

Magic Tropics, Aqua's *latino* twin, closer to the beach entrance on Mitla, plays Spanish beats. Cover 40 pesos. Open daily 10pm-5am in high season; W-Su low season.

POCHUTLA ☎9

The key thing to remember about Pochutla is that it is not Puerto Escondido. Though you may be disoriented after the long and terrifying bus trip through the mountains, and think that Pochutla's thick hot air hints at the proximity of the ocean, do not disembark. You will find yourself not in a beachside paradise but rather a transportation hub filled with buses, taxis, and dust. Come here only to stock up on money and other necessities.

Taxi colectivos headed to **Puerto Escondido** (50 pesos), **Puerto Ángel** (5 pesos), **Zipolite** (15 pesos), and beyond leave from the downhill part of town, across from the Estrella del Valle bus station. The most efficient way to travel between coast towns is by *camioneta* (every 20min. 6am-7pm, 3 pesos to Puerto Ángel, 5 pesos to Zipolite or Mazunte). Cristóbal Colón (☎584 02 74) on the left side of Cárdenas as you enter the city, sends buses to: **Bahías de Huatulco** (1hr., 5 per day 10am-10pm, 19 pesos); **Mexico City** (15hr., 7:45pm, 355 pesos); **Oaxaca** (12hr., 7:45 and 10pm, 165 pesos); **Puerto Escondido** (6 per day 7am-8:30pm, 29 pesos); **Tehuantepec** (4½hr.; 10am, 8:45, and 9:45pm; 85 pesos). It is fastest to get to **Oaxaca** with Estrella del Valle (7hr., several per day, 88 pesos).

Most banks, services, and shops, as well as the town's two bus stations are on **Cárdenas**, the main street. Bus stations and cheaper hotels are downhill, closer to the freeway entrance, while banks and supermarkets are farther uphill, where the road curves right. To reach the *zócalo*, church, and main outdoor market, follow Cárdenas uphill and turn right on Juárez a block after the area where the *colectivos* drop-off. **Inverlat,** just after Juárez branches off Cárdenas to the right, uphill from the bus stations, has a 24hr. **ATM** (open for exchange M-F 9am-5pm), as does Bital, north of the *zócalo* on Cárdenas. (Open for exchange M-F 8am-7pm, Sa 8am-3pm.) **Mercado 15 de Octubre,** 25m uphill from the Cristóbal Colón station on the right, sells mainly food. (Open daily 6am-9pm.) **Police:** in the Palacio Municipal to the left of the church. No English spoken. (☎584 01 59.) **Farmacias de Más Ahorro,** just before Juárez on Cárdenas, is open 24hr. **Hospital General,** also known as **SSA,** between Pochutla and Puerto Ángel. No English spoken. (☎584 02 19.) **Internet: Iguanet,** between the Cristóbal Colón station and the *colectivo* drop-off on Cárdenas, also has long-distance *casetas* and fax. 1 peso per minute. Open daily 7am-10pm. **Post office:** make a right on Juárez toward the *zócalo;* it's to the left of the church, behind the Palacio Municipal. (Open M-F 8am-3pm.) **Postal code:** 70900.

Hotel Santa Cruz, just up the street from the Cristóbal Colón station, has clean rooms for crashing in the event of a long layover. (Singles 70 pesos, doubles 120 pesos.) **Hotel Izalo,** on Cárdenas just past Juárez, is quieter and a bit fancier. (Singles 130 pesos; doubles 300 pesos.) **Cafe Cafe,** off Cárdenas on the far side of the zócalo, serves a small selection of baguettes, starting at 30 pesos. (Cafe americano 8 pesos. Open daily 8am-11pm.)

PUERTO ÁNGEL   ☎9

Between the more developed resorts of Huatulco and Puerto Escondido are Puerto Ángel, Zipolite, and Mazunte, none of which are directly accessible by bus. Unfortunately, Puerto Ángel and Zipolite bore the brunt of Hurricane Pauline in 1997. Since then, the towns have struggled to rebuild; construction continues on many streets, trash lines once picturesque pathways, and the dog population seems on the verge of conquest. In comparison to Huatulco's contrived opulence and Puerto Escondido's slightly affected hipness, Puerto Ángel is just a beach. Yet it is scenic, swimmable, and secluded—enough for most.

⌐ TRANSPORTATION. Puerto Ángel is 240km south of Oaxaca and 68km east of Puerto Escondido. All transportation in or out of Puerto Ángel passes the **sitio stand** on Uribe. Puerto Ángel is second in the great **camioneta** loop linking Pochutla, Zipolite, and Mazunte (every 20min. 6am-7pm, 3-8 pesos depending on which way you're going). **Taxis** link Puerto Ángel to: **Pochutla** (15min.; 50 pesos, 5 pesos shared) and **Zipolite** (25min.; 30 pesos, 15 pesos shared). They can be flagged down anywhere along Uribe or Principal.

WorldPhone. Worldwide.

MCIˢᴹ gives you the freedom of worldwide communications whenever you're away from home. It's easy to call to and from over 70 countries with your MCI Calling Card:

1. Dial the WorldPhone® access number of the country you're calling from.
2. Dial or give the operator your MCI Calling Card number.
3. Dial or give the number you're calling.

- Mexico   01-800-021-8000 Avantel
                 001-800-674-7000 Telmex
                 01-800-021-1000 Collect access in Spanish

Sign up today!

Ask your local operator to place a collect call
(reverse charge) to MCI in the U.S. at:

1-712-943-6839

For additional access codes or to sign up, visit us at www.mci.com/worldphone

www.mci.com/worldphone

It's Your World...

www.mci.com/worldphone

⚡🛈 ORIENTATION AND PRACTICAL INFORMATION. The *carretera* that connects Pochutla to Zipolite becomes Puerto Ángel's main drag as it runs through town, and later **Principal** as it descends the hillside from Pochutla; finally called **Uribe**, it curves 90 degrees to the right and hits downtown. The *sitio* stand and all the town's hotels lie directly on or close to this main road. After Uribe curves right, **Playa Principal** skirts the road on the left. The only significant side street, **Vasconcelos,** branches to the right off Uribe soon after the turn.

Services in Puerto Ángel are minimal; most must be begged, borrowed, or imported from nearby Pochutla. For **tourist information,** try the **Agencia Municipal,** next to the post office at the 90-degree turn. (☎584 31 30. Open daily 9am-2pm.) There is **no bank** in Puerto Ángel; several upscale hotels change money at exorbitant rates. A **market** 25m to the right on the street after Vasconcelos offers little more than produce. (Open daily 7am-8pm.) **Supermarket: Super Puerto,** in the turquoise and white building on the right as Uribe starts to climb. (Open daily 9am-9pm.) **Police:** can be reached through the Agencia Municipal. **Farmacia Villa Florencia,** attached to the hotel of the same name, on Uribe shortly past the turnoff for Vasconcelos. (☎584 30 44. Open daily 8:30am-9pm.) **Hospital General (SSA),** between Puerto Ángel and Pochutla, No English spoken. **Centro de Salud,** (☎584 02 19), at the top of Vasconcelos to the left on a dirt path, offers limited services. (Open daily.) **Telecomm,** next to the post office. (Open M-F 9am-3pm.) **Gel@net,** at Vasconcelos 3, just after Hotel Soraya, has a long distance **caseta.** (Internet 35 pesos per hr. Open daily 8am-10pm.) The town lacks **LADATELs;** several other *casetas* are farther up Uribe. **Post office:** at the 90-degree turn. No Mex Post. (Open M-F 8:30am-3pm.) **Postal code:** 70902.

🏠 ACCOMMODATIONS. Though prices rise during July and August, the city is filled with options year-round. Most hotels are on or right off Uribe. Reservations recommended during July, August, December, and *Semana Santa.*

Hotel Capy, on the left 5min. uphill, at the street leading to Playa Panteón, offers clean, well-maintained rooms, and private baths. Its impressive view of the cove is best appreciated while enjoying a moderately-priced meal in the quality balcony restaurant. Fish filet 35 pesos. Singles 90 pesos; doubles 130-148 pesos; triples 150 pesos.

El Peñasquito, on the left on the side street leading to Playa Panteón, offers a clean, safe bungalow with hammocks. 40 pesos per night.

La Buena Vista, (☎584 31 04), off Uribe before it starts climbing—watch for the sign. The adjoining restaurant is worth a visit even if you're not staying here. Vegetarian *tamales* 45 pesos, fish 55 pesos. Doubles 310 pesos; cabins 340 pesos.

Gundi y Tomas, (☎584 30 68; gundtoma@hotmail.com), is conveniently situated by the taxi stand. Clean, quirky rooms feature terraces with scenic vistas and hammocks. Kitchen, laundry, restaurant available. Doubles 130-150 pesos, with bath 170 pesos.

Puesta Del Sol Hotel, (☎584 30 96; puesta_del_sol@puertoangel.net), in an elegant old-school Mexican house, doesn't look like it would offer some of the cheapest rooms in the city. Look for the sign after Uribe starts to climb. Cheap meals, Internet available. Singles 90 pesos, with bath 180 pesos; doubles 120 pesos.

Casa Arnel Puerto Ángel, (☎584 30 51), has clean rooms with baths, and teenagers play Play Station. Laundry, Internet available. Singles 100 pesos; doubles 150 pesos.

🍴 FOOD. Much of the fish that fries in Zipolite first saw land in Puerto Ángel. Recently deceased, yet to be prepared fish pile up alongside many restaurants. On the main beach, **Restaurant Marisol** keeps prices low (25-40 pesos), and serves breakfast for under 10 pesos in an informal atmosphere. (Open daily 8am-9pm.) By the basketball court between Playa Principal and Uribe, the tasty seafood at **Restaurant Maca** compensates for the concrete atmosphere. Prices are moderate-to-high, but the fish are fresh to barely-dead and the serving sizes are big to enormous. (Fish filet 35-40 pesos. Seafood soup 50 pesos. Open daily 8am-11pm.)

SOUTHERN PACIFIC COAST

Beto's Restaurant Bar, on Uribe across from Hotel Capy. Excellent fish filets 27 pesos. (Open daily 4pm-midnight.) **Restaurant Villa Florencia,** at the Villa Florencia hotel on Uribe. A diverse menu features breakfast, tacos, seafood, spaghetti, and hamburgers. (Octopus 35 pesos. Open daily 7am-midnight.)

◢ **BEACHES.** Though Puerto Ángel's cove is small and slightly crowded, its beaches still have sparkling water and white sand. **Playa Principal,** off Uribe, is closest to the docks and fishing boats. Though slightly grimier, it offers a tad more breathing room than **Playa Panteón.** Ubiquitous refreshment stands envelop both beaches. The two beaches, connected by a stone walkway, encircle a harbor with superb snorkeling. Panteón is also accesible via a footpath entrance near the footbridge on Uribe, or by the paved side street branching left farther up Uribe. On Panteón, **Azul Profundo** rents snorkeling gear and leads tours. (☎ 584 31 09. Snorkeling tours 100 pesos, scuba tours 450-600 pesos, fishing tours 300 pesos per hour.)

For better sand and more space, head east to **Playa Estacahuite** (a-stack-o-wheatie). Over the headland from Puerto Ángel's bay, Estacahuite's three little beaches (the 3rd is to the right of the path) are pristine. Although they can be reached by *lancha* from Puerto Ángel (100-150 pesos) or taxi (starting at 40 pesos round trip), the walk is pleasant and easy (30min.). From Playa Principal, turn right on Uribe and walk uphill toward Pochutla. The dirt road to Estacahuite branches to the right as the road curves uphill, just past the telephone pole numbered E0034. Follow the road as it climbs and curves left around a hill and finally plunges steeply to the beach. Snorkeling is good and the beach is a beauty, but be careful—emergency services are far away. Farther down the coast is **Playa Boquilla,** the only other beach accessible by land. The sand is smooth and the waves small. The beach is difficult to reach without taxi or *lancha*. It's 4km on the road to Pochutla, then another 3km along a dirt road to the right (marked by a "Playa Boquilla" sign). Take a *camioneta* (3 pesos) or taxi *colectivo* (5 pesos) to the sign and walk, or take a snorkeling trip and remain at the beach, arranging to be picked up when the tour returns (100 pesos). Keep in mind that, like in Playa Estacahuite, services are nonexistent in Playa Boquilla. The walk back can be grueling, though many of the houses along the trail sell refreshments, proving yet again that the world's most intrepid travelers work for the Coca-Cola corporation.

ZIPOLITE   ☎ 9

Zipolite's reputation precedes it. Joints are rolled on the beach, at the dinner table, on hotel counters—you name it—while backpacks from around the world lean against countless *cabaña* doors. The town is a prime stop on the Euro-trail, and locals smile wistfully as foreigners parade nude up and down its beaches. When Hurricane Pauline hit Zipolite in 1997, government aid was slow to come, a fact attributed by some to resentment of the town's unrestrained tourist trade. Zipolite has indeed had problems with drug-related crime, and visitors here are wise to exercise their common sense. Since the hurricane, the town has rebuilt and regained all its scantily-clad glory. Zipolite is mostly patronized by backpackers, though this term misleadingly suggests the image of an intrepid youngster hiking miles each day and living on his wits alone. The most rigorous hike required of most is from the hotel to the bar, which is usually right in front of the hotel.

◪ **TRANSPORTATION.** Just 4km west of Puerto Ángel, Zipolite is easily accessible by any vehicle rumbling down the poorly paved coastal road. *Camionetas* (3 pesos), *taxi colectivos* (10 pesos), and *taxi especiales* (30 pesos) pass more frequently. From Pochutla, *taxi colectivos* are 15 pesos during the day. At night, take a private taxi (25min., 70 pesos).

◼◪ **ORIENTATION AND PRACTICAL INFORMATION.** Zipolite consists of one 2km stretch of beach and the roads that run behind it. Look for the beach sign pointing toward the waves; to get to the major hotels, go down the dirt road at the west end of the beach. While there is no **currency exchange** in Zipolite, most hotels and *cabañas* accept dollars and some of the bigger ones accept travelers checks. The nearest hospital, **General Hospital,** is between Puerto Ángel and Pochutla. No English spoken. (☎584 02 19.) **Farmacia Zipolite,** on the road across from the police station at the east edge of town, has limited medical supplies and houses a small general store. (Open daily 7am-10pm.) Supplies are cheaper in Pochutla. **Zipolnet Communications,** on a dirt road running perpendicular to west end of the beach has *casetas*, fax, and internet. (Internet 50 pesos. Open M-Sa 8am-10pm).

▐ ACCOMMODATIONS. Almost every *palapa* on the beach has huts out back, most with relatively clean shared baths. (*Cabañas* 80 pesos; hammocks 30 pesos.) Whichever you choose, be sure to put valuables in a safe box. Most of the nicer, more secure *cabañas* and rooms are on the west side of the beach. Almost to the west end of the beach, **Posada San Cristóbal,** a tree and hammock filled courtyard opening onto the beach, projects powerful lethargy rays. Communal bathrooms are clean and each bed comes with its own mosquito net. (☎584 31 91. Singles 60 pesos, with bath 100 pesos; doubles 120 pesos. Discounts for longer stays.) **Hotel Paraiso,** farther east, rents some of the nicest rooms in town, sparkling new and clean with bath and balconies looking out on the ocean. (☎014 31 88. Rooms 100 pesos.) For a more private experience, try **Lo Cósmico,** at the far west end of the beach, with rustic, Swiss-Family-Robinson-esque cabins perched on a hill over-looking the sea. Communal baths. (Rooms 90-150 pesos.) **La Choza,** a short walk east of Paraiso, rents budget rooms. (☎584 31 90. Hammocks 30 pesos; rooms 80 pesos, with bath 100 pesos.) On the east side of the beach, **Lyoban** rents cheap *cabañas* and hammocks, and features a lobby with restaurants, bar, a safe, and lockers. (Singles 70 pesos. Doubles 120 pesos; hammocks 30 pesos.)

▢ FOOD. Seafood and pasta restaurants abound, and the hordes of health-con-scious tree-huggers ensure that vegetarian dishes are easy to find. Most of the best restaurants are at the west end of the beach. **San Cristóbal** is a seafood-based breakfast (starting at 15 pesos) and lunch hot spot. Service at night is spotty. (☎584 31 91. Fish filets 35 pesos. Open daily 7am-11pm.) Your best bet for Italian is **El Alquimista Restaurant and Pub,** just past San Cristóbal. (☎584 31 70. Huge bowls of delicious spaghetti 30 pesos, pizza 45 pesos. Open daily 5pm-1am.) **3 de Diciembre,** about two blocks north of El Paraiso at the corner of two dirt roads, serves stellar vegetarian meals (35 pesos). Also popular is their extensive *pay* (pie) menu, ranging from all-natural fruit pies to the decadent *pay de chocolate*. (11 pesos per slice. Open W-Su 7pm-2am.)

▟▙ BEACHES AND WARNINGS. Besides the sea, the only sights in Zipolite are sunbathers, or waves coming in from two directions, creating a series of chan-nels that suck unsuspecting, naked swimmers out to sea. Although ferocious, these channels are not very wide. If you find yourself being pulled from shore, do not panic and do not attempt to swim directly toward the beach; rather, swim par-allel to the beach until clear of the seaward current. Also watch for red and yellow warning flags on the beach that mark especially dangerous areas. Many people have drowned at Zipolite, and warnings should be taken seriously. If you do swim, keep close to the shore in areas that are highly populated. Zipolite is unfortunately plagued by theft, so keep an eye on your valuables when you step in (naked) for a dip. Better yet, leave them locked somewhere. A final warning: **scorpions** are com-mon in Zipolite. Give your boots a good shake before plunging your feet in.

WEST FROM ZIPOLITE

The road west of Zipolite to Pochutla passes **San Agustinillo** and **Mazunte,** perfect stretches of sand growing in popularity with international backpackers and friendlier to swimmers than Zipolite's killer surf. The road also passes some very worthwhile ecotourism projects, **Museo de la Tortuga** and **Cooperativa Ventanillo,** dedicated to the preservation of native species. The following sites, listed from east to west, are all accessible via a "Mazunte" *camioneta* from Zipolite (every 20min. 6am-7pm, 3 pesos), or any Zipolite-bound *camioneta* from Pochutla.

EL MARIPOSARIO. An easy walk or short *camioneta* ride on the road to Mazunte leads to the Mariposario, the closest of three conservation-education centers. The netted sanctuary pays a much overdue tribute to the butterflies that flutter through Mexican forests like confetti. Frogs and iguanas are also on display. The preserve covers three hectares of land, and the butterflies get special attention from the guides, one of whom speaks English. The tour (20min.) includes a visit to the sanctuary. *(Open Tu-Sa 9am-4pm. 15 pesos.)*

SAN AGUSTINILLO. Four kilometers from Zipolite, the small town of San Agustinillo perches on a beach of the same name, where an European beach scene awaits under the *palapas*. Although developing, San Agustinillo remains less colonized and less hyped than Zipolite, if less lively and a little shabbier in terms of accomodations. The two coves that form the harbor have fairly manageable surf (stay away from the rocks), which can be harnessed with body boards, fins, or surfboards rented from **Mexico Lindo** (30-50 pesos per hr.). *Many beginners like to start here before braving the bigger waves at Zipolite. Mexico Lindo also rents some of the best rooms on the beach: new and clean with fans, private baths, and double beds. (Singles and doubles 100 pesos.) The restaurant serves a mean fish filet (50 pesos. Open daily 8am-10pm). Other accomodations in town are basically the same: slightly dingy cabañas 50 pesos, hammocks 20 pesos.*

MUSEO DE LA TORTUGA (NATIONAL MEXICAN TURTLE CENTER). Another bumpy kilometer down the road from Pochutla lies **Mazunte,** and first thing in town is the Museo de la Tortuga on the left. Though the number of people looking out for the health of the Oaxacan coast is still dangerously small, interest is growing. An anchor in the movement, the museum draws tour buses to Mazunte to observe: turtles large and small in outdoor tanks; the specialized aquarium containing seven sea turtle species, seven river species, and three land species; and the obligatory gift shop. The museum also serves as a research center, seeking new ways to protect the species—presumably the goal of a recent project documented with photographs and charts, that involved gluing large transmitters to the backs of sea turtles. *(Open Tu-Sa 10am-4:30pm, Su 10am-2:30pm. 20 pesos, children 6-12 10 pesos. Tours approx. every 10 min.)*

PLAYA MAZUNTE. A few blocks past the turtle center lies a short dirt path leading to Playa Mazunte. Less than a kilometer long, Mazunte is a quiet, secluded, and pretty and popular but not yet overrun by backpackers or besieged by *palapas* and refreshment stands. Good food and lodgings are easy to find.

The nicest accommodations on the beach are the wooden Cabañas Ziga, perched on a hill overlooking the beach. Private bathrooms and fans ensure a comfortable stay. (Singles 80 pesos; double 120 pesos. 30 pesos more in high season.) Ziga's also has a restaurant that fries up fish filets (35 pesos) and serves some of the best spaghetti (40 pesos) to be found on the whole Italophile coast. (Open Tu-Su 8:30am-10pm.) Although the rooms at Carlos Einstein's aren't quite as posh, they are cheap, and you're not going to meet such a character elsewhere on the coast. The owner looks like (surprise) a Mexican Einstein, but specializes in the science of herbal healing and brujería (witchcraft) instead of physics. (Breakfast included. Rooms 40 pesos per person; hammocks 40 pesos.) Palapa El Mazunte allows camping under its roof and also rents hammocks. Its cabañas have communal bathrooms. At the restaurant, breakfast starts at 15 pesos. (Restaurant open 9am-10pm. Hammocks 30 pesos; singles 80 pesos; doubles 100-200 pesos.) Many nearby palapas will allow tents under their awnings (20 pesos or less per person).

LA VENTANILLA. Playa Ventanilla, 1½km past Mazunte, has vicious, swimmer-hostile waves and dirty sand. The reason to make the trip is the **Cooperativa Ventanilla.** The *cooperativa* houses a small colony of families who work to preserve the wetland wildlife system at the mouth of the Tonameca River. The group runs amazing *lancha* tours (1hr.; 35 pesos, children 6-12 15 pesos) that pass through the mangrove swamps. Guides paddle through the lagoon in small boats, pointing out enormous crocodiles lurking only feet away. The tour includes a stop on an island in the middle of the lagoon which houses a mangrove farm, baby croc pens, and a refreshment stand. (*A 700m walk down the dirt path marked by the "La Ventanilla" sign. Open daily 6am-7pm.*)

PUERTO ESCONDIDO   ☎ 9

The narrow highway that runs into Puerto Escondido winds out of the mountains and parallels the coast. Lined on both sides by jungle, it rarely reveals the blue water to the south until the forest parts for the city, a thousand lights crawling out of the Pacific Ocean into the hills. This first impression may be the best thing about Puerto Escondido, but beaches and waves also await the surf-loving traveler. Playa Zicatela is considered one of the world's best surfing beaches. The rest of the city is tourist-generated sprawl, not particularly noteworthy, but not destructively gaudy or trashy either.

▐ TRANSPORTATION

Airport: (☎582 04 92) is best reached by taxi (20 pesos). **AeroCaribe** (☎582 20 23) flies to Mexico City, Oaxaca, and Bahías de Huatulco.

Buses: All of the bus stations are scattered uptown, just past the crucero. To get to the beaches and hotels, simply walk downhill. The parking lot of **Estrella Blanca** (☎582 00 86) can be seen across the freeway at the curve of Oaxaca. Buses go to: **Acapulco** (7hr., every hr. 5am-3pm, 126 pesos; semi-direct, 4 per day 4am-11:30am, 169 pesos); **Bahías de Huatulco** via **Pochutla** (2½ hr., 5 per day 2:30am-12:30am, 53 pesos); and **Mexico City** (12hr.; 7:30, 8, and 9pm; 360-380 pesos). **Oaxaca-Istmo** (☎582 03 92) on Hidalgo just behind the Estrella Blanca station, runs to **Salina Cruz** (6am and 1:30pm, 75 pesos). On Hidalgo 2 blocks to the right of Oaxaca is Estrella de Valle (☎582 00 50), with the best service to **Oaxaca** (6½ hr., 11 per day 7:30am-10:45pm, 80-405 pesos). Cristóbal Colón, 1 Nte. 207 (☎582 10 73) sends buses to: **Bahías de Huatulco** (2hr., 5 per day 8:45am-9:30pm, 47 pesos); **San Cristóbal de las Casas** (12hr., 8:45am and 9:30pm, 264 pesos); **Tuxtla Gutiérrez** (10hr., 8:45am and 9:30pm, 230 pesos). Cristóbal Colón also travels 1st-class to Oaxaca, but by a route that takes 5hr. longer than 2nd-class service. Micros to **Pochutla** leave from the crucero (1hr., every 30min., 12 pesos).

▐ ORIENTATION AND PRACTICAL INFORMATION

Built on a hillside 294km south of Oaxaca on **Mex. 175,** Puerto Escondido is bisected by **Mex. 200,** also known as **Carretera Costera,** which divides uphill from downhill. The main tourist corridor, known as the **Adoquín, Las Cadenas,** or **Gasga** at different sections, loops down from Mex. 200, scoops the main beach, and reconnects again at the **crucero.** Going east from the *crucero* will take you to **Zicatela.** Locals may insist that Puerto Escondido is safe, but recent assaults on tourists have prompted the tourist office to recommend that travelers stay in groups and avoid isolated beaches, even during daylight hours. **Taxis** can be found by the tourist information booth and along Carretera Costera and Calle de Morro in Zicatela; they are the safest way of getting around after nightfall (15 pesos).

Tourist Office: Módulo de Información Turística (☎582 01 75), the helpful booth at the beginning of the pedestrian walkway, down Gasga from the *crucero*. Advice in your language or something close to it. Open M-F 9am-2pm and 4-6pm, Sa 10am-1pm.

Currency Exchange: Banamex (☎582 06 26), on Gasga as it curves up from the tourist corridor, exchanges traveler's checks and has an **ATM**. Open M-F 9am-2pm. **Money Exchange** (☎582 28 00), on the Adoquín halfway up the hill, has bad rates but convenient hours. Open M-Su 8am-9pm. Good rates and **ATM** machines are available at **Bancrecer,** on Hidalgo between Oaxaca and 1 Pte. Open M-F 9am-5pm, Sa 10am-2pm. **Bital** (☎582 18 24), 1 Nte. at 3 Pte., also has **ATMs.** Open M-F 8am-7pm.

Markets: Mercado Benito Juárez, 8 Nte. at 3 Pte. Typical goods in an organized setting. Open daily 5am-8pm, but most busy W and Sa.

Supermarket: Ahorrara (☎582 11 28), at 3 Pte. and 4 Nte. Open M-Sa 8am-9pm, Su 8am-4pm.

Laundry: Lavamática del Centro, Gasga 405, uphill from the pedestrian walkway on the right. 15 pesos per kg. Open M-Sa 8am-8pm, Su 8am-5pm.

Library: IFOPE Library (ifope@yahoo.com), in Rinconada by Monte de Piedad. 900 books in English, French, German, and Spanish. Open W and Sa 10am-2pm.

Luggage Storage: None at the bus stations, but nearby Hotel Mayflower will guard your belongings. 6 pesos per day.

Car Rental: Budget (☎582 03 12), on Juárez at Monte Albán. **Alamo** (☎582 30 03), on Perez Gasga across from the tourist info booth.

Emergency: In an extreme emergency, contact Sheila Clarke (☎582 02 76) or Minnie Dahlberg (☎582 03 67), who head **Friends of Puerto Escondido International,** a neighborhood watchdog group of area expatriates. They will get you in contact with your embassy, the police, or medical help.

Police: (☎582 04 98), on the bottom floor of the Agencia Municipal, on 3 Pte. at the corner of Hidalgo. No English spoken.

Red Cross: (☎582 05 50), 7 Nte. between Oaxaca and 1 Pte. No English spoken. 24hr. ambulance service.

Pharmacy: Farmacia La Moderna 1 (☎582 06 98 or 582 27 80), at Gasga 203 as it curves down from the *crucero*. Open 24hr.

Medical Assistance: IMSS (☎582 01 42), Av. 2 Pte. and 7 Nte. **Centro de Salud,** Gasga 409 (☎582 23 60), is a small, minimal-expense medical clinic. No English spoken. Open 24hr. for emergencies.

Fax: Telecomm (☎582 09 57), next door to the post office. Open M-F 8am-7:30pm, Sa 9am-noon.

Internet: Tigre@zul, on the Adoquín near the tourist office, is also a bar and cafe. 25 pesos per hour. Open daily 8:30am-11pm.

Post Office: (☎582 09 59), 7 Nte. 701 at Oaxaca, a 15min. walk uphill from the *crucero*. Open M-F 8am-4pm, Sa 9am-1pm.

Postal Code: 71980.

YOUR CABBIE, YOUR FRIEND.

So they've nearly turned you into roadkill more times than you care to remember, and you're sure you've paid their "special" tourist rates more often than not. On August 12, however, forget your bitter memories and join in celebrating *el Día del Taxista*, the country-wide taxi holiday. The day begins with a special 8am mass and blessing of the cabs, guaranteeing their safe travels for the next year. Radiator grills are then strung with flowers as the cabs pass proudly through the city streets—hopefully a little more slowly than usual. Later in the day, cabbies celebrate among themselves, and you'll have a hard time finding a driver on the street. If you do manage to flag one down, be prepared to thank the driver profusely and offer a hefty *propina* (tip)—it is, after all, the day of the cabbie.

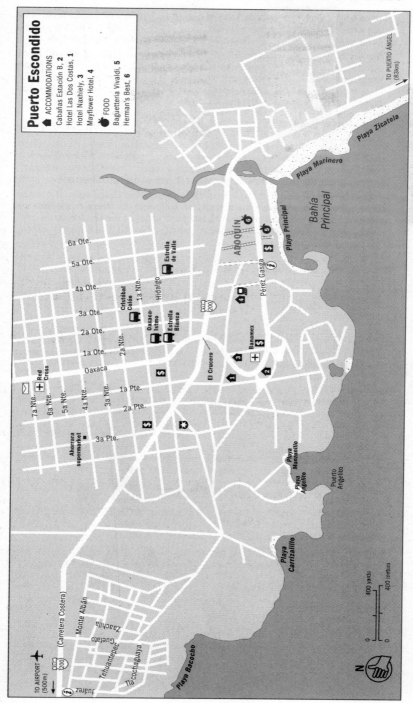

Puerto Escondido

▲ ACCOMMODATIONS
Cabañas Estación B, **2**
Hotel Las Dos Costas, **1**
Hotel Naxhiely, **3**
Mayflower Hotel, **4**

◆ FOOD
Baguetteria Vivaldi, **5**
Herman's Best, **6**

ACCOMMODATIONS

Budget accommodations in Puerto Escondido are bested in terms of location and ambience by comparably priced *cabañas* and hotels on Zicatela, which offer better access to beaches and beachfront bars. Prices fluctuate in Puerto Escondido, rising during the busy months of March, April, July, August, and December. During low season, many hotels have no officially posted rates. Reservations are recommended during *Semana Santa*, Christmas, July, and August.

Hotel Mayflower (☎582 03 67), on Libertad. From the bus station, cross the *crucero* and go left down a steep hill. The road ends, but stairs descend on the right to the entrance. Clean, tiled rooms with private baths and balconies, many with *vistas*, surround a common area with hammocks and shelves of books. The closest thing to a youth hostel in town, the hotel also has clean dorm rooms. Dorm beds 60 pesos; singles 160 pesos; doubles 200-240 pesos; each additional person 30 pesos.

Cabañas Estación B (☎582 22 51). From the *crucero*, follow Gasga down as it winds left and look for a sign on the right, a block after Banamex. Although their *cabañas* are on the shores of a gutter rather than the blue Pacific, Estación remains true to the original *cabaña* spirit. Each comes with mosquito netting, a hammock, and use of the clean communal baths. Complimentary breakfast during high season. *Cabañas* 60 pesos; hammock 20 pesos; camping 20 pesos.

Hotel Naxhiely, Gasga 301 (☎582 30 65). Not as cheap as Dos Costas or as nice to look at as the Mayflower, Naxhiely is still a reasonably priced option for those who prefer the institutional comforts of a hotel over the dangerous living of *cabañas*. Room price includes private bath and fan. Singles 150 pesos; doubles 180 pesos. Discounts in low season.

Los Dos Costas, Gasga 302 (☎582 0159), in the curve just down from the *crucero*. The best bargain in town, if you want your own room and a sandless front porch. Rooms are slightly run-down, but have private baths and are surprisingly clean. Singles 50 pesos; doubles 80 pesos; triples 120 pesos.

ON ZICATELA

Despite its location (15min. by foot from the tourist corridor), the many restaurants, bars, and *cabañas* on **Calle del Morro,** which runs in front of the beach, make Zicatela a self-sufficient neighborhood. The cheapest *cabañas* (around 50 pesos) might not be secure; lock your valuables if possible. Most safe *cabañas* have taken advantage of the tourist horde, and their rates are now higher than those at many budget hotels. During high season, make reservations several weeks in advance. Other than the first, *cabañas* below are listed east to west.

Hotel Buena Vista (☎582 14 74; buenavista101@hotmail.com), on Calle de Morros, is, with its spectacular view of the beach, good for people who have a hard time pulling themselves away from the surf. Some of the rooms come with kitchen, and all have clean private baths. Be sure to call several weeks in advance. Doubles 100-300 pesos depending on size and season; 50 pesos per additional person.

Cabo Blanco, some of the cheapest *cabañas* on the strip. Clean, pleasant rooms with fans. Its motto is: "where legends are born." Singles 80 pesos; doubles 125 pesos.

Las Olas, a bargain for all its amenities. Rooms have small kitchens, fans, personal security boxes, and private baths. All rooms 150 pesos.

Bungalows Zicatela (☎582 07 98). A laid-back atmosphere, pool, and high-class bungalows. Singles 120 pesos; doubles 200 pesos. Also rents pricey but very nice *cabañas* farther down the strip. Singles and doubles 400 pesos and up.

Hotel Acuario (☎582 10 27). Though on the expensive side, Acuario is a perennial favorite with surfers. Spend the extra pesos to frolic in the pool and support the hotel's conservation efforts—they've installed a special water purifier that cleans and reuses all hotel wastewater. Doubles 200 pesos, with A/C 250 pesos.

Buena Onda, possibly the best deal on Zicatela, a 20min. walk down the beach or an easy 2.5 peso bus ride. New *cabañas* sit right on the water. A great place for beginning surfers to practice, but swimmers should beware the choppy waters. 70 pesos.

🍴 FOOD

Though not so fish-crazy as cities like Veracruz, where vendors often wander the streets selling questionably sanitary sacks of recently-deceased shrimp, Puerto Escondido's proximity to the ocean means most restaurants add a seafood section to their otherwise standard Mexican menus. Most seafood entrees are slightly pricier than other options, but good deals can be found. The large expatriate community has brought a variety of international cuisine to Puerto Escondido, and Italian restaurants take up a good portion of Gasga. Swimwear makes for a health-conscious crowd, so vegetarian fare is also abundant, especially along Zicatela.

El Cafecito (☎582 0516). Across the street from Zicatela's best bakers, El Cafecito is frequented by European backpackers, beach babes, studly surfers, and hammock vendors. The slightly expensive menu makes everyone happy with garlic grilled shrimp (60 pesos; includes rice, vegetables, and bread), a variety of homemade breads, and vegetarian-friendly Mexican cuisine (30 pesos). Open daily 6am-10pm.

La Gota de Vida, on Zicatela, in front of Hotel Acuario. This veggie haven keeps prices low and veggies fresh. A selection from the huge vegetable and fruit salad menu (10-25 pesos) can be enjoyed on its own or with another entree. Vegetarian enchiladas (19 pesos), sandwiches (14 pesos), and homemade yogurt (12 pesos) keep customers coming back despite the somewhat slow service. Open daily 8am-10:30pm.

Baguettería Vivaldi, at the east end of the Adoquín. Tasty food for the homesick or anyone tired of the Mexican/Italian axis of grease. Vivaldi offers a number of standard ham-turkey-salami sandwiches starting at 21 pesos. Breakfasts and crepes start at 15 pesos. Menu in Spanish, English, and German. Open daily 8am-10pm.

Herman's Best, just past the east end of the tourist corridor. Herman may not know how to cook too many things, but if you've got a hankering for grilled fish, this is the place. Chat with the big man himself about his fish-flipping prowess and impressive collection of family photos. Slightly out of place in a line of wood-paneled Italian restaurants, Herman's serves savory, garlic-encrusted whole fish complete with rice, salad, and tortillas (25 pesos). Open daily 2-10pm.

Restaurante Vitamina T, on the east end of the Adoquín. Vitamina T is open just about all the time, and its cheap food is served hot and fast. Breakfasts 20 pesos. Fruit salads 10-15 pesos. The *tortas* are among the best in town (8 pesos). Open daily 7am-1am.

🏖 BEACHES

Snorkeling equipment may be rented from **Puerto Angelito** (30 pesos per hr.) or **Aventura Submarina,** on the Adoquín across from the tourist booth. (☎582 23 53. 70 pesos per day.) Aventura Submarina also leads diving trips (550 pesos). At most beaches, umbrellas can be rented from nearby restaurants (35 pesos per day); it probably makes more sense to buy a few drinks and use them for free. The following beaches are all established and considered relatively safe. Still, you should stay in a group and not visit at night unless at a restaurant. Adventurers exploring secluded beaches must exercise caution.

PLAYA PRINCIPAL. The main beach of Puerto Escondido, Playa Principal lies just beyond the stores and restaurants that line the Adoquín and is often crowded with *lanchas*, *palapas*, and cavorting families.

PLAYA MARINERO. Continuing east along the shore, you'll pass a small *laguna* on your left. Immediately after is Marinero, less crowded than Principal and good for swimming and sunbathing. Waves get more violent the farther along you go.

PLAYA ZICATELA. Stepping over the rocks will take you to Zicatela, reputedly the third-best surfing beach in the world. The talented surfer dudes bobbing up and down in the water waiting to ride the next killer wave all have many years of experience. Unless you are very well practiced, please don't try to partake of their fun—you will risk a fate worse than wiping out. The best times for surf-watching are around 7:30am and 6:30pm—times vary with the tide.

PLAYAS MANZANILLO AND ANGELITO. On the other side of Playa Principal, the clear, calm waters of Playas Manzanillo and Angelito attract snorkelers and swimmers alike. Both tend to be quite crowded in the early afternoon, with Manzanillo the quieter of the two. *Lanchas* from Playa Principal (15 pesos) or taxis (15 pesos) will bring you here. If you prefer to walk (20min.), go west on Gasga to Banamex and take a left; continue left toward the ocean when the road turns to dirt. You will come to a fork in the dirt path; the left path leads to Manzanillo, the right leads to Angelito. The two beaches are separated by an easily-crossed rock barrier.

■ **PLAYA CARRIZALILLO.** Farther west is Playa Carrizalillo, the best of Puerto Escondido's established beaches. Scenically secluded in a cove at the base of a steep hill, Carrizalillo's waters are calm enough for swimming or snorkeling, while offshore waves are substantial enough for surfing or body boarding. To get here, take a taxi (15 pesos). Because waters between Angelito and Carrizalillo are very rough, traveling by *lancha* may be a bad idea. To walk, continue straight on the dirt road instead of turning left for Angelito and Manzanillo until you come to the Rotary Club basketball courts. Make a left and keep walking downhill. Past Carrizalillo the waves again turn wild and dangerous—do not attempt to swim here.

PLAYA BACOCHO. Less scenic (and slightly dirtier) than other beaches, Playa Batocho is noteworthy because it provides the best sunset view around and features two beach clubs, **Coco's** and **Club de Playa Villasol,** which allow use of their bars and pools for 30 pesos per day. Bacocho is best reached by taxi (20 pesos).

◤ NIGHTLIFE

The Adoquín is the center of Puerto Escondido's nightlife, though even it can be a bit sparse in the off season. All the best places are right on the strip, eliminating the need for a taxi, or making for an easy ride from Zicatela (15 pesos).

BARS
In the early evening, every restaurant and bar has a Happy Hour, which usually lasts three or four hours and features cheap beers and two-for-one cocktails. Head to the tourist corridor for the ideal bar-hopping setting. The most popular, **Barfly,** in the middle of the strip, spins pounding techno music. (Beer 20 pesos, cocktails 30 pesos. Open daily 8pm-2am.) **Wipeout Bar,** just past Barfly on the right, plays similar blastingly loud techno and features an open-air second level. (Open daily 9pm-2am.) **Los 3 Diablos,** hosts a well-tanned crowd of youngsters who play pool and strain to hear over loud rap and rock. (Open Tu-Su 9pm-2am.) Farther down the strip, **La Terraza,** by virtue of music played at a slightly less than eardrum-piercing volume, seems comparatively peaceful. (☎582 19 17. Open daily during high season 8pm-3am.) Just past the strip, **Banana's** feels like a sports bar, with TV and a pool table. (☎582 00 05. Pool 30 pesos per hr. Open daily 8am-1am.)

CLUBS
After a day of surfing and sun, most are too wiped out to dance, leaving the disco scene a little weaker than one might expect. **El Tubo,** directly behind Wipeout Bar on Playa Principal, plays reggae, *salsa,* and rock. The crowd that gathers at this popular after-bar destination spills onto the beach by the end of the night. (Open daily 10pm-4am.) **Discoteque Bacocho,** in the Bacocho residential district, is the only full-fledged dance club. You'll have to shower and throw something nice over that thong bikini. Taxis whisk you there for 35 pesos. (☎582 21 37. Cover 30 pesos. Open F-Su 10pm-5am; daily in high season.)

ISTHMUS OF TEHUANTEPEC

East of Oaxaca, the North American continent narrows to a slender strip of land 215km wide, known as the Isthmus of Tehuantepec (tey-wan-teh-PECK) or *el istmo*. The region is home to patches of Zapotec culture, and many residents speak only a few Spanish words. In *el istmo*, the cultural way of life is not an act for tourists, which means the area is more authentic than most, but harder to find.

TEHUANTEPEC   ☎ 9

Tehuantepec (pop. 60,000) is the oldest and most historically significant of *el istmo's* three principal cities. Founded by Zapotec emperor Cosijoeza, it contains some of the first churches built by *indígenas*, a few from the 16th century.

▐ TRANSPORTATION. To get to town from the Cristóbal Colón/ADO bus station, 1.5km north of the *centro*, make an immediate left as you exit the station. This street becomes Héroes, veers to the right, and eventually dead-ends. Turn right and walk a few more blocks; make a left on Hidalgo and follow it to the *zócalo*. Taxis 15 pesos. From the station, Cristóbal Colón (☎715 01 08) travels to: **Huatulco** (3hr., 6am and 1:30pm, 51 pesos); **Mexico City** (11hr., 6:30 and 8:30pm, 409 pesos); **Oaxaca** (4hr., 2am and 1:30pm, 109 pesos); **Tuxtla Gutiérrez** (6½hr.; 12:30am, 2, 10pm; 108 pesos) and more. Buses also go to: **Juchitán** (30min., every hr., 8 pesos) and **Salina Cruz** (30min., 5 per day 5-8pm, 10 pesos). The fastest, cheapest way to travel to neighboring Juchitán and Salina Cruz is to walk west of the plaza for two blocks on 5 de Mayo to the *carretera*. Southbound buses to Salina Cruz stop frequently (7 pesos), as do northbound buses to Juchitán (8 pesos).

▟▛ ORIENTATION AND PRACTICAL INFORMATION. Most of Tehuantepec's action centers around the *zócalo*, which is bounded on the north by 22 de Mayo, the east by Juárez, the south by 5 de Mayo, and the west by Romero. Hidalgo runs north-south and begins on the north side of the plaza between the parallel streets of Romero and Juárez. The Palacio Municipal is on the south side of the *zócalo*. **Tourist information** is available at the Casa de la Cultura, two blocks north of the *zócalo*. The casa is 50m off the street. Turn right between the centro de salud and a refreshment stand. The *zócalo* is besieged by **banks: Serfín**, on the north side of the *zócalo*, has a 24hr. **ATM**, as does **Bital**, on Romero beside Hotel Oasis. **Farmacia El Pastillero** is south of the *zócalo* at Juárez 13. (Open daily 8am-9pm.) **LADATELs** are in the *zócalo*. **Police:** (☎715 00 01) around the back of the Palacio Municipal. **Centro de Salud:** (☎571 01 80) 2 blocks north of *zócalo*. **Telecomm:** next to the post office. (Open M-F 8am-6pm, Sa 9am-12pm.) **Post office:** on the north side of the *zócalo*. (Open M-F 8am-3pm.) **Postal Code:** 70760.

▟▛ ACCOMMODATIONS AND FOOD. Travelers to Tehuantepec should head straight to **Hotel Oasis**, a block south of the *zócalo* on Romero. Rooms are clean, sunny, and breezy, with fans, large beds, and firm mattresses, though the hotel's proximity to the noisy *zócalo* and railroad tracks is inhospitable to light sleepers. The real reason to go is the knowledgeable staff, who can tell you all about the history of the area. (☎715 00 08. Singles 100 pesos; doubles 130 pesos, 160 pesos with A/C.) The hotel also contains the **Restaurant El Almendro**, one of the nicer eating establishments (breakfasts 10-30 pesos) and an airy wood-furnished bar whose cheap beers and satellite TV draw a crowd in the evenings. **Hotel Posada Donaji**, Juárez 10, two blocks south of the *zócalo*, offers slightly higher quality rooms with TVs and fans. (☎715 00 64. Singles 105 pesos, with A/C 140 pesos; doubles 140-150 pesos, with A/C 190 pesos.) For budget meals, try the upper level **Mercado de Jesús Carranza**, on the plaza's west side. (Open daily 8am-8pm.) A quieter slightly over-priced option is the colorful **Cafe Colonial**, two blocks south of the *zócalo* at Romero 66. (☎715 01 15. Open daily 8am-10pm.)

◙ SIGHTS. Tehuantepec's most notable sight is also the best place to find tourist information; the morning library staff at the **Casa de la Cultura** will be happy to fill you in. (☎715 01 14. Open M-F 9am-2pm and 5-8pm, Sa 9am-2pm.) The *casa* is housed in the **Ex-convento Rey Cosijopi**, a 16th-century Dominican building named after the Zapotec leader who ordered its construction, and now holds a small wax museum (featuring such greats as Porfirio Díaz), a library, and diverse workshops and exhibits. A 15min. walk south of the *zócalo* will bring you to **San Blas,** where as in Juchitán's *mercado*, traditional dress and customs can be observed.

▣ ENTERTAINMENT. Between May and September, each of Tehuantepec's 14 communities holds its own week-long festival, beginning with a *baile velorio* at night, a special mass the next morning, and several days of parades, live music, dancing and extensive consumption of *cerveza* by all. Tourists are welcome, though a local chaperone is usually necessary to get into the primarily social events. Admission to the **Vela Sandunga,** in the last week of May, and the **Vela Tehuantepec** (Dec. 26), requires traditional dress for women and *guayáberas* for men, as part of the purpose of these *velas* is to preserve the culture of the town. At the Vela Sandunga, each *barrio* picks a representative to compete for the title of *Reina de la Vela*. The Vela Tehuantepec is a party, held in the main square, to which native *"tehunos"* return each year from all over Mexico and beyond.

NEAR TEHUANTEPEC: GUIENGOLA

From the carretera 2 blocks west of the zócalo in Tehuantepec take a southbound "Jalapa" bus, and ask the driver to drop you at the 3rd bridge, Puente de las Tejas (25min., every hr. 6am-5pm, 5 pesos). From the bridge, start down the dirt road to the right, marked by an archaeological zone sign. Walk 3½km (approx. 35min.) to a road branching to the left; it marks the beginning of the mountain. Alternatively, you can take a taxi from Tehuantepec to this point (60 pesos). Take the left road and walk until you reach a platform with a view (30 min.). At the far end of the platform, 2 paths branch; take the rougher one on the left. After another 30min., the path splits again; go right another 15min. to the ruins. "Jalapa" buses return from the bridge (every hr. until 5pm). "Oaxaca" buses run later and will get you back as well.

Approximately 15km southwest of Tehuantepec, the Zapotec ruins of Guiengola are little-visited, little-known, covered with plants, and for the most part still ruined. They lie a steep and rocky 3.5km up Monte de Guiengola. The trip to the top takes about 2hr. (if you're in shape and get a ride the first 3½km to the base). Regardless of walking prowess, start the day early, bring at least 3L of water, bug repellent, sunscreen, a hat, and long pants. The trip is best made in summer, when full foliage makes the heat more tolerable. Guides are required for solo trips and highly recommended otherwise. Trails on Guiengola are narrow and unmarked.

The main ruins of the Zapotec ceremonial center consist of two pyramids, the ceremonial plaza, a ballcourt, and the Palacio del Rey. Typical of Zapotec construction, all face southwest. Guiengola reached its peak at same time as Monte Albán (see p. 468), during the Classic period (AD 300-750), and was later the stronghold of King Cosijoez, who successfully repelled the Aztecs from the mountain around 1480. Relics of the battle can be seen on the way up the trail; at one point the path is lined by massive stones that were once a checkpoint for soldiers.

Arriving at the site after the grueling hike is probably the highlight of a Guiengola visit for the aerobically challenged. When you can walk again, directly on your left is a 25m long **ballcourt.** Unlike the Aztec ball games, which determined sacrificial victims, the slightly kinder Zapotecs played ball games primarily for sport. On the right of the path, just after the ballcourt, is the **larger of the two pyramids,** rising 9m. The pyramid was constructed in three sections and at one point had 35 stairs in the middle section, though these are now mostly eroded away. In front of the pyramid is the **ceremonial plaza,** which now contains ceremonial weeds, a ceremonial tree and a ceremonial trash can. The **second, smaller pyramid** sits to the left. Continuing straight on the path, you arrive at a rocky area, from which another path branches off to several nearby unexplored caves with impressive salt formations and plenty of bats. Caving opportunities exist for experienced spelunkers only. Backtrack on the main path 100m to a small path on the left, which leads to the **Palacio del Rey Cosijoez.** The palace once consisted of 64 rooms, but looks now more like 144 crumbling stone walls. The Palacio is still notable, though, for it's king's quarters, located at a *mirador* (lookout) so that he could keep watch over his kingdom. Other points of interest include the king's plump bathtub and dark, ancient storage cellar.

JUCHITÁN ☎ 9

If grandmothers ruled the world, it would probably look like Juchitán. One begins to suspect that there is some sort of government-sponsored flower subsidy as the open market would not seem to support the vast number of vendors that crowd the *zócalo*. There is also an unusually high incidence of ribbon-selling. Throughout, women wear traditional dress—loose fitting, embroidered shirts and long full floral skirts. Juchitán's traditional crafts are meant to be worn, and the aesthetic is an overwhelmingly important part of town life.

TRANSPORTATION. To get to town from the first-class bus station, follow **Prolongación 16 de Septiembre** to the right. It soon splits into **5 de Septiembre** and **16 de Septiembre,** which run parallel and eventually form the west and east sides of the *zócalo*, respectively. **Gómez** is the street to the north of the *zócalo*, **Juárez** is to the south. The *palacio municipal* and the market are to the east of the *zócalo* on 16 de Septiembre. Taxi *colectivos* run to the *centro* (3 pesos) from the left side of the bus station exit. **Local buses** connect Juchitán with the isthmus towns of **Tehuantepec** (30min., 10pesos) and **Salina Cruz** (1hr., 17 pesos). Cristóbal Colón (☎711 25 65) sends buses to: **Mexico City** (11½hr.; 8:30, 9:30, 10pm; 380 pesos); **Oaxaca** (4½hr., 8 per day midnight-4:05pm, 112 pesos); and other destinations.

PRACTICAL INFORMATION. The **tourist office** is on the first floor of the building to the north of the *zócalo* toward the west side. (☎710 19 71 or 715 54 13. Open M-F 9am-2pm and 5-8pm.) **Banamex,** 5 de Septiembre 12 on the *zócalo*, exchanges currency and has several 24hr. **ATMs.** (Open M-Sa 9am-5pm.) **Farmacia 24 Horas,** 2 de Abril at Gómez, one block east of the *zócalo*. (Open 24hr.) **Police:** (☎711 12 35), in the Palacio Municipal. No English spoken. **Telecomm:** across from post office, (Open M-F 8am-7:30pm, Sa-Su 9am-noon). **Post office:** Gómez and 16 de Septiembre. (Open M-F 8am-7pm.) **Postal code:** 70000.

ACCOMMODATIONS AND FOOD. Budget accomodations are available at **Hotel Modelo,** 2 de Abril 21, half a block from the market. Large rooms are spare with cold showers. Baths could be cleaner. (☎711 24 51. Singles 90 pesos; doubles 100 pesos.) **Hotel Don Alex,** 16 de Septiembre 48, is a tidier option. (☎711 10 64. Singles 150 pesos, with A/C and TV 250 pesos; doubles with A/C and TV 300 pesos.)

Juchitán is perhaps the best of the three principal *istmo* towns in which to sample regional cuisine. Unusual food prevails: iguana, deer, armadillo, and rabbit are plentiful and easy to catch, and often turn up stuffed into various tortillas, *tamales*, and tacos. The tame of heart can stick to *topotes*, an interesting variant on the *tostada*, with a frisbee-like airy corn patty as a base. While the town's **market** is a must-eat, **Los Chapulines,** 5 de Septiembre at Morelos, five blocks north of the *zócalo*, offers regional cuisine. Think rationally before ordering the house specialty, which is, not surprisingly, *chapulines* (grasshoppers; 50 pesos). Go for one of the non-insect entrees (45-55 pesos), which come with salad, rice, refried beans, bread, and tortillas. (☎712 01 96. Open daily 7am-11:30pm.)

SIGHTS. It could take a while to cover **Mercado 5 de Septiembre,** which consumes an entire block east of the *zócalo*. Support the flower market and if you are an old Mexican woman, share the latest gossip. Try on festival clothing on the second floor; the skirts and blouses are made of velvet and ornately embroidered with

Mooooore Room.

Real American Airlines deals for students and faculty, online at StudentUniverse. Earn AAdvantage miles and enjoy *more room throughout Coach only on American**.

 StudentUniverse.com

featuring
AmericanAirlines

WATCH FOR FALLING POTS Next time you're walking down a sidewalk, check out the amorous couple walking in front of you. More than likely, the woman will be walking on the inner part of the sidewalk and the man closer to the street. *Hombres* gallantly profess that they walk nearer the street to ensure that they, and not their *mujeres*, will be splashed by passing cars hitting puddles. However, a second, far less chivalrous theory exists...Many of the buildings in Mexico have balconies from which hang huge, heavy flowerpots, or *potes*. If one of the pots were to fall, it would land smack on the inner part of the sidewalk—where the women walk. In their more honest moments, some men confess that they walk nearer the street to avoid falling pots, not to protect their womenfolk from errant droplets of dirty street water. Gallant *caballeros* or sneaky, self-serving wretches...you decide.

flowers to represent women's connection with nature. Keep in mind that the vendors are interested in investigating the relationship between Zapotec clothing and your money. Haggling is advised. (Open daily 6am-8pm.)

At the corner of Domínguez and Colón, Juchitán's **Casa de Cultura** is filled with art and music workshops and home to a collection of regional archaeological artifacts. To get there, walk south on 5 de Septiembre from the *zócalo* toward the Banco Serfín sign. Turn right at Serfín and pass Parque Chariz on the left; the *casa* is on the right. (Open M-F 10am-3pm and 5-8pm, Sa 10am-2pm.) Before the *casa*, the church of **San Vincente Ferraro** is worth a peek. Constructed in 1528, the church has been remodeled many times but retains an ancient air. Most of the simple, whitewashed architecture dates from the 17th century.

NEAR JUCHITÁN: EL OJO DE AGUA

Across the highway from the 1st-class station in Juchitán, 2nd-class buses leave often for Ixtepec (30min., 8 pesos). In Ixtepec find the buses that go to Tlacotepec, which are right around the corner from the return buses to Juchitán. Tlacotepec buses sometimes drop off and pick up at the *balneario* (25min., every hr., 6 pesos). If not, get off at the "balneario" sign and take a 25min. walk. Balneario open 24hr. 10 pesos.

Approximately 1hr. northwest of Juchitán by bus, El Ojo de Agua, a bubbling *balneario* (natural spring), is the best way to beat the oppressive *istmo* heat that does not involve refreshing grain-based beverages. Cement walls have been erected at the source, directing the spring's flow through several large pools connected by small waterfalls. In contrast to most crusted-tile Mexican spas, small fish swim near the sand and rock bottom of the pools, and tree trunks jut from the sides. Beware assault by tadpoles. Though trash detracts from the scene, the water itself remains clean, clear, and cool—constantly replenished by the spring.

SALINA CRUZ ☎ 9

Salina Cruz offers little but oil refineries to tourists, but its central location makes it a convenient stop for buses. Cristóbal Colón (☎714 14 41) runs to: **Huatulco** (3hr., 6 per day 12:30am-4pm, 59 pesos); **Mexico City** (11½hr.; 7:30, 8:20, 9:15pm; 395 pesos); **Oaxaca** (5hr., 5 per day, 110 pesos); and elsewhere. The **Cristóbal Colón station** is a 30-min. hike from the *zócalo*. Spare yourself the trouble and walk until you hit the main street, then catch a blue *microbus* (2.5 pesos); taxis 10 pesos. Estrella Blanca sends second-class buses to **Acapulco** and all stops in between, including **Bahías de Huatulco** and **Puerto Escondido** (4 per day 6:15am-11pm). From Cristóbal Colón, walk right on the main street three blocks, then take another right. The Estrella Blanca station is half a block down on the right. To get from the second-class "istmo" stop to Cristóbal Colón, walk left past the buses to the first cross street and take a left. Walk approximately five blocks and hang a right; the station is near the corner on the left.

GULF COAST AND CHIAPAS

Tropical beauty, indigenous traditions, Caribbean music, and sweeping poverty unite the states of the southern Gulf Coast, which welcome travelers to beaches, natural reserves, and small towns aplenty.

Stretching 300km along the Gulf of Mexico, steamy **Veracruz** encompasses breathtaking beaches, burgeoning cities, and vast spaces filled only by roaming cattle and lush vegetation. The ancestral home of the Huastec, Totonac, and Olmec civilizations, Veracruz witnessed Cortés's first steps on American soil, and has since endured foreign intervention and invasion by the Spanish (1825), the French (1839), and the United States (1847 and 1914). Today, many residents continue to live off the land, cultivating tobacco and coffee, and running small-scale cattle ranches, but Veracruz's main income comes from oil and fishing. Still, the state that works hard also parties hard: *veracruzanos*, also known as *jarochos*, are renowned for their delightful sense of humor, wonderful seafood and coffee, and Afro-Caribbean inspired music. *Marimba* rhythms and Caribbean colors flow through the steamy port city of Veracruz day and night, and beautiful mountainous Xalapa overflows with art and culture.

Swampy **Tabasco** lies southeast of Veracruz along the Gulf of Mexico, dotted with lakes and swamps, criss-crossed by rivers, and swathed in dense jungle. Untouristed beaches line the northern coast, and the southern and eastern borders overflow with parks and nature sanctuaries. Once the center of Olmec territory, Tabasco gives a glimpse into its mother culture with the ruins at La Venta. Villahermosa, the capital, rises from the center of the jungle, its colonial identity battling the city's rapid modern growth.

Chiapas sits south of Tabasco, and for centuries has been known for environmental diversity—its cloud-enveloped heights contrast with dense, lowland rainforest. One of Mexico's most beautiful cities, San Cristóbal de las Casas, renowned for its cobblestone streets and surrounding *indígena* villages, rests high amid these peaks. The state forms part of the Maya heartland; the Lacandón Rainforest shields the remote ruins of Bonampak and Yaxchilán as well as fiercely traditional groups of Lacandón Maya. Chiapas's *indígenas* remain true to their roots—in many communities, schools teach in the local dialect as well as Spanish. The EZLN rebellion of 1994 drew the world's attention to Chiapas and the highland region's increasing land conflicts, which pit small-scale Maya farmers against wealthy ranchers and the national government.

HIGHLIGHTS OF THE GULF COAST

INHALE the rich vanilla aromas of **Papantla** (see p. 502), "the city that perfumes the world," and carry the scent with you to the awesome ruins at **El Tajín** (see p. 504).

STRIKE a pose at the stunning **Cascada de Texolo** (see p. 498), where movie stars galore have filmed famous scenes in the glistening falls.

GULP the thin air of **San Cristóbal de las Casas** (see p. 540), set atop lush green mountains in the Chiapan cloud forest.

TREK through the jungle to the archaeological sites of **Yaxchilán** (see p. 555) and **Bonampak** (see p. 557), home to some of Mexico's most well-preserved Maya ruins.

DROOL in amazement at the Olmec artifacts situated in a spectacular, outdoor jungle-setting in **Villahermosa's Parque-Museo La Venta** (see p. 526).

VERACRUZ

XALAPA

☎ 2

Drumming college students and packed cafes give Xalapa (hah-LAH-pah; pop. 420,000) a cosmopolitan vibe. The cool climate in this city of hills provides a welcome oasis in the muggy state of Veracruz. A self-proclaimed cultural center, Xalapa boasts a burgeoning university, an excellent orchestra, and one of the top archeological museums in the Americas. Conquered by the Aztecs in 1460, this Totonac city remained part of the empire until Cortés claimed the land for Spain. Though citizens spell their town's name (Náhuatl for "spring in the sand") with an "x," they struggle against the Hispanic "j" spelling. Name-game aside, the city thrives on debate. Even the cuisine is built upon contradictions: Xalapa is both the birthplace of the Xalapeño (jalapeño) pepper and the fertile soil for Mexico's rich, mellow coffee. Though the center bursts with commerce, even money takes a backseat to coffee-time, when groups of chattering friends overflow cafe tables. Xalapa's extensive blend of contrasts, culture, conversation, and cafe make the city's attractions as varied and topsy-turvy as its many rolling hills.

▐ TRANSPORTATION

The **train station** is at the extreme northeast edge of the city, a 40min. walk or 14-peso taxi ride from the *centro*. To get from the **bus station** to the *centro*, catch a bus marked "Centro" or "Terminal" (3 pesos); taxis cost 16 pesos. There are two

Veracruz State

bus stations. **CAXA,** 20 de Noviembre 571, east of the city center, services distant cities and has long-distance phones, telegraph and luggage service, shopping, and restaurants. **Terminal Excelsior** is a roundabout where you can catch buses to neighboring towns. Make sure to clarify which of these stations you wish to go to.

From CAXA, ADO (☎812 25 25) travels first-class to: **Catemaco** (5hr., 8 per day 7am-7:45pm, 119 pesos); **Mexico City** (5hr., 21 per day 1am-midnight, 147 pesos); **Papantla** (4hr., 8 per day, 114 pesos); **Puebla** (3hr., 9 per day, 84 pesos); **San Andrés Tuxtla** (3hr., 12 per day, 115 pesos); **Santiago Tuxtla** (3hr.; 10:15am, 2:05, 7:15, and 11:30pm; 109 pesos); **Tuxtepec** (5hr., 6am and 3:35pm, 119 pesos); **Veracruz** (2hr., 46 per day 5am-11pm, 49 pesos). Slightly slower, 10-pesos cheaper second-class service to nearly identical destinations is provided by **Autobuses Unidos (AU).**

✳ ⁊ ORIENTATION AND PRACTICAL INFORMATION

Located in the center of the state, Xalapa is 104km northwest of Veracruz on **Mex. 140** and 302km east of Mexico City. Downtown centers around the **cathedral** and the **Palacio de Gobierno. Enríquez,** which runs along **Parque Juárez,** separates the two. Streets that branch from Enríquez toward the park and the Palacio de Gobierno run downhill, while those that split from Enríquez on the cathedral side travel uphill to the market and main commercial district.

TOURIST, FINANCIAL, AND LOCAL SERVICES

Tourist Office: Dirreción de Turismo Municipal, Camacho 42 (☎818 66 22). English-speaking staff doles out maps and helpful information. Ask for Elsa. Open M-F 9am-3pm and 4-6pm.

Currency Exchange: Banks with **ATMs** line Enríquez and the surrounding streets. Most will change money, but better rates can be found at **Centro Cambio Jalapa** (☎818 68 60; Open M-Sa 9am-2pm and 4-6:30pm), or **Casa de Cambio Orisatal,** both down the road on Zamora. (Open M-Sa 9am-3pm and 4-7pm, Su 10am-1pm.)

American Express: Carrillo 24 (☎817 41 14), off Enríquez. Cashier open M-F 9am-1:30pm and 4-7pm, Sa 9am-1pm. **Viajes Xalapa,** a full-service **travel agency,** with English-language assistance, shares the office. Open M-Sa 9am-8pm.

Markets: Mercado Jauregui, 2 blocks behind the cathedral, sells fresh produce and a variety of other goods. Open M-Sa 7am-9pm, Su 7am-5pm. **Mercado San José,** northwest of La Iglesia de San José, off Zárate, is a 24hr. wonder of fruits and vegetables.

Supermarket: Chedraui is a **supermarket** and **pharmacy** on the corner of Lucio and Róa Bárcenas. Open daily 8am-9pm.

Laundry: Lavandería Express Salmones, Morelos 13 (☎818 52 15), between Guido and Camacho. 20 pesos per 3kg. Open M-F 8:30am-8:30pm, Sa 10am-6pm.

Luggage Storage: At the bus station. 30 pesos per day.

Bookstores: Several bookstores are located at Xalapeños Ilustres and Mata just past the Centro Recreativo. **Gandi Colorines** sells English-language books and magazines.

Cultural Centers: Centro Recreativo Xalapa, Xalapeños Ilustres 31, at Mata and Insurgentes, has art galleries, posts cultural information, and teaches classes on everything from *salsa* to political cartooning. Open M-Sa 10am-2pm and 4-8pm, Su 11am-5pm.

Car Rental: Alamo, 20 de Noviembre Ote. 522 (☎817 43 13). Exit to the right from the bus station, walk downstairs and through the small shopping center. On the opposite side of the street. Must be over 21. Open M-Sa 9am-2pm and 4-8pm.

EMERGENCY AND COMMUNICATIONS

Emergency: ☎060.

Police: (☎818 18 10 or 818 99 86), station at Cuartel San José, with offices at the intersection of Arteaga and Aldama.

Red Cross: Clavijero 13 (☎817 34 31 for emergencies or 817 81 58 for administration), 1 block uphill from Parque Juárez. No English spoken.

Pharmacy: Farmacia Reforma, Enríquez 41 (☎817 22 20). Open 24hr.

Hospitals: Hospital Civil, Pedro Rendón 1 (☎818 44 00), at Bravo. **IMSS,** Lomas del Estadio (☎818 55 55). No English spoken at either.

Fax: Telecomm, Zamora 70 (☎816 21 67), just before the Palacio Federal. Open M-F 8am-7:30pm, Sa 9am-5pm, Su 9am-1pm.

Internet Access: PC Manía, Rodríguez B. 29 (☎841 09 00), ½ a block east of the intersection of Morelos and Bravo, in the Zona Universitaria. Fast connections for 10 pesos per hr., 7 pesos before 1pm. Open M-Sa 9am-9pm, Su 10am-8pm. **Intercys** (☎818 52 31), outside the lower doors of the bus station to the right of the taxi stand. Slow computers. 15 pesos per hr., students 10 pesos per hr. Open daily 9am-2pm and 4-8pm.

Post Office: (☎817 20 21), at Zamora and Diego Leño in the Palacio Federal. Open M-F 8am-4pm, Sa 9am-1pm.

Postal Code: 91001.

ACCOMMODATIONS

For the peso-pinching traveler, Xalapa is a gold mine. Comfortable and convenient lodging can be found on **Revolución,** close to the *centro*, the market, and parks.

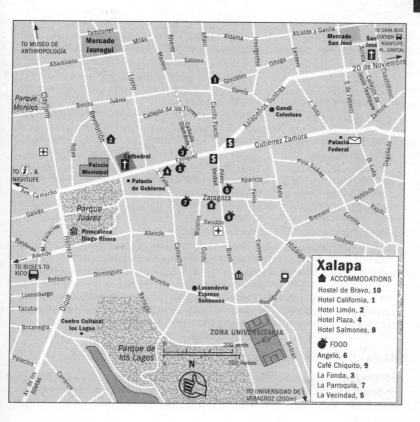

Xalapa

🏠 ACCOMMODATIONS

Hostel de Bravo, **10**
Hotel California, **1**
Hotel Limón, **2**
Hotel Plaza, **4**
Hotel Salmones, **8**

🍴 FOOD

Angelo, **6**
Café Chiquito, **9**
La Fonda, **3**
La Parroquia, **7**
La Vecindad, **5**

Hotel California, Gonzáles Ortega 1, on the north side of a small park, where Juárez intersects with Carrillo Puerto. Not exactly lovely, but it compensates with low prices. Rooms are spartan, white, and extremely clean. Singles 45 pesos, with bath 65 pesos; doubles 50 pesos, with bath 90 pesos.

Hostal de Bravo, Bravo 11 (☎818 90 38), below Zaragoza. Xalapa's only hostel has tidy rooms with large windows, fans, and TVs. The gorgeous patio has tables for chatting. Singles 165 pesos; doubles 190 pesos; each additional person 20 pesos.

Hotel Limón, Revolución 8 (☎817 22 04; fax 817 93 16), just past the cathedral. Brightly-covered tiles give the lobby and hallways a cheerful glow. Rooms are tidy and have TV. Singles 90 pesos; doubles 135 pesos; triples 170 pesos.

Hotel Plaza, Enríquez 4 (☎817 33 10; fax 818 27 14). If your room faces Enríquez, expect noise around the clock. Small rooms are bare except for TVs. Bathrooms in minor disrepair. Singles 148 pesos; doubles 173 pesos; each additional person 35 pesos.

Hotel Salmones, Zaragoza 24 (☎817 54 31). Those with a few pesos to spare will enjoy large carpeted rooms with A/C, phone, and TV. Ask for a room with a balcony. Singles 190 pesos; doubles 220 pesos; triples 250 pesos.

🍴 FOOD

Xalapeño food is cheap, plentiful, and always accompanied by *lechero (cafe con leche)*. Along with Xalapa's specialty *cafes*, visitors should be sure to sample regional foods: pickled chiles, jalapeño peppers, *picaditas* (flat corn cakes with mashed beans and cheese), and *garnachas* (bean-filled, fried corn cakes). Also, don't miss the *pambozo*, a sandwich-type food served on round bread and stuffed with beans, tomato, lettuce, and other goodies. Yummy tortillas are hand-patted in the corner of every restaurant. Many restaurants close before 6pm, so fill up early.

La Fonda, Callejón del Diamante 1 (☎818 72 82). Quite simply the best food around. Eat upstairs for better ambience, and don't leave without trying the cactus and egg soup and the cactus salad (20 pesos). Chicken *mole* and steak prepared *al gusto* are also fabulous (42 pesos). Open M-Sa 8am-5pm.

Cafe Chiquito, Bravo 3 (☎812 11 22), 2½ blocks south of Enríquez. A gorgeous open-air restaurant complete with gurgling fountain. 18 different types of coffee. *Enfrijoladas* and chicken *mole* (30 pesos). Open daily 8am-11:30pm. Live music M-Sa after 9pm.

Restaurant Rosalia, Abasolo 2 (☎817 56 38), 1 block past the north end of the market. Funny wooden booths and great food attract tired vendors to this 50-year-old market-side institution. 4 *super enchiladas* 7 pesos, *mole poblano* 10 pesos. Top it off with *cafe con leche* (3 pesos). Open M-Sa 9am-9pm, Su 9am-2pm.

La Vecindad, Enríquez 12 (☎818 32 65). Cheerful and central. At breakfast, eggs *al gusto* are 17 pesos, fruit salads 15 pesos. Come back later for *picadas* (17 pesos) and tacos *al pastor* (with ham; 20 pesos). Open M-Sa 9am-7pm.

Cafe de la Parroquia, Zaragoza 18 (☎817 74 01), a block downhill from Enríquez. The Parroquia is a 70s dream, with tinkling elevator music wafting through the tan, smoky interior. Wonderful coffee 9 pesos, famous *lechero* 12 pesos, succulent pastries, and *antojitos* 25-32 pesos. Open daily 7:30am-11pm.

Angelo, Casa de Té y Galletas, Primo 21 (☎817 61 71), below Zaragoza. The charming staff will brew one of 30 different teas just for you. Sip strawberries and cream or mango tea for a sweet treat (10 pesos). Open M-Sa 8am-9pm.

🔍 SIGHTS

■ **MUSEO DE ANTROPOLOGÍA.** The finest museum in the country after Mexico City's Museo Nacional de Antropología (see p. 108), Xalapa's museum focuses exclusively on the state of Veracruz. Start your visit in the front, with the 10 huge

Olmec heads, each of which weighs 20 tons, and work your way through the rectangular main gallery in chronological order. The museum is best viewed with one of the knowledgeable University of Veracruz students, who lead tours. *(Catch a yellow "Tesorería" bus on Enríquez (5 pesos), take a taxi (15 pesos), or walk on Enríquez/ Camacho away from the cathedral. Make a left on Av. Xalapa and continue for several blocks until you see the museum on your left (45min.).* ☎815 09 20 *or 815 07 08. Open daily 9am-5pm. 25 pesos. Camera 10 pesos, video camera 40 pesos. Free tours in Spanish given daily at 11:30am (1½ hr.). English tours can be arranged at any time for 100 pesos.)*

PARQUE ECOLÓGICO MACUITÉPETL. Xalapa's biggest, most beautiful park is Parque Ecológico Macuitépetl, where, with a little trekking, you can enjoy the flora and fauna native to the hills around the city. A brick path meanders past liplocked lovers to the summit of an extinct volcano 186m above Xalapa, where a spiral tower looks out over city and mountains. *(Take a "Mercado-Corona" colectivo (3 pesos) from Revolución and Altamirano, or hail a taxi (25 pesos). Open daily 6am-6pm.)*

UNIVERSITY OF VERACRUZ. The large, man-made "lakes" of **Paseo de los Lagos** lap against the university's hillsides below Enríquez. Not exactly an architectural gem, UV's institutional box-style buildings are painted in comely shades of blue and green. Still, pine trees and a lakeside path make it worth a visit. Pop into one of the art galleries for information on workshops and exhibitions.

PARQUE JUÁREZ. This park serves as Xalapa's surrogate *zócalo*. Relax, catch the breeze and take in the superb vista. Two staircases in the park's platform lead down to the **Agora de la Ciudad.** The center harbors a small cafe, several galleries, and a screening room where film festivals take place. *(Open Tu-Su 8am-9:15pm.)*

PINOCATECA DIEGO RIVERA. Xalapa's artistic gem is the Pinocateca, a small museum that houses many of Rivera's more experimental canvases—Impressionism, collage, Cubism, travel sketches, and a good dose of horse-human bestiality. *(Herrera 5, just below Parque Juárez.* ☎818 18 19. *Open Tu-Su 10am-6pm. Free.)*

CALLEJÓNES. Xalapa takes pride in its old cobblestone alleys, many of which are associated with gory love stories. **Callejón del Diamante,** off Enríquez, honors a diamond that could detect an unfaithful lover. Legend has it that a Spaniard gave the diamond to his Mexican wife, who then played hanky-panky with a local while he was away. The darkened diamond alerted the Spaniard who, enraged, slaughtered his wife. Off Rebsamen is **Callejón de la Calavera,** named for the legend of a wife who decapitated her cheating, drunken husband. As for **Callejón de Jesús te Ampare,** the lovers in question were killed by a widower who went mad with jealousy upon seeing the happy couple. *"Jesús te ampare"* (Jesus protect you) was the last thing the girl managed to say to her lover before their demise. Sanctuary from the carnage can be found next door at the 18th-century **Iglesia de San José.**

LOS MADRES CAPUCHINAS. If you're in the mood to satisfy your sweet tooth while getting a dose of religion, head to the convent of the **Adoratrices Perpétuas,** whose nuns have been making candy for the past 50 years. The easiest way to get there is by cab (12 pesos). At the store, pick up trinkets and *dulces de Jamoncillo*. Boxes of candy in the shape of fruits, vegetables, and birds cost 20-40 pesos. *(20 de Noviembre Ote. 150.* ☎817 37 51. *Open M-F 9am-6pm.)*

🎵 ENTERTAINMENT

Xalapa, in typical college-town fashion, has two varieties of nightlife: the cultural (theater, classical music, *ballet folklórico*) and the bawdy (drinking, dancing, sex). After attending a high-culture performance, bicker about the symbolic use of color in one of the city's cafes, most of which are full until about 11:30pm. **Cafe Lindo,** on Primo below Zaragoza, is one of the hottest. Later on, disco fever rages on **Camacho** and near the bus station on **20 de Noviembre.** Late night jaunts require a taxi (18 pesos), but it's a small price to pay for wild, sweaty fun.

CLUBS AND BARS

Discoteque La Estación, 20 Noviembre 571 (☎817 31 55), just below the 1st-class bus station. La Estación is reached by a dark, private road running through the chirping, whirring Xalapeño jungle. The Station pulsates with the almost 2000 bodies it takes to fill the exquisite wooden dance floor. An upper floor plays live rock, but is a bit more mellow. Casual dress. Cover 30 pesos, free 9-10:30pm. Open W-Sa 9pm-4am.

La Roka, Calzada del Tajar 2 (☎812 19 19), right across 20 de Noviembre from the bus station. Patrons are young, casually-dressed, and move to the beats of pop and rock. On F and Sa, *Grupo Salsa Picante* plays live *salsa,* complete with *sombreros* and traditional dress. Cover 30 pesos. Open Th-Sa 10:30pm-3am.

Bistro Cafe del Herrero, Camacho 8 (☎817 02 68), hosts a mature, bar-like scene with jam-packed passageways more conducive to pressing than dancing. Lighted aquariums house iguanas, who sway to the beat of Tex-Mex rock. Su-M live guitar music. Open daily 4pm-4am.

XCAPE, 20 de Noviembre 641 (☎812 50 75), 4 long blocks down 20 de Noviembre to the right of the station. A more sedate scene, with well-dressed patrons listening to live rock courtesy of a 3-band rotation. Cover 30 pesos. Open Th-Su 9pm-3am.

For information on cultural events, visitors should check listings in the local newspapers or head to the Centro Recreativo (☎817 31 10) to find out what's happening at Teatro del Estado. A 10min. walk up Enríquez and Camacho from Parque Juárez, the *teatro*, at the corner of Ignacio de la Llave, is the home of the Orquesta Sinfónica de Xalapa, which performs weekly. Performances by university students and professionals keep the stage lights warm all week long. Centro Cultural Los Lagos (☎812 12 99), four blocks off Camacho on Dique, also hosts concerts.

During the **Festival de Junio Musical** (late May-June), the symphony hosts concerts, and performers stage theater productions and recitals throughout the city. Xalapa also celebrates the month-long **Feria Internacional de Xalapa,** which features a variety of cultural, artisanal, and sporting events (April or May).

■ DAYTRIPS FROM XALAPA

▓ XICO'S CASCADA DE TEXOLO

To get to Xico from Xalapa, walk west on Allende until you reach Galeana and a large park (10 min.). From there, take any "Xico" bus (30min., 9 pesos). When you see a blue "Entrada de la Ciudad" sign on the right side of the road, alert the driver and exit the bus. From the main street, climb up the hill in front of you (a white building is to the left of the rocky path). After a 4min. walk, you will come to a wide, stone-paved road at the top. Turn left and continue walking on the street, which will change into a rocky stone road. The road forks at 2 points along the way—take the right fork both times. Taxis sometimes make the trip to the falls, but the ride is neither smooth nor quick.

In the town of Xico (HEE-koh), 19km outside of Xalapa, there are almost as many mules on the road as automobiles. Besides pastoral bliss, Xico has one huge selling-point—the dramatic waterfalls of **Texolo,** just 3km from town. If it looks like it's out of a movie, that's because it is. Several US movies were filmed here, including *Romancing the Stone* and *Clear and Present Danger.* Somewhat less glamorously, car and deodorant commercials have also been shot at the falls. In any case, Hollywood has left no trace of its presence, and few tourists frequent the site. The only sign of civilization is the conveniently placed **Restaurant El Mirador.** (Excellent *chiles rellenos* 18 pesos. Open daily 9am-7pm.) The best viewing area is located just beyond the restaurant. Head left before the footbridge crossing the gorge, and go down the cement steps with the blue railings. Take a right at the fork. The vista at the base of the falls is like something out of a fantasy book. The rocks are often slippery and deserted, so exercise caution and wear appropriate footwear. Also note that the walk to the falls is a long and lonely one: try not to go by yourself and don't hike to the falls at night. The insects are silent but ferocious—bring bug repellent.

TUXPAN (TUXPAM)   ☎ 7

Tuxpan (pop. 120,000) boasts a Caribbean vibe and attracts visitors eager to sample fresh seafood and relax amidst the jungle oasis. Just beyond the rows of seafood markets, couples amble along the Río Tuxpan, while heavy humidity in the mellow plaza encourages lovely, lethargic lounging. Much like their Olmec, Huastec, and Toltec predecessors, boys stand on the shore flinging fishing nets into the water, and fruit vendors traverse the streets selling bananas and mangoes by the bag. Tranquil and beautiful, Tuxpan makes for a great low-key getaway.

TRANSPORTATION. Tuxpan, 347km northwest of Veracruz, spreads along the northern bank of Río Tuxpan. Each bus line has its own station; to get to the town center from any one, first walk to the river. From the Estrella Blanca station, walk toward and past the bridge—from the other stations, walk away from the bridge for just a few blocks. ADO, Rodríguez 1 (☎834 01 02), close to the bridge, three blocks east of Parque Cano down Reyes Heroles, heads to: **Mexico City** (5hr., 13 per day, 172 pesos); **Papantla** (1½hr., 7 per day, 32 pesos); **Poza Rica** (1hr., every ½hr., 26 pesos); **Tampico** (3½hr., 1 per hr., 110 pesos); **Veracruz** (5hr., 13 per day, 140 pesos); **Xalapa** (5hr., 5 per day, 141 pesos). Estrella Blanca, Turistar, and Futura, at Cuauhtémoc 18 (☎834 20 40), two blocks past the bridge and two blocks inland, sends 1st-class buses to: **Matamoros** (12hr., 7 and 9:30pm, 351 pesos); **Mexico City** (6hr., 7 per day, 152 pesos); **Monterrey** (12hr., 9pm, 374 pesos); and second-class buses to most nearby destinations. Omnibus, Independencia 30 (☎834 11 47), under the bridge, goes to: **Guadalajara** (15hr., 5 and 9:15pm, 460 pesos) and **Querétaro** (10hr., 3 per day 5-9pm, 256 pesos).

ORIENTATION AND PRACTICAL INFORMATION. Reyes Heroles (or simply, "el bulevar," the boulevard) is Tuxpan's main thoroughfare, running along the river. One block north lies Juárez, followed by Morelos. Activity centers around two plazas: **Parque Rodríguez Cano** on the waterfront, just south of the busiest part of town, and **Parque Reforma,** the town's *centro*, between Juárez and Morelos a few blocks west of Parque Rodríguez Cano. The bridge marks the eastern edge of town, and streets parallel to the water run roughly east-west.

The **tourist office,** Juárez 20, on the floor floor of the Palacio Municipal in Parque Rodríguez Cano, has lots of maps and brochures. Enter on the Juárez side across from Hotel Florida. (☎834 01 77; www.tuxpam.com.mx. Open M-Sa 10am-5pm, Su 10am-2pm.) **Banco Serfín,** on Juárez between the two parks, exchanges traveler's checks and has a 24hr. **ATM.** (☎834 09 25. Open M-F 9am-3pm.) **Supermarket: Super Alan,** Ortega 11, entrance on Santander, off Morelos between the two plazas. (Open daily 8am-9pm.) **Lavandería Mejico,** Reyes Heroles 57, three blocks west of the *centro*, will wash, dry, and iron your clothes in 2hr. (☎834 27 08. 12 pesos per kg. Open M-Sa 8am-8pm.) **Emergency:** ☎060. **Police:** Galeana 38 (☎834 02 52), next to the Red Cross. **Red Cross:** Galeana 40 (☎834 01 58), 8 blocks west of the *centro* along the river, then four blocks up Galeana at the mini-bridge. English spoken. **Pharmacy: Benavides,** Rodríguez 9, on the bridge-side of the market one block in from the river. (☎834 12 41. Open daily 7am-10pm.) **FAX: Telecomm,** Ortega 20, 2 blocks off of Morelos. (☎834 01 67. Open M-F 8am-7:30pm, Sa 9am-5pm, Su 9am-noon.) **LADATELs** scattered around the two main plazas. **Internet: CyberSpace Snack and Net,** at the corner of Benito Juárez and Veracruz, blasts Spanish MTV on a large screen while patrons eat, drink, and type away. (12 pesos per hr. Open M-F 9am-10pm, Sa 10am-10pm.) **Post office:** Mina 16, has a **MexPost** inside. From Parque Reforma, follow Morelos toward the bridge, and take the first left onto Mina. (☎834 00 88. Open M-F 8am-6pm, Sa 8am-2pm.) **Postal code:** 92800.

ACCOMMODATIONS. Budget accommodations in Tuxpan cluster around the two central parks. **Hotel Riviera,** Reyes Heróes 17, across from the river, boasts clean, bright rooms with A/C, phone, and TV. Ask for a room facing the river.

(☎834 53 49. Singles 250 pesos; doubles 280 pesos.) **Hotel Parroquia**, Escuela Militar 4, left of the cathedral on Parque Rodríguez Cano, has musty rooms with fans, TV, and phone, all at rock-bottom prices. Ask for a room with a balcony. (☎834 16 30. Singles 153 pesos; doubles 179 pesos; triples 214 pesos; quads 234 pesos.) **Hotel El Huasteco**, Morelos 41, is a block left of Parque Reforma when facing the river. Claustrophobes may do well to skip the small, windowless rooms, but low prices and a good location make it comfortable enough for a night's stay. (☎834 18 59. Singles 130 pesos, with A/C 110 pesos; doubles 170 pesos; triples 210 pesos.) Those seeking budget luxury should head for **Hotel Plaza**, Juárez 39. Smack between Tuxpan's two main plazas, its large rooms come with beautiful wooden furniture, phones, TVs, A/C, and room service from the adjoining restaurant. (☎834 07 38 or 834 08 38. Singles 306 pesos; doubles 366 pesos.)

✿ FOOD. Along *el bulevar*, especially near the bridge, food vendors grill cheap seafood tacos and *gorditas*, and downtown itself has no shortage of small restaurants and *taquerías*. On a hot, humid evening in Parque Reforma, nothing is more refreshing than a *licuado* of fresh seasonal fruits (10-12 pesos). A great place to dine, **✿Los Girasoles** (The Sunflowers) is a dancer's paradise on weekends. This waterfront restaurant and bar, on Reyes Heroles at Hernandez, is decorated with phones, license plates, instruments, and bikes nailed to the wall. Everything, from steak entrees (40-60 pesos) to fried plantains (35 pesos), is delicious, and the wide screen TV is a great place to watch some *fútbol*. (☎834 003 92. Open Su-F noon-midnight, Sa noon-late.) **El Mejicano**, Morelos 49, opposite Parque Reforma, seats you among bright colors and imitation Riveras. The regional menu includes *enfrijoladas* (warm tortillas rolled in a black bean sauce and stuffed with cheese or chicken) and vegetarian options (32 pesos; ☎834 89 04. Open daily 6am-midnight). Yummy seafood in a serene setting can be found at **Las Canta Ranas** (The Singing Frogs), on Reyes Herdes, one block east of Hotel Riviera. A red brick patio, palm trees, and a view of the river add to the charm of this restaurant and bar. Twelve different shrimp dishes (75 pesos) and crab and octopus cocktails delight seafood lovers. (☎834 19 22. Open Tu-Su 1pm-late; kitchen closes 11pm.)

◉◀ SIGHTS AND BEACHES. *Tuxpeños* are justifiably proud of their beautiful river and scenic shores. Palm trees line the boardwalk, and at the market under the bridge, piles of well-priced pineapples, bananas, shrimp, and fish await.

Those interested in Mexico's somewhat intimate relationship with Castro should visit **◉La Casa de la Amistad Mexico-Cuba**, across the river via a blue ferry (2 pesos). Photos of a strapping, beardless Castro line the walls, taken during his stay in Tuxpan while exiled from Cuba in the late 1950s. From the ferry, walk two blocks from the river, then turn right on Obregón and follow it to its end; the museum is on your left. (Open daily 8am-7pm. Free.)

Twelve kilometers from the city center, Tuxpan's **Playa Azul** can be crowded with families and slightly dirty, but the fine sand stretches far enough for you to stake a claim somewhere under the wild coconut palms. Accessible by the "Playa" bus (½hr.; every 15min. 6am-10pm, last bus returns 8pm; 5 pesos).

✿ NIGHTLIFE. There are a number of bars in Tuxpan's *centro*, but problems with brawls and rowdy night owls are commonplace. The safest nightlife can be found after the crowds in the Parque Reforma thin out, a few blocks down the river at **Los Girasoles**, Reyes Heroles at Hernandez. Saturday nights, live rock draws the town's biggest crowds. (☎834 03 92. Open Su-Th 10am-midnight, F-Sa 10am-late. Cover Sa 40 pesos.) **Mantarraya**, Reyes Heroles, one block past the bridge, is the perfect place to break it down with a mixed-age crowd. Not-quite-current pop and techno hits. One Saturday a month, the club features "go-go dancers" (essentially, strippers who don't get all the way naked) of both the *chica* and *chavo* (male and female) variety, attracting straight and gay oglers. (☎834 00 51. Cover 20-40 pesos, including 2 drinks. Open Th-Sa 8:30pm-3am.)

FESTIVALS. Every Sunday night, townspeople crowd the two parks for **Domingos Familiares** (Family Sundays). In Parque Rodríguez Cano, little kids jump on mini-trampolines and drive bumper cars while adoring parents chat. In Parque Reforma, older couples prove romance never dies and dance to Latin classics, while teens try to look sexy as they down *liquidas frescas*. On a grander scale, August 15 marks the beginning of the **Feria Exposición**, a week-long display of town spirit. Traditional dance and song, cockfights, and open-air theater productions abound. On December 7, Tuxpan celebrates **El Día del Nino Perdido** (Day of the Missing Child), which remembers the oft-overlooked Gospel story of the day Mary and Joseph lost the child Jesus returning from the temple. In the evening, hundreds of local children light candles and walk the streets with colorful homemade cardboard "cars," to help Mary and Joseph find their missing son.

POZA RICA   ☎ 7

Known more for its industry than its history or culture, Poza Rica is one of the busiest oil centers in the country. Lush, green Poza Rica serves as a transportation hub for the northern part of the state, providing easy access to nearby Papantla and the ruins of **El Tajín.**

⊑ TRANSPORTATION. From the two adjoining bus stations in the northwest corner of town, the *centro* is accessible by "Centro" or "Juárez" minibuses (10-15min., 3 pesos). The station on the left is served exclusively by ADO, while the one on the right has several lines with less extensive service. ADO goes to: **Brownsville** (5 per day, 424 pesos); **Mexico City** (5hr., every hr., 127 pesos); **Papantla** (30min., every hr., 11 pesos); **Tampico** (5hr., every 30min., 136 pesos); **Tuxpan** (45min., every 30min., 24 pesos); **Veracruz** (4hr., 20 per day, 113 pesos); **Villahermosa** (10 per day, 377 pesos); **Xalapa** (4hr., 12 per day, 123 pesos). Estrella Blanca buses leave from the other station for: **Mexico City** (5hr., every 30min., 127 pesos) and **Tampico** (5hr., every hr., 136 pesos). Transportes Papantla motors to smaller regional destinations. Omnibus de México goes to **Tuxpan** (45min., every hr., 36 pesos) and **Guadalajara** (10hr., 3 per day 6:15-10:15pm, 435 pesos).

⋒ PRACTICAL INFORMATION. Poza Rica provides most services, but there is no tourist office. **Bank: Bital,** in Soriana Plaza next to the bus stations, exchanges traveler's checks and has a 24hr. **ATM.** (☎822 18 77. Open M-Sa 8am-7pm.) **Supermarket: Soriana,** the enormous shopping plaza is to the right as you exit the stations. (Open daily 8am-10pm.) **Luggage Storage:** In the bus station next to ADO, across from Turistar (3 pesos per hr.). **Emergency:** ☎060. **Red Cross:** ☎822 01 01. **Police:** ☎822 04 07. **Pharmacy:** in either station. (Open 24hr.) **FAX: Telecomm,** next to the post office. (Open M-F 8am-7:30pm, Sa 9am-5pm, Su 9am-noon.) **Post Office:** Calle 16 Ote., across from Parque Juárez, accessible by minibus to the *centro.* **MexPost** inside. (☎823 01 02. Open M-F 8am-4pm, Sa 9am-1pm.) **Postal code:** 93261.

⋒⋒ ACCOMMODATIONS AND FOOD. Should you decide to spend a night in town, several mid-priced to expensive hotels are available in the *centro,* along **Cortínez.** Near the stations resides the dirt-cheap **Hotel Farolito,** to the left as you exit either station. Only those desperate to save pesos could stand the small dark rooms with peeling paint and a musty smell. All rooms have TVs and fans. (☎824 34 66. Singles 100 pesos; doubles 120 pesos.) Nicer, clean rooms with A/C and TV await guests at **Auto Hotel Los Arcos** down the road. (☎822 16 00. Singles 200 pesos; doubles 250 pesos.) The restaurant and bar **Palma Sola** next door is an excellent place to relax and grab a bite. *Antojitos* 15 pesos, mixed drinks 20 pesos. (☎823 53 73. Open daily 8am-10pm.) Hidden inside Soriana Plaza is **Dona Torta's,** a counter-top restaurant that only serves *gorditas* (5-10 pesos. Open daily 8am-10pm).

◎ SIGHTS. The archaeological site of ▨**El Tajín** (see p. 504) is just 20min. from Poza Rica, halfway to Papantla. To get there from the bus station, take the minibus to the *centro*, and ask the driver to let you off at **Monumento a la Madre**, on the corner of Cortínez and Cárdenas. From there, hop on any bus that says "Papantla" or "Chote" (7.5 pesos), which will drop you right at the entrance.

PAPANTLA   ☎ 7

Papantla (pop. 81,293) is almost picture-perfect. Sprawling the green foothills of the Sierra Madre Oriental, it overlooks the magnificent plains of Veracruz. One of the few remaining centers of Totonac culture, Papantla sits 12km north of **El Tajín** ruins, an important Totonac city during the Classic Period. Conquered by the Aztecs in 1450, the Totonacs soon took revenge upon their enemies by joining Cortés in his march to Tenochtitlán. After the conquest, the Spanish discovered the city's delicious, long-cultivated vanilla and introduced it worldwide, titling Papantla "city that perfumes the world." Perhaps the most enduring mark of the city's indigenous history, however, is the flight of the *voladores*, a thrilling acrobatic ceremony laden with religious meaning, performed on weekends for delighted tourists.

▐ TRANSPORTATION. Papantla lies 250km northwest of Veracruz and 21km southeast of Poza Rica on **Mex. 180.** From the **ADO bus station,** Juárez 207 (☎842 02 18), to the *centro*, turn left on Juárez, and veer left at the fork. The walk is steep but short. Taxis (8.5 pesos) pass frequently along Juárez. If arriving at the **Second class bus station,** 20 de Noviembre 200, commonly called **Transportes Papantla,** turn left outside the station and ascend 20 de Noviembre three blocks, to the northwest corner of the plaza. ADO goes to: **Mexico City** (5hr., 9 per day 9:40am-12:45am, 137 pesos); **Tuxpan** (1½hr., 7 per day, 32 pesos); **Veracruz** (4hr., 7 per day, 104 pesos); **Xalapa** (4hr., 8 per day, 114 pesos). Call ahead—buses are often booked before they arrive in Papantla. The second class terminal sends buses to nearby **Poza Rica** (40min., every 20min. 4am-10pm, 11 pesos). Pay after boarding.

▣▐ ORIENTATION AND PRACTICAL INFORMATION. The central plaza, **Parque Téllez,** is bordered on the south by a white-washed cathedral on **Nuñez y Domínguez,** and on the north by **Enríquez.** The **tourist office** is in the Palacio Municipal, on the main plaza. Enter on the side of the building, around the block to the right if you're facing the Palacio. Knowledgeable staff provide maps. (☎842 00 26, ext. 714. Open M-F 9am-3pm and 6-9pm.) Banks on the northern side of the plaza, including **Banamex,** Enríquez 102, have 24hr. **ATMs.** (☎842 00 01. Open M-F 9am-5pm, Sa 9:30am-2pm; open for exchange M-F 9am-2pm.) **Supermarket: General de Muebles de Papantla,** Azueta 200, half a block from the main plaza. (☎842 00 23. Open M-Sa 8:30am-8:30pm, Su 10am-2pm and 4-8pm.) **Emergency:** ☎060. **Police:** (☎842 00 75), in the Palacio Municipal. **Red Cross:** (☎842 01 26), on Escobedo off Juárez. Some English spoken. **Pharmacy: El Fenix,** Enríquez 103E, at the north end of the plaza. (☎842 06 36. Open daily 8am-11pm.) **Hospitals: IMSS,** 20 de Noviembre (☎842 01 94), at Lázaro Cárdenas. From the ADO station, take a right and walk two blocks to Cárdenas, then turn left; IMSS is half a block up on the right. **Clínica del Centro Medico,** (☎842 00 82), on 16 de Septiembre near the tourist office. Little English spoken. **FAX: Telecomm,** on Olivo, off 20 de Noviembre near Hotel Totanacapán. (Open M-F 8am-7pm, Sa 9am-5pm, Su 9am-noon.) **LADATELS** stand along Enríquez in the main plaza. **Internet: Estación Web,** Juárez 201, downhill from the plaza. (☎842 15 48. 10 pesos per hr. Open daily 9am-10pm.) **Post office:** Azueta 198, 2nd fl., with MexPost, unmarked from the outside—head to the supermarket building General de Muebles. (☎842 00 73. Open M-F 9am-4pm.) **Postal code:** 93400.

▐ ACCOMMODATIONS. A few excellent budget lodgings exist in tiny Papantla. The lovely, economical **Hotel Totanacapán** is at 20 de Noviembre at Olivo, four blocks from the plaza. While it doesn't seem like much from the outside, hallway murals, bright colors, funky tiling, and large windows make it unintentionally retro-cool. (☎842 12 24. TVs, phones, and A/C. Singles 190 pesos; doubles 220 pesos.) A step up in ritz, **Hotel Tajín,** Núñez y Domínguez 104, half a block to the left from the plaza as you face the cathedral, has a stone-carved replica of El Tajín in the lobby. Shared balconies open to panoramic views. Perks include bottled water, cable TV, and phones. Guided horseback tours available with one-week advance notice. (☎842 01 21. Singles 265 pesos, with A/C 256 pesos; doubles 366 pesos, with A/C 478 pesos; each additional person 60 pesos. Horse tours US$30 per hr.) If these rates make you uneasy, head to **Hotel Pulido,** Enríquez 205, two blocks to the left of the main plaza, facing the cathedral. It has a tiled courtyard and sparkling rooms with fans and hot water. (☎842 00 36. Singles 130 pesos; doubles 190 pesos; each additional person 30 pesos.)

⊡ FOOD. Papantla's tourist-oriented downtown restaurants serve regional goodies—usually beef and pork. Specialties include *molotes,* Mexican dumplings of spiced meat wrapped in a boiled corn shell, and *bocoles,* stout fried tortillas filled with egg, cheese, sausage, or chicken. Papantla's delicious *tamales,* are served on weekends only. **Restaurant "Por Si a Caso Me Recuerdas,"** Juan Enríquez 102, sits to the left of the main plaza when facing the cathedral. Listen as the young cooks sing along to Spanish MTV, and enjoy the calm at this local hideaway. Its amazing food comes fast, hot, and cheap. (☎842 11 12. Four *bocoles* 12-16 pesos, chicken *mole* with rice 25 pesos. Open Su-W 7am-1am, Th-Sa 24hr.) **La Hacienda,** Reforma 100, overlooks the plaza. Families crowd this popular eatery for the great food and relaxing ambience. Healthy options include fruit salads, yogurt and granola, and *liquadas refrescas.* For dinner, don't miss the *enfrijoladas* (warm tortillas soaked in a black bean and cream sauce and stuffed with chicken or eggs, 21 pesos. Open daily 7:30am-11:30pm).

◪ SIGHTS. Papantla's biggest attractions are relics of its Totonac heritage. **Catedral Señora de la Asunción** overlooks the main plaza and has a remarkable 50m-long, 5m-high stone mural on its outer wall. Called *Homenaje a la Cultura Totonaca,* the mural—based on a relief from El Tajín—depicts eager Totonac ballplayers vying for the honor of ritualistic death and deification. On Sunday afternoons, the cathedral's spacious courtyard, **Plaza de los Voladores,** is where *voladores* (see **Fly Guys,** below) acrobatically entreat the rain god Tlaloc to water local crops. **Monumento al Volador,** Papantla's latest effort to enshrine its *voladores,* is a gigantic, flute-wielding *indígena* statue erected atop a hill in 1988 and visible all over town. To reach the monument, from which all of Papantla is visible, walk up Reforma, the road that passes the entrance to the cathedral (5-10min.). Both the view of the city and of couples making out at the statue's base are memorable. **La Casa de la Cultura,** the first right walking downhill on Pino Suárez off Enríquez, gives classes in Totonac language, dance, sculpture, and painting. The gallery upstairs shows a small but wonderful collection of paintings inspired by Totonac history. (☎842 24 27. Open M-F 8am-3pm.) **Museo de la Ciudad,** at Pino Suárez and Madero, displays murals on Totonac history, traditional clothing, and an impressive photographic time line of local history. (☎842 02 21. Open Tu-Su 10am-2pm and 4-8pm.)

⚐ SHOPPING. The town's two markets are situated next to the *zócalo.* **Mercado Juárez,** at Reforma and 16 de Septiembre off the southwest corner of the *zócalo,* specializes in fruits, vegetables, and freshly-butchered meat. **Mercado Hidalgo,** on 20 de Noviembre off the northwest corner, has fun *artesanía,* clothing, and souvenirs. This is the best place to buy Papantla's world-renowned **vanilla**—nearly every stand sells high-quality vanilla extract (20-100 pesos) and yummy vanilla liqueur (100 pesos per bottle). If you're counting pesos, shopkeepers are more than happy to give out small samples—hit every stand and you might get a buzz.

FESTIVALS. In early June, the 10-day Festival of Corpus Christi celebrates both the indigenous and Christian traditions of Papantla. Most of the action occurs at a

FLY GUYS The performance begins with five elaborately costumed men climbing a stationary pole to a platform at least 28m above the ground. Having consumed courage-enhancing fluids, the *voladores* (literally "fliers") begin by saluting the four cardinal points in a traditional dance around the pole. Four of the five then wind ropes around the pole, tie them to their waists, and start to "fly"—hanging from the ropes, spinning through the air, and slowly descending to earth. The fifth man plays a flute and dances on the pole's pin-head. Originally, each of the fliers corresponded to one of the four cardinal directions: the sun, wind, moon, and earth. Positions assumed during descent were related to requests for specific weather conditions. Now, the ritual has been commercialized: instead of performing once every 52 years, the *voladores* fly whenever tourists hand over pesos. You can watch the ceremony in Papantla during the festival of Corpus Christi in early June, at El Tajín whenever a crowd gathers, or in New York or Denmark when the *voladores* go on tour.

fair just outside town, with artistic expositions, fireworks, traditional dances, and cockfights. To get to the festival from the *centro*, flag down a taxi (15 pesos) or take any *pesero* (3 pesos) from 16 de Septiembre behind the cathedral and ask for the *feria*. In town, the *voladores* perform as often as three times a day, morning, afternoon, and evening. Once every 52 years, at the turning of the Totonac century, the festival takes on larger proportions.

NEAR PAPANTLA: ■ EL TAJÍN

El Tajín is accessible from Papantla via the white and blue peseros that stop at the corner of 16 de Septiembre and Reforma, next to the cathedral's courtyard (20min., every 15min. 5am-8pm, 7.5 pesos). Hop on a "Poza Rica" bus (it may also say "Chote" and "Tajín") and check with the driver to make sure it stops at El Tajín. The bus will pass through the town of El Chote, then stop at the entrance to El Tajín. To return to Papantla, catch a "Papantla" bus outside the museum (last bus at 5pm, 7.5 pesos). Ruins open daily 8am-7pm. 30 pesos, children under 13, adults over 60, and Su free.

Gazing at the impressive ruins of El Tajín, it's easy to imagine the thriving Totonac civilization that spread across modern-day northern Veracruz during the Classic Period. Though the ruins were "discovered" by the Spanish in 1785 (natives of the area always knew of its existence), restoration work did not begin until 1939. The area was probably settled around AD 100 by Huastec peoples before the Totonacs razed their structures and began seriously constructing the area early in the Classic Period (AD 300-400). The Totonac name is a Spanish derivative of the Náhuatl *Tutu Nacu*, which means "three hearts" and refers to the three major city centers of Totonac culture, of which El Tajín is one. In Totonac, "Tajín" means "thunder," "lightning," or "hurricane," and thus it is believed that the Totonacs dedicated this city to the god of rain. In the mid-Classic Period (AD 600-900), El Tajín was a Totonac capital, perhaps subservient only to Teotihuacán in the Valley of Mexico. For reasons still unclear, the area declined early in the Post-Classic Period, around AD 1200. Most archaeologists now believe the city was conquered and burned by invading nomadic tribes such as the Chichimecs. The Totonacs who remained in the area were brought under the control of the Aztecs in the late 15th century.

MUSEUM AND ENTRANCE AREA. Next to the entrance stands a large pole, the apparatus of *voladores* (performances June-Aug. every hr., Sept.-May weekends only). The daring acrobats typically request a 10-peso donation. A tiny but useful brochure and map about El Tajín in English or Spanish (6 pesos) can be purchased at the store adjoining the **information desk.** A small **restaurant** at the entrance makes seafood *comida corrida* (35 pesos). Entering the ruins, you pass **Museo de Sitio,** a museum featuring original mural fragments and a morbidly fascinating display of ancient skeletons, some with cracked skulls and visible bone injuries. From the museum, a straight path leads to the ruins, which are unlabeled or unexplained. The best sources of information are guidebooks or a guided tour (15 pesos).

PLAZA DE ARROYO. The Plaza, the central rectangle formed by four tiered pyramids, lies just to the left of the gravel road. Each pyramid points toward the northeast at a 20-degree angle, a common feature among the site's early buildings.

JUEGO DE PELOTA SUR (SOUTH BALLCOURT). Past the pyramids, two identical, low-lying, slanted constructions, to the left of the main path, form a central grass ballcourt where the famous one-on-one ball game was played. Every 52 years, a contest was held between the most valiant ballplayers. The winner earned the honor of being decapitated and deified, putting the World Cup to shame. Approximately 17 such courts grace the ruins of Tajín. This particular ballcourt is famous for its carved stone walls depicting the ball games in action.

THE CENTRAL ZONE. Across from the plaza stands an elevated central altar surrounded by two climbable temples. Left of the altar is a split-level temple that displays a statue of Tajín. This area, known as the Central Zone, is notable for the diverse styles and functions of its buildings.

LA PIRÁMIDE DE LOS NICHOS. To the northwest stands the Pyramid of Niches, El Tajín's most recognizable structure, with seven levels and a total of 365 niches corresponding to the days of the year. Each niche was once painted crimson and blue. The Totonacs kept time in 52-year epochs, during which a single flame was kept continuously burning. At the end of each epoch, the carefully nurtured flame was used to ritually torch many of the settlement's buildings. Each new epoch of rebuilding and regeneration was inaugurated by the lighting of a new flame. Ritual ceremonies are now held annually at the pyramid. During the vernal equinox, farmers place seeds in the pyramid's niches and later retrieve them for planting.

TAJÍN CHICO. Atop a hill to the north is **Tajín Chico,** accessible by a series of large stepping stones and a staircase to the west. While Tajín was a public religious and social center, archaeologists hypothesize that Tajín Chico provided shelter to the ruling class and political elite. One of the less-excavated areas, it is rimmed with "no access" signs. East of Tajín Chico, down the hill and around the curve, is the **Great Xicalcoliuhqui,** a recreational and religious area currently being unearthed.

VERACRUZ
☎ 2

The oldest port city in the Americas, Veracruz (pop. 327,500) is an assault on the senses. Intense humidity and often unbearable heat envelop the city, while a powerful scent of salt water and fish pervades the air. Small *marimba* bands and lone guitarists pop in and out of restaurants and bars, providing a constant sound track. The history of this strategically located state capital is appropriately bloody. After Cortés first landed at La Rica Villa de la Vera Cruz in 1519, the city was immersed in a swashbuckling era dominated by Spanish galleons, pirates, and the slave trade. Four subsequent invasions of Veracruz, the last ordered by Woodrow Wilson in 1914, didn't act to calm the steamy port. Today, residents, sailors, and tourists alike fill the streets—languishing by day and dancing by night. Locals and visitors alike love to indulge in nighttime strolls along the beach. Parked cars blare *marimba*, pick-up soccer games cover the sand, and nocturnal vendors promote their wares—Mexico's *sabor* has never been greater.

⊏ TRANSPORTATION

Airport: (☎934 37 74), 8km south of downtown Veracruz on Mex. 150. Taxis will take you there for 120 pesos. **Aeroméxico** (☎935 01 42) and **Mexicana** (☎932 22 42).

Buses: From Parque Zamora, Mirón connects the *centro* to the **Central de Autobuses Veracruz (CAVE),** Mirón 1698, which houses all the city's major bus lines. To get to the *centro* from the bus station, get on a "Díaz Mirón" bus headed north to Parque Zamora (4 pesos). Some buses run all the way to the *zócalo;* others stop at the park, 7 blocks south on Independencia. To return to the bus station, take a southbound "Díaz Mirón" bus from anywhere along 5 de Mayo. ADO (☎937 57 88) goes to: **Cancún** (21hr., 1am and 4pm, 720 pesos); **Catemaco** (3hr., 7 per day, 70 pesos); **Mexico City** (5½hr., 16 per day, 245 pesos); **Xalapa** (1¾hr., 50 per day 2:30am-11:30pm, 49 pesos). Cristóbal Colón (☎937 57 88) runs to **Oaxaca** (6½hr., 11pm, 282 pesos) and **Tuxtla Gutiérrez** (12hr., 4 and 8:15pm, 287 pesos). Cuenca (☎935 04 03) sends 2nd-class buses to **Oaxaca** (6hr., 8pm, 205 pesos) and **Tuxtepec** (3hr., every hr. 5am-8pm, 64 pesos). AU (☎937 57 32), 1 block behind the ADO station on the right side, offers 2nd-class service to: **Córdoba** (1½hr., 16 per day 6am-12:30am, 53 pesos); **Mexico City** (6hr., 16 per day 1am-midnight, 197 pesos); **Orizaba** (2½hr., 16 per day 6am-12:30am, 64 pesos); **Puebla** (4½hr.; 2, 8, 10:15am, 12:30pm; 140 pesos); **Xalapa** (1¾hr., 16 per day 6am-12:30am, 39 pesos).

✳🛈 ORIENTATION AND PRACTICAL INFORMATION

Veracruz sprawls along the coast in the southwest corner of the Gulf of Mexico, 104km south of Xalapa and 424km east of Mexico City. Along the south coast, Veracruz merges with the glam suburb **Boca del Río**. Home to luxury hotels, shopping malls, and sparkling shorelines, it is easily reached by the "Boca del Rio" buses which leave from **Zaragoza**, one block toward the bay from the *zócalo* (4 pesos). Buses are less frequent at night; taxis are a safer choice.

Tourist Office: (☎939 88 00, ext. 158), on the right side of the Palacio Municipal, facing the *zócalo*. Tons of brochures and a friendly staff. Open M-Sa 8am-8pm, Su 10am-6pm.

Currency Exchange: A slew of banks and *casas de cambio* pack the corner of Juárez and Independencia, 1 block north of the *zócalo*. **Banamex,** open M-F 8:30am-5pm, Sa 9am-2pm, and **Bital,** open M-Sa 8am-7pm, both have **24hr. ATM's.**

American Express: Camacho 221 (☎931 46 36), inside Viajes Olymar, across from Villa del Mar beach. Take a "Villa del Mar" bus. Open M-F 9am-8pm, Sa 9am-noon.

Markets: Mercado Hidalgo, Cortés at Madero, 1 block from Parque Zamora away from the Gulf, sells fruit, vegetables, *piñatas*, and more. Open daily 8am-8pm.

Supermarket: El Alba, Lerdo 270 (☎932 24 24), between Independencia and 5 de Mayo. Open M-Sa 9am-2:30pm and 5-9pm.

Laundry: Lavandería Ultra-Clean, Serdán 789, between Madero and 5 de Mayo. Same-day service. 7 pesos per kg. Open M-Sa 9:30am-7:30pm.

Luggage Storage: At the bus station. 5 pesos per hr.

Bicycle Rental: on Camacho at Bolívar, along Villa del Mar beach. 25-30 pesos per hr.

Emergency: ☎060.

Police: (☎938 06 64 or 938 06 93) at Colonial Palieno.

Red Cross: (☎937 55 00), on Mirón between Orizaba and Abascal, 1 block south of the Central de Autobuses, has **ambulance** service. No English spoken.

FOUR TIMES HEROIC Ravaged by pirates and disease, Veracruz has struggled against ill-fate since the time of its founding. After Mexico won its independence, the Spanish continued to attack the port city for 26 months—from September of 1823 to November of 1825. In 1838, during the Pastry War, Veracruz again had to withstand foreign invasion, this time from the French, who occupied the city and demanded reparation for damages suffered after the War of Independence. Santa Anna, the heroic general of the recent war with America, lost his leg here while trying to defend San Juan de Ulúa. American troops first occupied the city in 1847, when General Winfield Scott led an attack that felled the city and resulted in the deaths of more than 1000 Mexicans in just one week. In 1914, American marines again took control of the city, halting a shipment of arms to Mexican dictator Victoriano Huerta. For these four disastrous military encounters, Veracruz has christened itself *Cuatro Veces Heróica*. And heroic it is—after so many defeats, it's a wonder the city still stands.

Pharmacy: Farmacía del Ahorro, on Díaz Mirón, in front of the Social Security building. Open 24hr. Also on the *malecón* at Gómez Farías 2 (☎937 35 25).

Hospital: IMSS, Mirón 61 (☎932 19 20). **Sanitario Español,** 16 de Septiembre 955 (☎932 00 21), has a good reputation among travelers. No English spoken at either.

Fax: Telecomm (☎932 25 08), on Plaza de la República, to the left of the post office. Open M-F 8am-7pm, Sa 9am-5pm, Su 9am-noon.

Internet Access: Netchatboys, Lerdo 369, between Madero and 5 de Mayo. 15 pesos per hr., students 12 pesos per hr. Open M-F 9am-9pm, Sa-Su noon-8pm. **Webcafe,** Rayon 579A, is an easy step from Parque Zamora. 18 pesos per hr., students 15 pesos per hr. Open M-Sa 10am-10pm.

Post Office: Marina Mercante 213 (☎932 20 38), at Plaza de la República. Open M-F 8am-4pm, Sa 9am-1pm.

Postal Code: 91700.

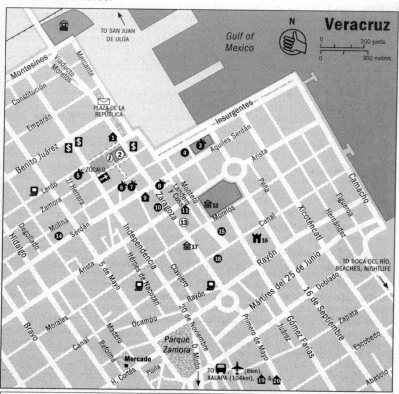

Veracruz

🔺 ACCOMMODATIONS
Hotel Amparo, **9**
Hotel Central, **19**
Hotel Latino, **20**
Hotel México, **1**
Hotel Santillana, **11**

🍎 ♪ FOOD AND NIGHTLIFE
Cochinito de Oro, **8**
El Alba Supermarket, **5**
Gran Cafe de la Parroquia, **3**
La Gaviota, **7**
Mariscos Tano, **6**

● 🏨 🏛 ○ SIGHTS AND SERVICES
Baluarte de Santiago, **16**
Casa de la Cultura, **15**
Casa de Salvador Díaz Mirón, **13**
Farmacia del Ahorro, **4**
Guayaberas Finas, **10**
Instituto Veracruzano de Cultura (IVEC), **18**
Lavandería Ultra Clean, **14**
Museo de la Ciudad, **17**
Museo Histórico Naval, **12**
Palacio Municipal, **2**

⚑ ACCOMMODATIONS

Veracruz has three high seasons: *Carnaval* (the week before Ash Wednesday), *Semana Santa*, and midsummer. Many hotels fill up well in advance during these times; expect to pay 20-100 pesos more for your room. The luxury of a room with A/C, much needed in this steamy city, ups the price even more.

NEAR THE CENTRO

Budget hotels line Serdán, two blocks from the *zócalo* and Morelos, just north of the *zócalo*. Both streets are fun, loud, and relatively safe.

Hotel Amparo, Serdán 482 (☎932 27 38), ½ block west of Zaragoza. If there are back-packers in Veracruz, they're probably here. Tiny rooms with heat and hot water are neat and inexpensive. Singles 120 pesos; doubles 180 pesos; TV 40 pesos extra.

Hotel México, Morelos 343 (☎932 43 60), across the street from the Aduanos building. Superb location. Bigger and nicer than Amparo. Brown, cabin-like rooms have fans and TVs. Singles 200 pesos; doubles 220 pesos.

Hotel Santillana, Landero y Coss 208 (☎932 31 16), at Dehesa. Small rooms with phones, TVs, and fans. The purple-green courtyard and caged parrots emanate a garish charm. Singles 200 pesos; doubles 350 pesos; each additional person 50 pesos.

NEAR THE BUS STATION

Convenience at a price—most hotels are on La Fragna, behind the ADO station.

Hotel Latino, La Fragua 280 (☎937 65 99). Exit left from the ADO station and walk 1½ blocks. The best bet for a stay near the station. Bare-bulb rooms don't exactly exude high class, but they are well-cleaned and have fans and TVs. Singles 150 pesos, with A/C 200 pesos; doubles 170-200 pesos, with A/C 200-270 pesos.

Hotel Central, Díaz Mirón 1612 (☎932 22 22), to the right of ADO. Modern-looking hotel with a faux-marble lobby and dim hallways. Big rooms have TV, phone, and bath. Singles 220 pesos, with A/C 260 pesos; doubles 270 pesos, with A/C 335 pesos.

⚑ FOOD

Small restaurants surround the fish markets on **Landero** and **Coss**. Eccentrically decorated, these are the places to dig into the mountains of fish, shrimp, octopus, and crab hauled out of the gulf on a daily basis. For a cheaper, slightly more frantic experience, try **Mercado Hidalgo,** where seafood stands sell fish and shrimp dishes for around 30 pesos. Restaurants under the *portales* in the *zócalo* offer yummy dishes and a *marimba* beat—for a price. Wherever you choose to dine, don't miss out on the distinctive *veracruzano* fare. Always steer clear of raw fish. Instead, order *huachinango a la veracruzana* (red snapper decked out in olives, capers, onions, and olive oil). Other regional specialties include *filete relleno* (fish fillet stuffed with *mariscos*), *arroz a la tumbada* (rice in a sauce that includes—of course—shellfish), and *jaiba* (large local crab).

🍴 **Gran Cafe de la Parroquia,** Farías 34 (☎932 35 84), on the *malecón*. A Veracruz tradi-tion, the entire town seems to gather here, and every president since 1810 has sipped the famous *lechero* (13 pesos). Entrees 14-70 pesos. Open daily 6am-1am.

🍴 **El Cochinito de Oro,** Zaragoza 190 (☎932 36 77), at Serdán. Cheap, excellent seafood explains El Cochinito's 50-year popularity with locals. Memorabilia scattered over the interior entertains as you wait. *Filete de pescado* and fish or shrimp stews average 35 pesos. Vegetarians can enjoy *huevos al gusto* (15 pesos). Open daily 7am-5pm.

Mariscos Tano, Molina 20 (☎931 50 50), 1 block south of the *zócalo*. A good place for anyone with limited Spanish proficiency. The menu is printed in English, and just about everything listed is stuffed and hanging from the ceiling. The *mariscos* (shellfish) are good, and the photo-history of *Carnaval* on the back wall is museum quality. A singing staff adds to the the laid-back atmosphere. Open daily 9am-10pm.

La Gaviota, Callejón de Trigueros 21 (☎932 39 50), ½ block from the intersection of Zaragoza and Serdán. The quiet, simple ambience and regional specialties are reminiscent of *zócalo* quality at more affordable prices. *Filete a la veracruzano* 48 pesos, *antojitos* 12-22 pesos. Open 24hr.

👁 SIGHTS

When it wasn't being blasted by bullets or mobbed by mosquitos, Veracruz had to contend with the fierce north wind known as *nortes*—both a curse and the reason the city rose to such importance as a center for Transatlantic trade. Most of the city's sites relate to one of its many military encounters, and young naval officers staff the museums, ready to offer official information.

■ **CASTILLO DE SAN JUAN DE ULÚA.** The fortress, Veracruz's most important historic site, rests on a fingertip of land jutting into the harbor. Using coral chunks as bricks, construction began sometime after Cortés's arrival under the order of Charles V. It was intended as part of the system of fortifications built to protect Spanish treasure from Caribbean pirates. However, after 1825, the building was used as a high-security jail for big-name political prisoners such as presidents Benito Juárez and Porfirio Díaz. Famous politicos aside, San Juan's best-known prisoner was the folk hero **Chucho el Roto,** a Robin Hood-like figure who stole from the rich and gave to the poor. El Roto's legend has grown to mythic proportions, as he is believed to have escaped from San Juan three times. *(Take a "San Juan de Ulúa" bus (3 pesos) in front of the Aduana building in Plaza de la República. Buses come infrequently and stop running at 5pm. Taxis charge around 40 pesos. ☎938 51 51. Open Tu-Su 9am-5pm. 20 pesos; Su free. Guided tours, 10 pesos in Spanish, 15 pesos in English, are well worth the cash.)*

■ **MUSEO HISTÓRICO NAVAL.** The museum, located on the grounds of Veracruz's Naval School, is a sailor's air-conditioned dream. Gallery after gallery of model ships, entertaining dioramas on man's seafaring history, and displays on Veracruz's naval successes and shortcomings make for an enjoyable navigation of Mexico's rich maritime history. *(Walk 3 blocks down Independencia and turn left on Arista for 2 blocks; the Naval School is on your right, occupying the entire block bordered by 16 de Septiembre, Arista, Montero, and Morales. ☎931 40 78. Open Tu-Su 9am-5pm. Free.)*

BALUARTE DE SANTIAGO. Built in 1526, the Baluarte is today the sole remnant of the stone wall that once encircled a good part of the city, protecting its inhabitants from pirates. The wall, along with the eight other *baluartes* (small forts), was torn down in the late 19th century. The museum inside displays a small and none-too-impressive collection of Pre-Hispanic gold ornaments called *Las Joyas del Pescador,* named for their rescue from the ocean by a lucky octopus fisherman. Around the back of the fort, a small spiral staircase leads to a pretty tower view. *(On Canal between 16 de Septiembre and Farías, 1 block from the Naval School. ☎931 10 59. Open Tu-Su 10am-4:30pm. 30 pesos; Su free.)*

MUSEO DE LA CIUDAD. Completely renovated in summer 2000, this vamped-up museum features paintings and dioramas depicting the history of the city from Pre-Hispanic times to the present. Television clips and guides help you as you go along. In the back stairwell, a stained-glass window tells the legend of Talinmasca, an orphan whose transgressions brought thunder, lighting, and the fierce autumn *nortes* to the area. *(Zaragoza 397. Down Canal away from the water, and right on Zaragoza. ☎931 84 10. Open W-M 10am-6pm. 25 pesos, students 10 pesos.)*

ACUARIO DE VERACRUZ. A popular family beachside attraction, the aquarium features fish, sharks, and turtles native to the gulf. *(In the Centro Comercial Plaza Acuario, a shopping mall on the left when facing the ocean at Villa del Mar. Catch a "Villa del Mar" bus on Zaragoza (3 pesos). ☎931 10 20. Open daily 10am-8pm. 20 pesos, children 10 pesos.)*

CASA DE SALVADOR DÍAZ MIRÓN. The famous *veracruzano* poet Díaz Mirón lived here for the final years of his life (1921-1928), and locals claim to still hear his ghost pacing the upper chambers. Today the house serves as a literary center for Veracruz. The renovated foyer holds temporary art exhibitions. Upstairs, a small museum replicates what the house looked like while occupied by Mirón. *(Zaragoza 332, between Morelos and Arista. ☎ 989 88 60, ext. 146. Open M-Sa 10am-8pm. Free.)*

🏖 BEACHES

The general rule for beaches in Veracruz is that the farther from the city, the nicer the beach, although it's practically impossible to escape the oil barges and tugboats in the distance. **Playa Villa del Mar** is a pleasant hour-long walk from the *zócalo* along the waterfront. It is also accessible via one of the frequent "Villa del Mar" or "Boca del Río" buses (4 pesos) that stop on Zaragoza behind the tourist office. Few people swim at Villa del Mar—restaurants have set up camp along the boardwalk, and their beachside presence makes frolicking in the sand almost impossible. Still, the restaurant huts and bars create a lively atmosphere at night.

The best beach in the Veracruz area (although that's not saying much) is **Playa Mocambo**, in the neighboring city of **Boca del Río.** Take a "Boca del Río" bus from Zaragoza and Serdán and get off at the mall, Plaza de Las Americas (30min.). The beach is on the other side of Hotel Torremar. Veer left for the beach or go straight into **Balneario Mocambo**, which has a clean, Olympic-sized public pool surrounded by artificial palm trees, changing rooms, and a pool side bar-restaurant. (☎ 931 02 88. Open daily 10am-6pm. 25 pesos, children 20 pesos.) Those who define their beach experiences by attitude rather than turquoise water will find plenty of laidback lounging in the residential area down the coast from the hotel.

🎵 🎭 ENTERTAINMENT AND NIGHTLIFE

In the evening, the hymns of the cathedral spilling out into the *zócalo* yield to the sexy rhythms of *marimbas*. Vendors spread their wares on the paths, and bars and restaurants fill with merry drinkers and *mariachi* bands. On weekend nights, some of the world's hottest senior citizens strut their stuff on the civic dance floor. Apart from this spontaneous merrymaking in the *zócalo*, most action takes place along **Camacho**, the seaside road connecting Veracruz and Boca del Río. Just before the purple high-rise landmark Hotel Lois, **Ruiz Cortínes** branches off Camacho, providing a great place to get off the bus.

BARS AND CLUBS

🏆**Aquarius Bar and Club,** Camacho 10 (☎ 959 55 06). Tiny tables, giant couches, and a beautiful view of the beach make Aquarius the city's premier choice for nightlife. The safe and very mellow atmosphere gives way to lots of activity on weekend nights. 2-for-1 drinks until 9pm, live music and karaoke at 10pm. Open daily 2pm-1am.

Carlos 'n' Charlie's, Camacho 26 (☎ 922 29 10), has been bestowed on Veracruz by Señor Frog's, the tourist-ridden franchise that just keeps on giving. The restaurant regularly fills to the point of immobility—but that's okay. Everyone sits, drinks, and sings along merrily with *salsa* music. Open Su-Th 9am-midnight, F-Sa 9am-2am.

Master Club Billar, Camacho 4 (☎ 937 67 48), is one of the friendliest, safest pool houses you'll ever see, with TV, music, bar, A/C, and tables for dominoes or cards. Pool 30 pesos per hr. Open daily 4pm-2am.

Zoo (☎ 921 79 35), on Camacho at Medica Militar. A step up in style and popularity, the monolithic stone zoo hosts trend-setters who blow air kisses, scrutinize each other's *haute couture*, and dance all night. Cover 40 pesos. Open F-Sa 10pm-5am.

El Palacio de la Salsa, Calle 12 #33, 4 blocks down Camacho from Cortínes intersection, 1 block right on Medico Militar and another block left on Calle 12. Cover 20 pesos. Open Th-Sa 10pm-6am.

IF IT'S GOOD ENOUGH FOR IKE...

A man can't claim to really know Veracruz until he's donned a traditional white shirt called a *guayabera*, named for the *guayaba* (guava). Cuban guava collectors were so tired of shimmying up and down trees countless times to harvest individual fruits, that they designed a shirt with four pockets to expedite the task. Originally from Cuba, the *guayabera* shirt found its way to Panama and then to Mexico, where Carlos Cab Arrazate added the thin pleats that form vertical stripes connecting the pockets. His grandson continues the family business, **Guayaberas Finas,** Zaragoza 233 (☎931 84 27), between Arista and Serdán, in Veracruz city. Everyone who's anyone has been seen in one of their high-quality, hot-weather shirts—check out US president Dwight D. Eisenhower's note of appreciation on the store's wall. A bit of fashion advice: shirts are not meant to be tucked in. (*Open M-F 9:30am-8pm, Sa 9:30am-7pm, Su 10am-4pm.*)

CULTURAL EVENTS

On any given night, *marimba* bands perform in the *zócalo*, while *mariachi* musicians hover nearby, ready to break into song at the sight of pesos. If you seek more structured entertainment, the **Instituto Veracruzano de Cultura (IVEC)** has weekly music, dance, and folklore performances in addition to movies, expositions, and art shows. Pick up a monthly schedule at IVEC or at the **Casa de la Cultura,** at the corner of Canal and Zaragoza. (☎931 43 96. Open M-F 9am-8pm, Sa-Su 9am-6pm.)

FESTIVALS

Every December 31, from midnight until dawn, *veracruzano* families dress in their Sunday best and fill Camacho, looking east to the Gulf of Mexico to witness the first sunrise of the year. With that auspicious start, a year of celebrations begins. The climax comes early, just before Ash Wednesday, when **Carnaval** invades the *zócalo* with nine days of festivities. The **Festival Internacional Afrocaribeño** takes place every July 11-21 and has a different theme each year—the 2001 festival used coffee as its inspiration. Enjoy music and dancing around the clock.

▶ DAYTRIPS FROM VERACRUZ

ZEMPOALA

From the 2nd-class bus station on La Fragua behind the ADO station, Autobuses TRV sends buses to **Cardel** (45min., 15 pesos). Exit out the right side of the station and walk 2 blocks to the right; the Zempoala bus pick-up is on the cross street at the T-intersection. From there, take a bus to **Zempoala** (25min., 6 pesos). Ask the driver to let you out at the ruins, at the intersection of Ruíz and Troncoso Norte. To return, stand across the street from where you were dropped off and hail a passing "Cardel" bus (6 pesos). From Cardel, catch a bus to Veracruz (45min; every 10min. midnight-8pm, every 15min. 8-10pm; 10 pesos). Site open daily 9am-4:30pm. 27 pesos; Su free.

The impressive ruins at **Zempoala** (sometimes spelled **Cempoala**) lie 40km north of Veracruz off Mex. 180. Zempoala was one of the largest southern Totonac cities and part of a federation that covered much of Veracruz. During its peak in the 14th and 15th centuries, the city may have had as many as 120,000 inhabitants, and many believe it to be the Totonac Post-Classic successor to El Tajín (see p. 504). In 1458, however, the Aztecs conquered the Zempoala and forced the Totonac to join the Aztec federation. When Cortés arrived in 1519, the humbled city had only about 30,000 residents and was eager to assist any enemy of the Aztecs, lending Cortés soldiers and supplies.

The site now consists of stone structures surrounding a grassy field next to present-day Zempoala. The palm trees and peaceful setting of the ruins seem incongruous with their bloody history. The structure closest to the entrance is the **Temple of Death.** To the left of the main path are three **pyramids.** The pyramid on the left is dedicated to Tlaloc (god of rain), the one on the right to the moon, and the one in the center, decorated with circular stone receptacles for the hearts of people sacrificed in religious offerings, to the sun. To the right of the main path is the **Templo Mayor,** the largest building on the site. When Cortés arrived, the Spaniards erected an altar to the Virgin on top of the temple, forcing Catholicism on the Totonacs. In front of the Templo Mayor is the **throne** where the king sat to observe sacrifices. The throne also faces the temple known as **Las Chimeneas,** next to which you will see a fenced-in structure. For the Totonacs, this area played a central role in the "New Five Ceremony," a five-day fast that took place every 52 years when a "century" of the ritual calendar ended. Every spring Equinox, people still come to the circle to expel negative energy and absorb positive energy.

LA ANTIGUA

Take a 2nd-class TRV bus from the Central, behind the ADO station (12 pesos). Tell the driver you want to get off at La Antigua—on the way to Cardel and Zempoala—and keep an eye out for the stop, marked by a tollbooth and a small sign. Cross the street and head up the main road for 15min. until you reach the town's main drag. To return, go back down the road; buses to Veracruz pass frequently from dawn to 9pm. You can also catch a bus from the TRV station in town, but that involves more waiting than it's worth.

When Cortés landed on the coast of Mexico in 1519, he and his army moved north, settling here, the first Spanish town in Mexico. Cortés named the town Villa Rica de la Vera Cruz, but when the city was reestablished in 1599 in its present location 28km away, the old town came to be known as just that—La Antigua. Dotted with overgrown ruins from centuries past, a walk through town is like entering a time warp, where buildings seem to range in age from the 16th to 21st century.

Unlabeled streets and the jungle's tendency to interrupt all things orderly make finding the town's 16th-century buildings something of a scavenger hunt. Crossing the street and taking the perpendicular road branching left of the main road, you'll come to the **Parroquia de Cristo del Buen Viaje,** which dates from the mid-17th century; the interior contains two 16th-century baptismal fonts carved by early indigenous converts. Passing the *zócalo* and continuing down the street, the famous **Casa de Cortés,** where the *conquistador* supposedly lived for a time, is back from the road on the left. The cannon was brought over from Spain by the man himself. Farther down the street, the monster tree that divides the road holds legendary status as the site where Cortés first armed himself for the fateful 1519 expedition. Built in 1523, the **Edificio del Cabildo** was the first office of the Spanish government in Mexico. The most beautiful of the buildings is the **Emerito del Rosario.** Finished in 1524, the building features stations of the cross rendered in Talvera tile. To find these buildings, it's best to ask locals to point the way.

After watching chickens scuttle in and out of the maze of old buildings, the best thing to do in La Antigua is to take a *lancha* ride around the area. After experiencing the novelty of the long **suspension bridge** that spans the Río Antigua, head down toward the deserted beaches at the river's mouth, an hour downstream by *lancha* (30 pesos, 120 pesos for a *lancha especial*). Though fishermen and impenetrable vegetation comprise most of the view, the cooling ride is worth the money.

CÓRDOBA   ☎ 2

Friendly, bustling Córdoba (pop. 200,000) feels like a rare Gulf breeze in comparison to the sweltering state capital nearby. The Spanish founded Córdoba in 1618, intending it to serve as a defensive post against anticipated slave rebellions at nearby sugarcane plantations. Instead, the city established itself as a place of freedom and compromise—the Treaty of Córdoba was signed here, granting Mexico independence from Spain.

■ **TRANSPORTATION.** All buses arrive at **Cordinados Córdoba** (☎ 727 04 68), 3km from the *zócalo* along Av. 4. To get to the *zócalo*, Plaza de Armas, from the bus station, exit to the right and take a "Centro" bus from the bus stand. ADO has 1st-class service to: **Mexico City** (4½hr., 24 per day, 161 pesos); **Oaxaca** (6hr., 12:10am and 10pm, 185 pesos); **Orizaba** (40 min., 19 per day, 11 pesos); **Palenque** (8½hr., 8:35pm, 335 pesos); **Puebla** (3hr., 14 per day, 98 pesos); **Tulum** (17½hr., 5:30pm, 607 pesos); **Tuxtepec** (3hr., 4:10pm, 67 pesos); **Tuxtla Gutiérrez** (11hr., 9:50 and 10:25pm, 342 pesos); **Veracruz** (1½hr., 22 per day, 59 pesos); **Villahermosa** (5½hr., 5 per day, 264 pesos); **Xalapa** (3hr., 10 per day, 81 pesos). Other lines offer 2nd-class service to some destinations. To reach Orizaba (7 pesos) or Fortín de las Flores (4 pesos) from Córdoba, hop on a westbound bus from anywhere on Calle 13.

ORIENTATION AND PRACTICAL INFORMATION.
Córdoba is 125km southwest of Veracruz, along Mex. 150. The city is easy to navigate; numbered *avenidas* run northwestern to southeast, with numbered *calles* crossing them at right angles. The *zócalo* is at the center, bounded by Calles 1 and 5 and Av. 1 and 3.

The **tourist office** (☎ 712 25 81) is under the *portales* in the Palacio Municipal, on the northwest side of the *zócalo*. (Open M-F 8:30am-7pm, Sa 9am-1pm.) **Casa de Cambio Puebla**, 117 Calle 2, between Av. 1 and 3, changes currency, as do many banks around the *zócalo*. **Iverlat**, on the corner of Av. 1 and Calle 3, and **Bital**, at Av. 1 and Calle 2, have 24hr. **ATMs**. The **market** is bounded by Calles 7 and 9 and Av. 6 and 8. (Open daily 7am-10pm.) **Luggage storage** at the bus station (3 pesos per hr.). **Emergency:** ☎ 060. **Police:** (☎ 712 67 20 or 712 1027), in the Palacio Municipal. **Red Cross:** (☎ 712 03 00 or 712 00 90), at Calle 9, #710, between Av. 7 and 9. **Farmacías de Dios,** at 510 Av. 1, between Calles 5 and 7. (☎ 712 00 64. Open 24hr.) **Hospital:** IMSS (☎ 714 38 00), on Av. 11 between Calles 1 and 2. **Internet Access: CETEC,** on Av. 3 across from the *zócalo*. Fast connections for 15 pesos per hr. (☎ 712 59 14. M-F 7am-10pm, Sa 8am-8pm, Su 9am-4pm.) **Post Office:** 303 Av. 3, one block southwest of the *zócalo*. (☎ 712 00 69. Open M-F 8am-4pm, Sa 9am-1pm.) **Postal Code:** 94500.

ACCOMMODATIONS AND FOOD.
Córdoba's many affordable restaurants and hotels, gathered on Av. 2 between Calles 9 and 11, make it ideal for a one-night stopover. **Iberiam**, 919 Av. 2, is the best bargain. Luxurious rooms feature TVs, phones, fans, reclining chairs, dark wood furnishings, and windows with a view of the courtyard garden. Lovers beware: sound travels through adjacent showers. (☎ 712 13 49. Singles 110 pesos; doubles 180 pesos; triples 240 pesos; each additional person 30 pesos.) For a cheap, no-frills stay, **Hotel Tres Caso** offers tiny, passable rooms. Walls are cracked and baths could be cleaner. (☎ 712 23 74. Singles 55 pesos; doubles 65 pesos; TV 10 pesos extra.) Indulge yourself at **Hotel Virreynal**, Av. 1 #309, across from the church in the *zócalo*. Spacious rooms include A/C, phone, and TV. The excellent adjoining restaurant provides room service. (☎ 712 23 77. Singles 220 pesos; doubles 240 pesos; each additional person 20 pesos.)

Casa de La Abuela (☎ 712 06 06), on Calle 1 between Av. 2 and 4, has cooked quality, affordable meals for two generations. Check out the family pictures on the wall as you munch on tacos (4 pesos), *antojitos* (6-17 pesos), and meat dishes (22-33 pesos). *Menu del día* 20 pesos. **Yang-Bara**, at Calle 1 and Av. 5, serves a vegetarian *menu del día* for 25 pesos. (☎ 712 69 34. Open M-Sa, 8am-8pm.) For *comida corrida* (15 pesos), try **Las Delicias** (☎ 714 86 51), on Av. 2 between Calles 5 and 7, where *antojitos* start at a low 2 pesos. **Restaurant Virreynal,** in Hotel Virreynal, offers a classier experience. At breakfast, families gather for *pan dulce, lechero,* fruit salads, and 20-pesos *huevos al gusto*. (☎ 712 23 77. Open daily 9am-11pm.)

SIGHTS.
Dominating the *zócalo*'s southeast side is the **Parroquia de la Inmaculada Concepción.** Constructed in 1621, the church combines both Baroque and Neoclassical styles. Now the city's primary place of worship, the *parroquia* is distinctive not only for the mango-colored exterior, but also for its infamous bells, which can be heard for miles around. Located under the *portales* on the *zócalo*'s northeast side is **Casa Zevallos.** Try to slip past the watchdog at the entrance to see the plaque in the courtyard that commemorates the site where Juan O'Donojú,

viceroy of Spain, and Augustín Iturbide, conservative rebel leader, agreed on the terms of Mexico's independence on August 24, 1821. Across the *zócalo*, half a block down Calle 3 to #303, lies **Museo de la Ciudad de Córdoba,** home to archaeological finds and historical documents. (Open daily 9am-2pm and 4-8pm. Free.)

ORIZABA   ☎ 2

At the base of Mexico's highest peak sits Orizaba (pop. 175,000). Formerly a center for sugarcane distillation, today Orizaba has turned to production, churning out barrels of beer and cement. The industrious city has long embraced workers; in 1906 President Porfirio Díaz ordered an unfavorable settlement for a labor strike, and Orizaba's residents took their protest to the streets. The government responded to this defiance with mass killings, and the city's tragedy cast a negative light on the dictatorial Porfiriato.

▐ TRANSPORTATION. Orizaba's two main bus lines maintain separate stations. To get to the *zócalo* from the **ADO station** (☎724 27 23), at Av. 6 Ote. 577, between Calles 11 and 13 Sur, exit to the left and walk to Calle 3 Sur; cross the road and continue 3 blocks to the *zócalo*. ADO has 1st-class service to: **Cancún** (19hr., 8:10pm, 667 pesos); **Córdoba** (40min., 28 per day, 11 pesos); **Mexico City** (4hr., 23 per day, 151 pesos); **Oaxaca** (6hr., 16 per day, 175 pesos); **Veracruz** (2hr., 22 per day, 69 pesos); **Villahermosa** (7hr., 4 per day, 282 pesos). From the 2nd-class **AU station** (☎725 19 79), at Calle 8 Pte. 425 between Calles 5 and 7 Nte., exit left and cross the bridge; take the first right and walk toward the church towers. To reach Orizaba from Córdoba, take a bus from the station or a westbound bus marked "Orizaba" or "Autopista" (7 pesos) from Av. 11 and Calle 13 to Av. 6 Ote. in Orizaba.

▰▱ ORIENTATION AND PRACTICAL INFORMATION. Orizaba lies 16km west of Córdoba and 25km northwest of Mexico's tallest mountain, **Pico de Orizaba.** Most points of interest are near **Parque Castillo,** bounded by Madero on the west, Colón on the south, Calle 3 Sur on the east, and Av. 3 Ote. on the north. **Av. 6 Ote.,** three blocks south of the *zócalo*, is the main thoroughfare.

The **tourist office,** in the Palacio de Hierro, at Madero and Av. 2 displays photos of Orizaba and arranges adventure tours. (☎726 58 61. Open M-Sa 8am-9pm, Su 9am-2pm.) Several banks south of the *zócalo* provide **currency exchange** and 24hr. **ATMs,** including **Banamex,** on the corner of Av. 2 Ote. and Madero, and **Serfín,** directly across the street. **Super Lavandería Orizaba,** Calle 11 Sur and Av. 4 Ote. **Mercado Melchor Ocampo,** between Av. 5 and 7 Ote. and Madero and Calle 3 Sur, sells fruits, vegetables, meat, and clothing. **Luggage storage** is available at the ADO station (5 pesos per 3hr.). **Emergency:** ☎060. **Police:** (☎724 38 84), at the corner of Circunvalación Nte. and Av. 5 Ote. **Red Cross:** Colón Ote. 253 (☎725 22 50), between Calles 5 and 7 Sur. **Farmacías Covadonga** at the corner of Calle 5 Sur and Av. 4 Ote. (☎725 74 33. Open 24hr.) **Hospital: IMSS,** at Gardenias. (☎726 30 69 or 725 85 51.) **LADATELs** are on the northwest side of the *zócalo*, just past the *parroquia*. **Internet Access: Cyber Cafe,** Colon Poniente 188, past the bridge. 9 pesos per hr. (☎726 57 66. Open daily 9am-10pm.) **Post office:** Av. 2 Ote. 282 (☎725 03 30), at Calle 7 Sur. (Open M-F 8am-4pm, Sa 9am-1pm.) **Mexpost** inside. **Postal Code:** 94300.

▮▢ ACCOMMODATIONS AND FOOD. The small rooms at family-run **Hotel Arenas,** Calle 2 Nte. 169, between Av. 3 and 5 Ote., are clean and come with TVs, fans, and access to the jungle-like courtyard. (☎725 23 61. Singles 110 pesos; doubles 150-160 pesos.) **Hotel San Cristóbal,** Calle 4 Nte. 243, between Av. 5 and 7 Ote., has spartan rooms with fans and hot water. (Singles 81 pesos, with TV 117 pesos; doubles 146 pesos, with TV 177 pesos.) More luxurious accommodations are available at **Grand Hotel de France,** Av. Oriente 6 #186. The giant stone courtyard boasts recently remodeled rooms with A/C, cable TV, and phones. Ask for a room with a balcony. (☎725 23 11. Singles 245 pesos; doubles 270 pesos.)

Always-crowded ■**La Hogaza,** Calle 4 Nte. between Av. 3 Ote. and Colón, has incredible food and a helpful staff. *Menu del día* 25 pesos. (☎726 05 29. Open daily 8am-7:30pm.) For a fast, cheap meal, visit **Antojitos Mexicanos,** Calle 2 Nte. 174. *Taquitos de pollo* 3 pesos; *tortas* 6 pesos; full-fledged meals of eggs, ham, tortillas, and refried beans 12 pesos. (☎723 47 24. Open daily 8am-11pm.)

🌅 **SIGHTS.** The ■**Museo de Arte del Estado,** Av. 4 Ote. between Calles 25 and 27, is a bit of a trek, but holds unforgettable works. If you prefer riding to walking, take an eastbound bus from Av. 6 Ote. The museum hosts fabulous rotating exhibits, featuring Mexico's best modern art. The pink colonial building also houses works by Diego Rivera and local artists. (10 pesos, students and teachers 5 pesos.) Follow Colón Pte. up to **Parque Alemeda,** where you can run, rent a bike, bounce on the giant trampoline, and snack on fried plantains and *papas fritas.*

🔳 **DAYTRIPS FROM ORIZABA**

CASCADA DE LA TROMPA DEL ELEFANTE

Catch an Estrella Roja bus at the corner of Av. 3 Ote. and Calle 2 Nte. and tell the driver where you want to go (20min., 6 pesos); he should let you off on Calle Isabel la Católica. Walk along the street as it turns into a dirt road and curves left around a small blue church. Following signs for Hotel Fiesta Cascada, continue over the autopista and then around a curve to the right. To return, retrace your steps and walk to the second intersection, where buses stop before returning to Orizaba.

The Cascada de la Trompa del Elefante (Waterfall of the Elephant's Trunk) offers scenic refuge from Orizaba's busy streets. Descend the famous **500 Escalones,** keeping an eye out for the waterfall, which will come into view on your right. Around the 250th stair, the path becomes crumbly and slick in places, so continue with care. At the bottom of the stairs, the path splits; the left fork follows the river for several kilometers, while the right fork crosses the river and continues past a power station up into the mountains. After the station is a small swimming hole.

LOS TUXTLAS

Calm, relaxing, and tourist-free, Los Tuxtlas nestle in the moist foothills of southern Veracruz. The region's three main towns—San Andrés Tuxtla, Santiago Tuxtla, and Catemaco—have distinct personalities. With quality cheap accommodations and transportation options, the fairly large town of **San Andrés** makes a good base for exploring the foothills. More touristed **Catemaco** is known for its *brujería* (witchcraft) and beautiful lagoon. Only 30min. from the Olmec site of Tres Zapotes, the small **Santiago Tuxtla** is primarily an archaeological stop.

SAN ANDRÉS TUXTLA ☎2

Lodged between the lush lakeside resorts of Catemaco and the Olmec artifacts of Santiago, San Andrés (pop. 125,000) is the tape that binds Los Tuxtlas. The tobacco and cattle-raising town offers a cache of budget hotels, an entertaining *zócalo,* and nearby natural attractions.

📧 **TRANSPORTATION.** Both the 1st- and 2nd-class **bus stations** are on Juárez, which branches off of Mex. 180. To get to the center from either station, exit left and follow Juárez as it descends a steep hill, crosses a small stream, and gradually ascends to meet the cathedral in the northern corner of the *zócalo.* Taxis travel the same 15min. route for 9 pesos. Autotransportes Los Tuxtlas (☎942 14 62), based in the 2nd-class station, sends buses to: **Catemaco** (20min., every 10min. 4:30am-6pm, 4 pesos); **Santiago Tuxtla** (20min., every 10min. 2:45am-6pm, 6 pesos); **Veracruz** (3½hr., every 15min. 4:30am-6pm, 56 pesos). ADO (☎942 08 71), at the 1st-class station, serves: **Mexico City** (7½hr.; 9:45, 10:30, and 11:10pm; 267 pesos); **Veracruz** (2½hr., 22 per day 12:20am-9:25pm, 66 pesos); **Villahermosa** (5hr., 11 per day, 141 pesos). AU (☎942 09 84) goes to **Puebla** (6hr., 9:50pm, 191pesos); **Veracruz** (2½hr., noon and 9:50pm, 66 pesos); **Xalapa** (4hr., 9:50pm, 115 pesos). Collective taxis *(colectivos)* also drive to Catemaco and Santiago Tuxtla (10 pesos).

❚❚❚ ORIENTATION AND PRACTICAL INFORMATION. San Andrés is located midway between Catemaco and Santiago. Before the cathedral, **Juárez** intersects **Constitución** to the left and **Madero** to the right, in front of the Palacio Municipal.

Exchange money at **Bancomer,** half a block south of the *zócalo* on Madero (open M-F 9am-5pm, Sa 9am-1pm), or **Serfín,** at Carranza as it curves to intersect 16 de Septiembre. (☎942 11 00. Open M-F 9am-3pm, Sa 10am-2pm.) Both have 24hr. **ATMs. Mercado 5 de Febrero** spills onto the streets several blocks from the *zócalo*. To get there, walk on Madero, turn right on Carranza, and walk uphill. (Open daily 6am-10pm; food stands close at 6pm.) **Laundry: Lava Maac,** Hernández 75, at Revolución. (☎942 09 26. 8 pesos per kg. Open M-Sa 8am-8pm.) **Police:** (☎942 02 35) in the Palacio Municipal. No English spoken. **Red Cross:** Boca Negra 25 (☎942 05 00), north of the *zócalo*. No English spoken. **Farmacía Garysa,** Madero 3, in the Canada building left of the Palacio Municipal. (☎/fax 942 44 34. Open 24hr.) **Hospital Civil** (☎942 04 47), at the edge of town. **SAT Internet** at the corner of Suárez and Argudín. (☎942 38 05. 15 pesos per hr. Open daily 9:30am-10:30pm.) **Post office:** at La Fragua and 20 de Noviembre, one block from the *zócalo*. (☎942 01 89. Open M-F 8am-3pm.) **Postal code:** 95701.

❚❚❚ ACCOMMODATIONS AND FOOD. San Andrés has great budget accommodations. Two of the best bargains are within spitting distance of each other on Suárez. To get there, walk left from the cathedral and turn right at the orange supermarket, continuing uphill past the movie theater. At **Hotel Colonial,** Suárez 7, you may never want to leave the mountain view balconies, small clean rooms, ceiling fans, comfortable lobby, and upstairs *sala*. (☎942 05 52. Singles 50 pesos; doubles 80 pesos.) **Hotel Figueroa,** Suárez 10, across the street, has portable fans, bigger, more comfortable rooms, and higher prices. (☎942 02 57. Singles 100 pesos; doubles 120 pesos; with cable TV 20 pesos more.) Those living in the A/C fast lane may upgrade to **Hotel Isabel,** Madero 13, to the left of Hotel Parque. Although the large rooms come with A/C and TV, the amenities do not warrant the price. (☎942 16 17. Singles 193 pesos; doubles 239 pesos.)

Several sidewalk cafes on the *zócalo* serve breakfast and coffee accompanied by a pleasant view of small-town life. Famous for elegant cakes and pies, **Winni's Restaurant,** south of the *zócalo*, across from Hotel Isabel on Madero, hosts chatting locals at its outdoor tables. (☎942 01 10. *Antojitos* 6-22 pesos. Open daily 8am-midnight.) Next door, **La Surianita** cooks cheap, filling meals. (☎942 44 42. *Antojitos* and egg dishes 10 pesos, meat entrees 25 pesos. Open daily 8am-10:30pm.) The older and more affluent **Restaurant del Parque,** on the ground floor of Hotel Parque in the *zócalo*, has a classier atmosphere and good coffee. (☎942 01 98. *Antojitos* 20 pesos. Open daily 7:30am-midnight.)

❚❚❚ SIGHTS AND ENTERTAINMENT. Even non-smokers will be impressed by the **Fábrica Tabacos San Andrés** (☎942 12 00), the birthplace of Santa Clara cigars. From the *zócalo*, walk up Juárez to the ADO terminal. Take a right around the corner, and continue about 200m down the street past the entrance to the bus parking lot. The management welcomes visitors, and, if you're polite, a staff member will walk you through the entire process. The store near the entrance sells the final product. Bottom of the line cigars are affordable (105 pesos and up), but a box of 25 of the finest *puros* goes for much more (1000 pesos). Note that customs regulations may limit the number of cigars you can take back into your country.

The sheer number of video rental stores clearly proclaim that San Andrés is not a town that parties until dawn. Most of the action centers in the *zócalo*, where folks gather to gossip, see, and be seen. **Cafe de la Cathedral,** to the right of the Singer store on the north side of the *zócalo,* used to be a coffee shop but now functions as the town's most popular bar, filling around 11pm and emptying only at dawn. **Cinemas San Andrés,** on Pino Suárez down the street from hotels Colonial and Figueroa, shows new American releases. (☎942 42 50. 15 pesos.)

SANTIAGO TUXTLA   ☎ 2

Of Tuxtla's three cities, Santiago (pop. 50,000) has the least to offer visitors. Its main attraction is the nearby Olmec ceremonial center of Tres Zapotes.

█ TRANSPORTATION. The **ADO station,** like everything else in Santiago, is just a few blocks from the *zócalo.* To reach the town center, walk downhill from Mex. 180 where the bus drops you. ADO (☎947 04 38) sends buses to: **Mexico City** (7hr., 30 per day, 270 pesos) and **Xalapa** (4½hr., 5 per day, 109 pesos). Autotransportes Los Tuxtlas buses leave from next to the ADO station for: **Catemaco** (40min., every 10min. 4:30am-7pm, 10 pesos) and **San Andrés** (20min., every 10min. 4:30am-7pm, 6 pesos). To reach other surrounding towns, take the taxi *colectivos* that leave from next to the market, a block from the *zócalo.*

▢ PRACTICAL INFORMATION. Inverlat, at the corner of the Palacio Municipal, has a 24hr. **ATM. Mercado Municipal Morelos** begins on the *zócalo* and continues one block downhill. (Open daily 5am-7pm.) **Police:** (☎947 00 92) downstairs in the Palacio Municipal. **Red Cross:** (☎942 05 00) in San Andrés. **Super Farmacía Roma:** 5 de Mayo just off the *zócalo.* (☎947 09 99. Open M-Sa 8:30am-9pm, Su 8:30am-3pm.) **Clínica Doctores Castellanos,** across from Hotel Castellanos. (☎947 02 60. Open daily 8am-8pm.) **LADATELs** are located across from Hotel Castellanos and in front of the Palacio Municipal. **Post office:** on the right side of the yellow building across the *zócalo* from the Palacio Municipal. (Open M-F 9am-4pm.) **Postal code:** 95830.

█▢ ACCOMMODATIONS AND FOOD. Built in the early 80s in a feeble government attempt to get Santiago's tourist industry ticking, **Hotel Castellanos,** at the far corner of the *zócalo* on the corner of 5 de Mayo and Comonfort, is not only a place to stay but Santiago's most interesting attraction. The tall cylindrical hotel has rooms that fit together like slices of a pie, each with A/C, phone, cable TV, and a balcony. (☎947 03 00. Singles 234 pesos; doubles 258 pesos.) Grub in Santiago is cheap, and sometimes is just that—grub. During the rainy season, small, winged insects seek refuge inside the *zócalo*'s street lamps. In the morning, the bugs are captured, de-winged, and sauteed with salsa to make the region's favorite taco filling. Besides the typical taco stands, there is also an upscale restaurant in Hotel Castellanos and a delicious bakery next to the bus station.

◎▢ SIGHTS AND ENTERTAINMENT. The largest **Olmec head** ever discovered (45 tons) sits complacently at the far end of Santiago's *zócalo,* shaded from the sun by a large cupola. The Cobata head, named for the place of its discovery, is distinctive not only for its size but for its closed eyes. The **Museo Regional Tuxteco,** to the left of the head, displays an Olmec head discovered at Tres Zapotes and other Olmec and Totonac artifacts from around the region. (☎947 01 96. Open M-Sa 9am-6pm. 27 pesos, Su free.) Celebrations for the fair in honor of Santiago's namesake and patron saint take place July 20-29 and include a choreographed fight between Christians and Moors and a *torneo de cintas* that features men dressed in medieval gear riding horses.

NEAR SANTIAGO: TRES ZAPOTES

From the Museo Regional Tuxteco in Santiago, take a right on Zaragoza. Walk 2 blocks to a T-intersection and cross the footbridge across the street to Morelos. From there, take a taxi colectivo to Tres Zapotes (30min., 22 pesos). Tell the driver that you want to go to the museo. Buses marked "Tres Zapotes" also pass through this stop, but while cheaper (8 pesos), they are also slower. Open daily 9am-6pm. 22 pesos; Su free.

Half an hour's ride from Santiago through small tobacco-growing towns is the site of Tres Zapotes. Along with San Lorenzo and La Venta, Tres Zapotes was a chief Olmec ceremonial center, peaking between 300 BC and AD 300, though evidence indicates that the area may have been occupied as early as 900 BC. The site itself remains largely unexcavated, but artifacts can be seen in the town's small museum. Most impressive is the large Olmec stone head. The first of the dozen or so Olmec heads ever found, it was discovered in 1862 by a *campesino* who first thought it was an overturned cooking pot. To the left of the head is **Stela C,** which, together with its more famous upper half (now at the Museo Nacional de Antropología in Mexico City; see **Mexico City: Sights,** p. 108), bears the oldest written date in the Americas—31 BC—inscribed in late Olmec, or Spi-Olmec, glyphs similar to those later used by the Maya. The date is depicted as a bar (representing "5") and two dots, totaling seven on the Olmec calendar. **Stela A** lies in the trancept to the left. Decorations on the stela include an Olmec face, a man holding an axe, and a serpent coiling in upon itself. **Stela D,** to the right of the head, depicts four people whose relative heights symbolize their power and importance.

NEAR SANTIAGO: CASCADA DEL SALTO DE EYIPANTLA

Take a micro labeled "El Salto" from the west side of the market (30min., 3.5 pesos). The micro drops off and picks up at the entrance to the falls; last return bus at 8:15pm. 5 pesos.

Although a bit touristy, with market stands and eating areas, the beautiful *cascada* is impressive for its force. At 40m across and 50m high, the Salto soaks viewers who stand at the end of the path, which is close enough to the falls to nearly be a part of them. And it's a good thing—after huffing down 262 stairs to see the falls, most visitors are ready for a heavy misting.

CATEMACO ☎2

The most touristed town in Las Tuxtlas, Catemaco (pop. 51,000), is surrounded by a gorgeous lagoon. Don't be surprised when you are approached by men anxious for you to "see the monkeys." They simply want you to take a *lancha* tour of the Laguna Catemaco, which passes by *la Isla de los Monos.* Fairly quiet in the off-season, Catemaco picks up during *Semana Santa* and during the celebration of the town's patron saint, Saint Carmen, when *gringos* and *chilangos* come to enjoy regional cuisine and Catemaco's much-hyped *brujería.*

☐ TRANSPORTATION. Catemaco lies on **Mex. 180** and is a popular bus stop. From the Autotransportes Los Tuxtlas 2nd-class stop, turn right and follow the curve of road past the "Bienvenidos a Catemaco" arches. Take a straight path for 10-15min. to the spires of the *basílica.* Autotransportes Los Tuxtlas travels to: **San Andrés** (20min., every 20min. 2am-7pm, 4 pesos) and other regional destinations. The **ADO** station is along the waterfront on the *malecón.* To get there from the church, take a right and follow the street for several blocks; take another right at Hotel Julita. ADO (☎943 08 42) heads to: **Mexico City** (9hr., 10pm, 281 pesos); **Puebla** (6hr., 10pm, 218 pesos); **Veracruz** (3hr., 6 per day 5:30am-5pm, 70 pesos); **Xalapa** (3hr., 4 per day 6:15am-5pm, 119 pesos). AU (☎943 07 77) goes to: **Mexico City** (9hr., 11:30am and 9pm, 252 pesos); **Veracruz** (3hr., 11:30am and 9:15pm, 562 pesos).

◢◤ ORIENTATION AND PRACTICAL INFORMATION. Streets are poorly marked, but the *basílica* in the *zócalo* is almost always visible. Using the *basílica* as a reference point, **Carranza** is the street to the left that runs past the Palacio Municipal. Straight ahead, the road becomes **Aldama.** One block downhill to the right is **Playa** and then the **malecón,** which follows the curve of the beach.

The **tourist office,** in the Palacio Municipal, offers maps of *pirata* routes, brochures, and helpful, though limited, advice. (☎943 00 16. Open M-F 9am-3pm.) **Currency exchange: Bancomer,** across Aldama from the *basílica,* has 24hr. **ATMs.** (☎943 03 17. Open M-F 9am-1:30pm.) **Market:** on Madero before the *zócalo.* (Open daily 6am-7pm.) **Police:** (☎943 00 55), in the Palacio Municipal on the *zócalo.* No English spoken. **Farmacía Nuestra Señora del Carmen,** at the corner of Carranza and Boettinger. (☎943 00 91. Open daily 7am-9pm.) **Centro de Salud** (☎943 02 47), on Carranza, in a white building with a blue roof, three blocks up from the *zócalo* on the left. Some English spoken. **Internet Access: PC Center,** Calle Matamoros 3, in a white and blue building five blocks up from the *zócalo* on the right. (☎943 01 70; www.gorsa.net.mx. Open M-Sa 9am-9pm.) **Post office:** on Aldama, two blocks past the *basílica* on the right. **Postal code:** 95870.

█▐█ ACCOMMODATIONS AND FOOD. Most hotels are situated around the *zócalo* and the waterfront. During Christmas, *Semana Santa,* and most of July, hotels fill up quickly, and prices generally rise 20-30 pesos. Crime makes it inadvisable to camp on the beaches. The **Hotel Julita,** Playa 10, one block downhill from the *zócalo,* is blessed with a kindly owner, unbeatable location, and large, clean rooms with fans. (☎943 00 08. Singles 70 pesos; doubles 120 pesos.) **Hotel Acuario,** at Boettinger and Carranza, across from the Palacio, provides large, slightly older rooms; some have balconies. (☎943 04 18. Singles 90 pesos; doubles 170 pesos.)

Lake views differ more than menu choices in Catemaco's waterfront restaurants. *Mojarra* and *topote* fish are endemic to the lagoon, as are *tegogolos,* the famous Catemaco sea snails. *Mojarra* is prepared in a variety of ways, while bite-sized *topote* is fried whole and often heaped with *tamales.* Amazing *mojarra* can be had at modestly-priced **Los Sauces,** on the *malecón* at Rayon, three blocks east of Carranza. (☎943 05 48. *Topotes* 15 pesos. Beautiful lakeside view. Open daily 8am-8:30pm.) **El Pescador,** on the *malecón* at Bravo, offers similar flavors, fares, and views. (☎943 07 05. *Mojarra* 40-50 pesos; *topotes* 12 pesos. Open daily 9am-8:30pm.) For something classier, head to **La Casona del Recuerdo,** across the *zócalo* on Aldama. A haven from aggressive *lanchistas,* the terrace overlooks a peaceful wooded garden. (☎943 08 22. *Tegogolos* 25 pesos. Open daily 8am-8pm.)

▣ SIGHTS. The rocky beaches of **Laguna Catemaco** are a refreshing break from the hot Veracruz sun. The water immediately in front of town is not safe for swimming, but a hiking path runs along the edge of the lake—walk down from the *zócalo* to the waterfront and turn left. The trail will guide you 1½km to **Playa Expagoya** and then another ½km to the more secluded and sandier **Playa Hermosa,** the first swimmable beach. The path is not safe at night. It's also possible to swim off a *lancha* in the deeper and sometimes clearer waters in the middle of the lake.

The best way to see Catemaco is on a ▣**lancha tour** that departs from the shore of the lagoon downhill from the *zócalo* (60 pesos on a *lancha colectiva* or 250 pesos for the whole boat). The tour lasts 1½hr.and takes you past several small islands and various attractions. Strange birds and water lilies aside, by far the most popular sight is **Isla de los Changos.** A group of wild, red-cheeked *changos* (mandrills, a type of baboon) was brought from Thailand for a scientific experiment at the University of Veracruz in 1979—scientists wanted to see if the animals could survive in a new environment. Lo and behold, 21 years later the *changos* are alive, well-fed, and posing for snapshots. En route to the island, you'll pass a cave-shrine that stands on the spot where the town's namesake and local fisherman, Juan Catemaco, had a vision of the Virgin Mary over a century ago. His statue, poised elegantly at the tip of the lagoon, overlooks the calm waters. Negotiate with the *lanchistas* for longer trips, including an exploration of the rivers that feed the lake or a trip past the nearby tropical forests.

▨▐ NIGHTLIFE AND ENTERTAINMENT. Catemaco's bars and discos are the best in the Tuxtlas, although nightlife only really heats up during high seasons. Many bars and clubs shut down or operate irregularly in low-season. Single women should exercise caution when out at night. The road along the beach dominates nightlife in Catemaco. Four blocks from Hotel Julita and one block from the water on Madero is **Jahac 45,** a video bar and disco that sometimes sponsors concerts by local bands and remains open faithfully all year. (☎943 08 50. Cover 25 pesos. Open Sa-Su 10pm-4am.) To experience the witching hour, head to **7 Brujas,** another video bar on the *malecón* near the corner of Playa. (☎943 01 57. Open Tu-Su 8am-3am.) **Chanequa's** (☎943 00 42 or 943 00 01), a video bar in Hotel Playa Azul, caters to the chic hotel crowd. Walking there at night is dangerous; a taxi will take you for 25 pesos. Catemaco's major secular celebration, **Day of the Fisherman,** occurs on May 30, when a procession of manually-powered *lanchas* parade across the lagoon and locals compete in a fishing tournament. The town also celebrates the day of its patron saint, **Saint Carmen,** on July 16.

NEAR CATEMACO: THE GULF COAST

Public transportation is limited to Transportes Rurales pick-up trucks, called piratas *by locals. Piratas depart from the eastern edge of town. To get there from the zócalo, cross Carranza, keeping the Palacio Municipal on your left, walk 6 blocks, and turn right onto Lerdo. From there, walk 5 more blocks until you pass the last restaurant. Turn left and walk until the intersection of a paved road, or take a taxi (10 pesos). Just outside town the road forks into 2 main routes. One heads north to Montepío on the Gulf Coast and the other goes east to Coyame on the opposite side of Lake Catemaco. Piratas depart for both (every 50min. 6am-7pm), but only when enough passengers have boarded.*

Catemaco entices travelers with its proximity to the secluded beaches of the Gulf Coast. Hiking, fishing, posh spas, rare wildlife, and miles of gorgeous beach await.

CATEMACO TO MONTEPÍO. On the way to Montepío is **Sontecomapán** (18km from Catemaco), a small town beside a saltwater lake that empties into the Gulf. *Lanchas* are available for excursions on the lake and down the coast (60 pesos per person on a *colectivo*; 250 pesos for a private boat). To the left of the *lanchas* is **Pozo de los Enanos** (Pond of the Midgets), a clear, fresh pond with an optical illusion that makes you appear half your size when you look into it. The next stop is **La Barra,** a fishing community where Laguna Sontecomapán empties into the Gulf. Take a *lancha* or *pirata* 8km beyond Sontecomapán until the road forks. Your *pirata* will normally follow the left fork; negotiate with the driver to take the right fork or hop off and hike the 5-6km to La Barra yourself. If you want to go to Playa Jicacal and Playa Escondida, you will have to ask the *lancha* driver to let you off and then walk 30min. to stony, empty **Playa Jicacal.** The pink *cabañas* of **Hotel Icacos,** near the entrance to the beach, contain two large beds, a fan, and little else. (☎942 05 56. *Cabaña* singles 120 pesos; doubles 150 pesos.) Instead of turning right to Playa Jicacal, you can walk uphill 10min. to the left to **Playa Escondida** and the simple, white **Hotel Playa Escondida.** (☎942 30 61 in San Andrés. Singles and doubles 200 pesos.) This beach offers the safest camping in the area; inquire at the hotel (25 pesos). Beach access for non-guests costs 10 pesos. Visitors who want a secluded beach without the walk through the jungle can have the *pirata* drop them off at the next stop, **Balzapote.** Farther down the road is a **biological research station** operated by the University of Veracruz, whose young scientists can show you the surrounding wildlife.

The *pirata* route ends on a bluff overlooking the beach at **Montepío** (2hr. from Catemaco), also home to a small fishing town. Susana Valencia Contreraz, the proprietor of **Loncheria Susi,** offers rooms with private bath. (Singles 40 pesos; doubles 80 pesos.) The new **Hotel Posada San José,** on the bank of the small river leading to the beach, is more expensive and more luxurious. (☎942 10 10 or 942 20 20 in San Andrés. Singles 200 pesos; doubles 240 pesos.) Montepío's biggest attractions are the **cascadas** up from the beach. The best way to reach the falls is with a guide; you can find one at the driveway to Posada San José. Most people go by horse, taking the guided trip to **Cascadas de Revolución,** inland and midway down the beach (80 pesos). Excursions to the other *cascadas* can be arranged, or you can rent a horse and try to find them by yourself (30 pesos per hr., 40 pesos with guide).

CATEMACO TO COYAME. *Piratas* also travel to Coyame (13km east of Catemaco), the underground springs that give birth to the soft drink "Coyame." Seven kilometers toward Coyame is the **Proyecto Ecológico Educacional Nanciyaga,** or **Nanciyaga** (☎943 01 99; *pirata* 3 pesos). From the road, turn right and walk in front of the "Nanciyaga" sign on a dirt path that leads toward the lake. *Lanchas* (60 pesos) or taxis (25 pesos) will also take you to Nanciyaga. To return to Catemaco, walk back to the road, cross the street, and flag down any *pirata* headed back to town; note that they usually only pass about once per hour. The "ecological educational park" is more like a spa than anything else. Guests stay overnight in candle-lit bungalows and enjoy the Olmec *temascal* sweat lodge, full-body mud baths, open-air concerts, and boat tours of the lake. (Singles 250 pesos; doubles 400 pesos. Hotel restaurant open 9am-4pm.) **Playa Hermosa** is another 8km down the beach from Montepío. Up a dirt road from the beach is **Cascada Cocoliso.** Turn right after the beer stand and follow the road to its conclusion. If you're too tired to walk back and no *colectivos* seem to be leaving from the docks, you can hire a private *lancha* (120 pesos). The Coyame area has plenty of decent hikes, but lacks tourist facilities. A good route begins from the town of **Tebanca,** near Coyame. Follow the cattle paths to explore **Cerro los Cumbres Bastonal,** a 4½hr. hike. Be careful in summer when paths may be covered in water. If you start early, you can climb Bastonal and return for the last *pirata* back to Catemaco at 7pm.

ACAYUCAN   ☎9

At the junction of Hwy. 180, which runs between Veracruz and Villahermosa, and Hwy. 185, which crosses the Isthmus of Tehuantepec, lies Acayucan (pop. 100,000), a transportation hub for southern Veracruz. The city lacks major sites, but its location, budget hotels, and dining options make it a key stopover point.

◰ TRANSPORTATION. Acayucan's **bus station** (☎245 11 42), on Acuña in Barrio Tamarindo, is on the eastern edge of the city. Tickets go fast and many are *de paso* so get to the station early. To get to the *zócalo*, exit right and walk straight to the town's main street, Hidalgo. Either turn left and walk straight for 10min. to reach the *centro*, or catch a westbound "Centro" *colectivo* (3 pesos). ADO goes to: **Mexico City** (7hr., 9 per day, 321 pesos); **Oaxaca** (4½hr.; 8, 10:15pm, and 1:10am; 162 pesos); **Palenque** (6hr., 4 per day, 164 pesos); **San Andrés Tuxtla** (2hr., 8 per day, 38 pesos); **San Cristóbal de las Casas** (10hr., 3am, 236 pesos); **Veracruz** (3½hr., 19 per day, 119 pesos); **Villahermosa** (4hr., 15 per day, 103 pesos); **Xalapa** (6hr., 7 per day, 166 pesos). *Urbanos* line the street outside and travel to nearby destinations.

⊟ PRACTICAL INFORMATION. Bital and **Serfín,** side by side at Victoria and Zaragoza on the plaza's south side, provide currency exchange and 24hr. **ATMs.** (Open M-Sa 8am-5pm.) **Emergency:** ☎060. **Police:** ☎245 10 78. **Red Cross:** Ocampo Sur 4 (☎245 00 28), between Victoria and Negrete. Some English spoken. **Internet Acayucan,** a block north of the *zócalo*, off Pipla at Guerrero Pte. 24. (☎245 12 70. Open daily 9am-9pm.) **Post office:** a block north on Moctezuma, and left on Guerrero. (☎245 00 88. Open M-Sa 8am-4pm.) **Postal Code:** 96001.

◰◲ ACCOMMODATIONS AND FOOD. Hotels and restaurants surround the *zócalo*. **Hotel Jesymar,** Moctezuma 206, one block north of the *zócalo*, is the best budget lodging in Acayucan. (☎245 02 61. Charming rooms with phones, TV, and balconies. Singles and doubles with fans 135 pesos, with A/C 170 pesos.) **Hotel Plaza,** Victoria 37, opposite 3 Hermanos, has large, tidy rooms overlooking the *centro*. (☎245 13 44. Singles and doubles with fan 117 pesos, with A/C and TV 234 pesos.)

After exiting the bus station and walking to the *zócalo*, you will encounter hordes of taco stands and *tortas* shops. **Obélix,** in the *zócalo* on Victoria, is known for quick and inexpensive *tortas* (13 pesos) and tacos (2.5 pesos). **Soyamar,** Guerrero 601, is a vegetarian oasis. (☎245 17 44. Tasty veggie burgers 10 pesos, fruit salad with granola, yogurt, and honey 15 pesos. Open M-F 7am-8pm)

NEAR ACAYUCAN: SAN LORENZO TENOCHTITLÁN

From the mercado in Acayucan, go to the line of regional buses and ask for one going to "Texistepec" (sometimes labeled just "Texi"), which will bring you to the town's bus depot (30min., 7.5 pesos). From Texistepec, catch a blue "Villa Alta" urbano, which stops in Tenochtitlán (45min., 10 pesos) and Zona Azuzul (1¼hr., 17 pesos). Buses leave at 8, 10am, 2, 3, and 5pm; last bus from Zona Azuzul back to Texistepec leaves at approximately 5:15pm. Taxis can be taken to the 2 sites (70 pesos and 120 pesos, respectively); if enough can be rounded up to go colectivo, fares are 14 and 21 pesos.

A pilgrimage best reserved for archaeology buffs, reaching the Olmec remains of San Lorenzo is a labor of love. San Lorenzo Tenochtitlán is the collective name given to the three Olmec sites of San Lorenzo, Tenochtitlán, and Zona Azuzul. Of these three centers, San Lorenzo is believed to have been the largest and oldest, flourishing between 1200 and 900 BC. Among the Olmec artifacts unearthed here are the earliest known ball player figurines, as well as those of serpentine and jadite. Though many of the artifacts found in the initial 1947 excavations have been relocated to museums elsewhere, finds from excavations in 1994 remain in the area and anchor the local collection. Today, the largest collection is in **Tenochtitlán**, where an assortment of artifacts are displayed under a protective shelter near the town's main dirt road. The exhibit includes a giant Olmec stone head, the only one of the 10 heads found at the three sites to remain in the area.

About 5km farther down the main dirt road lies the microscopic town of San Lorenzo. Several kilometers from the town are the actual ruins of **San Lorenzo,** but little remains to be seen. Approximately 3km past San Lorenzo is the third original Olmec ceremonial center, **Zona Azuzul.** Two small shelters atop the hill house the modest but remarkably well-preserved collection. The first hut holds four stone statues, two depicting kneeling human forms and two depicting jaguar forms. The second hut has larger jaguar figures. (Site open daily 8am-6pm. Free, except for a good tip to the site's caretaker.)

TABASCO

VILLAHERMOSA   ☎ 9

Villahermosa (pop. 1.6 million) is neither a *villa* (small village), nor is it *hermosa* (beautiful). The capital of Tabasco state is a metropolis whose growth has been driven by oil discoveries and its strategic location along the Río Grijalva, one of the few navigable rivers in the republic. Founded in 1519 as Santa María de la Victoria by Cortés, the city was an agricultural center of minor importance, accessible only by river. In the past 50 years, oil-spurred growth has created a dense and not particularly elegant forest of satellite dishes, luxury hotels, apartment complexes, and fast food restaurants. Villahermosa's proximity to the Palenque ruins and its position as a crossroads between Chiapas and the Yucatán make it a common stopover for travelers. Happy (and dry) is the well-prepared tourist: the weather behaves like clockwork--be prepared for showers every afternoon during the rainy season (June-Sept.).

▐ TRANSPORTATION

Airport: (☎356 01 56), on the Villahermosa-Macupana Highway, 14km from downtown. Taxis shuttle between the airport and the *centro* (40 pesos *especial,* 15 pesos *colectivo*). Most major airlines have offices in Tabasco 2000, including: **Aeroméxico,** Cámara 511 Locale 2 (☎01 800 021 40 00); **Aviacsa,** Via 3 #120 Locale 10 (☎316 57 33); **Aerocaribe,** Via 3 #120 Locale 9 (☎316 50 47); **Mexicana,** Via 3 #120 Locale 5-6D (☎316 31 32).

Buses: The **1st-class terminal** is on Mina at Merino. To reach downtown from the **ADO station,** walk 2½ blocks to your right on Mina to Méndez. From there, take a *combi*

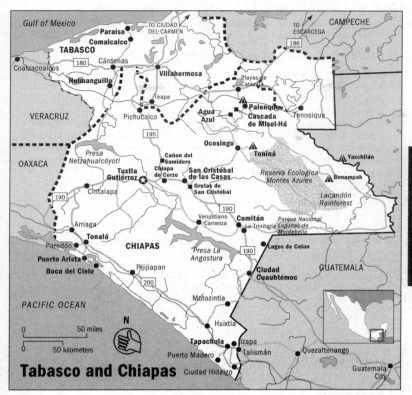

Tabasco and Chiapas

labeled "Pqe. Juárez" and get off a few minutes later at Parque Juárez. Most hotels are south of the park on either Madero or the parallel Constitución. Walking from the station to Parque Juárez takes 15-20min. Upon exiting the terminal, head right down Mina for 11 blocks, then turn left onto 27 de Febrero. 8 more blocks take you to the Madero intersection. ADO runs to: **Acayucan** (4hr., 16 per day 1am-9:25pm, 103 pesos); **Campeche** (5hr., 12 per day, 187 pesos); **San Cristóbal de Las Casas** (6hr., 7:35am, 137 pesos); **Cancún** (11hr., 8 per day, 386 pesos); **Xalapa** (9hr., 5 per day, 271 pesos); **Mexico City** (11hr., 20 per day, 424 pesos); **Oaxaca** (11hr.; 6, 7:55, and 9:25pm; 309 pesos); **Palenque** (2hr., 12 per day 2:55am-9:15pm, 62 pesos); **Puebla** (8hr., 4 per day, 361 pesos); **San Andrés Tuxtla** (4hr., 9 per day, 141 pesos); **Veracruz** (7hr., 15 per day, 206 pesos). Also serving the station are Cristóbal Colón, TRT, and Sur. Servicios Altos sends buses to **Tuxtla Gutiérrez** (6½hr., 6 per day, 100 pesos). To get downtown from the **2nd-class bus terminal,** located on Ruiz Cortines 2 blocks left of Mina, cross Grijalva on the pedestrian bridge left of the station exit, then hop on an "Indeco Centro" bus (3.5 pesos) and disembark at Parque Juárez on Madero. To make the walk from the station (25min.), cross the bridge and continue south on Mina for 3 blocks until you reach the ADO station (see above). A cab ride to the center of town costs 12 pesos. This terminal offers service to many regional destinations.

ORIENTATION AND PRACTICAL INFORMATION

Villahermosa is 20km from the Chiapan border. The spine of the downtown area is **27 de Febrero. Zona Luz,** the city's pedestrian-only downtown area, is bordered by **5** de Mayo, Zaragoza, Madero, and 27 de Febrero. Paseo Tabasco runs north-south and connects the Tabasco 2000 complex to the *centro*, intersecting 27 de Febrero in front of the cathedral. *Saetas* (public buses) and *combis* (4 pesos) run 6am-10pm.

TOURIST AND FINANCIAL SERVICES

Tourist Office: In Tabasco 2000, de los Ríos 113 (☎316 36 33 or 316 28 89), diagonally behind the Palacio Municipal. Open M-F 8am-4pm and 6-9pm, Sa 9am-1pm. Booths are located at the entrances of **Parque Museo La Venta** (open daily 8am-4pm), and the **airport**. Open daily 7am-8pm.

Currency Exchange: Banks abound in Zona Luz and on Paseo Tabasco. **Banamex,** on Madero at Reforma, has 24hr. **ATMs.** Open for exchange M-F 8am-1:30pm. **Bancomer,** on Madero next to VIPS near Reforma, has **ATMs.** Open for exchange M-F 8am-4:30pm.

American Express: Paseo Zabarco 715 (☎315 39 99), in the office of Turismo Creativo. Open M-F 9am-6pm, Sa 9am-1pm.

Radio Taxi: (☎314 34 56 in the *centro*, 316 64 21, in Tabasco 2000). On call 24hr.

Car Rental: Budget, 27 de Febrero 712 (☎314 37 90). Open daily 9am-2pm and 4-8pm. **Dollar,** Paseo Tabasco 600 (☎315 48 30). Open daily 8am-9pm. Chevrolets 551 pesos per day. **Alamo,** Paseo Tabasco 302-L. Open M-Sa 8am-8pm, Su 9am-2pm. Chevrolets 447 pesos per day.

LOCAL SERVICES

Luggage Storage: At the bus station. 3 pesos per hr. Open daily 7am-10pm.

Mercado: Pino Suárez, encompassed by Pino Suárez, Constitución, Hermanos Zozaya, and Grijalva, in the northeast corner of town. Open daily 5am-8pm.

Supermarket: Maz, on Madero at Zaragoza. Open daily 7am-9:30pm.

Laundry: Lavandería Top Klean, Madero 303, next door to Hotel Madero. 15 pesos per kg. Open M-Sa 8am-8pm.

EMERGENCY AND COMMUNICATIONS

Emergency: ☎060.

Police: Aldama 101 (☎315 26 33 or 315 26 30), in Zona Luz. The main office is at 16 de Septiembre at Periférico (☎315 25 17). No English spoken.

Red Cross: (☎315 56 00 or 315 55 55), on Sandino in Col. 1 de Mayo. Take a taxi. Some English. 24hr. ambulance service.

Pharmacy: Farmacias del Ahorro, Méndez 1405 (☎314 06 03 or 315 66 06 for delivery), after Pages Llergo. Open 24hr. Also in the Zona Luz near the corner of Reforma and Aldama, across from the Howard Johnson. Open daily 7am-10pm.

Hospital: IMSS, Sandino 102 (☎315 20 15 or 315 26 91). No English spoken. A better hospital: **ISSTE,** 27 de Febrero 1803 (☎315 06 19, 315 06 48, or 315 92 31).

Fax: Telecomm, Lerdo 601 (☎314 24 94), at Sáenz around the corner from the post office. Open M-F 8am-7:30pm, Sa 9am-5pm, Su 9am-1pm.

Internet Access: Several providers cluster around the intersection of Zaragoza and Aldama. **Hardware-Net,** Aldama 627-B (☎312 27 55). 12 pesos per hr. Open daily 9am-9pm. **Multiservicios Computacional,** Aldama 621 (☎312 21 66). 12 pesos per hr. Open daily 8:30am-9pm.

Post Office: Sáenz 131, at Lerdo. Open M-F 8am-3pm, Sa 9am-1pm.

Postal Code: 86000.

▌ ACCOMMODATIONS

In Villahermosa, any hotel wealthy enough to purchase more than a door-width space on the ground floor is probably out of the "budget" price range. The most inexpensive hotels are found in Zona Luz, but are very crowded so call ahead.

Hotel Oriente, Madero 425 (☎312 01 21 or 312 11 01). Couch potatoes will appreciate the TVs and access to VIPS across the street. Rooms are quiet and clean with fans. Singles 120 pesos, with A/C 200 pesos; doubles 180 pesos, with A/C 260 pesos.

Hotel del Centro, Suárez 209 (☎312 59 61), between Sánchez and Méndez. Neat rooms have TVs, fans, and memento graffiti scrawled by past tenants. Singles 110 pesos, with A/C 200 pesos; doubles 140 pesos, with A/C 230 pesos.

Hotel Madero, Madero 301 (☎312 05 16), near 27 de Febrero. Central location, but try to get a room away from the street. All rooms have fans and TVs, but vary in quality. Singles 170 pesos; doubles 200 pesos; triples 250 pesos; A/C 70 additional pesos.

Hotel Palma de Mallorca, Madero 510 (☎312 01 44 or 312 01 45), near the intersection of Zaragoza and Madero. Another hotel with tacky interior and cheap rooms. Singles 102 pesos, with mighty A/C 153 pesos; doubles 133 pesos, with A/C 184 pesos.

Hotel San Francisco, Madero 604 (312 31 98). Rooms with A/C: singles 163 pesos; doubles 198 pesos; triples 234 pesos.

FOOD

Villahermosa, like the rest of Tabasco, specializes in *mariscos* (seafood) and various swamp creatures. A typical *tabasqueño* dish—not for the faint of heart—is tortoise sautéed in green sauce and blood and then mixed with pickled armadillo. Another favorite is *pejelagarto* (lizardfish), a fish with the head of a lizard and the body of a fish, and *mojarra* (a local fish), flavored with ingredients like *chipilín*, *chaya* leaves, and *amashito* chile. To drink, try traditional *pozol*, made from

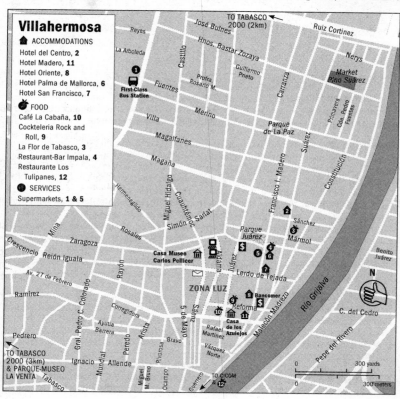

Villahermosa

🏠 ACCOMMODATIONS
Hotel del Centro, **2**
Hotel Madero, **11**
Hotel Oriente, **8**
Hotel Palma de Mallorca, **6**
Hotel San Francisco, **7**

🍴 FOOD
Café La Cabaña, **10**
Cockteleria Rock and Roll, **9**
La Flor de Tabasco, **3**
Restaurant-Bar Impala, **4**
Restaurante Los Tulipanes, **12**

⬤ SERVICES
Supermarkets, **1 & 5**

ground cornmeal, cocoa, and water. If someone offers you *venado* (venison) be aware that wetland deer are rare, and the hunting process is very destructive. Although *taquerías* litter the downtown area, most restaurants specializing in seafood are either far away or expensive. The best places to find regional foods are roadside restaurants and *palapas* along tourist routes such as the Teapa Comalcalco. For lovers of American junk food, there are McDonald's, Burger King, KFC, and Domino's Pizza in Zona Luz, and a Pizza Hut in Tabasco 2000.

■ **Restaurant Los Tulipanes** (☎312 92 17 or 312 92 09), in the CICOM complex, specializes in *comida tabasqueña*. Enjoy fresh seafood on the banks of the Río Grijalva in this local favorite. It's a tad expensive; seafood dishes start at 70 pesos, but the high cost means high quality, not tourist-inspired extortion. Open M-Sa 8am-11pm, Su 1-7pm.

Cockteleria Rock and Roll, Reforma 307 (☎312 05 93), across from Hotel Miraflores. The jukebox and swarm of customers make the "joint" a "hip scene." Cocktails are heavy on the cilantro. Cocktails 55-75 pesos. Open daily 10am-midnight.

La Flor de Tabasco, Madero 604 (☎312 48 97), your 1-stop fruit shop. A popular breakfast place, take your fruit cocktail (14 pesos) or *licuado de fruta* (12 pesos) to go and eat your meal across the street in Parque Juárez. Open daily 7am-9pm.

Cafe la Cabaña, Juárez 303 near 27 de Febrero. Drink coffee with the old folks of Villahermosa: frappuccino or cappuccino 11-13 pesos. Take-out coffee beans 80 pesos per kg. Open M-Sa 7am-10pm, Su 9am-9pm.

Tacolandia, Aldama in Zona Luz. Tacos for as little as 3.5 pesos. Flour tortilla with hot roast beef and cheese 12 pesos. Open M-Sa 7am-10pm.

Restaurant Bar Impala, Madero 421 (☎312 04 93). A cluttered hole in the wall with superb *tamalitos de chipilín, panuchos* (fried tortilla shells stuffed with meat and beans), and tacos for 4 pesos. Open M-Sa 9:30am-8pm.

🔄 SIGHTS

For a city unconcerned with tourism, Villahermosa has a surprising number of museums within walking distance of Zona Luz. Downtown is comprised of a series of pedestrian streets lined with specialty stores, *licuado* stands, gurgling fountains, shaded benches, and more hair salons than should be legal.

■ **PARQUE-MUSEO LA VENTA.** Located just south of Tabasco 2000, the park features 33 Olmec sculptures lifted from their original locations in La Venta, Tabasco, and western Veracruz and re-planted in Villahermosa by Carlos Pellicer Cámara. From the small museum at the entrance—less than a 1km walk along Ruiz Cortínes—enter the outdoor jungle-setting that reveals the impressive Olmec artifacts on a well-marked 1km path. The tropical setting is completed by wild animals in the park's zoo. *(Take a "Petrolera" bus (4 pesos) from Parque Juárez to the Pages Llergo and Ruiz Cortínez intersection. Walk northeast on Ruiz for 10min. until you reach the entrance. Alternatively, take a "Tabasco 2000," "Carrisal," or "Palacio" bus to the Tabasco and Ruiz Cortínez intersection, and cut through Parque Canabal to the entrance. Taxis 14-15 pesos. From Tabasco 2000, follow Paseo Tabasco to the intersection of Ruiz Cortínez; a 10-15min. walk. ☎314 16 52. Ticket office open daily 8am-4pm. 20 pesos. Museum open Tu-Sa 9am-4:30pm.)*

PARQUE TOMÁS GARRIDO CANABAL. Surrounding the museum is this sprawling park, complete with a large lagoon, landscaped alcoves, hidden benches and fountains, several concrete sculptures, and many teenage couples making out. While the *mirador* claims to offer a panoramic view of Villahermosa, all you get in reward for your 40m climb is a good look at a few treetops and the lagoon below. *(Main entrance is the corner of Tabasco and Grijalva.)*

MUSEO DE HISTORIA DE TABASCO. The small museum displays artifacts and pictures dealing with the history of the state, but the building itself is the most interesting exhibit. Known as **Casa de los Azulejos** (House of the Tiles), the famous blue edifice was built between 1889 and 1915 by a wealthy merchant and is decorated with Italian and Spanish baroque tiles; a different style adorns each room. Today, the house's occupants are old sewing machines and historical documents. Eleven classical sculptures sit atop the roof; the seated female figures are said to be members of the merchant's family. Also note the Egyptian tiles decorating the ledge on the outside walls. *(At the corner of Juárez and 27 de Febrero in Zona Luz. Open Tu-Sa 9am-8pm, Su 10am-5pm. 5 pesos.)*

CASA MUSEO CARLOS PELLICER. If you're wondering about the man whose name plasters every wall in town, head to this small museum, which features items such as a time line of Pellicer's life, furniture which belonged to his 19th-century *tabasqueño* family, and most importantly, his pants. Why other towns have not taken to displaying the pantaloons of famous citizens will forever remain a tourism-industry mystery. *(Sáenz 203. ☎312 01 57. Open M-Sa 10am-7pm.)*

CICOM. Carlos Pellicer's name graces yet another museum—the **Museo Regional de Antropología Carlos Pellicer Cámara,** the main attraction at Villahermosa's Center for the Investigation of Olmec and Maya Cultures (CICOM). The museum showcases Olmec and Maya artifacts from nearby archaeological sites La Venta and Comalcalco, including variations of favored Mesoamerican theme, "head sprouting several smaller heads." The center houses a public library, art school, theater, and traveling exhibits. *(From Zona Luz, the museum is a 15min. walk south along Río Grijalva. The #1 and "CICOM" buses pass often. ☎312 63 44. Open Tu-Su 9am-7pm. 10 pesos.)*

OVER 9 BILLION IGNORED

In Mexico, the line between work and home is often blurred. For many young clerks, so is the line between working and making out. To wring the precious drops of customer service from the mostly-dry towel of Mexican commerce, keep in mind the following facts:

—Most Mexican clerks were tragically born with a vision defect that allows them to see only straight ahead. Thus, customers not directly in front of a clerk will not be served. Stand proudly in front of the clerk and announce firmly yet politely what kind of business you would like to conduct.

—In Mexico, waiting in line requires concentration and quick reflexes. If there is even a small bit of space between you and the person you are waiting behind, someone else will fill it. This is common practice and is not considered "cutting." Keep close to the person you are following, perhaps attaching yourself to them with heavy-duty mountain-climbing equipment.

—Services advertised by Mexican businesses often bear no relation to the services offered. Frequently, clerks will tell you that only one employee of a given business has the authority to perform a certain transaction, such as money exchange or hotel room rental. Unfortunately, like the Mexican bird-god Quetzalcóatl, he is often "not in right now" (exiled on a raft made of snakes) and will "be back" (return with a blood-vengeance to claim his throne) in "a half hour" (in the year of One Reed). Remember that, like Quetzalcóatl, this employee is probably only mythical and may not return for a thousand eons.

—Never open your wallet/purse to reveal money before a price is set during a transaction, lest you unfortunately discover that the cost of the item in question is equivalent to the denomination of the highest bill you hold.

—Needless to say, in this sort of situation, *cambio* (change) will be hard to come by, as it always is in Mexico. Most establishments, even some hotels that ostensibly bring in thousands of pesos per day, keep only a tiny change jar that usually contains about 3 pesos. Prepare for this by using large bills to stock up on change at places such as supermarkets or bus terminals.

TABASCO 2000. Northwest on Paseo Tabasco, away from the city center and Río Grijalva, the complex features futuristically bland buildings and pedestrian-unfriendly streets light years away from the car-free walkways of Zona Luz. The long strip of stucco and concrete buildings includes the city's **Palacio Municipal**, a convention center, several fountains, a shopping mall, and a **planetarium** with **Omni Max** shows dubbed in Spanish. *(Take a "Tabasco 2000" or "Palacio" bus from Parque Juárez and get off by the Liverpool store, right smack in the middle of the complex. ☎ 316 36 41. Shows Tu-F 6 and 7pm, Sa-Su 5, 6, 7pm. 20 pesos.)*

YUMKÁ. Just 16km from the bustle of Villahermosa, animals run freely throughout the 101-hectare park, which mimics the four *tabasqueño* ecosystems: jungle, savannah, wetlands, and gift shop. Visitors view the animals in their natural habitats, traveling throughout the park in trolleys, boats, and by foot. *(To get there, take a combi marked "Ranchería Dos Montes" from the market on Suárez (4 pesos). Tell the driver where you want to get off. Combis are relatively infrequent; a taxi especial (70-80 pesos) is quickest. Open daily 9am-5pm. 30 pesos, children 15 pesos. 10 pesos extra for a lancha lagoon tour.)*

🎵📷 ENTERTAINMENT AND NIGHTLIFE

The Zona Hotelera in and around Tabasco 2000 is home to a number of discos and clubs. Here, Villahermosa's young and wealthy dress up and get down to a mix of *salsa* and tropical music. Taxi drivers are well-acquainted with disco hot spots, and their vehicles are the only safe means of reaching them at night.

BARS

Liquid o Solid Sports Bar, in the Zona Hotelera, next to the Hyatt. Food served in the "solid" portion of the bar, drinks in the "liquid" video-bar. Blue lighting, a lively social atmosphere, and bizarre videos such as "sports bloopers" found here. Solid bar open Tu-Su 6pm-2am; liquid bar open Th-Sa 9pm-2am.

Flambouyant (☎315 12 34), an elegant bar and club in the lobby of the 5-star Hyatt Hotel featuring a live band every night. 30-peso beers stage a frontal assault on the concept of supply and demand. Su-Th 7pm-1 or 2am, F-Sa 7pm-3am.

CLUBS

Disco Dasha (☎316 21 74 or 316 62 85), in front of Galerías Tabasco 2000 behind the government buildings. High prices and high security draw a slightly older and better-dressed crowd. Cover: Th men 70 pesos, women free; F men 60 pesos, women free; Sa men 160 pesos, women 110 pesos. Open Th-Sa 9pm-3am.

Ku Rock House, Sandino 548 (☎315 94 31 or 315 94 33), in Col. 1 de Mayo. The same rocking, sweaty, pounding atmosphere, but at a more manageable price. Cover W-Th 40 pesos, F-Sa 50 pesos. Open W-Sa 9pm-3am.

Factory Video Bar, Av. Méndez 1602. Cheap club features electronica and 20-peso beers. W-F no cover, Sa 30 pesos for men. Open W-Sa 9pm-3am.

CULTURAL EVENTS

Villahermosa presents a few "cultural" options. The **Centro Cultural Villahermosa** on Madero at the corner of Zaragoza, across from Parque Juárez, posts a weekly program of events around the city and at the *Centro* itself, including recitals and screenings. The cafe in the back of **Galería El Jaguar Despertado,** Sáenz 117, near Reforma in the Zona Luz, features live classical music or jazz. A weekly program of cultural events may be posted outside the door; performances are usually at 8pm. There is also a gallery upstairs. (☎314 12 44. Open M-Sa 9am-9pm, Su 9am-3pm.) Across the street, **Colégio de Arte Tabasco,** Sáenz 122, features contemporary *tabasqueño* artwork, much of it for sale. (Open M-Sa 9am-9pm, Su 9am-3pm.)

🏛 DAYTRIPS FROM VILLAHERMOSA

As the largest city in the mostly rural state of Tabasco, Villahermosa serves as a base for dozens of daytrips into the state's northern coast and southern jungle.

COMALCALCO

The ruins of Comalcalco are 3km outside the large and chaotic city of the same name, 52km northwest of Villahermosa. Though Comalcalco has a historic church and several budget hotels, it's better to skip the city altogether and make the visit directly from Villahermosa. Taxi colectivos to Comalcalco leave frequently from Alberto Reyes at Mina on the other side of Chedraui's from the 1st-class bus station (1hr., 30 pesos) and stop at the edge of Comalcalco's market, facing the zócalo. From there, take a taxi especial (25 pesos). Getting back is easier, especially toward closing time when the bus makes stops at the main gate (4 pesos). Site open daily 10am-5pm. 30 pesos; Su free. Guides are available in English, Spanish, and Italian; 150 pesos for 1½hr.

Unpublicized and generally ignored by backpackers, the Maya ruins of Comalcalco are surprisingly spectacular. Named somewhat mundanely after the *comale*, a dish used to make tortillas, the city, on the western frontier of Maya territory, was built during the Classic Period (100 BC-AD 800). Because the Tabasco Maya, known as Chontals, lacked stone to construct their temples, they used baked clay, making Comalcalco the oldest brick city in all the Americas.

To see the buildings themselves, follow the main road left from the museum entrance into the main plaza. With 10 levels, the 25m **pyramid** to the left of the entrance to the site is Comalcalco's landmark. Under an awning on the building's north face, the remains of a carving of a giant winged toad and several humans are all that's left of decorations that once covered the entire surface of the structure. Past temples II and III, a path leads to the **Gran Acropolis,** an 80m complex of temples and private residences. Look closely at the dilapidated walls and you can see the insides of Comalcalco's brickwork and oyster-shell mortar. Among the ruins is the precarious-looking **Palacio,** half of whose vault has somehow remained intact. The acropolis also contains what is thought to be a bathtub and cooling system. From the top of the acropolis it's possible to look out and see what the jungle looked like before deforestation and radio towers. Walk back down through the acropolis and keep an eye out for the sculptural remnants that have been preserved in protected corners of the structures. Especially interesting reliefs can be found on the east side in the **Tomb of the Nine Men of Night;** the figures are believed to represent the nine night gods of the Maya pantheon.

TEAPA AND LAS GRUTAS COCONÁ

To get to Teapa, take a taxi colectivo from the corner of Madero and Sánchez, past Parque Juárez (1hr., 30 pesos). 2nd-class buses travel between the 2 cities every 30min. (26 pesos 2nd-class, 27 pesos 1st-class), but take much longer to arrive. To return to Villahermosa, take 1 of the red taxi colectivos that gather on Teapa's main drag. Combis for the grutas leave from Bastar on the right-hand side of the church in Teapa (every 30min., 3 pesos). Taxis charge 15 pesos. Caves open daily 9am-4pm. 15 pesos, children 7 pesos. Guides cost about 20 pesos.

Located 52km south of Villahermosa amid countless farms and ranches, Teapa provides a pleasant base from which to explore nearby natural attractions. Several 18th-century churches in town, including the Franciscan **Temple of Santiago Apostol** and Jesuit **Temple of Tecomajica,** are also worth a visit. The real reason for traveling to Teapa, however, are **Las Grutas Coconá,** located just 2km outside of the city. Discovered in the late 1800s by two adventurous brothers hunting in the woods, the caves (or *grutas*) contain a lighted path that winds for 500m into the hillside, passing impressive caverns and underground lagoons along the way. Guides offer their services at the entrance; though unnecessary, they do point out formations that resemble other objects (the Virgin Mary, the head of a moose, etc.). The explanations are interesting, but your time may be better spent strolling through the *grutas* on your own. For some real spelunking, negotiate with the guides to take you to the unexplored *gruta* about 200m away. Tours of this *gruta* last anywhere from 1½ to three hours and are a bad idea for anyone claustrophobic or afraid of the dark. Try to pay less than 35 pesos for the tour.

EL AZUFRE

Take a combi from Teapa's market and tell the driver where you want to go (5 pesos). Taxis cost 40 pesos. Returning is more difficult: climb the hill from the spa to the main road, and flag down a taxi or bus. Open daily 6am-7pm. 10 pesos, children 5 pesos.

Another 15min. *combi* ride from Teapa is El Azufre, a spa with two large sulfur *albercas*. Although the pools could be better maintained, visitors claim the water has therapeutic qualities. Also available at the site are bathroom facilities, *palapas*, and a hotel. (Rooms 150 pesos; camping is free.)

TAPIJULAPA AND PARQUE NATURAL DE LA VILLA LUZ

2 buses serve the town, leaving every hour from Tacotalpa. To get to Tacotalpa, catch one of the taxi colectivos (1hr., 25 pesos) from the opposite side of Chedraui's next to the ADO station. 2nd-class buses leave for Tacotalpa every 30min. (PSI; 1½hr., 5:30am-9pm, 23 pesos). Colectivos stop on Tacotalpa's main drag. Half a block farther down on the same street, red and white buses leave for Tapijulapa plaza every hour (40min., 5am-6pm, 5 pesos). To reach the lancha dock, head straight 2 blocks past the plaza to the end of the street, turn right and head 1 block downhill. Return buses to Tacotalpa leave from the station, 2 blocks north of the plaza (every hr., last one at 7pm). Buses and taxi-colectivos returning to Villahermosa from Tacotalpa stop running around 8pm.

While traveling to Tapijulapa, 90km south of Villahermosa, the bus crosses into the state's highest mountains, where the humidity lets up and the distinction between slumber and consciousness becomes blurred.

Parque Natural de la Villa Luz, 3km from Tapijulapa, is reached by *lancha* (15 pesos roundtrip). Upon entering the *lancha*, climb the stairs in front of you to enter the park. Follow the cow path through a pasture until you come to a fence and go through one of the gates; guides can be found at the house just past the fence. Continue on and take the left fork to the abandoned home of former governor Tomás Garrido Canabal, whose name is plastered all over Villahermosa. The house has been outfitted with some token artifacts (an old sewing machine) and declared a museum. Continue along the path for 10min. and you'll arrive at the top of the *cascadas*. It is safe to bathe in the waist-high, sulfur-rich water, but you may want to wait until you reach the spas at the end, where you'll have surer footing.

The right fork will take you to another fork in the road. Stay right to reach **La Cueva de Las Sardinas Ciegas.** The cave's odd name comes from the sardines that, having adapted to their dark environment, are all blind. Every year on the Sunday before Easter, residents of Tapijulapa gather at the cave for the **Pesca de la Sardina.** While dancing to the music of the *tamborileros*, celebrants toss powdered narcotic plants into the water, which stun the fish and cause them to float to the top of the water for easy harvesting. The left fork leads to the spas—an area with several pools, all filled with therapeutic sulfur water. To return to the *lancha* dock, walk back retracing your steps (25min.). The entire trek takes approximately 2hr. Tip your guide at least 20-25 pesos.

OXOLOTÁN

From Tapijulapa, walk straight through the building opposite the plaza and climb the stairs on the opposite side of the street. Check out the view from the small courtyard at the top; the 17th-century Santiago Apostol church on the right side of the courtyard is also worth a visit. Walk through the courtyard and downhill 1 block to the main road. The green and white Oxolotán bus picks up here (40min., every hr., 5 pesos). Upon exiting the bus, with your back to the station, turn right and walk 2 blocks; the church is to your left on the cross street and the museum entrance is on the opposite side. Return buses to Tacotalpa leave every 1-1½hr., 5:30am-5pm. Museum open daily 9am-5pm. Free.

Farther down the road from Tapijulapa is Oxolotán (pop. 2000), a tiny, sleepy town in the middle of nowhere, albeit an exquisitely beautiful nowhere. The town's **Ex-convento de Santo Domingo** is a good excuse to visit, but the real reasons for going are the bus ride into the mountains and the amenity-free restfulness of the town. In 1550, when the Dominicans finally got around to evangelizing Tabasco, Oxolotán was an important trade center because of its position as the last navigable point on the Río Grijalva. When the ex-convento was finally finished in 1578, the town's importance had flagged, and the Dominicans relocated to Tacotalpa, leaving Oxolotán with a grand, empty parish church. The church has been in use for the last 400 years, and recent renovations have made the cloister a polished museum. The undecorated stone walls and quiet courtyards exude a tranquility that permeates the town, whose old *zócalo* consists of the ex-convento's ex-patio.

RESERVA DE LA BIOSFERA PATANOS DE CENTLA

Though Tabasco's eco-tourism industry has been slow and cumbersome in its attempts to take flight, the state's predominant feature (after its oil reserves) is its natural beauty. If you're willing to negotiate, it's possible to see the amazing jungle on a very limited budget. One of the best places to do this is the **Reserva de la Biosfera**, a preserve encompassing 302,000 hectares of the wetlands formed by the huge river systems that wind their way into the state. Set aside by the government in 1992, the land is home to 50,000 people, most of whom live in small fishing villages along the river systems deep inside the preserve. In addition to Centla's waterfalls, swamps, rivers, and the incredible variety of animals that inhabit them, the preserve represents a point of conflict between ecologists and the economic interests of the indigenous peoples who live here. Small turtles sell for 100 pesos in the open market, and rare venison goes for even more, giving residents a good reason to hunt many of the protected animals. This hunting is the bane of people who work at the preserve's station at **Tres Brazos.** The director of the program, Juan Carlos Romero, Paseo de la Sierra 613 (☎310 14 31), in the Colonial Reforma, will grant permission to stay at the Tres Brazos station, where visitors pay no more than the cost of gas and minimal fees for food in the cheery restaurant. The station has two clean, separate dorms for men and women, and a satellite TV that entertains attendants who keep the place open 24hr. When sending requests, explain that you'd like to stay at the station and see the *patanos* (wetlands) by *lancha*. Don't forget to drop the key word: *ecoturismo*. Once you have permission, the office will arrange transportation to the station just south of Frontera on the Río Grijalva, about 1½hr. northeast of Villahermosa. Exploring the reserve will take initiative, but *lanchistas* and locals will help you out, and the *crocodilos* will ensure an exciting time.

AGUA SELVA ECOTOURISM PROJECT

Reaching the project is a challenge. Buses to Herradura leave from the 2nd-class terminal in Villahermosa (11 per day, 43 pesos). Stop 1st in Huimanguillo (every 30min. 5:30am-9pm, 22 pesos) for a tour; Jorge Pagole del Valle (☎375 00 02), of the Hotel del Carmen at Morelos 39 (take a cab, 15 pesos), will guide you (100 pesos per day). From Herradura, pick-up trucks (pasajeras) leave for Malpasito daily at approximately 9am, noon, and 3pm (20min., 6 pesos). They return to Herradura from the town's main street 3 times a day. Pasajeras leave from Herradura to Francisco J. Mújica daily from 2-3pm (20 pesos). The only transportation returning to Herradura leaves at 4am the next morning. No transportation exists between Francisco J. Mújica and Malpasito, although it may be possible to rent a bike.

City-weary adventurers are drawn to Agua Selva, which encompasses 15,000 hectares of land bordering Chiapas and Veracruz. Located 142km southwest of Villahermosa, the project offers two main attractions: water and the jungle. With over 100 waterfalls, small mountains ranging up to 1000m, thick vegetation, and abundant wildlife (including armadillos, jaguars, and a wide variety of birds), the natural attractions necessary for the project's success are certainly there. Unfortunately, the human resources behind the project have so far been insufficient to maintain its infrastructure. Nonetheless, Agua Selva's natural beauty compensates for the hassle involved in reaching it, and locals eager to see the project succeed can help you upon your arrival.

MALPASITO. The tiny village of Malpasito is home to several not-to-be-missed attractions. Upon arriving, ask to be dropped off at the home of **Catalina Martínez,** who manages the flow of tourism into Agua Selva and is available for questions at any time. She can provide you with information about Malpasito and also arrange for a **guide** (50 pesos for a full day). The **Albergue Ecológico** is a rustic two-room lodging with beds and pillows for up to 13 people (35 pesos per person). Bath includes two toilets, a sink, and a bucket for bathing. Alternatively, **Guillermo Pérez Cajija** rents out a two-room *palapa* in his backyard. The *Señora* of the house prepares meals for a low price. Malpasito is a rural village with no services—accommodations are very basic. Do not expect blankets. Expect cockroaches.

A short 1km hike on a path just uphill from the *albergue* leads to the Post-Classic Maya ruins of **Zoque Ruins of Malpasito** (admission 22 pesos). Little is known about the Zoque Maya other than that they offered little resistance to the Spanish. Before entering the site, check out the **petroglyphs,** sketches of animals, birds, humans, and geometric shapes in rock, of which over 60 have been found so far. To your left after the short walk from the entrance to the clearing is the obligatory **ball court,** complete with what appears to have been a sort of locker room. On the plaza past the ball court, stairs lead to a second, smaller plaza, which offers a breathtaking view of the surrounding mountains. Ask your guide to lead you to the waterfall beyond the ruins, which has a pool at its base that is safe for swimming. From here, several trails lead farther into the mountains, where you can check out the rock formations of *La Pava* and *La Copa*. To find another waterfall, leave the site and walk down the hill until a road branches left. Follow this road up into the hills until it ends at a dilapidated shack. Follow the path on the inside of the fence leading away from the shack, cross the wooden footbridge and continue down the slope until the path splits. The right branch winds down to the base of a fall and the left to the top. The walk takes about 30min.

FRANCISCO J. MÚJICA. The other village providing accommodations and tourist resources near Agua Selva is Francisco J. Mújica, located approximately 20km west of Herradura. **Antonio Domínguez** manages an *albergue* nearly identical to that in Malpasito (35 pesos per person). Sr. Domínguez can help you find a trustworthy guide with whom to view the surrounding area. **Cascada Velo de Novia** (Bridal Veil Falls) is just an hour's hike from the village; beyond it is a steep canyon that you can descend (carefully and with the aid of the guide's rope) to a ledge that leads beneath the falls. The caves in the surrounding area contain petroglyphs as well, which guides can point out to you. If you can arrange an escort to the village of **Carlos A. Madrazo,** 4km beyond Francisco J. Mújica, **Raimundo Cruz,** a guide within the village, can lead you to several other noteworthy sites, including **Cascada de Aguaima,** another 4km from Madrazo. At this thundering *cascada*, two rivers converge to form the Río Pedregal.

PARAÍSO

1st-class buses from Villahermosa: 12:40, 4:50, 8:40pm, 44 pesos. 2nd-class buses run from Villahermosa to the 2nd-class terminal in Paraíso; the ride is long, bumpy, and hot (2¼hr., every hr. 6am-8pm, 25 pesos). Or, take a quicker taxi colectivo from the far side of Chedraui's (1¼hr., 30 pesos). Colectivos stop on 2 de Abril near Paraíso's zócalo. To reach the 2nd-class station from the zócalo, walk 2½ blocks away from Juárez, the main street, to Buenos Aires. The station is 9 blocks to the left.

Only 71km from Villahermosa, Paraíso and its beaches will help conquer the heat—if just for a day or two. The town is home to numerous seafood restaurants, and native oysters are sold on the streets. Other fresh seafood delicacies include crab, *mojarra*, and shrimp. There are several budget hotels, but your best option may be to sleep in a hammock on one of the beaches: many have facilities and *palapas* for hammock-hanging, and although the sand may not glitter as brightly as along the Caribbean, beaches are clean, uncrowded, and safe.

Public beaches lie to the east and west of the city. Beaches northwest of the city, including **Varadero, El Paraíso, Pal Mar,** and **Paraíso y Mar** can easily be reached by the "Playa" *combi* that leaves from the 2nd-class bus station (20min., every hr., 5 pesos). All lie around 500m right of the main road and have *palapas* in which visitors can hang their hammocks free of charge. Varadero and El Paraíso are by far the nicest of the four; both have restaurants, and El Paraíso has hotels and a pool (10 pesos, children 5 pesos).

Alternatively, an eastbound bus to Chiltepec leaves every 30min. from the second-class bus station. The first stop is **Puerto Ceiba** (15min., 3.5 pesos), a small fishing village on the edge of Laguna Mecoacán, a 51,000 hectare oyster breeding ground. Local fishermen give *lancha* tours of the lagoon; ask at any of the docks along the way. Across the bridge from Puerto Ceiba is **El Bellote,** another small fishing town located between the lagoon and the Río Seco. Although the town itself offers few attractions, it has several affordable, high-quality restaurants. Near the end of the route to Chiltepec and 27km east of El Paraíso is the town of **Playa Bruja;** just east is the beach itself, which has a restaurant and *palapas*.

CHIAPAS

TONALÁ ☎ 9

The beach towns in Oaxaca manage to be prettier, livelier, more secluded, and better serviced, but the Chiapan town of Tonalá (pop. 75,000) provides easy access to **Puerto Arista** and **Boca del Cielo,** lesser beaches that share a lazy vibe. Aside from *Semana Santa* and weekends in July and August, they are practically abandoned, with lights out by 8pm. The town is devoid of nearly all services save a public telephone, which can't be used for phone card calls, costs an unbelievable 12 pesos per minute, and sits beneath a sign that inexplicably declares that the telephone was "not invented to lengthen conversations." Tonalá proper is a giant sauna, unbelievably hot and humid, and offers little besides food and lodging for tourists.

▐ TRANSPORTATION

Autotransportes Tuxtla Gutiérrez, Hidalgo 56, five blocks south of the *zócalo*, has first-class bus service to: **Mexico City** (13hr., 5pm, 335 pesos) via **Puebla** (11hr., 285 pesos). First-class buses, including Maya de Oro (☎ 663 05 40), leave from the Cristóbal Colón station, six blocks north of the zócalo, for: **Mexico City** (13hr., 8pm, 444 pesos); **Oaxaca** (6½hr., 9:30pm, 180 pesos); **Puebla** (10hr., 8pm, 387 pesos); **Tapachula** (3hr., 20 per day 1am-7:40pm, 180 pesos); **Tuxtla Gutiérrez** (3hr., every hr. 3am-7:30pm, 65 pesos). **Taxis** (☎ 663 06 20) cruise up and down Hidalgo and hang out in the zócalo (40 pesos to Puerto Arista). If you're getting up early, the 24hr. radiotaxis (☎ 663 22 99) located on Hidalgo in the *zócalo*, will get you at your hotel. **Luggage storage** is 5 pesos per day, in the bus station.

▐ ORIENTATION AND PRACTICAL INFORMATION

Tonalá lies 223km northwest of Tapachula and 172km southwest of Tuxtla Gutiérrez. All **bus stations** are on **Hidalgo,** Tonalá's main street. To get to the *zócalo* from the Cristóbal Colón bus station, take a left and head six blocks south. Both the Autotransportes Tuxtla Gutiérrez and Fletes y Pasajes bus stations are south of the *centro*, so turn right and walk five blocks north. As the coastal highway, Hidalgo runs roughly north-south through town. To the east, **Rayón** parallels Hidalgo, while to the west run **Matamoros, Juárez,** and **Allende.** Listed from north to south, **Madero, 16 de Septiembre, 5 de Febrero, Independencia,** and **5 de Mayo** run east-west, completing the grid that composes the city center.

The **tourist office** is at Hidalgo and 5 de Mayo, two blocks south of the bus station, on the 2nd fl. of the Esmeralda building. (☎ 663 27 87. Open M-F 8am-4pm.) **Banamex,** Hidalgo 137 at 5 de Febrero, half a block south of the *zócalo*, exchanges currency and has a 24hr. **ATM.** (☎ 663 00 37. Open M-F 9am-3pm.) **Police:** (☎ 663 01 03), on Calle Libertad, two blocks north of Cristóbal Colón and to the right. **Farmacia El Pastillaero:** 16 de Septiembre, half a block west of Hidalgo. (☎ 663 31 98. Open 24hr.) **Hospital General:** (☎ 663 06 87), 27 de Septiembre at Mina, six blocks south of the *zócalo* and a turn three blocks east before the gas station. **Red Cross:** (☎ 663 21 21), on Joaquín Miguel Guttiérez. **Internet: Ciber Club Cafe** on Hidalgo, three blocks south of Cristóbal Colón and three blocks north of the *zócalo*. (10 pesos per hr. Open daily 9am-11pm.) **Post office:** 10min. walk west of Hidalgo on 16 de Septiembre. (Open M-F 9am-4pm.) **Postal code:** 30500.

◤ ACCOMMODATIONS AND FOOD

Maintaining health and sanity in sweltering Tonalá may require spending extra money for A/C. Cheaper rooms of comparable cleanliness and atmosphere are available in Puerto Arista. The **Hotel Tonalá,** a few blocks south of the Cristóbal Colón station, charges high rates for little space in its plains rooms. (☎ 663 04 80. Singles 160 pesos; doubles with TV and fan 200 pesos; triples with TV and A/C 280 pesos.) **Restaurant Sambors** at Madero and Hidalgo, on the *zócalo*, has good food and a wide-angle view of the *zócalo*, or at least the tin-roofed vendors' stands that surround it. (☎ 663 06 80. *Tortas* 12 pesos, *licuados* 9 pesos. Open daily 9am-1am.) **Restaurante Nora,** on Independencia 10, less than a block east of Hidalgo and a block from the *zócalo*, is a calm refuge from heat and sun. (☎ 663 02 43. 3-course *comida corrida* 45 pesos. Open M-Sa 8am-6pm.) For even cheaper meals, a number of small *comida típica* restaurants sell *pollo rostizado* for under 20 pesos.

◤ NEAR TONALÁ: PUERTO ARISTA

For most of the year, **Puerto Arista** is a ghost town. Hotel owners seem surprised to have guests, and restaurants shut before the posted closing for lack of customers. Among the few budget accommodations in the peaceful town is **Hotel Maracaino,** located a ways down the beach from the main road. This light clean hotel with sporadic views of the sea has singles for 150 pesos and doubles for 200 pesos. For a more upscale setting, try **Hotel Lizeth,** closer to the main intersection. (Singles with fan and TV 200 pesos; doubles with fan 230 pesos, with A/C 330 pesos. In the off-season, singles with A/C are 120 pesos.) Most hotels also serve moderately priced food. To get to Puerto Arista, catch a *combi* leaving from Juárez and 20 de Marzo, two blocks off Hidalgo (45 min., 10 pesos). From the same place, catch a *mini* heading to Boca de Cielo, a beachside estuary (1¼hr. from Tonalá).

TUXTLA GUTIÉRREZ ☎ 9

Energetic young Tuxtla Gutiérrez (pop. 466,495) is the capital of Chiapas and the focal point of commerce and transportation for most of southern Mexico. "Tuxtla" comes from the Náhuatl *tuchtlan*, meaning "place where rabbits abound," while "Gutiérrez" originates with Miguel Gutiérrez, a progressive *chiapaneco* governor who, rather than succumb to imperialist right-wing forces, wrapped himself in the Mexican flag and dramatically leapt to his death from a church spire.

Tuxtla Gutiérrez

🏠 ACCOMMODATIONS

Hotel Avenida, **4**
Hotel Del Pasaje, **8**
Hotel Don Candido, **9**
Villas Deportivas Juvenil, **6**

🍴 FOOD

La Antigua Fogata, **5**
Las Pinchachas, **7**
Restaurante Imperial, **1**
Restaurante Vegetariano Nah-Yaxal, **3**
Restaurante Tuxtla, **2**

📁 TRANSPORTATION

GETTING AROUND
Combis (VW van *colectivos*) run frequently throughout the city, east-west on Av. Central, north on Calle Central, east on Calle 1 Pte. Sur, and south on Calle 1 Sur Ote. (6am-10pm, 4 pesos).

GETTING AWAY
Airport: Aeropuerto Francisco Sarabia (☎ 615 05 37) is 15km southwest of town. Taxis 20 pesos. **Aerocaribe,** Av. Central Pte. 206 (☎ 612 00 20, or at the airport ☎ 612 17 72). **Aviacsa,** Av. Central Pte. 1144 (☎ 612 80 81, or at the airport ☎ 612 33 55).

Buses: To get to the *zócalo* from the **ADO/Cristóbal Colón bus station,** 2 Nte. Pte. 268, walk left on 2 Nte. Pte. (away from the buses) for 2 blocks. The *zócalo* is to your right along Calle Central. Cristóbal Colón (☎ 612 51 22) goes to: **Cancún** (18hr., 12:30pm, 460 pesos); **Mexico City** (15hr.; 2:30, 5:35, 8, 9:30pm; 490 pesos); **Oaxaca** (10hr.; 11:30am, 7:15pm, midnight; 218 pesos); **Palenque** (6hr., 6 per day 6am-11:30pm, 98 pesos); **Puebla** (13hr., 3 per day, 387 pesos); **Puerto Escondido** (11hr.; 5:30am, 12:30, 11:15pm; 230 pesos); **San Cristóbal de las Casas** (2hr., 6 per day 5:30am-11:15pm, 34 pesos); **Tehuantepec** (6½hr., 5 per day, 118 pesos); **Tapachula** (6hr., 14 per day 6am-midnight, 161 pesos); **Veracruz** (12hr.; 9:30pm, 287 pesos); and **Villahermosa** (7hr.; 11:15am, 3, 11:30pm; 125 pesos). Autotransportes Tuxtla Gutiérrez bus station, Av. 3 Sur 712, sits in a cul-de-sac at Av. 3 Sur and Calle 7 Ote. To get to the *zócalo*, exit right out of the station and make another right into the alley that doubles as a market. Make the 1st left onto Av. 2 Sur and continue west to Calle Central—the *zócalo* is two blocks to the right. Autotransportes Tuxtla Gutiérrez (☎ 612 03 22) has less frequent, slower buses at cheaper fares to similar destinations. Travelers from **Chiapa de Corzo** disembark at the small station at the corner of Calle 2 Ote. and Av. 2 Sur. To get to the *zócalo*, exit the station and walk right 2 blocks to Av. Central; the *zócalo* is 2 blocks to the left.

Local Transport: One of the cheapest ways to get to **San Cristóbal** is via Transporte Colosio, which sends *combis* from Av. 3 Sur between Calles 2 and 3 Ote., and Av. 2 Sur between Calles 3 and 4 Ote. (every 10min. 5am-9pm, 30 pesos). To reach **Chiapa de Corzo,** hop on a Transportes Chiapa-Tuxtla *microbús* at the station at Av. 2 Sur and Calle 2 Ote. (25min., every 10min., 6 pesos) or grab one leaving town on Blvd. Corzo.

✷ 🛈 ORIENTATION AND PRACTICAL INFORMATION

Tuxtla lies 85km west of San Cristóbal and 293km south of Villahermosa. *Avenidas* run east-west and *calles* north-south. The city's central axis, upon which the *zócalo* rests, is formed by **Av. Central** and **Calle Central**. Streets are numbered according to their distance from and geographical relation to the central axis. For example, Calle 2 Oriente Sur lies south of Av. Central and two blocks east of Calle Central. **Domínguez** is an east-west artery that runs south of the *zócalo*. Av. Central changes to **Corzo** in the east.

TOURIST AND FINANCIAL SERVICES

Tourist Office: Dirección Municipal de Turismo (☎ 612 55 11, ext. 214), 2 Nte. Ote. at Calle Central, on the street which runs under the public square. City maps and information. Open M-Sa 8am-8pm. The **State Tourism Office** is at Blvd. Domínguez 950, about 15 blocks west of the *zócalo*. There is a *modulo* open at this location M-F 9am-9pm.

Currency Exchange: Tuxtla's *parque central* and Av. Central are filled with banks and ATMS. **Bital,** on Calle Central, between Av. Central and Av. 1 Nte., across from the *zócalo*, has 24hr. **ATMs.** Open for exchange M-Sa 8am-7pm. **Bancrecer,** on the corner of Av. Central and Calle 1 Pte., also changes currency and has 24hr. **ATMs.**

LOCAL SERVICES

Luggage Storage: Free at the tourism office in the *zócalo*.

Markets: Tuxtla's crazy **Mercado Díaz Orden,** on Calle Central between Av. 3 and 4 Sur, has food and trinket stands. Open daily 6am-8pm. **Mercado Andador San Roque**, Calle 4 Ote. between Av. 3 and 4 Sur, has the best straw hats in town, oodles of wicker, and several cheap eateries. Open daily 7am-4pm.

Supermarket: Chedraui's, Blvd. Corzo, on the left just past the military base. Take an eastbound "Ruta 1" *combi* from a block west of the *zócalo* on Av. Central.

Car Rental: Hertz, Blvd. Domínguez 1195 (☎ 615 53 48), in Hotel Camino Real. Sedan 565 pesos per day. Open M-Sa 8am-8pm, Su 9am-5pm. **Budget Rent-A-Car,** Blvd. Domínguez 2510 (☎ 615 13 82). Sedans 573 pesos per day. Open daily 8am-7pm.

EMERGENCY AND COMMUNICATIONS

Emergency: ☎060, or call **Policía de Seguridad Pública** (☎612 05 30 or 613 78 05).

Police: Tourist assistance: ☎1 800 90 392 00.

Pharmacy: Farmacía del Ahorro, corner of Av. Central and Calle Central. Open 6am-midnight. For deliveries call 6 13 88.

Red Cross: 5 Nte. Pte. 1480 (☎612 00 96 or 614 28 31), on the west side of town. Little English spoken.

Hospital: Sanatorio Rojas, 2 Av. Sur Pte. 1487 (☎612 54 14). Some English spoken.

Fax: Telecomm (☎613 65 47; fax 612 42 96), Av. 1 Nte. at 2 Ote., next to the post office. Open M-F 8am-6pm, Sa 9am-5pm, Su 9am-1pm.

Internet Access: Internet cafes cluster on Calle Central past Av. 4 Nte., and on Av. Central east of the *zócalo*. **Ciber Cafe,** at Calle Central Nte. 402 (☎614 63 36), has fast connections and lots of computers. 8 pesos per hr. Open M-Sa 9am-9pm.

Post Office: (☎612 04 16), on Av. 1 Nte. at 2 Ote., on the northeast corner of the *zócalo* in the corridor to the right of the Palacio Municipal. Open M-F 9am-5pm, Sa 9am-1pm. **Mexpost** available.

Postal Code: 29000.

ACCOMMODATIONS

There are not enough backpackers in Tuxtla to support hostels or even hotels with hostel-like communal leanings, but cheap rooms abound, especially near the *mercado* around Av. 5 Sur. To avoid the mayhem of the market, head north to Av. Central Pte., where rooms are only slightly more expensive. Be aware that bathing in these places may be a lukewarm experience at best.

Villas Deportivas Juvenil, Blvd. Corzo 1800 (☎612 12 01), next to the footbridge over the road. From 1 block west of the plaza on Av. Central, catch an eastbound *combi* and ask the driver to let you off at INDEJECH (een-day-heche; rhymes with Anne Heche). A huge community sports center with 2 floors of dorm-style rooms on the east side. The beds are uncomfy, there are no toilet seats or doors for the toilet and shower stalls, and toilet paper is rare, but the price is a preposterously low 35 pesos per night. There is also a cafeteria open until 9pm M-Sa. Breakfast, lunch, and dinner 15 pesos each.

Hotel Del Pasaje, Av. 5 Sur Pte. 140 (☎612 15 50 or 612 15 52), ½ block west of Calle Central. Rooms are quiet, clean, and comfortable. The *mercado* lurks nearby. Singles 90 pesos, with A/C 140 pesos; doubles with A/C and TV 170 pesos.

Hotel Don Candido, Av. 5 Sur Ote. 142 (☎612 66 06), ½ block east of Calle Central. Slightly pricier with colorful decor and a sunny courtyard. Prime location minimizes the constant noise problematic in cheaper hotels. Singles 95 pesos; doubles 110 pesos.

Hotel Avenida, Av. Central 244 (☎612 08 07), between 1 and 2 Pte., has a nice central location and big rooms. Singles 100 pesos; doubles 150 pesos.

FOOD

Culinary miracles are rare in Tuxtla, but inexpensive eateries abound. *Carnes*, Chiapas-style, come prepared in *pepitas de calabaza* (squash seeds) or *hierba santa*. Other regional favorites include *pozol* and *tazcalate*, (two beverages with corn and cocoa bases). *Tamales* in Tuxtla come with every filling imaginable and can often be had for 5 pesos. For the gastronomically adventurous, *nucús*, edible ants, are plentiful at the start of the rainy season and come with everything from guacamole to taco fillings. Several new restaurants boldly proclaim their vegetarian leanings in this meat-lover's world.

☒ **Las Pichanchas,** Av. Central 837 (☎612 53 51), between Calles 8 and 9 Ote. Sharp waiters, traditional decorations, an upscale courtyard, *marimba* music, and nightly (9pm) *ballet folklórico* performances accompany reasonable prices for *carne salada con pepita de calabaza* (40 pesos), *tamales* (18 pesos), and *tazcalate* (10 pesos). Waiters shout *"¡Salió el pulpo!"* whenever someone rings a bell by the bar. Warning: do not order beer, which costs 14 pesos for a bottle that looks like the result of a government beer-shrinking project gone awry. Open daily noon-midnight.

Restaurante Vegetariano Nah-Yaxal, Calle 6 Pte. 124 (☎613 96 48), ½ block north of Av. Central. A leader in Tuxtla's vegetarian movement, Nah has colonized several storefronts around the *centro*. Full vegetarian *comida corrida* 38 pesos. Frozen yogurt mixed with fruit and grain 11 pesos. Open M-Sa 7am-10pm, Su 8am-5pm.

Restaurante Imperial, Calle Central Nte. 263 (☎612 06 48), 1 block north of the *zócalo*. Excellent *comida corrida* (26 pesos), *antojitos* (19 pesos), and breakfasts (8-18 pesos) are the secret to the imperialism. Open daily 7am-7pm.

La Antigua Fogata, Calle 4 Ote. 203 at the corner of 1 Sur, just off Av. Central. Greasy taco shack atmosphere, greasy taco shack prices, but much better than greasy taco shack food—especially with 25 years of experience behind the chicken *al carbón*. ¼ chicken 30 pesos. Open daily 8:30am-11:30pm.

Restaurante Tuxtla, 2 Norte and Calle Central. Big lunches with the fixings for 25 pesos. *Barbacoa de barrejo* is big and meaty. Open daily 7:30am-6:30pm.

👁 SIGHTS

MIGUEL ÁLVAREZ DEL TORO (ZOOMAT). The *zoológico* features more than 1200 animals in a natural Chiapan jungle. The quetzal and tapir are not found in any other zoo, and some endangered species, like the acrobatic spider monkeys, are hardly found anywhere. Some animals roam freely, as do numerous children and refreshment stands. *(From Calle 1 Ote. between Av. 6 and 7 Sur, take the "Cerro Hueco" or "Zoológico" bus (every 30min., 3 pesos). Open Tu-Su 8:30am-5:30pm. Free.)*

PARQUE MADERO. Many of Tuxtla's attractions can be found in Parque Madero. In the middle of the park is **Teatro de la Ciudad Emilio Rabasa.** Films by Latin American directors and performances of *ballet folklórico* dominate the schedule (hours vary; performances begin around 6pm on weekends and cost 20 pesos). To the north of the theater is a children's amusement park, **Conviviencia Infantil.** (Open Tu-Su 10am-10pm.) The far end of the amusement park holds the open-air **Teatro Bonampak,** which has free folk dance performances (Su 5pm). South of the *teatro* lies a broad concourse, lined with fountains and busts of famous Mexicans. Down the walkway on the right is **Museo Regional de Chiapas,** which displays regional archaeological finds along with Olmec and Maya artifacts. (Open Tu-Su 9am-4pm. 30 pesos; Su free.) Down the concourse on the left, you'll find **Jardín Botánico Dr. Faustino Miranda,** a mini-Chiapan jungle. (Open Tu-Su 9am-6pm.) Across the garden is **Museo Botánico.** (Open M-F 9am-3pm, Sa 9am-1pm.) *(Parque Madero begins in the northeast part of town at the intersection of 11 Ote. and 5 Nte. Walk, or take a "Km. 4-Granjas-5 de Mayo" combi from Calle 4 Ote. between Av. 4 and 5 Sur. 2.5 pesos.)*

THE ZÓCALO. Tuxtla's large *zócalo* (or **Parque Central**) is consistently packed with loitering crowds. Sit on benches, look at trees, and observe Mexican people. The surprisingly white **Catedral San Marcos** features a plaque on its north side commemorating Pope John Paul II's 1990 visit.

PARQUE DE MARIMBA. West of the *zócalo* at Av. Central and Calle 8 Pte., the park fills with people when live *marimba* plays (6pm).

⚡ DAYTRIPS FROM TUXTLA GUTIÉRREZ

SIMOJOVEL

From Tuxtla Gutiérrez, buses to Simojovel leave from Transporte. It is also possible to get there by taking a combi to Bochil from in front of the Transportation Station, then a camioneta or combi to Simojovel. Catch return buses at the station (3½hr.; 4:15, 5, 9:45, 11:45am, 1, 5:45 pm). To return to Tuxtla, it may be easier to take a combi or pasajera from 20 de Noviembre and Allende to Bochil, a town inhabited by Tzotzil Maya. From Bochil, buses, combis, and colectivos to Tuxtla leave frequently.

Simojovel is so high in the mountains, even *gringos* won't sweat. It also sits atop some fine amber mines which provide the small town with a tourist draw. Like many other Mexican craft towns, Simojovel lacks clear boundaries between residence, workshop, and store. Amber is sold out of homes and in odd locations, such as pharmacies. There are official stores such as the **Bazar Choj-choji** on 26 de Abril just past the far side of *zócalo* from the taxi/*camioneta* drop-off. Even at the Bazar prices are not marked. Be wary of *gringo* rates and, as in every Mexican business transaction, don't reveal your cash before the price is finalized.

CHIAPA DE CORZO   ☎ 9

Only 25 min. from Tuxtla, Chiapa de Corzo (pop. 120,000) draws tourists to Tuxtla's hotels and restaurants. In return, Tuxtla handles all the dust, exhaust, and teeming masses, allowing Chiapa to remain quaint and scenic. The city features an unusual 16th-century fountain, but the main attraction is **Cañon del Sumidero**, a canyon created by the **Río Grijalva**. The dam at the edge of the canyon has made it navigable for a fleet of motorboat *lanchas* that speed between the 1km-high walls.

⬕ TRANSPORTATION. Chiapa de Corzo overlooks Río Grijalva, 15km east of Tuxtla and 68km west of San Cristóbal de las Casas. Buses from Tuxtla drop you off in the *zócalo*. **Transportes Chiapa-Tuxtla** microbuses back to Tuxtla stop at the station at 2 Sur and 2 Ote. (25min., every 10min., 6 pesos.) **Boats** leave for **El Sumidero** from the riverbank two blocks southwest of the *zócalo*, on 5 de Febrero. Because Chiapa is the last stop on Mex. 190 before the mountains, most buses and *combis* headed north from Tuxtla pick up passengers along the way.

⬕⚡ ORIENTATION AND PRACTICAL INFORMATION. Plaza Ángel Albino Corzo is the town's *zócalo*, bounded by 21 de Octubre, La Mexicanidad, Madero/Grajales, and 5 de Febrero. Contact the **tourist office** in **Tuxtla** for tourist information on Chiapa; there is also a *módulo* with some pamphlets and a staffer available to answer questions on 5 de Febrero, just south of the *zócalo*. **Bancomer,** on the east side of the *zócalo*, has a 24hr. **ATM.** (☎686 03 20. Open M-F 8:30am-4pm.) Several other banks surround the *zócalo*. **Police station:** (☎686 02 26.) in the Palacio Municipal, on the northeast side of the *zócalo*. **Farmacia Esperanza**, on 21 de Octubre, one block east of the *zócalo*. (☎686 04 54. Open M-Sa 7am-11pm, Su 7am-2pm.) **Internet: El Parachico Cibernético,** on the north side of the *zócalo*. (10 pesos per hr. Open daily 8am-11pm.) **Telecomm:** On Mexicanidad, south of the *zócalo*. Open M-F 9am-3pm. **Post office:** on the north side of the plaza in the *Transito* building. (Open M-F 8am-3pm.) **Postal code:** 29160.

⬕⬕ ACCOMMODATIONS AND FOOD. Hotel Los Angeles, Grajales 2 at La Mexicanidad, on the southeast corner of the *zócalo*, is a good place to stay if a daytrip turns into a night. Rooms surround a spacious if sparse courtyard. The restaurant serves *comida corrida* for 35 pesos. (☎686 00 48. Singles 130 pesos; doubles 150 pesos; triples 175 pesos; quads 195 pesos.) The waterfront features several middle quality, middle-priced restaurants. **Restaurant Comitán,** to the left as you hit the dock, offers a breakfast special (40 pesos), occasional live *marimba* performances, and a partly-obscured view of the river. (Open daily 5am-6pm.) **Restaurant Veronica,** next door, has a better view, seafood for 50-65 pesos, and overpriced drinks. (Open daily 7am-7pm.) In the corner of the *zócalo* at Madero, **Restaurante Los Corredores** looks much more expensive than it is. A great place for seafood and regional dishes, the restaurant has a beautiful courtyard and a cool, colorful interior. Cheaper food can be found at the market to the left of the church. (Open daily 9am-6pm. Breakfasts 25 pesos, regional cuisine like *chiles rellenos de pollo* 40 pesos, fish fillets with all the fixings 45-50 pesos.)

◘ SIGHTS. Proper description of **Cañon del Sumidero,** an image of which adorns the Chiapas state seal, requires the invention of new, compound adjectives such as "super-huge-large" and "giganto-normous." A *lancha* journey through the canyon begins with views of cornfields, but shortly after the Belisario Domínguez bridge, the hills leap to form near-vertical cliffs, rising over 1200m above the water. Protected as a natural park, the steep walls are home to troupes of monkeys, hummingbirds, and falcons, while the murky waters harbor crocodiles and turtles. Along the river lie several caves and the park's most famous waterfall, **Árbol de Navidad,** which dashes over a series of vegetation-covered, scalloped rock formations (arranged in a pine-tree-like shape) before disintegrating into the fine mist that envelops passing boats. El Sumidero's northernmost extremity is marked by the 200m hydroelectric dam **Netzahualcóyotl,** which, along with three other dams on Río Grijalva, provides 25% of Mexico's electricity. When the Spanish defeated the Chiapa Indians in 1528, the Chiapa threw themselves from these cliffs rather than submit to capture and slavery. These days, people who are finished with colas and snacks heroically throw their detritus in the water.

Lanchas leave as soon as they're full from Chiapa's dock at the end of 5 de Febrero, two blocks from the southwest corner of the *zócalo* (2hr., 8am-5pm, 84 pesos per person). The trip down the river is best made during the month of August, at the height of the rainy season, when waterfalls are fullest.

Back in town, the *zócalo* contains two interesting colonial structures: a small **clock tower,** which is given excessive tourist-pamphlet coverage out of proportion with its relatively mundane appearance, and a **fountain** shaped like the crown of Queen Isabella of Spain. Often called **La Pila,** this famous Moorish fountain taps underground waterways 5km long and provided the town with fresh drinking water during a 1562 epidemic. Inside, tile plaques tell the story of Chiapa's colonial history. The red-and-white 16th-century **Catedral de Santo Domingo** sits one block south of the *zócalo* near Río Grijalva. The most famous of the four bells dangling in its tower, **Teresa de Jesús,** is named after a mystical Spanish saint. (Open daily 6am-2pm and 4-6:30pm.) Alongside the cathedral on La Mexicanidad, a 16th-century ex-convent houses the **Museo de la Laca,** which displays Mexican lacquer work, a handicraft practiced only in Chiapa de Corzo and five other Mexican cities. Interestingly, the practice originated in China. (Open Tu-Su 10am-6pm. Free.)

◫ ENTERTAINMENT. During Chiapa's **Feria de San Sebastián** (Jan. 6-23), *los parachicos*, men in heavy costumes and stifling masks, dance from dawn to dusk. The fair's grand finale is a mock **Combate Naval** between the *"españoles"* and *"indios."* More a beauty pageant than a battle, the event features fireworks to simulate cannons, decorated boats, and costumed sailors.

SAN CRISTÓBAL DE LAS CASAS ☎9

Most Mexican cities pack their charm into a pedestrian walkway or two lined with museums and cafes, while diesel-burning trucks circle the area, their loud horns threatening the cobblestone peace. But San Cristóbal is an entire city of charm dropped into a ring of green mountains. Founded in 1528, the city, named for its now-desanctified patron saint, St. Christopher, and Bartolomé de Las Casas, a cru-

INSURRECTION. On January 1, 1994, *indígena* Zapatista insurgents caught Mexico by surprise by overtaking parts of San Cristóbal. The situation is currently stable; tourists to the city and neighboring villages should not encounter problems so long as they carry their visa and passport. Those who come with political or human rights agendas, however, are unwelcome and could face deportation.

sader for indigenous rights, sits in the midst of several indigenous villages on the edge of the politically unstable Lacandon cloud forest. A fresh coat of paint on the Palacio Municipal covers slogans spray-painted by Zapatista rebels who overtook the buildings in 1994.

TRANSPORTATION

First and Second class bus stations are scattered along the Pan-American Highway near Insurgentes. To get downtown from the **Cristóbal Colón station**, take a right (north) on Insurgentes and walk seven blocks to the *zócalo*. Cristóbal Colón (☎ 678 02 91) sends buses to: **Cancún** (17hr., 2:30pm, 426 pesos); **Comitán** (1½hr., 10am, 35 pesos); **Mexico City** (18hr., 3:30 and 6pm, 502 pesos); **Oaxaca** (12hr., 5 and 10pm, 252 pesos); **Playa del Carmen** (2:30pm, 407 pesos); **Tuxtla Gutiérrez** (2hr.; 7:30, 11:30am, 12:15, 8:30pm; 34 pesos). Altos is your best bet for: **Mérida** (9:30am, 294 pesos); **Ocosingo** (2, 9:30, and 11:30am; 110 pesos); **Palenque** (9:30, 10:30, 11:30am, and 6:30pm, 79 pesos); **Tapachula** (6am and 5pm, 124 pesos); **Villahermosa** (11:30am, 120 pesos). From the other bus stations, walk east on any cross-street and turn left onto Insurgentes. **Taxis:** ☎ 678 93 40.

PRACTICAL INFORMATION

TOURIST AND FINANCIAL SERVICES

Tourist Office: Sedeatur (☎ 678 65 70), on Hidalgo, ½ block south of the *zócalo*. Open M-Sa 8am-8pm, Su 9am-2pm. **City office** (☎ 678 06 65) at the northwest end of the Palacio Municipal. Open M-F 8am-8pm, Sa 9am-8pm.

Currency Exchange: Bancomer, Plaza 31 de Marzo 10 (☎ 678 13 51), on the south side of the *zócalo*, has a 24hr. **ATM.** Open M-F 8:30am-4pm, Sa 10am-2pm.

Car Rental: Budget, Mazariegos 39 (☎ 678 31 00), 3 blocks west of the *zócalo*. At town travel agencies. VW Sedan 551 pesos per day. Open M-Sa 9:30am-2pm, and 4:30-7pm.

▨ **Bike Rental: Los Pinguinos,** 5 de Mayo 10-B (☎ 678 02 02), also at Ecuador 4-B. 20 pesos per hr., 90 pesos per day. Open M-Sa 10am-2:30pm and 3:30-7pm.

LOCAL SERVICES

English Bookstore: La Pared, Hidalgo 2 (☎ 678 63 67), ½ block south of the *zócalo*. Buys and sells new and used books. Open M-Sa 10am-2pm and 4-8pm.

Markets: between Utrilla and Domínguez, 7 blocks north of the *zócalo*. Best selection Sa. Open daily 6am-4pm. Huge **artisan's market** forms around the Santo Domingo Church, 5 blocks north of the *zócalo* on Utrilla. Open daily 8am-5pm.

Supermarket: Su Super, on Insurgentes across from the Iglesia de San Francisco. Open daily 9am-9pm.

Laundry: Lavomart, Real de Guadalupe 70A, 3½ blocks east of the *zócalo*. 1-5kg 40 pesos. 5-8kg 70 pesos. Open daily 8:15am-8pm. **Lavanderia,** Domínguez 8 (☎ 678 08 43). 30 pesos per kg. Open daily 8am-3pm, 5pm-9pm.

EMERGENCY AND COMMUNICATIONS

Emergency: ☎ 060.

Police: (☎ 678 05 54) in the Palacio Municipal. No English spoken.

Red Cross: Allende 57 (☎ 678 07 72), 3 blocks south of the Pan-American Highway. No English spoken.

Pharmacy: Farmacia del Ahorro (☎ 674 53 10), Mazariegos at Rosas. Open daily 7am-11pm.

Hospital: Hospital General, Insurgentes 24 (☎ 678 07 70), 4 blocks south of the *zócalo* in Parque Fray Bartolomé.

Internet: Cyber Cafe, just south of the *zócalo* on Hidalgo. 10 pesos per hr. Open M-Sa 11am-10pm. **El Puente,** Real de Guadalupe 55 (☎ 678 41 57), 2½ blocks east of the *zócalo*. 10 pesos per hr. Open daily 8am-11pm.

Post Office: (☎ 678 07 65), on Cuauhtémoc at Rosas, 1 block southwest of the *zócalo*. Open M-F 9am-5pm, Sa 9am-1pm. **MexPost** in the office. Open M-F 8am-2:30pm.

Postal Code: 29200.

ACCOMMODATIONS

An influx of backpackers has created a demand for cheap hotels and hostels, and San Cristóbal has responded with a plentiful supply, many conveniently near the *centro*. Camping is only available outside town (see below). Due to the altitude, the temperature often drops below 10°C (50°F), making blankets indispensable.

La Casa di Gladys, Cintelapa 6 (☎ 678 57 75), in El Barrio del Cerrillo, 7 blocks northeast of the *zócalo*. This "black hole hostel" sucks guests in. Halls are lined with hammocks and cozy alcoves, perfect for doing nothing, and the beer store is a block away. Internet 10 pesos. Breakfast 16 pesos. Beds 35-45 pesos; singles and doubles 100 pesos; triples 125 pesos; quads 140 pesos.

Youth Hostel, Juárez 2 (☎ 678 76 55), between Madero and Flores. The name says it all. Very cheap, clean rooms with spotless communal bathrooms and a TV in the common area. Beds 30-35 pesos, with private bath 40 pesos.

Hotel La Noria, Insurgentes 18-A (☎ 678 68 78). One of the cheaper high-end hotels around the *zócalo*. Rooms have cable TV and—prepare thyself, budget traveler—carpeted floors. Singles 200 pesos; doubles 280 pesos.

Posada Jovel, Paniagua 28 (☎ 678 17 34), northeast of the *zócalo*. Small rooms with colorful *serape* bedspreads, terraces with city views, and cozy reading areas. Singles 90 pesos, with bath 120 pesos; doubles 100 pesos, with bath 140 pesos; triples 120 pesos, with bath 160 pesos. The new annex across the street is free of tacky tiling and features TVs and terraces. Singles 150 pesos; doubles 200 pesos; triples 250 pesos.

Hotel Los Robles, Madero 30 (☎ 678 00 54), 2 blocks from the *zócalo*. Rooms come with private bath, and tiles cover the floors as far as the eye can see. Singles 100 pesos; doubles 120 pesos; triples 150 pesos. Discounts for larger groups.

Posada La Media Luna, Dr. José Flores 1 (☎ 678 88 14), between Insurgentes and Juárez. Pastel rooms have private baths. A 600-movie video library keeps guests occupied. Breakfast included. Singles 100 pesos; doubles 120 pesos; triples 160 pesos.

Rancho San Nicolás, Dobilla 47 (☎ 678 00 57), 1km east of town. A taxi is your best bet (15 pesos). If no one is around, ring the bell of the *hacienda* across the road. Rooms, camping, and a trailer park. During high season, (July-Aug. and Dec.-Feb.), call in advance. Horses 180 pesos per day. Parking 10 pesos. Bike rental 10 pesos per hr. Camping 30 pesos. Rooms 40 pesos per person.

FOOD AND CAFES

RESTAURANTS

San Cristóbal caters to international tourists, with several Italian restaurants, a few Chinese places, and a French bistro or two. Somehow prices have stayed low, and the *menu del día* usually costs 35 pesos or less.

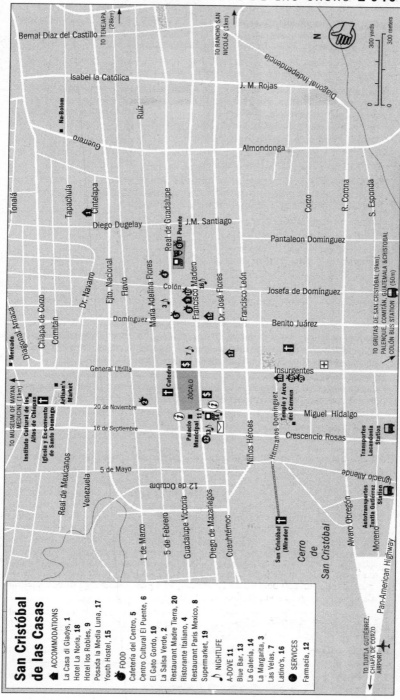

GULF COAST & CHIAPAS

San Cristóbal de las Casas

⌂ ACCOMMODATIONS
La Casa di Gladys, 1
Hotel La Noria, 18
Hotel los Robles, 9
Posada la Media Luna, 17
Youth Hostel, 15

♦ FOOD
Cafetería del Centro, 5
Centro Cultural El Puente, 6
El Gato Gordo, 10
La Salsa Verde, 2
Restaurant Madre Tierra, 20
Ristorante Italiano, 4
Restaurant Paris Mexico, 8
Supermarket, 19

♪ NIGHTLIFE
A-DOVE 11
Blue Bar, 13
La Galería, 14
La Margarita, 3
Las Velas, 7
Latino's, 16

● SERVICES
Farmacia, 12

■ **Centro Cultural El Puente,** Real de Guadalupe 55 (☎678 37 23), 2½ blocks from the *zócalo*. A leftist cafe/language school/cinema/restaurant/dance hall/Internet cafe. Breakfast 16 pesos. *Menu del día* 28 pesos. Open daily 8am-11pm.

■ **Ristorante Italiano,** Real de Guadalupe 40-L. Super-fine pasta prepared with several sauces or to special request (30 pesos), with splendid *tiramisu*. Open daily 1-10pm.

El Gato Gordo, Madero 28 (☎678 04 99), between Domínguez and Colón. Ideal for budget-style face-stuffing. *Menu del día* (17 pesos, available in vegetarian form) comes with enough food to feed a small family. Very rare selection of imported beer, including Guiness (35 pesos). Open W-M 9am-11pm.

Restaurante Madre Tierra, Insurgentes 19 (☎678 42 97), opposite the Iglesia de San Francisco, 2½ blocks south of the *zócalo*. Choose a corner and dig into the *menú viajero* (37 pesos). Open daily 8am-10pm.

La Salsa Verde, 20 de Noviembre 7 (☎678 72 80), 1 block north of the *zócalo*. It's hard to miss this taco diner with its red and green sign, red lamps, green tablecloths, and pine-covered floor. Tacos 4 pesos. Open daily 8am-midnight.

Restaurante París México, Madero 20 (☎678 06 95), half a block east of the *zócalo*. French *menu del día* 38 pesos, Mexican *menu del día* 32 pesos. Unholy "Francomex" *menu del día* 45 pesos. Open daily 7am-11pm.

Cafetería del Centro, Real de Guadalupe 15B (☎678 63 68), 1 block east of the *zócalo*. *Comida corrida* (soup, entree, rice or spaghetti, dessert, and coffee; 35 pesos) and breakfast (23 pesos) fill the tables. Open daily 7am-9:30pm.

CAFES

Proceeds from both of the following help indigenous coffee producers.

Cafe Museo, María Flores 10 (☎678 78 76), between Utrilla and Domínguez. A combination coffee museum, garden, and pastry shop. Live music almost every night from 8-10pm. Organic coffee 8-15 pesos. Open M-Sa 9am-10pm, Su 4-10pm.

La Selva Cafe, Rosas 9 (☎678 72 43), at Cuauhtémoc. A jungle patio and coffee production diagrams entice sippers and pastry enthusiasts. Desserts taste pre-fabricated. Organic coffee and tea 8-26 pesos; takeout 26 pesos per ¼kg. Open daily 9am-11pm.

◯ SIGHTS

■ **NA-BOLOM.** San Cristóbal's most famous attraction is the "House of the Jaguar," a private house that turns into a museum twice daily. Guided tours explore the estate of Frans and Trudy Blum, whose name was misinterpreted as Bolom (jaguar). The Boloms worked among the dwindling *indígena* communities of the **Lacandón Rainforest** on the Guatemalan border, from 1943 until Trudy's death in 1993. Today, international volunteers continue the Blum's work by conducting tours of their library and Neoclassical *hacienda*. The library's manuscripts focus on Maya culture, rainforest ecology, and the plight of indigenous refugees. The small **chapel** (originally intended to be a Catholic seminary) serves as a gallery of religious art. Other rooms are devoted to archaeological finds from the nearby site of **Moxviquil** (mosh-UEE-queel), religious artifacts from the Lacandón Rainforest, and a selection of the 50,000 pictures Trudy took of the jungle and its inhabitants during her life. Na-Bolom also rents rooms furnished by Frans and decorated by Trudy, complete with fireplace, mini-library, antique bath, and original black and white photos. *(Guerrero 33, in the northeast section of the city at the end of Chiapa de Corzo. ☎678 14 18; fax 678 55 86; nabolom@sclc.ecosur.mx. Guided tours at 11:30am and 4:30pm, followed by a 15min. film. 25 pesos. Shop open daily 9am-1pm and 4-8pm; library open M-Sa 11am-2pm. Dinner served daily 7pm; 77 pesos; make reservations 2hr. ahead. Singles 300 pesos; doubles 410 pesos; discounts for longer stays. Those interested in volunteering should contact the main office at least 2 months prior to arrival.)*

MUSEUM OF MAYA MEDICINE. Also called the **Centro de Desarrollo de la Medicina Maya (CEDEMM),** this museum features freaky life-sized models recreating Maya healing rituals, strong-smelling Maya herbs, hypnotic shaman prayers, and a display that explains the Maya use of black spider's teeth to treat inflammation of the testicles. Those with an iron stomach can view a video on Maya midwifery complete with graphic placenta footage. Medicine men are on hand to advise you on any problems you might have. *(Blanco 10, 1km north of the market. ☎/fax 678 54 38. Open M-F 9am-6pm, Sa-Su 10am-4pm. 15 pesos.)*

ZÓCALO. Since its construction by the Spanish in the 16th century, San Cristóbal's *zócalo,* **Plaza 31 de Marzo,** has been the physical and spiritual center of town. The **Palacio Municipal** stands on the west side of the plaza and the yellow **Catedral de San Cristóbal** dominates the north side of the plaza. Inside, the cathedral features a splendid wooden pulpit and chirping birds in the rafters. *(Open daily 7am-7pm.)*

IGLESIA Y EX-CONVENTO DE SANTO DOMINGO. The ex-convento's grounds make up the artisan market. The most beautiful church in San Cristóbal, Santo Domingo was built by the Dominicans from 1547-1560 and enlarged to its present size in the 17th century. The elaborate if poorly maintained stone facade houses an inner sanctuary, delicately covered in gold leaf and dozens of portraits, most anonymously painted in the 18th century. Inside the ex-convento, **Centro Cultural de los Altos de Chiapas** houses an excellent multimedia exhibit on the history of San Cristóbal and Chiapas, with colonial artifacts, photos, and *chiapaneo* textiles. *(On Utrilla beyond the Iglesia de la Caridad. Open daily 7am-2pm and 4-8pm. Centro Cultural open tu-Su 10am-5pm. 20 pesos; Su free. Tours in Spanish.)*

VISTA. Two hilltop churches overlook San Cristóbal. **El Templo del Cerrito San Cristóbal,** on the west side of town, is accessible by a set of stairs at the intersection of Allende and Domínguez. **El Templo de Guadalupe,** to the east, can be reached by walking west on Real de Guadalupe. Both areas are considered slightly unsafe—it's best to go during the day or with friends.

🔊 NIGHTLIFE AND ENTERTAINMENT

Both discoers and those with mellow tastes will enjoy a night on this town. For those with aching feet or technophobia, **Cinemas Santa Clara** (☎ 678 23 45), on 16 de Septiembre between Escuadrón and 28 de Agosto, shows US movies (18 pesos). **Cinema El Puente,** Real de Guadalupe 55 (☎ 678 37 23), three blocks from the *zócalo,* inside Centro Cultural El Puente, screens US and Mexican films and documentaries (10 pesos), and teaches **salsa lessons** (Tu, Th 7-8pm; 30 pesos).

BARS

La Galería, Hidalgo 3 (☎ 678 15 47), half a block south of the *zócalo.* Trendy furniture and live music, including jazz, fill the cavernous interior. Beer 18 pesos, cocktails 20 pesos. Live music 9:15pm-2am. Open nightly until late.

La Margarita, Real de Guadalupe 34A (☎ 678 09 57), 1½ blocks off the *zócalo.* An elegant, sit-down type of place. Beer 15 pesos. Live nightly music daily 9pm-midnight.

Latino's, Madero 23. Calls itself a restaurant-bar-club, offering food, pool tables, 19-peso beers, and live music after 10pm. Open M-Sa 8pm-3am.

CLUBS

Blue Bar, Rosas 2, one block west and half a block south of the *zócalo.* Guards pat down all men before letting them into this den of sinful pleasures. Live music morphs to thumping dance beats. 2-for-1 beers before 11pm. Open daily 9pm-6am.

Las Velas, Madero 14 (☎678 04 17), half a block east of the *zócalo*. Candles light the way to the bar and the stage, where the band jams after 11pm. 2-for-1 beers 9-11pm. F-Sa cover 10 pesos. Open daily 9pm-late.

A-DOVE, Hidalgo 2 (☎678 66 66), on the southwest corner of the *zócalo*. Music until the morning. Take a breather on the balconies overlooking the plaza. Open daily 8pm-4am.

SPORTS

San Cristóbal's most prized recreation is horseback riding. Guided rides to San Juan Chamula leave **La Casa de Gladys** (☎678 57 75; daily at 9:30am). **Rancho San Nicolás** (see **Accommodations**) rents horses, as does **Ranch Nuevo,** across from the entrance to Las Grutas de San Cristóbal (50 pesos per hr., 100 pesos with guide).

FESTIVALS

A schedule of events is posted at the Centro Cultural El Carmen, three blocks south of the *zócalo* on Hidalgo. August brings the month-long **Feria de Ambar** to the Centro Cultural, and artisans from all over Chiapas come to sell their amber. An annual **film festival** is held in Teatro Zebadúa (☎678 36 37), two blocks north of the *zócalo* on 20 de Noviembre. In San Cristóbal and nearby villages, hardly a week goes by without some kind of religious festival. On Easter Sunday, *Semana Santa* gives way to week-long **Feria de la Primavera y de la Paz.** Before riotous revelry begins, a local beauty is selected to preside over the festivities, which include concerts, dances, bullfights, cockfights, and baseball games. Hotel rooms must be reserved several months in advance. During the **Fiesta de San Cristóbal,** July 18-25, the city's desanctified saint is vigorously celebrated with religious ceremonies, concerts, and a staggering number of fireworks. In one of the more interesting traditions of the fiesta, a procession of cars, trucks, and *combis* from all over Chiapas crawl up the road to Cerro San Cristóbal. At the top, the driver opens the hood and door on the driver's side so that the engine and controls can be blessed with holy water by a Catholic priest, in the hope of avoiding accidents on the perilous mountain roads for another year.

▐▌ SHOPPING

San Cristóbal is a financial crossroads for the indigenous peoples of the Chiapan highlands. The daily **market** overflows with fruit, veggies, and assorted cheap goods. For souvenirs and jewelry, look to the market around **Iglesia de Santo Domingo** (open daily 8am-5pm). Try going Sunday, when *indígenas* from nearby villages turn out in droves, or visit the villages themselves (see **Near San Cristóbal** p. 547). **Utrilla** and **Real de Guadalupe,** the two streets radiating from the northeastern corner of the *zócalo*, are dotted with colorful shops that sell *típico* attire and amber. Tucked into the Ex-Convento is **San Jolobil,** "House of Weaving," a cooperative of 800 weavers from Tzotzil and Tzeltal villages in the *chiapaneco* highlands whose objective is to preserve and revitalize ancestral weaving techniques. While many top-quality *huipiles* cost more than your plane ticket home, Sna Jolobil is a good place to admire the area's traditional garments. (☎/fax 678 26 46. Open M-Sa 9am-2pm and 4-6pm. AmEx/MC/V.)

◤ DAYTRIPS FROM SAN CRISTÓBAL DE LAS CASAS

A host of indigenous villages lie within easy reach of San Cristóbal, all with their own unique history and traditions. Sunday morning is the best time to visit the markets of nearby villages, but, because all buses originate in San Cristóbal, visiting more than one village in a single morning is almost impossible. *Combis* leave various stands in the vicinity of the market. Destination signs are rarely accurate; always ask drivers where they're going.

Visiting on your own may give you more freedom, but guides will let you in on secrets you'd miss otherwise. Highly-regarded and knowledgeable **Mercedes Hernández Gómez** leads 5hr. tours. Look for her huge golf umbrella at the *zócalo*.

> **NO PICTURES, PLEASE.** The local Maya practice a unique fusion of Catholicism and native religion. In this system of faith, it is commonly believed that cameras capture a piece of the spirit. While visiting these villages, avoid taking pictures in churches and always ask before taking pictures of individuals; some may request a few pesos in return for a photo.

(Daily at 9am. 100 pesos for Chamula and Zinacantán tours.) **Raul and Alex** have a wealth of information on everything from regional customs to the Zapatista uprising. Look for their blue *combis* daily at 9:30am on the cathedral side of the *zócalo*. (☎678 37 41; 100 pesos for Chamula and Zinacantán tours.)

🖾 SAN JUAN CHAMULA

Combis to Chamula stop on Cárdenas, 1 block west and 1 block north of the market (15min., every 15min. 5am-6pm, 7 pesos). To reach Chamula by car, drive west from the zócalo on Victoria and bear right after crossing the small bridge on Diagonal Ramón Larraínzar. Go right at the fork; Chamula is at the end of the 4km road.

The community of San Juan Chamula (pop. 80,000), "the place of adobe houses" in Tzotzil, is the largest and most touristed village near San Cristóbal. The town, comprised of 110 *parajes* (clusters of 15-20 families), is known for its colors (black and blue), its carnival, and its shamanic-Catholic church. Chamulans expelled their last Catholic priest in 1867 and are legendary for their resistance to the government's religious and secular authority. Villagers have far greater faith in the powers of local shamans than in that of the regional Catholic church—the bishop is allowed into the church only once a month to perform baptisms. Similarly, the government medical clinic is only used after shamanic methods have failed. Before entering the chaotic **church,** which also functions as a hospital, you must obtain a permit (5 pesos) from the tourist office in the *zócalo*. At the front of the church is a sculpture of St. John the Baptist, who, after the Sun, is the second most powerful figure in the Chamulan religion. Jesus Christ, who is believed never to have risen, resides in a coffin. Chamulans take their religion seriously, and unholy residents are promptly expelled from the village. Separate shrines honor each saint, which occupy the residence of the current *cargo* holder (or *mayordomo*), responsible for that saint—look for the leaf arches outside signaling the house's holy function. Homes and chapels are generally not open to the public—you'll have to join an organized tour for a peek into private Chamulan life.

The best time to visit Chamula is one week before Ash Wednesday, during **Carnaval,** which draws approximately 70,000 *indígenas* and 500 tourists daily. The festivities originate in an ancient Maya ritual concerning the five "lost" days, or *wayeb*, at the end of a 360-day *tun* cycle. In addition to Chamula's *carnaval* and the charging of the *autoridades* (cargoholders; Dec. 30-31), the city celebrates the *fiesta* of **San Juan Bautista** (June 22-24), **San Sebastián** (Jan. 19-21), **San Mateo** (Sept. 21-22), and the **Virgen de Fátima** (Aug. 28).

SAN LORENZO ZINACANTÁN

Combis to Zinacantán (10 pesos) leave from the lot near the market (daily 6am-8pm). If driving, follow Victoria west from the zócalo and turn right after crossing the bridge on Diagonal Ramón Larraínzar. Turn left at the fork.

Eight kilometers from Chamula lies the colorful community of Zinacantán (pop. 38,000), comprised of a ceremonial center and outlying hamlets. Village women wear ribbons on each braid, and men flaunt dazzlingly red *chuj*. The village's flower industry has flourished of late, and Zinacantán has begun international exportation of its flowers. The many plastic-roofed structures that dot the hillsides are, in fact, greenhouses. Somewhat exceptional for a *chiapaneco* village is Zinacantán's acceptance of Catholic clergy. The village's handsome, white-washed **church** dates to the 16th century and, along with the small white convent, is used for both Catholic and Pre-Conquest forms of worship (admission 5 pesos). Animal sculptures lining the interior attest to the pervasive presence of *indígena* religion. The Catholic priest, independent of the village church, merely busies himself with confirmations, baptisms, and weddings. Zinacantán's festivals include **Fiesta de San Lorenzo** (Aug. 18-21), **Fiesta de San Sebastián** (Jan. 19-22), and **Semana Santa.**

SAN ANDRÉS LARRAÍNZAR

Combis *leave from the lot on the right side of the road after you cross the bridge north of the market on Utrilla (50min., 5am-4pm, 15 pesos). It's best to return before 2pm—the market shuts down and combis stop running soon after. By car, take the road northwest to Chamula and pass the village. On a curve 10km later, a sign reading "S.A. Larraínzar" points left to a steep road up the side of the valley; the village lies 6km beyond the fork.*

The site of the Zapatista negotiations in 1995 and 1996, San Andrés Larraínzar lies 26km northwest of San Cristóbal. Because there are no commercial tours to the village, its 5000 citizens are more disposed toward visitors. The village colors of red, black, and white, appear on most clothing and market items. Mexicans refer to the village as Larraínzar, but local Tzotziles prefer San Andrés. Since many villagers are loathe to carry their produce all the way to San Cristóbal, San Andrés's **market** (open F-Su until 1pm) is better stocked than the ones at Chamula or Zinacantán. For a panoramic view of the surrounding valleys and patches of cornfields, walk up the hill from the main church to La Iglesia de Guadalupe.

CHENALHÓ

Combis *for Chenalhó leave from an alley off the right side of Utrilla, 1 block before the bridge as you walk north from the market (75min., 6am-4pm, 15 pesos). If driving, continue on the road past Chamula for about 20km.*

Foreigners are rarely spotted at Chenalhó (pop. 10,000), which seems more remote from San Cristóbal than 32km would suggest. Typical dress for men varies from white or black ponchos worn over pants and bound with heavy belts to short, white tunics. Women who have not adopted more current fashions dress uniformly in dark blue skirts and white *tocas* (shawls) embroidered with bright orange flowers. The **market** spreads into the plaza in front of the church on Sunday and sells mostly foodstuffs, including *chiche*, a potent drink made from fermented cane. Villagers enthusiastically wave visitors into **San Pedro,** the church in the town's center and serves as both secular and religious meeting place. Chenalhó residents celebrate **Carnaval** and **La Fiesta de San Pedro** (late June). For a nice view of the town and mountains, follow the road on the far side of the *zócalo* up the hill to the blue and white church past the graveyard. For some do-it-yourself ecotourism, follow the highway back toward San Cristóbal. Just past the elementary school is a tiny path that winds along a fence and through a corn field, eventually reaching a scenic, climbable waterfall.

HUÍTEPEC ECOLOGICAL RESERVE

The reserve lies just off the road to Chamula, 3½km from San Cristóbal, and can be reached by any combi headed in that direction; ask the driver to let you off at the "Reserva Huítepec" (10min., every 15min., 6 pesos). Birdwatching tour daily 7am-10am. Su special plant-specific tour. To return, go 500m downhill toward San Cristóbal to a combi stop (2.5 pesos). Open Tu-Su 9am-4pm. 15 pesos. Guided tours for 2-8 people 200 pesos.

The Huítepec Ecological Reserve, on the east face of the **Huítepec Volcano,** provides a chance to explore an evergreen cloud forest ecosystem. Two trails wind around the park, home to over 100 species of birds and more than 300 species of plant. Those known for medicinal properties or religious importance are marked by small signs. The shorter of the two trails makes for an invigorating self-led, 2km hike, rising up 2390m. The longer 8km hike is led by a guide.

ROMERILLO AND TENEJAPA

Combis *and taxis to Romerillo and Tenejapa leave from Utrilla 1 block west and 1 block north of the market (15-20 pesos).*

Marked by 32 blue and green wooden crosses, **el Cementerio de Romerillo,** on the way to Tenejapa (pop. 5000), sits atop the Chiapan highlands. This local cemetery comes alive during **Día de los Muertos** (Nov. 2). The planks on each mound of dirt are pieces of a relative's bed or door, and old shoes are scattered around for the spirits' use. The town of Tenejapa, 28km from San Cristóbal, is surrounded by mountains, canyons, and corn fields. Crosses representing the tree of life stand at crossroads, near adobe homes, and in front of **La Iglesia de San Ildefonso.** The women's *huipiles* are replete with traditional symbols such as the sun, earth, frogs, flowers, and butterflies. Men wear black ponchos tied at the waist with a belt, red and white trousers, dark boots, and a purse diagonally across the chest. Religious and community leaders carry a staff of power and wear a long rosary necklace. Tenejapa's *mercados* (Th and Su mornings), the **Fiesta de San Alonzo** (Jan. 21), and the **Fiesta de Santiago** (July 23) attract crowds from near and far.

AMATENANGO DEL VALLE

Walk 2 blocks east of the bus station on the Pan-American Highway, and a small bus terminal will be on the right. Take a bus to Teopisca (10 pesos) and transfer to a bus headed for Amatenango del Valle (5 pesos).

Amatenango del Valle, known for its fine pottery, sits 37km southeast of San Cristóbal toward Comitán. Female artisans create the hand-molded pitchers, vases, pots, and jars that are traditionally baked with firewood. **La Casa de Juliana** is the most visited cooperative pottery house, with an original *temascal* (steam bath).

GRUTAS DE SAN CRISTÓBAL

Take the bus to Teopisca (see above) and ask to be let off at the grutas (6 pesos). To return, hop on any westbound combi. From the highway, a 5min. walk through the park brings you to the entrance. Open daily 9am-5pm. 10 pesos. Vehicle entrance 10 pesos.

From the small entrance at the base of a steep wooded hillside, a tall, narrow fissure, incorporating a chain of countless caves, leads almost 3km into the heart of the rock. A modern concrete walkway, up to 10m above the cave floor at points, penetrates some 750m into the caverns. The dimly lit caves harbor a spectacular array of stalactites, columns, and formations said to resemble objects such as Santa Claus. For a little post-cave recreation, the fellows from Rancho Nuevo, across from the entrance, offer horse-back riding.

OCOSINGO ☎9

The strategic importance of Ocosingo, the nearest large settlement to the Lacandón rainforest—the fringes of which harbor the majority of Zapatista rebels—is as obvious as the many military personnel who walk its streets. Ocosingo's residents still bear painful memories of the January 1994 uprising, when a shootout in the market between the army and Zapatista-friendly locals claimed dozens of lives. Despite the military backdrop, dusty streets, and ramshackle buildings, Ocosingo is a safe and quiet base from which to explore the nearby ruins of **Toniná.** Perhaps more importantly, the city is also the home of *quesillo*, huge balls of cheese that are sold from windows and doorways city-wide.

▐▀ TRANSPORTATION

Ocosingo lies 72km northeast of San Cristóbal and 119km south of Palenque. To get to the *zócalo* from the **Cristóbal Colón bus station** or the **Autotransportes Tuxtla station,** walk uphill three blocks and go left at the "Centro" sign. The *zócalo* is three blocks downhill. Autotransportes Tuxtla Gutiérrez (☎673 01 39), on the highway, motors to: **Campeche** (9pm, 170 pesos); **Cancún** (3pm, 300 pesos); **Mérida** (9pm, 225 pesos); **Palenque** (7 per day, 45 pesos); **Playa del Carmen** (3pm, 245 pesos); **San Cristóbal** (10 per day, 28 pesos); **Tulum** (3pm, 235 pesos); **Tuxtla Gutiér-rez** (10 per day, 50 pesos); **Villahermosa** (7 per day, 85 pesos). Cristóbal Colón (☎673 04 31), right next door, goes to **México City** (7pm, 448 pesos); **Palenque** (12 per day, 49 pesos); **Puebla** (7pm, 359 pesos); **San Cristóbal** (10 per day, 82 pesos) via **Tuxtla Gutierrez** (41 pesos).

✈✱ ⛴ ORIENTATION AND PRACTICAL INFORMATION

Ocosingo is laid out in the customary compass grid, with **avenidas** running east-west and **calles** running north-south. Street numbers increase from the intersection of **Av. Central** and **Calle Central**. From the *zócalo*, cardinal directions are marked by Hotel Central to the north, the Iglesia de San Jacinto to the east, and the Palacio Municipal to the west. **Banamex,** on the northwest corner of the *zócalo*, does not change currency, but will give cash advances on major credit cards and has a 24hr. **ATM.** (☎673 00 34. Open M-F 9am-5pm.) **Market:** four blocks downhill east on Av. 2 Sur. **Luggage storage:** at the Cristóbal Colón station (10 pesos per day). **Police:** (☎673 05 07 or 673 00 15), in the Palacio Municipal on the west side of the *zócalo*. **Pharmacy: Cruz Blanc,** Av. 2 Sur and Calle 1 Ote., one block south of the church. (☎673 02 33. Open daily 7am-10pm.) **Centro de Salud,** Av. Central 16, just west of the *zócalo*. No English spoken. **Telecomm,** on Av. Central, 2 blocks west of the *zócalo*. (Open M-F 9am-3pm, Sa 9am-1pm.) **Post office:** Av. 2 Sur 12, between Calle Central and Calle 1 Ote. 12, one block south of the *zócalo*. (Open M-F 9am-3pm, Sa 9am-1pm.) **Postal code:** 29950.

♒ 🍴 ACCOMMODATIONS AND FOOD

Ocosingo has a broad range of accommodations, and a few offer luxurious amenities at decent prices. **Hotel Central,** Calle Central 5, on the north side of the *zócalo*, is an oasis of clean, well-ventilated rooms with comfortable beds, spacious baths, bottled water, and cable TV. (☎673 00 24. Singles 140 pesos; doubles 180 pesos; triples 200 pesos.) **Hotel Bodas de Plata,** Av. 1 Sur at Calle 1 Pte., off the southwest corner of the *zócalo*, is a true budget hotel, with fans, private baths, and little else. (☎673 00 16. Singles 80 pesos; doubles 80 pesos; triples 100 pesos; quads 120 pesos.) **Hotel Nakum,** Calle Central Nte. 19, half a block north of Hotel Central, is newly renovated with firm beds, phones, TVs, and some fine-looking bathrooms. (☎673 02 80. Singles 175 pesos; doubles 210 pesos; triples 230 pesos.)

Restaurant La Montura, in Hotel Central, is overpriced, but the outdoor tables are the most pleasant in town. (Entrees 45-50 pesos. ☎673 05 50. Open daily 7am-11pm.) **El Buen Taquito,** on Calle Central on the north side of the *zócalo*, is everything a budget taco joint should be, replete with blaring TV and plastic tables. (Tacos 2.5 pesos. Open daily 6:30pm-midnight.) **El Desvan,** on the south side of the *zócalo*, overlooks the park. (Pizza 40-45 pesos. Open daily 9:30am-11pm.)

🏛 DAYTRIPS FROM OCOSINGO

TONINÁ RUINS

15km east of Ocosingo, the ruins are easily accessible by "Toniná" combis, which leave from the market (20min., every 30min., 10 pesos) and drop you at the newly-dedicated museum. The ruins are 500m farther down the road. Open daily 9am-4pm. 30 pesos; Su free. The lack of explanatory signs means a guide can be very helpful (about 150 pesos).

Encompassing 15 acres, Toniná was a huge fortress-like religious and administrative center that flourished during the Classic Period. The city was mysteriously abandoned in the 13th century. At the turn of the century, the governor of Ocosingo removed stones from the site to build roads, and thus the pyramids can never be fully restored. A museum featuring disturbing decapitated statues and recreations of the complex's appearance before it was abandoned marks the entrance.

The entrance path leads east of the ruins across the river up a small gully, emerging at the stone rings and five ground markers of the main **ballcourt**. Next to the ballcourt is the sacrificial altar, the **Temple of War**. Across the field, ruins of a smaller ballcourt lie near the steps of the giant **acropolis**. The first tier contains the **Palace of the Underworld**, with representations of Ik (god of wind) decorating its facade and inner walls. It was believed that those who made it through the labyrinth without man-made light would gain power from the gods of the underworld.

The fourth tier housed governors' bedrooms. On the far right of the fifth tier is the **Mural de las Cuatro Eras**. At the center is a royal grave where archaeologists discovered a stone sarcophagus, holding a king's body and two unidentified corpses. **The Altar de Monstruo de la Tierra** is on the right side of the sixth level. The seventh level of the pyramid, Toniná's religious focal point, supports four large pyramids. **The Temple of Agriculture,** right of the terrace, is decorated with roof combs. To the left is the **Temple of the Prisoners**. Despite the name, which comes from the reliefs of prisoners at the base, archaeologists believe that this mound once housed the king and royal family. Behind it are the **Pyramid of Finances** and the higher **Pyramid of War,** which served as an observatory and still offers a great view.

PALENQUE ☎9

In all of Mesoamerica, three sites are world-renowned for their expression of the beauty, power, and glory of the Maya Classic period. Honduras has Copán, Guatemala has Tikal, and Mexico has Palenque. These impressive ruins straddle a magnificent 300m-high natural palisade (*palenque*) in the foothills of the Chiapan highlands. Dense jungle meets the bases of Palenque's breathtaking pyramids, and the sounds of birds, monkeys, and crashing waterfalls echo off the walls. The town of Palenque (pop. 63,000) is not nearly as picturesque, but it serves as important crossroads for travelers who come to visit the ruins, sample the waters of the famous *cascadas* of Agua Azul and Misol-Ha, make forays into the heart of the Lacandón jungle, and begin excursions to Maya sites in Guatemala.

▐ TRANSPORTATION

All bus stations are five to eight blocks west of the *parque* on Juárez. To get to the *parque* from the stations, walk uphill (east) on Juárez. ADO (☎345 13 44) runs first class buses to: **Campeche** (6hr., 8am and 9pm, 153 pesos); **Cancún** (12hr., 8pm, 351 pesos); **Chetumal** (7½hr., 8pm, 200 pesos); **Mérida** (8hr., 8am and 9pm, 231 pesos); **Mexico City** (12hr., 6 and 8pm, 485 pesos); **Oaxaca** (13hr., 5:30pm, 356 pesos); **Playa del Carmen** (11hr., 8pm, 325 pesos); **Puebla** (10½hr., 7pm, 423 pesos); **San Cristóbal** (4hr., 10am, 70 pesos); **Villahermosa** (2hr., 9 per day, 62 pesos). Altos makes the run to **Tuxtla Gutiérrez** (112 pesos) and **Ocosingo** (49 pesos) at 4, 9:30am, noon, 6, and 8pm. **Taxis:** (☎345 01 12) are 40 pesos to the ruins, 15 pesos within town.

▐▐ ORIENTATION AND PRACTICAL INFORMATION

Palenque occupies the northeast corner of Chiapas, 274km from Tuxtla Gutiérrez. *Avenidas* run east-west, perpendicular to the *calles*.

Tourist Office: In the **Casa de las Artesanías**, at the corner of Juárez and Abasolo. Helpful staff speaks some English. Open M-Sa 9am-9pm, Su 9am-1pm.

Currency Exchange: Bancomer, Juárez 40, 2 blocks west of the *parque*. Open for exchange M-F 8:30am-4pm. **Banamex,** Juárez 62. Open M-F 9am-2pm. Both have 24hr. **ATMs.**

Luggage storage: At the Autobuses de Tuxtla Gutiérrez station, half a block toward town from the ADO station. 2 pesos per hr.

Police: (☎345 18 44), on Independencia, in the Palacio Municipal.

Pharmacy: Farmacia Central (☎345 03 93), Juárez near Independencia. Open daily 7:30am-10:30pm.

Medical Assistance: Centro de Salud y Hospital General (☎345 07 33), on Juárez near the main bus station, at the west end of town. No English spoken.

Fax: Buho's (☎345 01 95), near the tourist office on Juárez. Open daily 8am-9pm.

Internet: Cibernet (☎345 17 10), Independencia between 5 de Mayo and 20 de Noviembre. 10 pesos per 30min. Open daily 8am-11pm.

Post Office: Independencia at Bravo, north of the *parque.* Open M-F 9am-4pm, Sa 9am-1pm.

Postal Code: 29960.

ACCOMMODATIONS AND CAMPING

ON THE WAY TO RUINS

El Panchan, 1½km from the entrance. This backpacker's oasis is divided into 4 sections, each with its own accommodations. 3 have restaurants: 1 is vegetarian. ■**Don Mucho's** has delicious entrees for 30 pesos or less. Bag storage 5 pesos. Camping and hammock space 20 pesos. *Cabañas* with private bath 100 pesos.

Maya Bell Trailer Park and Camping (☎348 42 71), 6km from town and 500m from the ruins. Accessible by *combi* (7 pesos). Pitch a tent, string a hammock, or put down a sleeping bag (25 pesos per person). They also have trailer (35 pesos and up) and car space (20 pesos). The few rooms have fans, private baths, coordinated paint jobs and actual lighting fixtures. Singles 160 pesos; doubles 190 pesos; triples 220 pesos; quads 250 pesos; 150 pesos deposit.

Elementos Naturales (EN), between El Panchan and Maya Bell, slightly more rustic than both but also cheaper. Breakfast 20 pesos. Hammocks and camping 15 pesos.

IN TOWN

Canek Youth Hostel, 20 de Noviembre 43 (☎345 01 50). An average hostel with large rooms with fans, decent baths, and mountain views, but not much lounge space. Dorm beds 40 pesos; singles with bath 80 pesos; doubles 90 pesos; triples 120 pesos.

Posada Charito, 20 de Noviembre 15 (☎345 01 21), between Independencia and Abasolo, ½ block west of the *parque.* Local kids watch cartoons in the lobby. Rooms have private baths. Singles 50-100 pesos; doubles 80-120 pesos; triples 100-200 pesos; depending on season; each additional person 80 pesos.

Posada la Selva, Reforma 69 (☎345 06 41), between Allende and Calle 1a Pte., 5 blocks northwest of the *parque.* Green and white rooms with sparkling private baths, and if you're lucky, a jungle view. In-house agency organizes tours. Singles 100 pesos; doubles 120 pesos; triples 140 pesos.

Hotel Lacroix, Hidalgo 10 (☎345 00 14), just off the *parque* and next to Na Chan Kan Travel Agency and Restaurant. A large, gaudy Maya mural leads to cozy, cool, blue rooms with blue baths. No hot water. Singles 160 pesos; doubles 190 pesos; triples 220 pesos; quads 250 pesos. In low season, prices drop 40 pesos.

FOOD

Travelers have about as much chance of finding a cheap restaurant in Palenque as they do of discovering why the Maya abandoned the city. For cheap produce, try the **market** on Suárez, about seven blocks northwest of the *parque.*

Restaurante Las Tinajas, 20 de Noviembre 41, at Abasolo. Popularity has nudged up prices, but quality local dishes and large servings keep the tourists coming back. Breakfast specials 22 pesos. Open daily 6:30am-11pm.

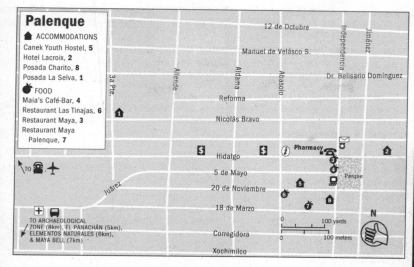

Palenque

▲ ACCOMMODATIONS
Canek Youth Hostel, **5**
Hotel Lacroix, **2**
Posada Charito, **8**
Posada La Selva, **1**

🍖 FOOD
Maia's Café-Bar, **4**
Restaurant Las Tinajas, **6**
Restaurant Maya, **3**
Restaurant Maya
Palenque, **7**

Restaurante Maya (☎ 345 00 42), Independencia and Hidalgo, at the northwest corner of the *zócalo*. Known as the "most ancient restaurant in Palenque," it's only 2050 years younger than the ruins. *Antojitos* from 26 pesos, *carne* dishes from 40 pesos, excellent lemonade 12.5 pesos. Open daily 7am-11pm.

Restaurant Maya Palenque, 20 de Noviembre 38 (☎ 345 07 81), between Restaurant Las Tinajas and Posada Charito, serves yogurt and fruit platters (18 pesos), salads (15-25 pesos), and local dishes (25-40 pesos). Open daily 7am-11pm.

Maia's Cafe-Bar Restaurante, corner of Juárez and Independencia. Popular due to its prime location—the food is good, too. *Pollo* tacos (30 pesos) avoid grease problems. *Comida corrida* 30 pesos. Open daily 7am-11pm.

👁 SIGHTS

🪨 THE ARCHAEOLOGICAL SITE OF PALENQUE

Ruins, 8km west of town, are most accessible by combis (6am-6pm, 10 pesos) which depart from Hidalgo on Allende. There are 2 entrances; the 1st is 50m from the site museum, 2km before the other. Take this entrance walking from Maya Bell or Panchan, and buy a ticket at the museum. **Visiting the ruins at night is prohibited and extremely unsafe.** *Do not take shortcuts to the back entrance from the campgrounds or the road—the dense jungle will isolate you from any other nearby tourists. Site open daily 8am-4:45pm. Museum open daily 9am-4pm. Crypt open daily 10am-4pm. 35 pesos; Su free. Guided tours available at main entrance (507 pesos for groups of 1-25).*

Palenque began as a small farming village in 100 BC, and grew steadily throughout the Pre-Classic Period. By around AD 600 Palenque had begun to flourish, reaching its zenith over the next 200 years. Palenque owes much of its success to the club-footed king **Pacal** ("sun shield" or "white macaw"), who inherited the throne from his mother **Zac-Kuk** in AD 615 at the age of 12. Pacal lived into his fifth *katun* (20-year period) and was succeeded in AD 683 by his elderly son **Chan-Bahlum** ("jaguar-serpent"), who celebrated his ascension by building a great pyramid-crypt (**Temple of the Inscriptions**) for his father. It was during the rule of these kings that most construction at Palenque took place. Soon after Chan-Bahlum's death in AD 702, Palenque slipped into oblivion, perhaps due to siege at the hands of the rival Totonacs or another Maya city. The site museum suggests an intriguing possibility: that Palenque was abandoned intentionally because elders felt its time was over.

The city was abandoned around AD 800, and when Cortés arrived in the 16th century, he marched right through without noting its existence. Today, though impressive, the ruins of Palenque merely hint at the city's former majesty.

TEMPLO DE LAS INSCRIPCIONES (TEMPLE OF THE INSCRIPTIONS). To the right of the entrance is the tomb of **Alberto Ruz,** one of Mexico's most famous archaeologists, who insisted on being buried there. Past the tomb lies the Temple of the Inscriptions, with 69 steps representing King Pacal's 69 years of reign. Named for its tablets, the temple was the tomb of King Pacal and the first substantial burial place unearthed in the Americas. After finding six skeletons, Ruz dug into the interior crypt, removing over 400 tons of rubble by hand. There he discovered the king's perfectly preserved, elaborately carved sarcophagus. The figure in the lower center of the tablet is Pacal himself, shown descending into the underworld with the *ceiba* tree directly over him. Visitors can view the royal crypt and sarcophagus. A hollow duct, designed to allow Pacal's spirit to exit the underworld and communicate with Palenque's priests, is on the right after the staircase.

TEMPLO DEL JAGUAR. A trail leads up the mountainside to the east of the Temple of the Inscriptions. About 100m along this trail, on the right, is the Temple of the Jaguar. Dare to descend the pitch-black stairwell inside the structure, and you'll come upon an old, slimy well.

EL PALACIO (THE PALACE). In the center, across from the Temple of the Inscriptions, is the trapezoidal, postcard-perfect Palace complex, a labyrinth of patios, rooms, and Palenque's signature three-story tower. The palace was most likely used for residential purposes, with royalty occupying the spacious quarters on the north side, and maids and guards occupying the cramped quarters on the south side. The tower, an unusual Maya construction, may have been for astronomical observation. T-shaped ducts throughout cooled the air and doubled as representations of Ik, the god of the breezes. Visitors can climb down the staircase from the top of the platform to explore the dimly-lit network of underground passageways.

PLAZA DEL SOL (PLAZA OF THE SUN). The path between the palace and the Temple of Inscriptions crosses the recently reconstructed aqueduct before leading to Plaza of the Sun, which is usually crowded with tourists seeking good views. The Plaza is made up of the **Temple of the Sun,** the **Temple of the Cross,** the **Temple of the Foliated Cross,** and the smaller **Temples XIV and XV.** The Temple of the Cross was

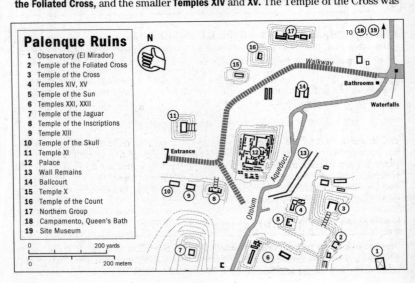

Palenque Ruins

1 Observatory (El Mirador)
2 Temple of the Foliated Cross
3 Temple of the Cross
4 Temples XIV, XV
5 Temple of the Sun
6 Temples XXI, XXII
7 Temple of the Jaguar
8 Temple of the Inscriptions
9 Temple XIII
10 Temple of the Skull
11 Temple XI
12 Palace
13 Wall Remains
14 Ballcourt
15 Temple X
16 Temple of the Count
17 Northern Group
18 Campamento, Queen's Bath
19 Site Museum

named for a stucco relief of a cross discovered inside, which inspired a flurry of hopeful religious theories among *conquistadores*. For the Maya, the cross represents the *ceiba* tree with a snake as its horizontal branch and a bird perched at the top. The outer layer of stucco has worn away, but the inner sanctum protects a large, sculpted tablet and reliefs on either side of the doors. About to be swallowed again by the jungle, the Temple of the Foliated Cross lies across the plaza from the Temple of the Sun. The inner sanctum contains a reddish carved tablet.

To the south of the plaza, through the wall of trees, several unreconstructed temples surround the uncleared **Plaza Maudslay**, including **Temples XVII, XX, XXI**, and **XXII**. Downhill from Temple XIV, past the palace, lie the vestiges of a **ballcourt**.

GRUPO NORTE (NORTH GROUP). Across the path from the ballcourt is the **Templo del Conde (Temple of the Count),** named after the kooky archaeologist Frederick Waldeck, who lived here for three years in the 1830s. The four other temples next to the Temple of the Count comprise the North Group.

QUEEN'S BATH AND MONTIEPA. After crossing the bridge, waterfall enthusiasts can shower and splash in the **Queen's Bath,** named for its exclusively female clientele. There are several small ruins between the main plaza and back entrance, around which the jungle has not been cleared. Overgrown banks and shallow water make swimming impractical. Palenque is full of paths leading to unrestored ruins and cascades; bring bug spray and a buddy if you want to explore.

⚡ DAYTRIPS FROM PALENQUE

CASCADAS DE AGUA AZUL AND MISOL-HA

The most painless way to visit Agua Azul and Misol-Ha is by joining Colectivos Chamblas, on Hidalgo at Allende where combis leave for the ruins. Tours leave at 9, 10am, and noon, spending 1hr. at Misol-Ha and 4 at Agua Azul. 80 pesos. Combis from the bus station in Palenque go to Misol-Ha (20 pesos) and Agua Azul (30 pesos). Agua Azul open daily 8am-5pm. 5 pesos, cars 20 pesos. Misol-Ha open 24hr. 5 pesos, cars 25 pesos.

These two large *cascadas* (waterfalls) have seduced many a tourist. **Agua Azul,** 58km south of Palenque, is a breathtaking spectacle. The Río Yax-Há jumps down 500 individual falls, slipping in and out of rapids, whirlpools, and calm spots. **Currents are extremely dangerous,** however, so swimming is only advisable in a few places. *Comedores* and gift shops cluster within a 20-min. walk of the entrance, and camping is available 10min. upstream from the entrance. (Tents 15 pesos; hammocks 20 pesos; beds 50 pesos.) Rather than numerous small falls, **Misol-Ha,** 20km south of Palenque, has one giant one. At its base is a pool for swimming. Bring a flashlight if you want to explore the cave behind the falls.

YAXCHILÁN

Rising from the banks of the Usumacinta River deep within the Lacandón jungle are the archaeological treasures of Yaxchilán, and, 8km away, **Bonampak.** Covering 8 sq.km and extending across the river into Guatemala, only one-fourth of Yaxchilán has been fully excavated. Already the vast number of stelae and hieroglyphics have revealed a rich history. The EZLN uprisings of the mid-90s postponed plans for a museum and development of the site, so a journey to Yaxchilán still resembles the archaeological expeditions of old. This ancient city is so remote, its carvings so clear, and the enveloping jungle so wild that families of toucans, spiders, and howler monkeys outnumber human visitors.

⚡ PRACTICAL INFORMATION

The nearest town to Yaxchilán, **Frontera Corozal,** is 197km southeast of Palenque. The site is a *lancha* cruise (40min.) down the Río Usumacinta, and the strong currents make it a longer trip back (1hr.). The road between Palenque and Corozal is a smooth ride, and constant patrolling by Mexican security ensures relative safety. The safest and cheapest way to reach Yaxchilán, however, is through a travel agency that is insured and familiar with the idiosyncrasies of Mexican security. Palenque travel agencies charge from 450 pesos for one-day trips to 650 pesos for two days, and usually include meals, boat fare, lodging, transportation, and a visit to Bonampak. If you want to venture off on your own, **Transportes Chancalan** runs *combi*s to Frontera Corozal (2½hr., every 2hr. 6am-4pm during high season, 80 pesos). Beware, however, that you will most likely face the military, pay many tolls, and have to shell out a hefty sum for a *lancha*. No matter how you choose to get to Yaxchilán, be sure to bring your passport and visa to deal with various army roadblocks. Also, make sure to get any errands done before leaving—the nearest services of any kind are in Palenque.

■ ACCOMMODATIONS

The handful of residents near the site entrance have recently begun to offer **camping** space for constantly changing prices. The new **Centro Ecoturístico Escudo Jaguar** in Frontera Corozal offers colorful *cabañas* with firm beds and fans. It also offers camping and a *palapa* with 15 hammock spaces and common bathroom. The Escudo runs *lancha* trips to the site. Arrangements are made at the hotel. (☎201 64 40. Singles and doubles 250 pesos; triples and quads 350 pesos; hammock and tent space 40 pesos. Tours 695 pesos for 1-6 people, 1000 pesos for 7-10 people.)

◉ SIGHTS

THE ARCHAEOLOGICAL SITE OF YAXCHILÁN
Tourist office ☎ 345 03 56. Open daily 8am-5pm. 35 pesos; Su free.

Yaxchilán ("Green Rocks") is famous for its thousands of glyphs, which almost completely narrate its history. The city began humbly around 350 BC as a fishing and farming village along the Usumacinta. Yaxchilán's emblem glyph began to appear at other places such as El Cayo, Piedras Negras, and Bonampak after AD 526, suggesting that it may have influenced those sites and perhaps been a regional capital. Years of bloody conquest and expansion during the reign of **Shield-Jaguar** (AD 726-742) made Yaxchilán one of the most important cities of the late Classic Maya. Shield-Jaguar's son, **Bird-Jaguar,** took the throne in AD 752, and, reinforced his rule by undertaking the greatest construction projects Yaxchilán had ever seen. It was during these years that Yaxchilán rose to the peak of its power through royal intermarriages and alliances with neighboring regions. Evidence of trade and iconographic exchange with cities as far as Teotihuacán have been found in this period. By AD 900, lesser nobles were flouting whatever ruling authority was left and began constructing their houses in the midst of old royal ceremonial centers. Along with many other Maya cities of this time, Yaxchilán was weakened and eventually abandoned.

Visitors enter Yaxchilán through the **Labyrinth,** a system of underground passageways symbolizing the underworld that have not yet been fully explored. Bring a flashlight to view the original stucco work. The end of the labyrinth opens into the vast **Grand Plaza.** Running west to east, the 500m long and 60m wide plaza was the monumental heart of the city, lined by temples and palaces on both sides. The first significant structure on the north side of the plaza, is **Building 16,** across from the Labyrinth. Three doorways are all that remain of the building, each with carved lintels. The middle one depicts a scene with Bird-Jaguar holding a ceremonial bar dated AD 743. Farther down the Grand Plaza is the **ballcourt,** built for two players during Shield-Jaguar's rule. Between Building 16 and the ballcourt on the south side of the plaza stands a 350 year-old *ceiba* tree of life.

Continuing east past the ballcourt, visitors arrive at **Stela 1,** dating from AD 782 and depicting the king and his wife undergoing a ritual self-sacrifice. Still on the

THE REAL PEOPLE The Lacandón Maya, or Winik (Real People) as they call themselves, have succeeded for centuries longer than any other Maya people in maintaining their traditional religious practices and beliefs. While other groups fused indigenous religion with Christianity during the first two centuries of colonial rule, the Lacandón refused to accept any facets of Christianity until the 1950s. At that time, the town of Lacanha Chan Sayab converted to Protestantism; in the 1970s, their neighbors in Mansabak adopted Seventh Day Adventism. However, the Lacandón of Nahá continue to live entirely outside Christianity to this day. Only a few hundred people still identify themselves as Lacandón (largely defined by speaking Lacandón Maya), and a good number live in **San Javier,** near Crucero Bonampak.

north of the plaza, past Stela 1, stands **Building 6,** also called the **Temple of Chac,** with original stucco still retaining some of its colors. A few meters past the Temple on the left lie remains of the hieroglyphic steps leading to the ancient bridge connecting Yaxchilán to Guatemala. Yaxchilán's most elaborate and important carving—**Stela 11,** to the east of Building 6, is engraved on four of its six sides and depicts the transfer of power from Shield-Jaguar to Bird-Jaguar. The monolith was originally found towering in front of Building 40 and eventually left here after numerous failed efforts to send it to the Museo Nacional de Antropología in Mexico City. Across from Stela 11 on the south side of the plaza, past some circular altars and another stela dedicated to Bird-Jaguar, is **Building 20.** Next door to the west is **Building 21,** with original stucco on its superior facade and an engraved lintel depicting the birth of Bird-Jaguar. Inside the building is a stela dating from AD 743 showing one of Shield-Jaguar's wives, **Lady Ik-Skul,** sacrificing her tongue. Stucco reliefs along the back wall retain some original red, blue, and green colors.

Some minor buildings round out the rest of the south side. Before them is a long, steep slope with lintels describing the rise of power of Shield-Jaguar and his first wife, **Lady Fist-Fish,** that climbs past **Buildings 25** and **26** on the left, reaching the immense **Building 33** at the top. The best-preserved of Yaxchilán's buildings, it was ordered by Bird-Jaguar IV, and is called the **House of Music.** Legend has it that as storms blow in from the north over Guatemala, the wind creates music as it passes over the building's openings. Inside sits a decapitated statue of Bird-Jaguar himself. No one knows how, when, or why his head came to rest in the next room, but when archaeologists attempted to replace it, they were stopped by the Lacandón Maya, who believe that at the moment the head is rejoined the end of the world will begin. The trail behind Building 33 leads to the opposite side of the grand acropolis composed of **Buildings 39, 40,** and **41.** To reach Building 41, cut through the small plaza. The unimpeded panoramic view of the Mexican jungle and Guatemalan highlands merits the 10min. hike. If you've got some energy left, take the detour up the mountain to the left to the **small acropolis,** which is composed of 13 buildings perched 75m above the grand plaza. The ruins themselves are not particularly striking, but a glimpse of the river below can be caught through the trees.

BONAMPAK

Transportes Chancalan runs combis from Palenque at 5 de Mayo between Allende and Juárez (45 pesos). They stop in San Javier, a 5km walk from Lacunjá, where you can catch a cab for the remaining 3km. Colectivos are not protected by Mexican security, making assaults easier and more frequent. Open daily 8am-5pm. 25 pesos; Su free.

Since their discovery in 1946, the murals of Bonampak ("Painted Walls"), 8km from Yaxchilán, have single-handedly changed scholars' conceptions of Maya civilization. The city was probably subordinate to Yaxchilán, and reached its peak late in the Classic Period, around AD 600-800. Most travelers visit Bonampak to see the spectacular murals. Despite 12 centuries and an ill-advised kerosene dousing by a restoration team, these one-of-a-kind *al fresco* paintings still leave visitors gaping.

Much of what is known about Bonampak pertains to a ruler known as **Chaan Muan II,** who is depicted on the 6m-high **Stela 1,** the first major sight in the **Great**

Plaza. Aligned with the central floor of the House of Paintings, the uppermost portion is in total disrepair. Enough remains to present the figure of the king holding spear and shield (dated AD 787). Two other important stelae are situated close to the plaza on the wide steps: **Stela 2,** on the left, depicts Chaan Muan II with two women performing a ritual self-sacrifice. **Stela 3,** on the right, features a richly attired Chaan Muan II standing over a prisoner. The prisoner's beard is a rarity in Maya art, which seldom portrayed facial hair. Stela 2 depicts Chaan Muan II and his mother initiating an alliance with his wife from Yaxchilán.

The **Temple of Paintings,** or **Building 1,** is a three-room building just above and to the right of the Great Plaza. Over the three doorways, from left to right, are lintels of Knotted-Eye Jaguar (an ancestor of Chaan Muan II), Shield-Jaguar II of Yaxchilán, and Chaan Muan II, all about to execute a prisoner. The two-headed serpent bar is a staff of rulership. Inside, the murals of the three rooms combine to form a narrative that reads from left to right. In Chamber 1, the murals depict a procession and the ascendence of an heir to the throne on the right side of the room. Note the musicians and lobster-costumed figure to the lower left. Chamber 2 shows a fierce battle in a forest—over the doorway is a display of tortured prisoners pleading for mercy from the jaguar-skin-robed royalty of Bonampak. The third chamber is a portrait of a victory celebration with dancers and musicians, as well as of the royal family undergoing self-sacrificial rituals. Behind and above the Temple of Paintings are a set of buildings numbered four to eight from right to left. Climb behind Building 4 to get a look at roofless Building 10.

COMITÁN ☎9

The last city on the Pan-America Hwy. before the Guatemalan border, Comitán (pop. 110,000) attracts visitors seeking visas and bus rides. Known in Maya as Balún Canan (Nine Stars), Comitán is close to many ecotourism attractions.

▐ TRANSPORTATION

The **bus station** (☎ 632 09 80), is at Domínguez 43. To reach the *zócalo*, cross the highway and turn left. After 200m, take the first right onto Calle 4 Pte. Sur. Walk five blocks to Central Benito Juárez, turn left and then walk three blocks north past the post office to the *zócalo*. **Taxis** (☎ 632 56 30) cost 15 pesos. Altos goes to: **Cancún** (1:30pm, 440 pesos); **Ciudad Cuauhtémoc** (6 per day, 32 pesos); **Mexico City** (1:10, 3:00, 4:45pm, 502 pesos); **Palenque** (3:30pm, 87 pesos); **Puebla** (5 per day, 449 pesos); **Ocosingo** (3:30pm, 40 pesos); **Tapachula** (6 per day, 91 pesos); **Tuxtla Gutiérrez** (35 pesos) via **San Cristóbal** (10am, 2, 6, 7pm; 64 pesos).

◢ ▐ ORIENTATION AND PRACTICAL INFORMATION

Blvd. Domínguez (the Pan-American Highway) runs north-south, passing the town to the west. Street numbers increase in all four directions away from the *zócalo*, and are named according to the quadrant in which they fall. **Avenidas** run north-south and **calles** east-west. If an address reads Av. 5 Pte. Sur between Calles 2 and 3 Sur Pte., it is 5 blocks west and 2½ blocks south of the northwest corner of the *zócalo*, which is the intersection of Calle Central (called Juárez) and Av. Central (called Domínguez, not to be confused with Blvd. Domínguez).

The municipal **tourist office, Codetur,** is on the 2nd fl. of the Palacio Municipal on the northern side of the *zócalo*. (☎ 632 62 13. Open M-F 9am-2pm and 5-7pm.) Another tourist office is at Central #6, next to the Palacio Municipal. (☎ 632 40 47. Open M-F 8am-4pm.) Guatemalan **visas** can be obtained from the **Guatemalan Consulate,** Av. 1 Sur Pte. #26, at Av. 2 Pte. Sur, marked by a blue and white flag. (☎ 632 04 91. Open M-F 9am-5pm.) Obtaining a visa will take 10-30 days (US$25). Visas not required for citizens of the US, UK, Australia, or EU. **Bancomer,** on the southeast corner of the *zócalo*, has a 24hr. **ATM.** (Open M-F 8:30am-4pm, Sa 10am-2pm.) **Market:** on Calle Central, just before Av. 2 Ote., one block east of the *zócalo*. (Open daily 6:30am-5pm.) **Supermarket: Supermás,** on Calle 2 Sur Pte. between Domínguez Sur and Av. 1 Pte. Sur. (☎632 17 27. Open daily 8am-9pm.) **Police:** (☎632 00 25), in the Palacio Municipal. No English spoken. **Red Cross:** (☎632 18 89) on Calle 5 Nte. Pte., 3½ blocks west of the highway. **Farmacia Esquivar,** on the south side of the *zócalo.* (☎632 43 50. Open daily 7am-10:30pm.) **Centro Médico de Comitán,** (☎632 00 67), on Av. 1 Pte. Sur between Calles 2 and 3 Sur Pte. Some English spoken. **Telecomm,** Domínguez Sur 47, 1½ blocks south of the *zócalo.* (Open M-F 8am-6pm, Sa 9am-5pm, Su 9am-1pm.) **Internet: Dante's Pizza,** one block north of east side of *zócalo.* (15 pesos per hr. Open daily 10am-10:30pm.) **Post office:** Domínguez 45. (Open M-F 9am-3pm, Sa 9am-1pm.) **Postal Code:** 30000.

ACCOMMODATIONS

Accommodations near the *zócalo* will go easy on your wallet. **Hospedaje San Francisco,** Av. 1 Ote. Nte. 13, one block from the *zócalo* on the corner of Calle 1 Ote. Nte., has a plant-filled *hacienda*-style courtyard and rooms with comfortable beds and private baths. (☎632 01 94. Singles 50 pesos; doubles 100 pesos; triples 150 pesos.) **Hospedaje Primavera,** Calle Central 2, has basic rooms with shared baths. (☎632 20 41. Singles 60 pesos; doubles 80 pesos; triples 100 pesos.) **Hospedaje Río Escondido,** Av 1 Pte. Sur 7, between Calle Central and Calle 1 Sur Pte., offers a colorful tile courtyard and matchbox size rooms with communal baths. (☎632 01 73. Singles 25 pesos; doubles 50 pesos; triples 65 pesos; quads 100 pesos.)

FOOD

For meals on the go, taco stands line the road in front of the market. Home-cooked *chiapaneco* cuisine, such as *butifara* (pork served cold), is available at restaurants. For elegant dining at bargain prices, try **Alis,** Calle Central 21 between Av. 1 Pte. Nte. and Av. 2 Pte. Nte. (☎632 12 62. *Huevos chiapanecos* 28 pesos, *filete oaxqueño* 39 pesos. Open daily 8am-6pm.) **Taco-Miteco,** Calle Central Nte. 5, near Palacio Municipal, serves tacos. (3 for 14.5 pesos. Open daily 8am-11pm.) **Cafe Quiptic,** housed in the Casa de Cultura on the east side of the *zócalo,* is always crowded. Drink coffee (7-18 pesos) or take home a kilo (70-100 pesos). Proceeds aid **La Sociedad Campesino Magisterial de la Selva,** a grassroots organization for farm workers. (Open daily 8:30am-11pm.)

SIGHTS

The **Casa Museo Dr. Belisario Domínguez,** Domínguez Sur 35, features 19th-century medical instruments and a re-creation of Dr. Belisario's pharmacy, including such products as Dr. Bell's Pine Tar Honey. (Open Tu-Sa 10am-6:45pm, Su 9am-12:45pm. 5 pesos.) The **Museo de Arte Hermila Domínguez de Castellanos,** Domínguez Sur 51, 1½ blocks south of the *zócalo,* is kitsch-free. Behind a colonial facade, the structure houses paintings, sculptures, and photography. (Open Tu-Sa 10am-6pm, Su 9am-1pm. 2 pesos.) The **Museo Arqueológico de Comitán,** Calle 1 Sur Ote. and Av. 2 Ote Sur, in the **Centro Cultural Rosario Castellanos,** houses prehistoric artifacts, information on Chinkultic, and flattened Maya skulls. (Open Tu-Su 10am-5pm.)

COMITÁN BLOODY MURDER Everything seems normal enough. Yet ask around discreetly; a good majority of Comitán residents will be able to direct you to the **Calle de Llorona** (Street of The Weeping One). Many are convinced that, late at night, you can hear the shrill cries of a mother who slaughtered her children in a fit of rage. And that door that just closed behind you? Well it could have been the wind, or it might have been the mischievous spirit of a **huérfano** (orphan child who perished before baptism), often blamed for minor mishaps by locals. From spirit-children to restless ghosts, Comitán's old stories have yet to bow to the modern age.

▶ DAYTRIPS FROM COMITÁN

PARQUE NACIONAL LAGUNAS DE MONTEBELLO

In Comitán, blue combis leave Av. 2 Pte. Sur 23 between Calles 2 and 3 Sur Pte. for either Bosque Azul or Tziscao (1hr., 5:30am-4:30pm, 15 pesos). Combis swing by the Cristóbal Colón bus station for those who want to head straight to the lakes.

A hop, skip, and a 58km *combi* ride from Comitán lie the pine-covered hills of the Parque Nacional Lagunas de Montebello, where 59 lagoons and lakes await exploration. Unfortunately, only 16 have trails from the main road, and some are notorious for **bandit attacks.** Inquire at the Comitán tourist office before undertaking hikes off the beaten path. Women traveling alone should consider taking *combis* to and from the lakes. The main destination for visitors is the **Lago Bosque Azul,** which has a few facilities, a restaurant (open daily 7am-10pm), and free camping. An onslaught of children will offer to lead you to **Las Grutas,** a cave with an underground lake. Horses and paddle boats are available for rent behind the restaurant.

Similar services can be found on the shores of **Lago Tziscao.** The *combi* will drop you off at the road into town; follow this road until just before it changes to dirt. Take a right over the hill, where the road will curve to the left, and continue along the shore for 500m to the **Hotel Tziscao,** with baths and showers for all. A large lobby for dining and socializing plays *ranchero* music or your own tapes. (☎633 13 03. Meals 30 pesos. Restaurant open daily 6am-10pm. Camping 10 pesos; outdoor cabins 40 pesos per person; hostel rooms 30 pesos per person.) Two nearby accommodations provide easy access to *lagos* and Maya site of **Chinkultic.** A few kilometers west of the park entrance at the access road to Chinkultic, **Doña María's** and **El Pino Feliz** rent *cabañas* at very reasonable prices.

LA CASCADA EL CHIFLÓN

Take a combi to El Puente de San Vincente en La Mesilla (not La Mesilla in Guatemala) from the La Angostura bus station on the highway between Calles 1 and 2 Sur Pte. (45min., every 20min. 5am-5pm, 16 pesos). From the bridge, follow the dirt road 500m before coming to a barbed-wire fence. Cross it (somehow) and continue along the road. The path becomes a narrow trail, skirting the banks of the river upstream to the falls (40min.). The trail is not marked but is fairly well-trod; if lost, follow the river downstream and you should soon spot the trail.

Named for their whistling sound, this series of waterfalls 45km west of Comitán on the Tzimol-Tuxtla road are an impressive 120m high. Hiking efforts will be rewarded when you set foot on the highest and nearest mount to the waterfall. **El Restaurante** serves fresh fish from the lake, and cooks meat from the ranch (20 pesos). Beer and *botanas* (appetizers) cost 10 pesos. (Open daily 8am-9pm.)

LAGOS DE COLÓN

Catch a lake-bound combi from the Transportes Mariscal station between Calles 1 and 2 Sur Pte. on the highway (every 20min. 6am-4pm, 20 pesos).

The warm, crystal-clear waters of the Lagos de Colón lie in a valley 70km southeast of Comitán and are connected by rushing streams and waterfalls. To reach the mouth of the waterfalls, follow the path, starting 100m before the lakes, into the woods for 15-20min. Lagos de Colón also houses a turtle pond near its entrance. Unfortunately, they must swim amidst soda bottles and beer cans. A Maya ruin, **Lagartero,** stands 2km from Lagos de Colón.

CHINKULTIC

"Montebello" combis drop you off at the access road; from there, it's a 2km walk or bike ride uphill to the entrance (local restaurant owners rent bikes for 20 pesos). Site open daily 9am-4pm. 23 pesos. Large groups free.

The ruins of Chinkultic lie 32km from the Pan-American Highway, on the way to Lagunas Montebello. The ruins date from the late Classic Period, and the city probably reached its peak in the 1st or 2nd century AD, making it one of the last western Maya settlements. Follow the *sacbé* road, traverse the jungle, cross the stone bridge, and climb the wooden steps to reach Chinkultic's 7th-century pyramid. Birds, lily pads, a cool breeze, and **Lago Tepancuapan** are among Chikultic's many virtues. Toward the entrance, on the left, is a quadrangle for religious sacrifices. Near the exit, stelae of victorious warriors and ball players guard the ballcourt.

TENAM PUENTE

Combis *leave the station at Av. 1 Pte. Sur between Calles 2 and 3 Sur Pte. and drop you at the ruins (every hr. 6am-6pm, 15 pesos). Site open daily 9am-4pm. Free.*

This white stone city, whose name means "fortification" in Náhuatl, commands two square kilometers encompassing a T-shaped ballcourt, burial palaces, *cruz de la madera* (wooden cross), and a tiered pyramid.

TAPACHULA   ☎ 9

Tapachula (pop. 300,000) bustles with sidewalk swapmeets, cheap diners, and *marimba* music echoing through the hazy afternoon and into the night. The gold and green *zócalo* provides a haven from Tapachula's loud, dirty daily life, where Guatemalan immigrants and *chiapanecos* sit, read, and socialize. As far as tourists are concerned, Tapachula is primarily a point of entry into Guatemala.

TRANSPORTATION. The **airport** is on the road to Puerto Madero, about 17km south of town. It's served by **Aeroméxico,** Av. 2 Nte. 6 (☎626 20 50), and **Aviacsa** (☎626 03 72). Tapachula's **first-class bus station** (☎626 28 91) is located northwest of the *zócalo* at Calle 17 Ote. and Av. 3 Nte. To get to the *zócalo*, take a left upon exiting onto Av. 17 Ote, walk 1½ blocks, take a left on Av. Central, and continue south six blocks. Take a right on Av. 5 Pte and go 3 blocks west to the northeast corner of the plaza. A *centro*-bound *combi* can be caught across the street from the bus station (2.5 pesos). Altos de Chiapas goes to **Comitán** (6 per day, 91 pesos) and **San Cristóbal de las Casas** (6am, 5pm; 124 pesos). Cristóbal Colón heads to **Mexico City** (18hr., 7 per day, 550 pesos); **Oaxaca** (11hr., 8pm, 333 pesos); **Puerto Escondido** (12hr., 10:45pm, 293 pesos); **Tuxtla Gutiérrez** (6hr., every 2hr., 198 pesos). Tika runs buses to **Guatemala City** (7am, 150 pesos).

ORIENTATION AND PRACTICAL INFORMATION. Tapachula is 18km from Talismán along the Guatemalan border and 303km west of Guatemala City. *Avenidas* run north-south, and *calles* run east-west. *Calles* north of **Calle Central** are odd-numbered; those south are even-numbered. Similarly, *avenidas* east of **Av. Central** are odd-numbered, while those west of it have even numbers. Tapachula's *zócalo* is at **Calle 3 Pte.** between **Av. 6** and **8 Nte.,** northwest of the intersection of Av. and Calle Central. Each street is divided by the axes centered at this intersection into Norte and Sur or Oriente and Poniente.

The **tourist office** is in the old Palacio Municipal, south of the Iglesia de San Agustín, on the west side of the *zócalo*. (☎626 14 85, ext. 140. Open M-F 8am-9pm, Sa 9am-1pm.) **Inverlat,** on the east side of the *zócalo* at Calle 5, has a 24hr. **ATM.** (Open M-F 9am-5pm.) **Mercado Sebastián Escobar,** 10 Av. Nte. between Calles 3 and 5 Pte., sells produce and baked goods. **Supermarket: San Agustín,** in the southwest corner of *zócalo*. (Open 24hr.) **Police: Base de Seguridad Publica,** km 2.5 on Carretera Antiguo Aeropuerto. (☎625 28 51) **Red Cross:** (☎626 19 49) across from post office. **Farmacia 24 Horas,** 8 Av. Nte. 25, at 7 Calle Pte. (☎628 64 48. Free delivery 7am-11pm.) **Hospital General,** (☎628 10 70), on the highway to the airport. **Internet access: Cyber City,** Av. 2 Nte. between Calle Central 1 Pte. (15 pesos per hr. Open M-Sa 9am-9pm.) **Telecomm:** next to post office. (Fax 626 10 97. Open M-F 8am-7:30pm, Sa 9am-5pm). **Post office:** at Calle 1 Ote. 32, between Av. 7 and 9 Nte. (☎626 24 92. Open M-F 8:30am-2:30pm, Sa 9am-1pm.) **Postal code:** 30700.

ACCOMMODATIONS AND FOOD. Due to border traffic, budget accommodations are a dime a dozen in Tapachula, especially near the market. Unfortunately, many hotel rooms are as noisy and dirty as the rest of the city. **Hotel Cervantino,** Calle 1 Ote. 6 between Av. Central and Av. 1 Nte, has clean and colorful rooms with private baths surrounding a pleasant atrium. (☎ 626 16 58. Singles 90 pesos, with TV 120 pesos; doubles 130 pesos, with TV 160 pesos.) **Hotel La Amistad,** Calle 7 Pte. 34, between Av. 10 and 12 Nte, has a verdant courtyard and peachy rooms with private clean baths. (☎ 626 22 93. Singles 75 pesos; doubles 100 pesos; triples 140 pesos; quads 185 pesos.) **Hotel Algarcas,** Av. 6 Nte. 12A, has rooms outfitted with fans, phones, cable TV, and very low ceilings. (Singles 125 pesos; doubles 170 pesos; triples 230 pesos; quads 300 pesos.)

Taco and pastry stands crowd near the *zócalo*, selling 4 to 8 peso tacos and *tortas*. Grab a meal at the **San Juan market** on Calle 17 Pte., north of the *centro* (open daily 6am-5pm). Typical Mexican restaurants line the southern edge of the *zócalo*; Chinese restaurants can be found on Calle 1 Pte. east of the *zócalo*.

CROSSING THE BORDER. The Maya may have known no borders, but tourists are not so lucky. Citizens of the US, Canada, and European Union countries do not need a visa to enter Guatemala for up to five months. Citizens from other countries will need a **visa,** which can be obtained from the Guatemalan consulate in Comitán. If you plan on staying longer than five months, check with an immigration office in Guatemala; otherwise, you might have to pay an additional fee when you leave. By far, the easiest and safest way to cross into Guatemala is to take a direct bus from Tapachula or Talismán to Guatemala City. If you choose to brave the crossing on foot, **Unión y Progreso** buses leave Calle 5 Pte., half a block west of Av. 12 Nte., for **Talismán** (30min., every 15min., 7 pesos). Tapachula buses drop passengers at the entrance to the Mexican emigration office. Present your **passport** and visa at the office, and follow the crowd across the bridge, where you'll need to pay a toll (approx. 65 pesos). Proceed to a small building on the left to have your passport stamped. A **taxi** from the zócalo to Talismán costs 60 pesos.

CIUDAD CUAUHTÉMOC ☎ 9

A popular border crossing to Guatemala, Ciudad Cuauhtémoc (kwah-TAY-moke) lies only 4km from the border. Travelers stuck overnight or waiting for buses will find only a few services in town. Altos (☎ 631 42 42) goes to: **Mexico City** (11:30am and 1:30pm, 516 pesos) via **Puebla** (465 pesos); **Tapachula** (10am, noon, 3, 5pm; 63 pesos); **Tuxtla Gutiérrez** (6 per day, 11:30am-9:30pm, 92 pesos) via **Comitán** (32 pesos) and **San Cristóbal** (63 pesos). The **bus station** is in the same building as the town's only hotel, **Hotel Camino Real,** which charges 100 pesos for a bed in spartan, airy, peach-colored rooms. There is a restaurant on the ground floor. *Especial* and *colectivo* taxis and *camionetas* leave from the front of the bus station for nearby **Comalapa** (6 pesos), **Comitán** (25 pesos), and **Guatemala** (*colectivo* 3-5 pesos, *especial* 15 pesos). About 25m down the road to Guatemala, a **doctor**'s office adjoins **Farmacia San Angel.** (Open M-Sa 8am-2pm and 4-8pm, Su 8am-noon.)

GULF COAST & CHIAPAS

YUCATÁN PENINSULA

The Yucatán Peninsula is a place where imagination meets reality, where tales of remarkably advanced ancient Maya civilizations, legends of pirates and Spanish conquistadors, images of steamy mosquito-infested jungles, and fantasies of the perfect vacation come together to form the ultimate travel experience.

At the extreme southeastern edge of Mexico, surrounded by the Gulf of Mexico and the Caribbean, the three distinct states of the Yucatán together evoke a comprehensive and satisfying taste of Mexico. Facing the Gulf of Mexico to the west, quiet **Campeche** inspires romantic images of history and legend. Savage pirate raids, brutal Spanish conquest, and ancient wars between Maya dynasties are enshrined in over two millennia of ruins. Ruling over the northern coast, the state of **Yucatán** overflows with cross-cultural treasures. Some of the world's most astonishing cathedrals, the stunning Maya ruins of Chichén Itzá and Uxmal, and the uncannily European metropolis of Mérida physically embody the unique culture of the *mestizo*—of a race apart, or of not a race at all. Finally, sublime **Quintana Roo**, bordering the Caribbean on the peninsula's eastern coast, exudes an unbridled hedonistic appeal. With its mega-resorts lining the Maya Riviera, world-renowned snorkeling and scuba diving in crystalline waters, the natural treasures of its luscious jungles and barrier reefs, and that ornate riot of US taste, Cancún—where the Garden of Eden meets Las Vegas on the beach—the state of Quintana Roo may very well be heaven on earth.

In the peninsula's small towns, where the only form of capitalism evident is the weekly visit from the Coca-Cola truck, the culture remains very traditional. Maya is still the primary language of many locals, and indigenous religious traditions persist within the boundaries of Spanish-instilled Catholicism. Yucatecan women still carry bowls of corn flour on their heads and wear embroidered *huipiles* (woven dresses), while modern Maya men fish and farm for subsistence. Increasingly, however, workers lured by the shine of pesos are moving to big cities to work in *gringo*-friendly restaurants, weave hammocks for tourists, or act as archaeological guides. The engineering of pristine pleasure-playgrounds throughout the peninsula has brought tourists in by the droves while unfortunately transforming much of the indigenous culture into little more than a gimmick for dollars, even as more and more tourists pour in to experience "authentic" Maya culture. The result is a modern-day twist on the age-old tension between native and foreign, reality and imagination.

HIGHLIGHTS OF THE YUCATÁN PENINSULA

SEE amazing Maya ruins at **Chichén Itzá** (see p. 591), and believe in their splendor.

GET DOWN with the young, the beautiful, and the very drunk in wild **Cancún** (see p. 604), Mexico's biggest resort, and the ruling king of US spring break.

BEHOLD thousands of brilliant orange-red flamingos at **Río Lagartos** (see p. 602).

CRUISE through the **Ruta Puuc** (see p. 573), an eclectic assemblage of relatively unexplored jungle ruins.

SOAK up the sun in the laid-back island of **Isla Mujeres** (see p. 612), which draws a hip, international crew of backpackers.

CLIMB the largest Maya structure ever built at the sweaty jungle-shrouded ruins of **Calakmul** (see p. 572).

Yucatán Peninsula

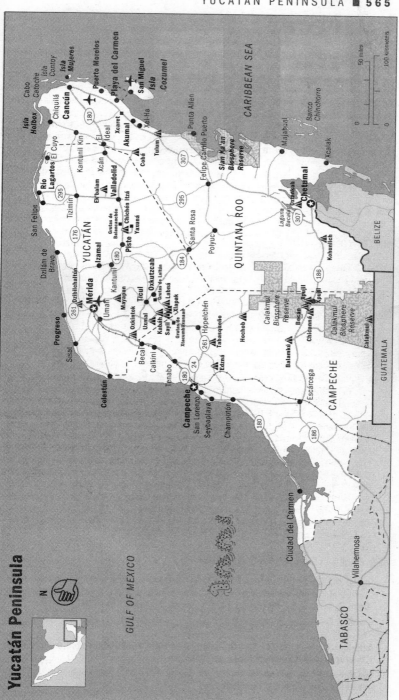

N

GULF OF MEXICO

CARIBBEAN SEA

Cabo
Catoche
Isla
Contoy
Isla
Holbox
Isla
Mujeres
Chiquilá
Cabo
Catoche
Puerto Morelos
Cancún
Playa del Carmen
San Miguel
Isla
Cozumel
El Cuyo
Kantunil Kin
Ideal
Xcaret
Xel-Ha
Akumal
Río
Lagartos
Tizimín
El
Xcán
Cobá
Tulum
Punta Allen
San Felipe
Ek'balam
Valladolid
Chichén Itzá
Yaxuná
Felipe Carrillo Puerto
Sian Ka'an
Biosphere
Reserve
Dzilám de
Bravo
Izamal
Gruttas de
Balancanché
Piste
Santa Rosa
QUINTANA ROO
Banco
Chinchorro
Progreso
YUCATÁN
Kantunil
Oxkutzcab
Polyuc
Laguna
Bacalar
Majahual
Acalak
Sisal
MÉRIDA
Umán
Mayapan
Ticul
Grutas de Loltun
Hopelchén
184
Bacalar
Chetumal
BELIZE
Celestún
Oxkintok
Uxmal
Kabáh
Sayil
Labná
Xlapak
Xtacumbilxunaah
Tabasqueño
Hochob
Kohunlich
295
Beca
Calkini
Tenabo
Edzná
Balamkú
Becán
Chicanná
Xpujil
Calakmul
Biosphere
Reserve
Calakmul
Biosphere
Reserve
Calakmul
Campeche
San Lorenzo
Seybaplaya
Champotón
Escárcega
CAMPECHE
GUATEMALA
Ciudad del Carmen
Villahermosa
TABASCO

180, 295, 176, 261, 24, 186, 307

YUCATÁN

50 miles
100 kilometers

CAMPECHE

CAMPECHE
☎ 9

At the western edge of the Yucatán, Campeche (pop. 200,000) has always seemed to exist only on the fringes. For the Maya, it was "Ah Kin Pech"—loosely translated as a mythical "Place of the Serpents and Ticks." For colonial Spaniards, it was the gateway into the untamed south, and from 1540, it was a chief port in the New World. Campeche soon became an easy prize for pirates, whose infamous raids mauled the city until the late 17th century, when the Spanish transformed it into a fortress of bulwarks, protective walls, cannons, and forts. Today, at the edge of the tourist boom sweeping the peninsula, Campeche draws quite a crowd. Out of fierce *mestizo* pride and wonderful Campechan amiability came a rich collective consciousness that transcends two races and four centuries.

⌐ TRANSPORTATION

GETTING AROUND

A confusing network of **buses** links Campeche's distant sectors to the old city (2.5 pesos). The market, where **Gobernadores** becomes the **Circuito,** serves as the hub for local routes. Buses can be flagged down, but do not run in the city center. **Taxis** (☎816 11 13) operate out of three stands: Calle 8 at 55, left of the cathedral; Calle 55 at Circuito, near the market; and Gobernadores at Chile, near the bus terminal. Intra-city travel is 15-20 pesos, more after dark.

GETTING AWAY

Airport: (☎816 31 09), on Porfirio, 13km from the city center. **Aeroméxico** (☎816 66 56). Taxis from the airport to the *centro* cost 35 pesos.

Buses: 1st and 2nd-class terminals stand at Gobernadores and Chile, ½km from the old city. To reach Parque Principal from the bus terminals, catch the "Gobernadores" bus (3 pesos) across from the station, and ask the driver to let you off at the Baluarte de San Francisco. Turn right into the old city and walk 4 blocks on Calle 57 to the park. Taxis run from the bus station to the *zócalo* (20 pesos). If walking (15min.), head left on Gobernadores and turn left when you reach the Circuito. 3 blocks later, turn right on Calle 57 through the stone arch and walk 4 blocks to the park. ADO goes to: **Cancún** (7hr., 10 and 11:30pm, 233 pesos); **Chetumal** (7hr., noon, 176 pesos); **Ciudad de Carmen** (11 per day, 95 pesos); **Mérida** (2½hr., 10 per day, 78 pesos); **Mexico City** (16hr., 4 per day, 611 pesos); **Oaxaca** (9:55pm, 480 pesos); **Palenque** (12:30, 2, and 10:30am, 153 pesos); **San Cristóbal de Las Casas** (9:45pm, 210 pesos); **Veracruz** (12hr., 1 and 9pm, 393 pesos); **Villahermosa** (7hr., 6 per day, 187 pesos); **Xpujil** (5hr., noon, 126 pesos). 2nd-class buses leave from the 2nd-class terminal (☎816 24 02, ext. 2405) for many of the same destinations.

⚡ PRACTICAL INFORMATION

Tourist Office: Calle 55 #3 (☎811 39 89), between Calles 8 and 10, right next to the cathedral. Some English spoken. Open M-F 9am-3pm and 6-9pm. You can also visit **Casa Seis,** Calle 57 #6 (☎816 17 82), across the *zócalo.* Open daily 9am-9pm.

Currency Exchange: Banamex (☎816 52 52), at the corner of Calles 53 and 10. Open M-F 9am-5pm, Sa 9:30am-2pm. 24hr. **ATM.**

American Express: (☎811 10 10), Calle 59 between 16 de Septiembre and the shore. Open M-F 10am-2pm and 5-7pm, Sa 9am-1pm.

Car Rental: Maya Rent-a-Car (☎816 22 33), Cortines 51., in the Hotel del Mar lobby. Open M-F 9am-8pm, Sa 9am-2pm.

Market: On Circuito Baluartes, between Calles 53 and 55. Open M-Sa sunrise-sunset, Su sunrise-3pm.

Supermarket: San Francisco de Asis (☎816 79 77), in Plaza Comercial A-Kin-Pech, behind the post office. Open daily 7am-10pm.

Laundry: Lavandería y Tintorería Campeche, Calle 55 #22 (☎816 51 42), between Calles 12 and 14. Same-day service. 12 pesos per kg. Open M-Sa 8am-4pm.

Police: (☎816 23 09), on Sierra, in front of El Balneario Popular. A more central station is at Calle 55 and the market.

Red Cross: (☎815 24 11), 1km up the coast from the old city. No English spoken.

Pharmacy: Farmacia Canto, Calle 18 #99 (☎816 31 65), at the market. Open daily 8am-10:30pm.

Medical Assistance: IMSS (☎816 52 02), Central at Circuito Baluartes. No English spoken. **Hospital General** (☎816 09 20), across the street.

Fax: Telecomm (☎816 52 10), in the Palacio Federal, opposite MexPost. Open M-F 8am-7:30pm, Sa-Su 8am-12:30pm.

Internet Access: The Password, Calle 12 #138B (☎811 19 84), between Calles 53 and 55. 15 pesos per hr., student ID discount. Open M-F 10am-9pm, Sa-Su 11am-8pm.

Post Office: (☎816 21 34), 16 de Septiembre at Calle 53 in the Palacio Federal. Open M-F 9am-3pm. **MexPost** (☎811 17 30) next door. Open M-F 9am-3pm, Sa 9am-1pm.

Postal Code: 24000.

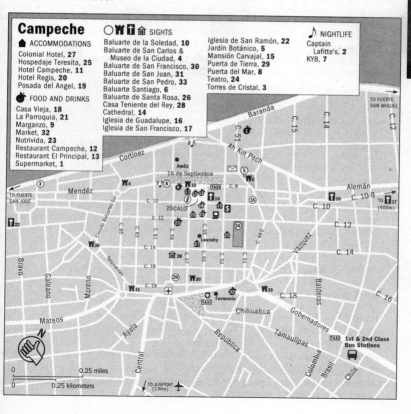

Campeche

▲ ACCOMMODATIONS

Colonial Hotel, **27**
Hospedaje Teresita, **25**
Hotel Campeche, **11**
Hotel Regis, **20**
Posada del Angel, **19**

🍴 FOOD AND DRINKS

Casa Vieja, **18**
La Parroquia, **21**
Marganzo, **9**
Market, **32**
Nutrivida, **23**
Restaurant Campeche, **12**
Restaurant El Principal, **13**
Supermarket, **1**

○ 🍴 🚻 🏛 SIGHTS

Baluarte de la Soledad, **10**
Baluarte de San Carlos & Museo de la Ciudad, **4**
Baluarte de San Francisco, **30**
Baluarte de San Juan, **31**
Baluarte de San Pedro, **33**
Baluarte Santiago, **6**
Baluarte de Santa Rosa, **26**
Casa Teniente del Rey, **28**
Cathedral, **14**
Iglesia de Guadalupe, **16**
Iglesia de San Francisco, **17**

Iglesia de San Ramón, **22**
Jardín Botánico, **5**
Mansión Carvajal, **15**
Puerta de Tierra, **29**
Puerta del Mar, **8**
Teatro, **24**
Torres de Cristal, **3**

♪ NIGHTLIFE

Captain Lafitte's, **2**
KY8, **7**

⚑ ACCOMMODATIONS

Campeche has thus far avoided the price boom that has swept most of the Yucatán Peninsula. Budget accommodations abound in the historic center, and an inexpensive hostel is located on the edge of downtown. During July and August, Campeche swells with Mexican and European tourists. Call ahead to make reservations.

Hotel Colonial, Calle 14 #122 (☎816 22 22), between Calles 55 and 57, 2½ blocks from the zócalo. A retro look saturates tall rooms and clean baths. Singles 123 pesos; doubles 152-164 pesos; triples 193 pesos; each additional person 24 pesos; A/C 64 pesos extra.

Posada del Ángel, Calle 10 #307 (☎816 77 18), between Calles 53 and 55, next to the cathedral. The white rooms are sparse and a little old, but nearly spotless. Singles 176 pesos; doubles 211 pesos; triples 246 pesos; A/C 82 pesos extra.

Hotel Regis (☎816 31 75), on Calle 12 between Calles 55 and 57. Large, white rooms with checkered floors, comfy beds, TV, fan, and A/C. Ask for a balcony. Singles 237 pesos; doubles 281 pesos; triples 325 pesos; each additional person 40 pesos.

Hospedaje Teresita, Calle 53 #31 (☎816 45 34), between Calles 12 and 14. The decor of these basic rooms leaves something to be desired, but the prime location compensates. Singles and doubles 60 pesos, with bath 70 pesos.

Villa Deportiva Universitaria (☎816 18 02), on Melgár, 1½ blocks from the coastal highway. From outside the north walls of the city (Calle 49C), catch a bus marked "Lerma," "Playa Bonita," or "ISSTE" heading toward the water. Clean, single-sex dorm rooms with 4 bunks and communal baths straight out of high school await. Often full July-Aug. and Dec. Call to reserve. Bunks 25 pesos; 25 peso deposit.

Hotel Campeche, Calle 57 #2 (☎816 51 83), between Calles 8 and 10, overlooking Parque Principal. The blue-green walls are a little cracked and soiled, but the baths are fairly clean and the location convenient. Singles 92 pesos; doubles 123 pesos.

◨ FOOD

Campechan cuisine is known for combining Yucatec specialties with European style and the flavors of the sea. Sample *pan de cazón* (stacked tortillas filled with baby shark and refried beans and covered with an onion, tomato, and *chile* sauce). Other local specialties include *pámpano en escabeche* (pompano broiled in olive oil and flavored with onion, garlic, *chile*, and orange juice), Campechan caviar, and *chicozapote*, a regional fruit. The city's cheapest food can be found at the numerous stalls and *loncherías* at the market.

Marganzo (☎811 38 98), on Calle 8 between Calles 57 and 59, is as fresh and colorful as its food. Something for everyone's budget (*tamales* 20 pesos, fish parmesano 58 pesos), and suave *mariachis* combine to make this one of the best dining experiences in town. Open daily 7am-11pm.

Restaurant La Parroquia, Calle 55 #8 (☎816 80 86), between Calles 10 and 12. Low prices and heaping portions. A cavernous and popular all-night local eatery with TV around the clock. Fat, steaming stacks of pancakes with honey 27 pesos. Open 24hr.

Nutrivida (☎816 12 21), on Calle 12 between Calles 57 and 59. Vegetarians rejoice! All-natural food such as apple yogurt (4.5 pesos) and meatless burgers (18 pesos) served fast. Open M-F 8am-2pm and 5:30-8:30pm, Sa 8am-2pm.

Casa Vieja, on Calle 10 between Calles 55 and 57. Slightly pricey menu but the balcony overlooking the zócalo provides an excellent place to dine. Baguette sandwiches 38-55 pesos, chicken fajitas 58 pesos. Open Tu-Su 9:30pm-2am, M 5:30pm-2am.

Restaurante Campeche, Calle 57 (☎816 21 28), between Calles 8 and 10. The A/C unit and futuristic blue lighting call the North Pole to mind. Complete the illusion with an ice cream dessert (15 pesos). Entrees 35-65 pesos. Open daily 6:30am-midnight.

Restaurant El Principal (☎811 12 11), in the gazebo of El Parque Principal, serves tropical ice cream (20 pesos), club sandwiches (38 pesos), pastas (40-55 pesos), and Campeche beer in a souvenir glass (15 pesos). Open Tu-Su 6pm-midnight. The only place in town that rents **bikes** (12 pesos per hr.).

Restaurante del Parque, Calle 8 #251 (☎816 02 40), at Calle 57. Tablecloths and cushioned chairs make this the height of budget elegance. *Tortas al pastor* 22 pesos and *pan de cazón* 35 pesos. Open daily 6:30am-11pm.

👁 SIGHTS

With ancient stone beautifully illuminated by the moonlight and myriad street lamps, Campeche's historical treasures are best viewed by night. The city has eight *baluartes* (bulwarks), visible along Circuito Baluartes or from the "Circuito Baluartes" bus. The convenient red "Tranvía" trolley tours major sights; catch it in Parque Principal on Calle 10 in front of the gazebo. (1hr.; M-F 9:30am, 6, and 8pm, Sa-Su 9:30am, 6, 7, and 8pm; 20 pesos. Tours in Spanish.) The green "El Guapo" trolley gives a guided tour on its way to Fuerte de San Miguel (Tu-Su 9am and 5pm) and Fuerte de San José El Alto (☎811 11 38. 1¼hr., Tu-Su 10:30am and 6:30pm, 20 pesos).

FUERTE DE SAN MIGUEL. Completed in 1801, this fort now houses the impressive **Museo Arqueológico de Campeche,** which has intriguing exhibits on the ruins in the state, ancient Maya city life, religion, and views of death and afterlife. On the top level, 19 cannons still protect the city. (Take a "Lerma" or "Playa Bonita" bus from Circuito Baluartes, half a block toward the sea from the market. Ask the driver to drop you off at the Castillo stop, then walk up the steep hill on the left until the road forks; the left turn leads to the fort. Open Tu-Su 8am-7:30pm. 17 pesos, students free; Su free.)

FUERTE DE SAN JOSÉ EL ALTO. Built in 1792, San Miguel's smaller fort stands guard on the opposite side of the city. The path leading to the drawbridge winds deliberately to prevent attacking pirates from using battering rams on the gate. Today, ships and armaments are exhibited inside. (The "Bellavista" or "San José El Alto" bus, caught at the same place as the bus for San Miguel, will drop you halfway up the hill, a 3min. walk from the fort. Open Tu-Su 8am-8pm. 25 pesos, students free; Su free.)

MUSEO DE LAS ESTELAS MAYA. Inside the **Baluarte de la Soledad,** the museum has a small collection of Maya stelae and reliefs from sites in Campeche state. (Off Calle 8 near Calle 57 behind Parque Principal. Open Su-M 8am-2pm, Tu-Sa 8am-8pm. 25 pesos.)

JARDÍN BOTÁNICO XMUCH'HALTUN. Enclosed by the walls of the **Baluarte de Santiago,** over 250 species of plant thrive in the tiny open-air courtyard shaded by trees and filled with benches, fountains, and frogs. (Calles 8 and 51. Open M-F 9am-8pm, Sa 9am-1pm and 5-8pm, Su 9am-1pm.)

LA PURÍSIMA CONCEPCIÓN. The construction of Campeche's cathedral was initially ordered by Francisco de Montejo in 1540, but builders did not complete the massive structure until 1705. (Open daily 7am-noon and 5-8pm. Free.)

IGLESIA DE SAN FRANCISCO. This church, built in 1546 on an ancient Maya foundation, marks the site of the first Mesoamerican mass, and the baptismal site of Hernán Cortés's grandson. The three bells toll for humility, obedience, and chastity. (About 1km from the center of town on Alemán. Open daily 8am-noon and 5-8pm.)

IGLESIA DE SAN ROMÁN. The church houses the image of **El Cristo Negro** (The Black Christ), greatly venerated by *campechanos* in Mexico. (A few blocks south of the centro on Calle 10. Open daily 6am-noon and 4-8pm.)

MUSEO DE LA CIUDAD. This small museum within Baluarte de San Carlos explains the history of the city from the 16th to the 18th centuries. (At the corner of Calles 8 and 65. Open Tu-Sa 8am-8pm, Su 9am-1pm, M 9am-2pm. Free.)

BEACHES. By any conceivable definition, downtown Campeche lacks a beach. For something prettier, catch a **"Playa Bonita"** bus to the beach of the same name.

🎵 ENTERTAINMENT

Traditional music and dance infuse Campeche's evening air and nourish its cultural roots nearly every night. The city sponsors various outdoor events. The **sound and light show** at Puerta de Tierra, Calles 59 and 18, tells the story of the *campechanos* staving off foolhardy pirates (Tu and F-Sa 8:30pm, 20 pesos, from July to mid-Aug.). Weather permitting, a *ballet folklórico* performance follows the show. **Sabadito Alegre en La Plaza de la República,** at Puerta de Mar, features *mariachi* and *danzones* (Sa 7-10pm). **Tradición y Folklore,** a celebration of *campechano* heritage, replete with music and dancing, is at Ex-Templo de San José (Tu 7pm). The state band strikes up *campechano* music in Parque Principal (Su 8pm). More events are scheduled during high season (July-Aug. and Dec.). Ask for a program at the tourist information center. *Campechanos* celebrate the feast of **San Román,** the city's patron saint, in the fall. (Sept. 14-30.)

On weekends, two clubs draw university students and a lively bar keeps the night active until early morning. See the Yucatán's hottest and sexiest (and perhaps wealthiest) under the colorful strobe of spacious **Azul Madrid,** at Urbina and Clausell, less than 16km east of the center of town. (Cover 50 pesos. Open F-Sa 10pm-3am.) Enormous crowds jammed on two floors in **KY8,** at Calles 8 and 59, break a few fire codes. The first floor tries to imitate Cancún clubs, while the second features live rock bands. (Cover 40 pesos. Open F-Sa 10pm-3am.) For an older crowd of Mexican and foreign tourists, try **Captain Lafitte's,** inside Hotel del Mar at Calle 59 and the shore. (☎816 22 33. Open daily 7pm-2am.)

🚌 DAYTRIPS FROM CAMPECHE

EDZNÁ

Catch a bus in the lot across the park from the market on República. The building at the entrance is marked "SUR" (7am and every hr. starting at 10am, 16 pesos). Be sure to ask the driver when he will return. Site open daily 8am-5pm. 30 pesos; Su free.

Edzná, "House of the Itzáes," named for Edzná's ruling family during its zenith in the late Classic Period (AD 600-900), was the most important Pre-Colombian city in western Campeche. The site covers 25 sq. km and had a unique rainwater distribution system, composed of an elaborate network of 29 canals, 27 reservoirs, and more than 70 *chultunes* (man-made water cisterns). The centerpiece of the ruins is the **Edificio de Cinco Pisos** (Building of the Five Floors), which, at 31m high, towers over the surrounding valley atop the magnificent **Gran Acrópolis.** Sixty-five stairs, some adorned with hieroglyphics over 1300 years old, lead to tiers of columns, crowned by a five-room temple, which once housed a stela with an engraving of the god of corn, illuminated twice yearly by the sun to signal planting and harvesting times. Next to the Edificio is the architecturally intriguing **Templo del Norte** that was remodeled at least four times over a period of 1100 years. The alterations and superstitions of this stylistically-varied temple are believed to correspond to the political circumstances in Edzná. The east side of Gran Acropolis faces the 135m-wide stairway of **Nohoch-Ná** (Large House), which functioned as a stadium for events in the principal plaza. Be sure to see the remains of the **ballcourt,** the **Small Acropolis** (the oldest building at the site), and the **Temple of Masks,** with its three-dimensional stucco masks representing sunrise and sunset.

GRUTAS DE XTACUMBILXUNAAN

The caves lie on Mex. 261, 30km north of Hopelchen and 8km south of Bolonchen. 2nd-class buses between Campeche and Mérida drop passengers at the access road (48 pesos). Open daily 8am-4pm. 22 pesos. Tours in Spanish only.

The **Grutas de Xtacumbilxunaan** (shta-koom-bill-shu-NAN, "Caves of the Sleeping Beauty") are 27km from the Yucatán-Campeche border. A guided tour leads down a stone stairway to several deep *cenotes*, a *ceiba* staff, and unusual rock formations. Spelunkers toting their own rock climbing equipment can take a two-day journey underground with guides to visit seven connected *cenotes* 150m below ground. Bring camping gear and stay in the outdoor *palapa* for free.

RÍO BEC AND XPUJIL   ☎ 7

The dozen or so Río Bec archaeological sites strewn over a stretch of **Mex. 186**, the Escárcega-Chetumal highway, occupy a total of 50 sq. km. From AD 400-800, before the rise of Uxmal and Chichén Itzá to the north, these former Maya cities formed the heart of human civilization in the Yucatán. The sites, which contain the largest Maya structure ever built, show great promise in untangling enigmas of Mesoamerican civilization, as the cities were a crucial intersection between the Yucatán Peninsula and the rest of Mexico and Central America. Organized tours of Río Bec are arranged in Campeche or Chetumal, but peso-pinchers should use **Xpujil** (ISH-poo-heel) as a base. The village straddles Mex. 186, a few kilometers west of the Campeche-Quintana Roo border, offering easy access to the sites.

TRANSPORTATION AND PRACTICAL INFORMATION

Xpujil is organized around the junction of Mex. 186 and the road to Dzibalchen. The **ADO bus station** (☎871 60 27) is on the north side of the highway, just east of the junction. *De paso* buses go to **Chetumal** (7am, 1:45, and 4:30pm; 51 pesos) and **Escárcega** (5 per day, 61 pesos). **Taxis** at the junction go to the ruins for hefty sums. *Combi*s are based in the same area and travel to **Becán** (5 pesos) and **Chicanná** (7 pesos), but service is infrequent. Take the 6 or 10am bus to either site (4 pesos), and catch the 1 or 4pm bus back to Xpujil (4 pesos). The blue *combi* will take 8-10 people from the junction to and from **Calakmul** (550 pesos).

A **pharmacy** (which also offers **medical services**) can be found at the southeast corner of the junction. (Open M-Sa 8am-1pm and 3-8pm, Su 8am-1pm.) **Telecomm** and the **post office** are at the southwest corner of the junction. **Postal code:** 24640.

ACCOMMODATIONS

Two options exist, each with decent restaurants and plenty of ants. **Hotel Calakmul,** in the pink building 600m west of the junction, has rustic *cabañas* with fans, mosquito nets, and shared baths. (☎/fax 871 60 29. Singles and doubles 200 pesos; each additional person 100 pesos; rooms with bath 350 pesos.) Atop a small hill 400m west, **Bungalows El Mirador Maya** has nicer *cabañas* with baths. (☎871 60 05. Singles and doubles 250 pesos, with A/C 300 pesos; each additional person 50 pesos.)

THE RÍO BEC RUINS

Río Bec was settled late in the Pre-Classic period, around 300 BC. The area reached its zenith some time later, in the middle of the Classic Period. Small and virtually ignored by tourists, the ruins are significant for the "Río Bec" architectural style, a mixture of Petén from the south and Chenes from the north, resulting in distinctively rounded corners and false front stairways on flanking towers.

XPUJIL. Christened after the cattail plant that grows there, Xpujil, across the street from the Mirador Maya, is the closest of the sites. Composed of 17 building groups, Xpujil most likely reached its peak around AD 500-750. The first ruin you will see is **Structure IV.** Note the holes in the interior walls, used to support curtain rods. Continue farther to **Structure I,** the centerpiece of the site. Deviating from typical Río Bec architecture, it has three towers instead of two. Enter the passage on the southeast side of the southern tower to climb the treacherous steps for a bird's-eye view of the site. *(Open daily 8am-5pm. 27 pesos; Su free.)*

BECÁN. Five km west of town, Becán ("Trench"), named for the 16m-wide, 2½m-deep defensive moat around it, was the region's political, economic, and religious capital from AD 600-800. As you enter the site, bear right after crossing the bridge and enter the 66m passageway. You will emerge near majestic **Structure VIII,** one of the largest examples of Río Bec architecture, and **Structure IX,** an immense 32m-high pyramid that once served as the religious center of the city. Scramble around to the northern tower of Structure VIII and try to find the secret staircase (unfortunately blocked off at the top). Continue on to **Structure X,** whose upper temple has representations of the god Itzamná, and to the **ballcourt** and elaborate maze-like courtyards behind it. An incredible frieze of a king emerging from a serpent's mouth is on the south side of Structure X. Before crossing the bridge on the way out, take a detour to the right to **Structures I-IV.** Here you'll find steam baths, examples of the Río Bec checkerboard motif, and a circular altar, erected AD 1100-1200 by the infiltrating cult of Kukulcán. *(Open daily 8am-5pm. 30 pesos, Su free.)*

CHICANNÁ. Named for the striking facade of its **Structure II,** Chicanná ("House of the Serpent's mouth") was a small elite center—a rich suburb of Becán. The ruins can be found 2km farther west and have their roots in the late Classic Period (300 BC-AD 250). The first building you will stumble upon is two-story **Structure XX,** whose masks at all four corners are typical of Chenes style. After passing the decrepit **Structure XI** you will arrive in the main plaza. **Structure I** is a fantastic example of Río Bec architecture. *(Open daily 8am-5pm. 27 pesos, Su free.)*

⬛CALAKMUL. Deep within the rain forests of the Calakmul Biosphere Reserve, only 30km from the Guatemalan border, lies the enormous archaeological site of Calakmul. Covering 25 sq. km, the site is still being excavated. Even at this early point, however, Calakmul was a city of profound importance in the Maya world, most likely a regional capital with anywhere between 60,000 and 200,000 people at its peak (AD 400-800). The jungle-shrouded ruins are eerily littered with 115 stelae, guarded by a wide variety of colorful, giant web-spiders. Calakmul's greatest claim to fame is its giant pyramid, the largest Maya structure ever built, a man-made mountain of stone towering 53m above the jungle floor and covering an area of five acres. The first plaza on the path was a center for astronomical observation. Bordering it are three structures used for recording the movements of the sun, moon, and stars. A path from the northwest corner of the plaza leads to the **grand acropolis, ballcourt,** and, farther on, **wall remains.** Southeast of the giant pyramid is another one, still being extracted from the surrounding jungle. *(The road to Calakmul branches off Mex. 186, 60km west of Xpujil. From there, it's a 65km ride on a paved road through the jungle. Leave early to see wildlife. Open daily 8am-5pm. 30 pesos; Su free. Toll 60 pesos.)*

BALAMKÚ. 1km west on Mex. 186 from the road to Calakmul, and 3km north, lies the newly discovered site Balamkú that boasts a remarkably detailed **frieze,** documenting the king's cycle of birth and death. The king emerges from the mouth of a crocodile, which, in turn, comes out of an earth-monster, linking the underworld to the earth. To see the frieze, follow the arrows to **Casa de Los Mascarones** and enter through the metal structure on its left side. *(Open daily 8am-5pm. Free.)*

YUCATÁN

LA RUTA PUUC

Dozens of exciting Maya ruins, collectively known as La Ruta Puuc, traverse the Puuc Hills between Mérida and Campeche. During the Classic period these sites were home to over 25,000 people. The ruins of **Uxmal** lie 80km south of Mérida on Mex. 261, and 16km south of Muna. The sites of **Oxkintok** and **Las Grutas de Calcehtok,** not properly part of the Ruta, are 20km northwest of Muna, and the ruins of **Mayapán** are 30km northeast of Muna. The town of **Santa Elena** sits 16km east of Uxmal, 8km north of **Kabah.** The Sayil-Oxkutzcab road branches to the east 5km south of Kabahto to **Sayil, Xlapac, Labná, Hacienda Tabí, Las Grutas de Loltún,** and ends up in **Oxkutzcab,** 19km east of **Ticul.**

GETTING AROUND LA RUTA PUUC . Renting a car in Mérida provides the easiest transportation, and travel agencies in Mérida and Campeche offer organized tours—inquire at a tourist office for the latest. Public transportation is the most difficult way to see the Ruta Puuc. 2nd-class **buses** traverse Mex. 261 frequently, and will stop when requested. None travel the Sayil-Oxkutzkub road with the exception of the **Autotransportes del Sur** "Ruta Puuc" bus that leaves Mérida at 8am and visits **Kabah, Sayil, Xlapac, Labná,** and **Uxmal,** returning to Mérida at about 4pm. If you don't mind a whirlwind tour of the sites, the bus is a bargain (40 pesos; admission to sites not included). The bus spends 30min. at each site and 90min. at Uxmal. *Combis* are most abundant in the mornings, and travel frequently between **Oxkutzcab, Ticul, Santa Elena,** and **Muna.** They will make almost any trip if paid enough. It is best, though not easy, to get a *combi* to Uxmal, Kabah, and other sites from the *zócalo* in Muna. Unfortunately, with both *combis* and buses, return trips are by no means guaranteed. Travelers who make the Ruta Puuc more than a daytrip often use **Ticul,** or more convenient **Santa Elena** as a base. From either of these towns, two to three days should provide ample time for exploration.

OXKINTOK

By car, follow the signs for Oxkintok as you approach the village of Maxcanú from the east. Some parts of the road are unpaved. Open daily 9am-6pm. 27 pesos; Su free.

Oxkintok lies 42km northwest of Uxmal, on the west end of the rolling Puuc hills. The ruins date from the Classic Period (AD 300-1050). By car, Oxkintok might merit a visit, as it is a well-maintained and thoroughly excavated site. Climb atop the **Ah May Pyramid,** the tallest building at 25km, and the **Ah Canul Palace** for a good view, or explore three-storied **El Laberinto** (The Labyrinth). Ask one of the workers to take you through its narrow corridors and 16 subterranean rows.

LAS GRUTAS DE CALCEHTOK

Follow the signs marked "Grutas" as you approach Oxkintok. A solitary guide mans the entrance. Take advantage of his services.

Only 2km southwest of Oxkintok are **Las Grutas de Calcehtok.** The extremely knowledgeable guide will take you deep inside the 2km-long pitch-black caverns, his lamps illuminating thousands of stalactites, stalagmites, and comically-shaped rock formations—the head of Frankenstein, a crocodile, etc.—on the way to Maya ritual and sacrificial grounds used 2000 years ago. 150 years ago, during the Caste War, a group of 60 Maya survived for months in the permanent darkness of the *grutas* while besieged by the Spanish Army who stood guard outside the entrance.

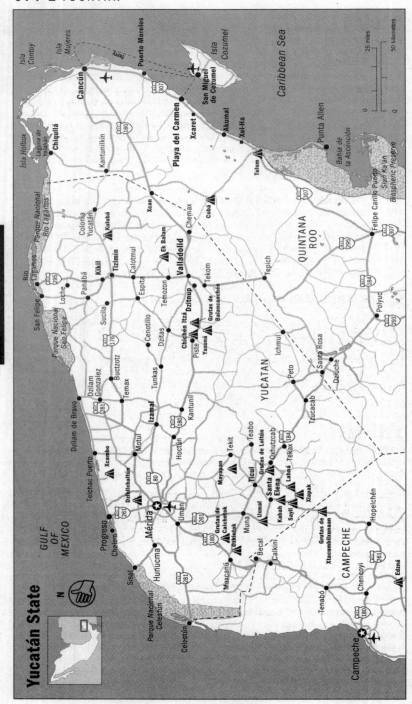

UXMAL

Uxmal will impress, if not astonish, with its enormous palaces, numerous legends, and breathtaking architecture. Despite painstaking restoration, its immense totality that once dominated the hills has yet to be fully realized, and travelers can venture into the surrounding jungle to see many as yet unexcavated structures.

TRANSPORTATION. Uxmal is 80km south of Mérida and 154km northeast of Campeche on Mex. 261. Autotransportes del Sur (ATS) goes from Mérida to Uxmal (1½hr., 6 per day, 35 pesos). The "Ruta Puuc" bus also stops here. From Campeche, take a Camioneros de Campeche bus to Mérida (3hr., 5 per day, 55 pesos). Ask the driver to stop at the access road to the ruins. To return, grab a passing bus at the crossing outside the entrance (last bus 8pm).

ACCOMMODATIONS AND FOOD. No budget accommodations are at Uxmal—only luxurious, multi-star hotels. However, 5km north of the ruins on Mex. 261 is **Rancho Uxmal,** which offers camping (20 pesos per person), pink rooms with clean bathrooms (singles 180 pesos; doubles 250 pesos), and a large *palapa*-covered restaurant/bar serving breakfast (30-50 pesos) and Yucatec favorites. (40-65 pesos. ☎ 977 62 54 or 977 56 21. Open daily 7:30am-8pm.) At the ruins, **Restaurant Yax-beh** makes sandwiches (33-43 pesos) and *comida típica* (48-60 pesos) in a colorful, air-conditioned setting. (Open daily 9am-8:30pm.) Budget accommodations and restaurants are also in nearby Santa Elena and Ticul.

THE ARCHAEOLOGICAL SITE OF UXMAL

Open daily 8am-5pm. Light and sound show 7pm in winter, 8pm in summer. 85 pesos, includes show. Show only 30 pesos. children under 13, holidays, and Su free. Parking 10 pesos. Guides about 350 pesos for 1-20 people.

Meaning "thrice built or occupied," Uxmal's tumultuous 2000-year history (800 BC-AD 1200) consisted of two major developmental periods. In the village stage, hydraulic projects, such as cisterns and mini-reservoirs, were built. These secure water sources allowed progression to the urban stage, when Uxmal became a city of 25,000 inhabitants that dominated southwestern Yucatán from AD 700-1000, and, along with Mayapán and Chichén Itzá, formed the Mayapán League. Although subordinate to the other two city-states, Uxmal was the largest of the Puuc sites and exercised control over the neighboring cities of Kabah, Sayil, and Labná. During the 10th century, neighboring Xius arrived in Uxmal, bringing the cult of Quetzcóatl, and merchants were the new city rulers. In the 12th century, Uxmal was mysteriously abandoned with many inhabitants moving to nearby Mani.

PYRAMID OF THE MAGICIAN (HOUSE OF THE SOOTHSAYER). According to legend, the 35m pyramid was built overnight by a dwarf-magician who hatched from a witch's egg and grew to maturity in a year. The legend of the dwarf-magician's birth struck terror into the heart of the governing lord, who challenged the dwarf to a contest of building skills. In reality, the pyramid was probably built over five construction stages between AD 600-1000.

QUADRANGLE OF THE BIRDS. To the immediate west of the pyramid lies the Quadrangle of the Birds, named for the bird sculptures that adorn its western side. The pyramid forms the eastern barrier of the quadrangle while the building to the north has a smooth facade, and the one to the south sports small columns.

QUADRANGLE OF THE NUNS. Continuing to the west is a large quadrangle—Uxmal's famed nunnery, constructed AD 900-1000, and misnamed by the Spanish who thought its many rooms resembled a convent. The four long buildings were built on different levels, and each has a distinctive decor. The northern building is adorned with masks of the rain god Chac; the eastern building has intricate lattice work and Venus symbols; the southern building contains a series of hut sculptures; and the western building shows kings and bound prisoners in high relief. The sizeable entryways of the southern building lead to the 34m-long **ballcourt.** Only one of the glyph-engraved stone signs remains, where well-padded players tried to knock a hardened rubber ball.

CEMETERY GROUP. Emerging from the ballcourt, head right down a narrow path to the Cemetery Group, a small, leafy plaza bounded by a pyramid to the north and a temple to the west. Stones that once formed platforms bear haunting reliefs of skulls and crossbones. To the west the pyramid looks down on the fretworks of the **Pigeon House.** Behind this lie the jungle-shrouded remains of the **Chenes Temple.**

PALACIO DEL GOBERNADOR (GOVERNOR'S PALACE). From the ballcourt, head south up the escarpment to this enormous palace. Replete with engravings and arches, it was one of the last buildings constructed, probably around AD 1000, and is considered by many to be Uxmal's finest example of architecture.

CASA DE LAS TORTUGAS (HOUSE OF THE TURTLES). The two-story house is on the northwest corner of the escarpment and is adorned along its upper frieze with a series of sculpted three-dimensional turtles, which symbolized rain.

GREAT PYRAMID. The dwarf's pyramid, comprised of nine levels and visible to the right of the Governor's Palace, easily out-classed the 30m-high Great Pyramid. On top sits the **Macaw Temple,** named for the many engravings of the bird on its facade, inside of which sits a Chac-motif throne. The spiteful ruler tried to undermine the legitimacy of the dwarf-magician's pyramid by complaining that its base was neither square nor rectangular (standard shapes) but oval with massive rounded ends, and proposed that he and the dwarf settle their quarrel by competing to see who could break a *cocoyol* (a small, hard-shelled fruit) on his head. The dwarf-magician slipped a turtle shell into his skull and easily cracked the *cocoyol,* while the unfortunate governor crushed his own unaltered skull.

CASA DE LA VIEJA (HOUSE OF THE OLD WOMAN). From the entrance, follow the trail south to five buildings surrounding a patio. Among these is the Casa de la Vieja, one of the oldest constructions in Uxmal, dating from AD 670-770. A 600m walk farther south brings you to **El Templo de los Falos** (the Temple of the Phalli). Phallic structures symbolizing fertility once adorned the top of the small structure.

SANTA ELENA
☎ 9

This tiny town of 4000 Maya residents lies 8km north of Kabah and 15km east of Uxmal. It has a park, soda shops, and an 18th-century church, which affords magnificent views from its roof. Ask the "sacristan" to show you the way up (open Su-F 3-6pm). Next to the church, a small museum showcases recently unearthed mummies that were interred under the church (open Tu-Su 10am-6pm). Santa Elena is home to the archaeological site of **Mulchic,** a small collection of platforms and substructures belonging to the late period. To reach the ruins, hike the 2km trail that branches off Mex. 261, 700m toward Mérida past the cemetery.

Buses leaving from Mérida bound for Campeche pass town on Mex. 261 (7:45, 10:30am, 1:30, and 6:30pm), as do buses bound for Mérida (6:30, 8, 8:45am, 2:45, 5:15, and 7:45pm). The "Ruta Puuc" bus stops at 9:30am and returns at 12:20pm. It proceeds to Uxmal, but doesn't return to Santa Elena. It is possible to return by hitching a ride with the workers who live in Santa Elena, or grabbing a *combi.* To reach **Grutas de Loltún** from Santa Elena, hop on the 7:30am bus bound for **Oxkutz- cab,** and then take a *colectivo.* The **police,** (☎992 10 15), are available at the north end of the *zócalo.* English spoken. **Farmacia Mirna,** one block west of the *zócalo* on Calle 20. (☎991 79 20. Open daily 8am-10pm.) Find Dr. Luis Sansores Mian next door to the pharmacy at **Consultario Medico** (☎991 79 20). Two fine budget **accom-**

modations lie along Mex. 261. **Sacbé Camping-Bungalows**, km 127, offers weary travelers pristine campgrounds with new solar showers and toilet facilities, outdoor grills, and a mosquito-netted thatched hut where the owners serve good meals. (sacbebungalow@hotmail.com. Breakfast 24 pesos, dinner 28-37 pesos. Campsites and hammock space 25 pesos per person; bunk bed in dormitory 50 pesos; small furnished bungalows with hot water, fans, and clean baths 120-140 pesos.) Only 150m north toward Uxmal, on the opposite side of the road, lies **Hotel/Restaurant El Chac-Mool**, with available hammock space (30 pesos) and four single rooms with clean, private baths and fans. (Rooms 160 pesos.) The adjacent restaurant is the best, and one of the only in town. (☎996 20 25. Large helpings of eggs, tacos, and sandwiches 30-40 pesos. Restaurant open daily 10am-8pm.)

KABAH

23km southeast of Uxmal, Kabah is bisected by Mex. 261, and can easily be reached by any 2nd-class bus running between Mérida and Campeche. Buses will stop here only if the driver is asked beforehand or if he sees a person wildly gesticulating on the shoulder of the highway. Traveling's easier with the "Ruta Puuc" bus. Open daily 8am-5pm. 27 pesos; Su free.

Once the second-largest city in the northern Yucatán, **Kabah** ("Sir of the Strong Hand and Powerful") was built with the blood and sweat of many slaves. The site's highlight is the incredible visual feast of the ◙**Codz Poop Temple** (or the Palace of the Masks), the single-most psychedelic piece of architecture on the Yucatán Peninsula. Close to 300 three-eyed faces of the rain god, Chac, protrude from the facade of the temple, staring, laughing, screaming, or grinning, depending on your state of mind. Unlike structures of pure Puuc style, characterized by plain columns and a superior decorative frieze, Codz Poop is covered with ornamental stone carvings of Chac from top to bottom, resembling more the Chenes style. Rain was extremely important for the inhabitants of Kabah, where none fell for half the year. Continue east and you will come across **El Palacio,** a two-story structure containing 30 rooms. Follow a path from the left side of the Palacio for 200m to **Las Columnas.** The site is thought to have served as a court where justices settled disputes, and gods comprised the jury. Across the street by the parking lot, a short dirt road leads to rubble (right), more rubble (left), and the famous **Kabah Arch** (straight). The arch marks the beginning of the ancient *sacbé* that ended with a twin arch in Uxmal. The perfect alignment of the archway with the north-south line testifies to Maya astronomical wisdom.

SAYIL

Sayil lies 5km off Mex. 261 on the Sayil-Oxkutzcab road, a stop on the "Ruta Puuc" bus. Buses between Mérida and Campeche stop here irregularly. Ask to be let off at the military checkpoint, then trek 5km to the site. Buses returning to Mérida come by about 3 times daily. Site open daily 8am-5pm. 27 pesos; Su free.

The **Palace of Sayil** stands out architectural among the region's ruins. The unique, three-story structure was constructed from AD 800-1000. It harbors 90 rooms, which served as storage, administrative space, and housing for 350 people. The foundation houses eight underground cisterns. The *sacbé* across from the Palace leads to **El Mirador,** a lofty pyramid-temple topped by a peculiar roof-comb. Left of El Mirador, a 100km path leads through the jungle to **Estela del Falo** (Stela of the Phallus), which was a tribute to Yum Keep, a Maya god of fertility. A few temples are visible through the undergrowth. Across the street up a dirt path is **El Templo de las Cabezas** (The Temple of Heads/Masks). The masks may be scarce, and the hike them steep and difficult, but the view of Sayil's palace is splendid.

XLAPAC

The "Ruta Puuc" bus stops here for 20min. To stay longer, hire a combi in nearby Oxkutzcab. Site open daily 8am-5pm. 22 pesos; Su free.

Xlapac ("Old Wall") lies between Labná and Sayil. The classic Puuc **El Palacio** pays homage to Chac with its impressive triple-decker masks of the rain god. 300m south of the palace is a partially-excavated stone structure, with the remains of fallen columns and carved stones lying along its perimeter.

LABNÁ

Labná lies 14km east of Mex. 261. No buses make the trip past Labná. Few combis come here, and hitching is reportedly tough. Try the "Ruta Puuc" bus or a private car. Open daily 8am-5pm. 27 pesos; Su free.

Labná was constructed toward the end of the Late Classic period (AD 700-1000), when the Puuc cities were connected by *sacbé* (paved, elevated roads). A short, reconstructed section of the *sacbé* runs between Labná's two most impressive sights: the palace and the stone arch. On the northern side to the left as you enter the site stretches the still-uncompleted **palace,** built over seven patios and two levels. Labná is famed for its picturesque **Arch of Labná,** 3m wide and 5m high. Archaeologists believe that the arch served as a ceremonial entry point for victorious returning warriors. Beyond the arch atop a rocky pyramid stands the observatory, **El Mirador.** The roof-comb of El Mirador was once magnificently decorated with stucco-modeled figurines. Back toward the palace, **El Templo de las Columnas,** one of the best examples of the Puuc style, is off the *sacbé* to the right.

HACIENDA TABI

The Hacienda is accessible only with a reliable car. On the Sayil-Oxkutzcab road, take the road that branches off at the Grutas de Loltún. The dirt access road to the Hacienda, goes straight (2km to the site) when the main road veers right. Open daily 8am-5pm. 22 pesos.

This *hacienda* was constructed as a sugar-producing facility in 1896, but the site was abandoned after a fire destroyed its machinery and church. The most impressive sights are the **Palacio,** which greets you while passing the gates, the gutted remnants of the church, and the two giant chimneys, used for burning sugar.

GRUTAS DE LOLTÚN

Snag a combi to Oxkutzcab from Calle 25A between Calles 24 and 26 (every 10min., 7 pesos); you'll be let off at the intersection of Calles 23 and 26. Combis and colectivos leave for Loltún from the lot across from Oxkutzcab's market, 20 de Noviembre. Ask to be dropped at the caves (10min., 3 pesos). Entrance with tours only. Tours daily 9:30, 11am, 12:30, 2, 3, and 4pm; available in both Spanish and poor English. 47 pesos; Su 20 pesos; guides ask for tips. Parking 10 pesos. Restaurant open daily 10am-6pm.

Winding through the rock for over 4km, the Grutas de Loltún comprise the largest cave system in Yucatán state. The word *loltún* means "stone flower" in Maya, and the fascinating, natural formations in the caves warrant the name. The enormous caverns hold the earliest evidence of humans in the entire Yucatán, as well as fossils of extinct mastodons and saber-toothed tigers from the Ice Ages. Around 2000 BC, the ancient Maya settled here to take advantage of the caves' water and clay. Thousands of years later, Maya *campesinos* returned seeking refuge from the Caste War (1847-48). Important caverns include the **Room of Inscriptions,** full of handprints, the **Na Cab** (House of the Bees), where you can see the forgotten grindstones, the **Gallery of Fallen Rocks,** and the Maya Gallery with Olmec-style sculpture known as "La Cabeza de Loltún." Several caves contain hollow stalactites and columns—strike each one with the heel of your hand and listen as a soft booming sound *("loltún...loltún...")* reverberates throughout the caves. Archaeologists speculate that the Maya used these formations as a means of underground communication—or perhaps as the first primitive discoteca.

TICUL ☎9

Ticul (pop. 35,000) is a convenient and inexpensive base for exploring the Puuc sites of Uxmal, Kabah, Sayil, Xlapak, and Labná, as well as the Grutas de Loltún and the ruins of Mayapán. For those with wheels, a number of *cenotes* and colonial buildings await exploration in the nearby towns of **Teabo**, 30km southeast, and **Holcá**, 105km to the northeast. **Maní**, 15km east of Ticul, features a colonial monastery; **Tekax**, 35km to the southeast, a hermitage; and **Tipikal**, an impressive colonial church. Ticul is home to the 17th-century **Templo de San Antonio** (open 8am-6pm), and hosts a **Tobacco Fair** starting in early April.

TRANSPORTATION. Ticul's **bus station** (☎972 01 62) is on Calle 24, behind the church. Trips are made to **Mérida** (every hr., 29 pesos). *Combis* leave from across Hotel San Miguel for **Muna** (7 pesos); for **Santa Elena, Uxmal,** and **Kabah** (10 pesos) from Calle 30, between Calles 25 and 25A; and for **Oxkutzcab** from Calle 25A, between Calles 24 and 26 (every 15min., 7 pesos).

ORIENTATION AND PRACTICAL INFORMATION. The main road, **Calle 23,** runs east-west, as do odd-numbered streets, increasing to the south. Even-numbered streets run north-south, increasing west. The *zócalo* is east of Calle 26, with most activity between the *zócalo* and Calle 30, three blocks west. Near the *zócalo*, on **Calle 25,** a strip of Maya statuettes pay tribute to ancient gods. **Currency Exchange: Bital,** Calle 23 #195, on the northeast corner of the *zócalo*, has a 24hr. ATM. (☎972 00 06. Open M-Sa 8am-7pm.) **Police:** (☎972 02 10) on Calle 23, at the northeast corner of the *zócalo*. No English spoken. **Farmacia Canto,** #202 Calle 23, at Calle 26. (☎972 05 81. Open M-Sa 8am-10pm, Su 8am-1pm and 5-9pm.) **Centro de Salud,** Calle 27 #226 (☎972 00 86), between Calles 30 and 32. No English spoken. **Fax: Telecomm,** Calle 24A between Calles 21 and 23, northeast of the *zócalo*. (☎972 01 46. Open M-F 9am-3pm, Sa 9am-1pm.) **Post office:** in Palacio Municipal, on the northeast side of the *zócalo*. (☎972 00 40. Open M-F 8am-2pm.) **Postal code:** 97860.

ACCOMMODATIONS AND FOOD. Hotel San Miguel, on Calle 28 half a block north of Calle 23, is inexpensive, and it shows. The rooms are not dirty, just old and worn. (☎972 03 82. Singles 59 pesos; doubles 76 pesos; triples 123 pesos.) **Hotel Sierra Sosa,** on Calle 26, near the northwest corner of the *zócalo*, has firm beds, clean baths, strong fans, and TV. (☎972 00 08. Singles 95 pesos, with A/C 140 pesos; doubles 125-135 pesos, with A/C 170-180 pesos; each additional person 20 pesos.) **Hotel Plaza,** Calle 23 #202, near the corner of Calles 23 and 26, has clean, luxurious rooms. (☎972 04 84. Singles and doubles 260 pesos, with A/C 300 pesos; each additional person 40 pesos.) After a hot day on the Ruta Puuc, Ticul is the place to refuel and rehydrate. Loncherías, along Calles 23 between Calles 26 and 30, serves the town's cheapest food. **Los Almendros,** Calle 23 #207, between Calles 26A and 28, is known for its *poc-chuc* (pork cooked with onions, beans, tomatoes, and dangerous Habañero peppers. ☎972 00 21. *Pollo pibil* 40 pesos. Open daily 9am-9pm.) **Restaurant Los Delfines,** Calle 27, between Calles 28 and 30, serves shrimp dishes, *chiles rellenos* (45 pesos), and jars of lemonade. (☎972 04 01. Open daily 11am-7pm.) **Pizzeria la Gondola** is a taste of Italy in the heart of the Yucatán. (☎972 01 12. Spaghetti 20 pesos, pizza 45 pesos. Free delivery. Open daily 8am-1pm and 5:30pm-midnight). Ticul's **market** is off Calle 23 between Calles 28 and 30. (Open daily 6am-2pm.)

MAYAPÁN

Mayapán is 50km southeast of Mérida on Mex. 18, and 26km northwest of Tekit on the same road. While not officially part of the Ruta Puuc, Mayapán is a 1hr. drive from Ticul. Combis make the trip between Mérida and Tekit. Open daily 8am-5pm. 22 pesos; Su free.

The ruins of Mayapán are not nearly as impressive as its history. From AD 1000-1200, the city was dominated by Chichén Itzá, which controlled the Mayapán League. After 1200, Mayapán overthrew Chichén Itzá and controlled the league until the arrival of the Spanish. The demise of Mayapán came in 1441, when Ah Xupan of Uxmal overthrew the Cocan dynasty. All that remains of the once-powerful city are the rubble of the main temple and the Caracol.

MÉRIDA

☎9

Hub of the Yucatán Peninsula, Mérida (pop. 725,000) is a rich blend of proud indigenous history, powerful colonial presence, and modern international flavor. The city was founded in 1542 by Francisco de Montejo atop what was once the Maya metropolis of T'ho. The Maya called the city "Place of the Fifth Point," to indicate that it was the center of the universe, the spot between the four points of north, south, east, and west. Modern Mérida continues to serve as a fifth point in the new Mexican cosmology of capitalism. The city's commercial centers burst with *jipis* (Panama hats) shipped from Campeche, hammocks from Tixcocób, and *henequén* (hemp) from all over the Yucatán Peninsula. The city attracts people as well, drawing visitors and immigrants from all over the world, but not yet succumbing to big-city indifference. While street cleaners struggle to maintain its reputation as "The White City," intimate conservations swirl about the ever-crowded *zócalo* and numerous city parks, the government sponsors nightly cultural performances, and every Sunday families come out to enjoy Mérida at its best.

▐ TRANSPORTATION

GETTING AROUND

Mérida's **municipal buses** run daily (6am-midnight, 3 pesos), and a bus headed in the right direction will usually drop you within a few blocks of your destination. **Taxis** do not roam the streets soliciting riders; call **Radio Taxi** (☎923 40 46) for a ride, or go to one of the stands along Paseo de Montejo, at the airport, or in the *zócalo*. Expect to pay at least 20-25 pesos for a trip within the *centro*. **Taxi-colectivos** (more commonly known as *combis*), charge 3 pesos for any destination in the city; drop-offs are on a first-come, first-serve basis.

GETTING AWAY

Airport: 7km southwest on Mex. 180. Taxis to the *centro* cost 85-135 pesos depending on the number of people and luggage. **Aerocaribe,** Paseo Montejo 500B x 45 y 47 (☎928 67 90). **Aeroméxico,** Paseo Montejo 460 x 35 y 37 (☎920 12 93). **Aviateca,** Paseo de Montejo 475 x 37 y 39 (☎925 80 59). **Mexicana,** Paseo de Montejo 493 x 43 y 45 (☎924 66 33). **Continental,** (☎926 31 00).

Buses: Mérida's 2 main terminals are southwest of the *centro*. To reach the *zócalo* from either, walk north to Calle 63 3 blocks away, turn right and walk another 3 or 4 blocks.

First-class terminal, Calle 70 #555 x 71 (☎924 83 91). **Campeche** (every 15min., 78 pesos); **Ticul** (7:30am, 36 pesos); **Cancún** (20 per day, 150 pesos); **Chetumal** (4 per day, 167 pesos); **Chichén Itzá** (4 per day, 56 pesos); **México City** (12:05 and 2:45pm, 689 pesos); **Palenque** (9:30pm, 257 pesos); **Playa del Carmen** (12 per day, 173 pesos); **San Cristóbal de las Casas** (9:30pm, 357 pesos); **Tulum** (3 per day, 114 pesos); **Valladolid** (14 per day, 75 pesos); **Veracruz** (10:30am and 9pm, 470 pesos); **Villahermosa** (10 per day, 265 pesos).

Second-class terminal, Calle 69 #544 x 68 y 70 (☎923 33 87), goes to most of the same places for less: **Campeche** (5 per day, 69 pesos); **Cancún** (15 per day, 109 pesos); **Chichén Itzá** (18 per day, 416 pesos); **Playa del Carmen** (6, 11am and 11pm, 101 pesos); **Tulum** (5 per day, 136 pesos); **Valladolid** (5 per day, 55 pesos).

To go to Progreso, head to the Autoprogreso station at Calle 62 x 65 y 67 (every 12min., 11 pesos). Buses to **Tizimín, Izamal,** and **Celestún** can be found at the Oriente station (Calle 50 x 65 y 67).

▐ ORIENTATION AND PRACTICAL INFORMATION

Mérida sits on the west side of Yucatán state, 30km south of the Gulf Coast. Even-numbered streets run north-south, with numbers increasing to the west; odd-numbered streets run east-west, increasing to the south. Addresses in Mérida are given using an "x" to separate the main street from the cross streets and "y" ("and" in Spanish) to separate the two cross streets if the address falls in the middle of the block. Thus "54 #509 x 61 y 63" reads "Calle 54 #509, between Calles 61 and 63."

TOURIST, FINANCIAL, AND LOCAL SERVICES

Tourist Information: Central Office (☎924 92 90), Calle 57A x 58 y 60, in Teatro Peón Contreras. Distributes *Yucatán Today*. Open daily 8am-9pm. Also at the **Palacio del Gobierno** (☎928 22 58. Open 8am-10pm) and in the **airport** (☎946 12 00).

Travel Agencies: Yucatán Trails, Calle 62 #482 x 57 y 59 (☎928 25 82 or 928 59 13; fax 924 19 28). Canadian owner Denis Lafoy is a good source of information and hosts a party for travelers at Restaurant Tango Gaucho, Calle 16 #114 at Calle 29, the first F of every month. Open M-F 8am-7pm, Sa 8am-1pm.

Consulates: UK, Calle 53 #498 x 58 y 56 (☎928 61 52; fax 928 39 62). Open M-F 9am-1pm. **US,** Paseo de Montejo 453 (☎925 50 11), at Colón. Open M-F 8am-1pm.

Currency Exchange: Banamex (☎924 10 11), in Casa de Montejo on the *zócalo*, has a 24hr. **ATM.** Walk through the courtyard. Open M-F 9am-5pm, Sa 9am-2pm.

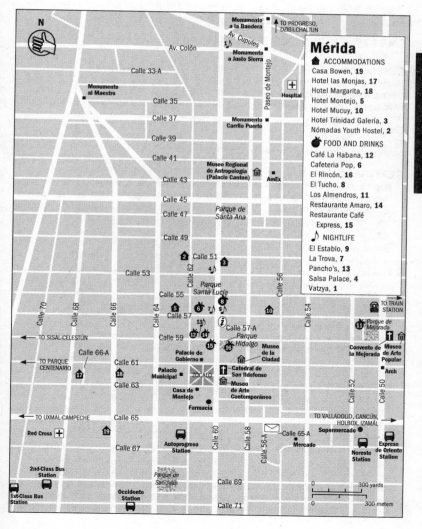

Mérida

🏠 ACCOMMODATIONS
Casa Bowen, **19**
Hotel las Monjas, **17**
Hotel Margarita, **18**
Hotel Montejo, **5**
Hotel Mucuy, **10**
Hotel Trinidad Galería, **3**
Nómadas Youth Hostel, **2**

🍎 FOOD AND DRINKS
Café La Habana, **12**
Cafetería Pop, **6**
El Rincón, **16**
El Tucho, **8**
Los Almendros, **11**
Restaurante Amaro, **14**
Restaurante Café
  Express, **15**

♪ NIGHTLIFE
El Establo, **9**
La Trova, **7**
Pancho's, **13**
Salsa Palace, **4**
Vatzya, **1**

YUCATÁN

American Express: Paseo de Montejo 492 x 41 y 43 (☎942 82 00 or 942 82 10). Open M-F 9am-2pm and 4-6pm, Sa 9am-1pm. Money exchange closes 1hr. earlier.

Car Rental: Mexico Rent-a-Car, Calle 57A #491 (El Callejón del Congreso) Dept. 12 x 58 y 60 or Calle 62 #483A x 57 y 59 (☎927 49 16 or 923 36 37). English spoken. VW Beetles, with unlimited kilometers, 250 pesos per day if paid with cash, 280 pesos per day if paid with credit card (subject to increase during high season). Open M-Sa 8am-12:30pm and 6-8pm, Su 8am-10am. **World Rent-a-Car,** Calle 60 #486A x 55 y 57 (☎924 05 87). English-speaking Mr. Mohan offers attractive rates on cars with automatic transmission and A/C.

English-Language Bookstore: (☎923 33 19), Calle 53 #524 x 66 y 68.

Laundry: La Fe, Calle 61 #518 x 62 y 64 (☎924 45 31), 1 block west of the *zócalo*. 40 pesos per 3kg. Open M-F 8am-7pm, Sa 8am-4pm.

Market: 4 square blocks south of Calle 65 and east of Calle 58. Open dawn to dusk.

Supermarket: San Francisco de Asís, (☎924 30 11), Calles 65 x 50 y 52, across from the market in a huge grey building. Open M-Sa 7am-9pm, Su 7am-3pm.

EMERGENCY AND COMMUNICATIONS

Emergency: ☎060

Police: (☎925 25 55), on Reforma (Calle 72) x 39 y 41, accessible by the "Reforma" bus. Some English spoken.

Red Cross: Calle 68 #533 x 65 y 67 (☎924 98 13). Some English spoken.

Pharmacy: Farmacia Canto, Calle 60 #513 x 63 y 65 (☎924 14 90). Open 24hr.

Hospital: Centro Médico de las Américas, Calle 54 #365 (☎926 21 11), at Calle 33A. **Clínica de Mérida,** Calle 32 #242 x 27 y 25 (☎920 04 11). English spoken at both.

Internet Access: Cybernet, Calle 57-A #491 (El Callejon de Congreso). 10 terminals. 20 pesos per hr. Open M-Sa 9am-9pm. **Cibercafe Sta. Luci@** (☎924 89 47), on the northwest corner of Calles 62 and 55. 20 pesos per hr. Open daily 8am-11pm.

Fax: (☎928 59 97), in the same building as the post office. Enter on Calle 56. Telegrams and internet access as well. Open M-F 8am-7pm, Sa 9am-4pm, Su 9am-noon.

Post Office: (☎928 54 04) on Calles 65 x 56 y 56A, in the Palacio Federal. Open M-F 8am-3pm. **Mexpost** next door. Open M-F 9am-5pm, Sa 9am-1pm.

Postal Code: 97000.

◪ ACCOMMODATIONS

Choosing budget accommodations in Mérida is like deciding in which bygone era to stay. Many once elaborate, private turn of the century mansions are now affordable hotels, clustering near the main bus station and the *zócalo*.

Nómadas Youth Hostel, Calle 62 #433 x 51 (☎924 52 23; nomadas1@prodigy.net.mx). A haven for backpackers, with clean facilities including full kitchen, Internet access (14 pesos per hr.), outdoor patio, travel agency, bike rentals, and Direct TV. However, mosquitoes abound and the men's dormitory has little protection from street noise. Bunks 65 pesos; doubles with private baths 195 pesos. Camping available.

Casa Bowen, Calle 66 #521B x 65 y 67 (☎928 61 09), between the main bus station and the *zócalo*. Large well-kept rooms in this beautiful colonial mansion have fans, firm beds, and clean bathrooms. Reservations recommended in Aug. and Dec. Singles 160 pesos; doubles 180 pesos, with A/C 230 pesos; each additional person 50 pesos.

Hotel Montejo, Calle 57 #507 x 62 y 64 (☎928 03 90), 2 blocks north of the *zócalo*. Large wooden doors face maroon arches and a lush garden. Fairly clean rooms have wooden ceiling beams, window porticos, and baths. Singles 190 pesos; doubles 250 pesos; each additional person 45 pesos. 10% discount with *Let's Go* in low season.

Hotel Trinidad Galería, Calle 60 #456 x 51 (☎923 24 63). Artists and eccentrics will feel at home in this quirky colonial mansion whose halls are crammed with artwork. Features an art gallery, fountain, and pool. The old rooms are fairly clean and, of course, decorated with plenty of art. Singles 250 pesos; doubles 320 pesos; triples 350 pesos. Rooms with A/C 400-450 pesos. Rooms with shared baths 150 pesos.

Hotel Mucuy, Calle 57 #481 x 56 y 58 (☎928 51 93), 2 blocks north and 2 blocks east of the *zócalo*. Comfy rooms with fans, spotless walls, and clean baths line a sunny courtyard that masks the hotel's central location. Glass doors enclose a reading room and piano in the lobby. Singles 180 pesos; doubles 220 pesos; triples 260 pesos.

Hotel Margarita, Calle 66 #506 x 61 y 63 (☎923 72 36). Small characterless rooms with slightly soiled walls, ultra-soft beds, and clean baths. Singles 90 pesos; doubles 100 pesos; triples 140 pesos.

Hotel Las Monjas, Calle 66A #509 x 63 y 61 (☎928 66 32). Plain blue rooms have fans and clean bathrooms. Singles 100 pesos; doubles 120 pesos; quads 145 pesos.

🍴 FOOD

Mérida's specialties make use of the fruits and grains that flourish in the Yucatán's hot, humid climate. Try *sopa de lima* (freshly squeezed lime soup with chicken and tortilla bits), *pollo pibil* (chicken with herbs baked in banana leaves), *poc-chuc* (pork steak with onions doused in sour orange juice), *papadzules* (chopped hard-boiled eggs wrapped in corn tortillas served with pumpkin sauce), *huevos motuleños* (refried beans, fried egg, chopped ham, and cheese on a crispy tortilla, garnished with tomato sauce, peas, and fried banana), and always satisfying *horchata* (rice and almond milk). Great meals can be found in the casual joints along the *zócalo*. The cheapest food in town is sold at the **market**, particularly on the second floor of the restaurant complex on Calle 56 at Calle 67 (Yucatec dishes 10-15 pesos; most stalls open M-Sa 8am-8pm, Su 8am-5pm).

▨ Restaurante Amaro, Calle 59 #507 x 60 y 62 (☎928 24 51). Exquisitely prepared dishes including delicious vegetarian options such as eggplant curry (42 pesos), *chaya* crepes (42 pesos), and fruit salads (38 pesos). Attentive service, and incredibly intimate candle-lit tables set in a quiet courtyard make for some of the finest dining on the Yucatán Peninsula. Open daily noon-midnight.

Restaurante "Cafe" Express (☎928 16 91), Calle 60 x 59 y 61, across from Parque Hidalgo. One of the oldest places in town, the service lives up to the name. Colorful paintings of Old Mérida decorating the walls and the view of Parque Hidalgo make for a visually stimulating dining experience. Breakfast and sandwiches 20 pesos, entrees 40-60 pesos. Open daily 7am-11pm.

Cafeteria Pop, Calle 57 #501 x 60 y 62 (☎928 61 63). This clean, air-conditioned cafeteria serves up cheap, simple food. Breakfast specials (20-35 pesos) served 7am-noon; other entrees (30-50 pesos) served noon-11pm. Open daily 7am-11pm.

El Rincón (☎924 90 22), Calle 60 x 59 y 61, on the east side of Parque Hidalgo. Set in a serene and pleasant outdoor courtyard. If in high spirits, the staff will sing and play the guitar. *Sopa de lima* 22 pesos, *arroz con plátanos* 20 pesos, fruit salads 28 pesos, *pollo pibil* 55 pesos. Open daily 7am-10:30pm.

Los Almendros and **Los Gran Almendros,** Calle 50 #493 x 57 y 59 (☎928 54 59) on Parque Mejorada, and at Calle 57 #468 x 50 y 52 (☎929 81 35), respectively. Upscale, but still affordable, the Yucatec food prepared here is world-famous, drawing both tourists and locals. Small portions allow you to enjoy several different dishes at a hefty price. *Poc-chuc* 62 pesos, *pavo* prepared in various ways 62 pesos. Los Almendros open daily 9am-11pm. Less touristy Gran Almendros open daily 1-5pm.

El Tucho, Calle 60 #482 x 55 y 57 (☎924 23 23). Wildly entertains customers with comedy troupes and musicians who perform while waiters ferry trays of free hors d'œuvres. Live music 2-4pm and 8pm. Meals 55 pesos. Open daily 11:30am-9:30pm.

Cafe la Habana, Calle 59 #511 x 62 (☎928 65 02). This air-conditioned cafe looks upscale and is one of the most popular places in town. A great place for great coffee. Breakfast specials 35 pesos. Open 24hr.

👁 SIGHTS

Mérida stands alone as a testament to the fascinating history of the Yucatán. Surrounded by historic palaces and a towering cathedral, the busy *zócalo* is renowned as the capital's social center. On Sundays, the streets are closed to traffic and vendors cram in dozens of stalls. Yucatec folk dancers perform in front of Palacio Municipal as crowds of people from all over enjoy *Mérida en Domingo*.

CATEDRAL DE SAN ILDELFONSO. Begun in 1563 and finished in 1598, the immense cathedral is the oldest on the American continent. The stone blocks of the cathedral were stolen from the Maya temples of T'hó, and the unusually barren interior was looted during the Mexican Revolution in 1915. Features an immense 20m wooden crucified Christ, the largest indoor crucifix in the world. *(On the east side of the zócalo. Open daily 6am-7pm.)*

■ **PALACIO DE GOBIERNO.** Built from 1883 to 1892, the *palacio* fuses two architectural styles—Tuscan (main floor) and Dorian (upper floor). A jail until the 1700s, the structure was rebuilt in 1735 with two stories of arches. It was here that Yucatecos declared their independence from Spain. Inside, giant murals painted by Mérida native Fernando Castro Pacheco in the 1970s dramatically chronicle the tumultuous history of the peninsula in several dimensions. Together with the eerily poetic paintings inside the Versailles-like *salon de historia*, the palacio offers one of the finest and most inspiring aesthetic experiences in the Yucatán. *(On the north side of the zócalo. Open daily 8am-10pm.)*

CASA DE MONTEJO. Probably begun by Francisco de Montejo, governor of Yucatán in 1549, this house was occupied by his direct descendents until 1980, whereupon it was sold to Banamex. Built with stones from the Maya temple T'hó, the carved facade follows the Toltec tradition of representing warriors standing on their conquerors' heads. *(On the south side of the zócalo. Open M-F 9am-5pm.)*

MUSEO DE ARTE CONTEMPORÁNEO (MACAY). The collection of modern Yucatec art is displayed around a central courtyard. *(On the east side of the zócalo, just south of the church. Open W-M 10am-5pm. 20 pesos; Su free.)*

EL MUSEO DE LA CIUDAD. This small museum provides a concise historical background of the White City and its colonial structures. It houses visual layouts and models of Mérida's most famous sights and also includes a bit of Pre-Hispanic history. *(Calle 58 x 61. Open Tu-F 10am-2pm and 4-8pm, Sa-Su 10am-2pm. Free.)*

■ **MUSEO REGIONAL DE ANTROPOLOGÍA E HISTORIA.** Mérida's most impressive museum is housed in a magnificent Italian Renaissance-style building, the **Palacio Cantón,** on the corner of Paseo Montejo and Calle 43. The collection includes Maya head-flattening devices, jade tooth inserts, sacrificial offerings recovered from the *cenote sagrado* of Chichén Itzá, and a Chichén Itzá *chac-mool*, in addition to highly intriguing exhibits on the Maya calendar, writing and numeric system, language, and distinctive notions of beauty. The museum shop sells small English-language guidebooks (6 pesos). Most exhibits are only in Spanish. *(☎923 05 57. Open Tu-Sa 8am-8pm, Su 8am-2pm. 20 pesos; Su free.)*

MUSEO DE ARTE POPULAR. The small museum has exhibits on modern-day Maya customs and handicrafts. Shares the building with a school of design and a relaxing student lounge. *(6 blocks east of the zócalo on Calle 59 x 48 y 50, behind Convento de la Mejorada. Open Tu-Sa 8am-6pm, Su 9am-2pm. 10 pesos; Su free.)*

CENTENARY PARK AND ZOO. The zoo is home to lions, tigers, jaguars, and other animals. A miniature train makes circuits of the park, but don't expect a quiet ride or a glimpse of many of the dozing creatures. *(On the corner of Calle 61 and Calle 86, Itzáces. Snag a bus at Calle 65 x 56 and ask to be let off at "El Centenario." 3 pesos. Park open Tu-Su 9am-6pm; zoo open Tu-Su 9am-5pm. Both free.)*

MUSEO DE HISTORIA NATURAL. Lodged within a 19th-century *hacienda*, this small but ambitious collection chronicles the history of life from the origin of the universe through the emergence of species. *(Main entrance on Calle 61 x 84, 1 block east of Itzáes. Back entrance accessible from the park. Open Tu-Su 9am-4pm. 15 pesos; Su free.)*

TEATRO PEÓN CONTRERAS. Named for the Mérida poet, José Peón Contreras, the beautiful building was built around the turn of the century and is notable for its marble Rococo interior. Frequent concerts and shows visit *el teatro;* stop by the box office for more information. *(On the corner of Calles 60 and 57. ☎923 73 54.)*

UNIVERSIDAD AUTÓNOMA DE YUCATÁN. The headquarters of the state's national university is housed in a Hispano-Moorish complex built in 1938. The ground floor has a gallery exhibiting works by local artists and a screening room for a variety of films. *(On Calle 57 x 60. Galería open M-F 9am-1pm and 5-9pm, Sa 10am-1pm, Su 10am-2pm. Movies Su 10:30am, F 5pm. Free.)*

PASEO DE MONTEJO. Aging French-style mansions and boutiques line the Paseo's brick sidewalks, culminating in the **Monumento a la Patria.** In faux-Maya style, the stone monument, built from 1945 to 1956, depicts major figures of Mexican history holding rifles and constitutions. On the other side of the monument, the *ceiba* (the Maya tree of life) stretches above a pool of water, enclosed by states' coats of arms. For an interesting detour from the Paseo, veer left (southwest) onto **Colón,** a street flanked by historic mansions in varying stages of decay.

OTHER SIGHTS. The many churches, statues, and parks scattered throughout Mérida's *centro* invite exploration. The old **Arco,** Calle 50 x 61, is one of the three remaining arches in Mérida, built at the end of the 17th century to mark the extent of the *centro.* **Iglesia Santiago,** on Calles 59 x 72, one of the oldest churches in Mexico, is worth a visit, as is **Iglesia de San Juan de Dios,** on Calle 64 x 67 y 71, and the Franciscan **Convento de la Mejorada,** at Calle 59 x 48 y 50.

🎵🎭 ENTERTAINMENT AND NIGHTLIFE

BARS AND CLUBS

For a less culture-filled evening, try one of Mérida's many excellent local beers, such as distinctive **Montejo León** and the darker **Negra León,** both tough to find in other parts of the country. Local establishments give free snacks after the purchase of a few beers. Live music and dance abound at **Pancho's,** Calle 59 #509 x 60 y 62, where sombrero-wearing hosts serve you free popcorn. (☎923 09 42. Happy Hour 6-8pm. Live music from 9pm. Open M-Sa 6pm-3am.) Three entertainment establishments are located next to each other on Calle 60 between Calles 55 and 57. Disco at **Ay Caray!** (cover 50 pesos); *salsa* at the **Azul Picante Salsa Bar** or **El Establo,** Calle 60 # 482A x 55 y 57, where young *merideños* and tourists shoot pool, play table hockey, and dance under sombrero lamp shades. (☎924 22 89. Cover men 40 pesos, women 30 pesos. Live music from 10:30pm.) A new place, **Salsa Palace,** Calle 60 #467 at Calle 53, boasts loud Cuban *salsa.* (Cover 40 pesos. Live music W-Sa 10pm-2am.) For more traditional music, head to dark and intimate **La Trova,** on the corner of Calles 57 and 60. (☎924 94 42. Live music M-Sa 9:30pm-1:15am.) Another option is the *salsa* bar of **Tulipanes,** Calle 42 #462A x 45 y 47. Multi-colored discos with A/C are far from the center; taxis run 50 pesos. **Vatzya** in Hotel Fiesta Americana, Colón x Calle 60, is where the young and trendy dance. (Cover 40-50 pesos. Open W-Sa 10pm-2am.)

FESTIVALS

When in Mérida, do as *merideños* do—keep your eyes peeled for announcements of upcoming events posted around the *zócalo* and in local magazine *Yucatán Today,* available free in the tourist office. Mérida's municipal government provides a repeating series of music and dance events organized by day:

Monday: Outdoor concerts with *yucateco* dancing in the Palacio Municipal (9pm).

Tuesday: 1940s big-band concerts in Santiago Park, Calles 59 x 72 (9pm).

Wednesday: Musical performances in the Maya House of Culture, on Calle 63 between Calles 64 and 66. Regional plays are also presented in the Jardín de los Compositores near the Palacio Municipal (9pm).

Thursday: The Serenade, the most historical event in Mérida, with music, poetry, and folklore, in Santa Lucia Park, Calles 60 x 55 (9pm).

Friday: University Serenade, in the main university building, Calles 60 x 57 (9pm).

Saturday: *Noche Mexicana*, a night of national dance performances and arts and crafts, on Calle 56A between Calles 47 and 49 (7pm).

⚑ Sunday: *Mérida en Domingo*, when the *zócalo* and surrounding streets are crowded with vendors, strollers, food stalls, and live music (9am-9pm).

⬛ SHOPPING

Mérida offers the best shopping in the Yucatán, which is both a blessing and a curse—nagging vendors and high-pressure salespeople accompany the good wares. The main **mercado** occupies the block southeast of the Palacio Federal, spreading outward from the corner of Calles 65 and 58. The ground floor of this behemoth center is occupied by **food vendors.** Oodles of fruits, vegetables, and meats await you. (Open M-Sa 8am-6pm.) The pricier second-floor **artisans' market,** part of the modern building behind and to the right of the Palacio Federal, sells trinkets, regional clothing, and the omnipresent hammock. White *huipiles* 250-350 pesos, *rebozos* (woven shawls) 220 pesos, *guayaberas* 150-250 pesos. Cheaper goods such as *huaraches* (hand-made leather sandals) are sold on the first floor of the market. Although jewelry stores line the streets, the best prices are at the smaller *prestas*, in the market, or at the *zócalo* every Sunday.

⬛ DAYTRIPS FROM MÉRIDA

DZIBILCHALTÚN

Combis *leave the Parque de San Juan in Mérida as soon as they fill up (about every 30min., 4 pesos). They will drop you off at the access road to the ruins, a 5min. walk from the entrance. To get back, walk back to the Conkal road and wait for a combi that runs between Mérida and the villages past Conkal. Some travelers hitch the 5km to the highway. Autoprogreso buses and Mérida-bound combis abound on Mex. 261, passing by in both directions every 15min. They are often full, and it can take a while to get back to Mérida. Site open daily 8am-5pm; museum open Tu-Su 8am-4pm. 50 pesos, children under 13 free; Su free; parking 7 pesos.*

Saying the name is half the fun. Situated 20km north of Mérida en route to the Gulf coast, Dzibilchaltún (dzib-ill-shahl-TOON; Place Where There Is Writing on Stones) sprawls over 60 sq. km of jungle brush. The site flourished as a ceremonial and administrative center from approximately 300 BC until the arrival of the Spanish in the 1520s, making it one of the longest continuously-inhabited Maya settlements. The excavated site now houses a 300m "ecological path" with nearly 100 different species of birds and labeled plants and houses **El Museo del Pueblo Maya,** which displays carved columns from Dzibilchaltún and Maya ceramics. The museum is the first building to the left of the entrance. The path leading to the museum is lined with an all-star gallery of Maya *stelae* with original sculptures from Chichén Itzá and Uxmal.

From the museum, follow the path to *sacbé* No. 1, the central axis of the site, and turn left. At the end of this road lies Dzibilchaltún's showpiece, the fully restored **Templo de las Siete Muñecas (Temple of the Seven Dolls),** constructed in the 5th century. The seven clay "dolls" discovered in this temple are on display in the museum. Shortly after sunrise, a huge shadow mask of the rain god Chac appears as the sun's rays pierce the temple during the spring and autumn equinox. The other end of *sacbé* No. 1 leads to a Maya temple converted into a chapel for Franciscan missionaries. Just beyond the eastern edge of the quadrangle is **Cenote Xlacah,** which served as a sacrificial well and source of water. Divers have recovered ceremonial artifacts and human bones from the depths of the 44m-deep *cenote.* While the *cenote* is not the most striking, the water invites a non-sacrificial dip. A path to the south leads past several smaller structures to the site's exit.

CELESTÚN ☎ 9

Celestún is an ideal vacation destination with seafood restaurants by the beach, inexpensive waterfront hotels, and pervasive *tranquilidad.* Many come for the warm shallow waters and refreshing breeze, or on day-trips from Mérida to visit the town's main attraction, **Río Celestún Biosphere Reserve,** home to 200 species of birds, including pelicans, cormorants, flamingos, and the occasional stork.

TRANSPORTATION AND PRACTICAL INFORMATION. Celestún lies 150km west of Mérida on the Gulf Coast. To get there by bus, go to the Oriente **bus station** in Mérida on Calle 50 between Calles 65 and 67. If you're driving, follow Mex. 281 into town; it becomes Calle 11, the main east-west street. Calle 11 passes the *zócalo* and hits the shore two blocks later after that. Odd numbers increase to the south, while even numbers decrease away from the sand. The *zócalo* is bounded by Calles 11, 13, 10, and 8. Autobuses de Occidente sends buses from a small booth at the corner of Calles 8 and 11, at the *zócalo*, to **Mérida** (2hr., 17 per day 5am-8pm, 31 pesos).

Police: (☎916 20 50) on Calle 13 side of the *zócalo*. English spoken. **Farmacia Don San Luis,** Calle 10 #108, between Calles 13 and 15. (☎916 20 02. Open daily 8am-11pm.) **Health center** on Calle 5 between Calles 8 and 10. No English spoken, but wild gesticulations understood. (☎916 20 46. Open M-Tu 8am-3:30pm, W-Su open 24hr.) **Telecomm,** on Calle 11 at the *zócalo*. (☎916 20 53. Open M-F 9am-3pm.)

ACCOMMODATIONS AND FOOD. Mexican tourists and biologists flock here in July and August; call ahead to make sure there's room. All budget accommodations are on Calle 12. **Hotel San Julio,** Calle 12 #93A between Calles 9 and 11, faces a sand patio that opens onto the beach. The blue rooms and baths are sparse, but clean. (☎916 20 62. Singles 80 pesos; doubles 120 pesos; each additional person 20 pesos.) **Hotel María del Carmen,** Calle 12 #111 at Calle 15, is right on the beach and has small golden rooms with sea views, balconies, and immaculate baths. They also rent bicycles. (☎ 916 20 61. Singles 170 pesos; doubles 200 pesos; each additional person 50 pesos; 10% student discount.) Vacationing *merideños* love the spotless rooms with TV and fans of **Hotel Sol y Mar,** on Calle 12 between Calles 11 and 13, one block from the beach. (☎916 21 66. Singles and doubles 150 pesos; with A/C 250 pesos; large suites with kitchen, fridge, and A/C 350 pesos. Prices rise 200-300 pesos in July and Aug.) **Hotel Gutiérrez,** Calle 12 #127 at Calle 13, lets you fit as many as you like in the brown stucco rooms with aqua tiles. Ask for a room with a view. (☎916 20 41 or 916 20 42. 200 pesos.)

Restaurants line Calle 12 and the beach, and *loncherías* cluster in the *zócalo*. At **Restaurant La Playita,** Calle 12 #99, between Calles 9 and 11, sumptuous plates of *jaiba frita* (fried blue crab) are 50 pesos. (☎916 20 52. Open daily 9am-7pm.) **Pelicano's,** Calle 12 #90 at Calle 9, has cheap fried fish (30 pesos) and crab claws (60 pesos), but sadly no pelicans. (☎916 20 37. Open Th-T 11am-7pm.) **La Boya,** Calle 12 #99 at Calle 11, has good, cheap seafood entrees like fried shrimp and fried crab (40 pesos), and a powerful sound system. (☎916 21 29. Open daily 10am- 6pm.)

SIGHTS. Celestún's estuary is a major wintering site on the central migratory bird flyway, and boat tours allow you to explore the exotic **Ría** the birds inhabit. The best tour takes you from the beach south along the coast until you enter La Ría, where you'll wind through a river tunnel of intertwined tree branches, pass petrified forests, and observe the abandoned fishing village of **Real de Salinas,** with a breathtaking view of the salt fields. Heading north through La Ría, you'll reach **Isla de Pájaros** (Island of Birds), an avian playground with, depending on your luck, hundreds to thousands of flamingos. The 2½hr. tour ends with a visit to a cold, freshwater *cenote* where you can take a refreshing dip. Tours operate daily 7:30am-4pm and can be arranged outside of **Restaurant Celestún** on the beach (150 pesos per person). Shorter and possibly cheaper tours can be arranged with *lancheros* at the bridge ½km before town. (1½-2hr. tours for 5-8 people 400 pesos.) **Celestún Expeditions,** on Calle 10 between 9 and 11, offers "Eco-tours with a difference," as well as birding, shelling, jungle walks, and anything else you could possibly dream of doing in Celestún. Birdwatching is US$100 for one person or US$140 for an all-day trip for 4 people. (☎916 20 49. Open M-Sa 7am-5pm.) On Saturday nights, bands from Mérida perform in Celestún's *zócalo*.

PROGRESO ☎ 9

Only 30 km north of Mérida on the northwestern Yucatec coast, Progreso entices weary Merideños seeking a convenient weekend retreat. For decades the seaside city with its 6km-long pier stretching indefinitely into the horizon acted as landlocked Mérida's port, exporting Yucatec *hequén* (hemp) to the world. Today, a different kind of cargo passes through the harbor—the city plays host to a never-ending stream of cruising tourists, courting docked foreigners with fresh seafood and soothing beaches. Progreso's cool evenings, colorful vistas of sea and sky, and pervasive tranquility provide a welcome change from big-city Mérida.

⌐ TRANSPORTATION. Autoprogreso Buses travel to Mérida's Autoprogreso station (40min., every 12min. 6am-10pm, 11 pesos). To get to the *zócalo* from the Progreso station (☎955 30 24), on Calle 20 between Calles 80 and 82, walk east on Calle 29 to the end of the block, turn right and walk one block on Calle 80. To reach the beach, follow Calle 80 in the opposite direction.

◼️🖬 ORIENTATION AND PRACTICAL INFORMATION. Calle 19, Progreso's turquoise *malecón* (boardwalk) runs east-west along the beach. Odd-numbered roads run parallel to the *malecón*, increasing to the south. Even-numbered streets travel north-south and increase to the west. Progreso's *zócalo* is bounded by Calles 31 and 33 on the north and south, and bisected by Calle 80.

The helpful **tourist office** sits in the northeast corner of Progreso's pinkish **Casa de la Cultura,** north of the lighthouse on Calle 80 between Calles 25 and 27. (☎935 01 04. Open M-F 8am-2pm and 4-8pm, Sa 8am-1pm.) **Banamex:** Calle 80 #126, between Calles 27 and 29, has a 24hr. **ATM.** (☎935 08 99. Open M-F 9am-5pm and Sa 9am-2pm.) **Laundry:** Calle 29 #132, between Calles 76 and 78, offers next day service. (☎935 08 56. 7 pesos per kg; 3kg minimum. Open M-Sa 8am-6pm.) **Supermarket: San Francisco de Asís,** at Calle 80 #144 between Calles 29 and 31. (☎935 37 60. Open daily 7am-9pm.) **Police:** (☎935 00 26), in the Palacio Municipal on the west side of the *zócalo*. **Farmacia Canto,** at the southwest corner of Calles 29 and 80. (☎935 11 03. Open daily 7am-10pm.) **Centro Médico Americano:** (☎935 09 51) at Calles 33 and 82. Some English spoken. **Internet Access: Inter Coffee del Sureste,** on Calle 80 between Calles 29 and 31. (☎935 07 46. 10 pesos per hr. Open daily 9am-midnight.) **Telecomm,** next door to the post office. (Open M-F 8am-7:30pm, Sa-Su 9am-noon.) **Post office:** Calle 31 #150, west of Calle 78, just off the *zócalo*. (☎935 05 65. Open M-F 8:30am-3pm.) **Postal code:** 97320.

🏠🍴 ACCOMMODATIONS AND FOOD. Encounter great value at **Hotel Miramar,** Calle 27 #124, between Calles 74 and 76, and sleep the night away in spacious, classy rooms with neat baths and skylights or four well-ventilated, fiberglass space-age rooms with escape-pod-like baths. (☎955 05 42. Singles 130 pesos; doubles 150-200 pesos, with A/C 260 pesos; each additional person 50 pesos.) For a few extra pesos, you can stay in spotless, newly remodeled wood-paneled rooms at **Hotel Progreso,** Calle 78 #142, near Calle 29. (☎935 00 39. Singles and doubles 190 pesos, with A/C 240 pesos; each additional person 40 pesos.) **Hotel Real del Mar,** Malecón 144, entrance on Calle 70, overlooks the beach, and has simple rooms with colorful beds; doubles with remodeled bathrooms tend to be the nicest. (☎935 07 98. Singles 200 pesos; doubles 240 pesos; each additional person 40 pesos.) Reservations recommended, especially during July and August.

The *pescado frito* signs on just about every corner prove the fact that Progreso is all about cheap seafood. Like fish with a view? Just take a stroll down the *malecón* to **Restaurant Los Cocos,** between Calles 76 and 78. Fresh fish are served hot and fried to a golden brown for 36 pesos. (Open daily 9am-7pm.) Brand-new **Riko Marea,** on the *malecón* between Calles 68 and 70, serves an array of seafood (40-60 pesos) and non-seafood specialties, like *milanesa marea* (a breaded pork chop topped with cheese, cream, and mushrooms, 38 pesos), while playing classic disco tunes. Entrees start at 28 pesos, pizzas 28-60 pesos, breakfast 20-32 pesos. (☎955 04 67. Open daily 8am-midnight.) You can't see the ocean from **El Cordobés,** Calle 80 # 150 at Calle 31, but a view of the peaceful *zócalo* accompanies solid *comida típica.* (29-60 pesos.☎955 26 21. Open daily 6am-midnight.)

◑◪ SIGHTS AND BEACHES. Progreso's shallow waters, beach boardwalks, and *palapas* attract hordes of visitors in August, but remain somewhat calm the rest of the year. For a more placid but perhaps less picturesque experience, try the beach at **Chelém,** 8km west of town, or the wind-sheltered beach at **Yucalpetén,** just before Chelém. *Combis* leave for Chelém from the parking lot outside Supermarket San Francisco on Calle 80 (every 15min., 3.5 pesos). Or you can take a bus from the local bus terminal (bordered by Calles 29, 31, 82, and 84). The custodian of **El Faro,** at Calle 80 near Calle 25, may let you climb the 120 steps to the top of the 19th-century lighthouse. Because the limestone shelf of the Yucatán peninsula descends so gradually into the sea, a 6km-long pier was constructed to reach deep water. Progreso's **Puerto de Altura** *muelle* (pier), Mexico's longest, appears to extend infinitely from the beach and is a great spot to reel in fish.

If sunbathing and fishing have you bored, a largely unexplored Maya site lies near **Xcambó,** at the end of a 2km access road that intersects the road to Telchac Puerto, 25km east of Progreso. The easiest way to get there is by taxi (200-250 pesos round-trip), as bus service is very spotty. The small, recently restored site consists of several structures and two pyramids—one of which supports two large, unidentified stucco masks and offers a panoramic view of the coast. A peculiar, still functioning church was built into the side of one of the pyramids. Small paths branch from the site to unexcavated ruins and tiny villages; the caretaker may be coaxed into acting as a guide. (Open daily 9am-5pm. Free.)

IZAMAL ☎9

Izamal ("City of the Hills" in Maya) and its 12 pyramids once were a central religious center of the Yucatec Maya. Also known as *La Ciudad Amarilla* (The Yellow City), Izamal's main buildings and world-famous convent are all painted a rich egg-yolky yellow with white trim. Yet another name, *La Ciudad de las Tres Culturas* (The City of the Three Cultures), begins to describe Izamal's harmonious blend of Maya pyramids, Spanish architecture, and *mestizo* character. The city's midday and evening tranquility is broken only by the occasional school-produced *ballet folklórico*, the clattering of *calesas victorianas* (horse-drawn carriages), and the whoops of children playing ball in the street.

▐ TRANSPORTATION. The **bus station** (☎954 01 07) is between Calles 31 and 33 on Calle 32, behind the municipal palace. Oriente and Autocentro buses leave from the terminal for: **Cancún** (5½ hr., 12 per day, 81 pesos); **Valladolid** (2½ hr., 12 per day, 30 pesos); **Mérida** (1½hr., every 30 min. 5:30am-7:30pm, 25 pesos).

▣▪ ORIENTATION AND PRACTICAL INFORMATION. The road from Hoctún, 24km to the southwest, turns into Calle 31, which runs east-west as do all odd-numbered streets, increasing to the south. Calle 31 runs past the convent (on the right going east), passing north-south streets with decreasing even numbers. Calles 28, 31, 32, and 33 frame the town's *zócalo*, municipal palace, and market.

For **tourist information**, head to the main office of the Palacio Municipal, just west of the *zócalo*. (☎954 02 41, ext 14. Open daily 8am-10pm.) Or direct your questions to any of the **Policía Turística** in brown and cream-colored uniforms patrolling the *zócalo*. **Currency exchange: Bancrecer,** on the corner of Calles 31 and 28, just north of the convent, has a 24 hr. **ATM.** (☎954 04 25. Open M-F 9am-3pm; Sa 10am-2pm.) **Police:** (☎954 00 09), across from the bus station in the Palacio Municipal. English spoken. **Market:** on the corner of Calles 30 and 33. **Farmacia Itzalana,** on the corner of Calles 31 and 32. Knock if closed. (☎954 00 32. Open 24hr.) **Medical Assistance: IMSS** (☎954 02 41), two blocks south and three blocks east of the *zócalo* at the corner of Calles 37 and 24. **Fax: Telecomm,** on the corner of Calles 31A and 32, behind the Palacio Municipal also has internet access. (☎954 02 63. Internet 15 pesos per hr. Open M-F 8am-8pm.) **LADATELs** are scarce, but one is in the post office. **Post office:** on the corner of 31 and 32A. (☎954 03 90. Open M-F 8am-3pm.)

▣▢ ACCOMMODATIONS AND FOOD. The best accommodations in the city are at beautiful ▣**Macan-Che Bed and Breakfast,** southeast of the *zócalo*. To get there, take one of the horse-drawn carriages waiting on the north side of the convent (5-10 min., 8 pesos). Twelve well-kept suites, with outdoor porch, fridge, fans, and *agua purificada*, nestle within a wonderful garden. A large and delicious freshly-made breakfast is prepared each morning on a *palapa*-covered patio. (☎954 02 87. Suite with breakfast 250-300 pesos.) For cheaper and far inferior rooms, look to **Hotel Kabul** and **Hotel Canto,** side by side on the northern edge of the *zócalo*, on Calle 31 between Calles 30 and 32. Kabul's run-down blue rooms have fans and hammock hooks. (☎954 08 14. Singles and doubles with shared bath 60 pesos. Singles with private bath 100 pesos.) Hotel Canto, next door, has old, soiled rooms with baths that don't keep bugs out. (Singles 80-100 pesos; doubles 120-150 pesos.)

Don't plan on late-night wining and dining in the Yellow City; most restaurants close by early evening. Locally lauded **Restaurant Kinich Kalemó,** Calle 27 #299, between Calles 28 and 30, makes regional dishes such as *pierna asada a la yucateca, escaseche oriental,* and *poc-chuc kinich kalemó* (45 pesos) under a plant-heavy *palapa*. (☎904 84 95. Open daily 9am-6pm.) The new and tranquil **El Toro** overlooks the convent on Calle 33 between Calles 30 and 32 and cooks up delicious beef filet *a la tampiqueña* (50 pesos) with freshly-made corn tortillas and big glasses of *agua de horchata* or lemonade (6 pesos). Also serves breakfast (20-30 pesos), sandwiches (25 pesos), and burritos (20 pesos). (☎967 13 47. Open daily 9am-11pm.) **Los Portales,** on the corner of Calles 30 and 31A next to the market, has the best view of the *zócalo*, but the cheap, filling meals will hold your attention. (☎954 03 02. Full breakfasts and lunches 25 pesos. Open Th-Tu 7am-9pm.)

▣ SIGHTS. The huge—and incredibly yellow—**Convento de San Antonio de Padua** consists of three main parts: the **church,** built in 1554; the **convent,** built in 1561; and the **atrium,** built in 1618 with 75 arches and second in size only to the Vatican. After the church entrance at the atrium, and a statue of the Pope, several original 16th-century frescoes hang on the facade. Inside the Baroque church is an ornate altar with a doorway at the top, through which Izamal's statue of the Immaculate Conception is wheeled out for every Mass. The room immediately behind the altar exhibits pictures and mementos of the Pope's August 1993 visit to Izamal. Continue up the stairs to arrive at Mexico's oldest *camarín*, where the statue of the Immaculate Conception rests when not in use. Fray Diego de Landa commissioned this statue in 1558 in Guatemala. There were originally two statues—called *Las Dos Hermanas*—one was sent to Mérida and the other to Izamal. In 1829, Izamal's statue was destroyed in a fire, and Mérida's copy was brought here. It is said, however, that the Izamal original was saved and taken to the nearby pyramid of Kinich Kakmó. Every December 8, at the climax of the town's week-long *fiesta*, the two switch places in *El Paso de las Dos Hermanas*. More legends are told at Izamal's small **museum,** on the north side of the Convent, on Calle 31. The museum details Izamal's three historical phases and has a model of the city in 500 BC. (Open Tu-W and F-Su 10am-1pm and 4:30-8:30pm. Free.)

Only after ascending the 34m high pyramid of **Kinich Kakmó** (temple of the fire and sun god) can visitors truly appreciate Izamal's most dominating structure. This massive pyramid, measuring 200m by 180m, is the fifth-tallest in Yucatán Peninsula. Yet even it was outclassed by **Pap-hol-chac,** the largest pyramid in ancient Izamal, whose remains lie under the convent. Kinich Kakmó was built during the Early Classic period (AD 400-600) and formed the northern border of the ancient city's central plaza. (Enter on Calle 27 between 28 and 28A.) Other pyramids dot Izamal, blending with the modern cityscape. **Itzamatul,** dedicated to the god Zamná, looms to the east and is accessible on Calle 26, between 29 and 31. **Habre** is the most removed, occupying the block encompassed by Calles 26, 28, 35, and 37. The most centrally-located pyramid, **Kabul,** or "working hand," is just north of the *zócalo*. Unfortunately, surrounding homes and businesses make it almost impossible to reach. (All pyramids open daily 8am-5pm. Free.)

CHICHÉN ITZÁ ☎ 9

Gracing hundreds of glossy brochure covers and suffering the footfalls of thousands of tourists, the Post-Classic Maya ruins at Chichén Itzá seem almost an archaeological cliché. Once here, however, the hype is understandable. Swarms of tourists surprisingly do not tarnish the history behind the magnificent, well-preserved site, and their presence evokes days a thousand years past when Chichén Itzá embodied all the political and cultural grandeur of ancient Maya civilization. Awesome stone structures with their faultless architecture and mystic decor, together with the sheer size of this former Maya capital, inspire awe for the skill and creativity of Maya builders. Yet more enigmatic is why this amazing ingenuity was devoted to horrific rites of human sacrifice practiced by the people of Chichén Itzá. A cliché they certainly might be, but the ruins still merit a long, loving visit from all who cross the Yucatán. Only 2.5km away, the town of **Piste** may merit a night's stay so as to enter Chichén Itzá at 8am and see it in relative peace. Avoid visiting around noon, when the sun scorches and the tourist wave peaks.

▐ TRANSPORTATION

The ruins of Chichén Itzá lie 1.5km from **Mex. 180,** the highway running from Mérida (119km west) through Valladolid (42km east) to Cancún (200km east). The two access roads are the main road from the west and another from the east. Mex. 180 becomes **Calle 15** in Piste, the town's main drag. Piste has two functionally equivalent bus stations, both on Calle 15. The main **bus station** (☎851 00 52) is between the Pirámide Inn and Posada Novelo on the eastern edge of town. ADO treks to **Cancún** (2½hr., 3:30pm, 110 pesos); **Mérida** (1½hr., 3 and 5:15pm, 56 pesos); **Playa del Carmen** (2:45pm, 115 pesos; 4:30pm, 140 pesos); **Valladolid** (1hr., 11am and 3pm, 24 pesos). Second-class buses run more frequently.

Reaching the ruins is easy. If you would rather skip the 20min. walk from Piste, catch a taxi (25 pesos) or wait in the bus station for an eastbound bus (every 30min., 5 pesos). To get to Chichén Itzá from other towns, see bus listings for Mérida (see p. 580), Cancún (see p. 604), and Valladolid (see p. 597). To return to Piste, wait in the bus parking lot until a taxi or bus swings by (every 45min.).

⚡ PRACTICAL INFORMATION

Piste and the ruins contain few services, so it's best to come prepared. Currency exchange: **Casas de cambio** congregate at the entrance to Chichén Itzá and near the Piste's *zócalo*. There are no **ATMs. Police:** (☎851 00 97), at the Camandancia on the east side of the *zócalo*. **Farmacia Isis,** Calle 15 #53, east of the *zócalo*, toward the ruins. (☎851 02 16. Open 24 hr.) **Medical care: Clínica Promesa,** Calle 14 #50 (☎851 00 05), in the blue-green building west of the *zócalo* and 100m north of Mex. 180. **Centro Telefónico,** across from the bus station, lets you phone home. (☎851 00 88. Open daily 9am-9pm.) **LADATELs** are along Mex. 180.

Services in Chichén Itzá are at the site's western entrance. Across from the ticket counter is a small **information booth**. The booth often has free **luggage storage.** (Open daily 8am-5pm.) The bus station also offers free luggage storage (6am-6pm). Restrooms, a restaurant, ice cream parlor, gift shop (which accepts US dollars), bookstore, small museum, and **parking** (10 pesos) are available at the site.

🏠🍴 ACCOMMODATIONS AND FOOD

Though luxury hotels have begun to invade, plenty of economical lodging remains in Piste. The extreme budget travelers can camp under a *palapa* at **Pirámide Inn** (40-50 pesos). For those desiring a bed, the accommodations below can be found either on or just off Mex. 180/Calle 15. **Posada Olalde,** left off Calle 15 across from Restaurant Carrousel and two blocks down the dirt road, is a pleasant stay and a great value with its large, spotless rooms in the main house and well-kept bungalows off the intimate courtyard. (☎851 00 86. Singles 135 pesos; doubles 180 pesos, with A/C 210 pesos; bungalows for two 140 pesos. Discounts for students and in low season.) Another option is **Hotel El Paso,** Calle 15 #48, across from El Carrousel. Bouncy beds make for good jumping and small windows ensure no one falls. (☎851 01 94. Singles 120 pesos; doubles 140 pesos.) The rooms are plain at **Posada Novelo,** next to the main bus station and closest to the ruins, but clean baths and a pool beckon exhausted explorers. (Singles and doubles 150 pesos.)

Those too engrossed with the ruins to think about eating should consider themselves lucky—pickings are slim in Chichén Itzá. The on-site **restaurant** specializes in *comida non-típica:* high prices and small servings. (Smoothies 30-40 pesos, entrees 45-60 pesos.) Picnickers save a few pesos by packing a lunch from one of the **small grocers** lining Calle 15 in Piste. **Las Mestizas,** across from Hotel Chichén Itzá, has good *comida regional* like *pollo* or *cochinita pibel* (baked chicken or pork wrapped in banana leaves, with tomatoes, onions, and salt—40 pesos) in an airy restaurant. (☎851 00 69. Open Tu-Su 7am-11pm.) Tasty and inexpensive food abounds at *palapa*-covered **Restaurant Carrousel.** *Chilaquiles con pollo* (fried tortillas with cheese, onions, and chicken) 20 pesos, enchiladas 20 pesos. (☎851 00 78. Open daily 7:30am-10:30pm.) **Los Pájaros,** a tad west of Restaurant Carrousel, is equally good and cheap. (☎858 12 87. Dishes 25-35 pesos. Open daily 8am-10pm.)

🔵 📖 THE ARCHAEOLOGICAL SITE OF CHICHÉN ITZÁ

Open daily 8am-6pm. 85 pesos; Holidays, children under 13, and Su, free. Documentary show times vary. Site museum and auditorium open daily 8am-6pm. Free. Light and sound show (in Spanish) daily 7pm in winter, 8pm in summer. Free with admission or 25 pesos without. Guided tours begin at the entrance and cost upwards of 400 pesos for groups of 1-20.

The settlement of Chichén Itzá took place over three periods; the first two are grouped together and called the **Maya Phase** (or **Chichén Viejo**), and the third called the **Toltec-Maya Phase** (or **Chichén Nuevo**). The name Chichen Itzá means "by the mouth of Itzá's well," implying that the area's earliest inhabitants were drawn here by two nearby freshwater *cenotes*. Settlers arrived in the first period around AD 700, the Maya Classic Period, during which Maya strength centered in Chiapas and Guatemala. These early settlers may have built the structures found today at

Chichén Viejo, though scholars disagree. The second period, in the late Classic or early Post-Classic Era around AD 900, saw more central construction, including the inner pyramid of El Castillo, original Temple of Chacmool (beneath Templo de los Guerreros). The last period began in the 11th century with the arrival of Itzá, a Maya group from Tabasco. A dwindling group of experts adheres to the traditional view that sometime before 1000, Toltec tribes of Tula infiltrated the Yucatán and overcame peaceful Maya settlements, bringing with them the cult of plumed serpent Quetzalcóatl (Kukulcán in Maya). The more widely accepted view, however, is Chichén Itzá, a crossroads of trade and ideas, eventually incorporated Toltec practices into its own culture. Toltec influence is evident in the distinctive reclining *chac-mools*, statues of the rain god Chac, with their heads turned sideways, holding forth plates to receive an offering or sacrifice. Gran Plaza, El Castillo, Templo de Guerreros, Observatory, and Juego de Pelota were all constructed during this period. In the 12th century, Chichén Itzá formed the powerful **Mayapán League,** through which it dominated the remaining Maya city-states in the Yucatán. In 1461, Chichén Itzá was abandoned due to war with rival city-state Mayapán, though religious pilgrimages to the site continued well after Spanish conquest.

For a more comprehensive (not to mention air-conditioned) understanding of Chichén and its people, visit **Centro Cultural Cecijema,** Calle 15 #45, just west of the bus station in Piste. The gray building houses a small selection of Maya ceramic replicas, a modest library, and rotating exhibits. (☎851 00 04. Open M-Sa 8am-5pm. Free.) The **information center** and a few services can be found at the main entrance to Chichén Itzá, on the western side of the ruins. A small **museum** presents the site history and displays sculptures and objects removed from the Sacred Cenote. The

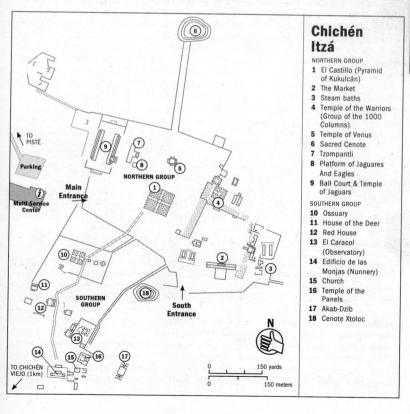

Chichén Itzá

NORTHERN GROUP

1 El Castillo (Pyramid of Kukulcán)
2 The Market
3 Steam baths
4 Temple of the Warriors (Group of the 1000 Columns)
5 Temple of Venus
6 Sacred Cenote
7 Tzompantli
8 Platform of Jaguares And Eagles
9 Ball Court & Temple of Jaguars

SOUTHERN GROUP

10 Ossuary
11 House of the Deer
12 Red House
13 El Caracol (Observatory)
14 Edificio de las Monjas (Nunnery)
15 Church
16 Temple of the Panels
17 Akab-Dzib
18 Cenote Xtoloc

YUCATÁN

PLAY BALL! The great ballcourts found at Chichén Itzá and other Maya cities were constructed for a specific game in which two contending teams endeavored to keep a heavy rubber ball (3-5kg) in constant motion using only their hips, knees, shoulders, and elbows. In this physically exhausting game, players scored by knocking the ball through small stone rings placed high on the court's side walls. Much more than a cultural pastime for the Maya, the ball game was both symbolic of the battle between good and evil and an important rite to keep the celestial bodies in motion (the ball represented the sun and its constant motion symbolized the movement of the sun through the heavens). The game also served as gory religious ceremony—at certain festivals, winning teams were honored with ritual decapitation and deification.

auditorium screens documentaries about the ruins in Spanish and English. Those green panels (whose purpose you'll be contemplating all day) pop open for the evening **light and sound show.** If you trust your bug repellent, the nighttime stroll from Piste is quiet and well-lit; otherwise take a taxi (25 pesos).

EL CASTILLO (THE CASTLE). Chichén's trademark edifice, El Castillo (also known as Pyramid of Kukulcán) stands as tangible evidence of the astrological mastery of the ancient Maya—and offers spectacular views of the site. The 91 steps on each of the four faces, plus the upper platform, total 365; 52 panels on nine terraced levels equal the years in a Maya calendar cycle. A staircase divides each face of the nine terraces, yielding 18 sections representing the 18 Maya *uinal* in each *tun* of the Long Count dating system. Even more impressive is the precise alignment of El Castillo's axes, which produce a bi-annual optical illusion. At sunrise during the spring and fall equinoxes, the rounded terraces cast a serpentine shadow down the side of the northern staircase. A light-and-shadow lunar serpent-god, identical to that of the equinoxes, creeps down the pyramid at the dawn of the full moon following each equinox. El Castillo was built atop an older Classic-era temple, which can be entered at the western side of the north staircase's base. After climbing the steps you'll be grimacing like the *chac-mool* in the ceremonial chamber. Check out the fanged jaguar throne with jade eyes behind the chamber. *(Inner temple open daily 11am-3pm and 4-5pm. Free.)*

JUEGO DE PELOTA (BALLCOURT). Northwest of El Castillo sits a playing field, bounded by high parallel walls, with temples at the north and south ends. Measuring 146m by 37m, Chichén boasts the largest ballcourt in Mesoamerica, and amazing side-to-side echoes. The elaborate game played here fascinated Cortés so much he took two teams back to Europe in 1528 to perform before the royal court.

TZOMPANTLI (PLATFORM OF THE SKULLS). A short distance from the ballcourt in the direction of the open grassy area is a platform typical of Maya-Toltec architecture that once exhibited the bare skulls of prisoners and enemies. The eerie columns of bas-relief skulls on the lower platform walls conjure horrific images of bloody skulls strung together vertically to strike fear in the hearts of enemies.

PLATFORM OF THE JAGUARS AND EAGLES. Next to Tzompantli, these animals represented the warrior castes, who were ordered to kidnap members of other tribes for sacrifices to their gods. To either side of the feathered serpent heads on the balustrades, reliefs of jaguars and eagles clutch human hearts in their claws.

TUMBA DEL CHACMOOL (TEMPLE OF VENUS). Directly north of El Castillo is the Temple of Venus, a square platform decorated with a feathered serpent holding a human head in its mouth. The temple's reliefs symbolize the planet Venus, other stars and planets, and give information on their motions.

CENOTE DE LOS SACRIFICIOS (SACRED CENOTE). Three hundred meters north of El Castillo and connected via a *sacbé*, this 60m-wide subterranean pool was

Chichén Itzá's most important religious symbol. The rain god Chac, believed to dwell beneath the surface, requested frequent gifts in exchange for good rains. Elaborate rituals, beginning atop El Castillo and culminating in the unfortunate victim's 25m plunge to death, appeased the god. In 1907, many sacrificial remains—including skulls, teeth, and jewelry—were dredged from the depths by anthropologist Edward Thompson. In the 1960s, scuba divers discovered more remains, suggesting that children and young men were the sacrifices of choice.

TEMPLO DE LOS GUERREROS (TEMPLE OF THE WARRIORS). On the left as you return from the *cenote* and northeast of El Castillo, this temple presents an array of carved columns that supported a perishable roof, but now stand like a great army. On the temple itself, before two great feathered serpents and several sculpted animal gods, is one of Chichén's best-preserved *chac-mools* and a table where human hearts were ritually extracted. This building's ornamentation shows heavy Toltec influence; a nearly identical structure stands in Tula, the former Toltec capital to the west. The temple was built over the former Temple of Chac-mool. *(Closed to the public.)*

GRUPO DE MIL COLUMNAS (GROUP OF A THOUSAND COLUMNS). Extending to the south and east of Templo de los Guerreros, the group of columns, believed to have been a civic or religious center, contains an elaborate drainage system that channeled rainfall into a depression on the complex's northeast side. The ruins extending southeast of the columns include several colonnades, a market, and steam bath. The bath house is split into a waiting room and interior, where water was poured over hot rocks, creating steam to purify those in religious ceremonies.

TUMBA DEL GRAN SACERDOTE. Also called the **Ossuary,** or **High Priest's Grave,** it is the first structure right of the path leading to the southern half of the site. The distinctive serpent heads mimic El Castillo, and a natural cave extends from within the pyramid 15m into the earth. The human bones and votive offerings of gold, silver, and jewels found in this cave are thought to have belonged to the ancient high priests of Chichén Itzá.

EL CARACOL (THE OBSERVATORY). One of few circular structures built by the Maya, this ancient planetarium consists of two rectangular platforms with large, west-facing staircases, and two circular towers. The tower's spiral staircase earned the name El Caracol (The Snail). The slits in the dome can be aligned with the major celestial bodies and cardinal directions, and the red handprints on the walls were supposedly made by the hands of sun god Kinich Ahau.

TEMPLO DE LOS TABLEROS (TEMPLE OF THE PANELS). Just south of the Observatory, this small ruin has carved panels and rows of columns. Though difficult to decipher, the panels on exterior walls contain emblems of warriors—jaguars, eagles, and serpents—in three rows. The upper part of the structure is believed to have been a site for fire-related ceremonies.

EDIFICIO DE LAS MONJAS (THE NUNNERY). At the southern extent of the South Group, this group of buildings, built over six phases, was probably the royal residence of a high priest. To the Spanish, however, the stone rooms looked suspiciously like a convent—hence the ruins' name. Above the entrance on the east side of the building, Maya glyphs are still visible. Also on the east side is the **annex,** which predates the rest of the nunnery. Above the doorway facing the small courtyard is a spectacular bas-relief of a seated royal-divine figure. Many rooms in the nunnery have doorways that lead to dark corridors, home to bats and frogs.

LA IGLESIA (THE CHURCH). For similar reasons, the elaborate building diagonal to the nunnery was misnamed the church. One of the oldest buildings at the site, its top-heavy walls are encrusted with intricate masks of hook-nosed Chac. The church fuses a variety of cultural styles: over the doorway are Maya stone lintels, while the use of wood and inclined edges indicate a Toltec influence. Above the door, the four *bacabs* that hold up the sky at four cardinal points are represented by a crab, a turtle, an armadillo, and a snail.

AKAB-DZIB. Sixty meters east of the nunnery, this complex earned its name for "dark writing" found in its 17 rooms. The oldest parts of this structure are believed to be Chichén's most ancient constructions—the two central rooms date to the 2nd or 3rd century, while the annexes on either side and to the east were added later. Inside, the small, red handprints of Kinich Ahau dot the ceiling.

CENOTE XTOLOC. The South Group ticket office hides the overgrown Cenote Xtoloc. To reach it from the office, take the first left 20m into the site. The *cenote* is in the hollow, beyond the ruined temple of Xtoloc, dedicated to that lizard god. No path goes down the slope through undergrowth, and swimming is prohibited due to dangerous currents. Secular counterpart to the holy waters of the Sacred Cenote, this pool at one time provided all of Chichén with drinking water. Follow *sacbé* No. 5, which becomes a narrow, winding trail, to get behind the observatory.

CHICHÉN VIEJO

Due to excavation and reconstruction, Chichén Viejo was closed to visitors in 2001 and will remain so for an indefinite period. Check with locals to find out the latest news.

Not many visitors to Chichén Itzá know that another adjacent site exists. Beginning about 1km south of the nunnery and spreading southwest from the main site, Chichén Viejo is so named because it was originally thought to contain the minor ruins of Chichén Itzá's first inhabitants. Recent work done at the site, however, suggests that this site was most likely inhabited around the same time as the rest of the city. Most of the ruins are unrestored and scattered throughout the jungle. To get to the **Group of the Initial Series** and the **Phallic Cluster,** follow the dirt road (simply marked with arrows) to the right of the nunnery past the intersection of other dirt paths to a deep well. Shortly beyond the well, a right at the T-junction brings you to the cluster, set in a clearing. Chichén Viejo carries the only dated inscriptions at Chichén Itzá, one of which is clearly visible on the only remaining lintel of the **Temple of the Initial Series.** Upheld by two columns, **The Temple of the Four Lintels** features a hieroglyphic inscription corresponding to July 13, 878. The rest of the temple stands in ruin. The main features of the appropriately named Phallic Cluster protrude from the interior walls of the temple, while nine warriors stand watch in the courtyard. The remaining ruins at Chichén Viejo, accessed by the path to the right of the **House of the Phalli,** following the rusted cart tracks, and cutting through the bushes, are best located with the help of a guide. In the **Principal Group of the Southwest,** glyphs depict the Maya practice of compressing children's foreheads with stone plates. The Principal Group contains a magnificently **ruined pyramid,** the restored **Temple of the Three Lintels** (dating to AD 879), and the **Jaguar Temple,** where a handful of columns salute the military order of the Jaguars.

◤ DAYTRIPS FROM CHICHÉN ITZÁ

GRUTAS DE BALANCANCHÉN

5km east of Chichén Itzá and 2km past the Dolores Alba Hotel, the caves are easily reached from Chichén or Piste by any eastbound bus on Mex. 180 (3 pesos). When boarding, be sure to tell the driver where you are headed. Or you can take a taxi (30 pesos one way, 50-60 pesos round-trip including wait). To get back, catch any westbound vehicle, but be prepared to wait a while. Tours in Spanish daily at 9am, noon, 2, and 4pm; in English at 11am, 1, and 3pm. 47 pesos. 2-person minimum. Guides required.

Descend into the ultra-humid corridors of the Maya underworld at the inner caves of Balancanchén, which were only rediscovered in 1959 when a local noticed the

HOLY WATER You may have noticed an absence of bridges on the lush Yucatán Peninsula, which lacks even a trickle of surface water. The whole peninsula rests on a porous limestone shelf, and rain water seeps right into the ground. The absorbed water finds itself in a complex network of underground rivers, all flowing to the ocean. Along the way, cracks break the surface of the earth, revealing the water beneath. These *cenotes* are great places for swimming and diving and the region's only source of fresh water. The ancient Maya, who relied heavily on the rains that fell from May to October, worshipped some *cenotes*, believing them to be the residences of the rain god Chac-mool and an important necessity for survival (and pleasure).

passageway blocked with stones. Further exploration opened 300m of caves filled with stalactites carved to resemble leaves, a huge treelike column representing the sacred *ceiba* tree, and three groups of ancient ceramic vessels and stone sculptures. Archaeologists believe the cave was a center for Maya-Toltec worship of the gods Chac (Tlaloc) and Kukulcán (Quetzalcóatl) during the 10th and 11th centuries. For unknown reasons, subterranean worship in Balancanchén stopped at the end of this period, and the offerings of pottery and sculpture rested undisturbed for nine centuries. The impressive stalactites and ceramics merit a visit, but be prepared for an almost incomprehensible sound and light show.

CENOTE SAGRADO AZUL

Across the street from the Dolores Alba Hotel, 3km east of Chichén Itza, the cenote can be reached from Chichén or Piste by any bus traveling east on Mex. 180 (3 pesos). Open daily 8am-6pm. 35 pesos.

After a long, sweaty trek through the ruins, nothing could be more refreshing than a dip in the clear waters of Cenote Sagrado Azul—unfortunately, nearly every other visitor to Chichén Itza will have the same idea.

YAXUNÁ

There is no public transportation to Yaxuná. Your options are either to rent a car or hire a taxi in Piste. There are 2 routes to Yaxuná. The better of the 2 takes you west on Mex. 180 to Libre Unión and then through Yaxcaba, a small town (300 pesos round-trip). The poorer road cuts through jungle, and taxistas charge more to cover possible damage to the car (450 pesos).

Thirty kilometers south of Chichén Itzá, Yaxuná is home to the ruins of yet another ancient Maya city. The temple was built by the Maya of Cobá, who were planning to declare war on the people of Chichén Itzá late in the Classic Period. To keep a close eye on their enemy, the Maya of Cobá aligned their temple with El Castillo. The most interesting feature of the site is the 100km *sacbé*, which connected Yaxuná to Cobá, making it the **longest in the peninsula**.

VALLADOLID   ☎ 9

In the middle of the Mérida-Cancún route and only 30min. from Chichén Itzá, Valladolid (pop. 52,000) ought to be jammed with tourists. Strangely enough, most bypass the beautiful city, ignorant of its colonial churches and natural *cenotes*. Formerly the Maya city of Zací, Valladolid was attacked in 1543 by the Spaniard Francisco de Montejo, and finally conquered several years later by a man of the same name, his nephew. The younger Montejo built imposing churches and gridlike streets as reminders of Spanish control, but the Maya were not so easily defeated. In 1848 they rose up and took the city hostage for several months in what is now known as the War of the Castes. The indigenous presence remains strong today; Maya is still heard among Indian women weaving *huipiles* (white dresses embroidered with colorful flowers), between vendors on street corners, and around the city's archaeological sites and *cenotes*.

YUCATÁN

◪ TRANSPORTATION

Traversed by Mex. 180, Valladolid lies in the heart of Yucatán state, midway between Mérida and Cancún. The **ADO station** (☎ 856 34 49) is on the northwest corner of Calles 54 and 37. To get to the *zócalo*, walk south one block on Calle 54 to Calle 39. Turn left and continue for six blocks. Better yet, you can get off before the bus station at the *zócalo* (look for a big twin-towered cathedral). ADO buses travel to: **Cancún** (2hr., 9 per day, 75 pesos); **Chichén Itzá** (1hr., every hr. from 5am, 14 pesos); **Mérida** (2½hr., every hr. from 6:30am, 75 pesos); **Playa del Carmen** (2½hr., 6 per day, 93 pesos); **Tizimín** (1hr., every hr. from 5am, 15 pesos); **Izamal** (1½hr., 12 per day, 30 pesos); **Chiquíla** (2½hr., 2:30am, 52 pesos). The **Oriente station,** on the northwest corner of Calles 39 and 46, goes to many of the same destinations.

◪ ? ORIENTATION AND PRACTICAL INFORMATION

Even-numbered streets in Valladolid run north-south, increasing to the west. Odd-numbered streets run east-west, increasing to the south. Except for Cenote X'keken, in the nearby village of **Dzitnup,** everything lies within walking distance of the *zócalo* (circumscribed by Calles 39, 40, 41, and 42). Blocks are spaced out, so what appears a short jaunt might really be a long haul.

Tourist Information: The **city hall** (☎ 856 20 63), on the corner of Calles 40 and 41, provides information and pamphlets. English Spoken. Open daily 6am-11pm.

Currency Exchange: Bancomer (☎ 856 21 50), on the Calle 40 side of the *zócalo* has a 24hr. **ATM** next door. Open M-F 8:30am-4pm, Sa 10am-2pm.

Bike Rental: Refaccionaria de Bicicletas Silva, and the sports store of Antonio Negro Aguilar (☎ 856 21 25), are both on Calle 44 between Calles 39 and 41. 5 pesos per hr. Open daily 8:30am-4pm.

Luggage Storage: At the ADO bus terminal. 3 pesos per hr.

Market: Fresh and cheap fruits, meats, and vegetables at the market 5 blocks northeast of the *zócalo*, bordered by Calles 30, 32, 35, and 37. Open daily 6am-2pm.

Supermarket: Super Maz (☎ 856 37 74), 3½ blocks west of the *zócalo* on Calle 39. Open daily 7am-9:30pm.

Laundry: Lavandería Tintorería Progreso, across from Super Maz. Full service, 2hr., 7 pesos per kg, 3kg minimum. Open M-Sa 8am-2pm and 5-8pm.

Emergency: ☎ 060.

Police: (☎ 856 21 00) Calle 41, 10 blocks east of the *zócalo*. Some English spoken.

Pharmacy: El Descuento, Calle 42 at 39, on the *zócalo*. Open daily 7am-10pm.

Hospital: (☎ 856 28 83), on the corner of Calles 51 and 52. English spoken.

Fax: Telecomm, on Calle 41, west of Museo San Roque, between Calles 38 and 40.

Internet Access: Xenyx Cybercafe, between Calles 37 and 39. 10 pesos per hr. Open M-Sa 9am-10 pm, Su 9am-3pm.

Post Office: (☎ 856 26 23) on the Calle 40 side of the *zócalo*. Open M-F 8am-3pm.

Postal Code: 97780.

◪ ACCOMMODATIONS

Penny-pinchers will want to stay away from the pricey hotels bordering the *zócalo*. Better bargains can be found one block west, especially on Calle 44.

◪ **Albergue La Candelaria Youth Hostel (HI)** (☎ 856 22 67), in Parque La Candelaria on the corner of Calles 35 and 44. A brand new hostel with a homely, laid-back atmosphere that features laundry areas, full kitchen, lunch patio, internet access (15 pesos per hr.), bike rentals (5 pesos per hr.), and free lockers. Bring mosquito netting or bug repellent. Bunk beds 65 pesos.

 Hotel Zací, Calle 44 #191 (☎856 21 67), between Calles 37 and 39, is a vacation from your vacation. Complete with restaurant, fountain, and glittering pool. Colonial rooms have blue curtains, carved dressers, and cable TV. Singles 188 pesos; doubles 246 pesos; triples 281 pesos. A/C 60-70 pesos extra.

 Hotel María Guadalupe, Calle 44 #198 (☎856 20 68), between Calles 39 and 41. Single rooms with clean bathrooms, colorful beds, ceiling fans, and dark wood furniture. Call in advance. Singles 110 pesos; doubles 130 pesos; triples 150 pesos.

 Hotel Mendoza, Calle 39 #204 (☎856 20 02), 1½ blocks west of the *zócalo*. A cheap, clean, satisfying option, as long as you don't mind the shared bath. Singles 50 pesos, with bath 80 pesos; doubles 70 pesos, with bath 100 pesos, with A/C, TV, and fridge 180 pesos; triples with bath 120 pesos.

 Hotel Lily, Calle 44 #192 (☎856 21 63), between Calles 37 and 39, across from Hotel Zací. 2 options available, both good values. Hotel-like accommodations with shared bathrooms and hammock holes: singles and doubles 90 pesos. Or nice rooms with private bathrooms: singles 110 pesos; doubles 140 pesos.

📇 FOOD

Comida yucateca, which blends European and Mexican flavors, tops every menu. Try *poc-chuc* (tender slices of pork marinated in a Yucatec sauce, covered with pickled onions), *panuchos* (tortillas filled with beans and topped with either chicken or pork, lettuce, tomato, and hot sauce), or *escabeche oriental de pavo* (a hearty turkey soup). *Xtabentun* is a delectable liquor of anise and honey.

 Restaurante Cenote Zací (☎856 21 07), on Calle 36 between Calles 37 and 39. Large and spacious restaurant underneath a giant *palapa*, surrounded by jungle trees, atop a *cenote*. Excellent *comida yucateca* (entrees 40-50 pesos) and liquor selection, including *xtabentum* (8 pesos). Sandwiches 18-24 pesos. Open daily 9am-6pm.

 Menyul (☎856 16 66), at the southeast corner of the *zócalo* across from the Casa de la Cultura. Traditional Mexican ambience, colorful murals, and a view of the *zócalo* complement a variety of Yucatec specialties (30-39 pesos) and *comida típica* (25-65 pesos). Breakfast specials 28-40 pesos. Open daily 9am-10pm.

 Bazar Municipal, Calle 39 at 40, right off the *zócalo*, is a narrow courtyard crowded with cafes serving *comida típica*, pizzerias, and juice bars. Prepare to be bombarded. Breakfast 15-20 pesos, *comida* 30-45 pesos. Hours vary by restaurant, but they are generally open daily 6am-midnight.

 Pollos Silvia Cocina (☎856 24 57), on Calle 46 between Calles 35 and 37. Small, outdoor *cocina económica* serves tasty, cheap food. *Salbute* (fried tortilla with *frijoles*, chicken, lettuce, cheese and cream) 3 pesos, 4 burritos 12 pesos, lunch specials and other dishes 20-25 pesos. Open daily 7am-3pm and 5-11pm.

 Restaurante María de la Luz (☎856 20 71), on the west side of the *zócalo*, in the Hotel María de la Luz. Eat *comida corrida* (35 pesos) in atypical surroundings as you observe the *zócalo* through breezy French bay doors. Open daily 6am-10pm.

 Restaurante del Parque, Calle 42 #199 (☎856 23 65), on the southwest corner of the *zócalo*. Situate yourself right and get an eyeful of the Franciscan Cathedral. *Comida yucateca* with sprinklings of US grub starts at 30 pesos. Open daily 7:30am-10pm.

🎯 SIGHTS

While most visitors take the next bus to Mérida or Chichén Itzá, those seeking a healthy dose of *cenotes* and cathedrals have come to the right place. The natural Yucatec jungle makes a steamy backdrop that blends seamlessly into the colonial city, creating a mix of natural and man-made beauty.

CENOTE ZACÍ. In the middle of the city, Cenote Zací (pronounced sah-KEY) is a cavernous hollow full of plunging stalactites and daredevil divers doing their best to imitate their Acapulco counterparts. *(3 blocks east of the zócalo, on Calle 36 between Calles 37 and 39. Open daily 8am-7:30pm. 10 pesos, children 5 pesos. Free view from the palapa restaurant on the edge.)*

SAN BERNARDINO DE SIENA. Affiliated with the **Ex-Convento de Sisal,** the church was built over a *cenote* in 1552 with stones from the main Maya temple. It is the oldest ecclesiastical building in the Yucatán. A large image of the Virgin of Guadalupe hangs on the altar at the rear of the church. *(On Calle 41A, 4 blocks southwest of Las Cinco Calles. Open W-M 8am-noon. 5 pesos.)*

CATEDRAL DE SAN GERVASIO. According to legend, two criminals who took refuge in the church were discovered and murdered by an angry mob. When the bishop learned of the mob's actions, he had the church destroyed. It was rebuilt in 1720-1730 facing north instead of east, the only church in all of Yucatán to be situated in this way. The massive colonial twin towers make this an unmistakable landmark. *(Over the zócalo on Calle 41. Open daily 9am-1pm and 5-8pm. Free.)*

EL PASEO DE LOS FRAILES (THE STREET OF THE FRIARS). This picturesque, colonial street provides the perfect setting for a stroll. Many residents leave their doors open, and you can catch peeks of interiors and courtyards—just don't be too nosy. *(Calle 41A between Las Cinco Calles and San Bernardino.)*

MUSEO DE SAN ROQUE. A relatively new addition to Valladolid's cultural scene, the museum features exhibits on the history of Valladolid and the surrounding area, with an emphasis on the civilization and culture of the Pre-Hispanic Maya. The courtyard makes for a good place to relax and admire sculptures. *(On the northwest corner of Calles 41 and 38. ☎856 25 51. Open daily 9am-9pm. Donation suggested.)*

🎵🎭 ENTERTAINMENT AND NIGHTLIFE

Valladolid is a small, quiet city that offers a small, quiet nightlife scene. Look to the *zócalo*, beautifully illuminated in the night, for strolling families, Maya vendors, friendly beggars, lively political oratory, guitar-strumming teens, and traditional dance shows on weekends at the **Casa de la Cultura** (on the *zócalo;* free). For later in the night, **Vaía Ral,** a new Cancun-style disco and the biggest in the Yucatán state, has recently opened a few blocks northwest of the ADO bus station (near the fairgrounds). There, all the area's youth get it on hard, dancing and romancing deep into the night. (Open F-Su 10pm-late. 80 pesos.)

🔲 DAYTRIPS FROM VALLADOLID

▨ CENOTE DZITNUP (X'KEKÉN)

6km west of town. To get there by car or bike, take Calle 39 to the highway toward Mérida. Make a left at the sign for Dzitnup and continue to the entrance plaza on your left (20min.). Without wheels, catch a colectivo (5 pesos) in the morning in front of the Hotel María Guadalupe. Open daily 7am-6pm. 12 pesos, children free.

The beautiful *cenote* with its refreshingly cold water is mostly underground. Visit before midday, when a beam of light slices through a circular hole in the roof and bathes the cavern in blue. Bring a towel, some warm clothes, and a swimsuit. Cenote Samila (10 pesos) is only 200m away.

EK' BALAM

The ruins are 25km northeast of Valladolid and accessible only by car, taxi, or organized tour buses. Taxis run about 200-225 pesos round-trip; the driver will wait up to 2hr. Open daily 8am-5pm. 22 pesos; holidays and Su free.

Ek' Balam ("Black Jaguar") was a Maya city that flourished in the late Classical period, around AD 700-1000. The site was discovered only 30 or so years ago. It contains several temples, a somewhat rare circular observatory, a ball court, a stone sacrificial table upon which the victorious ball team was beheaded, and a magnificent pyramid, all organized around a main plaza. The pyramid itself is one of the most massive in the Yucatan; it's not quite as tall as other Maya pyramids (35m), but its base is an astonishing 170m long. The unearthing of Ek' Balam is a work in progress. Note the two giant unexcavated mounds flanking the pyramid—archaeologists believe they hide even more intriguing structures including pyramids reaching 20-25m in height. The generally uncrowded ruins are being reconstructed and definitely merit a visit—if you can handle the hefty taxi fare.

TIZIMÍN ☎9

Faithful tourists flock to Tizimín (pop. 80,000) to take part in the many religious processions that culminate at the town's ambitiously restored colonial church and convent. The area's Maya congregate in the nearby village of Kikil to practice ancient religious ceremonies, and tourists from around the world take advantage of Tizimín's prime location to explore the eastern part of Yucatán state. Both colonial Valladolid and the nature reserves of San Felipe and Río Lagartos lie within an hour's drive on Mex. 295. The archaeological sites of Ek' Balam and Kulubá are also not far away. While Tizimín's mornings are big-city busy, things quiet down to small-town proportion in the sultry afternoons, and in the evenings, a cacophonous chorus of birdsongs around the carefully manicured Parque Principal seems to be the only thing stirring the warm air.

◪ **TRANSPORTATION.** Tizimín is located in the heart of eastern Yucatán, 55km north of Valladolid and 65km south of the Gulf Coast. Its **bus station** is on the northwest corner of Calles 46 and 47. Oriente travels to **Valladolid** (1 hr, 9 per day, 18 pesos); **Mérida** (3 hr., 5 and 8am, 66 pesos); **Izamal** (2½ hrs; 5:15, 11:20am, and 3:30pm; 47 pesos). Mayab goes to **Cancún** (3 hr., 8 per day, 66 pesos); **Playa del Carmen** (8:30am, 89 pesos). Noreste goes to **Río Lagartos** (45 min.; midnight, 10am, and 7:30pm; 17 pesos).

◪◪ **ORIENTATION AND PRACTICAL INFORMATION.** Tizimín's even-numbered streets run north-south, increasing to the west. Odd-numbered streets run east-west, increasing to the south. The city centers around the Parque Principal which is framed by Calles 50, 51, 52, and 53. To get to the Parque Principal from the bus station, walk two blocks west and two blocks south. **Currency exchange: Bancomer,** on the corner of Calles 48 and 51, exchanges currency and has a 24hr. **ATM.** (☎863 23 81. Open M-F 8:30am-4pm.) **Lavandería de los Tres Reyes** is three blocks south of the Parque Principal on Calle 57 between Calles 52 and 54. (☎863 38 83. 7 pesos per kg. Open daily 8am-1:30pm and 5-7:30pm.) **Police:** (☎863 20 13) in the Palacio Municipal on the corner of Calles 51 and 52. **Farmacia YZA,** on the corner of Calles 51 and 52. (☎863 44 62. Open 24hr.) **Hospital General San Carlos,** Calle 46 #461 (☎863 21 57). **Internet Access: Instituto de Computación,** on Calles 50 and 52. (10 pesos per hr. Open daily 8am-10pm.) **Post office:** Calle 53, south of the church. (☎863 32 10. Open M-F 8:30am-3pm.) **Postal code:** 97700.

◪◪ **ACCOMMODATIONS AND FOOD.** In Tizimín, going budget might be your only option, but watch out for big price increases in July and August. The rooms at **Posada Marian,** on Calle 51 between Calles 48 and 50, are large and slightly rundown, but most have remodeled bathrooms and cable TVs. (☎863 30 66. Singles and doubles 100 pesos, with A/C 130 pesos; each additional person 15 pesos.) Find nicer, bigger rooms at **Hotel San Jorge,** Calle 55 #412, on the southwest corner of the Parque Principal. (☎863 20 37. Singles 130 pesos; doubles 150 pesos; A/C 30 pesos extra.) **Posada María Antonia,** Calle 50 #408, sits directly behind the statue of a woman on the south side of the church. The small, clean rooms all have two beds, a TV, and A/C. (☎863 28 57. Singles and doubles 160 pesos.) **Hotel San Carlos,** Calle 54 #407, between Calles 51 and 53, is the farthest from the *zócalo*, but the most comfortable, with spotless rooms, private baths, and an inviting garden. (☎863 20 94. Singles 150 pesos; doubles 160 pesos; A/C 25 pesos extra.)

Dining options in Tizimín are limited, no matter what your budget. Booths selling tacos and tortas at the *mercado*, on the southwest corner of Calles 47 and 48, and scattered *loncherías* serve the city's cheapest food. The town's favorite is **Restaurant Tres Reyes**, which advertises "La Mejor Comida del mundo," and is owned by the lively and friendly Willy Canto. Delicious meals (45-75 pesos) are accompanied by a stack of tortillas. (☎863 21 06. Open daily 7:30am-midnight.)

◙ ♫ SIGHTS AND ENTERTAINMENT. Much work has recently been done to renovate the colonial structures that dominate Tizimín's center. On the east side of the Parque Principal stands the majestic **Iglesia de Los Tres Reyes,** still the city's main church. On the corner of Calles 48 and 51, the massive fortress-like **Ex-Convento de Franciscanos,** completed in 1599, perpetually reminds one of the city's great age. Those curious about Tizimín can find out anything they want to from one man—**Julio Caesar,** a fountain of information about the region's Maya ruins. Having himself written the first extensive documentation of the site of Kulubá, Caesar is eager to point tourists in its direction. Try finding him at his photography studio on Calle 50 #39A near Calle 49. (☎861 24 46. Studio open daily 8am-9pm.)

Tizimín's main attractions are two relatively underrated historical sights outside the town proper, **Ek' Balam** (see p. 600) and **Kulubá.** The ruins at Kulubá, 33km east of town, are being reconstructed and will not open to the public until early summer 2002. However, talk to Julio Caesar and he can help you get access to the site. Dating from the late Classic period (AD 800-1000), Kulubá represents the easternmost point of Puuc architectural influence. The *Edificio de Las Ues*, a structure 40m long, 8m high, and 7m wide, is carved with "U"s all along its facade. The original red stucco paint is still visible on the carved portions of the stone. The second partially restored building features two surprisingly well-preserved pairs of masks of the rain god Chac and other carved ornamentation.

The tiny town of **Kikil** (pop. 5000), 5km north of Tizimín, is home to the remains of the first colonial church in the area and the fresh waters of *Nohock Dzonot de Kikil*, a crystal clear *cenote*. To get there, take a taxi (85 pesos round-trip with wait) or to save pesos, get dropped off by a Río Lagartos-bound buses. Known to locals as **La Iglesia Kikil,** the church is just to the right of the highway as you enter Kikil from Tizimín. The church burned in the mid-19th century during the Caste War. Legend has it that years ago, residents threw a stone at a passing Catholic priest, who then predicted that the church would be laid to ruin. Just inside the gate of the small courtyard, to the left as you face the church, stands a carved stone baptismal font that rings like a bell when struck. Many Maya live in Kikil and you will not only find their language, but also many of their customs and rituals alive and well. To return to Tizimín, catch one of the southbound buses which pass only about every two hours.

The most important of the town's religious processions is the **Festival of the Three Kings** (Dec. 30-Jan. 12), when over one million pilgrims pour into Tizimín from surrounding towns and the countryside. While the parades, dancing, bullfights, and banquets of *comida típica* last for two weeks, the most important day of the festival is January 6, when the pilgrims file through the church to touch the patrons with palm branches. In May and June, visitors to Kikil can enjoy traditional Maya ceremonies such as the **Kaash Paach Bi,** a spiritual cleansing for the land, and the **Chaa-Chac,** a rain prayer. During January and June, Kikil participates in a **pig head dance ritual,** praising and giving thanks to Tsimin, a Maya deity.

RÍO LAGARTOS   ☎ 9

Known affectionately as *"La Ría,"* this 53km inlet of ocean water is much the same today as when Hernán Cortés mistook it for a river. Now a 60,000-hectare wild animal refuge, Río Lagartos National Park is home to a rare mangrove forest, over 300 different bird species, crocodiles, and 30,000 long-legged orange-red flamingos. The head of this inlet is commanded by the quiet village of Río Lagartos (pop. 3500), which is steadily adapting to its role as an ecotourist hotspot.

⊏⊐ TRANSPORTATION AND PRACTICAL INFORMATION. Perched on a tiny peninsula, standing guard over the entrance to *La Ría*, Río Lagartos lies on the northern shore of the eastern Yucatán, 65km north of Tizimín. Streets are numbered but change names frequently and point in every possible direction. Calle 10 is the town's main street and runs to the waterfront. A good reference point is the fountain at the southern edge of the main park. One block east of the fountain is the **bus station.** Noreste offers service to **Tizimín** (10 per day, last one at 5:30pm; 18 pesos) and **Mérida** (4 per day, 85 pesos). **Tourist information:** at the Restaurante Isla Contoy (below). **Police station:** (☎862 00 02), just south of the basketball court, 2 blocks north of the fountain. **Centro de Salud:** (862 00 33), on Calle 17 off Calle 10. (Open M-Sa 8am-noon and 3-7pm.) Río Lagartos lacks most other services.

⊓⊔ ACCOMMODATIONS AND FOOD. The clean, repainted rooms of **Posada Leyli** on Calle 14 at Calle 11 offer of the island's best values. (☎862 01 06. Singles without bath 120 pesos; doubles with bath 200 pesos. Prices rise 20-30 pesos in July and August.) **Posada Lucy,** on the northern waterfront (☎862 01 30), with its five brand new rooms with private bath, also provides a good value with singles and doubles at 200 pesos year-round. The colorful cabañas at **Restaurante Isla Contoy** provide simple, rustic lodgings of one bed, two hammock hooks, a fan, and private bath. (☎862 00 00. Cabañas 120 pesos, 150 pesos in July and August.) **Cabañas los Dos Hermanos,** two blocks east of the fountain on Calle 10, offers a variety of clean rooms with baths and fans that are not particularly nice, but will do for a night's stay. (☎862 01 28. Singles and doubles 150-250 pesos, depending on size.) **Restaurante Isla Contoy,** Calle 19 #134, west of the fountain (follow the signs), cooks seafood on the shore (tasty *filet a la veracruzana*, 45 pesos) and provides tourist information and boat tours. (☎862 00 00. Open daily 7am-10pm.) Relatively cheap seafood is served in a festive ambience at **Los Negritos** (☎862 00 22), on Calle 10 # 133, a little south of the flamingo fountain. Most dishes cost 35-45 pesos. To reach **Las Gaviotas,** walk north from the fountain until you reach the water, then turn left. Relax on the waterfront while enjoying *ceviche* and *sopa de mariscos*. (☎862 01 30. Open daily 10am-6pm.)

⊡♫ SIGHTS AND ENTERTAINMENT. The town's main attraction is the multitude of flamingos, one of the largest concentrations in the Western Hemisphere, that live in nearby **Ríó Lagartos National Park.** To see them, you must hire a boat captain. On the fascinating 2½hr. boat tour through mangrove forests and brackish swamps, you will encounter jumping fish, a crocodile or two, a host of extremely rare birds, and an amazing vista of hundreds, or perhaps thousands, of orange-red flamingos. The tour usually ends with a visit to the freshwater **Chiquilá cenote** where you can take a refreshing dip. The best time to see the flamingos is around 6:30am or near sunset when there are fewer boats in the water. To ensure a safe and ecologically responsible trip through this fragile wildlife reserve, make sure to choose a tour guide who is certified by the national park. To find one, visit the kiosk at the northern waterfront to arrange for a tour or head to the professional English-speaking folks at **Isla Contoy Tours,** Calle 19 #134, located in the restaurant. (☎862 00 00; diego2902@yahoo.com. 250 pesos and up.) **Union de Lancheros** (☎862 00 42), also offers flamingo tours (350 for 4 people per 2½hr.) as well as fishing trips (100 pesos per hr.). If you didn't see many crocodiles in the lagoon during the day, you might want to head out again in the evening when, with a flashlight, they'll be more visible. Isla Contoy Tours will take you for 500 pesos. With most people busy flamingo-watching and fishing during the day, the streets of Río Lagartos are perpetually quiet and empty. The one exception is the town **Fiesta,** which runs from the second Saturday in July to the end of the month, in honor of Santiago Aposto, the younger brother of Spain's patron saint.

QUINTANA ROO

CANCÚN ☎ 9

Perfectly situated on the sparkling Caribbean coast, the once modest city of Cancún (pop. 500,000) has erupted into a metropolis whose alcohol-soaked, disco-shaken, sex-stirred insanity surpasses any other in the Western Hemisphere. Ask any university student who's "done" Spring Break Cancún and their eyes will inevitably glass over while their heads shake in lingering disbelief as they recall night after night of drunken debauchery. Fear not, young party animal—this fishing village gone party town does not disappoint. However, budget travelers who seek culture and relaxation in Cancún will have to work a little harder and trek a little farther. Cancún's location serves as a great jump-off point for many budget-friendly excursions up and down the Turquoise Coast, to spots such as the nature preserves at Río Lagartos and Xel-Ha and the Maya ruins at Chichén Itzá and Tulum. Within Cancún proper, the party could leave you penniless. But who—except your liver and your peeling skin—would say no to the chance to get burned, hammered, and nailed again, and again, and again?

▛ TRANSPORTATION

GETTING AROUND

Getting around Cancún is a snap, as the city's public buses shuttle sunburned beachcombers to and fro with ease. Taxis operate within the Zona Hotelera (40 pesos), within downtown (20 pesos), and between the two (as much as 150 pesos). **Buses** marked "Hoteles" run between the bus station downtown and the Zona's tip at Punta Nizuc around the clock (5 pesos) and can be caught at any blue sign along Tulum and Kukulcán; alternatively, you can stick out your hand and wave like a madman when you see one passing by. To get off the bus in the Zona Hotelera, push one of the little square red buttons on the ceiling when in sight of your stop—if you don't know where you need to get off, mention the name to the bus driver, with a *por favor*. While many places rent **mopeds** (useful for exploring the 18km of beaches from the CREA hostel to Punta Nizuc), buses are much cheaper and nearly as convenient.

GETTING AWAY

Airport: (☎886 00 28). South of the city on Mex. 307. To reach either the downtown area or the Zona Hotelera, buy a ticket for the shuttle van **TTC** (75 pesos). **Taxis** will charge 150 pesos. Airlines include: **Aerocaribe** (☎884 20 00); **American** (☎883 44 60); **Continental** (☎886 00 06); **LACSA** (☎887 31 01); **Mexicana** (☎887 44 44); **Northwest** (☎886 00 46); **United** (☎886 00 25); **Lan Chile** (☎886 03 60); and **Martinair** (☎886 00 70).

Buses: (☎884 13 78). The bus station is downtown on the corner of Uxmal and Tulum, facing Plaza Caribe. Public buses are outside. ADO goes to: **Campeche** (6hr., 11:30am and 10:30pm, 170 pesos); **Valladolid** (2hr.; 11am, 1pm, and 10:30pm; 55 pesos); **Palenque** (14hr., 3:45 and 5:45pm, 325 pesos). Premier goes to: **Chichén Itzá** (2½hr., 9am, 50 pesos); **Playa del Carmen** (1 hr., every 15min., 20 pesos); **Chiquilá** (3hr., 6 per day, 45 pesos). 2nd-class buses leave from the curb, and go to **Mérida**, **Tulum**, and **Chetumal.**

Ferries: To get to **Isla Mujeres**, take a bus marked "Pto. Juárez" to the 2 ferry depots north of town (Punta Sam for car ferries, Puerto Juárez for passenger ferries, 15min.). Express service (20min., every 30min. 6am-9pm, 35 pesos) and regular service (45min., every 2hr. 8am-6pm, 18 pesos).

YUCATÁN

✦ 🏋 ORIENTATION AND PRACTICAL INFORMATION

Perched on the northeastern tip of the Yucatán Peninsula, Cancún lies 285km east of Mérida via Mex. 180 and 382km north of Chetumal and the Belizean border via Mex. 307. Cancún is divided into two areas: downtown Cancún, the *centro*, where you'll find more bargains but no beaches, and Isla Cancún, or the **Zona Hotelera**, with fewer bargains but oh-so-much beach and glam. The Zona is a slender "7"-shaped strip of land, and addresses along its one main road are given by kilometer number. Kilometer numbers increase from 1 to 20, roughly north to south.

TOURIST AND FINANCIAL SERVICES

Tourist Offices: Tulum 5 (☎887 43 29, ext. 114; relacionespublicas@cancun.gob.mx), inside the Ayuntamiento Benito Juárez. Open M-F 9am-3pm and 6-8pm. Another tourist office at the corner of Náder and Cobá (☎884 65 31) offers similar paraphernalia and help. Open daily 9am-8pm. Ask for **Cancún Tips**, a free English-language magazine full of useful information and maps. Also available at the airport and at Plaza Caracol.

State Secretary of Tourism: Pecari 23, S.M. 20 (☎881 90 00). Open M-F 9am-5pm.

Consulates: Canada, Plaza Caracol, 3rd fl. (☎883 33 60 or 883 33 61; fax 883 32 32), at km 8.5. Open M-F 9am-5pm. **UK**, in Royal Sands Hotel (☎881 01 00). Open M-F 9am-3:30pm. **US**, Plaza Caracol, 3rd fl. (☎883 02 72), at km 8.5. Open M-F 9am-1pm.

Currency Exchange: Bancomer, Tulum 20 (☎884 44 00) at Calle Claveles. Open M-F 9am-4:30pm, Sa 10am-2pm. **Banamex**, Tulum 19 (☎881 64 02) gives cash advances and has **ATMs**. Open M-F 9am-5pm, Sa 9:30am-2pm.

American Express: Tulum 208 (☎884 19 99), 3 blocks south of Cobá. Open M-F 9am-6pm, Sa 9am-1pm. In the Zona Hotelera an American Express (☎885 39 03) can be found on the 1st floor of Plaza Kukulcán at km 13. Open daily 10am-5pm.

LOCAL SERVICES

Luggage Storage: At the bus station. 4 pesos per hr.

English Bookstore: Fama, Tulum 105 (☎884 65 41), between Claveles and Tulipanes. Newspapers, magazines, guidebooks, and more. Open daily 9am-10pm.

Supermarket: Comercial Mexicana (☎880 91 64), across from the bus station on Tulum. Open daily 7am-midnight. Smaller but more centrally located is **Super San Francisco** (☎884 11 55), on Tulum next to Banamex. Open M-Sa 7am-10pm, Su 7am-9pm.

Laundry: Lavandería "Alborada," Náder 5 (☎884 15 84), behind the Ayuntamiento Benito Juárez. Self service 10 pesos. Open M-Sa 9am-8pm. **Tintorería Lavandería** (☎884 26 69) has dry cleaning. Open M-F 9am-8pm and Sa 9am-5:30pm.

Car rental: Rental options are everywhere in Cancún: along the Zona Hotelera, in the *centro*, and at the airport (look for the booths on your right as you exit customs). Prices range from US$40-55 for a car without A/C and US$50-80 per day with A/C. However, special promotions can push rental prices down to as low as US$25 per day. Most rental options offer free pick-up at your hotel. **Alamo**, at km 9.5 (☎886 01 68), has prices starting at US$43 per day. **Avicar**, Tulum 3 (☎886 02 21), has lots of locations with air-conditioned cars including insurance starting at US$53 per day.

Moped Rental: Look for vendors between Hotel Aquamarine and Hotel Costa Real. 100 pesos per hr., 500 pesos per day. **Bicycles** and **in-line skates** also for rent. 70 pesos per hr., 160 pesos per day.

EMERGENCY AND COMMUNICATIONS

Emergency:☎060.

Police:☎885 22 67.

Red Cross: Yaxchilán 2 (☎884 16 16). English spoken.

Pharmacies: Several along Tulum and Yaxchilán. **Farmacia Paris,** Yaxchilán 32 (☎884 30 05), at the intersection with Rosas. Open 24hr.

Medical Assistance: Hospital Americano, Viento 15 (☎884 61 33, after hours 884 63 19), 5 blocks south on Tulum after its intersection with Cobá. For an **ambulance,** call **Total Assist** (☎884 80 82), at Claveles 5 near Tulum. English spoken.

Fax: (☎884 15 29) next to the post office. Open M-F 8am-6pm, Sa 9am-1pm. Telegram service and Internet also available.

Internet Access: Internet cafes are springing up everywhere in the *centro*. Those listed charge 5 pesos per 15 min., 8-10 pesos per 30 min., and 15 pesos per hr. **Travel Internet,** Uxmal 19 (☎884 12 50). Open daily 9am-9pm. The office of **Moka's Cafe,** Uxmal 19 (☎892 38 54). Open daily 9am-midnight. **Internet Business Center,** Crisantemos 1 (☎ 887 04 84). Open daily 9am-9pm. **Silvernet Internet Cafe,** Sunyaxchén 49 (☎850

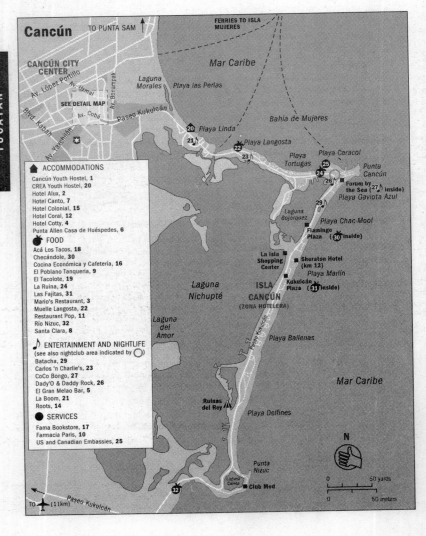

Cancún

TO PUNTA SAM

FERRIES TO ISLA MUJERES

Mar Caribe

CANCÚN CITY CENTER

Av. López Portillo
Av. Uxmal
Blvd. Kabah
Av. Cobá
Av. Yaxchilán
Av. Bonampak
Paseo Kukulcán

SEE DETAIL MAP

Laguna Morales
Playa las Perlas

Bahia de Mujeres

20 Playa Linda
21
22 Playa Langosta
23
Playa Tortugas
Playa Caracol
25 Punta Cancún
24
26
Forum by the Sea (27 inside)
Playa Gaviota Azul
29
Laguna Bojórquez
Playa Chac-Mool
Flamingo Plaza (30 inside)

La Isla Shopping Center
Sheraton Hotel (km 12)
Playa Marlin
Kukulcán Plaza (31 inside)

Laguna Nichupté

ISLA CANCÚN (ZONA HOTELERA)

Laguna del Amor

Playa Ballenas

Mar Caribe

Ruinas del Rey
Playa Delfines

N

Punta Nizuc

32
Club Med

Playa Kukulcán

TO ✈ (11km)
Paseo Kukulcán

Laguna Caleta

0   50 yards
0   50 meters

♠ ACCOMMODATIONS
Cancún Youth Hostel, 1
CREA Youth Hostel, 20
Hotel Alux, 2
Hotel Canto, 7
Hotel Colonial, 15
Hotel Coral, 12
Hotel Cotty, 4
Punta Allen Casa de Huéspedes, 6

🍅 FOOD
Acá Los Tacos, 18
Checándole, 30
Cocina Económica y Cafetería, 16
El Poblano Tanqueria, 9
El Tacolote, 19
La Ruina, 24
Las Fajitas, 31
Mario's Restaurant, 3
Muelle Langosta, 22
Restaurant Pop, 11
Río Nizuc, 32
Santa Clara, 8

♪ ENTERTAINMENT AND NIGHTLIFE
(see also nightclub area indicated by ◯)
Batacha, 29
Carlos 'n Charlie's, 23
CoCo Bongo, 27
Dady'O & Daddy Rock, 26
El Gran Melao Bar, 5
La Boom, 21
Roots, 14

● SERVICES
Fama Bookstore, 17
Farmacia Paris, 10
US and Canadian Embassies, 25

YUCATÁN

36 16). Open M-Sa 9am-9pm. **La Taberna,** Yaxchilán 23 (☎887 73 00) is also a sports bar and cafe. Open daily 10am-5am.

Post Office: (☎884 14 18), Xel-Ha at Sunyaxchén. From Tulum, cut through any street to Yaxchilán and go 4 blocks up Sunyaxchén. Open M-F 8am-6pm, Sa-Su 9am-12:30pm.

Postal Code: 77500.

ACCOMMODATIONS AND CAMPING

Trying to find cheap accommodations in Cancún is not for the faint of heart. The closest budget travelers will stay to the Zona Hotelera is the **CREA Youth Hostel,** located at the far end of the Paseo Kukulcán. All other budget options are located downtown; the new youth hostel four blocks west of the bus station is the cheapest. Hotels are scattered throughout the *centro,* but many cluster around Uxmal and Yaxchilán, and at about 250 pesos per person during the off season (spring and fall), are still far from budget. Keep in mind that prices generally rise during the summer and winter by 25%. As Cancún is regularly swamped by tourists, reservations are a good idea any time of the year.

Cancún Youth Hostel (HI), Palmera 30 (☎ 887 01 91). 4 blocks west of the bus station, off of Uxmal. This new, sparsely populated, multilevel hostel is friendly, well-equipped with full kitchens, private lockers, hot showers, and Internet (10 pesos per hour). Sleep indoors or under a *palapa* on the roof. There's no A/C, but powerful fans keep the 50 bunk beds well-ventilated. If you're alone this is the best value in Cancún at 100 pesos a night. Bring ear plugs to ensure a good night's rest.

YUCATÁN

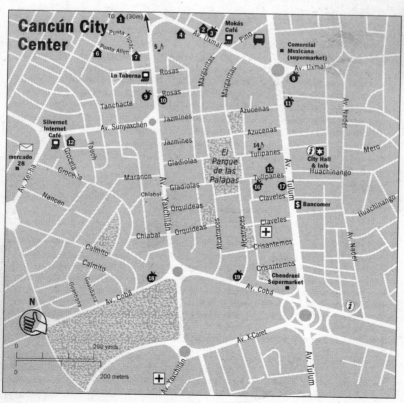

Cancún City Center

Suites Albatros, Yaxchilán 154 (☎884 22 42), 2 blocks south of Cobá and across the street from the Red Cross. It's easy to forgive the extra effort it takes to get here after walking through the shady courtyard into one of the apartment-like rooms. Full kitchens, A/C, and large beds and closets. Each room upstairs has a balcony with laundry lines and sink. Make reservations at least 3 days in advance. With doubles for 300 pesos, this is one of the best values in Cancún.

CREA Youth Hostel (HI), Kukulcán at km 3 (☎849 43 60). For those who plan to beach or club it, CREA is the cheapest place in the Zona Hotelera. Catch any "Hotelera" bus and ask to be let off at "CREA," where Mexican students on vacation will be your main company. 200 single-sex dorm rooms with 8 bunk beds apiece and personal lockers (bring your own locks). Sheets and pillows provided. Communal showers with no hot water. Beach volleyball, soccer field, ping-pong, and a small *cantina* in the lobby. 15-night max. stay. No curfew. Bunks with no A/C 100 pesos; cabins with A/C 400 pesos; pitch a tent on the back lawn for 50 pesos per person. Light breakfast 20 pesos.

Hotel Alux, Uxmal 21 (☎884 66 13), 1 block west of the bus station on the north side of the street. The pink facade covers a well-maintained establishment, with A/C, TV, hot water, and phones in the rooms (3 pesos per local call). Request a room away from the noisy street. One of the best values downtown. Singles 255 pesos; doubles 285 pesos.

Hotel Colonial, Tulipanes 22 (☎ 884 15 35), off of Tulum. 50 well-kept rooms with TV and hot water face a courtyard. Though somewhat pricey for the area, the Colonial's great location in the *centro* makes it a favorite among vacationing Mexicans. Doubles 400 pesos, with A/C 450 pesos.

Punta Allen Casa Huéspedes, Punta Allen 8 (☎884 10 01). Walk south from the intersection between Uxmal and Yaxchilán and turn right after 1 block. The hotel will be ahead on the left. Interior jungle theme decor and expansive lounge area plus hot water, *agua purificada*, A/C, TV, and free continental breakfast. Doubles 280 pesos, nicer and more spacious doubles with balcony 320 pesos.

Hotel Coral, Sunyaxchén 30 (☎884 20 97). Heading west from Yaxchilán, the hotel is 3 blocks down on the left; look for the red and white building with a garden inside. Supercharged fans make up for the sparse furnishings. The attentive staff keeps the bathrooms clean and the *agua purificada* cold. Doubles 200 pesos, with A/C 300 pesos.

Hotel Canto (☎884 12 67), on Yaxchilán. As you turn off Uxmal onto Yaxchilán, look for the faded pink building, 2 blocks down on your right. Besides A/C, TV, and hot water, the only benefit Hotel Canto offers is its downtown location. Doubles 250 pesos.

Hotel Cotty, Uxmal 44 (☎884 05 50). Simple but clean rooms with A/C, cable TV, and hot water recall an American motel. On top of the hotel is the Aries Disco Club. Light breakfast included. Singles 270 pesos; doubles 338 pesos.

Hotel María Isabel, Palmera 59 (☎884 90 15), 3 blocks west of the bus station. Although sparse, the 12 blue and yellow rooms are clean and peaceful. A/C, TV, and hot water. Singles 250 pesos; doubles 270 pesos.

⬛ FOOD

Although hard to find, a surprising number of affordable places in the resort-heavy Zona Hotelera serve tasty, authentic cuisine. Still, dining tends to be cheaper and of better quality in the *centro*. The bacteria-shy should avoid the many street vendors who follow few (if any) health codes. For some of the cheapest meals around, head to **Mercado 28** behind the post office and circumscribed by Xel-Ha, but make sure to eat only from the more sanitary stands. Otherwise, many restaurants between Tulum and Yaxchilán and in the center of *El Parque de las Palapas* serve authentic and relatively budget-friendly meals priced from 25-65 pesos.

El Tacolote, Cobá 19 (☎887 30 45), 2 blocks east of Yaxchilán toward the Zona Hotelera. Look for the sombrero-sporting yellow chicken out front. A wide menu of seafood available, but delicious tacos (14-44 pesos) and *quesadillas* (15-20 pesos) are great deals. Mention *Let's Go* for a complimentary drink with dinner. Open daily 1pm-1am.

Cocina Económica y Cafetería, Tulipanes 23 (☎884 13 39), near *El Parque de las Palapas*. Serves up salads, sandwiches (15-22 pesos), fresh juices, milkshakes, breakfast combos (25-55 pesos), and dinner specials (30-70 pesos). Open daily 7am-11pm.

El Tapatio (☎887 83 17), at the corner of Uxmal and Palmera. Cafe-style restaurant/bar offers variety of *comida típica*. Satiate your appetite with the *muy rico* Jalisco-style *pozole* (38-65 pesos) and a fruit smoothie (21-26 pesos). Open daily 8am-midnight.

Restaurante Río Nizuc, Paseo Kukulcán at km 22. Get on the "Hoteles" bus (4 pesos) and ask to be let off here. Look for the sign and be rewarded with shady *palapas* and a view of the river. Dip your feet while the cook prepares sizable servings of *tikin xic* (fresh barbecued fish; 60 pesos). Seafood entrees 60-70 pesos. A perfect place to escape Cancún chaos while still enjoying the tropical splendor. Open daily 11am-6pm.

Muelle Langosta, at km 5 (☎849 47 27). Good food near Playa Langosta. Fried fish and *tikin xic* are yummy at 55 pesos each. All-you-can-eat breakfast served 7:30am-noon (35 pesos). Open daily 7am-11pm.

Checándole, at km 11.5 in the Plaza Flamingo food court (☎885 13 02). Dishes out authentic Mexican and Yucatec food; the *tampiqueña* (a huge strip of steak served with beans and guacamole; 72 pesos) is a favorite. Tacos (26-52 pesos) and burritos (30 pesos) are tasty and inexpensive. Open daily noon-10pm.

La Ruina, at km 9 near Playa Terramar (☎883 38 48). This darkly-lit restaurant/bar blaring classic rock opens early and closes late, serving *fajitas*, burritos, and *quesadillas* (65 pesos each) that will bring your weight to *ruina*. The hamburgers and fried chicken attract droves of North American tourists. Open 8am-late.

Las Fajitas, at km 13 on the 2nd fl. of Plaza Kukulcán (☎885 21 99). Good Mexican fast food. Tacos 18 pesos, combo plates 45 pesos. Open daily noon-10 pm.

Restaurante Pop, Av. Tulum 25 (☎884 19 91), near the corner with Uxmal. About 1 block from the bus station. A/C and sizable helpings provide perfect recovery from a long bus ride. 3-course breakfast, lunch, or dinner 50-90 pesos. Open daily 8am-11pm.

Mario's Restaurant, Uxmal 21 (☎887 80 71), 1 block west of the bus station. Grab a hanging sombrero and dig into the seafood-heavy fare (entrées from 35 pesos). All-you-can-eat buffet served 7am-5pm (44 pesos). Open daily 7am-11pm.

El Poblano Taquería, on the corner of Punta Nicchehabi and Yaxchilán. Good tacos (15-20 pesos) and *gringas* (17 pesos) cooked late into the night. Open daily 6pm-4am.

Santa Clara, (☎889 95 48), at the southeastern corner of Tulum and Uxmal. Cool down with some of the best ice cream in Cancún. Single scoop 22 pesos; double scoop 42 pesos. Open daily 10am-10:30pm.

Acá Los Tacos, Cobá 43 (☎884 81 74), just west of Yaxchilán. Make your own *quesadillas* and tacos in this traditional Mexican joint. If it's your birthday, everything you put down your throat, including drinks, is on the house. Tacos, *quesadillas*, and *gringas* 10 pesos; flaming desserts 35 pesos. Open daily 7:30pm-3am.

◉ SIGHTS

Cancún does not obsess about museums, history, or culture. About the only educational thing around is the small archaeological site of **El Rey**, km 18, on the lagoon. The ruins were once part of a Maya fishing community that inhabited what is now the Zona Hotelera from AD 150-1200. When the Spanish arrived, bringing their lethal illnesses, the Maya buried their dead in the foundations of their houses and moved on. The centerpiece of the site is the lofty king's pyramid. (Ruins open daily 8am-5pm. 30 pesos. Tours in English or Spanish US$10.)

◉ BEACHES

The world famous beaches of Cancún are rightly renowned: multi-hued turquoise waters gently tickle the endless, sparkling Caribbean coastline covered with so much hot, tanned skin. Although you'll usually have plenty of company on the sands, Cancún's beaches are long enough (22 km!) and wide enough to accommodate swimming, napping, volleyball games, reading, meditating—you name it. And don't fret about the wall of luxury hotels standing between you and the glorious surf. All beaches in Mexico are public property, and there are regular public access points to the beaches along Kukulcán.

Stealing the show on the north side of the Zona Hotelera are **Playa Langosta** (at km 5) and **Playa Tortugas** (at km 5.5). Less spectacular but also less crowded are **Playa las Perlas** (at km 1.5) and **Playa Linda** (at km 3.5) to the west. On the east side of the Zona Hotelera, **Playa Chac-Mool** starts just south of Punta Cancún; the 1m high waves are as thrilling as Cancún's surf gets. Heading south, you'll come across pleasant **Playa Marlín** (at km 12) and quiet **Playa Delfines** (at km 17.8).

Water sports enthusiasts are in luck: Cancún offers opportunities to participate in nearly every aquatic sport known to mankind. Like in most resort areas, prices in Cancún are much higher than those in less-developed neighboring communities. Many organized recreational activities can be arranged through the luxury hotels lining the beaches or through private companies and tour guides:

Big Game Fishing, km 3.5 (☎884 16 17), next to the Blue Bay Hotel. Gives those interested a chance to kill their own dinner. Sunrise (7am-1pm; US$99) and sunset (2pm-6pm; US$79) trips. Beer and bait included.

Aqua World, km 15.2 (☎848 83 00). A popular choice for exploring Cancún's water paradise. Jungle tours (US$45) and waterskiing (US$38-50 per 30 min.) are offered in the oft-forgotten Laguna Nichuplé. Open daily 7am-10pm.

Scuba Cancún, km 5 (☎849 75 08). Offers 2hr. scuba diving lessons (US$77), snorkeling (US$24), kayak rentals (US$10-15 per hour), deep-sea fishing, and much more. Open daily 8:30am-8pm.

Aqua Tours, km 6.25 (☎883 04 00). Offers a range of aquatic adventures along with jungle tours (US$38.50), snorkeling tours (US$38.50), big game fishing (US$77-99), and waterskiing (US$1 per minute). Open daily 8am-8pm.

🎵🎭 ENTERTAINMENT AND NIGHTLIFE

As night descends, Cancún morphs from a beachgoer's playground into a hotspot for bars, clubs, and other nocturnal diversions. Out on the Zona, expect to see tipsy tourists parading down Kukulcán, drinks in hands and smiles on faces. If you have the money, don't miss some of the biggest and hottest clubs in the Western Hemisphere. Crowds in the Zona differ according to time and season. April hosts US college students, June welcomes high school and college graduates, and late night year-round belongs to the stream of wealthy international tourists. Experience more authentic Mexican sounds and crowds in the quieter *centro*. Locals favor bars and discos at the south end of Tulum near Cobá and at the north end of Yaxchilán near Sunyachén. Most establishments in Cancún open at 9pm, get going after midnight, and close when the crowds tire, around 5 or 6am.

BARS

Bars in the *centro* center around Yaxchilán and Tulipanes. Out on the Zona Hotelera, you'll be out of luck finding local bars—the party is at clubs and chains like Carlos 'n Charlie's, T.G.I. Friday's and Señor Frog's.

🎸 **Roots,** Tulipanes 26 (☎884 24 37; fax 884 55 47), between Palapas Park and Tulum. Caribbean-colored walls and eclectic artwork with a music motif set the stage in this superior jazz 'n blues joint. A motley crew populates the candle-lit tables. Live regional musicians Tu-Sa; shows go from 9pm to midnight Tu-Th, F-Sa 10pm-2am. No cover. Open Tu-Th 5pm-1am and F-Sa 5pm-2am. Menu until midnight Tu-Th, until 1am F-Sa.

El Gran Melao Bar, Yaxchilán 22 at Calle Punta Allen. A slightly older crowd dances and relaxes to live Caribbean, usually Cuban, music. No cover. Open M-Sa 9pm-3am.

Carlos 'n Charlie's, km 5.25 (☎849 40 52). Alcohol starts flowing early in the morning and never seems to stop here. Even at midday the place is packed with crowds of drunken Americans getting downright dirty by the lagoon. Live bands play in the evening and in the hot night air the makeshift dance floor becomes a sea of beer, sweat, and raging hormones. Open bar US$13. Open daily 10am-3am.

CLUBS

Most of the best clubs and discos are near the Zona's Punta Cancún, near **Playa Caracol** and **Forum by the Sea.** Older travelers beware: Cancún's glam clubs are usually teeming with US teenagers eager to indulge in sinful pleasures. Dress code for the discos is simple; less is more, tight is just right. Bikini tops often get women in for free, use your judgment in more laid-back clubs. US dollars rule in the Zona.

Coco Bongo, at km 9 in Forum By the Sea (☎883 05 92). Steamy, exhilarating, and unstoppable. Get down to rock, pop, and hip-hop at one of the hottest clubs in Cancún. Partiers dance on stage, on the bar, on the tables, and, yes, on the dance floor. Cover US$20, includes open bar.

Dady'O, km 9.5 in Forum by the Sea (☎883 33 33). The cave-like entrance lets you know you're headed into a disco inferno. The cave-scape continues through to a stage and dance floor streaking with lasers and pulsating with strobes, surrounded by winding, layered walkways whose crevices sport tables and chairs. A cafeteria in the club serves snacks (30-60 pesos). Bikini contests held regularly. Wristband-hawking staff outside will fill you in on the nightly special. Cover US$20. Open daily 10pm-late.

Dady Rock (☎883 33 33) next door to Dady'O. Provides the headbanging to complement Dady'O's hip-hopping. Hosts 2 live bands every night and offers open bar deals (US$15) several nights per week. Cover US$20. Open daily 6pm-late.

La Boom, km 3.5 near the CREA hostel (☎849 75 91). 2 nightclubs, a bar, and a pizzeria under the same roof. Serious dancers groove with lasers and phone booths. Ladies night and open bar vary week to week. Cover US$20.

Batacha, km 10 in the Hotel Miramar Misión (☎883 17 55). Dance under refreshing *palapas* to live *salsa* and *merengue* at this colorful local favorite. Cover 45 pesos. Open daily 10pm-late.

Bum-Bum, Yaxchilán 15 (☎884 13 09). High-powered Mexican music charges the stage at this local favorite for the youth of Cancún. 18+. Open daily 9pm-5am.

GAY AND LESBIAN NIGHTLIFE

There is little gay and lesbian nightlife in Cancún, with surprisingly none at all in the Zona. Karamba is pretty much the only happening gay bar and disco in town. Also on Tulum, a little north of Uxmal, is the much, much quieter bar, **Picante**.

Karamba, Tulum 9 (☎884 00 32) on the corner of Tulipanes. A spacious multilevel gay bar and disco with pop-art murals and a wide variety of dance music to complement the wild blue and purple lights. Action begins after 1:30 am. Open daily 9pm-late.

SPORTS

Death comes every Wednesday afternoon to the brutal **Plaza de Toros** (☎884 79 99), on Bonampak at Sayil. Tickets for the 2hr. bullfights—which always end with the bull's slaughter—are available at travel agencies on Tulum (300 pesos per person, children under 12 free; group discounts available) or at the bullring on a fight day.

SHOPPING

Cancún entices those not on a budget. Plazas Terramar, Caracol, Flamingo, and Kukulcán, between km 9 and 13, will swallow your dollars whole in the Zona. In the *centro*, artisan markets line Tulum, north of Cobá; be ready to bargain.

FESTIVALS

El Parque de las Palapas, between Tulum and Yaxchilán in the very center of town, hosts free regional music and dance performances during the weekends. The **Folkloric Ballet of Cancún** (☎881 04 00 ext. 193), located in the convention center on the Zona Hotelera puts on some excellent shows, occasionally in the Plaza de Toros. Admirable foresight or lucky timing could mean enjoying Cancún's celebrated **Jazz Festival** (mid- to late-May) or the refreshing **Caribbean Festival** (November). Check with the tourist office for more information and exact dates for this year.

ISLA MUJERES   ☎ 9

In 1517, Francisco Hernández de Córdoba happened upon this tiny island, looking for slaves to work in Cuban mines. He found instead hundreds of small female statuettes scattered on the beaches and named it Isla Mujeres (Island of Women). Hernández had stumbled upon a sanctuary for Ix Chel, the Maya goddess of fertility and the moon. For years Isla Mujeres (pop. 14,500) was a small fishing village whose culture centered around the sea. In the 1950s, vacationing Mexicans discovered the pristine island, and Australians, Europeans, and North Americans followed, transforming it into a hot spot for hippies and backpackers. While some locals still fish, most now cater to the daytrippers who arrive fresh from Cancún every morning or use the island as a jump-off point to explore **Isla Contoy,** a bird sanctuary 24km away. Although more and more tourists visit Isla Mujeres each year, they have yet to disrupt the tropical serenity of **Playa Norte** or disturb the carefree local life complete with daily *siestas* and late-night *salsa* dances.

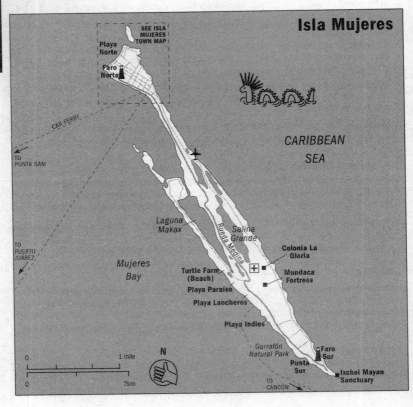

⊏▮ TRANSPORTATION

GETTING THERE AND AWAY

Isla Mujeres can only be reached by **ferry** from **Puerto Juárez**, 3km north of downtown Cancún, accessible by a "Puerto Juárez" bus (15min., 5 pesos) or by taxi (40 pesos) from Cancún. **Express service** boats (20 min., every 30 min. 6am-9pm, 35 pesos) are more expensive than **normal service** boats, which take much longer (45min., every 2hr. 8am-6pm, 18 pesos). Arrive early—ferries are notorious for leaving ahead of schedule when full. A **car ferry** runs to Mujeres from Punta Sam, 5km north of Puerto Juárez (5 per day; 12.5 pesos per person, 50+ pesos per car, depending on size). Come at least 30min. ahead of time for the car ferry.

GETTING AROUND

Walking is the best way to navigate the island's lovely *centro*. The best way to explore the ends of the island is by renting a moped, a bike, or a golf cart. Cars—with the exception of the occasional speeding taxi—are a rare sight on the island. Red **taxis** (☎877 00 66) line up at the stand directly to the right as you come off the passenger dock and zip to Playa Paraíso (10 pesos), Playa Lancheros (20 pesos), Garrafón (35 pesos), and the Maya sanctuary (40 pesos). Taxis also roam the length of Isla Mujeres; you should have no problem catching one elsewhere. Public **buses,** on the other hand, go only as far as Playa Lancheros (3 pesos).

Isla Mujeres Town

▲ ACCOMMODATIONS
Hotel Caribe Maya, **8**
Hotel Carmelina, **6**
Hotel Isleño, **9**
Hotel Marcianito, **4**
Hotel Xul-Ha, **1**
Poc-Na Youth Hostel, **5**

🍴 FOOD
Café Cito, **2**
Café Selva, **7**
Chen Huaye, **10**
El Poc-Chuc Lonchuría, **11**
French Bistro, **3**

CARIBBEAN SEA

Playa Panchalo

Tarzan Watersports
La Palapa

Mujeres Bay

Lavandería Angel
Coral Scuba Diving Ctr.

Pepe's Rentals

ZÓCALO

0   200 yards
0   200 meters

FERRY TO PUERTO JUÁREZ (CANCÚN)

CAR FERRY TO PUNTA SAM

TO PLAYA GARRAFÓN

🛈 PRACTICAL INFORMATION

Isla Mujeres is a narrow landmass (7.5km by 1km) 11km northeast of Cancún. The town—the *centro*—is located at the northwest corner of the island. The *centro* is laid out in a rough grid. Right in front and perpendicular to the dock is **Rueda Medina,** which runs the length of the island along the coastline, past the lagoon, Playa Paraíso, Playa Lancheros, and the Garrafón Reef.

TOURIST, FINANCIAL, AND LOCAL SERVICES

Tourist Office: (☎877 03 07), on Rueda Medina, take the 1st left after exiting the port, on the right-hand side. Open M-F 8am-8pm, Sa-Su 9am-2pm.

Currency Exchange: Bital (☎877 00 05), on Rueda Medina to the right after exiting the port. Has a 24hr. **ATM.** Open M-Sa 8am-7pm.

Books: Cosmic Cosas, Matamoros 82 (☎860 34 95). Buy, sell, and exchange books in many languages. Open daily 10:30am-10:30pm.

Laundry Service: Lavandería Tim Phó, Juárez 94 (☎877 05 29), at Abasolo. 40 pesos per 4kg. 2hr. turnaround. Open M-Sa 7am-9pm, Su 8am-2pm. **Lavandería Ángel,** Hidalgo local A-3 near the beach. 30 pesos per 4 kg. minimum. Open M-Sa 7am-9pm.

Rentals: Pepe's Rent, Hidalgo 19 (☎/fax 877 00 19), between Matamores and Abasolo. Golf carts 100 pesos per hr.; mopeds 50 pesos per hr., 200 pesos per day. Open daily 8am-6pm.

Police: Hidalgo at Morelos (☎877 00 98), in the Palacio Municipal. Open 24hr.

Red Cross: (☎877 02 80), at the Colonia la Gloria, toward the south end of the island.

Pharmacy: La Mejor, Madero 17 (☎877 01 16), between Hidalgo and Juárez. Open daily 9am-10pm.

Supermarket: Super San Francisco, Morelos 5 (☎ 887 10 94 and 887 10 92). Open M-Sa 7am-10pm, Su 7am-9pm.

Medical Assistance: Centro de Salud, Guerrero 5 (☎877 01 17), at Morelos. The white building at the northwest corner of the *zócalo.* Open 24hr. Some doctors speak English, such as **Dr. Antonio E. Salas** (☎877 04 77 or beeper 91 (9) 888 78 68, code 1465), at Hidalgo near Madero, who will make house calls.

Fax: Telecomm, Guerrero 13 (☎877 01 13), next to the post office. Open M-F 9am-3pm, Sa 9am-12:30pm.

Internet Access: Compucentro, Madero 14 (☎887 07 44). 25 pesos per hour. Open daily 10am-1am. **Cyber Bar and Cafe,** Hidalgo between Matamoros and López Mateos. 25 pesos per hour. Both offer free coffee with your email.

Post Office: Guerrero and López Mateos (☎877 00 85), at the northwest corner of town, 1 block from the Playa Norte. Open M-F 9am-4pm.

Postal Code: 77400.

🏠 ACCOMMODATIONS AND CAMPING

Prices increase by about 100 pesos during the high season (July-August and December-April). During those times, inquire ahead and consider making reservations. Many visitors stay in Cancún, where hotels are more plentiful and have A/C.

Hotel Xul-Ha, Hidalgo 23 (☎877 00 75), between Matamoros and López Mateos. Large rooms have ceiling fans and mirrors. Color TV, coffee machines, refrigerator, and books in the lobby. Singles and doubles with fan 150 pesos, with A/C 200 pesos.

Hotel Carmelina, Guerrero 4 (☎877 00 06), between Abasolo and Madero. Bright colors liven up the well-kept rooms. Reservations recommended Dec.-Jan. Singles with fans 180 pesos; doubles with A/C 280 pesos; triples 300 pesos.

Hotel Marcianito, Abasolo 10 (☎877 01 11). Recently remodeled, this hotel manages to avoid the faded blues, greens, and yellows of other Mexican budget hotels offering peaceful, well-kept rooms at a fair value. No A/C. Singles 250 pesos; doubles 300 pesos.

Poc-Na Youth Hostel, Matamoros 15 (☎877 00 90), near *Playa Norte*. An international assortment of weary backpackers, guitar-strumming Americans, and middle-aged card-playing Mexicans converge here to rest, relax, and enjoy the beaches. Bring your own hammock, tent, and lock. Restaurant open daily 7am-11pm. Hammock and tent space 25 pesos per person; bunk beds 39 pesos; private rooms 200 pesos.

Hotel Caribe Maya, Madero 9 (☎877 06 84), between Hidalgo and Guerrero. Small but suitable rooms. Singles and doubles with fan 170 pesos, with A/C 220 pesos. Additional persons 50 pesos each.

Hotel Isleño, Madero 8 (☎877 03 02), on the corner with Guerrero. Behind the pink facade are green and orange rooms. Singles and doubles with fans and shared bath 181.5 pesos, with private bath 252 pesos; each additional person 70 pesos.

🞇 FOOD

Seafood abounds in Isla Mujeres. Try *pulpo* (octopus) or *ceviche* (seafood marinated in lime juice, cilantro, and other herbs). Be wary of the restaurants near the plaza and along the Rueda Marina as they are a bit pricier. Also plan ahead—many restaurant owners close between lunch and dinner for siesta and relaxation.

▧ Chen Huaye, on Guerrero. Near the *zócalo*. This restaurant and bar with its elaborate blue and orange decor offers a cool place to enjoy traditional Yucatec cuisine and take refuge from the daytime heat. Platters of 5 *antojitos yucatecos* 30-34 pesos. Breakfast specials 25-35 pesos. Savor a refreshing fruit drink with milk before you go outside to brave the sun (23 pesos). Vegetarian options. Open daily 9am-11pm.

French Bistro Francais, Matamoros 29, at Hidalgo. Flavors from all over the world are blended together to create the most healthful menu on the island. Yogurt (32 pesos) and crepe specials (31 pesos) are popular morning picks, and yummy grilled seafood, cooked with a French flavor, satisfies all. Open daily 8am-noon and 6-10pm.

Cafe Cito, Matamoros 42 (☎877 04 38), at Juárez. Sand and shells under the see-through tabletops let patrons pretend they never left the beach. Replenish body and soul with freshly made crepes, sandwiches, and orange juice. Open high season 8am-2pm and 5-10:30pm; off season 8am-2pm.

El Poc-Chuc Lonchería, Juárez 5, on the corner with Abasolo. The colorful murals of sharks and Maya temples will soothe the senses as you dine relatively cheaply on traditional Mexican fare (20-40 pesos). Open M-Sa 8am-10pm.

Cafe Selva, Juárez 11 (☎877 12 45). For those missing the flavors of North American breakfasts, this new cafe specializes in bagel sandwiches (15-30 pesos), breakfast burritos (25 pesos), and fruit smoothies (25-35 pesos). Open daily 7am-10pm.

👁 🕭 SIGHTS AND BEACHES

Beaches in Isla Mujeres are peaceful and tranquil. The most popular and accessible beach is **Playa Norte** on the north shore, where gentle winds and waves lull sunbathers to sleep. Here one can wade fairly far out into the shallow water. On the west side of the island, **Playa Lancheros** and **Playa Paraíso** open onto Mujeres Bay, forming a smaller beachfront broken up by numerous boat docks. On the south end of the island, the **Faro Sur,** a lighthouse powered by an assortment of old car batteries, overlooks rocky bluffs, providing excellent views. Paths and stairways carved into the rock here allow you to descend the cliffs to meet the crashing surf.

A throng of vendors meets each ferry, offering bicycles (60 pesos per day) and mopeds for rent (80 pesos per hr.), as well as fishing and snorkeling trips to nearby **Isla Contoy,** a wildlife sanctuary reef with over 100 bird species. Captain **Ricardo Gaitan,** Madero 16, and many others can take you on a wonderful trip. (☎877 04 34.)

Includes equipment, breakfast, and lunch. Open daily 9am-4:30pm. 400 pesos.) The **Coral Scuba Dive Center**, Matamoros 13-A (☎877 07 63), has some of the cheapest scuba diving packages and lessons (US$59) and snorkel trips (US$14). **Tarzan Watersports**, on Playa Norte near Guerrero, offers an array of aquatic exploits and rents beach gear such as chairs and umbrellas. (☎877 06 79. Open daily 9am-5:30pm. Waterskiing US$50 per 30 min., kayaks US$15-20 per hr., 2hr. windsurfing lesson US$50.)

To support some dedicated individuals working to save the planet and see endangered sea turtles, head over to the **Turtle Farm**, across the *laguna* from the northern half of the island and northwest of **Playa Paraíso**. This biological research station breeds three species of sea turtles. Female turtles, captured by **Eco Caribe** in May, lay their eggs in the safety of the station's beach throughout the summer and are returned to the wild in October. The young are reared for a year before they, too, are released. (Open daily 9am-5pm. 20 pesos for a guide.)

Enjoy exciting cable rides, snorkeling, and an oceanside swimming pool at the **Garratón Natural Park,** located to the southeast of **Playa Lancheros** (US$10).

The Maya ruins of **Ixchel**—to which women made pilgrimages from all over to seek help from the goddess of fertility—are on the south tip of the island, accessible by taxi (40 pesos). Most of the site was reduced to rubble by Hurricane Gilbert in 1988, but a partially reconstructed one-room building and an awesome panorama of the Yucatán and the Caribbean await those who make the journey.

▣ NIGHTLIFE

Isla Mujeres offers relaxing nightlife for those wanting to escape the mega-resorts and throngs of drunken American teens in Cancún. Most of the best nighttime activity is concentrated at the north end of Hidalgo. Around sunset, tourists and locals bounce from one bar to the next toasting with half-price Happy Hour bargains. **Slices,** Hidalgo 14, with its pool table, balloon-strewn dance floor and hay, and massive speaker system exploding with techno and *salsa*, is the favorite of local youth. (☎ 877 10 35. Cover men 80 pesos, women 110 pesos. Open daily 8pm-3am.) For a slightly older feel, there's the two-story **Kokonuts,** Hidalgo 65, where patrons refresh themselves with tequilas and ice-cold beers and dance under a *palapa* to every strain of *música latina*. (☎877 07 97. Open daily 7pm-late.) Just across the street lies **Cafe Kokon.** For something closer to the beach, **La Palapa,** on **Playa Norte** to the right of Hidalgo, hosts a temporary dance floor on the sand adorned with lights and glow-in-the-dark artwork. (Open daily 11pm-6am.)

ISLA HOLBOX   ☎9

Isla Holbox (EES-la ohl-BOSH) was settled in 1873 by descendants of pirates who came to the isolated 40km finger-shaped island to start a new, more tranquil life of fishing. Almost 130 years later, the island remains a refuge—but not for those trying to make an honest living. Instead, nearby travelers in Cancún needing to get away from it all escape to Holbox's boat-lined shores, desolate sands, and the quiet village (pop 3,000), where all the people and all the dogs have known each other all their lives. Though this island is small and unbelievably slow-paced, that doesn't stop the *holboxeños* from enjoying themselves, nor should it stop you.

▣▣ TRANSPORTATION AND PRACTICAL INFORMATION

Isla Holbox lies just off the northern coast of Quintana Roo, in the Gulf of Mexico. Getting there requires planning. The easiest way is to take a **bus** from **Cancún** (8am and 12:45pm, 50 pesos) to **Chiquilá**, then hop on a "Los 9 Hermanos" *lancha* (approx. every 2hr. 6am-5pm, returning 5am-4pm; 30 pesos). There are two ways of getting to the ferry at Chiquilá from Valladolid. Either take a 1st-class bus directly to Chiquilá (2:30am, 52 pesos) or take a 2nd-class bus from the old bus station (at the corner of Calles 39 and 46), heading to Cancún. Stop in the town of El Ideal and either catch a 10am bus to Chiquilá (30 pesos) or take a *taxi colectivo* to Kantunil Kin (13 pesos), and then a bus to Chiquilá (4:30, 10:30am, and 3pm; 13 pesos). Return buses to Valladolid or Mérida meet the ferry (5:30am). The Cancún bus leaves Chiquilá at 7:30am and 1:45pm. If you miss the last ferry, Chiquilá's hotel **Puerta del Sol** (☎875 01 21) will welcome you for 100 pesos. The ferry dock is on the southwestern edge of the island.

In Holbox, a 24hr. **police** trio that speaks English may be found sitting on the benches of **La Alcaldia Municipal** (☎875 21 10), the light orange building on the corner of Juárez and Díaz. The **Centro de Salud,** a blue and white building 200m from the dock on the right side of the Juárez, houses a 24hr. doctor. There is **no bank** on the island. **Fax** and **telegram** service on the corner of Juárez and Díaz. (☎875 20 53. Open M-F 9am-3pm.) **Telmex** phones are scattered throughout the village and park.

ACCOMMODATIONS AND CAMPING

Finding cheap places to stay on Isla Holbox isn't a problem. Many family-run *posadas* cluster around the *zócalo* or Parque Juárez, which is about 500m north of the dock. Prices can rise 100-200% during high season. Free camping is available on the beach; just get a permit from the mayor's office, the Alcaldia Municipal (☎875 21 10), on the south side of the *zócalo*.

Posada D'Ingrid (☎875 20 70), 1 block northwest of the *zócalo*, at Morelos and Joaquín. Gleaming pink rooms with sparkling baths and fans open up to a *palapa*-roofed patio with speakers and card tables. A/C available. Singles and doubles start at 150 pesos; triples 175 pesos.

Posada La Raza (☎875 20 72), on the west side of Parque Juárez. The owners pride themselves on making their *posada* feel like home. Clean white rooms with new fixtures. Singles and doubles 150 pesos, with A/C 350 pesos; off-season singles and doubles 60 pesos. Discounts for longer stays.

Posada Los Arcos (☎875 20 43), next door to Posada La Raza. Clean, well-kept rooms have 2 beds and fans. A large, flamingo-filled courtyard. The only place in town to rent bikes (15 pesos per hr., 60 pesos per day). Singles 100 pesos; doubles 150 pesos, with A/C 250 pesos. Prices rise in April.

Posada Don Joaquín (☎875 20 88), just east of Parque Juárez, on Igualidad, the 3rd house on the left, with a Coca-Cola sign on the doorway. Adjoined to Abarrotes Addy. Large make-shift rooms with fans are the cheapest on *La Isla*. 50 pesos.

FOOD

The three best restaurants on the island all serve fresh seafood at budget prices. One block south of Parque Juárez on Palomino, excellent seafood dishes are prepared in the *palapa*-covered **Zarabanda,** named after a Caribbean rhythm. (☎875 20 94. Open daily 8am-9pm.) **Restaurant Edelyn,** Palomino, east of the park, grills large fish (40 pesos) and flips pizza in its two-story *palapa*. (☎875 20 24. Open daily 9am-11pm.) **Carocas Restaurant,** 1½ blocks east of the *zócalo* on the northern shores, carefully flavors the zesty fish filet *a la veracruzana* (grilled fish with tomatoes, onion, green peppers, bananas, and olives; 53 pesos) and the steak *a la Tampiqueña* (46 pesos) with beans and guacamole (☎875 22 10. Open daily 9am-10pm). For natural juices, a wide assortment of healthful and therapeutic shakes (13-20 pesos), and tropical fruit salads (25 pesos with either yogurt or granola), head to **La Isla del Calibri** (☎875 20 00), at the southwest corner of the *zócalo*.

BEACHES AND ENTERTAINMENT

New hotels have invaded the picturesque northshore of the island, but you can still soak up Isla's tranquility on some of its gorgeous sun-saturated beaches. The **Pla-**

yas de recreo, just north of town, are fairly crowded with fishing boats, but less than 1km east of town lie fairly desolate, seashell-covered sands and emerald-colored waters caressed by gentle winds. Or rent a bike for the 8km trek on the inland road to **Punta Mosquito,** where a 25km stretch of virgin beach begins.

Several tiny islands and an inlet on the mainland, only accessible by boat, will thrill admirers of nature, especially birdwatchers. **Isla de Pájaros,** home to nearly 40 species of birds, including flamingos and pelicans, lies a few kilometers southeast of the dock. On the mainland, west of Isla Holbox, is **Ojo de Agua,** an inlet fed by a subterranean freshwater spring. Finally across the lagoon that separates Isla Holbox from the mainland is **Isla Pasión,** named for the amorous pairs of both birds and humans that "relax" there off-season. Tours of the islands can be arranged through private fishermen, or at the **Delfín Artículos de Pesca** house, one block from the northern shores on Juárez. (☎875 20 18. 4hr. tour 600 pesos.)

The small size and relative isolation of Isla Holbox would seem to forecast a sleepy evening, but the locals are a rowdy bunch. To see *holboxeños* at their liveliest, cruise the brightly lit Parque Juárez at dusk, when friends and families gather to socialize, enjoy the playground, play the local *lotería,* and watch the basketball and volleyball games. Each month a creative group of local actors puts on a very interesting, though somewhat incomprehensible, experimental theatre performance free at **Diosakali,** a bar east of the *zócalo* on the northern shores. (☎875 20 69. Open daily noon-11pm.) During high season, Isla Holbox's restaurant/bar scene caters to tourists and a disco opens at **Cariocas Restaurant,** 1½ blocks east of the *zócalo* on the northern shores. (☎875 22 10. Margaritas and piña coladas 25 pesos.) For more natural entertainment, head to the north shore during the night. If conditions are right, you can witness *ardentía,* a rare and completely natural **phosphorescence.** Microorganisms respond to movement in the water by turning bright green; just kick the water or stir it with your hands to see the glow.

PLAYA DEL CARMEN   ☎9

People come for the beach; people stay at the beach; people eat, sleep, and party on the beach; people start new lives at the beach; it's said that a person once died for the beach; and many people from all over the world find, once there, that they simply don't have any reason to leave the beach. This is Playa del Carmen (pop. 20,000)—or as the locals know it, "Playa." Smack in the middle of Quintana Roo's legendary Maya Riviera, the rapidly growing town tempts travelers with its proximity to the dive sights of Cozumel, the shameless hedonism of Cancún, and the inland Maya ruins; however, the true seduction occurs on the long stretch of silky white beach married to spectacular turquoise surf. In the past decade, travelers en route to the reefs of Cozumel have "discovered" Playa and decided to stay, bringing with them the flavors, architecture, and spirit of their homes. The awesome beach, excellent food, sunset happy hours, burgeoning nightlife, and perfect location from which to explore the Yucatán make Playa an authentic tourist paradise.

▚ TRANSPORTATION

Buses: From the station (☎873 01 09) at the corner of Quinta and Juárez, ADO goes 1st-class to: **Chetumal** (4½hr., 12 per day, 128 pesos); **Mexico City** (25hr.; 7am, noon, and 7pm; 716 pesos); **Orizaba** (14hr., 12:15 and 7:15pm, 641 pesos); **Puebla** (23hr., 8:45pm, 720 pesos); **San Andrés** (9½hr., 3:45 and 10:15pm, 476 pesos); **Veracruz** (12hr., 3:45 and 10:15pm, 565 pesos); **Villahermosa** (12hr., 9 per day noon-9pm, 359 pesos). Cristóbal Colón goes to: **Ocosingo** (13hr., 4 per day, 336 pesos); **Palenque** (11hr., 4 per day, 289 pesos); **San Cristóbal** (15hr., 4 per day, 378 pesos); **Tuxtla Gutiérrez** (16hr., 3 per day, 410 pesos). ATS has 2nd-class service to **Tulum** (1hr., 10 per day, 28 pesos). Premier goes to **Mérida** (5hr., each hour, 178 pesos), via **Ticul** (3½hr., 127 pesos).

Playa del Carmen

⌂ ACCOMMODATIONS
Cabañas and Camping La Ruina, **12**
CREA Youth Hostel, **2**
Hotel Marinelly, **11**
Posada Freud, **3**
Posada Lily, **13**
Posada Papagayo, **7**
Urban Hostel, **6**

🍅 FOOD
Café Tropical, **5**
Media Luna, **4**
Restaurant La Tarranga, **10**
Sabor!, **9**
T'Amo Da Morire, **14**
Xtabentun Restaurant, **8**
Zas, **1**

Calle 14
Av. 1
Calle 12
Abyss Dive Shop
Calle 10
Calle 8
Lavandería Tintoría
Calle 6
Quinta (Av. 5)
Calle 4
Calle 2
CARIBBEAN SEA

Av. 40
Av. 35
Av. 30
Av. 25
Av. 20
Av. 15
Av. 10

Fama Bookstore
Bus Terminal
Maya Ruin
Juárez
Farmacia
ZÓCALO
Calle 1
Calle 1
Calle 1 Sur
TO COZUMEL →
Ferry Dock

0   300 yards
0   300 meters
N

🛈 PRACTICAL INFORMATION

Playa is located on the Maya Riviera, 34km south of Cancún and 90km north of Tulum. Two blocks south and one block east of the bus station, where Calle 3 hits the beach, the ferry to Cozumel docks at **Juárez** and **Quinta** (Av. 5) intersect here. Juárez runs west from the beach to the Cancún-Chetumal road, **Highway 307**, 1.5km away. Quinta is a pedestrian walkway lined by popular shops and restaurants running parallel to the beach. East-west *calles* increase by two in either direction; north-south *avenidas* increase by five.

Tourist Office: Information (☎873 28 04), on the corner of Juárez and Av. 15. English spoken. Open M-Sa 9am-9pm, Su 9am-5pm.

Currency Exchange: Bital (☎873 04 04), on Juárez, 1 block west of the *zócalo*. Exchanges currency and traveler's checks. 24hr. **ATM.** Open M-Sa 8am-7pm.

Book Store: Fama (☎873 09 39), on Juárez between Av. 10 and 15. Open daily 9am-2pm, 6pm-10pm.

Laundry: Lavandería Tintoría, on Calle 6 between Av. 5 and 10. Wash and dry for 15 pesos per kg. Open daily 7:30am-7:30pm.

Emergency: ☎060.

Police: (☎873 01 91), on Juárez, 2 blocks west of the plaza. English spoken.

Pharmacy: Farmacia del Carmen (☎873 23 30), on Juárez, opposite the bus station. Open 24hr.

Medical Assistance: Centro de Salud (☎873 03 14), on the corner of Juárez, across from the post office. Some English spoken.

Internet Services: La Taberna (☎803 04 47 or 803 04 48), on the corner of Calle 4 and Av. 10. 18 pesos per hour. Open daily 10am-3am.

Post Office: (☎873 03 00), on Juárez, 3 blocks from the plaza. Open M-F 9am-5pm, Sa 9am-1pm. **MexPost** in the same building. Open M-F 9am-3pm. **Fax:** (☎873 00 29), next to the post office. Open M-F 9am-3pm, Sa-Su 9am-12:30pm.

Postal Code: 77710.

ACCOMMODATIONS AND CAMPING

With Playa's stunning recent growth, budget accommodations are becoming more scarce. During high season (Dec. 21-Apr. 15 and July 15-Sept. 15), prices are especially high and reservations are necessary. Most establishments lie along Quinta or Juárez, near the beach.

Posada Freud (☎873 06 01), on Quinta, between Calles 8 and 10. Palm trees and colorful hammocks persuade passersby to lounge in one of Freud's 11 unique pastel abodes. Rooms start at US$25. Call ahead to make reservations.

Posada Papagayo (☎873 24 97), Av. 15 between Calles 4 and 6. Spacious, nicely furnished rooms await the traveler who goes the extra mile to find Papagayo. Singles and doubles 150 pesos; triples 200 pesos. Prices rise 100 pesos in high season.

Posada Lily, the flaming pink building on Juárez, 1 block west of the plaza. Small, cushy beds in clean rooms with fans can be found at this noisy but convenient location near the bus stop. Singles 120 pesos; doubles 150 pesos; triples 200 pesos.

Hotel Marinelly (☎873 01 40), the yellow and blue building on Juárez, 1½ blocks west of the *zócalo*. Ask for one of their newly renovated rooms. Noise can be a problem here. Singles 150 pesos; doubles 200 pesos; triples 250 pesos. A/C 50 pesos extra. Prices rise 50 pesos in the high season.

Cabañas and Camping La Ruina (☎873 04 05). This eclectic and colorful place is almost perfectly located. Beachfront *cabañas* and camping space, 200m north of the ferry dock, are a hop, skip, and jump from Juárez and Quinta. Popular with Europeans, the hostel-style *cabañas rústicas* have ceiling fans and tiny, stiff military beds, communal bathrooms, and cooking facilities. Lockers 10 pesos. Singles and doubles 160 pesos. Hammock-space and camping 50 pesos each. Beachside cabaña with A/C 359 pesos. Each additional person 60 pesos.

Urban Hostel (☎879 93 42), on Av. 10 between Calles 4 and 6. This new hostel, 2 blocks from the beach, offers single-sex bunk beds under a giant *palapa*, ceiling fans, lockers, and a full kitchen for an almost unbeatable US$10 per person.

CREA Youth Hostel (☎873 15 08), near the corner of Av. 30 and Calle 8, about ½km northwest of the *zócalo*, CREA has a spacious lot with a soccer field and basketball courts. Single-sex dorms with bunk beds and communal showers. 40 pesos per person. *Cabañas* with private bathrooms and A/C 200 pesos per person. Lockers available—bring your own lock.

FOOD

It can be hard to find a bargain amongst the distinctly French and Italian flavors of Quinta's flashy restaurants which cater to a growing European ex-patriot population. While Playa is definitely the place to splurge on a meal, if you decide not to, the host of *loncherías* west of Av. 10 that serve inexpensive *tortas* and regional cuisine will take care of you.

Sabor! (☎873 26 50), on Quinta, 1½ blocks north of the *zócalo*. Locals and tourists enjoy vegetarian platters (35-50 pesos), tequila shrimp (65 pesos), and healthy breakfast specials (24 pesos) under vines and a blossoming tree. Open daily 6:30am-11pm.

Restaurant La Tarranga (☎873 20 40), at the end of Calle 2 right on the beach. This budget-friendly restaurant and bar is perfect if you don't want to leave the beach, even for a second. Breakfast ranges from 12-30 pesos. Fish filet Tilei-nix (barbequed fresh fish) 40 pesos. Open daily 7am-10:30am and noon-9pm.

Xtabentun Restaurant (☎803 11 25), on Calle 2 between Av. 10 and 15. This new Mexican restaurant with a jukebox serves omelettes for breakfast (20-25 pesos), tacos (30 pesos), and 14 different kinds of sandwiches representing everywhere in the world (25-30 pesos). Open daily 7am-10pm.

Media Luna (☎873 05 20), on Quinta between Calles 8 and 10. Whether you're digging into a healthful breakfast or simply sipping a frothy *frapuccino helado* (frozen frapuccino), you'll want to linger in the padded booths. Tasty tropical fruit crepes 49 pesos, luscious fruit platters topped with granola 30 pesos, creative salads 54 pesos. Open daily 8am-midnight.

Cafe Tropical (☎873 21 11), on Quinta, across from Media Luna. Enjoy the generous portions served underneath a gigantic shady *palapa*. Smoothies 25 pesos, sandwiches 35 pesos, omelette 36 pesos, other entrees 40-60 pesos. Open daily 7am-1am.

T'Amo de Morire (☎877 54 49), on Calle 1 between Av. Quinta and the beach. Come here for a romantic evening overlooking the beach and enjoy food that is truly to die for. Shrimp tacos 50 pesos, grilled red snapper filet 60 pesos, spaghetti with octopus 65 pesos. Open M-Sa 4pm-11:30pm.

Zas (☎873 05 26), on Quinta, between Calles 12 and 14. For a classy, jazzy dining experience, savor gourmet food with pizzazz at Zas. Although somewhat hidden and on the upscale side, it is well worth the 1-time splurge. Entrees average 70 pesos. Try the caramelized bananas in brandied butter (40 pesos). Open daily 5pm-11:30pm.

◧ BEACHES AND WATERSPORTS

Lined with palm trees and fringed by the turquoise waters of the Caribbean, Playa's beaches are sandy, white, and oh-so-relaxing. They are relatively free of seaweed and coral, strewn instead with scantily (if at all) clad tourists. In search of an aquatic escape? Depending on your bargaining ability, 120-160 pesos will buy you an hour's worth of windsurfing. Windsurfing equipment and other gear can be rented from some of the fancier hotels just south of the pier, or from shacks a few hundred meters north. The **Abyss Dive Shop**, on the beach at Calle 12, will fulfill all your diving and snorkeling desires. It services 15-18 different dive sites and caters to all skill levels. (☎873 21 64. "Discover" scuba diving trips US$69. Open water courses US$350. 2-tank dive US$59. 2½ hr. snorkeling trips 250 pesos. Snorkeling equipment 60 pesos. Open M-Sa 8:15am-9pm, Su 8:15am-6pm.)

◧ ◧ NIGHTLIFE AND ENTERTAINMENT

Come nightfall, the shops on Quinta close and the street is transformed from a busy thoroughfare of vendors into a glitzy nightlife hotspot. Sun-lovers recuperate from the day's rays by swaying in hammocks and jiving to guitar-strumming, flute-playing locals. At **Karen's Grill**, on Quinta, 1½ blocks north of the plaza, waiters start the party by escorting women to the dance floor and pouring cafe flambe in a waterfall style, all to the rhythms of *salsa* and *merengue*. (☎879 40 64. Live South American music daily 6pm-midnight. Happy Hour 10am-1am.) Swings replace the conventional bar stools at the always crowded **Blue Parrot Inn Palapa,** on the beach at Calle 12, which was voted one of the 10 best bars in the world by *Newsweek* magazine in 1996. Rock in your seats to the live music, which starts up every afternoon. (☎872 00 83. Open 24hr.) All the youngest and hottest staying or living in Playa del Carmen come to **Tequila,** on the beach between Calles 4 and 6. Amidst the colorful lights, strobe, and energetic *música Latina*, people can't help going wild. (Open daily 10pm-2:30am.) If the party's not at Tequila, then it's probably at neighboring **Capitan Tutix's,** Tequila's less raucous cousin on the beach at Calle 4, where guests shake and groove to Latin and international dance hits. (☎873 17 48. Cover 40 pesos, includes 1 drink. Ladies free after 11:30pm. Open daily 10pm-late.) Indulge your hankering for Hollywood at **Cinema Playa del Carmen,** four blocks west of the *zócalo* and one block north of Juárez. (Tickets 10-15 pesos.)

XCARET: XCELLENT BUT XPENSIVE. Legend has it that the Maya bathed themselves in the clear sacred water of this *cenote* during their pilgrimage to Cozumel. Fifty kilometers south of Cancún and just south of Playa del Carmen, XCARET is a privately owned and operated theme park dedicated to Maya culture, the natural splendor of the Maya Riviera, and its own profit. A hefty US$39 entrance fee will admit you to a massive seaside complex, complete with underground rivers, reconstructed Maya villages, archaeological ruins, an aviary, a museum, a beach, a lagoon, wading pools, dolphins, snorkeling and scuba diving tours, stables, botanical gardens, jungle cats, monkeys, and bats, and even a mushroom farm. It doesn't stop there. At night, XCARET puts on a variety of shows, from folkloric dances to ancient Maya rituals. Buses to XCARET leave from the XCARET information center opposite Plaza Caracol in Cancún (9, 10, and 11am) or from Tulum (8:15am). Call (9) 883 31 43 or (9) 883 31 44 for more information, or visit www.xcaretcancun.com.

AKUMAL ☎9

Akumal, "Place of the Turtles" in Maya, is a high-class, luxury resort catering to an older wealthier crowd who are drawn to its older, wealthier activities. Don't let this deter you, oh fearless budget traveler, as there do remain some deals to be had, as well as world-class diving and snorkeling at the biggest living reef in the Western hemisphere. The town is a string of fancy, upscale hotels lining the bay but budget travelers should make a beeline for CEA, the **Centro Ecológico Akumal,** where an interesting international assortment of scientists and students will teach you the latest about Caribbean hurricanes, endangered sea turtles, environmentally-beneficial toilets, and coral ecosystems.

█▓ TRANSPORTATION AND PRACTICAL INFORMATION. Akumal is located on the Maya Riviera, 37km south of Playa del Carmen and 30km north of Tulum. There is a small pueblo located to the west of Mex. 307, but the Akumal resort area is a short 1-2km toward the ocean. Taxis are also available at the highway and can take you to the resort area for 10-15 pesos. To get to either Tulum or Playa del Carmen, you can try to flag a bus down on Mex. 307, but it's probably easier to take the white vans going north or south that generally pass each hour (10 pesos).

Travel Agency TSA, right outside CEA, has it all: car and bike rental, telephone, fax and email, money exchange, airport transportation, and tours to nearly every sight. (☎875 90 30. Open M-Sa 9am-6pm, Su 8:30am-1:30pm. Exchange closes M-Sa 1-2pm.) The supermarket **Super Chomak,** on the right as you approach the main gates, stocks all the essentials but prices can be outrageous. (☎875 90 16. Open daily 7am-9pm.) For better prices but less selection try the mini-super across the street. **Laundry: Lavandería,** to your left 100m from the arch. (15 pesos per kg, 2kg min. Open M-Sa 7am-1pm and 5-7pm.) **Emergency:** ☎060. **Farmacia Tomy III,** on your left as you approach the gates, next to the basketball courts. (☎876 90 49. Open daily 9am-9pm.) **Postal Code:** 77760.

▛▟ ACCOMMODATIONS AND FOOD. The Centro Ecólogico Akumal, or **CEA,** is the only budget option in Akumal. The center is a research facility where university students from both Mexico and the United States spend their summers taking tropical marine science classes. Student rooms are sometimes available for rent.

DON'T HURT THE TURTLES Sea turtles are a natural attraction of the Maya Riviera. Unfortunately, the unfettered development and legions of tourists flooding the region haven't been as attractive to the turtles. The creatures nest through the summer, but, as of late, they haven't had much luck—encroaching hotels and beachfront properties have disturbed their nesting grounds. "What can I do to help?" you may ask. The best thing you can do is to give the turtles that are alive a greater chance of surviving. When you see a turtle while snorkeling, stay 5-6m away, or you may scare it from its food source. Also, do not litter on the beach as the turtles often mistake plastic waste for jellyfish and choke when they try to eat them.

The large, well lit rooms (four beds in each) have private baths and some come with A/C. During university breaks, the Ecocenter gets busy and fills up fast. Email or call ahead to make reservations. (☎875 90 95; mul@caribe.net.mx. 100 pesos per night. 50 peso deposit for reservations.)

Like the hotels, most restaurants in Akumal go straight for the wallet. But a couple of places do serve budget-friendly food. **Ecocina,** just outside the CEA to the left of the welcoming arch, is popular with students from the CEA and workers from the resorts. (Breakfast 25 pesos, lunch specials 45 pesos, milkshakes 20 pesos. Open daily 8am-3pm.) **Lonchería Alenmalito,** right next to Super Chomate, also offers decent food at decent prices. (Breakfast 30 pesos. Lunch and dinner 35-65 pesos. Open daily 6am-9pm.) For a more expensive treat, try **La Cueva del Pescador,** near CEA. Grab a table outside, sliced from a giant tree trunk, or eat indoors and dig your toes into the sand. Seafood is on everybody's plate, and entrees average a hefty 80-100 pesos. (☎875 92 05. Open M-Sa 7am-10pm.)

◄⊙BEACHES AND SIGHTS. The beach of Akumal Bay is famed for its white sands and the clarity of its tranquil waters, buffered by the offshore reef. Shallow waters close to shore contain a remarkable variety of animal life in the sea grass and in the areas just seaward of the sea grass. Coral, inch-long lettuce slugs, sleeping fish, and large sea turtles are just a few of the creatures you might come across. Although snorkelers, divers, and sunbathers litter the beach and bay, there still seems to be room for all. The **Akumal Dive Shop** rents snorkeling equipment (US$8 per day), and organizes snorkeling and scuba trips to the ocean, caverns, and caves. Certification courses available. (☎875 90 32. Open daily 8am-5pm. US$35 for 1 tank dive, US$62 for 2.) In the mood to expand your environmental horizons? The Centro Ecológico Akumal hosts lectures on a wide range of topics, from sea turtles to the modern Maya to theories of dinosaur extinction. (☎875 90 05; www.ceakumal.org. Open M-F 4:30pm. Free, but donations accepted.) CEA also offers night walks to the nesting beach of Akumal where sea turtles lay their eggs. Bring water, a flashlight, and a camera. (Make reservations at the CEA office. Walk leaves at 9pm from the Akumal Dive Shop. 80 pesos.)

COZUMEL

☎9

The calm diving mecca of Cozumel—"land of the swallows" in Maya—has seen its share of history. Ever since French diver Jacques Cousteau called attention to the amazing coral formations and colorful marine life of **Palancar Reef,** the second-largest barrier reef in the world, divers from all over the world have flocked here. Today the calm tropical island, with its turbulent history of vanquished Maya, conquering Spaniards, pirate bases, tragic mass desertions, and recent tourist build-up, is a popular getaway for those wishing to explore Mexico's natural beauty without saying goodbye to luxury resorts and eager service. Much of the island remains undeveloped and ripe for exploration. Miles of empty white beach, Maya ruins, and lagoons full of crocodiles greet tourists motivated enough to leave the island's city, San Miguel de Cozumel (pop. 80,000), and explore the island itself.

YUCATÁN

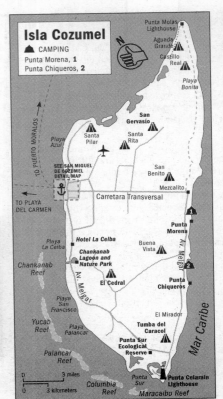

Isla Cozumel

▲ CAMPING
Punta Morena, **1**
Punta Chiqueros, **2**

Punta Molas
Lighthouse
Aguada
Grande
Castillo
Real
Playa
Bonita
San
Gervasio
Santa
Pilar
Santa
Rita
Playa
Azul
SEE SAN MIGUEL
DE COZUMEL
DETAIL MAP
San
Benito
Mezcalito
Carretara Transversal
TO PUERTO MORELOS
TO PLAYA
DEL CARMEN
Punta
Morena
Playa
La Ceiba
Hotel La Ceiba
Chankanab
Lagoon and
Nature Park
Buena
Vista
Chankanab
Reef
El Cedral
Punta
Chiqueros
Av. Melgar
Av. Melgar
Playa
San
Francisco
El Mirador
Yucab
Reef
Playa
Palancar
Tumba del
Caracol
Punta Sur
Ecological
Reserve
Mar Caribe
Palancar
Reef
Punta
Sur
Punta Celarain
Lighthouse
Columbia
Reef
Maracaibo Reef

0   3 miles
0   3 kilometers

▤ ■ TRANSPORTATION

GETTING THERE

Most people reach the island via ferry from Playa del Carmen (to the west) or Puerto Morelos (to the north). Ferries from **Puerto Morelos** transport cars to and from Cozumel (☎871 03 55. 2½hr.; Sa-M and W-Th 5am and 5pm; 55 pesos, with car 735 pesos). While tourist vehicles supposedly have priority, the car ferry is nevertheless inconvenient and unpredictable. If you're set on it, the tourist office recommends securing a spot in line 12 hours in advance. Ferries between **Playa del Carmen** and Cozumel run frequently. Tickets can be bought at the dock in Cozumel or from the booth on Playa's plaza (45min., 12 per day, round-trip 146 pesos). If you are coming from Cancún, an alternative to the bus-ferry ordeal is the 20min. **air shuttle** operated by Aerocaribe (☎872 34 56).

GETTING AWAY

Airport: (☎872 04 85), 2km north of town. **Aerocaribe** (☎872 34 56), **Continental** (☎872 04 87), and **Mexicana** (☎872 29 45) serve Cozumel.

Ferries: Passenger ferries leave for **Playa del Carmen** from the dock at the end of Juárez (every hr. starting at 4am, one-way 61 pesos). Arrive early; ferries sell out several minutes before departure. Buy tickets at the corner of Melgar and the dock. Car ferries (☎872 08 27) leave from the dock south of the main dock bound for **Puerto Morelos.**

◪ ⚇ ORIENTATION AND PRACTICAL INFORMATION

The island of Cozumel is 18km east of the Quintana Roo coast and 85km south of Isla Mujeres. At 53km long and 14km wide, Cozumel is Mexico's largest Caribbean island. The main town, **San Miguel de Cozumel** (home to the island's ferry docks), is located in the middle of the west coast. Downtown streets are clearly labeled and numbered with stubborn logic. Beaches lie both to the north and south of town, and the rest of the island is relatively untouristed and easily explored by bike, moped, or safari. Catch a **taxi** (☎872 02 36 or 872 00 41) easily as you come off the dock to the airport (40 pesos) or to Punta Moreno (100 pesos).

TOURIST, FINANCIAL, AND LOCAL SERVICES

Tourist Office: (☎872 75 63), on the 2nd fl. of Plaza del Sol, to the left of Bancomer, on the plaza. English spoken. Open M-F 9am-3pm and 6-8pm.

US Consulate: (☎872 45 74, emergencies 87 261 52), on the 2nd fl. of Plaza Viamar, in the northwest corner of the zócalo. Open M-F noon-2pm.

San Miguel de Cozumel

♠ ACCOMMODATIONS
Hotel Flores, **17**
Hotel Pepita, **16**
Hotel Posada Edém, **3**
Posada Letty, **15**

● FOOD
Casa Denis, **11**
The Coffee Bean, **19**
El Abuelo Gerardo, **8**
La Parroque, **9**
Mi Chabelita, **14**
Rock-n-Java Caribbean
Café, **21**

♪ NIGHTLIFE
Bar Romance, **12**
Carlos 'n Charlies, **2**
Coco Wook, **5**
Fat Tuesday, **4**
Havana Club, **1**

● SERVICES
Aqua Safari Melgar, **20**
Blue Bubble Dive Shop, **18**
Fama Bookstore, **6**
Farmacia Kiosco, **10**
Laundry, **13**
Le$$ Pay Car Rental, **22**
Moped Rental, **7**

Currency Exchange: BanNorte (☎872 03 18), Av. 5 Norte, between Juárez and Calle 2, exchanges traveler's checks. Open M-F 9am-4pm. **Bancomer** (☎872 15 50), on the plaza, has the same rates but charges a flat fee of US$0.50 per check. Open M-F 8:30am-4pm, Sa 10am-2pm. **BITAL** (☎872 01 42), on the plaza, has a 24hr. **ATM.** Open M-Sa 8am-7pm.

Car Rental: LE$$ Pay (☎872 47 44 or 872 19 47), on Melgar 628, about 1km south of town. VW Safaris (US$30 per day), jeeps, and mopeds (250 pesos per day) available. Discounts for multiple-day rentals. Open daily 8am-8pm. **Executive** (☎872 13 08), Calle 1 Sur #19, between Av. 5 and 10. Rentals with insurance from US$45-65 per day. 15% off if you grab a coupon book from the ferry. Open 8am-8pm. **Budget** (☎878 40 30), on Av. 5 between Calle 2 and 4. US$33 per day, with A/C US$38-50 per day. Open daily 7:30am-2pm and 4-7pm.

Moped Rental: Rentadora Sol y Mar (☎869 05 45), across from Hotel Posada Edem on Calle 2. 100 pesos per hr., 250 pesos per day. Open daily 9am-6pm.

Bike Rental: Rentadora Cozumel (☎872 11 20 or 872 15 03), on Av. 10 between Calle 1 and Salas. 50 pesos per day. 7pm return. Open daily 8am-8pm.

Bookstore: Fama (☎872 50 20), on Av. 5, between Juaréz and Calle 2 Norte. CDs, books, magazines, and maps in English. Open daily 9am-10pm.

Supermarket: Sedenu (☎872 05 72), Av. Melgar and Calle 12 Norte, 6 blocks north of the dock. Open M-Sa 6:30am-10:30pm, Su 8am-6pm.

Laundry: Express Lavandería (☎872 29 32), Salas, between Av. 5 and Av. 10. Washer 15 pesos, dryer 11 pesos per 10 min. Open M-Sa 8am-9pm, Su 8:30am-3pm.

EMERGENCY AND COMMUNICATIONS

Emergency: ☎060.

Police: (☎872 04 09) on Calle 11 Sur near Rafael Melgar, in the Palacio Municipal. Some English spoken.

Red Cross: (☎872 10 58), on Av. 20 Sur at Salas. Open 24hr.

Pharmacy: Farmacia Kiosco (☎872 24 85), on the *zócalo* near Hotel López. Everything for the sun-happy or sun-sick tourist. Open M-Sa 8am-10pm, Su 9am-10pm.

Medical Assistance: General Hospital (☎872 01 40), Calle 11 Sur and Av. 20.

Fax: (☎872 00 56), next to the post office. Open M-F 8am-7:30pm, Sa-Su 9am-12:30pm.

Internet Access: Modutel Communicaciones (☎869 01 00), on the corner of Juárez and Av. 10. 20 pesos per hr. Open daily 8am-4am.

Post Office: (☎872 01 06), off Melgar, just south of Calle 7 Sur along the sea. Open M-F 9am-4pm, Sa 9am-1pm.

Postal Code: 77600.

▗ ACCOMMODATIONS AND CAMPING

Since they cater primarily to foreign divers with cash to burn, hotels in Cozumel are generally more expensive than those on the mainland, and extra pesos do not guarantee higher-quality rooms. Resist being roped into a pricey package deal when stepping off the ferry. Try to secure a room before noon, especially during high season. Camping, particularly on the secluded spots at **Punta Morena** and **Punta Chiqueros** on the east side of the island, may be the best option. Those thinking about camping should check in with the naval headquarters on Melgar near the post office, as a permit may be required.

Hotel Posada Edém, Calle 2 #12 (☎872 11 66), between Av. 10 and 5, across from the taxi station. From the dock, go left 1 block, turn right, and walk 2 blocks. Small, slightly run-down but functional pink rooms with 2 beds, fans, and *agua purificada* in lobby. One of the cheapest places in town where the friendly *señora* will call you *jefe*. Singles 150 pesos; doubles 180 pesos; each additional person 50 pesos.

Posada Letty, Calle 1 #272 (☎872 02 57), between Av. 10 and 15. Their business card promises "Cleanliness-Order-Morality." We can only vouch for the first. Well-kept green and blue rooms have big windows with big beds and feel more like a house than a hotel. Singles 180 pesos; doubles 200 pesos; each additional person 50 pesos. Prices rise 10% in high season.

Hotel Flores, Salas 72 (☎872 14 29), on Av. 5, 50m from the sea. Clean white rooms; ask for one with an ocean view. Singles and doubles 200 pesos, with A/C 250 pesos. Prices rise 10% in the high season.

Hotel Pepita, 15 Av. #120 (☎872 00 98), just south of Calle 1 Sur. It might cost you a little extra, but private bath, refrigerator, A/C, and free coffee make this a very good value. Singles and doubles 279 pesos; 50 pesos per additional person.

Hotel Cozumel Inn, Calle 4 #3 (☎872 03 14). Clean rooms with green tiles overlook a swimming pool and courtyard. Singles and doubles 280 pesos. Larger doubles with A/C and balconies 336 pesos.

▗ FOOD

Like any Caribbean island, Cozumel serves up plenty of seafood, but prices indicate that seafood is intended more for the resort-vacationer than the budget traveler. Moderately priced restaurants can be found a few blocks from the *centro*, and small cafes are tucked away on side streets. The **market** at Salas between Av. 20 and 25 Sur, has fresh meat, fish, and fruit. The *loncherías* next door are the most authentic and cheapest places in town. For a sweet treat, stroll into **Panificadora Cozumel**, on Calle 2 Nte. between Av. 5 Nte. and Melgar, where pastries melt in your mouth for pocket change. (☎872 00 58. Open daily 6am-10pm.)

Casa Denis (☎872 00 67), on Calle 1 between Av. 5 and 10, across from the flea market on the *zócalo*. Become a part of *La Familia Denis*, while enjoying home-cooked recipes, attentive staff, and photos of Che Guevara fishing with Fidel Castro. Breakfast 25 pesos, sandwiches 13-34 pesos, Maya pork tacos 27 pesos, other *comida regional* 50-70 pesos. Open M-Sa 7am-10:30pm, Su 5-10:30pm.

Mi Chabelita (☎872 08 96), on Av. 10 between Calle 1 and Salas. A variety of regional favorites at favorable prices (33-43 pesos) make this *cocina económica* the best deal in town. Don't miss out on their refreshing milkshakes (23 pesos). Open M-Sa 8am-9pm.

El Abuelo Gerardo (☎872 10 12), on Av. 10 between Juárez and Calle 2 Nte., near the church. A mellow, spacious place to grab an ice-cold afternoon beer, watch TV, and enjoy generous portions of *antojitos* (20-40 pesos) and fish fillet (45 pesos). Or, if you prefer, sit down to a hearty breakfast (25 pesos). Open daily 7:30am-7:30pm.

La Parroque, on Av.10 #40 between Calle 1 and Juárez. Chill with the locals on this 2nd floor restaurant and bar overlooking Av.10, and enjoy 3 tacos con carne (36 pesos), *quesadillas* (28 pesos), or the seafood soup (45 pesos). Open daily 11am-2am.

San Francisco Restaurant, on the southwest coast of the island at km 15. Grab chilled drinks or freshly squeezed tropical drinks with chips, guacamole, and salsa. *Antojitos* (15-37 pesos). *Pescado entero* (whole fish) is cooked in 10 different styles.

Rock-n-Java Caribbean Cafe, Melgar 602 (☎8724 40 5), near LE$$ Pay between Calle 9 and 11 Sur. Healthy breakfasts with fruit-topped multi-grain French toast (40 pesos), fresh salads (25-50 pesos), homemade soups (30 pesos), and flavored coffee (25-45 pesos) are all served with a view of the Caribbean, surrounded by crusty black and white sailor photos. Vegetarian food offered. Open Su-F 7am-11pm, Sa 7am-2pm.

The Coffee Bean, (☎872 77 48), on Calle 3 next to Pizza Hut and the shore. An American-style espresso bar infused with the Caribbean. Freshly baked homemade desserts include strawberry cheesecake, pecan pie, apple pie, and brownies. Espresso ice cream and coffee from Chiapas and Veracruz 19-25 pesos. Open 7:30am-11pm.

BEACHES AND SIGHTS

DIVING

Many visitors make the trek to Cozumel with one goal in mind: diving and snorkeling in the beautiful coral reefs around the island. If you arrive *sans* equipment, have no fear: dive shops proliferate like bunnies in Cozumel. Over 100 shops operate out of the island concentrating on the waterfront and along Calle 3 Sur between Melgar and Av. 10. The standard rate for snorkeling equipment is US$4-8 per day. Scuba gear is, of course, more expensive (US$30-60 per day). Always consider safety before price; look for shops with **ANOAAT** (Asociación Nacional de Operadores de Actividades Aquaticas Turístico) affiliation.

Del Mar Aquatics (☎872 19 00), 200m north of La Ceiba Hotel, 7km south of town. Rents snorkeling (US$6 per day) and scuba equipment (US$34 per day), and offers deep-sea fishing, night and day dives, and snorkeling trips. Open daily 7am-7:30pm.

Blue Bubble Divers, Calle 3 #33 (☎872 18 65; www.bluebubble.com), has a friendly, English-speaking staff and a choice of 20 reefs to visit. Snorkeling equipment US$6 per day. 2-tank dive US$70. Open M-Sa 7am-9pm, Su 7am-7pm.

Aqua Safari (☎872 01 01), Melgar at Calle 5 Sur. Single-tank dive US$30; 2hr. snorkeling boat trip US$20. Open daily 7am-2:30pm and 4-6:30pm.

Studio Blue Dive Center (☎872 44 14), on Salas near Av. 5. Scuba diving lessons US$60. Snorkeling trips US$30-45. Open daily 8:30am-9pm.

YUCATÁN

DON'T TOUCH THE CORAL! We repeat: don't touch the coral! You will kill the coral. Then you'd feel pretty bad about yourself, wouldn't you?

Once you have your equipment ready, mopeds or bikes are the best way of getting to the ideal spot. Otherwise, you might have to fork over money for an expensive taxi. Snorkelers will want to head south of town, toward **Playa La Ceiba** and **Chankanaab National Park.** Divers should head toward one of the reefs that hug the southeast side of the island. Note that some reefs (like the Colombia and Maracaibo reefs) have strong currents and should only be attempted by more experienced divers. Be sure to ask before diving. Those looking to expend minimal effort might consider joining a pre-packaged excursion. (US$25-35 per day for snorkeling trips; US$60 and up for scuba dives, depending on skill level; US$350 for 4-day full certification courses. US$180 for referral certification dives.)

BEACHES

Beachcombers should not be disheartened by the beaches near San Miguel. The island's true treasures lie to the north, east, and south of town. While those looking to swim may be disappointed by the sharp coral underneath Cozumel's waves, sunbathers and snorkelers will find paradise. From San Miguel, traveling 7km south on Melgar will bring you to the small **Playa La Ceiba,** the beachfront of the Hotel La Ceiba. The clear waters off the beach have excellent snorkeling—less than 100m offshore lurks the underwater grave of the plane wreck from the James Bond film "Survive." Several kilometers farther south off Melgar past the Chankanaab National Park, the uncrowded **Playas Francisco** and **Palancar** are regarded as the best beaches on the island, and serve as jumping-off points for exploring the Palancar Reef. The east coast of the island is lined with dozens of beautiful and less touristed beaches that make good picnic and camping spots. While many beaches tempt with magnificent turquoise waters, please remember the water has a strong undertow and can be turbulent. Always exercise caution.

SIGHTS

Chankanaab National Park, 9km south of downtown off Melgar, contains a beautiful bay circled by a botanical garden, museum, dolphin pen, and restaurant. The clear, oval lagoon nearby used to be open to swimmers, but the excessive traffic was found to be damaging to the coral, and the lagoon has since been declared off limits. The real attractions are now the abundant fish and stunning coral formations in the bay, which is open to snorkelers and scuba divers. Equipment facilities lie in the park. The park's small museum focuses on natural resources, and houses photographs of the underwater caves in the lagoon. (☎872 29 40. Open daily 7am-7pm. Admission US$10.) At the southern tip of the island, 27km from downtown, the recently opened **Punta Sur Ecological Reserve** wows visitors with boat rides through crocodile-infested lagoons, snorkeling (equipment rental included in admission), and the small ruins of a Maya tomb. The lighthouse at Punta Celerain, within the reserve, overlooks sand dunes that buffer the beach and presents a thrilling view of Cozumel's southern shores. (☎872 29 40. Open daily 8am-4pm. 150 pesos.)

CORAL GRIEFS The Palancar Reef of Cozumel, part of the second-largest reef system in the world, draws legions of scuba fanatics eager to explore its colorful depths. However, few visitors realize the biological importance of the majestic coral pillars. Coral is to a reef as soil is to a rainforest; if the coral is destroyed, the entire ecosystem disintegrates. International law prohibits the harvesting of coral, but it does not forbid the purchase or exportation of coral-derived crafts. Several shops in Cozumel sell goods made from coral. By patronizing these establishments, tourists heighten the demand for coral, and contribute to the destruction of the splendid reefs they have come to see. So no matter how cute a trinket they're selling, **don't buy coral.**

A former Maya trading center, Cozumel is littered with dozens of ruins. None of them, unfortunately, are well preserved. The very small **El Cedral**, the oldest ruins on the island, are located on a road off Melgar a few kilometers south of Playa San Francisco. (Open daily 8am-5pm. Free.) The only excavated and reconstructed ruins are the ones at **San Gervasio**, which include the remains of an observatory and several houses, temples, and arches that together form what was once the most prominent community in Cozumel. (Take Juárez out of town; after 8km, a "San Gervasio" sign marks a gravel road branching to the left. Follow the road another 6km. ☎800 22 15. Open daily 9am-6pm. 50 pesos.) The air-conditioned **Museo de la Isla de Cozumel**, on the waterfront between Calles 4 and 6, may be small but is well-worth a visit. The museum's four themed rooms are filled with photographs, poetry, coral, marine and jungle trivia, and artifacts. The Coral and Reefs room, with its colorful exhibits and wealth of information on Cozumel's marine treasures, may especially enrich the underwater experiences of prospective snorkelers and scuba divers. (☎872 14 75 or 872 14 34. Open daily 9am-6pm. US$3.)

◗ NIGHTLIFE

Like almost everything else on the island, the nightlife in Cozumel is both relaxing and tourist-heavy. Around the *zócalo* in downtown San Miguel, divers kick back after a day at the reefs, and docked tourists unload their cash. If you're looking for a party, Carlos n' Charlie's and Neptuno are typically where it's at.

Carlos n' Charlie's (☎872 15 05), on Melgar, 2 blocks north of the dock. Perhaps the most happening place in all of Cozumel, this restaurant/bar entertains North Americans with drinks, slammer contests, and ridiculous rules of the house, the last of which is "there are no rules." Open daily 10am-1am.

Neptuno, Calle 11, 5 blocks south of the plaza, has multi-level dance floors, blasting lasers, and throbbing bass. Cover 75 pesos. Open daily 9pm-late.

Havana Club (☎872 20 98), on Melgar between Calles 6 and 8, on the 2nd fl. of Diamonds International. This upscale waterfront cafe/bar features live bands playing the finest in Cuban *salsa* and jazz. Cuban cigars available. Open M-Sa 9am-11pm.

Fat Tuesday (☎872 51 30), right off the dock, 50m in on Juaréz. Ever wonder where the tourists get their tall, fluorescent drinks? This is it. The staff cracks jokes over the speakers and boozers belt it out on the karaoke machine. Open daily 10:30am-2am.

Coco Wook (☎872 03 16), on Melgar, across from the dock. Get hypnotized by the nonstop techno and the jungle decor. No cover. Open daily 6pm-2am.

Bar Romance, on Calle 1 between Av. 5 and 10 inside Plaza California. A sleepy karaoke bar and dance floor with a local clientele. Open daily 7pm-2am.

PUERTO MORELOS ☎9

Even the gods would be content with the unspoiled coral reef and pristine white sand beach of Puerto Morelos (pop. 4000). The serene beauty and sleepy peace inspire pride in the townspeople, and locals do everything they can to preserve this calm. Waterskiing and parasailing are forbidden here, as are resort hotels and other Cancún-style hedonism. Friendly Puerto Morelos has become a popular vacation destination for Mexicans in need of relaxation and tourists tired of frenetic city life. Stop for a day here to enjoy meditating on the beach, exploring the reef, or kicking back in a bar, and you may decide never to leave.

◗ **TRANSPORTATION.** Catch buses at Mex. 307, 2km west of town, to **Playa del Carmen** and **Cancún** (every 10 min, 16 pesos). To get to the *centro*, take a taxi (13 pesos) from the highway. A car ferry leaves for Cozumel from the port ½km south of the *zócalo*. (☎871 03 55. 3hr.; 5am and 2pm every day except Tu and F; 55 pesos, with car 735 pesos.) Those with cars should arrive 2hr. in advance.

📋🛈 ORIENTATION AND PRACTICAL INFORMATION. Puerto Morelos is located on the east coast of Quintana Roo, 30km south of Cancún and 30km north of Playa del Carmen. Mex. 307 runs north-south, and passes 2km west of the town center. The town itself is laid out in a simple grid, organized around a central *zócalo*, which borders the beach. **Marant Travel**, Tulum 1 (☎871 03 32), on the southwest corner of the *zócalo*, offers **tourist information**, bike rentals (10 pesos per hr., 50 pesos per day), car rentals (550-2200 pesos per day), and **Internet** access (45 pesos per hr.). **Mor Ex**, at the southwest corner of the *zócalo*, provides currency exchange; an **ATM** is located on the north side, under Restaurant El Pescador. **Emergency: ☎**060. **Farmacia San José Obrero**, Rojo Gómez 2, is on the west side of the *zócalo*. (☎871 00 53. Open 8am-2pm and 4-10pm). For medical assistance, visit the **Centro de Salud**, southeast of the *zócalo*. (Open M-F 8am-1pm and 5-8pm, Sa 9am-1pm.) The **police** are at the northwest corner of the *zócalo*. (☎871 01 17. Some English spoken.) Puerte Morelos has no post office. **Postal Code:** 77580.

📋🏠 ACCOMMODATIONS AND FOOD. Budget accommodations are scarce in Puerto Morelos; the best option may be camping on the beach. Ask the police for permission. **Amar Inn**, between Mexicano and Cárdenas, a walk north of the *zócalo*, sits right on the beach. Run by the gracious Ana Luisa, the inn has three private cabins and three rooms surrounding a shady courtyard. (☎871 00 26. Cabins come with fridges and fans. US$30-55.) **Posada Amor**, on Rojo Gómez, south of the *zócalo*, is a small inn with an adjoining restaurant, set in a maze of brightly colored courtyards. The simple rooms with fans vary in quality. (☎871 00 33. Singles 168-224 pesos; doubles 224-336 pesos.) Budget-friendly restaurants are rare in Puerto Morelos. **Torteria El Pirata**, on the northwestern corner of the *zócalo*, offers the best deals with its seafood and chicken plates and 35- to 40-peso sandwiches. (☎871 04 89. Open daily 7:30am-10:30 pm.) **Las Palmeras**, southeast of the *zócalo*, is a roomy, airy restaurant overlooking the beach. Have a drink and dine under a shady *palapa* outside while enjoying the Caribbean breeze and great seafood. (40-80 pesos. ☎871 01 63.) Restaurant and bar **Don Pepe**, Rojo Gómez 4, northwest of the *zócalo* also serves fresh seafood (45-65 pesos) in addition to 18-peso coconut creams. (☎871 06 02. Open daily 1pm-1am. Karaoke starts 6pm.)

🔲🏖🎉 SIGHTS, BEACHES, AND NIGHTLIFE. Snorkeling and scuba diving are the best way to explore the coral reef, which was designated a national park in 2000. Several dive shops along the *zócalo* rent equipment. **SubAqua Explorers** (☎871 00 12; open daily 9am-4pm and 6-9pm) and **Snorkeling Sea Blue** (☎871 00 37) will gladly indulge your aquatic interests. (2hr. snorkeling trips with equipment 200-250 pesos.) Consider yourself more of a landlubber? Look no farther than **Goyo** and his **Custom Jungle Adventures** (☎871 01 78), on Rojo Gómez just north of the *zócalo*. Goyo will lead you inland and show you Maya villages, trees with medicinal properties, and refreshing *cenotes*. Tours leave from his *palapa* (US$40-80).

While waves crash into the popular coral reef 600m off shore, the ocean waters gently massage the uncrowded beach. White sands, emerald waters, and Mexican children improvising watery playgrounds around the docks make a day at the beach here virtually unforgettable.

Nightlife in Puerto Morelos is refreshingly different than in other places on the Maya Riviera. Rather than multitudes of bars packed with drunken tourists and clubs that loudly pulsate late into the night, Puerto Morelos hosts lone mariachi bands wandering from bar to bar on the beachfront. Many people choose to spend evenings on the beach, sipping tequila and watching the clear sky until sunrise.

TULUM   ☎9

On the edge of the *Etaib* (Black Bees) jungle, atop a rocky seaside cliff, stands the walled Maya "City of the Dawn." While the ruins do not rival those of Uxmal or Chichén Itzá in terms of scale, many of the buildings are still intact, and their towering presence above the breaking waves of the Caribbean is unforgettable. First settled in the 6th century AD, Tulum (pop. 16,000) was the oldest continuously inhabited city in the New World when the Spanish arrived. Today, sun worshippers of a different kind tramp to the ancient port, complementing their sightseeing with healthy doses of swimming, sunbathing, and living at civilization's edge on the white beach. With an unparalleled natural backdrop, Tulum's temples attract an increasing number of daytrippers from Cancún. There are two bases for exploring the ruins, beaches, and numerous cenotes of Tulum: either the village of Tulum or the many *cabañas* lining the beach for 9km south of the ruins.

⌐ TRANSPORTATION

GETTING AROUND
Getting around the Tulum area can be time-consuming and expensive. Although numerous taxis are readily available at the crossing point - the *crucero* - in Pueblo Tulum, along Mex. 307, and at various *cabañas*, their relatively pricey fares can add up fast. The best budget option is to rent a bicycle and give your legs an old-fashioned workout. To get to any of the sites near Tulum, wave down one of the many white *colectivo* vans (10 pesos) as it passes on Mex. 307. Some travelers successfully hitchhike from site to site along the highway.

GETTING AWAY
Buses: There are two **ADO** bus stations. The main one (☎871 21 22) is on the east side of Mex. 307, right in the middle of the Pueblo. The small waiting room is sandwiched between two currency exchange booths. Buses head to: **Cancún** (2hr., every hr., 55 pesos); **Chetumal** (3hr., 5 per day, 104 pesos); **Chichén Itzá** (3hr., 8:30pm, 66 pesos); **Cobá** (1hr., 4 per day, 21 pesos); **Mexico City** (24hr., 1:10pm, 760 pesos); **Palenque** (12hr., 5:45pm, 292 pesos); **Playa del Carmen** (1hr., every hr., 22 pesos); **Mérida** (4hr., 2:30am, 114 pesos); **San Cristóbal de las Casas** (14hr., 5:45pm, 380 pesos); and **Veracruz** (21hr., 4:30pm, 542 pesos). There is also an ADO terminal located at the *crucero*, next to the Hotel Copal.

⚡ 🔒 ORIENTATION AND PRACTICAL INFORMATION

Located 42km southeast of Cobá and 127km south of Cancún, Tulum is the southernmost tourist attraction on the Caribbean coast of Quintana Roo, known as the **Maya Riviera,** and the easternmost of the major Maya archaeological sites. Tulum sprawls over three separate areas: the **crucero** (crossroads), which is near the ruins, the beach *cabañas*, and Pueblo Tulum. Arriving in Tulum from the north on Mex. 307, you will come first to the *crucero*, about 3km before town. Here, several restaurants, hotels, overpriced minimarts, and a gas station huddle about 800m west of the ruins. 1km south of the *crucero* is a turnoff leading to food and lodging at the beachside *cabañas*, about 2-3km from Mex. 307. Pueblo Tulum, about 3km south of the *crucero*, also offers a handful of roadside restaurants, hotels, and services.

Tourist Office: There is no official tourist office, but the Weary Traveler Backpacker's Center (☎871 24 61), across the street from the bus station, offers maps and information about lodging and sights. Open 24hr.

Currency Exchange: At the *crucero* in the Hotel Acuario or next to the bus office in Pueblo Tulum. There are currently **no banks** or ATMs in Tulum.

Police: (☎871 20 55), in the Delegación Municipal, 2 blocks past the post office. English spoken.

Pharmacy: La Salud Farmacia (☎871 23 19), on the west side of Mex. 307, across the street from the bus station. Open daily 7am-11pm.

Supermarket: Super Marcaribe (☎871 22 26), 4 blocks north of the bus station. Open daily 7am-11pm. **Mini-Super El Pipazo** (☎871 22 71), south of Cabañas Copal, next to the Nohock Tunich Cabañas. Open daily 7:30am-9pm.

Laundry: Lavandería Burbujas (☎871 24 65), 2 blocks east of the bus station. Wash and dry 12 pesos per kg. Express service is an additional 20 pesos per kg. Open M-F 8am-7pm, Sa 8am-2pm.

Bike Rental: La Estación (☎871 22 57), 20m north of the bus station. 70 pesos per 24hr. Open daily 8am-10pm.

Car Rental: Cabañas Playa Mambo (☎287 20 30), across the street from the bus station. Rental rates 350 pesos per day. Open daily 8am-8pm.

Medical Assistance: Centro de Salud, take the 1st left heading south from the bus station, and then another quick left. Open 24hr. for emergencies.

Internet Access: The Weary Travelers Backpacker's Center (☎871 24 61), across the street from the bus station. 0.5 pesos per min. Open 24hr.

Post Office: a few hundred meters into town on Mex. 307. Open M-F 9am-4pm.

Postal Code: 77780.

ACCOMMODATIONS AND CAMPING

The *cabañas* of Tulum are deservedly world-famous and offer a unique experience that shouldn't be missed. Cheap, right on the sandy beach, made of sticks, without electricity (bring a flashlight and some candles), with little clean water, and populated by hippies and mellow backpackers from around the world, the *cabañas* demonstrate how it is possible to live fruitfully without modern civilization—at least for a few days. Chill on the pristine beaches, listen to local singers, revel at late-night beachside fires, and perfect your tan. Bring mosquito netting and repellent; the bugs are nasty. During the high season (mid-Dec. to Apr. and July and Aug.), arrive early in the morning or make reservations.

Cabañas Copal (☎871 24 81), 5km south of the ruins on the beachfront road. Perched atop cliffs overlooking crashing waves, these relatively well-furnished *cabañas* are quiet and civilization-free. *Cabañas* with common bath and shower 100-150 pesos, with private bath 200-250 pesos. Prices rise 200-300 pesos in the high season.

Cabañas Santa Fe, off the paved road about ½km south of the ruins. Follow the signs to Don Armando's and turn left. If you don't mind getting sand everywhere, shack up with backpackers from all over the world at these very primitive *cabañas* on the beach. Long lines during high season; no reservations allowed. Hammocks 25 pesos; camping 30 pesos; *cabaña económica* (i.e. an empty room) 100 pesos; beds 140 pesos.

Don Armando Cabañas (don_Armando_mx@yahoo.com), on the access road less than 1km south of the ruins. A humble paradise with a basketball court. The *cabañas* are solid and secure, and the communal facilities are more than outhouses. *Cabañas* 100-145 pesos, with private bath 280 pesos. No seasonal price changes.

Hotel Copal (☎871 24 79), located 800m west of the ruins at the junction with Mex. 307. Great location if you've to see the ruins. Simple run-down rooms keep mosquitos out and won't dent your wallet. Call ahead in high season. Single bunks with common bath 70 pesos; doubles with private bath 150 pesos. Prices rise in the high season.

FOOD

Although points of interest in Tulum tend to be rather spread out, hearty and inexpensive food is never too far away. The *pueblo* has plenty of cheap *loncherías* and mini-supers not too far from the bus station, while the *crucero* and the beachside *cabañas* offer satisfying budget-friendly restaurants.

Son y Cafe (☎871 22 72), on Orion, 2 blocks east of Don Cafetos. This colorful new restaurant serves fresh and tasty vegetarian food in addition to *comida típica*. Don't miss the Natilla Maya vanilla pudding (16 pesos), the excellent creamy vegetable soup (23 pesos), or the super-refreshing Chaya fruit drink (21 pesos), made with Chaya (a therapeutic green, leafy vegetable) grown on the premises. Open daily 8am-11pm.

Restaurante Santa Fe, at the Cabañas Santa Fe. Reggae tunes, *salsa* rhythms, and local guitarists are the perfect compliment to the fresh fish (40-60 pesos) and breakfasts (30-40 pesos). Happy Hour 8-10pm. Open daily 7am-11pm. Kitchen closes at 9pm.

Don Cafetos (☎871 22 07), just north of Crocodilos. The green-checked table cloths and more-than-ample bar encourage guests to lounge and enjoy the shrimp cocktails (50 pesos) and tacos (32 pesos). Open daily 7am-11pm.

El Gaucho Ilegal (☎871 24 79), located in the Hotel Copal at the *crucero*. Listen to some well-chosen tunes as you dig into a giant, all-inclusive breakfast (45 pesos) or fresh seafood (45-70 pesos). Open daily 8am-6pm.

ⓩ BEACHES

THE BEACH. Swimming, splashing, and tanning on the beach are popular ways to end a hot day in Tulum, and nude bathing is no longer a rare phenomenon. Off-shore, waves crash over Tulum's **barrier reef,** the largest in the Americas; it runs the full length of the Yucatán Peninsula and Belize. Although the water is not as clear as at Xel-Ha or Akumal, the fish are just as plentiful. To mingle with them, rent scuba and snorkeling equipment from **Dive Tulum** at Cabañas Sante Fe. The shop also plans trips to the reef and a nearby *cenote*. (☎871 20 96. Snorkeling US$5 per day, trips US$10-20; 1-tank dive US$30, 2-tank dive US$50. Open daily 8am-5:30pm.) Another option is **Punta Piedra,** 5km south of the ruins, a bit past Cabañas Copal. They rent snorkeling equipment (50 pesos per day) and tanks (US$35 for 1, US$60 for 2). They also offer bike rental (60 pesos per day, 50 per day for 2 or more days) and a spectacular jungle tour (200 pesos), which includes visits to multiple *cenotes*. (☎876 91 67. Open daily 7:30am-7pm.)

CENOTES. The hidden treasures of Tulum are its numerous *cenotes*, sunk into the jungle throughout the area. *Cenotes* are places where the ground opens up to reveal a pool of fresh water below, actually part of a massive underground network of rivers, which work their way through the limestone shelf on which the Yucatán Peninsula sits and out to the sea. **Cenote Escondido** and **Cenote Cristal** are both 3km south of the intersection of Mex. 307 and the road to Cobá (admission 40 pesos, divers 60 pesos). Here you will find freshwater tropical fish, green underwater vegetation, and cool, crystal clear waters. Following the road to Cobá west out of town, you will come across the **Cenote Calaveras**—also called the Temple of Doom—after 1.6km. (Free.) Look for a newly constructed house on your right, and follow the path through the roads behind it. Continue on the road to the mini-paradise of **El Gran Cenote,** 1.5km farther on and clearly marked with a sign (admission 40 pesos, divers 60 pesos). Regarded as the best *cenote* in the area—for snorkeling (equipment rental 40 pesos). The *cenote's* unforgettable beauty is like something out of a fairy-tale—bats, birds, and butterflies flutter over the cold, clear blue waters filled with friendly fish and green lilypads. Discovered less than 15 years ago and less crowded than its more famous neighbor, **Cenote Dos Ojos,** it is still invaded by proliferating tourist groups in the afternoon. *Cenotes* are generally open from 8am to 4pm. You must be an experienced open water diver to dive alone, but the calm and clear waters offer a great place to learn how to dive.

ⓞ THE ARCHAEOLOGICAL SITE OF TULUM

The ruins lie a brisk 10min. walk east of Mex. 307 from the crucero; the amusement park-style train (15 pesos) covers the distance in slightly less time. Tickets are sold at a booth to the left of the parking lot and at the entrance to the ruins. Open daily 8am-6pm. 35 pesos; Su free. Guided tours available in several languages (45 min. tour for 5 people 250 pesos); inquire at the crucero.

Perched on a cliff overlooking the calm, blue Caribbean, the beautiful ruins at Tulum ("Wall" or "Fortification" in Maya) are what remains of one of the last Maya cities to be inhabited. The city was first constructed around AD 500, in the middle of the Maya Classic Period, but its strategic position on a seaside cliff, where it was easily defended, kept it inhabited for over a millenium. Not until well into the Post-Classic Period, in the 15th and 16th centuries, did Tulum reach its zenith as a fortification and religious center. Most of the 50 or so structures at the site are temples dedicated to religious ceremonies and living quarters for nobles and priests. In 1544, the city fell to Spanish conquerors, but even after its defeat, Tulum was used as a Spanish base to fend off English, Dutch, and French pirates. As late as 1847, Tulum provided refuge for Maya fleeing government forces during the Caste War. Today the ruins are infested with mosquitos and tourists—many of whom cool off at the small beach located within its site.

THE WALL. The first thing visitors see in Tulum is the impressive wall surrounding the city center's three landlocked sides. The wall, made of small rocks wedged together, was originally 3.6m thick and 3m high. It shielded the city from aggressive neighbors from other Maya city-states and prevented all but the 150 or so priests and governors of Tulum from entering the city for most of the year. Representations of the Maya "Descending God" cover the western walls and are illuminated every evening by the rays of the setting sun.

HOUSE OF THE HALACH UINIK AND THE PALACIO. To the left of the entrance lie a grave and the remains of platforms that once supported huts. Behind these are the House of the Halach Uinik (House of the Ruler), characterized by a traditional four-column entrance, and the Palacio, Tulum's largest residential building.

TEMPLO DE LOS FRESCOS (TEMPLE OF THE PAINTINGS). The temple is a stellar example of Postclassic Maya architecture and was most likely built in three separate stages. Well-preserved 600-year-old murals inside the temple depict deities intertwined with serpents, fruits, and flowers. Masks of Itzamná, the Maya Creator, occupy the northwest and southwest corners of the building.

EL CASTILLO (THE CASTLE). The most prominent structure in Tulum, El Castillo looms to the east over the rocky seaside cliff, commanding a view of the entire walled city. The pyramid was built in three separate stages, and was probably not intended to be a pyramid after all. What is now visible was most likely built around the 12th or 13th centuries AD. A double-headed, feathered serpent sprawls across the facade, with a diving god in the center. This icon contains bee-like imagery, perhaps alluding to the importance of honey in Caribbean trade. In more recent times, El Castillo served as a lighthouse, aiding returning fishermen in finding the gap in the barrier reef just off the shore. In front of the temple is the **sacrificial stone** where the Maya held battle ceremonies and prisoners of war were sacrificed.

TEMPLO DE LA SERIE INICIAL (TEMPLE OF THE INITIAL SERIES). On a plaza to the southwest of El Castillo is the Temple of the Initial Series. Named after a stela found here, the temple bears a date that corresponds to the beginning of the Maya religious calendar in the year AD 761.

TEMPLO DEL DIOS DESCENDENTE. The Temple of the Descending God, with a fading relief of a feathered, armed deity diving from the sky, stands on the opposite side of the plaza. Archaeologists believe that this figure, seen at various buildings in Tulum, symbolized the setting sun.

TEMPLO DE VIENTOS (TEMPLE OF THE WINDS). Perched on its own precipice on the northeast side of the beach, the Temple of the Winds was designed with special acoustics to act as a storm-warning system. Sure enough, before Hurricane Gilbert struck the site in 1988, the temple's airways dutifully whistled their alarm.

DAYTRIPS FROM TULUM

SIAN KA'AN BIOSPHERE RESERVE

Follow the coast road 7km south of Tulum to the "Maya Arch," at the entrance. The Amigos de Sian Ka'an, who work to maintain the reserve, lead the best tours, departing from Tulum. Call their offices in Cancún (☎880 60 24; open M-F 10am-6pm.), Felipe Carrillo Puerto (☎834 08 13), Chetumal (☎837 16 37), or at Cabañas Ana y José in Tulum (☎880 60 22) for more information and to reserve a place. The main office for the reserve is in Cancún at Kukulcán km 4.5 (☎849 75 54).

Sian Ka'an ("Birth of the Sky") comprises roughly 10% of the state of Quintana Roo (1.6 million acres) and is Mexico's largest coastal wetland reserve. Protected by federal decree on January 20, 1988, the immense reserve was Mexico's first UNESCO Natural World Heritage site and encompasses tropical forests, *cenotes*, savannas, mangroves, lagoons, and 112km of coral reef. It is home to 1200 species of flora, 339 species of birds, 103 species of mammals, and 23 Maya archaeological sites. The best way to see Sian Ka'an is by boat. You can drive a car along the poorly-maintained coastal road for 57km before arriving in Punta Allen, but all you will see is a wall of dense jungle on either side.

XEL-HA

Xel-Ha lies 15km north of Tulum. Get on any northbound bus and ask to be let off at Xel-Ha (10 pesos). Taxis charge exorbitant rates. Getting back to Tulum at the end of the day, when buses begin to come less and less frequently, can be challenging. Vigorously wave down a bus on its way to Tulum or Cancún. Locals will usually be able to tell you when the next one is due to pass. ☎(9) 875 40 70; www.xelha.com.mx. Open daily 8:30am-6pm. US$25; all-inclusive (restaurants, snorkel gear, lockers, and towels) US$49.

Xel-Ha (SHELL-ha; "where the water is born") is Disneyland set in the Yucatec jungle. Famous for its natural aquarium, almost 2m deep, nestled amidst jungles, caves, and coves, Xel-Ha allows visitors to admire parrot fishes and meter-long barracudas and splash around in the nearby *caleta* (inlet). For relative peace during busy times, cross the inlet and explore the underwater caves, or stay dry and visit the sea turtle camp. Use caution and don't go diving under overhangs alone. Xel-Ha also contains two *cenotes*, a natural river, and underground sea caves. Try arriving before noon, when busloads of tourists from the resorts overrun the place. If you don't get the all-inclusive admission, you can rent towels (US$3) and snorkel gear (US$9), available at the shower area. Xel-Ha also maintains a small archaeological site on the highway, 100m south of the entrance to the inlet. **El Templo de Los Pájaros** and **El Palacio,** small Classic and Post-Classic ruins, were only recently opened to the public. The former (the ruin farthest into the jungle) overlooks a peaceful, shady *cenote* where swimming and rope swinging are permitted. (The jungle at Xel-Ha is rife with mosquitoes, so bring insect repellent.)

CENOTE DOS OJOS

3 trips daily from Dos Ojos Dive Center, several hundred meters south of the park entrance (9, 11am, and 1pm; ☎879 72 84). Trips also leave from the Cabañas Santa Fe. Getting to Dos Ojos requires the same patience as getting to Xel-Ha. Hop on a combi or a colectivo after waving it down from the side of the road (every 10 min. or so).

Cenote Dos Ojos, 1km south of Xel-Ha, is the one of the longest and most extensive underwater caverns in the world, stretching 33,855m. Originally a dry cave system with limestone formations in shades of amber as well as calcic stalactites, stalagmites, and natural wind-etchings, the system was flooded long ago. Snorkelers and divers find a haven in "the place of hidden waters," along with tetras, mollies, and swordfish. You must be an experienced certified open water diver to dive in the sometimes crowded Dos Ojos (1-tank US$50, 2-tank US$80).

COBÁ

The Maya ruins of Cobá are located less than 50km northwest of Tulum. To get to the ruins from the Cobá bus station, walk south on the main street in town as far as the T-junction at the lake. Take a left on Voz Suave; the ruins are a 5min. walk down this road. Remember to bring a water bottle, hat, and plenty of mosquito repellent. Ruins open daily 7am-6pm. 35 pesos; Su free. Parking 10 pesos. Tour guides can be found at the entrance. A 45min. tour for 1-6 people starts at 250 pesos. Cheaper tour guides can be found just inside the entrance. Allow at least 2hr. to see most of the site.

Stretching over 70 sq. km deep within the jungle, the ruins of Cobá testify to what was perhaps the largest of all Maya cities. Inhabited at various intervals for over a millenium, the population reached 55,000 at Cobá's peak, from AD 800 to 1100. The city flourished in the Classic Period as a crossroads of the entire Yucatán Peninsula, connecting distant Maya cities through its vast network of *sacbé*, ancient Maya roadways. By the Post-Classic Period, Cobá had mysteriously lost its power to nearby cities such as Tulum and Xcaret. Today, the tranquil, shaded ruins, guarded by several shallow lakes, receive far less attention than others at Chichén Itzá and Tulum. The government has poured less money into the site, leaving an estimated 6,500 buildings unexcavated. Yet work slowly continues at Cobá, each year revealing structures that have been hidden from human eyes for centuries.

Once through the gate, the site's main attractions are laid out in a Y-shaped formation, with the entrance and the ruins of Grupo Cobá, dating from the Early Classic Period (AD 300-600), at the base of the "Y." Past the entrance, and after an immediate right, looms the impressive 28m high **Temple of the Churches,** built over seven 52-year periods, each one associated with a new chief priest. Only the front face of the temple has been excavated, revealing a corbel-vaulted passageway that you can explore. In front of the structure is a stone **sacrificial table**, upon which animal offerings were made to Chac, the rain god. Follow a second passageway farther south to **Plaza del Templo,** where assemblies were once held. The red plant dye still visible on the walls of the passageway dates from the 5th century. A mortar here was used to prepare maize, the staple food of the Maya. Return to the main path for a look at the **ballcourt** with its intact stone arches.

A 1km walk up the "trunk" of the "Y" takes you to the other sites. Follow the right branch for 1km to reach the eight stelae of the **Grupo Macanxoc.** On the way, a well-engineered Maya *sacbé* awaits. This particular road is 20m wide and raised 4m from the jungle floor. The ornate stone slabs of the Grupo Macanxoc were erected as memorials above the tombs of Maya royals, but unfortunately, their pictorial secrets are now barely discernible, with one exception. The first slab, the impressive and well-preserved **Retrato del Rey**, portrays a king standing on the heads of two slaves, bow and arrow in hand, wearing a *quetzal*-feather headdress.

Taking the left-hand branch of the "Y," you will encounter the **Temple of Paintings,** named for the richly colored frescoes that once adorned the building. Follow an unmarked trail northwest of the temple to the three stelae of **Chumuc Múl.** The first depicts a kneeling Maya ballplayer and is the tomb of a victorious captain; you can make out the ball in the upper-left-hand corner. The second stela depicts a princess, while the third portrays a priest. His seal is stamped on top of the slab, along with a jaguar's head, a common Maya symbol of worship. Two hundred meters farther up, you'll run into **sacbé No. 1,** a road that ran from Cobá all the way to Chichén Itzá, 101km west. Runners were posted every 5km to deliver messages via a series of quick dashes. Images of the honeybee god around the site are a reminder of Coba's past as an economic hub. The Maya used honey (along with salt, coconuts, and jade) as a medium of exchange.

Several hundred meters farther toward the pyramid, **Nohoch Múl,** you'll pass another ballcourt, Temple 10, and the well-preserved Stela 20. Finally, you will see towering Nohoch Múl, the tallest Maya structure in all the Yucatán, rising out of the jungle. A climb up this breathtaking 42m high stone pyramid will make the entire visit to Cobá worth your while. The pyramid's nine levels and 127 steps, where Maya priests once led processions, display carvings of the "diving god" similar to the ones in Tulum. A spectacular view of Lake Cobá, Lake Macanxoc, and the surrounding area awaits you at the top level. When coming down, be cautious not to lose your footing—several people have slipped and died during the descent.

CHETUMAL

☎ 9

Residents of Quintana Roo are proud of Chetumal (pop. 200,000), the relatively new capital of Mexico's youngest state, which hugs the Belizean border. The city, founded in 1898 to intercept arms shipments to Maya insurgents and prevent illegal timber harvesting, was leveled by a hurricane in 1955. The reconstruction produced the wide avenues, modern architecture, and waterfront boulevard. The city is also home to an extensive shopping district and world-class Maya museum.

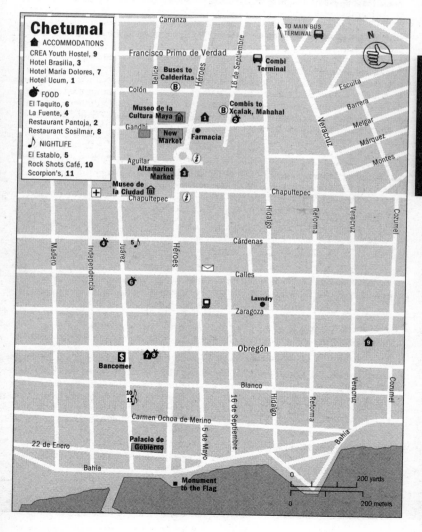

Chetumal

🏠 ACCOMMODATIONS
CREA Youth Hostel, **9**
Hotel Brasilia, **3**
Hotel María Dolores, **7**
Hotel Ucum, **1**

🍴 FOOD
El Taquito, **6**
La Fuente, **4**
Restaurant Pantoja, **2**
Restaurant Sosilmar, **8**

🎵 NIGHTLIFE
El Establo, **5**
Rock Shots Café, **10**
Scorpion's, **11**

YUCATÁN

☐ TRANSPORTATION

Airport: (☎832 04 65), 5km southwest of the city on Aguilar. **Aerocaribe** and **Mexicana,** (☎832 66 75). **Aviacsa** (☎832 76 76), Cárdenas at 5 de Mayo.

Buses: (☎832 51 10) Insurgentes at Belice. To reach the *centro* from the station, your best bet is a taxi (10 pesos). Buses go to: **Campeche** (7hr., noon, 176 pesos); **Cancún** (5½hr., 18 per day, 155 pesos); **México City** (22hr., 4:30 and 9pm, 658 pesos); **Mérida** (8 per day, 167 pesos); **Playa del Carmen** (4½hr., 18 per day 12:30am-11pm, 115 pesos); **Tikal** (7am and 4pm, 380 pesos); **Tulum** (3½hr., 8 per day, 104 pesos); **Villahermosa** (9hr., 6 per day 7am-9pm, 234 pesos); **Xcalac** (4hr., 3pm, 50 pesos); **Xpujil** (2hr., 5 per day, 51 pesos); **Belize City** (3hr.; 11:45am, 3pm, and 6pm; 60 pesos). Cristóbal Colón leaves at 9:15pm for: **Ocosingo** (251 pesos); **Palenque** (198 pesos); **San Cristóbal de las Casas** (287 pesos); **Tuxtla Gutiérrez** (320 pesos).

☐☐ ORIENTATION AND PRACTICAL INFORMATION

Tucked into the Yucatán's southeastern corner, Chetumal is just north of the Río Hondo, the natural border between Mexico and Belize. The thriving shopping district lines **Héroes**, starting at **Mercado Viejo** and extending 1km south to the bay. At the southern terminus of Héroes lies **Bahía**, a wide avenue flanked by statues, small plazas, and playgrounds that follows the bay for several kilometers. From here you can see part of Belize, the long, distant spit of land to the right as you face the sea. **Taxis** will take you anywhere in town (7-10 pesos).

Tourist Offices: Information booth (☎832 36 63), Héroes and Aguilar. Open M-Sa 9am-2pm and 6-9pm. **Secretaría Estatal de Turismo** (☎835 08 60), north on Héroes, 4km from the *centro*. Huge packets of information. English spoken. Open M-F 8am-5pm.

Currency Exchange: Bancomer (☎832 53 00), on Juárez at Obregón, has good rates and a 24hr. **ATM.** Open M-F 8:30am-4pm, Sa 10am-2pm.

Consulates: Belize, Carranza 562 (cell ☎044 983 8 77 28). To enter Belize for 30 days, US, Canadian, and EU citizens need only a valid passport and a bus ticket. Open M-F 9am-2pm and 5-8pm, Sa 9am-2pm. **Guatemala,** Chapultepec 354 (☎832 30 45), at Cecilio Chi. US, Canadian, and EU citizens don't need a visa. For those who do, the process is quick (US$15). Open M-F 10am-2pm.

Market: Altamarino (or **El Mercado Viejo**), on Aguilar at Héroes. Open daily 6am-6pm.

Laundry: Lavandería "Rot Yeg" Zaragoza 141 (☎832 03 78), at Hidalgo. 11 pesos per kg., 3kg minimum. Same-day service. Open M-Sa 8am-8pm.

Emergency: ☎060.

Police: (☎832 15 00), on Insurgentes at Belice, next to the bus station. English spoken.

Red Cross: (☎832 05 71), on Chapultepec at Independencia, 2 blocks west of Héroes.

Pharmacy: Farmacia Canto, Héroes 99 (☎832 04 83), at the north end of the market. Open M-Sa 7am-11pm, Su 7am-5pm.

Hospital: Hospital General, Quintana Roo 399 (☎832 19 32), at Sordio.

Fax: Telecomm (☎832 06 51), by the post office. Open M-F 8am-6pm, Sa-Su 9am-12:30pm.

Internet: Compucentro (☎832 80 38), on Zaragoza at Cinco de Mayo. 10 pesos per hr. Open daily 9am-10pm. **Cafe Internet,** Veracruz #451 (☎832 91 45), at Gonzales. 10 pesos per hr. Open 24hr.

Post Office: Calles 2 (☎832 25 78), 1 block east of Héroes. Open M-F 9am-4pm, Sa 9am-1pm.

Postal Code: 77000.

ACCOMMODATIONS

Chetumal's budget accommodations are far from fancy, but they score points for location. A stroll down Héroes, south of the market, will open up many options.

Hotel María Dolores, Obregón 206 (☎832 05 08), half a block west of Héroes. Donald Duck image points the way to clean aqua rooms with strong fans and private baths. Restaurant inside. Singles 120 pesos; doubles 135-180 pesos; triples 180 pesos.

Hotel Ucum, Gandhi 167 (☎832 07 11 or 832 61 86). Spotless rooms have tile floors and modern bathrooms. Singles and doubles 150 pesos, with cable TV 170 pesos, with A/C 220 pesos; triples 170 pesos.

CREA Youth Hostel (HI) (☎832 34 65). From Héroes, walk east on Obregón for 5 blocks to the end—take a left and a right and you're there. Pool, lobby with *agua purificada*, and TV. Fills July-Aug.; call to reserve. Small but neat single-sex dorms with 3-4 bunks each and institutional bathrooms. Bed with sheets, pillow, and locker 30 pesos.

Hotel Brasilia, Héroes 157 (☎832 09 64), across from the market. Ask to see a room, as all are decent but some are cramped. Friendly management stores backpacks. Singles 90 pesos; doubles 120-130 pesos; triples 155 pesos; quads 175 pesos.

FOOD

Chetumal offers a spicy blend of Mexican and Belizean cuisine. *Loncherías* at the market on Héroes and Aguilar, and on Obregón, west of Héroes, are the best deals.

Restaurante Pantoja, Gandhi 181 (☎832 39 57), past Hotel Ucum, northeast of the market. An extremely popular family restaurant. Delicious and piping hot *comida casera* (homemade food) 28-32 pesos. Drink options rotate daily. Open M-Sa 7am-9pm.

Restaurant y Cocktelería Sosilmar (☎832 63 80), on Obregón, in Hotel María Dolores. Tasty fish filets 50 pesos, *milanesa de puerco* 42 pesos. Open daily 8am-10:30pm.

Machachado Pinocho, at the corner of Morelos and Camelias. This local favorite will reward your 7-peso taxi ride with cheap *antojitos*, ice-cold *machachados* (ice cream shakes; 18 pesos), and plenty of company. Open daily 6am-midnight.

El Taquito, on Calles between Juárez and Héroes. Chew on tacos and *antojitos* under the fan-cooled *palapa*. 5 beef and cheese tacos 21 pesos. Open M-Sa 6:30pm-midnight.

Restaurante Vegetariano La Fuente, Cárdenas 222 (☎832 53 73), between Independencia and Juárez. A small and bland dining area at the rear of a health food store. Full vegetarian meals Mexican-style 35 pesos. Open M-F 9am-6pm, Sa 9am-2pm.

SIGHTS AND ENTERTAINMENT

At the northern end of the market is the **Museo de la Cultura Maya,** on Héroes between Ghandi and Colón. The high-tech, interactive museum explores the Maya's three-leveled cosmos—the earth, underworld, and heavens—with glyphic text, sculptures, stelae, and models of famous Maya temples. (Open Tu-Th 9am-7pm, F-Sa 9am-8pm, Su 9am-7pm. Shows Sa 6pm and Su 11am. 50 pesos, students 20 pesos; Su free.) Before you leave, check out the free art galleries next door showcasing the work of regional artists. The informative **Museo de la Ciudad,** in the **Centro Cultural de las Bellas Artes,** Héroes 68, south of the market, details the short history of Chetumal. (Open daily 9am-7pm. 10 pesos.) The nearest beach is the *balneario* at **Calderitas.** Buses leave from Colón, between Héroes and Belice. (15min., every 30min. 7am-9pm, 4 pesos.) Although the water is turbid and the shores rocky, the beach draws crowds during summer and school holidays.

Chetumal's young nightlife scene is growing along with the rest of the city. A 20-something crowd frequents **El Establo,** on Cardenás between Héroes and Juárez, rocking to live music on the packed dance floor. (☎832 91 01. Cover men 80 pesos, women 60 pesos. Open Th-Su 10pm-4am.) Chetumal's youngest and sexiest get down Cancún-style at **Rock Shots Cafe,** on Juárez between Blanco and Merino. (☎832 97 12. Cover 30 pesos after midnight. Open Th-Su 10pm-4am.) Next door is less-happening **Scorpion's.** (Cover men 30 pesos, women 15 pesos. Open F-Su 10:30pm-3am.) **Caribbeans Cat's,** Veracruz 451, at Gonzales, a short taxi ride from the *centro*, is the newest disco in town. (☎832 91 45. Cover 40 pesos.)

🔁 DAYTRIPS FROM CHETUMAL

YUCATÁN

BACALAR

Buses leave the station at the corner of Hidalgo and Verdad. (45min., every hr. 6am-9pm, 10 pesos.) The route passes Laguna Milagros and Cenote Azul before reaching Bacalar.

Much nicer than Calderitas, both for atmosphere and for swimming, are the *cenotes* near the town of Bacalar, 36km away. The bus route passes beautiful **Laguna Milagros** and serene **Cenote Azul** before reaching the town. Quieter than those at Bacalar, both have bathing areas, dressing rooms, and *cenote*-side restaurants. Past the **Fuerte de San Felipe** in Bacalar is one of the largest and most picturesque lakes in all of Mexico, **Laguna de Siete Colores** (or **Laguna Bacalar**), so named for the seven hues reflected in its depths. The fresh water is warm, clear, and carpeted by powdery limestone, making it excellent for swimming. Nearby are bathrooms, dressing rooms, fruit vendors, expensive dockside restaurants, and a campground.

MAHAHUAL AND XCALAC

Buses to Mahahual (3hr., 40 pesos), 154km from Chetumal, and Xcalac (4hr., 60 pesos), another 100km away, depart daily at 6am, 7:30am, and 3pm from the station. A combi leaves at 5:30am from 16 de Septiembre at Gandhi, 20m past Restaurante Pantoja.

La Costa Maya, the stretch of idyllic coast running from Mahahual to Xcalac, provides a fairly good idea of what Cancún looked like 40 years ago. The quietest of the seaside fishing villages, Mahahual, with its newly-built pier for Caribbean cruise ships, and Xcalac, the southernmost community on the narrow peninsula extending south from the Sian Ka'an Biosphere Reserve, are considered "the next big thing" in Quintana Roo and offer mellow bungalows, restaurants, snorkeling, and boat rentals. Luxury resorts are a few years in the making, and savvy travelers can still savor affordable deep-sea fishing and pristine, palm-lined beaches with clear, turquoise waters perfect for sunning, swimming, and snorkeling. Nearby off the coast is enticing **Banco Chinchorro,** Mexico's largest atoll, a dream-come-true for snorkelers and experienced divers. Sharks, sea turtles, fish, and a multitude of corals coexist with the second-largest shipwreck site in the world.

KOHUNLICH

Kohunlich is 67km west of Chetumal on Mex. 186. Ride any combi from the terminal at Hidalgo and Verdad heading toward Villa or Bravo (1hr., every hr., 30 pesos). Ask to be let off at the crucero of Kohunlich, and make your way—hitch, walk, or crawl 9km down a bumpy dirt road to the entrance. Those with cars will have an easier go.

Kohunlich, an ancient Maya ceremonial center of the early Classic Period famed for its stucco masks, is a garden of palm trees and wild flowers. Its name originates from the English "Cohune Ridge," a tropical palm with copious foliage. More than 200 Petén and Río Bec style structures await excavation within the depths of the jungle. The **Pirámide de los Mascarones** (Pyramid of the Masks) is lined with several impressive 5th-century masks portraying the sun god Kinich Ahau, whose thick eyebrows and lips recall Olmec sculptures. To the west is **Plaza de las Estelas** (Plaza of the Stelae), a huge ceremonial center. To the east of the plaza stands the **acropolis,** the largest building at the site, with 8m vaults, and the half-demolished rooms of the **residential complex** and **palace.** To the south of the plaza lies a **ballcourt,** stripped of stone arcs and markers. The farthest excavated structure is the **Building of the 27 Steps,** a residence for the Maya elite from AD 600-1200. Niches once used to store incense canisters and furnishings line the walls.

DZIBANCHÉ

Several km west of the crucero of Kohunlich on Mex. 186 is the Morocoy turnoff (km 58). The turnoff for Dzibanché is 36m north of Morocoy.

Dzibanché was a powerful city, flourishing from AD 300-1200. The highlight of the site is the Early Classic pyramid, **Temple I,** or Temple of the Owl, which was once adorned with giant masks.

APPENDIX

NATIONAL HOLIDAYS

Most Mexican businesses close to observe national holidays, and hotels and sights flood with vacationing families. It's a good idea to make reservations in advance when planning to travel during these times. Official holidays are in **bold.**

January 1: Año Nuevo (New Year's Day)

January 6: Día de los Reyes (Three Kings' Day; Epiphany)

January 17: Día de San Antonio de Abad (Feast of the Blessing of the Animals)

February 2: Día de la Candelaria (Candlemas)

February 5: Día de la Constitución (Constitution Day)

February 24: Día de la Bandera (Flag Day)

🖼 Late February or Early March: Carnaval

March 21: Día del Nacimiento de Benito Juárez (Birthday of Benito Juárez, 1806)

Late March or Early April: Semana Santa (Holy Week)

May 1: Día del Trabajo (Labor Day)

May 5: Cinco de Mayo (Anniversary of the Battle of Puebla, 1862)

May 10: Día de las Madres (Mother's Day)

August 15-16: Feast of the Assumption

September 1: Informe Presidencial (Presidential State of the Union Address)

🖼 **September 16: Día de la Independencia (Anniversary of the Cry of Dolores, 1810)**

October 12: Día de la Raza (Day of the Race, or Columbus Day)

November 1: Día de Todos Santos (All Saint's Day)

🖼 November 2: Día de los Muertos (Day of the Dead)

November 20: Día de la Revolución (Anniversary of the Revolution, 1910)

December 12: Día de Nuestra Señora de Guadalupe

December 16: Posadas (Candlelit processions celebrating the journey of Mary and Joseph to Bethlehem)

December 24-25: Christmas Eve and Christmas Day

MEASUREMENT CONVERSIONS

1 inch (in.) = 25.4 millimeters (mm)	1 millimeter (mm) = 0.039 in.
1 foot (ft.) = 0.30 m	1 meter (m) = 3.28 ft.
1 yard (yd.) = 0.914m	1 meter (m) = 1.09 yd.
1 mile = 1.61km	1 kilometer (km) = 0.62 mi.
1 ounce (oz.) = 28.35g	1 gram (g) = 0.035 oz.
1 pound (lb.) = 0.454kg	1 kilogram (kg) = 2.202 lb.
1 fluid ounce (fl. oz.) = 29.57ml	1 milliliter (ml) = 0.034 fl. oz.
1 gallon (gal.) = 3.785L	1 liter (L) = 0.264 gal.
1 acre (ac.) = 0.405ha	1 hectare (ha) = 2.47 ac.
1 square mile (sq. mi.) = 2.59 sq. km	1 square kilometer (sq. km) = 0.386 sq. mi.

SPANISH QUICK REFERENCE

PRONUNCIATION

Each **vowel** has only one pronunciation: A ("ah" in father); E ("eh" in pet); I ("ee" in eat); O ("oh" in oat); U ("oo" in boot); Y, by itself, is pronounced the same as Spanish I. Most **consonants** are pronounced the same as in English. Important exceptions are: J, pronounced like the English "h" in "hello"; LL, pronounced like the English "y" in "yes"; Ñ, pronounced like the "gn" in "cognac." R at the beginning of a word or RR anywhere in a word is trilled. H is always silent. G before E or I is pronounced like the "ch" in "chutzpah"; elsewhere it is pronounced like the "g" in "gate." X has a bewildering variety of pronunciations: depending on dialect and word position it can sound like English "h," "s," "sh," or "x." Spanish words receive **stress** on the syllable marked with an **accent** (´). In the absence of an accent mark, words that end in vowels, "n," or "s" receive stress on the second to last syllable. For words ending in all other consonants, stress falls on the last syllable. The Spanish language has masculine and feminine nouns, and gives a **gender** to all adjectives. Masculine words generally end with an "o": *él es un tonto* (he is a fool). Feminine words generally end with an "a": *ella es bella* (she is beautiful). Pay close attention—slight changes in word ending can have drastic changes in meaning. For instance, when receiving directions, mind the distinction between *derecho* (straight) and *derecha* (right).

PHRASEBOOK

ENGLISH	SPANISH	ENGLISH	SPANISH
PHRASES			
Yes/No.	Sí/No.	**Hello/Goodbye**	Hola/Adiós.
Please.	Por favor.	**I'm sick/fine.**	Estoy enfermo(a)/bien.
Thank you.	Gracias.	**Could you speak more slowly?**	¿Podría hablar más despacio?
You're welcome.	De nada.	**I don't speak Spanish.**	No hablo español.
Do you speak English?	¿Habla inglés?	**How are you?**	¿Qué tal?/¿Cómo está?
Can you repeat that? Again?	¿Lo puede repetir? ¿Otra vez?	**Where are (the mummies)?**	¿Dónde están (las momias)?
What?	¿Cómo?/¿Qué?/ ¿Mande?	**Where is (the center of town)?**	¿Dónde está (el centro)?
I don't understand.	No entiendo.	**Good morning. (Good afternoon/night.)**	Buenos días. (Buenas tardes/noches.)
What is your name?	¿Cómo se llama?	**My name is Inigo Montoya.**	Me llamo Inigo Montoya.
You killed my father...	Mató a mi padre...	**Prepare to die.**	Prepárese para morir.
How do you say (ice cream) in Spanish?	¿Cómo se dice (helado) en español?	**Why (are you staring at me)?**	¿Por qué (está mirandome)?
I am hot/cold.	Tengo calor/frio.	**I want/would like...**	Quiero/Me gustaría...
How much does it cost?	¿Cuánto cuesta?	**That is cheap/expensive.**	Es muy caro/barato.
Excuse me.	Perdón.	**Sorry.**	Lo siento.
Closed/Open.	Cerrado(a)/Abierto(a).	**Let's Go is the best.**	Let's Go es el mejor.

YOUR ARRIVAL

ENGLISH	SPANISH	ENGLISH	SPANISH
I am from the US/Europe.	Soy de los Estados Unidos/Europa.	What's the problem, sir?	¿Cuál es el problema, señor?
Here is my passport.	Aquí está mi pasaporte.	I lost my passport.	Perdí mi pasaporte.
I will be here for less than 6 months.	Estaré aquí por menos de seis meses.	I don't know where the drugs came from.	No sé de donde vinieron las drogas.
I have nothing to declare.	No tengo nada para declarar.	Please do not detain me.	Por favor no me detenga.

GETTING AROUND

ENGLISH	SPANISH	ENGLISH	SPANISH
How do you get to (the bus station?	¿Cómo se va a (la terminal de autobúses)?	Is there anything cheaper?	¿Hay algo más barato/económico?
Does this bus go to (Guanajuato)?	¿Este autobús va a (Guanajuato)?	On foot.	A pie.
Can I buy a ticket?	¿Puedo comprar un boleto?	How can you get there?	¿Cómo se puede llegar?
How long does the trip take?	¿Cuánto tiempo dura el viaje?	Is it near/far?	¿Está cerca/lejos de aquí?
I am going to the airport.	Voy al aeropuerto.	The flight is delayed/cancelled.	El vuelo está retrasado/cancelado.
I lost my baggage.	Perdí mi equipaje.	Is it safe to hitchhike?	¿Es seguro pedir aventón?
Turn right/left.	Doble a la derecha/izquierda.	Stay straight.	Continua al derecho.
I would like to rent (a car).	Quisiera rentar (un carro).	Please let me off at ...	Por favor, déjeme en...
How much does it cost per day/week?	¿Cuánto cuesta por día/semana?	Does it have air-conditioning?	¿Tiene aire acondicionado?

ACCOMODATIONS

ENGLISH	SPANISH	ENGLISH	SPANISH
Is there a cheap hotel around here?	¿Hay un hotel económico por aqui?	Are there rooms with windows?	¿Hay habitaciones con ventanas?
Do you have rooms available?	¿Tiene habitaciones libres?	I am going to stay for (four) days.	Me voy a quedar (cuatro) días.
I would like to reserve a room.	Quisiera reservar una habitación.	Are there cheaper rooms?	¿Hay habitaciones más baratos?
Can I see a room?	¿Puedo ver una habitación?	Do they come with private bath?	¿Vienen con baño privado?
Do you have any singles/doubles?	¿Tiene habitaciones sencillas/dobles?	I'll take it.	Lo tomo.
The bathroom is broken.	El baño está roto.	Can I borrow a plunger?	¿Me prestas una bomba?
There are cockroaches in my room.	Hay cucarachas en mi habitación.	They are biting me.	Están mordiendome.

EATING OUT

ENGLISH	SPANISH	ENGLISH	SPANISH
I am hungry/thirsty.	Tengo hambre/sed.	Do you have hot sauce?	¿Tiene salsa picante?
Where is a good restaurant?	¿Dónde hay un restaurante bueno?	Table for (one), please.	Mesa para (uno), por favor.
Can I see the menu?	¿Puedo ver el menú?	Disgusting!	¡Guácala!/¡Que asco!
This is too spicy.	Pica demasiado.	I am going to be sick.	Voy a vomitar.
I would like to order ...	Quisiera...	Delicious!	¡Qué rico!
Where is the bathroom?	¿Dónde está el baño?	Check, please!	¡La cuenta, por favor!
Do you have anything vegetarian/without meat?	¿Hay algún plato vegetariano/sin carne?	Do you take credit cards?	¿Aceptan tarjetas de crédito?

EMERGENCY

ENGLISH	SPANISH	ENGLISH	SPANISH
Help!	¡Auxilio!/¡Ayúdame!	Call the police!	Llame a la policía!
I am hurt.	Estoy herido(a).	Leave me alone!	¡Déjame en paz!
It's an emergency!	¡Es una emergencia!	I have been robbed!	¡Me han robado!
Fire!	¡Fuego!/¡Incendio!	They went that a-way!	¡Fueron en esa dirección!
Call a clinic/ambulance/doctor/priest!	¡Llame a una clínica/una ambulancia/un médico/un padre!	How can we solve this problem? [suggesting a bribe]	¿Cómo podemos resolverlo?
I need to contact my embassy.	Necesito contactar mi embajada.	I will only speak in the presence of a lawyer.	Sólo hablaré en presencia de un abogado(a).

MEDICAL

ENGLISH	SPANISH	ENGLISH	SPANISH
I feel bad/better/worse.	Me siento mal/mejor/peor.	I have a cold/a fever/diahrrea/nausea.	Tengo gripa/una calentura/diarrea/náusea.
I have a headache.	Tengo dolor de cabeza.	I have a stomach ache.	Tengo dolor de estómago.
I'm sick/ill.	Estoy enfermo(a).	It hurts here.	Me duele aquí.
I'm allergic to (cows).	Soy alérgico(a) a (las vacas).	Here is my prescription.	Aquí está mi receta médica.
What is this medicine for?	¿Para qué es esta medicina?	I think i'm going to vomit.	Pienso que voy a vomitar.
Where is the nearest hospital/doctor?	¿Donde está el hospital/doctor más cercano?	I haven't been able to go to the bathroom in (four) days.	No he podido ir al baño en (cuatro) días.

INFORMAL (PERSONAL) RELATIONSHIPS

ENGLISH	SPANISH	ENGLISH	SPANISH
What is your name?	¿Cómo se llama?	Pleased to meet you.	Encantado(a)/Mucho gusto.
Where are you from?	¿De dónde es?	I'm (twenty) years old.	Tengo (veinte) años.
This my first time in Mexico.	Este es mi primera vez en Mexico.	I have a boyfriend/girlfriend.	Tengo novio/novia.
What's your sign?	¿Cuál es tu signo?	I'm a communist.	Soy comunista.
I am gay/straight.	Soy gay./No soy gay.	Would you like to go out with me?	¿Quieres salir conmigo?
Do you have a light?	¿Tiene fuego?	It's true. Politicians can never be trusted.	De verdad. No se puede confiar en los políticos.
I had the very same dream!	¡Tenía el mismo sueño!	No thanks, I have many diseases.	No gracias, tengo muchas enfermedades.
Please stop kissing me.	No me besas más, por favor.	I love you.	Te quiero.
Marrying me will not make you a US citizen.	Casarte conmigo no te hara un ciudadano de los Estados Unidos.	What a shame: you bought Lonely Planet!	¡Qué lástima: compraste Lonely Planet!

NUMBERS AND DAYS

0	cero	21	veintiuno
1	uno	22	veintidos
2	dos	30	treinta
3	tres	40	cuarenta
4	cuatro	50	cincuenta
5	cinco	100	cien
6	seis	1000	mil
7	siete	1 million	un millón
8	ocho	Sunday	Domingo
9	nueve	Monday	Lunes
10	diez	Tuesday	Martes
11	once	Wednesday	Miércoles

ENGLISH	SPANISH	ENGLISH	SPANISH
12	doce	Thursday	Jueves
13	trece	Friday	Viernes
14	catorce	Saturday	Sábado
15	quince	today	hoy
16	dieciseis	tomorrow	mañana
17	diecisiete	day after tomorrow	pasado mañana
18	dieciocho	yesterday	ayer
19	diecinueve	day before yesterday	antes de ayer/anteayer
20	veinte	weekend	fin de semana

GLOSSARY OF TERMS

aduana: customs
agua (purificada): water (purified)
ahora: now
al gusto: as you wish
almuerzo: lunch
amigo/a: friend
andador: pedestrian walkway
antojitos: appetizers
arroz: rice
artesanía: artisanry
avenida: avenue
bahía: bay
balneario: public pool
bandidos: bandits
baños: bathrooms
barato/a: cheap
barranca: canyon
barrio: neighborhood
batido: milkshake
basílica: basilica
biblioteca: library
bistec/bistek: beefsteak
bonito/a: pretty/beautiful
borracho/a: drunk
buena suerte: good luck
buen provecho: bon appetit
burro: donkey
caballero: gentleman
cabañas: cabins
cafe: coffee, cafe
cajeros automáticos: ATM
caldo: soup, broth, or stew
calle: street
callejón: little street; alley
cara de cholita: slutface
caro: expensive
cascadas: waterfalls
camarones: shrimp
cambio: change
camión: bus
campo: countryside
cantina: saloon-type bar (mostly-male clientele)

capilla: chapel
carne asada: roast meat
caro/a: expensive
carretera: highway
casa de cambio: currency exchange booth
caseta: phone stall
catedral: cathedral
cena: dinner
cenote: freshwater sinkhole
centro: center (of town)
cerro: hill
cerveza: beer
chicharrón: bite-sized pieces of fried pork rind
chicle: chewing gum
chuleta de chancho: pork chop
chupacabra: demon that sucks goat blood
colectivo: shared taxi
colonia: neighborhood
combi: small local bus
comedor: small diner
comida corrida: fixed menu
consulado: consulate
correo: post office
crucero: crossroads
cuadra: street block
cuarto: room
cuenta: bill/check
cucaracha: cockroach
cueva: cave
cuota: toll
dama: lady
de paso: bus that picks up passengers by roadsides
desayuno: breakfast
dinero: money
dulces: sweets
embarcadero: dock
entrada: entrance
extranjero: foreign/foreigner
farmacia: pharmacy
faro: lighthouse
fiesta: party; holiday

frijoles: beans
frito/a: fried
frontera: border
fumar: to smoke
fútbol: soccer
glorieta: traffic circle
gobierno: government
gratis: free
gringo: North American
grutas: caves
güera: blond
hacienda: ranch
helado: ice cream
hombre: man
iglesia: church
isla: island
jarra: pitcher
jugo: juice
ladrón: thief
lago: lake
lancha: boat
lavandería: laundromat
licuado: smoothie
loma: hill
lonchería: lunch place
malecón: promenade, boulevard
mar: ocean; sea
maricon (slang): homosexual
mariscos: seafood
matrimonial: double bed
menso: idiot; asshole; Josh Davis
menú del día: pre-set meal
mercado: market (often outdoor)
merienda: afternoon snack
microbús: minibus
enano: midget
migra: immigration
mirador: viewpoint
mordida: bribe
muelle: wharf
mujer: woman
niño: child
norte (Nte.): north
novio/a: boyfriend/girlfriend; fiancé/fiancée
oriente (Ote.): east
palapa: palm-thatched beach bungalow
panadería: bread shop
panga: motorboat
parada: a stop (on a bus or train)
parque: park
paseo: promenade
pescado: fish
picante: spicy
pesero: local bus
peligro: danger
pirámides: pyramids
playa: beach
plaza: square

pollo: chicken
pollero (slang): person who transports illegal immigrants
poniente (Pte.): west
posada: inn
postre: sweet; dessert
poza: well; pool
primera clase: first-class
pueblo: village; community
puerta: door
puerto: port
queso: cheese
refrescos: refreshments; soft drinks
ropa: clothes
ruinas: ruins
ruta: local bus
sábanas: sheets
sabor: flavor; taste
sacbe (Maya): upraised, paved road
sacerdote: priest
salida: exit
salud: health
segunda clase: second-class
selva: jungle
semana: week
servicio de lujo: luxury service
SIDA: the Spanish acronym for AIDS
simpático: friendly/nice
stela: upright stone monument
supermercado: supermarket
sur: south
taqueria: taco stand
talavera: white, glazed earthenware produced in Puebla
tarifa: fee
tejano: Texan
telenovela: soap opera
templo: church; temple
tienda: store
típico: typical; traditional
tipo de cambio: exchange rate
toalla: towel
torta: sandwich
turismo: tourism
turista: tourist; diarrhea
tranquilo: peaceful
vaquero: cowboy
valle: valley
zócalo: central square
zona: zone; region

DISTANCES (KM) AND TRAVEL TIMES (BY BUS)

	Acapulco	Chihuahua	Cancún	El Paso	Guadalajara	La Paz	Mazatlán	Mérida	Mexico City	Monterrey	Oaxaca	Puebla	San Cristóbal	San Luis Potosí	Tijuana	Veracruz
Acapulco		2440km	1938km	2815km	1028km	4917km	1429km	1779km	415km	1402km	700km	544km	1036km	828km	3228km	847km
Chihuahua	24hr		3262km	375km	1552km	3237km	1031km	2945km	1496km	834km	2154km	1625km	2785km	1195km	1548km	1841km
Cancún	33hr	47hr		3637km	2442km	6499km	2963km	319km	1766km	2506km	1693km	1895km	902km	2267km	4810km	1421km
El Paso	29hr	5hr	54hr		1549km	3009km	1406km	3320km	1871km	1209km	2529km	2000km	3127km	1569km	1320km	2216km
Guadalajara	15hr	17hr	45hr	25hr		4159km	521km	2125km	676km	885km	1222km	805km	1853km	348km	2340km	1021km
La Paz	60hr	46hr	96hr	41hr	60hr		3508km	6180km	4733km	4071km	5279km	4862km	5883km	4283km	1689km	5050km
Mazatlán	21hr	15½hr	53hr	25hr	8hr	50hr		2646km	1197km	940km	1743km	1326km	2374km	799km	1819km	1542km
Mérida	29hr	42hr	4hr	47hr	40½hr	92hr	40hr		1449km	2189km	1374km	1791km	743km	799km	4491km	1104km
Mexico City	6hr	20hr	26hr	25hr	10hr	68hr	18hr	22hr		950km	546km	129km	1177km	413km	3044km	345km
Monterrey	18hr	12hr	38hr	17hr	11hr	60hr	17hr	32hr	12hr		1533km	1116km	1918km	537km	2382km	1085km
Oaxaca	9hr	29hr	29hr	34hr	17hr	77hr	27hr	24½hr	9hr	21hr		417km	631km	959km	3590km	450km
Puebla	7hr	22hr	24hr	27hr	12hr	71hr	20hr	20hr	2hr	14hr	4hr		1048km	542km	3285km	303km
San Cristóbal	16hr	39hr	17hr	44hr	28hr	88hr	19hr	12½hr	18hr	30hr	12hr	16hr		1590km	4193km	833km
San Luis Potosí	10hr	14hr	31hr	18hr	6hr	60hr	12hr	27hr	5hr	7hr	20hr	16hr	23hr		2743km	846km
Tijuana	46hr	22hr	72hr	17hr	36hr	24hr	26hr	66hr	44hr	36hr	53hr	46hr	62hr	36hr		3361km
Veracruz	13hr	28hr	21hr	33hr	17hr	76hr	26hr	13hr	8hr	17hr	8hr	4½hr	13hr	13hr	52hr	

INDEX

MAPS

ABOUT LET'S GO

FORTY-TWO YEARS OF WISDOM

For over four decades, travelers crisscrossing the continents have relied on *Let's Go* for inside information on the hippest backstreet cafes, the most pristine secluded beaches, and the best routes from border to border. *Let's Go: Europe*, now in its 42nd edition and translated into seven languages, reigns as the world's bestselling international travel guide. In the last 20 years, our rugged researchers have stretched the frontiers of backpacking and expanded our coverage into the Americas, Australia, Asia, and Africa (including the new *Let's Go: Egypt* and the more comprehensive, multi-country jaunt through *Let's Go: South Africa & Southern Africa*). Our new-and-improved City Guide series continues to grow with new guides to perennial European favorites Amsterdam and Barcelona. This year we are also unveiling *Let's Go: Southwest USA*, the flagship of our new outdoor Adventure Guide series, which is complete with special roadtripping tips and itineraries, more coverage of adventure activities like hiking and mountain biking, and first-person accounts of life on the road.

It all started in 1960 when a handful of well-traveled students at Harvard University handed out a 20-page mimeographed pamphlet offering a collection of their tips on budget travel to passengers on student charter flights to Europe. The following year, in response to the instant popularity of the first volume, students traveling to Europe researched the first full-fledged edition of *Let's Go: Europe*. Throughout the 60s and 70s, our guides reflected the times—in 1969, for example, we taught you how to get from Paris to Prague on "no dollars a day" by singing in the street. In the 90s we focused in on the world's most exciting urban areas to produce in-depth, fold-out map guides, now with 20 titles (from Hong Kong to Chicago) and counting. Our new guides bring the total number of titles to 57, each infused with the spirit of adventure and voice of opinion that travelers around the world have come to count on. But some things never change: our guides are still researched, written, and produced entirely by students who know first-hand how to see the world on the cheap.

HOW WE DO IT

Each guide is completely revised and thoroughly updated every year by a well-traveled set of nearly 300 students. Every spring, we recruit over 200 researchers and 90 editors to overhaul every book. After several months of training, researcher-writers hit the road for seven weeks of exploration, from Anchorage to Adelaide, Estonia to El Salvador, Iceland to Indonesia. Hired for their rare combination of budget travel sense, writing ability, stamina, and courage, these adventurous travelers know that train strikes, stolen luggage, food poisoning, and marriage proposals are all part of a day's work. Back at our offices, editors work from spring to fall, massaging copy written on Himalayan bus rides into witty, informative prose. A student staff of typesetters, cartographers, publicists, and managers keeps our lively team together. In September, the collected efforts of the summer are delivered to our printer, who turns them into books in record time, so that you have the most up-to-date information available for your vacation. Even as you read this, work on next year's editions is well underway.

WHY WE DO IT

We don't think of budget travel as the last recourse of the destitute; we believe that it's the only way to travel. Our books will ease your anxieties and answer your questions about the basics—so you can get off the beaten track and explore. Once you learn the ropes, we encourage you to put *Let's Go* down and strike out on your own. You know as well as we that the best discoveries are often those you make yourself. When you find something worth sharing, please drop us a line. We're Let's Go Publications, 67 Mount Auburn St., Cambridge, MA 02138, USA (feedback@letsgo.com). For more info, visit our website, www.letsgo.com.

Will you have enough stories to tell your grandchildren?

Yahoo! Travel

Do You Yahoo!?

CHOOSE YOUR DESTINATION SWEEPSTAKES

No Purchase Necessary.

**Explore the world with Let's Go® and StudentUniverse!
Enter for a chance to win a trip for two to a Let's Go destination!**

Separate Drawings! May & October 2002.

GRAND PRIZES:
Roundtrip StudentUniverse Tickets

✓ Select one destination and mail your entry to:

☐ Costa Rica
☐ London
☐ Hong Kong
☐ San Francisco
☐ New York
☐ Amsterdam
☐ Prague
☐ Sydney

* **Plus Additional Prizes!!**

Choose Your Destination Sweepstakes
St. Martin's Press
Suite 1600, Department MF
175 Fifth Avenue
New York, NY 10010-7848

Restrictions apply; see offical rules for
details by visiting Let'sGo.com or sending SASE
(VT residents may omit return postage) to the address above.

Name: _____

Address: _____

City/State/Zip: _____

Phone: _____

Email: _____

Grand prizes provided by:

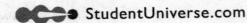

StudentUniverse.com   Real Travel Deals

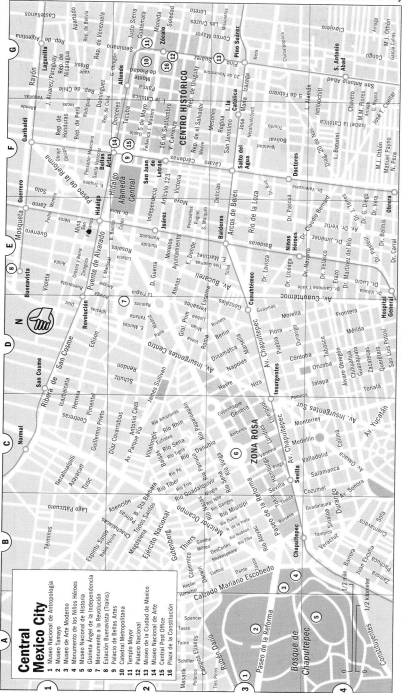

Central
Mexico City

1 Museo Nacional de Antropología
2 Museo Tamayo
3 Museo de Arte Moderno
4 Monumento de los Niños Héroes
5 Museo Nacional de Historia
6 Glorieta Ángel de la Independencia
7 Monumento a la Revolución
8 Estación Buenavista (Trains)
9 Palacio de Bellas Artes
10 Catedral Metropolitana
11 Templo Mayor
12 Palacio Nacional
13 Museo de la Ciudad de Mexico
14 Museo Nacional de Arte
15 Central Post Office
16 Plaza de la Constitución

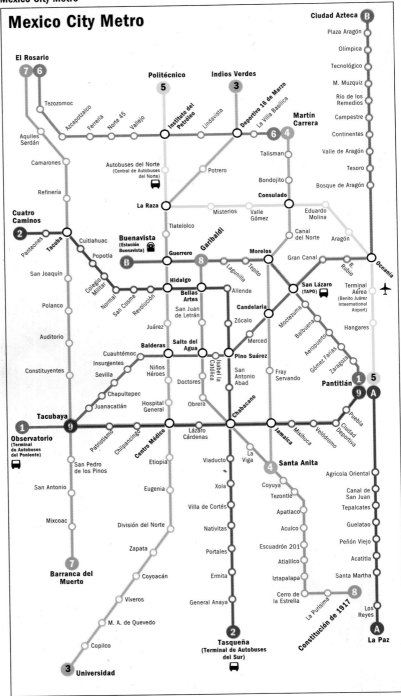